# THE DICTIONARY OF
# CLEVELAND BIOGRAPHY

# THE
# DICTIONARY OF
# CLEVELAND
# BIOGRAPHY

David D. Van Tassel, *Editor*

John J. Grabowski, *Managing Editor*

PUBLISHED IN ASSOCIATION WITH
CASE WESTERN RESERVE UNIVERSITY AND
THE WESTERN RESERVE HISTORICAL SOCIETY

*The Encyclopedia Project is an official project of
the Cleveland Bicentennial Commission*

INDIANA UNIVERSITY PRESS

*Bloomington & Indianapolis*

The paper used in the publication meets the minimum
requirements of American National Standard for Information
Sciences-Permanence of Paper for Printed Library
Materials, ANSI Z39.48–1984

MANUFACTURED IN THE UNITED STATES OF AMERICA

**Library of Congress Cataloging–in–Publication Data**

Dictionary of Cleveland biography / David D. Van Tassel, editor; John
  J. Grabowski, managing editor.
     p.    cm.
   "An official project of the Cleveland Bicentennial Commission."
   Includes bibliographical references and index.
   ISBN 0–253–33055–6 (cloth  :  alk. paper)
   1. Cleveland (Ohio)—Biography—Dictionaries. 2. Cleveland Region
(Ohio)—Biography—Dictionaries.   I. Van Tassel, David D. (David
Dirck), date.   II. Grabowski, John J.   III. Case Western Reserve
University.   IV. Western Reserve Historical Society.   V. Cleveland
Bicentennial Commission (Cleveland, Ohio)
F499.C653.A23   1996
920.0771'32—dc20

                                                      95–45459

    2   3   4   5   01   00   99   98   97   96

# CONTENTS

# City of Cleveland

### MICHAEL R. WHITE, MAYOR

Dear Reader:

In the last two hundred years, Cleveland has grown from a small frontier outpost to one of America's major metropolitan centers. Today, with a score of reinvigorated urban neighborhoods, a newly revitalized downtown, unparalleled cultural amenities, and one of the most diverse populations in the nation, Cleveland is looked upon as a model for what can be accomplished in urban America. The future of Cleveland is bright. It is one closely linked to the evolving global economy and to the new spirit of American enterprises in the coming 21st century. It is however, a future that rests upon the unique combination of individual, neighborhood and community that characterizes our city today.

The creation of that important combination of people, neighborhood and community is the core of our city's history. That history, the story of the beginning of our city, of the contributions of hundreds of thousands of people, of our successes and of our failures, is the foundation for the future to which we look forward. To know that story of the past, of good times and bad, of prejudice and achievement, of dreams and despair, is to understand who we are today and what we can become tomorrow. Although much of our bicentennial celebration looks forward, an important part of it must look toward the past.

The Encyclopedia of Cleveland History and the Dictionary of Cleveland Biography are our city's primary review of the foundation of our city. In nearly four thousand separate entries, they detail the stories of men and women, of the organizations and events that have created the city in which we live. These volumes tell us not only who we were, but hint at what we might aspire to become.

These two volumes contain the true legacy of our city: the story of people of every race and background from every part of the world who came to settle on the shores of Lake Erie and who built one of the nation's and world's most notable cities. In reading through these volumes, I hope that you will join me in celebrating the achievements of all Clevelanders past & present in creating a city that has captured the imagination and attention of the world.

Michael R. White
Mayor of Cleveland

# Preface

The *Dictionary of Cleveland Biography* is the outgrowth of the first edition of the *Encyclopedia of Cleveland History,* published in 1987, containing over 2,500 entries, of which more than 900 consisted of biographical sketches of individuals who had made a contribution to the growth and development of the Greater Cleveland community. In addition, many of the other entries which concerned businesses, social service agencies, clubs, and churches also contained a good deal of biographical information about their founders and leaders. In compiling the *Encyclopedia* we learned quite quickly that the history of the city really is the history of its people.

Given the importance of biography and the great interest people have in other people, we decided that the second edition of the *Encyclopedia of Cleveland History* would be expanded into two volumes, one of which would be totally devoted to biography. This new volume, *The Dictionary of Cleveland Biography,* contains over 1,500 entries detailing the lives of individuals who have contributed to the growth, well-being, fame and social conscience of Greater Cleveland. All of the biographical sketches contained in the first edition of *The Encyclopedia of Cleveland History* are to be found in *The Dictionary of Cleveland Biography,* rewritten, condensed and checked for accuracy. In addition, over 600 new sketches have been added.

*The Dictionary of Cleveland Biography* is the latest addition to a genre stretching back to the late 19th century of biographical directories of "representative Clevelanders." This volume is not just the latest, but is new in a very different and important sense. Unlike its predecessors, the *Dictionary* includes sketches of Clevelanders who achieved in a wide variety of endeavors, ranging from neighborhood leadership to industrial capitalism, and who are broadly representative of the racial and ethnic makeup of Cleveland.

Guided by the advice and nominations of more than 100 community members who attended planning conferences and assisted by a representative editorial advisory board, we hope we have made the new *Dictionary* representative of a broad spectrum of the city's people. The sketches of individual achievement span dozens of nationalities, scores of endeavors, and more than 200 years of history. The criteria for inclusion were complex and sometimes arbitrary. We know many worthy people are not to be found in these pages, but had we included all of those whom we and others deemed worthy, this project would have run to several more volumes. The first criterion for inclusion was that the person had to have died prior to 1 June 1995. The second was that the person had to have lived in Cleveland for a substantial amount of time; long enough to have made a major contribution to the city's lore and long enough for the city's environment to have had an impact on the individual's development and subsequent career. There were many other specialized criteria, such as Hall of Fame recognitions for sports figures, and national or international recognition through showings and peer awards for artists, physicians, and others. But always we have attempted to keep the general reader in mind and select subjects whom he or she might be interested in looking up. community. The final choice was then made by the editors.

Published along with the new, illustrated version of *The Encyclopedia of Cleveland History, The Dictionary of Cleveland Biography* has its own index and stands by itself, yet it is linked by cross references to its companion volume. The new *Dictionary* provides a wealth of information for planners, fund raisers, and genealogists; but more important, we hope it presents a series of role models for the generation that will move Cleveland toward its 300th anniversary.

David D. Van Tassel, Editor
Case Western Reserve University

John J. Grabowski, Managing Editor
Western Reserve Historical Society

# ADVISORY BOARD

# STAFF

# Acknowledgments

The process of preparing for the second edition of the *Encyclopedia of Cleveland History* began almost immediately after the publication of the first edition as we assembled corrections from friends and critics and sought to keep abreast of the rapid changes in the business and cultural communities. The pace began to quicken nearly four years prior to publication as we assembled a staff of writers and researchers, many of whom were veterans of the first edition. During the course of these last nine years, we have accumulated a host of debts to a great variety of people in the Greater Cleveland area and to some outside the community. Although the official staff has always been small, the number of volunteers has grown over the years so that this has become truly a community endeavor. We cannot acknowledge all of the people who have helped us, but we hope that they know that they have our appreciation and take satisfaction in having contributed their part to securing the future of Cleveland's past.

We would like to thank, first, Agnar Pytte, president of Case Western Reserve University and executive director emeritus, Theodore A. Sande, and Richard Ehrlich, executive director of the Western Reserve Historical Society, for lending their personal and institutional support to this project. It could not have succeeded without the vastly important intellectual and institutional resources of Case Western Reserve University or the magnificent manuscript and photographic collections of the Western Reserve Historical Society, as well as the many contributions of its staff. We would like to thank those often unsung heroes of the CWRU Development Office who helped raise the funds that made the preparation of the manuscript possible. Special thanks go to Martha Gibbons, past associate director of Foundation Relations, who worked indefatigably, her enthusiasm never flagging despite obstacles and some disappointments along the way. We thank Bruce Loessin, vice-president of Development and Alumni Affairs, John Glasson, director of Foundation Relations, Carol Elliott Giltz, assistant vice-president of Development and Alumni Affairs, trustees Allen Ford and Lainie Hadden, and Karen Horn in soliciting corporate and personal donations. Special thanks to our good friend Henry Foltz, who played an important role in the final days of the fund raising effort. David Abbott, executive director, and other members of the Cleveland Bicentennial Commission not only named this an official project of the Bicentennial year, but made possible the funding for completion of the pre-publication work on the completed manuscript. The Cleveland Foundation, however, comes in for the bulk of the credit for not only funding the launching of the first edition but contributing sustaining funding to ensure that there would be a second edition. Steven Minter, director, and Susan LaJoie, associate director, have kept an ever-watchful eye over the project that they were so influential in launching many years ago. The Gund Foundation was another important original supporter and David Bergholtz (who was first introduced to Cleveland by a gift of the first edition of the *Encyclopedia*) has ever since been an enthusiastic supporter of the project. We, of course, have listed all of the foundations, corporations, and individuals who have offered their donations and support.

As the project came closer to publication, we were again fortunate to have the advice and assistance of John Gallman, Director of the Indiana University Press; Roberta "Bobbi" Diehl, Senior Copy Editor; her assistant, John Vollmer; and the press's thoroughly professional editorial, design, and production staffs. Their patience in wading through and helping to standardize the thousands of pages of manuscript was appreciated by all of us on the "Cleveland end" of the project.

The editors' deep appreciation goes to Sarah Snock, project coordinator, and to Michael Morgenstern, assistant editor. Sarah Snock, as coordinator for the project, played an essential role in synchronizing every aspect of this complex and wide-ranging enterprise. Her genial spirit and enthusiasm for the project, with gentle prodding when necessary, kept morale high and things moving along according to schedule. Michael Morgenstern supervised a number of research assistants, researched all of the photographs for this project and several ancillary projects along the way, checked all of the information for updating articles, and worked many overtime hours. Both Sarah and Mike performed a wide range of necessary tasks and assumed a great deal of responsibility for getting things done and spotting things that needed to be done.

Throughout the project the editors have enjoyed the constant support of their colleagues and families as the enormity of this sprawling enterprise overwhelmed their offices, homes, and leisure time. The Department of History of Case Western Reserve University has endured the intrusions the project has created within the teaching and professional schedule of the editor without complaint. The managing editor owes a debt to Drs. Theodore A. Sande and Richard Ehrlich, executive directors of the Western Reserve Historical Society, and to Kermit Pike for approving his participation in this project. Helen Van Tassel and Diane Ewart Grabowski not only have endured the disruptions of home and family but also have assisted their husbands editorially in the compilation of this volume. To them and to the legion of writers, supporters, and helpful critics, we can only extend a heartfelt thank you for assistance, patience, and understanding in our effort to portray the history of a great and complex city in the best manner possible.

In addition, there were many institutions, archives, and libraries that not only welcomed us into their collections, but their staff members' unstinting help in finding materials was indispensable. Many of their names are listed below. To them we owe a great debt of gratitude:

*Case Western Reserve University—Archives, Library & Special Collections:* George Barnum; Nora Blackmun; Helen Conger; Sue Hansen; Dennis Harrison; Jill Tatum

*Western Reserve Historical Society:*; Ann Ameling; Barbara Billings; Samuel W. Black; Leslie Graham; David Holcombe; Michael McCormick; Kermit J. Pike; Nancy Schwartz; Ann Sindelar; A. Joseph Zawatski

*Western Reserve Historical Society—Genealogical Advisory Committee:* Donna Agan; Mary Lou Bregitzer; Ellie Brucken; Thomas Frye; Duncan Gardiner; Jeannette Grosvenor; Bernice Hess; Marilyn McCleod; Sheldon McCleod; G. L. Moore; Mary Jean Neiswander; Bruce Reed; Carol Reed; Mary Clare Yarham

*Cleveland Artists Foundation:* Ann Caywood Brown; Rota Sakerlotsky

*City of Cleveland, City Council Archives:* Martin Hauserman

*City of Cleveland Department of Vital Statistics:* Mark Kassouff

*Cleveland Bicentennial Commission:* Ann Zollar

*Cleveland Clinic Foundation Archives:* Fred Lautzenheiser; Carol Tomer

*Cleveland Museum of Natural History:* Joe Hannibal; Anita Weber

*Cleveland Public Library:* Joan Clark

*Special thanks to the staffs of the following Cleveland Public Library Departments: Main Reference, Photograph Collection, Newspapers, Art History, History, Social Sciences, Foreign Literature.*

*Cleveland State University Archives—Cleveland Press Collection:* William Becker

*Cuyahoga County Archives:* Judith Cetina

*Dittrick Museum of Medical History:* Jennifer Simmons

*Jewish Community Federation of Cleveland:* Judah Rubinstein

*Jewish Genealogical Society of Cleveland:* Arlene Rich

*Lake View Cemetery:* Katherine Kohl

*Mayfield Cemetery:* Pat Corrigan

*Oberlin College—Archives:* Roland Baumann; Tammy Martin

*The Plain Dealer:* Bill Barnard; Genevieve Barnard; Patty Gratsiano; Alex Machaskee; William Miller; Ernie Rocco; Amy Rosewater

David D. Van Tassel
John J. Grabowski

# DONORS—1987 EDITION

## Foundations

Cleveland Foundation
National Endowment for the Humanities
Bolton Foundation
William Bingham Foundation
George Gund Foundation
Ohio Humanities Council
Martha Holden Jennings Foundation
Kelvin and Eleanor Smith Foundation
Treuhaft Foundation
Forest City Enterprises Charitable Foundation
Nathan L. Dauby Charity Fund
George M. and Pamela S. Humphrey Fund
Louise H. & David S. Ingalls Foundation
H.M. O'Neill Charitable Trust
George W. Codrington Charitable Foundation
Elizabeth Ring Mather and William Gwinn
   Mather Fund
Bicknell Fund
Firman Fund
Lucile & Robert H. Gries Charity Fund
Kulas Foundation
John P. Murphy Foundation
Britton Foundation
Harry K. and Emma R. Fox Foundation
Laub Foundation
Hadden Foundation
S. Livingston Mather Charitable Trust
Wolpert Fund

## Companies

Cleveland Electric Illuminating Company
Leaseway of Ohio Incorporated
Standard Oil Company
Chessie System Railroads
M.A. Hanna Company
TRW Incorporated
Ferro Corporation
Eaton Corporation
The Higbee Company
Jones, Day, Reavis & Pogue
Oglebay Norton Company
Ohio Bell Telephone Company
Premier Industrial Corporation
Squire, Sanders & Dempsey
White Consolidated Industries, Inc.
East Ohio Gas Company
May Company
Parker Hannifin Corporation
Sherwin-Williams Company
SIFCO Industries
Van Dorn Company
AmeriTrust Company
Huntington National Bank
Lubrizol Corporation
Plain Dealer Publishing Company
Centran Corporation
Society National Bank
Baker Hostetler
Bearings, Inc.
Ernst & Whinney
Hauserman, Inc.
Reliance Electric Company
Cleveland Cliffs Incorporated
Arthur Andersen & Co.
Calfee, Halter & Griswold
Spieth, Bell, McCurdy & Newell
Price Waterhouse
Standard Products Company
Stouffer Corporation

## Individuals and Associations

Mrs. C. Baldwin Sawyer
Mrs. Ralph S. Schmitt
S. Sterling McMillan
Early Settlers Association
Robert M. Ginn
Anonymous
David W. Swetland
Edward E. Worthington
James P. Conway
Ralph M. Besse
Betty Del Duca
Robert E. Glazer
Curtis Lee Smith
Michael Altschul
Founders and Patriots
William S. Burton

# DONORS—BICENTENNIAL EDITION

## Foundations

Cleveland Foundation
Cleveland Bicentennial Commission
George Gund Foundation
Abington Foundation
Firman Fund
Lucile & Robert H. Gries Charity Fund
Payne Fund
Sherwick Fund
Elizabeth Ring & Wm. Gwinn Mather Fund
Forest City Enterprises Charitable Fund
Perkins Charitable Foundation
Premier Industrial Foundation
Cleveland Cliffs Foundation
Helen & Joseph Lewis Fund
Peter B. Lewis Philanthropic Fund
S. Livingston Mather Charitable Trust
Wm. J. & Dorothy K. O'Neill Foundation
Standard Products Foundation

## Companies

Baker & Hostetler
Cole National Corporation
Progressive, Inc.
TRW
Lincoln Electric Company
Squire, Sanders & Dempsey
Cleveland Electric Illuminating Company
Ferro Corporation
Thompson, Hine & Flory

## Individuals

Charles Bolton
Werner D. Mueller
Given in Honor of Richard F. and Virginia H.
  Outcalt:
  Mr. and Mrs. Richard F. Outcalt, Jr.
  Mr. and Mrs. Robert H. Outcalt
  Mr. and Mrs. Jim Beck
  Mr. and Mrs. Jon H. Outcalt
  Mr. David B. Outcalt
  Mr. and Mrs. C. Henry Foltz
  Miss Allison Foltz
  Mr. Richard F. Outcalt, III
  Miss Dana Outcalt
  Mr. and Mrs. Jeffrey King
  Mr. and Mrs. Jon H. Outcalt, Jr.
  Mr. Kenneth W. Outcalt
  Mr. and Mrs. W. Price Foltz
Arthur Holden
Dorothy Humel-Hovorka
Frances Wragg Ingalls
Melissa Arnold

# AUTHORS

*The following individuals have written articles for the* Encyclopedia of Cleveland History *and* Dictionary of Cleveland Biography *either as staff members, contractual agents, students, or volunteers. An asterisk denotes authors who worked on the 1996 edition.*

Abrams, Sylvia
Alewitz, Sam
Alexander, J. Heywood
Altschul, Michael
Ameling, Ann*
Anderson, Fleka J.
Baldanza, Lawrence
Ballenger, Jesse*
Banks, James
Barloon, Marvin
Barnum, George
Barrett, Timothy
Barrow, William*
Beach, David*
Beal, Carol A.
Beal, Eileen*
Becker, Thea*
Becker, William*
Bellamy, Paul
Bergheger, Brian
Boieru, Olga
Borchert, James
Brachna, Gabor S.
Brinnon, Lillian
Brose, David
Brown, Jeffrey P.
Busch, Jane
Callahan, Nelson
Campbell, Thomas F.
Cauffield, Jane H.
Cetina, Judith G.
Chang, K. Laurence
Cheney, Nina
Chernen, June
Cimperman, John D.
Clemenson, Barbara*
Cline, Scott
Cohen, Paula
Colombi, Christopher A., Jr.
Connell, Timothy C.
Conti, Deborah
Copeland, Helen
Cross, James
Danielson, Elizabeth

Dardis, Kenneth
Dawson, Virginia P.
Day, Charles
Day, Jack G.
Deal, Mary
Decker, Timothy
Diaconoff, Peter
Dolezal, Brian J.
Duino, Russell
Durnbaugh, Linda
Edmonson, James
Eiben, Christopher J.*
Erdey, Nancy*
Farnham, Eleanor
Ferroni, Charles D.
Fertel, Eileen
Fischer, Scott
Ford, Amasa*
Freer, Frederick S.
Fugita, Stephen S.
Gaines, Ervin J.
Garfinkel, Stanley
Gerstner, Patsy
Gibans, Nina
Goetz, Heidi
Goodwin, Shawn*
Goretta, Laura*
Gorn, Cathy
Grabowski, Diane Ewart
Grabowski, John J.
Graham, Martin F.
Grant, H. Roger
Greppin, John
Grossberg, Michael
Haddad, Gladys
Halasa, Joyce*
Hall, Maria
Hamerla, Rich*
Hammack, David C.*
Hannibal, Joe*
Harris, Jill
Harrison, Dennis I.*
Hategan, Vasile
Hatfield, Thomas P.*

Hauserman, Martin
Hehr, Russell
Herrick, Clay
Higgins, Bette Lou*
Hoagland, Dorothy
Hruby, Frank
Hudson, Jean
Jackle, Robert C.
Janice, Christina
Jaquay, Robert
Johannesen, Eric
Johnson, Becky*
Johnston, Chris
Jones, Adrienne
Jones, Robert L.
Kabalan, Said S.
Karipides, Kathryn*
Kastner, Christine K.
Kelling, Amy
Kelly, Karen
Kipel, Vitaut
Klein, Richard
Klyver, Richard
Kollar, Mary Ellen
Kolson, Kenneth
Koozer, Sandra
Kosman, George
Kotrba, Karen
Krosel, Christine
Krumholz, Norman
Krzywicki, Marianne
Kuby, Donald J.
Kulchytsky, George P.
Kusmer, Kenneth
Landau, Earl
Lavelle, Kenneth
Laverty, Harriett
Lawler, Patrick
Lawson, Ellen*
Leahy, John A.
Lee, Nancy A.
Leonard, Henry
Linke, Daniel
Loranth, Alice

Lupold, Harry
Lutz, Evelyn
Maciuszko, Jerzy*
Mack, Wayne
Mansfield, Herbert H.
Manthey, Ethel
Marley, Wendy
Marsalek, Daniel E.
Masek, Linda
Maxwell, Marilyn J.
McCormick, Michael
McCracken, Martha G.
McNally, Edith
McTighe, Michael
Mercer, Patricia
Metzger, Lynn
Meyer, Jimmy E.W.*
Miggins, Edward M.
Miller, Carol Poh*
Miller, Craig S.
Miller, Genevieve
Miller, Ivan
Miller, Michael A.
Milner, Zelda
Morgenstern, Michael*
Morton, Marian J.
Mossbrook, Joe*
Musgrave, Tina
Nelson, Paul
Owen, Charles
Palermo, Anthony
Paley, Liz
Papp, Susan
Pappas, Thomas
Pauly, Dorothy R.
Perry, Richard
Pershey, Edward J.
Peters, Frances
Pfenninger, Allen
Pike, Kermit J.
Poole, Sarah
Porter, Roderick Boyd
Prpic, George J.

Psuik, Robert
Rarick, Holly M.
Reisman, Ellen
Reznik, Claudia
Rhoades, Camille
Richardson, James F.
Rodgers, Elizabeth G.
Rodis, Themistocles
Rolik, Drew*
Rose, Kenneth*
Rose, Mark H.
Rosenblum, Evy*
Rosenblum, Lou*
Ross, David
Ross, Hugh
Rothstein, Jane*
Ruksenas, Algis
Ryan, Patrick*
Sabo, Gerald
Salgia, Tansukh
Sande, Theodore A.
Sanders, James W.
Sanko, Helene
Scharf, Lois
Schickler, Mildred J.
Schuld, Fred N.
Shaland, Irene*
Shelley, James
Sherrill, Charles
Shoup, Debbie
Sibley, Willis
Sidley, John David
Siney, Marion
Singer, Geoffrey A.
Sinnema, John R.
Solotko, Leslie Ann
Sords, Virginia A.
Sparrow, James
Spittler, Ernest
Stapleton, Darwin
Stark, Barbara
Stark, William*
Stavish, Mary Ellen

Stavish, Mary B.*
Steirer, Michael D.
Strasmyer, Robert
Susel, Rudolph M.
Swierenga, Robert P.
Szabo, Stephen
Szaniszlo, Elaine M.
Tanaka, Henry T.
Thrower, Glennis
Tipka, Donald
Toman, James A.*
Topp, Walter
Traks, Andreas
Tussey, Jean Y.
Tuve, Jeanette
Ubbelohde, Carl*
Vacha, John*
Valencic, Joseph*
Van Aken, William R.
Van Tassel, David D.
Vasilakes, Michael
Venkateswaran, Uma
Vourlojianis, George*
Wallen, Harold E.
Weber, Marc
Weeks, Phillip
Weiner, Ronald
Wells, Michael
Wertheim, Sally
Weymueller, Carl
Wheeler, Robert
Williams, John
Williams Morgan, Regennia*
Wilmer, Kathryn
Wing, Marie
Wollons, Roberta
Wood, James M.
Worthington, Edward W.
Wright, Richard
Wyatt-Brown, Bertram
Young, Dallas
Zentos, Nicholas J.
Zwolak, Loretta

# The
# Entries

# Readers' Guide

**Entry Structure.** The entries in this volume are designed to indicate the importance of the person's role in the growth and development of Greater Cleveland and to provide certain basic information about each. In almost all cases this includes full birth and death dates; place of birth; names of parents; educational background; name of spouse; children's names; and place of burial. The club or organization affiliations given with various biographees are not to be considered complete—rather, they represent those organizations in which the individual served as an officer or in which he/she played a founding or prominent role. Similarly, only the most significant awards or honors given to any biographee have been selected and listed.

**Cross-Referencing.** Within each entry we have capitalized the names of individuals who are the subject of other entries in the volume. We have also capitalized the names of organ-izations and events that constitute entries in the companion volume, *The Encyclopedia of Cleveland History* (second edition, 1996). In this latter instance we have followed each capitalized term with a "dagger" (†) to clearly distinguish the fact that the entry is not located in the volume at hand. In both instances, capitalization replaces the more standard "q.v." notation. A comprehensive index provides access to personal names (including those of living individu-als), events, organizational names, and major subject areas found within the entries.

**Bibliographic Citations.** Bibliographic citations are provided to direct the reader to other sources, both published and manuscript, relating to the subject of an entry. Citations for books and articles are given in short title form to save space. Provision of a bibliographic citation with any entry does not necessarily indicate that the resource was used in the writingof the entry. Several abbreviations relating to local libraries and archives have been used in the bibliographic citations. These include CPL (Cleveland Public Library), CWRU (Case Western Reserve University), CSU (Cleveland State University), and WRHS (Western Reserve Historical Society).

**Style.** In order to conserve space, we have made several deviations from standard style. This includes using European date citation and the abbreviation of both terms and names. Similarly, numbers are given in figures rather than being spelled out.

**Author Credits.** In the instances where an entry represents the work of a single writer, that person's initials follow the entry. A key to authors' initials is provided in the listing of authors elsewhere in the front matter. Entries without initials represent the work of several authors.

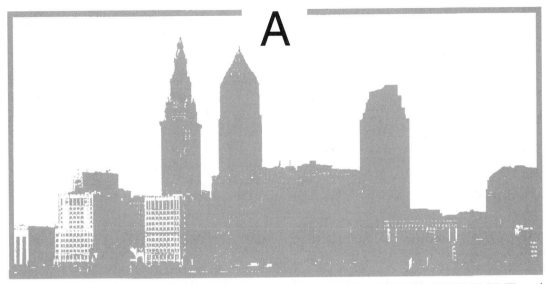

**ACKLEY, HORACE A.** (Aug. 1810–26 Apr. 1859) was a surgeon, the first local physician to use ether in surgery, and a founder of the Cleveland Medical College, now the medical school of CASE WESTERN RESERVE UNIV.† Born in Genesee County, NY, he attended lectures at the College of Physicians & Surgeons of the Western District of the State of New York from 1833–34, a student of JOHN DELAMATER and classmate of JOHN LANG CASSELS.

After being licensed in 1834, Ackley moved to Akron, OH, in 1835, then to Toledo, and in 1839 to Cleveland. He performed the first ether-assisted operation in the WESTERN RESERVE† only 3 months after it was first publicly demonstrated in Boston in 1847. By 1850 Ackley confined his practice to surgery, becoming so well known that in 1855 Stephen A. Douglas had him operate on his throat, removing his uvula. In addition to his practice, Ackley worked at Cleveland's City Hospital and U.S. Marine Hospital and helped found the Northern Ohio Insane Asylum in Newburg in 1851.

Ackley demonstrated anatomy at Willoughby Medical College from 1835 to 1842 when, due to a dispute among the faculty, he and Drs. Cassels, Delamater, and JARED POTTER KIRTLAND left, founding the Cleveland Medical College under the charter of Western Reserve Univ. Ackley taught surgery and conducted clinics in surgery and medicine until his resignation in 1856.

Ackley was a member and warden of Trinity Church. In 1837 he married Sophia Howell of Willoughby. They had a son, Horace Hall Ackley (1846–1905). Ackley, first buried at Erie St. Cemetery, was reinterred at Lake View Cemetery in 1915.

**ADAMS, ALMEDA C.** (26 Feb. 1865–8 Sept. 1949) overcame sightlessness to help found the CLEVELAND MUSIC SCHOOL SETTLEMENT and achieve a long career as a teacher, author, and lecturer. Born in Cohernton, PA, to James and Katherine (Ketchum) Adams, Almeda lost her sight at the age of 6 months and was educated at the State School for the Blind in Columbus. Her father's calling as an itinerant preacher led her to homes in Tiffin, Toledo, and Columbus. As a reward in a contest in which she sold 2,000 subscriptions to the *Ladies' Home Journal,* Adams completed her education with 2 years at the New England Conservatory of Music in Boston, which had to be pressured by the magazine into accepting a blind pupil. She then taught piano and voice at the Univ. of Nebraska.

Returning to Cleveland in 1901, Adams taught music in local social settlements such as HIRAM HOUSE, where she directed an annual operetta for 10 years. A suggestion from her father led her to secure the assistance of ADELLA PRENTISS HUGHES and the FORTNIGHTLY MUSICAL CLUB† to establish the Cleveland Music School Settlement in 1912. She made the first of three European tours in 1926 as chaperone for a voice student. As a result, she wrote a book in the form of letters to friends at home, *Seeing Europe Through Sightless Eyes* (1929). In it she described her reactions to the continent's great art, much of which had been allowed to handle by such museums as that of the Vatican. From 1918 to 1931, Adams organized and directed the Schumann Society, a choral group for working girls. Never married and survived by only a cousin, she continued teaching and lecturing to within a year of her death. Adams was buried in Lake View Cemetery.

**ADAMS, SEYMOUR WEBSTER** (1 Aug. 1815–27 Sept. 1864), pastor (1846–64) of Cleveland's FIRST BAPTIST CHURCH,† was born in Vernon, NY. His father, a farmer, was a deacon in the Baptist church, and his mother was a niece of Noah Webster. Adams decided on the ministry as a youth, attending Hamilton Theological Seminary after graduating from Hamilton College. Ordained in 1843, Adams served in 3 churches in New York before accepting First Baptist's second call to him, serving there from Nov. 1846 until his death. Adams was a carefully prepared sermonizer and an active pastor who oversaw the growth of First Baptist and the new congregations that spun off from it. He was perceived by his contemporaries as scholarly, shy, and retiring, yet an example of moral rectitude and high purpose to his fellow citizens so potent that he was still mourned 50 years after his death. During 1858–59, he wrote a memoir of Dr. Nathaniel Kendrick, founder of the Hamilton Theological Seminary.

Adams married 3 times: first to Caroline E. Griggs, who died in 1847; then in 1849 to Mrs. Cordelia C. Peck, a widow, who died in 1852; and finally to Augusta Hoyt in 1855. In the summer of 1864, he joined other volunteers of the U.S. Christian Commission in nursing Union soldiers in Washington, DC, where he contracted a fatal case of typhoid.

———

Bishop, J. P. *Memoir of Rev. Seymour W. Adams, D.D.* (1866).

**ADDAMS, GEORGE STANTON** (23 Feb. 1869–15 Apr. 1933) was juvenile court judge in Cleveland from 1905–26; during these years he was prominent in making the juvenile court the central coordinating organ for dependent and delinquent youth services. His efforts served as a model throughout Ohio and the entire U.S. Addams was born in Conotton, OH. He earned a B.A. from Oberlin College in 1890 and an LL.B. from Cincinnati Law School in 1892. After a year as clerk of the Ohio legislature, he set up private practice in Cleveland, where he lived the remainder of his life. He was an associate of TOM L. JOHNSON, and when Johnson became mayor in 1901, Addams served as assistant director of Cleveland's law department under NEWTON D. BAKER. He wrote the bills that eliminated sheriff fees and created police powers of juvenile probation officers. He led the reform campaign behind the 1913 Ohio Child Welfare Code that mandated juvenile courts in every county and strengthened Mother's Pensions. In 1913 Addams presided over the National Conference on Charities and Correction and wrote an essay, "Recent Progress in Training Delinquent Children," for the U.S. Bureau of Education. He created a detention home for Cleveland's children in 1906 and later established Cleveland's Child Guidance Clinic (see GUIDANCE CENTERS†). Addams insisted on the cooperation of all child welfare

agencies in Cuyahoga County and worked to make the juvenile court the center of this network. He served as the Cuyahoga County Probate Court judge from 1926–33.

Addams married Florence Farrand and had 2 sons, Carl and Stanton. He died in Atlantic City, NJ, but was buried in Cleveland.—P.R.

**ADDISON, HIRAM M.** (21 Nov. 1818–14 Jan. 1898) was an early Cleveland settler, educator, and reformer. He was born to the pioneer Western Reserve family of William and Hannah Addison in EUCLID,† educated in local schools, and began teaching in eastern Ohio and western Pennsylvania, where he achieved a considerable reputation as an educator. He married Anna McCaslin, one of his pupils, in Pennsylvania in 1844 and moved first to Warrensville, settling in Cleveland in 1856. Addison ventured into journalism, writing for the *Ohio Farmer* in the 1850s. He founded, edited, or was associated with several ill-fated newspapers before the Civil War, including the *American Advertiser,* the *Temperance Banner,* the *Harpoon* (a temperance paper), and the *Cleveland Commercial.* Addison was interested in various social causes, particularly ABOLITIONISM† and the plight of poor urban children, to the extent that he was known as "Father Addison." In 1874 he began his summer Fresh Air Camp in Warrensville Twp. for indigent city children, hoping to influence them through exposure to nature, and organized recreation to strive for higher goals than their backgrounds allowed, an idea that was copied and continues as a part of urban social work today. In 1879 Addison founded the EARLY SETTLERS ASSN. OF THE WESTERN RESERVE.† He also originated the idea for erecting the log cabin on PUBLIC SQUARE† that became a focal point of the city's centennial festivities. Addison and his wife had no children. He was buried in Woodland Cemetery.

**ADOMEIT, GEORGE GUSTAV** (15 Jan. 1879–22 Nov. 1967) was a prominent Cleveland businessman, artist, and founder of the CLEVELAND SOCIETY OF ARTISTS.† Adomeit was born in Memel, Germany, the son of George and Anna (Glozat) Adomeit. His family moved to Cleveland when he was 3. In 1887, when his parents bought a forested home in Woodland Hills, Adomeit became interested in drawing. In 1894 Adomeit won a competition for a 4-year scholarship to the Cleveland School of Art, where he attended Saturday classes until graduating from high school. While at the Cleveland School of Art, Adomeit secured an apprenticeship in lithography, afterwards becoming head of the school's photoengraving shop.

In 1902 Adomeit and W. H. Webster bought the

Mason Engraving Co., renaming it the Caxton Engraving Co. and growing in one year from 5 to 25 employees. Incorporating as Caxton Co., Printers & Engravers, in 1905, by the 1920s they were one of the 5 outstanding printing concerns in the country. In 1925 Adomeit became an honorary member of the Society of Calligraphers based on his accomplishments in the graphic arts. Adomeit was president and art director of the Caxton Co. from 1937 until his retirement in 1956.

Adomeit was a founder of the Cleveland Society of Artists. His paintings and drawings were exhibited at 40 consecutive MAY SHOWS,† winning 24 awards, and in major art galleries, including the CLEVELAND MUSEUM OF ART.† In 1932 his painting "Hills of Ohio" was one of 46 gathered from various regions of the U.S. to showcase contemporary American painting.

Adomeit and his wife, Ida Von Den Steinen, are buried at Lake View Cemetery. They are survived by a daughter, Ruth.

**AIKEN, SAMUEL CLARK** (21 Sept. 1791–1 Jan. 1879), the first resident pastor of Cleveland's FIRST PRESBYTERIAN (OLD STONE) CHURCH,† was one of the most prominent clergymen in the city in the mid-19th century. Born in Windham, VT, the son of Nathaniel and Betsy (Clark) Aiken, he entered Middlebury College in 1813 and then studied for the ministry at the Andover Theological Seminary. Ordained as a Presbyterian pastor in Utica, NY, in 1818, Aiken followed some of his flock to Cleveland in 1835, accepting their call to the pastorate of First Presbyterian, which he guided until 1861 with his commanding presence and conservative outlook. While Millerism, Mormonism, Universalism, skepticism, and the debate over slavery threatened the solidarity of many churches, Aiken's church, while debating these issues, with one exception did not divide over them.

Besides pastoring his church, Aiken was active in the affairs of Cleveland. He presided at the organizational meeting of the Cleveland YMCA (1854), and his addresses on topics such as theaters, public education, CRIME,† and TEMPERANCE† were important opinion pieces. A supporter of public improvements, Aiken spoke at the opening of the Erie Canal. He also preached a well-publicized sermon to Gov. Reuben Wood and other notables on the importance of railroad improvements in Ohio (1851). Aiken's denunciation of slavery before the 1857 Presbyterian General Assembly, meeting in Cleveland, helped the church on a national level decide that accommodation on slavery was no longer possible.

Aiken was married twice; his first wife, Deliah Day, whom he married in 1818, died in 1838. They had 7 children: Samuel C., Deliah, Henry, Helen, Henrietta, and 2 others who died in infancy. Aiken's second marriage was in 1839 to Deliah's sister, Henrietta Day. They had 2 children, Helen and Charles. He died at his home on Woodland Ave. and is buried in Erie St. Cemetery.

*Annals of the First Presbyterian Church of Cleveland, 1820–1895* (1895).

**AKRAM, WALI A.** (4 Aug. 1904–1 Aug. 1994) was the founder of First Cleveland Mosque, the first official home to Muslims in Cleveland. He remained its imam for 52 years.

Born Walter Gregg to Clarence and Leah Brown Gregg in Bryan, TX, he completed his general education and then studied electrical engineering at Prairie View State College in Texas. He attended Lane Seminary in Nashville, TN, but while there became interested in Islam. Moving to St. Louis, MO, in 1923 he converted to Islam, adopted his Islamic name, and began teaching Arabic.

On 25 July 1925 he married Kraeema, the former Hannah Dudley. They raised 13 children: Mahmoud, Ali, Rasoul, Ahmad, Khalid, Abdullah, Ameer, Hussain, Maryam, Khadija, Kamelah, Nurah, and Mubarka.

In Cleveland in 1925, he became involved with visiting Muslim missionaries, and when they departed, he became de facto leader of the city's fledgling Muslim community.

First Cleveland Mosque was established in 1937, with Akram as imam. Originally located at 7605 Woodland Ave., the mosque moved several times; it was at 3615 East 131 St. in 1995.

Akram continued teaching Arabic, and in 1946 produced the volume *Arabic Made Easy*. In 1957 he made the first of two pilgrimages to Mecca. His second trip came in 1986. From 1947 to 1962 he operated the Akram Family Store next to the mosque on Woodland Ave. Besides his devotion to Islam, Akram retained his interest in engineering, and liked tinkering with various inventions.

Akram became imam emeritus in 1989. He is buried in Cleveland's Evergreen Cemetery.—J.T.

**ALBL, MICHAEL ALBERT** (8 Oct. 1869–19 Feb. 1944) was a doctor prominent in Cleveland's CZECH† community. He was born in Cleveland and was one of six sons of Michael and Katherine (Peck) Albl. His father, who arrived in the U.S. in 1850, was well known in the Czech community of Cleveland, especially due to his involvement in numerous organizations.

Michael Albert Albl was educated at Cleveland public schools, including CENTRAL HIGH SCHOOL.† He graduated from the School of Pharmacy of Western Reserve Univ. in 1888, and from Western Reserve Univ.'s medical school in 1892. He began practicing medicine that same year. Albl had a combined office and residence at 5074 Broadway, directly opposite ST. ALEXIS HOSPITAL,† for many years. His brothers all had either offices or stores along this section of Broadway.

Albl was on the consulting staff and was vice chief of staff at St. Alexis Hospital, the same hospital where he took his internship. He remained associated with the hospital for 52 years, until his death. He also served as a director of the Crescent Realty Co. He belonged to several medical and fraternal organizations and was known as a devotee of hunting and fishing.

Michael Albl married Francis Stadnik in Cleveland on 25 Aug. 1892. They had three children: Frances Waugh, Oswald M. Albl, and Jasmine Soetga Gadke. Albl died in Cleveland.—D.R.

**ALBRITTON, DAVID** (13 April 1913–14 May 1994) made his mark as a high jumper in the Olympic Games and as a pioneering African American in the Ohio General Assembly. He was born in Danville, AL, which was also the home town of JESSE OWENS, the son of Peter and Josephine Albritton. Like Owens, Albritton was raised in Cleveland and became a track star at EAST TECHNICAL HIGH SCHOOL.† He also accompanied Owens to Ohio State Univ. and the 1936 Olympic Games in Berlin. During tryouts for the latter he and teammate Cornelius Johnson tied for a world record of 6' 9½" in the high jump. In Berlin, however, Albritton finished 2nd to Johnson for a silver medal. In the early 1940s he became an industrial arts teacher and athletic coach at Dunbar High School in Dayton, OH. His teams won 3 state titles, and Albritton himself won or tied for 7 AAU outdoor titles in a personal track career lasting until 1950. From 1954–57, Albritton worked for the U.S. State Dept., setting up athletic programs in Iran, Iraq, Pakistan, and Turkey. He also operated an insurance agency in Dayton, and in 1960 won election as a Republican to the Ohio House of Representatives. Named to chair the House Interstate Cooperation Committee in 1969, Albritton was the first African American in Ohio history to head a house committee. He was a member of the National Track and Field Hall of Fame, the Ohio Sport Hall of Fame, and the Ohio State Athletic Hall of Fame. Albritton married Margaret Ann Holliday in 1937. He died in Dayton, survived by a son, David II.—J.V.

**ALBURN, WILFRED HENRY** (20 April 1877–9 Sept. 1952) was an author, editor, publisher, journalist, and historian. With his wife, Miriam, he wrote a 4-volume history, *This Cleveland of Ours* (1933) (see HISTORIES OF CLEVELAND†). Alburn was born in Lawrence County, PA, to John Frederick and Cecelia Luebben Alburn. He grew up in Youngstown, OH, and graduated from Rayen High School. In 1902 he graduated from Adelbert College, Western Reserve Univ. (WRU, see CASE WESTERN RESERVE UNIV.†). Alburn then worked for the *PLAIN DEALER,†* first as a reporter, then as Sunday editor, and finally as editorial writer. In 1910 he joined the staff of the *Boston Traveler.* On 17 May 1911, Alburn married Miriam Russell of Cleveland; they had 2 children, David and Miriam. In 1914, while living in New York, the couple founded the Alburn Bureau, an independent, nonpartisan syndicate that provided editorial services for subscribing daily papers. The Alburns moved to ROCKY RIVER† in 1917 and expanded the enterprise from their home, located first on Frazier Dr. and later on West Lake Ave. The bureau distributed articles and commentary on world and domestic affairs, features, and human-interest editorials 3 times a week to papers in over 120 cities. The bureau's client papers had a combined circulation of over 1.6 million. Alburn retired from the Alburn Bureau toward the end of his life due to illness. Miriam Alburn continued the bureau until selling it in 1956. Wilfred Alburn, who wrote the words to "Dear Old Reserve," WRU's alma mater, died in Cleveland.

**ALEXANDER, WILLIAM HARRY** (10 Nov. 1916–24 Aug. 1988) served as president and co-publisher of the *CLEVELAND CALL & POST†* (1981–88) and presided over the board of the REGIONAL TRANSIT AUTHORITY† (RTA, 1979–84). A Washington, DC, native, son of William and Mary Alexander, he came to Cleveland in 1935 to work single-handedly as the circulation department for the *Call and Post,* then a new weekly newspaper, directed toward and run by AFRICAN AMERICANS†. He claimed to have delivered papers to distributors by streetcar. By 1979, he was the growing paper's business manager and corporate secretary. Under Alexander's presidency, the *Call and Post* expanded to Dayton, Youngstown, Warren, and Akron; it became known for mentoring other black newspaper workers.

Alexander was appointed to the RTA board in 1975 and made vice-president in 1976. As board president, he was a controversial figure, condemning the media and holding closed-door meetings. In 1981 he charged the RTA with excluding African American firms in the awarding of contracts. He continued to serve on the board after his presidency (1984–87); he was next appointed to the board of the Northeast Ohio Regional Sewer District.

Alexander was married twice. His first marriage was in 1942 to Marion Mills; they divorced in 1965. They had 3 children: Carlos, Anthony, and Marilyn. His second marriage was to Ethel Stewart. He died in St. Luke's Hospital of a heart attack and was buried in Highland Park Cemetery.—J.M.

**ALGER, HENRY** (30 Oct. 1789–2 April 1862) and his family were the first permanent settlers in the part of Rockport Twp. which became LAKE-WOOD† and were the earliest settlers to travel over the Indian path that became Detroit Ave.

Born in Warren, CT, Henry was the eldest son of Nathan and Prescilla (Peet) Alger. The Algers moved to Ohio, settling in Rockport on 7 June 1812. Traveling westward along one Indian trail (Detroit Rd.), the Algers turned south at another Indian trail (Warren Rd.). Settling in the area south of Madison Ave., the Algers founded what became known as the Alger settlement, a tract of land on Warren Rd. south of Detroit Ave., in sections 12–13 of Rockport Twp.

The Algers built a 13' x 15' log cabin. When Nathan Alger died in 1813, Henry became head of the family. In April 1819, Henry represented his household at the first election in Rockport Twp., in which he was elected a trustee. Alger's history of the early Rockport settlement, *The First Settlement of Rockport up to 1821*, was first published in the *Cleveland Morning Leader* in 1858.

Alger married Susan Nichols. Their daughter, Philana, was the first white girl born in Rockport. An Episcopalian, Alger is buried in Alger Cemetery. There is a street in Lakewood named for the Alger family.—T.B.

**ALI-BEY, OMAR** (17 Oct. 1954–3 Sept. 1994), a leader in Cleveland's African American community, was an example of how a person can convert a life of crime into one of social service.

Born Harold Iverson in Cleveland, son of Harold McBride and Louise Iverson, he attended local schools, but dropped out before graduation. In 1972 he moved to Chicago, IL, where he became involved in street gang culture. In 1973, facing a jail sentence, he opted to enlist in the U.S. Army, but his life further deteriorated. He became a heroin addict and served time in the army stockade.

In 1979 Iverson returned to Cleveland. In 1981, to support his addiction, he was involved in a robbery. Seeking to elude police capture, he was seriously injured in an automobile crash. The near-fatal accident prompted a decision to change his life. He converted to Islam and adopted his Muslim name in 1982.

On 16 Jan. 1983 he married Linda Perry (Kalima), and they had 3 children: son Mandela,

and daughters Jamilah and Zafirah. Ali-Bey also had another son, Bilal, by a previous union.

Ali-Bey resumed his schooling at CUYAHOGA COMMUNITY COLLEGE† and DYKE COL-LEGE,† where he earned a degree in marketing. He also became an activist in the African American community.

Through the Coalition for a Better Life, he campaigned to improve conditions in the city's subsidized housing tracts. His efforts were aimed at both physical conditions and at making the environment safer and drug-free. A gifted speaker, he worked with youths, helping them see the dangers of drugs and gang involvement. His work to help the community was acknowledged by the Cleveland chapter of the Southern Christian Leadership Conference in 1990, and again in 1993 by the caucus of Black Elected Democrats of Cleveland.

Ali-Bey is buried in Evergreen Cemetery in Cleveland.—J.T.

**ALLEN, DUDLEY PETER** (25 Mar. 1852–6 Jan. 1915) was one of the founders of the CLEVELAND MEDICAL LIBRARY ASSN.† and an eminent surgeon and professor. Born in Kinsman, OH, the son of Dudley Allen and grandson of PETER ALLEN, both doctors, in 1862 he went to Oberlin to study, receiving his A.B. in 1875 and his M.D. from Harvard Medical School in 1879. He settled in Cleveland in 1883.

Allen was one of the first Cleveland physicians to confine his practice to surgery. He wrote articles on surgery and medical ethics, and a history of medicine in the WESTERN RESERVE.† Allen taught surgery at Western Reserve Medical College from 1884–90, became Professor of Principles & Practice of Surgery in 1893, Professor Emeritus of Surgery in 1910, and Senior Professor of Surgery in 1911.

A connoisseur of fine arts and an expert in Chinese porcelain, Allen was one of the first trustees of the CLEVELAND MUSEUM OF ART.† Oberlin, where he was a trustee from 1898 until his death, honored him with an M.A. in 1883 and an LL.D. in 1908. Allen was a founder of the Cleveland Medical Library Assn. in 1894, served as president from 1903–06, and donated his entire library upon his retirement. The Allen Memorial Library building was a gift of his widow, Elisabeth Severance Prentiss, whom he married on 4 Aug. 1894. They had no children. Allen was also active in the Second Presbyterian Church. In 1910 he resigned all his positions and retired from practice.

Allen Memorial Library Archives.

**ALLEN, FLORENCE ELLINWOOD** (23 Mar. 1884–12 Sept. 1966) was a jurist whose career marked a series of firsts for women. Born in Salt Lake City, UT, to Clarence Emir and Corrine M. (Tuckerman) Allen, she majored in music at WRU from 1900–04, studying piano from 1904–06 in Berlin while also working as a music journalist. After a nerve injury ended her music career, she returned to Cleveland as the *PLAIN DEALER's*† music critic and a teacher at LAUREL SCHOOL.† Law became her main interest; she received an M.A. in political science and constitutional law from WRU in 1908.

Rejected by WRU's law school because of her sex, Allen attended the Univ. of Chicago (1909–10) and New York Univ. (1911–13), and after receiving her law degree was admitted to the Ohio bar in 1914. Allen was an ardent suffragist and successfully defended women's municipal suffrage before the Ohio Supreme Court in 1917.

Allen's career marked firsts for women: her appointment as asst. county prosecutor in 1919; her election as common pleas court judge in 1920, and as Ohio Supreme Court judge in 1922 and 1928; and her appointment by Pres. Roosevelt as Judge of the U.S. 6th Circuit Court of Appeals in 1934. Presidents Roosevelt and Eisenhower both considered her for a Supreme Court appointment. In 1958 Allen became the first woman chief judge of any federal court, the 6th Circuit. She retired in 1959.

Allen wrote *This Constitution of Ours* (1940), *The Treaty as an Instrument of Legislation* (1952), and her autobiography, *To Do Justly* (1965). She spoke on human rights, cultural relations, and international law. Never married, Allen died in Cleveland and is buried in Waite Hill Cemetery.

Tuve, Jeanette. *First Lady of the Law* (1984).
Florence E. Allen Papers, WRHS.

**ALLEN, JOHN W.** (1802–5 Oct. 1887) was a railroad developer, lawyer, editor, and mayor of Cleveland from 1841–43. Born in Litchfield, CT, to John and Ursula (McCuroy) Allen, he graduated from Harvard in 1825 and came to Cleveland in 1826 to study law under Judge Samuel Cowles. In 1828 he married Anna Marie Perkins, who died a few months later. Allen married Harriet C. Mather in 1830; they had 3 children: James, William, and Louisa.

In 1831 Allen became editor of the Whig's *CLEVELAND ADVERTISER.†* From 1832–42 he directed the COMMERCIAL BANK OF LAKE ERIE.† He funded various railroad ventures: the CLEVELAND & NEWBURGH RAILROAD† in 1834; the Columbus & Cincinnati Railroad in 1835; and the Ohio Railroad Co., which failed during the Panic of 1837. He was president of the CLEVELAND INSURANCE CO.† and in 1849

became president of the Society for Savings. He assisted in the incorporation of the Trinity (Episcopalian) Parish of Cleveland in 1828 and was vestryman and warden of the parish. In 1933 he incorporated the CLEVELAND LYCEUM.†

Allen's public career began in 1828, when he petitioned Congress for aid to build a harbor in Cleveland. In 1832 he established the city's first board of health during the CHOLERA EPIDEMIC.† From 1831–35 he was president of the village of Cleveland's Board of Trustees. He was elected to the Ohio senate in 1835, and beginning in 1836 served 2 terms in Congress. In 1841 Allen became Cleveland's fourth mayor. Eventually he became a Republican. In 1879 he helped form the EARLY SETTLERS' ASSN.† of Cuyahoga County. Allen died in Cleveland and is buried in the Erie St. Cemetery.

**ALLEN, PETER** (1 July 1787–1 Sept. 1864) was a prominent doctor in the WESTERN RESERVE.† Born in Norwich, CT, he obtained a preliminary education at the Norwich Academy, where he later taught for 2 years. He received his medical education under Dr. Phineas Tracy in Norwich. In 1838 he received an honorary degree from Jefferson College. He married Charity Dudley on 13 May 1813. Their only child, Dudley Allen, succeeded his father in his practice.

Allen began practice in the Kinsman, OH, area in 1808. In 1812 he was appointed surgeon in the Western Army under Gen. Simon Perkins and served in the campaign on the Maumee River. He was censor at the Medical College in Willoughby and later at the Cleveland Medical College. In 1835 he was elected the first president of the Ohio Medical Convention, which later fostered the Ohio State Medical Society, of which he was president in 1856.

Dr. Allen's practice at one time covered 12 townships in northeastern Ohio and western Pennsylvania. In addition to the general practice of medicine, he performed various surgical operations, including ligation of the femoral artery for aneurysm; tracheotomies; amputations of the leg, thigh, arm, and shoulder joint; and operations for strangulated hernia and removal of tumors. These were performed without the use of an anesthetic. Before the establishment of medical schools, Allen usually had 3 or 4 students studying under him. His saddlebags and their contents are exhibited at the HOWARD DITTRICK MUSEUM OF HISTORICAL MEDICINE† in Cleveland. Allen died at the family home in Kinsman, OH, and is buried at the Kinsman Cemetery.

**ALLYNE, EDMUND E.** (25 Dec. 1874–18 Aug. 1961), prominent in the foundry industry and in automotive and refrigeration development, was born in Cleveland, the son of Joseph H. and Anna M. (Wightman) Allyne and attended public schools. After five years with the Ohio National Guard, 1893–98, he organized and operated Allyne Bros. Foundry, 1900–09, selling it in order to form the Aluminum Castings Co., which adopted production methods to make aluminum castings in large quantity, sufficient to supply castings for Liberty airplane engines during World War I. The company, with plants in six states, became one of the largest in the country. He and Daniel Ryan also founded the Allyne-Ryan Foundry Co. in 1913 to produce gray iron castings. After resigning as president of Aluminum Castings in 1920, Allyne organized the Allyne-Zirk Co. to market a lubrication system for automobiles he had developed, selling it to the Alemite Co. in 1924. Interested in refrigeration, Allyne developed a refrigerator unit that used kerosene instead of electricity, which he patented in 1932. It was manufactured by Midland Steel Products Co. of Cleveland. He organized Allyne Laboratories, Inc. in early 1935 with Walter Guzik as his chief engineer and designed a refrigerator cabinet to house the mechanism. Sears, Roebuck and Co. marketed Allyne's household refrigerator under the trade name "Coldspot" to homeowners without electricity.

Allyne married Mildred M. Ford 14 May 1902, and they had three children: sons Rollin Ford and Edmund E. Jr., and daughter Mrs. Vernon Stolte. A resident of UNIV. HTS.,† he died in Cleveland and was buried at Lake View Cemetery.—M.S.

**AMBLER, HENRY LOVEJOY** (10 Sept. 1843–14 June 1924) earned distinction as a practitioner, teacher, and historian of dentistry. Born in Medina, he received an M.S. from Hillsdale College in Michigan before graduating from the Ohio College of Dental Surgery in Cincinnati, earning an M.D. from Cleveland's Western College of Homeopathic Medicine in 1868. He began lecturing on oral surgery at the latter school while establishing a dental practice in Cleveland. He moved to New Hampshire in 1886 but returned 6 years later to become Professor of Operative Dentistry at the Dental College of Western Reserve Univ. (see CASE WESTERN RESERVE UNIV.†). Ambler served as dean of the dental school from 1893–1906, a period marked by deteriorating relations with the university's medical school, possibly due to Ambler's background in homeopathy. During his tenure the dental school moved into separate quarters from the medical school and saw its students closed out of the latter's science courses and labs. Ambler resigned at the time that the dental school was sold to a private operator. More successful as a dental innovator, Ambler invented several

dental instruments and wrote a book on *Tin Foil and Its Combinations for Filling Teeth* (1897). A global trip resulted in another book, *Around the World in Dentistry* (1910). Noted for his scholarship, Ambler produced a *History of Dentistry in Cleveland, Ohio* (1911) and served for 21 years as Critic of the Cleveland Dental Society, becoming the arbiter on the pronunciation of terms and historical facts. Following the death of his first wife, Annie Jenness Ambler, he married Juliet A. Ambler. Ambler was buried in Lake View Cemetery.—J.V.

Henry Lovejoy Ambler Papers, Dittrick Museum of Medical History.

**AMBLER, NATHAN HARDY** (Sept. 1824–19 Nov. 1888), dentist in California and Ohio and purveyor of lucrative real estate deals, bought property on the Cleveland city limits and resold it as the city pushed outward. A millionaire, he once owned much of AMBLER HEIGHTS.† Born in Huntington, VT, to Selah and Charlotte Caswell Ambler, Ambler began to study DENTISTRY† in 1841. He joined the California Gold Rush in 1849 and amassed a small fortune as a dentist there (he was paid in gold dust) before opening a practice in Cleveland (1852). Ambler's Cleveland office was first located on the corner of Erie (E. 9th) and Bond (E. 6th) streets, and later in the Northrup & Harrington building on Superior Ave. One of a family of dentists, Ambler trained his nephew, HENRY LOVEJOY AMBLER, who practiced for a time with his uncle (1866–68). In 1868 Nathan Ambler turned to real estate full-time.

He married Martha S. Buell on 4 July 1845. Their home, called Rock Rest, sat on a hill between the present Fairhill Blvd. and Cedar Ave. (at the later site of the Baldwin Filtration Plant). With partner Daniel O. Caswell (1857–1906), Ambler developed a water cure establishment, the BLUE ROCK SPRING HOUSE† (see HYDROTHERAPY†). Childless (a daughter died as a toddler), the Amblers made Daniel Caswell, Jr., their heir. Ambler is buried in Lake View Cemetery. In 1894 Martha Ambler donated 25 acres to the city of Cleveland for Ambler Park.—J.M.

Henry Lovejoy Ambler Papers, Dittrick Museum of Medical History.

**AMES, LYDIA MAY** (1863–1 Oct. 1946) was a distinguished landscape painter and one of Cleveland's first woman artists. Born in NEWBURGH,† she was the daughter of Ashley Ames, who operated a livery service. May Ames (as she was known) studied art in New York and Cleveland, graduating from the Cleveland School of Art (see CLEVE-

LAND INSTITUTE OF ART†) in 1900 with a major in pictorial art. She taught for 27 years at the School of Art, where she became recognized as an authority on the history and development of art. Oil landscapes were her own medium, in which she specialized in postcard-sized miniatures and earned the title of "Cleveland's first impressionist painter." Her work was chosen for the inaugural exhibit in a 5th-floor gallery opened in the Lindner Coy department store in Aug. 1925 (see STERLING-LINDNER CO.†). Ames also exhibited in New York, Philadelphia, Buffalo, Detroit, and Mansfield, OH. At one time she was the only woman member of the New York Art Club. She also belonged to a group of Ohio-born women painters who annually sent out a traveling exhibition of their work across the state. For the last 20 years of her life, May Ames owned her own studio, where she continued teaching classes. She lived on Miles Ave., and scenes from nearby GARFIELD PARK† constituted one of her favorite subjects. Unmarried, Ames was preceded in death by only a few months by her sister, Sara, a Cleveland librarian.—J.V.

**ANDORN, SIDNEY IGNATIUS** (25 Sept. 1906–25 Sept. 1981), worked in newspapers, radio, and television during a journalism career spanning over 50 years. Born in Newark, OH, he moved to Cleveland in 1912. After graduating from Western Reserve Univ. with a degree in English, he joined the *CLEVELAND PRESS†* in 1929, soon writing Cleveland's first gossip column, "The Minute Review." In 1935 Andorn moved to radio, doing a gossip program for WGAR.† Over the next 15 years he also did news commentaries and a ground–breaking "Open Forum" program, in which listeners phoned in questions on civic issues to experts in the studio. In 1944 he won a commendation for his coverage of the EAST OHIO GAS CO. EXPLOSION AND FIRE.†

Andorn entered television in 1950 as program director for WXEL (later WJW†). Later in his career he returned to Channel 8 as host of the "Cleveland Caucus" civic affairs program. Andorn wrote a column for the *CLEVELAND NEWS†* from 1954 until its demise in 1960, when he returned to WGAR, doing news commentaries and the "Open Forum." A City Club member, he instituted its summer outdoor debates in the Cleveland Public Library's Eastman Garden. He also taught broadcast journalism and mass communications at CUYAHOGA COMMUNITY COLLEGE.† Late in his career, Andorn's news commentaries were heard over WCLV-FM† and his newspaper column appeared in the Sun suburban chain. Andorn was married to Jessie Brown Semple on 13 Aug. 1938. He died in CLEVELAND HTS.† and was survived

by his second wife, the former Miriam Cramer, and a daughter, Dr. Anne Andorn.

**ANDREWS, SAMUEL** (10 Feb. 1836–15 Apr. 1904) was a poor English immigrant who became a pioneer in the oil industry and cofounder of the STANDARD OIL CO.† Born in Oaksey, England, a candlemaker by trade with little formal education, Andrews arrived in Cleveland in 1857. In 1859 he married Mary Cole; they had six children: Charlotte, Lillian, Bertha-Belle, Mary, Horace, and John. By 1859 he was an assistant to Chas. A. Dean, an oil supplier who refined lard oil and manufactured coal oil from cannel coal. With Andrews's help, Dean's company became the first in Cleveland to refine kerosene from crude oil. Understanding the commercial possibilities of kerosene, in 1863 Andrews decided to establish his own production company, Andrews, Clark & Co., convincing Maurice B. Clark and JOHN D. ROCKEFELLER to provide financial support. With Andrews's practical knowledge and Rockefeller's financial handling, the firm grew quickly, increasing production and taking on new partners. In 1870 it became the Standard Oil Co., with Andrews as works superintendent. Andrews often disagreed with Rockefeller and sold his interest in Standard Oil to Rockefeller in the spring of 1874 for $1 million. Andrews's fortune helped support several educational institutions in Cleveland, helping build BROOKS MILITARY SCHOOL† in 1875. He served as a trustee of Adelbert College of Western Reserve Univ., and was also a member of the Erie St. Baptist Church. Andrews used his fortune to build one of the city's largest mansions. Known as ANDREWS'S FOLLY,† it was inefficient and costly to maintain and was razed in 1923. Andrews died in Atlantic City, NJ, and is buried at Lake View Cemetery.

**ANDREWS, SHERLOCK JAMES** (17 Nov. 1801–11 Feb. 1880), one of Cleveland's first lawyers, was considered the father of the Cleveland Bar. Andrews was born in Wallingford, CT, the son of John and Abigail Andrews. After graduating with high honors from Union College in 1821, Andrews studied law at New Haven Law School. He came to Cleveland in 1825, forming a law partnership with Judge Samuel Cowles until Cowles's retirement in 1832; then working with JOHN A. FOOTE and JAS. M. HOYT (Andrews, Foote & Hoyt). He was elected president of Cleveland's first city council in 1836 and served as the prosecuting attorney for Cuyahoga County.

In 1840 Andrews was elected to the U.S. House of Representatives, retiring after a single term due to poor health. Returning to his law practice still in poor health, he pleaded only important cases. The Ohio General Assembly appointed Andrews to the Cuyahoga County Superior Court in 1848. The next year, he was a leading member of the Ohio Constitutional Convention. Since the new constitution abolished the superior courts, Andrews again returned to his practice. He also served as president of the Merchants Bank and the Society for Savings. In 1873, when another convention was called to revise the Ohio constitution, Andrews was elected as a delegate and head of the Cleveland district delegation, receiving both the Republican and Democratic nominations. Andrews married Ursula Allen of Litchfield, CT, in 1828. Her father, John Allen, was a member of Congress. The Andrewses had 11 children, 5 of whom, Sarah, Ursula, Harriet, Cornelia, and William, survived to adulthood. Andrews died in Cleveland and was buried in Lake View Cemetery.

**ANDRICA, THEODORE** (9 Aug. 1900–1 Mar. 1990) chronicled the affairs of Cleveland's diverse ethnic population for 46 years as Nationalities Editor of the *CLEVELAND PRESS.†* Born in Radna, Romania, he emigrated to the U.S. in 1920. He began writing nationality news for the *Canton Daily News* before being hired in 1927 by the new editor of the *Press,* LOUIS B. SELTZER, to cover the same beat in Cleveland. With Seltzer's encouragement, Andrica literally invented the field of "ethnic journalism." Naturalized in 1928, he married Mary P. Patrilla of Cleveland the following year. In pursuit of material for his "Around the World in Cleveland" column, he conversed in 6 languages and claimed to have attended an estimated 14,000 banquets. Affectionately dubbed the "Broken-English Editor" by his colleagues, he promoted a series of All-Nations exhibitions in PUBLIC AUDITORIUM† and in 1932 sold Seltzer on the idea of sending him on annual visits to the homelands of their readers. He took thousands of messages, culled from mail-in coupons printed in the *Press* before his departure, from Clevelanders to their relatives in Central and Eastern Europe. After World War II and a year at Harvard in 1943 on a Nieman Fellowship, Andrica resumed his European tours in 1945. Expelled by the Communist government of his native Romania, he chartered a jetliner to fly tons of clothing from Clevelanders to refugee camps in Austria following the 1956 Hungarian uprising. Retiring from the *Press* in 1973, Andrica edited a Romanian quarterly and authored *Romanian Americans and Their Communities of Cleveland* in 1977.—J.V.

Theodore Andrica Papers, WRHS.

**ANISFIELD, JOHN** (5 Mar. 1860–22 Apr. 1929), successful clothing manufacturer and real-estate executive, was a leader in the Fed. of Jewish Charities and active in other civic and Jewish communal organizations. He was born in Cracow, in what was then Austria, son of Isaiah and Amelia Anisfield. He was educated in the public schools of Europe, studying engineering. Arriving in America in 1876, Anisfield settled in Cleveland to work for his uncle, Dr. Jas. Horowitz, a partner in the D. Black Cloak Co. Anisfield worked there for 6 years, attaining the position of manager. In 1882 he started his own cloakmaking business, employing 700 workers at his factory at E. 22nd St. and Superior by the early 1900s. In 1909 he erected the Anisfield Bldg. at E. 9th St. and Huron. Anisfield also served as president of the Garfield Realty, Anisfield Realty, and Broadway-Hamm companies.

Although he became active in Jewish communal organizations late in life, Anisfield held many high offices, including president of MT. SINAI HOSPITAL,† the Jewish Orphan Home, and the HEBREW FREE LOAN ASSN.† At the time of his death, he was treasurer of the Fed. of Jewish Charities and one of 2 Jews appointed to the Committee on Benevolent Assns. of the Chamber of Commerce. Anisfield was married twice. In 1886 he married Daniela Guttenberg of Vienna, who died 10 years later. In 1904 he married Alice Strauss, the daughter of Adolph Strauss, an influential Jewish leader in New York. Anisfield had a daughter, Edith, by his first marriage. He died in New York City and is buried in Mayfield Jewish Cemetery.

**ARBUTHNOT, MAY HILL** (27 Aug. 1884–2 Oct. 1969) was a nationally known educator and author on early childhood education and children's books. Born May Hill in Mason City, IA, to Frank and Mary E. (Seville) Hill, she received a B.A. from the Univ. of Chicago in 1922 and an M.A. from Columbia Univ. in 1924. Her first teaching experiences were at the State Teachers College in Superior, WI, and the Ethical Culture School in New York City. In 1922 she came to Cleveland as principal of the Cleveland Kindergarten–Primary Training School, later part of Western Reserve Univ., where she was associate professor of education until her retirement in 1946. Arbuthnot wrote articles for *Parents,* the *National Education Assn. Journal,* and *Elementary English Review,* while also editing *Childhood Education.* She gave lectures on education and children's books into her eighties. Two of her many books, *Children and Books* and *The Arbuthnot Anthology of Children's Literature,* remained standard texts in children's literature long after her death. Among her other books were *Time for Fairy Tales* (1952), *Time for True Tales* (1953), and *Children's Books Too*

*Good to Miss* (1948). She co-authored a series of reading texts for the Scott-Foresman Co., and in 1969 the company established a lectureship at CASE WESTERN RESERVE UNIV.† in her honor. Arbuthnot received an honorary Litt.D. degree from WRU in 1961 and the Constance Lindsey Skinner Award for Children's Literature in 1959. May Hill married Chas. Arbuthnot, chairman of the Economics Department at WRU for 38 years, on 17 Dec. 1932. She died in CLEVELAND HTS.†

**ARMINGTON, RAYMOND Q.** (12 Jan. 1907–19 Apr. 1993) was an engineer and executive with the Euclid Rd. Machinery Co., a founder and chairman of the Webb-Triax Co., and headed numerous business, educational, and civic organizations.

Born in Wickliffe to George and Clara (Pritchard), Armington earned a bachelor's degree in industrial engineering from Ohio State Univ. (1928) and a law degree from Pepperdine Univ. (1932).

Armington worked from 1928–30 for two Akron rubber companies before joining his brothers in 1931 at the Armington Engineering Co., an outgrowth of a crane and hoist manufacturing firm founded by their father in 1899. In 1931 Armington Co. was absorbed by Euclid Rd. Machinery and Armington served as vice-president and general manager, 1937–51, and president, 1951–53. After General Motors Corp. acquired the company in 1953, Armington remained as general manager of the Euclid Division.

Armington left GM in 1960 to establish Triax Co. in Cleveland, serving as president, 1960–67, and chairman, 1967–77, when Triax became Webb-Triax. He also was chairman of Willoughby's Ranpak Corp. from 1972 until his death.

Armington was a director of numerous corporations, including Addressograph-Multigraph, Glidden, and White Motor Co. He was a trustee of CWRU, Univ. Circle Inc., Hiram House, Hawken School, and Lakeland Community College.

He received the first Free Enterprise Fellow Award from the Heritage Foundation, Washington, D.C., in 1984.

Armington married Elizabeth Rieley in 1932 (d. 1988). They had four children: Charles (deceased), George, Steven, and Linda. In 1990 he married Elizabeth Steck. Armington was a Presbyterian, lived in Willoughby, and is buried in Lake View Cemetery.—T.B.

**ARMSTRONG, WILLIAM W.** (18 Mar. 1833–21 Apr. 1905) was a local newspaper publisher and Democratic party political leader. He was born in New Lisbon, OH, and lived there until moving to Tiffin, OH, in 1854, where he bought and published a local newspaper. In 1857 he married Sarah Virginia Hedges; they had one daughter, Isabella. After serving as a registrar in the state treasurer's office in Columbus, Armstrong was elected secretary of state—the youngest man to hold that office in the history of Ohio (1862). He moved to Cleveland in 1865, bought the *PLAIN DEALER†*, and edited it until 1883. In 1868 he testified at the impeachment trial of Pres. Andrew Johnson. Armstrong served as a delegate to the Democratic Natl. Conventions in 1868, 1880, and 1884. He also served on the Democratic Natl. Committee. In 1881 he declined the nomination to run for governor of Ohio. In 1891 the Democratic party adopted his rooster design as the party symbol. Although often referred to as "Major" or "General," Armstrong never served in the military. The titles dated from his youth, when he was a member of a military organization for young boys. The fact that his father, Gen. John Armstrong, had been a military officer enhanced William's reputation of possessing a military background. Armstrong died at his home in Cleveland and was buried in Tiffin, OH.

**ARTER, CHARLES KINGSLEY** (24 Apr. 1875–22 Mar. 1957) was a senior partner in the Cleveland-based firm of ARTER & HADDEN,† founded in 1843 as Willey & Cary, the oldest law firm in Ohio.

Born in Cleveland to Frank and Eliza (Kingsley), Arter attended Cleveland public schools, graduating from Amherst College in 1898, and Harvard Law School in 1901. He was admitted to the Massachusetts bar in 1901, then returned to Cleveland where he was admitted to the Ohio bar and began his practice as a firm member of Smith, Taft & Arter.

Arter left Smith, Taft & Arter in 1918 to join the firm of Hoyt, Dustin, Kelley, McKeehan & Andrews. He turned down a federal judgeship in 1920 to continue his practice, specializing in corporation, bankruptcy, and labor law (representing employers). In 1929 Arter's name was added to the firm which became known as Dustin, McKeehan, Merrick, Arter & Stewart. In 1951 the firm merged with Andrews, Hadden & Putnam to create Arter, Hadden, Wykoff & Van Duzer. In 1969 the firm went simply by the name of Arter & Hadden.

Arter was a board of trustee member of St. Luke's Hospital, CHILDREN'S AID SOCIETY,† PHILLIS WHEATLEY ASSN.,† the Welfare Federation, the CLEVELAND MUSEUM OF NATURAL HISTORY,† and BALDWIN-WALLACE COLLEGE.† He was president of the Cleveland Chamber of Commerce (1935), vice-president of the Ohio Rubber Co., and director of the Land Title Guarantee & Trust Co.

Arter married Grace Denison in 1902. They had three children: Elizabeth, Charles Jr., and Calvin.

Arter was a Methodist and is buried in Lake View Cemetery.—T.B.

O'Hara, Janet. *Arter & Hadden, 1843–1993 Anniversary Book.*

**ARTHUR, ALFRED F.** (8 Oct. 1844–20 Nov. 1918) was a noted tenor, cornetist, conductor, educator, composer, and compiler. Son of Hamilton and Margaret (Hanna) Arthur, he was born in Pittsburgh and received his early training in Ashland, OH, and at the Boston Music School. Following further education in Europe and service in the Civil War (1861–65), he moved to Cleveland in 1871. He was active as a choral conductor, most notably with the CLEVELAND VOCAL SOCIETY,† which he founded in 1873 and conducted through 29 seasons. Arthur also conducted a short series of purely orchestral concerts at Brainard's Piano Rooms in 1872, which mark a real beginning for orchestral music in Cleveland. These programs included vocal solos, waltzes, and other light pieces by Strauss, along with overtures and parts or all of symphonies by Haydn, Beethoven, and Mendelssohn.

As an educator, Arthur founded the Cleveland School of Music (inc. 1875), to which he gave considerable attention and which continued under the management of Arthur's son until his death in 1938. As a composer, Arthur wrote a number of songs and 3 operas, *The Water Carrier* (1875), *The Roundheads and Cavaliers* (1878), and *Adaline* (1879), none of them published. He authored several technical studies and compiled 2 hymnals, *The Evangelical Hymnal* and *The Spirit of Praise*, as well as a popular choral collection, *Brainard's Choir Anthems* (1879). In 1871 Arthur married Kate Burnham. They had 3 children: a daughter, Ada, and 2 sons, Edwin and Alfred F. He died at his home in LAKEWOOD† and is buried in Woodland Cemetery.

**ARTL, JOSEPH A.** (31 Jan. 1893–23 June 1970) was one of Cuyahoga County's most respected public officials in a career spanning 4 decades. A product of Cleveland's Fleet Ave. neighborhood, he was the son of Bohemian immigrants, Mr. and Mrs. John Artl. After graduating from South High School, he worked as an accountant at the Newburgh Works of the American Steel & Wire Co. while attending Cleveland Law School (see CLEVELAND STATE UNIV.†). He received his law degree and was admitted to the bar in 1923. Artl was elected to CLEVELAND CITY COUNCIL† in 1932, serving as Democratic minority leader and briefly, in 1936, as council president. Although he withdrew from the 1935 mayoral election in the interest of party harmony, he was appointed in 1936 to Cleveland Municipal Court, where he presided for the next decade. In 1947 Artl was elected judge of the Common Pleas Court, where one of his most notable decisions was the issuance of an order in 1949 enjoining employees of the CLEVELAND TRANSIT SYSTEM† from continuing a work stoppage. Named the county's outstanding Democrat by the 33rd Ward Democratic Club in 1961, Artl was elected in 1963 to the 1st of 2 terms on the Ohio Court of Appeals (8th Dist.). He was married twice: in 1915 to Sadie Sue Minarik, who died in 1957; and in 1959 to Ethel Placek, a widow who predeceased him by a few months in 1970. Artl died in Cleveland, survived by sons Adelbert J., and Lawrence J., and stepdaughter Mrs. John Zuber. —J.V.

**ASHMUN, GEORGE COATES** (31 Jan. 1841–25 June 1929) became a distinguished medical professor and civic official while remaining one of Cleveland's most illustrious CIVIL WAR† veterans. Born to Russell Atwater and Maria (Wright) Ashmun and educated in Tallmadge, OH, he served as a musician in the 2ND OHIO VOLUNTEER CAVALRY† before being recruited for a special Ohio company assigned as personal bodyguard to President Abraham Lincoln. He served as lt. in that unit, where he was a highly visible participant in Lincoln's 2nd Inauguration. Following the war he earned a medical degree in 1873 from the Cleveland College of Medicine, where he became professor of children's diseases. After that institution merged in 1893 into Western Reserve Univ. (see CASE WESTERN RESERVE†), he served the latter institution as professor of hygiene and preventive medicine and professor of jurisprudence and medical ethics until retirement in 1925. Ashmun served Cleveland as a health officer in the 1880s, when he was credited with ridding the city of its backyard pig sties. He contributed several articles during the period to the *Cleveland Medical Gazette*. Ashmun also served for 2 terms on the city council and several on the Board of Education, including president in 1910. He served as a surgeon in the 5th Ohio Infantry during the SPANISH-AMERICAN WAR† and with the Case School unit of the Students Army Training Corps during WORLD WAR I.† Believed to be the last survivor of Lincoln's bodyguard unit, Ashmun was widely consulted by Civil War scholars and made local appearances at Lincoln Day observances. Married in 1880 to Laura J. Post (d. 1886) and then to Alice Ford in 1888, he left 4 children: Russell Ford, Louis Henry, George Slaght, and Bernice. He died at home in CLEVELAND HTS.† and was buried in Lake View Cemetery.—J.V.

**ATKINS (NUSBAUM) LARRY (LAWRENCE)** (3 Mar. 1903–24 July 1981) was a nationally known boxing matchmaker and fight promoter from the 1930s to the 1960s. Atkins was born in Cleveland to Michael and Fannie Pasternak Nusbaum. He attended East Tech and Glenville High School and was a batboy for the CLEVELAND INDIANS,† as well as a boyhood friend of Bob Hope. He studied at Ohio Business College and John Marshall Law School. In the early 1920s, he worked for the *CLEVELAND NEWS†* and *PLAIN DEALER†* sports departments. Moving to Chicago, he helped Frank Churchill promote prizefights. During a 3-year period, which included the second Tunney fight in 1927, Atkins was Jack Dempsey's personal press agent. Returning to Cleveland in 1929, Atkins began promoting fights in the city. When CLEVELAND MUNICIPAL STADIUM† opened, he became the public relations director and asst. matchmaker for the facility. He lived in St. Louis from 1936–39, but returned to Cleveland, joining the new boxing promotion firm headed by Bob Brickman. During the next 25 years, he promoted boxing matches for firms including Natl. Sports Enterprises, Cleveland Sports Promotion, and Buckeye Sports Enterprise. For 19 years he was the matchmaker for the News Christmas Toyshop Fund boxing show. Realizing that televised fights were damaging live boxing promotions, Atkins became a pioneer in lining up closed-circuit television for championship bouts. Married during the 1930s, Atkins was divorced by his wife, Molly. The couple had a daughter, Marcy. Atkins died in SHAKER HTS.† and is buried in Lansing Cemetery.

**ATKINSON, DR. WILLIAM HENRY** (23 Jan. 1815–2 April 1891), an early Cleveland dentist, was a pioneer in dental surgery and the first president of the American Dental Assn.

Born in Newtown, PA, to David and Mary (Margerum) Atkinson, William worked as a farmhand and tailor's apprentice. He began studying medicine in 1840 with Dr. William Woodruff in Meadville, PA. Atkinson received his M.D. from Willoughby Univ. (1847), and an honorary D.D.S. degree from the Ohio College of Dental Surgery (1859).

Atkinson practiced first in Meadville before moving to Norwalk, Ohio, where a traveling dentist inspired him to choose dentistry as a profession.

When Atkinson came to Cleveland in 1853, he was the first dentist to demand a higher standard of fees for dental surgery and place his services on the time basis. He is credited with a number of important methods used in dentistry. He reintroduced the hand mallet to condense gold fillings and designed new instruments to build contour fillings.

A student of microscopy and the natural sciences,

Atkinson was a tireless researcher and prolific writer who contributed substantially to dental literature. In 1857 Atkinson was present at the organizational meeting of the Northern Ohio Dental Assn. In 1860 Atkinson was elected as the first president of the American Dental Assn. at the first regular meeting in Washington, where the constitution and bylaws were adopted.

Atkinson married Martha Woodruff on 17 May 1840. They had eight children. Atkinson moved his practice to New York City in 1861. He died there and was buried in Woodlawn Cemetery.—T.B.

**ATWATER, AMZI** (23 May 1776–14 (22) June 1851) was employed by the CONNECTICUT LAND CO.† to help survey the Western Reserve in 1796 and 1797 and recorded the events of the undertaking in his journal.

Atwater, one of five children, was born in New Haven, CT, to Enos and Lois Atwater. After attending school briefly, Amzi worked as a hired hand to help support the family. In 1795 he lived with his uncle, Rev. Noah Atwater, in Westfield, MA, and learned the art of surveying. The following year he traveled to Canadaigua, NY, where he joined General MOSES CLEAVELAND's surveying party as an assistant in June 1796. On their way to survey the Western Reserve lands, Atwater was among the group of young men who demanded higher wages from Cleaveland, who instead offered them a township of land (Euclid) in the Reserve at a stipulated price. Atwater's 2-year journal gave a detailed description of the land and its suitability for farming as well as the daily working life of a surveyor in the wilderness. The Cleaveland party left the Reserve in Oct. 1796, and Atwater returned with the second party in the spring of 1797, this time as an asst. surveyor. In 1798 and 1799 he surveyed for the Holland Land Co. in western New York. The land in Euclid he had bought in 1796 proved to be of poor quality, and in 1800 he purchased land in Mantua, OH, and remained there for the rest of his life.

Atwater married Hulda Sheldon 21 Nov. 1801. They had a daughter, Cleona, born 4 Dec. 1802. After his wife's death in Oct. 1845, Atwater married Mrs. Rebecca Paine. Atwater died in Mantua at age 75. His second wife lived until Feb. 1854.—M.S.

Amzi Atwater Field Notes, 1797, WRHS.
Atwater Journal, WRHS.

**AUSTIN, SAMUEL** (16 June 1850–23 May 1936), founder of the AUSTIN CO.,† worldwide builder of factories and public buildings, was born in the village of Orton, Waterville, in England, the son of Thomas and Mary Austin. An apprentice carpenter and joiner in England, he came to Cleveland in 1872 where he practiced his trade, becoming an independent carpenter-contractor in 1878 and establishing a shop at Broadway and Gallup streets (4401 Broadway) about 1883. By the turn of the century, Austin was building manufacturing plants across northern Ohio and as far away as Chicago, including plants for CLEVELAND WORSTED MILLS† and CANFIELD OIL CO.† When his son, WILBERT J. AUSTIN, joined him in 1901 they formed a stock company, and 3 years later incorporated as the Samuel Austin & Son Co. with capital of $25,000, joining construction expertise with his son's engineering background. In 1913 the company constructed its general headquarters at Euclid Ave. and Noble Rd., and the firm officially became the Austin Co. on 11 Apr. 1916. Samuel Austin was president of the company from 1878 to 1924, when he became chairman of the board, a position he held until he died.

In 1874 he married Sarah Gynn. They had a son, Wilbert John Austin, and four daughters: Mrs. William Manchester, Mrs. Lillian Ferguson, Mrs. John Shimmon, and Mrs. Herbert Whiting. Two years after Sarah's death on 3 June 1933, Samuel married Louise Allen. Austin died at his residence in Willoughby and was buried at Lake View Cemetery.—M.S.

Shirk, Charles A. *The Austin Co.: A Century of Results,* WRHS.
Greif, Martin. *The New Industrial Landscape* (1978).

**AUSTIN, WILBERT JOHN** (2 Nov. 1876–4 Dec. 1940), a prominent engineer and builder, was one of five children born in Cleveland to Sarah Gynn and SAMUEL AUSTIN. After receiving a B.S. degree in engineering from Case Institute of Applied Science in 1899, he spent a year of travel and graduate work before joining his father to form the Samuel J. Austin & Son Co. in 1901. Wilbert persuaded his father to combine construction with his own design and engineering abilities in order to offer clients a full range of service for their entire projects. He was credited with originating the standard steel-frame factory building, forerunner of the prefabricated steel building. An aviation enthusiast, Austin developed a canopy door for airplane hangars which led to the company's leadership in the design and construction of airports and other air transport facilities. He succeeded his father as president of the AUSTIN CO.† in 1924 and initiated an intensified program of engineering research. Austin also was president of Advance Properties Co. and was a member of the first Board of Directors for the NATIONAL AIR RACES† in 1929.

Austin married Ida Stewart 13 Sept. 1903, and they had 3 children: Allan Stewart, Donald Gynn, and Margaret Louise (Mrs. Clarence Williams). He died in a commercial airline crash in Chicago and was buried in Cleveland's Lake View Cemetery. —M.S.

Shirk, Charles A. *The Austin Co.: A Century of Results,* WRHS.
Greif, Martin. *The New Industrial Landscape* (1978).

**AVERILL, HOWARD EARL** (21 May 1902–17 Aug. 1983), the "Earl of Snohomish," was centerfielder for the CLEVELAND INDIANS† from 1929–39, and a consistent .300 hitter during the 1930s. Averill was born in Snohomish, WA, completing 9 years of school and working at various jobs, from construction camps to sawmills. He married Gladys Loette Hyatt on 15 May 1922, and they had 4 sons: Earl D., Jr., who played in the major leagues from 1956–63, Howard, Bernie, and Lester.

Averill played for semi-pro teams in central Washington before signing with the San Francisco Seals of the Pacific Coast League in 1926. After 3 successful seasons, his playing contract was sold to Cleveland in 1928. In his first time at bat in the major leagues, he hit a home run. On 17 Sept. 1930, Averill hit 4 home runs in a doubleheader, 3 in the first game. He played in the first All-Star game in 1933 and in 4 later. His highest batting average was .378 in 1936, 2nd in the league. His lifetime home run total of 238 is the career record for an Indian. Averill was traded to Detroit in 1939 and completed his playing career in 1941 with Boston in the Natl. League, with a .318 lifetime batting average. After retiring from baseball, he operated a greenhouse and later owned a motel. In 1975 Averill was elected to the Baseball Hall of Fame at Cooperstown, NY. He died in Everett, WA.

**AVERY, ELROY MCKENDREE** (14 July 1844–1 Dec. 1935), author, historian, lecturer, scientist, and educator, was born in Erie, Monroe County, MI, to Caspar H. and Dorothy Putnam Avery. At 17, he volunteered as a private in the Civil War, also serving as a war correspondent for the *Detroit Daily Tribune*. Avery entered the Univ. of Michigan in Sept. 1867, earning his Ph.B degree in June 1871. He married educator Catherine Hitchcock Tilden on 2 July 1870. Soon after graduation, Avery was appointed superintendent of E. Cleveland (Ohio) schools, becoming principal of East High School in 1872, and principal of Cleveland Normal School in 1878.

Avery wrote high school textbooks on physical science, as well as several histories, including *Cleveland in a Nutshell* (1893), and *History of Cleveland and Its Environs* (3 vols., 1918). He served on city council (1891–92) and in the Ohio state senate (1893–97). He founded the Children's Fresh Air Camp in 1890, serving as its president for 13 terms, beginning in 1895. In 1905 Avery and 11 others studied the Cleveland public schools, making recommendations that were distributed throughout the country. He was founder and first president of the Western Reserve Chap. of the Sons of the American Revolution (chartered 5 May 1906). Avery received honorary degrees from the Univ. of Michigan (1874), Hillsdale College (1881), Wilberforce Univ. (1894), and Hillsdale College (1911). After Catherine died on 22 Dec. 1911, Avery married Ella Wilson on 15 June 1916; the couple had no children. They moved to Florida in 1919, where Avery died. He is buried in Knollwood Cemetery, Cleveland.

**AYERS, LEONARD PORTER** (15 Sept. 1879–29 Oct. 1946), nationally known educator, economist, and statistician, was vice-president and chief economist of the Cleveland Trust Bank for 26 years. Ayers, born in Niantic, CT, the son of Milan Church and Georgiana (Gall) Ayers, was educated in the public schools of Newton, MA. After graduating from Boston Univ. in 1902, he taught school in Puerto Rico, becoming superintendent of the island's school system in 1906. Returning to Boston, he earned a Ph.D. degree from Boston Univ. in 1910. He was made director of the Department of Education and Statistics at the Russell Sage Foundation in 1908, where he applied statistical methods to a number of educational studies, including the Education Survey of the Cleveland School System conducted under the auspices of the CLEVELAND FOUNDATION† from 1915–17. During World War I, Lt. Col. Ayers organized the Division of Statistics for the military.

Ayers joined the Cleveland Trust Co. (see AMERITRUST†) in 1920, where he edited the bank's "Business Bulletin." While there, he acquired a national reputation for his economic opinions and predictions through his writings. In his book, *The Economics of Recovery,* published in 1933, Ayers correctly assessed the severity of the Depression compared with past U.S. economic downturns. Reports in his Cleveland years included "The Automobile and Its Future" (1921) and "Business in Two War Periods" (1945). During his career, he published 7 books, numerous articles, and reports.

In 1940–42 Ayers returned to active service in the military as a brigadier general. In 1946 he died in Cleveland of a heart attack and was buried in Arlington National Cemetery.—M.S.

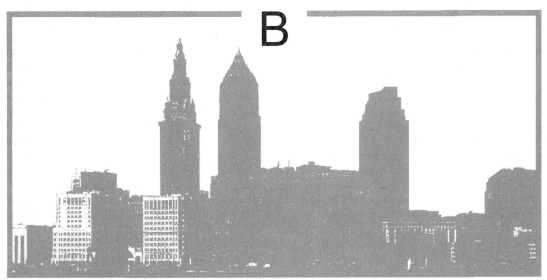

# B

**BABCOCK, BRENTON D.** (2 Oct. 1830–9 Jan. 1906) was an entrepreneur, mayor of Cleveland (1887–88), and founder of Cleveland's Scottish Rite Masonry. Born in Adams, NY, to William and Elvira (Gaylord) Babcock, he attended Adams Seminary and graduated from Watertown College, NY. In 1855 he became a clerk with the Erie Railroad Co. in Buffalo, coming to Cleveland in 1865 as a bookkeeper for Cross, Payne & Co., a local coal dealership. Staying in the coal industry, Babcock became a partner in Chard & Babcock in 1869; then in 1875 he became a traveling salesman for the firm of Tod, Morris & Co., which three years later became Babcock, Morris & Co. Babcock joined the Freemasons in 1859, rising to a 33rd degree Mason and becoming a member of the Supreme Council for the Northern Masonic Jurisdiction of the USA. He served as grand commander of the Knights Templar of Ohio, as well as the Oriental Commandery. He was high priest of the chapter, member of the Royal Order of Scotland, and founder of the Scottish Rite. The Democratic party nominated Babcock as its mayoral candidate to defeat Republican Wm. M. Bayne in 1886. As mayor, Babcock supported reorganizing the city government on the Federal Plan, but otherwise served only as a titular leader. On 6 Nov. 1867, Babcock married Elizabeth C. Smith (1837–1926) of Buffalo. They had no children. In 1900 the Babcocks donated several hundred volumes to the Adams Free Library, NY. The Babcock private library was donated to the Masonic Temple Assn. of Cleveland. Babcock died in Cleveland and was buried in Lake View Cemetery.

**BABIN, VICTOR** (13 Dec. 1908–1 Mar. 1972), pianist, composer, and teacher, was the director of the CLEVELAND INSTITUTE OF MUSIC† for 11 years. Born in Moscow, son of Heinrich and Rosalie (Wolk) Babin, he studied in Riga before studying composition with Franz Schrecker and piano with Artur Schnabel in Berlin at the Hochschule fur Musik. He came to the U.S. in 1937 and taught at the Aspen School of Music in Colorado, which he also directed; the Berkshire Music Festival at Tanglewood, MA; and the Cleveland Institute of Music, becoming director there in 1961. As director, Babin brought distinguished musicians to the CIM faculty, broadened the course offerings, and established a cooperative relationship between CASE WESTERN RESERVE UNIV.† and the Institute. He was made an adjunct professor at the university in 1969.

In 1933 Babin married another Schnabel student, Vitya Vronsky (see VICTORIA VRONSKY BABIN). They formed probably the best known duo-piano team of their day. Their U.S. premiere was in New York in 1937, and they continued an active concert and recording career throughout their married life. A planned European tour was canceled by Babin's death in 1972. Babin's compositions included concerti for 2 pianos and orchestra, chamber music, and songs. A song cycle, "Beloved Stranger," was set to texts by Witter Bynner. Babin was honored with the Cleveland Women's City Club Music Award and received an honorary doctorate from the Univ. of New Mexico. The Babins had no children.

Grossman, F. Karl. *A History of Music in Cleveland* (1972).

**BABIN, VICTORIA (VITYA) VRONSKY** (22 Aug. 1909–28 June 1992) was a distinguished pianist and teacher long associated with the CLEVELAND INSTITUTE OF MUSIC.† A native of Yevpatoria in the Russian Crimea, she was the daughter of Michel and Sophia Blinkoff Vronsky. Graduating from the Kiev Conservatory of Music at 15, she went to

Berlin to study piano under Artur Schnabel, whose students at the time also included another Russian, VICTOR BABIN. Vronsky appeared as soloist with the leading orchestras and conductors of Europe before marrying Babin in 1933 and becoming half of the piano duo of Vronsky and Babin. They toured and recorded extensively for the next quarter century, making their American debut in 1937. When Babin came to Cleveland as CIM director in 1961, Vronsky accompanied him as a member of the piano faculty and an artist in residence. Dividing their time between a summer home in New Mexico and a SHAKER HTS.† apartment, they maintained friendships with such artists and musicians as Marc Chagall, Darius Milhaud, and Igor Stravinsky. After Babin's death, Vronsky remained at CIM as Distinguished Professor of Piano and, from 1977–85, head of the Piano Dept. She began playing again in 1975, performing one of her husband's compositions with his successor as CIM director, Grant Johannesen. She was awarded the rank of Chevalier of the Order of Arts and Humanities by the French government in 1972 and served as a judge for the Robert Casadesus International Piano Competition (see CLEVELAND INTERNATIONAL PIANO COMPETITION†). With no children, she died in her Shaker Hts. apartment, leaving no survivors. —J.V.

BABKA, JOHN JOSEPH (16 Mar. 1884–22 Mar. 1937) was a leader in Cleveland's CZECH† community who served a single term in Congress. Born in old NEWBURGH,† he was the son of Bohemian immigrants Frank and Mary Babka. He completed his education at night while working in a foundry, graduating from Cleveland Law School (see CLEVELAND STATE UNIV.†) and being admitted to the bar in 1908. After serving as special counsel for the Ohio Attorney General in 1911–12, he became an asst. prosecuting attorney in Cuyahoga County from 1912–19. A Democrat, Babka was elected to the 66th Congress in 1918 and defeated for reelection in 1920. He also served as a delegate to Democratic National Conventions in 1920 and 1932. He became president of the League of Czech Democratic Clubs in 1934. He was appointed deputy superintendent of buildings and loans in 1935 to assist in liquidating the City Savings & Loan Co. Buried in Calvary Cemetery, Babka was survived by his wife and 3 children: Mrs. Virginia Tomasch, Mrs. Hortense Horak, and John J., Jr. His widow, Marie H. Babka, served as a member of the Ohio House of Representatives in the late 1940s and a member of the Electoral College in 1948. John J. Babka, Jr., was also a state representative in the early 1940s.—J.V.

BACHER, OTTO HENRY (31 May 1856–16 Aug. 1909) was one of Cleveland's first artists to travel to Europe and attain a national and international reputation. The Cleveland native was born on River St. near St. Clair Ave., son of Henry and Charlotte Bacher. He attended the Cleveland public schools. After working as a decorator of lake vessels and local mansions, he began art studies under De Scott Evans in 1874, and became one of the founders of the ART CLUB.† In company with fellow Clevelanders Willis Seaver Adams and Sion Wenban, Bacher left in 1878 for Europe, where he studied at the Royal Academy in Munich and with Cincinnati artist Frank Duveneck. Following Duveneck to Italy, he became a friend of James MacNeill Whistler, who printed some of his Venetian etchings on Bacher's press. Bacher was also highly regarded for his etchings, many of them depicting scenes from his early years in Cleveland. He returned to Cleveland twice in the 1880s, teaching at the Art Club and during the summer in Richfield, OH. He married a former Cleveland art student, Mary Holland, in 1888. By that time he had settled in New York City, where his paintings reflected the preoccupation with light embraced by the Impressionist movement. In 1908 he published *Whistler in Venice,* which appeared first as a serial in *The Century* magazine. Bacher died in Bronxville, NY, survived by his wife and 4 sons: Robert, Otto, Eugene, and Will.—J.V.

Sackerlotzky, Rotraud. *F. C. Gottwald and the Old Bohemians* (1993).

BACKUS, FRANKLIN THOMAS (6 May 1813–14 May 1870), a prominent Cleveland lawyer, was born in Lee, Berkshire County, MA, to Thomas and Rebecca (Couch) Backus. He was completely self-taught and was admitted as a junior-year student to Yale in 1834. In 1837 Backus came to Cleveland and opened a school for the classics. After studying law with the firm of Bolton Kelley, he was admitted to the bar in 1839, forming a law partnership with Jesse P. Bishop in 1840. In 1841 Backus was elected prosecuting attorney for Cuyahoga County, reelected in 1843. He was elected to the Ohio House of Representatives in 1846, and in 1848 became a state senator. In 1858 Backus, with 3 other prominent lawyers, RUFUS SPALDING, ALBERT G. RIDDLE, and Seneca O. Griswold, acted for the defense in the OBERLIN-WELLINGTON RESCUE† case. As a Republican, Backus ran unsuccessfully for the Ohio Supreme Court and the U.S. House of Representatives. In 1868 he ran as a Democrat for Congress and lost. Despite these losses, Backus was considered an excellent lawyer, with the Cleveland Bar stating he had "sound judgement, vigorous intellect and unsurpassed integrity." In 1869 Backus helped establish the Cleveland Law Library; after his death, his law books were donated there. He was also a founding member of the WESTERN RESERVE HISTORICAL SOCIETY.† In 1892 his wife, Lucy (Mygatt), whom he married in 1842, donated $50,000 to Western Reserve Univ. to found a law school named after her husband. Backus adopted his niece, Fanny, as his daughter. Backus died in Cleveland and was buried in Woodland Cemetery.

**BADGER, JOSEPH** (28 Feb. 1757–5 Apr. 1846), the first missionary sent to the WESTERN RESERVE† by the Connecticut Missionary Society and founder of the first Congregational church in the Western Reserve (in Austinburg), was one of the earliest clergymen in the area and, traditionally, preacher of the first sermon in Cleveland. Badger was born in Wilbraham, MA, to Henry and Mary Langdon Badger and after service in the Continental Army, worked as a weaver, but quit to attend Yale, graduating in 1785. Ordained a Congregational minister in 1786, Badger arrived in the Western Reserve in late 1800, after a 13-year career in a Massachusetts church, to serve both Congregationalists and Presbyterians under the Plan of Union, the first Congregational effort to cooperate with Presbyterians in missionary activities on the frontier. His wilderness travels gave him a knowledge of the frontier, which brought him to the attention of Wm. Henry Harrison and led to his appointment as a brigade chaplain during the War of 1812. He spent 35 years in the Western Reserve as a missionary and resident minister, organizing churches and schools. Interested in education, in 1801 Badger tried to secure a charter from the Territorial Assembly for a college, and in 1803 he sponsored the plans of the Erie Literary Society for an academy in Burton. Badger's retirement in 1825 was interrupted by another 8-year tenure as pastor of a new congregation. Badger was married in 1784 to Lois Noble (d. 1818). He married Abigail Ely in 1819. Badger had six children from his first marriage: Henry, Lucius, Joseph, Sarah, Juliana, and Lucia. He died in Perrysburg, OH, and was buried in the Fort Meigs Cemetery there.

Weimer, Gary Wilfred. *Man of God in New Connecticut* (Senior Thesis, Princeton Univ., 1966).
Badger, Joseph. *A Memoir of Joseph Badger* (ed. by Henry Noble Day, 1851).

**BADGLEY, SIDNEY R.** (28 May 1850–29 Apr. 1917) was a prominent church architect in the U.S. and Canada, active in Cleveland from 1887 until his death. Born at Ernestown, Ontario, Canada, son of William Edwin and Nancy Rose Badgley, he was educated at public schools and private academies in Canada and served as an apprentice in a Toronto architectural office. He came to Cleveland in 1887 and practiced under his own name and in partnership with Wm. Nicklas. Several churches and a former orphanage designed by Badgley were still extant in 1995, including the former Jones Home for Friendless Children (1903) at 3518 W. 25th St., the former Fourth Reformed Church (1909) at Woodbridge Ave. and W. 32nd St., the Lakewood United Methodist Church at 15700 Detroit Ave., and PILGRIM CONGREGATIONAL CHURCH† (1894) at W. 14th St. and Starkweather Ave. The Pilgrim Church is one of Badgley's finest structures and one of the first church buildings designed in the U.S. to function as both a religious and community-service center. Badgley's pioneering design was exhibited at the Paris Exposition of 1900. Badgley was a vice-president of the Equity Savings & Loan Co. He was married twice. His first marriage, to Alma A. Clark in 1872, ended with her death 2 years later. He married Charlotte J. Gilleland of St. Catherines, Ontario, on 21 Sept. 1876. They had no children. Badgley died at his home in Wickliffe and is buried in St. Catherines Cemetery.

**BAEHR, HERMANN C.** (16 Mar. 1866–4 Feb. 1942), a businessman and politician, served as county recorder (1904–09) and mayor of Cleveland (1910–12). He was an officer of the CLEVELAND-SANDUSKY BREWING CO.,† vice-president of the Forest City Savings & Loan, and a director of Cleveland Trust bank. Baehr was born in Keokuk, IA, the son of Jacob and Magdalena Zipf Baehr. His parents had lived in Cleveland from 1850–62 before moving to Iowa and returned here shortly after the Civil War. He was educated in public schools, quitting school at 14 to join his father's brewing company. He later attended Lehman's Scientific Academy at Worms-on-the-Rhine, and graduated from the First Scientific Station of New York in 1887. Baehr received an M.B. degree. After returning to Cleveland, Baehr was an official of the Baehr Brewing Co., which his father had founded, and became secretary and treasurer of the Cleveland-Sandusky Brewing Co. when it took over Baehr Brewing. He married Rose Schulte in 1898. Interested in Republican party politics, Baehr was elected county recorder, serving for 5 years, and defeated TOM L. JOHNSON for mayor in 1909. He declined to seek reelection in 1912, becoming first vice-president and director of the Forest City Savings & Trust Co. He became a director of the Cleveland Trust Bank (see AMERITRUST†) when it took over Forest City Savings. He was also president of the Langenau

Mfg. Co. Baehr had no children and died in Los Angeles, CA.

---

Hermann Baehr Papers, WRHS.

**BAER, ALICE DOROTHY** (2 Mar. 1911–24 Feb. 1993) was a publishing company executive and founder of Modern Curriculum Press of Cleveland.

Born in Coloma, MI, to George and Elizabeth Breidinger Lorenz, Baer attended Coloma elementary school and graduated from Coloma High School in 1929. She received her B.A. from Western Michigan Univ. in 1933 and her M.A. in mathematics from Loyola Univ., Chicago, graduating with honors, Kappa Rho Sigma, in 1939. She then taught high school in Chicago at Convent Sacred Heart, 1934–38 and Loretto High School, 1938–42.

From 1942–44 Baer worked as a civilian inspector in the U.S. Army Ordnance Department in Chicago, and later as a production planner for the Container Corp. of America, also in Chicago, from 1944–49.

Baer began working as a part-time editor at Reardon Baer & Co., her husband's publishing firm in Cleveland, and served as secretary from 1962–71. The company published a wide range of phonics educational materials used extensively in U.S. Catholic schools during the 1950s. In 1961 Baer founded Modern Curriculum Press, located at 13900 Prospect Road, Berea, to publish elementary school books and phonics materials for public schools. She continued to serve as company president after selling MCP to Esquire, Inc. in 1972, until her retirement in 1975.

Alice married Frederick William Baer on 14 May 1949. They had two children: Mary Alice and William Gerard. Baer, a Roman Catholic, is buried in St. Mary's Cemetery in Elyria, OH.—T.B.

**BAESEL, ALBERT E.** (1892–27 Sept. 1918) was 1 of 3 World War I soldiers from Ohio awarded the Congressional Medal of Honor. Albert, the son of Henry and Caroline Baesel, was born and raised in Berea. During World War I, 2nd Lt. Baesel was serving with the 148th Infantry Regiment, 37th Division, when he was killed on 27 Sept. 1918, while rescuing Cpl. Sterling S. Ryan near Ivoiry, France. A newly chartered American Legion post was named in Baesel's honor at a welcome-home celebration held in Berea 4 July 1919, and his posthumously awarded Congressional Medal of Honor was presented to his widow, Lydia Cole Baesel, on 23 Dec. 1922. Hastily buried during the war, Baesel's body was returned to the U.S. and reinterred in Woodvale Cemetery, Middleburg Hts., 11 April 1926.

**BAGE, HELEN** (29 Aug. 1901–26 July 1992) was one of the first women in the U.S. to own and operate a lighting-fixture manufacturing company—Bage Lighting Co., in Cleveland (est. 1940s). Born in Windber, PA, to Frank and Susan (Cheek) Bage, she moved with her family to Cleveland when a child. In the early 1920s she began working in the offices of Hinckley Lighting Co., where she later became office manager. Upon Hinckley's death, she opened her own company, part-time at first due to the metals shortages of World War II. While establishing her business, Bage also worked for Jack & Heintz (see LEAR SIEGLER, INC. POWER EQUIPMENT DIV.†). Bage Lighting Co., located first at E. 55th St., later on Chester Ave., and finally on Cedar Rd., eventually served the eastern U.S. Bage retired in 1977, after the company's building was leveled by fire.

In the 1920s and 1930s, Bage won several amateur tennis tournaments. A single woman, she lived in SHAKER HTS.† and gardened on her rural property in Hiram, OH. She belonged to the Shaker Hts. Republican Club and Plymouth Congregational Church (United Church of Christ). Bage is buried in Knollwood Cemetery in MAYFIELD HTS.†—J.M.

**BAILEY, REV. DR. HORACE CHARLES** (15 Aug. 1860–16 Feb. 1942) was the first pastor of ANTIOCH BAPTIST CHURCH† (1903–23) who led Antioch through a period of tremendous expansion, growth, and activity.

Born in Natchez, MS, to Nicholas and Mary (Hall) Bailey, Horace graduated from Natchez College, served several pastorates in the South, and did graduate work at the Univ. of Chicago. On 1 Mar. 1903, Bailey was installed as Antioch's pastor.

Bailey faced several problems, including sparse membership, a $17,000 debt, and the need for a permanent church home. An outstanding administrator and businessman, Bailey enlisted the aid of the CLEVELAND BAPTIST ASSN.† and JOHN D. ROCKEFELLER to build a new church at Central Ave. and E. 24th. Costing $16,000, the church was dedicated in Nov. 1905, 2 years after Bailey's arrival.

Bailey established the West Park Baptist Mission (which became the Second Calvary Baptist Church of LINNDALE†), and led the church in raising sufficient funds to clear its indebtedness. Church membership increased to about 1,200.

Bailey made Antioch a center of interracial activity by cooperating with Cleveland's white Baptists. In 1916 he was president of the NAACP, Cleveland branch. Bailey was president of the Independent Voters League, which supported Robert LaFollette in the 1924 national election, and sponsored meetings in Cleveland's black district. Bailey resigned in

1923 due to declining health. He returned as supply pastor, 1927–28.

Bailey married Sarah Mitchell (3rd wife) on 10 Aug. 1904. He had two children, Horace Jr. (d. 1936) and Lottie (Patterson). Bailey is buried in Lake View Cemetery.—T.B.

**BAKER, EDWARD MOSE (MAX)** (18 Aug. 1875–17 Feb. 1957), broker and philanthropist, was one of the founders of the Fed. of Jewish Charities. Born in Erie, PA, to Isaac and Bertha (Ernhorn) Baker, he received his bachelor's degree from the Univ. of Chicago in 1898, afterward studying philosophy, sociology, and for the rabbinate under his uncle, renowned Reform rabbi Emil Hirsch. Baker went to Temple Israel in Chicago in 1901, coming to Cleveland only 6 months later upon the death of his brother-in-law, Jacob Mayer, to take over Mayer's brokerage business. Before the year was over, he was elected vice-president of the Cleveland Stock Exchange, later serving 15 years as its president.

A product of both the Progressive Era and Reform Judaism, placing emphasis upon ethical monotheism and social reform, Baker believed the test of wealth was how it was used. He helped found several charitable and social-service agencies, including Associated Charities, the LEGAL AID SOCIETY,† and the Community Fund. In 1903 he cofounded the Fed. of Jewish Charities, serving as its first secretary, as president for four years, and on the Board of Trustees for 50 years. From 1907–08 he was chairman of the Republican Executive Committee for Cuyahoga County. In 1912 he was a founder and 1st vice-president of the CITY CLUB OF CLEVELAND,† subsequently serving as president. Baker argued that Judaism and Americanism were compatible, sharing similar principles, in "Judaism and the American Spirit," published in 1904 in *Arena* and later issued as a pamphlet. Never married, Baker died in Cleveland.

**BAKER, ELBERT H.** (25 July 1854–27 Sept. 1933) was the "fourth founder" of the *PLAIN DEALER.†* Born in Norwalk, OH, to Henry and Clara Maria (Hall) Baker, his family came to Cleveland in 1865, moving to Kansas City in 1870. Baker returned to Cleveland in 1873, working for the *CLEVELAND HERALD†* in 1877, moving to the *CLEVELAND LEADER†* in 1882. In 1897 Baker followed CHAS. E. KENNEDY to St. Louis to work for Joseph Pulitzer's *Post-Dispatch,* returning the following year to take over the *Plain Dealer* under a lease signed with owner LIBERTY E. HOLDEN. Kennedy assumed editorial control, while Baker became business manager. Baker's reforms included compiling reliable circulation figures and adopting uniform advertising rates. He and Kennedy also

eliminated partisan bias from news stories and expanded national and foreign news coverage.

When Kennedy withdrew in 1907, Baker also assumed editorial direction of the *Plain Dealer* as general manager. Baker personified the *Plain Dealer* and became an influential civic leader. He arranged the compromise that ended Cleveland's 10-year traction war under Mayor TOM L. JOHNSON, and later twice orchestrated settlements between the city and the EAST OHIO GAS CO.,† where he became chairman of the board in 1930. He was a director of the Associated Press and the American Newspaper Publishers' Assn., serving as president from 1912–14. Married in 1876 to Ida Smith, Baker had 2 daughters, Louise and Mary, and 3 sons, Frank, Elbert, and Alton. In partnership with 2 of his sons, he became co-publisher of 3 newspapers on the West Coast. Baker died in Cleveland and was buried in Lake View Cemetery.

Kennedy, Charles E. *Fifty Years of Cleveland* (1925).
Shaw, Archer H. *The Plain Dealer* (1942).

**BAKER, HENRY M.** (2 Jan. 1856–12 Aug. 1929), active in Jewish benevolent associations, was born in Erie, PA, the son of Kennard and Barbara Beitman Baker. He came to Cleveland in 1886, and after the turn of the century became involved in real estate. Baker was interested in progressive philanthropy, particularly as it related to the welfare of Jewish children, and he joined the COUNCIL EDUCATIONAL ALLIANCE† where he helped many boys and girls secure funds to develop their talents and found them employment. He served as president of the CEA for 10 years and was instrumental in establishing the Mt. Pleasant settlement house and in organizing Camp Alliance in 1924 to provide a summer program for the CEA children. The 25-acre camp, located adjacent to CAMP WISE† in Painesville, had a sliding scale of fees based on what a family could afford to pay. Baker himself spent time there to ensure that it was operated in the interests of the young campers it served. In 1930 the facility was renamed Camp Baker in his honor.

Baker was married to Sarah Mandelbaum, and they had two children, H. Clay and James M. A resident of CLEVELAND HTS.,† Baker died in Cleveland and was buried at Mayfield Cemetery. —M.S.

**BAKER, NEWTON DIEHL** (3 Dec. 1871–25 Dec. 1937) was mayor of Cleveland (1912–16) and secretary of war under Pres. Woodrow Wilson. Born in Martinsburg, WV, to Newton Diehl and Mary Ann Dukehart Baker, he graduated from Johns Hopkins Univ. in 1892, and received his law degree from Washington & Lee Univ. in 1894. He returned to

Martinsburg in 1897 to practice law before coming to Cleveland in 1899 to work in the law office of MARTIN FORAN. He was appointed asst. law director under Mayor TOM L. JOHNSON in 1902 and city solicitor in 1903. After Johnson's death, he became the leader of the county Democratic organization until 1924, remaining chairman of the County Central Committee until 1936.

Active in promoting municipal HOME RULE,† Baker helped write the 1912 Ohio constitutional amendment giving municipalities the right to govern themselves. As mayor, he was influential in selecting the commission to write Cleveland's first home rule charter, campaigning for its passage in 1913. He oversaw construction of a new municipal light plant (1914). Declining to run for a 3rd term as mayor in 1916, he retired to practice law, founding the law firm of Baker, Hostetler & Sidlo (see BAKER & HOSTETLER†).

Baker supported Woodrow Wilson in 1912; however he declined Wilson's offer to be secretary of the interior in 1913, preferring to remain Cleveland's mayor. Two months after his retirement in 1916, he accepted appointment as secretary of war in Wilson's cabinet. When the U.S. entered World War I, Baker was responsible for drafting, organizing, and outfitting an army of 2 million men as quickly as possible, and demobilizing the troops and negotiating the cancellation of war contracts when the war ended. Baker left Washington in the spring of 1921, returning to his law firm in Cleveland.

Baker championed the cause of the League of Nations. He also was active on many institutional, charitable, educational, and corporate boards and committees. He received the Cleveland Chamber of Commerce Medal for public service in 1927, and the U.S. Distinguished Service Medal in 1928. He authored *Why We Went to War* (1936). Baker married Elizabeth Wells Leopold in June 1902, and they had 3 children: Elizabeth (Mrs. John Phillips McGean), Newton D. Baker III, and Margaret (Mrs. Fulton Wright). Baker died in Cleveland.

---

Newton D. Baker Papers, WRHS.
Cramer, Clarence H. *Newton D. Baker* (1961).

**BAKER, WALTER C.** (27 June 1868–26 Apr. 1955), an engineer, helped found the American Ball Bearing Co. and developed automobile parts. Born in Hinsdale, NH, to George W. and Jeanette Rowene (Hall) Baker, the family came to Cleveland in 1871. Baker's father, an inventor, helped organize the White Sewing Machine Co. and the Cleveland Machine Screw Co., which Baker joined after graduating from Case School of Applied Science in 1891.

In 1895 Baker, John Grant, Rollin C. White, and F. Philip Dorn organized the American Ball Bearing Co. to produce axles for horse-drawn vehicles, but supplied the automobile industry by 1898. Baker was president from 1895–1918, when the firm and 13 others merged to form the Standard Parts Co., which Baker served as consulting engineer. Baker also developed a steering knuckle for front wheels and a full-floating rear axle, and introduced the left-handed steering system. Baker and Dorn built an electrically powered automobile in 1897, organized the Baker Motor Vehicle Co. in 1898, and advertised their $850 car as "the Most Elegant Automobile Made."

By 1905 annual production was 400 cars. A truck model was introduced in 1907. In June 1915, the company merged with the Rauch & Lang Carriage Co., forming the Baker, Rauch & Lang Co. The last Baker cars were produced in 1916; the company was sold to the Stevens-Duryea Co. in 1920. Walter Baker was vice-president of the car company until 1912, when he became supervisor of General Electric's Owen Magnetic Co.'s electric car construction.

Baker married Fannie Elizabeth White in 1891. They had two children, Elizabeth and Robert. Baker died in Cleveland and was cremated.

**BALDWIN, CHARLES CANDEE** (2 Dec. 1834–2 Feb. 1895) was a corporate lawyer, circuit judge, and founder of the WESTERN RESERVE HISTORICAL SOCIETY.† Born in Middletown, CT, to Seymour Wesley and Mary (Candee) Baldwin, he and his family moved to Elyria, but returned to Connecticut in 1847. Baldwin graduated from Wesleyan Univ. in 1855 and from Harvard Law School in 1857. That year he moved to Cleveland, was admitted to the Ohio Bar, and began working with Samuel B. and F. J. Prentiss, being made an equal partner in 1863. Over the years, he had successive partnerships with all 3 Prentiss brothers.

As a lawyer, Baldwin achieved expertise in corporate law. Despite ill health later in life, in 1884 Baldwin was elected to the first of 3 terms as a judge of the circuit court. Almost all his time was spent hearing appeals, with few of his decisions being overturned. Baldwin was civically active. In 1882 he was chiefly responsible for the funds raised to secure a site in Cleveland for Western Reserve College of Hudson. He was also active in the Library Assn., and from 1875–78 was president of the Cleveland Board of Underwriters. In 1867, with CHAS. WHITTLESEY, Baldwin organized what soon became the Western Reserve Historical Society, serving as secretary for many years and in 1886 succeeding Whittlesey as president, leaving his important cartographic collection to the WRHS. He authored many works on Ohio history and genealogy.

Baldwin married Caroline Prentiss in 1862 and had 4 children, two dying in infancy. The surviving children were Mary Candee (Sawyer) and SAMUEL P. BALDWIN. Baldwin was buried in Lake View Cemetery.

**BALDWIN, JOHN** (ca. 13 Oct. 1799–ca. 28 Dec. 1884) was a successful businessman and educator who used his wealth to promote righteous and intellectual living. Baldwin was born in North Branford, CT, the son of Joseph and Rosanna (Meloy) Baldwin. Although largely self-taught, he acquired enough academic training to hold several teaching positions. He and his bride came to the Berea area in 1828 to farm 200 acres of land he had purchased. About 1833, Baldwin discovered high-quality sandstone on his property, which he fashioned into a crude grindstone to sharpen tools and utensils. Baldwin leased his lands to others for the quarrying operations, and the income from the sandstone leases and the manufacture and sale of grindstones provided him with enough money to pay off his debts and to pursue his benevolent interests.

A believer in moral living, Baldwin donated land in June 1836 to establish the Lyceum Village—a utopian community and schools where a lifestyle of simplicity and self-denial was practiced. By 1839 the community had dwindled, and Baldwin assumed its debts and remaining assets. Still anxious to organize a school, he gave land to the North Ohio Conference of the Methodist Episcopal Church in 1845 to establish the Baldwin Institute as a coeducational preparatory school combining education and work experience for its students. Ten years later he underwrote the Institute's rechartering as Baldwin Univ., the predecessor of BALDWIN-WALLACE COLLEGE†. He also established schools in Baldwin, KS, Baldwin, LA, and Bangalore, India.

Baldwin married Mary Chapel in January 1828, and they had seven children: Milton, Rosanna, Hulda, Newton, John, Mary, and Martha. He died in Baldwin, LA.—M.S.

John Baldwin Papers, 1827–1902, WRHS.

**BALDWIN, LILLIAN LUVERNE** (1888–11 Sept. 1960) served the CLEVELAND PUBLIC SCHOOLS† for a quarter century as supervisor of music appreciation. She was born in Marion, IN, and received her undergraduate education at Glendale College. After teaching singing at Harcourt Place School in Gambier, OH, she returned to Glendale as an instructor and then went to New York to continue her studies at Columbia Univ., where she eventually earned B.S. and M.A. degrees. She had also been head of the vocal school at Hood College in Frederick, MD, before coming to Cleveland in 1929. Her principal duty with the Cleveland school system was to supervise the annual series of children's concerts on assignment with the CLEVELAND ORCHESTRA.† Working with associate conductor RUDOLPH RINGWALL, she would help plan the programs and then write study booklets for the 50,000 or more students who attended the concerts. Some of her study materials were published by the KULAS FOUNDATION† as *A Listener's Anthology of Music* (2 vols.) in 1946. Miss Baldwin resigned from her position in 1956, the same year that Ringwall was replaced as associate conductor by Robt. Shaw. Her departure was the culmination of an altercation with principal conductor GEORGE SZELL, who had criticized what he deemed the "trashy" nature of the children's concerts. Never married, Baldwin conducted workshops and lectured until her death in her CLEVELAND HTS.† apartment.—J.V.

**BALDWIN, NORMAN C.** (29 July 1802–12 June 1887), a prominent businessman and politician in Cleveland and OHIO CITY† during the mid–1800s, was born in Goshen, CT, to Stephen and Susannah (Adams) Baldwin. He came to Hudson at 15 and opened a general store there. His experience as a merchant led him, in 1829, to form a partnership with Noble H. Merwin in the produce commission business. Later he formed Giddings, Baldwin & Co., which owned one of the first and largest steamship lines on the lake, with a fleet of steamers and packets known as the Troy & Erie Line, moving goods, primarily wheat and passengers, from Portsmouth on the Ohio River, via the Ohio Canal to Lake Erie, and then to New York and the Erie Canal. Baldwin moved to Cleveland in 1830 and began developing land on the west side of the Cuyahoga River in Ohio City as a member of the Buffalo Land Co., formed in 1833 to drain and improve land for houses and factories. In 1836 he retired from the mercantile business to concentrate on real-estate speculation, at one time owning land in Cuyahoga, Summit, and Lucas counties with his brother, Frederick. Baldwin was elected a councilman in Ohio City's first election in 1836; from 1838–39 he was Ohio City's third mayor. In 1834 Baldwin became the first president of the Bank of Cleveland; running it until it closed in 1843. Baldwin moved from Ohio City to Cleveland, into a large house on Euclid Ave.

Baldwin married Mary H. Palmer in 1829 and had 9 children: Eliza, Mary, Norman A., Charlotte, Elizabeth, Henry P., N. C., Ellen, and Henry, who died in infancy. Baldwin died in Cleveland and was buried in Lake View Cemetery.

**BALDWIN, SAMUEL PRENTISS** (26 Oct. 1868–31 Dec. 1938) was a noted ornithologist, naturalist, and lawyer. He established the BALDWIN BIRD RESEARCH LABORATORY† and helped organize the CLEVELAND MUSEUM OF NATURAL HISTORY.† He was the leading expert on the house wren, a pioneer in bird banding, and an author of numerous monographs on birds.

Born in Cleveland to CHARLES C. BALDWIN and Caroline Sophia (Prentiss), Samuel received an A.B. (1892), A.M. (1894) and a D.Sc. (1932) from Dartmouth College, and an LL.B. (1895) from Western Reserve Univ. Admitted to the Ohio Bar, Baldwin practiced law until illness forced his retirement in 1902. He then entered business, becoming chairman of the Williamson Co. and president of the New Amsterdam Co.

In 1914 Baldwin founded and directed the Baldwin Bird Research Laboratory at Hillcrest, his GATES MILLS† estate, to study live wild birds. From 1914–19 Baldwin pioneered a method of bird banding, adopted by the U.S. Biological Survey, which enabled scientists to study the migratory habits of individual American birds. Baldwin developed the wrenograph and the potentiometer to study the house wren's temperature and to prove it a cold-blooded animal.

Baldwin's most significant contribution was studying the body temperature of birds and proving their reptilian ancestry. Baldwin was a biology research associate at Western Reserve U., and a trustee of the CLEVELAND MUSEUM OF NATURAL HISTORY.†

Baldwin married Lilian Converse Hanna on 15 Feb. 1898. They were childless. Baldwin, a Presbyterian, is buried in Lake View Cemetery.—T.B.

**BALDWIN, SAMUEL S.** (ca. 1776–12 July 1822), was an early Cleveland and Cuyahoga County public official. Born in Ridgefield, CT, to Samuel and Hannah (Northrup) Baldwin, he moved to a farm in NEWBURGH† in 1808 and dabbled in real estate with LEONARD CASE. Baldwin's short public career revolved around politics. In 1809 he was elected justice of the peace in Cleveland. In 1810 he became the first surveyor and may have been sheriff of Cuyahoga County. (Several sources indicate Smith S. Baldwin was the first sheriff.) As surveyor he relaid the road between Cleveland and Aurora, and from Mantua to Warren, as a state road. Sheriff Baldwin officiated at the murder trial and hanging of JOHN O'MIC. In 1812 he served in the state assembly. The next year, he was elected to the Board of County Commissioners and appointed by the board to act as clerk. Baldwin married Sarah Camp of Ridgefield, CT, who died in 1818 at the age of 36. They had 6 daughters and 2 sons. In 1819 Baldwin married Rhoda Boughton of Grafton, OH. They had 8 children: Philander, Lucretia, Caroline, Julia, Sarah, Emily, Henry, and Edward. Baldwin died in Cleveland but his burial site is unknown.

**BALL, ERNEST R.** (22 July 1878–3 May 1927), composed many popular songs from 1904–27. Born in Cleveland to Anna (Kocker) and Ernest Adelbert Ball, he studied at the Cleveland Conservatory before moving to New York, where he became a vaudeville pianist, and traveled throughout the U.S. Later, Litmark Music Publishing House hired him as a demonstrator and staff composer. Ball's first successful composition was "Will You Love Me in December As You Do in May?" which he wrote with Jas. J. Walker, later mayor of New York. He next composed musical scores for Broadway shows, including *Barry of Ballymore* (1910), *The Isle of Dreams* (1913), and *Heart of Paddy Whack* (1914) for Irish tenor Chauncey Olcott, with whom he collaborated. His other collaborators included Geo. Graff, Darl MacBoyle, J. Kiern Brennan, Arthur Penn, Annelu Burns, and David Reed.

Ball composed "Mother Machree," "When Irish Eyes Are Smiling," "A Little Bit of Heaven," "Dear Little Boy of Mine," and "Let the Rest of the World Go By." His ballad "Mother Machree" became associated with Irish tenors such as John McCormack. Ball also had a successful touring career as a singer of his own ballads, with his sentimental music appealing to cultured musicians as well as the general public. Ball was a charter member of ASCAP in 1914. While on tour in Santa Ana, CA, in 1927, he suffered a fatal heart attack. He was married twice. First in 1898 to Jessie Mae Jewett; they had three children: Roland A., Ruth Mary, and Ernest A. His second marriage beginning and ending in 1911 was to Maude Lambert, a vaudeville entertainer. Ball is buried in Lake View Cemetery.

———

Ernest R. Ball Papers, WRHS.

**BALL, WEBB C.** (6 Oct. 1846–6 March 1922), regulated the watches of most of the nation's railroads as a sideline of his Cleveland jewelry business. Born on a farm in Knox County, OH, he was the son of Aaron and Sidney Ann Clay Ball. He began his jewelry apprenticeship in 1869 in Fredericktown, OH, and joined the Deuber Watch Case Co. of Cincinnati in 1874. Coming to Cleveland in 1879, Ball bought an interest in the firm of Whitcomb & Metten Jewelers, which in 2 years became the WEBB C. BALL CO.† He was consulted as a "time expert" by the Lake Shore & Michigan Southern Railroad in 1891, after an accident due to an inaccurate watch claimed 13 lives. Developing specifications for an accurate, dependable railroad watch, Ball produced and patented several distinct watch movements adapted to the industry's requirements. He also organized the Railroad Time and Watch Inspection Service to enforce standards of accuracy. Administered nationally from his Cleveland jewelry establishment, the system was eventually extended to three quarters of the nation's railroads, covering a total of 125,000 miles of track. It was credited with saving hundreds of lives, in recognition of which Ball was elected an honorary member of the BROTHERHOOD OF LOCOMOTIVE ENGINEERS† in 1921. He was also a member of the UNION CLUB OF CLEVELAND† and a former president of the Cleveland Convention Board. Married since 1879 to the former Florence I. Young of Kenton, OH, he died at their home in CLEVELAND HTS.† He was survived by her, his son Sidney Y. Ball, and daughters Wilma Ball, Florence Ball, and Alice Andrews.—J.V.

**BANDLOW, ROBERT** (4 June 1852–29 Jan. 1911) was an organizer for the Central Labor Union, predecessor to the CLEVELAND FED. OF LABOR,† and for many years the business editor of the *CLEVELAND CITIZEN.†* Born in Germany to Henry and Caroline Bandlow, the family immigrated to Cleveland in 1854. After a public-school education, Bandlow became a typesetter for the *Wachter am Erie* newspaper and an early participant in the labor movement. First organizing Local 16 of the German Typographical Workers in the 1870s, he quickly gained a reputation as a leader who could balance long- and short-term goals. When the CLU was formed in 1887, Bandlow worked days as a printer and nights and weekends as an organizer for this infant AFL affiliate. Within 2 years, he organized 26 unions linked to their respective internationals, and built CFL membership up to 500. His constant theme at union meetings, labor forums, and the FRANKLIN CLUB† was the education of the worker, which he felt to be the best hope for instilling the discipline necessary to attain labor goals. By 1891, Bandlow, a Socialist, supported Henry C. Long and MAX S. HAYES in founding the *Citizen,* which Bandlow regarded as a solid educational tool, mobilizing CLU support in the form of guaranteed subscriptions. Within 2 years, he was the business editor. To the time of his death in 1912, Bandlow shaped the *Citizen* into a powerful organizing and educational tool for Cleveland labor.

Bandlow and his wife, Barbara (Kachel) had four children: Lissing, Karl, Robert, and Walter. Bandlow died in Cleveland and was buried in Lake View Cemetery.

**BANG, EDWARD F. "ED"** (28 Apr. 1880–27 Apr. 1968) was sports editor of the *CLEVELAND NEWS†* for 53 years. Born in Sandusky, OH, to Charles and Rose Bang, he worked at the *Sandusky Register* and then in Youngstown before he was hired by the *News.* He became sports editor in 1907. Bang was influential on the local and national sports scene. A founder of the Baseball Writers' Assn. of America, he also helped organize the Cleveland Baseball Fed., which sponsored sandlot baseball programs. In 1916 he played a persuasive role in the trade bringing outfielder TRIS SPEAKER from Boston to the CLEVELAND INDIANS.† Bang wrote the daily column "Between You and Me," and assembled a strong staff, including Herman Goldstein, ED MCAULEY, and Regis McAuley. He promoted professional basketball exhibitions and the 1931 SCHMELING-STRIBLING FIGHT† in Municipal Stadium.

Bang also sponsored the annual News Toyshop Fund Boxing Show, which raised $500,000 over 30 years to provide Christmas presents for underprivileged youngsters. He was a founder of the "Round Table," an informal gathering which met daily at the Statler Grill and included I. S. (NIG) ROSE and Judge SAMUEL H. SILBERT. Bang retired shortly after the *News* was sold to the *CLEVELAND PRESS†* in 1960. From 1955–77, members of the Round Table sponsored an "Ed Bang Journalism Scholarship" which was awarded annually in his honor to 2 area high school graduates.

Bang married Rose Schneider (d. 1950) in 1904. They had 4 children: Charles N., Ernest, Regina, and Betty. He died in Kirtland and is buried in Lake View Cemetery.

**BARBER, GERSHOM M.** (2 Oct. 1823–20 July 1903) was an educator, lawyer, and judge who also served in the CIVIL WAR.† Born in Groton, NY, to Phineas and Orpha Barber, he came to Berlin Twp., OH, with his family at age 7. At 15 he enrolled in Norwalk Seminary and, after teaching in Kentucky for a few years, attended Western Reserve College in Hudson, transferring to Michigan Univ., graduating in 1850. From 1850–56, Barber was a professor of mathematics and languages at Baldwin Institute; serving the last 2 years as principal. He resigned to study law under Samuel B. Prentiss in Cleveland, and was admitted to the bar in 1857.

Barber entered the Civil War as a 2nd lt. in Oct. 1862. From Mar. 1863-Apr. 1865 he commanded a battalion of sharpshooters, attaining the rank of captain. Toward the war's end, he was promoted to lt. col. and was recommended by Gen. Thomas for a brevet commission of brigadier general. In June and July 1865, Barber served as president of the Military Examining Court. After the war, Barber developed a successful law practice in Cleveland with W. W. Andrews. He was a Cleveland city councilman from 1872–73, and in 1873 was elected a judge of the 2nd Superior Court. In 1875 Barber was elected to a 5-year term in the Common Pleas Court; he was reelected in 1880. Barber made notable gifts to the Cleveland Law Library. He married Huldah Lavinia Seeley in 1851 and had 5 children: Clarence, Ida, Marion, Arthur, and Earnest. Barber died in Cleveland and was buried in Woodland Cemetery.

**BARBER, JOSIAH** (1771–10 Dec. 1842), the first mayor of OHIO CITY† and son of Capt. Stephen and Alice (Cass) Barber, was a prime mover in west side residential, commercial, and industrial development. In 1809, when the last division of WESTERN RESERVE† lands was made in Connecticut, Barber, his father-in-law, Samuel Lord, and brother-in-law, RICHARD LORD,† received the portion along the western border of the CUYAHOGA RIVER† to the lake. They arranged for a survey and sale of lands to settlers in the BROOKLYN† section through the Lord & Barber Realty Co. In 1818 Barber constructed a log house at Pearl (W. 25th) and Franklin overlooking the river valley, which he later replaced with the first brick house in Cleveland. To entice settlers, Barber operated a store at Pearl and Lorain. In 1840 he and his partners dedicated a large portion of land for an open-air market that was the forerunner of the WEST SIDE MARKET.† In 1834 Barber was among the incorporators of the CUYAHOGA STEAM FURNACE CO.,† the first manufacturing concern in Cleveland. By the mid-1830s, Barber was active in Brooklyn Twp. politics. Appointed a circuit judge in 1834, he stepped down to become the first elected mayor of Ohio City. Barber was an incorporator of Trinity Parish in downtown Cleveland and St. John's Parish at W. 26th and Church. As the vice-president of the CUYAHOGA COUNTY COLONIZATION SOCIETY,† he favored gradual abolition of slavery and the colonization of blacks in Africa or South America.

Barber married twice. His first marriage was to Abigail Gilbert; they had a daughter, Abigail G. His second marriage was to Sophia Lord. Together they had 4 children: Epiphras, Harriet, Sophia L., and Jerusha. Barber died in Cleveland.

**BARDOUN, FRANK J.** (3 Oct. 1905–3 Dec. 1988) was prominently involved in the affairs of Cleveland's CZECHS† for more than half a century. A native Clevelander, the son of Louis and Mary Plantner Bardoun, he was a graduate of EAST TECHNICAL HIGH SCHOOL.† After further study at the JOHN HUNTINGTON POLYTECH-

NIC INSTITUTE,† he embarked on a 43-year career as a metallurgist for the Park Drop Forge Co. (see PARK-OHIO INDUSTRIES, INC.†). From c. 1930 to the paper's demise, he was editor of the English-language page of the Czech socialist weekly, *AMERICKE DELNICKE LISTY.†* At about the time of his marriage to Anne E. Prudek in 1936, he undertook a lifelong service as secretary of the WORKERS GYMNASTIC UNION.† For most of that period he was also secretary for the group's Taborville committee. Bardoun also served from 1944 to his death as president of Paramount Lodge #372 of the Czechoslovak Society of America. For much of that period he was on the board of trustees of the national organization. Bardoun collected and preserved a remarkable body of manuscripts and papers relating to Cleveland's Czech community which are now housed in the WESTERN RESERVE HISTORICAL SOCIETY.† Predeceased by a son, Allen E., he was survived by his wife and another son, Donald F.—J.V.

---

Frank Bardoun Papers, WRHS.

**BARNARD, MAXWELL ("MAX") VOSPER** (6 April 1884–3 Feb. 1978), became known through his primitive artwork as the "Grandpa Moses" of CHAGRIN FALLS.† Born in Auburn Twp., Geauga County, he was the son of Jay and Lena Barnard and grandson of one of the early settlers of Chagrin Falls. He quit school after the 6th grade to take up his father's trade of housepainter and paperhanger, being credited with covering most of Chagrin Falls during a career of more than half a century. Following the death of his first wife, Margaret, Barnard and his second wife, Carlotta (Lottie), in the 1930s moved back to his grandfather's house on Orange St. in town. In the 1940s he began painting primitive scenes recalled from his childhood on spare pieces of lumber and plasterboard. Completely unschooled in technique, he won a first prize in the prestigious MAY SHOW† for a scene painted on a window-shade. Using ordinary housepaint for the most part, he turned out more than 2,000 primitive paintings over a period of 30 years, pricing them according to the size of the picture. He also covered the walls of his home with landscapes. His work was shown at the Chagrin Valley Art Club in 1973 and the Heartland Museum in Harvard, MA, in 1986. Barnard also made uniquely designed birdhouses which were highly prized. He left a sketchbook containing 300 pen-and-ink drawings, with written commentaries, of early Chagrin Falls residents. He died in Millersburg, OH, and is buried in Chagrin Falls. Having outlived both his wives and a daughter from the first marriage, Jane Budnick, he was survived by a granddaughter, Beverly Myers.—J.V.

**BARNETT, JAMES** (21 June 1821–13 Jan. 1911), a businessman, politician, soldier, and philanthropist, organized many charities. Born in Cherry Valley, NY, to Melancthon and Mary (Clark), the family moved to Cleveland in 1825. After attending Cleveland public schools, Barnett clerked in Potter & Clark's store for 3 years before going to GEO. WORTHINGTON's store, eventually becoming president and director on the board of the GEO. WORTHINGTON CO.† He was president and director of several banks, including GUARDIAN SAVINGS,† as well as the Big Four Railroads and Cleveland Iron Mining Co. In 1839 Barnett joined the CLEVELAND GRAYS,† fighting as colonel of the CLEVELAND LIGHT ARTILLERY† in the CIVIL WAR.† Barnett was promoted to general and chief of artillery on Gen. Thos. Rosecrans's staff—the highest rank of any soldier from Cuyahoga County. In 1862, while visiting Cleveland, he opened an office to help enlisted men find homes for their children.

In 1856 Barnett helped organize the Republican party in Cleveland. He was appointed police commissioner in 1866, and served from 1873–74 on city council. Barnett was most satisfied working with charities. He served on the board of managers for the Soldiers' & Sailors' Orphan Home in Xenia, OH, and the Natl. Homes for Disabled Soldiers. In 1881 he helped create the Society for Organizing Charity, which merged with Bethel Mission in 1886 to form the Bethel Associated Charities, forerunner of the ASSOCIATED CHARITIES OF CLEVELAND†, of which Barnett was honorary president.

On 12 June 1845, Barnett married Maria H. Underhill. They had 5 children: Mary C., Carrie M., Laura, Lanny, and George. Barnett died at his Euclid Ave. home and was buried in Lake View Cemetery.

---

Barnett, James. *Reminiscences of the Cleveland Light Artillery* (1906).
Jas. Barnett Papers, WRHS.

**BARNUM, FRANK SEYMOUR** (25 Nov. 1850–17 Dec. 1927) was an architect who designed and supervised the construction of over 75 Cleveland public school buildings, and was among the first architects to utilize modern building techniques in his designs.

Born in Norwalk, OH, to David and Virginia (Lambert) Barnum, Frank was educated in Norwalk common and high schools. He came to Cleveland in 1871 and worked as a draftsman for architect JOSEPH IRELAND.

In 1876 Barnum opened his own office. From 1878–97 Barnum practiced with FORREST A. COBURN in the firm COBURN & BARNUM,† designers of the WESTERN RESERVE HISTORI-CAL SOCIETY BUILDING† (1898), buildings for WESTERN RESERVE UNIV. and Case Institute of Technology, and numerous churches and residences. The firm also included architects BENJAMIN HUBBELL and W. DOMINICK BENES.

After Coburn's death, Barnum formed F. S. Barnum & Co. with Albert Skeel, Harry Nelson, Herbert Briggs, and Wilbur Hall. In 1901 Barnum designed the CAXTON BUILDING† (completed 1903), an 8-story steel-frame building in the Chicago commercial style, for AMBROSE SWASEY. Barnum designed the Park Building on PUBLIC SQUARE† (1904), one of Cleveland's first buildings to utilize reinforced concrete floor slabs. After Barnum's retirement in 1915, the firm continued as Briggs & Nelson.

Barnum's appointment as architect and superintendent of buildings for the CLEVELAND PUBLIC SCHOOLS,† 1895–1915, marked the era of modern school construction. The new buildings pioneered fireproof construction, had flat roofs, electric light, steam heat, and used space efficiently.

Barnum married Jeannette May (d. 1921). They had one son, W. Hamilton. Barnum moved to Coconut Grove, FL, died in Miami, and is enurned in Lake View Cemetery.—T.B.

**BARR, JOHN** (26 Jan. 1804–24 Jan. 1875), Cleveland's first magistrate and local historian, was born in Hartford, Trumbull County, the son of Thomas and Suzanna Barr. The Barr family came to Euclid Twp. in 1810 when Thomas Barr was appointed the first pastor of the FIRST PRESBYTERIAN CHURCH OF EAST CLEVELAND.† John came to the village of Cleveland in 1828 and was appointed county sheriff, serving from 1830–34. He became an attorney and was a partner in the law firm of Sullivan, Barr & Stetson. When the Ohio legislature established municipal police courts in 1853, Barr was elected Cleveland's first judge. A tireless promoter of Cleveland as a rail center, he compiled and published statistics to demonstrate the city's commercial growth, substantiating the area's need for rail transportation, and served as a delegate to the Nov. 1838 meeting in Harrisburg, PA, where construction of the Cleveland and Pittsburgh railroad was discussed. A historian as well as a statistician, Barr wrote an account of the early settlement of the Western Reserve ca. 1843, and was a leader in historical preservation, serving as the first secretary of the Cuyahoga County historical society in 1858. He also helped organize the WESTERN RESERVE HISTORICAL SOCIETY† in May 1867.

Barr married Delia M. Bush 21 Oct. 1845, and they had a daughter, Nellie. He died at his residence

in Cleveland and was buried at Erie St. Cemetery.
—M.S.

**BARRICELLI, GIOVANNI ALFONSO** (22 Feb. 1873–16 Apr. 1934) was a cardiopulmonary specialist, but is best known as one of the early leaders of the Italian community in Cleveland. Born in Benevenuto, Italy, to Pietro and Lucia (Cangelicri) Barricelli, he attended the Univ. of Naples, completing courses in physics and chemistry. In 1889, at the age of 16, he arrived in the U.S., remaining in New York City for 8 years after passing his pharmacy examination, where he owned and operated 3 drugstores. He studied medicine at St. Francis College of New York and completed his studies at the Univ. of Illinois in Chicago, receiving his M.D. degree in Nov. 1902. In Cleveland, following postgraduate work in New York, Barricelli opened his cardiopulmonary practice at 419 Woodland SE in the area known as BIG ITALY.†

Barricelli originated the Cleveland chapter of the Order of the Sons of Italy and was its Grand Commander for a period of time. During World War I, he served as a member of the U.S. Volunteer Medical Corps, as head of the Roman Legion in Cleveland, and as chairman of all the Liberty Loan campaigns among the Italians in Cleveland. He was made a Knight of the Crown of Italy for his services rendered to the Allies during the war. On 1 Sept. 1923, Barricelli married Orfea Malpezzi (d. 1981) known in Italy and America as a scholar of philosophy and literature. The Barricellis had a son, Gian Piero. Barricelli died in Cleveland and was buried in Lake View Cemetery.

**BARRY, FRANK T.** (9 Feb. 1881–31 Jan. 1956), a minister and social worker, founded and directed Woodland Ctr. Neighborhood House for over 30 years. Born in Lincoln, NE, and growing up in Topeka, KS, he graduated from Lake Forest College, Lake Forest, IL (1905); from McCormick Theological Seminary, Chicago (1908); and from Northwestern Univ. (1912). He pastored Presbyterian congregations in Chicago, Evanston, IL, and Minneapolis, KS, before coming to Cleveland in 1918 as associate pastor and director of religious education at Woodland Ave. Presbyterian Church, becoming senior minister in 1923. Barry was named minister in 1925 when the congregation of Woodland Ave. united with Kinsman</->Union Congregational Church to form WOODLAND HILLS (COMMUNITY) UNION CHURCH.† He developed Woodland Ctr., a social settlement house, as part of the church program and served as its director, creating social and recreational programs for people of all ages and ethnic backgrounds which at one time served over 4,000 neighbors. In May 1938, Woodland Ave.

Presbyterian Church was razed, and in Mar. 1941, Woodland Ctr. Neighborhood House, renamed Garden Valley Neighborhood House, moved to E. 71st St. and Kinsman Rd. Barry pastored Woodland Hills from 1925–44, and directed Woodland Ctr. until 1948, when he retired and moved to Florida.

Barry married Sarah Prince McArthur in 1908 and had 4 children: Mary K. (Mrs. Raymond Gladieux); Dr. Frank McArthur Barry, a Cleveland physician; Martha Isabel (Mrs. Allen Mark); and Rev. David W. Barry. Barry was buried in Florida.

**BARTON, THOMAS C.** (b. 1831), a U.S. Navy seaman who received the Congressional Medal of Honor during the CIVIL WAR,† was born in Cleveland. Barton was on board the USS *Hunchback* when it attempted to rescue an army detachment surrounded by Confederate troops near Franklin, VA. During a ship-to-shore bombardment 3 Oct. 1862, Barton threw a pail of water on a live shell on the ship's deck to prevent it from exploding. He was awarded the Medal of Honor on 3 April 1863 for his quick action.

**BATES, KENNETH F.** (24 May 1904–24 May 1994), a long-time member of the faculty of the CLEVELAND INSTITUTE OF ART,† specialized in enamel work and was nationally recognized for his achievements in the field.

Born to Francis and Winnette Litchfield Bates in North Scituate, MA, Kenneth pursued his art education at the Massachusetts School of Art and earned his bachelor's degree there.

He came to Cleveland in 1926, and one year later joined the faculty of the Cleveland School of Art. During his forty-three years at the Institute, he taught every class of the required course in basic design. He also taught advanced courses in enameling. He became professor emeritus in 1971.

In 1927 Bates submitted his first enamel work to the MAY SHOW† of the CLEVELAND MUSEUM OF ART†; it received first prize. Bates continued to submit entries to the annual May Show for the next 62 years, garnering a long list of prizes. In 1946 he was awarded first prize in the national enameling competition. His works have been displayed in many museums and were featured in one-man shows in Brooklyn and Chicago. In 1987 the National Society of Enamelists honored him with the title Dean of American Enamelists.

Bates authored three books: *Enameling: Principles and Practice*, 1951; *The Enamelist*, 1967; and *Basic Design*, 1970.

Bates was also an accomplished horticulturist, and in the greenhouse of his EUCLID† home, he raised prize-winning dahlias and roses.

Bates married Charlotte Young in May 1930, and

they raised three children: Cornelia, Katherine, and Benham. Bates is buried in Lake View Cemetery. —J.T.

**BATTISTA, JOSEPH "PIPP"** (4 Nov. 1908–16 May 1993) was a community leader in the LITTLE ITALY† neighborhood and a member of the Mayfield-Murray Hill District Council. Battista owned and operated Pipp's Hardware (Murray Hill & Edgehill) for 35 years and was a trustee and president of ALTA HOUSE.†

Battista lived with his brothers and earned money caddying at Oakwood Country Club (see OAKWOOD CLUB†), where he developed a life-long love of GOLF.† He later competed in Ohio Hardware Assn. tournaments and won its 1961 championship.

Battista purchased his hardware store in 1945. As a member of the Mayfield-Murray Hill District Council, Battista assisted in building relationships between the neighborhood and surrounding institutions, including CASE WESTERN RESERVE UNIV.† and UNIV. CIRCLE, INC.†

Battista was involved with Alta House for 28 years as a trustee and president. He established the Alta House golf association, sponsoring the annual Alta golf tournament, which attracted top amateur golfers in the Greater Cleveland area.

Battista was also a lay minister at HOLY ROSARY† Catholic Church, where he helped organize the parish council and church credit union. He also worked on the Feast of the Assumption celebration that brought thousands of people to Little Italy each August.

Battista married Margaret Chiocchio on 8 Aug. 1931 and had three children, Marylou (Strathers), Joseph Jr., and Bruce. He is buried in the Western Reserve Memorial Gardens.—T.B.

**BATTISTI, FRANK JOSEPH** (4 Oct. 1922–19 Oct. 1994) was a federal judge for the U.S. District Court, Northern District of Ohio, who presided over the landmark Cleveland school desegregation case resulting in crosstown busing.

Born in Youngstown to Eugene and Jennie (Dalesandro) Battisti, Frank served in the army (1943–45) and graduated from Ohio Univ. (B.A., 1947), and Harvard Law School (LL.B., 1950). In 1950 Battisti was admitted to the Ohio Bar and served as Ohio asst. attorney general.

From 1951–52 Battisti was legal adviser to the Army Corps of Engineers. In 1952 he entered into private practice in Youngstown and taught as an instructor at the Youngstown College law school (Youngstown State Univ.). Battisti was Youngstown's first asst. law director, serving 1956–59.

In 1959 Battisti became judge of Mahoning County's Common Pleas Court. In 1961 Battisti became the youngest U.S. federal judge when he was appointed to the northern Ohio bench by Pres. John F. Kennedy. He became chief judge in 1969.

On 31 Aug. 1976, Battisti ruled in *Reed v. Rhodes*, the Cleveland public school desegregation case, that the schools had practiced racial segregation. His comprehensive order contained 14 components intended to bring an equal education to all Cleveland students.

Battisti presided over other high-profile cases, including the integration of public housing in Cleveland and PARMA,† the acquittal of eight former Ohio National Guardsmen in the 1970 Kent State Univ. student killings, and the deportation hearing of John Demjanjuk.

Battisti married Gloria Joy Karpinski on 10 Aug. 1963. They had no children. Battisti, a Roman Catholic, is buried in Calvary Cemetery.—T.B.

**BAUDER, LEVI F.** (28 Jan. 1840–1 Oct. 1913), was a CIVIL WAR† soldier, civic official, and permanent secretary of the Soldiers & Sailors Monument Commission. Born in Cleveland to Levi and Eliza (Phillips) Bauder, he graduated from CENTRAL HIGH SCHOOL.† Bauder attended Oberlin College for 1 year and taught school in Pickaway County until the outbreak of the CIVIL WAR.† He enlisted on 20 July 1861 in the Sprague Cadets, which became Co. B, 7TH OHIO VOLUNTEER INFANTRY,† and was promoted to 1st sgt. on 30 Sept. He served as company commander during the Chattanooga, TN, campaign of 1863, although he was never promoted to the rank of captain. After the war, Bauder married Elizabeth Page in 1866. They had 5 children: Arthur, Frank, Theresa, Walter, and Blanche. He practiced law and served as Cuyahoga County auditor (1877–83) and justice of the peace (1886–92). He maintained the records of the Soldiers & Sailors Monument Commission for 15 years. Bauder published a book of poems in 1880, *Passing Fancies*. He died in Cleveland and was buried in Lake View Cemetery.

William P. Palmer Manuscript Collection, WRHS.

**BAYLESS, WILLIAM NEVILLE** (6 Mar. 1912–9 Aug. 1992), known as Neville, won awards from the American Assn. of Advertising Agencies and maintained an interest in history, as a published writer and founding member of the Cleveland Civil War Roundtable (see Civil War ROUNDTABLES†). Born in Toledo, OH, to Bertha Snyder and William Niven Bayless, he was the younger of two children. Bayless moved to Lakewood at 8 years of age; he graduated from Lakewood High School, then from Adelbert College of Western Reserve Univ. (WRU, later CASE WESTERN RESERVE UNIV.†) in 1933, cum laude. After receiving a master's from WRU in 1934, Bayless joined his father's business, the Bayless-Kerr Advertising Agency. He served as agency president from 1956 until retiring in 1974. After retirement, Bayless did extensive genealogical research and frequently contributed acerbic letters to the editors of local newspapers.

Bayless directed the City Club of Cleveland and was president of the Cheshire Cheese Club of Cleveland. On 3 Apr. 1937, he married Margaret Falke (d. 1979); they had five sons: William, Robert, Ronald, Thomas, and David. In 1984 he married Jean Poser. Bayless died in his home in ROCKY RIVER† and was buried in Crown Hill Cemetery in Twinsburg, OH.—J.M.

**BEACH, CLIFTON BAILEY** (16 Sept. 1845–15 Nov. 1902), congressman and businessman, was born in Sharon, Medina County, the son of Israel Bailey and Emily C. (Wiggin) Beach. He moved with his parents to Cleveland in 1857, attending public schools and Western Reserve College in Hudson, where he graduated in 1871. After studying law, he was admitted to the bar in 1872 and practiced with several firms until 1884, when he joined the partnership of Terrill, Beach & Cushing. He also became president of the H. P. Nail Co., which was organized by his father-in-law, HENRY CHISHOLM, in 1877 to produce wire, nails, staples, and rods. Beach also served two terms as congressman from Cleveland's 20th district (4 Mar. 1895–3 Mar. 1899); he was not a candidate for renomination in 1898.

After living in Cleveland for many years, Beach purchased a 427-acre estate along the lake shore in 1888 from George Merwin and ex-Ohio governor Reuben Wood, where he lived for the rest of his life. In 1897 Beach donated land to Rockport Twp. for an elementary school, which was named Beach School. The Beach Cliff area of ROCKY RIVER† originally was part of his property. The Rocky River Clock Tower at Avalon Dr. and Lake Rd. was rebuilt and rededicated in 1987; built in 1912, it had been the ornamental entrance marker for the Beach estate.

Beach married Janet Chisholm 15 Oct. 1873, and they had a son, Chisholm. After her death on 21 Sept. 1890, he married Adelaide Thow of St. Louis. Beach died at his home in Rocky River and was buried at Lake View Cemetery.—M.S.

**BEARD, CHARLES AUGUSTINE** (15 Dec. 1923–4 Feb. 1993), held key positions in the city's urban renewal and housing agencies from the 1950s through the 1980s. The son of Chappell and Aria Thomas Beard, he was born in Macon, GA, and raised in Newport, RI. He studied drafting at the

Rhode Island School of Design and also attended Springfield College in Springfield, MA. During World War II he became a fighter pilot with the 99th Pursuit Squadron at Tuskegee, AL. Coming to Cleveland in 1945, he went to work for the Cleveland Urban Renewal Agency. During the 1950s he became the first African American to fill the position of chief planner for the Cleveland City Planning Commission. Among the projects for which he was responsible was the ST. VINCENT CHARITY HOSPITAL/CUYAHOGA COMMUNITY COLLEGE† Metro Campus area. In 1967 he joined the staff of PATH (Plan of Action for Tomorrow's Housing), becoming executive director in 1970. As head of the private advocacy group for low-income housing, he provided testimony which was instrumental in a federal lawsuit against PARMA,† which paved the way for PUBLIC HOUSING† in the suburbs. After PATH† closed down due to lack of funding, Beard became a government liaison with the FEDERATION FOR COMMUNITY PLANNING† from 1974 until his retirement in 1983. He was one of the founders of Friends of SHAKER SQUARE,† serving as vice-president and helping the group obtain its first planning grant. He also helped organize the North Coast Chapter of the Tuskegee Airmen. Beard married the former Peggy Lanton in 1960. Survived by her and 3 children, Hilary, Alison, and Jonathan, he was buried in Lake View Cemetery.—J.V.

**BEAUFAIT, HOWARD G.** (15 Oct. 1904–3 Nov. 1976) was the "big story" reporter of the *CLEVELAND NEWS†* during its last quarter-century. He was born in Detroit, MI, son of Louis and Dorothy (Johnson) Beaufait. He was educated in New York and England, and broke into journalism as editor of a small Maine weekly. When his English stepfather, an airplane pilot named Rex Uden, came to work in Cleveland, Beaufait followed and joined the staff of the *News* in 1928. During the 1930s he became one of the country's first aviation writers and later turned out a daily column, "Here Today." After serving as city editor of the *News* during World War II, he covered such national stories as the McCarthy hearings and the executions of Ethel and Julius Rosenberg. His coverage of the Korean War in 1953 earned him an award from the CLEVELAND NEWSPAPER GUILD,† while the National Headliners Club honored him for a beat on the starvation deaths of American prisoners of war. Always noted as a crime specialist, Beaufait was the first reporter on the scene of the SHEPPARD MURDER CASE.† He served as president of the Cleveland Newspaper Guild in 1954. Following a 1956 divorce from his first wife, the former Hazel J. Krauss, whom he married on 8 Dec. 1928, Beaufait married Doris

O'Donnell, a reporter for the *News* and the Cleveland *PLAIN DEALER*,† on 14 Sept. 1957. When the *News* ceased publication in 1960, he became assistant executive secretary of the Cleveland Area Heart Society. Later he returned to journalism with jobs on the *Lake County News-Herald* and the *Tribune-Review* of Greensburg, PA. He died near his home in Ligonier, PA, survived by 3 children: Howard, Jr., Elaine Owen, and Janis Corso.—J.V.

**BEAUMONT, LOUIS D.** (26 April 1857–1 Oct. 1942), a cofounder of the May Co. (see KAUFMANN'S, A DIVISION OF THE MAY CO.†), also created the LOUIS D. BEAUMONT FOUNDATION.† For his work in France during World War I, he was made a Chevalier of the Legion of Honor (1920). Called "Commodore" because of his affinity for yachting, Beaumont was born Louis Schoenberg in Dayton, OH, one of 6 children. After attending public school, he traveled west, settled in Leadville, CO, and opened a general store with his two brothers. The brothers later joined brother-in-law David May to form the May Shoe and Clothing Co., predecessor of the nationwide May Dept. Store chain. Beaumont came to Cleveland in 1899 when the company opened its first local store. He retired from the May Co. in 1912 but remained a vice-president until his death. After retiring, he moved to France, where, because of intense anti-German feeling, he changed his last name to Beaumont. During his travels in Europe, Beaumont supervised the company's foreign interests. He continued to maintain U.S. citizenship and, after 1939, lived in Palm Beach, FL, and New York City.

Interested in aviation as well as boating, Beaumont was president of the Aero Club of America in France and organized aviators' clubs along the front lines during World War I. Beaumont generously supported the American Hospital in Neuilly, France, and the National Jewish Hospital (for tuberculosis) in Denver, among other efforts. Locally, he donated money to Western Reserve Univ. for research on high blood pressure.

Beaumont was married twice. His first wife, and son, Dudley, died in the early 1900s. He married Helene M. Thomas in France. Beaumont died in a New York hospital and was buried in Salem Fields, Brooklyn, NY, in the family mausoleum.—J.M.

**BECK, CLAUDE SCHAEFFER** (8 Nov. 1894–14 Oct. 1971), a surgeon, achieved worldwide recognition for his work in heart surgery and cardiopulmonary resuscitation. Born in Shamokin, PA, to Simon and Martha Schaeffer Beck, he graduated from Franklin & Marshall College (Lancaster, PA) in 1916, receiving his M.D. from Johns Hopkins Univ. in 1921. He trained at Johns Hopkins, New Haven

(CT), Peter Bent Brigham (Boston), and Lakeside hospitals, and worked under Dr. HARVEY CUSHING at Harvard in 1923–24. Beck came to Cleveland in 1924, joining UNIV. HOSPITALS† as resident and Crile Research Fellow in Surgery. He was associate surgeon from 1928 until he retired in 1965. Western Reserve Univ. School of Medicine appointed him demonstrator of surgery in 1924–25; professor of neurosurgery in 1940; and the first professor of cardiovascular surgery in the U.S. from 1952 until 1965. He was a surgical consultant in the army from 1942–45, receiving the Legion of Merit.

Beck's greatest contributions were in the surgical treatment of heart disease. He assisted Dr. ELLIOT CUTLER in the first mitral valve operations in the 1920s. He performed the first surgical treatment of coronary artery disease in 1935; the first successful defibrillation of the human heart in 1947; the first successful reversal of an otherwise fatal heart attack in 1955; and the first successful removal of a heart tumor. Beck and his colleagues developed cardiopulmonary resuscitation techniques that they began teaching medical professionals in 1950, training more than 3,000 doctors and nurses in less than 20 years. In 1963 a course in closed-chest cardiopulmonary resuscitation for lay persons was added.

Beck married Ellen Manning in 1928. They had three daughters: Mary Ellen, Kathryn, and Martha.

Claude S. Beck Papers, Univ. Hospitals Archives.
*Centennial Celebration: Claude S. Beck, 1894–1971* (Univ.Hospital Archives, 1994).

**BECK, JOHANN HEINRICH** (12 Sept. 1856–26 May 1924) was a noted conductor, composer, teacher, and violinist. Born in Cleveland to Charles and Rebecca (Butter) Beck, he completed his musical education in Europe at the Leipzig Conservatory (1879–82), where he premiered his own String Quartet in C Minor at the Gewandhaus. Returning to Cleveland, he was active in music in the city for many years. Heard frequently in concert as a violinist, he organized the Schubert String Quartet in 1877 and later the BECK STRING QUARTET,† which gave frequent concerts during the 1880s. He directed the Detroit Symphony, 1895–96, and appeared with other important orchestras, conducting his own works. Together with EMIL RING, he led local orchestras under various names, preluding the formation of the CLEVELAND ORCHESTRA† in 1918.

As a composer, Beck produced an unfinished opera, *Salammbo* (1887-), and over a dozen orchestral works. The Cleveland Orchestra included his *Lara* overture in a concert on 18 Dec. 1919, to critical acclaim. His chamber works include various piano pieces, songs, choral pieces, and string quartets. Beck's bust now stands at the entry to the Fine Arts Div. of the CLEVELAND PUBLIC LIBRARY,† which houses an extensive collection of his manuscripts. Beck married Mary Blanding Fellar of Tiffin, OH, in 1890. They had a son, Henry J., and a daughter, Hildegarde. Beck was buried in Woodland Cemetery.

**BECKWITH, ADA BEL** (27 Feb. 1886–17 May 1964) was regarded as an innovative educator during a long tenure as art supervisor in the LAKEWOOD† Public Schools. Daughter of Havel and Alida (Haight) Beckwith, Ada was born and educated in Cleveland, graduating from CENTRAL HIGH SCHOOL† and Cleveland Normal School. She studied art at the Pratt Institute and also attended Western Reserve Univ. (see CASE WESTERN RESERVE†) and Columbia Univ. Beginning her career in the CLEVELAND PUBLIC SCHOOLS† in 1906, she taught elementary art and was made asst. supervisor of art from 1913–18. Beckwith became supervisor of art in Lakewood in 1918 and remained in that position until her retirement in 1956. Her philosophy of allowing children to express themselves with a minimum of teacher guidance became standard practice in art education, promoted in part by her many articles in educational journals. Beckwith was also a practicing artist, exhibiting in the MAY SHOW† at the CLEVELAND MUSEUM OF ART.† She was a vice-president of the Lakewood Society of Artists and a director of the WOMEN'S ART CLUB OF CLEVELAND.† In retirement, she taught summer sessions at BALDWIN-WALLACE COLLEGE.† She never married.—J.V.

**BECKWITH, CHARLES G.** (19 Apr. 1870–26 (27), Sept. 1933), electrical engineer and expert in operation of municipal light plants, was born in Dowagiac, MI, the son of Edwin W. and Clara L. (Sullivan) Beckwith. The family moved to Cassopolis, MI, where he graduated from high school, and took a special course at the Univ. of Michigan at Ann Arbor. Leaving the university in 1892, he built and operated a small municipal light plant in his home town, and was in charge of the Montpelier, OH, light plant from 1895–1900. Collinwood Village hired Beckwith to construct and operate a municipal light plant for them in 1900, and when Collinwood was annexed to Cleveland in 1910, he was employed by the city. In 1914, Beckwith, as superintendent of Cleveland's new municipal light plant at E. 53rd St. and Lakeshore, personally planned and supervised the installation of a modern system of street lighting, which used tungsten lamps for the first time to create the effect of a great "White Way."

He also became an expert in setting electric rates, crucial to the plant's operation, since it was expected to sell current at a rate not to exceed $.03 per kilowatt hour. His expertise helped ensure that Muny Light customers initially would pay less than half the rates charged by the CLEVELAND ELECTRIC ILLUMINATING CO.†

Beckwith married Belle N. Norton 19 February 1895, at Cassopolis, and they adopted a son, Raymond N. Ellis. Beckwith died in Cleveland and was buried at his home town in Michigan.—M.S.

**BEDELL, GREGORY THURSTON** (27 Aug. 1817–11 Mar. 1892), bishop coadjutor of the Protestant Episcopal Diocese of Ohio (1859–73) and third bishop of Ohio (1873–89) was born in Hudson, NY, to Rev. Gregory Townsend and Penelope (Thurston) Bedell. He graduated from Bristol College in 1836 and from the Theological Seminary of Ohio in 1840. Ordained in 1841, he was Bp. Chas. McIlvaine's assistant for 14 years, then worked in New York City before becoming bishop coadjutor in Ohio. In the early 1870s, Bedell was involved in an evangelical-versus-tractarian dispute that decimated the administrative, faculty, and student ranks at Bexley Hall, the Episcopal seminary at Kenyon College. He eventually reconciled to high church practices, accepting vested choirs, hymn singing, surplices for the clergy, and a cross and flowers on the altar in the chancel. Ill health led to his retirement to New York City in 1889.

During the Civil War, Bedell and Bishop McIlvaine preached loyalty to the Union and urged Episcopal clergymen to stay out of politics. In 1874 he presided over a statewide convention that divided Ohio into 2 dioceses. Between 1881–87, when the Ohio Episcopal Church faced a crisis in church growth, Bedell traveled to counter the slump. He also worked on a financial assistance plan for the diocese and began the annual parish sermon on endowing the episcopacy. He advocated an Episcopal central cathedral, leading to the development of Cleveland's TRINITY CATHEDRAL† (consecrated 1907). He was married to Julia Strong. Bedell died in New York City and was buried in Gambier, OH.

**BEEMAN, EDWIN E.** (Mar. 1839–6 Nov. 1906), a physician, became "the Chewing Gum King" after introducing "Beeman's Pepsin Gum." Born in LaGrange, OH, son of Julius and Margaret Beeman, he grew up in Lorain and Erie counties. After 2 years at Oberlin College, at 18 he started reading medicine under his father and joined him in the drug business in Cleveland in 1863–64. Beeman then practiced medicine in Birmingham, OH, for 12 years, and in Wakeman, OH, for 6 years. A specialist in digestive disorders, Beeman discovered that pepsin, an extract from hogs' stomachs, provided relief from indigestion. By 1883 Beeman returned to Cleveland to manufacture pepsin.

Beeman produced pepsin on a small scale until 1888, when he organized the Beeman Chemical Co. with Albert C. Johnson, Chris Grover, and Wm. Cain. In Jan. 1890, the company's bookkeeper, Nellie M. Horton, suggested that Beeman add pepsin to chewing gum. Using WILLIAM J. WHITE's† chewing gum recipe, the following month "Beeman's Pepsin Gum" appeared. Its success led to a company reorganization in 1891; Beeman's earlier partners sold their interests to Geo. H. Worthington, Jas. M. Worthington, and Jas. Nicholl, with Nellie Horton becoming a stockholder and asst. secretary and treasurer. By 1898 the company's gum sales totaled $408,685, pepsin sales were $1,449, and profits totaled $131,487. In June 1899, the directors authorized the sale of the company to the American Chicle Co. Besides his business and medical interests, Beeman served 4 terms on CLEVELAND CITY COUNCIL† and was a Royal Arch Mason. Beeman married Mary Cobb in 1862. They had 2 children, Harrie L. and Lester A. Beeman died in Cleveland and was buried in Harvard Grove Cemetery.

**BEGIN, FLOYD L.** (5 Feb. 1902–26 April 1977) served the Roman Catholic church (see CATHOLICS, ROMAN†) in various capacities, including pastor of Cleveland's St. Agnes Parish (23 January 1949–21 February 1962), and then as the first bishop of the diocese of Oakland, CA. Begin was born in Cleveland, the oldest of 7 children of Stella McFarland and Peter Begin. He attended St. Columbkille and St. Thomas Aquinas elementary schools, CATHEDRAL LATIN SCHOOL,† and Loyola High School. He then studied at St. John Cathedral College in Cleveland and at North American College in Rome, Italy. Ordained in Rome 31 July 1927, Begin served there as asst. to the rector of North American College while completing doctorates in philosophy, theology, and canon law.

Returning to Cleveland in the 1930s, Begin was personal secretary to Bp. JOSEPH SCHREMBS, and vice-chancellor and pro-vicar general for the diocese. He was named monsignor in 1934. In 1938 Begin was appointed Officialis of the Diocesan Tribunal (Diocese of Cleveland) and director of both the Diocesan Council of Catholic Men and the SEVENTH NATIONAL EUCHARISTIC CONGRESS.† He was consecrated by Archbishop EDWARD FRANCIS HOBAN on 1 May 1947 and became his auxiliary. Begin was appointed vicar general of the diocese on 30 March 1948. While serving St. Agnes Parish in HOUGH during a critical transition, he advocated more city services for

and local acceptance of the AFRICAN AMERICANS† who were his parishioners. Begin belonged to the board of the AMERICAN RED CROSS, CLEVELAND CHAPTER,† and co-chaired the Hough Area Council. He is buried in Holy Sepulchre Cemetery in Oakland, CA.—J.M.

St. Agnes Parish Records, Diocese of Cleveland Archives.

**BEIDLER, JACOB A.** (2 Nov. 1852–13 Sept. 1912), a prominent coal merchant and politician, was a pioneer in the "back-to-the-farm" movement. Born near Valley Forge, PA, son of Israel and Mary (Latshaw) Beidler, he graduated from Lock's Seminary at Norristown, PA, at 21. He then came to Cleveland and began a coal dealership. He was active in the coal business over 40 years as president of the East Goshen Coal Co.; the Burton-Beidler-Phillips Coal Co.; and the Rhodes & Beidler Coal Co. He also organized the Belle Vernon-Mapes Dairy Co.; was vice-president of the CLEVELAND, PAINESVILLE & EASTERN RAILWAY†; and was a director of the *Painesville Telegraph-Republican.*

Beidler began his Republican political career during Jas. G. Blaine's 1884 presidential campaign; later he served on CLEVELAND CITY COUNCIL.† A political feud between Beidler and JAS. R. GARFIELD resulted in Beidler's election to Congress representing Cuyahoga, Lake, and Medina counties in 1900. Beidler had already moved to Belle Vernon, his Willoughby, OH, farm, where he raised Guernsey cattle in advocacy of the back-to-the-farm movement, which stressed the value of a rural, agrarian lifestyle. As a congressman, Beidler obtained 75 rural free delivery routes for his district; supported the good-roads movement; and helped veterans obtain their pensions. Beidler was reelected in 1902 and 1904 but retired in 1907, when he was appointed to the Ohio Board of Agriculture.

He married his wife, Hannah, in 1885 or 1886. They had 4 children: Mary, Mabel, Joseph, and Dudley. Beidler died in Cleveland and was buried in Lake View Cemetery.

**BELL, ARCHIE** (17 Mar. 1877–26 Jan. 1943), covered drama and music for Cleveland newspapers for over 30 years. Born in Geneva, OH, to Samuel A. and Sarah Jane (Soden) Bell, he began working shortly after graduation from Geneva High School as secretary to the *CLEVELAND WORLD's*† publisher, B. F. Bower, becoming a reporter, Sunday editor, and finally managing editor before Bower persuaded him to become the drama critic. When the *World* merged into the *News* in 1905, Bell continued as drama and literary editor, taking some time off to serve as publicity director for the HIPPODROME THEATER† and manage tours for actress

Olga Heghersole and soprano Ernestine Schumann-Heink.

In 1910 Bell joined the *PLAIN DEALER†* as drama and music critic, moving to the *Leader* about 1914, and to the *News* in 1917. Bell brought Fr. John Powers of St. Ann's Church together with ADELLA PRENTISS HUGHES of the MUSICAL ARTS ASSN.† for the benefit concert marking the birth of the CLEVELAND ORCHESTRA† in 1918. He also persuaded Morris Gest to bring "The Miracle" to Public Hall, paving the way for later visits of the Metropolitan Opera Co.

Bell, a world traveler, wrote travel books, as well as *The Clyde Fitch I Knew* (1910), and the fictional *The Clevelanders: An Expose of High Life in the Forest City* (1906), which is set mainly in Florida. Bell retired from the *News* in the mid–1930s because of a heart ailment. A bachelor, he died of pneumonia and was buried in Highland Park Cemetery. His books and theatrical memorabilia were donated to the Geneva Public Library.

**BELL, MYRTLE JOHNSON** (17 Nov. 1895–2 Sept. 1978), teacher, administrator and community activist, was the first African American asst. high school principal in the Cleveland Public Schools, where she taught mathematics, black history, and human relations. Bell was born in Warrensville, OH, the 3rd youngest of 8 children, and moved to Cleveland when she was 7. She graduated from CENTRAL HIGH SCHOOL† at 16 and from the College for Women, Western Reserve Univ. (WRU) in 1916. Bell taught mathematics at the Tuskegee Institute in AL and in Clarksburg, WV before returning to Cleveland. Denied a permanent teaching position on the basis of her race, she substituted in the Cleveland Public Schools for a few years. Her first regular assignment came in the late 1920s. While a teacher at Kennard Junior High, Bell created the Question Mark Club (1930s) where black students could study "Negro life and history." She later introduced a similar organization at Central High School (1942).

After her marriage in 1934 to L. Frank Bell, she lost her full-time position at Central: school policy prohibited married women from teaching if their husbands could support them. Substituting at first, Bell managed to secure a permanent contract before the fall 1935 semester ended. She received a Masters' degree from WRU in 1937. The next fall, Supt. Chas. Lake appointed Bell Central High Asst. Principal for Girls, a position she held until retirement (14 yrs. at Central and 14 yrs. at East Tech, after the schools' merger). Most of that time Bell was the system's only black asst. high school principal.

Bell participated actively in community affairs, serving on the city's advisory board on playgrounds (1936), on the Community Relations Board (1945–49), as special projects committee chair for the BUSINESS & PROFESSIONAL WOMEN'S CLUB,† and, with her husband, on the Glenville YMCA board. Bell died at the Margaret Wagner House of the BENJAMIN ROSE INSTITUTE.† —J.M.

---

Myrtle J. Bell Papers, WRHS.

**BELL, NOLAN D.** (7 July 1920–26 Feb. 1976), a veteran of the Karamu Theater, was one of the best nonprofessional actors-comedians in America. He worked full-time for the Cleveland Sanitation Dept. to support his wife, Viola, and their 7 children (Robert, Charles, Nolan, Russell, Rowena, Denise, and Caree), while acting in more than 200 plays. Born in Gary, IN, to Edward and Marie (Westbrook) Bell, his family moved to Cleveland, where Bell appeared in his first production with the Karamu Children's Theater in 1926. A graduate of CENTRAL HIGH SCHOOL,† in 1935 Bell and a friend, Joseph Singleton, won roles on radio station WGAR† portraying "Pin and Willie." After 2 years at the City College of Indiana and 1½ years at Indiana Univ., Bell served in the army from 1940–46, studying for a year at the Univ. of Manila. In 1946 Bell resumed his acting career at KARAMU HOUSE,† starring in many LANGSTON HUGHES productions. He also performed operatic roles, and appeared at the MUSICARNIVAL† in Cleveland and Florida, the DOBAMA THEATER,† and the Chagrin Valley Little Theater. Talent scouts from Hollywood and New York tried to lure him, but Bell preferred sharing his talents within his own community. In 1968 he became the first African American to join the regular staff at the CLEVELAND PLAY HOUSE† and was honored with a listing in *Who's Who in America;* he was the only actor–garbage collector to be so listed. In 1972 he starred in an episode of the television series *Maude.* Bell died at his home in CLEVELAND HTS.† and was buried in Highland Park Cemetery.

**BELLAMY, GEORGE ALBERT** (29 Sept. 1872–8 July 1960), founded HIRAM HOUSE,† the first social settlement in Cleveland. Born in Cascade, MI, to William and Lucy Stow Bellamy, his family's involvement in the Disciples (Christian) Church led him to enter the ministry. While studying at Hiram College from 1892–96, he became interested in settlement work (see SETTLEMENT HOUSES†) and joined students in establishing Hiram House in Cleveland in 1896, assuming its control in 1897 and developing it into the largest and most financially secure settlement in the city.

Bellamy was early interested in urban, environmental reform, working for housing code regulation and serving on the Cleveland Chamber of Commerce's Public Bath House Committee (1901) and Committee on the Housing Problem (1903). Later he became interested in recreational work, overseeing the city's first night-lighted playground at Hiram House in 1900, promoting a recreational bond issue in 1912, and named unpaid supervisor of the city's playgrounds. Bellamy lectured for the Natl. Playground Assn., and directed the establishment of recreational facilities at military camps during World War I.

Bellamy's social-work philosophy changed after the war. In the 1920s he evolved a "Child Growth and Development Program," directed toward molding individual character traits, to which he committed a large portion of Hiram House's resources. Bellamy became increasingly conservative, opposing Franklin Roosevelt's welfare programs. He retired from Hiram House in 1946. Bellamy was married twice; first to Hiram House co-worker Marie Laura Parker, who died in 1909: then Clara Horn in 1912. He had four children: Laura (Cole), Alice (Benham), Ester (Anderson), and Betty (Pempin). Bellamy died in Cleveland and was cremated.

Hiram House Records, WRHS.
Grabowski, John J. "A Social Settlement in a Neighborhood in Transition, Hiram House, 1896–1926" (Ph.D. diss., Case Western Reserve Univ., 1977).

**BELLAMY, PAUL** (26 Dec. 1884–12 Apr. 1956), was editor of the *PLAIN DEALER†* from 1928–54. Son of utopian author Edward Bellamy and Emma (Sanderson) Bellamy, he was born in Chicopee Falls, MA, graduated from Harvard (1906), and worked a year on the Springfield (MA) *Union* before coming to Cleveland as a reporter for the *Plain Dealer*. Two years later he became the youngest city editor in the paper's history. Leaving the *Plain Dealer* briefly for work in Chicago and service in World War I, Bellamy returned in 1919, was managing editor the following year, and took over editorially in 1928 until Jan. 1954, when he became editor emeritus.

Bellamy was president of the American Society of Newspaper Editors in 1933 and helped write the Natl. Recovery Act code for newspapers. A director of the Associated Press for 18 years, he warned against excessive wartime censorship in 1943. Although he was a Democrat and knew Pres. Franklin Roosevelt, Bellamy became critical of the New Deal and the Democratic *Plain Dealer* endorsed Wendell Willkie in 1940. Nonetheless, Roosevelt made Bellamy head of a wartime committee formulating policies governing occupational draft deferments for federal employees.

Bellamy was a charter member of the CITY CLUB OF CLEVELAND.† His first marriage, to Marguerite Scott Stark in 1908, ended in divorce in 1941 after producing 4 children: Peter, Richard K., Joan B. May, and John. Bellamy subsequently married Mrs. Mary Mitchell Henry on 21 Nov. 1941. He died in his Bratenahl home at age 72. His son, PETER BELLAMY, was a critic and columnist for the *CLEVELAND NEWS†* and the *Plain Dealer*. Bellamy was buried in Lake View Cemetery.

Paul Bellamy Papers, WRHS.
Porter, Phillip W. *Cleveland: Confused City on a Seesaw* (1976).

**BELLAMY, PETER** (9 Nov. 1914–6 Jan. 1989) covered many beats during a journalism career of 50 years, but was best remembered as drama critic of the *PLAIN DEALER.†* He was a native of Cleveland and the son of PAUL BELLAMY, editor of the *Plain Dealer* from 1928–54. Educated at HAWKEN SCHOOL,† Shaw High, and Harvard Univ., Bellamy began his own newspaper career in Iowa with the Des Moines *Register-Tribune* in 1936. Two years later he returned to Cleveland to join the staff of the *CLEVELAND NEWS,†* where he served as drama and film columnist before seeing service in the navy during World War II. Following the war he returned to the *News,* which gave him a daily column, "Bellamy Around," in 1956 and made him, reportedly, Cleveland's first male society editor in 1959. With the expiration of the *News* in 1960, Bellamy moved to the *Plain Dealer* and became its drama critic, succeeding Harlowe Hoyt in 1962. During his 14 years on the drama desk, he once even covered a professional wrestling match at the instigation of *Plain Dealer* sports editor GORDON COBBLEDICK, who held that such exhibitions were, properly speaking, more theatrical than sporting in nature. At the other extreme of the drama spectrum, he also lectured on Shakespeare during a summer session at Western Reserve Univ. (see CASE WESTERN RESERVE†). In the decade prior to his retirement in 1986, Bellamy served as the paper's critic-at-large. He died in his home in CLEVELAND HTS.,† survived by his wife, the former Jean Dessel, and 5 children: Sheila J., Stephen P., John S., II., Christopher, and Nicole B. (Loughman). Bellamy was buried in Lake View Cemetery.—J.V.

**BEMIS, EDWARD W.** (7 Apr. 1860–25 Sept. 1930), a college professor, expert on public taxation, and proponent of municipal ownership, was a political ally of TOM L. JOHNSON, serving as superintendent of the Cleveland Water Works from 1901–09.

Born in Springfield, MA, Bemis, son of Daniel W. and Mary W. Tinker Bemis, was educated at Amherst College (A.B., 1880; A.M., 1884) and Johns Hopkins (Ph.D., 1885), studying history and economics. He reportedly taught the first university extension course in America, at Buffalo, NY, in 1885, then taught economics at Amherst (1885–86); Vanderbilt (1888–92); the Univ. of Chicago (1892–95), which he had to leave because of his "radical" views; and Kansas State Agricultural College (1897–99). Bemis wrote prolifically about local government, tax policy, municipal ownership of utilities, working conditions, labor strikes, trade unions, socialism, and religion and social problems.

Tom Johnson gave Bemis an opportunity to enact his reforms as head of the municipal waterworks, a department described as "a nest of party hacks." Bemis replaced the spoils system with the merit system, unleashing protests from both the department and the local Democratic organization. Bemis ran the department in a businesslike manner, installing a record 70,000 meters and reducing rates. The elimination of graft and incompetent workers enabled completion of the water-intake tunnel. Bemis also crusaded for higher tax evaluations on properties owned by utilities and railroads. After 1909, Bemis moved to New York City, where he served in similar capacities and worked as a consultant.

Married on 28 Oct. 1889 to Annie L. Sargent, Bemis had three children: Walter S., Alice L., and Lloyde E. He died in Springfield, MO, and was buried in New York City.

Biographical Notes on Edward W. Bemis, WRHS.

**BEN** was a fugitive slave who spent several months in Cleveland in 1806. In the spring of 1806, a small boat transporting a man named Hunter, his family, and Ben, was upset and driven ashore just east of ROCKY RIVER.† Hunter, from Michigan, hoped to resettle in the WESTERN RESERVE.† Ben was the only survivor; the others drowned or died of exposure. After 3 or 4 days, French trappers en route to Detroit rescued Ben, returning to Cleveland and leaving him in the care of Lorenzo Carter.

That October, 2 men from Kentucky, one claiming to be Ben's owner, demanded to see Ben. Carter purportedly stipulated that Ben must consent to the meeting, which he did. As a precaution, Carter had Ben on one side of the CUYAHOGA RIVER† and the 2 men on the other. The owner reportedly reminded Ben of his former good treatment and Ben consented to return to him. After the men left with Ben, they were confronted in INDEPENDENCE† by 2 men carrying rifles, who ordered Ben to flee into the woods, which he apparently did. These men, John Thompson and Jas. Geer, were considered employees of Carter's, or at least frequenters of his tavern, so Carter was credited with arranging the affair. Unable to find Ben, the slave owners returned to Kentucky. For a while it was believed that Ben lived in a hut, in either Independence or BRECKSVILLE.† He eventually made his way to Canada, and nothing more is known of him thereafter.

**BENADE, ARTHUR H.** (2 Jan. 1925–4 Aug. 1987), physicist and recognized expert on the acoustics of musical instruments, was born in Chicago, the son of James Martin and Miriam McGaw Benade, who shortly returned to India with their son to resume their careers as teaching missionaries. Arthur went to school in Lahore (now Pakistan) and after completing high school he returned to the U.S., where he served in the Army Air Force (1943–45) and subsequently as an electronics specialist at Los Alamos (1945–46). He resumed his education in physics, receiving an A.B. degree in 1948 and a Ph.D. in 1952 from Washington Univ. in St. Louis. He joined the faculty of Case Institute of Technology in Cleveland the same year, where he combined work in low-energy atomic and nuclear physics with the study of musical instruments. In his pioneering research on brass and woodwind instruments, Benade effectively combined theory and engineering practice in his study of their acoustics, tone production, and response, becoming an international authority in the field. He also was a skilled woodwind instrument maker and a practiced amateur performer on the flute and clarinet, enabling him to work closely with many professional musicians as a consultant. His two major works in the field were *Horns, Strings, and Harmony* (1960) and *Fundamentals of Musical Acoustics* (1976), which dealt with all aspects of musical acoustics, including the performing techniques, concert hall acoustics, and listener responses.

Benade married Virginia Lee Wassall 9 June 1948, and they had two children, Judith and Martin. A resident of SHAKER HTS.,† he died in Cleveland and was cremated.—M.S.

**BENDER, GEORGE HARRISON** (29 Sept. 1896–18 June 1961) was powerful in Republican politics in Cuyahoga County for many years. Bender was born in Cleveland to Joseph and Anna Sir Bender. After public school education and service in World War I, he became advertising manager for the BAILEY CO.† in 1920, and later general manager of the Bedell Co. He founded the G. H. Bender Insurance Co. in the 1920s. Bender married Edna B. Eckhardt in June 1920, and they had 2 children, Barbara (Mrs. Ernest B. Stevenson) and Virginia (Mrs. Dorsey Joe Bartlett).

Bender was elected to the Ohio senate in 1920, serving there until 1930. During the 1930s, Bender published 2 Republican party magazines and authored a book promoting Wendell Willkie for president in 1940. He chaired the Republican Central Committee of Cuyahoga County from 1936–54 and controlled Republican affairs there.

After 4 unsuccessful attempts, Bender was elected to the U.S. House of Representatives as a congressman-at-large in 1938, remaining until defeated in 1948, but returning again in 1950. When Robt. Taft died in 1954, Bender won the election to finish his Senate term, narrowly defeating THOS. A. BURKE. He lost his Senate seat in 1956 to Frank Lausche. In 1958 Jas. Hoffa hired Bender to chair a commission investigating racketeering in the Teamster's Union. The Senate Rackets Committee and court-appointed Teamster monitors denounced the Bender commission as a whitewash, and he resigned from the commission in Jan. 1960, returning home to CHAGRIN FALLS,† where he died.

George Bender Papers, Ohio Historical Society.

**BENEDICT, DANIEL** (20 Mar. 1776–16 Nov. 1840) was a pioneer settler and the first permanent resident of BEDFORD.† At the time the township was organized in 1823, it was Benedict who proposed the name Bedford, in honor of his home town.

Born in Bedford, CT, Benedict first moved to Vermont before settling in the wooded wilderness of the Bedford area in 1821. Here he built a sawmill at TINKER'S CREEK,† a tributary of the CUYAHOGA RIVER,† providing power for early industries.

Benedict was active in the township's government during its early years. On 7 April 1823, he was elected to the first Board of Trustees for Bedford Twp., serving until 1825. He was also appointed as judge.

Daniel and Catharine Benedict had nine sons: Julius, Darius, Ralph, Sillock, Judson, James, Rodolphus, Phinamber, and Allison. Benedict belonged to the Bedford Methodist Episcopal Church, having been among the first church members when it was formed in 1833. Benedict is buried in Bedford Cemetery.—T.B.

**BENEDICT, GEORGE A.** (5 Aug. 1812–12 May 1876) was the editor of the *CLEVELAND HERALD*† from 1857–76. Born in Watertown, NY, to Amos and Ann (Stone) Benedict, he moved to Cleveland in 1835, shortly after his admittance to the bar. He practiced law for several years, also serving briefly as city attorney and president of the city council. In 1848 he was appointed clerk of the superior court, which he filled until the court's

abolition under the Ohio Constitution of 1851. In 1853 Benedict purchased an interest in the *Cleveland Herald,* to which he had previously contributed articles. When JOSIAH A. HARRIS left the *Herald* in 1857, Benedict succeeded him as editor, forming a new partnership with the paper's other proprietor, A. W. Fairbanks, as Fairbanks, Benedict & Co.

Benedict kept the *Herald* on a course of conservative Republicanism through the Civil War and Reconstruction years. He was rewarded in 1865 with an appointment as postmaster of Cleveland, a position he held for 4 years. However Benedict's cautious stewardship of the *Herald* was no match for the aggressive Republicanism of EDWIN COWLES of the *CLEVELAND LEADER,*† and by the end of the war, the *Herald* had surrendered its competitive advantage to the upstart *Leader.* A vestryman of ST. PAUL'S EPISCOPAL CHURCH,† Benedict was married on 12 July 1839, to Sarah Rathbone. They had one son, George, and 2 daughters, Mary and Harriett. After his son's death in 1871, Benedict's health began to deteriorate, and after a long illness he died. His executor sold his interest in the *Herald* to his partner, Fairbanks. Benedict is buried in Lake View Cemetery.

**BENES, W. DOMINICK** (14 June 1857–15 May 1935), a prominent architect, was, with BENJAMIN S. HUBBELL, responsible for some of Cleveland's most splendid classical revival buildings, including the CLEVELAND MUSEUM OF ART† (1916), as well as major early modern commercial structures, including the Ohio Bell Telephone Co. (1927). Born in Prague, Bohemia, to Joseph M. and Josephine Nowak Benes, his family emigrated to the U.S. in 1866. At 15 Benes left high school in Oberlin, OH, to begin a 3-year (1873–76) apprenticeship with Bohemian-born architect, ANDREW MITERMILER.

In 1876 Benes joined the Cleveland architectural firm of COBURN & BARNUM,† later Coburn, Barnum, Benes & Hubbell (1896). Benes and Hubbell subsequently established their own partnership, HUBBELL & BENES† (1897–1939), whose major projects included the Citizens' Bldg. (1903); the Cleveland School of Art (1905), demolished; the Mather College Gymnasium (1908); the WEST SIDE MARKET† (1912); the YMCA (1912); the Illuminating Bldg. (1915); the Masonic Auditorium (1921); the current business wing (1922) of the CLEVELAND PUBLIC LIBRARY†; the PHILLIS WHEATLEY ASSN.† (1927); and St. Luke's Hospital (1927). Benes was the "personal architect" to JEPTHA H. WADE, and Hubbell & Benes designed the WADE MEMORIAL CHAPEL† (1901) in

LAKE VIEW CEMETERY.† Benes alone designed the Centennial Arch erected in PUBLIC SQUARE† during 1896.

Benes was president of the AMERICAN INSTITUTE OF ARCHITECTS, CLEVELAND CHAP.† and the CLEVELAND ARCHITECTURAL CLUB.† He married Matilda F. Nowak on 9 Mar. 1881 and had 4 children: Grace, Clara, Matilda, and Jerome H. Matilda's father, Frank Nowak, erected the first meeting house for various Bohemian societies. Benes died in Cleveland and was buried in Highland Park Cemetery.

Johannesen, Eric. *Cleveland Architecture, 1876–1976* (1979).
Hubbell & Benes Records, WRHS.

**BENESCH, ALFRED ABRAHAM** (7 Mar. 1879– 21 May 1973) was an active community leader and senior partner in one of Cleveland's most prestigious law firms, Benesch, Friedlander, Coplan & Aronoff. Born in Cleveland to Isidore J. and Bertha Federdian Benesch, he received his law degree from Harvard in 1903 and established a practice with Benjamin Star. Among his clients was the predominantly Jewish Peddlers' Self-Defense Assn., for whom Benesch obtained better police protection and fair treatment in the courts.

In 1912 Benesch was elected to the city council. In 1914 Mayor NEWTON D. BAKER appointed him as public safety director. Benesch was state director of commerce from 1935–39 and area rent director for northeastern Ohio from 1942–45. He was a member of the Cleveland Board of Education from 1925–62, including 2 terms as its president, 1933– 34. Benesch was active in B'NAI B'RITH† and, representing that organization, successfully fought to remove the quota system at Harvard Univ. that restricted Jewish admissions to 10%.

Benesch was a founder of the BUREAU OF JEWISH EDUCATION† in 1924 and an active or honorary member of its Board of Trustees until his death. He also served on the boards of the JEWISH FAMILY SERVICE ASSN.,† the JEWISH COMMUNITY FED.,† BELLEFAIRE,† MT. SINAI HOSPITAL,† and the Natl. Jewish Hospital in Denver, serving that institution for over 50 years, including as a vice-president during the 1950s and 1960s. In 1955 Benesch received the Eisenman Award from the Jewish Community Fed. for his civic and humanitarian activities. He married Helen Newman of Chicago in 1906. They had no children. Benesch died in Cleveland and was buried in Mayfield Cemetery.

Alfred A. Benesch Papers, WRHS.

**BENJAMIN, CHARLES H.** (29 Aug. 1856–2 Aug. 1937), a mechanical engineer and educator at Case School of Applied Science from 1889–1907, established that school's mechanical engineering department. Benjamin was born in Patten, ME, the son of Samuel E. and Ellen Fairfield Benjamin. He attended Patten Academy and served as a machine shop apprentice before receiving his bachelor's degree from Maine State College (now the Univ. of Maine) in 1879. After a year at a machine shop in Lawrence, MA, he returned to his alma mater, earning a master's degree in 1881 and teaching there, leaving in 1886 to become asst. manager at the McKay Bigelow Machine Co. in Boston. In 1889 he accepted the professorship of mechanical engineering at Case and became head of that new department, creating the curriculum, supervising plans for the department's new building (1892), and acquiring the necessary laboratory equipment. Benjamin was professor of mechanical engineering and department head from 1889–99 and from 1903–07; between 1899–1903, professor of applied mechanics was added to his title. In 1907 he left Case to become dean of the School of Engineering at Purdue Univ., until 1921, when he became director of the Engineering Experiment Station at Purdue. While at Case, Benjamin gave public lectures and wrote 2 books, *Modern American Machine Tools* (1906) and *Machine Design* (1906); he later wrote *Steam Engine* (1909). He also served the city of Cleveland as supervising engineer in 1901 and as a smoke inspector. Benjamin married Cora L. Benson on 17 Aug. 1879; they had no children. He died in Washington, DC.

**BENN, REV. LUTHER** (28 Oct. 1910–15 Aug. 1993) was the founder of St. John Missionary Baptist Church, known as a place where the hungry could go to get food and clothing. Benn was noted for his encyclopedic knowledge of the Bible and he was often sought out for advice on secular as well as religious matters.

Born in Dry Branch, GA, Benn joined the navy in 1932. Trained as a cook, he was promoted to officer's chef. Benn sailed across the Atlantic Ocean 19 times and around the world 7 times. Benn left the navy in 1937 and moved to New York City. In 1941 Benn moved to Cleveland, taking a foundry job with Republic Steel Corp., from which he retired in 1973.

In June 1941 Benn joined Second Mount Sinai Baptist Church, where he became a deacon and taught Sunday school. He took courses with Moody Bible Institute and Cedarville Baptist College and was ordained as a minster in 1950.

Benn served as pastor of Second Mount Zion Junior Church for two years, before founding the St. John Missionary Baptist Church with 7 members.

They held their first service in a funeral home at E. 46th St. and Cedar Ave. in 1953. Two years later, the congregation moved to a basement on E. 100th St. and built a church on the site. St. John Missionary Baptist Church disbanded with Benn's death.

Rev. Benn married Estella Moss in 1934. They had a son, Bernard. Benn lived in CLEVELAND HTS.† His remains were shipped to Macon, GA. —T.B.

**BENTLEY, REVEREND ADAMSON** (4 July 1785–2 Nov. 1864) was a minister of the DISCIPLES OF CHRIST,† a banker and merchant, and the first settler in BENTLEYVILLE,† which he founded in 1831.

Born in Allegheny County (currently Bentleyville), PA, to Benjamin and Mary (Baldwin) Bentley, Adamson moved with his family to Brookfield, Trumbull County, OH. Here Bentley made public confessions of his faith in Jesus Christ in the Baptist order. His guardians advised him to prepare for the ministry and at age 19 he began preaching, continuing for the next five years as a licentiate.

In 1810 Bentley settled in Warren, OH, and became an ordained minister. In 1811 Bentley served as pastor of Bethany Baptist Church in Warren. In 1830 Bentley received a grant of 2,000 acres of land in the Western Reserve about 20 miles southeast of Cleveland. This area today is located on Miles Road.

In 1831 Bentley settled in the area presently known as Bentleyville, and founded a town which included a dam, saw mill, grist mill, woolen mill, carding mill, race mill, a bridge, handle factory, a barn for his cattle, and his home. The Village of Bentleyville was incorporated on 27 February 1929.

In 1832 Bentley became the first pastor of the Disciples of Christ Church (now the Federated Church) in CHAGRIN FALLS,† serving until 1852. Bentley traveled a great deal to merchandise his cattle and preach sermons.

Bentley married Mary Brooks in 1811. They had nine children: Benjamin, Stoughton, Martin, May, Laura, Emily, Martha, Lorinda and Lucretia. Bentley is buried in Evergreen Hills Cemetery in Chagrin Falls.—T.B.

**BENTON, ELBERT JAY** (23 Mar. 1871–28 Mar. 1946) was an author, educator, historian, and college administrator. Born in Dubuque, IA, to Oliver Dustin and Sarah Proctor Benton, Elbert grew up in Kansas where he received his A.B. degree from Campbell College, Kansas City Univ. He taught in high schools while doing graduate work at the Univ. of Chicago and at Johns Hopkins Univ., from which he received his Ph.D. in 1903, when he was appointed instructor of history at Adelbert College.

He became asst. professor in 1906; full professor in 1909; and the first dean of the newly organized Graduate School in 1925, although he continued to teach. He retired in 1941, becoming dean emeritus. In 1942, Benton, who had served as secretary and trustee of the WESTERN RESERVE HISTORICAL SOCIETY† since 1913, became acting director, and subsequently director. Benton wrote several books, including *Peace without Victory* (1918) and *A Short History of the Western Reserve Historical Society, 1867–1942*, both published by the society. He co-authored several histories with Western Reserve Univ. professor HENRY E. BOURNE, and also wrote the 3-volume *Cultural History of Cleveland*. He was an editor of the *American Historical Review* and contributed articles to the *Dictionary of American Biography* and the *Dictionary of American History*. In 1959 the Elbert Jay Benton Chair in History was established in his honor at Western Reserve Univ.

Benton married Emma Kaul in June 1895. She died in May 1925. In 1927 he married Emma's sister, Irene J. Kaul (d. 22 Nov. 1977). Benton had no children. He died in SHAKER HTS.† and was buried in Knollwood Cemetery.

**BERGENER, ALBERT EDWARD MYRNE (A.E.M.)** (5 Sept. 1875–14 May 1950) was, in the words of one of his reporters, the "cussing, shouting, reporter-insulting, hard-boiled" city editor of the *CLEVELAND NEWS.†* The son of Henry and Katherine (Casyl) Bergener, he was born and raised in Chicago. He dropped out of the Univ. of Notre Dame at 19 to commence his journalism career with several Chicago papers. Brought to Cleveland in 1912 to become city editor of the *CLEVELAND LEADER,†* Bergener sent back for his fiancee, Maud Woodruff, who became his 2nd wife on 12 Apr. 1913. He became city editor of the *News* when the *Leader* ceased publication in 1917. He personally obtained a murder confession from local gangster Leonard "Kid" Lyons in 1917 and uncovered a bootlegging scandal in the LAKEWOOD† police dept. which resulted in a dozen federal indictments during the Prohibition era. Tracking down fugitive embezzler Geo. J. J. McKay in 1927, Bergener kept him under wraps and milked him for several exclusives before turning him over to police. Described as possessing "a granite face and eyes like drills," he advised such cub reporters as HOWARD BEAUFAIT, LOUIS CLIFFORD, and JACK CLOWSER to "make yourself a human question mark." Bergener was made managing editor in 1931 but left in 1934 to serve the *News* as Washington correspondent. He tried retirement in Florida in 1935 but returned to Cleveland 2 years later to become public relations consultant for businessman ARTHUR B.

MCBRIDE. He died in his Lakewood home, survived by his wife and 2 sons in Chicago from his first marriage, Wallace and Elbert.—J.V.

**BERNARDI, GIACOMO** (3 Jan. 1888–12 Aug. 1966), brought some of the greatest names in music to Cleveland in his career as impresario of more than 1,000 concerts. Born Jacob Moses Schwartz in Galati, Romania, he emigrated to the U.S. in 1906 and soon found employment in a Cleveland clothing factory. His ambition was to become a singer, however, and he left on the recommendation of no less than Enrico Caruso to study voice in New York. He returned to Cleveland in 1913 as a featured singer in *Robin Hood* at the EUCLID AVE. OPERA HOUSE,† but his career was soon aborted by an unsuccessful sinus operation. He turned to booking concerts under his adopted name of G. Bernardi in 1919, taking over a function formerly performed by ADELLA PRENTISS HUGHES, founder of the CLEVELAND ORCHESTRA.† When the Depression cramped the concert business, Bernardi concocted a patent sinus medicine with the aid of Cleveland pharmacist Henry Sherwood and marketed it under the name Benaris. Having been divorced from Bessie S. Bernardi ca. 1925, Bernardi married Harriet Dragon in 1940 and resumed the promotion of concerts under the title of Cleveland Concert Assn., and later Cleveland Opera Assn. The list of performers appearing under his aegis, usually in PUBLIC AUDITORIUM† or Music Hall, included Sergei Rachmaninoff, Jascha Heifetz, the Bolshoi Ballet, Artur Rubinstein, Marian Anderson, and the New York Philharmonic. Reflecting changing public tastes, he also began booking more popular acts in the 1960s. He was survived by his wife, Harriet, and 3 children: Victoria Schultz, Gloria, and Franklin. They continued the concert agency for several years, becoming inactive around 1971. —J.V.

Giacomo Bernardi Papers, WRHS.

**BERNON, (BERNSTEIN) MAURICE** (24 Aug. 1885–23 Mar. 1954), political activist and philanthropist, was born in Cleveland, the son of polish immigrants David J. and Augusta Jacobs Bernstein. Educated at CENTRAL HIGH SCHOOL,† Bernstein entered Western Reserve Univ. Law school at age 18 and received an LL.B. degree in 1906. After graduation he practiced law and held a succession of elected and appointed positions in local government, including Cleveland City Councilman, representing the 15th Ward on lower Woodland Ave. 1908–09, and asst. city solicitor, 1910–11. As a member of the Ohio Senate 1913–14, Bernstein promoted legislation in the tradition of Cleveland

Mayor Tom Johnson who sought to improve the quality of urban life in Cleveland; he also was Asst. Attorney General, Ohio 1917–18. Changing his name to Bernon about 1919, he was elected judge of the Cuyahoga County Common Pleas Court in 1920, serving until 1924. At that time he was the senior partner in the firm of Bernon, Mulligan, Keeley & LeFever. Bernon was one of the principal strategists for the Cuyahoga County Democratic Party 1928–34, the period when the ward-mayor form of government replaced Cleveland's CITY MANAGER PLAN.† He was elected to the party's Executive Board in 1936. Active in the JEWISH WELFARE FEDERATION,† Bernon was the first campaign chairman of the Jewish Welfare Fund organized to provide money for local, national, and international Jewish causes outside the scope of local welfare activities.

Bernon married Minnie Reiss 25 Dec. 1912, and they had two children, Howard of Roslyn, NY, and George. A resident of Cleveland when he died, Bernon was buried at Mayfield Cemetery.—M.S.

**BERNSTEIN, HARRY** (1856–1920), known as "Czar" Bernstein, was an entrepreneur and Republican political ward boss who could, according to contemporary accounts, deliver the votes he promised from his ward to a man. Born in Poland to Berman and Rosa Bernstein, he was brought to Cleveland in 1868, and educated in the public schools. During his career, Bernstein owned theaters, a restaurant, a saloon, a pool hall, and a hotel; established a neighborhood bank; and operated a junk business. He established the People's, and less successful Perry theaters in the 1890s to present Yiddish entertainment in the heavily East European Jewish Woodland neighborhood. His Perry Bank, which later merged with the Cleveland Trust Co., was established specifically to serve the immigrant neighborhood.

Bernstein's businesses, and providing favors for needy immigrants in the 16th (later 12th) ward, provided the base for his political power. Beginning ca. 1888 as an operative for the Hanna machine, he became one of Cleveland's most effective ward bosses, although his influence was confined to the immigrant district. In the 1890s, Bernstein groomed a young protege, MAURICE MASCHKE, who within a decade became a leader of the county's Republican party. In 1903 Bernstein was elected to the city council, the only time he held elective office. Although he supported Mayor TOM L. JOHNSON, Bernstein did not curry favor with the reformers. With the ascendancy of the Progressives and the beginning of a population shift in his ward, Bernstein lost much of his influence during the first decade of the 20th century.

Bernstein married Sarah Trilling on 21 Oct. 1888. They had five children: Alex, Hyman T., Charles, Fannie, and Rose. He died in Cleveland.

**BERTMAN, JOSEPH** (1902–20 Oct. 1988), noted for his mustard, first used at LEAGUE PARK in the late 1920s and then at CLEVELAND MUNICIPAL STADIUM† for many years, was born in Lublin, Poland, in 1902 and came to this area with his parents as a child. Working as a deliveryman for William Edwards Co. and Halle Bros., he established Bertman Pickle Co. in 1925 at his home on E. 147 St. near Kinsman, where he developed a variety of choice pickles, salad dressings, mustard, and other items based on his own recipes.

In the mid–1930s he established Joseph Bertman Inc., a wholesale food business first located at E. 103 St. and St. Clair and then at 2180 E. 76th St. His mustard, made from a secret recipe, was also popular at Euclid Beach, the Arena, the Coliseum, and area race tracks. It was known as Bertman's Stadium Mustard until 1982 when it became Ball Park Mustard.

Bertman, who was married to Edith Gutermann Bertman for many years, was survived by his son Philip and daughter Patricia (Mrs. Marvin) Mazoh of Cleveland.—M.S.

**BICKFORD, CLARA L. (GEHRING)** (25 Sept. 1903–13 Dec. 1985), musician, teacher, and collector, founded and served as the first president (1933–35) of the Women's Committee of the CLEVELAND INSTITUTE OF MUSIC† (CIM). A pianist, Bickford collected music manuscripts, letters, autographs, and photographs relating to music. She donated that collection to the CIM, which exhibited it late in 1986. Bickford was born in the Cleveland area to Emma Motz and Frederick Gehring. She graduated from LAUREL SCHOOL† and Bryn Mawr College. Bickford taught piano at CIM and served on its board for many years. Her other activities reflected her musical interest, including serving on the board of the CLEVELAND ORCHESTRA,† as president of the orchestra's Women's Committee, leading the Lecture Recital Club, and presiding over the Music Therapy Committee of the Cleveland State Hospital. She belonged to the Cleveland Friends of Music and the board of Amateur Music Makers, and performed with the Two Piano Club. Bickford also belonged to the Women's City Club and served as president of its foundation in 1950. She volunteered for and donated to the above groups as well as the CLEVELAND MUSEUM OF ART.†

Bickford married GEORGE P. BICKFORD on 6 Apr. 1933; they had a daughter, Louise Boyd. The family lived in CLEVELAND HTS.† CIM held a memorial concert for Bickford on 8 Oct. 1986. —J.M.

———

Cleveland Institute of Music Archives.

**BICKFORD, GEORGE P.** (28 Nov. 1901–14 Oct. 1991), a Cleveland attorney, became a noted authority on Indian and Far Eastern art through the process of acquiring an extensive personal collection in the field. A native of Berlin, NH, he was raised in Washington, DC. Following his graduation from Harvard in 1922, he traveled to China, where he studied Chinese and taught in a missionary school in Shanghai. Bickford then returned to earn a degree from Harvard Law School, graduating in 1926 and joining the Cleveland law firm later known as ARTER & HADDEN.† In 1933 he married Clevelander Clara Gehring (see CLARA GEHRING BICKFORD), a piano instructor at the CLEVELAND INSTITUTE OF MUSIC.† Mrs. Bickford, who later became president of the Women's Committee of the CLEVELAND ORCHESTRA,† and of the Women's City Club Foundation (see WOMEN'S CITY CLUB†), acquired through the years an impressive collection of musical autographs. Bickford conceived his own interest in Indian art as a result of army service in the Judge Advocate General's Dept. during World War II, where he served in the India-Burma Theater. Upon his return, the collection he had begun was displayed in the CLEVELAND MUSEUM OF ART† in 1946, and later in 1975. He made bi-annual postwar trips to India and in 1964 was appointed honorary consul for India for the Cleveland area. For 35 years, he also served as trustee for the Cleveland Museum of Art. Active in Republican politics, Bickford was a founder of the Republican Ripon Club and served as general counsel to the Federal Housing Administration in 1958–59. Long a resident of CLEVELAND HTS.,† he was survived by a daughter, Louise G. Boyd.—J.V.

**BICKNELL, WARREN, JR.** (5 Sept. 1902–23 April 1975), leader in both business and PHILANTHROPY,† founded the BICKNELL FUND† with his wife, Kate Hanna Bicknell. He was born in Wheaton, IL, to Ann Guthrie Bicknell and Warren Bicknell, Sr. By the fourth grade, his family lived in CLEVELAND HTS.† and he attended UNIV. SCHOOL. He graduated from Taft School (CT), and Williams College (1925). Bicknell served as president of his father's business, the Cleveland Construction Co. from 1940 until retiring in 1969. President of the BUILDERS EXCHANGE† (1945–46), he was also a director of the M. A. HANNA CO.,† Union Salt, the National Acme Co. (see ACME-CLEVELAND†), the Cleveland Storage

Co., and the Society for Savings Bank (see SOCI-ETY NATIONAL BANK†), among other corporations, and of philanthropic entities such as Advisory Services, Inc. In the realms of EDUCATION† and HIGHER EDUCATION,† Bicknell served as a trustee of Williams College, LAUREL SCHOOL† and the Western Reserve Academy in Hudson, OH. He was a life member of the BOY SCOUTS OF AMERICA.†

Bicknell married Kate Hanna, granddaughter of Howard M. Hanna, Sr. They lived in Chardon with children Constance Reynolds, Kate Kirkham, Wendy, and Warren, III. Buried in Thomasville, GA, Bicknell has a memorial headstone in Lake View Cemetery.—J.M.

**BIEHLE, AUGUST FREDERICK JR.** (13 Jan. 1885–7 Feb. 1979) emerged from the artistic background of the BIEHLE FAMILY to become a recognized member of the "Cleveland School" of artists (see ART†). Born in Cleveland, the son of Christina (Mussler) and August F. Biehle, Sr., Biehle trained as an apprentice decorator with his father for the firm of Rorimer Brooks (see LOUIS RORIMER). He went to Europe in 1903 to study painting in Paris and at the Kunstgeverbeschule in Munich. Absorbing the work of the Blue Rider, German Expressionist, and French Fauve schools, he developed a distinctive style of flat decorative patterns. Upon his return to Cleveland in 1905 Biehle went to work for the SHERWIN-WILLIAMS CO.† He continued his studies at night with F. C. GOTTWALD and returned to Munich in 1910 to study at the Royal Academy. Back in Cleveland in 1912, he was persuaded by CARL MOELLMAN and WILLIAM SOMMER to become a lithographer for Otis Lithography and Continental Lithography Corp., where he remained from 1913–52. Married in 1921 to the former Mary Theresa Wessler, Biehle continued with his own painting, studying with HENRY KELLER at his Berlin Hts. summer school and exhibiting with FRANK WILCOX, PAUL TRAVIS, and Sommer. Known for landscapes, he also did portraits and painted murals for the WPA. By 1955 he was working abstractly. Biehle's paintings were so frequently selected (25 yrs.) for the MAY SHOW,† that he was awarded Emeritus Nonjury Entrant status, allowing him to bypass the normal competition. A member of the KOKOON KLUB,† he was survived by his wife and 3 children: Marie Scott, Reta Alder, and Frederick A.—J.V.

Landau, Ellen (ed.). *August F. Biehle, Jr.: Ohio Landscapes* (1986).

The **BIEHLE FAMILY** were designers and painters who worked on frescoes and decorative painting for such clients as the Chamber of Commerce, churches, and several of Cleveland's foremost families. August Frederick Biehle, Sr. (4 July 1856–10 Nov. 1918), the senior family member, was born in Freiberg, Baden. His father, a manufacturer of costume jewelry, died when he was 4. Until he was 14, he attended school in his home town and sang in the choir of Freiberg Cathedral. He was apprenticed with a "master painter" and went to a trade school, where he focused on drawing. After working in other European cities and completing a 3-year military service, he emigrated to America in 1880. Biehle came directly to Cleveland and ultimately took a position with L. Cooks (later called Cooks Bros.), where he stayed for 16 years, the last 8 as chief designer and painter. In 1897 he went into business for himself and contracted to do work for the firm of L. Rohreimer and L. H. Hays (later Rorimer Brooks Co.). His work appeared in the Chamber of Commerce and many mansions and churches in the northeastern part of the country. Of Biehle's 5 children, AUGUST F. BIEHLE, JR., achieved distinction as an artist in his own right. The Biehle Bros. firm was formed by 3 of the children of the elder Biehle's brother, Frederick A. Biehle, Sr. (1857–1916), a master decorator of mansions. The firm decorated in the Cleveland area ca. 1920–50 under the leadership of August W. Biehle (1882–1961), whose apprenticeship and college degree were received in interior design. Other members were his brothers, Karl (1897?–1949), and Frederick A., Jr. (1881–1945). A 4th brother, William A. Biehle (1890–1979), formed his own decorating business in Chicago. Carrying on the family tradition into a 3rd generation were a son and daughter of August F. Biehle, Jr. Frederick August Biehle became an artist and art educator, while Reta Biehle Alder was active in Cleveland's music community as a pianist, organist, and choir director. —J.V.

**BIELEN, CASIMIR** (10 Feb. 1925–2 Sept. 1992), educator and clean-air activist, participated in more than 80 organizations, including nationality groups and political and educational organizations. The Nationalities Services Center recognized Bielen's fundraising efforts in 1977. Bielen was born in Cleveland's SLAVIC VILLAGE† to Martin and Josephine (Schotka) Bielen. He attended South High School and Denver Univ. and, after a stint in the U.S. Air Force during World War II (1943–46), graduated in 1951 from the Cleveland College of Western Reserve Univ. (later CASE WESTERN RESERVE UNIV.†). He later received a master's degree from Kent State Univ. (1964). On 9 June 1951, Bielen married Valera P. Japel.

Bielen worked as an elementary and junior high school principal in GARFIELD HTS.† and as executive assistant to the state auditor. On the board of the Polonia Foundation, he also served as spokesperson for the COSMOPOLITAN DEMOCRATIC LEAGUE OF CUYAHOGA COUNTY,† the Polish American Congress, and the Cleveland Society of POLES.† He worked for the CLEVELAND CULTURAL GARDENS FEDERATION,† coordinated ethnic affairs for the MAYORAL ADMINISTRATION OF DENNIS J. KUCINICH,† and was secretary of both the Southeast Air Pollution Committee (1950–56) and the Air Pollution Committee of the Southeast Community Council (1956–59). In 1959 he was made executive secretary of the Ohio Pure Air Assn., located in Cleveland. Bielen donated $5,000 in 1980 to the family of his deceased friend, Olympian STELLA WALSH, to help clear her name after media reports questioned her gender.—J.M.

Casimir Bielen Papers, WRHS.

**BILL, ARTHUR HOLBROOK** (10 Nov. 1877–11 Mar. 1961) was an innovator in hospital obstetrics and helped establish Cleveland's reputation for low maternal mortality. Born in Cleveland to Herbert Weston and May McIlewain Bill, he received his B.A. from Adelbert College (1897), his M.A. from Western Reserve Univ. (1898), and his M.D. from WRU Medical School (1901). Bill interned at Lakeside Hospital; at Johns Hopkins Hospital in 1902; at Vassar Hospital in 1903; and at New York Lying-in Hospital in 1904, specializing in obstetrics. In 1905 he studied in Berlin, Vienna, and Paris, returning to WRU in 1906 as an asst. in obstetrics, becoming demonstrator in 1907, instructor in 1908, and associate professor and head of the department in 1909. In 1906 Bill became associated with Maternity Hospital and began an outpatient clinic in his home. In 1911, when Bill became chief of staff, he moved Maternity and helped affiliate it with WRU. In the early 1920s, he campaigned for a larger and better hospital, which climaxed with the development of the UNIVERSITY HOSPITALS OF CLEVELAND† complex and the opening of the new Maternity Hospital on 30 Nov. 1925. Bill structured the obstetrics training program at WRU so that students did not simply witness confinements, but helped deliver as many as 40 babies and attend innumerable labors. By his retirement in 1948, Bill had trained over 2,000 obstetricians-gynecologists and had developed techniques to relieve childbirth pains. Bill was survived by his wife, Gladys Buttermore Bill, whom he married in 1923. He was buried in Oakwood Cemetery in Cuyahoga Falls.

**BINGHAM, CHARLES W.** (22 May 1846–3 Mar. 1929) was a businessman active in Cleveland cultural institutions. Born in Cleveland to William and Elizabeth Beardsley Bingham, he graduated from Yale with a B.A. in 1868. Bingham spent 3 years in Europe studying geology, mining, and chemistry. He earned his M.A. from Yale in 1871 and began working in Cleveland, perhaps at the Cleveland Iron Co., of which his father, WM. BINGHAM, was president. In 1879 he was a member of Wm. Bingham & Co., and from 1881 until his death, was president of the Standard Tool Co. He served on several banking boards and arranged business matters for family members, for which he established Perry-Payne Co. On 8 June 1876, Bingham married Mary Perry Payne. They had 5 children: Oliver Perry, William II, Elizabeth Beardsley (Blossom), FRANCES PAYNE (BOLTON), and Henry Payne.

From 1892 until his death, Bingham was a trustee of the WESTERN RESERVE HISTORICAL SOCIETY.† He was treasurer of the Case Library and president of the Case Library Assn. He was an original trustee conducting the Huntington Art & Polytechnic Trust, and was a trustee of the Horace Kelley Art Foundation. He chaired the building committee representing these 2 trusts in the construction of the CLEVELAND MUSEUM OF ART,† of which he was a trustee from 1913–20. A trustee of the Lake View Cemetery Assn., Bingham was also a member of the FIRST PRESBYTERIAN (OLD STONE) CHURCH† from 1862, and a trustee from 1909 until his death. He was buried in Lake View Cemetery.

**BINGHAM, FLAVEL W.** (15 May 1803–1867) was a lawyer and politician who served 1 year as mayor of Cleveland. He was born in New York to Flavel and Fanny White Bingham and came to Cleveland in 1837, where he set up the law practice of Collins & Bingham. He was elected councilman and chosen city council president in 1845. In 1847 and 1848, he was elected as an alderman and again served as city council president. In 1849 he became mayor. Bingham was elected the city's first probate judge, serving from 1852–55. When his term expired, he returned to private law practice, forming the partnership Bingham & Hovey. He served as president of the Society for Savings bank and was well connected with local business interests. He left Cleveland for New Orleans in 1863, where he died. He and his wife, Emmeline, had 3 children: Frances, Charles, and Edward.

**BINGHAM, WILLIAM** (9 Mar. 1816–17 Apr. 1904), a prominent Cleveland businessman, was born in Andover, CT, to Capt. Cyrus and Abigail

Foote Bingham. He was educated in Andover and Monson, MA, schools before coming to Cleveland when he was 20. His father helped him establish a hardware business with GEO. WORTHINGTON, and in 1841 he purchased the firm of Clark & Murfey, organizing it as Wm. Bingham & Co., dealing not only in hardware but also in metals. In 1846–47 Bingham served on CLEVELAND CITY COUNCIL,† initiating the establishment of a city waterworks system and supervising construction of the first tunnel into the lake for drinking water. In 1862 he was appointed to the city board of sinking fund trustees. During the Civil War, he raised volunteers, relieved disabled soldiers and their families, and raised money for the Union. It appears he was considered for the Republican nomination for mayor of Cleveland in 1865 and 1867, but he apparently avoided the honor. In 1873 he was elected Senator, and in 1876, Pres. Grant appointed him to the Board of Indian Commissioners, from which he resigned in 1877, apparently because he had to make good on a defaulted note he had endorsed for a colleague. Bingham was also involved in banking and railroads; and served as the first president of the UNION CLUB† (1870). He was a trustee of the Case Library Assn. and of the FIRST PRESBYTERIAN CHURCH.† On 2 Jan. 1843, Bingham married Elizabeth Beardsley. They had 3 children: Caroline Elizabeth, CHAS. WILLIAM, and Cassandra Hersh. Bingham died at his home in Cleveland and was buried in Lake View Cemetery.

**BINKLEY, ROBERT CEDRIC** (10 Dec. 1897–11 April 1940), professor and chairman of the Department of History at Flora Stone Mather College of Western Reserve Univ. (WRU, 1932–40), earned a national reputation as a historian pioneering and advocating archival preservation methods such as the Photostat, microphotography, and mimeography. As technical advisor for work relief projects operated through the Federal Emergency Relief Administration (1933–35), and then the WORKS PROGRESS ADMINISTRATION† (1935–40), he helped establish Cleveland as a national center for project standards and development for the national HISTORICAL RECORDS SURVEY.†

Binkley was born in Mannheim, PA, the oldest of 11 children of Mary Engle Barr and Christian Kreider Binkley. He served in the U.S. Army in France during World War I. After the war, he assisted Professor Ephraim D. Adams in developing the Hoover War Library at Stanford Univ. in Palo Alto, CA. He received an A.B. (1922), A.M. (1924), and Ph.D. (1927) in history from Stanford. Before coming to WRU as acting professor in 1930, Binkley taught at New York Univ. (1927–29), Smith College

(1929–30), and Stanford (1930); he later served as visiting lecturer and professor at Harvard Univ. (1932–33) and Columbia Univ. (1937–38). Binkley also worked with the Library of Congress, attempting to save wartime documents and helping draft national copyright legislation. While chair of the Joint Committee of the American Council of Learned Societies and the Social Science Research Council (1932–40), Binkley proposed that relief labor be utilized in a variety of archival surveys. In his advisory affiliation with the WPA and Historical Records Survey National Director Luther H. Evans, Binkley devised techniques by which white-collar relief workers sorted, correlated, and catalogued public and private archival records. One of the major results of this project was the *ANNALS OF CLEVELAND*† series (see HRS). These *Annals* served as models for similar projects around the country and embodied Binkley's desire to make a community's cultural resources more democratic through their accessibility to scholars, students, and citizens.

On 13 Sept. 1924, Binkley married Frances Williams in CA. The couple had three children: Barbara (who died in infancy), Robert Williams, and Thomas Eden. Binkley died at Lakeside Hospital and was buried in California. In his memory, WRU set up the Committee on Private Research, with a $10,000 grant from the Carnegie Corp.—M.M.

Fisch, Max H., ed. *Selected Papers of Robert C. Binkley* (1948).
McDonald, Wm. *Federal Emergency Relief and the Arts* (1969).

**BIRD, PHILIP SMEAD** (9 Nov. 1886–10 June 1948), a clergyman and civic leader, was born in Newtonville, MA, the son of Joseph Edward and Gertrude Hubbard Smead Bird. He graduated with an A.B. from Pomona College, Claremont, CA (1909); from the Univ. of California with a Master of Literature degree (1910); and from Union Theological Seminary, New York, in 1913.

Bird was ordained on 11 May 1913, and served as pastor and teacher of biblical literature at churches and schools in Claremont, CA, and Dobbs Ferry and Utica, NY, before his installation as pastor of the CHURCH OF THE COVENANT† in Cleveland on 20 Feb. 1928. During his ministry, membership increased from 1,733 to 2,500; Christ Chapel was created; the Williamson Chancel was restructured; and the Student Christian Union on the Western Reserve Univ. campus was established. Bird was president of the Cleveland Church Fed. (1931–33); chairman of the Church Extension Committee of the Presbytery of Cleveland (1929–33); and moderator of the Presbytery (1942–43). In 1933 he organized the interfaith Cleveland Peace Committee, and was elected its chairman in 1936. He was also on the board of numerous civic and social service organizations.

Dr. Bird received honorary degrees from Hamilton College, Clinton, NY (1924); from WRU (1928); and from the College of the Ozarks, Clarksville, AR (1933). Dr. Bird married Margaret Hubbell Kincaid of Utica, NY, on 11 July 1922; and had a daughter, Mrs. Joseph (Margaret Elizabeth) Kuder. Dr. Bird died in Cleveland and is buried in Lake View Cemetery.

---

Philip Smead Bird Papers, WRHS.

**BIRINYI, LOUIS KOSSUTH** (19 Apr. 1886–3 Sept. 1941) was a prominent member of the Cleveland Hungarian community. Author, journalist, and lawyer, Birinyi was an articulate spokesman on behalf of his native Hungary.

One of five children of Joseph and Susanna Birinyi, Louis was born in Damak, Hungary. His parents emigrated to the U.S. when Louis was two years old, leaving him behind with his grandparents. His parents returned to Hungary eleven years later. By then Louis himself wanted to come to the U.S., and his father made that possible in 1902.

Settling in Pittsburgh, Birinyi supported himself as a steel worker until 1907, when he moved to Crescent, NC, in the hopes of studying there for the ministry of the Hungarian Reformed Church. Changing career goals, in 1909 he moved to Lancaster, PA, where he earned his B.A. degree from Franklin and Marshall College. In 1913 he came to Cleveland to study law at Western Reserve Univ. He received his law degree, was admitted to the bar in 1916, and set up his first office at East 89th St. and Buckeye Rd.

In 1924 Birinyi wrote his first book, *The Tragedy of Hungary,* an attack on the provisions of the Versailles Treaty, which had split apart the Austro-Hungarian empire. The book was widely read on both sides of the Atlantic and earned Birinyi membership in the Hungarian Academy of Science. In 1938 he wrote a second book, *Why the Treaty of Trianon is Void.*

In addition to his books, Birinyi was a frequent contributor and correspondent for several U.S. Hungarian-language newspapers.

In 1917 Birinyi married Anna Lemak. They had two children, Louise and Louis K., Jr.—J.T.

**BIRNS, ALEX "SHONDOR"** (21 Feb. 1905–29 Mar. 1975), a notorious criminal, was involved in rackets, prostitution, theft, assault, and murder from the days of Prohibition until his death. Born to Herman and Illon Birn, the family emigrated to Cleveland from Austria-Hungary in 1907. He grew up on Woodland Ave., an accomplished athlete, quick with his fists, and with a volatile temper. He enjoyed notoriety, treating journalists who labeled him "Public Enemy No. 1" very well. Birns dropped out of school after 10th grade in 1922, enlisting in the navy in 1923 but discharged 6 months later because he was underage. He began selling bootleg whiskey. Birns's criminal record was extensive, ranging from vagrancy to murder. He was first arrested, for car theft, in 1925, serving about a year in Mansfield Reformatory. Birns was afterwards arrested a number of times but served little time in jail, having friends among lawyers, judges, and policemen, and buying off or silencing witnesses. Birns operated the Ten-Eleven Club and the Alhambra Restaurant, often treating off-duty policemen, lawyers, and journalists. In 1942 he was arrested by U.S. immigration officials as an enemy alien, since he was still a Hungarian citizen, and for years officials tried to deport Birns; however, no country would accept him.

Birns married twice. His first marriage was in 1952. He and his wife, Jane, had one son, Michael (d. 1978). They divorced in 1964 and Birns then married Allene Leonards. In the spring of 1975, Birns was released from a short stay in jail and announced that he was going to go straight, but he was killed by a bomb planted in his automobile. No one was arrested for his murder.

**BISHOP, ROBERT H., JR.** (22 Aug. 1879–29 Sept. 1955), a Cleveland physician, was a leader in hospital administration, in anti-tuberculosis (TB), and other public health issues. Born in Mankato, KS, he graduated in 1903 from Ohio's Miami Univ. where his great-grandfather had been the college's first president, and his grandfather a Latin professor. Bishop went to Western Reserve Medical School, and in 1909 finished his internship under Dr. DUDLEY P. ALLEN. He was director of Lakeside Hospital (1920–24), then worked for its consolidation with Maternity Hospital and Babies & Children's Hospital into UNIV. HOSPITALS,† of which he was director from 1932–47. He then headed the new Joint Commission for Advancement of Medical Education & Research at Western Reserve Univ.

A founder of the Anti-TB League, Bishop established the bureau of TB in the Cleveland Health Department in 1914, setting up 8 TB control centers and special treatment programs. He served as health commissioner during World War I. In 1918, with Prof. John H. Lowman, Bishop organized and took to Italy the first overseas TB unit of the American Red Cross. He also promoted a bond issue for a sanatorium at Sunny Acres, where he served as chairman of the board.

Throughout his career, Bishop was a member of many civic organizations and worked to implement public-health programs. He was trustee of the Cleveland Welfare Fed., director of the Natl. Social Hygiene Assn., American Hosp. Assn., president of the American College of Hospital Admins., and on the Board of Trustees of Miami Univ. Bishop was awarded the American Social Hygiene Assn.'s William Freeman Snow Medal for distinguished service to humanity.

Bishop married Constance Mather in 1914; they had four children: Robert III, William M., Amasa S., and Jonathan S.

Mather Family Papers, WRHS.

**BLACK, HILBERT NORMAN** (3 Oct. 1929–25 Nov. 1981), earned a reputation as one of the top police reporters in the city's history during his 29-year career with the *CLEVELAND PRESS.†* He was a native of St. Louis, MO, the son of Robert and Mary Black. After service with the U.S. Army, he earned a journalism degree from Bowling Green State Univ. in 1952. He joined the *Press* that summer as a copy aide and was assigned to the police beat the following year. By 1955 his reputation for accuracy and gaining the confidence of sources resulted in his promotion to chief police reporter. He headed the paper's 7-man police beat for 15 years, until becoming asst. city editor in 1970. In that position, he was a key member of a team which won a CLEVELAND NEWSPAPER GUILD† award for best news story in 1976 for its coverage of the Eddie Watkins bank robbery, siege, and capture. Black maintained his old network of contacts in his work on the city desk and took a special interest in the training of young African American reporters. He was also noted by fellow workers for his hobbies of woodworking and gourmet cooking. Black was a member of MT. ZION CONGREGATIONAL CHURCH† and the NATIONAL ASSN. FOR THE ADVANCEMENT OF COLORED PEOPLE.† He died of cancer, survived by his wife Judith, son Alan, and daughter Cristi. Buried at Highland Park Cemetery, he was inducted posthumously into the CLEVELAND JOURNALISM HALL OF FAME.†—J.V.

**BLACK, COL. LOUIS** (24 Dec. 1844–12 Jan. 1919) was a civic and business leader best known as president of the BAILEY CO.† A native of Hungary, he was the son of Morris and Rose Black, reputed to be Cleveland's first Hungarian family when they immigrated to the city in 1854. Louis was one of the first Hungarians naturalized in Cuyahoga County and served in the 150TH OHIO VOLUNTEER INFANTRY REGIMENT† during the CIVIL WAR.† He entered business in Cleveland with the D. Black Cloak Co., where he remained until 1896. He then joined C. K. Sunshine in assuming control of the Bailey department store, which they incorporated in 1899 as the Bailey Co. Black remained with the store until his death, filling the positions of treasurer and president. Active in Republican politics, he served 2 years on CLEVELAND CITY COUNCIL† and became the city's first fire director under Mayor WILLIAM GREY ROSE. He was a long-time member of the CLEVELAND GRAYS,† being a trustee during construction of GRAYS ARMORY.† His honorific title of Col. was evidently acquired from his membership in the Knights of Pythias. Black was also a director of the Cleveland Jewish Hospital Assn. and a president of the Hungarian Benevolent Assn. Besides the Bailey Co., his business interests included real estate and banking. He indulged his hobby of gardening at his EUCLID AVE.† home in EAST CLEVELAND† and a country home on Lake Shore Blvd. Survived by his wife of 51 years, Anna, and 2 children, Roy Black and Mrs. Victor Sincere, Black was buried in Lake View Cemetery.—J.V.

**BLACK, MORRIS ALFRED** (31 May 1868–23 Apr. 1938) was an influential businessman and civic leader. Born in Toledo, OH, to Hungarian immigrants Herman and Eva Judd Black, in 1892 the Blacks moved to Cleveland, where Herman's uncle and aunt were the pioneer Hungarian family. Black graduated from Harvard Univ. with an A.B. in 1890, and became a designer in the H. Black Co. (founded in 1883 by Herman), manufacturers of women's "Wooltex" coats and suits.

Succeeding his father as company president, 1903–22, Black made Cleveland a national garment center. Employing around 1,000 workers, Black believed factories should not only be efficient but also attractive and pleasant work places. In 1922 H. Black merged with the PRINTZ-BIEDERMAN CO.† In 1923 Black became president of the Lindner Co., a garment manufacturer he founded in 1913. He was also president of the Blackmore Co. and the Cleveland Garment Mfrs. Assn. Black attempted to stabilize the garment industry by making agreements for impartial arbitration. Resigning as president of Lindner in 1936, he worked until his death as a business consultant.

Black helped found the Civic League in 1903, predecessor of the CITIZEN'S LEAGUE,† serving on its executive board until 1921. Interested in housing and city planning, he organized and chaired the City Plan Commission from 1915–25, and was vice-president from 1915–20. From 1914–19, he was president of the Cleveland Chamber of Commerce. He married Lenore E. Schwab on 21 Mar.

1898, and they had a son, Herman. Black died of a heart attack in Aurora, OH, and was cremated.

**BLACK HAWK** (1767–3 Oct. 1838) was an American Indian chief of the Sauk and leader of the Black Hawk War against the U.S. in 1832. Born in a Sauk village on Rock River, IL, near the present day city of Rock Island, IL, he came to Cleveland in 1833 to visit his mother's grave on the CUYAHOGA RIVER.† Although some men from Cleveland served in the Black Hawk War, the village was unaffected directly by the war, although indirectly 50 Clevelanders died from an epidemic of cholera brought by a troop boat returning from the war. The boat had been denied docking in Detroit, but after consultation was allowed to stop in Cleveland, where the epidemic spread.

After the war, Black Hawk was taken into custody by the U.S. government and brought east to meet with President Andrew Jackson. Returning westward, he asked to stop in Cleveland for a day in order to visit his mother's grave. In Cleveland, Black Hawk was given a canoe or boat, and he paddled up the river alone to a bluff overlooking the valley (possibly from the southeast corner of RIVERSIDE CEMETERY†). He remained there for a short time and upon returning he reportedly had tears in his eyes. After stopping in Cleveland, Black Hawk was brought west to the Sauk reservation in Iowa, where he was buried. His body was stolen in 1839, mutilated, and burned in a fire at the Historical Society of Burlington, IA, where it had been placed after it had been recovered.

Black Hawk (M. M. Quaife, ed.). *Life of Black Hawk* (1932).

**BLANCHARD, FERDINAND Q.** (23 July 1876–4 Mar. 1968), a clergyman, poet, author, and civic leader, was born in Jersey City Hts., NJ, to Edward Richmond and Anna Winifred Quincy Blanchard. He received his A.B. from Amherst College (1898) and his B.D. from Yale Divinity School (1901). He was ordained in 1901, and pastored churches in Southington, CT (1901–04), and East Orange, NJ (1904–15), before becoming the minister of the EUCLID AVE. CONGREGATIONAL CHURCH† on 25 Mar. 1915.

Blanchard was president of the Cleveland Church Fed. (1919–20); and served the AMERICAN RED CROSS, CLEVELAND CHAP.†; the Associated Charities; the URBAN LEAGUE OF CLEVELAND†; KARAMU HOUSE†; the Maternal Health Assn.; Schauffler College; the Missionary Assn.; and Fisk Univ. as trustee or board member. He founded (Jan. 1920) the Alathian Club, an ecumenical group of Cleveland clergy, and received honorary D.D.

degrees from Amherst College (1918), and Oberlin College (1919).

On 14 June 1942, Blanchard became moderator of the General Council of the Congregational Christian Churches of the U.S., and from 1944–50, was national chairman of the Congregational Commission of Interchurch Affairs. He worked for the June 1957 union of the Congregational and the Evangelical & Reformed churches, which established the United Church of Christ. Blanchard also wrote articles, poems, and hymns, as well as several books. He retired in 1951.

Blanchard married Ethel Hebard West in 1901; they had 2 children, Edward R. and Virginia (Mrs. Chas. S. Becker). A memorial plaque was dedicated to him at the Euclid Ave. Cong. Church after his death. He was buried in Lake View Cemetery.

*From Village Green to City Center, 1843–1943* (Centennial of the Euclid Ave. Congregational Church, Cleveland, OH, 1943).

**BLEE, ROBERT E.** (31 Jan. 1839–26 Feb. 1898), a railroad superintendent, was mayor of Cleveland from 1893–95. Born in Glenville, OH, to Bridget and Hugh Blee, who were early settlers of Cuyahoga County, Blee attended district schools and Shaw Academy at COLLAMER,† and was inspired by a graduation speaker to pursue a career in railroading. At 15 he became a brakeman for the Cleveland, Columbus & Cincinnati Railroad, the "Bee Line." During the Civil War, Blee supervised troop transportation for the army between Cleveland's Camp Chase and Columbus' Camp Dennison. After the war, he returned to the Bee Line, and by 1888 was its general superintendent. Blee organized and was president for 22 years of the Bee Line Insurance Co.; was president of the Ohio Natl. Bldg. & Loan Co.; and was a director for several other corporations. He never married.

Elected as a Democrat, Blee was Cleveland's police commissioner from 1875–79 and is credited with ending the unpopular "star chamber sessions" that typified police arrests until that time (police board policy of keeping the press out of hearings). As the result of a Republican split in 1893, Blee was elected mayor of Cleveland. During his term, he advocated harbor improvements and dock building to maintain the city's position as a Great Lakes port. The police department also tried to register local prostitutes, but Blee was forced to stop them because of public outrage. Blee was defeated for reelection by ROBT. E. MCKISSON in 1895.

**BLISS, STOUGHTON** (18 Feb. 1823–19 Sept. 1896) was a Cleveland businessman and army officer during the Civil War. Son of William and

Cynthia (Wolcott) Bliss, he was born in Cleveland and worked as a post office clerk until he went into the hat and fur business in 1846. Between 1850 and the outbreak of the Civil War, he was appointed colonel and served as asst. quartermaster of Ohio, a position that he held throughout the war. After the war he went into the stone business. At his death, he was affiliated with the Diamond Stone Quarry in BEREA,† and was treasurer of the Grafton Stone Co. He was 1st vice-president of the Cleveland Light Artillery Assn. Bliss married Mary Sweet in 1849. He never remarried after her death in 1851. There were no children. He is buried in Woodland Cemetery.

**BLOCH, ERNEST** (24 July 1880–15 July 1959), was an internationally known composer, conductor, and teacher recruited to found and direct the CLEVELAND INSTITUTE OF MUSIC† in 1920. Bloch was born in Geneva, Switzerland, the son of Sophie (Brunschwig) and Maurice (Meyer) Bloch, a Jewish merchant. Bloch showed musical talent early and determined that he would become a composer. His teen years were marked by important study with violin and composition masters in various European cities. Between 1904 and 1916, he juggled business responsibilities with composing and conducting. In 1916 Bloch accepted a job as conductor for dancer Maud Allen's American tour. The tour collapsed after 6 weeks, but performances of his works in New York and Boston led to teaching positions in New York City. During the Cleveland years (1920–25), Bloch completed 21 works, among them the popular Concerto Grosso, which was composed for the students' orchestra at the Cleveland Institute of Music. His contributions included an institute chorus at the CLEVELAND MUSEUM OF ART,† attention to pedagogy especially in composition and theory, and a concern that every student should have a direct and high-quality aesthetic experience. He taught several classes himself. After disagreements with Cleveland Institute of Music policymakers, he moved to the directorship of the San Francisco Conservatory. Following some years studying in Europe, Bloch returned to the U.S. in 1939 to teach at the Univ. of California at Berkeley. He retired in 1941. His students over the years included composers Roger Sessions and HERBERT ELWELL. Bloch composed over 100 works for a variety of individual instruments and ensemble sizes and won over a dozen prestigious awards. In 1955 a bronze sculpture of Bloch was dedicated in the Hebrew Cultural Garden in ROCKEFELLER PARK.†

Bloch married Margarethe Schneider on 13 Aug. 1904. They had 3 children: Suzanne, Lucienne, and Ivan. Bloch spent the later years of his life in Agate Beach, OR; he died in Portland, OR.

**BLODGETT, WALTER** (28 May 1908–25 Oct. 1975), an organist and teacher, was curator of musical arts at the CLEVELAND MUSEUM OF ART† (CMA) from 1943–74. Born in Grand Rapids, MI, the son of Arthur W. and Asenath (Harvey) Blodgett, he was a graduate of Oberlin College and the Juilliard School of Music. He also studied organ design and construction in Germany before coming to Cleveland in 1931. As a career organist, he directed music at EPWORTH EUCLID METHODIST CHURCH,† St. James Episcopal, the First Unitarian Church, and ST. PAUL'S EPISCOPAL CHURCH,† the latter for 25 yrs. His choir gave the Cleveland premiere of Beethoven's Missa Solemnis. As curator of musical arts at CMA, he played nearly 1,200 organ recitals and helped design the museum's Gartner Auditorium, where he rebuilt the P. J. McMyler Memorial Organ. He initiated the May Festival of Contemporary Music and is credited with generating considerable funds for the museum from endowments. During World War II, Blodgett was music critic for the CLEVELAND PRESS.† He contributed articles to various music magazines and was a faculty member at Western Reserve Univ. from 1957–62. In 1974 he became dean of faculty at the CLEVELAND MUSIC SCHOOL SETTLEMENT.† The same year, he won the Cleveland Arts Prize "for support and promotion for the creation and performance of new works, and encouraging and sustaining musical life in Cleveland." A resident of SHAKER HTS.,† Blodgett was unmarried.

**BLOSSOM, DUDLEY S.** (10 Mar. 1879–7 Oct. 1938) was a Cleveland businessman and philanthropist whose charitable activities eventually led him to civic office as city welfare director. Blossom, the son of Henry S. and Lela Stocking Blossom, after earning an A.B. degree from Yale, became associated with the Perry-Payne Corp., Payne-Bingham Co., Standard Tool Co., Cleveland Hobbing Machine Co., Blossom Lock Co., and Central Natl. Bank, serving each as a director or officer. He served with the Red Cross in France during World War I, and in 1919 was appointed Cleveland city welfare director, a position he retained until 1921, then again from 1924–32. As welfare director, Blossom was a progressive innovator, gaining national attention for city human services projects, including City Hospital and Blossom Hill Home.

As a substantial contributor to the Community Fund, Blossom became fund chairman in 1934 and was appointed honorary chairman for life in 1938. He headed the campaign that raised the funds required to match JOHN L. SEVERANCE's $2.5

million donation to build SEVERANCE HALL.† Blossom served as president of the MUSICAL ARTS ASSN.† and was a trustee of the Negro Welfare Fund, UNIV. HOSPITALS,† and Cleveland College. In the mid–1930s he was chairman of the GREAT LAKES EXPOSITION,† and also served a term as state representative. Blossom married Elizabeth Bingham, heiress to Oliver Hazard Payne's Standard Oil fortune, on 29 Sept. 1910. They had 2 children, Dudley S., Jr., and Mary.

Dudley S. Blossom Papers, WRHS.

**BLOSSOM, EMILY ELKINS** (7 May 1913–21 Dec. 1991) was awarded the Medal of Merit from the Garden Club of America in 1973 for helping to create, beautify, and sustain Blossom Music Center, the CLEVELAND ORCHESTRA's† summer home. On 11 July 1992 the center dedicated the Emily Blossom Garden, established in 1990 in her honor. Blossom was born in Waycross, GA, the daughter of James and Mary (DeFord) Elkins. She married A. Davis Gale in 1934 and moved to Cleveland. They had two daughters, Sylvia G. Oliver and Emily G. McCartney. In 1954, two years after Gale died, Blossom married Dudley S. Blossom, Jr., becoming stepmother to Laurel Blossom, Elizabeth Hefferman-Meers, C. Bingham Blossom, and Dudley S. Blossom III. Her husband died in 1961.

Blossom became a trustee of the MUSICAL ARTS ASSN.† in 1968 and served as vice-president from 1982–88. In 1990 the association named her honorary trustee for life. She was also honorary chair of the Blossom Women's Committee. Among other horticultural and cultural activities, Blossom served on the boards of the Cleveland Guidance Center, the GIRL SCOUTS,† the NORTHERN OHIO OPERA ASSN.,† the LAKE ERIE OPERA THEATER,† and Cleveland Metroparks. In addition, she volunteered for PLANNED PARENTHOOD OF GREATER CLEVELAND† and supported conservation projects. She was living in LYNDHURST† when she died. Blossom was buried in Lake View Cemetery. —J.M.

**BLOSSOM, HENRY C.** (16 Nov. 1822–18 Aug. 1883) was a business leader and life member of the WESTERN RESERVE HISTORICAL SOCIETY† and the Northern Ohio Historical Society. He was born in Chester, GA, to Orrin and Laura Fellows Blossom. Blossom came to the Cleveland area in the 1830s to work in a hardware store, first in Painesville. In a few years, he joined the William Bingham & Co. (forerunner of the W. BINGHAM CO.†) as a clerk. By the early 1840s Blossom had become a partner; he remained with the firm for 35 years. He belonged to Second Presbyterian Church.

In 1850 Blossom married Amma Louisa Nash of Willoughby; the couple had 2 children, Henry S. and Josie (Mrs. C.) Clark. Blossom died in Hamburg, Germany; he is buried in Lake View Cemetery.—J.M.

**BLYTHIN, EDWARD** (10 Oct. 1884–14 Feb. 1958) was a Cleveland law director, mayor, and judge. Born in Newmarket, Wales, to Peter and Elizabeth Roberts Blythin, he worked 2 years as a bookkeeper for an English coal firm before coming to Cleveland in 1906, where he worked as bookkeeper for the Walton Realty Co. for 10 years, while studying law nights at Cleveland Law School. After receiving his LL.D. in 1916, he practiced law from 1916–41 and 1942–43, specializing in municipal law. He was appointed Cleveland asst. law director in 1935, law director in 1940, and succeeded HAROLD H. BURTON as mayor of Cleveland when Burton became a U.S. Senator in 1941, serving 11 months before losing the election to FRANK LAUSCHE. As mayor, Blythin mobilized manpower for the national defense, and urged companies and unions to remove barriers to black employment.

From 1943–48, Blythin was financial vice-president and secretary of Western Reserve Univ. He was elected judge in the common pleas court in 1949, presiding at the trial of Dr. Samuel H. Sheppard for the murder of Sheppard's wife, Marilyn, in 1954 (see SHEPPARD, SAMUEL, MURDER CASE†). With the widespread publicity, the defense maintained that Sheppard had not received a fair trial, but Blythin defended both his conduct of the case and the propriety of holding the trial in Cleveland. He remained judge until his death at age 73. Blythin married Jane Rankin 5 Apr. 1913, and they had 5 children:Robert, Arthur, Glen (dec.), Jane (Mrs. Robt. Drake), and William.

Harold Burton and Edward Blythin Papers, WRHS.
"In Memory of Judge Edward Blythin" (paper delivered to the Philosophical Club of Cleveland, 14 Jan. 1958, WRHS).

**BOARDMAN, WILLIAM JARVIS** (15 Apr. 1832–2 Aug. 1915), was a lawyer active in Cleveland business, civic, and political affairs before moving to Washington, DC, in the late 1880s. Son of Henry Mason and Sarah Hall Benham Boardman and born in Boardman, OH, William Boardman spent 3 years at Kenyon College before transferring to Trinity College in Hartford, CT, where he graduated in 1854. He then entered Yale Law School and transferred to Harvard a year later. After graduating from Harvard Law School in 1856 he moved to Cleveland, working briefly in the law offices of Samuel B. and Frederick J. Prentiss before being admitted to the bar and opening his own law office. In 1859 Boardman began a long tenure as a director of the Commerce Branch Bank of Cleveland and its successor in 1865, the Commercial Natl. Bank. In 1877 he became a director and general counsel of the Valley Railway Co. In the 1860s he served as president of the CLEVELAND LIBRARY ASSN.,† later the Case Library; and in 1869 he became president of the Cleveland Law Library Assn., later serving as a trustee. He was a trustee of both Kenyon College and Adelbert College of Western Reserve Univ., and was also active in Trinity Church and in political organizations in the 5th Ward. On 20 Dec. 1859, Boardman married Florence Sheffield. They had 6 children: Mabel Thorp, William Henry, Joseph Sheffield, Elijah George, Josephine Porter, and Florence. In 1887 the Boardmans moved to Washington, DC, where Boardman died and was buried. Upon his death in 1915, Wm. J. Boardman was identified by newspaper headlines as the father of the leader of the Red Cross, Mabel Boardman.

**BOCK, JOSEPH COURTNEY** (24 Sept. 1913–14 Feb. 1992), musical prodigy and outstanding amateur tennis player, was born in Cleveland, the son of Peter D. and Laura Henrich Bock. He attended Western Reserve Univ. studying the liberal arts. Bock also was an accomplished musician, playing the piano and violin at a young age. He performed as a piano soloist at the CLEVELAND INSTITUTE OF MUSIC† at age 13 and two years later was playing the piano for his own radio program on WHK.†

Bock began his tennis career in the 1930s and won several area championships, including Cleveland's Municipal Tennis Title in Sept. 1936, when he defeated Gene Vash in the men's singles event. In his late 40s and early 50s, Bock and his partner, Edward DiLeone, won the men's doubles in the Senior National Public Parks tennis championship in 1961, 1962, 1964, and 1965. Adept at languages, he learned to speak Polish, German, and Spanish in his work with community groups in Cleveland. Bock, who never married, died in Cleveland at age 78 and was buried at Calvary Cemetery.—M.S.

**BOEHM, CHARLES** (1853–9 Apr. 1932) was a missionary to Hungarian immigrants in America. Born in Selmecbanya, Hungary, to Felez and Julia Boehm, he entered the minor seminary at Esztergom, and was sent to the Univ. of Vienna, where he completed his studies for the priesthood. He was ordained on 16 July 1876.

Boehm pastored at Maria Nostra and Nagy-Modro before 1892, when he was the first Hungarian priest chosen by Kolos Cardinal Vaszary to

work among Hungarian Catholics in America. Boehm arrived in Cleveland in Dec. 1892, and established ST. ELIZABETH'S CHURCH,† making provisions for a school that opened in 1893 under lay direction, until Fr. Boehm gained the services of the URSULINE SISTERS† in 1895. Boehm started the newspaper *Katolikus Magyarok Vasarnapja* (Catholic Hungarian Sunday) and also organized a number of spiritual and fraternal organizations.

In 1907 Fr. Boehm left St. Elizabeth to devote himself to missionary work. Using Buffalo as his headquarters, he traveled throughout the eastern U.S. and Canada, ministering to Hungarian communities. In 1923, he resumed the pastorate of St. Elizabeth's. In recognition of his many services, Fr. Boehm was declared a domestic prelate by the Vatican and given the title of monsignor. Msgr. Boehm resigned his parish in 1927 because of advancing age, but took on a new apostolate, visiting CLEVELAND STATE HOSPITAL† for five years and serving as its unofficial chaplain. He died in St. Vincent Charity Hospital in 1932 after a brief illness. Boehm is buried in Calvary Cemetery.

Papers of St. Elizabeth Parish Archives, Diocese of Cleveland.

**BOHM, EDWARD H.** (7 Feb. 1838–7 May 1906) was a CIVIL WAR† officer, newspaper publisher, and public official. Born in Alstedt, Saxe-Weimar, Germany, his family settled on a farm in NEWBURGH,† in 1851. Bohm left the farm in 1856 to work on the Cleveland & Toledo Railroad until the Civil War broke out. He enlisted in Co. K, 7th Ohio Volunteer Infantry, on 18 Apr. 1861. Captured by Confederates on 20 Aug. 1861 on the Gauley River in western Virginia, he was imprisoned until 30 May 1862, when he was released at Washington, NC. He was commissioned a 2nd lt. in Co. D, 7th OVI, in Jan. 1863, and was wounded at Chancellorsville (May 1863). He was mustered out with the 7th on 6 July 1864.

In the postwar years, Bohm prosecuted soldiers' claims against the U.S. government. He was elected to the school board in 1870 and served as Cuyahoga County recorder from 1870–76. He founded the *Cleveland Anzeiger,* a German daily newspaper, but was forced to relinquish the paper after 4 years because of financial difficulties. He was president of the North American Saengerbund and the Saengerfest of 1874. A Republican, he served as presidential elector-at-large for Ohio in 1876 and was elected justice of the peace in 1885. He served as a member of the Soldiers & Sailors Monument Commission, 1896–1906.

Bohm married Alvina F. Jassvard in 1865 and had

3 children: Alvina, Antoinette, and Edward. After her death in 1875, he married again. He and his wife, Hedwig, had 3 children: Hedwig, Arno, and Erwin. Bohm died in Cleveland and was cremated.

**BOHN, ERNEST J.** (1901–15 Dec. 1975) was a nationally known expert on PUBLIC HOUSING.† Born in Hungary, the son of Frank J. and Juliana (Kiry) Bohn, he came to Cleveland with his father in 1911, graduating from Adelbert College in 1924 and Western Reserve Law School in 1926. In 1929 he was elected to the Ohio House as a Republican, then served as city councilman until 1940. Active in housing reform, he authored the first state housing legislation, passed in 1933. As president and organizer of the Natl. Assn. for Housing & Redevelopment Officials, Bohn helped pass the U.S. Housing Act of 1937.

Bohn directed the Cleveland Metropolitan Housing Authority (CUYAHOGA METROPOLITAN HOUSING AUTHORITY†) from its founding in 1933 until 1968, and chaired the City Planning Commission from its founding in 1942 until 1966. His work included slum clearance and redevelopment. Following World War II he focused on housing for the elderly, building the Golden Age Ctr. at E. 30th St. and Central Ave., the first such housing development in the U.S. Deterioration of central-city housing in the mid–1960s led to charges that Bohn neglected meeting the needs of poorer people and promoted racial discrimination in filling CMHA units.

Following his retirement, Bohn lectured at CASE WESTERN RESERVE UNIV.† and was on the Board of Directors of the Natl. Housing Conference and the Ohio Commission on Aging. Bohn Tower and the Ernest J. Bohn Golden Age Ctr. were named in recognition of his contributions to Cleveland. Bohn never married. He died in Cleveland and was buried in Calvary Cemetery.

Ernest J. Bohn Collection, Freiberger Library, CWRU.

**BOIARDI, HECTOR** (1897–21 June 1985), known to millions as Chef Boy-ar-dee, began as a local restaurateur. Boiardi, son of Joseph and Mary (Maffi) Boiardi, began cooking in Italy at age 10. He left for New York about 1914 to work at the Ritz Carlton. He came to Cleveland 3 years later as chef at the Hotel Winton, where his spaghetti dinners became the talk of the Midwest. Boiardi married Helen Wroblewski on 7 April 1923. In 1924 they opened their first restaurant, the Giardino d'Italia. By 1928 their dine-in and carry-out operation required factory production, and their products were sold in stores over an expanding geographic area, prompting the name change to the phonetic Chef Boy-ar-dee, with the chef's picture as the trademark.

Producing tasty and inexpensive meals, the Boiardi company prospered in the Depression. To be close to tomato fields, Boiardi moved the company to Milton, PA. During World War II Boiardi developed field rations for the armed services. By war's end, sales of Chef Boy-ar-dee Quality Foods were $20 million annually, and the operation was sold to American Home Foods for $6 million. The chef was a company consultant until 1978.

Boiardi remained in local restaurants, opening Chef Boiardi's in 1931, and also acquiring interests in other restaurants. A talented businessman, after a venture in 1946 to produce animal food from restaurant scraps, Boiardi bought the Milton Steel Co. after a strike, and sold it for a large profit in 1951. When this pioneer in convenience foods died in 1985, Boiardi's former company's sales were $500 million a year.

The Boiardis had one son, Mario. Boiardi died in PARMA† and was buried at All Souls Cemetery.

**BOLE, ROBERTA HOLDEN** (30 Sept. 1876-28 Oct. 1950) was a philanthropist who helped establish Holden Arboretum, classes for gifted children in the CLEVELAND PUBLIC SCHOOL† system, and helped preserve DUNHAM TAVERN.† She was also cofounder of HAWKEN SCHOOL† for boys (1915) and a children's author (*The Aunt's Cookbook* and *Poor Richard*).

Born in Salt Lake City, UT, to Delia Elizabeth (Bulkley) and LIBERTY EMERY HOLDEN, Roberta came to Cleveland with her family at age 15. She was a graduate of Miss Mittleberger's School.

Roberta began her civic improvements in 1905 by finding a permanent home for the Cleveland School of Art. She became a trustee of the CLEVELAND MUSEUM OF ART† and served on its advisory council. In 1928 she presented the statue "Night Passing Earth to Day" to the museum and, in 1932, together with her siblings, presented Filippino Lippi's great painting, "The Holy Family with St. Margaret and St. John."

Roberta was a benefactor of the CLEVELAND MUSEUM OF NATURAL HISTORY.† In the 1930s she donated the original 100 acres on which Holden Arboretum in Kirtland was located.

In 1936 Bole and Ihna Thayer Frary helped found the Dunham Tavern Corp. to collect funds to save the historic tavern from destruction.

In 1937 the Boles's established the $50,000 FREDERICK HARRIS GOFF educational scholarship, which enabled Cleveland's public schools to establish classes for gifted children.

Roberta married Benjamin P. Bole (d. 1941) on 2 Sept. 1907, and had one son, Benjamin, Jr. Roberta belonged to the Unitarian Church and is buried in Lake View Cemetery.—T.B.

**BOLLES, JAMES A.** (2 May 1810–19 Sept. 1894), controversial rector of Trinity Church from 1855–59, was born in Norwich, CT, the son of Ralph and Happy (Branch) Bolles. After graduating from Trinity College in Hartford (1830) and studying at the General Seminary in New York, in 1834 Bolles became an Episcopal priest and rector of St. James Church in Batavia, NY. In 1853, primarily through Samuel L. Mather, Bolles became rector of Trinity Church in Cleveland. Opposed to the evangelical movement, Bolles advocated written sermons and practices associated with the Catholic Church, strongly objecting to the mass conversions of revival meetings and arguing against the interdenominational movement, which he considered superficial. Bolles engaged in public, published debate with the Episcopal bishop of Ohio over such issues, drawing national church attention.

Within a few months of Bolles's coming to Trinity, the church burned down. Bolles provided the leadership to rebuild it. During his ministry, Bolles emphasized charity and implemented systematic giving and the founding of 2 mission churches. He advocated the free church system, including free (as opposed to rented) pews, and in 1859 resigned when the vestry refused to make Trinity a free parish, with his congregation already divided over his advocation of daily services and other Catholic practices. In 1859 Bolles became rector of the Church of the Advent in Boston, but returned to Cleveland in 1871 as a senior canon at Trinity Church for many years. Bolles wrote *Vade Mecum: A Manual for Pastoral Use*, used by a generation of pastors.

Married twice, Bolles's first marriage was in 1833 to his cousin, Mary Frances Bolles (d. 1849); they had 3 children: Abby, Constance, and Kendrick. His second marriage was to Martha Elizabeth Evans in 1850; they had a daughter, Mary Frances. Bolles was buried in Lake View Cemetery.

---

Pierce, Roderic Hall. *Trinity Cathedral* (1967).

**BOLT, RICHARD ARTHUR** (12 Mar. 1880–3 Aug. 1959), a physician and director of the CLEVELAND CHILD HEALTH ASSN.,† was born in St. Louis to Richard Orchard and Mary Virginia Belt Bolt. He studied at Washington Univ. before transferring to the Univ. of Michigan, earning his A.B. in 1904 and his Ph.D. in 1906, afterward doing postgraduate work. Bolt came to Cleveland in 1907 to St. Vincent's Charity Hospital as an intern, then

pathologist, and later visiting physician in the Gynecological Out-Patient Department. During 1909–10, he was acting medical director of the Babies' Dispensary and Hospital. From 1911–16, Bolt was medical director of the U.S. Indemnity College of the Tsing Hua College at Peking, China; returning to Cleveland in 1917 as chief of the city's bureau of child hygiene and instructor of pediatrics at Western Reserve Univ. Medical School. From 1918–20, he served public health organizations in Italy and California, and from 1920–25, lectured at Johns Hopkins. Bolt returned to Cleveland in 1929 as Director of the Child Health Assn. and associate in hygiene, public health, and pediatrics at Western Reserve. Bolt pioneered expectant mother classes and maintained the babies' dispensaries' free milk program and the CLEVELAND PUBLIC SCHOOLS'† dental program. As early as 1945, he advocated using fluoride in the city's water. Bolt retired in 1945 to organize the Univ. of California's public health school. He married Rebecca Beatrice French on 21 July 1908, and had 4 children: Elizabeth, Richard, Marrion, and Robert. Bolt died in California.

**BOLTON, CHARLES CHESTER** (23 March 1855–31 July 1930) was a distinguished Cleveland businessman, civic leader, philanthropist and member of a prominent Cleveland pioneer family. He was a partner in M. A. HANNA CO.,† and was a charter member of TROOP A.†

Born in Cleveland to Judge Thomas and Emeline (Russell) Bolton, he attended Miss Guilford's Cleveland Academy, Cleveland High School and Philips Exeter Academy in NH. He received his B.A. from Harvard College in 1877, then traveled abroad for 2 years. In 1879 Bolton began working as a clerk for Rhodes & Co. (predecessor to M. A. Hanna & Co.) and remained with the firm after its reorganization under Marcus Hanna in 1885. Bolton rose to partner, and retired from the firm and business life in 1904.

In 1889 Bolton became the first treasurer of the COUNTRY CLUB†. He was also an organizer and early member of Troop A and moved up the ranks, becoming captain in 1892.

Bolton was a director of the Brown Hoist Machine Co., Bourne-Fuller Co., National Refining Co., Guardian Trust Co., and Society for Savings (also vice-president). He was a trustee and vice-president of the Associated Charities and active in the Community Fund. In 1903 Bolton received an honorary M.A. degree from Kenyon College.

Bolton married Julia A. Castle (the daughter of WILLIAM B. CASTLE) on 24 Nov. 1880. They had five sons: Chester Castle (see CHESTER CASTLE BOLTON), Kenyon Castle, Irving Castle,

Newell Castle, and Julian Castle. An Episcopalian, Bolton is buried in Lake View Cemetery. —T.B.

**BOLTON, CHESTER CASTLE** (5 Sept. 1882–29 Oct. 1939), an industrialist, Ohio senator, and U.S. congressman, was born in Cleveland to CHARLES C. and Julia Castle Bolton. His father was a prominent Cleveland businessman and philanthropist, and his mother was the daughter of former Cleveland mayor WM. B. CASTLE. He attended UNIV. SCHOOL† and received an A.B. degree from Harvard Univ. in 1905, before returning to Cleveland as asst. treasurer of the Bourne-Fuller Co. In 1917 he joined the army, attaining the rank of lieutenant colonel in the Army Ordnance Dept. After World War I, Bolton began his political career as a member of the municipal council of Lyndhurst Village from 1918–21. He was elected as a Republican to the Ohio senate in 1922, serving from 1923–28; and to Congress from the 22nd district in 1928. As chairman of the Natl. Republican Congressional Campaign Committee, he was instrumental in bringing the REPUBLICAN NATL. CONVENTION OF 1936† to Cleveland. A critic of the New Deal, he lost his congressional seat in the 1936 election, but was elected again to Congress in 1938. Bolton married Frances Payne Bingham in 1907, and they had 3 sons: Chas. B., KENYON C., and Oliver P., and a daughter, Elizabeth. Upon his death, his wife, FRANCES PAYNE BOLTON, was elected to serve out his term in Congress. Bolton was buried in Lake View Cemetery.

Chester C. Bolton Papers. WRHS.

**BOLTON, FANNY MANN HANNA** (6 Dec. 1907–9 May 1980) was a major contributor to and trustee of UNIV. HOSPITALS† and was the founder of the Bolton Foundation.

Fanny Bolton was born in Cleveland to Jean Claire and Howard Melville Hanna, Jr., president of the M. A. Hanna Mining Co. Fanny attended Laurel School and completed her education in New York by attending Miss Masters School at Dobbs Ferry, and the French School.

Fanny married Julian Castle Bolton on 27 April 1929. They had two daughters: Clair Hanna Bolton Jonklaas, and Betsy Hanna Bolton Schafer. Julian Bolton was vice-president of the Hanna Co. when he died suddenly on 24 Feb. 1944.

In 1952 Fanny Bolton established the Bolton Foundation, to which she was a major contributor. There were no restrictions on the use of income, and it primarily supported Cleveland hospitals and health services. While the Bolton Foundation still exists on record, the foundation funds were equally distributed in 1988 into two new Ohio foundations: the Eliza-Bolton Foundation and the Kerridge Fund.

Fanny Bolton spent much of her life at Melrose Plantation in Thomasville, GA. She died at Hanna House and is buried in Lake View Cemetery.—T.B.

**BOLTON, FRANCES PAYNE** (29 Mar. 1885–9 Mar. 1977) served as Republican congresswoman for 29 years and supported projects in nursing, health, and education. Born in Cleveland to banker-industrialist Chas. W. and Mary Perry Payne Bingham, and educated at HATHAWAY-BROWN† School and in New York City, in 1904 she began volunteering with the Visiting Nurse Assn., which sparked her lifelong interest in nursing.

During World War I, Bolton persuaded Secretary of War NEWTON D. BAKER to establish an Army School of Nursing rather than rely on untrained volunteers. Believing that nurses should have college educations as well as nursing training, Bolton funded a school of nursing at Western Reserve Univ., enabling WRU to raise the school from a department of the College of Women to a separate college in 1923, which was renamed the Frances Payne Bolton School of Nursing in June 1935.

In 1907 she married CHESTER CASTLE BOLTON, and had 4 children: Chas. B., Oliver P., KENYON C., and Elizabeth. When her husband, a Republican congressman from the 22nd district, died in 1939, she served out his term and was elected to the seat in her own right in 1940. During her long tenure in the U.S. House of Representatives, her major interests were nursing and foreign affairs. She sponsored the Bolton Bill, creating the U.S. Cadet Nurse Corps in World War II. As a long-time member of the House Foreign Affairs Committee, she was the first woman member of Congress to head an official mission abroad, to the Middle East in 1947. In July 1953, Pres. Eisenhower appointed her a congressional delegate to the U.N. She was defeated for reelection by Chas. Vanik in 1968 and returned to Cleveland. In addition to nursing, Bolton also founded the Payne Study & Experiment Fund in 1927 to finance projects benefiting children, and donated the land in LYNDHURST† for HAWKEN SCHOOL.† She died at her home in Lyndhurst and was buried in Lake View Cemetery.

Loth, David. *A Long Way Forward* (1957).
Frances Payne Bolton Papers, WRHS.

**BOLTON, KENYON C.** (29 Mar. 1912–14 July 1983), philanthropist, military officer, and diplomat, served as special assistant to the U.S. ambassador to France (1949–52) and as Honorary French Consul (1975–80), among other positions. He was awarded military honors by four countries, including the U.S. Bronze Star, the French Legion of Honor (1961), and the French Colonial Medal (1945). Bolton was born in Cleveland to FRANCES PAYNE BOLTON and CHESTER CASTLE BOLTON. He was educated at HAWKEN SCHOOL,† Milton Academy in Massachusetts, St. Stephens at Columbia Univ., and the Consular Acadamie in Vienna, Austria. During World War II, he served the U.S. Army as liaison officer in France and with the Joint Chiefs of Staff in Germany. Beginning in 1946, he was appointed to various overseas positions in the U.S. Department of State and served as secretary to the U.S. delegation at five postwar conferences. In the 1950s, Bolton presided over Cleveland Air Taxi, a helicopter shuttle service.

Among his myriad community activities, Bolton helped create and chaired the Nationalities Services Center (see INTERNATIONAL SERVICES CENTER),† was president of the CLEVELAND COUNCIL ON WORLD AFFAIRS† (1953–63), and actively supported the CLEVELAND PLAY HOUSE† for over 30 years, serving 8 years as president of the board of trustees, on the board's advisory committee and chair of the Play House Foundation. He served on the boards of over 50 other organizations, both national, such as the National Endowment for the Arts, and local, such as the MUSICAL ARTS ASSN.† and JOHN CARROLL UNIV.† He represented the third generation to serve as a trustee of Kenyon College. At least 2 theaters are named for Kenyon Bolton, at the Cleveland Play House and at Kenyon College.

On 22 June 1940, Bolton married Mary Idelle Peters of Lancaster, OH; they had five children: Thomas C., Kenyon C., III, John B., and Phillip P. Bolton and Mary B. Hooper. Bolton died of cancer in his Shaker Hts. home.—J.M.

Kenyon C. Bolton Papers, WRHS.

**BOLTON, SARAH KNOWLES** (15 Sept. 1841–21 Feb. 1916) was a prolific writer of biographical studies, poetry, and a temperance novel. Born in Farmington, CT, the daughter of John Segar and Mary Elizabeth Miller Knowles, she came to Cleveland in 1866 after marrying Chas. E. Bolton, a Cleveland businessman and active worker in temperance activities. All of her books, regardless of type, reflect her contention that despite hardships, life can be worth living if one works hard and believes in God. Her own experiences as associate editor of the *Congregationalist* (1878–81), a Boston publication, and her husband's experiences as he labored for the cause of the workingman and the discouraged in heart served as subject matter for her books. Her stories were published in 2 volumes: *A Country Idyll* and *Other Stories*. Bolton wrote sev-

eral juvenile biographies, which revealed her own and her readers' judgements about what they admired in women. Her *Lives of Girls Who Became Famous* (1897) included essays on novelist Harriet Beecher Stowe, humanitarian and reformer Helen Hunt Jackson, abolitionist and woman's rights advocate Lucretia Mott, author Louisa May Alcott, educator Mary Lyon, and nurse Florence Nightingale. The most professional and prolific of local writers, her biographies received rightful acclaim, but her other books less.

Bolton had one child, Charles Knowles Bolton. She was buried in Lake View Cemetery.

Bolton, Charles K. *Sarah K. Bolton: Pages from an Intimate Autobiography* (1923).

**BOLTON, THOMAS** (29 Nov. 1809–1 Feb. 1871), a prominent lawyer, was born in Scipio, NY, to Thomas and Hannah (Henry) Bolton. He attended Harvard Univ. (1829–33), there meeting his future partner, Moses Kelley. Bolton studied law in Canandaigua, NY; came to Cleveland in Sept. 1834; and was admitted to the bar in 1835. In 1836 he and Kelley formed the firm of Bolton & Kelley.

In 1835 Bolton helped draft Cleveland's city charter, and was clerk for the first elections. He was a councilman in 1839, and served in the Office of the Judiciary then and for the 1841–42 term. He was also an alderman and on the city's Claims Committee in 1841–42. In 1841 he became president of the city council, and gained attention and criticism for defending 3 slaves who were accused by their captors of having escaped from their plantation. Despite threats, Bolton proved the captors had kidnapped the slaves and then claimed ownership.

Disillusioned with Democrats, after joining the Free-Soilers in 1848 Bolton attended the Pittsburgh convention to organize the Republican party in 1856, serving as a delegate to that year's Republican Natl. Convention in Philadelphia. In 1856 he left legal practice to become judge of the Court of Common Pleas, remaining until his retirement 10 years later. Bolton was a founding member of the private Cleveland City Guard (1837), and cofounded ST. PAUL'S EPISCOPAL CHURCH† (1846). In 1838 he married Elizabeth L. Cone, who died in 1846; then on 1 Dec. 1846, Bolton married Emeline Russel. From his first marriage, Bolton had four children: Thomas, Elizabeth, Fesius Cone, and James; from his second, he had a son, Charles C. Bolton died in Cleveland and was buried in Lake View Cemetery.

**BOND, DOUGLAS DANFORD** (2 July 1911–30 Oct. 1976) was a prominent psychiatrist, educator and dean of Western Reserve Univ.'s School of

Medicine (1959–66) and director of psychiatric services at UNIV. HOSPITALS OF CLEVELAND† (1946–69).

Born in Waltham, MA, to Dr. Earl Danford and Grace (Newson) Bond, Douglas graduated from Harvard College (A.B., 1934), and the Univ. of Pennsylvania Medical School (M.D., 1938). He took his psychiatric training at Bryn Mawr and Butler Hospitals (1938–40). Bond was a fellow in psychiatry at the Institute of Pennsylvania Hospital (1940–41) and Harvard Medical School (1941–42). He was a Diplomate of the American Board of Psychiatry and Neurology and a graduate of the Detroit Psychoanalytic Institute. During World War II, Bond was chief consultant for the U.S. Army Air Force.

Bond came to CWRU in 1946. With Bond as chairman (1946–69) of the psychiatry department, and professor (1946–76), patient care, physical facilities, teaching, and research activities were developed. The field of psychiatry assumed new importance throughout CWRU's four-year medical curriculum.

In 1950, together with the WOMEN'S CITY CLUB,† Bond created a course to help parents in raising children. In 1969 Bond retired from administrative duties to continue teaching and maintain a private practice. He belonged to numerous professional organizations and government institutions.

Bond married Helen Cannon on 3 July 1937. They had four children: Peter, Thomas, Sharon, and Barbara. Bond died of a heart attack and was cremated. The Douglas Danford Bond Chair was approved in 1978 as the first professorship established at CWRU's psychiatry department.—T.B.

**BOND, ROBERT L.** (17 Jan. 1917–19 April 1990) spent his life in social work, and was a leader in the activities of Cleveland's neighborhood centers.

Bond was born in New York City, son of Sam and Rose Bellows Bond. Following schooling in NYC, he completed undergraduate work in history at the Univ. of Michigan, before returning to NYC for his master's degree in adult education at Columbia Univ. As part of his graduate program, Bond became involved with a settlement house and there he met his future wife, Anna Muelberger. They were wed on 1 March 1941, and raised three children: Lynne, Gary, and Brooks.

The settlement house experience determined Bond's future. After he returned from World War II, during which he served in North Africa and Europe, the Bonds moved to Riverside, CA, where he and his wife established a settlement house for HISPANICS† and AFRICAN AMERICANS.† They moved to New Orleans for a year, before coming to Cleveland in 1951.

In Cleveland, he first worked at the GOODRICH-GANNETT NEIGHBORHOOD CENTER.† He then became the director of United Neighborhood Centers. In 1963 he secured a grant, and helped merge his organization and the Neighborhood Settlement Assn. into the GREATER CLEVELAND NEIGHBORHOOD CENTERS ASSN.† He became that group's first executive director, helping it grow from 13 members to 25. When Bond retired in 1988, it was then the largest voluntary association of its kind in the U.S.

Bond was honored many times: In 1985 by the Northeast Ohio Chapter of the American Society for Public Administration, in 1987 by United Neighborhood Centers of America, and in 1990 by the Ohio Chapter of the National Assn. of Social Workers.

In his retirement, Bond wrote a book about the settlement house experience, *Focus on Neighborhoods*. Bond was cremated, and his remains were not interred.—J.T.

**BONE, JOHN HERBERT ALOYSIUS (J. H. A.)** (31 Oct. 1830–17 Sept. 1906), upheld literary standards on 2 Cleveland newspapers for half a century. The son of a British army officer, he was born in Penryn, Cornwall, and diverted from a similar career by a boyhood accident which left his right arm crippled. He married Ellen Carpenter and brought her directly to Cleveland in 1851. First settling in OHIO CITY† as a bookkeeper, Bone then moved to the east side and began contributing articles to the *CLEVELAND HERALD.†* He joined the paper's staff as city editor in 1857 and soon became its lead editorial writer. Bone also contributed articles to such national publications as the *Atlantic Monthly*, *Knickerbocker Magazine*, and *Godoy's Lady's Book*. Noted locally as an Elizabethan scholar, he wrote a series on English history for *Our Young Folks*. In the late 1850s, he published a small volume of poems, followed in 1865 by *Petroleum and Petroleum Wells*, a book on the oil regions. When the *Herald* was sold to the *CLEVELAND LEADER†* and the *PLAIN DEALER†* in 1885, it fell to Bone to write his paper's obituary. He then went to work for the *Plain Dealer*, serving as managing editor to 1893, and thereafter as editorial writer and literary editor. A close friend of Cleveland's scholar-philanthropist LEONARD CASE, JR., Bone belonged to the Cleveland Library Assn. and the WESTERN RESERVE HISTORICAL SOCIETY.† Afflicted with cancer, he retired from active duties in March 1906, although he continued to send book reviews to the *Plain Dealer* from his Vienna St. residence until his death. He was survived by a daughter, Estelle J. Bone, who also worked for the *Plain Dealer*, and a son, Aubrey.—J.V.

**BOURKE-WHITE, MARGARET** (14 June 1904–27 Aug. 1971) was a prominent photojournalist who began her career in Cleveland. Born in New York, she graduated from Cornell Univ. in 1927 and after a failed first marriage came to Cleveland, where her widowed mother had moved. Here she explored the FLATS,† which she called "a photographic paradise," and photographed stately homes for the local social publication *Town & Country Club News.* She also photographed the newly completed Terminal Tower, where she opened her first studio. Her curiosity and interest in steelmaking led her to seek permission from ELROY J. KULAS to photograph in his mill, the Otis Steel Co. Pleased with the results, Kulas had them published in *The Story of Steel,* a booklet distributed to Otis Steel stockholders.

Bourke-White left Cleveland for New York in 1929, when Henry Luce hired her for his new publication, *Fortune,* on the basis of her steel pictures. He later chose her as one of the 4 original staff photographers for *Life.* Ultimately, Bourke-White became the first woman accredited as a war correspondent (1942), traveled with Gen. Geo. Patton's 3rd Army through Germany (1945), and photographed Gandhi in India a few hours before his assassination (1948). She married novelist Erskine Caldwell in 1939 but was divorced in 1942. She died at the age of 67 in Stamford, CT.

**BOURNE, HENRY E.** (13 Apr. 1862–19 June 1946), an expert on the French Revolution and history professor at Flora Stone Mather College, was born in East Hamburg, NY, son of James and Isabella (Staples) Bourne. He earned his B.A. (1883) and B.D. (1887) from Yale Univ. Bourne also received an L.H.D. degree from Marietta College and an L.L.D. degree from Western Reserve College. He taught history for 3 years before becoming professor of history and registrar at the four-year-old Mather College in 1892. As registrar (i.e., dean of the faculty), he raised the college's standing to one of the highest in the nation among women's colleges. Bourne also developed new teaching standards in history. Working with the American Historical Assn., he helped establish standards for preparing all levels of history teachers, suggested material for students in the various grades, and espoused the use of primary source material at the undergraduate level, writing the standard teacher's guide, *The Teaching of History and Civics in the Elementary Schools* (1902). In association with ELBERT J. BENTON, he also wrote textbooks on American history, showing the interplay of American and European history. Bourne served on the Mather faculty until 1930.

Between 1930–36, he was a history consultant to the Library of Congress and managing editor for the *American Historical Review.* He returned to Cleveland in 1936. Bourne was founder and first secretary of the Municipal League (later the CITIZENS LEAGUE OF CLEVELAND†), and for 20 years president of the Goodrich Settlement. Upon his retirement, he presented the Mather College library with a valuable collection of books on the French Revolution.

Bourne married Margaret Anne Mason on 2 April 1890. They had 2 children: Margaret and Richard. Bourne died at his home in CLEVELAND HTS.† and was buried in Knollwood Cemetery.

**BOYD, ALBERT DUNCAN "STARLIGHT"** (14 Feb. 1872–8 Dec. 1921) was a colorful Republican businessman whose association with Republican county chairman MAURICE MASCHKE and control of Ward 11 politics ranked him among the most powerful local AFRICAN AMERICANS† in the early 20th century. Born on a plantation in Oak Grove, MS, the son of Walker and Hannah (Caleman) Boyd, he came penniless to Cleveland in his teens, soon becoming a handyman, clerk, and bookkeeper in a lodging house. By 25, he purchased his own tavern on Canal Rd., beginning a career as a tavernkeeper and real-estate speculator that netted him a small fortune. Boyd's tavern became a popular center of political activity. Following the drift of the black population to the lower Central-Scovill district, he built more elaborate quarters at E. 14th St. and Scovill Ave. His Starlight Cafe, remodeled in 1907 to include a barber shop, bath facilities, and a pool room, became the unofficial headquarters for the Republican party in Ward 11. Boyd gained the loyalty of a growing black population by providing aid to needy families. His control of ward voters was well respected despite charges of vice and corruption in his businesses. Boyd's support for THOS. W. FLEMING, the city's first black councilman, was the center of controversy during Fleming's campaigns for election, especially between 1917–21. Black political and religious leaders charged that under Boyd and Fleming's control, the ward was the vice center of the city. The Republican party, however, continued to support Fleming with Boyd's active endorsement until Boyd's death at age 50.

Boyd and his wife, Isabel, had 2 children, Isabel D. and Albert, Jr. He died surrounded by his wife and his son. Boyd is buried in Lake View Cemetery.

**BOYD, ELMER F.** (19 Mar. 1878–12 Feb. 1944), son of William F. and Anna Mariah Waters Boyd, was a native of Urbana, OH. He came to Cleveland in 1898 and entered one of the few professions open to blacks at the turn of the century—undertaking—

operating a funeral home in Cleveland from 1905 until his death. Boyd learned his profession at Clark's College of Embalming in Cincinnati and Meyer's Embalming School in Springfield, passed the state examination on 5 June 1905, and that fall opened an office at 2604 Central Ave. in Cleveland. In Apr. 1906, he took on a partner, Lewis J. Dean, opening an establishment described as "a combination funeral parlor and haberdashery." In 1911 Dean left the business. Boyd continued alone, moving his business several times and, by 1938, changing its name to E. F. Boyd & Son. The son, Wm. F. Boyd, continued the business after his father's death.

Elmer F. Boyd was active in a number of local civic and fraternal organizations, as well as local, state, and national professional organizations. He founded the Cleveland Funeral Directors' Assn. and was a trustee of ST. JOHN'S AME CHURCH.† His obituary reports that he gave generously to charitable and religious institutions. In 1910 Boyd married Cora Stewart (1875–4 Jan. 1960) of Salem, OH. A schoolteacher for 15 years early in her career, Cora Boyd was active in the PTA in the Central area and was a member and officer in the local, state, and district branches of the Fed. of Colored Women's Clubs.

**BOYER, WILLIS BOOTH** (3 Feb. 1915–31 Jan. 1974), board chairman and chief executive officer of Republic Steel and civic leader, was born in Pittsburgh, the son of Pearce F. and Hester Booth Boyer. He graduated from Lafayette College and came to Cleveland in 1937, joining Republic Steel as a clerk in the cold strip mill. After holding various positions at the company, Boyer joined Republic's finance department, serving as asst. treasurer, treasurer, and becoming vice-president and treasurer like his father before him. By 1964 Boyer was vice-president of Finance and Administration and a member of the Board of Directors. He was made president in 1968, chief executive officer in 1971, and was elected chairman of the board in May 1973. During his rise in the executive ranks, he completed the advanced management program at Harvard Univ.

Boyer also used his financial abilities as treasurer of the Welfare Federation and United Torch, and served on the Executive Committee of the GREATER CLEVELAND GROWTH ASSN.† As trustee of UNIV. HOSPITALS OF CLEVELAND,† he was active in raising funds to further the patient care programs there and aided diverse local organizations including the Cleveland Development Foundation, Bluecoats, Inc. and the Educational TV Assn.

Boyer died at age 58 in Cleveland. He was survived by his wife, Esther Greenwood Boyer, and sons Willis B. Jr., Jonathan Greenwood, and Paul Christopher; a sister, Hester B. Tucker (Mrs. Carl C.), and brother Pearce F. Jr. of Litchfield, CT. —M.S.

**BRADBURN, CHARLES** (16 July 1808–12 Aug. 1872) was a merchant and leader in the organization and development of CLEVELAND PUBLIC SCHOOLS,† called the "Father of Cleveland Schools," who worked from 1841–61 as a member of the school board and/or city council to establish Cleveland schools.

Born in Attleboro, MA, to Sarah Leach Hovey and cotton manufacturer James Bradburn, Charles graduated from the Middlesex Mechanics Assn. and attended a classical school at Ashfield, MA. Coming to Cleveland in 1836, Bradburn became a pioneer in the local wholesale grocery business, building the first riverfront grocery warehouse on St. Clair St. in 1843.

In 1841 Bradburn was elected by the city council to the first Board of School Managers and served until 1853 when the council replaced school managers with a Board of Education. In 1854 Bradburn was elected to the city council, becoming council president in 1855. Bradburn returned to the board, serving as president in 1856 and 1858. On 5 Apr. 1859 Bradburn won election to the first Board of Education elected by the public.

Bradburn devoted one-fourth of his time to provide free secondary education at public expense. He chaired the committee on schools in the city council and greatly influenced public-school development. He helped to establish Cleveland's first public high school, CENTRAL HIGH SCHOOL,† which opened in 1846. He was concerned with the physical requirements of schools and even created the "Bradburn schoolhouse," a simply designed building equipped with the furniture and heating a proper school required.

Bradburn married Eliza Stone of Lowell, MA, in Jan. 1831. They had 6 children: Charles Jr., George, Sarah Eliza, Helen E., Anna M., and Lydia. Bradburn is buried in Erie St. Cemetery.—T.B.

**BRADLEY, ALVA** (27 Nov. 1814–28 Nov. 1885) was a sailor, ship owner, and shipbuilder, who helped develop Great Lakes shipping. Born in Ellington, CT, to Leonard and Roxanne Thrall Bradley, he moved to Brownhelm, OH, in 1823. At 19 Bradley left home to become a sailor on the Great Lakes. After time on numerous ships, Bradley became master of the 15-ton "Olive Branch," running trade from the islands to Lake Erie's southern ports, then the 47-ton schooner "Commodore Lawrence." In 1853 Bradley, in partnership with Ahira Cobb, formed Bradley & Cobb, shipbuilders with yards in

Vermilion. In 1859 Bradley moved to Cleveland, moving all his interests, including his shipyards, to Cleveland in 1868. Building at least 1 vessel each year, Bradley built 18 vessels between 1868–82, and had such extensive and efficient business operations that he carried his own insurance. He never wrecked as a sailor and lost only 5 vessels as an owner. Much of his estimated wealth of $10 million was invested in real estate. In 1880 Bradley helped found the Cleveland Vessel Owners Assn. and became its first president. This group combined with its Buffalo counterpart to form the LAKE CARRIERS ASSN.† in 1892. Bradley was an original incorporator of Case Institute of Technology and a trustee of the EUCLID AVE. CONGREGATIONAL CHURCH.† He was also active in temperance. Bradley married Helen M. Burgess of Milan, OH, in 1851 and had 4 children: Elizabeth, Eleanor, Minetta, and Morris. Bradley was buried in Lake View Cemetery.

**BRAINARD, SILAS** (19 Feb. 1814–8 Apr. 1871) turned an avocation for music into a business that supplied Cleveland with much of its early musical scores and instruments. He was born in Lempster, NH, the son of merchant Nathan and Fanny (Bingham) Silas. He was educated at New Hampton, NH. He came to Cleveland in 1834 with his father and started in the grocery business as N. Brainard & Son. An accomplished flutist, the younger Brainard also became active in the city's embryonic musical circles. He joined the CLEVELAND MUSICAL SOCIETY† and began arranging music for its members. In 1836 he started his own music business, which eventually became an institution under the name S. BRAINARD'S SONS.† Beginning with the retailing of music and musical instruments, Brainard added a publishing business in 1845 and purchased Watson's Hall at the same time, running it as Melodeon Hall and later Brainard's Hall (see GLOBE THEATER†). A house organ which he began in 1864 as *Western Musical World* became one of the country's leading music publications under the name *Brainard's Musical World*. Although once regarded as having few peers as a flutist, he apparently subordinated his performing talents to the demands of his business. He was noted as the author of a *Violin Instruction Book* and numerous musical arrangements, some of which appeared under an assumed name. Brainard married Emily C. Mould and had 7 children: Charles, Henry, George, Fanny, Emma, Annie, and Laura. He died of inflammatory rheumatism in his residence at 348 Prospect Ave., survived by at least 3 sons: Charles, George, and Henry. Brainard was buried in Woodland Cemetery.—J.V.

**BRAMLEY, MATTHEW FREDERICK** (4 Jan. 1868–30 May 1941) was an influential businessman who organized and was president of the CLEVELAND TRINIDAD PAVING CO.,† Templar Motors Co., Bramley Storage Co., and was an original investor and owner of the Luna Park Amusement Co.

Born in Independence, Bramley lived on a farm and attended Cleveland public schools. At age 19 Bramley drove a team for paving contractors and learned about the business. He advanced to foreman, first for the Claflin Paving Co., then for J. F. Siegenthaler, whose daughter, Gertrude, he married in 1891.

Shortly thereafter Bramley moved to Cleveland and worked at the Produce Bank. Impressing his superiors, Bramley was offered financing if he could obtain paving contracts. He secured three and from these he organized the Cleveland Trinidad Paving Co. in 1894. He built it into the largest paving corporation in the world. In 1910 Bramley purchased LUNA PARK. He installed many new attractions and the park thrived until the Depression brought it to a close in 1930. In 1916 Bramley organized and was general manager of Templar Motors, which operated successfully until World War I when he was forced, under government contract, into manufacturing ammunition. After the war the factory became Bramley Storage, one of Ohio's largest furniture storage plants.

Bramley served two terms in the Ohio House of Representatives (1898–1902), and served on the City Hall Commission of Cleveland (1898–1908), and the Cuyahoga County Building Commission (1905–1908).

Bramley had two children, John and Margaret. He is buried in Riverside Cemetery.—T.B.

**BRAVERMAN, LIBBIE LEVIN** (20 Dec. 1900–10 Dec. 1990) was a teacher, educational consultant, and writer. Braverman was born in Boston, MA, to Rabbi Morris A. and Pauline Drucker Levin. She and her brothers, Sol and Harry, attended school in various locations. When her father became director of Community Hebrew Schools in Cleveland, she came to this city and graduated from CENTRAL HIGH SCHOOL.† Braverman studied the Talmud, often the only girl in the class, and began teaching Hebrew school as an adolescent, first in Chicago and then in Cleveland at the Euclid Ave. Temple (see ANSHE CHESED†) and B'NAI JESHURUN.† On 23 Nov. 1924, she married architect SIGMUND BRAVERMAN; they lived at 2378 Euclid Hts. Blvd. in CLEVELAND HTS.† She received a certificate from Cleveland Normal School in 1920 and a Bachelor of Science in education from Western Reserve Univ. in 1933, and took graduate courses at

Harvard, the Univ. of Pittsburgh, and the Cleveland School of Art. After a brief stint of public school teaching, Braverman became education director for the Euclid Ave. Temple (1946–52). She designed and published curriculum and books of educational activities for religious school, collaborating with people such as NATHAN BRILLIANT. Her works included *Children of Freedom* (1953) and the two-volume *Teach Me to Pray* (1955, 1957). Braverman served on the faculty of the Cleveland College of Jewish Studies (1945–ca. 1960); the school made her an honorary board member and in 1981 presented her with an honorary doctorate. Braverman lectured for the Jewish Chatauqua Society, belonged to the America Israel Public Affairs Committee, and served as regional president and board member of Hadassah, among other activities. Braverman died at the MARGARET WAGNER HOME.† She was buried at Hillcrest Cemetery.—J.M.

Libbie Levin Braverman Papers, WRHS.
Braverman, L.L. *Libbie: An Autobiography* (1986).

**BRAVERMAN, SIGMUND** (22 May 1894–27 Mar. 1960) was a prominent Jewish architect who designed more than 40 synagogues in the U.S. and Canada, and many diverse structures in Cleveland. Born in Austria-Hungary, to Bernard and Fannie (Weiss) Braverman, he came to the U.S. at age 10 and settled with his family in Pittsburgh. Braverman received a B.S. from the Carnegie Institute of Technology in 1917, and served in the military during World War I. In 1920 he came to Cleveland and opened an architectural practice. His work included apartments, theaters, shopping centers, schools, and hospitals. From 1932–35, he was assistant, then acting Cleveland city architect. Among Braverman's best known local designs are the Brantley Apts. (1937), the Cleveland Hebrew Schools, Shaker-Kinsman Branch (1951), the BUREAU OF JEWISH EDUCATION† (1952), Fairmount Temple, designed in association with Percival Goodman (1957), and Warrensville Ctr. Synagogue (1958). Active in Jewish community affairs, Braverman was director of the Bureau of Jewish Education, trustee of the Cleveland Jewish Welfare Fed., and vice-president and director of the JEWISH COMMUNITY CTR.† He was a leader in Cleveland's Zionist movement. On 23 Nov 1924 he married Libbie Levin (see LIBBIE LEVIN BRAVERMAN); they had no children. In June 1978, their CLEVELAND HTS.† residence at 2378 Euclid Hts. Blvd. was designated a city landmark.

Sigmund Braverman Papers, WRHS.

**BREED, WALTER** (1867–9 Mar. 1939) was the rector of ST. PAUL'S EPISCOPAL CHURCH† for over 30 years, leading the church's move from E. 40th and Euclid to Fairmount and Coventry in CLEVELAND HTS.,† and guiding 2 generations of parishioners with his intellectual spirituality compressed into his hallmark 18-minute sermons. A descendant of the rector of Old North Church in Boston, Breed was born in Lynn, MA, to Joseph and Frances (Burrall) Breed. With an evangelical liberal point of view, he was ordained in May 1891 at Tarrytown, NY, after graduating from Wesleyan Union in Connecticut and Episcopal Theological Seminary in Cambridge, MA. He received his D.D. at Harvard. In 1907, after serving parishes in New England, he was assigned to St. Paul's, the fashionable Episcopal church in Cleveland's social center of Euclid Ave. St. Paul's congregants included the Devereuxs, Mathers, Boltons, Seymours, and Scovills. Breed won their loyalty with enlightened sermons grounded in the humanities and with his fresh readings of familiar prayers. As downtown became less residential, Breed negotiated a merger with St. Martin's Episcopal Church and arranged the move to Cleveland Hts. At the suburban church, Breed developed a church school. Particularly interested in children's religious education, he frequently taught classes, talking to children as young adults. Breed's philosophy for keeping perspective in his many duties was "Take long vacations and keep sermons short." Breed married Ellen Brodrick Zehner on 4 June 1895. He died of pneumonia, leaving his wife and son, William Zehner.

**BREITENSTEIN, JOSEPH C.** (30 July 1884–19 Aug. 1974), attorney, served as special asst. U.S District Attorney (15 Nov. 1922–15 Mar. 1923) and was a leader in the CUYAHOGA COUNTY DEMOCRATIC PARTY† and the Ohio Democratic party. As asst. district attorney, he handled *U.S. v. Eugene Debs,* among other cases. Breitenstein was born in Canton, OH, to Louis and Mary Shane Breitenstein; his first job was news reporter for the Canton *Repository.* He graduated from St. Francis Solanius' College, Quincy, IL (1910), and Georgetown Univ. Law School (1914). Breitenstein was secretary to U.S. Senator ATLEE POMERENE (1911–15), secretary of the Ohio Democratic party executive committee (1916), and chief asst. U.S. District Attorney (May 1915—November 1922) for the Northern District of Ohio. While maintaining a law practice in Cleveland (Wertz & Breitenstein), he presided over the local Georgetown Univ. alumni association and the Cuyahoga Club (1929–30), a group of young Democrats working to oust W. BURR GONGWER and NEWTON D. BAKER as party heads. In 1934 Breitenstein ran unsuccessfully for Congress from the 20th district, against incumbent MARTIN L. SWEENEY. The next year, Ohio governor Martin Davey named him special counsel to investigate the fees paid to bank and building and loan liquidators and their attorneys.

In 1931 Breitenstein married Zita Marie Clarke; the couple had no children. He is buried in Cleveland's Holy Cross Cemetery.

---

See also POLITICS.†

**BRETT, WILLIAM HOWARD** (1 July 1846–24 Aug. 1918), librarian of CLEVELAND PUBLIC LIBRARY† and founder of the Western Reserve Univ. Library School, was born in Braceville, OH, to Morgan Lewis and Jane Brokaw Brett. He became the school librarian at Warren High School at 14. He fought in the Civil War before entering the Univ. of Michigan and later WRU, but was forced by poverty to abandon his studies. Brett settled in Cleveland and worked for the bookdealer, Cobb & Andrews Co., becoming acquainted with bibliophiles, including JOHN G. WHITE, who helped appoint Brett as librarian of the CPL in 1884. Brett contributed to cataloguing, and by 1890 developed the concept of the open-shelf library.

Brett published the first issue of his *Cumulative Index to the Selected List of Periodicals* in 1896, a publication that eventually became the *Reader's Guide to Periodical Literature*. That same year he was elected president of the American Library Assn. Brett campaigned vigorously for children's libraries and established an alcove for juvenile books in the CPL. Under his leadership, the first branch libraries were opened in Cleveland. Staff training occupied a large place in Brett's thinking; he realized the importance of specialized education for library work. His interest led to the formation of a library school at WRU in 1904, with Brett as its first dean, although he remained head of the public library. During the years before his death, Brett developed plans for the main library building on Superior Ave., which, although not opened until 1925, bore the imprint of his thought.

Brett married Alice L. Allen on 1 May 1879. They had five children: Morgan Lewis, Allen, William, Edith, and George. Brett was buried in Lake View Cemetery.—J.M.

---

Eastman, Linda A. *Portrait of a Librarian* (1940).

**BREWSTER, WILLIAM H.** (16 June 1813–7 Mar. 1894), a Methodist minister who guided a Congregational church in Cleveland (1859–68), was a prominent advocate of abolition and temperance. Born in New Hampshire, son of Isaac and Betsey (Dike) Brewster, he bucked many of the city's clergy and left Euclid Ave.'s Wesleyan Methodist Episcopal Church to become the first pastor of the Univ. Hts. Congregational Church—an amalgam of Episcopal Methodists, EPISCOPALIANS,† PRESBYTERIANS,† CONGREGATIONALISTS,† and Wesleyan Methodists. Instead of bestowing an authoritative orthodoxy on this congregation, Brewster relied upon common moral precepts and a recognition of Jesus as the Christ to keep the flock together. Abolition and temperance were primary concerns of Brewster's. He championed the Sunday closing of saloons in deference to the moral and religious rights of the community, and accepted civil disobedience as appropriate in opposing slavery. He also served as pastor of HUMISTON INSTITUTE.† A popular lecturer, Brewster inaugurated a series of talks on the Bible (1859) and even during the Civil War selected political topics for speeches to Cleveland literary societies. He was executive secretary of the Cuyahoga County Temperance Society (1862), vice-president of the 1st General Conference of the Methodist Church (1867), and a trustee of CLEVELAND UNIV.† Brewster led the non-Episcopal and antislavery Methodists who split from the Episcopal branch of the church to organize (1842–43) the Wesleyan Connection of America. He was compared to Henry Ward Beecher for his vehement attacks on slavery. Brewster married Catherine Hoyt Turner in 1838 and had 6 children: Ellen Maria, Henrietta, George Henry, Abbie Jane, Catherine Lenora, and Mary Louisa. He left Cleveland for Wheaton, IL, and died there.

**BRICKNER, BARNETT ROBERT** (14 Sept. 1892–14 May 1958), the rabbi at ANSHE CHESED† for 33 years, was born in New York City to Joseph and Bessie (Furman) Brickner. He received his bachelor's (1913) and master's (1914) degrees from Columbia Univ. Teachers College; and was ordained in 1919 following graduation from the Hebrew Union College. He received a Ph.D. in social science in 1920 from the Univ. of Cincinnati.

Nationally, Brickner helped found Young Judea (Zionist, 1910), cofounded the Natl. Jewish Education Assn., and directed training of Jewish welfare workers during World War I. As rabbi at Holy Blossom Congregation in Toronto (1920–25), Brickner led the congregation from Orthodoxy to the Reform movement.

Becoming rabbi of Anshe Chesed in 1925, Brickner increased its membership from 700 to over 2,500 families, making it the largest Reform congregation in the country. He created the first Young People's Congregation, reinstituted Hebrew in the Sunday school curriculum, and also established an annual institute on Judaism for Christian religious educators. From the late 1920s until World War II, he had a weekly radio program.

Brickner debated attorney Clarence Darrow at the Masonic Auditorium on "Is Man a Machine?" in Feb. 1928. Between 1928–36, he was a labor arbitrator. Brickner succeeded Rabbi ABBA HILLEL SILVER† as president of the BUREAU OF JEWISH EDUCATION† (1932–40), and in 1935 co-chaired with Silver the reorganized fundraising Jewish Welfare Fund. Brickner was also the president of the Cleveland Zionist District, the local branch of the Zionist Organization of America.

During World War II, Brickner chaired the Conference Committee on Chaplains and was administrative chairman of the Committee on Army & Navy Religious Activities of the Natl. Jewish Board, for which, along with his visits to camps, Brickner received the Medal of Merit in 1947 from Pres. Harry Truman.

Brickner married Rebecca Ena Aaronson, a co-worker at the Bureau of Jewish Education in New York, on 10 Aug. 1919. They had 2 children, Joy Marion and Arthur James Balfour. Brickner was buried in Mayfield Cemetery.

---

Barnett R. Brickner Papers, WRHS.

**BRIGGS, JAMES A.** (6 Feb. 1811–22 Aug. 1889), an attorney active in local and national politics, was credited by some with creating Gen. William Henry Harrison's successful 1840 presidential campaign slogan, "Tippecanoe and Tyler, too." After leaving Cleveland for New York (1857), Briggs was influential in the nomination of his friend Abraham Lincoln as the Republican party's presidential candidate (1860).

Briggs was born in Claremont, NY. Moving to Cleveland at age 22, he served as a notary public for Cuyahoga County (1835, 1838, 1841, 1847, and 1852), and was county auditor (1842, 1844, and 1846) (see CUYAHOGA COUNTY GOVERNMENT†). Briggs became the first attorney of the rechartered Cleveland, Columbus & Cincinnati Railroad (see RAILROADS†). During 1848–49, he published and edited the *DAILY TRUE DEMOCRAT,†* which promoted the ideals of the FREE SOIL PARTY.† Briggs worked with CHARLES BRADBURN to establish the Cleveland high school system in 1847 (see CLEVELAND PUBLIC SCHOOLS†); he replaced Bradburn on the Cleveland Board of Education in 1854. He was among the original incorporators of the Society for Savings Bank (1849) (see SOCIETY CORP.†) and was the first president of the Mercantile Library Assn. (1852) (see LIBRARIES, ARCHIVES, AND HISTORICAL SOCIETIES†). In the realm of welfare and relief, Briggs helped organize the Cleveland

Protestant Orphan Asylum (see BEECH BROOK†), participated in the movement for TEMPERANCE,† and served as vice-president of the SOCIETY FOR THE RELIEF OF THE POOR.† He belonged to the CLEVELAND BAR ASSN.†

In 1857 Briggs moved to Brooklyn, NY, where he became an assessor and a special correspondent to several newspapers, including the *Cleveland Leader*. Briggs married Margaret Bayard in 1842. After she died, he married Catherine Van Vechten.

**BRIGGS, JOSEPH W.** (5 July 1813–23 Feb. 1872) instituted free home mail delivery in Cleveland and was later appointed to a postal job in Washington to establish this system throughout the U.S. Born in Claremont, NY, and raised by his uncle, Geo. Nixon Briggs, governor of Massachusetts, Briggs, in the early 1860s, was appointed clerk and assistant to the postmaster of Cleveland's first and only post office, on PUBLIC SQUARE.† At this time, mail was handed out on request at windows and was not delivered to specific addresses unless by paid private carriers. Briggs claimed he thought of free delivery during the winter of 1862–63 while watching how women, coming for letters from soldiers, were exposed to the cold while waiting in slow-moving lines. Briggs's plan was approved by the postmaster, EDWIN COWLES, publisher of the *CLEVELAND LEADER,†* who believed his paper's circulation might also benefit from free delivery. The U.S. postmaster granted Briggs permission to implement his system in Cleveland. Initially, the mail was sorted and taken to grocery stores throughout the city, where it was distributed; later it was delivered to specific addresses. Briggs's system caught the attention of Congress, which on 3 Mar. 1863 passed a bill authorizing free mail delivery in cities throughout the country. Briggs was appointed special agent to implement the new system and was later made national superintendent, responsible for organizing free mail delivery in 52 cities throughout the U.S. Before he died, Briggs helped design the first mailman's uniform.

Briggs married Harmony Gilmore in 1836. They had nine children: Mary, Nancy, Rufus, Laura, Alfred, Isabella, Emma, Leonard, and Kate. He died in Cleveland and was buried in Woodland Cemetery. A bronze plaque in the lobby of the Cleveland Federal Bldg. honors his achievements.

---

Joseph Wm. Briggs Papers, WRHS.

**BRIGGS, PAUL WARREN** (23 Nov. 1912–10 Nov. 1989), superintendent of the CLEVELAND PUBLIC SCHOOLS† (1964–78), made physical improvements and recruited blacks as teachers and administrators, but opposed integration by busing.

Briggs was born in Mayville, MI, and graduated from Western Michigan College. He taught in Brown City, MI, and served as superintendent of Bay City, MI, schools before coming to the PARMA† schools as superintendent in 1957. During his tenure with Cleveland Public Schools, Briggs oversaw the construction of 40 new buildings, expanded vocational schools, created schools for the hearing-impaired, and, assisted by the PACE ASSN.,† added libraries to over 100 elementary schools. He also helped create the Master of Arts in Teaching degree at JOHN CARROLL UNIV.† In 1978 Briggs tendered his resignation shortly after a federal court order established an independent body to implement desegregation. He then accepted a position as visiting professor at Arizona State Univ.

Briggs married Arvilla Moran on 18 June 1933. They lived on Edgewater Dr. while in Cleveland and had two children, James and Betty Ann B. Washburn. Briggs died in Tempe, Arizona.—J.M.

Gorn, Cathy. "Achieving 'Comfortableness': Private Action and Public Educational Policy in Cleveland, 1962–74" (Ph.D. thesis, CWRU, 1992).

**BRILLIANT, NATHAN** (4 Sept. 1894-Nov. 1983) was a leader in Cleveland's Jewish educational activities for more than 3 decades. He came from New York, where he had graduated from the City College of New York, and earned a master's degree in education from Columbia Univ. Besides teaching English for 6 years in the New York City Public Schools, he served as teacher and administrator in 2 Jewish schools there. He came to Cleveland in 1927 to become educational director at the Euclid Ave. Temple (see ANSHE CHESED†). He remained in that post 19 years, overseeing a 1,000-pupil Sunday school and co-authoring *Religious Pageants for Jewish Schools* in 1941 with Mrs. LIBBIE BRAVERMAN, who became his successor. In 1946 Brilliant became director of Cleveland's BUREAU OF JEWISH EDUCATION,† where he coordinated the activities of all the religious schools in the Jewish community. One of his accomplishments was a unified school transportation system made necessary by the increasing dispersion of the Jewish population. Brilliant also lectured on Jewish contemporary philosophy at Western Reserve Univ. (see CASE WESTERN RESERVE†) and was elected president of the National Council for Jewish Education in 1956. He was co-author of several other texts on Jewish education and a frequent contributor to periodicals on the subject. On the occasion of his retirement in 1960, he was presented with a trip to Israel. A lifelong bachelor, Brilliant died in Miami Beach, FL.—J.V.

**BRITTON, BRIGHAM** (20 June 1907–12 Nov.1979) was a businessman and philanthropist who helped found and was board chairman of CARLON PRODUCTS CORP.,† the first American company to produce plastic pipe. He also helped establish the BRITTON FUND.†

Born in Cleveland to Charles S. and Ann (Brigham) B., Britton graduated from UNIV. SCHOOL† (1925) and Yale Univ. (1929). Britton worked briefly in his father's printing business while establishing his own company. On 1 May 1929 Britton and his brother, Philip (with help from Chas. Britton and attorney George Quinn), started Carter Products Corp. to make metal specialties. In the 1940s they switched to plastics and pioneered the extrusion field. Carter Products became the first company in America to make the lightweight plastic pipe used widely by oil and gas industries. Much of the special machinery and equipment used for making plastic pipe and fittings was designed by Philip Britton.

On 9 Aug. 1950, Carter became Carlon Products Corp. to match the plastic pipe's trade name, and by that time it had become the world's largest manufacturer of plastic pipe. Britton remained Carlon's president until 1957 when he chaired the board. Britton retired in 1959. On 4 May 1986, Carlon became a division of the LAMSON & SESSIONS CO.†

In 1952 Britton helped establish the Britton Fund to support charitable organizations, particularly the United Way Services, and other social agencies, education, hospitals, health services, and youth agencies.

Britton married Gertrude Haskell (see GERTRUDE HASKELL BRITTON) on 10 Oct. 1931. They had two sons: CHARLES S. and Coburn H. Britton was Episcopalian, lived in BRATENAHL† and is enurned in Lake View Cemetery.—T.B.

**BRITTON, CHARLES SCHUYLER II** (6 July 1932–13 May 1993) was a ship manufacturer and founder of Douglass & McLeod Plastics Co., later known as Tartan Marine Co., the world's first fiberglass-sailboat manufacturer. He also served as president of the BRITTON FUND,† incorporated in 1952 by his parents and M. J. Mitchell.

Born in Cleveland to BRIGHAM and GERTRUDE HANNA (HASKELL) BRITTON, Charles attended school in BRATENAHL,† graduating from UNIV. SCHOOL (1951) and Trinity College (1955). Charles served as an operations officer in the U.S. Navy (1956–58).

As a child Britton competed in the "snipe" class races at the Mentor Yacht Club. He was captain of Univ. School's sailing team and competed in intercollegiate racing. In 1958, while stationed at Tokyo

Bay, Britton built his first sailboat, "Temba," a 42-foot ocean-going craft. In 1959, along with two friends, he completed a 204 day, 22,000 mile voyage from Japan to New York. He continued to sail competitively throughout his life, winning every major offshore sailboat race on Lake Erie, as well as world class events.

In 1960, with Ray McLeod of Douglass and McLeod Inc., Britton founded the Douglass & McLeod Plastics Co., in Grand River, changing its name to the Tartan Marine Co. in 1971. The company became the world's sixth largest builder of fiberglass sailboats complete with onboard engines. Britton sold the company in 1983 following disputes with the United Steelworkers of America, and the National Labor Relations Board.

Britton married Lynda Rounds on 27 April 1961. They had three children, Schuyler, Terence, and Timothy. Britton, an Episcopalian, is buried in Lake View Cemetery.—T.B.


**BRITTON, GERTRUDE HASKELL** (21 May 1909–18 July 1992) was a philanthropist, civic and social leader, volunteer with many civic organizations, and an artist. She was a founder of the BRITTON FUND,† and a founder and president of the CLEVELAND MUSEUM OF NATURAL HISTORY† Women's Committee.

Born in Cleveland to Gertrude (Hanna), niece of MARCUS A. HANNA, and COBURN HASKELL, inventor of the modern golf ball, Gertrude was privately tutored until she attended boarding schools in Toronto and Massachusetts. She studied art education in New York, then returned to Cleveland.

Gertrude enjoyed interior and exterior decoration and designed and restored homes as a hobby. She designed a halfway house for clients of HILL HOUSE,† a mental health organization, and helped build and restore a number of area homes. As an artist, Britton worked with ceramics and modeling clay, and enjoyed boat building.

Britton served as a volunteer, teaching arts and crafts to patients at the U.S. Marine Hospital on Fairhill Rd. She was also involved with the Natural History Museum, the JUNIOR LEAGUE OF CLEVELAND,† Planned Parenthood, Blue Hill Memorial Hospital, and the United Negro College Fund.

In 1952 she helped establish and served as vice-president of the Britton Fund, which makes grants to United Way Services and other charitable organizations in Ohio.

Gertrude married BRIGHAM BRITTON, a founder of CARLON PRODUCTS,† on 10 October 1931. They had two sons, CHARLES SCHUYLER II, and Coburn. Britton lived in BRATENAHL† and is buried in Lake View Cemetery.—T.B.

Britton Family Papers, WRHS.


**BROADBENT, BIRDSALL HOLLY** (27 Sept. 1894–23 Dec. 1977), a Cleveland dentist and orthodontist, invented a head positioning device used in taking radiographs of the face and teeth. Born in Lockport, NY, to James F. and Mabel Holly Broadbent, he graduated from Western Reserve Univ. Dental School in 1919 and began specializing in orthodontia. During the 1920s, Broadbent and Dr. T. Wingate Todd developed the cephalometer, which holds a patient's head stationary when x-rays are taken. The cephalometer gave dentists a practical method of diagnosing abnormal growth. For his work, Broadbent received the Ohio Dental Assn.'s 1952 John R. Callahan Memorial Award. In 1929 Broadbent became director of the Bolton Fund of Western Reserve, the world's largest individually endowed fund for dental research. He helped assemble the world's largest collection of serial cephalometric records, and in 1933 the results of his study of facial development were displayed at the Chicago World's Fair. In 1948 Broadbent became clinical professor of dental facial anatomy at WRU. In 1960 Broadbent received an honorary degree from Dublin Univ.; in 1966, he became an honorary fellow in dental surgery at the London Royal College of Surgeons; and in 1967, he received an honorary Doctor of Science from WRU. As a youth Broadbent was among the first joiners of the Boy Scouts in America in 1910, beginning a 60 year association with Scouting. He received the Silver Beaver Award in 1952.

Broadbent married Bernice Mathews in 1921 and had four children: Ann Holden, Jane Paisley, Frances Philbrick, and Dr. Birdsall Holly Broadbent, Jr. He died in Kirtland and his ashes were buried in the Brooklyn Hts. Cemetery.


**BROCK (SLOMOVITZ), PHILIP** (ca. 1890–?), one of the finest lightweight boxers in the early 1900s, was the son of Russian immigrants Abraham and Anna Slomovitz. Brock, who fought in the era of the padded glove, was noted for the effectiveness of his left-hand punch and his staying power in the ring. Managed locally by Dave Langdon, Brock participated in boxing matches all over the country. As championship contender in the lightweight division (135 lbs.), he went to Los Angeles in 1907 to train for a bout with British champion Freddie Welsh. In an epic 25-round fight 30 May 1908, Brock lost to Welsh on points, and the following year he lost to Welsh again in Boston. Later, he became a favorite of the bettors when he defeated both Welsh and contender Packy McFarland in a lightweight elimination tournament held on the West Coast. In Cleveland, Brock boxed world champion Willie Richie 22 February 1912 at LUNA PARK,† where they fought to a draw in 12 rounds. He remained in the city after his boxing career was over, and in 1930 he and his wife, Myrtle, were living on E. 85th St.

In 1976 Brock was inducted into the GREATER CLEVELAND SPORTS HALL OF FAME.†—M.S.

**BROEMEL, CARL WILLIAM** (5 Sept. 1891–23 May 1984) was noted as a watercolorist associated with the Cleveland School of artists. The son of Anna (Vlasteck) and Fred Charles Broemel, an architectural sculptor, Carl was born in Cleveland's old German district around Scovill and East 22nd St. He became the youngest student in the Cleveland School of Art (see CLEVELAND INSTITUTE OF ART†), where he studied decorative design and graduated in 1909. After further study in Europe and New York, he returned to Cleveland and established a commercial art studio in the Hanna Bldg. Broemel exhibited watercolors and oils annually in the MAY SHOW† from 1923–40. His watercolors were also shown locally in such venues as the WEBB C. BALL CO.† and the KORNER & WOOD† bookstore. In Oct. 1935 Broemel became the first supervisor of the WPA Federal Art Project's District 4 in Cleveland. Prior to his resignation in Feb. 1937, he instituted a "guild system" for his unit in which artists of varying degrees of training and accomplishment worked together in a single studio to produce art works in a cooperative manner. He then served as a regional art juror for the 1939 New York World's Fair and the following year opened a studio in New York. Moving to Sharon, CT, he exhibited in such places as the Albany Institute of History and Art and also served as a staff artist for the U.S. Air Force. With his wife, Ruth, Broemel had 3 children: Phyllis, Carl Broemel, Jr., and Charlotte. Broemel, a past president of the CLEVELAND SOCIETY OF ARTISTS† and the New York Artists Guild, moved to Daytona Beach, FL, shortly before his death. —J.V.

---

Marling, Karal Ann. *Federal Art in Cleveland, 1933–1943* (1974).

**BROOKS, CHARLES STEPHEN** (25 June 1878– 29 June 1934) was an essayist and playwright who was instrumental in the founding of the CLEVELAND PLAY HOUSE.† A Cleveland native, and the son of Stephen E. and Mary (Coffinberry) Brooks, he graduated from WEST HIGH SCHOOL† and Yale Univ. (1900) and then entered the family printing and stationery business. After rising to the rank of vice-president, he retired in 1915 to devote himself to a literary career that produced more than a dozen volumes. Most of these consisted of essays gleaned from numerous bicycle travels in England and elsewhere, of which the first, *Journeys to Baghdad*, was published in 1915. He indulged in a leisurely style on such fanciful topics as "The Decline of Night-Caps" and "In Defense of Plagiarism." He also wrote plays, of which *Wappin' Wharf*, a pirate comedy, had received 150 presentations by 1931. Brooks was a founder and first president of the Cleveland Play House (1915), which produced 2 of his plays and named one of the theaters in its first permanent home after him. Brooks headed the theater's building campaign and at his death was president of the Play House Foundation. During World War I he had served on the House Commission gathering data for the use of the American peace delegation at Versailles. He also lectured on English literature at Western Reserve Univ. (see CASE WESTERN RESERVE†). Brooks married Minerva Kline (see MINERVA K. BROOKS) in 1907. Following a divorce from her in 1925, he married Mary S. Curtis Brown in 1929. Together they produced several of his short plays in their home on Magnolia Dr. One of Brooks's last works, *Prologue*, is a memoir of his childhood on the near west side. Brooks had no children and is buried in Lake View Cemetery.—J.V.

**BROOKS, MINERVA KLINE** (1833–5 May 1929) campaigned for suffrage for women in the 1910s, helped organize the precursor of the CLEVELAND PLAY HOUSE† (1915), and introduced interpretive dance in both Cleveland and New York City. Born in Cleveland to Virgil P. Kline (attorney to JOHN D. ROCKEFELLER) and Minerva E. Cozens Kline, she graduated from HATHAWAY BROWN SCHOOL† (1899) and from Vassar College (1903). On 12 October 1907 Brooks married writer CHARLES S. BROOKS. In 1910 she became a charter member of the Cleveland chapter of the National College Equal Suffrage League. Brooks belonged to the Cleveland Suffrage Assn., presided over the Cleveland Suffrage Party (1914), and published articles on suffrage in local newspapers. She participated in the successful effort to attain municipal suffrage for women in EAST CLEVELAND† in 1914. In the fall of 1915, Brooks and her husband invited 8 friends to their home on E. 115 St. to discuss formation of an Art Theatre; in November 1915 the organization elected her as secretary. In May 1916, Brooks participated in the first production of the Cleveland Play House, a puppet show. Late in 1916, Minerva and Charles Brooks left Cleveland for New York City, he to pursue his literary career and she to expand her interest in dance. They later returned to their hometown but Minerva Brooks divided her time between locales. In the fall of 1919, the *New York Times* called her "an exponent of interpretive dance"; in the early 1920s, with Winifred Lawrence Ingersoll, she taught interpretive dance at the Cleveland branch of the Noyes School of Rhythm. In 1925 Brooks and her husband divorced. At her death Brooks lived on Beacon St. in Boston.

**BROOKS, OLIVER KINGSLEY** (21 May 1845–14 Sept. 1914) was a prominent Cleveland businessman who had served in the Union Army during the CIVIL WAR.† His father, Oliver Allen Brooks, was a grandson of Joshua Brooks, who was a Minuteman—one of those who "fired the shot heard round the world"—at Concord Bridge on 19 Apr. 1775. Oliver Allen, at the age of 20, traveled with his widowed mother from Burlington, VT, in 1834 by stage coach and canal to Buffalo and from there by lake to Cleveland. Here his mother opened a boardinghouse, and he started a hardware and crockery business, Huntington and Brooks, which was the first to import Staffordshire pottery direct from Liverpool to Cleveland. The successor firm, Rorimer Brooks Co., became nationally known for interior design and furniture making.

Oliver Kingsley had artistic ambitions. After high school he studied with Thomas Hicks in New York, but the Civil War brought his studies to an end. At the age of 18 he enlisted in the 150TH OHIO VOLUNTEER INFANTRY† as one of the "Hundred Days Men," participating in the defense of Washington, DC. Returning home with a near-fatal case of malaria, he decided to enter his father's business. In 1880 he joined the newly organized Cleveland Malleable Iron Co., later merged into the National Malleable and Steel Castings Co. There he served as secretary-treasurer until his death.

Oliver Kingsley Brooks married Harriet Ellen Gill of Meadville, PA, in 1884. They had two daughters, Katherine Gill Brooks (1888–1981) and Elizabeth Kingsley Brooks (1896–1990) who married DAVID K. FORD in 1920. Oliver's brother, William Keith Brooks, became the first Professor of Zoology at Johns Hopkins Univ. and was noted for his studies of the Chesapeake Bay oyster. William Keith returned to Cleveland to dedicate the Biology Building at Western Reserve Univ. in 1899.

Oliver K. Brooks was a lifelong member of TRINITY CATHEDRAL,† where he served as vestryman and warden of Trinity Parish for 25 years. He was a friend of the Cleveland artist OTTO BACHER and encouraged the development of sketching and painting, serving as vice-president of the CLEVELAND ART CLUB† in 1881. He later became a serious collector of autographs and first editions and was an early and active member of the ROWFANT CLUB.†—A.F.

**BROUGH, JOHN** (17 Sept. 1811–29 Aug. 1865) was a newspaper publisher, state auditor, railroad president, and Civil War governor of Ohio. Brough was born in Marietta, OH; orphaned at 11, he became an apprentice printer. After paying his way through Ohio Univ., he edited and published newspapers in West Virginia and Ohio. A Democrat, Brough was elected state representative of the Fairfield-Hocking district at age 26 and served 1838–39. As auditor for the State of Ohio between 1839 and 1845 Brough prevented a repudiation of the Ohio debt, which would have endangered interest payments on the OHIO & ERIE CANAL† bonds. Brough founded the *Cincinnati Enquirer* in 1841, publishing it and practicing law until 1848, when he sold it. Shortly afterward, he established residence in Cleveland and became president of the Bellefontaine and Indianapolis Railroad, which later joined the Big Four (the Cleveland, Columbus, Cincinnati & Indianapolis Railroad Co.). He also served as president of the Madison & Indianapolis Railroad.

In 1863 Unionist Republicans in Ohio convinced Brough to run for governor, and he won over Clement L. Vallandigham. Although he raised 34,000 militia troops for Civil War service, his policy of promoting army officers according to seniority generated so much discontent that he decided not to run for reelection in 1865.

Before his term was up, he died at age 53 in Cleveland and was buried in Woodland Cemetery. His first wife, Achsah P. Pruden of Athens, OH, whom he had married in 1832, died 8 Sept. 1838; they had a son, John, and a daughter, Mary. His second wife, Caroline A. Nelson, of Columbus, OH, whom he married in 1843, bore him three daughters: Caroline, Emma, and Anna.—M.S.

**BROWN, ALEXANDER EPHRAIM** (14 May 1852–26 Apr. 1911), inventor of the Brown Hoist, which revolutionized the lake shipping industry, was born in Cleveland, the son of FAYETTE and Cornelia Curtis Brown. He graduated from CENTRAL HIGH SCHOOL† and completed a course in civil engineering at Brooklyn Polytechnical Institute in 1872. While employed as chief engineer at the Massillon, OH, Bridge Co. in 1873–74, Brown devised a method of building bridge columns from scrap iron and steel. Returning to Cleveland, he continued to work as a mechanical engineer, but also experimented with ways to facilitate the unloading of bulk cargo on the Great Lakes by partially automating the process. Brown designed a cantilevered crane, rigged with wire cable to convey an automatic clamshell bucket to and from the ship's hold, removing the cargo. His hoist, first set up on the Erie docks, reduced lake transportation costs and greatly shortened the turn-around time of the vessels. He and his father, FAYETTE BROWN, organized the Brown Hoisting & Conveying Machinery Co. in 1880 with a capital of $100,000, incorporating it in 1893. Brown secured several hundred patents on his invention, which was distributed all over the world. The firm also produced other materials handling equipment for docks, railroads, and coal and steel plants.

Alexander Brown married Carrie M. Barnett 14 Nov. 1877, and they had 2 children, Alexander Cushing and Florence Cornelia. Brown died in Cleveland and was buried at Lake View Cemetery. —M.S.

Fayette Brown Papers, WRHS.

**BROWN, ANNA V.** (1914–12 Nov. 1985) developed Cleveland's Office on Aging in 1971, heading it until her death. Born in Vivian, WV, to physician Joseph E. and Hattie Brown, the family moved to Cleveland in 1941. Brown received her bachelor's degree from Oberlin College (1938) and her master's degree from New York Univ. She worked as an auditor in the General Accounting Office, then as assistant executive secretary of the PHILLIS WHEATLEY ASSN.† In 1946 she became manager of her father's office.

From working with patients, Brown became an advocate for the elderly. In Feb. 1971, Mayor Carl Stokes appointed her executive director of the Mayor's Commission on Aging, which became a city department in July 1981. Her office brought in $2 million in 2 years; assembled a list of services for the elderly; supported Community Responsive Transit and winter assistance heating; and developed programs such as CareRing, checking on those living alone. Brown participated in the 1971 and 1981 White House Conferences on Aging, and in 1984 became president of the Natl. Council on Aging. She was president of the Urban Elderly Coalition and the Ohio Chap. of the Caucus on the Black Aged; was a consultant to the Congressional Black Caucus Brain Trust; and served on the boards of the ELIZA BRYANT HOME† and the CLEVELAND CLINIC FOUNDATION.† Brown received honorary degrees from Oberlin College and Miami Univ. (1985). Brown's husband, Elmer Brown, whom she married on 7 June 1943, was the artist responsible for the freedom mural in the CITY CLUB OF CLEVELAND† and worked for AMERICAN GREETINGS CORP.† They had no children. Brown died in Cleveland.

**BROWN, FAYETTE** (17 Dec. 1823–20 Jan. 1910) was a Cleveland businessman who served as a U.S. Army paymaster during the CIVIL WAR.† Born in N. Bloomfield, OH (Trumbull County), to Ephraim and Mary (Buckingham Huntington) Brown, he worked for his brother at a wholesale dry goods store in Pittsburgh, PA, after completing his schooling, and became a member of the firm in 1845. He moved to Cleveland in 1851, formed a banking partnership with Geo. Mygatt under the name of Mygatt & Brown, and took over the business in 1857, when Mygatt retired. Brown closed his business at the outbreak of the Civil War, serving as paymaster, U.S. Army, 1861–62, before resigning his commission to return to private life. He returned to Cleveland to become general agent of the Jackson Iron Co. In the following years he became a powerful force in the iron industry, serving as president of the Union Steel Screw Co.; general manager of the Stewart Iron Co.; president of the Brown Hoisting & Conveying Machine Co.; and receiver of the Brown, Bonnell Co. of Youngstown, OH. Brown married Cornelia C. Curtiss of Allegheny City, PA, on 15 July 1847, and had 3 sons: ALEXANDER E., William F., and Harvey H.; and 2 daughters, Florence C. and Mary L. Because of Brown's military service, he was frequently referred to as "Major" or "Colonel." Brown was buried in Lake View Cemetery.

Brown Family Papers, WRHS.

**BROWN, JERE A.** (1841–28 Mar. 1913), a black Republican politician, was born in Pittsburgh, PA, attended Avery College in Allegheny, PA, and lived in Canada and St. Louis before arriving in Cleveland in 1870 or 1871, becoming active in politics here to improve his status. He was appointed bailiff for Judge Daniel R. Tilden, and in 1877, deputy sheriff, the first African American to receive political appointment in Cuyahoga County. He served as clerk for the Board of Equalization & Assessment; and in 1881 became a letter carrier, an elite occupation, resigning after 4 years because it kept him from politics. In 1885 he was elected a state representative and served 2 terms (1886–87, 1888–89).

Brown sponsored legislation preventing life insurance companies from discriminating against blacks (see AFRICAN AMERICANS†), helped secure funds for Wilberforce College, and repealed Ohio's BLACK LAWS.† He supported organization of the militant civil-rights group, the Afro-American League, in 1890. Later Brown became more interested in partisan politics, working for Republican candidates and expecting rewards. For supporting U.S. Sen. John Sherman, he became a customs inspector (1890), later gaining appointment to the

Ohio Dept. of Insurance, becoming the first black to serve there. Brown served in the Dept. of Internal Revenue in Washington, DC, before returning to Cleveland as immigration inspector. Brown, married to Nina L., had 2 children, Frances and Jere. He was active in the Prince Hall Masons, was a member of the Republican State Executive Committee, and a trustee of Wilberforce College, where he was buried.

**BROWN, JOHN** (ca. 1798–30 March 1869) reputedly became Cleveland's wealthiest African American citizen during a 40-year career as the city's most notable barber. Born of free parents in Virginia, he came to Cleveland in 1828 and in barbering took up a trade nearly monopolized in the 19th century by AFRICAN AMERICANS.† He married the widow of an established barber, Henry F. Stanton, ca. 1838. Until its destruction by fire in 1854, Brown was the proprietor of the barber shop in one of Cleveland's finest hotels, the New England House. Widely known as "John Brown the barber," he parlayed his earnings through real estate investments into an estate estimated to be worth from $35,000–40,000. Joining JOHN MALVIN and other Cleveland blacks in organizing a school for the city's African American children, Brown for a period maintained the resultant schoolhouse almost entirely at his own expense. He was also active in the black community's social life, participating in debates before the colored Young Men's Union Lyceum. Brown was acknowledged as an intelligent and formidable barber shop conversationalist on politics, religion, and philosophy. Less known at the time were his activities in the Underground Railroad, in which his downtown shop often served as the last stop for fugitive slaves before embarking on a lake vessel to freedom. In the face of Ohio's initial reluctance to recruit black troops during the Civil War, his 2 sons, John and Charles, went to join a black regiment in Massachusetts. Dying during a visit to Akron, Brown was survived by his wife, the 2 sons, and 2 daughters. His stepdaughter, Lucy Stanton (see LUCY ANN STANTON), was the first black woman to complete the Ladies Course at Oberlin College, and became the wife of WILLIAM HOWARD DAY.—J.V.

**BROWN, LLOYD ODOM** (12 Dec. 1928–3 May 1993) was the first African American elected as a Cleveland Municipal Court judge and the second to sit as an Ohio Supreme Court Justice. He also served on Cuyahoga County's Common Pleas Court and with the firm of Weston, Hurd, Fallon, Paisley & Howley.

Born in Little Rock, AR, Brown moved with his family at age 2 to Cleveland. He attended Gladstone Elementary School and graduated from East Technical High School in 1946. After 4 years in the Coast Guard, Brown enrolled at Ohio State Univ. and earned both a B.A. in political science and a law degree in 1955. Admitted to the Ohio Bar in 1956, he practiced with the Cleveland firm of Charles V. Carr & Associates.

Brown served as an Ohio Assistant Attorney General, 1958–59, and as a trial lawyer in the Cuyahoga County prosecutor's office, 1959–67. Brown was elected as a municipal court judge in 1967, where he instituted a $5 reduction in fines in traffic court for those found wearing a seat belt at the time the citation was issued, the first such program in the country.

Appointed to the Ohio Supreme Court by Gov. John Gilligan in 1971, Brown served until defeated in the 1972 general election. In 1973 Gilligan appointed Brown as a Cuyahoga County Common Pleas judge. He remained on the bench until 1986, when he joined the firm of Weston, Hurd, Fallon, Paisley & Howley where he remained until his death.

Lloyd and Phyllis Brown married in 1951. They had three children: Lloyd Jr., Raymond, and Leslie. Brown is buried in Highland Park Cemetery.—T.B.

**BROWN, PAUL E.** (7 Sept. 1908–5 Aug. 1991) was the head coach of the CLEVELAND BROWNS† from its beginnings in 1946 through 1962. An innovative and highly successful coach at all levels, Brown developed coaching procedures that revolutionized modern football and earned him election to the Pro Football Hall of Fame in 1967. Brown was born in Norwalk, OH, the son of Ida (Sherwood) and Lester Brown. He moved with his family to Massillon, OH, where Brown became the quarterback of the high school football team. Considered too small for football at Ohio State Univ., he transferred to Miami Univ. in Oxford, OH, and played quarterback there in the 1920s. Brown began his coaching career in 1930 at Severn Prep School in Annapolis, MD. He returned to Massillon in 1932 as head coach at Washington High School. In 9 seasons his teams won 80 games, including a 35-game winning streak. In 1941 Brown became head football coach at Ohio State, where his team won the national championship in 1942. During World War II Brown was the head coach at the Great Lakes Naval Training Ctr. near Chicago. In 1945 he agreed to become head coach and 5% owner of a new professional franchise being formed in Cleveland. Brown was able to recruit the best players he had seen in his years at Ohio State and Great Lakes for the team which was named in his honor. Beginning in 1946, the Browns won 4 consecutive All-America

Football Conference championships (1946–49) and 3 National Football League title games (1950, 1954, and 1955), while compiling a record of 158–48–8 during his tenure. Nine of the Browns' players were inducted into the Hall of Fame. Nevertheless, a new team owner, Art Modell, fired Brown on 7 Jan. 1963. Brown returned to coaching in 1968 after establishing the Cincinnati Bengals. Retiring as coach after the 1975 season, he continued as the team's vice-president and general mgr. Among his coaching innovations were the use of intelligence tests for players, the creation of written playbooks, the calling of plays through messenger guards, the grading of players after the review of game films, and the adoption of the protective face mask.

Brown was first married in 1929 to his high school sweetheart, Kathryn (Katie) Kester. After her death in 1969, he married his former secretary, Mary Rightsell, in 1973. He died in Cincinnati, survived by 2 sons, Mike and Pete. He is buried in Rose Hill Memorial Park, near Massillon.—J.V.

Grabowski, John J. *Sports in Cleveland: An Illustrated History* (1992).

**BROWN, REV. RUSSELL S.** (31 Aug. 1889-Aug. 1981), pastor of MT. ZION CONGREGATIONAL CHURCH† (1925–33) was elected to fill the unexpired term of THOMAS W. FLEMING on CLEVELAND CITY COUNCIL† (1929). The first pastor and the second African American to serve on the council, he sat on the judiciary, finance, and steam RAILROADS† committee. Brown was born to Bartlett and Alice Brown in London, KY, the youngest of 11 children. The family moved to Kansas when he was 14. Brown attended public schools and Washburn College, Topeka, KS, and graduated from Payne Theological Seminary (1915), Xenia, OH. He served churches in Butte, MT, Memphis, TN (1917–20), Atlanta, GA (1920–25), and Washington, DC, and, during World War I, worked as a chaplain at Camp Funston, KS. Brown also served as jail chaplain (Fulton County, GA) and chaired a race relations committee on church cooperation (Atlanta) before coming to Cleveland.

At Mt. Zion, Brown directed a successful campaign to raise $50,000 to pay off church debts. Brown served on the executive committee of the Federated Churches (later INTERCHURCH COUNCIL OF GREATER CLEVELAND†), presided over the local Congregational ministers' club, and chaired the Willson District of ASSOCIATED CHARITIES.† A Republican who did not believe in mixing religion and politics, he reluctantly accepted the city council position and did not seek a second term. Brown left Mt. Zion in 1933 to take a pastorate in Denver, CO.

Brown married Floy Zxlema Smith of Oberlin, OH, on 24 June 1915, and they had 3 children: Alice Elaine, Charles Shelton, and Russell, Jr.—J.M.

**BROWN, WENDELL PHILLIPS** (27 Nov. 1866–31 Jan. 1951) was especially noted as a designer and builder of bridges during an engineering career of half a century. He was born in Hopkinton, RI, the son of George and Martha Brumley Brown. From Phillips Andover Academy he went to Yale, where he received his engineering degree in 1890. Brown immediately proceeded to Cleveland to join the engineering staff of the KING IRON BRIDGE & MANUFACTURING CO.† He married the former Hattie Sanger of Connecticut in 1893. In 1912 he joined WILBUR J. WATSON & Associates as vice-president and chief civil engineer. He left Watson in 1922 to form his own company, the Wendell P. Brown Co., serving as president and chief engineer until his retirement in 1940. Among the bridges designed by Brown were the Mahoning River viaduct in Niles, OH, and the Fulton Rd. Bridge in Cleveland (1932). During World War I he had designed and built factories for the manufacture of trucks by the WHITE MOTOR CORP.† He served on a citizens committee to determine the location and estimated cost of the Lorain-Carnegie (see HOPE MEMORIAL†) Bridge. His last major project was the design and construction in 1938 of the Upper West Third St. Bridge in the FLATS,† Cleveland's first roller bearing, vertical lift bridge. Brown was a past president of the CLEVELAND ENGINEERING SOCIETY† and a member of the New England Society of Cleveland (see PATRIOTIC SOCIETIES†). He died in Grosse Pointe Park, MI, and was buried at Lake View Cemetery. His wife having died in 1939, he was survived by a son, M. Sanger, and 2 daughters, Marjorie Blair and Mary Carter.—J.V.

**BROWNE, CHARLES FARRAR [ARTEMUS WARD, PSEUD.]** (26 Apr. 1834–6 Mar. 1867), a nationally known journalist and humorist, spent only 3 years in Cleveland but here invented his alter ego, "Artemus Ward." Born in Waterford, ME, to Levi and Caroline Farrar Brown, he moved to Ohio in 1854, working for papers in Tiffin and Toledo before JOSEPH W. GRAY recruited him for the *PLAIN DEALER†* on 30 Oct. 1857.

Browne's first "Artemus Ward" letter appeared in the *Plain Dealer* on 30 Jan. 1858. Ostensibly written from Pittsburgh by an itinerant showman and waxworks proprietor, it requested information and publicity for a forthcoming Cleveland appearance and closed with the tag line, "P.S. pitsburg is a 1 horse town. A.W." Further communications traced

Ward's peregrinations over the next 2 years. Turning his humor to other subjects, such as the "three tigers of Cleveland journalism" (Joseph Gray, GEO. A. BENEDICT, and JOSIAH A. HARRIS), Browne began sending copies of his material to *Vanity Fair* in New York, leading to friction with Gray, who wanted Browne's exclusive services but declined to pay Browne what he thought he was worth. They parted on 10 Nov. 1860.

Browne became editor of *Vanity Fair*; lectured as Artemus Ward; and published *Artemus Ward: His Book* in May 1862, from which Abraham Lincoln entertained his cabinet prior to announcing issuance of the Preliminary Emancipation Proclamation. Nothing came of Browne's offer to purchase the *Plain Dealer* after Gray's death, and Browne died of tuberculosis on the Isle of Jersey while lecturing in England. Never married, Browne was buried in Waterford, ME.

Shaw, Archer H. *The Plain Dealer: One Hundred Years in Cleveland* (1942).

**BROWNE, MARY KENDALL "BROWNIE"** (3 June 1891–19 Aug. 1971), championship golfer and tennis player, was born in Ventura County, CA, the daughter of Albert William and Neotia Rice Browne, and attended high school in Los Angeles. Only 5 ft., 2 in., she learned the man's all-court tennis game from her brother, Nat, and developed into a sound shotmaker and an aggressive player. In a memorable athletic career, Browne was three times national singles champion (1912–14), five times ladies doubles champion, and twice captain of the U.S. Wightman Cup team. She joined the first professional tennis tour, 1926–27, and was one of the first women enshrined in the Tennis Hall of Fame. In the early 1930s, Browne operated a sporting goods store in Cleveland and was an insurance agent with Wilson McBride & Co. She won the Cleveland Women's Amateur Championship four times (1931; 32; 34; 35) and was Ohio Women's titlist three times. A resident of Waite Hill, Browne was a part-time tennis instructor at Lake Erie College, 1930–41, and a physical education instructor at the college, 1945–51. She was a self-taught artist who received commissions to paint portraits of Clevelanders, including one of Mrs. George I. Vail. During World War II, she served with the American Red Cross at General Douglas MacArthur's headquarters in Australia.

Browne married Dr. Kenneth Smith in 1958. Subsequently they divorced, and she returned to southern California. She died at Laguna Hills and was buried at Forest Lawn Memorial Park in Glendale.—M.S.

**BROWNELL, ABNER** (1813–1857), a member of the city council and mayor of Cleveland from 1852–55, was born in Massachusetts, the son of Nathan C. and Elizabeth Adams Smith Brownell. He was educated in local schools, and came to Cleveland in the 1840s while in the employ (1846–49) of the W. A. Otis Co. as a dealer in iron and glass. From 1849–53 he was a partner in the banking firm of Wick, Otis & Brownell. His Massachusetts upbringing played a great role in shaping his personal and community life, and in 1853 he became president of the New England Society. In 1849 Brownell ran as a Democrat for city council, a post he held through 1852, when he successfully ran for mayor with no opposition. He became the first Cleveland mayor to serve 2 terms in office (until 1855). While mayor, he supported city departments, new schools, new sewers, and loans for area roads. After leaving office, he became a commission merchant until his death in 1857. Brownell and his wife, Eliza, were married in the early 1830s, shortly before he settled in Cleveland. They had four children: Charles W., Cornelia G., John, and Wilford S.

**BRUDNO, EZRA** (1877–12 Dec. 1954), attorney and author, was one of the most notable Jewish writers in Cleveland during the first 2 decades of the 20th century. Born in Lithuania to Isaac and Hannah (Model) Brudno, he was educated in a private European school and brought to America in 1891 by his parents. He continued his studies at CENTRAL HIGH SCHOOL,† Yale Univ., and Western Reserve Univ., receiving a law degree. Brudno began his law practice in 1900 and continued to practice until his retirement in 1949. Soon after entering the legal profession, he began writing. By 1910 he had 3 novels published: *The Fugitive, The Tether,* and *The Little Conscript.* In addition, his fiction and nonfiction were published in national magazines, such as *Lippincott's,* and locally in the *Jewish Review & Observer.* Although some of Brudno's fiction advocated shielding the young from the influence of America, he promoted the assimilation of Jews into Western civilization in his nonfiction. He wrote that there was little, if anything, of value in Judaism and Jewish culture worth preserving. In 1920 he published a novel about the legal profession, *The Jugglers,* which met with little success. Fifteen years later, he wrote his only full-length piece of nonfiction, *Ghost of Yesterday: A Reappraisal of Moral Values and of Accepted Standards in This Changing World.*

Brudno married Rose Hess and had two children: Lincoln and Emily. He died in his home in SHAKER HTS.†

**BRUSH, CHARLES FRANCIS** (17 Mar. 1849–15 June 1929), one of America's most distinguished inventors, was born in Euclid Twp. to Isaac Elbert and Delia Williams Phillips Brush. He received his mining engineering degree from the Univ. of Michigan in 1869. He worked 4 years in Cleveland as a chemist, then formed an iron dealing partnership with Chas. E. Bingham. In 1875 Brush married Mary Ellen Morris, and had 3 children, EDNA BRUSH PERKINS, Helene, and Charles.

In 1876 Brush received one of his 50 career patents, for the "perfect" open coil-type dynamo, a predecessor of the modern generator. His arc light (1878), demonstrated in Cleveland's PUBLIC SQUARE† in 1879, made Brush world-famous, and by 1882 "Brush Lights" were used throughout the world. In 1880 Brush formed the Brush Electric Co., which was bought by Thomson Houston Electric Co. in 1889, merging with Edison General Electric Co. in 1891 to form General Electric Co. Brush spent the rest of his life pursuing interests in gravitation and heat, writing articles published by the American Philosophical Society and the Royal Society.

Brush maintained various business interests. He was founder and president of the Linde Air Prods. Co., helped form the Sandusky Portland Cement Co. (later Medusa), and was president of the Cleveland Arcade Co., the Euclid Natl. Bank, and the Cleveland Chamber of Commerce. He was a trustee of Adelbert College, the Cleveland School of Art, and LAKE VIEW CEMETERY.† Brush received many honorary degrees; was made a chevalier of the Legion of Honor of France (1881); and received medals from the American Academy of Arts & Sciences (1899), the American Institute of Electrical Engineers (1913), and the Franklin Institute (1928). He founded the BRUSH FOUNDATION† following the deaths of his son and 6-year-old grandson in 1927. Brush died in Cleveland and was buried in Lake View Cemetery.—J.M.

Charles F. Brush Papers, Freiberger Library, CWRU.
Perkins, Charles Brush. *Ancestors of Charles Brush Perkins and Maurice Perkins* (1976).
*A Concise Genealogy of Isaac Elbert Brush & Delia Williams Brush, His Wife, and Their Descendants* (1932).

**BRUSH, DOROTHY ADAMS HAMILTON** (14 Mar. 1894–21 June 1968) was a reformer in the area of birth control for over 30 years. She helped found the Maternal Health Assn. (MHA, later PLANNED PARENTHOOD OF GREATER CLEVELAND†), managed the BRUSH FOUNDATION,† and served as founding editor of the International Planned Parenthood Federation's (IPPF) newsletter and as IPPF's Honorary Adviser for Field Work. Brush was born in Cleveland, daughter of Walter J. and Jane Adams Hamilton, and sister of actress MARGARET HAMILTON.† She received a B.A. from Smith College in 1917 and married Charles Francis Brush, Jr., the same year. After a brief military stint, the Brushes settled in Cleveland Hts. In May 1927, Brush's 6-yr.-old daughter, Jane, died, and a week later her husband succumbed to complications from blood transfusions to his daughter during her illness. In her husband's memory, Brush donated funds to open the MHA birth control clinic in Cleveland (1928), a project which she and others had been planning since 1921. In 1929 Brush's father-in-law, inventor CHAS. F. BRUSH, SR.,† appointed her to the Board of Managers of his newly created Brush Foundation.

Although Brush did not live in Cleveland after 1928, she remained active on the boards of both the Brush Foundation and the MHA throughout her life. The foundation funded the planning, creation, and early years (1949–1966) of the New York-based IPPF, largely because of Brush's international work with birth control activist Margaret Sanger, with whom she was a close friend for over 30 years.

Brush married two more times: Alexander C. Dick (3 Jan. 1929, div. 1947) and Louis C. Walmsley (1 Dec. 1962). She died in 1968 and was survived by two children, Chas. F. Brush III and Sylvia Dick (Mrs. Athan Karas).—J.M.

Perkins, Charles Brush. *Ancestors of Charles Brush Perkins and Maurice Perkins* (1976).
Dorothy H. Brush Papers, Sophia Smith Library, Smith College.

**BRYANT, ELIZA** (1827–13 May 1907) was the founder of the Cleveland Home for Aged Colored People (The ELIZA BRYANT CENTER†) in 1897. It was the first nonreligious welfare institution supported by Cleveland's African American community, and quickly became the most widely supported institution of the black community.

Eliza was born in North Carolina to Polly Simmons, a slave, and her master. In 1848 Polly Simmons was freed and moved north with her family, purchasing a home in Cleveland with funds from her master.

Once in Cleveland, Eliza, like her mother, opened her home to newcomers until they found work and could support themselves. Around 1893 Eliza became aware of the need to care for aging AFRICAN AMERICANS† left alone due to slavery. Denied admission to white homes for the aged, Eliza related their plight to her female church members. Aided by Sarah Green and LETHIA FLEMING, they tapped into the network of women in the churches and clubs of Cleveland. Their appeals for humane treatment won supporters as volunteers and as contributors. In January 1895 the board of trustees was selected, with Emman Ransom as president over the all-female trustees. They met in each other's homes to make plans for the future.

Incorporated on 1 Sept. 1896, the Cleveland Home for Aged Colored People opened on 11 Aug. 1897 at 284 Giddings (East 71st) St.

In 1960, under reorganization, the institution was renamed the Eliza Bryant Home to honor its founder.

Bryant married and had several children. She is buried in Woodland Cemetery.—T.B.

**BUCK, REV. FLORENCE** (19 July, 1860–12 Oct. 1925) served with MARIAN MURDOCH from 1893–99 as joint ministers of the First Unitarian Society of Cleveland.

Born in Kalamazoo County, MI, to Samuel P. and Lucy (Reasoner) Buck, Florence attended Coldwater and Kalamazoo schools. She became head of the science department and principal of Kalamazoo High School. Raised a Methodist, Buck was converted to Unitarianism by her friend, Marian Murdoch. Buck attended Meadville Theological School and studied for a year at Manchester College in Oxford and at Oxford Univ. in England before graduating from Meadville in 1894.

Buck was ordained on 24 Sept. 1893 in Chicago. In 1893 Buck and Murdoch were called by the First Unitarian Society of Cleveland to serve as joint ministers of the First Unitarian Church (Unity Church). During their tenure the church prospered, growing to 80 members.

In 1899 Buck and Murdoch resigned in order to travel and study in Europe. In 1901 Buck moved to Michigan as a field worker for the American Unitarian Assn. (AUA). Later that year she went to work in Kenosha, WI, remaining until 1910. She moved to Palo Alto, CA, in 1910, then on to Alameda from 1911–12. Buck served as associate secretary of the AUA's Department of Religious Education in 1912 and the department's executive secretary in 1925.

In 1920 Buck was honored for her work in religious education by becoming the first woman ever to receive a Doctor of Divinity degree from the Meadville Theological School.

Buck died in Boston, MA, following a bout of typhoid fever.—T.B.

Morton, Marian. *Women in Cleveland: An Illustrated History* (1995).

**BUHRER, STEPHEN** (25 Dec. 1825–8 Dec. 1907), Democratic mayor of Cleveland from 1867–71 and 4-term city councilman (1855–57, 1863–67, 1874–76) was born to Johann Casper and Anna Maria Miller Buhrer on the Zoar farm in Tuscarawas County, OH. When his father died in 1829, he was bound to the Society of Separatists, who operated the communal farm at Zoar, until he came of age. Buhrer received education in evening classes and Sunday school, learned the coopering trade when he was 12, and left Zoar at 17 to work as a cooper in Cleveland. After a time as a traveling salesman, he returned to Cleveland in the late 1840s and opened his own coopering shop. He sold the shop in 1853, and by 1856 was in business rectifying and distilling alcohol, expanding that business to manufacture gentian bitters and sewer gas traps, and bottled mineral waters. By the turn of the century, he was a wholesale distributor of alcoholic beverages.

Buhrer served 3 terms on the city council and was elected mayor of Cleveland in 1867. He urged the building of the Cleveland House of Correction & Workhouse, later serving on its Board of Directors. After his second mayoral term, Buhrer returned to the city council for another term. He remained in business until he died in Cleveland. Buhrer married Eva Maria Schneider in 1848, and had 3 children: John, Mary Jane, and Lois Catherine (Mrs. Frank Q. Barstow). After the death of his wife in Mar. 1889, he married Marguerite Paterson.

**BULKLEY, ROBERT JOHNS** (8 Oct. 1880–21 July 1965), a prominent banker and businessman, was a Democratic U.S. Representative from 1910–14, and U.S. Senator from 1930–39. Born in Cleveland to Charles Henry and Roberta Johns Bulkley, he received an A.B. (1902) and M.A. (1906) from Harvard, and studied law for a year. Bulkley was admitted to the Ohio Bar in 1907.

Urged by Mayor TOM L. JOHNSON to run for Congress, Bulkley was elected in 1910. As a member of the Banking & Currency Committee, he helped frame the Federal Reserve Act of 1913, but lost his bid for reelection in 1915. During World War I, he served the legal departments of several federal boards. Returning to Cleveland, he headed the Bulkley Bldg. Co. and helped found the Morris Plan Bank of Ohio, serving as president and chairman of the board for over 30 years. He was a founder of the NORTHERN OHIO OPERA ASSN.† in 1927.

In 1930 Bulkley ran to fill the unexpired term of Sen. THEODORE BURTON. Advocating Prohibition's repeal, he won and was reelected in 1932. He supported the New Deal and also backed Roosevelt's plan to enlarge the Supreme Court, which contributed to his defeat by Republican Robt. A. Taft in 1938. He then became senior partner in the Cleveland firm of Bulkley & Butler.

Bulkley married Katherine C. Pope (d. 1932) on 17 Feb. 1909 and had 3 children: William Pope,

Robt. Johns, and Katharine. In 1934 he married Helen Graham Robbins; they had one child, Rebecca Johns. Bulkley died in Cleveland.

Robert J. Bulkley Papers, WRHS.

**BUNDY, LEROY N.** (14 Apr. 1873–28 May 1943), a Cleveland dentist, was also a politician who served 4 terms as the black Republican councilman of Ward 17, and was an early leader of the Cleveland branch of the UNIVERSAL NEGRO IMPROVEMENT ASSN.† Born in Hamilton, OH, to Rev. Charles and Eliza Bundy, he moved to Cleveland at an early age and was educated at CENTRAL HIGH SCHOOL.† Bundy graduated from the Dental School of Western Reserve Univ. in 1904. He practiced his profession in Cleveland until the 1920s, when he entered politics, using the opportunity to oversee the newly formed local branch of the Universal Negro Improvement Assn. to increase his influence. Elected to the city council in 1929, in 1930 Bundy sponsored legislation to prevent the spread of tuberculosis in the E. 55th St. area and called upon city health authorities to clean up the junkyards in his ward. He was chairman of the council's Utilities Commission and wielded great influence in council later as a veteran member. In 1933 Bundy began studying law at the Law School of WRU, earning his law degree in 1936. By 1936 the dominating influence Bundy exerted at council meetings gave him power in the local Republican organization and won him recognition at the REPUBLICAN NATL. CONVENTION OF 1936,† where he organized delegates from the southern states. Dr. Bundy and his wife, Vella, had no children. He died in Cleveland and was buried in Highland Cemetery.

**BUNTS, FRANK E.** (3 June 1861–28 Nov. 1928) was one of the 4 founders of the CLEVELAND CLINIC FOUNDATION† and the first president of the ACADEMY OF MEDICINE† in Cleveland. Born in Youngstown, OH, to William C. and Clara E. Bunts, he graduated from the U.S. Naval Academy at Annapolis in 1881 and received his M.D. from the Western Reserve Univ. School of Medicine in 1886, serving as house officer at Charity Hospital in Cleveland. Along with GEO. W. CRILE, SR., Bunts assisted Dr. Frank Weed in his practice on Cleveland's west side and did casualty work for the railroads and shipyards. He took additional medical training in Europe and served in the Spanish-American War before returning to practice medicine in Cleveland in 1896. He was Professor of Principles of Surgery and Clinical Surgery at WRU, and in 1902 became the first president of the Academy of Medicine in Cleveland. In 1921 Bunts joined Geo.

W. Crile, Sr., JOHN PHILLIPS, and WM. E. LOWER in establishing the Cleveland Clinic Foundation, patterned after the group-practice model of the Mayo brothers in Rochester, MN. Bunts continued performing most of his surgery at Charity Hospital (1885–1928) and was its chief of staff (1913–28). His main surgical-medical interests were gallbladder disease, breast tumors, and cancer. Bunts also wrote a small volume of short stories entitled *The Soul of Henry Huntington*. In 1888 Bunts married Harriet Taylor and had 2 children, Alexander Taylor Bunts and Clara Louise Bunts (Dauost). Bunts is buried at Lake View Cemetery.

Bunts, Alexander T., and George W. Crile, Jr., eds. *To Act as a Unit* (1971).
Crile, George W., Jr. *George Crile* (1947).

**BURCHFIELD, CHARLES EPHRAIM** (9 Apr. 1893–10 Jan. 1967) was probably the most renowned graduate of the Cleveland School of Art (see CLEVELAND INSTITUTE OF ART†) and maintained Cleveland ties even after settling in Buffalo, NY. Born in Ashtabula, OH, the son of Wm. Charles and Alice (Murphy) Burchfield, he moved to Salem, OH, at age 5, following his father's death. In 1912 Burchfield entered the Cleveland School of Art, where he was a student of HENRY KELLER and FRANK WILCOX. He served in the army in World War I, after which he exhibited paintings at LAUKHUFF'S BOOKSTORE† in the Taylor Arcade and won first prize in a CLEVELAND SOCIETY OF ARTISTS† exhibit in 1921. He moved to Buffalo that year to work as a wallpaper designer, and in 1922 he married Bertha Kenreich of Greenford, OH, with whom he had 5 children. Burchfield earned a reputation as a regional realist during the decades between the 2 world wars for his watercolors of small town life, reportedly inspired by his reading of Sherwood Anderson's *Winesburg, Ohio*. Between 1930–41 he had 8 one-man shows at the Rehn Gallery in New York City. During World War II his interest shifted from town scenes to subjects of nature, and after the war he also began to teach on a limited scale. He had one-man shows at the Cleveland School of Art in 1940 and the Cleveland Town and Country Gallery in 1948, while the CLEVELAND MUSEUM OF ART† held a retrospective exhibit of his drawings in 1953. He continued to paint up to his death from a heart attack near his home. Burchfield was buried in W. Seneca, NY. —J.V.

**BURDICK, HAROLD BENNETT** (5 Oct. 1895–24 May 1947) was an eclectic architect who designed some 28 homes in SHAKER HTS.† and whose own residence represented the first complete architectural statement of the modern house in Greater Cleveland.

Born in Cleveland to Dr. Halbert and Mariette (Bennett) Burdick, Harold graduated from Cornell Univ.'s School of Architecture and then served as a second lieutenant during World War I.

Returning to Cleveland after the war, Burdick worked for the architectural firms of WALKER & WEEKS† and Mead & Hamilton before establishing his own firm. His first major design, completed in 1924, was a French Provincial house at 19000 South Woodland Road. Burdick designed in Colonial, English Tudor, French, Georgian, Neo-Classical and Jacobethan Revival styles. His period of greatest activity occurred during 1928–29.

During 1938–39 Burdick built a glass block house for his own residence at 2424 Stratford Road, CLEVELAND HTS.† It was one of the few local homes designed in the International Style and it reflected the "streamlined" look popular in the 1930s. Featuring an all-electric kitchen and possibly the first domestic use of fluorescent lighting, Burdick planned it as a prototype for a quality house in an economical price range.

Burdick helped design the Cleveland FEDERAL RESERVE BANK† and the Moreland Courts Apartments in Shaker Hts.

Burdick married Marjorie Donnell on 29 June 1932. Burdick had two children, John (previous marriage) and Ellen. Burdick belonged to the First Baptist Church and is buried in Lake View Cemetery.—T.B.

**BURKE, EDMUND STEVENSON JR.** (1 Feb. 1879–7 April 1962), wealthy banker and sportsman, was born in Cleveland, the son of Edmund S. and Julia Fritz Burke. He graduated from UNIV. SCHOOL† in 1896 and attended Princeton Univ. for 4 years, where he played baseball and football. Burke studied law for a short time before joining the Corrigan McKinney Steel Co., where his grandfather, STEVENSON BURKE, was a major stockholder. When the Union Trust closed in 1933, Burke was a member of the group that sought to resurrect the company. He served as chairman of the Federal Reserve Bank in Cleveland 1934–38 and was a member of the Securities Exchange Commission in the 1940s.

A skilled yachtsman, Burke was best known for the 140-ft. long yacht "Josephine," built in 1926 at a cost of $500,000. He also raised horses on his estate, his trotters and pacers winning the local harness racing challenge cup in 1907, 1908, and 1909. Burke, along with Corliss Sullivan, introduced the game of polo to Cleveland in 1911, providing a polo field on his estate, assembling a team for the matches, and importing expert Earl

Hopping to teach the game. In 1938 he sold his 30-room townhouse to the CLEVELAND MUSIC SCHOOL SETTLEMENT.†

Burke married Josephine Brainard Chisholm 22 Oct. 1924, and they had four children: Stevenson Burke, Mrs. Josephine Gillespie, Mrs. Parthenia de Muralt of New York, and Mrs. Kathleen Sherwin of Cleveland. He died at his home in CLEVELAND HTS.† and was buried at Lake View Cemetery. —J.M.

**BURKE, STEVENSON** (26 Nov. 1826–24 Apr. 1904), noted jurist and expert railroad litigator, was born in St. Lawrence County, NY, son of David and Isabella Burke. He was 8 years old when his family moved to North Ridgeville in Lorain County, OH, where he received his early education. After attending Ohio Wesleyan Univ., he studied law with Horace D. Clark in Elyria and was admitted to the bar in 1848. He practiced law there and was elected judge of the Common Pleas Court in 1861, serving until 1869 when he came to Cleveland. In Cleveland he joined in partnership first with FRANKLIN T. BACKUS and E. J. Eastep, and after 1870, with WILLIAM B. SANDERS and Jonathan E. Ingersoll, where he was instrumental in effecting a number of railroad mergers.

In addition to his legal representation, Burke took an active part in the management of several railroads, including the Cleveland, Columbus, Cincinnati & Indianapolis, the Cleveland and Mahoning Valley roads, and Central Ontario Railways, serving as their president. He is perhaps best known for his 1881 purchase of controlling interest in the NICKEL PLATE RAILROAD,† acting as the agent for William K. Vanderbilt, who owned the competing Lake Shore and Michigan line.

Burke married Parthenia Poppleton 28 Apr. 1849. After her death in 1878, he married Mrs. Ella M. Southworth, 22 June 1882. Burke died in Washington, DC.—M.S.

**BURKE, THOMAS A. (ALOYSIUS)** (30 Oct. 1898–5 Dec. 1971) served as Cleveland law director and mayor. Born in Cleveland to Thomas A. and Lillian McNeil Burke, he received his B.A. from Holy Cross College (1920), and his LL.B. from Western Reserve Univ. School of Law (1923). He was asst. county prosecutor from 1930–36; in 1937, the state attorney general appointed him special counsel to prosecute vote fraud. Burke became Cleveland law director under Mayor FRANK LAUSCHE in 1941, and mayor when Lausche became governor in 1945. As an independent Democrat, Burke was elected mayor in 1945 and served 4 terms. During his administration, he presided over a large capital-improvement program, including a lakefront airport built on landfill, the first downtown airport in the country (see BURKE LAKEFRONT AIRPORT†). He campaigned for a charter amendment, passed in 1951, giving the mayor power to appoint and dismiss the police chief, and helped establish a free municipal parking lot adjacent to the shoreway.

When U.S. Sen. Robt. Taft died in 1953, Gov. Lausche appointed Burke to fill Taft's Senate seat. In the 1954 election, Burke lost his bid for the seat to Congressman GEO. H. BENDER. He retired from politics but continued practicing law as senior partner in the law firm Burke, Haber & Berwick. Burke married Josephine Lyon in 1923 and had 2 daughters, Barbara (Mrs. Terrence J. Martin) and Jo Anne (Mrs. Stanley L. Orr). After Mrs. Burke's death in 1964, he married Evelyn Sedgwick. Burke was buried in Calvary Cemetery.

Thomas Burke Papers, WRHS.

**BURKETT, JESSE CAIL "CRAB"** (12 Feb. 1870–27 May 1953), a left-handed outfielder for the CLEVELAND SPIDERS† from 1891–98, holds the record with Ty Cobb and Rogers Hornsby for hitting .400 or over during 3 seasons. Born in Wheeling, WV, to Granville and Eleanor Burkett, he began in 1888 as a pitcher with Scranton, was transferred to the outfield by the New York Giants, and by 1891 was playing for the Spiders. Batting .423 in 1895 and .410 in 1896, Burkett helped the Spiders in the Temple Cup series, the equivalent of the World Series, with the Spiders defeating Baltimore 4 games to 1 for the league championship in 1895. In 6 seasons, Burkett never hit below a .345 average, leading the league 3 times in total base hits. At the beginning of the 1899 season, Frank De Haas Robison, who owned 2 clubs, transferred CY YOUNG and Burkett to St. Louis, where the outfielder hit .402. After leading the NL in hitting during the 1901 season, Burkett jumped to the American League St. Louis team, three seasons later being traded to the Boston Red Sox, finishing his career in 1905 with a .342 lifetime batting average. Burkett was the owner and manager of Worcester in the New England League from 1906–13, and also coached Holy Cross College (1917–20) and Assumption College (1928, 1931, 1932). In 1946 he was elected to the Baseball Hall of Fame at Cooperstown, NY. Burkett and his wife, Ellen, had a daughter, Anna, and a son, Howard, who played minor-league ball. Burkett was buried in St. John's Cemetery in Wooster, MA.

**BURNHAM, THOMAS** (18 June 1808–7 Apr. 1898), a founder of the malleable iron business west of the Allegheny Mts. and mayor of OHIO CITY† from 1849–50, was born in Moreau, NY, son of James and Miriam Burnham. He was master of a freight boat on the Champlain Canal before settling in Brooklyn Twp., OH, in 1833. He took a job as a schoolteacher, and the following year became one of the proprietors of the Burton House, a hotel at the corner of Pearl and Detroit streets. In 1834 Burnham was employed by the Troy & Erie Line, a company doing a large business on the Ohio Canal, Lake Erie, and the Erie Canal shipping wheat. Burnham acquired an interest in the company and took control of a grain elevator on the CUYAHOGA RIVER,† above the Superior St. viaduct. In 1851 he purchased the Erie elevator, one of the largest in Cleveland. He continued in the elevator business until 1871. Burnham was active in local government, in both Ohio City and Cleveland. Mayor of Ohio City when it was consolidated into Cleveland, Burnham was elected to CLEVELAND CITY COUNCIL† and later served as council president. A founder of the Cleveland Malleable Iron Co., Burnham served as its president for 5 years. He was also one of the founders of the Chicago Malleable Iron Co. In addition, he was the president of several smaller manufacturing interests in the Midwest.

Burnham married Maria Louisa White in 1833 and had 4 children: Matilda, Harriet, Thomas, and Charles. Burnham died in Glens Falls, NY, and was buried in Lake View Cemetery.

**BURROWS, GEORGE HOWARD** (25 Aug. 1893–11 Aug. 1970) was an architect who designed nearly 1,000 homes in SHAKER HTS.,† CLEVELAND HTS.,† and other eastern suburbs in various sizes and styles, and also designed numerous commercial structures.

Born in Cleveland to George Humphrey and Ida (Folliette) Burrows, George graduated from the Univ. of Michigan School of Architecture (1920), then taught high school in Cleveland (1920–21).

Burrows started his architectural practice in 1922. His partners included Chester Lowe (1923), Philo Brooke (1923–29) and Urban Schwerzler (1928–42). Brooke and Burrows designed numerous homes in the Van Sweringen (see VAN SWERINGEN, ORIS, AND MANTIS†) tradition. These were finely detailed, two-family homes designed to resemble single family residences.

Burrows was senior partner and principal designer in the firm of Burrows, Hinman, and Gabriel (1950–58), which became George Howard Burrows & Charles Hinman Associates.

Burrows's commercial structures included numerous buildings on the south side of Chagrin Blvd. between Lee and Avalon. He received a patent on a split-level apartment design, examples of which remain on Van Aken Blvd. between South Woodland and Drexmore.

Burrows belonged to the Univ. Club of the American Institute of Architects and the Ohio Society of Architects.

George and Irene L. Burrows were married in 1917 (div. 1928). They had a daughter, Lenore. Burrows married Phoebe Brooke Wolfe on 3 Aug. 1928. They had two daughters, Phoebe Tritton (stepdaughter), and Mrs. Clay Murray. Burrows was cremated.—T.B.

**BURTEN, LONNIE L. JR.** (20 Oct. 1944–29 Nov. 1984) was a Cleveland city councilman and community activist who worked toward revitalizing the inner city. Outspoken, unconventional, and determined to provide decent housing, Burten created the Central Area Development Corp. to finance construction of single-family homes in the Central-Woodland area. Burten's opposition to public housing projects led to his being threatened and burned out.

Born in Shaw, MS, to Lonnie and Grace Arrington Burten, Burten was raised in Cleveland's Central area. He attended Cuyahoga Community College, received his B.A. from Central State Univ. in 1967, and his M.A. from (Clark) Atlanta Univ. in 1971. He was elected Democratic Ward 12 councilman in 1975, unseating 30-year veteran CHARLES CARR in 1981.

Never married, Burten was a full-time councilman. Instrumental in securing a $255,000 grant from HUD to build new homes for the inner city, Burton also used his council salary to buy foreclosed property and renovate the homes, something his ward had not seen in over sixty years. If not working on a home himself, Burten supplied building materials to low-income residents.

Burten's political style put him at odds with council president George Forbes. In 1976 Burten was suspended for one week without pay for refusing to heed council rules. In 1981 Burten led an unsuccessful campaign to replace Forbes as council president. Burten rose above controversy to give his constituents the kind of grass-roots, personal representation needed to rebuild the community. Burten was murdered at age 40. A Baptist, he is buried in Highland Park Cemetery.—T.B.

**BURTON, COURTNEY, JR.** (29 Oct. 1912–19 Aug. 1992), chairman of OGLEBAY NORTON CO.† for 35 years and active in national Republican party affairs, was born in Cleveland, the son of Courtney Burton, Sr., and Sarita Oglebay Burton. He attended Hawken School and from 1932–34

studied at the Michigan College of Mining and Engineering in Houghton, MI. Burton was closely associated with the Ferro Machine and Foundry Co. at 3155 E. 66th St. and by 1940, the foundry, employing 3,500 people, was wholly owned by his family. After the death of Crispin Oglebay in 1949, Burton was elected vice-president of Oglebay Norton and from 1957 until shortly before his death, he served as chairman of the board.

Burton served as special assistant to Nelson Rockefeller in the Office of Interamerican Affairs until receiving his commission as a navy officer in 1944. After World War II, he was mayor of Gates Mills from 1948–61. Active in raising money for the Republican party, he served as vice-president of the party's National Finance Committee, 1952–61, and was in charge of its operations for Ohio, West Virginia, and Kentucky. As a lifelong conservationist, Burton headed the Cleveland Zoological Society for 9 years, served on the Metropolitan Park District board for 8 years, and played a significant role in the formation of the CUYAHOGA VALLEY NATIONAL RECREATION AREA† in 1973.

Burton married Marguerite Rankin 7 Sept. 1933, and they had 2 daughters, Sarita Burton Frith and Marguerite Burton Humphrey. After his wife's death in 1976, Burton married Margaret Leitch on 20 Dec. 1978.—M.S.

Jonovic, Donald J. *Iron, Industry, and Independence: A Biographical Portrait of Courtney Burton, Jr., American Industrialist and Patriot* (1986).

**BURTON, HAROLD HITZ** (22 June 1888–29 Oct. 1964), mayor of Cleveland, U.S. Senator, and Associate Justice of the U.S. Supreme Court, was born in Jamaica Plains, MA, to Dr. Alfred Edgar and Gertrude Hitz Burton. He graduated from Bowdoin College (1909), and received his LL.B. from Harvard Law School (1912), then came to Cleveland to work for two years. He served during World War I, receiving a citation from the U.S. government, the Purple Heart, and the Belgian Croix de Guerre.

Burton practiced law in Cleveland after the war. He was elected to the Ohio state legislature in 1928 as a Republican. From 1930–31 he was Cleveland law director, becoming acting mayor from Nov. 1931–Feb. 1932, and in 1935 was elected mayor for the first of 3 terms. During his administration, the rackets in Cleveland were broken up. The mayor promoted Cleveland as a convention center, hosting the REPUBLiCAN CONVENTION OF 1936.† Burton acquired $40 million from the state for relief assistance. When there were strikes, the mayor encouraged negotiations, but did what was necessary to preserve order.

In 1940 Burton was elected Senator, serving until 1945 when Pres. Truman appointed him to the Supreme Court. In 1951 he wrote the Court opinion outlawing racial segregation in railroad dining cars, and he participated in the *Brown v. Board of Education* decision outlawing school segregation. He retired from the Court in 1958, living in Washington, and occasionally presided as judge. He married Selma Florence Smith on 15 June 1912 and had 4 children: Barbara (Mrs. H. Chas. Weidner), Deborah (Mrs. Wallace Adler), William, and Robert. He died in Washington, DC.

Harold H. Burton Papers, WRHS.

**BURTON, LEWIS** (3 July 1815–9 Oct. 1894) was a prominent Episcopal rector in the Cleveland area for 47 years, where he founded or managed a number of parishes. Born just south of Erie, PA, the son of John and Hannah (Miller) Burton, he followed his brother into the Episcopal priesthood, graduating from Allegheny College in 1837. He married Jane Wallace in 1841; they had 3 children: Amelia, Eliza, and Lewis.

Burton was known as a handsome, dignified, genial, and able man. He used these qualities and a head for business to help his church meet the needs of its membership as it followed the southern and western expansion of Cleveland. Moved by the condition of a parishioner, Burton and his sister-in-law, ELIZA JENNINGS, combined her gift of 7½ acres of land with community financial support to start the ELIZA JENNINGS HOME† in 1888; it eventually became a well-endowed social-service agency for needy women.

Succeeding his brother as rector of Ohio City's St. John's parish in 1847, Burton led a successful rebuilding effort after fire destroyed the church in 1866. He started All Saints' and St. Mark's as missions of St. John's. He resigned from St. John's (1871) to take charge of both missions as they became full-fledged parishes. He led All Saints' until 1875 and was rector at St. Mark's until his retirement in 1887. He also developed a former Trinity mission into the Church of the Ascension (1875) and served as its first rector. Burton was buried in Lake View Cemetery.

**BURTON, THEODORE ELIJAH** (20 Dec. 1851–28 Oct. 1929) served as a Republican in the U.S. House of Representatives (1889–91, 1895–1909, 1921–28) and U.S. Senate (1909–15, 1928–29). Born in Jefferson, OH, to Rev. Wm. and Elizabeth Grant Burton, he attended Grinnell Academy & College in Iowa 2 years before returning to Ohio, earning an A.B. from Oberlin College (1872), studying law with Lyman Trumbull in Chicago, and

coming to Cleveland to practice law after being admitted to the Ohio Bar in 1875. He served on the city council (1886–88) before being elected to Congress. Defeated for reelection by Democrat TOM L. JOHNSON in 1890, he resumed law practice, being elected again to Congress in 1894, serving 7 terms.

With Cleveland improving the CUYAHOGA RIVER† and its harbor, Burton promoted development of the Great Lakes waterways, serving and later chairing the Rivers & Harbors Committee in the House of Representatives.

In 1907 Burton returned to Cleveland, challenging Tom L. Johnson in the mayoral election. After his defeat, Burton returned to Congress and chaired the new Inland Waterways Commission and its successor, the Natl. Waterways Commission (1908–12). From 1908–12 he also studied worldwide banking systems on the Natl. Monetary Commission. Elected to the U.S. Senate in 1909, Burton retired in 1915, becoming president of Merchants' Natl. Bank in New York City (1917–19). He was again elected to the House of Representatives in 1921 and served on the World War Foreign Debt Commission, which restructured payments of wartime loans made to foreign countries. Burton was active in the peace movement, was president of the American Peace Society for many years, and gave up his seat in the House in 1928 to pursue this cause before being elected to the U.S. Senate. Never married, Burton died in Washington, and was buried in Cleveland in Lake View Cemetery.

Burton authored several books. On 16 Apr. 1928, the Cleveland Chamber of Commerce awarded him the Cleveland Public Service Medal in recognition of his service.

Theodore E. Burton Papers, WRHS.
Crissey, Forest. *Theodore E. Burton, American Statesman* (1956).

**BUTKIN, NOAH L.** (26 June 1918–11 Feb. 1980) was an internationally known chemical engineer and metals executive. Born in New York City to Louis and Edith Butkin, Noah Butkin grew up in Oklahoma and was educated at the Univ. of Oklahoma (B.S., 1941), where he played violin with the Oklahoma City Symphony Orchestra. After a brief U. S. Army stint in World War II, Butkin went to work for the Continental Can Co. in Terre Haute, IN, then did research for the Indianapolis-based P. R. Mallory and Co. In 1947 he cofounded (with Sidney Danziger) and became president of the Alloys and Chemical Corporation (inc. 1950) in Cleveland, an international metal business. Butkin later opened a smelting company. In 1964 Alloys and Chemicals became part of Rio Tinto Zinc (RTZ) Corp. of England; Butkin retained his position as president. In 1969 he was named president of RTZ Aluminum Industries Inc., and the following year became managing director of RTZ Aluminum Industries Inc. In 1973 he was president and chair of Rio Indal, Inc., a metals, marketing, and trading office of RTZ.

Butkin belonged to several professional organizations and served on the boards of trustees of the CLEVELAND MUSEUM OF ART† and the WESTERN RESERVE HISTORICAL SOCIETY.† Works of art which Butkin donated to the Cleveland Museum of Art include a harbor scene by Allaert van Everdingen, a Willem van der Velde seascape, and the salon landscape by Jean Victor Bertin. He married Muriel Spiro of Waynesboro, PA; they lived in SHAKER HTS. The couple had no children. Butkin was buried in Lake View Cemetery.

**BUTLER, MARGARET MANOR** (1 Mar. 1898–2 Oct. 1971), turned her curiosity about the history of her adopted community of LAKEWOOD† into a major avocation. A native of Cleveland and graduate of Smith College, she married Clyde H. Butler and moved to Lakewood in the 1920s. Her husband was an aerial photographer, a profession he pursued in the armed forces in both world wars. It was during World War II, with its gas rationing, that Mrs. Butler began exploring the streets of Lakewood on walks with her 2 sons. Investigating the histories of some of the homes she passed, she began a series of stories on local history for the weekly *Lakewood Post*. These were turned into a book, *The Lakewood Story* (1949), for which Butler was named Lakewood's outstanding citizen of the year. Three years later she began a campaign to save an 1838 sandstone house on Detroit Ave. from demolition. With the aid of the Lakewood City Council and the LAKEWOOD HISTORICAL SOCIETY,† which she organized that year, she succeeded in having the structure moved to Lakewood Park. It was restored as a museum under the management of the society, which Butler served as first president. Mrs. Butler turned another newspaper series into a second book, *The Romance of Lakewood Streets,* which was followed in 1963 by *A Pictorial History of the Western Reserve.* She also served as president of the Radio-Television Council of Greater Cleveland and organized the Lakewood chapter of the Smith Alumnae Club. Upon her death, a memorial service was held in the Stone House in Lakewood Park.—J.V.

Margaret Manor Butler Papers, WRHS.

**BYERS, EDGAR S.** (10 Apr. 1876–21 Feb. 1963), an attorney and outspoken liberal, was born in Sharpsville, PA, to Orsamus and Elizabeth Mitchell Byers. He came to Cleveland at age 10, graduated from Western Reserve Univ. Law School, and in 1901 formed a law partnership with CARL D. FRIEBOLIN, which lasted until 1947. In 1915 Byers joined the City Club, and with JACK RAPER, Ed Doty, PETER WITT, and others who formed the Soviet Table, a lunch group whose name exaggerated its members' liberal views. Byers spoke for the table, protesting proposals he thought were contrary to the public interest. He directed the City Club from 1927–30. In 1924 Byers managed Sen. Robt. La Follette's area presidential Progressive party campaign, carrying the county by 10,000 votes, while spending only $10,000.

Byers protested the original plans for the Main Ave. Bridge, Municipal Stadium, and many other civic projects. Byers and the Soviet Table were criticized by CITIZENS LEAGUE† director MAYO FESLER after successfully campaigning to eliminate Cleveland's CITY MANAGER PLAN† of government. Byers objected to city manager WM. HOPKINS's use of authority and many of his land purchases, including the site that later became CLEVELAND HOPKINS INT'L. AIRPORT.† Byers also opposed construction of Union Terminal, the claim of railways to lakefront public property, and the 1942 sale of the CLEVELAND RAILWAY CO.† to the city, believing private interests were benefiting from publicly owned resources. Byers also opposed tax writeoffs for industrial facilities and tax credits on security dividends. Byers married Birja Wilkins in 1902 and had 3 daughters: Elizabeth, Nancy, and Barbara. Byers died in Cleveland and was buried at Lake View Cemetery.

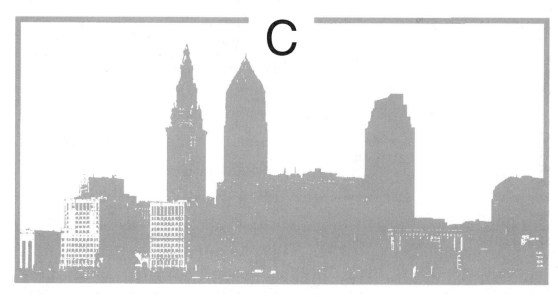

# C

**CADWALLADER, STARR** (11 June 1869–2 June 1926), a prominent social worker during the Progressive Era, was born in Howard, NY, and graduated from Hamilton College (1893) and Union Theological Seminary (1897) before coming to Cleveland as the first head resident of the newly established Goodrich Social Settlement, serving until 1905. He worked there with NEWTON D. BAKER, FREDERIC C. HOWE, and other young men who later became prominent in local reform and political affairs. Because of his interest in young people, Cadwallader helped establish a juvenile court in Cleveland (1902). From 1902–04, Cadwallader directed schools under Mayor TOM L. JOHNSON, with his no-politics policy in appointing teachers and administrators causing many ward bosses to dislike him. He then became superintendent of the Cleveland Dept. of Health (1908–09) and was a member of the Ohio Board of Administration (of state institutions) under Gov. Jas. Cox.

During World War I, Cadwallader headed the Cuyahoga County Draft Board, and in 1917 became director of the Lake Div. of the American Red Cross. He was a member of the realty firm Stein, Cadwallader & Long, which was the agent for the VAN SWERINGEN brothers in the sale of SHAKER HTS.† property from 1910–17. He married Harriet E. Gomph in Utica, NY, on 30 July 1896; she died in New York in 1935. They had a son, Starr, Jr. Cadwallader died at his Shaker Hts. home.

**CADWELL, DARIUS** (3 Apr. 1821–26 Nov. 1905), an attorney, state legislator, Union Army officer, and judge, was born in Andover, OH, in Ashtabula County, son of Roger and Caroline Cadwell. He attended county and select schools, and completed 1 year at Allegheny College in 1841. After teaching county schools for several years, he studied law

under Benjamin Wade (later U.S. Senator) in Jefferson, OH, and was admitted to the bar in 1844. In 1847, Cadwell joined the firm of RUFUS P. RANNEY and Charles Simmonds of Jefferson, OH. He was a deputy clerk in Jefferson and in 1850 a census agent in Ashtabula County. He served from 1856–58 as state representative, and from 1858–60 as state senator, representing Lake, Geauga, and Ashtabula counties in Columbus. Turning down a captaincy in the Regular Army in 1862, Cadwell instead accepted the position of provost marshal of the 19th district, which had its headquarters in Youngstown, OH. In the fall of 1865, the 19th district was consolidated with the 14th, 16th, and 18th provost marshal districts, with headquarters in Cleveland. Cadwell maintained this position until the Cleveland provost marshal's office was closed in Dec. 1865 (see 18TH PROVOST MARSHALL DISTRICT OF OHIO†). In 1873 he was elected to the Cuyahoga County Court of Common Pleas and served until 1884. Having opened a law office in Cleveland in the early 1870s, he practiced there after his second term expired.

Cadwell married Ann Eliza Watrous 13 Apr. 1847. They had four children: Frank W., Mrs. Richard Hubbard, Florence, and James R.

Darius Cadwell Papers, WRHS.

**CAFARELLI, CARMELA** (1889–1 Sept. 1979) kept the flame of grand opera burning in Cleveland as impresario of the Cafarelli Opera Co. Born in Cleveland, she was the daughter of Rocco G. Cafarelli, an Italian who immigrated to Cleveland ca. 1887 to become the city's first harpist. She studied the instrument under her father and Henry B. Fabiani, playing from the age of 12 for visiting opera companies in need of a harpist. From 1918–21, she was the first harpist for the newly founded CLEVELAND OR-CHESTRA.† Armed with a recommendation from Arturo Toscanini, Cafarelli went to Italy to study singing. Making her operatic debut in Florence in 1923, she toured opera houses in Italy for the following 3 years, but also became involved in a passport wrangle that left her "a woman without a country." The State Dept. refused to grant her an American passport on the grounds that her 1918 marriage to an Italian citizen, Allesandro Chiostergi, had made her an Italian subject. Italy also denied her a passport because her husband had become a naturalized American in the meantime. Re-entering the U.S. on a visitor's passport, she regained her American citizenship and divorced Chiostergi in 1932. After numerous local singing appearances, Cafarelli formed the Cafarelli Opera Club (later Co.) to present *Madame Butterfly* in 1934. For the next 3 decades she presented an annual opera in Masonic Auditorium, concentrating on the standard repertoire and, in the early years, portraying the leading soprano roles herself. In the 1940s and 1950s, her company constituted the principal local alternative to the annual visits of the Metropolitan Opera (see OPERA†). Cafarelli also taught voice and harp in her CLEVELAND HTS.† home until 1976. She died in the Margaret Wagner House, leaving no immediate relatives. —J.V.

CAHILL, VAUGHN DABNEY (29 Dec. 1889–29 July 1973) drew upon his musical training and accounting experience to head the Federal Music Project in Cleveland during the Depression. A native of Fairfield, OH, he was the son of Rev. Issac J. Cahill and Lillian Skidmore Cahill. He studied music at Hiram College, his instruments being violin and viola. Marrying Louise Ruth Wells in 1911, he taught music at BALDWIN-WALLACE COL-LEGE† and Rice Univ. in Texas. During the 1920s he moved to Galion, OH, where he worked as an accountant for the North Electrical Manufacturing Co. Cahill maintained his interest in music, composing various works, including a symphony, a sonata for violin and piano, and an orchestral work entitled "Bolivar Road." Appointed to direct the Federal Music Project (see WORK PROJECTS AD-MINISTRATION) in 1935, Cahill commuted to Cleveland from Galion for the next 5 years. Following the death of his first wife, he married Ivana Perdan, a music project singer, in 1940 and moved to CLEVELAND HTS.† Of the 12 children from his first marriage, 6 sons served in the Armed Forces during World War II: Eric, Kevin, Phadrig, Quentin, Timothy, and Jerold. Cahill joined the CLEVITE CORP.† as an accountant in 1942 and eventually became procedures director. After retiring, he served

as a systems analyst for National City Bank (see NATIONAL CITY CORP.†) and comptroller for the FOREST CITY HOSPITAL.† He also continued teaching music privately until moving to Mantua, OH, in the 1960s. Dying there, he was buried in Galion. Besides the 6 sons mentioned above, he was survived by his second wife, sons Larry and Martin, and daughters Patricia Berry, Lillian Basil, and Sheila Streenberg.—J.V.

CAHOON, JOSEPH (28 Aug. 1762–16 Mar. 1839), the first settler of Dover Twp. (BAY VILLAGE), was the son of Reynolds and Rebecca Cahoon. He was born in Rhode Island and settled in Vergennes, VT, before emigrating to the Western Reserve. He was primarily a miller, but also invented a cotton compress, a tie buckle machine, a grape hoe (drawn by 1 horse), and a shingle-making machine.

With his family, Cahoon left Vergennes for the WESTERN RESERVE† in 1810 after visiting Ohio in 1799 and buying land west of the Cuyahoga near the lakeshore, where the climate seemed favorable for fruit trees. On 10 Oct. 1810 the family arrived in Dover Twp., and in 4 days erected a log cabin on Lot #95 (north of Lake Rd., at the mouth of Cahoon Creek). Within the first year, Cahoon planted seeds for apple and peach trees. On 10 Sept. 1813, the family erected the first gristmill in the Western Reserve west of the Cuyahoga, as they heard the distant guns of Perry's fleet off Put-in-Bay. Cahoon later built a sawmill, enabling him, with his son, Joel, to build a frame house in 1818. When his fruit trees matured, Cahoon built a distillery to manufacture peach brandy. Around 1786 Cahoon married Lydia Kenyon and had 12 children: Samuel, Amos, Mary, Joel, Abigail, Rebecca, Daniel, Benjamin, William, Joseph, and a pair of twins who died in infancy. The family remained in their original frame house, Rose Hill, until 1917, at which time the house was deeded to the community and used as a library until 1960, when it became the Rose Hill Museum. It is maintained by the BAY VILLAGE HISTORICAL SOCIETY.† Cahoon died in Dover Twp. and was buried in the Dover Twp. Cemetery.

CAIN, FRANK C. (6 May 1877–7 Nov. 1967) placed his stamp on the suburb of CLEVELAND HTS.† during a record 32-year tenure as mayor. Born in Springfield, OH, he came to Cleveland in 1895 and went into business as a grain broker. He moved to Cleveland Hts. on 1 Aug. 1900, the day of his marriage to Alma Lambert. In 1909 he was elected to the village council, and became mayor in 1914. When Cleveland Hts. became a city in 1921, Cain headed a charter commission that installed a mayor–city manager plan of government. Technically elected mayor by the council, Cain headed a slate of councilmen that went undefeated for 18 elections. In his last election he received a record total of 81% of the vote. Under his mayoralty Cleveland Hts. enacted the state's first comprehensive zoning laws and developed the wooded park at Lee Rd. and Superior Ave., later named in his honor. Cain's influence was credited with inducing the Rockefellers to donate part of their FOREST HILL† estate for more parkland and the CLEVELAND RAILWAY CO.† to replace streetcar lines with express buses on Cedar Rd. and Fairmount Blvd. Even ORIS and MANTIS VAN SWERINGEN were said to have chosen undeveloped SHAKER HTS.† for their model suburb rather than battle Cain's Cleveland Hts. for partially subsidized street improvements. Cain became a recognized spokesman for all Cuyahoga County suburbs in his fierce opposition to the sacrifice of their independence to any plan of REGIONAL GOVT.† Long a member of the CITY CLUB OF CLEVELAND,† he served as president in 1922–23 and was later treasurer of its Forum Foundation Fund. He retired from city government in 1946 and died 4 years after his wife, survived by their 3 children: Donald L., Dorothy Caulkins, and Lucile Dalzell.—J.V.

Campbell, Thomas F. *Freedom's Forum: The City Club, 1912–1962* (1962).

**CAMPANARO, DOROTHY** (19 Feb. 1915–23 Sept. 1993) was an industrial editor on the public relations staff of the Ohio Rubber Division of Eagle Picher Co. and cofounder of the Willoughby Printing Co.

Born in Cleveland to Alex and Mary (Pietriacovo) Campanaro, Dorothy received her B.A. from Notre Dame Univ. in 1937, and her teaching certificate from Western Reserve Univ. in 1940.

Campanaro taught junior high classes in Cleveland public schools before joining Ohio Rubber in 1940, where she became an industrial editor.

In 1947 Campanaro helped found the Willoughby Printing Co. She remained a partner in the printing company and an editor at the rubber company until she quit working in 1967 to care for her ailing mother. Following her mother's death, Campanaro became the asst. to the fire chief of the Cleveland Hts. Fire Department, becoming the department's first female employee in the late 1960s. Campanaro gradually retired in the early 1980s.

Campanaro was recognized at a national convention during World War II by the American Red Cross for her successful efforts in selling war bonds. Campanaro was a member of the American Assn. of Industrial Editors, serving as secretary from 1955–56, and a member of the Northern Ohio Industrial Editors Assn.

Campanaro was Roman Catholic. Never married, she lived in CLEVELAND HTS.† and is buried in Lake View Cemetery.—T.B.

**CAMPBELL, MARION WINTON STRONGHEART** (ca. 1897–1944) was a composer of operas, a crusader for Native American rights, and the 3rd wife of ALEXANDER WINTON. A native of Bellefontaine, OH, she first attracted local notice as the composer and librettist of *Love's Wishing Well*, a light opera given its premiere by the original CLEVELAND OPERA CO.† on 7 March 1927. Based on Irish folklore, the work brought Campbell to the attention of automobile magnate Winton, who married her later that year. Campbell became interested in the history of the American Indian, which became the inspiration for another opera, *The Seminole*. It received its premiere on 12 June 1929, in concert form, under a tent on the Winton estate in CLIFTON PARK.† Among the first-nighters were Gov. and Mrs. Myers Y. Cooper of Ohio, CHIEF THUNDERWATER of Cleveland, and Samuel Insull of Chicago, the utility tycoon and opera impresario. On 18 Sept. 1929 Campbell founded the Women's National League for Justice to American Indians, but her crusading zeal on behalf of Native Americans contributed to her estrangement from Winton. Following her divorce in 1930, she married Chief Nipo Strongheart, a Yakima Indian from Washington state. She and Strongheart were divorced in 1933. After living in the Los Angeles area, she apparently spent her last years in Florida.—J.V.

**CANFIELD, MARTHA ANN ROBINSON, M.D.** (10 Sept. 1845–3 Sept. 1916), homeopathic physician, was among the earliest women in Northern Ohio to practice MEDICINE† as a profession. She followed MYRA MERRICK as the second president of the Women's and Children's Free Medical and Surgical Dispensary Society (1900) and helped create its successor, WOMAN'S GENERAL HOSPITAL.† Canfield presided both over the hospital and its Board of Trustees (1912–16), was a charter member of Maternity Hospital (see UNIV. HOSPITALS OF CLEVELAND†), and directed the Canfield-White Hospital. Born in Freedom (Portage County), OH, to Henry and Eliza Brown Robinson, Canfield attended Hiram College and graduated from Oberlin College in 1868. She taught school in Oberlin before entering the Medical College of CLEVELAND HOMEOPATHIC HOSPITAL,† where she studied with Dr. Charles Morrell. After graduating in 1875, she began practicing in Cleveland. She also studied in Germany and France. Canfield blended her teaching and medical interests, becoming a professor of gynecology at the Homeopathic College (1890–97). She was also active in PHILANTHROPY,† especially with the Federated Charities (see FEDERATION FOR CHARITY AND PHILANTHROPY†). Canfield belonged to the Cleveland Hospital Council, CLEVELAND SOROSIS,† the Women's Press Club of Cleveland, and the COLLEGE CLUB OF CLEVELAND. Canfield was a member of the Euclid Ave. Congregational Church.

In 1869 Canfield married attorney Harrison Wade Canfield; the couple had 4 children. One son, Charles, died at an early age; the others were Hiram H. Canfield, Elma (Mrs. H. B.) Cody, and Mary (Mrs. J. R.) Ewers. Canfield is buried in Lake View Cemetery.—J.M.

**CANFIELD, SHERMAN BOND** (25 Dec. 1810–5 Mar. 1871) was the first pastor of the Second Presbyterian Church of Cleveland, later to become CHURCH OF THE COVENANT.† Canfield was born in Chardon, OH, the son of Norman and Susannah Bond Canfield. He attended Western Reserve College, receiving his master's degree in 1838. Hamilton College conferred a Doctor of Divinity degree upon him in 1857. Canfield spent his career as a Presbyterian minister in Ohio and New York. His first pastorate (1839–41) was in OHIO CITY,† and he followed his service at Second Presbyterian with a long tenure (1854–70) as a pastor in Syracuse, NY. Although not physically prepossessing, he was a powerful speaker.

The Second Presbyterian Church of Cleveland was organized around a membership largely derived from the Old Stone Church, with Canfield the unanimous choice as pastor of the new congregation. He was astute enough to realize that limited pew space caused bruised feelings and church divisions in many of Cleveland's rapidly growing houses of worship, so he insisted that the new structure for Second Presbyterian be roomy enough to accommodate an increase in membership, resulting in one of the largest churches in the city. An ally of SAMUEL AIKEN in doctrinal matters, Canfield chaired an 1841 Cleveland Presbytery investigation into Chas. Finney's philosophy of Perfectionism (Oberlinism). On 4 July 1837, he performed the first marriage in CHAGRIN FALLS.† Canfield married his first wife, Delia Slater, in 1836 and had a son, Sherman. In 1843 he married Sarah Winston White and had 2 children, Frederick and Edward.

**CANNON, AUSTIN VICTOR** (9 June 1869–27 Sept. 1934) was a well-known lawyer, businessman, and leader in securing much needed relief funds for Cleveland during the Depression. Cannon was born in Streetsboro, OH, the son of Artemus M. and Lenora (Wells) Cannon. Educated at Buchtel Col-

lege (now the Univ. of Akron), he received a B.S. degree in 1892. After passing the bar, Cannon was made a partner in the law firm White, Johnson, McCaslin & Cannon in 1896. An expert on bankruptcy and equitable receivership law, Cannon served as commissioner on Uniform Laws from Ohio for more than 15 years and lectured on bankruptcy at Western Reserve Univ. He utilized his legal skills in business as vice-president and director of the Electric Vacuum Cleaner Co., and secretary-treasurer and director of the National Woolen Co., among others.

Perhaps Cannon's most outstanding contribution to the community was his effort to obtain adequate relief money for the needy in the early 1930s. Cannon lobbied the Ohio legislature vigorously for more emergency relief funds and served as chairman of the Joint Relief Commission 1932–33, a period when an estimated 219,000 people in Cuyahoga County were out of work. Cannon helped administer relief as chairman of the Cuyahoga County Relief Commission, from 1933 until his death. In April 1935, he was posthumously awarded the Cleveland Medal for Public Service. Cannon married Marian E. Cook, and they had 3 children: sons, Rudolph A. and Victor M. and daughter Josephine Cannon Watt. Cannon died suddenly of a heart attack while attending a welfare workers party at NELA PARK.† He is buried in Lake View Cemetery.

**CARABELLI, JOSEPH** (9 Apr. 1850–19 Apr. 1911), a skilled stonemason and influential businessman, son of Carolina (Sartori) and Carlo Carabelli, was one of the first lay leaders in the LITTLE ITALY† section of Cleveland. Unlike many other residents of Little Italy, Carabelli was a northern Italian Protestant. A native of Porto Ceresio, Como Province, he emigrated to America in 1870 at the age of 20, following an apprenticeship as a stonecutter. He spent 10 years in New York City as a sculptor, where he carved the statues for the city's Federal Bldg. Carabelli came to Cleveland in 1880 and established the Lakeview Granite & Monumental Works, near LAKE VIEW CEMETERY,† which soon attracted a large group of stonecutters from the province of Campobasso, who settled Mayfield Rd. near the cemetery.

Carabelli was responsible for the creation of a nursery and kindergarten in 1895 for the children of working mothers in this neighborhood. With his financial assistance, and that of JOHN D. ROCKEFELLER, the nursery grew into ALTA HOUSE.† Carabelli also played a major part in the creation of the first Cleveland Italian mutual benefit society, the Italian Fraternal Society, in 1888. This society served as the model for many other Italian benevolent groups, and by the mid–1890s it functioned as the arbiter. Carabelli was elected to the Ohio House of Representatives in 1908 on a Republican ticket. He capped his career by pushing a bill through the legislature proclaiming Columbus Day an official holiday in 1910.

Married in Torino, Italy, in 1875, Carabelli and his wife, Annetta, had 3 children who survived to adulthood: Joseph, Charles A., and Lillian (Bailey); 2 children died as infants, Charles M. and Irene. Carabelli died in Cleveland and was buried in Lake View Cemetery.

**CARR, CHARLES VELMON** (9 October 1903–30 Apr. 1987), influential Democratic member of CLEVELAND CITY COUNCIL† and promoter of black civil rights, was born in Clarksville, TX. His parents, Will and Pauline Carr, were educators who traveled, and he often lived with his grandfather who brought him to Cleveland briefly to attend East Technical High School. He graduated from Fisk Univ. in Nashville, TN, returning to Cleveland to attend John Marshall Law School (see CLEVELAND-MARSHALL LAW SCHOOL†). After passing the Ohio Bar he practiced law, establishing the firm of Carr, Jackson and Payne in 1954. In his early days as a lawyer, he was legal counsel to the FUTURE OUTLOOK LEAGUE† and served as a member of their Board of Trustees.

Interested in politics, Carr ran unsuccessfully for Cleveland City Council in 1939, but succeeded WILLIAM O. WALKER as 17th Ward councilman in 1945. The following year, he assisted in gaining council approval of a civil-rights ordinance which revoked the license of any public business convicted of discrimination against blacks. He also fought for fair housing ordinances, and was co-sponsor of the first Fair Employment Practices legislation in the state. A master of political compromise, Carr was elected Democratic majority leader of the city council in 1959, serving for 13 years. After losing his council seat to LONNIE BURTEN in 1975, Carr was appointed to the Regional Transit Authority's Board of Trustees in 1977, where he served until his death.

Carr died in Cleveland at age 83. He was survived by his wife, Hortense Leverett Carr, daughters Carole J. Bush, Cathleen V. Willis and Leah P.; son, Charles O., and stepson Michael K. King.—M.S.

**CARROLL, GENE** (13 Apr. 1897–5 Mar. 1972), had one of the longest-running television shows in Cleveland. A native of Chicago, he dropped out of high school and performed in amateur shows to compete for cash prizes. He joined Jack Grady of Chicago in a successful song-and-dance act in 1924. When Grady became ill in 1929, Carroll teamed up with Glenn Rowell of Cleveland. Known as Gene &

Glenn, they appeared in vaudeville and on the radio, performing in Cleveland on station WTAM† from 1930–35. In 1934 NBC began broadcasting a 15-minute version of the act "Gene & Glenn," including the characters of Jake and Lena, which were created by Carroll. When Jake was to marry Lena in 1935, crowds gathered around the WTAM building in anticipation of a glimpse of the couple. Carroll and Rowell left Cleveland in 1935, performing out of Des Moines, Chicago, and Boston until 1943. After Rowell's departure for war work, Carroll appeared on the "Fibber McGee & Molly Show" on NBC for 1 season. He returned to Cleveland in Apr. 1948 to establish a talent school and begin a television variety show on WEWS,† continuing these projects until his death. The television program, originally known as the "Giant Tiger Amateur Hour" and then the "Gene Carroll Show," was continued by his widow. After his first two marriages ended in divorce, Carroll married Helen Olsen in 1940.

**CARTER, LORENZO** (1766–8 Feb. 1814), frontiersman, community leader, and tavernkeeper, was Cleveland's first permanent settler, arriving in Cleveland on 2 May 1797 with his brother-in-law, Ezekiel Hawley (Holley, Holly), and their families. Lorenzo was born in Warren, CT, and on 28 Jan. 1789 married Rebecca Fuller. Until Apr. 1800, the Carters were the only white family in Cleveland, with other families who settled briefly there soon moving to Newburgh or Doan's Corners to escape the swampy environment. The Carters built a pretentious log cabin, used as an inn, with a garret, serving as a jail, on the east bank near the mouth of the CUYAHOGA RIVER.† Cleveland's first wedding, of the Carters' house helper, Chloe Inches, and Wm. Clement of Ontario, on 4 July 1797; and the first social dance, on 4 July 1802, took place in Carter's home.

Carter, a Baptist, operated a ferry at the foot of Superior St.; constructed the first tavern in the city; and built the 30-ton schooner, the *Zephyr*, a lake trading vessel (1808). He purchased 23½ acres of land in 1802, and built the first frame house in Cleveland, which was destroyed by fire before completion. In 1802 he also built a blockhouse containing Carter Tavern, and constructed the first log warehouse in the city in 1810.

Carter was a constable for Cleveland Twp. and a major in the state militia. The Carters had 9 children: 3 boys, Alonzo, Henry, and Lorenzo; and 6 girls, Laura, Rebecca, Polly, Rebecca (2nd), Mercy, and Betsy. Lorenzo and Rebecca died in infancy; Henry drowned in the river at age 10. The Carters purchased a large farm on the west side of the Cuyahoga River in 1810 which later became the property of Alonzo Carter. Carter died at age 47. His wife, Rebecca, died on 19 Oct. 1827. Both are buried in the Erie St. Cemetery.

**CARTER, WILFRED CARLYLE "WHIZ BANG"** (15 or 16 May 1905–26 Apr. 1982) used the skills acquired in his own boxing career to become one of Cleveland's most successful boxing trainers. Originally from Mt. Vernon, OH, the son of Edward and Grace Carter, he received his first instincts for self-defense from defending his turf as a shoeshine boy in a barber shop across from Cleveland's LEAGUE PARK.† He began boxing in 1921, acquiring the nickname "Whiz Bang," after a contemporary humor book, because of his hard and fast hitting style. Although he won the city and state welterweight amateur championships in 1928, he retired from the ring after only 6 professional bouts in 1932 because of the low Depression-era prize purses. Married since 1924 to the former Mary Moore, Carter earned his living as a letter carrier for the U.S. Post Office. He began coaching neighborhood boys at the Portland-Outhwaite Recreation Center and at one time had a field of 70 boxers in the northeastern Ohio district A.A.U. competition. One of his charges, Jackie Wilson, fought on the 1936 American Olympic boxing team, while another, heavyweight Jimmy Bivens, was named "duration champion" during World War II, in the absence of Joe Louis. Following his retirement from the Post Office, Carter operated a poolroom on Central Ave. and in 1968 was named secretary of the Cleveland Boxing and Wrestling Commission by another of his former pugilistic pupils, Mayor Carl B. Stokes. He died as the result of burns from a fire that destroyed his home on Montgomery Ave., survived by a son, Robert E.—J.V.

**CASE, LEONARD, JR.** (27 Jan. 1820–6 Jan. 1880), a philanthropist who endowed Case School of Applied Science, was born to Elizabeth Gaylord and LEONARD CASE in Cleveland and educated in law at Yale. Sickly all his life, he neither married nor practiced his profession, but devoted himself to scholarly pursuits. Along with his brother, WM. CASE, Leonard was an Arkite, a group of prominent Clevelanders who conversed about natural science in a small building (the ARK†) filled with specimens they shot and mounted. Case helped form the CLEVELAND LIBRARY ASSN.† Inheriting $15 million in 1864, Case regarded his wealth as a trust to be used for good. In 1859 the Case brothers constructed Case Hall, a civic and cultural center which housed the CLEVELAND ACADEMY OF NATURAL SCIENCES,† the Cleveland Library Assn., and the Ark club, as well as theater productions and lectures. Case built the commercial Case Block in 1875.

Case anonymously gave $1 million to establish a technical school to teach pure science, an orientation that attracted support from local businesses, permitting the institution to become an important center for industrial research. To provide annual revenues, Case bequeathed the rental income from his downtown properties to the school. The Case School of Applied Science, as it became known, opened in 1881 on Rockwell Ave. and moved to UNIV. CIRCLE† in 1885. Case left the city 200 acres for industrial plants and railroad rights-of-way, which became the city's first comprehensive industrial district. Other beneficiaries were the Old Stone Church, the Cleveland Orphan Asylum, the Industrial Aid Society, and the CLEVELAND FEMALE SEMINARY.†

**CASE, LEONARD, SR.** (29 July 1786–7 Dec. 1864), a businessman and philanthropist, was born in Westmoreland County, PA, son of Meshack and Magdalene (Eckstein) Case. He moved in Apr. 1800 to Warren Twp., Trumbull County. In 1806 he became clerk of the Court of Common Pleas for Trumbull County, later becoming clerk to Gen. Simon Perkins of the CONNECTICUT LAND CO.† He studied law, passed the bar in 1814, and moved to Cleveland in 1816 when the COMMERCIAL BANK OF LAKE ERIE† was formed, as the cashier. After the bank failed, Case stayed in Cleveland practicing law. From 1821–25, as president of the Cleveland Village council, he was responsible for planting shade trees along streets, earning Cleveland the nickname "FOREST CITY."† From 1824–27, he served in the Ohio legislature, drafting laws taxing land according to value rather than size. He advocated railroads and canals.

From 1827–55, Case was an agent for the Connecticut Land Bank, acquiring large amounts of land from debtors during the Panic of 1837. In 1832 Case reorganized the Commercial Bank of Lake Erie and became its president. He was also an investor in the Cleveland-Columbus-Cincinnati Railroad. Case married Elizabeth Gaylord in Stow, Portage County, in 1817, and in the late 1840s turned his affairs over to his sons William and Leonard, Jr. Case gave to many charitable organizations, including Cleveland's first school for the poor, the Cuyahoga County Historical Society, the Cleveland Medical College, and the city's first lyceum for the arts. Case died in Cleveland and was buried in Lake View Cemetery.

**CASE, WILLIAM** (10 Aug. 1818–19 Apr. 1862), son of Elizabeth Gaylord and LEONARD CASE, SR., was a prominent businessman, politician, and civic leader. Born in Cleveland, he received his education locally at Rev. Colley Foster's school and privately (1836–38) with FRANKLIN T. BACKUS, who urged him to attend Yale Univ.; but Case chose to attend to business activities in Cleveland. However, he was also ambitious in other areas: natural history, architectural research, horticultural experiments, politics, and founding library and educational institutions.

Case helped form and was first president (1846) of the CLEVELAND LIBRARY ASSN.† (later the Case Library); founded CLEVELAND UNIV.† (1850); and chaired the national meeting in Cleveland of the American Assn. of the Advancement of Education (1851). Case was president of the Cleveland, Painesville & Ashtabula Railroad, securing the financing allowing the line to complete its Chicago-to-Buffalo route (1852). He was president of Lake Shore Railroad (1855–57) was elected to the city council (1846), and served as an alderman (1847–49). He was the first Cleveland-born citizen to become mayor (1850–52), and organized the city workhouse, poorhouse, and house of refuge, as well as the city finances. His large real estate holdings combined with his horticultural interests in a tree-planting campaign (1852), similar to his father's in the 1820s, firmly established Cleveland's reputation as the "FOREST CITY."† Case was the moving spirit of the ARK,† an informal organization that was a precursor to the CLEVELAND MUSEUM OF NATURAL HISTORY.† In 1859 he built CASE HALL,† modeling it on Boston's Faneuil Hall. Case never married.

**CASSELS, JOHN LANG** (15 Sept. 1808–11 June 1879), a founder of Cleveland Medical College, now the medical school of CASE WESTERN RESERVE UNIV.,† was born in Glasgow, Scotland, attended the Univ. of Glasgow (1824–26), and emigrated to Utica, NY, in 1827. He enrolled at the College of Physicians & Surgeons of the Western District of the State of New York in 1831, meeting Dr. JOHN DELAMATER, and receiving his medical degree in 1834. He taught anatomy, chemistry, geology, mineralogy, and botany. In the 1830s, Cassels became a professor at Willoughby Medical College, resigning in 1843 to establish, with Delamater, HORACE ACKLEY, and JARED POTTER KIRTLAND, the Cleveland Medical College under the charter of Western Reserve Univ. Cassels taught chemistry, pharmacy, materia medica, toxicology, and botany for 30 years, and was also dean.

Cassels studied chemistry, concentrating on toxicology, often serving as an expert witness at criminal trials. He also studied food and water, checking Lake Erie water purity. Cassels was also a geologist employed by Cleveland industrialists to explore for deposits, and in 1846 claimed large deposits of iron ore on the southern shore of Lake Superior. Known as Cleveland Mountain, this provided the city with the ore necessary to begin its iron and steel industries.

Cassels lectured and published many articles. He never practiced medicine privately in Cleveland. Suffering a stroke in 1873, Cassels retired and was made professor emeritus of WRU. He was married in 1838 to Cornelia Olin of Vermont; they had a daughter.

**CASSESA, DOMINIC** (27 April 1925–8 March 1993) was a union organizer and an international representative whose career in union politics spanned 5 decades. As assistant regional director of UAW Region 2, Cassesa successfully organized more than 15 new plants, bringing thousands of members into Region 2.

Born in Cleveland to Victor and Lena (Gentile) Cassesa, Dominic grew up in LITTLE ITALY† and attended Murray Hill Elementary, Fairmount Jr. High, and East High Schools. He served in Europe during World War II with the Army Corps of Engineers.

Cassesa's union career began in 1946 at Eaton Manufacturing Co. (see EATON CORP.†) as a steward for UAW Local 307. After 17 years as the union's benefits representative, he became local president, serving from 1961–1967. In 1967 he was appointed to the staff of Region 2 by Regional Director PATRICK O'MALLEY. As assistant director of the UAW's Eaton Department, Cassesa led the UAW's Eaton National Bargaining Committee in 1968. He served 16 years on the Region 2 staff before UAW Regional Director Warren Davis appointed him assistant regional director in 1983, a post he held until his retirement in 1986.

Cassesa married Rosa Borgini in 1949 (div. 1959) and had a daughter, Carla. Cassesa married Shirley Bockmann in 1969 (div. 1973), then married Joyce Hoffman. His fourth wife was Mary Catherine, from whom he had 4 stepdaughters. Cassesa lived in Seven Hills and Ashtabula before retiring to Florida. Cassesa died in Davenport, FL, and is buried at Greenlawn Memorial Garden.—T.B.

**CASTLE, WILLIAM BAINBRIDGE** (30 Nov. 1814–28 Feb. 1872), a businessman and mayor, was born in Essex, VT, moved to Toronto in 1815, and settled in Cleveland in 1827 (one source indicates 1832). Later that year, Castle, his father, and Chas. Giddings opened Cleveland's first lumberyard. Upon his father's death (either 1829 or 1832), Castle returned to Ontario, moving to Ohio City in 1839 and in 1840 forming the hardware partnership of Castle & Field. Castle joined the CUYAHOGA

STEAM FURNACE CO.† as an accountant in 1843, became manager in 1859, and was with the company until his death.

For many years, Castle was a member of the Ohio City Common Council and was mayor in 1853–54, when he helped write the 1854 agreement merging Ohio City into Cleveland. Upon consolidation, Castle resigned as mayor, but was elected in 1855 as mayor of Cleveland, when he directed cutting a shorter channel between Lake Erie and the Cuyahoga, opening the river to larger ships; and building a suitable harbor on the lakefront. He promoted and became a trustee of the city's water-works, which began in 1856. Castle was defeated for reelection in 1857.

Castle was a director of the finance boards of the Peoples Gas & Light Co., the Citizens' Savings & Loan Co., and various railroads. Castle married twice. In 1836 he married Mary Derby, who died a year later. In 1840 he married Mary Newell; the Castles had a son and 3 daughters.

William B. Castle (1872).

**CASTO, FRANK M.** (30 May 1875–25 April 1965), a noted dentist and educator at the Western Reserve Univ. Dental School from 1904–37, was born in Blanchester, OH, and graduated from the Ohio State Univ. Dental School with a D.D.S. degree in 1898, from the OSU Medical School with an M.D. degree in 1900, and from the OSU Pharmacy School with a Ph.D. degree in 1902. As a junior in dental school, Casto passed the Ohio state dental boards and opened a private practice in 1897 in Plain City, OH. He began teaching in 1899 as an instructor at the OSU Dental School. In 1904 he became professor of orthodontics at the WRU Dental School, where he organized its first orthodontic clinic. In 1917, when Casto was appointed dean of the school, dental schools demanded only a high school education of their first-year students. Casto raised the program of instruction to a 4-year curriculum, and in 1922, WRU raised its entrance requirement to 1 year of college. By Casto's retirement in 1937, WRU and all leading dental schools demanded at least 2 years of preprofessional college training for admission. Casto also maintained a private practice in Cleveland and served as president of the local and state dental societies. He married Florence M. Andrus on 20 Feb. 1902, and had 3 children: William, Ruth, and Florence. Awarded emeritus status in 1937, Casto moved to California, where he practiced dentistry and medicine with his son.

**CATHCART, WALLACE HUGH** (2 Apr. 1865–6 Sept. 1942), prominent bibliophile, is best known for his association with the WESTERN RESERVE HISTORICAL SOCIETY† of Cleveland, first as its president and then as its director. Born and raised in Elyria, OH, son of S. H. and Eliza (Chamberlain) Cathcart, he first became fascinated with books as a bookstore clerk. Upon his graduation from Denison Univ. in 1890, he came to Cleveland to aid a book-dealing company, Taylor & Austin, during the holiday rush. After 7 years there, he joined the Burrows Bros. Co., where he quickly ascended from secretary to vice-president and general manager. As a prominent member of the book trade, Cathcart was one of the founders and later vice-president of the American Booksellers & Publishers Assn. Cathcart also served as an officer in several of Cleveland's civic and mercantile organizations and as president of the Baptist City Mission Society for 7 years. Civic-mindedness and love of books attracted Cathcart to the WRHS where he acted as the organization's secretary (1894–97), president (1907–13), and finally the society's first full-time director (1913–42). As a book collector, Cathcart concentrated his energies in developing one of the best historical libraries in the nation. Many major, comprehensive collections were acquired, such as the Cathcart Shaker collection, considered the largest of its kind in existence. In addition to expanding the society's library, Cathcart broadened its educational and cultural programs and participated in the movement of both the museum and the library to new locations on East Blvd. in the late 1930s. Cathcart and his wife, Elsie, raised 2 daughters, Genevieve and Evelyn.

In Memory of Wallace Hugh Cathcart, WRHS (1942).
Wallace Hugh Cathcart Papers, WRHS.

**CATTON, BRUCE** (9 Oct. 1899–28 Aug. 1978), went from a Cleveland newspaper career to become an authority on the CIVIL WAR† and one of America's most honored popular historians. Born in Petoskey, MI, Catton broke into journalism on the *CLEVELAND NEWS†* in 1920, after attending Oberlin College and serving in the navy during World War I. After a year with the *Boston American*, he returned to Cleveland to work for the *PLAIN DEALER.†* Probably his first published Civil War writing was a series on local Northern veterans that he did for the *Plain Dealer* in 1923. Following his marriage to Hazel H. Cherry in 1925, Catton switched to a job in the Cleveland office of Scripps-Howard's Newspaper Enterprise Assn. (NEA), supplying news, features, editorials, and book reviews for clients throughout the country. Leaving Cleveland in 1939, Catton moved to NEA's Washington office and later worked for the Dept. of Commerce. His first book, *The War Lords of Wash-*

*ington,* appeared in 1948, followed by a trilogy on the Army of the Potomac. The last of this series, *A Stillness at Appomattox,* brought him the 1954 Pulitzer Prize for History. From 1954–59, he served as the first editor of *American Heritage* magazine. Catton's later books included *The American Heritage Picture History of the Civil War* (1960) and the 3-vol. *Centennial History of the Civil War (1961–65).* Continuing his association with *American Heritage,* Catton was a senior editor from 1959 until his death at his summer home in Frankfort, MI. He had a son, Wm. Bruce Catton.—J.V.

**CELEBREZZE, ANTHONY.** See **MAYORAL ADMINISTRATION OF ANTHONY CELEBREZZE.†**

**CELEBREZZE, FRANK D.** (12 May 1899–21 Aug. 1953), asst. county prosecutor, safety director, and municipal court judge, was born in Cleveland, son of Rocco V. and Dorothy (Marcogiuseppe) Celebrezze (Cilibrizzi). The family returned to Italy in 1908 to find employment and Frank attended Italian schools. After they returned to Cleveland in 1912, Frank enrolled in Brownell School. Encouraged by a teacher to continue his schooling, he graduated from East Technical High School, enrolled in St. Ignatius College (now JOHN CARROLL UNIV.†) for a year, and attended Notre Dame Univ. for 3 years, receiving an LL.B. degree in 1925. He was admitted to the bar in 1926 and went into private practice. He married Mary Delsander, 24 Nov. 1927, and had 6 children: Frank D., Jr., Gerald, Dorothy, Joanne, Monica, and James P.

Democratic party politics attracted Celebrezze, and he was appointed asst. county prosecutor in 1929. While in the prosecutor's office, he spearheaded a successful drive to break up racket operations in Cleveland, assisting Judge FRANK LAUSCHE in closing the large gambling clubs. He went to Italy to try Angelo Amato in connection with the SLY-FANNER MURDER CASE.† Amato was sentenced to prison for 30 years. In 1942 Celebrezze was appointed safety director, replacing ELIOT NESS, and remained there until 1947, with a brief stint in the army during World War II. He was elected judge of the municipal court in 1947 and reelected in 1951. Celebrezze was buried in the Holy Cross Cemetery of Cleveland.

Frank D. Celebrezze Papers, WRHS.

**CELESTE, FRANK PALM** (24 March 1907–9 Nov. 1988) was a real estate developer, housing expert, and mayor of LAKEWOOD† from 1956–64.

Born to Samuel and Carolina Santora Celeste in Cerisano, Italy, Celeste was ten months old when his family came to the U.S. He was raised in Monessen, PA, and graduated from Monessen High School in 1924. He received the A.B. degree from Wooster College in 1928, and the LL.B. from Western Reserve Univ. Law School in 1931. He passed the Ohio Bar in 1932 and began his law practice in Cleveland.

With Democratic party backing, Celeste ran a nonpartisan campaign to become Lakewood's mayor in 1955 and break the Republican party's hold on city hall. Once in office, Celeste helped to amend Lakewood's charter to provide for partisan elections. Running as a Democrat, Celeste was reelected in 1959. Celeste's tenure marked the development of high-rise apartment buildings along Lakewood's Gold Coast, which increased Lakewood's tax base by $30 million. Celeste also led in promoting housing for the elderly with the Westerly Apartments, opening in 1963.

After two terms, Celeste returned to private practice and his business, National Housing Consultants & Management, Inc., which developed condominiums and federally subsidized housing for the elderly. Celeste's final political campaign, the 1967 Cleveland mayoral primary, ended with Celeste finishing third to Carl Stokes and Ralph Locher.

Celeste married Margaret Louis on 1 Oct. 1932. They had three children: Richard, Mary Patricia, and Theodore. A Methodist, Celeste is buried in Lakewood Park Cemetery.—T.B.

Borchert, Jim & Susan. *Lakewood: The First Hundred Years* (1989).

**CERMAK, ALBINA** (4 Apr. 1904–22 Dec. 1978) was a lifelong Republican and the first woman to run for mayor of Cleveland. Born in Cleveland to Frank J. and Rose Cermak, she dropped out of nursing school to become bookkeeper-secretary-buyer in the family Cermak Dry Goods Co. In 1933 she became a bookkeeper for the city public utilities department; within 2 years, she was supervisor. Active as a Republican precinct committeewoman from 1925–53, Cermak served as vice-chairman and secretary of the Cuyahoga County Republican Central & Executive Committee and chairman of the Republican Women's Organization of Cuyahoga County from 1939–53. From 1946–53 she was a member of the Board of Elections and was a delegate to the Republican Natl. Conventions in 1940, 1944, and 1952.

In 1953 Cermak resigned from many offices to become U.S. collector of customs, stepping down to run against Anthony Celebrezze in 1961 as the first woman to run for mayor. She predicted that Celebrezze, if elected, would abandon Cleveland for a cabinet post. As expected, she lost, while Celebrezze became secretary of HEW in 1962. Cermak was rewarded for party loyalty with choice and historic appointments. She was the first woman appointed bailiff to the common pleas court in 1964. In 1965 State Auditor Roger Cloud selected her as an administrative specialist, while Gov. Jas. Rhodes named her vice-chairwoman of the Ohio Status of Women Committee in 1966. Single by choice, she was considered among Cleveland's top career women and was a sought-after speaker.

Albina Cermak Papers, WRHS.

**CERRI, NICOLA** (30 Mar. 1875–4 Nov. 1954), widely known physician and Italian consul in Cleveland, was born in Avezzano, Italy, the son of Antonio and Mariannina (Jetti) Cerri. After graduating from Victor Emanuel College at Naples in 1892, he attended the Univ. of Rome, receiving his medical degree in 1898, and practiced in Rome for a year. Cerri came to Cleveland in December 1899, opened his medical practice on Prospect Ave., and helped found the ACADEMY OF MEDICINE† in 1902. He served as Italian Consul, 1900–26, aiding many immigrants who settled in Ohio, Kentucky, and West Virginia. Italian immigration to the Cleveland area increased dramatically after the turn of the century, and for a time Cerri scaled back his practice in order to fulfill his consular duties. In 1930 he helped found the Democratic League of Ohio and was appointed U.S. commissioner general, in charge of all federal exhibits at the GREAT LAKES EXPOSITION† 1936–38. He also was appointed supervisor of the census for Ohio in 1940.

Cerri married Josephine Grace Rittman of Washington DC, in Dec. 1903, and they had a son, Nicola Jr. A resident of Cleveland, he died in Washington DC, and was buried at Lake View Cemetery.—M.S.

**CERUTI, JOSEPH** (7 May 1912–26 Nov. 1993) was a renowned architect who designed numerous apartment buildings, homes, industrial complexes, libraries, schools and public housing projects (King-Kennedy) and a founding member who served 45 years on Cleveland's Fine Arts Advisory Committee (Design Review Committee).

Born in New York City to Antonio and Luisa (Forte) Ceruti, Joseph came to Cleveland with his family at age two. He graduated from East Technical High School (1929), and received his bachelor of architecture from Western Reserve Univ. (1934), a diploma from the School of Fine Arts in Fontainebleau, France, and a certificate from the Beaux-Arts Institute of Design, New York. He was a registered architect with Ohio, and the National Council of Architectural Registration Boards.

Ceruti began his career in 1936 and, through 1947, was associated with several prominent Cleveland architectural firms. From 1941–45 he was principal architect for the WARNER & SWASEY CO.† and, in 1952, designed the company's plant in New Philadelphia.

In 1947 Ceruti opened his own office on Euclid Ave. His more notable designs include an office and laboratory building for the HARSHAW CHEMICAL CO.† (1946), the 12-story Shaker Towers apartments at Coventry Rd. and Shaker Blvd. (1951), and rehabilitation of the WEST SIDE MARKET† (1949).

Ceruti taught architecture and interior design at John Huntington Polytechnic (1939–40, 1946–47), Cleveland College (1948–49), and the CLEVELAND INSTITUTE OF ART,† (1947–49). Ceruti was elected to the College of Fellows of the American Institute of Architects.

Ceruti married Dorothy Parma on 17 Jan. 1959. They had four children: Lisa, Anne, Joseph, and Mary Ellen. Ceruti is buried in Lake View Cemetery.—T.B.

Joseph Ceruti Papers, WRHS.

**CHADSEY, MILDRED** (6 June 1884–3 Apr. 1940), prominent in local reform work, came to Cleveland in 1912 after graduating from the Univ. of Chicago as the city's first housing commissioner, which included the duties of sanitary inspector. She used her authority and uniformed sanitary police to force landlords to repair plumbing, clean buildings, and provide fire protection. In her first year, she caused over 200 tenements to be demolished or vacated. In 1913 Chadsey formed the Cleveland Bureau of Sanitation to oversee housing and sanitation and served as director. A political move by the city council in 1915, by officials who owned tenements, threatened her job; but citizens FREDERICK H. GOFF and SAMUEL MATHER vowed to pay Chadsey's salary if the council would not.

Chadsey worked for progressive legislation, including the city's dance hall ordinance of 1911 and housing code; was active in the labor movement and the CONSUMERS LEAGUE OF OHIO†; and was a founder of the WOMEN'S CITY CLUB.† During World War I Chadsey managed Red Cross activities in Italy. From 1921–24 she edited the Cleveland Year Book, an annual report of events outlining social progress.

In 1919 Chadsey was hired by Western Reserve Univ. to teach social work administration, later becoming director of the group work services division of the School of Applied Social Sciences, continuing until 1924. Chadsey helped found and directed the Adult Education Assn. in 1925. She was also active in the CLEVELAND PLAY HOUSE,† CLEVELAND PUBLIC LIBRARY,† and LEAGUE

FOR HUMAN RIGHTS.† Born in Cherokee, KS, Chadsey was the daughter of Asa Newton and Selina Elizabeth (Adams) Chadsey. She never married. She died in Cleveland and was buried in Lake View Cemetery.

**CHADWICK, CASSIE L.** (1857–10 Oct. 1907), Cleveland's most famous con artist, whose trial drew worldwide attention, was born Elizabeth Bigley in Eastwood, Ontario, Canada. At 22 she was arrested in Woodstock, Ontario, for forgery, escaping conviction on grounds of insanity. In 1882 Bigley married Dr. Wallace S. Springsteen of Cleveland, but after 11 days was thrown out when her background was revealed. She became a fortuneteller, known as Lydia Scott, in 1886, and in 1887 assumed the name Madame Lydia DeVeré. In 1889 she was sentenced to 9½ years in the state penitentiary for forgery in Toledo. Four years later, after being paroled by then-governor Wm. McKinley, she returned to Cleveland, living as Mrs. Hoover. In 1897, "Hoover" married Dr. Leroy Chadwick, who knew nothing of her criminal activities. Between 1897–1905, Chadwick borrowed vast sums of money from Cleveland banks, claiming to be the illegitimate daughter of Andrew Carnegie, and using $5 million in securities and certificates forged with Carnegie's name as security. She accumulated over $1 million in debts, but was exposed on 2 Nov. 1904 when H. B. Newton brought suit to recover $190,800. She fled to New York, was arrested, stood trial in Cleveland, and on 10 Mar. 1905 was convicted on 7 counts of conspiracy against the government and conspiracy to wreck the Citizens Natl. Bank of Oberlin. She was sentenced to 14 years in prison and fined $70,000. Chadwick was jailed on 12 Jan. 1906, dying a year later.

**CHALOUPKA, ALOYSIUS W.** (2 July 1886-May 1961), attorney, served as asst. prosecutor for Cuyahoga County (1919–20). Chaloupka was born in Austria-Hungary to Joseph and Anna Pleticha Chaloupka and came to Cleveland as a child. He attended St. Prokop's Parochial School and St. Ignatius College. In 1917 he received a law degree from the Cleveland Law School and began his law practice. By 1927 his offices were located in the Society for Savings Building (see SOCIETY NATIONAL BANK BUILDING†). In the 1920s Chaloupka taught English for the Cleveland Board of Education and citizenship classes for the Citizens' Bureau.

On 10 Nov. 1910, Chaloupka married Hermina Vanera; they lived in Cleveland with their children, Lawrence, Eleanor, and Robert. He belonged to the Cuyahoga County Democratic Club, the K. of C.,

and the Fraternal Order of Eagles. Chaloupka is buried in St. Mary's Cemetery.—J.M.

**CHAMBERLAIN, SELAH** (4 May 1812–27 Dec. 1890), a railroad developer involved in the iron industry and banking, was born in Brattleboro, VT, to Selah and Abigail (Burnett) Chamberlain. He moved to Boston at age 21 where he obtained business training as an apprentice in a grocery store. In 1835 Chamberlain formed his own company and was contracted to complete construction on an extension of the Erie & Pennsylvania Canal. He received larger contracts for the Wabash & Erie Canal, and in the 1840s supervised improvements on the St. Lawrence River. In 1847 he returned to Vermont and contracted to build segments of the country's emerging railroad system. He was largely responsible for the construction of the Rutland & Burlington Railroad to Boston, and the Lake Champlain Railroad. In 1849 Chamberlain moved to Cleveland to take advantage of Midwest railroad expansion. In Cleveland, Chamberlain also co-founded the private banking house of Chamberlain, Gorham & Perkins, which in 1880 merged into Merchants Natl. Bank. Related to his railroading, in 1850 he was a founder of the Cleveland Iron Mining Co. (later to become CLEVELAND CLIFFS†). Chamberlain's railroad interests included the entire contract to construct the Cleveland & Pittsburgh Railroad (1849), railroad building in Iowa and Wisconsin, and being a major stockholder in several railroads. He was an incorporator of the Cleveland, Lorain & Wheeling Railroad Co., helped form the Cleveland Transportation Co., and for many years was its president. Chamberlain married Arabella Cochran in 1844 and had 2 children, James and William. They were one of the first families to own a mansion on "Prosperity Row" on Euclid Ave. Chamberlain was buried in Lake View Cemetery.

**CHAMPA, FRANK A.** (2 Sept. 1908–24 Mar. 1993) was an area musician and accordionist who is enshrined in the Polka Hall of Fame in EUCLID.† As a tavern owner, Champa helped to promote the Slovenian Hour, which has played on various radio stations around Cleveland since 1961.

Born in Cleveland to Anton and Frances (Sager) Champa, Frank attended Cleveland schools. Frank first taught himself to play the button-box accordion and later the German chromatic or 120 base accordion. At the age of 5, Frank and his brother, Tony, made the rounds of their E. 61st St. and St. Clair Ave. neighborhood playing for weddings, parties, and other events.

Champa owned the Glen Park Cafe on E. 185th St. from 1943–61. It had a polka stage and dance floor. After freeway construction displaced his tavern, Champa opened Champa's Lounge (LaMalfa Party Center) in Eastlake.

Champa played the polka circuit with his son, Raymond, and the Ray Champa Band. They performed on WSRS-AM from 1949–50 and recorded together in the mid–1950s. In 1977 Champa and his son were named Co-Polka Musicians of the Year at the Holmes Ave. Slovenian Home's annual celebration. In 1992 Champa was placed on the Polka Hall of Fame honor roll for his contributions as a musician and promoter.

Champa married Olga, his wife, on 2 Feb. 1928. They had a son, Raymond. Champa, a Roman Catholic, lived in Euclid and is buried in All Souls Cemetery.—T.B.

**CHANDLER, NEVILLE (NEV) ALBERT JR.** (2 Oct. 1946–7 Aug. 1994) possessed one of the most familiar voices in Cleveland broadcasting during his career as a radio and television sportscaster. He was born in LAKEWOOD,† the son of Neville and Dorothy Chandler. Following his graduation from Rocky River High School, he earned a journalism degree in 1968 from Northwestern Univ. He broke into television broadcasting with WVIZ† and WKBF in Cleveland and WTVN in Columbus. He married the former Cynthia Weber in 1971, the year he became the weekend television sports anchor for Cleveland's WEWS.† By 1979 Chandler was also hosting a radio call-in show called Sportsline over WWWE. In 1980 he temporarily left television to become the radio announcer for the baseball games of the CLEVELAND INDIANS† over WWWE, serving also as the station's sports director. He returned to television as sports director and weekday sports anchor for WEWS in 1985. Later that year he became the "radio voice of the CLEVELAND BROWNS,†" as he assumed the weekly play-by-play broadcasting duties for the football games. From 1987–89, and again in 1993, Chandler was named "Ohio Sportscaster of the Year" by the Ohio chapter of the National Sportswriters and Sportscasters Assn. He died of cancer at his home in ROCKY RIVER.† Buried at Lakewood Park Cemetery, he was survived by his wife, son Scott, and daughter Ashley. Chandler was elected posthumously to the CLEVELAND JOURNALISM HALL OF FAME.†—J.V.

**CHAPIN, HERMAN M.** (29 July 1823–24 May 1879), a businessman interested in libraries, was born in Walpole, NH, to Nathaniel and Fanny Bowen Brown Chapin. He came to Cleveland in 1848 as a partner in the wholesale grocery warehouse of Chas. Bradburn & Co. In 1852 he started his own business as a provision dealer and beef and pork packer, moving to Chicago in 1862, but re-turning to Cleveland a few years later. In 1865 he helped form and became president of the Hahnemann Life Insurance Co., which later merged with Republic Life Insurance Co. and moved to Chicago.

During the Civil War, Chapin raised money and equipment for the Union; and while away in the spring of 1865, he was elected mayor of Cleveland, not even knowing he was nominated. During his term, the Metropolitan Police Act was passed, transferring police powers of the mayor, police marshal, and city council to a new board of police commissioners consisting of the mayor and 4 others appointed by the governor. In 1872 the act was changed, allowing for the commissioners' election.

In 1854 and 1858, Chapin was president of the CLEVELAND LIBRARY ASSN.,† putting the organization on a sound fiscal base, and became a director for life in 1870. He was a founder of the First Unitarian Church in 1854, and that year built the Chapin Block at the Square, whose third floor housed the elegant public Concert Hall, later renamed Chapin Hall. Chapin married Matilda Fenno of Boston on 15 Oct. 1849, and had 5 children: Erving, Matilda, Fanny, Jeanie, and Agnes. He died in Cleveland and was buried in Lake View Cemetery.

**CHAPMAN, EDMUND HAUPT** (14 Aug. 1906–14 Oct. 1975) was a professor of Art History and chairman of the department of Art & Architecture at CASE WESTERN RESERVE UNIV.† (1946–72), and author of Cleveland: Village to Metropolis.

Born in New Haven, CT, Chapman received his Ph.B (1928) and A.M. (1930) from Yale Univ. and his Ph.D. (1951) from New York Univ. He taught at the Univ. of Colorado (1930–35), the City Univ. of New York's Hunter College (1939), and Goucher College in Baltimore, MD (1939–42). During World War II Chapman served as a lieutenant commander in the Navy Air Combat Intelligence (1942–46).

Chapman's book, Cleveland: Village to Metropolis, published in 1964 in cooperation with the WESTERN RESERVE HISTORICAL SOCIETY,† was based on the thesis for his doctoral degree. He also contributed articles to the Journal of the Society of Architectural History and the College Journal.

Chapman belonged to the Society of Architectural Historians, the American Assn. of Univ. Professors, and the College Art Assn. and was a former chairman of the zoning board of Munson Twp.

Chapman married Affa Gray in 1930. They had a daughter, Dr. Gretel Chapman. Chapman lived in Chardon. He was cremated.—T.B.

**CHAPMAN, RAYMOND JOHNSON "RAY"** (15 Jan. 1891–17 Aug. 1920), a Cleveland Indian between 1912–20, was the last major league player to die as a result of being hit by a pitched baseball. Born in Beaver Dam, KY, but growing up in Herrin, IL, during 1910–11 he played baseball with Springfield and Davenport in the Three III League. He joined the Toledo Mud Hens of the American Assn. in 1911, and in August 1912, his contract was purchased by Cleveland, where Chapman was the Indians' shortstop. More interested in team wins than his own accomplishments, Chapman led the league in sacrifice hits 3 years, setting a major-league record with 67 sacrifices in 1917. His team record of 55 stolen bases in 1917 was not broken until Miguel Dilone's mark of 61 in 1980. A competent fielder, Chapman was the league leader in putouts 2 seasons, and assists 1 year. In 1,303 baseball games with Cleveland, he had a batting average of .278. While playing at the New York Polo Grounds on 16 Aug. 1920, Chapman was hit in the head by a pitched baseball from Carl Mays, an underhand Yankee pitcher, dying at a New York hospital 12 hours later. His funeral at St. John's Cathedral was one of Cleveland's largest. Chapman's teammates dedicated the season to him and, led by their playing manager, TRIS SPEAKER, won the league and world championships for the first time. Chapman was married on 29 Oct. 1919, to Kathleen Marie Daly.

**CHASE, RUSSELL N.** (18 Feb. 1900–24 April 1980) was a lawyer active in the defense of accused communists and in the affairs of the American Civil Liberties Union. A native Clevelander, the son of William and Edna Thomas Chase, he was a graduate of Asheville School for Boys in Asheville, NC. After brief service in the army during World War I, he completed his undergraduate education at Cornell Univ. and earned a law degree from the Western Reserve Univ. School of Law (see CASE WESTERN RESERVE†) in 1925. Chase set up his own law practice in Cleveland ca. 1927, handling for the most part estates and civil liberties cases. During the Spanish Civil War he was active in organizations sending aid to Loyalist Spain. He toured the Loyalist area in 1937, reporting his experiences in 2 articles printed in the *CLEVELAND PRESS.†* By 1940 he was chairman of the ad hoc Cleveland chapter of the American Civil Liberties Union. He was also executive secretary of the Cleveland Council of the American Peace Mobilization. Chase married Virginia Hatch Combs in 1942. Following World War II he served as president of the Cleveland chapter of the National Lawyers Guild, which was cited as a subversive organization by the House Un-American Activities Committee in 1950. He defended Communists as well as persons ac-

cused of communist activities during the McCarthy era. A past president of the Cleveland Cornell Club, Chase died at his home in HUNTING VALLEY.† He was survived by a daughter, Amanda Madar, and 5 stepsons.—J.V.

Russell N. Chase Papers, WRHS.

**CHAUNCEY, HERBERT S.** (16 Apr. 1887–22 June 1930), business and civic leader, was appointed in 1929 as the first African American member of the Cleveland City Planning Commission (see CITY PLANNING†). Born in Eastman, GA, to Coleman and Marietta Chauncey, he was educated at Talladega College. After becoming a railway postal clerk, he transferred to Cleveland. He attended law school at night and later left the mail service to open a law office. In 1919 Chauncey obtained a state charter for the African-American-owned EMPIRE SAVINGS AND LOAN CO.,† with shareholders such as NORMAN L. MCGHEE, SR. He also created the People's Realty to serve AFRICAN AMERICANS.† Chauncey organized two mutual societies, the Modern Crusaders of the World (1926), and the Crusaders Mutual Insurance Society (1927), which provided sick, accident, and death benefits to members. These societies later consolidated with others into the Dunbar Mutual Insurance Society (1935, acquired by the SUPREME LIFE INSURANCE CO. OF AMERICA† in 1960). Chauncey convened the Cleveland Businessmen's Assn. in 1925, the forerunner of the Progressive Business Alliance (1939, later the Cleveland Business League). Chauncey and his wife, Benton, had a daughter, Rose Marie (d. 1943). He died in Cleveland and was buried at Highland Park Cemetery.—J.M.

**CHESNUTT, CHARLES WADDELL** (20 June 1858–15 Nov. 1932), a novelist, short-story writer, and lawyer, was the first black writer to deal with race from the African American point of view. Born in Cleveland to Andrew J. and Maria Chesnutt, the family moved to Fayetteville, NC, where Chesnutt grew up. He graduated from Howard School at 16 and augmented his education with study in German, French, and Greek. He taught himself stenography to make a living. Chesnutt became a teacher in black schools in North Carolina, and at 19 was asst. principal of the New Fayetteville Normal School, and later its principal. He kept a journal, from which he would draw for his writing. Chesnutt came to Cleveland in 1883. He studied law and was a stenographer for Judge SAMUEL WILLIAMSON. He was admitted to the Ohio Bar in 1887 and served as a court reporter to support his family and writing.

Chesnutt depicted AFRICAN AMERICANS† as human beings, new in American literature, where blacks had been portrayed as stereotypes or subtypes. He attempted to bridge the race gap and raise the issue of civil rights and equal opportunity for blacks. In 1887 the *Atlantic Monthly* published its first Chesnutt story, "The Goophered Grapevine." In 1899 selected stories were published in *The Conjure Woman*. Another volume of short stories and several novels followed, the most popular being *The House behind the Cedars* (1900), about intermarriage. Later, Chesnutt's popularity waned as white readers grew tired of his themes. He continued to write and lecture, and was active in the Chamber of Commerce.

In 1878 Chesnutt married Susan Perry; they had 4 children: Ethel, Helen, Edwin, and Dorothy. Chesnutt died in Cleveland and was buried in Lake View Cemetery.

Charles W. Chesnutt Papers, WRHS.

**CHIEF THUNDERWATER** (10 Sept. 1865–10 June 1950), whose Indian name was Oghema Niagara, was a Native American Indian chief who worked to preserve his people's rights and culture, and improve their welfare and image among white Americans. Born on the Tuscarora Indian reservation near Lewistown, NY, to Au-Paw-CheeKaw-Paw-qua (Woman-Whose-Name-Shall-Never-Die), an Osaukee, and Jee-wan-gah, a Seneca, little is known about him between 1875–1910, when he apparently appeared in Buffalo Bill Cody's Wild West shows for about 9 years. He began working for AMERICAN INDIANS† after 1883. In the early 1900s, Niagara settled in Cleveland, becoming president of the Preservative Cleaner Co., manufacturers of polish; and selling his own Thunderwater's Mohawk Oil, for rheumatism and arthritis, and Jee-wan-ga tea.

On 10 Mar. 1917, Niagara helped incorporate the Supreme Council of the Tribes, a revival of the League of the Confederacy of Iroquois Nations, formed to assist Indians, promote their welfare and legally protect their rights, and teach temperance and education. As chief of the Supreme Council, Niagara operated "the Council Sanctuary" in his home at his own expense, housing, feeding, clothing, and providing medical attention for hundreds of destitute and sick Indians and persons of all races.

Niagara's efforts to educate white Americans included being active in the EARLY SETTLERS ASSN. OF THE WESTERN RESERVE,† appearing at public ceremonies in full headdress, and holding an annual ceremony at the grave of JOC-O-SOT in the Erie St. Cemetery. Niagara remained active until ca. 1942, when illness forced him to give up many public appearances.

Niagara was married once; his wife's name is not known. He had one son, Louis Keokuk. Niagara died in Cleveland and was buried in Erie St. Cemetery.

Chief Thunderwater Papers, WRHS.

**CHISHOLM, HENRY** (22 Apr. 1822–9 May 1881), the primary stockholder of the Cleveland Rolling Mill that eventually became part of U.S. STEEL,† was born in Lochgelly, Fifeshire, Scotland, apprenticed as a carpenter at 12, and emigrated to Montreal, Canada, establishing himself as a contractor. In 1850 he came to Cleveland to build a breakwater. His reputation as a technical genius and superb handler of men attracted DAVID and JOHN JONES, owners of the Jones & Co. Mill. Chisholm invested heavily in the firm, renamed Chisholm, Jones & Co., and reoriented operations toward rerolling worn-out rails. By 1858 the plant produced 50 tons of rerolled rails daily, with Chisholm personally managing the operations and finances. To preserve scarce cash, he offered company-owned housing and company-store benefits to the workers, whom he knew and regarded as important to the company's success. Seeing steel would be the metal of the future, Chisholm sent his best ironmaster to learn the Bessemer process, and in 1868 Cleveland Rolling Mill was the 5th American plant producing Bessemer steel, producing rails for $225 a ton, compared to $250 for French or English rails.

Chisholm diversified operations to manufacture wire, screws and nuts, and tools, buying Newburgh Wire Mill in 1867, and with others organizing the American Sheet & Boiler Plate Co. (1866), the Union Steel Screw Co. (1872), and the H. P. Horse Nail Co. (1877). Chisholm died at 59, leaving 5 children and his wife, the former Jean Allen. Upon his death, his workers contributed to a monument for him in Lake View Cemetery. His passing ended paternalistic labor relations and progressive mill management. Wm. Chisholm, who succeeded his father, provoked major strikes (see CLEVELAND ROLLING MILL STRIKES OF 1882 & 1885†) and alienated Wm. Garrett, inventor of a new rodmaking process the company needed to remain a leader. Aside from his Cleveland interests, Henry Chisholm held stock in the Union Steel Co. of Chicago, Indiana blast furnaces, and Lake Superior ore.

**CHURCH, HENRY JR.** (20 May 1836–17 April 1908), a CHAGRIN FALLS VILLAGE† blacksmith, achieved a posthumous reputation as an American primitive for his avocation of painting and sculpting. He learned the blacksmithing trade from his father, one of the founders of Chagrin Falls. The younger Church was born in Chagrin Falls and educated largely by his mother. He married Martha Prebble in 1859 and set up his own blacksmith shop in the village, setting aside the second floor as a studio, where he experimented with painting and later sculpting. He was entirely self-taught, not even meeting another artist until the 1870s, when he traveled to Cleveland to watch ARCHIBALD WILLARD at work. In the 1880s Church began carving bas relief figures in Squaw Rock on the bank of the CHAGRIN RIVER.† Variously interpreted as a memorial to the rape of the Indians or an allegorical depiction of the progress of U.S. civilization, the work is today part of the South Chagrin reservation of CLEVELAND METROPARKS.† Church was unsuccessful in his efforts to support himself by his art, which included the operation of a museum at Geauga Lake Park in 1888. His painting, *The Monkey Picture* (ca. 1895) was sold by his daughter for $12 in the 1930s before becoming part of the permanent collection of the Abbey Aldrich Rockefeller Folk Art Center in Williamsburg, VA. Having previously carved his own tombstone, Church preached his own funeral sermon by means of a pre-recorded wax cylinder. He was survived by his daughter, Mrs. Jessie Sargent, and a son, Austin Church, cofounder of the Brewster & Church dept. store in Chagrin Falls.—J.V.

Lipman, Jean and Tom Armstrong (eds.). *American Folk Painters of Three Centuries* (1980).
Theis, Jana M. "Chagrin Falls' Henry Church," in *Western Reserve*, vol. XI, no. 1 (1983).

**CLAPP, NETTIE MACKENZIE** (22 Aug. 1868–30 July 1935), the first woman elected to the Ohio House of Representatives from Cuyahoga County, was born in Cincinnati and attended public and private schools there, including the Cincinnati School of Art. She came to Cleveland in 1911 and during World War I helped organize the Cleveland Hts. auxiliary Red Cross. Her interest in politics grew out of her work for woman's suffrage. She was elected to the Ohio House of Representatives as a Republican in 1922, where she served for 3 terms. As chairperson of the Committee on Benevolent & Penal Institutions, she supported a bill to establish the London prison farm. She was the only woman to serve on the executive committee of the REPUBLICAN NATL. CONVENTION of 1924, which was held in Cleveland. Her bid for election to the Ohio senate in 1928 was unsuccessful. She married Harold T. Clapp, M.D., in 1912 and had a daughter,

Dorothy Annette (Mrs. Daniel H. Petty). She died in Cleveland at age 66.

**CLARK, HAROLD TERRY** (4 Sept. 1882–31 May 1965), a Cleveland lawyer and philanthropist, was born in Derby, CT, son of William J. and Mary J. (Terry) Clark. He graduated from Yale College with an A.B. (1903) and from Harvard Law School with an LL.B. (1906). Admitted to the Connecticut and Ohio bars, Clark settled in Cleveland in 1906, working with SQUIRE, SANDERS & DEMPSEY,† becoming a member of the firm in 1913. In 1937 Clark opened his own law office, specializing in corporate and probate law. During World War I he served the U.S. War Industries Board and, after the war, the American Commission to Negotiate Peace. Clark designed the corporate structure of the Glidden Co. and Fisher Bros. Foods, and served as a director for CLEVELAND QUARRIES,† FISHER FOODS,† the CLEVELAND ELECTRIC ILLUMINATING CO.,† and the Cleveland Chamber of Commerce, and as a trustee of Society Natl. Bank.

Clark guided millions of dollars to institutions. During the Depression and World War II, Clark kept the CLEVELAND MUSEUM OF NATURAL HISTORY† in operating funds. He preserved Mentor Marsh, promoted relocation of Holden Arboretum to Kirtland, helped transform BROOKSIDE PARK† into a fine zoo, and influenced formation of the Metropolitan Park System. As vice-president and trustee of the CLEVELAND SOCIETY FOR THE BLIND,† Clark promoted sight-saving and Braille classes. Clark was the 1958 recipient of the Charles Eisenman Award for Civic Service to Cleveland, awarded by the JEWISH COMMUNITY FEDERATION.† In 1961 the Cleveland Museum of Natural History began awarding the Harold T. Clark Medal to those "whose achievements inspire a love and respect for nature." The HAROLD T. CLARK TENNIS COURTS† were named in his honor. Clark married Mary Sanders in 1911. She died in 1936, leaving 6 children: David, Mary, John, William, Annie, and Margaret. In 1940 Clark married Marie Odenkirk. He died in Cleveland and was buried in Lake View Cemetery.

Harold T. Clark Papers, WRHS.

**CLARK, MAURICE B.** (6 Sept. 1827–9 March 1901) was a Cleveland businessman remembered chiefly as the first partner of JOHN D. ROCKEFELLER. Clark was a native of Malmesbury, Eng., who emigrated to America in 1847 and soon made his way to Cleveland via Boston. In 1853 he married another English immigrant, Mary Clement. A job on the OHIO AND ERIE CANAL† led him into the grocery and grain business, and he went to work for the commission house of Otis, Brownell & Co. on River St. In 1859 he and Rockefeller, a former fellow student at FOLSOM'S MERCAN-TILE COLLEGE,† established their own commission business, Clark and Rockefeller. With the sociable Clark handling most of the outside buying and selling, and the industrious Rockefeller in charge of the office and books, the company did $1/2 million of business in its first year. The partners then joined with Clark's brothers, James and Richard, and SAMUEL ANDREWS to enter the oil business in 1863 as Andrews, Clark & Co. Rockefeller and Andrews bought out the Clarks 2 years later, after which Clark and Col. OLIVER H. PAYNE formed the rival works of Clark, Payne & Co. This firm was merged into Rockefeller's STAN-DARD OIL CO.† in 1872. Clark later organized and served as president of the Co-operative Stove Co. An active abolitionist prior to the Civil War, he ran unsuccessfully for mayor in the 1860s and served a term on CLEVELAND CITY COUNCIL† in 1872–73. Following the death of his first wife in 1881, he married Mary Semlow and built a large house in GLENVILLE.† Buried in Lake View Cemetery, he was survived by his second wife and 2 daughters, Mrs. Bell Teagle and Mrs. Emeline Coit.—J.V.

**CLARK, MERWIN** (5 Nov. 1843–30 Nov. 1864), a volunteer soldier and commissioned army officer in the CIVIL WAR,† was born in Cleveland, attended local public schools, and enlisted in the Sprague Zouave Cadets on 22 Apr. 1861, when the war broke out. The Cadets became Co. B, 7th Ohio Volunteer Infantry, serving a 3-month enlistment through 12 Oct. 1861. After campaigning in western Virginia, Clark reenlisted for 3 years on 19 June 1861. He survived the campaigns of 1862–63 in central Virginia and those in Georgia in 1864, to be mustered out with the 7th Regiment in Cleveland on 8 July 1864. He was promoted to captain on 1 Sept. 1862.

In Cleveland, Clark enlisted in the Regular Army as a private. Gov. Brough of Ohio ordered his discharge from the Regular Army and appointed him lieutenant colonel of the 183rd OVI on 12 Nov. 1864. Three weeks later, the 183rd was assigned to the 2nd Div., 3rd Brigade of the 23rd Army Corps (Army of the Ohio) commanded by Maj. Gen. John M. Schofield, near the center of the federal line at the Battle of Franklin, TN, on 30 Nov. 1864. During the battle, Clark was killed while rallying his regiment. He was only 21 and was referred to as "the boy officer." His body was buried in the field but was later removed to Cleveland for burial at Wood-land Cemetery. His bust stands in the SOLDIERS & SAILORS MONUMENT† on PUBLIC SQUARE.†

**CLARKE, JOHN HESSIN** (18 Sept. 1857–22 Mar. 1945), practiced law and rose through Democratic ranks to the U.S. Supreme Court, crusading after retirement for world peace. Born in Lisbon, OH, to John and Melissa (Hessin) Clarke, he attended Western Reserve Univ., earning an A.B. (1877) and A.M. degree (1880). Admitted to the Ohio Bar in 1878, he moved to Youngstown in 1880, after practicing law in Lisbon. In 1882 he became part-owner of the Youngstown *Vindicator*. Through his editorials, he supported civil service reform and workmen's compensation.

In 1898 Clarke moved to Cleveland. He was counsel for the NICKEL PLATE ROAD† (1899–1912), and later for the Pullman Co. Not solely a corporate lawyer, he also fought for a $.02/mi. railroad fare in Ohio. Active in Democratic party politics, Clarke worked for a short ballot in Ohio and, in 1904, at the party's request, ran a hopeless campaign against Sen. MARCUS A. HANNA. Clarke's political ambitions were directed toward the judiciary. Woodrow Wilson appointed him U.S. district judge for the Northern District of Ohio in 1914, and an Associate Justice of the U.S. Supreme Court in 1916. After retiring from the Court in 1922, Clarke became president of the League of Nations Non-Partisan Assn. of the U.S. and a trustee for the World Peace Foundation, believing it was vital for the U.S. to join the League of Nations. In 1942, admitting the peace movement's failure, Clarke hoped America would learn from its failure to join the league.

Never married, Clarke died in San Diego, CA. He was buried in Lisbon, OH.

**CLARKE, MELCHISEDECH CLARENCE** (10 Nov. 1889–9 May 1956), known as M. C. or Mel, founded and developed agencies which enabled AFRICAN AMERICANS† in Cleveland to obtain insurance and loans. He was the first African American member of the Cleveland Chamber of Commerce and served on Cleveland's city planning commission (1946). Born in Lewiston, NC, son of Barbadres (Jesse) Clarke and Elydia (Pew) Clarke, he was educated at Franklin Normal School, Kittrell College (NC), and the Univ. of Cincinnati. An insurance salesman and deputy county clerk in Cincinnati, he came to Cleveland in 1923 as district manager of the Supreme Life and Casualty Co. (later the SUPREME LIFE INSURANCE CO. OF AMER-ICA†). A few years later, he created the Imperial Finance Corp. in Cincinnati. In 1934 Clarke organized the Dunbar Mutual Insurance Society in

Cleveland out of 4 struggling fraternal insurance societies which he had investigated in 1930 as state insurance examiner. Clarke served as president of Dunbar after leaving state office in 1937. He founded the Bardun Mortgage and Investment Co. in 1939. In 1943 Clarke expanded, incorporating the Dunbar Life Insurance Co., opened in April 1945. Thirteen years later, the statewide company had assets of over $7.5 million. After Dunbar merged with Supreme Life Insurance (1960), Clarke became president of that company's Ohio Division. In 1954 he purchased the ailing QUINCY SAVINGS & LOAN† and, as president, quickly developed it into a thriving concern.

Clarke was married on 28 June 1913 to Callie Mack Clarke. Clarke converted to Catholicism in 1924. The Catholic Interracial Council of New York named him Negro Catholic Layman of 1947 and awarded him the James J. Hoey Award for Interracial Justice in 1949. A trustee of Central State College, Wilberforce, OH, Clarke received honorary degrees from that institution as well as from Morris Brown College in Atlanta, GA. He is buried in Calvary Cemetery in Cleveland.—J.M.


**CLAASSEN, EDO NICHOLAUS** (1833–12 July 1932) was a Cleveland pharmacist who published more than 100 articles, most on pharmacological and botanical topics, and assembled an important plant collection. A son of the burgomaster of Hage, Prussia (now Germany), Claassen studied at a Gymnasium and obtained an apprenticeship as a pharmacist. At 24, he began study at the Univ. of Gottingen, where one of his professors was the famous chemist Friedrich Wohler. Claassen emigrated to the U.S. in 1867 and soon afterward moved to Cleveland, where he opened a drugstore on Woodland Ave. in 1868. He married his wife, Juliana, in 1870.

Claassen moved to EAST CLEVELAND† later in life. Over a period of many years, he assembled a large collection of plants, mounted on paper in herbarium style. The majority of his specimens were collected in northern Ohio; many were also collected in Europe. He also assembled a collection of minerals. Claassen published many articles on mosses, liverworts, and lichens, as well as grasses and other types of plants found in northern Ohio. He was survived by only one of his 4 children, Mrs. Julia C. Steinke. He donated his plant collection, consisting of about 10,000 specimens, to Western Reserve Univ. It was later transferred to Holden Arboretum and then, in 1986, to the CLEVELAND MUSEUM OF NATURAL HISTORY.† His collection has great regional importance, as it documents past occurrences of various plants in northern Ohio, some of which no longer are found in the same areas due to changes in the environment.—J.H.

**CLEAVELAND, MOSES** (29 Jan. 1754–16 Nov. 1806), founder of the city of Cleveland, was born in Canterbury, CT, son of Thankful (Paine) and Col. Aaron Cleaveland. In 1777 Cleaveland began service in the Revolutionary War in a Connecticut Continental Regiment, and graduated from Yale. Resigning his commission in 1781, he practiced law in Canterbury, and on 21 Mar. 1794 married Esther Champion; they had four children: Mary Esther, Francis Moses, Frances Augustus, and Julius Moses. As one of 36 founders of the CONNECTICUT LAND CO.† (investing $32,600), and one of 7 directors, in 1796 Cleaveland was sent to survey and map the company's holdings.

When the party arrived at Canandaigua, NY, Cleaveland spoke with representatives of the Six Nations and convinced them their land had already been ceded through Gen. Anthony Wayne's Treaty of Greenville. Although they had not signed the treaty, the Indians relinquished their claim to the land to the CUYAHOGA RIVER.† At the mouth of Conneaut Creek, on 27 June 1796 his party negotiated with the MASSASAGOES† tribe, who challenged their claim to their country. Cleaveland described his agreement with the Six Nations, promised not to disturb their people, and gave them trinkets, wampum, and whiskey in exchange for safety to explore to the Cuyahoga River. Cleaveland arrived at the mouth of the Cuyahoga on 22 July 1796, and believing that the location, where river, lake, low banks, dense forests, and high bluffs provided both protection and shipping access, was the ideal location for the "capital city" of the Connecticut WESTERN RESERVE,† paced out a 10-acre New England-like Public Square. His surveyors plotted a town, naming it Cleaveland. In Oct. 1796, Cleaveland and most of his party returned to Connecticut, where he continued his law practice until his death, never returning to the Western Reserve. A memorial near his grave in Canterbury, CT, erected 16 Nov. 1906, by the Cleveland Chamber of Commerce, reads that Cleaveland was "a lawyer, a soldier, a legislator and a leader of men."

Moses Cleaveland Papers, WRHS.


**CLEMENS, CHARLES EDWIN** (1858–26 Dec. 1933) was an internationally recognized organist who inaugurated the Department of Music at Western Reserve Univ. He was born in Devonport, England, where he was the regular organist of Christ Church by the age of 11. He furthered his musical education at London's Royal College of Music, where Sir Arthur Sullivan singled him out to serve as accompanist for a special performance of the Mikado. Clemens was active in several musical organizations in the Devonport region until a breakdown sent him to Germany in 1889 to recuperate. There he attracted the notice of the Empress Victoria, daughter of England's Queen Victoria, who invited Clemens to become organist at St. George's Royal Chapel. He also taught at the Klindworth-Scharwenka Conservatorium and married a young English widow living in Berlin. In 1895 Clemens came to Cleveland to become organist of ST. PAUL'S EPISCOPAL CHURCH.† He began teaching courses in harmony and music history at WRU's College for Women (later Flora Stone Mather College) in 1899, several years after the lapse of the school's affiliation with the Cleveland Conservatory of Music. Clemens instituted weekly Vesper Services at Harkness Chapel and also, despite the frowns of conservative faculty members, worked Gilbert and Sullivan excerpts into the concerts of the Mather Glee Club. Upon its completion in 1911, he became music director at the CHURCH OF THE COVENANT.† Clemens also served on the faculty of the Cleveland School of Music and as conductor of the SINGERS CLUB.† Awarded the degree of Doctor of Music in 1915, he became professor emeritus at CWRU upon his retirement in 1929. He was survived by his wife, Alice, and 3 stepdaughters.—J.V.


**CLEMENT, KENNETH W.** (24 Feb. 1920–29 Nov. 1974), a physician and civic leader, born in Vashti, Pittsylvania County, VA, to Harry Leonard and Inez Mae Clement, was a leading advisor in the election of Cleveland's first black mayor, Carl B. Stokes. Clement came to Cleveland as a child. He graduated from CENTRAL HIGH SCHOOL† as class president and valedictorian (1938), from Oberlin College (1942), and from Howard Medical School (1945). After internship and residency, and service in the U.S. Air Force, Clement returned to Cleveland. He was asst. clinical professor of surgery at Western Reserve Univ., guest lecturer in intergroup relations in the School of Applied Social Work, and practiced at FOREST CITY HOSPITAL,† MARYMOUNT HOSPITAL,† ST. LUKE'S HOSPITAL,† and Metropolitan General Hospital.

Clement served as the first black layman elected president of the CLEVELAND BAPTIST ASSN.,† as national director of the NAACP and Urban League, and as national president of the Natl. Medical Assn., supporting civil rights and Medicare legislation. Pres. Kennedy appointed him the first black and first physician to the Natl. Social Security Advisory Council in 1963. Pres. Johnson appointed him to the Advisory Committee to the Disability Operation of Social Security, the Agency for International Development, the Presidential Appeals Board of the Natl. Selective Service System, and the Hospital Insurance Benefits Advisory Council, which helped draft the original Medicare regulations. Active in politics, Clement's guidance led Cleveland to become the first major American city to elect a black mayor.

Clement married Ruth Doss on 22 Aug. 1942. They had 4 children: Michael, Craig, Leslie Denise, and Lia Deborah. Clement died in Cleveland and was buried in Highland Park Cemetery.


**CLIFFORD, CARRIE WILLIAMS** (Sept. 1862–10 Nov. 1934), noted orator, poet, and activist for women and AFRICAN AMERICANS† helped found the Ohio State Federation of Colored Women in 1900 and served as its first president while she lived in Cleveland. Clifford was born in Chillicothe, OH, and educated in Columbus. She taught school in Parkersburg, WV, before she married Ohio state legislator WILLIAM H. CLIFFORD in 1886 and moved to Cleveland. The couple had two sons, Joshua and Maurice.

Clifford founded and edited the official publication of the Ohio State Federation of Colored Women, the *Queen's Garden,* and *Sowing for Others to Reap,* a federation-sponsored compilation of essays. She served as editor of the women's department of the *CLEVELAND JOURNAL,†* a black newspaper. Among her publications was an essay entitled *"Cleveland and its Colored People"* (*Colored American,* July 1905). Clifford also recruited African American women for the Niagara movement, a predecessor of the NATIONAL ASSN. FOR THE ADVANCEMENT OF COLORED PEOPLE† (NAACP).

In 1908 the Cliffords moved to Washington, DC. Clifford later published two volumes of poetry, *Race Rhymes* (1911) and *The Widening Light* (1922) and served the local and national NAACP. —J.M.


**CLIFFORD, LOUIS L.** (24 June 1906–25 May 1968), city editor of the *CLEVELAND PRESS†* during the post-World War II hegemony, was born in Wabash, IL, moved to Cleveland, and graduated from CATHEDRAL LATIN HIGH SCHOOL† in 1924. He began working as a police and criminal-courts reporter for the *CLEVELAND NEWS†* under city editor A. E. M. BERGENER. Joining the *Press* in 1928, Clifford earned a reputation as a human-interest writer. After service as asst. city editor, he was named city editor in 1943. Clifford's 25-year tenure at the city desk coincided with the *Press's* domination of Cleveland politics and journalism. He trained and directed the strong local staff, which executed the political campaigns of editor LOUIS B. SELTZER, and pursued the "big" stories of crime and corruption that interested Clifford. Both friendly and rival journalists extolled Clifford as the best city editor. Unlike Seltzer, Clifford maintained a low profile outside of his job. He eschewed the flamboyant theatrics of traditional city editors such as Bergener in favor of a lower-key, but no less authoritative, approach. A resident of Euclid, Clifford married Patricia Sloan and had 3 children: John E., Thos. S., and Mrs. Donna O'Donnel. He served on the Euclid Charter Commission and the Euclid Glenville Hospital board. He died of a heart attack in the *Press* parking lot as he was preparing to leave for a week's vacation.

**CLIFFORD, WILLIAM H.** (8 Apr. 1862–10 Jan. 1929), a black Republican politician, as an Ohio legislator played an important role in electing MARCUS A. HANNA to the U.S. Senate, casting the deciding vote in Hanna's favor in Jan. 1898. A native Clevelander, Clifford worked 7 years for the Woodruff Palace Car Co. before embarking in public service and politics. In 1888 he took a job in the county clerk's office; in Sept. 1888 he became cost clerk, the highest-paid black man in local, county, or state government up to that time. He held various offices in the Republican party, served as asst. sergeant-at-arms at the 1896 and 1900 Republican national conventions, and served in the Ohio House of Representatives twice (1894–95, 1898–99). In 1902 he graduated from Cleveland Law School, and ca. 1908 was appointed to a position in the auditor's office in the War Dept. in Washington, DC, which he held until his death.

Clifford married CARRIE WILLIAMS CLIFFORD in 1886; they had two children, Joshua and Maurice. Clifford was buried in Woodland Cemetery.

**CLINGMAN, ANDREW R.** (1844–14 May 1864), a soldier depicted by LEVI T. SCOFIELD in the infantry sculpture group, The Color Guard, on the SOLDIERS & SAILORS MONUMENT,† enlisted in Co. E, 103rd Ohio Volunteer Infantry, on 8 Aug. 1862 in Cleveland. Clingman (sometimes spelled Klingman), son of Andrew and Maria Clingman, was described as being 5' 7¹/₂" tall, of dark complexion with hazel eyes and brown hair. His place of birth was listed as "Atlantic Ocean," and his occupation as sailmaker. He was one of the color guard killed during an assault at the battle at Resaca, GA, on 14 May 1864. Capt. Scofield, XXIII Army Corps engineers, observed the assault and claimed to have seen Clingman carried off the field in a blanket.

After the war, Scofield depicted Clingman in the Color Guard group as the soldier on the right flank, lying on his back, suffering from a mortal wound. He was one of 2 103rd soldiers depicted by name. (See also MARTIN STREIBLER.)

Board of Monument Commissioners. *Brief Historical Sketch of the Cuyahoga County Soldiers and Sailors Monument* (1965).
Members of the One Hundred and Third Ohio Volunteer Infantry. *Personal Reminiscences and Experiences, Campaign Life in the Union Army, 1862–1865* (1900).

**CLOWSER, JACK** (8 March 1901–19 March 1983), specialized in the coverage of track and intercollegiate football during his journalism career on the 2 Cleveland afternoon dailies. His family brought him from his native Barnet, England, to Philadelphia in 1910 and then to ROCKY RIVER,† where in 1920 he was a member of Rocky River High School's first graduating class. After attending Ohio Wesleyan Univ., Clowser broke into journalism with the *CLEVELAND TIMES,†* followed by 3 years with the *Lakewood Post*. In 1926 he joined the *CLEVELAND NEWS,†* where he became one of the first sports writers to discover Cleveland's track great, JESSE OWENS. Clowser became one of 8 founders of the CLEVELAND NEWSPAPER GUILD† in 1933, serving as its first treasurer. In 1942 he resigned from the *News* to become publicity director for Case School of Applied Science (see CASE WESTERN RESERVE†), but a few months later he became a member of the *CLEVELAND PRESS†* sports staff. His scoops included a prediction in 1945 of the Rose Bowl agreement between the Pacific Coast and Big Ten football conferences. Clowser also helped discover another scholastic track runner, Harrison Dillard of BALDWIN-WALLACE COLLEGE,† whom he followed to London to cover in the 1948 Olympics. A charter member of the Cleveland Touchdown Club, Clowser also served 6 years on the executive board of the Football Writers Assn. Following his retirement from the *Press* in 1966, Clowser wrote for the SUN NEWSPAPERS† and waged a personal letter-writing campaign against U.S. involvement in Vietnam. Married to the former Mabel Neate, he was the father of 2 children.—J.V.

**COACH, RICHARD J.** (22 July 1866–4 July 1922), founded the R. J. Coach Detective Service Co., which was based in Cleveland for 23 years and had offices in 15 major cities in the U.S. Richard was born in Galveston, TX, the son of Jacob and Charlotte Pole Coach, both of whom had come to this country from Austria. He entered the detective business in 1884 and was well established by the time he arrived in Cleveland in 1899. The agency, which was located in the Coach Building at 1301–05 Prospect Ave., was incorporated in 1904, specializing in service to corporations. Agency advertisements made it clear that no divorce cases would be accepted. The firm also had offices in New York, Cincinnati, Chicago, Pittsburgh, Kansas City, and Denver, among others. In the early 1920s, Coach, who resided in Cleveland, consolidated his company with the Keystone Secret Service Bureau, and William Bidlingmyer became principal and general manager of both companies.

Coach, who was married, died in Cleveland and was buried at Woodland Cemetery.—M.S.

## COAKLEY, JOHN ALOYSIUS (22 Sept. 1881–18 May 1950), manufacturer, was both an authority on industrial transportation and a philanthropist. For his contributions as a Catholic layperson, he was made Master Knight of the Sovereign Military Order of Malta. Coakley was born in Pittsburgh to Thomas F. and Agnes (Quinn) Coakley (originally from Vermont). Educated in parochial grammar school, he began working at age 11 as an office boy for the Pennsylvania Railroad in Pittsburgh. After several promotions, Coakley moved to Cleveland in 1904 as Division Freight Agent for American Steel & Wire. He attended night school and graduated from BALDWIN-WALLACE COLLEGE† with an A.B. (1908) and from Cleveland Law School with an LL.B. (1912). He passed the bar that year, although he never practiced law. Coakley became vice-president in charge of traffic for American Steel & Wire in 1927; in 1932 he became General Traffic Manager for Operations of U.S. Steel. In 1937 Coakley resigned to become president and chair of the "Automatic" Sprinkler Corp. of America (later FIGGIE INTERNATIONAL, INC.†), which he helped create, along with George A. Neracher. With offices in the Perry-Payne Building in Cleveland, he also supervised the company's Youngstown, OH, plant.

A Republican, Coakley chaired the boards of directors of the Marjon Co. of Delaware and the Cleveland Stevedore Co. of Ohio, and served on the boards of New Castle Refractories (PA), the Swindell Dressler Corp. (PA), the Midland Bank, and other companies, some of which he founded. He was a trustee of the CATHOLIC CHARITIES CORP.† (which he helped organize) and a member of the boards of Associated Charities and St. Ann's Hospital (see SAINT ANN FOUNDATION†), among others. Georgetown Univ. awarded him an honorary doctorate posthumously in 1950.

On 23 Jan 1912, in Cleveland, Coakley married Marie Louise Beckman. They lived on Berkshire Rd. in CLEVELAND HTS.† and maintained a country home in Huron, OH. The couple had 11 children: John A., Jr.; Mary V. (Mrs. Tomas E.) Morton; Agnes R. (Mrs. John J.) Power; Ann (Mrs. Edward) Egan; Henry B.; Sister Margaret Mary; 2 sons named Thomas F. (one deceased); William D.; Ellen T. (Mrs. Michael) O'Neil; and Joseph C. In his son's memory, Coakley established the Henry Beckman Coakley Foundation for education.—J.M.

Coakley, Thomas. Letters of John A. Coakley to his Family and Friends (1957), WRHS.

## COATES, WILLIAM R. (14 Nov. 1851–20 Feb. 1935), teacher and author, was a leader in the local Republican party (see CUYAHOGA COUNTY REPUBLICAN PARTY†). He wrote such local history titles as *The Brecksville Centennial, 1811–1911* (1911) and the 3-volume *A History of Cuyahoga County and the City of Cleveland* (1924) (see HISTORIES OF CLEVELAND†). The son of Lucy (Weld) and Col. John Coates III, he was born in North Royalton in a log cabin built by his great-grandfather, John Coates, a pioneer settler of Cleveland. He attended public schools in Brecksville, where his family had moved soon after his birth. Coates then attended Oberlin College, taught school in Brecksville and Independence for 12 years, and managed a farm. Interested in politics, he was deputy clerk (1884) for Cuyahoga County, then County Clerk (1889) (see CUYAHOGA COUNTY GOVERNMENT†). As mayor of Brooklyn Village, he helped to annex the village to Cleveland in 1890 and 1894. Coates served in the 67th Ohio General Assembly, was a director of the Cleveland Chamber of Industry (1918) and presided over both the Brecksville and the Brooklyn Village school boards, and the Cuyahoga County Teachers Institute. Coates belonged to the EARLY SETTLERS' ASSN. OF THE WESTERN RESERVE† (secretary and president) and the Republican Tippecanoe Club of Cleveland. He authored the history of the club. Coates contributed numerous historical articles to newspapers and magazines.

Coates married Celestia Stacy White (d. 1934) on 22 Feb. 1872; they had 3 children: Mary, Mildred, and Herbert.

## COBBLEDICK, GORDON (31 Dec. 1898–2 Oct. 1969), sports writer for the *PLAIN DEALER,†* was born in Cleveland and studied mining engineering at Case School of Applied Science before joining the *Plain Dealer* in 1923, covering the police beat and city hall. He worked for the *CLEVELAND TIMES†* in 1926, but shortly returned to the *Plain Dealer,* succeeding Henry P. Edwards as the baseball writer. His coverage of the CLEVELAND INDIANS† throughout the 1930s culminated in exposure of the

"players' rebellion" in 1940 against manager Oscar Vitt. As a war correspondent in the Pacific Theater during World War II, Cobbledick's V-E Day dispatch from Okinawa, contrasting the news from Europe with the costly campaign still continuing against Japan, was widely reprinted and eventually canonized in Richard Morris and Louis Snyder's *A Treasury of Great Reporting.*

Although Cobbledick was rewarded with a general column upon returning to the *Plain Dealer,* he was called back to athletics in 1946 upon the death of sports editor Sam D. Otis. "Cobby" edited the sports section, and his "Plain Dealing" column was a popular feature, despite (or because of) such whimsical conceits as his insistence that golf was not a "sport" but merely a "game." Retiring in 1964, Cobbledick conducted a sports program on WEWS-TV† for a time and authored a 1966 biography of Indians slugger Rocky Colavito, entitled *Don't Knock the Rock.* He married Doris V. Mathews and had 2 sons, William and Raymond. He died shortly after moving to Tucson, AZ, in 1969.


**COFALL, STANLEY B.** (5 May 1894–21 Sept. 1961), outstanding football player and manager, was born in Cleveland, the son of Fred and Ida Bingham Cofall. He played football at EAST TECHNICAL HIGH SCHOOL† in 1910, then moved to East High School, where he became all-scholastic in football and hockey. Cofall attended Notre Dame, where he played halfback, and was named to several All-America teams in 1916. After graduation he played and coached the Massillon Tigers professional football team in 1917, and served in World War I 1918–19. Cofall organized the Cleveland Indians football team in 1919, and the following year he and owner JAMES O'DONNELL attended the Canton, Ohio, meeting where the American Professional Football Assn. (forerunner of the National Football league) was organized, with Cofall as league vice-president. Later, Cofall coached various professional and college teams, returning to Cleveland in the early 1930s. He founded Stanco Oil Co. in 1935, which merged with the National Solvent Corp., manufacturer of greases and oils, in 1937, with Cofall as president-treasurer. Active in the Cleveland sports scene, he helped bring the Notre Dame-Navy football game to Cleveland in 1942, was a founder of the Cleveland Touchdown Club, and served as chairman of the Cleveland Boxing Commission.

Cofall was married to Irene Held, and they had three children: Jack, Stanley Jr., and Mrs. Blossom Cummings. After their divorce in 1953, he and his second wife, Louise, moved to Peninsula, OH.

Cofall died at home and was buried at Union Cemetery in Peninsula.—M.S.

**COHEN, GUSTAVE M.** (26 Mar. 1820–13 Dec. 1902), leader at ANSHE CHESED CONGREGATION† from 1861–73, was probably the first musically trained cantor in America. Born in Walsdorf, Meinengen, Germany, Cohen was educated in music, pedagogy, Hebrew, and German at Heidelberghausen in Meinengen. He emigrated to America in 1844, becoming chazan at Temple Emanu-El in New York City, organizing the first choir and introducing organ music to the service. In 1856 he moved to Chicago, then to Cincinnati before coming to Anshe Chesed in 1861. Although he promised not to introduce any reforms at the still-Orthodox congregation, he opened the 1863 Rosh Hashanah service with a German song and used an organ and choir.

Late in 1865, 30 members of Anshe Chesed petitioned Congregation Tifereth Israel for membership, provided that Cohen be hired as cantor. The congregation refused. The following year, 34 members of Anshe Chesed again petitioned Tifereth Israel for membership under the same conditions. The congregation agreed, and Cohen accepted the Tifereth Israel offer until his release in 1867, when Tifereth Israel hired an ordained rabbi. Cohen returned to Anshe Chesed until 1873, when Rabbi Michael Machol was hired.

Cohen composed and published collections of musical works. He was active in Jewish communal organizations, and in 1861 founded the ZION MUSICAL SOCIETY,† probably the first Jewish musical society in America. After leaving Anshe Chesed, Cohen worked as a grocer, bailiff, music teacher, and insurance agent. He lived his last decade at the MONTEFIORE HOME.†

Cohen married his wife, Caroline, before he settled in Cleveland. They had 6 children: Dora, Celina, Viola, Hattie, George, and Harriet. He was buried in the Willet Street Cemetery.

**COLE, ALLEN E.** (1 Sept. 1883–6 Feb. 1970), a professional photographer in Cleveland's black community, generated over 27,000 negatives during his life, a collection acquired by the WESTERN RESERVE HISTORICAL SOCIETY† and selectively published in a book entitled *Somebody, Somewhere, Wants Your Photograph* (1980), which was Cole's business motto. Son of Allen and Sara Cole, he was born in Kearneysville, WV. Cole graduated from Storer College and worked as a waiter in Atlantic City and a railroad porter and cook in Cincinnati until he was injured in a train accident. He moved to Cleveland, worked as a waiter at the CLEVELAND ATHLETIC CLUB,† and eventually became head waiter there for over 10 years.

At the Athletic Club, Cole met Joseph Opet, manager of Frank Moore Studios, who introduced him to photography. He assisted at Opet's studios for 6 years, then decided to live as a photographer, opening a studio in his home in 1922. When individual orders declined in the Great Depression, Cole did commercial work and commission work for 8 white studios. Cole contributed photographs to the *CLEVELAND CALL & POST,†* and his work earned prizes at state and local exhibitions. Cole also was a founder and treasurer of the Progressive Business League, an officer of the Dunbar Life Insurance Co., a member of ST. JAMES AME CHURCH,† and was active in the Elks and MASONS.† For years he was the only black member of the Cleveland Society of Professional Photographers. His wife, Frances T. Cole (1 Jan. 1889–29 Apr. 1979) was his assistant and business manager. Cole was buried in Highland Park Cemetery.

*Somebody, Somewhere, Wants Your Photograph* (1980), WRHS.
Allen E. Cole Papers, WRHS.

**COLKET, MEREDITH BRIGHT JR.** (18 Aug. 1912–19 May 1985), archivist and genealogist, was born in Strafford, Chester County, PA, son of Meredith Bright and Alberta (Kelsey) Colket. He earned his B.A. (1935) and M.A. (1940) in history at Haverford College, and received an honorary Litt.D. from BALDWIN-WALLACE COLLEGE† in 1974. Colket joined the Natl. Archives in Washington, DC, in 1937 as staff specialist, becoming genealogy and local-history specialist in 1950. He co-compiled *A Guide to the Genealogical Records in the National Archives* (1964), the first comprehensive finding aid of that institution. In 1957 Colket assumed the directorship of the WESTERN RESERVE HISTORICAL SOCIETY,† becoming director emeritus upon his retirement in 1980.

Colket believed citizens could understand their American heritage through studying their family history. He published genealogical accounts of Anne Hutchinson and Katherine Marbury Scott (1936), the Fairbrothers (1939), Pelhams (1940–43), Jenkses (1956), Pelots (1980), and Chisholms (1984). His *Creating a Worthwhile Family Genealogy* (1968) is still a model for those publishing a family history. Colket also published *Founders of Early American Families, Emigrants from Europe, 1607–1657* (1975, rev. ed. 1985). During Colket's tenure, the WRHS expanded its main plant on East Blvd. and acquired outlying properties, including the Jonathan Hale farm in Bath, OH. The library became one of the foremost local history and genealogy research centers in America. Colket was a founder (1940) of the Assn. for State & Local

History and founder and first director (1950–60) of the Natl. Institute for Genealogical Research. In 1992 Colket was inducted into the National Genealogical Hall of Fame.

Colket married Julia Beatrice Pelot in 1945. They had three sons: William Currie, Meredith Bright III, and John Pelot. He was buried in Laurel Hill Cemetery, Philadelphia, PA.

**COLLINS, JAMES WALTER** (16 Sept. 1889–16 Aug. 1971), filled what he regarded as the most important job in metropolitan journalism for 33 years, as city editor for the Cleveland *PLAIN DEALER.†* Born in Portland, ME, he was the son of James and Olive Fogelin Collins. While still in high school, he began writing for the *Brockton* (MA) *Times*. In 1911 he became a sports writer, and later telegraph editor, for the *Providence Journal* in R.I. He was hired to direct the *Plain Dealer's* copy desk by ERIE C. HOPWOOD in 1919 and became day city editor 2 years later. In 1921 he married Lora Montgomery, a former *Plain Dealer* secretary and Kentucky school teacher. His tenure as city editor began in 1929, during which time he violated all stereotypes of the position by never yelling or even swearing. Nevertheless, he headed a news team which won an award from the CLEVELAND NEWSPAPER GUILD† for its coverage of the SHEPPARD MURDER CASE.† He also shared a Sigma Delta Chi National Public Service Award for exposing a gypsy-chasing racket by the Teamsters Union. In retirement, Collins worked for the reelection of Ohio governor Michael DiSalle and headed a Cuyahoga County Grand Jury in 1965. Predeceased by his wife and a daughter, Ruth, he was survived by another daughter, Virginia, and a son, Philip. He was buried in Lakewood Park Cemetery and inducted posthumously into the CLEVELAND JOURNALISM HALL OF FAME.†—J.V.

**COLMAN, CHARLES CECIL** (23 July 1890–13 July 1978), born Colman Schwarzenberg, left many landmarks in his native Cleveland as a practicing architect for 4 decades. The son of Ephraim A. Schwarzenberg and Mollie Colman, he graduated from CENTRAL HIGH SCHOOL† and studied architecture at Cornell Univ. and the Cleveland School of Art (see CLEVELAND INSTITUTE OF ART†). Following U.S. Army service during World War I, he married Fanny Freedman in 1921. As a member of the local firm of WALKER AND WEEKS† in the 1920s, he designed the East Cleveland Public Library. His residential designs were well represented in the suburban developments of CLEVELAND HTS.† and SHAKER HTS.,† and his plans for the Neal Storage Co. on Detroit Ave. and the TELLING-BELL VERNON CO.† on Carnegie earned Colman awards from the CLEVELAND CHAMBER OF COMMERCE.† From 1935–43 he was the chief architectural supervisor for the Federal Housing Administration in northern Ohio. After World War II, his plans for drive-in theaters, represented locally by the Euclid Ave. Drive-In in Wickliffe, gained him an appointment as consultant in designing similar theaters for the Belgian govt. He also served as supervising architect under Eric Mendelsohn for PARK SYNAGOGUE.† Colman retired from private practice in the 1960s. An avid stamp collector, he was also active in Cornell Univ. alumni affairs. He was survived by his wife, daughter Kip Bachman, and son John C.—J.V.

Charles C. Colman Oral History (1972), WRHS.
Colman Family Papers, WRHS.

**COMBES, WILLARD WETMORE** (23 Dec. 1901–17 Jan. 1984), balanced dual careers as a teacher at the Cleveland School of Art (see CLEVELAND INSTITUTE OF ART†) and editorial cartoonist for the *CLEVELAND PRESS.†* A lifelong Clevelander, he had already won an art contest in the *Press* for his caricature of JOHN D. ROCKEFELLER before his graduation from Glenville High. Upon graduation from the Cleveland School of Art in 1924, he completed a European tour before joining the CSA faculty and becoming head of the Department of Illustration. He remained on that faculty for 22 years, during which time he also taught 10 years (1926–36) at the Western Reserve Univ. School of Architecture (see CASE WESTERN RESERVE†). When none of his students was able to satisfy the requirements of the *Cleveland Press* for a new cartoonist in 1934, Combes himself took the job at the urging of the "dean" of Cleveland artists, HENRY KELLER. Combes specialized in local and state issues during his 28 years as *Press* cartoonist, since the Scripps-Howard chain generally supplied the paper with national cartoons. He won a Pulitzer Prize honorable mention in 1938 for a cartoon on a cemetery lot racket. Also known as a portraitist, Combes served 2 terms as president of the CLEVELAND SOCIETY OF ARTISTS.† He executed murals for such local institutions as Lutheran High School East and St. Luke's Church in LAKEWOOD,† and in 1953 started his own stained glass business. Married twice, to Vivian C. Kepler, and Mary Jean McCready Bissett, he was survived by 4 children.—J.V.

Feingold, Rachel G. (ed.). *Provocative Pens: Four Cleveland Cartoonists, 1900–1975* (1992).

**COMODECA, CHARLOTTE** (1 Aug. 1940–11 Feb. 1993), achieved a distinguished record as a volunteer who collected and distributed aid to various Native American groups, Indian Reservations and the inner city needy.

Born outside Birmingham, AL, to Albert and Ores Hancock, Charlotte received her Native American heritage through both parents, counting Cherokee and Seneca Indians among her ancestors. She was 16 when her family settled in Cleveland, where she graduated from West Technical High School. Charlotte married James Comodeca on 1 Aug. 1959.

Comodeca began her career as a volunteer by meeting the needs of local Native Americans (see AMERICAN INDIANS†). She expanded her efforts into a year-long drive, helping needy Native Americans locally and nationally. She organized annual mitten drives with various school groups, mailing boxes of donated mittens and coats to the Rosebud Reservation in the Dakotas. Comodeca also obtained enough dental equipment from a retiring dentist to start a clinic at Rosebud.

Comodeca helped start a pre-school program at St. Anthony of Padua Catholic Church, Parma, and served as an administrator. She also opened her home to international students attending BALDWIN-WALLACE COLLEGE† who were unable to return home for the Thanksgiving and Christmas holidays.

The Comodecas had four children: Theresa (Schmalz), Lisa (Nickle), James, and Christopher. A Roman Catholic, Charlotte Comodeca is buried in Holy Cross Cemetery. After her death the Lake Erie Native American Council (LENAC) held a Pow Wow in which she was honored, the first time a non-full-blood Indian had been recognized.—T.B.

**CONNERS, WILLIAM RANDALL** (4 Oct. 1878–22 Jan. 1942) was founder and first executive secretary of the Negro Welfare Assn. (URBAN LEAGUE OF CLEVELAND†) who gained national attention for his efforts to improve conditions for AFRICAN AMERICANS.†

Conners was born in Augusta, GA. He graduated from Biddle College (Johnson C. Smith Univ.) Charlotte, NC, in 1897 and received his M.A. in 1903. He received his Ph.D. from the Univ. of Pennsylvania.

Conners taught at Livingston College in Salisbury, NC, and was later principal of the Gay St. Training School in Westchester, PA.

Coming to Cleveland in 1917 Conners became executive secretary of the Negro Welfare Assn., founded with the purpose of ending employment discrimination against blacks. He held the position until his retirement in 1940.

During his early years with the Negro Welfare Assn., Conners focused on convincing Cleveland industries to accept black labor in their factories and mills. He established an employment agency at the Assn.'s headquarters on East 40th St.

During the 1930s, Conners, who was a longtime housing advocate, changed the Assn.'s primary goal from employment to improved housing conditions. The Assn.'s programs would center around better housing, improved sanitation, domestic relations counseling and promoting racial understanding to end employment and housing barriers.

Long active in civic work Conners founded and served as secretary (until 1936) of the Lower Woodland Community Council, which included civic, religious, and educational leaders of the district.

Conners married Nathalie Mikell. They had two daughters, Lauretta and Nellie. Conners was Presbyterian and is buried in Lake View Cemetery.—T.B.

The Urban League of Cleveland Records, WRHS.

**COOLEY, HARRIS REID** (18 Oct. 1857–24 Oct. 1936), minister and reform leader, was born to Laura Reid and LATHROP COOLEY in Royalton, OH, graduated with a B.A. from Hiram College in 1877, and with an M.A. from Oberlin College in 1880. Following postgraduate work at Oberlin, he served 1-year pastorates in DISCIPLES OF CHRIST† churches in Brunswick and Aurora, OH. In 1882 Cooley became pastor of Cedar Ave. Christian Church in Cleveland, retaining that position for 21 years. Among his large congregation was TOM L. JOHNSON, who became a close friend, especially when Johnson became ill with typhoid fever. They shared ideals in politics and reform, with Cooley being almost alone among the city's Protestant clergy supporting Johnson's radical democracy. When Johnson was elected mayor in 1901, he appointed Cooley director of charities and correction, which he held for 10 years. Cooley created the farm colony on 2,000 acres in WARRENSVILLE TWP.,† purchased in 1902 for $350,000, which housed the CLEVELAND WORKHOUSE,† the county poorhouse, and a tuberculosis sanatorium. "Cooley Farms" was considered an outstanding example of progressive penology and health care. In 1903 Cooley supervised the opening of the City Farm School, popularly known as the CLEVELAND BOYS' SCHOOL,† in Hudson, OH, which provided a rehabilitative setting where orphaned or incorrigible boys under 14 could be guided by a professional staff. Cooley also served on the City Plan Commission (1915–34). In 1900 Cooley married Cora Clark, a Hiram College professor and suffragist; they had no children. He died in Cleveland and was buried in Woodland Cemetery.

**COOLEY, LATHROP** (25 Oct. 1821–2 Jan. 1910), a DISCIPLES OF CHRIST minister, was born in Genesee County, NY, to a family that moved to Portage and then Lorain County, OH. He attended Brooklyn Academy and finished studying in Bethany, WV. Although he taught school, Cooley began preaching in 1843 at N. Eaton in Lorain County and, except for one year in Chicago, he was an active minister for 60 years in the WESTERN RESERVE.† Cooley, interested in business, made sound real estate investments, was a director of the Citizens Savings & Trust Co., and was involved in other Cleveland businesses. His interest in education led to a 30-year tenure as benefactor and trustee of Hiram College. Cooley eloquently supported ventures he considered important for Cleveland's public good. He preached in the workhouse, the city jail, and the Aged Women's Home. In 1880 he was appointed superintendent and chaplain of the Cleveland Bethel Union, a reorganized seamen's mission that eventually sheltered women, offered an outdoor work-relief program, and conducted missionary services. In 1877 Cooley founded the Disciples Mission, which in 1883 became the Cedar Ave. Church of Christ, attended by TOM L. JOHNSON. His business investments led a legacy establishing what became HURON RD. HOSPITAL.† Cooley was responsible for financing a chain of Disciples of Christ missions around the world. He was twice married; his first wife, Laura Reid, whom he married in 1848, died in 1893. They had five children, including Almon B. and HARRIS REID COOLEY. In 1895 he married Letta E. Searles.

**COON, JOHN** (28 July 1822–24 Sept. 1908) was an attorney, businessman, city official, newspaper publisher, and a leading politician in the local Whig and early Republican parties.

Born in Ballston Spa, NY, to Mathew and Albacinda (Lyon), Coon's family moved to Cleveland in 1832. He served as an apprentice to Cleveland jeweler, N. E. Crittenden, and graduated from Yale Univ. in 1847. Returning to Cleveland, Coon was elected city clerk in 1847. He studied law with the firm of Andrews & Foot and was admitted to the Ohio Bar in 1848.

Coon worked as a clerk for Secretary of the Interior Thomas Ewing, from 1848–50. As superintendent, he oversaw the opening of the U.S. Marine Hospital, Cleveland, in 1852. In 1853 Coon became joint owner and publisher of the *Cleveland Herald*. He served as city solicitor from 1855–57.

Coon interrupted his law practice to become Paymaster, Army of the Cumberland, during the Civil War. In 1868 Coon was an incorporator of the Cleveland Railway Motor Co. In 1874 he was president of the Broadway & Newburgh St. Railroad Co.

Coon was a leading figure in local politics, first in the Whig party, and later the Republican party, serving as a delegate to the county convention in 1855, and chairing the Republican county executive committee in 1860.

Coon was an original member of THE ARK† and a trustee of the Cleveland Library Assn.

Coon married Martha Ann Elisabeth Howe of Worcester, MA. They had two sons, George and John, Jr. Coon died in Lyons, MI, and is buried in Highland Park Cemetery.—T.B.

**CORBUSIER, JOHN WILLIAM CRESWELL** (31 Oct. 1878–8 June 1928), a national authority on church architecture who helped design the CHURCH OF THE COVENANT† in UNIV. CIRCLE† and the CHURCH OF THE SAVIOUR† in CLEVELAND HTS.,† was born to Francis H. and Mary Nagle Corbusier of Rochester, NY. Educated in Rochester and in Paris at L'Ecole des Beaux Arts, he moved to Cleveland in 1905 and practiced architecture under his own name, as well as in a partnership called Corbusier, Lenski & Foster. Corbusier was the architect for at least 30 churches throughout the U.S. Two examples of his work extant in Cleveland in 1995 are the Church of the Saviour (1928) at 2537 Lee Rd. in Cleveland Hts., and the Church of the Covenant (1911) at 11205 Euclid Ave., a design in which he was associated with the national architectural firm of Cram, Goodhue & Ferguson. Corbusier, Lenski & Foster were the architects for the home of SALMON P. HALLE, a prominent Cleveland department store owner who built a grand French provincial villa on Park Rd. in SHAKER HTS.† A resident of Hudson from 1913–28, Corbusier was an elder at the First Congregational Church of Hudson, a former director of the choir at the Church of the Covenant, and a member of the Chamber of Commerce and the Cleveland Athletic, Kiwanis, and Hudson clubs. He married Katherine Lyman (1881–1932) in 1905. Both are buried in Hudson, OH. They had four children: Henry L., Margaret, John W. C., and Philip Giles.

**CORCORAN, CHARLES LESLIE** (8 Sept. 1878–22 Dec. 1958) was a banker, businessman, prominent Catholic layman and original board and founding member of the CATHOLIC CHARITIES CORP.,† where he served as president.

Charles was born in Cleveland to Hugh and Mary (Manning). He graduated from (Cleveland) CENTRAL HIGH SCHOOL and attended St. Ignatius College, but did not graduate. Corcoran joined Central National Bank in 1899 and worked his way up to senior vice-president in the banking division.

He remained with Central National until his retirement in 1947.

When Catholic Charities was incorporated in 1919, Corcoran was named as a member of the original Board of Trustees. Already a prominent businessman, Corcoran was one of several Catholic laymen recruited to help the financially troubled diocese. He served as its first secretary until 1927, became the organization's first vice-president in 1930, and served as president in 1931. Corcoran continued to remain active on the advisory board of Catholic Charities until his death.

Corcoran's involvement with numerous Catholic agencies and his lifelong work for the church won him appointment by Pope Pius XII as a Knight of St. Gregory the Great. He was a member of the Assn. of Reserve City Bankers, a director of the Dobeckmum Co., Cleveland, and served on the Community Fund's hospital budget committee.

Corcoran married Anne O'Rourke on 6 Sept. 1905. They had four children: Mary, Elizabeth, Margaret, and G. Robert. Corcoran is buried in Calvary Cemetery.—T.B.

**CORCORAN, MICHAEL** (1848–3 Oct. 1919), Congressional Medal of Honor recipient for service rendered during the Indian wars, was born in Philadelphia, PA. Corporal Corcoran, a member of the 8th U.S. Cavalry operating out of Camp Whipple, AZ, was among those who engaged a band of Indians between the Aqua Fria and Rio Verde rivers on 25 Aug. 1869. He received the Medal of Honor 3 March 1870, for "gallantry in action" during the skirmish.

After military service, Corcoran resided in Johnstown, PA, moving to Cleveland after the 1889 flood. Residing in the city, he earned a living as a railroad worker while raising a family. Corcoran died in Cleveland and was buried at Calvary Cemetery. —M.S.

**CORLETT, SELENE** (13 Oct. 1864–8 Feb.1943) was a milliner and dressmaker who organized a training school which prepared 260 women to work in hospitals, factories, at the AMERICAN RED CROSS, CLEVELAND CHAPTER,† and on streetcars during World War I. A suffragist who picketed the White House and Capitol in 1916, she volunteered and raised funds for many other local efforts to improve the status of women. Corlett was born in England to Thomas and Caroline Griffiths James. The family came to America while Corlett was young; she attended the CLEVELAND PUBLIC SCHOOLS† and studied law at the Pittsburgh College for Girls.

On 4 March 1884, Corlett married city engineer

Walter H. Corlett; the couple lived in SHAKER HTS.† with daughter Blanche (d. 9 Feb. 1943). Corlett was president of the board of the Women's Civic Assn. and chaired the Welfare Federation committee which improved conditions at the police station for women witnesses. She claimed to have been the first in Cleveland to suggest hiring women officers at the CLEVELAND POLICE DEPARTMENT† (see WOMEN'S BUREAU OF THE CLEVELAND POLICE DEPARTMENT†). An activist, she urged the adoption of codes of sanitation in the suburbs. Corlett presided over the local branch of the National Woman's Party, served on the Shaker Hts. school board, and belonged to the Welsh Women's Assn., the WOMEN'S CITY CLUB OF CLEVELAND,† the Republican Women's Club of Ohio, and the Susan B. Anthony Club. Corlett is buried in Highland Park Cemetery in Cleveland. —J.M.

**CORLETT, WILLIAM THOMAS** (15 Apr. 1854–11 June 1948), a physician and dermatologist who introduced new methods to treat skin and venereal diseases, and researched the effect of climate, particularly cold, on skin diseases, was born in Orange, OH, to William and Ann (Avery) Corlett. He attended Oberlin College from 1870–73, and graduated with an M.D. from Wooster Univ. Medical College (College of Wooster) in 1877. After teaching 2 years at Wooster, Corlett studied skin diseases in London and Paris, qualifying as a fellow in the London Royal College of Physicians. Returning to Cleveland, in 1882 Corlett was appointed lecturer, then, in 1884, professor on skin and genito-urinary diseases at Wooster. He resigned to take a lectureship in the same branch at Western Reserve Univ. Medical School. He was appointed professor of dermatology in 1887. Returning to Europe in 1889, Corlett visited medical centers in Vienna, Berlin, London, and Paris. In 1890 his title at WRU was changed to professor of dermatology and syphilology, a chair he held until 1914, when he was appointed senior professor. In 1924 he became professor emeritus. Corlett was on staff at Charity, ST. ALEXIS,† Lakeside, and City (Metropolitan General) hospitals. He brought the first x-ray machine to the area from Vienna. As a member of the Board of Health in 1893, Corlett fought for better lighting and ventilation in public schools, as well as instituting health board visits to the schools.

Corlett married Amanda Marie Leisy at Rheinpflatz, Germany, on 28 June 1895. They had five children: Christine (Mrs. Horace F. Henriques), Ann (Mrs. Daniel B. Forn), Helen, Thomas, and Edward. Corlett died in Cleveland and is buried in Riverside Cemetery.

**CORRIGAN, JAMES W. JR.** (7 Apr. 1880–23 Jan. 1928), who inherited the Corrigan-McKinney Steel fortune, was born in Grybow, Polish Austria, the son of Capt. James C. and Ida Allen Corrigan. He was educated at the Michigan Military Academy at Orchard Lake, MI, and Case School of Applied Science. Corrigan's father, with STEVENSON BURKE, founded the Corrigan-Ives Steel company in the early 1890s. Price McKinney became a partner in 1894. Young James left for the west after his mother and 3 sisters drowned, 7 July 1900, when their yacht capsized during a storm. He attended Falkenou's School of Assaying & Mill Tests in San Francisco, worked for a telegraph office in Goldfield, NV, and later supervised Corrigan-McKinney properties in Mexico. When his father died in 1908, James received $15,000 in cash and 40% of the Corrigan McKinney stock, to be held in trust until he reached age 40. McKinney, who was trustee of James's stock, received a 30% stock interest of his own, giving him majority ownership of the company. Hostilities between James and Price McKinney surfaced in 1917 when McKinney dropped the name Corrigan from the firm. Corrigan ousted him as a trustee and took control of his interest but did not try to take over the company. He had married Laura Mae MacMartin 2 Dec. 1916 in New York and opted instead to support her efforts to break into society (see LAURA MAE CORRIGAN). After buying another 13% of the McKinney Steel Co. stock, he returned to Cleveland from abroad in May 1925, and with his 53% majority, took over the presidency from McKinney. In charge of the renamed Corrigan-McKinney Steel, he ran the company until his untimely death. He is buried in Lake View Cemetery.—M.S.

**CORRIGAN, LAURA MAE** (2 Jan. 1879–22 Jan. 1948), an international socialite, was born in Wisconsin, the daughter of Charles and Emma Whitlock. She married, then divorced, physician Duncan R. MacMartin in Chicago. In 1917 she married JAMES W. CORRIGAN, son of a founder of the Corrigan-McKinney Steel Co. Possibly because of her divorce, Laura was never really accepted into Cleveland society, so the Corrigans spent their time in Europe. Corrigan's lavish parties were covered in society columns in both Europe and the U.S., as her guests included the Prince of Wales and the Duchess of York. In 1925 Jas. Corrigan returned to Cleveland and took control of Corrigan-McKinney Steel, although Laura, except for visits, remained in Europe. James died in 1928.

After James died, Corrigan resided in Europe. In Paris when World War II broke out, she escaped to England via Portugal. During the war she worked for French soldiers and refugees, organizing the aid group of French women known as La Bien Venue. Corrigan also helped U.S. citizens financially stranded in Europe. In Buckinghamshire, England, she ran the popular officers' Wings Club. Before the war, Corrigan received an annual income of $800,000. During the war, the U.S. State Dept. allowed her only $500/month, so she sold her jewelry, tapestries, and furniture to finance her activities. After the war, she received the Croix de Guerre, Legion of Honor, and Croix de Combattant from the French government, and the King's Medal from the British government. Corrigan had no children by either marriage and was buried in Lake View Cemetery.

**COVELESKI, STANLEY ANTHONY "STAN"** (13 July 1889–20 Mar. 1984) was a major league baseball pitcher for the CLEVELAND INDIANS† between 1916–24, his 3 victories in the 1920 World Series helping the team win its first world championship. Born in Shamokin, PA, to Anthony and Antoinette Coveleski, he worked in the coal mines at age 12. He was one of 5 brothers who played baseball; his older brother, Harry, was a pitcher for Philadelphia and Detroit. In 1908 Coveleski signed to pitch for Lancaster, but he did not make the major leagues as a regular pitcher until 1916. Coveleski's best pitch was a spitball, which he could make break down or up. From 1917–21 he won 20 or more games a season, with 24 victories in the 1920 championship season his best mark. His 3 wins in the World Series were each 5-hit complete games. Traded to Washington in 1925, Coveleski won 20 games for the Senators and pitched in another World Series. He ended his major league career in 1928 after pitching for the Yankees. Coveleski won 215 and lost 141 games during his 14-year career and posted a low 2.88 ERA. He was elected to the Baseball Hall of Fame at Cooperstown, NY, in 1969. Following his baseball career, Coveleski owned and operated a gas station in South Bend, IN.

Coveleski married Frances Chivetts in Jan. 1922; they had 2 children: Jack and William. He died in South Bend, IN, and was buried in the St. Joseph Cemetery there.

**COVERT, JOHN CUTLER** (11 Feb. 1837–14 Jan. 1919) answered to the callings of journalist, politician, diplomat, and civic leader during a lifetime of 8 decades. He was born in Norwick, NY, and brought in his youth to Cleveland, where he learned the printing trade in the job office of TIMOTHY SNEAD and EDWIN COWLES. His education was supplemented by a residence of 7 years in Europe, where he traveled and learned several languages. He returned to Cleveland and in 1868 became a reporter for Cowles's CLEVELAND LEADER,† where he advanced through the positions of editorial writer, associate editor, and managing editor, succeeding to the editorship upon the death of Cowles in 1890. Covert also served 2 terms in the Ohio House of Representatives, and during the national election of 1896 published a volume entitled The A.B.C. of Finances. Pres. Wm. McKinley appointed him U.S. consul at Marsailles in 1897, which took him to France for the following 12 years. Transferred later to Lyons, Covert was decorated by the French government for his lectures on literature and America. He returned to spend his final decade in Cleveland, where he was honored as the founding president of both the PRESS CLUB OF CLEVELAND† (1887) and the ROWFANT CLUB† (1892). As a member of the EARLY SETTLERS ASSN.,† he had sponsored the original resolution leading to the observance of the Cleveland Centennial in 1896 (see CLEVELAND ANNIVERSARY CELEBRATIONS†). Although married, he had no children.—J.V.

**COWAN, R. (REGINALD) GUY** (1 Aug. 1884–10 March 1957) established and operated COWAN POTTERY, Cleveland's only major pottery, which earned a national reputation for its ceramic sculpture in the 1920s. Descended from a family of potters, he was born in East Liverpool, OH, and learned his craft at the New York State School of Clayworking and Ceramics. In 1908 he came to Cleveland, where he introduced pottery making in the CLEVELAND PUBLIC SCHOOLS† as an instructor at EAST TECHNICAL HIGH SCHOOL.† With the encouragement of the CLEVELAND CHAMBER OF COMMERCE,† Cowan opened his first studio on Nicholson Ave. in LAKEWOOD† in 1912, using the area's natural gas for his kilns. Incorporated in 1913 as the Cleveland Pottery and Tile Co., the studio first won recognition with a first place for pottery at the Art Institute of Chicago's 1917 International Show. Following service as a captain in the U.S. Army during World War I, Cowan moved his studio in 1921 to 19633 Lake Rd. in ROCKY RIVER.† Known after 1927 as the Cowan Pottery Studio, Inc., the company employed such local artists as Alexander Blazys, Edris Eckhardt, Thelma Frazier, and Viktor Schreckengost to create Art Deco designs. Under business manager Wendell G. Wilcox, Cowan ceramics were marketed in 1,200 outlets nationwide until the Depression forced the company into receivership in 1930. It continued under court supervision for another year before closing. Cowan, who also taught ceramics at the Cleveland School of Art (see CLEVELAND INSTITUTE OF ART†) since ca. 1918, joined the Onondaga Pottery Co. in Syracuse, NY, in 1933. He assisted the Syracuse Museum of Art in establishing the Ceramic Nationals exhibition and became a museum trustee. Married to Bertha G. Bogue of Cleveland, he was survived by 3 children.—J.V.

**COWGILL, LEWIS F.** (2 July 1910–4 Oct. 1988), inventor and school teacher, contributed to the fields of automation and educational television. Lewis was born in Lewisburg, OH, the son of William F. and Gula Schwartz Cowgill. He earned a bachelor's degree in education from Ohio State Univ. in 1933 and began his teaching career the next year at Rawlings Junior High and Tremont Elementary schools in Cleveland. During World War II he worked at the Cleveland Tank plant (see I-X CENTER†) as a quality assurance engineer. After the war he embarked on a new career at Acme Billiard and Bowling Supply Co., where he invented an innovative type of automatic control for use in bowling alleys. His invention was a contribution to the automation of bowling alley operations led by the introduction of automatic pinspotters by AMF in 1946. Cowgill patented his invention and became president of the company.

In 1954 he returned to teaching science in the Parma school system, becoming an audiovisual aid specialist. He furthered his expertise in the field by receiving a masters degree from Miami Univ. in 1962. Returning to the Parma schools, he took the lead in founding station WTIP, the first high school–operated television station in greater Cleveland. After retirement in 1975, he collected and restored antique clocks. Cowgill married Carol L. Hand 14 June 1936; they had 2 daughters, Janet Grambo of Indianapolis and Karen Borkenhagen of Lafayette, CA, and a son, Charles F., of Houston. A resident of PARMA,† Cowgill died at PARMA COMMUNITY GENERAL HOSPITAL† and was cremated.—M.S.

**COWLES, EDWIN W.** (19 Sept. 1825–4 Mar. 1890), a prominent newspaper editor, was born in Austinburg, OH, and came to Cleveland in 1839 as a printing apprentice. In 1844 Cowles and TIMOTHY SMEAD formed a printing partnership. Cowles printed the *OHIO AMERICAN†* and *True Democrat,* acquiring an interest in the latter when it merged into the *Forest City Democrat* in 1853, making it the *CLEVELAND LEADER†* in 1854.

Cowles led the Republican party in Cleveland, hosting, with his new partner, Joseph Medill, a meeting calling for the first Republican Natl. Convention, held in Pittsburgh in 1855. Cowles secured sole control of the *Leader,* became its editor, and made it the area's leading radical Republican voice. After the Republican victory in 1860, Cowles was rewarded with the Cleveland postmastership, where he pioneered free mail delivery. However, under Pres. Andrew Johnson he was replaced as postmaster by GEO. A. BENEDICT, editor of the more moderate *Herald.*

Cowles was as outspoken a nativist as he was a Republican, heading the Cleveland chapter of the anti-Catholic Order of the American Union, and carrying on an editorial war with MANLY TELLO, editor of the *Catholic Universe.* He was the city's last representative of the era of personal journalism and was eulogized even by rivals. Cowles married Elizabeth C. Hutchinson in 1849 and had 3 sons and 2 daughters. When two of his sons invented a new melting process for aluminum, Cowles devoted his declining energies to promoting a company to exploit their discovery. He died at home.

**COWLES (COWLS), SAMUEL** (ca. 1774–22 Nov. 1837), pioneer Cleveland lawyer and businessman, was born in Simsbury, CT, the son of Joseph and Sarah Mills Cowles. A graduate of Williams College, he practiced law in Connecticut for some 15 years before coming to Cleveland in 1818. In 1819 he and ALFRED KELLEY organized the Kelley & Cowls law firm, which was dissolved in 1822. In 1825 Cowles formed a partnership with SHERLOCK ANDREWS which lasted until he retired in 1832. As a lawyer, Cowles acted as an agent for land sales in the area, which included choice lots on Ontario, Lake (Lakeside), and Water (W. 9th) sts. and almost 4,000 acres of farm land in Rockport Twp. Cowles himself acquired extensive landholdings and was one of the early settlers who profited from the city's growth. His home on Euclid Ave. near E. 6th St was a village landmark. After his death, his widow sold the property, which extended from Euclid to Prospect aves., for $7,000. By 1915 its value had increased to about $900,000. Actively involved in organizations that served to knit the community together, Cowles helped found the First Presbyterian Society of Cleveland, the Cuyahoga County Colonization Society, and the Cuyahoga County Agricultural Society, among others. He also served on the board of school managers which monitored the progress of Cleveland's early public school system. A month before Cowles died in 1837, he was appointed judge of the Common Pleas Court.

Cowles married Cornelia Whiting of Lenox, MA, in 1832. They had no children. He died in Cleveland and was buried in Erie St. Cemetery.—M.S.

**COX, JACOB DOLSON** (15 May 1852–23 Feb. 1930), cofounded the Cleveland manufacturing firm of Cox and Prentiss, an ancestor of the ACME-CLEVELAND CORP.† He was born in Warren, OH, to Jacob Dolson and Helen Finney Cox. His father, a lawyer, was the 22nd governor of Ohio

(1865–67) and secretary of the interior under Pres. Grant. Educated in public schools, at 17 Cox began learning the iron business, working at the Cleveland Iron Co. and the CUYAHOGA STEAM FURNACE CO.† In June 1876 he became a partner in a twist drill manufacturing concern in Dunkirk, NY, which moved to Cleveland a few months later; in 1880 the firm became Cox and Prentiss. Although he retired from the business in 1905, Cox succeeded partner FRANCIS FLEURY PRENTISS as president of the company, then called Cleveland Twist Drill.

Cox married Ellen Atwood Prentiss in 1878 in Cleveland. The couple lived on EUCLID AVE.† with their 3 children: Jeannette P. (Mrs. Gordon) Morrill, Samuel H., and JACOB DOLSON COX, JR. Cox served on the boards of directors of the Cleveland Trust Co. (see AMERITRUST†) and the Cleveland & Pittsburgh Railroad Co., was a trustee of Case School of Applied Sciences (1898–1918, see CASE WESTERN RESERVE UNIV.†), and was among the original members of the Chamber of Commerce. Cox enjoyed yachting, photography, and travel. He died at his winter home in Pasadena, CA, and is buried in Lake View Cemetery.

**COX, JACOB D., JR.** (1 Nov. 1881–16 Feb. 1953), president of the Cleveland Twist Drill Co., was a pioneer in profit sharing and employee stock participation planning. Born in Cleveland to Ellen Prentiss and JACOB D. COX, SR., founder of Cleveland Twist Drill (see ACME-CLEVELAND†), his grandfather had served as governor of Ohio. Cox grew up in the family mansion on Euclid Ave. and attended Williams College. After college, Cox spent several years working in the western logging industry, but his work was often interrupted by poor health. In 1911 he became assistant to his father, and in 1919 succeeded him as president of Cleveland Twist Drill, holding that position until his death. Cox was interested in relations between management and labor; while he was president, there was never a work stoppage due to a labor dispute. Cox introduced many employee benefits that are standard today, including 2 weeks of vacation (after 2 year's service); a share in the company's profits at Christmas; profit sharing and participation in the company's investment; old-age pension on retirement at age 65; a sickness and accident fund; payment for suggestions leading to better efficiency and increased production; group life insurance; discussion groups in the factory; and promotion from the ranks. Cox formulated his profit-sharing plan in 1915. He later wrote a book, *The Economic Basis of Fair Wages*. Cox's innovative policies, which also included hiring handicapped persons whenever possible, served as models for similar programs throughout the country. He married Phyllis Graves on 23 Nov.

1937. They had no children. Cox died in Cleveland and was buried in Lake View Cemetery. —J.M.

**COYLE, GRACE LONGWELL** (22 March 1892–8 March 1962), sociologist, author, and educator, specialized in social reform through group activity while professor at the School of Applied Sciences of Western Reserve Univ. for almost 30 years. She served as president of the National Conference of Social Work (1940), the American Assn. of Social Workers (1942–44), and the National Conference of Social Work Education (1958–60); WRU named the Grace Longwell Chair in social work in her honor (1961). Coyle was born in North Adams, MA, to Mary Cushman Coyle and John Patterson Coyle, a Congregational minister. She received a B.A. from Wellesley College in 1914 and a master's degree in economics and a Ph.D. in sociology from Columbia Univ. She belonged to Phi Beta Kappa. Her doctoral dissertation, *Social Progress in Organized Groups,* published in 1930, was a widely used text. Before joining the WRU faculty in 1934, Coyle worked in SETTLEMENT HOUSES† in Penn. and New York.

Coyle advocated for expansion of government services to help solve social problems, and, in 1942, was appointed to the federal War Relocation Authority. She continued to publish works such as *Study in Group Behavior* (1937) and *Group Work with American Youth (1948).* Another book, *The Social Sciences in the Professional Education of Social Workers* (1957) was based on a study funded by the Russell Sage Foundation. She served locally and nationally with the YOUNG WOMEN'S CHRISTIAN ASSN.† (YWCA). Coyle, a single woman, lived on East 124th St. in Cleveland.—J.M.

Case Western Reserve Univ. Archives.

**COZAD, SAMUEL III** (4 April 1794–23 May 1870), WESTERN RESERVE† pioneer who settled the Euclid Ave.–Wade Park area, was born in New Jersey, the son of Samuel Jr. and Jane McIlrath Cozad. He and his family arrived in the Western Reserve in 1806 to settle land purchased by his father at $1 an acre, extending from DOAN'S CORNERS† (E. 107th St.) to LAKE VIEW CEMETERY,† on the south side of Euclid Ave. Later, Samuel III purchased 100 acres in EAST CLEVELAND† Twp., on the north side of Euclid, from Doan's Corners eastward beyond Wade Park. His nearest neighbor was Job Doan, who kept a tavern at the corner of Euclid and E. 107th St. Cozad turned the woods, undergrowth, and marsh into farmland, and built a log cabin in the area of Wade Park lagoon. He and Mary Condit were married in

1816, and they had a son, Newell, born in 1830. Pioneer farming was backbreaking work, and predators roamed the area, making it necessary to guard their domesticated animals. Later in life, Newell recalled how they hunted bear near the campus of Western Reserve Univ. As the area grew in population, land values increased, and Cozad built a frame house on the site of SEVERANCE HALL.† By 1860 his property was valued at $20,000. Cozad died at his residence in East Cleveland Twp. and was reinterred at Lake View Cemetery in 1878.—M.S.

**CRAIG, LILLIAN** (12 June 1937–14 Nov. 1979), a leader in the local welfare-rights movement and founder of the Natl. Welfare Rights Organization (1967), was born in Cleveland to an abusive, alcoholic father, placed in foster care at age 14, after her mother's death, then sent to Marycrest School for Girls. She had to refuse a scholarship to St. John's College because it made no allowances for living expenses.

As a divorced mother of 3, Craig found it too difficult to work and care for her children, so she applied for welfare. She found support at St. Paul's Community Church, a member of INNER CITY PROTESTANT PARISH† (ICPP), with Clevelanders United for Adequate Welfare (CUFAW), a group of welfare mothers who helped each other and by the mid–1960s became politically active, working for larger welfare payments, free school lunches, and better treatment from the welfare bureaucracy. Along with STUDENTS FOR A DEMOCRATIC SOCIETY† members Carol McEldowney and Kathy Boudin, Craig wrote *The Welfare Rights Manual,* in "people terms."

Craig engaged in sit-ins, marches, and public confrontations, making national headlines in 1966 when she grabbed a microphone from Sargent Shriver, head of the Office of Economic Opportunities, confronting him about welfare policies. Her actions made it difficult for her to secure employment. She worked at the McCafferty Health Ctr. from 1971–79, and in 1976 became director of the Near West Side Multi-Service Ctr. She also volunteered at the Crisis Ctr. and served on a child abuse task force.

Grevatt, Marge. *Just a Woman* (1981).

**CRAMER, CLARENCE HENLEY** (23 June 1905–15 Mar. 1982), author, dean, and professor of history, was born in Eureka, KS, to Rev. David and Erma Henley Cramer. The family settled in Mt. Gilead, OH, and Cramer received his B.A. (1927), M.A. (1928), and Ph.D (1931) in history from Ohio State Univ. From 1931–42 he was associate professor of history at Southern Illinois Univ. at Carbondale. During and after World War II, he served in various governmental posts.

Cramer came to Cleveland in 1949 as associate professor of history and business at WRU. After serving as acting dean of the School of Business from 1952–54, he became dean of Adelbert College from 1954–69, afterwards returning to teaching. "Red" Cramer was always accessible to the students, and was known for his wise counsel and ability to uncover financial resources for promising students. He specialized in economic and diplomatic history, and wrote biographies of Robt. G. Ingersoll and NEWTON D. BAKER, *American Enterprise—Free and Not So Free* (1972), and *Open Shelves and Open Minds: A History of the Cleveland Public Library* (1972). After his retirement in 1973, he published *Case Western Reserve Univ.: A History of the Univ., 1826–1976* (1976), and *Case Institute of Technology: A Centennial History, 1880–1980* (1980). He also wrote histories of the law school, the school of library science, and the school of dentistry at CWRU. He married Elizabeth Garman in Dec. 1949. He died in Cleveland.

**CRANE, HART** (21 July 1899–27 Apr. 1932), a modern, lyrical poet of the 1920s, was born in Garretsville, OH, to Grace Hart and C. A. Crane, millionaire candy manufacturer. In 1909, after his mother and father separated, he and his mother moved to Cleveland. Crane began writing verse at age 13, publishing his first poem at 16 (1915) in Bruno's *Weekly* while attending East High School. He attempted a college education but was mainly self-taught. While writing and studying, he held jobs with advertising companies in Cleveland and served a brief stint as a *PLAIN DEALER†* reporter. Moving to New York, Crane published poems in the small-press literary magazines *Dial, Seven Arts, Poetry,* and others. His first collection, *White Buildings* (1926) was well received. A wild life, including alcoholism and homosexual behavior, established him as a legendary figure. He traveled through California (1927–28) and Europe (1928–29). In 1930 he published *The Bridge,* his most famous collection, using the Brooklyn Bridge as a metaphor for American life and destiny, which won him critical acclaim and a Guggenheim Fellowship in 1931. In 1931 Crane lived in an artists' colony outside of Mexico City and worked on an epic poem about the conquest of Mexico, which he never finished. In 1932 Crane's depression, alcoholism, and the feeling he had lost his poetic powers led him to jump ship while sailing to America to settle his father's estate. His body was never recovered. His collected poems were published posthumously in 1933.

**CRANE, ORRIN J.** (1828–27 Nov. 1863), a volunteer CIVIL WAR† Army officer, was born in Troy, NY, and at the war's outbreak was employed as a carpenter for a Cleveland shipbuilder. He enlisted on 17 Apr. 1861 as a private, was elected 1st lt. when his company became Co. A, 7TH OHIO VOLUNTEER INFANTRY,† and was appointed captain on 14 May 1861. He learned the rudiments of military science from Col. WM. R. CREIGHTON and excelled in supervising the building of bridges, barracks, and corduroy roads. He participated in the campaigns of the Army of the Potomac in Virginia during 1862–63.

Crane was promoted to lt. col. on 6 Oct. 1862 and commanded the 7th Ohio on 27 Nov. 1863 when ordered to assault Taylor's Ridge, a 500' summit near Ringgold, GA, being forced to move through a ravine where the brigade was mauled by enfilading Confederate fire. The brigade failed to occupy the summit, suffering heavy casualties. Crane was killed near the top. Col. Creighton tried to retrieve Crane's body but failed and was himself mortally wounded. Both Crane's and Creighton's remains were transported back to Cleveland, where they lay in state at City Hall. After a memorial service at the Old Stone Church, where Crane was a member, both were deposited in Erie St. Cemetery in the Bradburn family vault. Thousands of citizens lined the street for the procession. In July 1864, both bodies were buried in Woodland Cemetery, side by side.

**CRAWFORD, FREDERICK COOLIDGE** (19 March 1891–9 Dec. 1994) successful businessman, promoter of aviation, and collector of vintage automobiles, was born in Watertown, MA, the son of Fred E. and Mattie Coolidge Crawford. He attended Harvard Univ., graduating in 1913, and received a masters degree in Civil Engineering from the school the following year. In 1916 Crawford took a job at Cleveland's Steel Products Co., which manufactured auto parts, beginning as a millwright's helper and working his way into a management position. When he was sent to close the company's Detroit plant in 1922, Crawford became its manager instead and transformed it into a profitable operation. Steel Products changed its name to Thompson Products, Inc. in 1926, and when Crawford became vice-president in 1929, he returned to Cleveland as general manager of the Cleveland plant. After president Charles E. Thompson died in 1933, Crawford succeeded him as president, continuing the company's promotion of the NATIONAL AIR RACES.† Vehemently opposed to labor unions, Crawford tried to maintain a good working relationship with his own employees and encouraged the development of an independent company union. He also opposed high taxes and increasing government regulation of business, although his company augmented its output of aircraft engines with government help during World War II.

Crawford was instrumental in bringing what would become the NASA LEWIS RESEARCH CENTER† to Cleveland in 1940 and was an incorporator of the AIR FOUNDATION† which returned the air races to Cleveland 1946–60. Recognizing the historic influence of the automobile on American society, Crawford combined his interest in antique cars and aviation to organize the Thompson Auto Album and Aviation Museum in 1937. He arranged to have the collection turned over to the WESTERN RESERVE HISTORICAL SOCIETY† in 1963 and led the fundraising campaign to erect a building to house the collection at the society. The structure was named the Frederick C. Crawford Auto Aviation Museum in his honor.

A long-time member of the Case Institute of Technology Board of Trustees, and board chairman 1955–64, Crawford helped develop the school as a major force in science and engineering education and research, leading two successful fundraising drives to expand its facilities. Crawford Hall was named in his honor in 1969. Active in the Cleveland Zoological Assn., he helped organize a safari in 1945 and donated animals collected on the expedition to the Cleveland Zoo (see CLEVELAND METROPARKS ZOO†). He also provided assistance to families of policemen and firemen killed in the line of duty as a charter member and president of Bluecoats, Inc., founded in 1956.

Crawford married Audrey C. Bowles 17 Oct. 1932. There were no children. After her death in Nov. 1971, he married Kathleen M. Saxon on 28 May 1975. A resident of BRATENAHL,† Crawford died in a hospital near his summer home at Cotuit, MA, and was buried in Lake View Cemetery in Cleveland.—M.S.

Crawford, Frederick C. (Christopher Johnston, ed.). *Selected Speeches of Frederick C. Crawford* (1993).
Crawford, Frederick C. (Christopher Johnston, ed.). *Storyettes: Reminiscences of Frederick C. Crawford* (1992).
Frederick C. Crawford Papers, WRHS.

**CREECH, HARRIS** (26 Feb. 1874–18 May 1941) was president of the Cleveland Trust Co. for 18 years; his leadership during the Depression ensured the company's continuance as the premier banking institution for many years. Creech was born in Cleveland, the son of James and Carabelle Simmons Creech, and was educated in the city's public schools. He went to work for the Garfield Savings

Banks as a utility clerk when it opened in 1892, and rose through the ranks to become president in 1916 at age 42. Following the merger of Garfield Savings with Cleveland Trust in 1922, Creech became vice-president of the combined institution. When FREDERICK GOFF died in March 1923, he was named president of the trust company.

A strong advocate of branch banking from his days at Garfield, Creech actively pursued the extension of Cleveland Trust offices throughout the area. When the Trust Co. reopened after the national bank holiday in 1933, Creech personally reassured jittery depositors seeking to withdraw their money that the company was sound financially. In 1936 he was awarded the Cleveland Chamber of Commerce Medal for Public Service for his successful efforts to maintain public confidence in the banking community during the crisis. While he was president of Cleveland Trust, its deposits increased by about $270 million, and it became the largest commercial bank and trust company in Ohio.

Creech died in Cleveland at age 67 and was buried in Lake View Cemetery. He was survived by his wife, Carlotta, a son, James Pope, and a daughter, Mrs. Edward T. Bartlett II.—M.S.

**CREIGHTON, WILLIAM R.** (June 1837–27 Nov. 1863), a volunteer CIVIL WAR† officer born in Pittsburgh, PA, was a printer at the *CLEVELAND HERALD†* when war began. Creighton recruited a company of infantry on 17 Apr. 1861, mustered as Co. A, 7TH OHIO VOLUNTEER INFANTRY.† Elected lt. col., he was promoted to col. on 23 Mar. 1862 after meritorious service at the Battle of Winchester, VA. On 9 Aug. 1862, he was severely wounded at Clear Mountain, VA, and did not rejoin the 7th until Sept. 1862.

On 27 Nov. 1863, Creighton, in command of the 1st Brigade, was ordered to assault 500' Taylor's Ridge near Ringgold, GA. The brigade struggled and Creighton, rallying his former regiment, commanded by Lt. Col. ORRIN J. CRANE, was shot trying to rescue the body of Crane. He was carried down the ridge, dying 6 hours later.

Creighton's and Crane's remains were transported back to Cleveland, kept at City Hall the night of 7–8 Dec. 1863, and taken to Old Stone Church for a memorial service on 8 Dec. They were transported to Erie St. Cemetery and temporarily deposited in the Bradburn family vault. Later, both Creighton and Crane were buried side by side in Woodland Cemetery. Ft. Wood at Chattanooga, TN, was renamed Ft. Creighton in the col.'s honor. Creighton was survived by his widow, the former Eleanor L. Quirk, whom he had married on 2 May 1861. A bust of Creighton is displayed in the SOLDIERS & SAILORS MONUMENT.†

Wm. R. Creighton Papers, 1862–64. In Regimental Papers of the Civil War, WRHS.

**CRILE, GEORGE, JR.** (3 Nov. 1907–9 Sept. 1992), an honorary member of the English Royal College of Surgeons (elected 1978), served the CLEVELAND CLINIC FOUNDATION† for over half a century and campaigned against unnecessary surgery. His advocacy modified the treatment of breast cancer across the U.S. Crile, called Barney, was born in Cleveland, the third child (and first son) of GEORGE CRILE and Grace McBride Crile. Crile attended UNIV. SCHOOL,† graduated from Hotchkiss boarding school and Yale Univ., and received his medical degree from Harvard in 1929. He joined the surgical staff of the Cleveland Clinic in 1937, following a residency there, and became head of the Department of General Surgery in 1957. During World War II, Crile served with a Cleveland Clinic mobile unit in the U.S. Navy. He retired from the clinic in 1968 but remained active, first as senior consultant, and after 1972, as emeritus consultant. He also served on the clinic's Board of Governors from 1955 until 1958 and from 1962–66.

In his first research effort, Crile discovered that less-intrusive procedures often counteracted thyroid cancer as well as surgery. He then studied breast cancer and published a paper in 1961 to demonstrate that a combined treatment of lumpectomy and radiation had a survival rate comparable to the commonly used, more complicated, and disfiguring radical mastectomy.

In addition to research and surgery, Crile traveled and wrote extensively, both scientific and popular works, including an autobiography. Crile married Jane Halle on 5 Dec. 1934. They lived on Kent Rd. in CLEVELAND HTS.† and had four children: Ann C. Esselstyn, Joan C. Foster, Susan Crile, and George Crile, 3rd. Jane died in 1963. On 9 Nov. 1963, Crile married editor and author Helga Sandburg, whose father, poet Carl Sandburg, performed the ceremony. Crile died at the Cleveland Clinic of lung cancer.—J.M.

George Crile, Jr. Papers, Cleveland Clinic Foundation Archives.
Crile, George, Jr. *The Way It Was: Sex, Surgery, Treasure and Travel, 1907–1987* (Kent State Univ., 1992).

**CRILE, GEORGE WASHINGTON, SR.** (11 Nov. 1864–7 Jan. 1943), surgeon, researcher, and a founder of the CLEVELAND CLINIC FOUNDATION,† was born in Chili, OH, to Michael and Margaret Deeds Crile. He received his A.B. from Ohio Northern Univ. (1885), his medical degree from Wooster Medical College (1887), and addi-

109

tional training in Europe. Along with FRANK E. BUNTS, he worked for Dr. Frank Weed and served several Cleveland hospitals, including Lakeside Hospital, where he served as chief of surgery. He is reputed to have performed the first successful human blood transfusion at ST. ALEXIS HOSPITAL† in 1906. During the Spanish-American War, Crile worked in the U.S. Army Medical Corps and studied military surgery, field sanitation, and tropical diseases. During World War I, he served in army hospitals in France and researched war neurasthenia, shell concussion, effects of poison gas, wound infection, and shock. He received the French Legion of Honor (1922). Along with Drs. WM. E. LOWER, Frank E. Bunts, and JOHN PHILLIPS, Crile founded the Cleveland Clinic, a medical group practice modeled after Mayo Clinic. Crile was president (1921–40) and trustee (1921–36) of the foundation. Crile perfected operations for goiter and thyroid disease and also studied intelligence and personality, theorizing that the human organism is an electrochemical mechanism. Crile was a founding member and second president (1916–17) of the American College of Surgeons, and taught at the Univ. of Wooster (1890–1900) and Western Reserve School of Medicine (1900–43). He married Grace McBride of Cleveland and had 4 children: GEORGE, JR., Robert, Margaret, and Elizabeth. Crile was buried in Lake View Cemetery.

Crile, George. *An Autobiography* (1947).
Geo. W. Crile, Sr. Papers, WRHS.

**CROGHAN, GEORGE** (1720–31 Aug. 1782) was a frontiersman, trader, and Indian agent who was born in Ireland and came to Pennsylvania in 1741. He served as a captain under Gen. Braddock, and later as Sir Wm. Johnson's deputy superintendent of Indian affairs. Before the French & Indian War (1754–63), Croghan established trading posts throughout the upper Ohio country in the present states of Ohio, Indiana, and Illinois. When not representing his own interests, he served those of the British, often facilitating negotiations with the Indians who opposed them to the French. Croghan is significant in Cleveland's history as the first identifiable white man to maintain a trading post at the mouth of the CUYAHOGA RIVER.† He visited there periodically between 1745–48. Little is known of Croghan's private life. He had one white daughter, Susannah, and later was said to have fathered children with a Mohawk Indian woman. Croghan, an Episcopalian, died in Passyunk, Pennsylvania.

Volwiler, A. T. *George Croghan and the Westward Movement, 1741–1782* (1926).

**CROSSER, ROBERT** (7 June 1874–3 June 1957), congressman for 38 years (1912–54), believed in equal rights and was dedicated to eliminating poverty. Born in Holytown, Lanarkshire, Scotland, to James and Barbara C. Crosser, his family emigrated to Salineville, OH, in 1881. Crosser graduated from Kenyon College with an A.B. in 1897 and attended Columbia's and Cincinnati's Law Schools, earning his LL.B. in 1901, when he was admitted to the Ohio Bar.

Crosser practiced law in Cleveland from 1901–23. Politically, he worked for Mayor TOM L. JOHNSON in 1910 was elected to the Ohio House of Representatives; and in 1912 was a delegate to Ohio's 4th constitutional convention. Crosser won election as congressman-at-large in 1912 and as representative of Ohio's 21st congressional district in 1914 and 1916. He was defeated in 1918 and 1920, largely because he opposed the draft. In 1922 Crosser was reelected to Congress, holding the seat until 1954, when he was defeated by Chas. Vanik in the primary.

Although a Democrat, Crosser followed his conscience even though his independence resulted in his being passed over for powerful congressional leadership positions. Crosser was chairman of the Interstate & Foreign Commerce Committee (1948–52) and the first congressional Flood Control Committee. He supported postal and railroad workers, authoring railroad workers security benefit legislation; and enjoyed support from both groups. Crosser married Isabelle D. Hogg and had 4 children: Justine, Barbara, Robert, and James. Crosser suffered from arthritis and from 1934 on was confined to a wheelchair. He died in Cleveland and was buried in Highland Park Cemetery.

**CROWELL, BENEDICT** (21 Oct. 1869–8 Sept. 1952), asst. secretary of war under NEWTON D. BAKER during World War I, was born in Cleveland, the son of William and Mary Benedict Crowell. He attended Case Institute of Technology, and earned his Ph.B. (1891) and M.A. (1918) in chemistry from Yale. Crowell worked for Otis Steel Co. as a chemical engineer and was a mining engineer in Brazil, Mexico, and Alaska before starting Crowell & Little Constr. Co. In 1938 he became president of Central Natl. Bank, remaining until shortly before his death. He was also a director of the Nickel Plate Railroad.

Newton D. Baker appointed Crowell to the Civil Service Commission. When war began, Crowell supervised artillery castings as a major of ordnance, and headed the Washington office of the Panama Canal Zone. In 1917 Baker appointed him asst. secretary of war, and later, director of munitions. In 1922 a Washington grand jury indicted Crowell and 6 aides with altering contract bidding to enrich construction firms in which they had interests, but charges were dropped in 1925 for lack of evidence. Between the wars, Crowell served several government organizations. In 1931 Pres. Hoover promoted him to brigadier general, and during World War II he was special consultant to the secretary of war. Crowell was founder and first president of the Army Ordnance Assn., advocating national defense preparedness, and president of the Natl. Rifle Assn. He married Julia Cobb and had 2 children, Florence and Benedict. Crowell is buried in Arlington Natl. Cemetery.

Benedict Crowell Papers, WRHS.

**CROWELL, JOHN** (15 Feb. 1801–10 Mar 1883) was a well-known attorney, supporter of the Republican party, and public speaker.

Crowell was born in East Haddam, CT. His family moved to Ashtabula County, OH, where his father farmed. In 1822 he entered an academy in Warren, OH, leaving it in 1825 to teach school and study law. After being admitted to the Ohio Bar in 1827, he bought part interest in and wrote articles for the *Western Reserve Chronicle* of Warren.

He was elected to the Ohio State Senate in 1840 and to the U.S. Congress, as a Whig, in 1846. He won reelection twice and retired from Congress in 1852, at which time he moved to Cleveland, where he practiced law. Shortly after arriving, he began lecturing on commercial law at Forsom Business College.

Crowell held the position of president of Cleveland's Ohio State and Union Law College from 1862 to 1876. He edited the *Western Law Monthly* and was instrumental in the formation of the law library of the CLEVELAND BAR ASSN.† in 1866.

A supporter of the Federal Union, Crowell spoke and worked for the candidacy of Abraham Lincoln. After the outbreak of war he used his oratorical skills to garner support for the Union cause, raising both funds and recruits through his efforts. He was called "General" Crowell because of his service as commander of the 20th Division, Ohio Militia, in the 1840s. He did gain the rank of major general.

He remained active in politics in the postwar years, being elected chairman of the Cuyahoga County Republican Committee in 1868 and serving as the secretary of the Republican Congressional Convention in 1870.

Crowell married Eliza B. Estabrook in 1833. They had 4 children. Crowell is buried in Lake View Cemetery.

**CROWLEY, JOSEPH HERRON** (23 Dec. 1893–16 Nov. 1984), chief legal council for the City of Cleveland for 24 years and scholar in the field of municipal law, was born in Long Island City, NY, the son of John Francis and Elizabeth Herron Crowley. After his father's death, his maternal grandfather, Patrick Herron, brought Joe, his older brother, John Francis, and his mother to Cleveland in 1895. He attended Central High School, and Adelbert College, graduating in 1916. He received an LL.B. and LL.M. from Ohio Northern Univ. in 1921 and 1923 respectively. In 1923 he was named attorney for the Cleveland Humane Society.

Crowley joined the city law department in 1929 as asst. police prosecutor, and the following year he was appointed asst. law director. He became chief counsel of the city in 1938, serving in that capacity until his retirement at the end of 1962. Six mayors, from Ray T. Miller to Ralph Locher, sought his legal advice. He did legal work for the Great Lakes Exposition, the ERIEVIEW† project, and creation of the Public Defender's Office and also taught at John Marshall Law School. The three volumes of his authoritative *Crowley's Ohio Municipal Law, Procedure and Forms* were published by BANKS-BALDWIN LAW PUBLISHING CO.† in the 1960s.

Crowley married Margaret Comyns 1 Sept. 1923, and they had three children: Joan Margaret (Mrs. Edward Svetina), Virginia Helen (dec.), and Denis Joseph. Crowley, a resident of CLEVELAND HTS.† was buried at Calvary Cemetery.—M.S.

Joseph Crowley, Law Director Files WRHS.

**CUDELL, FRANK (FRANZ), E.** (1844–25 Oct. 1916), of the important architectural firm of Cudell & Richardson, was born at Herzogenrath, near Aachen (Aix-la-Chapelle), Germany, to Dr. Karl and Louise Krauthausen Cudell. He emigrated in 1866, came to Cleveland in 1867, and formed a partnership with John N. Richardson (1837–1902) in 1870. Cudell & Richardson designed a series of churches in the Victorian Gothic style: St. Joseph Catholic Church (1871–99), St. Stephen Catholic Church (1873–81), and FRANKLIN CIRCLE CHRISTIAN CHURCH† (1874–75). They also designed institutional buildings, such as the Jewish Orphan Asylum (1888); and residences for the wealthy, of which the TIEDEMANN HOUSE† (1881), and Jacob Goldsmith house (1880) were standing in the 1980s.

They also designed commercial buildings embodying lighter structure, more open walls, and the use of cast and wrought iron, demonstrated in the Geo. Worthington Bldg. (1882), the Root & McBride-Bradley Bldg. (1884–85), and the PERRY-PAYNE BLDG.† (1889)—the first building in Cleveland to use iron columns, not a steel frame, throughout all 8 stories, and celebrated for its interior light court. The firm dissolved following completion of the Perry-Payne Bldg., and Cudell retired in 1903.

He was interested in the Group Plan, pointing out flaws in the Group Plan Commission's plans. Cudell was a liberal thinker, pamphleteer, and inventor. He bequeathed the property for the Cudell Ctr. to the city (see CUDELL†). Cudell was married twice. His first wife was Marie Heffenmuller (d. 1887). He married Emma Mueller, daughter of former lieutenant governor JACOB MUELLER, in 1889. Cudell died in Cleveland and was buried in Lake View Cemetery.

**CUNIN, JOHN** (11 Sept. 1924–18 July 1993), chairman and chief executive officer of BEARINGS, INC.,† was also known for his involvement with numerous civic and charitable causes.

Cunin was born in Akron, the son of Earl and Mary (McAlonan) Cunin. He graduated from St. Vincent High School and then served in the 8th Air Force in Europe during World War II. Afterwards he attended the Univ. of Akron and JOHN CARROLL UNIV.† He majored in business and marketing, but left before graduation.

In 1948 he began working at Bearings as an order clerk and advanced to salesman. In 1973 he became general sales manager and then president in 1980. He served the company as chairman and chief executive officer from 1983 to 1989. Under his leadership the company expanded and its revenues doubled, making it the largest firm of its kind in the nation. After his retirement he served as a member of the Board of Directors, and returned to John Carroll Univ. to finish his degree.

Cunin was a founder and director of the MIDTOWN CORRIDOR ASSN.† He also served as chairman of CLEAN-LAND, OHIO† and VOCATIONAL GUIDANCE SERVICES.† He served as a trustee for numerous civic and humanitarian organizations, as well as on the board of CLEVELAND TOMORROW.† He also served as the chairman of the Bruening Foundation (see EVA L. AND JOSEPH M. BRUENING FOUNDATION†), a director of Society National Bank (see SOCIETY CORP.†), and a trustee of John Carroll and NOTRE DAME COLLEGE.†

He married Marilyn McGulgan in 1952. They had 5 children: John, Thomas, William, Mary Catherine, and Jane. Cunin died in CLEVELAND HTS.† and is buried at All Souls Cemetery, Chardon, OH.—D.R.

**CUSHING, ERASTUS** (15 July 1802–4 Apr. 1893), one of Cleveland's most respected physicians, was born in Cheshire, MA, to David, Jr. and Freelove Brown Cushing. He attended New York College of Physicians & Surgeons in New York City, and was certified to practice in 1823. He continued his education at Berkshire Medical Institute of Williams College, a student of JOHN DELAMATER, receiving his medical degree in 1824. Cushing practiced in New England and attended lectures at the Medical Dept. of the Univ. of Pennsylvania in Philadelphia between 1834–35, moving to Cleveland in Oct. 1835 for health reasons. He opened a practice on PUBLIC SQUARE† as a family physician, eventually in partnership with his son, HENRY KIRKE CUSHING. In 1837 Cushing helped organize the Willoughby Medical College in Willoughby, OH, inducing his former professor, Dr. John Delamater, to teach there. Dr. Cushing was also involved in forming Cleveland Medical College under the charter of Western Reserve College, and was appointed to a committee charged with presenting the WRU board with suitable candidates for the M.D. degree. Known as a kind and distinguished gentleman, easily recognizable by his long black cape, Cushing continued in his lucrative private practice until age 62, when he went into semi-retirement, retiring fully at 70. Cushing married Mary Ann Platt in 1826 had 3 children: Henry Kirke, William David, and Cornelia. Cushing died in Cleveland and was buried in the Erie St. Cemetery. His son, Henry Kirke, grandsons Edward F. and HARVEY W. CUSHING, and great-grandsons E. H. and Kirke W. Cushing, all received medical degrees.

**CUSHING, HARVEY W.** (8 Apr. 1869–7 Oct. 1939), son of Betsey M. Williams and HENRY CUSHING, was America's first neurosurgeon. He was born in Cleveland and received his medical degree from Harvard in 1895. He began as a general surgeon, only gradually becoming interested in brain and spinal cord surgery. After study in England and Germany, he became an associate professor of surgery of the central nervous system at Johns Hopkins Univ., where he came into contact with Sir Wm. Osler, a Canadian physician renowned for his work on malaria, cerebral palsy, and diseases of the spleen, heart, and blood. Cushing later wrote a biography of Osler, which won him a Pulitzer Prize in 1926. From 1912–32, Cushing was professor of surgery at Harvard Medical School, and from 1932–37 was the Sterling Professor of Neurology at Yale. Cushing introduced a method of operating on the brain with local anesthesia. Through preoperative studies, the use of tourniquets and silver clips to control bleeding, and checks on blood pressure and oxygen levels, he reduced mortality from brain surgery to 10%, when most doctors were losing 33 to 50%. Cushing first used electrocautery in brain surgery, classified brain tumors, and was first to link them with gastric ulcers. An expert on the pituitary gland, in 1931 he discovered a new disease, Cushing's disease, in which the basophil cells of the pituitary are overstimulated. A plaque on PUBLIC

SQUARE† honors Cushing as America's first neurosurgeon. He married Katherine Crowell. They are buried together in Lake View Cemetery. The Cushings had four children: Mary Benedict, Bebey, Henry Kirke, and Barbara.

**CUSHING, HENRY KIRKE** (29 July 1827–12 Feb. 1910), a prominent Cleveland physician active in raising the professional and educational standards of the medical profession, was born in Lanesboro, MA, to Mary Ann Platt and Dr. ERASTUS CUSHING. The family moved to Cleveland when Cushing was 8. He graduated from Union College in 1848 and studied medicine under his father while also attending lectures at Cleveland Medical College. He received his medical degree in 1851 from the Univ. of Pennsylvania in Philadelphia and soon after returned to Cleveland. In 1856 Cushing became a faculty member of the Western Reserve Medical Dept., staying until 1883, primarily teaching obstetrics and gynecology. During the CIVIL WAR† he served as surgeon-major in the 7TH OHIO VOLUNTEER INFANTRY.† Through his involvement in medical societies, Cushing helped promote a more scientific approach to the study and practice of medicine. He was an organizer of the (early) Cleveland Academy of Medicine in 1867 and later was president of the CUYAHOGA COUNTY MEDICAL ASSN.† In 1887 Cushing became the first president of the Cleveland Society of Medical Sciences. He served on the joint committee of 3 Cleveland medical societies which led to the founding of the CLEVELAND MEDICAL LIBRARY ASSN.† in 1894. In 1906 the Dept. of Experimental Medicine was formed at the WRU Medical School and named in honor of Cushing. He married Betsey M. Williams in 1852; they had 8 children: Edward, HARVEY W. CUSHING, WILLIAM ERASTUS, Alice Kirke, HENRY PLATT CUSHING, Edward Fitch, George Briggs, and Alleyne Maynard. Cushing died at his home in Cleveland.

**CUSHING, HENRY PLATT** (10 Oct. 1860–14 April 1921) was a prominent geologist who taught for 30 years at Western Reserve Univ. (see CASE WESTERN RESERVE†). He was born into a prominent Cleveland family, being the grandson of early settler Dr. ERASTUS CUSHING and the son of physician HENRY K. CUSHING and Betsey Williams Cushing. His brother, HARVEY W. CUSHING, became one of America's most prominent physicians. Henry P. Cushing studied geology at Cornell Univ., where he graduated in 1882, and later added master's and doctor's degrees. He also studied at the School of Mines at Columbia Univ. and in Europe at the Univ. of Munich. In 1886 he

married Florence E. Williams of Ithaca, NY, and from 1885–91 he taught at the State Normal School at Mankato, MN. Cushing came to Western Reserve in 1892, becoming full professor of geology in 1895 and eventually head of the department. From 1893 he was also a geologist on the New York State Geology Survey, carrying out field work in the Adirondack Mts. His principal legacy to Western Reserve was the geological collection he left to the university, consisting of the paleontological collection inherited from his father-in-law, Prof. S. G. Williams, as well as his own specimens culled from the Cleveland and Adirondack regions. Cushing was a charter member of the Geological Society of America and a trustee of the CLEVELAND MUSEUM OF NATURAL HISTORY.† He died in Cleveland, survived by his wife and a daughter, Cornelia Cushing Peterson.—J.V.

**CUSHING, WILLIAM ERASTUS** (23 Sept. 1853–19 Dec. 1917), a lawyer, served on the Ohio State Board of Commissioners on Uniform Laws (1902–05) and on the American Bar Assn. committee on uniform state laws. He was related to at least 6 Cleveland physicians. Cushing was born in Cleveland, one of 9 children (and the oldest son) of Betsey M. Williams and HENRY KIRKE CUSHING, and the grandson of ERASTUS CUSHING. (Other physicians in the family included Edward F., E. H., Kirke and HARVEY W. CUSHING.) He graduated from Western Reserve College in Hudson, OH, in 1875 with a B.A. and was elected to Phi Beta Kappa. In 1878 he received an LL.B. from Harvard Law School and was admitted to the bar. Cushing first practiced with the firm of Terrell, Beach & Cushing and later formed a law partnership with Judge Samuel E. Williamson, Williamson, Cushing & Clarke. By 1910 he was a senior partner with Cushing, Siddall & Palmer and later, in 1913, with Cushing, Hopkins & Lamb. Cushing preferred the study of law, especially corporate law, to litigation.

A Republican, Cushing supported Pres. Rutherford B. Hayes and George William Curtis in their struggle to reform the Civil Service. He belonged to the WESTERN RESERVE HISTORICAL SOCIETY† and the Cleveland Chamber of Commerce, among other organizations, served as secretary of the board of UNIV. SCHOOL† since its founding, and was trustee of the Society for Savings and Adelbert College of Western Reserve Univ. (see CASE WESTERN RESERVE UNIV.†). Cushing was also a member and trustee of FIRST PRESBYTERIAN (OLD STONE) CHURCH.† On 4 June 1884, in Pittsfield, MA, Cushing married Carolyn Kellogg; she later served on the founding board of the FORTNIGHTLY MUSICAL CLUB.†—J.M.

**CUTLER, CARROLL** (31 Jan. 1829–25 Jan. 1894), presided over Western Reserve College (see CASE WESTERN RESERVE†) during that institution's removal from Hudson, OH, to Cleveland. The son of Rev. Calvin and Rhoda Little Cutler, he was a native of Windham, NH. A graduate of Yale College and Yale Divinity School, he married Frances Gallagher of Orange, NJ, in 1858. Cutler then continued his studies for a year in Germany before joining the Western Reserve faculty in 1860. Regarded as the faculty's foremost scholar, he taught philosophy and natural theology, among several other subjects. His publications included *Purposes of College Studies* (1874), *A History of Western Reserve College in Its First Half Century* (1876), and *The Beginnings of Ethics* (1889). After a year as acting president, Cutler was appointed as the college's 4th president in 1871. Although he liberalized the curriculum in the direction of increased emphasis on sciences and modern languages, he was less successful as an administrator and fundraiser. His most memorable initiative was the admission of women to the student body on equal terms with men. One of those who benefited was his only child, Susan Rhoda Cutler, who graduated as valedictorian of her class in 1885. Cutler personally would have preferred to see the college remain in Hudson, but supported the trustees once the decision to move to Cleveland in 1882 had been reached. Resigning the presidency in 1886 following a faculty rebellion against co-education, he left the university in 1889. Cutler had always been an ardent abolitionist, and he spent his remaining years teaching at small Negro colleges in Charlotte, NC, and Talledega, AL. He died in the latter town, survived by his wife and daughter, and was returned for burial in Hudson.

**CUTLER, ELLIOT CARR** (30 July 1888–16 Aug. 1947), internationally known for his work in heart and brain surgery, was born in Bangor, ME, to George Chalmer and Mary Franklin Wilson Cutler. He received his A.B. from Harvard Univ. in 1909 and his M.D. degree in 1913. He was a surgeon at Peter Bent Brigham Hospital, and in 1915, at Massachusetts General Hospital, both in Boston. In 1916 he took an assistantship working in immunology and bacteriology at the Rockefeller Institute in New York City. During World War I, Cutler was a captain in charge of Base Hospital No. 6. Later promoted to major, he received the Distinguished Service Medal for his work in the evacuation hospital in Boulogne, France. He returned to Harvard and Peter Bent Brigham Hospital in 1919, beginning his private practice in 1921. In 1924 Cutler was appointed professor of surgery at Western Reserve Univ. Medical School and director of surgery at Lakeside Hospital, serving until 1932, when he became the Moseley Professor of Surgery at Harvard and director of surgery at Peter Bent Brigham Hospital. While in Cleveland, Cutler, collaborating with CLAUDE BECK, developed a surgical treatment, cardiovalvulotomy, for the heart condition mitral stenosis, a thickening and narrowing of the valve between the left auricle and ventricle, which hampers blood circulation. Used only 6 years, this procedure opened the field of direct surgical approaches to not only chronic valvular disease but also other congenital and acquired mechanical heart abnormalities. Cutler married Caroline Pollard Parker and had 4 children: Elliot, Thomas, David, and Marjorie Parker. He died and was buried in Boston.—J.V.

**CUTLER, JAMES ELBERT** (24 Jan.1876–29 Oct. 1959), taught the first formal courses in sociology at Western Reserve Univ. (WRU, 1907–46, see CASE WESTERN RESERVE UNIV.†) and, with CHARLES THWING, cofounded and served as the first dean of WRU's pioneering School of Applied Social Sciences (1916–41). Cutler was born in Princeville, IL, to Francis Wilson and Antonaiah Hoag Cutler. After his mother died, he was raised by an aunt in Colorado. He attended Princeville public schools, went to the State Preparatory School in Boulder, CO (1894–96), and received a B.A. from the Univ. of Colorado (1900) and a Ph.D. from Yale Univ. (1903). He taught at Yale (1903–04), Wellesley College (1904–06), and the Univ. of Michigan (1906–07). Cutler first held the position of associate professor of sociology at WRU until 1910, when he became Selah Chamberlain Professor. During World War I, he served as captain, then major, with the Military Intelligence Division of the U.S. Army's office of the Chief of Staff (1918–19) in Washington, DC. In 1941 Cutler retired as dean and cut down to part-time teaching. Five years later he retired entirely and was made dean emeritus.

Cutler married Carolena D. Sperry (d. 1945) on 25 June 1903; the couple lived in Cleveland. On 2 Aug. 1946 he married Ida May Devine; they lived in SHAKER HTS.† Cutler had no children. A charter member of the American Sociological Society and president of the Ohio Valley Sociological Society (1939), he served locally as a trustee of the Welfare Federation, the Goodrich Social Settlement (see GOODRICH-GANNETT NEIGHBORHOOD CENTER†), UNIV. SOCIAL SETTLEMENT,† and CLEVELAND ASSOCIATED CHARITIES.† He helped organize the Federation for Charity and Philanthropy (see FEDERATION FOR COMMUNITY PLANNING†). Cutler served as president of the New England Society of Cleveland & the Western Reserve (1926–27, see PATRIOTIC SOCIET-

IES†). Cutler, a Republican, was a member of the CHURCH OF THE COVENANT.†—J.M.

James Elbert Cutler Papers, CWRU Archives.

**CUTTER, ANNIE SPENCER** (20 Feb. 1877–26 Mar. 1957), teacher and librarian, extended CLEVELAND PUBLIC LIBRARY† services to junior and senior high schools throughout the city. Cutter was born in Cleveland to Charles Long and Annie Spencer Cutter. She grew up on Woodland Ave. and attended CENTRAL HIGH SCHOOL.† In 1899 she graduated from the College for Women (later Flora Stone Mather College, CASE WESTERN RESERVE UNIV.†). After two years abroad, Cutter taught at Univ. School (1902–05). She then joined the Cleveland Public Library staff, where she remained until retiring on 1 Sept. 1942. Under director WILLIAM HOWARD BRETT, she helped establish the library's Stevenson Room for young people. During World War I, Cutter set up a library for soldiers in France. In 1920 director LINDA EASTMAN appointed Cutter head of the school library activities; in this capacity, she not only established libraries in city schools but also selected the schools' librarians. Cutter also served as Asst. Professor of Library Science at Western Reserve Univ. (1920–43), as a trustee of the WOMEN'S CITY CLUB,† and on the advisory board of the American Library Assn.

Possessing an adventurous spirit, Cutter spent a summer teaching in a 1-room school in Labrador. She continued her activities after retirement; presiding, for example, over the Mather Advisory Council (1945–48) and organizing a library at CALVARY PRESBYTERIAN CHURCH,† where she was a lifelong member. Both Western Reserve Univ. and Wooster College awarded her honorary doctorates. Cutter died in her CLEVELAND HTS.† home, which she had shared with a sister, Rose, also unmarried. Another sister, Elizabeth (Mrs. Dwight) Morrow, was the mother of Anne Morrow (Mrs. Charles) Lindbergh.—J.M.

**CZOLGOSZ, LEON F.** (1873–29 Oct. 1901), the assassin of Pres. Wm. McKinley, was born in Detroit to Polish immigrants. The family settled in Cleveland in 1891. With less than 6 years of schooling, Czolgosz found work in the Newburgh Wire Mill in 1891, participated in a failed strike in 1893, and subsequently grew bitter toward religion and capitalism, quit the mill in 1898, and did not work again. Czolgosz attempted to join the Liberty Club, a local anarchist group, but its leaders did not trust him. He apparently got the idea of shooting McKinley after reading of an anarchist's assassination of King Humbert I of Italy in 1900, although he later claimed a speech by noted anarchist Emma Goldman delivered at Cleveland's FRANKLIN CLUB† in May 1901 incited him.

Knowing through advertisements that McKinley would visit the Pan-American Exposition in Buffalo in Sept. 1901, Czolgosz left Cleveland in mid–1901 and on 31 Aug. rented a room in Buffalo. On 6 Sept., among a crowd waiting for the president in the exposition's Temple of Music, Czolgosz, who had concealed a revolver under a handkerchief wrapped about his hand, fired twice, hitting the president in the breastbone and abdomen. He was captured immediately. McKinley died of the abdominal wound 8 days later. Czolgosz was tried by the Supreme Court of the State of New York and found guilty of murder in 2 days. He was electrocuted at the Auburn, NY, State Prison on 29 Oct. 1901 and buried in an unmarked grave on the prison grounds.

Johns, A. Wesley. *The Man Who Shot McKinley* (1970).

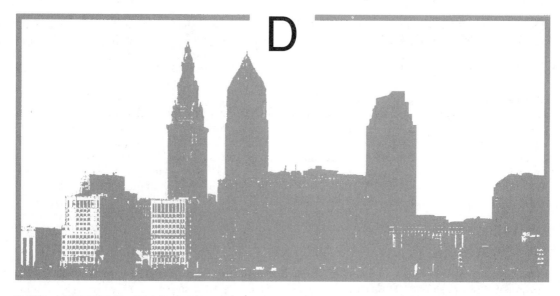

D

**DALL, ANDREW, JR.** (30 Mar. 1850–4 Feb. 1923) was a building contractor who, with his father, ANDREW DALL, SR. (1821–87), formed ANDREW DALL & SON,† prominent building contractors during the late 19th- and early 20th-century Cleveland.

Born in Markinch, Scotland, to Elizabeth (Davidson) and Andrew Dall, Sr., Andrew Jr. came to America with his family in 1852. He attended Cleveland public schools and studied the building trade under his father.

In 1874 he and his father formed Andrew Dall & Son. By 1875 they were well established as a contracting and building firm, having built the Randall Wade and Backus houses on EUCLID AVE.† They also built the EUCLID AVE. OPERA HOUSE† (1875), St. Paul's Episcopal Church (1876), Adelbert College (1881), and the Wilshire Building (1881). Other Euclid Ave. mansions the firm erected were those of SYLVESTER T. EVERETT, Samuel Andrews, CHARLES BRUSH, and CHARLES BINGHAM.

When his father died, Dall Jr. worked independently until, in 1888, Dall formed a partnership with Arthur McAllister to establish the firm of McAllister & Dall. This firm was responsible for erecting the BRATENAHL† residence of Samuel Mather, the SOLDIERS & SAILORS MONUMENT† (1894), and the SOCIETY FOR SAVINGS BUILDING† (1889–90), in PUBLIC SQUARE.†

In 1899 the firm became Andrew Dall & Son, as Dall formed a partnership with his son, William. The firm was responsible for building the UNION CLUB† (1905), the CUYAHOGA COUNTY COURTHOUSE† (1912), and other buildings throughout Ohio. In 1913 the firm was dissolved.

Dall married Alice Bennett in 1873. They had six children: Emma, William, Elizabeth, John, Joseph,

and Irene. Dall is buried in Lake View Cemetery. —T.B.

**DALL, ANDREW SR.** (ca. 1821–22 Nov. 1887) was a building contractor, stone cutter, and mason who, together with his son, ANDREW DALL, JR. (1850–1923) formed ANDREW DALL & SON,† building contractors, prominent during late 19th-century Cleveland.

Born in Markinch, Scotland, Dall served an apprenticeship of 7 years in the stone-cutting trade, becoming thoroughly familiar with all the details of the trade before moving to the U.S. with his family in 1852. Settling in Cleveland, Dall, an ambitious, enterprising, and skilled tradesman, plied his trade and was soon contracting work and establishing his own accounts. He was successful from the beginning and became identified as a leading contractor and citizen of Cleveland.

In partnership with his architect son, Andrew Dall, Jr. (who joined his father in business in 1874 to form Andrew Dall & Son) he erected the Randall Wade and FRANKLIN THOMAS BACKUS residences on Euclid Ave., ST. PAUL'S EPISCOPAL CHURCH† (1876), and the dormitory at Adelbert College (1881). He also erected the EUCLID AVE. OPERA HOUSE† (1875) E. 4th & Euclid, and the Wilshire Bldg. (1881). Other Euclid Ave. mansions erected by the Dalls were those of SYLVESTER EVERETT, SAMUEL ANDREWS (Andrew's Folly), CHARLES BRUSH, and CHARLES BINGHAM. They also erected many other buildings of note in Cleveland and neighboring cities and were considered one of the most important building contractor firms in late 19th-century Cleveland.

Dall married Elizabeth Davidson in Scotland. They had six children: Andrew Jr., Robert, and Mrs. John Protheroe (remaining three deceased).—T.B.

**DALTON, HENRY GEORGE** (3 Oct. 1862–27 Dec. 1939) was an industrialist, business and civic leader, and philanthropist.

Dalton was born in Cleveland to Frederick and Ellen (Gordon). He attended Cleveland public schools until age 14, when he went to work on WHISKEY ISLAND† for the New York, Pennsylvania & Ohio Railroad.

Dalton's industriousness caught the attention of Samuel Mather, who hired Dalton as a clerk in the newly formed PICKANDS, MATHER & CO.† in 1883. Dalton quickly moved up to bookkeeper, and in 1893 became the firm's fourth general partner. He became senior partner following Mather's death in 1931. Dalton honored his friend and partner in 1924 and 1925, when he gave Kenyon College $400,000 for the Samuel Mather Science Hall.

In 1925 and 1930, Dalton was appointed by the president to analyze the U.S. Shipping Board's merchant marine policies. As a director of both Bethlehem Steel Corp. and Youngstown Sheet & Tube, Dalton clashed with CYRUS EATON in a legal battle over a proposed merger of the two companies in 1930.

Dalton was a patron and supporter of the CLEVELAND ORCHESTRA,† and a vice-president, trustee, and executive committee member of the CLEVELAND MUSEUM OF ART.† In 1936 Dalton became the first recipient of Western Reserve Univ.'s doctor of humanities honorary degree and in 1938 he was presented with the Cleveland Chamber of Commerce's Public Service Medal.

Dalton married Julia Kaufholz on 19 Jan. 1886 (d. 1935). Their two children died at an early age. Dalton, an Episcopalian, lived in Cleveland and is buried in Lake View Cemetery.—T.B.

---

Pickands, Mather and Co. Records, WRHS.

**DANDRIDGE, DOROTHY** (9 Nov. 1923–8 Sept. 1965), Cleveland-born black nightclub entertainer and movie actress, who earned a Best Actress Oscar nomination in 1954, was influenced by her mother, Ruby, a screen and radio actress. Dorothy entered show business at age 5 as part of a singing trio with her mother and sister, Vivian. She also performed acrobatic ballet at Cleveland churches and schools, becoming known, with her sisters, as the Wonder Children. The family moved to Los Angeles when Dorothy was 9. Dorothy dropped out of high school and formed a trio with her sister, Vivian, and friend Etta Jones, singing with big band leader Jimmy Lunceford, winning small parts in movies, and in 1940 opening at the Cotton Club in New York City, where Dandridge met dancer Harold Nicholas. They married in 1941 and had a daughter, Harolyn, in 1944. They divorced in 1951.

After singing with the Desi Arnaz band at Hollywood Mocambo, and successes on the supper-show circuit, she starred opposite Harry Belafonte in *Carmen Jones,* a black Broadway musical based on Bizet's opera, which appeared in Cleveland at the Palace in 1954. In 1959 she costarred with Sidney Poitier in *Porgy and Bess.* On 30 June 1959, Dandridge married Jack Dennison, a Las Vegas nightclub owner. They had no children and divorced in 1962. In 1963, Dandridge filed for bankruptcy, with debts over $100,000. In 1965 she collapsed in her West Hollywood apartment from a rare complication resulting from a fractured foot.

**DA SILVA, HOWARD** (4 May 1909–16 Feb. 1986) regarded his native Cleveland as a "second city" long after he had left to achieve stardom as an actor on Broadway and in films. Moving with his family from Cleveland at the age of 1, he was raised in the Bronx, NY, and completed his education at Carnegie Institute in Pittsburgh. In 1928 he returned to New York to join Eva Le Gallienne's Civic Repertory Theater, where he played the classics for 6 years. Da Silva returned to Cleveland in 1935, becoming director of the Peoples Theatre, a labor theater that presented the local premiere of Odets's *Waiting for Lefty* and other socially conscious works. He also starred in several productions at the CLEVELAND PLAY HOUSE† before returning to New York to join the Federal Theatre Project. He originated the lead in Marc Blitzstein's *The Cradle Will Rock,* the "runaway opera" that broke away from the FTP and led to Orson Welles's Mercury Theatre. Da Silva also created the role of Jud in *Oklahoma!* and picked up Academy Award nominations for his film work in *Lost Weekend* and *Two Years Before the Mast.* His refusal to cooperate with the House Un-American Activities Committee in 1951, however, led to his being blacklisted. During that period he again returned to Cleveland, where he was invited to direct the 1958 season of the Chagrin Falls Summer Valley Playhouse. Da Silva later appeared on Broadway in such musicals as *Fiorello!* and *1776,* and made a film comeback in *David and Lisa.* He was coauthor of the anti-apartheid play, *The Zulu and the Zayda* (1965). Dying of lymphoma in Ossining, NY, he was survived by his wife, Nancy, and 5 children.—J.V.

**DAUBY, NATHAN L.** (31 May 1873–17 May 1964), who built the May Co. (see KAUFMANNS†) into the city's largest department store, was born in Cleveland to David and Lena Loeb Dauby. He started work at 15 as a clerk in a shoe store, and became its manager 2 years later. In 1892 Dauby and Emil Strauss opened Dauby & Strauss, the city's first one-price shoe store. Dauby bought Strauss out in 1898, and around 1902 the May Co. leased him its shoe department. In 1904 he became manager of the entire Cleveland May Co. store, serving as both general and merchandise manager until 1933, and as general manager until 1945, leaving the organization in 1961.

Dauby convinced May Co. to build a 6-story, $2.5 million building on PUBLIC SQUARE,† completed in 1914, and introduced the first escalator (1914) and parking garage for patrons (1925), and a children's playground (1904). Dauby also enticed customers by offering Eagle Trading Stamps, and later double stamps. Dauby became director of the national May Co. operation in 1910 and by 1918 was a vice-president. From 1945 until his death, Dauby concentrated on philanthropic work, especially the LOUIS D. BEAUMONT FOUNDATION.† In 1952 he donated his Euclid Ave. mansion to the CLEVELAND HEARING AND SPEECH CENTER.† Upon his death, he left an estate of $10 million; $1.5 million went to local institutions. In 1946 the Chamber of Commerce awarded Dauby its Medal for Public Service. Dauby and his wife, Bessie, married 2 Oct. 1901, had a son, David, and a daughter, Mrs. Lucile D. Gries.

**DAVIES, THOMAS D.** (3 Nov.1914–21 Jan. 1991) set a long distance aviation record in 1946 by flying nonstop from Perth, Australia, to Columbus, OH, and invented the sky compass for navigation near the Earth's magnetic poles.

Born in Cleveland to Katherine (Smith) and David Austin Davies, Thomas graduated from East High School and attended Case School of Applied Science before entering the U.S. Naval Academy. He graduated and was commissioned an ensign in 1937. He also graduated from the National War College and earned an M.A. from George Washington Univ.

Davies served on the USS *Portland* (1937–39), and the USS *Wichita* (1939–42). He completed flight training at Pensacola, FL, becoming a naval aviator on 24 July 1942.

Davies commanded a four-man navy crew that flew "The Truculent Turtle," a PV2 Neptune bomber, 11,237 miles non-stop in 55 hours, 15 minutes from Perth to Columbus on 1 Oct. 1946, setting a world's distance record unbroken for almost 16 years. Davies also held the transcontinental east to west speed record.

Davies developed a new system for sight reduction for celestial navigation and held a patent for the invention of nose wheel catapulting for aircraft carriers.

Davies advanced in rank to rear admiral on 1 July 1965. Retiring from the navy in 1973, Davies became asst. director of the U.S. Arms Control and Disarmament Agency. He later served on the Committee for National Security and as president of the Navigation Foundation.

Davies married Eloise English on 27 Apr. 1945. They had four children: Thomas Jr., Douglas, Ronald, and Meredith. Davies lived in Maryland and died in the Netherlands. He was buried at the Naval Academy Cemetery in Annapolis, MD.—T.B.

**DAVIS, HARRY EDWARD** (26 Dec. 1882–4 Feb. 1955), a lawyer active in Republican party politics and black community affairs, was born in Cleveland to Jacob Henry and Rosalie Dete Davis. He attended Hiram College (1904–05), and earned his LL.B from the Western Reserve Univ. Law School in 1908, being admitted to the bar and beginning private practice. In 1909, using the 1896 Ohio civil-rights law, Davis brought racial discrimination charges against a Burrows Store seller who refused to sell to him. Although the seller was found guilty, the jury denied Davis civil damages.

In 1920 Davis was elected to the first of 4 terms in the Ohio general assembly. He introduced a referendum removing a provision limiting the elective franchise to "white male citizens" from the Ohio constitution, which passed in 1923. In 1928 Davis became the first black elected by the city council to the Cleveland Civil Service Commission, serving as president from 1932–34. Elected to the Ohio senate in 1947, Davis was the first black legislator to preside over that body, and with his reelection in 1953 was the only successful black candidate for the Ohio legislature during the 1950s. Davis married Louise Wormley in 1917. He was a trustee of KARAMU HOUSE† and EUCLID AVE. CHRISTIAN CHURCH,† a 33rd-degree mason, and authored a manuscript on blacks (see AFRICAN AMERICANS†) in Masonry. His work on the history of blacks in Cleveland was completed by his brother, RUSSELL H. DAVIS. The Cleveland Board of Education named Harry E. Davis Jr. High School in his honor in 1962.

Russell H. Davis Papers, WRHS.

**DAVIS, HARRY LYMAN** (25 Jan. 1878–21 May 1950), 4-term mayor of Cleveland (1916–20, 1933–35) and governor of Ohio (1921–23) was born in NEWBURGH† to Evan and Barbara Jones Davis. He left school at 13 to work in the steel mills, studying at home and night school. At 21, he became a solicitor for the Cleveland Telephone Co., and 3 years later founded the Davis Rate Adjustment Co., selling telephone securities. He later established the Harry L. Davis Co., selling insurance. He married Lucy V. Fegan in 1905 and had a son, Harry L., Jr.

Davis was elected Republican city treasurer in 1909. In the 1915 mayoral election, the preferential election process used (see HOME RULE†) gave his opponent, PETER WITT, more first-place votes; however, Davis won with a plurality of over 2,800 on a combination of first, second, and other choice votes. Davis established the MAYOR'S ADVISORY WAR COMMITTEE,† and was reelected for 2 more terms, but resigned in May 1920 to campaign successfully for governor. During his term, he restructured the executive branch to include a cabinet of 7 directors to help administer state affairs. He did not run in 1922, but campaigned in 1924, losing to incumbent Vic Donahey. Returning to Cleveland, Davis opposed the CITY MANAGER PLAN,† and worked unsuccessfully for passage of an amendment to abolish it in 1927, 1928, and 1929. He took little part in the successful 1931 attempt, although afterwards he was again elected mayor (1933–35). Davis died in Cleveland.

Harry L. Davis Papers, WRHS.

**DAVIS, RUSSELL HOWARD** (29 Oct. 1897–14 Nov. 1976), teacher, administrator, civic activist, and historian of Cleveland's black community, was born in Cleveland to Jacob and Rosalie (Dite) Davis. He earned his bachelor's degree from Adelbert College of Western Reserve Univ. (1920), a degree in chemical engineering from Case School of Applied Science (1922), and a master's degree in education from WRU (1933). Davis worked as a chemical engineer for the GRASSELLI CHEMICAL CO.† before becoming a math and science teacher at Kennard Jr. High School, the first black male to serve in Cleveland's secondary schools. In 1932 he transferred to CENTRAL HIGH SCHOOL,† remaining as principal of Central Jr. High in 1940, when the new Central High was built. In 1951 he transferred to Rawlings Jr. High, and in 1962 became the principal of the new Harry E. Davis Jr. High School, named for his brother. He retired in 1965.

In 1943 Davis spearheaded the Welfare Fed.'s Central Area Social Study, creating the Central Area Community Council, of which he was an executive committee member. He also helped organize and was first president of the Glenville Area Community Council, and was an incorporator and executive committee member of the Neighborhood Settlement Assn. Davis chronicled the history of Cleveland's black community in newspaper columns and books, writing *Memorable Negroes in Cleveland's Past* and completing a project begun by his brother, the encyclopedic *Black Americans in Cleveland* (1972). Davis married Claire Richardson in 1923. They had a son, Russell Lee (b. 1924; d.

1933). Russell died in Cleveland and was buried in Lake View Cemetery.

Russell H. Davis Papers, WRHS.

**DAVIS, SYLVESTER SANFORD, JR.** (24 June 1925–17 Aug. 1989), an obstetrician, gynecologist, and surgeon, directed the division of gynecology and reproductive health at ST. LUKE'S MEDICAL CENTER† (1958–82) and participated in the NATIONAL ASSN. FOR THE ADVANCEMENT OF COLORED PEOPLE† (NAACP) for over 40 years. He served as president of the Cleveland Branch (1981–83) and on the national board, and testified at Senate subcommittee hearings on health reform (1979). Davis was born in Cleveland to teacher Amaza Dewey Weaver Davis and postal clerk Sylvester Sanford Davis. He attended local public schools, graduating from East High School. As a youth he worked as a page at the CLEVELAND PUBLIC LIBRARY† and maintained a large route for the *CLEVELAND CALL & POST.†* World War II interrupted his studies at Adelbert College of Western Reserve Univ. (WRU, see CASE WESTERN RESERVE UNIV.†); he served in the Army Air Corps (1943–46). Upon discharge as first lieutenant, Davis finished his degree (1949) at WRU and graduated from medical school at Howard Univ. in Washington, DC (1953). After interning at City Hospital of Cleveland (later MetroHealth Medical Center), he entered private practice in 1958 in Cleveland.

Davis was a clinical instructor at the CWRU School of Medicine (1958–89). He belonged to the ACADEMY OF MEDICINE† of Cleveland, the Cleveland Society of Obstetrics and Gynecology, the CUYAHOGA COUNTY MEDICAL SOCIETY,† the CLEVELAND MEDICAL READING CLUB,† among numerous other medical associations.

Davis married three times: Beverly Ann Yancey in 1953, they divorced in 1970; Estelle Jasper on 29 May 1971, they were divorced in 1977; and on 26 Mar. 1983 he married Muriel Johnson. He had 3 sons: Sylvester III, Carl, and Kerrick. Davis, who lived in SHAKER HTS.,† belonged to the ANTIOCH BAPTIST CHURCH† and was buried in Highland Park Cemetery.—J.M.

**DAVY, WILLIAM MCKINLEY** (9 June 1895–5 Sept. 1973) headed the CLEVELAND NEWSPAPER GUILD† for its first 30 years and became a leader in the local councils of LABOR. The son of a Welsh coal miner in Tuscarawas County, he was born in Midvale, OH, to William B. and Rachel (Herron) Davy. He quit school in the 6th grade to enter the mines but soon left to come to Cleveland in

1912. Working first in a hat factory and as a cab driver, he completed his education through extensive reading and married Clevelander Catherine Wallace in 1917. He entered newspaper work as an office boy and later reporter and columnist for the Central Press Assn., a news syndicate. Unemployed as a result of the Depression, Davy assisted in the founding of Local 1 of the American Newspaper Guild and was hired as its first executive secretary on 1 Dec. 1933. Besides heading the Cleveland local, Davy also served the national as an organizer and international representative. Twice he was executive secretary of the CLEVELAND INDUSTRIAL UNION COUNCIL,† from which he campaigned to expel communists, as he had from the American Newspaper Guild. In his home community of LAKEWOOD,† Davy was a trustee of Lakewood Hospital and member of the Lakewood Civil Service Commission. He was survived by his wife and 2 daughters, Ruth Murray and Dorothy Inklebarger.—J.V.

**DAWE, CHARLES DAVIS** (16 Mar. 1886–24 Aug. 1958), found a career as a choral conductor in Cleveland, where he was best remembered as founder of the ORPHEUS MALE CHORUS.† A native of Port Talbot, S. Wales, he studied music in London and began conducting choirs in Wales by the time he was 18. In 1912 he emigrated to Cleveland with his wife May and infant son, Chas. Gounod Dawe, securing an appointment as choirmaster at Calvary Anglican Church on EUCLID AVE.† On his way back to England in 1918 for service in World War I, he survived the torpedoing of his ship. Returning to Cleveland after the war, he founded the Orpheus in 1921 and conducted several other choirs such as the Cleveland Railroad Male Chorus, WTAM† Cathedral Choir, SHERWIN-WILLIAMS† Glee Club, and EPWORTH-EUCLID† Choral Society. At one time in 1930, he was directing 450 singers in 11 different groups each week. Besides the Orpheus, he was most visible as director of the OHIO BELL† Chorus in both Cleveland and Akron. He founded the Cleveland Bell group in 1922 and continued to direct it even after relinquishing the Orpheus baton in 1957. Following World War II, Dawe returned to Wales to assist in reviving the Eisteddfod choral competition with the help of a bequest from Cleveland industrialist Edwin S. Griffiths. Dawe often acted as an adjudicator in the Eisteddfod, which his Orpheus Chorus had won in 1926. A resident of CLEVELAND HTS.,† he relaxed by raising English pigeons and collecting Staffordshire china. He died shortly after retirement in St. Petersburg, FL.—J.V.

**DAY, WILLIAM HOWARD** (16 Oct. 1825–3 Dec. 1900) was an abolitionist, editor, publisher, printer, teacher, lecturer, civic leader and clergyman who devoted his life to improving the conditions of his fellow AFRICAN AMERICANS.†

Born in New York City to John and Eliza (Dixon) Day, William was educated at a private school and attended high school in Northampton, MA, where he learned printing at the *Northampton Gazette*. He was the only black graduate from Oberlin College (1847), where he received his M.A. (1859). Day received the D.D. degree from Livingstone College, Salisbury, NC, in 1887.

Day moved to Cleveland in 1847 where he worked to repeal the BLACK LAWS,† chaired the NATIONAL CONVENTION OF COLORED FREEDMEN† (1848), and helped organize the Negro Suffrage Society. Day edited the Cleveland *DAILY TRUE DEMOCRAT†* (1851–53) and published the *ALIENED AMERICAN†* (1853–54), Cleveland's first black newspaper, later editing its successor, the *People's Exposition* (1855).

In 1854 Day, who taught Latin, Greek, math, and rhetoric, was appointed librarian of the CLEVELAND LIBRARY ASSN.†

Day left Cleveland in 1856 for Buxton, Canada, to teach fugitive slaves fleeing north. In 1859 he visited Great Britain, raising over $35,000 for schools and churches for Canadian blacks. Returning to America after the Civil War, Day worked with the Freedman's Aid Assn., lectured, inspected freedmen schools, worked for black voter registration, and held various educational positions. In 1866 Day was ordained a minister of the African Methodist Episcopal Zion church.

Day married LUCY ANN STANTON on 25 Nov. 1852 (div. 1872). They had one child, Florence. In 1873 Day married Georgia F. Bell. He died in Harrisburg, PA.—T.B.

Davis, Russell H. *Memorable Negroes in Cleveland's Past* (1969).
Lawson, Ellen N. *The Three Sarahs: Documents of Antebellum Black College Women* (1984).

**DAY, WILLIAM L.** (13 Aug. 1876–15 July 1936), lawyer, U.S. district attorney, and federal judge, was born in Canton to William R. and Mary E. (Schaeffer) Day. He attended Williston Academy in E. Hampton, MA, and received his LL.B. degree from the Univ. of Michigan in 1900. He was then admitted to the Ohio Bar and practiced law in the firm of Lynch, Day & Day in Canton. In 1908 Day moved to Cleveland, having been appointed U.S. district attorney for northern Ohio by Pres. Theodore Roosevelt. He served in that office until 1911, when he was appointed U.S. district court judge. Day resigned the bench in 1914 because the low salary did not allow him to adequately support his family. Day joined the firm of SQUIRE, SANDERS & DEMPSEY,† remaining until 1919, when he left to join the firm of Day, Day & Wilkin. From 1925 until his death, Day practiced with his brother, Luther, in the firm of Day & Day. In 1919, Day & Wilkin were appointed special assistants to the Ohio attorney general to investigate crime in Cleveland. Conducting thousands of interviews with people involved in gambling, vice, and other criminal activities, Day & Wilkin were instrumental in uncovering bail-bond scandals and securing an indictment for the murder of a Cleveland police patrolman. Day married Elizabeth E. McKay on 10 Sept. 1902 and had 2 children, Wm. R. and Jean C. He died in Cleveland and was buried in Canton, OH.

**DEARING, ULYSSES S.** (25 June 1903–24 June 1984) was the first African American restaurateur to own a major restaurant in Cleveland and manage some of the city's most popular night clubs.

Born in Washington, PA, Dearing was named and raised by an uncle. Reared in poverty, Dearing received little formal education and left home when young to work at odd jobs. At age 15 he worked in the Carnegie steel mills. By 19 he was a chef in Wilkinsburg, PA. At 21, Dearing had saved enough money to open a small hotel and restaurant, but saw it destroyed by a flood.

Arriving in Cleveland in the early 1930s, Dearing first worked as a short order cook until hired as manager of the popular Cedar Gardens night club at E.79th and Cedar Ave. by owner, Jack Hecht.

In 1946 Dearing opened his first (of six) restaurant at 1930 E. 105th St. His second opened around 1953 at 10932 Superior Ave., and included a catering business. Dearing also opened one of Cleveland's first carry-out diners, "The Carry Out" at E. 97th St. and Cedar, which he sold in 1958 to open a Dearing's at 10930 Superior. In 1969 he opened a restaurant at 17234 Harvard. At the time of his death, one Dearing restaurant remained, at E. 110th St. and Superior Ave.

Dearing's civic involvement in the community spanned 50 years, including membership in the NAACP (lifetime), the URBAN LEAGUE,† and the GREATER CLEVELAND GROWTH ASSN.†

Dearing married Roberta Walker in 1936 and had two children, Ulysses Jr., and Sandra. Dearing is buried in Highland Park Cemetery.—T.B.

**DE CAPITE, MICHAEL** (13 April 1915–21 Jan. 1958) drew upon his Cleveland background to launch a promising though short career as a novelist. The son of Italian immigrants on the near west side, he played baseball in the shadows of industrial smokestacks in the FLATS and graduated from Lincoln High School. He attended Ohio Univ. in Athens, OH, where he met his future wife, Natalie Whiting, and graduated in 1938. De Capite broke into writing as a newspaperman, serving as feature editor of the Claremont (NH) *Daily Eagle* and as a police reporter in Chicago. During World War II he joined the U.S. Army, where he became a writer for *Yank* and the Army News Service. His first novel, *Maria* (1943) was based upon his memories of immigrant life during his Cleveland childhood. It was followed in 1944 by *No Bright Banner,* for which he drew upon his Chicago experiences. His last novel, *The Bennett Place* (1948), set in a fictitious Ohio college town suggestive of Athens, was awarded a $1,000 prize by the Friends of American Writers. Following the war, De Capite went to work in 1947 as an information officer for the United Nations. He was Chief of Editorial Services of the UN's Department of Public Information when he died from injuries received in an automobile accident near Mexico City. Buried near his home in Hastings-on-Hudson, NY, he was survived by his wife and 2 children, Philip and Suzanne. —J.V.

**DECKER, EDGAR** (18 Feb. 1832–1 Dec. 1905), one of Cleveland's earliest and most prominent photographers, grew up in New York state and was largely self-taught. At 13, he became a clerk in a store, after 7 years managing his own store, where he developed an interest in photography. He moved to Cleveland in 1857 and worked in various studios for 2 years before opening his own on Superior St. in 1859, moving it to the more fashionable EUCLID AVE. in 1883. Decker maintained a studio in Cleveland for over 40 years, producing an enormous volume of work that included portraits of old pioneers, lawyers, businessmen, physicians, society women, and families. In 1862 he photographed Cleveland regiments encamped outside the city prior to their involvement in the Civil War. Decker won many prizes for his portraits of famous statesmen, soldiers, diplomats, and actors and actresses. Among these were 4 presidents—Garfield, Grant, Hayes, and McKinley—as well as Gen. Sheridan. His original photographic portraits were tipped in the book *Cleveland, Past and Present; Its Representative Men* (1869). Active in photographic societies, in 1887 Decker was elected president of the Natl. Photographic Assn. His work was continued by his protege GEO. EDMONDSON, who also became a well-known Cleveland photographer. Edmondson acquired Decker's studio at the turn of the century. Decker also served on city council from 1878–82. He married Julia English on 2 Feb. 1857. They had a son, Edgar, Jr. Decker was buried in Lake View Cemetery.

**DEGRANDIS, PAUL J., JR.** (12 Nov. 1929–3 June 1993), politician, businessman, and labor leader, helped develop UNIV. CIRCLE† as the representative of the former Ward 19 on CLEVELAND CITY COUNCIL† (1958–61). He also presided over Local 100 of the American Federation of State, County and Municipal Employees (AFSCME) (1966–67), and the Board of Trustees of the CLEVELAND PUBLIC LIBRARY† (president, 1992–93, vice-president, 1991, board member, 1981–93), and served as district director for AFSCME (1967–68). He was widely recognized as a strong force in state and local politics and in the CUYAHOGA COUNTY DEMOCRATIC PARTY.† DeGrandis was born to Ruth and Paul J. DeGrandis, Sr. (d. 1994), both deputy clerks in the Cleveland Municipal Court. A graduate of CATHEDRAL LATIN SCHOOL,† he attended JOHN CARROLL UNIV.† before working for such officials as the Cuyahoga County engineer and the county recorder. DeGrandis served the U.S. Army in Europe during the early 1950s. In 1967 he became the deputy director of the Cuyahoga County Board of Elections. Four years later, over political differences, he left that position and joined the Ohio Department of Transportation as personnel director.

DeGrandis was also a successful businessman. In the 1960s he presided over DeGrandis Associates bonding agency, and in 1975 he created a coal brokerage which sold fuel to industries. In 1981 the Cleveland Public Library appointed him to its board. DeGrandis met Rita C. Feller at a meeting of the Democratic party and married her on 22 June 1957. The couple lived in Cleveland with their 7 children: Mary Anne Baucco, Mary Ruth Andrews, Mary Catherine, Mary Jane Garris, Mary Rita, Paul II, and David. DeGrandis belonged to Our Lady of Peace Catholic Church.—J.M.

**DEHARRACK, CHARLES PERETZ** (10 Sept. 1881–24 June 1985) was a pianist, composer, and choral director active in both Cleveland and international music circles. He was born in Brest-Litovsk, Russia. Brought to Cleveland at the age of 4, he attended local elementary schools before returning to Europe for musical training, which included piano lessons from Xaver Scharwenka and Theodore Leschetizky. He spent most of the following decade in Europe, teaching and giving concerts. He was the court pianist to King Peter I of Serbia and an accompanist for tenors Leo Slezak and Beniamino Gigli. Returning to Cleveland, De-Harrack became organist and choir director at the Temple on the Heights (see B'NAI JESHURUN†). He was also director of the Nyegosh Serbian Choir and the Yiddish Gesang Verein, as well as music critic for the German-language daily, *WAECHTER*

*UND ANZEIGER.* As pianist, he performed locally in such venues as Masonic Hall, PUBLIC AUDITORIUM,† and the HIPPODROME THEATER.† He composed extensively, winning a composition prize in 1905 at Leipzig and being published there and in Vienna. Among his compositions were an "Allegorical Poem" dedicated to the ORPHEUS MALE CHORUS† and a song, "Lights," set to lyrics by Cleveland journalist EDWIN ("TED") ROBINSON. He also wrote religious music for Jewish synagogues. His wife, Cecile, preceded him in death by 4 years.—J.V.

Charles DeHarrack Papers, WRHS.

**DEIKE, CLARA L.** (1881–13 March 1964) was a distinguished Cleveland artist and art teacher. Born in Detroit, MI, she came to Cleveland as a child to receive her education at CENTRAL HIGH SCHOOL,† the Cleveland Normal Training School, and the Cleveland School of Art (see CLEVELAND INSTITUTE OF ART†). Her art training was later supplemented by study with Hans Hoffman in Munich and Capri and with Diego Rivera in Mexico. Deike taught art for 30 years in the CLEVELAND PUBLIC SCHOOLS,† notably at Central High School, John Adams, and WEST HIGH SCHOOL.† She also pursued an active avocation as a painter, exhibiting regularly in the MAY SHOW† and holding 1-person shows in Cleveland, Columbus, and Washington, DC. "She never was in the flow of what became known as the Cleveland School of artists, though historically she belongs in the fold," said art critic Helen Cullinan. Her style ranged from still lifes and landscapes to abstract experimentation in her later years. A founding member of the WOMEN'S ART CLUB OF CLEVELAND,† Deike served as the group's president in 1919–20. Never married, she maintained studios in her LAKEWOOD† residence and in a summer home in Gloucester, MA.—J.V.

**DELAMATER, JOHN** (18 Apr. 1787–28 Mar. 1867), a teacher of medicine and founder of 3 medical colleges, was born in Chatham, NY, son of Jacob and Elizabeth (Dorr) Delamater. He studied medicine with his uncle from 1804–07, and was licensed in 1807, practicing privately between 1807–22. Delamater began teaching in 1823 at the newly established Berkshire Medical Institute at Williams College, receiving an honorary M.D. in 1824. Between 1823–43, Delamater held professorships at numerous colleges, including Willoughby College in Akron, of which he was a founder in 1837. He also conducted a private medical school in Palmyra, NY, several months each year.

In 1840 Delamater moved to Willoughby, OH,

leaving for Cleveland in 1842 and founding, along with Drs. Ackley, Cassels, and Kirtland, Cleveland Medical College, where he was dean and professor for 17 years. Delamater was a member of many professional organizations, and in 1819 helped organize the Berkshire District Medical Society. Delamater was a deacon of the Congregational church and an elder of the Presbyterian church. He was politically outspoken, especially against slavery, and lectured on temperance. When he retired in 1860, Western Reserve elected him their first professor emeritus and awarded him an honorary LL.D. He continued in private practice and filled temporary teaching vacancies nearly until his death. Known for his charity and negligence in collecting fees, he retired in near-poverty. His colleagues collected funds to furnish him with a home in Cleveland. Married to Ruth Angell in 1811, Delamater had 8 children: Mehitable, Elizabeth, Jacob, Gertrude, John, Mary, Eliza, and Martha. Delamater died in East Cleveland.

**DELANEY, JOHN (JACK) F.** (3 Oct. 1913–4 Feb. 1990), Cleveland policeman for 41 years, organized the department's ports and harbor unit and wrote the city's first Water Traffic Code. He was born in Cleveland, the son of John and Gertrude (Dahm) Delaney, and attended EAST TECHNICAL HIGH SCHOOL.† He joined the police force in 1937. In addition to writing Cleveland's first water traffic code, he was credited with the idea of using an orange fluorescent flag as a distress signal for boaters—a symbol that became Ohio law in the early 1960s and was adopted elsewhere in the country. He organized the department's ports and harbors unit in 1962 and was the unit's commander until he retired in 1978. In the mid–1980s a Port Authority boat was named after him.

A boater all his life, Delaney was an active volunteer in the Greater Cleveland chapter of the American Red Cross, serving as a water safety and first aid instructor for the chapter. He also trained prospective sailing instructors and helped maintain and repair Red Cross sailing equipment. In 1982, the Red Cross Safety Programs presented him with its Hall of Fame Award.

Delaney married Lucretia K. Holobosh 20 Nov. 1937, and they had 5 children: two sons, Jack C. Jr. and Timothy J., and daughters Carol Fisher, Eileen Kohut, and Peggy Masin. A resident of Cleveland, Delany died here at age 76 and was interred at All Souls Cemetery in Chardon.—M.S.

**DELANEY, RALPH DAVID** (22 April 1933–27 April 1990) was a social activist who dedicated his life to serving the poor and the homeless. Born in Cleveland to Ralph and Ann (Yaniko) Delaney, Ralph attended CATHEDRAL LATIN SCHOOL, leaving in 1949 to join the Marianist Order in Cincinnati, where he became a teaching brother. Delaney graduated from the Univ. of Dayton (B.A., 1955) and CASE WESTERN RESERVE UNIV.† (M.A., 1961).

Delaney left the Marianist order after eleven years to become a teacher, community organizer, and worker with Cleveland's needy. Delaney collected food each night to feed the street people around PUBLIC SQUARE.† He also took clothing to the poor, and would take them on outings such as the KARAMU HOUSE.†

Delaney organized and directed the Collinwood Arts Center, teaching classes in drama, video production, writing, poetry, art therapy, art education, photography, mathematics, and philosophy. He organized and directed the Gandhi-King Peace Center, was asst. chaplain at the Cuyahoga County Jail, participated in the Catholic Worker Movement and worked at the RAINEY INSTITUTE.†

On 19 April 1990, as Delaney was videotaping evidence of dilapidated living conditions at CMHA apartments, he was robbed and savagely beaten. He died from massive head injuries several days later at ST. VINCENT CHARITY HOSPITAL AND MEDICAL CENTER.† More than 1,200 mourners, including Cleveland Mayor Michael White (see MAYORAL ADMINISTRATION OF MICHAEL WHITE†), attended his funeral liturgy at ST. JOHN CATHEDRAL.† Delaney, who never married, is buried in Holy Cross Cemetery.—T.B.

**DE LERY, JOSEPH GASPARD CHAUSSEGROS** (21 July 1721–11 Dec. 1797), a French lieutenant, described in his private journal the earliest recorded account of the complete transit of the south shore of Lake Erie. In it, he noted the first recorded encampment at the CUYAHOGA RIVER,† on 2 Aug. 1754, and drew a sketch of the river, which he called "Riviere a Seguin or Blanch, also Goyahague." The transit of the south shore occurred in the summer of 1754. In the latter part of Apr. 1754, de Lery was ordered by the Marquis Dequesne to journey to Detroit to reinforce the garrison and to serve there as second in command under Sieur Pierre Joseph de Celoron de Blainville. He departed Presque Isle on 30 July 1754 with a force of 285 men in 27 canoes and arrived at Ft. Detroit on 6 Aug. His journal includes detailed directions, distances, descriptions of the shoreline, and drawings of numerous rivers and creeks. While earlier descriptions of the south shore of Lake Erie exist, they are limited to either end of the lake and exclude the Cuyahoga River.

**DEMAIORIBUS, ALESSANDRO LOUIS "SONNY"** (25 Apr. 1898–5 May 1968), a member of CLEVELAND CITY COUNCIL† for 20 years and longtime leader in Cuyahoga County Republican affairs, was born in Cleveland, son of Domenic and Lucia DeMaioribus. He lived behind the grocery store operated by his father at 1930 Coltman Rd. Nicknamed "Sonny" as a child, he attended Murray Hill School and East High School. He went to work for the CLEVELAND HOME BREWING CO.† in 1925 as a bookkeeper, becoming general manager by 1934 and eventually president of the firm, until it was liquidated in 1952. Attracted to politics, DeMaioribus was first elected to the city council in 1927. At that time, the Republican party was in the majority, and he gained political influence serving as council president from 1934–42. Resigning from the council in 1947, he worked at the Cuyahoga County Republican headquarters until 1955, when he became party chairman, succeeding GEO. BENDER. During this time, the Democratic party was in the ascendancy, and the Republicans suffered electoral defeats consistently. By cooperating with the Democrats, however, DeMaioribus was able to obtain some of the available patronage for his party. Unmarried, DeMaioribus was preparing to retire as county chairman when he died suddenly. DeMaioribus was buried in Lake View Cemetery.

**DEMMY, OLEAN WELLS** (8 Jan. 1913–23 June 1993) capped a long career in community service with the revival of the old Hruby Conservatory as the Broadway School of Music. A native of frontier Oklahoma, she was the daughter of Joseph and Hadie Savage Wells. She earned a teaching certificate from South Eastern College of Oklahoma, adding a master's degree later from Oklahoma A&M. While teaching in Alaska she met Pennsylvania native Nicholas Demmy, whom she married in 1946. The couple moved from Baltimore to Portland, OR, to San Francisco while Demmy pursued a medical education. They came to Cleveland in 1956, and Dr. Demmy served on the staff of the FAIRHILL MENTAL HEALTH CTR.† Mrs. Demmy became involved in the CLEVELAND COUNCIL ON WORLD AFFAIRS,† teaching English and American culture to wives of foreign doctors. She was also president of the Women's Auxiliary of the ACADEMY OF MEDICINE OF CLEVELAND.† When Dr. Demmy joined the staff of ST. ALEXIS HOSPITAL,† she became president of the St. Alexis Hospital Medical Auxiliary. She determined to restore the Hruby Conservatory of Music building (see HRUBY FAMILY) near St. Alexis after her husband had purchased it as an investment. Taking charge of cleaning and repairs, she induced the CLEVELAND MUSIC SCHOOL SETTLEMENT† to operate a branch there in 1980. It became independent as the Broadway School of Music in 1983, with Mrs.

Demmy serving as chairwoman until her resignation for health reasons. She died in Cleveland and was buried at Lake View Cemetery. Besides her husband, she was survived by 2 daughters, Elizabeth Anne Delton and Mary Kathryn Demmy.—J.V.

**DEMORE, MATTHEW** (Apr. 1903–18 Mar. 1976), a labor leader active in the Internatl. Assn. of Machinists for 4 decades, was born and raised in LITTLE ITALY,† son of Dominick and Carmella (DeBaise) DeMore. He quit school at 16 to work as a machinist's apprentice for the Michigan Central Railroad in Detroit. He returned to Cleveland in 1920 to work for the maintenance department at General Electric, a position he held until 1926, when he became active in the fledgling IAM. Within 3 years, he headed a reform slate of officers on a platform to streamline the operations of District 54, which included Cleveland. Under his leadership, the district was practically free of strikes, and membership jumped from 4,500 to 6,000. He led the district as president from 1938–61. While DeMore participated in strikes, he advocated them only as a last resort. He was regarded as fair and honest, leading to his appointment to many government boards. In 1946, he unsuccessfully challenged incumbent FRANCES P. BOLTON for Congress. He was vice-president of the Ohio and Cleveland AFL-CIOs, and director for the State Council for Machinists. In 1961, DeMore was elected an international vice-president of the IAM and moved to New York. Within 3 years, he was a regional vice-president at the IAM Washington office, and was elected general secretary-treasurer in 1965. When his 4-year term expired, DeMore devoted his time to the Natl. Council of Senior Citizens and other activities for seniors. He and his wife, Mary, had 5 children: Dorothy, Marie, Delores, Alice, and Matthew. DeMore died in Washington, DC, and was buried in Cleveland's All Soul's Cemetery.

**DEMPSEY, JAMES HOWARD** (29 Mar. 1859–2 May 1920), a lawyer and founding partner of SQUIRE, SANDERS & DEMPSEY,† was born in Shelby, OH, to John and Martha (Davis) Dempsey. He graduated from Kenyon College in 1882, and went to study law at Columbia Univ. The summer following his first year at Columbia, Dempsey gained employment at the Cleveland firm of Estep, Dickey & Squire. Persuaded to stay, he continued his studies under Judge Estep, the senior partner. Upon passing the bar in 1884, Dempsey became a partner. He stayed with the firm until 1890, when he left with ANDREW SQUIRE† to establish, along with Judge WM. SANDERS, the firm of Squire, Sanders & Dempsey. Devoted to improving education, Dempsey was on the board of trustees of

UNIV. SCHOOL and his alma mater, Kenyon College, which bestowed him with an LL.B. degree in 1912. He was also on the board of trustees of Lake View Cemetery. Dempsey was president of the Factory Site Co. and director of many Cleveland companies, including the Union Commerce Natl. Bank, GRASSELLI CHEMICAL CO.,† and Bourne-Fuller Co.

Dempsey married twice. His first wife, Emma Norris Bourne, whom he married on 24 Sept. 1885, died on 14 Mar. 1893. They had 2 sons, John Bourne and Ernest Cook. He married Ada Hunt on 30 Oct. 1915. They had 2 children, Jas. H., Jr., and Isabel. Dempsey died in Cleveland and was buried in Lake View Cemetery.

**DEPAOLO, LOUIS** (1894–5 Dec. 1977), a businessman and leader who earned the title "mayor of LITTLE ITALY,†" was born in Italy, son of Alex and Lena (Truisonno) DePaolo. He left Campobasso to join 4 uncles in Cleveland in 1910. He studied 2 years at night school and was trained as a tailor by an uncle. He worked as a tailor, then a bank clerk, before opening his own business: first a bookstore, then a confectionery, then a paint store, and finally an insurance and real estate agency. Italian immigrants found more than books or paint in DePaolo's stores and offices. He spoke 18 Italian dialects and was often a translator for the Dept. of Justice. He helped with visas, coached those preparing for citizenship examinations, offered advice about income taxes, sold Alitalia airline tickets, and, beginning in the 1950s, led an annual tour of Italy. From 1941 until ca. 1975, DePaolo produced, directed, and hosted the "Italian Radio Hour"; he also published the Italian weekly newspaper *L'ARALDO* (the Herald) from 1952–59. In addition, DePaolo was active in civic and Democratic political affairs. He was a trustee of ALTA HOUSE,† and president of the Mayfield Merchants Assn., the Mayfield-Murray Hill District Council, and the Democratic Italian League; he ran for state representative in 1952. After World War II, he received the Star of Solidarity from the Italian government for his work in helping rebuild his native country. DePaolo married Theresa Arietta on 12 July 1917; they had two children, Madeline and Allessio. DePaolo was buried in Lake View Cemetery.

**DE SAUZE, EMILE BIALS** (7 Dec. 1878–11 July 1964), director of foreign languages for the CLEVELAND PUBLIC SCHOOLS† from 1918–49 and developer of the conversational teaching method, was born in Tours, France, and graduated from the Univ. of Poitiers (1900) before coming to the U.S. in 1905 and receiving a Ph.D. from St. Joseph College. He came to Cleveland in 1918.

The de Sauze method, or "Cleveland Plan," emphasized listening and speaking as well as reading and writing, using the target language exclusively in the classroom, a departure from the traditional grammar-translation method. Under de Sauze's direction, his textbook *Cours pratique de Francais* (lst ed. 1919) was the beginning text, later supplemented by advanced-level readers de Sauze either authored or edited from 1924–39. During the 1920s, French was added to the curriculum for gifted elementary school children with classwork, entirely oral and in French, based on active participation. De Sauze trained his teachers, contributing to his method's success. He founded, and for many years directed, the School of French of Western Reserve Univ., as well as the Demonstration School of Foreign Languages where, during the summer, educators from all over the world came to observe his methodology. He founded the MAISON FRANCAISE,† a cultural organization for the Cleveland Francophone community. De Sauze died in Cleveland. His wife, Melanie Philips, whom he married in 1903, and their daughter, Marcelle (Mrs. Oliver J. Deex), preceded him in death.

**DEUTSCH, SAMUEL H.** (2 Apr. 1892–4 Sept. 1958) prominent sportsman and jeweler, was born in New York City, the son of Rudolph and Hulda Heimlich Deutsch. The family moved here in 1899, and after finishing school, he entered the Rudolph Deutsch Co., his father's jewelry firm, where he learned the art of diamond cutting. He succeeded his father as company president and became chairman of the board in 1956, with his son Robert as president. In local sports, Deutsch was primarily known as owner of the Cleveland Indians, an early professional football team in the National Football League. Deutsch bought the defunct Cleveland franchise in 1923, continuing the Indians name, and finishing fifth in the 20-team league. The NFL champion Canton Bulldogs lost money that year, and Deutsch purchased the team for $1,500 from a group of Canton businessmen. He switched the best Canton players to Cleveland and renamed the team the Cleveland Bulldogs, leaving the Canton franchise inactive. Cleveland's Bulldogs won the 1924 NFL championship, and Deutsch sold the inactive franchise back to Canton for $3,000. With key players returning to Canton in 1925, the Cleveland Bulldogs finished 12th in the NFL. After a hiatus in 1926, Deutsch revived the Cleveland Bulldogs. Although the team finished fourth in 1927, it was unsuccessful financially, and Deutsch sold the franchise to Elliot Fisher of Detroit at the end of the season.

Deutsch married Martha S. Leibel 29 June 1919; they had 2 children, Robert and Mrs. Shirley Feder.

A resident of SHAKER HTS.,† he died in Cleveland.—M.S.

**DEVEREUX, HENRY KELSEY "HARRY K."** (10 Oct. 1859–1 May 1932), son of Antoinette (Kelsey) and JOHN H. DEVEREUX, made his greatest contributions to harness racing, although he was an able business follower of his father. At 16, he attended Brooks Military Academy and was chosen as the drummer boy model in ARCHIBALD WILLARD's painting *THE SPIRIT OF '76.†* After graduating from Yale in 1883, he worked for the Cleveland, Columbus, Cincinnati & Indianapolis Railroad, and later managed the Chicago-Cleveland Roofing Co. Devereux was fascinated with harness racing. Never a bettor, he invested in horses and drove them in amateur races at the GLENVILLE RACE TRACK.† He won over 3,000 cups and ribbons and accumulated 14 records.

Devereux devoted both time and capital advancing harness racing. In 1895 he organized the Gentlemen's Driving Club of Cleveland, which competed with other clubs through the League of American Driving Clubs, which Devereux organized in 1901, professionalizing the sport and focusing attention on Cleveland. When a proponent of the Glenville Race Track died, the mayor of that village declared betting illegal, assuring the closing of the track (1909). So in 1908, sportsmen organized the village of N. RANDALL, and Devereux financed the building of RANDALL PARK† Race Track and was its first president. When Devereux died, he left his horses and racing paraphernalia to a pair of faithful stablemen. Devereux married Mildred French on 11 Feb. 1885 and had 2 children, Julian French and Aileen (Mrs. Lanier Winslow). He died at his winter home in Georgia and was buried in Lake View Cemetery.

Devereux Family Papers, WRHS.
Gentlemen's Driving Club of Cleveland Records, WRHS.

**DEVEREUX, JOHN H.** (5 Apr. 1832–17 Mar. 1886), a civil engineer and leading Midwest railroad manager, was born in Boston, son of John and Matilda (Burton) Devereux. He attended Portsmouth Academy in New Hampshire, and at 16 came to Cleveland as a construction engineer on first the Cleveland, Columbus & Cincinnati Railroad, then the Cleveland, Painesville & Ashtabula Railroad. From 1852–61 he worked in Tennessee, joining the Union Army when the CIVIL WAR† began. In 1862, as a colonel, he was in charge of all Union rail lines in Virginia, in disarray because of damage inflicted by Confederates and conflicts between various army and government departments using the lines. Devereux improved efficiency, orga-

nized inspection and repair units, obtained equipment, enforced use rules, and smoothed differences between departments. Under his supervision, the trains moved large amounts of troops, artillery, and the sick. Devereux resigned as a general in the spring of 1864.

After the war, Devereux returned to Cleveland as general superintendent, and later vice-president, of the Cleveland & Pittsburgh Railroad. In 1868 he became vice-president, then president, of the Lake Shore Railroad, and became general manager when the company consolidated into the Lake Shore & Michigan Southern. In 1873 he became president of the Cleveland, Columbus, Cincinnati & Indianapolis Railroad and the Atlantic & Great Western Railroad Co. and several smaller companies. The Devereux residence, built in 1873, was part of "Millionaires Row" on EUCLID AVE.† Devereux was twice defeated for Congress. In 1851, Devereux married Antoinette Kelsey. They had 4 children: Mary, John, Antoinette, and HENRY K. DEVEREUX. Devereux is buried at Lake View Cemetery.

Devereux Family Papers, WRHS.

**DEVINE, MARGARET CRILE GARRETSON** (2 Feb. 1901–17 Jan. 1993), civic leader, helped train women to work in war plants during World War II. Devine was born in Cleveland, the 3rd child and oldest daughter of Grace McBride and GEORGE W. CRILE, SR. She attended LAUREL SCHOOL,† Bryn Mawr College, and Garland School in Boston, MA. Devine worked at the JOHN HUNTINGTON POLYTECHNIC INSTITUTE† during and after World War I. She was also employed as a secretary and editorial assistant in the astronomy and humanities departments of the Case Institute of Technology (later CASE WESTERN RESERVE UNIV.†). In 1922 Crile married Hiram Garretson (d. 1967). They lived in Cleveland with their 2 children, Richard C. Garretson and Ann E. Ford. The couple supported the local art community. She was vice-president of the PRINT CLUB OF CLEVELAND† and he was president; they both belonged to the Cleveland Society for Contemporary Art. Crile married Charles Devine (d. 1986).

Devine was a trustee of Laurel School (1933–47) and president of its alumnae board (1940–42). She also was a board member of the Rainbow Hospital for Crippled and Convalescent Children (see UNIV. HOSPITALS†), the JUNIOR LEAGUE OF CLEVELAND, INC.,† and the Children's Asylum (later BEECH BROOK, INC.†). Devine presided over the RECREATION LEAGUE OF CLEVELAND† before World War II. She loved the outdoors and shot a moose herself on one of many hunting trips with her brother Barney (GEORGE W. CRILE, JR.). Devine died at the MARGARET WAGNER HOME.†—J.M.

**DEWALD, LOUISE** (3 Nov. 1877–12 Oct. 1954) was for many years the highest-ranking woman in Cleveland's city government. She rose through the department ranks to become Commissioner of Cemeteries (1925–42), possibly the only woman cemetery commissioner in the U.S. Daughter of William and Catherine (Klump) Dewald, she was a Cleveland native and public school graduate. Dewald began with the department in 1900 at Woodland, supervised by her brother. In 1911 a high civil service exam score placed Dewald on a classified list, from which she was picked for departmental secretary in 1912. In Mar. 1917 she was appointed supervisor of cemeteries, becoming commissioner of cemeteries in 1924. Popular with employees and the press, Dewald strove to enhance the department's self-sufficiency, promoting the nation's first municipally owned mausoleum and crematory at Highland Park in 1928.

In 1932 Mayor RAY T. MILLER, wanting to distribute patronage, fired officeholders, including Dewald, who immediately petitioned the Ohio Supreme Court for reinstatement, which the justices unanimously granted. "Woman Upsets Democratic Machine in Court Test," announced the CLEVELAND PRESS† in this vindication of municipal civil service. In June 1934, Dewald drew bipartisan criticism from the city council's finance committee for exploiting women when it discovered she employed them for $.37$\frac{1}{2}$ per hour versus the men's $.60 per hour rate. In late 1941 and early 1942, this survivor of 12 mayors was accused of embezzling over $19,000, allegedly for gambling. After restoring the funds by May 1942, she was placed on 5 years' probation for technical embezzlement.

Unmarried, Dewald died in Cleveland and was buried in Highland Park Cemetery.

**DICK, MARCEL** (18 Aug. 1898–13 Dec. 1991) provided Cleveland with a link to the Austrian musician Arnold Schoenberg, as head of the advanced theory and composition dept. of the CLEVELAND INSTITUTE OF MUSIC.† A great-nephew of Hungarian violinist Edward Remenyi, Dick was born in Miskolc, Hungary, and studied under composer Zoltan Kodaly at the Royal Academy of Music in Budapest. After serving in the Austrian army during World War I, he became a member of the Kolisch String Quartet and first violist of the Vienna Symphony. He lived for nearly 2 years in the same apartment building with Schoenberg and participated in the world premiere of the latter's *Serenade*. Dick came to the U.S. in 1934, about the same time

that he married Ann Weil. He became principal violist of the Detroit Symphony and served the CLEVELAND ORCHESTRA† in the same capacity from 1943–49. He began teaching at CIM in 1946, becoming head of composition 2 years later. Among his students were Donald Erb and Hale Smith. In his own works, Dick exemplified the 12-tone serial techniques of Schoenberg. His *Symphony* was performed by the Cleveland Orchestra under Dimitri Mitropoulos in 1950, and Dick himself led the orchestra in his *Capriccio for Orchestra* in 1957 and the *Adagio and Rondo for Orchestra* in 1963. In 1962 he received one of the Fine Arts Awards presented by the WOMEN'S CITY CLUB.† Although he gave up the chairmanship at CIM in 1973, he continued to teach and compose. A volume of essays, *Studies in the Schoenbergian Movement in Vienna and the United States,* was published in his honor by colleagues and former students in 1990. He was survived by his wife and a daughter, Suzanne Wolfe.—J.V.

**DIETZ, DAVID** (6 Oct. 1897–9 Dec. 1984), covered science and medicine for the CLEVELAND PRESS† and all Scripps-Howard newspapers for over 50 years. Born in Cleveland, the son of Henry W. and Hannah (Levy) Dietz, he graduated from Central High School in 1915 and began writing for the *Press* while attending Western Reserve Univ., being designated science editor for the Scripps-Howard chain in 1921. His daily science column began appearing in papers the following year. In 1934 he was a charter member and first president of the Natl. Assn. of Science Writers. Their coverage of the scientific meetings held in conjunction with the Harvard tercentenary brought Dietz and 4 other science correspondents the 1937 Pulitzer Prize in reporting.

During World War II, Dietz served as consultant to the surgeon general of the army and on a committee of the Office of Scientific Research & Development. His book *Atomic Energy in the Coming Era* appeared in 1945, and after the war he covered the atom bomb tests at Bikini Atoll. Respected for rendering scientific jargon into readable prose, Dietz was also science correspondent for the NBC radio network in the 1940s. Dietz received honorary doctorates from WRU and Bowling Green State Univ., and was granted many awards. Among his 9 books, at both adult and young-reader levels, *All about Satellites and Space Ships* (1958) sold over 250,000 copies. Dietz married Dorothy Cohen on 26 Sept. 1918 and had 3 children: Doris (Turner), Patricia (Morris), and David, Jr. After an estimated production of 9 million column words, he retired to his home in SHAKER HTS.† in 1977. Dietz died at the MARGARET WAGNER HOUSE† of the BENJA-

MIN ROSE INSTITUTE†and was buried in Lake View Cemetery.

**DINARDO, ANTONIO** (1887–29 June 1948) was an architect active in Cleveland from 1921–48, born in Pennapiedimonte, Italy, son of Domenico and Rosina Augeta Domenica (Guilante) DiNardo. After coming to America, DiNardo attended the Univ. of Pennsylvania and the Beaux-Arts Institute of Design in Philadelphia. He then studied in Europe. Upon his return, he worked in the office of Paul Cret, and later in the New York office of Arnold Brunner, who planned the Federal Bldg. in Cleveland and was a member of the Group Plan Commission. While in Brunner's office, DiNardo designed a building for the north end of the Mall, which was apparently the earliest conception of the tower design that became the Terminal Tower.

DiNardo came to Cleveland in 1921, becoming a designer in the office of HUBBELL & BENES†; among other buildings, he designed their Pearl St. Bank. His own work included St. Augustine Academy in LAKEWOOD,† St. Margaret of Hungary Church, portions of the McGregor Home for the Aged, and St. Augustine Church in Barberton. He planned a number of private residences, one for Robt. Black in Mansfield among the most notable. In 1936, DiNardo designed the Transportation Bldg. for the GREAT LAKES EXPOSITION.† Also an artist in both oil and watercolor painting, DiNardo exhibited frequently in the Cleveland MAY SHOW.† He published a volume of lithographs in 1924 entitled *French Farmhouses, Churches, and Small Chateaux.*

His wife, Alida, whom DiNardo married on 15 Sept. 1918, preserved many of his architectural drawings. The couple had no children. DiNardo died in Cleveland and was buried in Lake View Cemetery.

**DITTRICK, HOWARD** (14 Feb. 1877–11 July 1954) was a Cleveland physician and medical writer. With his wife, Gertrude, he collected and cataloged medical artifacts which provided the basis for the DITTRICK MUSEUM OF MEDICAL HISTORY,† which he curated (1928) and then directed (1935–54). Dittrick edited the Bulletin of the ACADEMY OF MEDICINE OF CLEVELAND† (1934), *Current Researches in Anesthesia and Analgesia,* and the *Cleveland Clinic Quarterly* (1944–48) (see CLEVELAND CLINIC FOUNDATION†) and compiled a book on local medical history. He was born in St. Catherines, Ontario, Canada, to Duncan and Martha Harper Dittrick and graduated from St. Catherines Collegiate Institute. After earning both his M.B. (1900) and M.D. (1927) at the Univ. of Toronto, Dittrick practiced obstetrics and gynecol-

ogy in Cleveland from a Prospect Ave. office. In 1925 he began teaching at the School of Medicine of Western Reserve Univ. (see CASE WESTERN RESERVE UNIV.†) and continued to teach there until 1944. Associate Gynecologist for UNIV. HOSPITALS OF CLEVELAND,† Dittrick presided over the Cleveland Medical Examiners Society and belonged to numerous state and national professional associations. He represented the U.S. twice at the International Congress of History of Medicine (1935, 1938). Outside the medical realm, Dittrick belonged to the CLEVELAND MUSEUM OF ART† and chaired a local intermuseum advisory group.

On 29 Jan. 1907 Dittrick married Gertrude B. Moore; the couple lived in CLEVELAND HTS.† with their 6 sons: Douglas, John, Lawrence, Alan, Howard, and Paul. Dittrick is buried in Lake View Cemetery.—J.M.

Howard Dittrick Papers, Dittrick Museum of Medical History.

**DIVELY, GEORGE SAMUEL** (17 Dec. 1902–1 Nov. 1988) was a prominent business and civic leader in Cleveland. He led the HARRIS CORP.† from 1941–72 from a small manufacturer of printing presses to a multinational producer of high-technology communications and information processing equipment.

Born in Claysburg, PA, to Michael and Martha (Dobson), Dively attended Lock Haven State College, earned a B.S.E.E. at the Univ. of Pittsburgh (1925) and an M.B.A. from Harvard Univ. (1929). After graduation he worked at North American Refractories, in investment banking, and at Republic Steel Corp.

Dively joined Harris-Seybold-Potter Co. of Cleveland in 1937 as an asst. to the secretary. He became a director in 1941, vice-president and general manager in 1944, and president in 1947. He served as both president and chairman from 1954–61 when he resigned the presidency, continuing as board chairman until his retirement in 1972.

Under Dively's leadership, Harris' annual sales increased from $10 million to $2 billion. He also orchestrated a series of acquisitions, including a merger with Radiation Inc. (1967) and the relocation of company headquarters to Florida, where Harris became the largest industrial employer.

Dively was cofounder of the Cleveland One-Percent Plan to encourage corporate support for higher education and participated in leadership of CLEVELAND NOW!,† CLEVELAND TOMORROW,† and other urban improvement efforts. In 1956 he endowed the GEORGE S. DIVELY FOUNDATION† to assist various charitable and educational interests.

Dively married Harriet Seeds (d. 1968) in 1933. They had one son, Michael. Dively married Juliette Gaudin in 1969. He died in Florida and was cremated.—T.B.

George S. Dively Papers, WRHS.
George S. Dively Foundation Records, WRHS.

**DIXON, ARDELIA BRADLEY** (3 June 1916–16 Oct. 1991) served on the CLEVELAND PUBLIC LIBRARY† (CPL) Board of Trustees (1980–88), as chair of both the personnel and community services committees and as secretary. She worked as a secretary at ANTIOCH BAPTIST CHURCH,† CENTRAL HIGH† John Hay High School, and volunteered for countless local and national organizations, including the INTERCHURCH COUNCIL OF GREATER CLEVELAND† and the National Council of Churches. Dixon was born in Atlantic City, NJ, to Oscar and Ardelia (Jackson) Bradley and moved to Cleveland as a child. She graduated from John Hay High School, attended Fenn College (1940–41, see CLEVELAND STATE UNIV.†) and received a B.A. from the Cleveland College of Western Reserve Univ. (later CASE WESTERN RESERVE UNIV.†) in 1948.

Dixon married Henry George Dixon (d. 1991) in 1945. They lived in Cleveland; there were no children. Dixon was a life member of the NATIONAL ASSN. FOR THE ADVANCEMENT OF COLORED PEOPLE† (NAACP) and served on many NAACP committees. She marched in Washington, DC, for civil rights in 1963. In the 1980s she frequently expressed support of CPL in letters to the editor, published in the *PLAIN DEALER.†* A volunteer at FAIRHILL PSYCHIATRIC HOSPITAL† and the PHILLIS WHEATLEY ASSN.,† Dixon belonged to Alpha Kappa Alpha sorority for 47 years. She died in BEACHWOOD's† Parkland Nursing Home.—J.M.

**DOAN, NATHANIEL** (1 June 1762–29 Nov. 1815) was a blacksmith and in charge of the cows, oxen, and horses of the 1797 second surveying expedition of the Connecticut Land Co. Doan, son of Seth and Mercy (Parker) Doan, was born in Middle Haddam, CT, where, on 29 Nov. 1785, he married Sarah Adams (d. 4 Mar. 1853). Along with JAS. KINGSBURY, JOB STILES, and others, he received city lots from the CONNECTICUT LAND CO.† In 1798 he returned to Connecticut and brought his wife and 6 children back on a 92 day trip. Doan was required to set up a blacksmith shop on his property on Superior St., Cleveland's first light industry. Doan shod pack horses and also made tools. Within months, the Doans were forced out of the area by the scourge of fever, ague, and mosquitos, and in

1799 Doan bought 100 acres in Euclid Twp. (later E. Cleveland, now part of Cleveland) for $1 an acre. He built a hotel and tavern, a landmark for almost 50 years, on the northwest corner of what is now Euclid Ave. and E. 107th, which he occupied until his death. Doan added a store, saleratus factory, and blacksmith shop. Doan served as justice of the peace, postmaster, and clergyman. When the first military company was organized in Cleveland in 1804, he was elected first lieutenant, and captain the following year. He was town clerk for many years, and in 1809 he became an associate judge of Cuyahoga County.

Doan and his wife had six children, though only the names of five are known: Sarah, Job, Delia, Mercy, and Rebecca. Doan died in Cleveland and his burial site is unknown.

Post, Charles Asa. *Doan's Corners and the City Four Miles West* (1930).

**DOCKSTADTER, NICHOLAS** (4 Jan. 1802–9 Nov. 1871), pioneer, merchant, banker, and mayor of Cleveland from 1840–41, was born in Albany, NY, to Jacob and Angelica (Hanson) Dockstadter. Educated locally, he came to Cleveland in 1826 with 2 of his brothers, Richard and Butler. Once in Cleveland, Dockstadter embarked on an independent dealership in hats, caps, and furs, which he received in trade with local Indians. He soon became the leading fur trader in the region. In 1834 he became treasurer of the CLEVELAND & NEWBURGH RAILWAY.† In 1835 Dockstadter was chosen treasurer of the village of Cleveland. The following year, he was elected alderman of the newly incorporated city, elected again in 1838. During 1837–38, Dockstadter was chosen as a delegate to the county and state Whig conventions. His popularity brought him a victory in the 1840 election for mayor. He served only 1 term, after which he returned to private business.

Dockstadter was married to Harriett Judd (1805–37). The couple had 5 children: William, Richard, Charles, Julia, and Elisabeth. He died in Cleveland and was buried in Woodland Cemetery.

**DONAHEY, JAMES HARRISON "HAL"** (8 Apr. 1875–1 June 1949), chief editorial cartoonist of the *PLAIN DEALER†* for half a century, was born to John Coulter and Catherine Chaney Donahey of West Chester, Tuscarawas County, OH. His first newspaper experience was with the *Ohio Democrat* (New Philadelphia), before coming to Cleveland to study at the Cleveland School of Art. In 1896 he became an illustrator for the *CLEVELAND WORLD,†* and began drawing for the *Plain Dealer* on 1 Jan. 1900. During the mayoral campaign of

1907, Donahey won an artists' duel with Homer Davenport, whom the *Leader* borrowed from New York to battle Mayor TOM L. JOHNSON. On 23 Apr. 1910, Donahey published his most famous cartoon at the death of Mark Twain, depicting 2 somber boys rafting a flower-draped bier "Down the River." Some of his originals were prominently displayed in the GREAT LAKES EXPOSITION† of 1936.

His national reputation brought Donahey an invitation to work for the *New York Journal* in 1911, but after a week he returned to Cleveland. Combining work with his love of travel, Donahey provided the paper with pictorial accounts of such diverse locales as Egypt and Alaska. Donahey was also active in community affairs, receiving the Cleveland Community Fund's Distinguished Service Award in 1938. After his first wife, Beatrice, died in 1939, Donahey married Mrs. Josephine Rhodes, a widow. He had one stepdaughter, Mrs. K. M. Haber, but no children of his own. After the 1920s, he lived on a farm in Aurora, dying shortly after suffering a stroke. He was buried in New Philadelphia.

---

James H. Donahey Collection, WRHS.

**DONAHUE, MYRON MICKEY** (16 Nov. 1927–5 Nov. 1993) was a leader of Cleveland's labor community and active in community affairs.

The son of Myron T. and Eleanor (Bradley) Donahue, Mickey (as he was always known) was born and educated in Cleveland. Upon graduating from EAST TECHNICAL HIGH SCHOOL,† he joined the U.S. Navy and served aboard an aircraft carrier during the last months of World War II. On 11 June 1949 he married Ruth Fox, and together they raised three children: Kathleen, Theresa, and Michael.

In 1952 Donahue joined Local 120 of the United Assn. of Journeymen and Apprentices of the Plumbing and Pipefitting Industry of the U.S. and Canada (commonly known as the Pipefitters Union). In 1960 he was named vice-president of the local, and in 1962 he became its business representative. He continued in that position until 1988. From 1988 until the time of his death he served as an international representative for the Pipefitters. He also served on the international's apprenticeship board.

In addition to his duties for the Pipefitters, Donahue devoted many hours to the community in a variety of service roles. He was president of the Cleveland Building Trades Council 1981–88, and served for three years on the Ohio state executive board of the AFL-CIO. In 1974 he was appointed to the board of the CUYAHOGA METROPOLITAN HOUSING AUTHORITY,† and in 1979 he became a member of the Board of Building Standards and

Appeals. In 1978 the Irish Good Fellowship Club honored him by naming him Irishman of the Year.

Donahue is buried in Holy Cross Cemetery in Cleveland.—J.T.

**DORR, DAVID,** was the author of the first book known to be published by an African American in Cleveland. His travelogue, *The Colored Man around the World,* was published in 1858. Dorr traveled to Europe, North Africa, and Asia as a slave. He escaped after his arrival back in the U.S. when the freedom he had been promised by his master was denied. The diary of his experiences during this journey formed the content of the book. Little more is known of Dorr except that he served as a soldier in the 7TH OHIO VOLUNTEER INFANTRY† during the CIVIL WAR.†

**DOW, HERBERT H.** (26 Feb. 1866–15 Oct. 1930), developer of Dow Chemical Co., was born in Belleville, Ontario. The son of Joseph H. and Sarah Bunneil Dow, he moved with his family to Cleveland, and graduated with a B.S. from Case School in 1888. His senior thesis, which he presented that summer at the Cleveland meeting of the American Assn. for the Advancement of Science, dealt with brines in Ohio.

From 1888–89, when Dow was professor of chemistry at the Huron St. Hospital College, he developed a process for manufacturing bromine from brine, receiving a patent on 12 Apr. 1892. In 1889 he organized a company to work with brines in fields near Canton. That venture failed, however in 1890 he started Dow Process Co. in Midland, MI, where the brines contained heavy concentrations of bromine. Dow organized Midland Chemical Co. in 1892 and in 1895 began manufacturing chlorine and its derivatives. He formed Dow Chemical Co. in 1897 to manufacture chlorine and caustic soda; in 1900, Dow Chemical absorbed Midland Chemical Co. In establishing his companies, Dow was financially and technically assisted by Case classmate ALBERT W. SMITH. Dow was president and general manager of Dow Chemical, responsible for developing new chemical processes, for which more than 100 patents were granted. He received honorary degrees from the Case School of Applied Science (1924) and the Univ. of Michigan (1929) and the Perkin Medal from the Society of the Chemical Industry in 1930.

On 16 Nov. 1892, Herbert Dow married Grace A. Ball of Midland, MI. They had no children. He died in Rochester, MN, and was buried in Midland, MI.

**DOWELL, DORSEY MAXFIELD** (28 Apr. 1903–3 Apr. 1964) was rector (1942–64) of Christ Episcopal Church in SHAKER HTS.† He was affiliated with the Church of the Epiphany, St. Mark's Church, the Church of the Redeemer, and St. Thomas Church. Dowell was born in Clarksburg, WV, the son of Olive A. and Creetus A. Dowell, an Episcopal clergyman. He received a degree from Kenyon College and then attended Bexley Hall, graduating in 1928. Ordained a priest in 1929, Dowell, except for a stint in Piqua, OH, spent his entire life in the Cleveland area. Reflecting his times, he was concerned about racial and religious harmony within the church and community. As a counselor for Alcoholics Anonymous, Dowell saw the AA unit at Christ Episcopal develop 12 sister units. He was also known as a builder of churches, organizing the Church of the Epiphany in EUCLID† (1928–29), leading St. Mark's and the Church of the Redeemer's unification to form a new St. Mark's, and serving as rector of St. Thomas in BEREA† (1938–42). He guided Christ Episcopal through a disastrous fire, and the flooding of its replacement, as the church's congregation grew from 125 to 1,100 families. At the time of his death, he was president of the standing committee of the diocese.

Dowell married Elizabeth Hubbard in 1928. They had no children. Dowell died in Shaker Hts. and was buried in Chestnut Grove Cemetery, Ashtabula, OH.

Clergy Records, Episcopal Diocese of Ohio Archives.

**DOWLING, JAMES** (b. Ireland), Congressional Medal of Honor recipient for service during the Indian wars, was born in Ireland. He was a Cleveland resident when he enlisted in the 8th U.S. Cavalry. From Aug. to Oct. 1868, Cpl. Dowling participated in patrols and scouts operating out of Camp Whipple in the Arizona territory (west of Prescott), which skirmished with the Hualapais and Tonto Apache Indians on the Santa Maria and Verde rivers. His Medal of Honor was awarded 24 July 1869 for "bravery in scouts and actions against the Indians."

**DRIMMER, MELVIN** (2 Nov. 1934–17 June 1992), educator, author, and civil-rights activist, was a Jew who pioneered African American history courses at Spelman College in Atlanta, GA (1963–72), and taught African American and African History at CLEVELAND STATE UNIV.† (1972–92). He made 21 trips to Africa as director of the American Forum for International Study and focused on relations between AFRICAN AMERICANS† and Jews (see JEWS AND JUDAISM†). Drimmer was born in New York City to Oscar and Nettie (Natille) Drimmer. He graduated from the City College of New York (Phi Beta Kappa), attended Oxford Univ.,

and received his doctorate in history from the Univ. of Rochester, NY (1965). He began his career at Hunter College in New York City and served as visiting professor at other institutions, such as New York Univ. and Dillard Univ., New Orleans, LA.

Inspired by Martin Luther King, Jr., Drimmer believed in acting on his beliefs: he was once jailed in an Atlanta civil rights demonstration. He unsuccessfully sought to enter politics, losing both a Congressional seat in the 19th District (1982) and a seat on the Cleveland Board of Education (1985, see CLEVELAND PUBLIC SCHOOLS†). In 1985, Drimmer married Lillian Boehmer; they had 2 children, Alan Stessin and Barbara.—J.M.

**DRURY, FRANCIS EDSON** (20 Aug. 1850–3 April 1932), earned a fortune from the manufacture of stoves and dedicated a good part of it to Cleveland's cultural institutions, notably the CLEVELAND PLAY HOUSE.† He was born in Pittsfield, MI, the son of DeWitt and Sarah Dimmick Drury. Entering the hardware business after a public school education, he invented the first internal gear lawnmower while employed in Springfield, OH. He brought his invention to Cleveland in 1870 and arranged for its manufacture by the Taylor & Boggis Foundry Co., becoming the firm's vice-president and general manager. Drury married Frances Perkins of Michigan in 1872 and, following her death, married Clevelander Julia Robinson in 1882. He joined H. P. Crowell of Chicago in organizing the Cleveland Foundry Co. in 1888 to begin the manufacture of oil heating and cooking stoves. The company's fortune was assured when the Standard Oil Co. (see BP AMERICA†) undertook to market its product in an effort to increase the consumption of its surplus kerosene. It became the Cleveland Metal Products Co. in 1910 and the Perfection Stove Co. in 1921, by which time it was the largest manufacturer of its kind in the world. In 1910 Drury built one of the last mansions on EUCLID AVE.† at the northwest corner of E. 87th St., also acquiring the old Ammon estate across Euclid to indulge his hobby of landscape gardening. In 1916 he invited the newly organized Cleveland Play House to use the Ammon property for its first productions, and in 1925 he donated a portion of the property for a permanent theater. One of the Play House stages is named in his honor. Though the Drurys moved from the Euclid Ave. mansion by 1926, they had a replica built in GATES MILLS,† where it was eventually acquired by GILMOUR ACADEMY.† Drury was also a founder of the CLEVELAND MUSIC SCHOOL SETTLEMENT† and a benefactor of the CLEVELAND ORCHESTRA,† Western Reserve Univ., and Case Institute of Technology (see CASE WESTERN RESERVE†). He died in Augusta, GA, and was buried in Lake View

131

Cemetery, survived by his second wife and a son from his first marriage, Herbert R.—J.V.

**DUMOULIN, FRANK** (9 July 1870–9 July 1947), Episcopal priest, third dean and rector of TRINITY CATHEDRAL† (1907–14), and bishop coadjutor of the Protestant Episcopal Church of Ohio (1914–24) was born in Montreal, Canada, son of John Philip and Frances Mary (Brough) DuMoulin. He received his B.A. and M.A. degrees from Trinity College, Univ. of Toronto (1894), and was ordained a deacon (1894) and priest (1895) of the Church of England. DuMoulin had several positions before coming to Trinity. Plagued with ill health, DuMoulin resigned and spent 1924–25 in Egypt and Asia Minor, resuming his career in 1925 with rectorships in Philadelphia, North Carolina, and New York before retiring in 1943.

DuMoulin was interested in uniting his church with social and welfare needs. He helped organize the Fed. for Charity & Philanthropy, and in 1913 was appointed by Mayor NEWTON D. BAKER as a delegate to a conference discussing the rights of cities under the new Ohio constitution. He also worked with the CITY MISSION.† While dean, he chaired the social betterment committee of the Pastors' Union and was first president of the Federated Churches of Cleveland. He continued the cathedralization of Trinity, began a vacation Bible school, and established a playground for underprivileged children. DuMoulin chaired the Federal Council of Churches of Christ in America committee on motion pictures, which in 1936 submitted a report condemning movies that were morally harmful to young people. DuMoulin married twice: to Ethel King (d. 1928) in 1901, and to Cora Stiles in 1929. DuMoulin had three children: Francois, Rockwell, and Emily. He was buried in Philadelphia, PA.

**DUNCAN, WILLIAM McKINLEY** (19 May 1873–5 Sept. 1945) was a nationally known railroad executive with the WHEELING & LAKE ERIE RAILROAD† for thirty years, and senior partner in the law firm of SQUIRE, SANDERS & DEMPSEY.† During the late 1920s, Duncan's legal work on behalf of the W&LE helped clear obstacles for construction of the Cleveland Union Terminal Tower complex.

Nephew to Pres. William B. McKinley, Duncan was born in Pittsburgh, PA, to Andrew Jackson and Sarah McKinley Duncan. He attended public school in Pittsburgh, Rayen High School in Youngstown, OH, and Cornell Univ. Duncan was admitted to the Ohio Bar in 1894 and began his legal career as an associate with the Cleveland firm of Squire, Sanders & Dempsey.

Duncan devoted much of his 50 year career with Squire Sanders to supervising the firm's railroad business. He was appointed chief counsel for the Wheeling & Lake Erie in 1905 and a receiver for the railroad in 1912. Over the next four years Duncan's corporate skills and knowledge of railroad law combined to pull the W&LE out of receivership. From 1916–45 Duncan continued his association with the railroad as president and then chairman of the board. Duncan retired from Squire Sanders on 13 December 1944, following a disagreement with Sterling Newell, who supervised the firm's corporate practice, over the makeup of a reorganized firm.

Duncan married Viola Deetrick in Youngstown, OH, on 18 Oct. 1899. They had three sons: William McKinley, Jr., John Allison, and Andrew Jackson III. Duncan is buried in Poland, OH.—T.B.

Gibbons, Ralph H. ed. *A Century of Change: Squire, Sanders & Dempsey* (Wheeler Communications, Cleveland, 1990.)

**DUNKLE, DAVID HOSBROOK** (9 Sept. 1911–3 Jan. 1984) was an internationally known paleontologist. Born in Winnipeg, Manitoba, he grew up in Indiana and attended the Univ. of Kansas. After receiving his Ph.D. from Harvard in 1939, where he studied under famed paleontologist Alfred S. Romer, Dunkle joined the staff of the CLEVELAND MUSEUM OF NATURAL HISTORY.† There he turned his attention to the Museum's collection of arthrodires (a type of extinct armored fish) from Devonian age rocks of the Cleveland area. He soon began to publish a series of papers, most in collaboration with assistant Peter A. Bungart (1876–1948), describing these fish. He also led two western trips in the 1940s in order to collect dinosaurs and fossil animals for the museum. Dunkle left Cleveland for a position as a vertebrate paleontologist at the U.S. National Museum of Natural History in 1946. While at the national museum, he continued an association with the Cleveland museum and, during the 1960s, acted as advisor for that museum's Interstate–71 fossil salvage operation. He retired from the National Museum in 1968 and returned to the Cleveland museum. He again retired in 1975 and moved to Burgess, VA. Dunkle died in Tappahannock, VA and his ashes were placed in a family plot in Linden, IN. He was survived by his wife, Helena (Heckart) Dunkle, and his daughter, Ann David. Dunkle's greatest legacy is his published work, consisting of about 50 scientific and nontechnical papers, most dealing with fossil fish. Dunkleosteus, a genus of large armored fish found in the Cleveland shale, is named in his honor.—J.H.

**DUNMORE, WALTER T.** (15 July 1877–23 Jan. 1945), a noted law professor, was born in Cleveland to Thomas and Elizabeth (Wright) Dunmore. He grew up in Norwalk and graduated from Oberlin College with an A.B. (1900). From 1900–02, Dunmore clerked in the Norwalk probate court, which led to his enrollment in the Western Reserve Univ. Law School where he earned his LL.B. (1904). He returned to Oberlin, completed his A.M. degree (1905), and was admitted to the Ohio Bar in 1904. Dunmore was appointed an instructor of his specialty, real property law, at WRU Law School in 1905. Later he taught evidence, wills, and conflicts of law. In 1911 he was appointed dean of WRU's law school, serving until his death.

Dunmore was a critic of the American legal-education system, feeling too many graduating lawyers' chief aim was profit. Instead of training students to think, he believed schools attempted to "pour" legal training into their students and hope for the best. Dunmore served on the executive committee of the Cleveland LEGAL AID SOCIETY,† devoting much time and greatly aided the society's effort to help the underprivileged be aware of and secure in their legal rights and protection. Dunmore wrote extensively on legal matters. His book, *Ship Subsidies,* was awarded the Hart, Shaffner & Marx Economic Prize. He assisted ARCHIBALD THROCHMORTON in preparing the Ohio General Code (1921).

Dunmore was first married to Mabel Curtis (d. 1921) on 10 Nov. 1904. They had 2 daughters, Marjorie Curtis Oliver and Helen Elizabeth Ayres. In 1939 Dunmore married Kathleen Townsend Firestone. He died in Cleveland and was buried in Milan, OH.

**DUNN, DANIEL A. "DANNY"** (17 Sept. 1884–17 Jan. 1968), noted Cleveland boxing trainer, promoter, and manager during the 1920s and 1930s, whose most famous boxer, JOHNNY RISKO, fought and defeated several heavyweight contenders, was born in New York City to Charles and Sarah (Sheady) Dunn. As a newsboy, he learned to fight early in order to protect his business on the city's west side. A 5' 2", 120-lb. contender, he fought as an amateur and professional in and around New York City, receiving $2 for his first match in Harlem. In 1910 Dunn came to Cleveland and continued his professional boxing career. He taught boxing and operated health clubs at the CLEVELAND ATHLETIC CLUB† and in the Sloan Bldg. In 1923 he opened a gym in an old building at 2861 Detroit Ave. One day Johnny Risko came in to learn boxing, and Dunn became his trainer and manager. Although Risko's first fight paid him only $2, before his career finished, Risko and Dunn earned over $250,000. Several times Risko was only a bout away from a championship fight. Dunn

invested in real estate and advised Risko to establish a $100,000 trust fund. When Dunn suggested Risko retire from boxing, the fighter dropped him as his manager in 1935. Dunn never found another Risko, and closed his gymnasium. By 1942 he was working as a laborer in the Cleveland Service Dept. for $.72 per half-hour. He was married to Gerda Marie Bergland on 28 Oct. 1924. They had no children. Dunn was buried in Lakewood Park Cemetery.

**DUPERTUIS, CLARENCE WESLEY** (2 June 1907–5 Sept. 1992) was a prominent physical anthropologist who devoted his career to somatology (the study of body types), with an emphasis on investigations of possible relationships between physiques and susceptibility to disease. Son of Samuel and Myra (Kinney) Dupertuis, he was born in Yacolt, WA, but spent much of his childhood in the Boston area. Dupertuis studied at Harvard Univ., graduating in 1929. In 1934 he married Helen Stimson, who would help him with his scientific work over the years. Dupertuis received his Ph.D. from Harvard in 1940 and joined the faculty of the School of Medicine at Western Reserve Univ. in 1948. During his long career he authored or coauthored a number of scholarly papers and reports, ranging from a study of the physique of coronary patients to a study of sex differences in pubic hair distribution. He also wrote portions of several books. His research and consulting projects took him around the world, including countries in Africa and Asia. He was a consultant to the military and had a small role in picking out the original U.S. astronauts. Dupertuis died in Cleveland, survived by his wife, his son, William S., his daughter, Lucy Gwyn Dupertuis, and two grandchildren. He was interred at Hillcrest Cemetery.—J.H.

**DU PONT, ZARA** (24 Feb. 1869–1 May 1946), reformer, helped underprivileged children and youth and actively supported rights for labor and suffrage for women in Cleveland and elsewhere. She was a sister of Senator Thomas Coleman du Pont and cousin of other Delaware du Ponts—Lammot, Irenee, and Pierre—and also of Cleveland mayor TOM L. JOHNSON. Born in Louisville, KY, to Antoine Bidermann du Pont and Susan Coleman du Pont, du Pont attended private school in Philadelphia, PA. In an early act of defiance, she refused the coming-out party typical of other debutantes. Instead, she joined the board of the Children's Free Hospital (Louisville). In Ohio, du Pont worked with ELIZABETH HAUSER to include woman suffrage in the new state constitution (1910). She joined the Cuyahoga Women's Suffrage Assn. (1911) and served on the board of the state suffrage organization. While less daring local women turned their backs to the camera, du Pont and Grace Treat posed for a full-face photograph publicizing the Votes for Women pageant and parade in New York City (1912). Du Pont traveled throughout northeast Ohio, often in a red Winton automobile, speaking on behalf of woman's suffrage, until she moved to Cambridge, MA, where she continued to protest against injustice and prejudice. For example, as a stockholder, she advocated pro-labor policies in the boardroom of the Bethlehem Steel Co. (1941) and signed resolutions in a proxy statement against Montgomery Ward's labor policies (1945). Du Pont died in Cambridge, MA.

**DURDEN, EDWARD** (5 Apr. 1932–6 Mar. 1993), was a local civil rights activist. He was born to Arthur and Mae (Moon) Durden and educated in Birmingham, AL. He moved to Cleveland after high school and worked for a variety of factories, including Day-Glo Color Corp. In his activism for equal rights, Durden participated in the NAACP, the United Freedom Movement, CORE (Congress on Racial Equality), and the Freedom Fighters. He also worked against crime, patrolling EAST CLEVELAND† neighborhoods and marching against drugs in that city. Committed to social change, he educated people about critical issues, sometimes via loudspeakers on his car. In 1984 he led an effort to recall an East Cleveland city commissioner. At the time of his death, Durden was involved in the Grassroots Political Action Committee and the Concerned Citizens of East Cleveland.

In 1955 Durden married Mary Alice Lee (d. 1989); they had a daughter, Dr. Faith Marie, and 2 sons, David, and Jerome A. The family moved to East Cleveland in the 1960s, where Durden became president of the Bender Ave. St. Club. He also taught Sunday school at the Greater Abyssinia Baptist Church. Fellow activists honored Durden with vigils and rallies after his death. He was buried in Highland Park Cemetery.—J.M.

**DU SHATTAR, JOSEPH** was an early fur trader who established a trading post on the CUYAHOGA RIVER† ca. 1790. According to Charles Whittlesey, the youthful Du Shattar worked for the North-West Fur Co. along Lake Erie. About 1790 he married Mary Pornay of Detroit and opened a trading post about 9 miles from the mouth of the Cuyahoga River, probably in old Brooklyn on the west bank, across the river from NEWBURG.† While there, his second child was born, in 1794. Traders John Baptiste Flemming and Joseph Burrall were also at the post from time to time. Although Whittlesey noted a quarrel with Indians over a rifle at the river, peaceful trade with the Wyandot, Delaware, Chippewa, and Ottawa Indians was possible. The

1790–95 warfare between settlers and Indians over Northwest Territory lands did not disturb the unsettled area along Lake Erie at the Cuyahoga River, whose commercial possibilities were already well known.

Du Shattar was still alive in 1812, having helped capture JOHN O'MIC, who murdered two trappers in Sandusky.—M.S.

Whittlesey, Charles. *Early History of Cleveland, Ohio, Including Papers and Other Matters Relating to the Adjacent Country.*

**DYER, J. MILTON** (22 Apr. 1870–27 May 1951), a prominent architect who designed Cleveland's CITY HALL† (1916) on Lakeside Ave., was born in Middletown, PA, to Cyrus and Eliza Dyer. He moved with his family to Cleveland in 1881. He graduated from CENTRAL HIGH SCHOOL,† attended a local training school for machinists, and studied at the Cleveland Institute of Technology and L'ecole des Beaux Arts in Paris (1900). After returning to Cleveland from Europe, Dyer had an active practice in the first 2 decades of the 1900s. Some of his major commissions were the Brooklyn Savings & Loan Assn. (1904) at W. 25th St. and Archwood Ave.; the TAVERN CLUB† (1905) at E. 36th and Prospect Ave.; the First Methodist Church (1905) at Euclid Ave. and E. 30th St.; the PEERLESS MOTOR CAR CO.† (1906), later C. Schmidt's & Sons brewery at E. 93rd St. and Quincy Ave.; the CLEVELAND ATHLETIC CLUB† (1911); and City Hall (1916). After a period of inactivity, Dyer designed the U.S. Coast Guard station (1940) on WHISKEY ISLAND† at the mouth of the CUYAHOGA RIVER.† Early residences designed by Dyer include one for Edmund Burke (1910) on Magnolia Dr. in UNIV. CIRCLE† (now used by the CLEVELAND MUSIC SCHOOL SETTLEMENT†) and the Lyman Treadway house (1911) at E. 89th St. and Euclid Ave. (now part of the HEALTH MUSEUM†).

Unmarried, Dyer died in Cleveland and was buried in Woodland Cemetery.

**DYKSTRA, CLARENCE ADDISON** (25 Feb. 1883–6 May 1950) was a political scientist who promoted the city manager form of government. Born in Cleveland to Lawrence and Margaret Barr Dykstra, he grew up in Chicago. Dykstra received a B.A. from the Univ. of Iowa in 1903 and then held teaching positions at the Univ. of Chicago, in Florida, at Ohio State (1908–09), and at the Univ. of Kansas (1909–18). He became nationally known as a leader in state and municipal administration. Dykstra returned to Cleveland in 1918 as executive secretary of the Civic League and started the movement for instituting a city manager form of government in Cleveland. He served on the 1919 committee to improve Cleveland's city charter; he also drafted an unsuccessful amendment allowing county home rule in Ohio and consolidating city and county governments. He unsuccessfully fought the Van Sweringen proposal to put CLEVELAND UNION TERMINAL† on PUBLIC SQUARE.† The Civic League did not rehire Dykstra as executive secretary in 1920; many attributed this decision to the Van Sweringens' opposition.

In Chicago and then Los Angeles, Dykstra held similar positions to his Civic League position. He became the second city manager of Cincinnati in 1930 and returned to academia as president of the Univ. of Wisconsin until 1945, when he returned to UCLA as provost, a post he held until his death. On 31 July 1903 Dykstra married Ada Hartley (d. 1926); the couple had a daughter, Elizabeth. Dykstra married Lillian K. Rickaby on 25 Dec. 1927 and adopted her son, Franz Rickaby. Dykstra was buried in Inglewood, CA.

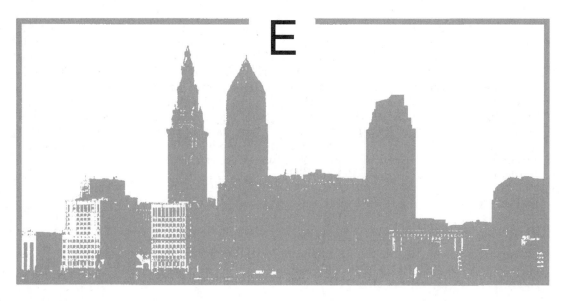

**EARNEST, G. (GEORGE) BROOKS** (2 Oct. 1902–13 Sept. 1992), dean of engineering and president of FENN COLLEGE, oversaw the transfer of the school to the State of Ohio in order to form CLEVELAND STATE UNIV.† Born in Mifflintown, PA, Earnest graduated from high school in Altoona, PA, and attended Case Institute of Technology, receiving a Civil Engineering degree in 1927. After graduation, he served as a field engineer for construction of the Terminal Tower. In 1930 he joined the faculty of Case Institute as an instructor of engineering, earning his M.S. in 1933. Rising through the academic ranks, he became professor of engineering surveying and director of Camp Case in 1948. Earnest left Case in 1951 to become dean of engineering at Fenn College and was made president of the college in 1952. During his first 10 years as president, a substantial endowment was established, new programs were instituted, and enrollment increased by about 70%. In 1965 Fenn College became the nucleus of Cleveland State Univ. The following year, Earnest became director of the Fenn Educational Foundation, a nonprofit corporation. Under his leadership, nearly half a million dollars was contributed for the development of cooperative education programs in Northeast Ohio. Earnest retired to Florida in 1980.

Earnest married Mary Alice McKeighan 28 Feb. 1928; they had 2 sons, Samuel Allen of Murrysville, PA, and David Brooks of West Bloomfield, MI. He died in West Bloomfield.—M.S.

---

Earnest, G. Brooks. *A History of Fenn College* (1974).

**EASTER, LUSCIOUS "LUKE"** (4 Aug. 1915–29 Mar. 1979), a 6' 4", 240-lb. first baseman for the CLEVELAND INDIANS† between 1949–54, was born in St. Louis, MO, and was a softball player until signed by the Cincinnati Crescents of the Negro American League in 1946. During 1947–48, he was a member of the Homestead Grays. Bill Veeck, owner of the Indians, purchased his contract in 1949 and sent him to San Diego. After 80 games in the Pacific Coast League, Easter had a .363 average and 25 home runs. Recalled to play for the Indians in Aug. 1949, he began a 6-year major league career, limited to 491 games with Cleveland due to chronic knee problems. Although Easter hit only 93 major league home runs, called by radio announcer JACK GRANEY "bazooka blasts," his long drives made him a fan favorite. On 23 June 1950, Easter hit a baseball into the upper deck measured at 477' from home plate, considered the longest home run hit at CLEVELAND MUNICIPAL STADIUM.† After leaving the majors, Easter played in the Internatl. League until 1966. He returned to Cleveland and worked as a polisher at TRW in EUCLID.† The Indians hired him as a batting coach in 1969. By 1979 Easter was a shop steward at TRW.† On 29 Mar. 1979, he was killed by bank robbers while cashing his fellow workers' paychecks. Easter married Virgil Lowe in 1948 and had 4 children: Luke, Terry, Gerald, and Nana.

**EASTMAN, HARRY LLOYD** (9 Apr. 1882–7 July 1963), judge of Cuyahoga County Insolvency & Juvenile Court from 1926–60, was responsible for innovations that made the court a model for the country during the 1940s. He was born to Oliver H. and Clara (Bond) Eastman in Butler, PA, but grew up in Findlay, OH. He became a photoengraver, inventing a "perfect ratio rule" measuring device for photoengravers. After working at the *PLAIN DEALER†* and *CLEVELAND LEADER†* a few years, he did odd photoengraving jobs to work his way through the Western Reserve School of Law, receiving his LL.B. degree and being admitted to the Ohio Bar in 1913. He was asst. U.S. attorney for the Northern District of Ohio from 1919–21, and practiced law with several Cleveland firms until 1926. He married Marcella J. Dalgleish on 30 Sept. 1922. They had no children.

In May 1926, Eastman was appointed judge of the Cuyahoga County Insolvency & Juvenile Court, and was reelected to hold that position for 34 years. During Eastman's terms of office, the County Detention Home and Juvenile Court buildings were built (completed in 1932); Juvenile Court became an independent branch of the court system (1934); and changed and added services made the court one of the most progressive in the nation. Eastman improved personnel standards by raising the requirements for civil service, cooperation with schools of social work, and instituting professional casework training for probation officers. He established the first Juvenile Court psychiatric clinic and founded a department of child support. Judge Eastman retired in May 1960. He died in his SHAKER HTS.† home and was buried in Lake View Cemetery.

---

Harry Lloyd Eastman Papers, WRHS.

**EASTMAN, LINDA ANNE** (17 July 1867–5 Apr. 1963), the fourth librarian of the CLEVELAND PUBLIC LIBRARY,† succeeding her friend and mentor WM. HOWARD BRETT, was the first woman in the world to head a library of that size. Eastman was born in Oberlin, OH, daughter of William Harley and Sarah Ann (Redrup) Eastman. Her family moved to Cleveland when she was 7 and Eastman attended public school, graduating with honors from West High. Completing a course at Cleveland Normal School, Eastman began teaching but soon found herself attracted to library work. She became an assistant at the CPL in 1892 and was promoted to vice-librarian under Brett in 1895. Eastman was named librarian in 1918, a position she held until her retirement 20 years later. Her first years were dominated by the construction and occupancy of the $4.5 million main library building, opened in 1925. Later in her tenure, she developed several specialized operations, including a travel section, a business information bureau, and services to the blind and handicapped. Eastman's achievements within her profession were highly regarded and recognized nationally. She was president of both the Ohio Library Assn. and the American Library Assn. and held a professorship at the Library School of Western Reserve Univ. She retired as librarian in 1938, when she was 71. Eastman died in CLEVE-LAND HTS.† and was buried in Riverside Cemetery.

---

Archives, Cleveland Public Library.

**EATON, CYRUS STEPHEN** (27 Dec 1883–9 May 1979), a controversial capitalist who promoted better U.S.-Soviet relations, was born in Pugwash, Nova Scotia, son of Joseph H. and Mary A. (McPherson) Eaton. He graduated from McMaster Univ. (1905) and came to Cleveland to work for the EAST OHIO GAS CO.† With the help of JOHN D. ROCKEFELLER, he went into business in 1907, securing natural gas franchises in Manitoba, Canada, for a New York banking syndicate, which collapsed. With the franchises, Eaton organized the Canada Gas & Electric Corp., consolidating his companies into the Continental Gas & Electric Corp. in 1912. Eaton settled in Cleveland in 1913 and diversified, in 1916 joining Otis & Co. banking firm, in 1926 organizing Continental Shares, Inc. investment trust, and in 1929 consolidating the REPUBLIC STEEL CORP. His 1929 wealth was an estimated $100 million, most of which he lost in the Great Depression.

Eaton rebuilt his fortune in the 1940s and 1950s, becoming a director (1943), then board chairman (1954), of the Chesapeake & Ohio Railroad, and also board chairman of the West Kentucky Coal Co. (1953). In 1955 Eaton transformed his boyhood home in Pugwash into a "Thinker's Lodge," inviting scholars for a week's retreat. He invited a Soviet scholar in 1956, and in 1957 the first Pugwash Conference of Nuclear Scientists brought scientists from around the world to discuss international issues. During the Cold War, Eaton cultivated friendships with Soviet leaders and urged the U.S. and Soviet Union to develop better relations, receiving the Lenin Peace Prize in 1960.

Eaton was active in Cleveland. He was a founder and trustee of the CLEVELAND MUSEUM OF NATURAL HISTORY†; helped transform the YMCA night school into FENN COLLEGE†; and was a trustee and benefactor of Case School of Applied Science. Eaton married twice; first, in 1907, to Margaret House, then to Anne Kinder Jones in 1957. He had seven children: Margaret Grace, Mary Adelle, Elizabeth Ann, Anna Bishop, Cyrus S., Jr., Augusta F., and MacPherson. Eaton died at his home and was buried in Nova Scotia.

---

Cyrus S. Eaton Papers, WRHS.

**EDMONDSON, GEORGE MOUNTAIN** (23 Aug. 1866–8 Nov. 1948), a portrait photographer, was born in Norwalk, OH, son of George William and

Mary Jane (Mountain) Edmondson. He was educated in the public schools and at age 16 began to study photography with his father, a well-known photographer. After working for his father, he moved to Cleveland in 1887, becoming assistant to veteran photographer JAS. F. RYDER in his Superior St. studio. Edmondson used his knowledge of enlarging on the new bromide paper for Ryder, and in turn, the studio won several prizes. After a year and a half, he joined the studio of Decker & Wilbur (see EDGAR DECKER). Edmondson remained when the firm dissolved partnership in 1891 due to Wilbur's retirement and 6 years later became a partner. In 1903 he succeeded to the business and moved to larger facilities at 510 Euclid Ave. Edmondson concentrated on portrait photography, receiving numerous medals and awards for his work. He kept his studio up to date in equipment and technique and was in the forefront of color photography in the early 1900s. In 1902 Edmondson became president of the Photography Assn. of America. He was also president of the Photographers Assn. of Ohio, and secretary and treasurer in 1910 of the Professional Photographers Society of Ohio. He belonged to the Unitarian church. He married Wilhelmina Neason in 1901 and had 2 children, Geo. Mountain, Jr., and Ivy Jane. Edmondson died in Venice, FL, and was buried in Sarasota.

EELLS, DAN PARMELEE (16 Apr. 1825–14 Aug. 1903), a banker and financier born in Westmoreland, NY, to the Rev. James and Mehitable (Parmelee) Eells, moved with his family to Ohio in 1831, settling in Amherst in 1837. Eells entered Oberlin College in 1843, transferred to Hamilton College in Clinton, NY, in 1844, but left college in 1846 to support himself, teaching and then working as a bookkeeper in a Cleveland commission house. He continued studying by correspondence, however, graduating from Hamilton in 1848. Eells became a bookkeeper in the Commercial Branch of the State Bank of Ohio in Cleveland in 1849, a teller in 1853, and a cashier in 1858. When the bank reorganized as the Commercial Natl. Bank of Cleveland in 1865, Eells became vice-president, and was president from 1868 until his retirement in 1897. Eells was a director of 32 firms, and held interests in oil, iron, steel, cement, coke, gas, and railroads.

Eells was active in civic and religious organizations. He was a trustee of several colleges; president and trustee of the Cleveland YMCA; president of the Cleveland Bible Society; treasurer of the Protestant Orphans' Asylum and the Home for Aged Women; and treasurer and vice-president of the CHILDREN'S AID SOCIETY† and the BETHEL UNION.† In 1882 Eells bought land and built the

Willson Ave. Presbyterian Church, renamed the Eells Memorial Presbyterian Church in 1903. In Sept. 1849 Eells married Mary M. Howard, who died in 1859. He married Mary Witt in Jan. 1861. Eells's son was Howard Parmelee Eells. Eells is buried in Lake View Cemetery.

───────────

Howard P. Eells, Jr., Family Papers, WRHS.

EINSTEIN, RUTH WEINER (Oct. 1882–20 June 1977), Jewish community leader for over half a century, was born in Cleveland, daughter to Abraham and Belle Aub Weiner. She graduated from the College for Women of Western Reserve Univ. Einstein joined the Board of Trustees of the NATL. COUNCIL OF JEWISH WOMEN, CLEVELAND SEC.,† in 1920, remaining a trustee until her death. In 1920 she was a founder of the NCJW Jewish Big Sisters Assn. affiliate. In 1922 she suggested training volunteers, which became a major part of the NCJW program. During the Depression, she helped establish educational and vocational classes for the unemployed through NCJW and proposed Council Thrift Shops, which became a major fundraiser. In 1954 Einstein developed the idea for a low-rent, nonsectarian apartment complex for the healthy elderly. Through her fundraising and lobbying efforts, the Council Gardens project started in 1960 with the units opening in 1963. Einstein chaired the Council Gardens Board of Directors from 1960–64. Einstein was also a board member of BELLEFAIRE,† the JEWISH COMMUNITY FED.,† the JEWISH FAMILY SERVICE ASSN.,† and the MONTEFIORE HOME.† In 1964 she received the Chas. Eisenman Service Award for community service from the JCF. She received a special citation for service from United Appeal in 1965, and the Hannah Solomon Award by the national office of the NCJW for service in 1972. Ruth Weiner married Jacob L. Einstein (d. 1919) on 21 Oct. 1903. They had 3 children: Paul Eden, Edith Freedlander, and Jane Gross.

EISENMAN, CHARLES (1865–9 March 1923), clothing manufacturer and organizer and first president of the Fed. of Jewish Charities, was born in New York City, son of Isadore and Caroline (Rosenblatt) Eisenman. He moved to Cleveland as a young man, and cofounded the K & E Co. (later the Kaynee Co.), manufacturing shirts and blouses. Eisenman believed good working conditions and fair treatment of employees encouraged productivity, and opposed trade unions as an infringement on the rights of employers. After accumulating considerable wealth, Eisenman retired in 1906 to devote himself to PHILANTHROPY.†

In 1903 Eisenman was one of 9 who formed the

Fed. of Jewish Charities, organizing the local Jewish organizations to facilitate fundraising and curtail duplication of services. He was elected president, remaining that until his death. Eisenman opposed including organizations in the FJC that could not demonstrate an ability to raise funds from their constituents, and proposed including only "matured" immigrant organizations. Eisenman was a principal supporter of the establishment of MT. SINAI HOSPITAL,† and was active in the American Jewish Committee and the American Jewish Relief Committee, created to assist European Jews who suffered during World War I. He was an organizer and active member of the Cleveland Community Fund Council until his death. During World War I, he chaired the Council of the Natl. Defense Committee on Purchases & Supplies and was awarded the District Service Medal for his work.

In honor of his charitable works, the Charles Eisenman Award for Outstanding Community Service was inaugurated in 1924 by the JEWISH COMMUNITY FED.† Eisenman married Bertha Hays on 16 Sept. 1891. They had no children. Eisenman died in St. Augustine, FL, and was buried in Mayfield Cemetery.

Eisenman, Charles. *Everybody's Business: A Businessman's Interpretation of Social Responsibility* (1916).

**EISENMANN, JOHN** (26 Mar. 1851–6 Jan. 1924), architect of the ARCADE† and author of Cleveland's first comprehensive building code, was born in Detroit, son of Christian and Anna (Schubert) Eisenmann. He graduated from the Univ. of Michigan in 1871, and headed the U.S. geodetic survey of the Great Lakes and St. Lawrence and Mississippi rivers until contracting jaundice and being forced to take a 2-year leave of absence. He then studied architecture at the polytechnics of Munich and Stuttgart, graduating from the latter institution, before returning to his former post. He came to Cleveland in 1882 as Professor of Civil Engineering at Case School of Applied Science. When Case moved to UNIV. CIRCLE,† Eisenmann drew plans for the first building (1885). In 1880–90 he designed, with GEO. H. SMITH, the Arcade; and in 1904, under Mayor TOM L. JOHNSON, Eisenmann wrote Cleveland's first comprehensive building code (see BUILDING CODE 1904†).

Eisenmann, a member of the Wade Park Commission, participated in planning the Wade Park area. He is also credited with designing the Ohio state flag. A pioneer of structural-steel construction, Eisenmann invented and patented "Mannel," a hollow building tile. Upon his death in 1924, his widow, Anna M., revealed Eisenmann had mortgaged their home to raise funds to draw up plans for the Perry Memorial at Put-in-Bay. However, another plan had been chosen, and, disappointed, Eisenmann began failing in health. Before he died, he requested that his ashes be scattered from the top of the Perry monument.

Young, Herbert R. "John Eisenmann, First Case Professor of Civil Engineering and Drawing" (WRHS, 1962).

**ELDREDGE, HEZEKIAH** (3 April 1795–25 Aug. 1845) was an architect and master builder in OHIO CITY,† and the architect-builder of the historic ST. JOHN'S EPISCOPAL CHURCH† on West 26th St., Cleveland's oldest standing church.

Born in Salisbury, CT, to Micah and Ann (Hanks) Eldredge, Hezekiah was raised in Weedsport, NY. In 1815 he joined the state militia, rising to the rank of captain. Eldredge left the militia in 1824, working first as a carpenter, then as an architect and builder. He moved to Rochester in 1825, where he constructed houses, banks, and stores in western New York and repaired boats for the Erie Canal trade.

Eldredge came to Cleveland in May 1834, settling in Ohio City, and established his own building business, including a shop and lumberyard. Among his more important projects were the Ohio City Exchange (1835), the Cleveland Center Block (1836), the Baptist Meeting House in Brooklyn (1836), the Pearl St. House (1837), and numerous warehouses on the river's edge. He became chief engineer of Ohio City in 1837.

In 1836 Eldredge became a charter member of St. John's Church and contracted with St. John's Building Committee to construct the church. Completed in 1838, it is the sole remaining example here of Eldredge's work.

The panic of 1837 damaged Eldredge's career, and in 1841 he declared bankruptcy. His last major project was the Merchants' Hotel, built in 1844.

Eldredge married Fanny Maria Lacey on 18 Dec. 1814 (d. 1833). They had eight children: George, Alonzo, Fanny, Hiram, Sarah, Helen, Ann, and Celia. Eldredge married Eunice Kellogg on 5 Nov. 1833. They had three children: Hezekiah Jr., Mary, and Franklin.—T.B.

Rusk, Sarah E. "Hezekiah Eldredge, Architect-Builder of St. John's Church, Cleveland, Ohio." *Journal of the Society of Architectural Historians* (1966).
Hezekiah Eldredge Family Papers, WRHS.

**ELLIOTT, CAMPBELL W.** (25 June 1913–9 May 1990) was vice-president of public affairs for the VAN DORN CO.† from 1977 until his death. He was president of the GREATER CLEVELAND GROWTH ASSN.† from 1973–77 and was active in community affairs.

Born and raised in St. Louis, MO, Elliott received an LL.B. from the City College of Law (1936). He joined General Motors Acceptance Corp. in St. Louis as sales promotion manager (1936–42), moved to Philadelphia as asst. to the president of Cramp Shipbuilding Co. (1942–45), and then to Minneapolis as vice-president and director of industrial and public relations for Minneapolis-Moline Co. (1945–56).

In 1956 Elliott came to Cleveland to join Midland-Ross Corp. as senior vice-president until 1970. From 1970–73 he was president and chief executive officer of AMERICAN SHIP BUILDING† Co. As Growth Assn. president, Elliott transformed the organization's image from conservative and business-dominated to one uniting big and small business, labor and government in working together to build a greater Cleveland.

He was named Man Of The Year by the CLEVELAND AREA BOARD OF REALTORS† (1976) and Variety Club's Super Citizen (1977).

Elliott was an active fund raiser for several Catholic charities and served on numerous boards and executive committees, including Clark Consolidated Industries, the American Red Cross, and Medical Mutual of Ohio. He was past council president of Junior Achievement of Greater Cleveland and a member of Marymount Hospital's advisory committee.

Elliott married Dorothy Mueller on 30 Jan. 1937. They had four children: George, Michael, Mary, and Carol (dec.). A Catholic, Elliott is buried in Calvary Cemetery.—T.B.

**ELLIOTT, FRANKLIN REUBEN** (27 April 1817– 10 Jan. 1878) was an early horticulturalist and fruit farmer who wrote and conducted research on fruit trees and who helped expand local awareness of the area's great variety and excellent quality of its fruit.

Son of Rubin and Grace (Fairchild) Elliott, he came to Cleveland from Guilford, CT, in 1842 and entered into the seed and implement business. He opened F. R. Elliott & Co. nursery, two miles west of Cleveland, and was proprietor of the Forest City Agricultural warehouse and seed store in Cleveland. Elliot also established the Lake Erie Nursery between Detroit and Lorain St., the most elaborate and widespread nursery in the county. Here he built the home that was later to become the CUDELL ARTS AND CRAFTS CENTER.†

The hard winter of 1856, combined with the Panic of 1857, resulted in the collapse of Elliott's agricultural and seed warehouse business. In 1858 Elliott left temporarily for St. Louis. When Elliott returned he was elected secretary of the Ohio Grape Growers Assn. in 1862, and appointed to prepare a report about the vineyards of northern Ohio. From 1862–69 Elliott provided the U.S. Department of Agriculture with research and background information on fruit trees.

Elliott helped organize the Cleveland Horticultural Society in 1844 and the Cuyahoga County Agricultural Society in 1846. In 1845 he became editor-publisher of the *Western Reserve Magazine of Agriculture and Horticulture*. Elliott also authored several popular books on fruit-growing, deciduous trees and evergreens, and ornamental landscaping.

Elliott married Sophia Hopkins on 17 Feb. 1846 (separated 1875). They had five children: Frank, Katherine, Cara, Cora, and HENRY WOOD ELLIOTT.—T.B.

The Elliott Family Papers, Lakewood Historical Society.

**ELLIOTT, HENRY WOOD** (13 Nov. 1846–25 May 1930) was an internationally known conservationist, naturalist, artist, and scientist. He authored the first international wildlife conservation treaty, the Hay-Elliott Fur Seal Treaty of 1911.

Born in Cleveland to Franklin and Sophia (Hopkins) Elliott, he attended West High School, yet was self-taught in art and science. From 1862–78 he worked for the Smithsonian Institution, studying and sketching natural history. In 1864 he traveled to British Columbia in his first field expedition. From 1869–71 Elliott worked on the U.S. Geological Survey out West.

In 1872 Elliott visited Alaska to investigate seal conditions on the Pribilof Islands, Bering Sea, following reports of depredations by open sea sealers. Elliott returned in 1874 and 1890. His sketches of St. Paul's Island provided persuasive evidence of the need to stop the seal slaughter.

When not in Alaska, Elliott lived in Cleveland, tending to local business matters and his vineyards. He kept up with reports on Alaska and contributed many articles to leading magazines such as *Harper's* and *Scribner's*.

A prolific artist, Elliott made between two and three hundred sketches of the Pribilofs between 1872–74. Many of his finished watercolor sketches are in the Smithsonian and the CLEVELAND MUSEUM OF NATURAL HISTORY.†

Elliott married Aleksandra Melovidov on 10 July 1872. They had 10 children: Grace, Flora, Marsha, Frank, Ruth, Edith, Narene, Lionel, John, and Louise. Elliott retired to Seattle, WA. His ashes were scattered over Mt. Rainier.—T.B.

**ELLSLER, EFFIE** (4 Apr. 1854–8 Oct. 1942), a member of the famous Ellsler theatrical family and known as "Cleveland's Sweetheart" from the 1870s to 1900s, learned to perfect the art of emotional distress and extravagant gesture so popular during the pre-Ibsen period of stage and screen. Ellsler was named for her mother, Euphemia Emma Ellsler, who, with her husband, JOHN A. ELLSLER, performed on stage as "Uncle John A. and Effie E." Little Effie's first stage appearance was portraying Little Eva in Harriet Beecher Stowe's *Uncle Tom's Cabin,* and later playing Cricket in *The Cricket on the Hearth.* Trained in the dramatic arts by her father, and later at Ursuline Academy, at 18 she took the role of Virginia in a production called *Virginius.* On 6 Sept. 1875, her father opened the EUCLID AVE. OPERA HOUSE† with Bronson Howard's play *Saratoga,* in which he performed and Effie was leading lady. On 1 Dec. 1880, Effie performed as Hazel in Steele MacKaye's melodrama *Hazel Kirke,* playing her best remembered role when it opened in Madison Square Theater on 4 Feb. 1880. The play made a record run on Broadway that was not surpassed until 1906. Ellsler's last appearance in Cleveland occurred on 29 May 1919 at the Shubert-Colonial Theater in a play called *Old Lady 31.* She was married in May 1881 to Frank Weston, an actor who appeared with her in *Hazel Kirke* and many other plays. They had no children. Ellsler was buried in Los Angeles.

**ELLSLER, JOHN ADAM** (26 Sept. 1821–21 Aug. 1903), actor, producer, manager, and theater builder, was born in Harrisburg, PA, but moved to Baltimore, working in a printing shop that published programs and posters for theaters. Responsible for delivery, Ellsler stayed for performances and decided to devote himself to the theater. Returning to Philadelphia, he worked as asst. treasurer of Peale's Museum, and as a property man while acting in minor roles. In 1846 he became a member of Arch St. Theater, then moved to Chatham St. Theater in New York, where he married the actress Euphemia Emma Myers. They remained at Chatham until Dec. 1849, when they began traveling.

The Ellslers first came to Cleveland in the mid–1850s, for 3 months at the Cleveland Theater. Ellsler subsequently assumed management of the ACADEMY OF MUSIC† and established a full-time theatrical company that began its schedule in Cleveland, moved to Columbus during legislative sessions, returned to Cleveland until the 4th of July, and ended with road trips to nearby cities such as Akron and Canton. He also attracted prominent figures from THEATER, opera, and burlesque to the academy's stage from 1855–73, and assisted new actors, including his daughter EFFIE ELLSLER, get started. Ellsler constructed the EUCLID AVE. OPERA HOUSE† in 1873, but cost overruns and the financial panic of 1873 forced him to sell to MARCUS HANNA in 1879. Ellsler became manager of

the Park Theater until 1886, when he moved to New York, continuing his acting career until his death. Euphemia and John Ellsler had 4 children: Effie, William C., John J., and Annie. Ellsler died in New York City and was buried in Lake View Cemetery.

*The Stage Memories of John A. Ellsler* (WRHS, 1950).

**ELSON, WILLIAM H.** (22 Nov. 1854–2 Feb. 1935), a progressive educator, served as superintendent of the CLEVELAND PUBLIC SCHOOLS† 1906–12. He was also author of several popular series of textbooks which were adopted by many school systems both throughout the nation and overseas.

Born to Thomas and Hannah (Alexander) Elson in Carroll County, OH, William and his family moved to Indiana, where he received his early schooling. He then moved on to Indiana Univ. and the Univ. of Chicago to earn his teaching credentials.

His years as a classroom teacher were few. By 1881 he was already a superintendent of schools in Parke County, IN. He moved on to Superior, WI, and then to Grand Rapids, MI, before coming to Cleveland in 1906.

In Cleveland he provided for the quarterly promotion of students, instituted one of the first technical high schools in the country (EAST TECHNICAL H.S.† in 1908), and started a program of elementary vocational education at Brownell School. Though his contributions in Cleveland were enduring, his leadership suffered a blow when a deadly fire struck Collinwood School (see COLLINWOOD SCHOOL FIRE†). Critics held him responsible for inadequate safety provisions at the school. Elson resigned from the superintendency in 1912, and then went to Cornell Univ. as a professor.

Elson's most lasting fame came from "The Elson Readers," a series of reading texts first published in 1909, which eventually achieved sales exceeding 50 million copies. They were in use in 34 countries.

Elson married twice, first to Minnie Trueblood on 20 June 1974. They had one son, Carl. On 19 Nov. 1879 he married Mattie Welch, with whom he had another son, Frank. Elson died in Chicago, IL.—J.T.

**ELWELL, HERBERT** (10 May 1898–17 Apr. 1974), composer and *PLAIN DEALER†* music critic, was born in Minneapolis to George and Belle (Horn) Elwell. He studied 2 years in New York with ERNEST BLOCH, and went to Paris in 1921, joining Aaron Copeland and Virgil Thomson and studying under Nadia Boulanger. In 1923, with a fellowship from the American Academy in Rome, he conducted the premiere of his ballet suite *The Happy Hypocrite.* Elwell came to Cleveland in 1928 to head the CLEVELAND INSTITUTE OF MUSIC's† composition and advanced theory department, and was also asst. director during his 17 years there. He also taught at Oberlin Conservatory of Music and the Eastman School of Music in Rochester, and directed the composition department of the CLEVELAND MUSIC SCHOOL SETTLEMENT.† From 1930–36, he was program annotator for the CLEVELAND ORCHESTRA.†

As music critic for the *Plain Dealer* from 1932–64, he held even the most popular artists to exacting standards, observing of Geo. Gershwin that "as a pianist he is a good composer." He was not beyond breaking into the middle of a concert with a "Bravo!" for an unexpectedly harmonic chord. His Sunday writings fulfilled the educational function of criticism. Nothing else Elwell wrote as a composer equaled the success of *The Happy Hypocrite*, which was programmed by GEO. SZELL on the Cleveland Orchestra's 1965 European tour. His *Lincoln Requiem Aeternam* for chorus and orchestra received the Paderewski Prize and a nationwide radio presentation in 1947. He resided in CLEVELAND HTS.† with his wife, Maria, whom he married on 27 July 1927. They had no children. Elwell was buried in Calvary Cemetery.

**ELWELL, JOHN JOHNSON** (22 June 1820–16 Mar. 1900), physician, attorney, and Union Army officer, was born in Warren, OH, to Samuel and Anna (Reeves) Elwell. He practiced medicine after graduating from Cleveland Medical College in 1846. Following 9 years in Orwell, OH, he served in the Ohio legislature (1853–55) was admitted to the Ohio Bar in 1855, and practiced law in Cleveland, publishing the *Western Law Monthly*, teaching at Ohio & Union Law College and Cleveland Medical College, and authoring a text on medical jurisprudence.

After the outbreak of the CIVIL WAR,† Elwell was appointed quartermaster, equipping the 2ND OHIO VOLUNTEER CAVALRY† of Cleveland, the 3rd Ohio Volunteer Cavalry of Huron County, and the Sherman Brigade. Elwell was volunteer aide-de-camp to Gen. Henry W. Benham at the Battle of Secessionville, SC, on 16 June 1862; and at the assault of Ft. Wagner, 18 July 1862, rallied troops in battle. Elwell was promoted to lt. colonel, serving as chief quartermaster of the Dept. of the South until 1 Feb. 1864. Because of yellow fever, Elwell was removed to Elmira, NY, where he purchased horses for the cavalry and supplied Elmira Prison and the rendezvous at Elmira for drafted men. Elwell was breveted 4 times for gallantry in battle and received the Gillmore Medal for meritorious conduct. His brevet generalship dated from Mar. 1865. After the war, he returned to Cleveland, resuming his careers and becoming editor of John Bouvier's *Law Directory*. Elwell married Nancy Chittenden in 1846; they had four children, all of whom died in infancy. He is buried in Woodland Cemetery.

**EMENY, BROOKS** (29 July 1901–12 July 1980) became president of the Foreign Policy Assn. on the basis of his reputation as director of the CLEVELAND COUNCIL ON WORLD AFFAIRS.† Born in Salem, OH, he graduated from Princeton Univ. in 1924 and continued his studies in Europe in preparation for a career in government service. A talk with Clevelander MYRON T. HERRICK, U.S. Ambassador to France, helped to steer Emeny's aspirations from the diplomatic service toward education in public affairs. Returning to the U.S., he became an instructor in political science at Yale Univ., where he also received his doctorate in international relations. He was the author of *The Strategy of Raw Materials: A Study of America in Peace and War* and coauthor, with Frank H. Simonds, of *The Great Powers in World Politics*. In 1935, at the instigation of NEWTON D. BAKER and others, he came to Cleveland to assume the unpaid position of director of the local Foreign Affairs Council, which became the Council on World Affairs under his tenure. During his 12 years as director and later president, he transformed the organization from a circle of 300 members to a potent 5,000-member interest group. Emeny also served as an associate professor of international relations at Cleveland College (see CASE WESTERN RESERVE UNIV.†) and as foreign affairs adviser for Republican presidential candidate Wendell L. Willkie in 1940. He left Cleveland in 1947 to become president of the Foreign Policy Assn. in New York, serving in that position until 1952. After the death of his first wife, Winifred Rockefeller, Emeny married Barbara Cox in 1954. He was survived by her and a daughter from his first marriage.—J.V.

**EMERSON, OLIVER FARRAR** (1860–13 March 1927) was head of the English department at Adelbert College (see CASE WESTERN RESERVE UNIV.†) and an internationally recognized scholar on Chaucer. The son of a New England missionary, he was born in Traer, IA, and received his bachelor's degree from Grinnell College. After serving as superintendent of the Grinnell schools, he proceeded to Cornell Univ., where he earned his doctorate and taught English. From Cornell he was called to Adelbert College in 1896, becoming Oviatt Professor of English in 1906. An authority in the fields of Old and Middle English, Emerson was the author of *A History of the English Language* and *A Middle*

*English Reader*. He also edited several volumes of English authors and contributed regularly to scholarly journals. A resident of EAST CLEVELAND, from where he habitually walked to and from the Adelbert campus, he also maintained a summer home in Mentor Headlands. Locally, he was a founder of the NOVEL CLUB.† Nationally, he served as president of the American Dialect Soc. and the Modern Language Assn. of America. He died in Ocala, FL., having gone there in an unsuccessful attempt to recover from a heart condition and Bright's disease. Married to Annie Laurie Logan of St. Louis, he was survived by her, a son, and a daughter. His library was donated to the university, and a memorial volume consisting of his Chaucer essays was published by the Western Reserve Univ. Press.—J.V.

Oliver Farrar Emerson biographical file, CWRU Archives.

**ENGEL, ALBERT JOHN** (12 May 1879–30 Dec. 1978) was among the first Clevelanders to own a plane and the first Clevelander to fly one extensively. In 1978 he became the first inductee to the Western Reserve Aviation Hall of Fame.

Born in Cleveland to John and Mary (Billenstein), Engel was raised on the west side and worked for the Water Works Department from 1906–10. Intrigued by flight, Engel attended the Curtiss Airplane Co. flying school at Hammondsport, NY. By 1911 Engel was airborne.

Engel crashed his first airplane near Cleveland in the fall of 1911. After working for Curtiss in San Diego, he returned to Cleveland in 1912, buying a new hydroaeroplane (seaplane) from Curtiss for about $6,000. Engel promoted a contest, for ladies only, to name the new plane. "Bumble Bee" was chosen and the winner received a free flight. He flew exhibition and passenger flights throughout northeast Ohio, and air meets in Chicago and Buffalo. During the summer of 1914, Engel flew "Aeroplane Mail" (airmail) across Lake Chautauqua, NY. Engel retired the "Bumble Bee" after the 1u914 season and continued with Curtiss in Buffalo.

During World War I he taught flying to army recruits in Spain. In 1918 he opened the Engel Aircraft Co., acting as vice-president. The business collapsed in 1919 and Engel stopped flying.

During World War II Engel built army gliders as general manager of the National Aircraft Co. After the war Engel retired to Cleveland. In 1946 he sold the "Bumble Bee" to the Thompson Products Museum. The restored plane now rests in the Crawford Auto-Aviation Museum of the WESTERN RESERVE HISTORICAL SOCIETY.†

Engel was twice married. He married Nettie Stanek in 1899 (div. 1903). In 1906 he married Elizabeth Schroeder (d. 1956). Engel was childless. He is buried in Sunset Memorial Park.—T.B.

**EVANS, DINA REES (DOC)** (19 June 1891–20 Jan. 1989) trained a generation of actors as a drama instructor at Cleveland Hts. High School and the founding director of CAIN PARK THEATER.† She was born in Chicago and received her bachelor's degree from the Univ. of South Dakota. During the 1920s she taught languages in Bozeman, MT, while pursuing graduate degrees at the Univ. of Iowa. Her doctorate (1932) was the first granted for theater in the U.S. Evans meanwhile had moved to Cleveland, where she taught English and directed the Heights Players at Cleveland Hts. High from 1930–58. In 1934 she staged a summer production in a wooded ravine soon named Cain Park. A permanent amphitheater was built there in 1938, and Evans served as its managing director until 1950. She remained involved in Cain Park's activities until her retirement from teaching in 1958. Her alumni at Hts. High and Cain Park included Joel Gray, Jack Weston, John Price of MUSICARNIVAL,† and Wm. Boehm of the SINGING ANGELS.† Evans moved to Arizona in retirement, where she bought and ran a local newspaper, organized a theater group, and married Harvey Shaw at the age of 72. She occasionally returned to Cleveland, notably in 1980 for the publication of her book on *Cain Park Theatre: The Halcyon Years*. Hts. High renamed its auditorium after her in 1976, and Cain Park similarly renamed its main amphitheater in 1989. Following her death in Sun City, AZ, her ashes were interred in the family plot in Gallipolis, OH.—J.V.

**EVERETT, HENRY A.** (16 Oct. 1856–10 Apr. 1917) was a street railway magnate involved with the financing, construction, and operation of many early electric railways in Cleveland and Ohio.

Born in Cleveland to Dr. Azariah and Emily (Burnham) Everett, Henry was educated in Cleveland public and private schools.

Everett turned his interest in electricity into a career. He figured prominently in public utilities, having organized and financed independent telephone companies and being associated with electric lighting corporations in numerous Midwestern cities.

In 1893 Everett became president of the CLEVELAND ELECTRIC RAILWAY CO.† In 1895, Everett became president of Ohio's pioneer interurban line, the Akron, Bedford & Cleveland Railway Co., which in 1899 consolidated with the Akron Traction & Electric Co. to form a new company operating 60 miles of track. This company reorganized in 1892 as the Northern Ohio Traction &

Light Co. when several Akron and Canton lines were acquired. Everett was president.

In 1896 Everett's efforts to build 3-cent fare lines were followed by an ordinance to reduce Woodland Ave. fares from 5 to 4 cents at stated hours, and 3 cents during other hours of the day.

Everett formed the Everett-Moore Syndicate with EDWARD MOORE in 1901 to operate the LAKE SHORE ELECTRIC RAILWAY CO.,† formed through the merger of four interurban railways, including the Lorain & Cleveland Railway Co. and the Sandusky, Milan & Norwalk Railway. The syndicate also owned the CLEVELAND, PAINESVILLE & ASHTABULA† and CLEVELAND, PAINESVILLE & EASTERN† lines.

Everett married Josephine Pettengill on 2 June 1886. They had two children, Leolyn and Dorothy. Everett lived in Willoughby. He died in Pasadena, CA.—T.B.

**EVERETT, MORRIS SR.** (14 Feb. 1910–20 March 1993) was recognized as the dean of area investment counselors, served three terms as mayor of Hunting Valley, and was a trustee of numerous organizations.

Born in Cleveland, Everett attended HAWKEN SCHOOL,† graduated from Kent School (Lakeville, CT) in 1929, and received his A.B. from Yale Univ. in 1933. He then worked for Republic Steel in Cleveland, 1933–36; Murray Ohio Manufacturing Co., 1936–40; and Pan American Air Ferries in New York, 1940–42. During World War II Everett served as an Air Force Major.

In 1946 Everett became office manager in the investment management firm of Scudder, Stevens & Clark. He opened the firm's Cleveland office and became a general partner in 1967. When he retired from the firm in 1975 he was national vice-president.

Everett was treasurer of the John Huntington Fund for Education from 1975–92, providing scholarship funding to area colleges, and was a trustee of the fund at his death.

Everett first entered politics prior to World War II as treasurer of HUNTING VALLEY. After the war he served as village councilman until he was elected to the first of three consecutive terms as mayor in 1957.

Everett was a national expert on Confederate philatelic history, gathering one of the largest and finest collections of Confederate covers in the world. He was a trustee of the WESTERN RESERVE HISTORICAL SOCIETY.†

Everett married Eleanor Egan in 1934. They had three children: Chandler, Morris Jr., and Mrs. Anne Kucklick. An Episcopalian, Everett is buried in Lake View Cemetery.—T.B.

**EVERETT, SYLVESTER T.** (27 Nov. 1838–13 Jan. 1922), Cleveland financier, was born in Liberty Twp., to Henry and Sarah (von Piteil) Everett. At 12 he joined an older brother in Cleveland. At 13 he became a messenger for the banking house of Brockway, Wason, Everett (an older brother) & Co., becoming a cashier in a few years before leaving in 1858 to work briefly in a bank in Philadelphia. He was then superintendent of a petroleum company, returning to Cleveland in 1868 to manage Everett, Weddell & Co. (previously Brockway, Wason, Everett & Co.). In 1876 he became president of Second Natl. Bank, and then organized the Union Natl. Bank, which became one of the city's leading financial institutions.

Everett had interests in mining and transportation. He was also active in city government, serving 7 terms as city treasurer between 1869–83, when he enormously increased public investment in municipal bonds. A staunch Republican, he attended conventions and was a friend of JAS. A. GARFIELD and Wm. McKinley. Pres. Garfield appointed Everett U.S. government director of the Union Pacific Railroad; McKinley offered him the ambassadorship to Austria-Hungary. Everett financed and built 2 of the first street railways (electric) in the U.S.—in Akron and in Erie, PA. Everett was an art collector, owning some of Europe's finest art treasures. He was also a founder and charter member of the UNION CLUB.† His home at Euclid and East 40th St. was one of the largest on "Millionaires Row." Everett married Mary Everett in 1860. They had 3 children: Katherine, Eleanor, and Marguerite. After Mary's death in 1876, Everett married Alice Wade, the granddaughter of JEPTHA WADE, I, in 1879. They had 5 children: Esther, Alice, Ruth, Randall, and Homer. Everett died in Cleveland and was buried in Lake View Cemetery.

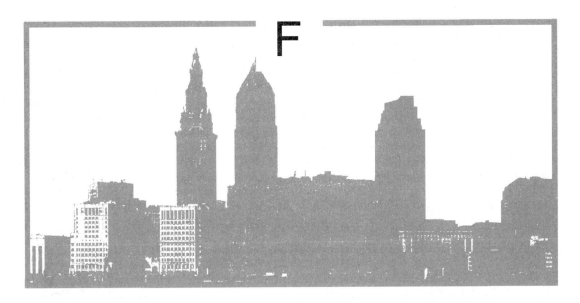

F

**FAGAN, HARRY** (15 Dec.1939–9 Dec. 1992), social activist, influenced community development and politics as director of the Commission on Catholic Community Action in the Diocese of Cleveland (1976–83). Fagan was born in Cleveland; his Irish parents, Harry and Jane Fagan, ran Fagan's Tavern in the FLATS.† After graduating from John Carroll Univ. (1961), he worked in advertising at the Cleveland *PLAIN DEALER†* and volunteered at St. Henry Catholic Church. Fagan first joined the Commission on Catholic Community Action full-time in 1971 as associate director. He trained people to create and lead neighborhood coalitions (such as the Buckeye–Woodland Community Council and the St. Clair–Superior Coalition) which attacked social problems and played key roles in local elections. Other positions Fagan held included: chair of the Social Concerns Department of the Ohio Catholic Conference and of the national Catholic Committee on Urban Ministry (1978–80); director of the Heights Community Congress; and board member of the Cuyahoga Plan, the Cleveland Tenants Organization, and the INTERCHURCH COUNCIL OF GREATER CLEVELAND.† In 1983 Fagan left Cleveland to help develop the National Pastoral Life Center in New York City. He became associate director there and organized and served on the board of the nationwide Roundtable of diocesan social action directors (1984–92).

In June 1963, Fagan was married to Sheila Fitz-Simmons; the couple lived in CLEVELAND HTS.† They had two daughters, Alison Soler and Jocelyn. Fagan died in New York.—J.M.

Fagan, Harry. *Empowerment: Skills for Parish Social Action* (1979).

**FAIRFAX, FLORENCE BUNDY** (24 Dec. 1907–6 Mar. 1970), a long-time African American employee of the city's Recreation Dept., was born in Cleveland to George and Florence (Wilson) Bundy. She graduated from the College for Women of Western Reserve Univ. In 1928 she became physical-education director in the city's Div. of Recreation, and following college graduation in 1929, became physical-education director of the Central Recreation Ctr. In 1934 she was appointed playground supervisor in the Central District, becoming superintendent of the Bureau of Recreation Ctrs. in 1944. On 16 Aug. 1953, Fairfax suffered severe injuries in an automobile accident which took the life of her husband, Lawrence E. Fairfax. After 7 months she returned to work, and in May 1954 was appointed superintendent of the new Bureau of Special Activities, which was designed to help "the unattached youngster or independent street club or gang . . . find better ways and better places to play" and to help solve the problem of juvenile delinquency by guiding problem youth to appropriate social agencies. She hoped the bureau would be able "to help children to form good social patterns of behavior through recreation." In recognition of her years of devotion to the recreational needs of Cleveland's inner-city youth, the Fairfax Recreation Ctr. was dedicated in her honor in 1959. In 1966 Mayor Ralph Locher appointed her assistant commissioner of recreation, a position she held until her death.

Fairfax was married twice. Her first marriage was to William Wright on 29 June 1929; the second was to Lawrence Fairfax. There were no children from either marriage. Fairfax died in Cleveland and was cremated at Highland Park Cemetery.

**FAIST, RUSSELL** (6 Sept. 1922–5 Jan. 1990) spent the greater part of his journalistic career of 4 decades as an editor with the *CATHOLIC UNIVERSE BULLETIN.†* A Cleveland native, he was the son of Edward and Helen Bringman Faist. After graduating from ST. IGNATIUS HIGH SCHOOL,† he earned a degree in English from JOHN CARROLL UNIV.† In 1943 he married Dorothy Jean Benes and enlisted for a 2-year stint in the U.S. Maritime Service during World War II. Faist joined the *CLEVELAND NEWS* in 1945 as a copyboy, advancing to reporter, and by the late 1950s, to city editor. He worked on 2 award-winning series, one on inadequate welfare relief and the other on abuses in liquor licensing. Only 2 weeks before the *News* folded, Faist moved to the *Universe Bulletin*. Soon promoted from reporter to city editor, he won 5 PRESS CLUB OF CLEVELAND† awards for his columns on such topics as racial justice and world peace. From April 1986 to his retirement the following November, he served as editor of the Catholic Press Union, publisher of the *Universe Bulletin* as well as sister papers in Toledo and Youngstown. Among his innovations was an updated graphic and editorial style for the *Universe Bulletin*. Faist died at his home in ROCKY RIVER.† Buried at Lakewood Park Cemetery, he was survived by his wife and 6 children: Kathleen, Diane, Margaret, Mary, Jerome, and Frank.—J.V.

**FARLEY, JOHN HARRINGTON** (5 Feb. 1846–10 Feb. 1922), a member of the city council (1871–77) and Cleveland mayor (1883–85, 1899–1901), was born in Cleveland to Patrick and Ann Schwartz Farley. He received a public-school education. Interested in politics, he was elected to city council in 1871 as a Democrat and served 3 terms. Known as "Honest John" Farley, he was elected mayor in 1883. After 1 term in office, he was appointed collector of internal revenue by Pres. Grover Cleveland and was made director of public works in Cleveland under Mayor ROBT. BLEE in 1893. With the support of the Municipal Assn. (now the CITIZENS LEAGUE†), he defeated incumbent Republican mayor ROBT. MCKISSON in Apr. 1899. During his term in office, Farley had to request the state militia to support Cleveland police in maintaining order during the STREETCAR STRIKE OF 1899.† In business, Farley was a contractor and president of the Mutual Bldg. & Investment Co. He participated in founding the Central Natl. Bank and also was an officer of the GUARDIAN SAVINGS & TRUST CO.† Farley married Margaret Kenney on 23 Nov. 1884; they had no children. He died of a stroke.

**FARMER, JAMES** (19 July 1802–17 Mar. 1891) was a businessman closely identified with Cleveland's earliest manufacturing, mining, railroad, and banking interests. He founded the Cleveland & Pittsburgh, and the Valley Railroad companies and, with his wife, MERIBAH BUTLER FARMER, founded Cleveland's original evangelical Quakers organization and the FIRST FRIENDS CHURCH.†

Born near Augusta, GA, to John and Mary (Taylor) Farmer, James and his family moved to Columbiana County, OH, in 1805, then to Salineville in 1818. From 1818–1924 James worked in his father's business as a salt manufacturer.

In 1828 James began his own mercantile career by opening a general store. In 1838 he built the first flour mill in Ohio, and in 1844 he built a steamer to carry goods down the Ohio and Mississippi rivers. In 1846 he secured a charter for the Cleveland & Pittsburgh Railroad Co., serving as its first president until 1859, and on the Board of Directors until ca. 1866.

Farmer moved to Cleveland in 1856. In 1871 he secured the charter and organized the Valley Railroad from Cleveland through the Cuyahoga Valley to Akron and Canton. Farmer was president of the Ohio National Bank, and helped organize the State National Bank, serving as president until his death.

In 1871 the Farmers opened their home to the first meeting of the Cleveland Friends. As an elder and honored member of the Society of Friends, Farmer was instrumental in building the Friends' Church on Cedar Ave. in 1874.

Farmer married Meribah Butler on 1 Oct. 1834. They had seven children: Elihu, Beulah, Ellen, Lydia, Laura, Elizabeth, and James. Farmer is buried in Lake View Cemetery.—T.B.

Painter, Lydia Ethel Farmer. *The Memoirs of James and Meribah Farmer* (1900).
Malone, J. Walter. *The Autobiography of an Evangelical Quaker* (1993).

**FARMER, MERIBAH BUTLER** (14 July 1805–4 April 1898) was a Quaker minister and philanthropist who, together with her husband, JAMES FARMER, helped found Cleveland's original evangelical Quakers organization and the FIRST FRIENDS CHURCH.†

Born near Philadelphia, PA, to Benjamin and Hannah (Webster) Butler, Meribah and her family moved to Salem, OH, in 1811. She married James Farmer on 1 Oct. 1834, and they settled in Salineville, OH. In 1856 the Farmers became the first members of the Society of Friends (Quakers) to settle in Cleveland.

Meribah was accepted early in life as a Quaker minister. Always wearing her bonnet and unostentatious attire, Meribah adhered strictly to the dress and manners of the Quakers, and, in meetings for worship, ministered in the spirit with great strength and sweetness.

The Cleveland Friends meeting first began in 1871 in the Farmer's home, located at the corner of Superior Ave. and East 6th St. (former HOL-LENDEN HOTEL† site). It was here the idea for a First Friends Church was born. In 1874 a modest church was built on Cedar Ave. Meribah was one of four resident ministers, and James Farmer was an elder.

Meribah devoted herself to various charities, including the Cleveland Protestant Orphan Asylum, the Aid Society of the Civil War, the Homeopathic Hospital, the Retreat (a home for the mentally disabled), and always provided aid for the Freedmen and the Native Americans through the board of the Society of Friends.

The Farmers had seven children: Elihu, Beulah, Ellen, Lydia, Laura, Elizabeth, and James. Meribah is buried in Lake View Cemetery.—T.B.

Painter, Lydia Ethel Farmer. *The Memoirs of James and Meribah Farmer* (1900).
Malone, J. Walter. *The Autobiography of an Evangelical Quaker* (1993).

**FARRELLY, JOHN PATRICK** (15 Mar. 1856–12 Feb. 1921), fourth bishop of Cleveland, was born in Memphis, TN, to John Patrick and Martha Moore Clay Farrelly. He converted to Catholicism as a child. Farrelly was educated at Georgetown Univ., the Jesuit College at Nemur in Belgium, and North American College in Rome, and was ordained to the priesthood on 22 May 1880 in Rome, then studying 2 years in Palestine. He was a noted Scripture scholar, linguist, and archeologist. In 1882 Farrelly was assigned to the Cathedral in Nashville, and became chancellor of the diocese in 1883. In 1887 Farrelly became secretary to the rector of North American College, whose staff, prior to the founding of the Apostolic Delegation, was the intermediary between Rome and the American bishops. In 1894 he became spiritual director of the college. He was named bishop of Cleveland on 16 Mar. 1909 and was consecrated in the chapel of North American College on 1 May 1909.

Farrelly was concerned over the inefficient fundraising of various charitable organizations, and so established the Board of Charities (forerunner of Catholic Charities) in 1910. Farrelly built new buildings for health-care facilities in the diocese, established a ministry to the deaf and hearing-impaired, and opened MERRICK HOUSE† and the Catholic Young Women's Hall. He established the office of superintendent of schools to standardize parochial education and opened several secondary schools, including CATHEDRAL LATIN.† Farrelly planned to build a new seminary, but died suddenly while visiting Knoxville, TN, where he contracted a fatal case of pneumonia.

**FAWICK, THOMAS L.** (14 Apr. 1889–8 Jan. 1978), industrialist, inventor, and art collector, was born in Sioux Falls, SD, son of Thomas and Lena Fawick. He quit school at 15, and at 20 built what was reportedly the first 4-door touring car in America. Fawick patented over 250 inventions, but disparaged the use of books as an impediment to ingenuity. In 1917 Fawick was one of 3 incorporators of Twin Disc Clutch Co. in Racine, WI, selling his interest in 1936 to organize the Fawick Clutch Co., which he moved to Cleveland in 1942. For the airflex clutch, used in industry and naval landing craft during World War II, Fawick in 1949 received the Franklin Institute's John Price Wetherill Medal. Fawick also invented in other fields, patenting a handgrip for golf clubs in 1965 and establishing an Akron company to manufacture it. He also designed and improved sound systems for Public Hall and the stadium.

A self-taught violinist, Fawick composed and published numerous pieces and owned 2 Stradivarius violins. Interested in making violins, he developed a treatment that accelerated wood aging and kept the instrument even-tempered during temperature fluctuations. His Fawick violin gained international acceptance. In 1968 the Fawick Corp. merged with EATON CORP.† and Fawick retired to devote his time to his private Fawick Museum, containing art he had collected; following his death in 1979, it was auctioned for $1.2 million, two-thirds of which went to the CLEVELAND MUSEUM OF ART† and the remainder to BALDWIN-WALLACE COLLEGE.†

Fawick and his wife, Marie, had one child, Florence. He was buried in Lake View Cemetery.

Depke, John E. *The Tom Fawick Story* (1972).

**FEATHER, WILLIAM A.** (25 Aug. 1889–7 Jan. 1981) founded a successful printing business but was best known as editor of the company's *The William Feather Magazine*. A native of Jamestown, NY, he was brought to Cleveland in 1903 and graduated in 1906 from South High School. After earning an A.B. from Western Reserve Univ. (see CASE WESTERN RESERVE†) in 1910, he spent 5 years as a reporter for the *CLEVELAND PRESS.†* Feather then worked a year in public relations and in 1916 started *The William Feather Magazine* in the printing shop of a friend, David Gibson. Having married Ruth Presley (1888–1965) in 1912, he borrowed from her inheritance to buy out Gibson and start the WILLIAM FEATHER CO.† in 1919. During the 1920s, Feather gained a national reputation as a "benevolent iconoclast" through his writings in his own organ and for such magazines as H. L. Mencken's *The American Mercury*. He maintained personal friendships with such opposites as Mencken and advertising executive Bruce Barton. As a member of the CITY CLUB OF CLEVELAND,† he enjoyed arguing with the radicals at the "Soviet Table," but he later joined the UNION CLUB† to press his single-tax views on a more conservative audience. His books included *As We Were Saying* (1921), *Haystacks and Smokestacks* (1923), *The Ideals and Follies of Business* (1927), and *The Business of Life* (1949). In 1941 he was separated, but never divorced, from his wife, Ruth Feather, who had pursued her own career as an actress at the CLEVELAND PLAY HOUSE.† Although he retired as president of the Wm. Feather Co. in favor of his son, Wm. Jr., in 1959, he continued to function as editor of his magazine. He was survived by his son and a daughter, Judith Carey. —J.V.

**FEDER, MARK** (7 July 1907–3 July 1992) was a leading figure in Cleveland theatrical circles. He was the founder of the Jewish Community Theatre of the JEWISH COMMUNITY CENTER† (JCC), serving as its drama director from 1948 until his retirement in 1972.

One of ten children of Hirsch and Toby Feder, Mark was born in Minsk, Russia (now Belarus). At age 11, he emigrated to the U.S., joining his older brother, Joseph, then living in Cleveland. After graduation from John Adams High School, he moved to Chicago, where he attended Jewish People's Institute and studied acting. He continued his education at Carnegie-Mellon Univ. in Pittsburgh, where he majored in directing.

His interest in the theater took him to New York City, where he attended classes at New York Univ. and gained acting experience at the Yiddish Art Theatre. During World War II, he toured extensively, performing for the Armed Services.

Following the war he returned to Cleveland and began his association with the Jewish Community Center. Before the JCC opened its own theater in 1960, he produced his plays on various stages around the city. Altogether, in his 24 years with the JCC he directed over 100 plays, occasionally acting in some as well.

Prior to his return to Cleveland, Feder was also active as a writer. For several years in New York he authored a syndicated column on Jewish humor, "Live and Laugh," from which he later produced a book, *It's a Living*, which was published in 1948.

In 1943 he wed Ethel Grumer. They had one daughter, Tova.

Following his retirement in 1972, Feder moved to San Diego, CA, where he died and is interred.—J.T.

**FEIGHAN, MICHAEL ALOYSIUS** (16 Feb. 1905–19 March 1992) was a 14-term Democratic congressman for the 20th District of Ohio, and the chief architect of the Federal Immigration Act of 1965 which abolished the system of quotas by national origin.

Born in LAKEWOOD, OH, to John T. and Mary (English) Feighan, he attended St. Ignatius High School, JOHN CARROLL UNIV.† (for one year), and graduated from Princeton Univ. in 1928. He received his law degree from Harvard Univ. in 1931 and practiced law in Cleveland with his 4 brothers in the firm of Feighan, Feighan, Feighan, Feighan & Feighan.

He began his political career in 1937 with the Ohio state legislature and rose to Democratic minority leader in 1939. In 1942 he was elected congressman for the 20th District of Ohio. In 1953 he became chairman of the Immigration and Nationality Subcommittee of the Judiciary Committee. Regarded as a staunch anti-communist, Feighan introduced and guided legislation over a 12-week period which eliminated the monopoly northern and western European immigrants held in entering the U.S., in favor of opening the door to more eastern Europeans burdened by Soviet control. Feighan left office in 1971 when Cleveland Council president James V. Stanton won the 1970 Democratic primary. He then became a political consultant.

Feighan married Florence J. Mathews on 21 June 1930 (d. 1980) and they had three children: Michael A. (dec.), William Mathews, and Fleur. He was buried in Calvary Cemetery. His nephew, Edward F. Feighan, was a Democratic congressman for the 19th District of Ohio in 1993.—T.B.

**FEIKERT, WILLIAM FREDERICK** (8 June 1851–7 Oct. 1896), and **ADELAIDE DYBALL** (ca. 1860–3 Jan. 1942), were both active in the confectionery and chewing gum business in Cleveland. William Feikert was born in Cleveland, the son of Christian and Sadie (Fuchs) Feikert; attended public schools here, and graduated from Univ. School. By that time both his natural parents were dead and he went to work for his stepfather, Nathan Heisel, who was a manufacturing confectioner. In 1871 he set up his own manufacturing and wholesale confectionery firm and also opened several retail stores in the city.

His chemical experimentation yielded a new chicle paste used in the manufacture of chewing gum, and this became a major part of his successful operation, headquartered at 11 Woodland Ave.

Feikert married Adelaide DyBall of Cleveland 20 Mar. 1876. Adelaide, the daughter of Edmond and Martha Elizabeth (Curtis) Dyball, was orphaned at an early age. She lived with her guardian, P. S. Bosworth, attending Mayflower grammar school, and graduating from Central High School. Of the Feikerts' 4 children only William Eugene reached adulthood. In the early 1890s William Sr.'s poor health led his wife, Adelaide, to take over the business. After his death in 1896, Adelaide disposed of the wholesale and retail businesses, organized the Cuyahoga Chemical Co. to manufacture the chicle paste her husband had invented, and made her son William a partner in the firm. For nearly 20 years she expanded the company's chicle sales throughout the country and gained a reputation as an astute businesswoman among her peers. Later she built a factory in her garage on E. 84th St. and continued selling the paste. She died at her residence in Cleveland at age 82.—M.S.

FEISS, PAUL LOUIS (3 June 1875–20 Jan. 1952), business executive and bibliophile, pioneered methods of scientific management as vice-president and general manager of JOSEPH AND FEISS† clothing store. Kent State Univ. acquired his 5,000-volume library in 1952; his 450 rare books formed the basis for the university library's department of special collections. Born in Cleveland, son of Julius F. and Carrie (Dreyfuss) Feiss, he graduated from UNIV. SCHOOL† in 1890. He did not attend college but began a lifelong avocation of reading and book collecting. He acquired the major portion of his library between 1895 and 1915. Feiss soon became an expert in incunabula, early printing, and rare 16th and 17th century editions. With a working knowledge of Latin, he also spoke and wrote fluent German. During World War I, Feiss served as the federal representative of the Division of Housing of the Department of Labor for the Cleveland District. Shortly after the war, Feiss was named a member of Pres. Woodrow Wilson's Industrial Conference.

Feiss served as president of the Cleveland Chamber of Commerce (1917–18), helped organize the CLEVELAND ORCHESTRA†, and was a member of the Board of Advisors of the CLEVELAND MUSEUM OF ART† (1914–52). The ROWFANT CLUB,† of which he was president and a board member, made him a fellow. From 1950 until his death, Feiss served on the CLEVELAND HTS.† Planning Commission. Married to Edith Lehman on 2 June 1903, Feiss had 4 children: Julian W., Carl L.,

Caroline B., and Gertrude L. Feiss died at his Cedar Rd. home in Cleveland Hts.—J.M.

Joseph and Feiss Company Records, 1847–1960, WRHS.

FELTON, MONROE H. (30 Mar. 1902–22 Jan. 1989) was an entrepreneur in Cleveland's African American community following World War II. He was active in both the real estate and entertainment fields.

Born in Americus, GA, Felton was educated there and at Morris Brown College in Atlanta, where he majored in mathematics. He married Vivian D. Martin there, and he and his wife moved to Cleveland in 1923. They had no children.

At first Felton worked as a waiter at Hotel Cleveland and then for the White Motor Co. His ambition, however, was to secure a real estate license, and he devoted his free time to studying for it. He earned the Ohio salesman's license in 1941, and followed that up with a broker's license in 1946. In that year, together with some associates, he organized the Manhattan Realty Co. Its offices were located at 4000 East 104th St. He mixed business with compassion, often surrendering a part of his commission to enable his customers to afford the price of a home.

Besides his interest in real estate, Felton was also fascinated by the entertainment world, and he was active in booking black entertainment groups. He was successful in bringing to Cleveland such ensembles as the Ink Spots and the Mills Brothers. Most frequently, the cabaret-style programs he sponsored were held at the old Majestic Hotel on East 55th St. and Central Ave.

Felton retained his real estate business until 1986. Then in 1988, his health failing, he became a resident at the Willow Park Convalescent Home. He died in 1989. Interment was at Highland Park Cemetery.—J.T.

FENN, SERENO PECK (25 Apr. 1844–3 Jan. 1927), prominent in the SHERWIN-WILLIAMS CO.,† was born in Tallmadge, OH, to Sereno and Elizabeth Carrothers Fenn. He arrived in Cleveland in 1862 to attend HUMISTON INSTITUTE.† In 1864 he served 4 months in the Ohio 164th Infantry. In 1865 Fenn began as a clerk in the Cleveland, Columbus & Indianapolis Railroad freight office, but rather than violate his religious convictions by working on Sundays, he quit the railroad in 1870.

In 1869 Fenn attended an international YMCA convention, meeting fellow delegate Henry A. Sherwin. In Apr. 1870 Sherwin hired Fenn as cashier-bookkeeper in the new partnership of Sherwin-Williams & Co. In 1880, Fenn became a partner and treasurer. In 1884 the partnership was incorporated, with Fenn as an incorporator and significant stockholder. He was vice-president from 1921 until his death. Fenn was a director of the Cleveland YOUNG MEN'S CHRISTIAN ASSN.† from 1868–1920 and its president for 25 years, with special interests in educational programs. In 1930, the Cleveland YMCA School of Technology was re-named Fenn College in his honor. Fenn was an active member of the FIRST PRESBYTERIAN (OLD STONE) CHURCH† from 1865 to his death, serving as elder, trustee, and superintendent of the Sunday school. He married Mary Augusta DeWitt in May 1870, who died in 1917. He married Helen Barry Wright in July 1918, who died in June 1923. Fenn had no children of his own. His stepdaughter, Elizabeth Huntington DeWitt, married JOHN L. SEVERANCE.

**FENSTER, LEO** (1904–22 Sept. 1984), a UAW activist, was born in New York, the son of Polish immigrants Samuel and Jennie Fenster. He moved to Cleveland as a child and attended a year at Western Reserve Univ. As a clerk at the Coit Rd. Fisher Body Plant, he helped organize Local 45 of the CIO-Auto Workers' Union (later the Cleveland District Council-UAW), and over the years held many offices. Fenster's leftist influence (he declared himself a Communist in 1942) was prominent in the *Eye Opener,* the local's paper, which was critical of both UAW and government policies.

Fenster came under increased attack in the late 1940s as "right-wing" union forces tried to oust "left-wing" forces, charging funds had been di-verted to political causes and that the *Eye Opener* was too costly, although it cost less than half what the official UAW paper cost. In Oct. 1950, Fenster was replaced as *Eye Opener* editor for refusing to run a column supporting the Korean War. The international tried unsuccessfully to remove him from any local power; he ultimately resigned. Like many early Communist supporters, Fenster grew disenchanted with Kremlin power abuses but re-mained a leftist critic of social policy. He advocated Vietnam troop withdrawal by 1968, and in 1970 joined a citizens' committee that met with peace negotiators. After a stroke in 1968, Fenster retired to write and lecture about the history of the labor movement. In 1971 he edited the autobiography of Wyndham Mortimer. Fenster died after another stroke. He left his wife, Bertha Blank, and 4 chil-dren: Eric, Marc, Dale, and Russ. Fenster was bur-ied in Hillcrest Cemetery.

Leo Fenster Papers, WRHS.
Leo Fenster Papers, Walter Reuther Library.

**FERRELL, FREDERIC LEONARD** (21 May 1915–23 Dec. 1992), attorney, pioneered interracial law practice and defended unpopular cases, such as women against abusive husbands and members of the Black Panthers. Born in Danville, VA, to Isaac and Martha Jackson Ferrell, he was raised in BEREA† after his father died. Ferrell graduated from Berea High School and Wilberforce Univ. (1939). The armed services would not accept Ferrell despite his ROTC training, citing a full quota of African American officers; however, he enlisted in the Army Air Corps. After World War II, Ferrell worked at the WARNER AND SWASEY CO.† while attending the Cleveland Marshall Law School of (see CLEVELAND STATE UNIV.†, graduating in 1953). His defiance of lunchroom segregation at the factory led to the demise of such separation there. In his Cleveland law practice, Ferrell allowed new graduates of any race to use his office free of charge but held them to standards of excellence.

Ferrell married Mollie Thomas on 8 Jan. 1943; they lived with their 7 children (Emile Betterson, Louise Franklin, Sandra Woodall, Janice Rabb, Linda, Frederic L., Jr., and Charles) first in GLEN-VILLE,† then in EAST CLEVELAND.† Ferrell moved back to Berea shortly before his death. He was a member of the MASONS.†—J.M.

**FESLER, MAYO** (19 Nov. 1871–6 May 1945), reformer and director of the CITIZENS LEAGUE,† was born in Morgantown, IN, to Peter and Emma (Collitt) Fesler. He attended DePaul Univ. and the Univ. of Chicago, graduating in 1897. He taught high school before becoming secretary of the St. Louis Civic League in 1903. In 1910 the Cleveland Municipal Assn. hired him as secretary. Fesler, NEWTON D. BAKER, and A. R. Hatton cam-paigned for municipal home rule, Fesler as secretary of the Ohio Municipal League, formed to promote the cause. HOME RULE† was adopted in the 1912 state constitution, and Fesler helped draft Cleve-land's first city charter. He encouraged implementa-tion of the merit system for city employees and the general assembly's passage of a civil service act in 1914. In 1913 he changed the name of the Munici-pal League to the Civic League. Fesler helped orga-nize the CITY CLUB OF CLEVELAND† in 1912 and was its first secretary.

Fesler left Cleveland in 1917 to become secretary of the Brooklyn, NY, Chamber of Commerce; in 1922 he became secretary of Chicago's city club. The Civic League was reorganized as the Citizens League in 1923, and Fesler returned to Cleveland as its first director, retiring 2 months before his death. Fesler started the movement leading to recodification of Ohio's election code in 1929, and often lobbied before CLEVELAND CITY COUN-

CIL† and the Ohio general assembly. Fesler married Gertrude Fails in 1903; they had 1 daughter, Jean Louise. Fesler died in Cleveland and was buried in Highland Park Cemetery.

**FETZER, HERMAN** (24 June 1899–17 Jan. 1935), better known as "Jake Falstaff" to *Akron Times* and *CLEVELAND PRESS†* readers, was born in Maple Valley, OH, to Levi E. and Lydia Fetzer. After graduating from Akron's West High School, he worked as suburban reporter for the *Akron Times*, where in 1920 he began his column "Pippins and Cheese," taking its title and his pen name from Shakespeare's *Merry Wives of Windsor.* Except for a short sabbatical serving as managing editor of the *St. Petersburg (FL) Times* and head of the Cleveland *PLAIN DEALER's†* Akron bureau, Fetzer remained with the *Times* until its merger into the *Akron Times-Press.* He worked briefly for the *Akron Beacon Journal* and published 3 books, 2 of them based on his Teutonic folk hero, Reini Kugel.

Fetzer's reputation spread as he published articles, poems, and stories in the *New Yorker,* the *Nation, Collier's,* and *Liberty.* In the summers of 1929 and 1930, he wrote the "Conning Tower" column for the vacationing Franklin Pierce Adams in the *New York World.* Lured to the *Cleveland Press* early in 1930, Fetzer not only contributed "Pippins and Cheese" but also did rewrites, editorials, and features until his early death from pneumonia. Largely through the efforts of his widow, the former Hazel Stevenson of Akron, several volumes of his work were published posthumously: *The Bulls of Spring: Selected Poems* (1937); 3 volumes of Ohio farm stories culled from a "Rural Vacation" series composed for the *Press;* a representative Fetzer anthology, *Pippins and Cheese* (1960); and *Jake Falstaff Selections to Make You Thirsty* (1969). Fetzer had no children and was buried in Canaan, OH.

**FINKELSTEIN, LOUIS,** aka "Louie the Dip" (Aug. 1894–1 Jan. 1964) was Cleveland's "prince of pickpockets." His 50-year career record of over 120 arrests and 20 sentences served made him the most frequently arrested pickpocket in Cleveland's history.

Born in Odessa, Russia, Finkelstein came to Cleveland in 1909. His first arrest occurred in March 1909 for picking a woman's purse in the Grand Theater lobby. Between 1909–15, Finkelstein was arrested three times, serving terms in the Ohio Reformatory and the Warrensville Workhouse.

Between 1915–33 Finkelstein was arrested 46 times (convicted 23) for numerous offenses. The highlight of this period occurred in 1933 when he picked the Parma police chief's pocket, and once

spent a Saturday night in two jails, in Chardon and Cleveland. Finkelstein picked his bail bondsman's pocket, and even that of a reporter covering one of his trials.

Sentenced to the workhouse in 1933, Finkelstein escaped but was recaptured in New York while working the crowd at a revival meeting. Convicted of grand larceny, he was given an 8–10 year sentence at Sing Sing. The U.S. government unsuccessfully attempted to deport Finkelstein as a habitual criminal.

Paroled in 1941, Finkelstein returned to Cleveland and the workhouse. A 1942 city investigation found that Finkelstein was the workhouse "boss," avoiding all tough jobs and arranging for money and favors for prisoners.

In 1954, arthritis forced Finkelstein into early "retirement." He tried gambling, but failed. Finkelstein applied for relief and received his first payment in 1959.

Finkelstein married Annabelle Morris. They had no children. Finkelstein died penniless and is buried in Ridge Rd. No. 1 Cemetery (Chesed Shel Emeth). —T.B.

**FINKLE, HERMAN** (Apr. 1891-Oct. 1952), "Little Napoleon of Ward 12," was city councilman for 35 consecutive years and considered a ruthless, corrupt sergeant of the Republican machine. By his death he was recognized as a most knowledgeable and able councilman. Born in Detroit, MI, son of Samuel and Sara Epstein Finkle, he moved at age 11 to Cleveland, graduating from Cleveland Law School in 1913. Finkle became law partner and brother-in-law to Republican organizer "Czar" ALEX BERNSTEIN, and was the protege of boss MAURICE MASCHKE. In 1917 Finkle ran for council in the 12th Ward, easily winning with Republican machine support, which helped him get reelected 18 times. In 1921 Finkle became Republican floor leader, holding that position until the Democrats took over city hall in 1932. Finkle was associated with land, patronage, and financial scandals, and several unsuccessful attempts were made by the CITIZENS LEAGUE† to oust him from the council.

Finkle's behavior seemed to change soon after the death of his only daughter, Betty Jane, in the mid–1930s. His interests extended to city-wide problems such as street lighting, establishing health centers, mass transportation, airport development, and minority-rights issues. As minority leader of the council, he was able to successfully pass legislation. Finkle's expertise was in city finances, and he served many years as chairman of the powerful Finance Committee. By the 1940s, many, including the Citizens League, lauded Finkle as a respectable political leader. He declined to run for mayor several times, and was still a member of the council at the time of his death.

He married Delia Gold on 20 June 1917. Finkle was buried in Mayfield Cemetery.

Herman Finkle Vertical File, WRHS.

**FISHER, EDWARD BURKE** (ca. 1799–ca. 1859) was a lawyer involved in several publishing enterprises in Cleveland during the 1840s. He came to Cleveland in 1839 from Pittsburgh, PA, where he had edited *The Literary Examiner and Western Monthly Review*. In Cleveland he began the *DAILY MORNING REVIEW†* in partnership with Calvin Hall in Sept. 1841, which was merged into the *DAILY MERCURY AND NEWS†* 2 months later. While editing the latter, Fisher also began publishing and editing the *CLEVELAND GATHERER†* in Dec. 1841. Neither paper likely survived the following year, and Fisher apparently began practicing law. Using the pen name of Timothy Jenkins, he wrote 2 locally published satires: *The Bench and Bar of Cuyahoga County: A Modern Epic* (1843), and *Wars of the Barn-Burners of Cuyahoga County: An Epic Extraordinary* (1844). Possibly as a consequence of these "epics," he later became a journalist in Columbus, OH. His death is reported to have occurred in South Bend, IN.—J.V.

**FISHER, EDWARD FLOYD** (2 Aug. 1925–1 Feb. 1993) kept work-bound Clevelanders company for 20 years as the "morning man" on RADIO† station WJW.† A native of Butler, OH, he was raised in Mansfield, OH, and graduated from Mansfield High School before seeing service with the U.S. Marines in World War II and the Korean War. Fisher broke into RADIO† with WMAN in Mansfield and later worked for WHIZ in Zanesville, OH. He married Nancy Snider of Zanesville in 1949. After freelancing for such local radio stations as KYW (see WWWE), WERE, and WGAR,† he moved to Cleveland in 1958 to take over the morning program for WJW. Fisher's show maintained a low-key format featuring his own piano playing and interviews with such guests as Benny Goodman, MARGARET HAMILTON, and Frank Sinatra. During the 1960s he also worked in TELEVISION,† entertaining children as "Bozo the Clown" on WJW-TV. His radio program was dropped by WJW in 1978, after which he worked for WBBG and WEOL in Willoughby. He left radio in 1986 to become a partner in Artco, Inc., a printing company in his home suburb of NORTH ROYALTON.† Fisher also did some acting in local theaters, teaming with children's television personality Lynn Sheldon for an appearance in Neil Simon's *The Odd Couple* at the Cabaret dinner theater. Divorced from his first wife in 1976, Fisher later married and divorced Laura Fisher. He was survived by 5 children.—J.V.

**FITCH, JABEZ W.** (1823–5 April 1884), son of Gurdon and Hannah (Peck) Fitch, was a native Cleveland attorney who served as commandant of Camp Taylor in Cleveland during the CIVIL WAR.† In 1852 Fitch served as Cleveland fire chief; he was appointed U.S. marshal in 1855 when the seat of the Northern District of the U.S. Federal Court was established in Cleveland. In the spring and summer of 1861, he served as commandant of Camp Taylor, a camp of rendezvous and preliminary instruction. He later enlisted as a private in the 19th Ohio Volunteer Infantry and served as quartermaster. After the Civil War, Fitch returned to Cleveland and sold real estate. In 1873 he was elected president of the Cleveland Society for the Prevention of Cruelty to Animals, which later became known as the Cleveland Humane Society. In 1874 he became president of a statewide humane society. The following year, he was elected lt. governor of Ohio under Gov. Bishop. Fitch married Mary J. Dolman; they had no children. He died in Cleveland and was buried in Erie St. Cemetery.

*Annals of the Early Settlers Association of Cuyahoga County* (1886).

**FITCH, SARAH ELIZABETH** (14 March 1819–10 April 1893) helped organize and served as the first president of both the Women's Christian Assn. (WCA, 1867) (see YOUNG WOMEN'S CHRISTIAN ASSN.†) and the Women's Temperance League of Cleveland (March 1874). Born in Cherry Valley, NY, daughter of Gurden and Hannah (Peck) Fitch, her family moved to Cleveland in 1827. She was a local pioneer in kindergarten education and in 1837 opened a school at Huron and Erie streets, which was notable for its approach to teaching small children. In 1867, concerned about the religious and moral lives of young women working away from home, she helped create the WCA, the 6th such association in the U.S. Fitch was president of the organization until her death in 1893. Her interests in TEMPERANCE† and early childhood education shaped the work of the WCA. In 1882 the organization incorporated the Young Women's Temperance League and formed the Young Ladies Branch of the WCA, which focused on CHILD CARE† and kindergartens. A decade later it became the independent CLEVELAND DAY NURSERY & FREE KINDERGARTEN ASSN.† In her temperance work, Fitch participated in a prayer meeting outside a brewery in Berea, and in a 6-week appeal to bar owners to cease serving strong drink. She also taught Sunday school at First Presbyterian (Old Stone) Church.

**FITCH, ZALMON** (1785–28 Apr. 1860), a leader in Cleveland and Warren financial circles, was born in Norwalk, CT, to Haynes and Ann (Cook) Fitch. Little is known about his education or early life. In 1810 he established a general store in Canfield, OH, the second one in the WESTERN RESERVE.† He moved to Warren in 1813 and became a leading businessman. When the Western Reserve Bank was established in 1816, he became a cashier, holding that position until he became president 23 years later. He also served as land agent for several original stockholders of the CONNECTICUT LAND CO.† In 1838, the receivers of the then-closed Bank of Cleveland appointed him trustee to settle its affairs after it collapsed in the Panic of 1837. Fitch served on the Board of Trustees of the new Western Reserve College in Hudson in 1826; as a trustee of the Warren Municipal Court in 1836, 1842, 1847–48, and 1854–55, even after moving to Cleveland in 1838. He was a member of the Board of Agency of the Cleveland Medical College in 1843 and of the Warren Board of Education in 1849. He was a founding member of the Euclid St. Presbyterian Church in 1853. He was on the Board of Directors of the Cleveland & Pittsburgh Railroad in 1859. Fitch married Betsey Mygatt of Canfield, OH, in 1808 and had 3 children: Lucy, Grant, and Laura. When his first wife died in 1838, Fitch married Rebecca H. Salter of New Haven, CT. Fitch died in Cleveland and was buried in the Erie St. Cemetery.

Zalmon Fitch Papers, WRHS.

**FITZGERALD, WILLIAM SINTON** (6 Oct. 1880–3 Oct. 1937), a member of the city council for 4 years and appointed mayor by HARRY L. DAVIS in 1921, was born in Washington, DC, to David and Esther Sinton Fitzgerald. He was educated in Washington's public schools, and received a Master of Laws degree from Geo. Washington Univ. in 1903. He came to Cleveland in 1904, was admitted to the Ohio Bar that year, and practiced law. In 1911 he was elected to the city council from the 11th Ward as a Republican and served 2 terms. Fitzgerald was appointed law director by Mayor Harry L. Davis, and when Davis resigned in 1920 to campaign for governor, Fitzgerald became mayor. He was defeated in his mayoral bid by FRED KOHLER in 1921 and afterward resumed his law practice. He died in N. ROYALTON† at age 56. He married Margaret Chilton Tucker on 14 Jan. 1920 and they had a son, Wm. Sinton, Jr. They were divorced in 1922, and he married Carolina Granger on 23 Mar. 1933.

**FLAGLER, HENRY M.** (2 Jan. 1830–20 May 1913), a developer of STANDARD OIL CO.,† was born in Hopewell, NY, to Elizabeth Harkness and itinerant Presbyterian minister Isaac Flagler. He attended school through the 8th grade, and at 14 went to live with his Harkness relatives in Republic, OH. In 1852 he joined Dan and Lamon Harkness in buying out F. C. Chapman's interest in Chapman & Harkness, forming Harkness & Co., a distillery which made $50,000 for Flagler by 1863. During the Civil War he worked as an agent dealing in provisions. After losing $100,000 in the salt industry in Michigan, Flagler moved to Cleveland in 1866, briefly selling barrels to oil refiners, then becoming a commission merchant. By 1867 he had enough money to establish H. M. Flagler & Co.

In 1867 STEPHEN HARKNESS invested $100,000 in JOHN D. ROCKEFELLER's oil business, placing Flagler in charge of his investment; the firm became Rockefeller, Andrews & Flagler. Flagler developed the idea of absorbing smaller refineries, and of replacing the partnership with a joint stock company in 1870 and with the Standard Oil trust in 1879. Flagler was secretary and treasurer of the corporation, and vice-president of Standard Oil until 1908 and a director until 1911, but ceased playing an active role after ca. 1881, when he moved to New York and began investing heavily in Florida, developing Palm Beach and Miami. Flagler married 3 times: Mary Harkness in 1853; Ida Alice Shourds in 1883 after Mary's death; and Mary Lily Kenan in 1901 after divorcing Ida. He had 3 children: Jennie Louise, Carrie, and Harry. Flagler died in West Palm Beach and was buried in the Flagler Mausoleum in St. Augustine, FL.

Chandler, David Leon. *Henry Flagler* (1986).
Akin, Edward N. *Flagler* (1988).
Martin, Sidney W. *Florida's Flagler* (1949).

**FLEMING, LETHIA COUSINS** (7 Nov. 1876–22 Sept. 1963), directed national campaign efforts among African American women for three Republican presidential candidates—Warren G. Harding (1920), Herbert Hoover (1936), and Alfred M. Landon (1940); she also led the National Assn. of Republican Colored Women (1920) and women's activities in Cleveland's 11th Ward for almost a decade (1920s). Born in Tazewell, VA, to James Archibald Cousins and Fannie Taylor Cousins, Fleming attended high school in Ironton, OH, and Morristown College in Tennessee. She then taught school in Virginia and West Virginia, where she was an active suffragist. On 21 February 1912 Fleming married THOMAS WALLACE (TOM) FLEMING and moved to Cleveland. It was his second marriage; he and Lethia had no children. By 1914 Lethia

Fleming chaired the board of Lady Managers of the Cleveland Home for Aged Colored People (see the ELIZA BRYANT CENTER†). In 1929, after her husband's imprisonment, Fleming made a short-lived attempt to run for his seat on CLEVELAND CITY COUNCIL.† That election ousted her from ward leadership. From 1931–51, Fleming worked for the Cuyahoga County Child Welfare Board while continuing her involvement in politics on a national level.

Fleming was a life member and local and national officer in the Improved Benevolent Protective Order of Elks of the World. She was a charter member of such local organizations as the TRAVELERS' AID SOCIETY,† the NATIONAL ASSN. FOR THE ADVANCEMENT OF COLORED PEOPLE,† Cleveland branch, and the PHILLIS WHEATLEY ASSN., and served on the first board of the Negro Welfare Assn. (see URBAN LEAGUE OF CLEVELAND†). The first woman trustee of MT. ZION CONGREGATIONAL CHURCH,† Fleming also maintained an interest in the Baha'i faith. She is buried in Lake View Cemetery.—J.M.

Thomas and Lethia Fleming Papers, WRHS.

**FLEMING, THOMAS WALLACE (TOM)** (13 May 1874–18 Jan. 1948), the first black elected to CLEVELAND CITY COUNCIL† and an active Republican until 1929, was born in Meadville, PA, son of Thomas and Lavina (Green) Fleming. He arrived in Cleveland in 1893 to work as a barber. He became active in Republican politics as a protege of HARRY SMITH, challenged established black Republicans when they failed to endorse a black as candidate for city council, and began attending council meetings to learn "the art of government." He attended Cleveland Law School in the evening, and in 1906 he passed the teachers' and bar examinations. Appointed a member of the Republican State Executive Committee that year, he was unsuccessful gaining a council seat in 1907, but was elected councilman-at-large in 1909. He was elected councilman from Ward 11 in 1916, serving until his indictment in 1929 on a much-disputed charge of unlawful soliciting and corruption in office, for which he served 3 years in the Ohio Penitentiary. While on the council, Fleming facilitated the appointment of blacks to city jobs, and introduced ordinances to build a public bath house, gymnasium, and swimming pool in the Central area and to prevent organization of a Ku Klux Klan chapter in Cleveland. Fleming cofounded the *CLEVELAND JOURNAL†* in 1903, and with ALBERT D. "STARLIGHT" BOYD formed the Starlight Realty & Investment Co. in 1919, to buy and rent properties in the Central area. Fleming's first marriage, to Mary Ingels Thompson, ended in divorce in 1910. He had 3 sons: Russell, Lawrence, and Wallace. In 1912 he married Lethia Cousins (see LETHIA COUSINS FLEMING). Fleming is buried in Lake View Cemetery.

Thomas and Lethia Fleming Papers, WRHS.
Fleming, Thomas W. "My Rise and Persecution," (WRHS, 1932).

**FLINT, EDWARD SHERRILL** (3 Jan. 1819–29 Jan. 1902), a railroad executive, banker, and mayor of Cleveland (1861–63) was born in Warren, OH, but the early deaths of both parents left him to be raised and educated by his grandparents in Vermont. He initially worked as a bookkeeper, but by 1851 relocated himself and his family to Cleveland to start a real estate firm. Finding his interest to be railroads, Flint served as superintendent of the Cleveland, Columbus, Cincinnati & Indianapolis Railroad from 1859–78. In 1860 Flint became a member of the Cleveland School Board and the following year was elected mayor. The outbreak of the Civil War made Flint decide to become a Republican, although he later became a War Democrat. During his term in office, he supported the cause of the North in the Civil War and took measures for the city to aid the families of local soldiers. Flint was defeated in his second mayoral election by IRVINE MASTERS. He retired from public life, remaining in the railroad business until his retirement in 1879. At that time he remained as a trustee of the Society for Savings. Flint was married to Caroline E. Lemen (d. 1899) of Cleveland. The couple had 3 children: Carolin, Fanny, and William. Flint died in Cleveland and was buried in Lake View Cemetery.

**FLYNN, EILEEN ELEANOR FINLIN** (13 June 1915–11 Oct. 1992), attorney, civic leader, and social activist, was asst. attorney general to Ohio attorney general William Saxbe (1957–59) and a member of the Cleveland Board of Zoning Appeals in the 1960s (see ZONING†). She served as president of the diocesan council of the National Council of Catholic Women (NCCW, 1956–58) for the Diocese of Cleveland (see CATHOLICS, ROMAN†) and the youngest head of the Catholic Federation of Women's Clubs. Born in Cleveland to Honor Graham and John Frank Finlin, Flynn graduated from Flora Stone Mather College (1937) of Western Reserve Univ. with a home economics major. After her marriage on 17 September 1936, she studied law at the Cleveland Marshall Law School of CLEVELAND STATE UNIV.† (LL.B., 1947) with her husband, James P. Flynn, Jr. In 1948 they opened their law practice, Flynn & Flynn, with Eileen Flynn specializing in probate law. She held national chairs in legislation for both the National Assn. of Women Lawyers and the NCCW, organizing workshops for the council in 100 dioceses. Flynn also served on a Presidential Committee for Traffic Safety, the juvenile court committee of the CLEVELAND BAR ASSN.,† and the legislative committee for the Welfare Federation. She edited the journal of the National Assn. of Women Lawyers (1950–51).

In addition to professional groups, Flynn actively participated in welfare organizations, for example, as trustee of the INTERNATIONAL SERVICES CENTER† and MERRICK HOUSE,† and as president of the CHRIST CHILD SOCIETY.† She had 1 child, John Colman; the family lived in Cleveland. Flynn is buried in Calvary Cemetery.—J.M.

**FOGG, WILLIAM PERRY** (27 July 1826–8 May 1909), an adventurer and writer, was born in Exeter, NH, the son of Josiah and Hannah (Pecker) Fogg. He moved to Cleveland as a child. A transplanted "Yankee," he was an early member and president of the New England Society, which promised to promote a kindred spirit among the offspring of New England pioneers. Initially a chinaware merchant, Fogg became active in city affairs and was appointed to the Board of Commissioners in 1866. Cleveland Mayor HERMAN M. CHAPIN, Fogg, and the other commissioners drafted the Metropolitan Police Act of 1866. In 1868 Fogg began his round-the-world travels, being one of the first Americans to travel through the interior of Japan. The *CLEVELAND LEADER†* published his letters; they were later published as the book *Round the World Letters*, which also included his letters from China. His second book, *Arabistan, or The Land of the Arabian Nights* (England, 1872), was an account of his journey through Egypt, Arabia, and Persia to Baghdad. His final book was the revised American edition of *Land of the Arabian Nights*. When he returned to America, Fogg and Richard C. Parsons acquired the Herald Publishing Co. in 1877. The venture failed, leaving lawyer Parsons to go back to his practice and Fogg to go abroad again. Fogg returned to the U.S. and lived in Roselle, NJ, from 1901–08, then living in Morris Plains for the last year of his life. He married Mary Ann Gould on 20 May 1852; they had 2 children, Annie and Helen.

**FOOTE, JOHN A.** (22 Nov. 1803–16 July 1891), reformer and politician, was born in New Haven, CT, to Samuel A. and Eudocia (Hull) Foote. His father was governor of Connecticut and a member of both the U.S. House of Representatives and the U.S. Senate. Foote was also the elder brother of Adm. Andrew H. Foote, of naval fame during the

Civil War. After graduating from Yale (1823), he practiced law in Litchfield before coming to Cleveland in 1833, when he formed a partnership with SHERLOCK J. ANDREWS. He was also director of the Cleveland, Columbus & Cincinnati and the Cleveland & Pittsburgh railroads. A member of the WHIG PARTY,† Foote served in the Ohio legislature (1837–39), and in 1839 became president of city council. In 1844 Foote ran unsuccessfully for mayor, but was elected to the Ohio state senate in 1853. He became a Republican after 1854.

Foote worked for juvenile education and reform, in 1839 helping make the first land purchases for schools; and in 1856 being a state commissioner studying reform schools, adopting the European "family" system reform farm for Ohio. With HARVEY RICE, he started the Industrial School of Cleveland and the CHILDREN'S AID SOCIETY.†

Foote was president of the Cleveland Temperance Society, and proposed ordinances against liquor; in 1839 proposing creation of a committee on licenses to regulate "dram shops," which passed in 1840. He also opposed slavery and was an officer of the CLEVELAND ANTI-SLAVERY SOCIETY† and the CUYAHOGA COUNTY ANTI-SLAVERY SOCIETY.† Foote was a member of the FIRST PRESBYTERIAN CHURCH† of Cleveland. He married twice: first to Frances A. Hitchcock, of Cheshire, CT, who died in 1855, leaving 7 children: Samuel, Louisa, Mary, Frances, Cornelia, John, and Andrew; and then, in 1858, to Mary S. Cutter of Cleveland.

**FORAN, MARTIN A.** (11 Nov. 1844–28 June 1921), U.S. Congressman, county prosecutor, and judge of the Court of Common Pleas, was born in Choconut Twp., Susquehanna County, PA, to James and Catherine O'Donnell Foran. He learned the coopering trade, and attended St. Joseph's College in Susquehanna County for 2 years. During the Civil War, he served in the 4th Pennsylvania Cavalry. In 1868 Foran came to Cleveland as a cooper, serving as president of the Coopers International Union and editor of the *Coopers' Journal* (1870–74). He meanwhile studied law, was a member of the Ohio Constitutional Convention in 1873, and after being admitted to the Ohio Bar in 1874, practiced law in Cleveland.

Active in Democratic party politics, Foran was prosecuting attorney for Cuyahoga County from 1875–77. He supported the KNIGHTS OF LABOR† and was considered a moderate reformer. With labor support, he served 3 terms in Congress, beginning in 1883. He wrote a novel, *The Other Side: A Social Study Based on Fact*, describing a working man's life. Declining to run for a 4th term, in 1888 Foran returned to Cleveland to practice law.

He brought NEWTON D. BAKER to the attention of Mayor TOM L. JOHNSON, and was elected judge of the Court of Common Pleas in 1910, where he served until his death in Cleveland. On 29 Dec. 1868, Foran married Kate Kavanaugh. They had 2 children, Gertrude M. (Mrs. Franklin A. Handrick) and Margaret O. (Mrs. Jas. Connolly). After Kate died in 1893, he married Emma Kenny that same year.

**FORD, DAVID KNIGHT** (10 Feb. 1894–28 Oct. 1993) was a lawyer, businessman, and churchman who took pride in his family roots in New England and early Cleveland. He incorporated the LUBRIZOL CORP.,† was a director and served as a trustee of its foundation continuously from its founding until his death. Ford was a lifelong member and major benefactor of the EUCLID AVE. CONGREGATIONAL CHURCH.† His support of and service to CASE WESTERN RESERVE UNIV.† (as a member of the university's Board of Overseers, 1978–81, and the law school's visiting committee) earned him the Western Reserve College Medal for Distinguished Achievement (1982). Ford was born in Cleveland to Ida May Thorp and HORATIO CLARK FORD. Ford attended East High School (1911) and Yale Univ., where he graduated Phi Beta Kappa (1915). He served on the Mexican border with TROOP A† (1916). During World War I he served in France as a captain in the 813th Pioneer Infantry. Ford received a degree in law from WRU's law school in 1921 and then entered practice with his father's firm. He later became partner in several other firms, and he was of counsel with Spieth, Bell, McCurdy, and Newell at the time of his death. Ford served in various positions at Lubrizol, as general counsel (1934–63), asst. secretary (1934), secretary (1935–58), and director (1935–63). During World War II, he acted as counsel for local draft boards and recruited ambulance drivers, while also volunteering with his wife at UNIV. HOSPITALS.† He served on the executive committee (1952–55) of the CLEVELAND BAR ASSN.†

Ford married Elizabeth Kingsley Brooks (d. 1990) on 12 June 1920. They had four sons: Amasa B., David K., Allen H., and Oliver M. Ford. Ford moderated the Cleveland Congregational Union for 5 years and presided over the Cleveland Church Federation (see INTERCHURCH COUNCIL OF GREATER CLEVELAND†). He was president of GOODWILL INDUSTRIES,† the Western Reserve Chapter of the Sons of the American Revolution, the WOMEN'S PHILANTHROPIC UNION,† and the board of trustees of the SCHAUFFLER COLLEGE OF RELIGIOUS AND SOCIAL WORK.† He was also a trustee of Defiance College and Deaconess

Hospital and a director of the Williamson Co. Ford was buried at Lake View Cemetery.—J.M.

CWRU Archives.
David Knight Ford Papers, WRHS.
Horatio C. Ford Family Papers, WRHS.

**FORD, HORATIO** (23 June 1881–28 Nov. 1952), a banker and lawyer involved in the BOY SCOUTS OF AMERICA† and in forest conservation, was born in Cleveland to Ida May Thorp and HORATIO CLARK FORD. He earned his A.B. from Yale Univ. in 1904, his LL.B. from Western Reserve Univ. Law School, and was admitted to the Ohio Bar in 1907. In 1906, Ford started as a cashier in the Garfield Savings Bank, serving as bookkeeper, secretary, attorney, and director by the time Garfield merged with Cleveland Trust Bank in 1922. After the merger, he continued as a co-trustee for certain trusts, attorney, director, and asst. vice-president for Cleveland Trust. A member of the law firm of Snyder, Henry Thomsen, Ford & Seagrave from 1913–26, Ford retired from banking in 1940 to return to law, joining the firm of Ford & Reece, later Ford, Reece, Baskins & Howland.

In 1910 Ford helped organize the Boy Scouts in the Cleveland area, serving on the area executive committee from 1910–20. Ford qualified 1,500 acres of family-owned Whitfield Woods property in Middlefield, OH, as one of the first tree farms in Ohio. From 1950 until his death, he was president of the Ohio Forestry Assn. Ford married Ella Almira White on 7 May 1908, and they had 6 children: Horatio, Andrew, Thomas, Jonathon, Baldwin, and Almira.

**FORD, HORATIO CLARK** (25 Aug. 1853–25 Aug. 1915), a descendant of early settlers of New England and Cleveland, was a prominent lawyer, entrepreneur, banker, and civic leader. His father, Horatio Cyrus Ford, came from Cummington, MA, with his parents in 1847 to (old) East Cleveland, where he married Martha Cordelia Cozad, granddaughter of SAMUEL COZAD. Horatio Clark was born in the family farmhouse, on the corner of Euclid Ave. and Adelbert Rd., where he also died, on his 62nd birthday, in the same room where he was born. He married Ida May Thorp in 1877. They had six children: Mildred (Cobb), HORATIO, Lauretta, Cyrus, DAVID, and Baldwin. The Ford house and land were later acquired by Western Reserve Univ. Flora Stone Mather College (1888), the Franklin Thomas Backus School (1892), and the School of Applied Social Science (1916) were all started in the former Ford home.

"Clark" Ford was educated in CLEVELAND PUBLIC SCHOOLS,† attended Oberlin College, graduated from the Univ. of Michigan in 1875, and was admitted to the Ohio Bar in 1878. Active as a lawyer from then on, he was senior partner of Ford, Snyder, and Tilden when he died. He was a banker and a street railway and real estate developer. He developed the Cleveland and Eastern Railway Co., was active in the street railway business in Syracuse, NY, and became an officer of the Wheeling, WV, Traction Co. In real estate, he was responsible for the building of the Williamson Building, then the tallest building in the state. In related activities, he was a director of the Cuyahoga Telephone Co.

In banking, he founded or was a director of the Garfield Savings Bank, the Western Reserve Trust Co., the Metropolitan National Bank, and the East End Savings and Trust Co., which later merged with the Cleveland Trust Co., where he became a charter director (1894). Ford was elected to the Cleveland Common Council (1879–1885) and served as its vice-president. Ford was a lifelong member of the EUCLID AVE. CONGREGATIONAL CHURCH.† He held national offices in this denomination, organized the Congregational City Missionary Society, and was a trustee of Oberlin College.—A.F.

**FORD, LEONARD "LENNY"** (18 Feb. 1926–13 Mar. 1972), defensive end for the CLEVELAND BROWNS† from 1950–57 and Pro Football Hall of Famer (1976) was born in Washington, DC, to Lenny Guy and Gerlean Ford. He was captain of the football, baseball, and basketball teams his senior year at Armstrong High School. Ford began college at Morgan State, but transferred to the Univ. of Michigan where he was a football All-American in 1946 and 1947 and played in the 1948 Rose Bowl. He began his professional career playing both offensive and defensive end for the Los Angeles Dons of the All-America Football Conference in 1948 and 1949, catching 67 passes on offense.

The Browns acquired Ford after the 1949 season in the draft held to allocate players from failed AAFC teams. Coach PAUL BROWN used Ford strictly on defense, and although he missed most of the 1950 season with a fractured jaw, Ford returned during the 1950 championship game to tackle Los Angeles Rams ball carriers for losses on 3 successive plays. An excellent pass rusher, standing 6' 5" and weighing 260 lbs., Ford was named to the All-NFL All-Star team each year from 1951–55. On 19 May 1958, however, the Browns traded Ford to the Green Bay Packers, for whom he played 1 season before retiring. During his 11-year professional career, Ford recovered 20 fumbles. After his retirement, Ford lived in Detroit and studied law, working as the asst. director of the Considine Recreation Center at the time of his death. Ford married Geraldine Bledsoe in 1951. His wife went on to

become a municipal judge in Detroit. The couple had two children, Anita and Deborah; they divorced in 1959. Ford is buried in Washington, DC.

**FORSYTH (MYERS), JOSEPHINE** (ca. 1890–24 May 1940) was a Cleveland singer, composer, and musical patron. Born on the city's south side, she received vocal training from Marcella Sembrich and former Clevelander Rita Elandi. Making her New York debut in the light opera *Listen Lester* in 1919, she expanded her repertoire to opera and folk songs in costume. For her marriage to pump manufacturer Philip A. Myers of Ashland, OH, in 1924, she composed and sang a musical setting of "The Lord's Prayer." It achieved international popularity, from the Easter Sunrise Service in Hollywood Bowl to the 1938 Wales Eisteddfod. Following her husband's death in an automobile accident in 1932, Forsyth resided chiefly in Wade Park Manor and continued to promote the city's cultural life. A member of the FORTNIGHTLY MUSICAL CLUB,† she was survived by a daughter and stepson.

**FORTE, ORMOND ADOLPHUS** (17 Dec. 1887–14 Jan. 1959) earned the honorary title of "dean of Cleveland Negro newspapermen" for his efforts in publishing 3 black weeklies over a span of 4 decades. A native of Barbados, British West Indies, he was educated at Harrison College. Fluent in Spanish, Portuguese, and French as well as English, he served as commercial representative for several European firms before coming to Cleveland in 1910. Forte married Ida Grant soon after his arrival and took a position with Cleveland businessman DANIEL R. HANNA. With the backing of Hanna, who at the time published 2 Cleveland dailies, Forte began the *CLEVELAND ADVOCATE†* in 1914 and ran it for 10 years. In 1925 he began a new weekly, the *CLEVELAND HERALD,†* which lasted only 2 years before suspension due to a shortage of funds. After a hiatus of several years, he published the *Cleveland Eagle* from 1935–38 and then revived the *Herald,* which he maintained until his retirement, due to failing health, in 1954. In all his journalistic endeavors, Forte took a moderate stand on racial issues and tended to support the Republican party. He served as a trustee of the GREATER CLEVELAND HOSPITAL ASSN.† and the Normal School of Wilberforce Univ. Dying at FOREST CITY HOSPITAL† after a stroke, he was survived by his wife and 5 children: Mrs. Hilda Walker, Mrs. Thelma Pruitt, Mrs. Edna Lockhart, Ormond A., Jr., and Frederick J.—J.V.

**FOSTER, CLAUD HANSCOMB** (23 Dec. 1872–21 June 1965), automotive inventor, industrialist, and philanthropist, was born in the Cleveland suburb of Brooklyn to George and Julia Wells Foster. In 1891 he opened a machine shop, playing the trombone for 11 years in the Euclid Ave. Opera House orchestra to support his business. In 1896 Foster became an automobile dealer, selling the Cleveland-built General, also acquiring in 1900 the Peerless and Ajax automobile agencies. Foster developed the Gabriel Horn, a multitone automobile horn powered by exhaust gases, starting the successful Gabriel Co. in 1904. Foster then patented his "Snubber" automotive shock absorber in 1914, capitalizing its production at $1 million.

From 1920–25, the Gabriel Co. earned annual profits of more than $1 million, selling 75% of all shock absorbers marketed in the world. Foster developed an employee profit-sharing incentive program, between 1917–25 paying his employees more than $600,000 in addition to their salaries. He sold the Gabriel Co. in 1925 to Otis & Co. for $4 million, only half the company's evaluated price, and remained company chairman until 1928. Known as the "Doctor of Car Riding," Foster was often consulted by manufacturers when new car models developed riding difficulties. Throughout his career, Foster made numerous large anonymous gifts to hospitals and charitable institutions. On 22 July 1952, he announced to the heads of 16 educational and charitable institutions that he was dividing the bulk of his wealth, almost $4 million, among them. Married to Emma Schultz on 2 May 1894, Foster had 2 sons, Earl and Daniel. Foster is buried in Riverside Cemetery.

Thomasson, Wayman H. *Claud Foster: A Biography* (1949).

**FOSTER, LEONARD GURLEY** (10 Sept. 1840–13 Dec. 1937) was a CIVIL WAR† veteran whose avocation brought him the epithet "the Buckeye poet." Born on the family homestead in the Cuyahoga Valley near Denison Ave., he was educated at HUMISTON INSTITUTE† and Berea College. He was principal at Tremont School from 1860–64, after which he served with the 8th Ohio Battery on Johnson's Island. Foster also actively worked the family farm, which inspired many of his verses on nature. A veteran of the first Chautauqua meeting in 1874, he remained active in the movement as a speaker and contributor of poetry. He wrote an estimated 80,000 verses in his lifetime, including 47 volumes of poems in manuscript which he presented to the WESTERN RESERVE HISTORICAL SOCIETY.† His published volumes included *Whisperings of Nature* (1893) and *The Early Days: A Pioneer Idyl* (1911). Many of his poems were also published in the CLEVELAND NEWS† and the CLEVELAND TIMES† (1922). He was the first clerk of the Brooklyn Village council and the second-to-last survivor of the Brooklyn Post, G.A.R. Married to Lyde Holmden, Foster was survived by one of their 3 children. His brothers, Edwin J. and Henry E., were Cleveland lawyers, the former having published verse and the latter a 1900 political campaign tract. His sister, Hanna Alice Foster, was a temperance worker and poet as well.—J.V.

**FOSTER, WILLIAM ADELBERT** (17 Feb. 1915–2 May 1945) was a private in the U.S. Marine Corps during World War II, posthumously awarded the Congressional Medal of Honor on the island of Okinawa. William, one of 6 children, was born in Cleveland to Charles J. and Alma Messzik Foster. After graduation from Garfield Hts. High School in 1933, he worked at various jobs, including one at Cleveland Automatic Screw Machine Co., and was a member of the National Guard. As the sole support of his family during the war, he was exempt from service, but chose to enlist in the Marine Corps in 1944. On 1 May 1945, while on active combat duty with Co. K, 3rd Battalion, 1st U.S. Marine Div., on Okinawa, Foster dove onto a live Japanese hand grenade that landed in a foxhole he shared with another Marine, and it exploded. Mortally wounded, but having saved the life of his fellow Marine, Foster gave up his 2 remaining hand grenades to his fellow comrades-in-arms to continue the fight against infiltrating Japanese soldiers. The Medal of Honor was presented to Foster's parents by U.S. Marine Commandant Gen. Alexander Vandegrif in a ceremony at Cleveland City Hall on 20 Aug. 1946. Foster's remains were returned to Cleveland for reinterment at Calvary Cemetery, 5 March 1949. An elementary school in his hometown of GARFIELD HTS.† was named in his honor in 1957. Also, a Marine Camp on Okinawa was named Camp Foster in his honor. On 5 May 1990, a special headstone for recipients of the Medal of Honor was placed on his gravesite at Calvary Cemetery. Foster never married.—J.V.

**FOX, BEATRICE WRIGHT** (16 Mar. 1903–1 Aug. 1988), educator and the first African American administrator in the MT. PLEASANT† area, and an advisor-director with the PHILLIS WHEATLEY ASSN.†

Born in Cleveland to Walter and Sarah (Johnson) Wright, Beatrice attended Cleveland public schools and completed teacher training at the Cleveland Normal School (1922). She received her B.S. from Cleveland College (1949) and her M.A. in Education from Western Reserve Univ. (1958).

Precluded by law from teaching because she was married, Wright became a group leader at the

Kingsley Arter Branch of the Phillis Wheatley Assn. During her 11 years at Wheatley, she became director of the Kingsley Arter Center and Camp Mueller. She also served as advisor of the Assn.'s Junior Board.

In 1945 Beatrice returned to teaching. She taught at Mayflower, Orchard, and Doan schools and later became an asst. principal. In 1961 she became principal of Andrew J. Rickoff School—the first black administrator in Mount Pleasant. She retired in 1973.

Beatrice was active in MT. ZION CONGREGA-TIONAL CHURCH.† She served as a Church School teacher, Church School superintendent, president of Women's Fellowship, and was church clerk from 1978 until her death. Beatrice also founded the Mt. Zion Congregational Ceramics Class which included church and non-church members and generates sales to provide funds for the church.

Beatrice married Morris W. Fox on 30 June 1931 (Dec. 1981). They had no children. She is buried in Lake View Cemetery.—T.B.


**FRANCE, MERVIN BAIR** (31 Mar. 1901–16 Feb. 1970) was a Cleveland banker and civic leader who orchestrated the unification of the SOCIETY FOR SAVINGS† into SOCIETY NATIONAL BANK† and helped found SOCIETY CORP.,† a bank holding company.

Born in Harlem Springs, OH, to William and Elizabeth (Atwell) France, Mervin was raised in Alliance and graduated from Alliance High School. From 1920–23 he attended Ohio State Univ., leaving in his senior year due to a family illness.

In 1925 France sold bonds for a Canton investment firm. In 1927 he became the Ohio representative of Pittsburgh's Union Trust Co., making his office in Cleveland.

In 1934 France joined the Society for Savings as asst. vice-president and asst. secretary in charge of the investment and collateral loan departments. He advanced to bank vice-president in 1936, first vice-president in 1941, and president in 1947, making him one of the youngest top bank executives in the nation.

As president, France oversaw Society's restructuring from a mutual savings and loan into a nationally chartered bank. He presided over the transformation of the company into the parent holding company, Society Corp., and the birth of its wholly owned banking subsidiary, the Society National Bank, of which he was cofounder and president in 1956 (resigned 1968). France was SNB chairman from 1968–69 and, in January 1970, he was appointed an honorary director.

France was a director of several companies and a member of numerous civic and social organizations.

France married Berenice Renkert on 12 Oct. 1927. They had two children, William and Elizabeth. France is buried in Lake View Cemetery.—T.B.

Mervin B. France Papers, WRHS.

**FRARY, IHNA THAYER** (13 Apr. 1873–18 Mar. 1965), author, lecturer, and teacher of architecture and architectural history, was born in Cleveland to George S. and Caroline Frary. He studied at the Cleveland School of Art (see CLEVELAND INSTI-TUTE OF ART†) and in 1894 became an interior designer for the Brooks Household Art Co. (later Rorimer Brooks), remaining there until 1914 when he became an independent designer. During his association with Rorimer Brooks, Frary designed furniture, including that for 2 Statler hotels. For a time he worked for the F. B. STEARNS CO.† designing auto interiors, and in 1918 he worked for the American YMCA as educational director for the southwest region, based in San Antonio, TX. In 1920 Frary returned to Cleveland to become membership and publicity secretary for the CLEVE-LAND MUSEUM OF ART,† a position he occupied until his retirement in 1946. He was a member of the faculty of the Cleveland School of Art and a lecturer at the Cleveland School of Architecture of Western Reserve Univ. and at the JOHN HUNTINGTON POLYTECHNIC INSTITUTE.† He served as a trustee for the Museum of Art and the WESTERN RESERVE HISTORICAL SOCIETY.† His interest and study in architectural history brought forth his books: *Thomas Jefferson, Architect and Builder* (1939), *Early Homes of Ohio* (1936), *Early American Doorways* (1938), *They Built the Capitol* (1940), and *Ohio in Homespun and Calico* (1942). Frary married Mabel Guild on 2 June 1904, and had 2 sons, Spencer G. and Allen T.

Ihna Thayer Frary papers, WRHS.

**FRASCH, HERMAN** (25 Dec. 1851–1 May 1914), chemical engineer and inventor whose work proved valuable to the STANDARD OIL CO.,† was born in Gaildorf, State of Wurttemberg, Germany, and apprenticed to a druggist before coming to Philadelphia in 1868, working at the College of Pharmacy before opening his own shop in 1873 to apply chemistry to industrial problems. In 1876 he developed a new process for refining paraffin wax from petroleum, which he patented and sold to the Cleveland Petroleum Co., a subsidiary of Standard Oil. Impressed, Standard Oil officials offered Frasch a position in the research department in Cleveland, and Frasch moved there in 1877. Although working mostly with petroleum, Frasch also developed a new oil lamp, a process to produce white lead, and methods to manufacture salt and carbonate soda.

In 1885 Frasch purchased high-sulfur, low-quality crude oil fields near Ontario, Canada, establishing Empire Oil Co. He developed a process to desulfurize crude petroleum, receiving 21 U.S. patents. He sold his Ontario operations and patents to Standard Oil, enabling Standard Oil to produce high-quality refined oil from poor-quality crude supplies. In 1891 Frasch patented a process for mining sulfur, organizing the Union Sulfur Co. the following year. Frasch moved to Paris after retiring from business. His innovations were honored in 1912, when he received the Perkins Gold Medal in chemistry. While living in Philadelphia, Frasch married Romalda Berks (d. 1889); they had two children, George and Frieda. In 1892 he married Elizabeth Blee of Cleveland.

Sutton, William Ralph. "Herman Frasch" (Ph.D. diss., Louisiana State Univ., 1984).

**FRAZEE, JOHN N.** (3 Sept. 1829–21 Jan. 1917), a volunteer CIVIL WAR† officer and law-enforcement official, was born in Wyantskill, NY, came to Cleveland in 1850, and took a job as a west side patrolman with the CLEVELAND POLICE DEPARTMENT. Following a reorganization of the department, he was appointed chief of police in 1852—the first chief in the department's history. Frazee served as a cpl. in the CLEVELAND GRAYS† before the outbreak of the Civil War, and left the police department to enlist in Co. E, 1st Ohio Volunteer Infantry, on 16 Apr. 1861. He was promoted to sgt. on 21 Apr. 1861, 1st sgt. on 1 June 1861, and 2nd lt. on 2 July 1861. He was mustered out with Co. E (mostly Cleveland Grays) on 1 Aug. 1861. Frazee then served 4 months as a captain in the 84th OVI. In Aug. 1863, he was appointed lt. col. of the 29th Ohio Volunteer Militia. In May 1864, he was appointed to the 150th OVI and saw service around the defenses of Washington, DC, being mustered out with that regiment in Cleveland on 23 Aug. 1864. After the war, Frazee was captain of the Cleveland Grays. In 1888 he established a successful laundry business, retiring in 1915.

Frazee was married to Louise Littlejohn in 1853. They had a son, Henry. Frazee's funeral was held at GRAYS ARMORY† on 23 Jan. 1917. He is buried in Woodland Cemetery.

**FREED, ALAN** (15 Dec. 1922–20 Jan. 1965) is credited with the invention and development of ROCK 'N' ROLL.† He was born to Charles and Maud Freed in Johnstown, PA. The family moved to Salem, OH, in 1924, where Alan graduated from Salem High School. Freed attended Ohio State Univ. for two quarters and then enlisted in the army in 1941.

After attending broadcasting classes at Youngstown's WKBN-AM, he worked as a news and sports announcer at WKST-AM in New Castle, and then at WKBN. In Jan. 1945, he started at WAKR-AM in Akron as a play-by-play announcer for Akron Univ.'s basketball games, a news reporter, and then as the afternoon disc jockey.

Freed met LEO MINTZ in 1948 and saw how Mintz's customers at Cleveland's Record Rendezvous enjoyed Rhythm & Blues records. Mintz called it Rock 'n' Roll. Soon after, Freed started playing a rock 'n' roll tune as a novelty record on his afternoon show at WAKR. He left WAKR in Dec. 1949 and started in the Cleveland market on WXEL-TV (Channel 9) in April as the afternoon movie show host.

With Mintz's sponsorship, Freed started in July 1951, at WJW-AM† (850) with a late night radio show called "The Moondog Rock & Roll House Party." Later that year, Freed promoted dances and concerts featuring the music he was playing on the radio. With Lew Platt of Akron, Freed promoted a large, five-act concert at the CLEVELAND ARENA† on 21 Mar. 1952 called the Moondog Coronation Ball, which is considered to have been the first rock 'n' roll concert.

After the Moondog Ball, Freed's radio program was syndicated in 8 markets and on the Armed Forces Network in Europe. Freed moved to WINS-AM in New York City in Aug. 1958.

Freed's TV show on WNEW-TV, his four movies, and records on his label, End Records, made him a world-wide personality. He promoted successful concerts and toured throughout the eastern states.

On 3 May 1958, Freed was fired from WINS after a riot at a dance in Boston featuring Jerry Lee Lewis. Freed immediately moved to rival WABC-AM. He was fired from WABC on 21 Nov. 1959 when he refused to sign an FCC statement that he never received funds or gifts for playing records on the air. Freed's refusal and his high profile made him the main scapegoat at the FTC congressional hearings concerning payola in the record industry. Freed's radio career and concert business was over after the payola hearings. He was blackballed from the music business.

After a short stint at WQAM-AM in Miami, Freed moved to Palm Springs, where he died of cancer. He was survived by his 3 children: Sieglinde, Alana, and Lance.—J.H.

**FREEDHEIM, EUGENE HEITLER** (16 Mar. 1900–19 Dec. 1984), attorney, presided over the CLEVELAND BAR ASSN.† during its controversial defense of 11 accused communists (1955–56), a local case which signaled the beginning of the demise of McCarthyism nationally. Freedheim was born in Leadville, CO, to Carrie H. and Alfred A. Freedheim. His father ran a men's clothing store. Freedheim attended Denver public schools and graduated from the Univ. of Colorado (A.B. 1921) and Harvard Univ.'s School of Law (LL.B. 1924), where he edited the *Harvard Law Review*. Admitted to the bar in 1924, he first worked as a law clerk in the Supreme Judicial Court of Massachusetts. In 1925 Freedheim came to Cleveland and joined the Mooney, Hahn, Loeser & Keogh law firm; by 1930, he was a partner. A Democrat (see CUYAHOGA COUNTY DEMOCRATIC PARTY†), he served as precinct committeeman to SHAKER HTS.†

On 2 Mar. 1927 Freedheim married Mina Koperlik; the couple had twin sons, Donald K. and David E., and one daughter, Joan Kraus Collins. A member of the Ohio State Bar Assn., Freedheim served as trustee of the Jewish Welfare Federation (see JEWISH COMMUNITY FEDERATION†), the FAMILY SERVICE ASSN.† of Cleveland (1945–49), the Youth Bureau, and as national president of the Family Service Assn. of America (1957–59). In 1956, Freedheim won the first Distinguished Service Award of the Community Chest Campaign and in 1970 he was presented with the CHARLES EISENMAN Award of the JCF.—J.M.

**FREEDLANDER, SAMUEL OSCAR, M.D.** (30 July 1893–4 Jan. 1971), Cleveland's first thoracic surgeon (1922), was chief of surgery and chief of thoracic surgery at Mt. Sinai Hospital (1946–59) (see MT. SINAI MEDICAL CENTER†), chief surgeon at KAISER PERMANENTE† (1960s), and chief of surgery and of thoracic surgery at City Hospital (1932–53). He established the division of surgery at City Hospital, pioneered a surgical treatment for tuberculosis, and, with CARL H. LENHART, determined the physiology of pneumothorax (collapsed lung). An authority on the treatment of pulmonary thrombosis, Freedlander instituted the internationally known technique of thoracoplasty. After retiring from Mt. Sinai, he lobbied the Ohio legislature to establish the Community Health Foundation, Kaiser's predecessor.

Freedlander was born in Wooster, OH, to David L. and Anna Arnson Freedlander. He earned both his A.B. (1915) and M.D. (1918) from Western Reserve Univ. (WRU; see CASE WESTERN RESERVE UNIV.†) and did post-graduate work in Vienna, Austria. Trained at City Hospital (1918–21), Freedlander taught surgery at the WRU School of Medicine (1925–59). In 1939 he maintained an office on Carnegie Ave.; later his office was located on EUCLID AVE.† Freedlander served other hospitals as visiting surgeon, including Lakeside Hospital (see UNIV. HOSPITALS OF CLEVELAND†), FOREST CITY HOSPITAL,† and ST. LUKE'S HOSPITAL AND MEDICAL CENTER.† In addition, he was director of surgery at the Sunny Acres Sanatorium. His medical affiliations included the American Assn. for Thoracic Surgery and the American Medical Assn.

On 5 January 1931, Freedlander married Adeline Kaden; they lived on Cedar Rd. with their 2 children, Nina and Jean. A member of EUCLID AVE. TEMPLE,† Freedlander also belonged to the CITY CLUB OF CLEVELAND.† He served on its Board of Directors and as president (1961–62).—J.M.

**FREEMAN, ERNEST (ERNIE)** (16 Aug. 1922–15 May 1981), arose from Cleveland's big band scene to become one of Hollywood's leading composers and arrangers. A native Clevelander, he was the son of Ernest and Gertrude Freeman and a graduate of CENTRAL HIGH SCHOOL.† Earning a bachelor's degree from the CLEVELAND INSTITUTE OF MUSIC,† he also played in the "Swing Club," a dance band organized by his sister, Evelyn Freeman. He married Clevelander Isabelle Collier and in 1942 enlisted in the armed forces. During World War II he was stationed with the U.S. Navy Band at Bunker Hill Naval Air Station in Indiana. After the war Freeman went to the West Coast, where he obtained a master's degree from the Univ. of Southern California. He worked on the road as a pianist-arranger for Dinah Washington and DOROTHY DANDRIDGE. Freeman eventually won 3 Grammy awards as an arranger, for "Strangers in the Night" with Frank Sinatra, "Everybody Loves Somebody" with Dean Martin, and "Bridge Over Troubled Water" with Simon and Garfunkel. Over the course of his career he amassed a total of 60 gold albums and 150 gold singles. Among the other artists he arranged and conducted for were Paul Anka, Rosemary Clooney, Sammy Davis, Jr., Johnny Mathis, Mel Torme, the Four Aces, the Mills Brothers, and the Platters. His movie scores included "The Cool Ones" and "The Pink Jungle." He also conducted Dick Clark's Hollywood Bowl Concerts for 3 years and worked on television specials for Carol Channing and Leslie Uggams. Freeman died in North Hollywood and was interred at Forest Lawn. He was survived by his wife and a daughter, Janice Carter. His niece, Claire E. Freeman, was director of CUYAHOGA METROPOLITAN HOUSING AUTHORITY† in 1995.—J.V.

**FREEMAN, HARRY LAWRENCE** (9 Oct. 1869–24 March 1954) became the first African American to compose an opera, adding nearly a score of works

161

in the same genre during a long career as teacher and composer. The son of soprano Agnes Sims Freeman, he was born in Cleveland and educated in its public schools, where he learned to sight-read music. He organized a boys' quartet at the age of 10 and became assistant organist at his family church at 12. Following his high school graduation, Freeman went to Denver, CO, where he composed and produced his first opera, *The Martyr* (1893). The first opera ever written by an African American, it was also produced in Chicago and at the German Theater in Cleveland in 1904. After writing a second opera, *Nada* (1898; later retitled *Zuluki*), Freeman returned to Cleveland to study composition and theory under JOHANN BECK. Excerpts from Freeman's *Nada* were also performed by the Cleveland Symphony Orchestra under Beck in 1901. Freeman went on to teach at Wilberforce Univ. from 1902–04, and later in New York, where he founded the Freeman School of Music in 1914. He continued to compose operas to his own librettos, the majority of them centered around African American, Native American, or Mexican characters. Several of them´ were never performed, although *Valdo* (1906) had its premiere in Cleveland's Weisgerber's Hall, and *Voodoo* (1914) became the first African American opera to be performed in New York's Broadway theater district, on 10 Sept. 1928. Those that were performed were generally produced by Freeman himself, often with the participation of his soprano wife, Carlotta, and son, Valdo L., a baritone. Freeman died at his home in New York City.—J.V.

**FREESE, ANDREW J.** (1 Nov. 1816–2 Sept. 1904), first superintendent of Cleveland schools, was born in Levant, Penobscot, ME. Determined to become a teacher, Freese attended college irregularly for about 3 years, teaching to finance his education. He traveled throughout New England and consulted with Horace Mann to learn about existing school systems. Freese came to Cleveland in 1840 and taught at Prospect St. School, later becoming division principal. Supported by the Board of Managers, he helped effect changes in state laws that led to a graded school system, better textbooks, and the establishment of public high schools, including Ohio's first free public high school, which became CENTRAL HIGH SCHOOL,† opening in Cleveland on 13 July 1846 with Freese as principal. In 1847 Western Reserve Univ. conferred an honorary M.A. degree upon Freese.

In June 1853, the Board of Education (formerly the Board of Managers) created the office of superintendent of instruction, appointing Freese, who also continued as Central High principal, until 1861 when he resigned due to ill health. He taught at Eagle School and in 1868 became principal of Central High School, resigning in 1869 because of illness. He then originated a series of outline maps, assisted editing the Ohio Journal of Education, and authored books on education, as well as the *Early History of Cleveland Public Schools* (1896). On 17 June 1847, Freese married Elizabeth Merrill; they had one child, Elmira. Freese is buried at Lake View Cemetery.

**FREIBERGER, ISADORE FRED** (12 Dec. 1879–27 Apr. 1969), a banker active in social, educational, and civic activities, was born in New York City to Esther and Samuel Freiberger. He moved with his family to Cleveland when he was 3. Freiberger attended CENTRAL HIGH SCHOOL,† then worked his way through Adelbert College, graduating in 1901. He worked as a clerk at Cleveland Trust Co. but attended BALDWIN-WALLACE COLLEGE† at night, earning an LL.B. in 1904. Freiberger was promoted steadily at Cleveland Trust, eventually becoming chairman of the board in 1941. He was also a director for the FOREST CITY PUBLISHING CO.,† which published the *PLAIN DEALER†* and *CLEVELAND NEWS,†* becoming its president in 1943, and was a director of 9 other businesses. He was president of the Cleveland Chamber of Commerce in 1927 and vice-president of the GREAT LAKES EXPOSITION† in 1936. During his life, he was a member of over 50 religious, civic, business, and charitable organizations, and was a trustee of MT. SINAI HOSPITAL,† the Playhouse Foundation, Western Reserve Univ., Cleveland-Marshall Law School, and the JEWISH COMMUNITY FED.† He was awarded the Cleveland Chamber of Commerce Medal for Public Service, the American Heart Assn.'s Award of Merit for Distinguished Service (1957), an honorary doctorate of humanities from WRU (1947), and Adelbert College's Distinguished Alumnus Award (1968). He helped the university with a $20 million development program, and in 1956 the school named its new library in his honor. He married Fannie Fertel in 1903 and had 2 children, Lloyd Stanton Freiberger and Ruth Gilbert.

**FRENCH, WINSOR** (24 Dec. 1904–6 Mar. 1973), society columnist for the *CLEVELAND PRESS,†* was born in Saratoga Springs, NY, to Winsor P. and Edith French. He became the stepson of Joseph O. Eaton, founder of the EATON CORP.,† after his father's death. French moved to Cleveland with his family in 1915. After sporadic education, he worked for the *CLEVELAND NEWS†* and *TIME†* magazine. In 1933 he joined the *Press* and married Margaret Hall Frueauff. A year later Mrs. French obtained a divorce, becoming a noted actress under the name Margaret Perry.

French wrote some drama criticism for the *Press*, but found his calling as a society reporter. His friends included Lucius Beebe, Marlene Dietrich, Clark Gable, Libby Holman, John O'Hara, and Cole Porter. He left the *Press* to live in New York in 1941 but returned at the conclusion of World War II. Sent to Europe to report on the condition of the average European in 1946, he cabled interviews with Noel Coward, Beatrice Lillie, and Somerset Maugham. Never remarried, French lived like the people he wrote about, partly through the gift of IBM stock from Clevelander Leonard Hanna. Failing in health and confined to a wheelchair late in his career, French campaigned for the rights of the handicapped, resulting in Mayor Ralph Locher ordering City Hall and other city buildings to be made accessible to handicapped persons, and in French's receiving a presidential citation in 1966. He retired from the *Press* in 1968, and is buried with his parents in Williamstown, MA.

**FREY, FRANZ (FRANK) XAVIER** (8 Dec. 1837–13 March 1900), recipient of the Congressional Medal of Honor for service during the CIVIL WAR,† was born in Zurich, Switzerland, emigrated to the U.S. prior to the war, and settled in Cleveland. He enlisted in the 37th Volunteer Infantry at Cleveland 16 Oct. 1861 and was promoted to cpl. 25 July 1862. Frey participated in the campaign to capture Vicksburg, MS, in May 1863 as one of 150 volunteers who stormed the Confederate earthworks north of the city. Although the storming party failed to achieve its objective, party members, including Frey, received the Medal of Honor 14 Aug. 1894 for gallantry during the assault. He finished the war as a commissary sgt. and was discharged at Camp Cleveland, OH, in 1865. He remained in the city after the war, marrying three times. His third wife, Margaret Heinkleman, bore him a son, Franz, on 23 Dec. 1885. Frey died in Cleveland at age 62 and ultimately was buried at Lake View Cemetery.

**FRICKE, OTTO L.** (1886–4 June 1951), a lawyer who supported GERMANS† and German-Americans, was born in Germany, came to the U.S. in 1909, and graduated from Cleveland Law School. He worked as a clerk, bookkeeper, auditor, and treasurer before entering real estate. By 1926 he established a law practice with Joseph C. Calhoun, Jr. and Henry W. MacLeod.

Active in German-American organizations, Fricke was president of the national German-American Congress, and was national secretary of the German-American Natl. Alliance of Philadelphia. Locally, for 10 years he was president of the German Central Organization, and a founder and first president of the Cleveland Stadtverband.

Fricke's identification with his heritage made him controversial in the 1930s and 1940s. Speaking at a German Day celebration in June 1940, Fricke attacked newspapers, politicians, and all "who foment hatred against Americans of German descent," asserting "Americans of German stock are Americans first, last and all the time." Yet Fricke was counsel to the German consulate in Cleveland until June 1941; was chairman of the Cleveland chapter of American Aid for German War Prisoners; and represented Karl Zanzinger, the only Clevelander arrested in the 1941 national roundup of suspected German agents accused of recruiting skilled craftsmen to work in factories in Nazi Germany. In 1945 the *WAECHTER UND ANZEIGER†* published his letter urging German-Americans to protest Allied postwar policies as detrimental to Germans and Germany's future. Fricke married twice: first to Lucy Fricke (d. 1926), with whom he had two children, Alex L. and Robert O.; and then to Serena Cooks (d. 1973). Fricke is buried at Lakewood Park Cemetery.

**FRIEBOLIN, CARL DAVID** (19 Jan. 1878–2 Sept. 1967), lawyer, teacher, federal bankruptcy referee, and well-known wit and satirist who wrote the CITY CLUB OF CLEVELAND's ANVIL REVUE† for years, was born in Owatonna, MN, to Rev. William and Kate Dennerline Friebolin. The family moved to Cleveland in 1885. Friebolin attended CENTRAL HIGH SCHOOL,† received his law degree from Western Reserve Univ. in 1899, and practiced law in Cleveland. With the encouragement of Mayor TOM L. JOHNSON, he was elected to the Ohio House of Representatives in 1911, and to the Ohio senate in 1913. Before his senate term was completed, he was appointed to the common pleas bench but lost when he ran for election to the post. In 1916 he was appointed federal bankruptcy referee, continuing in that position until his death. He became a nationally known expert on bankruptcy law, helping draft the 1938 Natl. Bankruptcy Act, and also drafting the rules of uniform procedure adopted by the Natl. Assn. of Referees. From 1934–59 he taught bankruptcy law at WRU. In Cleveland, Friebolin is perhaps best known as the author of the Anvil Revue, a satiric look at Cleveland put on each year by the City Club. For the revue, he created the character Ben Sapp, the confused ordinary citizen who "got over the fence last." Friebolin died in Cleveland at age 89. After his death, the Carl Friebolin Memorial Scholarship was established at Case Western Reserve Law School. He married Florence Brookes on 30 June 1906, and had a son, Brookes, born in 1910.

---

Carl Friebolin Papers, WRHS.

**FRIEDLAND, ABRAHAM HAYYIM** (1891–3 Aug. 1939), educator, author, and first director of the BUREAU OF JEWISH EDUCATION,† was born in Gorodok, Lithuania, to Leah Friedland. He received a traditional yeshiva education. His family came to New York when he was 14, and he studied at the Isaac Elchanan Yeshiva in addition to public high school. Following graduation from Columbia Univ., Friedland helped establish the Natl. Hebrew School for Girls in New York in 1911, remaining there until 1920, when he became superintendent of the CLEVELAND HEBREW SCHOOLS.† In 1924, when the Bureau of Jewish Education was established to coordinate institutions offering Jewish education, Friedland became its first director, establishing teacher training, youth clubs, children's theater, advanced Hebrew studies, and the Institute for Jewish Studies—building a network of 8 Hebrew and 5 religious schools, and an adult institute. An ardent Zionist, Friedland was criticized by those who believed he taught secular Jewish nationalism. In 1926 he declined an invitation to become director of the Jewish educational system in Palestine.

Friedland was president of Cleveland Zionist District, Ohio Region of the Zionist Organization of America, Histadrut Ivrith, and Natl. Council of Jewish Education. Interested in aids to teach Hebrew to children, he wrote *Torah-Li, Shiron, Sippurim Yofim,* and coauthored *Gilenu.* He also wrote *Sonettot;* poetry, published as *Shirim;* and coauthored *Hashvil* with Rabbi SOLOMON GOLDMAN. He translated Hebrew literature into English and English poets into Hebrew. He married, Yonina, a native of Palestine, in 1916. They had 1 daughter, Aviva.

Bureau of Jewish Education Records, WRHS.
Abraham H. Friedland Papers, American Jewish Archives, Cincinnati, Ohio.

**FRIEDMAN, ALLEN** (1921–13 Oct. 1992), a labor organizer and vice-president of Teamster Local 507, was born in Cleveland, the son of Louis and Teresa Friedman. The youngest of 5 children, Allen grew up in the Glenville area, attending school through the 7th grade. After his father's death in 1934 and his mother's death in 1935, Allen lived with his sister and brother-in-law, William and Faye Presser. By 1939 he was acting as an enforcer for WILLIAM PRESSER's union organizing activities. Friedman organized Local 274 Hotel and Restaurant Workers for JACKIE PRESSER in the mid–1950s, and developed the persuasive skills needed to recruit union members, using violence or the threat of violence to make his point.

Beginning in 1966, Friedman recruited warehouse workers for Teamster Local 507 and served as the union's vice-president. After a heart attack in 1969, however, he broke with Local 507 and started his own independent warehouse workers Local 752. With his life threatened by another heart attack in 1976, Friedman turned his union over to Local 507 in return for a monthly salary for which no work was required. A federal investigation of this illegal arrangement led to Friedman's conviction for embezzling $165,000 as a ghost employee of Local 507 in 1983. He spent 11 months in prison. He died in Cleveland at age 71.

Friedman was married and divorced several times. His former wife, Nancy Friedman, survived him, as did 4 daughters: Toni Friedman and Michalene Martin (Mrs. Edward), both of Denver, and Jacqueline Friedman and Tami Kowit (Mrs. Brad) of Cleveland.—M.S.

Neff, James. *Mobbed Up* (1989).

**FRIEDMAN, BENJAMIN "BENNY"** (18 Mar. 1905–23 Nov. 1982), a native Clevelander, born to Louis and Mayme Friedman, was a college and professional quarterback. He was a football star at Glenville High School and led the team to an undefeated season and city championship in 1922. He played football at the Univ. of Michigan in 1924, 1925, and 1926, and was All-American the latter 2 years. Friedman returned to Cleveland to play professional football in 1927 for the CLEVELAND BULLDOGS,† receiving a seasonal $18,000 salary and $750 for each postseason game, when most players made about $150 per game. In addition to quarterbacking, he promoted upcoming games. He played for the Detroit Wolverines in 1928, and in 1929 New York Giants owner Tim Mara bought the entire Detroit team to obtain Friedman. Friedman also played for the Brooklyn Dodgers (1932–34) before retiring. Friedman's specialty was accurate passing, but he ran with the ball, did place-kicking, and played defense as well as offense. During his professional career he threw 71 touchdown passes and scored 179 points.

Friedman became head football coach at City College of New York (1934–41) and head football coach and athletic director at Brandeis Univ. (1949–63). For many years he operated a summer camp in Oxford, ME. Friedman was inducted into Glenville High School's Hall of Fame (1980) and the College Football Hall of Fame (1952). He married on 12 Feb. 1931. He and his wife, Shirley (Immerman), had a son, Leslie. In 1982 Friedman, suffering from cancer and a circulatory ailment and having lost a leg to amputation, took his own life.

**FRIEDMAN, HAROLD J.** (25 Dec. 1905–7 Jan. 1993), allergist, developed Cleveland's monitoring of the pollen count. Having proved that both household dust and silk could also trigger allergic reactions, he spurred drug manufacturers to eliminate silk fibers from typhoid vaccine production. A winner of the Distinguished Service Award from the American Academy of Allergy (1972), Friedman published research and served as associate editor of the *Journal of Allergy and Immunology*. Born in Ashtabula, OH, to Goldie and Abraham Friedman, he was raised in Cleveland and graduated from East High School and Ohio State Univ., where he received both a B.S. and an M.D. (1932). Friedman interned and spent his residencies in City Hospital, New York City before returning to Cleveland in 1940. He served on the staffs of the MT. SINAI MEDICAL CENTER† and the MERIDIA HURON HOSPITAL,† where he headed the allergy department.

Friedman married Judith Steiner on 24 Nov. 1943; they lived in BEACHWOOD† with 3 daughters, Elizabeth, Nancy Zavelson, and Kathleen Kirchner.—J.M.

**FRIEDMAN, MAX R.** (11 Nov. 1918–24 Sept. 1993) was a former president of the JEWISH COMMUNITY FEDERATION† (1967–70), Fairmount Temple (see ANSHE CHESED†), and the JEWISH COMMUNITY CENTER,† (JCC). He was also a civic leader, civil-rights advocate, philanthropist, and cofounder of the Friedman Buick Co., one of the nation's most successful Buick dealerships. Friedman, born in Allentown, PA, to Sam and Rose (Klein) Friedman, moved to Cleveland when he was an infant. He graduated from John Adams High School and attended Ohio State Univ. During World War II he served in the army.

In 1946 Friedman and his brothers, Allen and Robert, opened State Auto Sales, a used car lot on Euclid Ave. In 1957 they acquired the Ralph Stewart Buick Co. and, in 1959, founded Friedman Auto Lease, considered the largest leasing company in Ohio and operating in 40 states. In 1967 their Buick dealership, located on St. Clair Ave., was ranked 12th nationwide. In 1970 a new showroom opened in MAYFIELD HTS.† In 1973 Max Friedman was named New Car Dealer of the Year.

Friedman was long active in Jewish community organizations. He chaired the United Jewish Appeal's Cleveland campaign (1969), and helped raise millions for Israel as chairman of the Cleveland Committee for State of Israel Bonds (1971). He was a JCC Board of Trustee member since 1959 and on the executive committee. He was a life trustee with the Jewish Community Federation.

Friedman helped raise money for leading Democratic party candidates and was a life member of the NAACP.

Friedman was married three times. He and his first wife, Sylvia Jacobs, were married on 27 Nov. 1946. After divorcing in 1947, Friedman married Gloria May Stotter on 23 Nov. 1951; they divorced in 1953. Friedman's third marriage was on 15 Aug. 1954 to Jane Gilbert; they had three children: Nancy, Steve and Suzy. Friedman lived in PEPPER PIKE† and is buried in Mayfield Cemetery.—T.B.

**FRITZSCHE, ALFRED** (21 May 1869–18 Jan. 1944), industrialist and leader in Catholic charitable organizations, was born in Cleveland, the son of Alfred and Carolyne (Snyder) Fritzsche. Educated in Cleveland public schools, he went to work at age 12 as a typesetter for the *Penny Press*, forerunner of the *CLEVELAND PRESS.†* Fritzsche was associated with the Grinnell Co. as vice-president and general manager and later in the same positions with "Automatic" Sprinkler, organized in 1910 to manufacture equipment for fire control. He also was president of the Twin High Transmission Co.

Fritzsche was a member of the first CATHOLIC CHARITIES CORP.'s† Board of Trustees, when it was founded in April 1919, and served in that capacity until he died in 1944. He was board president in 1935. Fritzsche was especially concerned for the needs of children, particularly those who were handicapped or orphaned, and was active in securing funds for them as a trustee of the Rose-Mary Home (see ROSE-MARY CENTER†), Parmadale Children's Village (see PARMADALE FAMILY SERVICES†), and the CATHERINE HORSTMANN HOME.†

Fritzsche married Clara Neracher 6 June 1894, and they had four sons: Allan, Alfred, Jr., Paul, and William. A resident of SHAKER HTS.,† he died in New York City and was buried in Lake View Cemetery.—M.S.

**FULDHEIM, DOROTHY** (26 June 1893—3 Nov. 1989), entered the field of television at an age when most people begin to plan their retirement, and lasted there long enough to become a living legend. She was born Dorothy Violet Snell in Passaic, NJ, and grew up in Milwaukee, WI, where she attended Milwaukee College and entered teaching. Following her marriage to Milton H. Fuldheim, she moved to Cleveland in the 1920s and pursued a career in lecturing. She also gained experience in radio, including a local historical biographical series on WTAM† and a weekly editorial over the ABC network. Joining Cleveland's first television station, WEWS,† 2 months before it went on the air in Dec. 1947, Fuldheim became the first woman in the country with her own news show. Unhampered by any hardened format, she devised one which worked commentary and interviews into the straight news summary.

Eventually others took over the "anchor" chores, leaving her free to concentrate on analysis and interviews and to co-host a long-running afternoon show, "The One O'Clock Club." Among her estimated 15,000 interviews by 1974 were Helen Keller, Anastas Mikoyan, and the Duke of Windsor. WEWS also used her as a roving reporter on assignments ranging from the Mideast to Northern Ireland. An interview she did in Hong Kong with 2 American prisoners released by Communist China in 1955 brought her a National Overseas Press Club award. After the death of her first husband in 1952, Fuldheim married William L. Ulmer. Her only child, Dorothy Fuldheim-Urman, a professor of Russian at CASE WESTERN RESERVE UNIV.,† died in 1980, and her own career was finally ended at age 92, after a crippling stroke suffered on the job on 27 July 1984. Named one of America's Most Admired Women by a Gallup Poll, Fuldheim was the only active journalist included among the charter members of the CLEVELAND JOURNALISM HALL OF FAME,† established by the PRESS CLUB OF CLEVELAND.† She wrote 2 autobiographical reminiscences, *I Laughed, I Cried, I Loved* (1966) and *A Thousand Friends* (1974).—J.V.

Fuldheim, Dorothy. *I Laughed, I Cried, I Loved: A News Analyst's Love Affair with the World* (Cleveland, 1966).

**FURDEK, STEPHAN** (2 Sept. 1855–18 Jan. 1915), a priest who worked with Czech and Slovak immigrants, was born in Trstena, Slovakia. Cleveland Bp.

RICHARD GILMOUR wrote to the Prague Seminary asking them to locate a priest fluent in Czech and Slovak who could come to Cleveland to work with the immigrants, and Furdek, nearing the end of his studies for the priesthood, was chosen. He arrived in Mar. 1882, studied at ST. MARY SEMINARY,† and was ordained by Bishop Gilmour on 2 July 1882 and assigned to ST. WENCESLAS CHURCH.† Fr. Furdek worked there until May 1883, when he organized another parish for CZECHS† residing near E. 55th and Broadway.

The new parish was placed under the patronage of Our Lady of Lourdes. Fr. Furdek quickly built a small church and school. He was briefly assigned to St. Procop's, but the parish of Our Lady of Lourdes demanded his return, and he spent the rest of his priestly ministry there. In 1888 he organized ST. LADISLAUS CHURCH,† the first parish to serve both SLOVAKS† and HUNGARIANS† in Cleveland. In 1891 Furdek founded the national fraternal insurance organization, the FIRST CATHOLIC SLOVAK UNION,† whose membership was 45,000 by 1915. He was the founder and publisher of *Jednota,* its journal. Furdek wrote numerous books and pamphlets on religious and educational themes in Slovak and Bohemian, and published a reader for Slovak students. He served as a diocesan consulter and advisor to the bishop. Furdek died in Cleveland and is buried in Calvary Cemetery.

Archives, Diocese of Cleveland.
Furdek, Stepan. *Kde se vzel svet? Napsal Stepan Furdek* (1911).

**GAERTNER, CARL FREDERICK** (1898–4 Nov. 1952), a nationally known landscape artist whose best medium was watercolor, son of Nellie and H. Frederick Gaertner, manager of BURROWS BROS. CO.,† was born in Cleveland, graduated from EAST TECHNICAL HIGH SCHOOL,† began attending Western Reserve College in 1918, finishing at the CLEVELAND INSTITUTE OF ART.† In 1918, while still a student, he began instructing at South High School in Willoughby. In 1925 Gaertner started teaching at the Cleveland Institute of Art, Western Reserve College, and JOHN CARROLL UNIV.† Gaertner exhibited in 27 Cleveland May Shows and his paintings hang in galleries throughout the country, including the CLEVELAND MUSEUM OF ART,† Metropolitan Museum, Chicago Art Institute, and Whitney Gallery. He painted the fresco in the Cleveland Greyhound bus station. Gaertner is best known for his Ohio landscapes, with their dark, dramatic skies. He traveled frequently to Cape Cod, Hudson River Bay, the Allegheny Mts., and the Monongahela Valley to find variety in landscapes, but always returned to the Chagrin Valley and his farm in Willoughby. Gaertner won the Natl. Academy of Design Award in 1953 for an oil painting entitled "Barge Men." His portrait hangs there in tribute to him. He was president of the CLEVELAND SOCIETY OF ARTISTS† and the Carl Gaertner Memorial Prize in painting is offered at the Institute of Art. A retrospective of Gaertner's work was held at the Cleveland Museum of Art in June 1953. Gaertner married Adelle Potter in 1938 and had 2 sons, Frederick and Carl.

**GAHN, HARRY C.** (26 Apr. 1880–2 Nov. 1962), lawyer, councilman, congressman, and public official, was born in Elmore, OH, to Dr. Louis and Esther Knight Gahn. He graduated from the Univ. of Michigan with an LL.B. degree, and was admitted to the Ohio Bar in 1904, working with Wm. Patterson (1904–06) and with the law firm of THEODORE BURTON (1906–08), specializing in trial practice. In 1909 Gahn became legal counsel for the LEGAL AID SOCIETY,† serving until 1912, while working in the law office of Harry Howell.

Elected from the 14th Ward to CLEVELAND CITY COUNCIL† (1911–21), Gahn served as council president between 1918–19. As a member of the Cleveland River & Harbor Commission, 1911–21, he studied Cleveland harbor development, port administration, and the merchant marine, advocating public ownership of harbor facilities to make them the best on the Great Lakes, so that when the St. Lawrence River became navigable to ocean vessels, Cleveland would become an important world seaport. In 1921, Gahn was elected to the U.S. Congress from Ohio's 21st district. Defeated for reelection in 1923, he returned to practicing law, especially handling estates and personal-injury cases. He became counsel for the Methodist Children's Home in Berea in 1913 and was president of the Cleveland Chevrolet Dealers' Assn. (1924–37). In 1936, he became solicitor for the city of INDEPENDENCE,† retiring after 20 years in 1956. Gahn married Grace Gerrard in June 1917. They were divorced in 1929. He had 2 daughters, Marjorie and May.

Harry C. Gahn Scrapbook, WRHS.

**GAINES, ERVIN J.** (8 Dec. 1916–21 June 1986), CLEVELAND PUBLIC LIBRARY† director (1974–85) was born in New York City to Ervin J. and Helen Hennessey Gaines. He graduated from Columbia Univ. (1942) before joining the navy. He returned to Columbia as an English instructor (1946–53), and earned his master's degree (1947) and doctorate (1952). From 1953–56, Gaines worked for the anti-Soviet Radio Liberation in Munich; then entered personnel management, including work with the Boston Public Library, which led to a position as asst. director there (1958–64). From 1964 to 1974 he directed the Minneapolis Public Library.

In Cleveland, Gaines found declining circulation, a large underpaid staff, a divided board, outmoded operations, physically deteriorating libraries, and public displeasure, resulting in a 1974 levy defeat. Gaines quickly eliminated little-used programs and books to cut costs, increased salaries 20%, consolidated branch libraries, and implemented use of the Library of Congress book numbering system. To finance such changes, he directed a successful levy campaign in 1975. Branch libraries were reduced from 39 in 1974 to 31 in 1984, with 8 new and 10 remodeled buildings; through attrition, library employees were reduced from 649 to 451; and after declining to 2.6 million items in 1978, circulation increased to 4.1 million in 1984. Gaines replaced the card catalog with a computerized system, and launched the valuable index of local papers (1976-) and the Cleveland Heritage Project. As executive director of the Urban Libraries Council, Gaines supported federal aid to libraries. Gaines married Martha Zirbel on 11 Feb. 1938 and had two children, Colleen and Sanford. He died in Cleveland and was cremated.

**GAMMETER, HARRY C.** (ca. 1870–11 Apr. 1937), the inventor of the modern multigraph and one of the founders of the American Multigraph Co., was one of 8 children. Although little is known of his early life, as an adult he worked as a sales engineer for the United Typewriter and Supply Co. of Louisville, KY. On a sales trip to Cleveland, he observed a stenographer endlessly copying circular letters and wondered if it was possible to devise a machine that would print a complete line or page of type with a single stroke. In 1900 he built a crude model of such a machine, demonstrating its feasibility to Clevelander Henry C. Osborn, of the Osborn-Morgan Co. consulting engineers. Osborn designed, produced, and financed a duplicating machine based on the rotary drum principle, which was patented 10 March 1903.

In the meantime, Gammeter and Osborne had organized the American Multigraph Co. in 1902, manufacturing the machine in a small, unsightly one-story wooden structure at E. 40th St. and Kelley Ave. Gammeter's duplicator, often referred to as the "waffle iron," evolved into a broad line of sophisticated multigraph equipment. Soon after the company was founded, Gammeter's health began to fail, and in an effort to recover he developed Green Springs, OH, as a health spa, while maintaining his residence in Cleveland Hts.

Gammeter was married to Maude Fry and they had two children, Electa and Harry F. He died in Cleveland at age 67 and was buried in Green Springs.—M.S.

Brainard, George C. *A Page in the Colorful History of Our Modern Machine Age* (1950).

**GANNETT, ALICE** (1876–23 May 1962), prominent settlement-house worker and reformer, was born in Bath, ME, to Henry and Mary Chase Gannett. She attended schools in Washington, DC, and earned a degree from Bryn Mawr College. She taught school 3 years before traveling to New York City in 1906, where she took a room in a tenement among poor social conditions, there becoming devoted to the settlement-house idea and the promotion of social welfare. She served briefly at Welcome Hall in Buffalo, NY, before returning to New York City, where she headed Lenox Hill House for 6 years. She also served as associate director of the Henry St. Settlement in New York for many years. Gannett came to Cleveland in 1917, heading Goodrich House (see GOODRICH-GANNETT NEIGH. CTR.†) at 1420 E. 31st St. for 30 years. During her tenure, the settlement established a tradition of free thought and speech, commitment to neighborhood, and improved working conditions. Gannett was president of the Cleveland Fed. of Settlements for 5 years, of the Natl. Fed. of Settlements for 2 years, and headed the CONSUMERS LEAGUE OF OHIO† for 8 years. She was also a trustee of the Welfare Fed. of Cleveland. In the 1950s she founded the Neighborhood Group, a senior citizens' organization for civic improvement. Gannett died in Harrisburg, PA, and is buried in Washington, DC.

**GARDNER, GEORGE W.** (7 Feb. 1834–18 Dec. 1911), businessman, councilman, and mayor of Cleveland, was born in Pittsfield, MA, to James and Griselda Porter Gardner. The family came to Cleveland in 1837. Leaving school at age 14, Gardner sailed the Great Lakes for 5 years before returning to Cleveland to work for the private banking house of Wick, Otis & Brownell (1853–57), after which he became a junior partner in Otis, Brownell & Co., grain dealers. Gardner joined grain merchants M. B. Clarke and JOHN D. ROCKEFELLER to found Clarke, Gardner & Co. in 1859. Two years later, with Peter Thatcher, Geo. H. Burt, and A. C. McNairy, he built the Union Elevator, the largest grain elevator in the area. Later the firm became Gardner & Clark and added the manufacture of flour to their elevator business with the purchase of Natl. Flour Mills in 1878. Gardner was an incorporator of the Cleveland Board of Trade, which later became the Chamber of Commerce, and its president in 1868. He was also president of Buckeye Stove Co., Buttman Furnace Co., and Walker Mfg. Co., as well as a director of Merchants Natl. Bank. Gardner was an organizer of the CLEVELAND YACHT CLUB,† and was active in Republican politics, serving as city councilman 1863–64 and 1876–81, and as council president 1879–81. He was mayor in 1885–86 and 1889–91. He died in Dayton, OH, but is buried at Woodland Cemetery in Cleveland. He married Rosaline (or Rosilda) Oviatt in 1857, and had 7 children: Ellen, George, Burt, James, Anna, Kirtland, and Ethel.

**GARDNER, W. JAMES, JR., M.D.** (12 June 1898– 29 Jan. 1987), called the "grandfather of neurosurgery" in Ohio because he trained so many neurosurgeons, served as chief of neurosurgery at the CLEVELAND CLINIC FOUNDATION† (1929–62, emeritus 1974–87) and at FAIRVIEW GENERAL HOSPITAL† (1964–67), and also practiced at the LUTHERAN MEDICAL CENTER† and Huron Rd. Hospital (1964–74, see MERIDIA HURON ROAD HOSPITAL†). Gardner developed the Gardner neurosurgical chair to facilitate brain surgery (1938); he helped develop a pneumatic suit to maintain blood pressure (1956); and numerous other devices and methods. Gardner was born in McKeesport, PA, to Sara Lucy Gongaware and W. James Gardner, Sr., a general surgeon. He attended public school and graduated from Washington and Jefferson College, Washington, PA (1920), and the Univ. of Pennsylvania's medical school (1924).

WILLIAM EDGAR LOWER hired the young physician to replace Dr. Charles E. Locke, who had perished earlier that year in the CLEVELAND CLINIC DISASTER.† Gardner served as a founding member of the Cleveland Clinic's Board of Governors (1955–59), the Northern Ohio Neurological Society (est. 1968), and the American Assn. of Neurological Surgeons, which awarded him the Cushing Medal (1982). He presided over the Society of Neurological Surgeons and was vice-president of the Harvey Cushing Society. In retirement, he consulted for Euclid General Hospital (see MERIDIA EUCLID HOSPITAL†), ST. ALEXIS HOSPITAL,† ST. LUKE'S MEDICAL CENTER,† and MT. SINAI MEDICAL CENTER.† The Congress of Neurological Surgeons honored him (1967), and the Cleveland Clinic created a lectureship in his name (1985).

Gardner married Ann Ray Kieffer in 1928, and they had 3 children: June Mallinckrodt, Dr. W.

James, III, and Hugh Blaine. Gardner died in Ogden, UT.—J.M.

W. James Gardner, Jr., Papers, Cleveland Clinic Foundation Archives.

**GARFIELD, ABRAM** (21 Nov. 1872–16 Oct. 1958), son of Lucretia Rudolph and president JAS. A. GARFIELD, was born in Washington, DC, moving to Cleveland after his father's death in 1881. He received a B.A. from Williams College (1893) and a B.S. from MIT (1896), beginning his architectural practice in 1897. In 1898 he formed Meade & Garfield with FRANK MEADE, becoming premier residential designers.

From 1905–22, Garfield practiced as Abram Garfield, Architect, adding partners as the firm expanded. Garfield was personally responsible for Mrs. John Hay's residence (1910), now part of the WESTERN RESERVE HISTORICAL SOCIETY†; large homes in SHAKER HTS.† and BRATENAHL†; the original Babies & Childrens and Maternity Hospital (1923); Bratenahl School (1901); and the Woodhill and Seville homes for the CUYAHOGA METROPOLITAN HOUSING AUTHORITY.† He was a founder and first president of the Cleveland School of Architecture (1924–29), and vice-president and vice-chairman of the board (1929–41) when the school became part of Western Reserve Univ. Garfield became a trustee of WRU in 1941, was elected an honorary lifetime member in 1943, and received an honorary Doctor of Humanities degree from the university in 1945.

An advocate of CITY PLANNING,† Garfield served on the Group Plan Commission and the Cleveland Planning Commission (1928–42), as chairman in 1930–42. He helped found with ERNEST BOHN, and was president of, the Regional Assn. of Cleveland. Garfield married Sarah Grainger Williams (d. 1945) on 14 Oct. 1897 and had two children, Edward W. and Mary Louise. Garfield married Helen Grannis Matthews in 1947. Garfield died at his home in Bratenahl and is buried in Lake View Cemetery.

Mary Garfield Stanley Brown Papers, WRHS.

**GARFIELD, JAMES ABRAM** (19 Nov. 1831–19 Sept. 1881), 20th president of the U.S., was born in Orange Twp., Cuyahoga County, OH, to Abram and Eliza Ballou Garfield. Fatherless at age 4, Garfield worked as a farmer, carpenter, and canal boatman. He studied at Geauga Seminary in Chester, OH, Western Reserve Eclectic Institute (now Hiram College) from 1851–54, and graduated from Williams College in Massachusetts in 1856. He returned to Hiram to teach classics and served as its president (1857–61), while also being a lay minister in the DISCIPLES OF CHRIST church. In 1859 he was admitted to the bar and elected to the Ohio senate. Garfield was commissioned as lt. colonel in the 42nd Ohio Regiment in 1861. After defeating superior forces at Middle Creek, KY, in 1862, he was promoted to brigadier general, and after winning distinction at Chickamauga, became a major general. Garfield resigned his commission in Dec. 1863 after being elected to the U.S. House of Representatives, where he served for 17 years. In Jan. 1880, Garfield was elected to the U.S. Senate, but before his term began attended the Republican convention in Chicago as campaign manager for John Sherman of Ohio. Garfield, however, became the candidate for president, nominated on the 36th ballot as a compromise between former president Ulysses S. Grant and Sen. Jas. G. Blaine. Chester Alan Arthur of New York was his running mate, opposing Democratic candidates Winfield Scott Hancock and Wm. H. English. Headquarters for the campaign were in Cleveland, but Garfield spent most of the time receiving delegations at his home, "Lawnfield," in Mentor, OH. Garfield won the election by fewer than 10,000 votes, but garnered 214 of the 369 electoral votes. Garfield, confronted with problems of patronage, spent most of his time in office trying to ameliorate the two conflicting factions within his party. Indebted to Blaine for election support, Garfield appointed him secretary of state, angering Roscoe Conkling, who unsuccessfully attempted to block Senate approval; the Senate confirmed the appointment and Conkling resigned from the Senate. On 2 July 1881, while on his way to a Williams College reunion, Garfield was shot at the Washington, DC, railroad station by Chas. Julius Guiteau, a disappointed office seeker. Garfield suffered agonizing attempts by various physicians to save his life before he died on 19 Sept. 1881 at Elberon, NJ. He was buried at Lake View Cemetery in Cleveland, and the GARFIELD MONUMENT was erected to his memory in May 1890. Garfield married Lucretia Rudolph in 1858 and had seven children: JAMES R., Harry A., Irving M., Edward, Eliza A., Mary (Mollie), and ABRAM.

Peskin, Alan. *Garfield* (1978).
James A. Garfield Papers, WRHS.
James A. Garfield Papers, Library of Congress.

**GARFIELD, JAMES RUDOLPH** (17 Oct. 1865–24 Mar. 1950), lawyer and son of Lucretia Rudolph and president JAS. A GARFIELD, was born in Hiram, OH, and received his B.A. from Williams College (1885), and his LL.D. from Columbia Univ. Admitted to the Ohio Bar in 1888, Garfield started his 60-year practice in Cleveland with his older brother, Harry. He became the senior partner in the firm of Garfield, Baldwin, Jameson, Hope & Ulrich.

From 1896–1900, Garfield served in the Ohio senate, authoring an election reforms bill. In 1902, Pres. Roosevelt appointed him to the Federal Civil Service Commission, established because of his father's assassination. He was appointed to the U.S. Commission of Corp.s (1903), and became Roosevelt's secretary of the interior in 1907, spearheading Roosevelt's conservation efforts and active in Indian affairs. He was later associated with the Progressive party.

Returning to his Cleveland law practice in 1909, during World War I he served on the Cleveland War Council. Pres. Coolidge appointed him to the emergency board investigating railroad labor disputes, and Pres. Hoover appointed him chairman of the Federal Commission of the Conservation of the Public Domain. Garfield was a founder and trustee of the Community Fund; the first legal counsel for the CLEVELAND FOUNDATION,† vice-president of the Cleveland Welfare Fed. from 1917–20, and trustee of the Speech & Hearing Clinic, the Humane Society, the Lake View Cemetery Assn., Lake Erie College, and the WESTERN RESERVE HISTORICAL SOCIETY.† Garfield married Helen Newell in 1890 and had 4 sons: John, Rudolph H., James A., and Newell.

James R. Garfield Papers, WRHS.

**GARLICK, THEODATUS A.** (30 Mar. 1805–9 Dec. 1884), surgeon, sculptor, photographer, and fish breeder, was born in Middlebury, VT, to Sabra S. Kirby and Daniel Garlick. In 1818 he joined his brother, Abel, producing Cleveland's first shipped goods, burr millstones. He worked as a blacksmith and tombstone carver in Cleveland, NEWBURGH,† and Brookfield (Trumbull Co.), while studying medicine with local physicians. He graduated from the Univ. of Maryland in 1834 and practiced surgery in Youngstown until 1852, when he became a partner of Dr. HORACE A. ACKLEY at the Cleveland Medical College. Garlick developed new procedures in plastic and facial surgery and operative midwifery, and invented splints and instruments for amputation, trepanning, and obstetrics. His skill in surgery and sculpture made him an adept portraitist: Pres. Jackson, Henry Clay, and JARED KIRTLAND posed for him. He also made precise painted plaster anatomy models for medical schools.

Garlick and his brother excavated a Cleveland Indian mound in 1820. Following Daguerre's methods, Garlick built a camera and, in Dec. 1839, made the first photograph in the WESTERN RESERVE† using a silvered brass plate. He made Cleveland's first daguerreotype on 9 Sept. 1841. Garlick fished, coauthored essays on angling, and in 1853 successfully artificially fertilized trout eggs in vitro and built the country's first fish hatchery. At 75, Garlick took up Greek, translating the Bible within 2 years. He died in Bedford. He married 3 times: his first 2 wives, Amanda and Sylvia Flowen, were daughters of Brookfield mentor, Dr. Elijah Flowen; he married Mary M. Chittenden in 1845. He had two children with Sylvia: a daughter, Frances, and a son, Wilmot, a physician and cofounder of the CLEVELAND ACADEMY OF NATURAL SCIENCES.† Garlick had one child with Mary, a daughter, Marietta.

Theodatus A. Garlick, "Nineteenth Annual Meeting of the Western Reserve and Northern Ohio History Society" (May 1869).

**GARLOCK, ANNA JANSEN CORDON** (12 June 1878–11 Nov. 1958), masseuse and specialist in HYDROTHERAPY† and physiotherapy, served as superintendent of the hydrotherapy department of WOMAN'S GENERAL HOSPITAL† from 1919 until that department closed in 1924. Garlock was born in Copenhagen, Denmark, to John P. and Augusta Borman Jansen. She attended private schools there and immigrated to the U.S. in 1891, graduating from a New York City nursing school (1899). She later studied massage, electrotherapy, and physiotherapy in Germany. From 1908–18 she directed the hydrotherapy department at the YOUNG WOMEN'S CHRISTIAN ASSN.† in Cleveland. Garlock was manager and treasurer of the Cordon Hydrothertic Co. (1918–21) and owned and managed the Physiotherapy Institute in the late 1920s. In 1927 she maintained a private practice on EUCLID AVE.†

Garlock married C. R. Cordon on 18 November 1908; they had one son, Christian. She was widowed by 1920. On 30 October 1922 Garlock married Silas Ledrew Garlock (d. 1944), who had one son, George, by a previous marriage. President of the Danish Sisterhood, Anna Garlock was a charter member of both the BUSINESS AND PROFESSIONAL WOMEN'S CLUB† (which she also served as president) and the Zonta Club of Cleveland. —J.M.

**GARVIN, CHARLES H.** (27 Oct. 1890–17 July 1968), physician, civic leader, and businessman interested in black social and economic programs, was born in Jacksonville, FL, and graduated from Howard Univ.'s medical school in 1915. He practiced medicine in Cleveland from 1916 until his death. During World War I, he became the first black physician commissioned in the U.S. Army, serving in France as commanding officer in the 92nd

Div. Garvin's interest in medicine extended beyond his practice to research and writing, especially tracing the history of Africans and AFRICAN AMERICANS† in medicine. He amassed an important collection of books on the black experience and also completed a manuscript (unpublished as of 1994) and wrote several articles on the subject. His account of the history of blacks in medicine in Cleveland was published in 1939 in the *Women's Voice*, a national women's magazine. Garvin was a founder of the Dunbar Life Insurance Co. and helped organize QUINCY SAVINGS & LOAN CO.,† serving as a director and board chairman. He also pioneered integrated housing during a period of intense racial separation in the city, living in the home he built on Wade Park Ave., an exclusive allotment, despite threats of violence and 2 bombings. Garvin was a trustee of KARAMU HOUSE,† the URBAN LEAGUE OF CLEVELAND,† the Cleveland branch of the NAACP,† and the CLEVELAND PUBLIC LIBRARY.† He was also national president of the Alpha Phi Alpha fraternity.

Chas. Garvin Papers, WRHS.

**GASSAWAY, HAROLD T.** (5 Aug. 1893–13 Apr. 1952), black lawyer and Republican politician, was born in Anderson, SC, to Carrie P. Walls and Mark Gassaway. He was a sergeant in the 349th Field Artillery during World War I, serving in France and the western front. He graduated from Clark Univ. and Howard Univ. in Washington, DC, where he received his law degree in 1922. Admitted to the Ohio Bar in 1923, Gassaway opened his first office in Cleveland, practicing in all the courts.

By the late 1920s, the growing black population east of E. 55th between Euclid and Woodland avenues enabled black leaders to take control of the Republican party organization in that area, including wards 17, 18, and 19. Gassaway entered politics, struggling in 1928 for control of Ward 18 with CLAYBORNE GEORGE, for Gassaway had been elected president of the Ward 18 Republican Club over George's opposition. Together with L. L. Yancy, then ward leader, Gassaway assumed control of Ward 18 and backed John Hubbard for council. From 1939 until his retirement from politics in 1951, because of declining health, Gassaway was councilman from Ward 18. When not in the political limelight, Gassaway busied himself as senior partner of the firm of Gassaway, Collum, Tyler & Kellogg. In addition, he was president of his own business, the Gassaway Broom Mfg. Co. Gassaway married former schoolteacher Ethel Sutton of Pomeroy, OH, on 27 Nov. 1926. He was survived by her and their 2 daughters, Margaret and Carol. Gassaway was buried in Highland Park Cemetery.

**GATES, HOLSEY (HALSEY)** (1 Jan. 1799–2 Nov. 1865) was an early settler of the WESTERN RESERVE† and the founder of the village of GATES MILLS† in Mayfield Twp. Born in East Haddam, CT, to Nathaniel and Hannah Knowlton Gates, the family moved to Delhi, NY in 1815 following Nathaniel's death. During this time Gates's brother and sister (Jeremiah Gates and Clarissa Gates Brainerd) moved to northeastern Ohio, with Jeremiah eventually settling in the village of BROOKLYN† and opening a sawmill with the assistance of brother Nathaniel, who permanently settled there ca. 1824.

Holsey Gates, the youngest of the 3 brothers, arrived in the area in 1825. A master miller who had accumulated much capital and milling equipment, he surveyed and purchased a 130-acre mill site in the Chagrin River Valley in Mayfield Twp. In 1826 Gates relocated with wife Lucy Ann and mother Hannah to a log cabin at the site, and over the next year he dammed the river, dug a mill race, and erected a sawmill and gristmill. The operation of these water-powered industries stimulated the development of Gates Mills. Over the next quarter-century, Gates designed and built structures in and around the village, including a school and the Gates Mills Inn (part of the CHAGRIN VALLEY HUNT CLUB,† which burned down in 1994). In 1844 he constructed a larger, more "modern" gristmill on the Chagrin River, powered by four water wheels. The original mill was converted into a rake factory. Gates also helped to fund, design and build the Gates Mills Methodist Episcopal church. The Greek Revival structure (now known as St. Christopher's by the River) was completed in 1855. Gates married Lucy Ann Bradley prior to moving to Ohio. The couple had 10 children; 7 survived to adulthood. Holsey Gates was buried in Woodland Cemetery.

Gates's most prolific offspring was his son, Washington Gates (4 August 1827–12 Aug. 1897), a prominent architect, builder and water power industrialist who helped to develop CHAGRIN FALLS† and BEDFORD.† Born in Gates Mills, Washington Gates apprenticed under his father. In all, the Gates family designed and erected 18 structures in Gates Mills. After 1865 Washington built and operated a rake factory (with brother William) in Toledo; he moved to Chagrin Falls in 1868, where he purchased a grist mill. As a prominent businessman, Gates was soon a member of the Chagrin Falls Village Council. In 1873 Gates began construction of an Italianate Victorian residence on the corner of Pearl (now Washington) and Walnut streets in Chagrin Falls, which was purchased by the village in 1938 for use as the Village Hall. Gates, along with his son Holsey M [sic] (29 June 1855–21 Sept. 1914), also constructed a grand residence in Bedford, where "W. Gates & Son" had opened and operated the Bedford Roller Mills in 1890, following a significant modernization of the Chagrin Falls and Bedford mills. In 1891 Holsey M (with a group of Bedford businessmen) organized the Bedford Electric Light Co., and began construction of a small hydroelectric generating plant adjacent to the Roller Mills. It was one of the first hydro-powered plants in the nation, utilizing the only form of water-powered industry which would survive into modern times. The Gates-Handyside House was finished ca. 1894, and was the first house constructed in Bedford that was wired for electricity. The house was placed on the National Register of Historic Places in 1975.

Handyside, Holsey Gates. "The Gates Family: Millers and Builders," published as *Facade Monograph No. 7,* Cleveland Restoration Society (1991).
Gates Family materials, WRHS.

**GAYLE, JAMES FRANKLIN** (5 Feb. 1920–1 July 1991) was one of the first 2 African American photographers to work for a Cleveland daily newspaper. He was born in Tuskegee, AL, the son of James and Bessie Gayle. His father, who taught physical education at Tuskegee Institute, moved the family to Cleveland when James was 3. After graduating from East High School, Gayle served as a musician in the U.S. Navy during World War II. A saxophonist, he also played and toured with the Ernie Freeman dance band (see ERNEST FREEMAN) following the war. He developed an interest in photography through a subsequent job in a photography shop. After marrying the former Juanita Wade in 1958, he opened a studio in Cleveland and began selling pictures as a free lancer to the *CLEVELAND CALL AND POST,†* the *PLAIN DEALER,†* and *Ebony* and *Jet* magazines. Among his subjects were such national figures as Dr. Martin Luther King, Jr., and Malcolm X. He also photographed local inventor GARRETT A. MORGAN, along with his patented traffic light, shortly before Morgan's death. Soon after Van Dillard broke the color barrier on the photography staff of the *CLEVELAND PRESS,†* Gayle was hired by the *Plain Dealer* in 1968. He retired for health reasons 22 years later. Buried in Woodland Cemetery, Gayle was survived by his wife and a daughter, Gina.—J.V.

James F. Gayle Photograph Collection, WRHS.

**GAYLOR, VERNA FRANCES** (23 Feb. 1925–18 Feb. 1993) was a pioneer and an acknowledged authority in the field of analytical chemistry and research, who held five patents and spent her 40-year career with BP Research at SOHIO (see BP AMERICA†).

Born in Charleston, WV, Gaylor was raised in Nitro, WV, and graduated from Nitro High School (1942), Ohio Univ. (B.S. chemistry, 1946), and Western Reserve Univ. (M.S. chemistry, 1954).

Gaylor joined Standard Oil's research & development department in 1946 as an analytical chemist. She advanced to group supervisor of chemical analysis by 1971, and in 1979 moved to the research side of her field. Gaylor retired as a senior chemist and researcher in 1987 and continued working as a consultant for several years.

Gaylor conducted some of the early, fundamental research of voltammetry with solid electrodes. One of her earliest contributions was the invention of the wax impregnated graphite electrode, which was used for over 30 years and pointed the way toward better materials for electrodes. She participated in the development of numerous methods used in various aspects of production, including polymers and electrochemistry.

A highlight of her career was spearheading a large-scale program that led to the successful commercialization of a plastic material known as Barex, used in food packaging.

Gaylor authored and coauthored numerous papers in the chemical analysis and electrochemical fields and made over 20 presentations at professional symposiums. In 1963 she presented a paper on crude oil assay at the World Petroleum Congress in Frankfurt, Germany. Gaylor never married, lived in PARMA,† and was cremated.—T.B.

**GAYLORD, GLADYS** (28 July 1888–1 Jan. 1985), social worker, promoted FAMILY PLANNING† in Ohio and Puerto Rico as the first executive secretary (1929–48) of the Maternal Health Assn. (MHA, see PLANNED PARENTHOOD OF GREATER CLEVELAND†), Cleveland's pioneer birth control clinic. She spoke at national conferences, such as a New York City roundtable sponsored by the American Eugenics Society and the American Birth Control League (1938), and published articles in such journals as *The Journal of Contraception* (1938). Gaylord was born in Detroit, MI, to Annie Gere Gaylord and Frank Bourne Gaylord. (Her father joined the administrative staff of Cleveland's Lakeside Hospital in 1920). After graduating from the School of Social Work of Simmons College (1914), Gaylord held various positions in New England before coming to Cleveland. She managed the MHA clinic and promoted its activities locally and around the state and nation. The BRUSH FOUNDATION† contributed substantially to her salary and later paid her pension. In 1934 and again in 1935 she traveled to Puerto Rico to help set up

contraceptive clinics there. Gaylord helped organize the Maternal Assn. of Ohio (1933) and served as field secretary for the state group, which was based in Cleveland.

A Presbyterian and a Democrat, Gaylord lived in Cleveland until she retired and moved to Maine. She belonged to the CONSUMERS LEAGUE† and the AMERICAN RED CROSS, CLEVELAND CHAPTER.† She did not marry.—J.M.

**GEBHARD, BRUNO** (ca. 1899–12 Jan. 1985), a leader in public health education in Germany and the U.S., was the first director of the Cleveland Health Museum (see HEALTH MUSEUM†). Gebhard was born in Rostock, Germany, and studied medicine there, where his father was a hospital administrator. He completed his studies in Berlin and Munich, receiving his medical degree in 1925. Although Gebhard's internships were in pathology and pediatrics, his real interest was in public health, and he served as curator of the German Hygiene Museum in Dresden from 1927 until he and his wife, Gertrude Herrmann Gebhard, fled Germany in 1937. Invited to the U.S. by the Carl Schurz Memorial Foundation to plan and design health exhibits, Gebhard established health museums at hospitals in Philadelphia and Reading, PA. He also planned and designed the health exhibit at the 1939–40 New York World's Fair. At the same time, he developed future plans for the Cleveland Health Museum, coming to Cleveland in the summer of 1940 to prepare for the museum's Nov. 1940 opening. As director of the first permanent health museum in the country, he practiced his philosophy of educating museum visitors by direct participation in exhibits.

Gebhard was the author of numerous articles in professional journals concerning family life, education, and geriatrics, as well as museum planning and management. After his retirement as director of the museum in 1965, he continued as a consultant, residing in SHAKER HTS.† until his wife died in 1975. He then moved to California, where he died in 1985. Gebhard was survived by daughters Ursula Fink of Rye, NY, and Suzanna Goodman of Roosevelt Island, NY.—M.S.

**GEHRING, ALBERT** (21 Mar. 1870–25 Feb. 1926) was an author and teacher equally at home in the fields of philosophy and music. A Cleveland native, he received bachelor's and master's degrees from Harvard ca. 1894 and lectured in philosophy at the College for Women (see CASE WESTERN RESERVE UNIV.†) in 1900–02. From 1902–04 he was a member of the Cleveland school board (see CLEVELAND PUBLIC SCHOOLS†), serving as president for the final year. Among his published books were *Racial Contrasts: Distinguishing Traits of the Graeco-Latins and Teutons* (1908), *The Basis of Musical Pleasure* (1910), *Mozart* (1911), *The Appreciation of Music* (1913), and *The Religion of Thirty Great Thinkers* (1925). His marionette play *The Soul of Chopin* was performed at the CLEVELAND PLAY HOUSE† in 1918. Gehring also composed numerous musical pieces for voice and piano. His song "In Mai" was sung in PUBLIC AUDITORIUM† by Metropolitan Opera baritone Lawrence Tibbett in 1927, during the last of the 5 SAENGERFESTS† hosted in Cleveland. Married to the former Irma Mueller on 10 Feb. 1889, he was survived by her and 3 children: Waldo E., Hermine B., and Mrs. Charles H. Reed.—J.V.

Flory, Julia McCune. *The Cleveland Play House: How It Began* (1965).

**GENTRY, MINNIE LEE WATSON** (2 Dec. 1915–11 May 1993), "The First Lady" of Karamu Theater (see KARAMU HOUSE†) was an original member of the Gilpin Players, who appeared in numerous dramatic, musical, and operatic productions. A critically acclaimed artist, Gentry received a Tony nomination in 1972 and the Outstanding Pioneer Award for her contributions to black theater in 1985.

Born to Taylor and Mincie Watson in Norfolk, VA, Minnie came to Cleveland's Central area with her family at age 5. At 9 she studied piano in the Phillis Wheatley School of Music. She sang in St. John's A.M.E. church choir and began acting at the Friendly Inn Settlement.

In 1931 Minnie met Lloyd Gentry, who introduced her to Karamu. They married in 1932 and Minnie joined the Gilpin Players. Later she worked on the Federal Theater project at Karamu and sang in *Tom Tom,* one of four operas performed at Cleveland Stadium.

Moving to New York in 1946, Gentry performed in her first Broadway production, *Lysistrata.* Gentry returned to Karamu, performing in numerous productions between 1949–60. In 1961 Gentry returned to Broadway for Genet's production of *The Blacks.*

In 1982 Gentry was the guest artist in Karamu's production of *A Raisin in the Sun.* (She had appeared in Karamu's original 1961 production). Her last Karamu appearance was in 1990 in *Dreams of Callahan.*

Gentry appeared in over fifteen movies, including *School Daze* and *Jungle Fever.* Her television credits include *The Cosby Show* and *All My Children.*

The Gentrys (divorced) had one daughter, Marjorie Hawkins. Gentry died in Manhattan and is buried in Evergreen Memorial Cemetery.—T.B.

The Minnie Gentry Files, Karamu House, Inc.

**GENUTH, DAVID L.** (12 Apr. 1901–23 Feb. 1974), one of Cleveland's most influential Orthodox rabbis for 4 decades, was born in Marmoresh Sziget, Hungary, to Elka and Isaac Genuth. He received a traditional yeshiva education before coming to the U.S. in 1924, continuing his studies at Yeshiva Univ. in New York and Yale Univ. Divinity School in New Haven, CT. Genuth was ordained in 1926 and accepted a pulpit in South Norwalk, CT. In 1931 he moved to Cleveland, where in 1933 a group of Marmoresher landsmen called him to serve as rabbi at the newly established KINSMAN JEWISH CTR.† He combined a modern view of Orthodoxy with an ability to cope with the radical labor element at the KJC to forge the center into an important Orthodox congregation. In 1948 Genuth left KJC, and with 8 families established Temple Beth El, the first congregation in SHAKER HTS.† Beth El, a family-centered congregation, had 500 families by 1966. An ardent Zionist, Genuth was a member of the Cleveland Zionist Society and an active supporter of the Jewish Natl. Fund and Bonds for Israel. He was also an organizer of the Jewish Community Council and a representative to its delegate assembly. Additionally, he was chaplain for Jewish patients at Highland View Hospital, gave monthly lectures at the MONTEFIORE HOME,† and provided bar mitzvah lessons for the deaf and mentally retarded. Genuth married Anne Einhorn, daughter of Rabbi Henry Einhorn of New Haven, on 2 Feb. 1929. They had 3 children: Saul, Phyllis, and Esther.

**GEORGE, CLAYBORNE** (26 Mar. 1888–24 Dec. 1970), councilman and Civil Service Commission member, was born in Surry, VA, to Bolling T. and Cornelia Brown George. He received his bachelor's degree from Howard in 1915 and graduated from that law school in 1917. George served in France as a 1st lt. in World War I. In 1920 he received his master's in law from Boston Univ., was admitted to the Ohio Bar that year, and began practice in Cleveland. He became active in politics and the local NAACP, serving as president from 1924–26. He ran unsuccessfully for city council in 1925, then established the East End Political Club as a political base, becoming an advocate of independent politics for the black community. George successfully ran for city council in 1927, 1929, and 1931; with LAWRENCE O. PAYNE and LEROY N. BUNDY he constituted the "black triumvirate" on the council, using political disputes and power struggles to make gains for the black community. George became a Republican ward leader in 1930. In Aug. 1933 he resigned from the council to run for municipal court judge, losing; but in 1934 Mayor HARRY L. DAVIS appointed him to the Civil Service Commission, where he served until 1969. In Jan. 1970 he retired from law practice. He was a founder of the John M. Harlan Law Club, first chairman of the Negro College Fund in Cleveland, and 3-term president of the Central Areas Community Council. George and his first wife, Enola, had a daughter, Hossie Gilchrist. Enola George died in 1941. He married ZELMA WATSON GEORGE in 1944.

Obsequies in Memory of Clayborne George, March 26, 1888–December 24, 1970 (1970).

**GEORGE, ZELMA WATSON** (8 Dec. 1903–3 July 1994), became a symbol of African American achievement in several fields, ranging from operatic diva to United Nations diplomat. A native of Hearn, TX, she was the daughter of Samuel and Lena Thomas Watson. Moving with her family to Chicago, she earned a sociology degree from the Univ. of Chicago and studied voice at the American Conservatory of Music. Later she added advanced degrees in personnel administration and sociology from New York Univ. After experience as a social worker in Illinois and a dean at Tennessee State Univ., she married and moved to Los Angeles, where she founded and directed the Avalon Community Ctr. (1937–42). As her first marriage ended in divorce, she obtained a Rockefeller Foundation grant to study African American music. Coming to Cleveland to examine the JOHN G. WHITE Collection of the CLEVELAND PUBLIC LIBRARY,† she met attorney CLAYBORNE GEORGE, whom she married in 1944. She wrote a musical drama based upon her research, "Chariot's A'Comin!", which was telecast by WEWS-TV† in 1949. That year George also assumed the title role in Gian-Carlo Menotti's opera, *The Medium,* at Karamu Theater (see KARAMU HOUSE†). She was selected by Menotti himself to repeat her triumph in an off-Broadway revival of the work where, as an African American appearing in a role not written for one per se, she was likely New York's first example of nontraditional casting. During the 1950s George was asked to serve on several government committees at the national level, culminating in a world lecture tour as good-will ambassador and an appointment as U.S. alternate delegate to the United Nations General Assembly (1960–61). From 1966–74 she served as director of the CLEVELAND JOB CORPS.† Following her retirement and the death of her husband, she lectured, wrote, and taught at CUYAHOGA COMMUNITY COLLEGE.† Among numerous honors were the Dag Hammerskjold Award, the Edwin T. Dahlberg Peace Award, and selection by the Greater Cleveland Women's History Committee as one of the "Women Who Shaped Cleveland." A resident of SHAKER HTS.,† she died childless. —J.M./J.V.

Zelma George Papers, WRHS.

**GERBER, SAMUEL R., M.D.** (22 Aug. 1898–16 May 1987), modernized the office of the Cuyahoga County Coroner during his long tenure (1937–15 Dec. 1986, afterwards, coroner emeritus) and contributed to such celebrated cases as the TORSO MURDERS† and the SHEPPARD MURDER CASE.† He was honored as Mr. Coroner of North America by the International Assn. of Coroners and Medical Examiners (1976). Gerber was born in Hagerstown, MD, to Bessie (Nachenson) and Julius H. Gerber, and studied at Valparaiso Univ. before enrolling at Cincinnati Eclectic Medical College, where he graduated in 1922. After an internship and residency in New York City, Gerber served as a cruise ship physician, and then had a private practice in Scott, OH, in Van Wert County, where he was elected mayor.

Gerber came to Cleveland in 1925 as a member of the city's Department of Health and Welfare, first as physician of the Warrensville Workhouse and, 3 years later, of the city's parochial schools. For 15 years he also maintained a private practice. In March 1933 Gerber was named physician in charge of the Wayfarers Lodge. Although he lost his first bid for coroner on the Democratic ticket in 1934, he won 13 consecutive elections thereafter. In 1949 Gerber graduated from the Cleveland Marshall Law School of CLEVELAND STATE UNIV.† and passed the bar, becoming qualified to practice before the U.S. Supreme Court (1955) and the U.S. District Courts (1961). He served on the faculty of the medical school of Western Reserve Univ. (WRU), as associate professor of legal medicine (1952–67), and of CASE WESTERN RESERVE UNIV.,† as asst. clinical professor of legal medicine (1967–81) and professor emeritus (1981–87). Gerber presided over the GREATER CLEVELAND SAFETY COUNCIL† and the medical-legal committee of the ACADEMY OF MEDICINE OF CLEVELAND.†

Gerber was first married on 4 Oct. 1926 to Myrtle M. Norcross. They divorced in 1935. His second marriage was to Alma Lee Quartullo on 1 Mar. 1939; the couple divorced in 1948. They had one daughter, Roberta Lee.—J.M.

Gerber, Samuel R. *Statements and Exhibits of S. R. Gerber, Coroner, Cuyahoga County, Ohio: Hearings* (1975).

**GERFEN, ELIZABETH H.** (1901–14 June 1984), nicknamed Tante Litz, chaired the foreign language department at LAUREL SCHOOL† (1940s–71) and was known as "La Grande Dame de E. 115th Street" for her activism on behalf of UNIV. CIRCLE† residents. Gerfen was born in Gibsonburg, OH, to immigrants from Alsace, France, who originally spelled their name Gerven. She graduated from the Western College for Women at Oxford, OH, and also studied at the Sorbonne, Paris. While teaching French and Spanish at Laurel School (1939–71), Gerfen designed the school's first language lab (1950s), pioneering that concept in the area. In 1987 the school named its new language lab for Gerfen. She led popular tours to Europe and served on the boards of *La Maison Francaise* and *Le Cercle des Conferences Francaises.* After retiring in 1971, Gerfen worked on her memoirs while living in Aix-en-Provence for a year. She also served as substitute teacher and did translations, being fluent in German as well as French.

A single woman, Gerfen lived on E. 115th St. in Univ. Circle from 1939 until her death. In the 1970s and 1980s, she fought the development of UNIV. HOSPITALS† and other institutions which encroached on her home (a historic landmark) and other residential properties. Gerfen was a founder of the Univ. Circle Tenants' Union (1972). As an appointee to the board of UNIV. CIRCLE, INC.,† Gerfen complained about neglected housing stock and lack of attention to tenants' concerns.—J.M.

**GERSTENBERGER, HENRY JOHN** (9 Jan. 1881–24 June 1954), a pediatrician who helped establish Babies & Childrens Hospital and develop SMA (Synthetic Milk Adapted), an artificial milk formula, was born in Cleveland to John H. and Clara E. Schake Gerstenberger. He received his M.D. from Western Reserve Univ. Medical School in 1903. Encouraged to study pediatrics abroad, Gerstenberger went to Berlin and Vienna, but his studies were interrupted when he contracted tuberculosis. Gerstenberger returned to Cleveland in 1906 as head of the pediatrics department at City Hospital (Metropolitan General Hospital); director of the Tuberculosis Contact Clinic, the first of its kind in the Western Hemisphere; and professor of pediatrics at Western Reserve Univ. Medical School. Recognizing the need for inner city infant and child care, he was instrumental in creating the Bureau of Child Hygiene as part of Cleveland's Dept. of Health. When Babies' Dispensary & Hospital formally opened in 1911, Gerstenberger was its first medical director. Located on Euclid Ave. near E. 30th St., the dispensary was open 6 days a week, with physicians donating their service. Partly financed by income from the production of SMA

formula, Babies & Childrens Hospital relocated on Univ. Hospitals' new campus in 1925. As professor of pediatrics, Gerstenberger found that a combined treatment of cod liver oil and ultraviolet light eased symptoms of spasmophilia, a convulsion caused by reaction to slight amounts of sunshine in springtime by children who suffer from rickets. Gerstenberger married Else B. Schweitzer on 28 Mar. 1913, and had 4 daughters: Paula Ruth, Else Louise, Gretel, and Katherine.

**GETZ, HESTER ADELIA** (23 March 1869–4 June 1948), who began her lifelong work as a florist as a child, opened a shop on EUCLID AVE.† and Huntington St. with Anna Westman (d. ca. 1911) about 1902. She continued to run Westman & Getz, Florists, until retiring in 1941. Getz was born in Columbus, OH, the youngest of 4 children of Israel S. and Margaret Shaffer Getz. She attended public schools there and began making bouquets and selling them to passersby near state government buildings; she claimed to have had William McKinley (later U.S. president) as a customer. Getz, who owned her own store in Columbus by age 18, came to Cleveland in 1900. Five years after opening their shop, Getz and Westman, in debt and struggling with prejudice against women in business (see BUSINESS, RETAIL†) moved to 5923 Euclid Ave. (Due to their sex, they reportedly had to pay twice the normal security deposit.) The business (which at first served only women) thrived at the new location. Westman & Getz introduced Sunday closings in the floral business and sold pottery and glassware in addition to flowers. Getz chaired the Retail Florists' Exhibition at least 3 times. A member of the advisory council of the CITIZENS' LEAGUE,† she also served on the board of directors, and as vice-president (1930) and treasurer (1931) of the WOMEN'S CITY CLUB,† of which she was a charter member. In her leisure time, Getz, a single woman who resided on Cleveland's east side, pursued travel and photography. She died in Coral Gables, FL, where she moved after retirement. —J.M.

**GIDDINGS, HELEN MARSHALL** (16 May 1870–5 July 1950), osteopathic surgeon, served as president (1934–36) and later chair of the finance and budget committee of the Osteopathic Women's National Assn. She was born in Green Springs, OH, to Frederick S. and Mary Elizabeth Marshall Giddings. Educated at Green Springs Academy, she received her medical degree from the American School of Osteopathy (1899, also called the Kirksdale College of Osteopathy and Surgery) in Kirksdale, MO. Giddings opened a private practice in an office on EUCLID AVE.,† which she later shared with her sister, MARY GIDDINGS (d. 1940), also an osteopathic physician. In addition to the national association, Giddings belonged to local and state osteopathic groups as well as the American Electronic Research Assn. and the American Society of Ophthalmology and Otolaryngology.

Giddings was also active in organizations for women, as a charter member of the WOMEN'S CITY CLUB OF CLEVELAND† and a member of groups such as the LEAGUE OF WOMEN VOTERS,† the Women's Civic Club of Cleveland Hts., the Federation of Women's Clubs on local, state and national levels, and the Women's International League for Peace and Freedom. A Unitarian, she worked with the local VISITING NURSE ASSN.† and LEGAL AID SOCIETY,† was a life member of the CLEVELAND MUSEUM OF ART,† and belonged to the Cleveland Foreign Affairs Council and the Consumers' League. Unmarried, Giddings resided with her sister in Cleveland Hts., and later in the New Amsterdam Hotel in Cleveland.—J.M.

**GIDDINGS, JOSHUA REED** (6 Oct. 1795–27 May 1864) represented Cleveland for about half of his 20-year tenure as one of the most renowned antislavery leaders in the U.S. Congress. Born in Tioga Point (later Athens), PA, in infancy he moved with his parents, Joshua and Elizabeth Pease Giddings, to Canandaigua, NY. In 1805 the family moved again to Ashtabula County, OH, where Giddings completed his common-school education and saw service in the WAR OF 1812. In 1819 he married the former Laura Waters and 2 years later, after reading law with Elisha Whittlesey of Canfield, OH, was admitted to the bar. He opened a law office in the Ashtabula County seat of Jefferson, taking Benjamin F. Wade as a partner and serving a term (1826) in the Ohio House of Representatives. Not long after his conversion to the antislavery movement, Giddings was elected as a Whig in 1838 to succeed Whittlesey in the U.S. House of Representatives. He joined a small group of like-minded Congressmen in the Washington boarding house of Mrs. Spriggs and in 1842 was censured by the House for offering a series of resolutions in support of the slave mutineers on the coastwise slaving vessel *Creole*. Immediately resigning his seat, Giddings returned to the WESTERN RESERVE† and was vindicated by an overwhelming reelection. Congressional redistricting brought Cleveland and Cuyahoga County into his district from 1844–53. During that period, Giddings left the Whigs for the Free Soil party and sponsored national Free Soil conventions in Cleveland to formulate policy and strategy in 1849 and 1851. Following the Kansas-Nebraska Act of 1854, he helped draft the "Appeal of the Independent Democrats" and assisted in the formation of the Republican party. Although denied renomination in 1858, Giddings secured the affirmation of the principles of the Declaration of Independence in the 1860 Republican national platform by threatening a one-man bolt of the convention. In 1858 he published *The Exiles of Florida,* which was followed in 1864 by *History of the Rebellion: Its Authors and Causes.* Appointed U.S. Consul General to Canada by Pres. Lincoln in 1861, Giddings died in Montreal. He was survived by his wife and 5 children: Comfort, Joseph, Lura Maria, Grotius, and Laura Ann.—J.V.

Stewart, James Brewer. *Joshua R. Giddings and the Tactics of Radical Politics* (1970).

**GIDDINGS, MARY** (d. 9 Oct. 1940) was an osteopathic physician, a charter member of the WOMEN'S CITY CLUB,† and the sister of osteopath HELEN MARSHALL GIDDINGS.

Born in Green Springs, OH, to Frederick S. and Mary Elizabeth (Marshall) Giddings, Mary attended Green Springs Academy and studied piano and voice. She worked as a secretary and public stenographer. Mary received her D.O. in osteopathic medicine in 1905 from the American School of Osteopathy. She established a private general practice in osteopathy.

Mary was a member of the Osteopathic Women's National Assn., and was national program chairman in 1936; the Cleveland Osteopathic Society; the Ohio Society of Osteopathic Physicians and Surgeons; and the American Osteopathic Assn.

Mary belonged to the Unitarian church. She died in Hamilton, OH, and her remains placed in Cincinnati.—T.B.

**GILCHRIST, MARIE EMILIE** (4 Jan. 1893–9 Nov. 1989) was a local poet whose poems appeared in numerous periodicals, including the *Nation,* the *Saturday Review of Literature,* the *New Yorker,* the *Forum,* and the *Book of Rhymers' Club.* Gilchrist was also a researcher for several years and, later, editor for *Reader's Digest.*

Born in Vermillion to Joseph and Emilie (Martin) Gilchrist, Marie attended Froebel School, graduated from HATHAWAY BROWN SCHOOL† (1910), attended Western Reserve Univ., then graduated from Smith College (1916). Gilchrist worked for the CLEVELAND PUBLIC LIBRARY† until 1918, then for an insurance office, followed by publicity service for the American Red Cross. She returned to Smith College where she held a fellowship in English (1920–21), and received her M.A. (1921). She worked in the Hampshire Bookshop at Northampton, MA, during 1922, then returned to Cleveland.

In 1926 Gilchrist rejoined the Cleveland Public Library as assistant in the Stevenson Room for Young People, where she helped to organize and direct the Stevenson Room Poetry Group in 1927. After a year in the Stevenson Room, Gilchrist became an assistant in the Popular Library section. Gilchrist left the library in 1930.

Gilchrist's first book of poems, *Wide Pastures,* was published by Macmillan in 1926. Her contribution to the book, *Writing Poetry,* published by Houghton Mifflin in 1932, contained work from the Stevenson Room Poetry Group. In 1942 Gilchrist wrote *The Story of the Great Lakes* about shipping on the Great Lakes, during the period of 1835–1905.

Never married, Gilchrist retired to the MARGARET WAGNER HOME† in CLEVELAND HTS.† Gilchrist is buried in Maple Hill Cemetery in Munson Twp.—T.B.

**GILLESPIE, CHESTER K.** (4 Apr. 1897–22 Mar. 1985), lawyer and Republican politician known as "Mr. Civil Rights," and part of Cleveland's black community agitating for immediate integration, was born in Home City, OH, to Warren and Lulu Trail Gillespie. The family moved to Cleveland about 1909. After attending Ohio State Univ., Gillespie earned a law degree from Baldwin-Wallace College Law School in 1920. He was asst. law director for Cleveland in 1921 and soon became the leading civil-rights attorney in Cleveland, bringing antidiscrimination suits against theater, restaurant, and amusement park owners.

Many of Gillespie's antidiscrimination suits were unsuccessful, influencing him as he served 3 terms in the Ohio general assembly (1933–34, 1939–40, 1943–44). He sponsored legislation extending Ohio's civil-rights law to prohibit discrimination in retail establishments, and also included in the liquor law a provision making racial discrimination grounds for revoking a liquor license. He assisted Central State Univ. in Wilberforce, OH; was president of the local NAACP (1936–37); and along with fellow attorney CLAYBORNE GEORGE, led the fight for downtown office space for black lawyers and other professionals in the 1930s and 1940s.

Gillespie was a member of the Republican State Central Committee and a delegate to national conventions (1948, 1968). He was appointed to the State Board of Education in 1963; later winning election to complete that term. Gillespie retired from law and politics in 1971 and moved to Los Angeles. On 27 Sept. 1924, he married Dorothy Thomas. Both were members of the CLEVELAND COUNCIL ON WORLD AFFAIRS.†

Chester K. Gillespie Scrapbooks, WRHS.

**GILMOUR, RICHARD** (24 Sept. 1824–13 Apr. 1891), second bishop of Cleveland, was born in Dumbarton, Scotland, to John and Marian Gilmour. His family emigrated to Nova Scotia, then to Pennsylvania, when he was a child. Gilmour, of Scotch-Presbyterian background, decided in 1842 to convert to Catholicism and study for the priesthood, completing his studies at Mt. St. Mary Seminary in Emmitsburg, MD. He was ordained on 30 Aug. 1852 and named pastor of St. Mary in Portsmouth, OH. In 1857 he was assigned to St. Patrick Church in Cincinnati, starting a model school. Gilmour translated a popular Bible history, winning papal commendation, and authored readers used in Catholic schools. From 1868–69 he was a seminary professor before being transferred to St. Joseph Church in Dayton. Gilmour was consecrated bishop of Cleveland on 14 Apr. 1872.

Gilmour defended Catholics' rights against prejudice, founding and subsidizing the *Catholic Universe* newspaper in 1874. He also defended PAROCHIAL SCHOOLS† when in 1877 the Cuyahoga County auditor declared them taxable and demanded the buildings be sold at auction, resulting in a bitter though successful 6-year court battle. Gilmour endorsed church schools and established a school board to maintain uniformity and high standards. He expanded services to the poor and sick, with St. Ann's Asylum & Maternity Home, ST. ALEXIS HOSPITAL,† and ST. JOHN HOSPITAL† founded with his support. Nationally, Gilmour served as an expert on the legal aspects of church property. He traveled to Florida to recuperate from deteriorating health in Mar. 1891, dying in St. Augustine in April.

**GINN, FRANK HADLEY** (25 Feb. 1868–6 Feb. 1938), corporation lawyer and patron of music and art, was born in Fremont, OH, to Francis Marion and Millicent Ophelia Pope Ginn. He earned his Ph.B. from Kenyon College (1890). Coming to Cleveland in 1890, Ginn studied law and was admitted to the Ohio Bar in 1892. In 1899 he became a member of Blandin, Rice & Ginn, which joined with Kline, Tolles & Morley in 1913 to form TOLLES, HOGSETT, GINN & MORLEY.† Appearing in court infrequently, Ginn worked in his office building a wide holding of stocks and connections. He was reportedly an officer or on the board of more companies than anyone else in Ohio, although he made few public appearances and had little open involvement in politics. However, he was intimately involved with many of Cleveland's powerful financial figures, including the Van Sweringen brothers.

Ginn was an active music and art patron, although most of his activities received no public recognition as he studiously avoided publicity. Ginn was a founder and officer of the MUSICAL ARTS ASSN.† and a prime mover in founding the CLEVELAND ORCHESTRA† and CLEVELAND STRING QUARTET,† as well as being a financial supporter. He was chairman of the building committee for SEVERANCE HALL† and on the Cleveland Committee of the NORTHERN OHIO OPERA ASSN.† Privately, Ginn gathered a large collection of paintings and tapestries. Ginn married Cornelia Root on 25 June 1899 and had 2 sons, Francis and Alexander, and 2 daughters, Mrs. W. Powell Jones and Barbara Root Ginn.

**GIRDLER, TOM MERCER** (19 May 1877–4 Feb. 1965), steel industrialist and labor and New Deal critic, was born in Silver Creek Twp., Clark County, IN, to Lewis and Elizabeth Mercer Girdler, graduating from Lehigh Univ. (1901) in mechanical engineering. Girdler worked for Buffalo Forge (1901–02), Oliver Iron & Steel (1902–05), Colorado Fuel (1905–07), Atlantic Steel (1908–14), and Jones & Laughlin Steel (1914–29) before accepting an offer from CYRUS S. EATON and WM. G. MATHER to assist negotiations leading to the formation of the REPUBLIC STEEL CORP.† in Cleveland in 1929, then become the company's first president and board chairman. Republic became a major producer of light alloys, with profits exceeding $87 million between 1936–43. Girdler first supported Pres. Roosevelt's Natl. Industrial Recovery Act, establishing a representation plan for Republic's employees, but when the Wagner Act outlawed such plans and promoted negotiations with regular unions, Girdler lost all affinity for the New Deal. He refused to bargain with the CIO; though conceding the need for collective bargaining, Girdler refused to do so by government edict. Republic's refusal to bargain and allow union elections resulted in the LITTLE STEEL STRIKE† in May 1937. In 1942, under order of the War Labor Board, elections were held and the CIO organized Republic. Girdler resigned from Republic's presidency in 1937 but continued as board chairman, later becoming board chairman and chief executive officer of Vultee and Consolidated, engineering their merger in 1943. He retired from Republic in 1956. Girdler was married four times: first to Bessie (Mary Elizabeth) Hayes (d. 1917) in 1903; Clara Astley; Lillian Snowden in 1924; and Helen Brennan in 1942. Girdler had two sons: Tom M., Jr. and Joseph; and two daughters, Mary Elizabeth and Jane. He died at his estate in Easton, MD.

Girdler, Tom M. *Boot Straps* (1943).

**GITLIN, DAVID** (14 July 1924–20 Mar. 1994) was a doctor and social activist known for his advocacy work on environmental issues.

Gitlin was born in Brooklyn, NY, the son of Isidor and Rebecca (Chase) Gitlin. He graduated from City College of New York and earned a medical degree at the Univ. of Lausanne in Switzerland. He began practicing medicine in MAPLE HTS.† before moving his practice to Westgate in FAIRVIEW PARK.†

Gitlin's involvement with environmental issues grew out of his career as a doctor, and specifically his work as an allergist. He spoke out against chemical lawn sprays, nuclear power, air pollution, and smoking, and is said to have helped start the movement against smoking on planes. He served on several boards and committees relating to environmental issues, and was an officer of the Citizens for Clean Air and Water and the Northeast Ohio Area Conservation Coalition. Gitlin also served on environmental committees for both BROOK PARK† and BEREA.†

In the 1960s, he played an important role in forming an advocacy movement for Jews in the Soviet Union and was credited with convincing Jewish organizations to take a stand on that issue. He was also a social activist in several areas, including civil rights and housing discrimination, and worked with such organizations as the Berea Area Council on Human Relations.

He married Christine Miles in Cuyahoga County on 6 Mar. 1960; they had 3 children: Donald, Deborah, and Darryl. Gitlin was cremated.—D.R.

**GITTELSON, BENJAMIN** (1853–1 Jan. 1932), rabbi and scholar, was born in Lithuania, son of Judah Leib Gittelson. He was descended from a long line of rabbis, but fatherless and impoverished, he wandered from town to town for charitable donations enabling him to receive a traditional yeshiva education. He became rabbi of Avanta in 1878, leaving in 1883 to become rabbi of Trashkun. He remained very poor, because the Jewish community was unable to pay an adequate salary. In 1890, Gittelson was asked to settle in Cleveland by the growing community of Lithuanian Jews in the city, becoming rabbi at Beth Hamidrosh Hagodol, serving that congregation until 1901. He then assumed the pulpit of Oer Chodosh Anshe Sfard and remained its rabbi until his death. Gittelson was a quiet, learned man who eschewed an active communal role among Cleveland's Orthodox Jews. However, his religious knowledge as Cleveland's first rabbinic scholar led him to become the spiritual authority for other small congregations, among them Ohave Emuna Anshe Russia, Shaari Torah, and Agudath Achim. Gittelson provided the community with responsa and discourses on Jewish law and custom. He published 2 scholarly works: *Ha-Poteah ve-ha-Hotem* (New York, 1898), a collection of Talmudic discourses, many given before Cleveland congregations; and *Seder Haggada shel Pesah 'im Be'ur Nagid ve-Nafik* (Jerusalem, 1904), a detailed commentary on the Passover Haggadah. Additionally, he wrote a commentary on the prayerbook, which was never published. Gittelson married Celia "Sippa" Alenik while still in Lithuania. They had 12 children: Louis, Abraham David, Reuben, Rachel (Klein), Rose, Lena, Albert, Minnie (Broida), Jack, Nathan, Sarah, and Rebecca. He is buried in Cleveland's Lansing Cemetery.

**GLASS, MYRON E.** (1 Aug. 1900–16 Dec. 1987), businessman and leader in the Jewish community, was born in Manchester, England, the son of Nathan and Etta Mendelsohn Glass, who came to Cleveland in 1906. He attended public schools and CLEVELAND MARSHALL LAW SCHOOL.† In 1927 Glass incorporated the Texas Distributing Co. with capital of $50,000. He and his partners, Milton and David Myers, established the company offices at 6504 Union Ave., from which it operated a number of gas stations throughout the Cleveland area. At one time Glass was also manager of the Ohio Division of Texaco Inc. After retiring in 1946, he organized the Texby Co., a real estate investment firm. Noted for his leadership in raising money for construction projects, Glass headed Mt. Sinai Hospital's (see MT. SINAI MEDICAL CENTER†) successful fundraising drive to build a new 12-story addition while serving as president of its Board of Trustees, 1952–59. He also was a leader in raising money for building PARK SYNAGOGUE,† and Glass Auditorium was named in his honor. During his presidency of the JEWISH COMMUNITY FEDERATION,† 1962–64, construction began on the federation's new headquarters building at E. 18th and Euclid Ave. He received their Charles Eisenman Award in 1965 for leadership in the health, welfare, and religious life of the community.

Glass and his wife, Rose, were married in 1926, and they had a son, Herbert. A resident of BRATENAHL† and Palm Springs, CA, he died at his California home and was buried at Park Cemetery in Cleveland.—M.S.

**GLASSER, OTTO** (2 Sept. 1895–11 Dec. 1964), pioneer in radiology, radium therapy, and nuclear medicine, was born in Saarbrucken, Germany, to Alexander and Lina Gentsch Glasser. He received his Ph.D. in physics from the Univ. of Frieberg (Germany) in 1919. In 1922 Glasser married Emmy von Eherenberg and emigrated to the U.S., serving at Howard Kelly Hospital, Baltimore (1922–23);

the Dept. of Biophysical Research, Cleveland Clinic (1923–24); and New York Postgraduate Medical School, Columbia (1925–27), before returning to Cleveland in 1927 as head of the Dept. of Biophysics at the CLEVELAND CLINIC FOUNDATION† (1926–61); and as emeritus consultant from 1961–64.

In collaboration with Dr. U. V. Portmann and Valentine B. Seitz, Glasser developed the condenser dosimeter to measure x-rays and radiation. Following World War II, he was interested in the medical applications of radioactive isotopes, being one of the first scientists to measure radioactive fallout and helping standardize the measurement of radioactivity. In addition, Glasser, with Dr. Irvine Page, worked in hemorrhagic shock and arterial transfusions; was one of the first to work in aviation medicine; and with Dr. GEO. W. CRILE, SR., simulated "bends" in animals to test physiologic results and treatments. Glasser was the world's authority on Wilhelm Conrad Roentgen, the discoverer of x-rays, publishing a life of Roentgen in 1931 in German and in English in 1933 and 1934. He published over 100 scientific articles and several books and received many honors. Otto and Emmy Glasser had a daughter, Hannelore Glasser.

Otto Glasser Papers, Archives, Cleveland Clinic Foundation.

**GLEASON, WILLIAM J.** (2 June 1846–20 Jan. 1905), volunteer CIVIL WAR† soldier and first president of the Soldiers & Sailors Monument Commission, was born in County Clare, Ireland. His parents, Patrick and Margaret Gleason, moved to Vermont when he was 6 months old, and shortly thereafter to Cleveland. Fifteen when the Civil War broke out, he left his job as a printer's "devil" for the *PLAIN DEALER,†* bought a drum, and drilled for 3 months with troops gathering at Camp Taylor in Cleveland. The following year he lied about his age and enlisted in the 60TH OHIO VOLUNTEER INFANTRY,† serving 1 week before his parents obtained a writ of habeas corpus and brought him home. His parents allowed him to join the 29th Regiment, Ohio Natl. Guard, Co. E, as a drummer boy. He continued working at the *Plain Dealer* but ran away to enlist in the 150TH OHIO VOLUNTEER INFANTRY REGIMENT† at 17, serving in the defenses of Washington, DC, in the summer of 1864. After the war, Gleason worked as a compositor in the printing trade and in the insurance business. He served on the board of elections and as secretary of the CLEVELAND PUBLIC LIBRARY† board, Cleveland controller, president of the Irish Natl. League, and nationally as a staff member of the commander of the Grand Army of the Republic.

He also served on the Soldiers & Sailors Monument Commission, 1894–1905.

On 15 Feb. 1870, Gleason married Margaret Gleason. They had 7 children: Agnes, Katherine, Alma, Florence, Charles, Edward, and William. Gleason is buried in Calvary Cemetery.

Gleason, William J. *History of the Cuyahoga County Soldiers and Sailors Monument* (1894).

**GLENNAN, THOMAS K.** (8 Sept. 1905–11 Apr. 1995) was a leading figure in the national scientific community, as well as president of Case Institute of Technology (see CASE WESTERN RESERVE UNIV.†).

The son of Richard H. and Margaret Laing Glennan, Thomas was born in Enderlin, SD, but raised in Montana and Wisconsin. He began college at Eau Clair Teachers College before transferring to Yale College, where he received his bachelor's degree in electrical engineering in 1927.

After college, Glennan moved to Hollywood, CA, where, for 8 years, he worked for the Sam Goldwyn and Paramount Studios. He then moved east to work for Ansco Corp. in Binghamton, NY. The war years found him at Columbia Univ.'s Division of War Research.

In 1947 he became president of Case Institute of Technology. During his eighteen years as president, however, he twice took leaves of absence for government-sponsored scientific assignments. In 1950–52 he served on the U.S. Atomic Energy Commission and from 1958–61 he was the first administrator of the National Aeronautics and Space Administration.

During his tenure at Case, 12 new buildings were erected on campus, graduate students increased tenfold, and the faculty by 60%. In 1960 Case admitted women for the first time. Glennan, together with Western Reserve Univ. president JOHN MILLIS, laid the foundation for the merger of the two institutions.

He announced his retirement at the end of the 1964–65 term, but remained with Case until a permanent successor was chosen in 1966. He then moved to Reston, VA, where he headed the Associated Universities, a research consortium.

Glennan received honorary degrees from JOHN CARROLL UNIV.† and FENN COLLEGE.† In 1969 CWRU honored him by naming a building for him, the Glennan Space Engineering Laboratories.—J.T.

**GLOVER, VERA ABAGAIL** (24 Nov. 1897–24 Sept. 1988), public health nurse, directed the nursing services for the Cuyahoga County Health Department from 1937–65. In 1951 she was elected the first woman and first non-physician president of the Ohio Public Health Assn. Glover was born in Van Wert, OH, to Della Squibb and Isaac Porter Glover. She attended school in Scott, OH, where she worked as a post office clerk, and Van Wert, OH, where she graduated in 1915. She received a nursing degree from Lakeside Hospital Training School in 1920 and later attended the Univ. of Michigan (1923), Wittenberg College (1926–27), Cleveland College (1930s), and Fenn College (1939–41). Glover received a B.S. in Nursing (1942) from Western Reserve Univ.'s Frances Payne Bolton School of Nursing, with a certificate in Public Health Nursing.

Before coming to Cleveland, Glover worked for county health departments in Van Wert (1921–25), Dayton (1925–28), and Hillsboro, OH (May 1928–June 1929), and the Ohio Department of Health (Jan.–May 1928). In July 1929 she joined the Cleveland Department of Health and the next April, the Cuyahoga County Department of Health, where she remained until retiring. A member of the American Nurses Assn., she became the county's Supervisor of Nurses in 1937. A single woman, Glover lived in CLEVELAND HTS., before moving to Canton, OH, in 1983. Glover was buried in Woodland Union Cemetery in Canton.—J.M.

**GOETZ, BERNICE** (4 May 1909–30 Dec.1958) was not content with roles traditionally open to women. Though a secretary by profession, she became famous for her expeditions into the jungles of Central and South America.

Born in Cleveland to Henry G. and Sophia Goetz, Bernice graduated from West Commerce High School before securing a job with the Brooks and Stafford insurance agency. She saved as much of her salary and vacation time as she could, and in 1931 was ready for her first expedition, to explore ruins in the Mexican jungles.

That first trip provided her with an additional resource for funding future expeditions. She found that she enjoyed lecturing, and she became a popular public speaker. She also found herself involved in teaching poetry through a program at the CLEVELAND PUBLIC LIBRARY.† Later she worked for the Red Cross and for an oil exploration firm in order to facilitate further travel.

Ultimately she was to make 13 personally planned and self-financed trips to South America, exploring regions in Peru, Brazil, Bolivia, Columbia, Ecuador, and Guatemala.

Each visit increased her popularity as a lecturer, and she was invited by local newspapers, as well as *National Geographic* magazine, to write of her travels. She also brought back to Cleveland many artifacts, donating them to the Cleveland Public

Library and the CLEVELAND MUSEUM OF NATURAL HISTORY.†

Goetz died from cancer shortly after returning from an expedition. She is buried in Brooklyn Hts. Cemetery.—J.T.

**GOFF, FREDERICK H.** (15 Dec. 1858–14 Mar. 1923), lawyer, banker, and civic leader, was born in Blackbury, IL, to Frederick C. and Catherine Brown Goff. He moved with his family to Cleveland. Goff earned a Ph.B. from the Univ. of Michigan (1881), then worked in the Cleveland Law Library, studied law, and was admitted to the Ohio Bar in 1883 or 1884.

Goff worked primarily in corporate law, specializing in reorganization and financial problems. In 1908 Goff became president of the Cleveland Trust Co., increasing its offices from 15 to 52, its depositors from 70,000 to 397,000, and its resources from $30 million to $176 million by 1923.

As a lawyer and banker helping Clevelanders plan their estates, Goff developed the living and community trusts. A living trust conveys property to a trustee prior to death, specifying its management. A community trust places property in a central community fund administered by trustees. Goff helped establish the CLEVELAND FOUNDATION† community trust in 1914.

Goff was mayor of GLENVILLE† in 1903, ending gambling at the local racetrack and endorsing Glenville's annexation to Cleveland. He represented the CLEVELAND ELECTRIC RAILWAY CO.† during 1907 negotiations with Mayor TOM L. JOHNSON over the street railway controversy. During World War I, he served on the MAYOR'S ADVISORY WAR COMMITTEE† and was appointed by Pres. Woodrow Wilson as vice-chairman of the War Finance Corp.'s capital issues committee. He served as director or officer in railroad, manufacturing, and service companies. He married Frances Southworth on 16 Oct. 1894, and they had three children: Frederika, William S., and Frances M. Goff died in Cleveland and was buried in Lake View Cemetery.

**GOLDBLATT, HARRY** (14 Mar. 1891–6 Jan. 1977), internationally recognized for his research in high blood pressure, was born in Iowa, the son of Phillip and Jennie Spitz Goldblatt. He grew up in Canada, received a B.A. from McGill Univ., and graduated from its medical school in 1916. After serving at Royal Victoria Hospital, Montreal, the Medical Reserve Corps of the U.S. Army (1917–18), and as resident pathologist of Lakeside Hospital, Cleveland, Goldblatt continued his education in Europe. From 1924–27 he was asst. professor of pathology at Western Reserve Univ., and assoc. professor from 1927–35. Between 1935–46 he was professor of experimental pathology and director of WRU's Institute of Pathology. After 7 years as director of medical research at Cedars of Lebanon Hospital, Los Angeles, Goldblatt returned to Cleveland, becoming Mt. Sinai's director of laboratories. From 1961 he was director of the Louis D. Beaumont Research Laboratories.

Goldblatt experimented in the early 1930s to discover the cause of essential hypertension, learning that clamping off part of the main arteries to the kidneys caused high blood pressure. Goldblatt tried to prove that renin, in normal kidneys, was the origin of essential hypertension. In 1965, with Dr. Erwin Haas, he isolated 4,000 ampoules of renin and Goldblatt units became the international standard of measurement of human renin. Later, with Drs. Haas and Sharad Deodhar, Goldblatt produced antirenin with acetylated homologous renin. Goldblatt received many honors, most significantly the Scientific Achievement Award of the American Medical Assn. in 1976. Because of the implications of his work, the American Heart Assn. established the Dr. Harry Goldblatt Fellowship. Goldblatt married Jeanne Rea on 25 June 1929; they had 2 children, David and Peter. Goldblatt died in Cleveland.

Goldblatt File, Stanley A. Ferguson Archives, Univ. Hospitals.

**GOLDENBOGEN, ELLEN MAY DURSCHIAG** (1890-?), attorney, was elected president of the city council of LAKEWOOD† (1928–29), among the first women to hold similar office elsewhere in Ohio. During her term of office, under Mayor Edward Wiegand, the suburb built a new fire station and a shelter in Lakewood Park, among other accomplishments. Goldenbogen was born in Cleveland to Christine Bozold and Ernest A. Durschiag. She attended Cleveland Public Schools and the Cleveland School of Education, and received a degree from the Cleveland Law School. She was first elected to the Lakewood City Council in 1926. With a law practice in Lakewood, Goldenbogen unsuccessfully entered the mayoral race in 1929 as Lakewood's second woman mayoral candidate (the first being BERNICE SECREST PYKE).

In 1922 Goldenbogen married railroad attorney Norman Edward Goldenbogen; the couple lived in Lakewood. A member of the CLEVELAND BAR ASSN.,† Goldenbogen was elected president of the newly formed Lakewood Bar Assn. in 1928. Other club affiliations included the Republican Women of Ohio, the LEAGUE OF WOMEN VOTERS† (second vice-president in 1927), the YOUNG WOMEN'S CHRISTIAN ASSN.,† the WOMEN'S

CITY CLUB OF CLEVELAND,† and the Lakewood Women's Club.—J.M.

**GOLDHAMER, SAMUEL** (1884–28 Feb. 1982) was the executive director of the JEWISH COMMUNITY FEDERATION† (JCF) from 1907–48 who initiated a community fund to expedite fundraising, a concept which spread throughout the country. Goldhamer was born in Cleveland to Max and Lena (Keller) Goldhamer. He attended Brownell School and CENTRAL HIGH SCHOOL.† Goldhamer worked for various clothing firms before joining the JCF as its first paid employee (a clerk) in 1907. Under Goldhamer's direction, the number of agencies represented by the JCF surpassed 100 by the 1940s.

On 5 Oct. 1907 Goldhamer married Lena Klein (d.1976); the couple lived in SHAKER HTS.† with sons Morton L., Walter M., and Robert H. In his free time, Goldhamer traveled and painted in watercolors and oils. Goldhamer died at his home.—J.M.

Goldhamer, S. *Why Doncha Write a Book? A Half-Century of Experience in Jewish Communal Life* (1963).

**GOLDMAN, SOLOMON** (18 Aug. 1893–14 May 1953), religious leader and educator, was born in Kozin, Poland, to Abraham Abba and Jeanette Grossman Goldman. He was brought to New York as a child and received a traditional Jewish education at Orthodox Yitzchak Elchanan Yeshiva, then entered the Conservative Jewish Theological Seminary. He was ordained in 1918, coming to Cleveland's B'NAI JESHURUN,† increasing its membership and making it Conservative. But internal resistance to his attempts at making it a Jewish center led Goldman to resign in 1923. He accepted the pulpit at ANSHE EMETH,† which less than a year earlier dedicated the Cleveland Jewish Ctr., which Goldman made a focus for the Jews of GLENVILLE,† and the largest such institution in the U.S.

Goldman was opposed by the Orthodox within the congregation, who challenged him concerning mixed seating for men and women and appealed to the Union of Orthodox Rabbis, which called Goldman to a rabbinical court. Goldman refused, since he and his congregation were Conservative. The dissidents then filed complaints in court, which refused to intervene, allowing mixed seating to remain. The dissidents joined OHEB ZEDEK.†

Goldman advocated Hebrew education, collaborated with A. H. FRIEDLAND in developing educational materials, and supported CLEVELAND HEBREW SCHOOLS† and the BUREAU OF JEWISH EDUCATION.† Goldman also had a national reputation in the Zionist movement. He was a Biblical scholar and published several works, including a pageant, "Romance of a People," performed at the Chicago Century of Progress Exposition in 1934.

Goldman married Alice M. Lipkowitz on 23 June 1908. They had two children, Geulah Judith and Naomi Ramah. He left Cleveland in 1929 to become Rabbi of Congregation Anshe Emet in Chicago, serving there until his death.

**GOLDNER, JACOB H.** (8 Aug. 1871–30 Dec. 1949), pastor of EUCLID AVE. CHRISTIAN CHURCH† for 45 years, one of the longest DISCIPLES OF CHRIST† pastorates, was born in Beaver, PA, to George and Caroline Vogt Goldner. He graduated from Hiram College in 1896. While a student he ministered at Austintown Church; his first full pastorate, at Chagrin Falls Church (1896–98), was followed by graduate studies at the Univ. of Chicago Divinity School. Before graduating he accepted the pastorate of Euclid Ave. Christian Church. The 400-seat structure was soon too small for the increasing membership, so a 1,100-seat church was dedicated in 1908. Soon after beginning at the church, Goldner embarked on an experiment in personal evangelism, calling on people within the community. Hundreds were received into membership, and church evangelism replaced revival meetings.

Dr. Goldner was on the committee organizing the Cleveland Fed. of Churches (later Cleveland Church Fed.) and was its president (1921–22). He was president of the Ohio Christian Missionary Society (1920), served as a commissioner of the Assn. for the Promotion of Christian Unity, and in 1924 became president of the Internatl. Convention of the Disciples of Christ. Goldner did graduate work at Harvard (1897) and Western Reserve Univ. (1903). Goldner resigned in 1945, was named pastor emeritus, and acted as ad interim pastor of 7 churches. He died right before his ministry's 50th anniversary celebration. Goldner married Harriet Marks Goldner 10 Aug. 1904 and had 2 sons, Jacob H., Jr., and Gerould R.

**GOLDSMITH, JONATHAN** (1783–1847), a master builder active in Lake County and Cleveland between 1819–43, was born in Milford, CT, the son of Jonathan Gillett and Anna (Beers) Goldsmith. After a brief apprenticeship as a shoemaker, he apprenticed himself to a carpenter-joiner at age 17. He worked in Hebron, CT, and Berkshire County, MA, before moving to Ohio in 1811. Goldsmith's known buildings include 30 homes and commercial buildings in Painesville, another handful around Lake County, and 10 houses in Cleveland. The Cleveland residences, none of which are extant, were all built between 1830–37 on Euclid Ave.

when it was a prime residential street, and were built for prominent citizens such as SHERLOCK J. ANDREWS, PETER WEDDELL, Samuel Cowles, and TRUMAN P. HANDY. All were executed in the late Federal and early Greek Revival styles; some, especially Handy's and Judge Thos. Kelly's homes, were mansions with colossal Ionic porticoes. Goldsmith's apprentice and assistant in Cleveland was his son-in-law CHAS. W. HEARD, who continued to practice architecture in Cleveland until 1876. Goldsmith is better-documented than most early 19th-century master builders, because many of his drawings, as well as account books, contracts, and letters, have survived and are in the WESTERN RESERVE HISTORICAL SOCIETY.† His drawings were included in the Metropolitan Museum's exhibition "The Greek Revival in the U.S." in 1943.

Goldsmith married Abigail Jones ca. 1808. They had ten children: Caroline, Eliza, Lucia, Frank, Anna, Gillett, Delos, and Augusta; two other children died in infancy. Goldsmith died in Painesville and was buried in the Painesville Township Cemetery.

Hitchcock, Elizabeth G. *Jonathan Goldsmith, Master Builder in the Western Reserve* (1980).

**GOLLMANN, JULIUS** (unknown–5 Aug. 1898) was a German painter who worked in Cleveland around the Civil War era. A native of Hamburg, he was active in the U.S. by the early 1850s. He worked principally in New York City, where he often exhibited portraits at the National Academy of Design. In the late 1850s, however, he was a member of the small art colony of Cleveland. His most significant contribution to the city's cultural heritage was the commission he undertook in 1858 to paint "A Meeting at the Ark." WM. CASE paid Gollmann $400 for the group portrait, which depicted 14 members of the early intellectual circle known as "Arkites" (see ARK†) and which eventually became part of the collection of the WESTERN RESERVE HISTORICAL SOCIETY.† After another sojourn in New York, Gollmann returned to Cleveland at least once again ca. 1872 before going back to Germany. Much of his later career was spent in Berlin, where he exhibited at the Berlin Academy in 1878 and 1890, prior to his death in that capital.—J.V.

Henderson, Walter B. *The Arkites, and Other Pioneer Natural History Organizations of Cleveland* (1962).

**GOMBOS, ZOLTAN** (21 Jan. 1905–26 Nov. 1984) was the publisher of the Hungarian daily *SZABADSAG* and the son of Samuel and Peti (Rubenstein) Gombos. He emigrated from Hungary in 1925, came to Cleveland as a student at Western Reserve Univ., and graduated in 1929. While a student, he worked as a sports columnist for a Hungarian paper. Gombos became one of Cleveland's first foreign-film exhibitors in rented theaters and opened a Gypsy theme restaurant at the 1936 GREAT LAKES EXPOSITION.† Beginning in 1932, he covered sports and amusements for *Szabadsag*, before being promoted to city, then managing editor in 1939. As president of Liberty Publishing Co., he also acquired the New York Hungarian daily *Amerikai Magyar Nepszava* (American Hungarian People's Voice), moving its printing to Cleveland and acquiring several Cleveland English neighborhood papers, including *Buckeye Press*. In the 1950s he published the national Hungarian weekly *A Jo Pasztor* (The Good Shepherd). Nationally prominent, Gombos was on the delegation that returned St. Stephen's Crown from the U.S. to Hungary in 1978, and received the American Hungarian Foundation's Geo. Washington Award in 1978. He served on Cleveland's zoning board for 11 years and was chairman of the Ohio Racing Commission from 1953–58. An original member of the Playhouse Square Foundation, he often sponsored appearances of attractions such as the Budapest Symphony. By the time Gombos sold his publishing interests in Sept. 1984, both *Szabadsag* and the New York paper were weeklies. Gombos married twice. His first marriage was to Madeline "Magda" Koloszi on 27 Oct. 1936; they divorced on 7 Nov. 1974. He then married Lenke Schaar, a Hungarian actress and singer, on 13 Nov. 1974. He had a stepdaughter, Suzanne Webster. Gombos died in Cleveland.

Zoltan Gombos Papers, WRHS.

**GONGWER, W. BURR** (1873–28 Sept. 1948), Democratic party boss for 35 years, was born near Mansfield, OH, the son of Louis and Irena Gongwer. He began as a journalist there before coming to Cleveland in 1899 as political reporter for the *PLAIN DEALER.† In 1900 he interviewed Democrat mayoral candidate TOM JOHNSON. They became friends and Mayor Johnson made Gongwer his secretary, although Gongwer was a Republican. Johnson so inspired Gongwer that he turned Democrat and, as Johnson's secretary for 8 years, Gongwer began gaining power as he was entrusted with party details, including patronage distribution.

Gongwer became deputy clerk of the Board of Elections in 1910 and chief clerk 2 years later. From 1915–21, he was collector of customs. With Johnson's death, party leadership passed to NEWTON D. BAKER, but he gradually relinquished party duties to Gongwer, his chief lieutenant, until by 1915 Gongwer was practically party boss, although he didn't become executive committee chairman until 1924. In the 1920s, when the Democrats were weak, Gongwer kept the party alive by implementing the "60–40 deal," allowing Democrats a portion of jobs under the Republican-controlled, CITY MANAGER PLAN.† In the early 1930s, Gongwer produced Democratic victories and ruled one of the strongest political organizations in Cleveland's history. However, a 5-year internal debate between Gongwer, MARTIN SWEENEY, and ROBT. BULKLEY again debilitated the party. Gongwer lost his position to RAY MILLER in 1940, retired from politics, and spent his remaining years in the insurance business he established in the 1920s.

Gongwer and his wife, Nona Cappeller, had a daughter, Dorothy. He died in Cleveland and was buried in Mansfield, OH.

W. Burr Gongwer Papers, WRHS.

**GONZALEZ, LOUIS A.** (15 Dec. 1916–22 Aug. 1993), achieved national recognition as a chef in several leading Cleveland restaurants. Born to Manuel and Filomena Alvarez Gonzalez in Tampa, FL, he moved to Cleveland as a boy and attended East High School. He began his career in the kitchen of the HOLLENDEN HOTEL† in the 1930s, lighting ranges as a "fireman" during his culinary apprenticeship. During World War II, he practiced his skills as a cook in the U.S. Army, serving in Europe after the Normandy invasion. Following the war he worked for the Hotel Cleveland (see STOUFFER'S RENAISSANCE CLEVELAND†), the Hickory Grill, Somerset Inn, and Sahara Hotel. His specialties included the paella of his Spanish heritage as well as such mainstream traditions as Beef Wellington. Besides mentoring many of Cleveland's younger chefs in his kitchens, he also taught briefly at CUYAHOGA COMMUNITY COLLEGE.† He appeared on the "Mike Douglas Show" during the television program's Cleveland period (see WKYC†) and on numerous local radio talk shows. His national honors included the Escoffier Medallion and induction into the exclusive Royal Order of the Golden Toque. Gonzalez retired as executive chef at the CANTERBURY GOLF CLUB† in 1981. Married twice, to the former Betty Carballada of Lorain, OH (1947), and to Irene Toth (1970), he was survived by his second wife, son Carl Gonzalez, stepson Edward Acocella, and stepdaughter Mary Wintucky.—J.V.

**GOODMAN, ALFRED THOMAS** (15 Dec. 1845–20 Dec. 1871), historian and secretary of the WESTERN RESERVE HISTORICAL SOCIETY,† was born in Washington, PA, the son of John and Ann (George) Goodman. They came to Cleveland so that Alfred could attend primary and secondary school in the city. Shortly after high school graduation in 1864, he enlisted in the Union Army, serving in the 150th Regiment of the Ohio National Guard in Washington, DC. After the war, he worked as a reporter on the *Daily Patriot and Union* in Harrisburg, PA, returning to Cleveland in 1868. He studied law with Judge RUFUS RANNEY for a time and was elected Secretary of the Western Reserve Historical Society, then a branch of the Cleveland Library Assn. Goodman began the society's autograph collection with the signatures of all U.S. presidents and acquired coins, maps, pamphlets, and books for the society. A gifted writer, he contributed more than 100 sketches for *Drakes American Dictionary of Biography*. Through his extensive acquaintance with manuscript sources, he prepared the *Journal of Captain William Trent* through Ohio in 1782, published by William Dodge of Cincinnati and wrote a history of General Harmar's campaign to the Maumee River in 1790. He also contributed several tracts to the Western Reserve Historical Society's publications before his untimely death at age 26. Goodman never married.—M.S.

**GOODMAN, LESTER** (18 June 1927–12 Apr. 1993) was a pioneer researcher in biomedical engineering who worked on perfecting the pacemaker and led early development of the artificial heart.

Born in Cleveland to Albert and Shirley (Itskovitz) Goodman, Lester graduated from Glenville High School (1945) and received his B.S. (1956), M.S. (1959), and Ph.D. (1962) from Case Institute of Technology.

Returning to Cleveland in 1949 after serving as a navy radar technician, Goodman helped in his father's business, Goodman Salvage Co., and attended Case. He was a research assistant in mechanical engineering (1956–57) and one of the first to earn a doctorate in the newly emerging field of biomedical engineering.

Remaining at Case Institute of Technology, Goodman advanced from engineering instructor (1957) to asst. professor, then associate professor (1965). From 1962–65 he was asst. director of the Systems Research Center.

In 1965 Goodman joined the National Institute of Health and worked on developing the synthetic materials used in the first experimental artificial hearts. In 1967 he announced the discovery of a plastic material which promised to be useful in biomedicine. He became chief of the Biomedical Engineering and Instrumentation Branch of the NIH, serving until 1975.

Goodman was president (1969) of the newly formed Alliance for Engineering in Medicine and Biology, became an international lecturer, and was awarded numerous honors. He was director (1975–

83) of the Biomed Engineering Division, Meditronics Inc. of Minneapolis, perfecting new designs for pacemakers. He was a visiting professor (1980–81), and associate director of the Engineering Design Center, CWRU.

On 1 July 1951 Goodman married Jacqueline Arnoff. They had three children: Clifford, Kenneth, and Rebecca. Goodman died in Alexandria, VA. —T.B.

**GORDON, HELEN** (20 Oct. 1906–4 Dec. 1989), award-winning business leader, operated Helen Gordon Advertising (1947–82) in the ARCADE,† among the first women to open such an agency in Cleveland. She was also a painter and volunteered for welfare organizations. Gordon was born in Pittsburgh, PA, to David and Catherine Martin Gordon, and graduated from the Pennsylvania College for Women (later Chatham College). Before opening her own agency, Gordon managed advertising for Stearns Co. and served as executive vice-president of Fran Murray, Inc., both in Cleveland. She presided over the Women's Advertising Club of Cleveland (1948–52) and penned scripts for its Gridiron Shows. Gordon received the Erma Proetz Award for radio copy written by a woman and was selected as Cleveland's Advertising Woman of the Year (1950s).

A single woman, Gordon volunteered for a variety of organizations, including the YOUNG WOMEN'S CHRISTIAN ASSN.† (YWCA), the Welfare Federation, the Central Volunteer Bureau, and the CITIZENS' LEAGUE.† She belonged to the CLEVELAND MUSEUM OF ART,† the CLEVELAND MUSEUM OF NATURAL HISTORY,† and the WOMEN'S CITY CLUB.† For the last 5 years of her life, Gordon lived at the LUTHERAN HOME† in WESTLAKE.† She is buried in North Braddock, PA.—J.M.

**GORDON, WILLIAM J.** (30 Sept. 1818–23 Nov. 1892), wholesale grocer and iron-ore dealer, best remembered for his gift of GORDON PARK† to Cleveland, was born in Monmouth County, NJ, to Jonathan and Mary Conover Gordon. He learned the wholesale grocery business in New York City and arriving in Cleveland in 1839, he started W. J. Gordon & Co., the largest grocery establishment in Ohio within a few years. In 1856 Gordon became partners with Geo. Fellows to conduct business in New York City, later adding Solomon D. McMillan and Martin R. Cook as partners.

In 1853 Gordon and Samuel Kimball shipped the first load of iron ore from the Lake Superior region to Cleveland. Convinced that iron ore could serve Cleveland's manufacturing interests, Gordon helped establish the Cleveland Iron Mining Co., serving as president from 1856–66. With John H. Gorham, he

also founded the first woodenware manufacturing firm in Cleveland. In 1865 Gordon began purchasing land east of Cleveland and laying out a 122-acre park which, at his death, was deeded to Cleveland provided it be forever maintained and kept open to the public under the name of Gordon Park. In 1872 Gordon began improving large tracts of unused land on both sides of the CUYAHOGA RIVER.† He purchased the tracts, laid out streets, and erected houses built with economy and taste. These he sold at moderate prices and on easy payment terms, enabling many Clevelanders to afford comfortable homes. Gordon married Charlotte Gertrude Champlin in 1843 and had 4 children: George, Ella, Georgina, and Charles, the latter two survived to adulthood. Gordon died in Cleveland and was buried in Lake View Cemetery.

**GOTTWALD, FREDERICK CARL** (15 Aug. 1858–23 June 1941), painter, instructor at Cleveland School of Art (later CLEVELAND INSTITUTE OF ART†), and sometimes referred to as the dean of Cleveland painters, was born in Austria to Frederick and Caroline Grosse Gottwald and came to Cleveland before his first birthday. His first artistic training was in 1874 with ARCHIBALD M. WILLARD, whom he joined in 1876 in founding the ART CLUB.† Gottwald earned money to study art by painting landscapes in the cabins and salons of lakeboats and by gilding figureheads for boats. He studied at the Cooper Institute in New York City, the Art Students' League in Munich, and the Julien Academy in Paris. Returning to Cleveland in the late 1880s, he accepted a post on the staff on the newly formed School of Art, with which he would be associated for 41 years. He also taught at Western Reserve School of Design, the JOHN HUNTINGTON POLYTECHNIC INSTITUTE,† and Oberlin College. On 22 Nov. 1899, Gottwald married Myria Scott. He and his wife traveled, particularly in Europe, and many of Gottwald's landscapes are based on scenes in Italy, England, and Germany. In 1921 he spent his sabbatical year in Italy, moving there after his retirement in 1926. He returned to Cleveland for a short time in 1930 before retiring to California in 1932, where he spent the remaining years of his life. In 1919 Gottwald received the Penton Medal at the Cleveland Museum of Art MAY SHOW† for his work entitled "The Thinker." He died in Pasadena, CA.

**GOULDER, HARVEY DANFORTH** (7 Mar. 1853–14 June 1928), maritime lawyer and onetime sailor, advocated harbor improvement and advised those engaged in widening the CUYAHOGA RIVER.† He served on both the Cleveland Board of Industry and the Cleveland Board of Trade (later the

GREATER CLEVELAND GROWTH ASSN.†), and acted as counsel to the Cleveland Vessel Owners' Assn. and the LAKE CARRIERS' ASSN.† Goulder was born in Cleveland to Barbara Freeland Goulder and Christopher D. Goulder, a captain on the Great Lakes. He graduated from CENTRAL HIGH SCHOOL† in 1869. In the summers during and after high school, he sailed on his father's ships. Goulder studied law first with the firm of Tyler & Dennison and later with admiralty lawyer John E. Cary. He was admitted to the bar in 1875 and entered into practice first with John H. Weh, then with ALEXANDER HADDEN, specializing in maritime and marine insurance law. Goulder practiced with various Cleveland firms, including Goulder & Lee (1890), Goulder & Holding (1892), Goulder, Holding & Masten (1896), Goulder, Day, White, Garry & Duncan (1914), and Goulder, White & Garry (1920s). He belonged to the American Bar Assn., the Cleveland Bar Assn., the Society of Naval Architects and Marine Engineers, and the Cleveland Chamber of Commerce.

On 11 Nov. 1878 Goulder married Mary F. Rankin. She died in 1913, and in 1915 he married Mrs. Seabury Ford. Goulder died at his CLEVELAND HTS.† residence and is buried at Lake View Cemetery.—J.M.

**GOULDER-IZANT, GRACE** (27 Mar. 1893–17 Nov. 1984), was a writer on Ohio history and lore, widely known for her long-running column in the *Plain Dealer Magazine* and for several books. She was born in Cleveland to Charles and Marian (Clements) Goulder, and graduated from Vassar College in 1914, afterward becoming the *PLAIN DEALER's*† society editor. With the outbreak of World War I, she worked for the national board of the YMCA in New York and Europe. After her marriage in 1919, she ceased working full-time until her article on the Ohio state capitol was bought by the *Plain Dealer* and became the first of her "Ohio Scenes and Citizens" columns, featuring an interesting person, historical sidelight, or unusual place in Ohio, which ran weekly in the Sunday Magazine until 1969. Goulder wrote *This is Ohio* (1953, rev. 1965), a collection of brief anecdotal histories of each Ohio county; *Ohio Scenes and Citizens* (1964), a collection of her magazine pieces; and *John D. Rockefeller, The Cleveland Years* (1972), documenting the oil tycoon's earlier life and Cleveland connections. A history of Hudson, OH, where Goulder lived from 1923 on, was in preparation at the time of her death. Goulder received many awards, including the Martha Kinney Cooper Ohioana Award and the Cleveland Women's City Club Creative Fine Arts Prize. She was a trustee of the WESTERN RESERVE HISTORICAL SOCIETY.† Goulder mar-

ried Robt. Izant (a vice-president of Central Natl. Bank) on 18 Oct. 1919. The couple had three children: Robt. J., Jonathan G., and Mary. Goulder was buried in Hudson, OH.

Grace Goulder-Izant Collection, Hudson Library and Historical Society.

**GRABER, BELLE (ISABEL) TAYLOR** (13 Sept. 1873–14 April 1957) was a civic and cultural leader who served as the first woman member of the Lakewood Board of Education and helped found both LAKEWOOD HOSPITAL† and Lakewood Public Library.

Born in Canada, Belle Graber came to the U.S. with her family as a young girl. She graduated from Ohio Northern Univ. in 1896, then taught school in Michigan before her marriage to Dr. C. LEE GRABER on 11 Oct. 1899. They had no children.

Mrs. Graber helped her husband establish Lakewood Hospital. On 27 Jan. 1908 the Lakewood Hospital Charitable Assn. was created out of her determination to help raise funds for the new hospital, supplement maintenance costs, and maintain three charity beds. Later the association became known as the Woman's Board of Lakewood Hospital.

Mrs. Graber served on the Lakewood Board of Education from 1912–17. Together with board member BERNICE PYKE, they raised civic support to secure a $45,000 grant to establish a library. The City of Lakewood purchased land in 1915 and construction began at the corner of Detroit and Arthur avenues for Lakewood Public Library, which formally opened in May 1916.

Mrs. Graber was active in the Cleveland Sorosis Society, serving as its president from 1914–16, and on the Executive Board from 1917–33. She was also an organizer of the Cleveland Music School Settlement when it began in 1912, and an early member of the Cleveland Academy of Medicine, Ladies Auxiliary.

Belle and C. Lee Graber were both longtime members of the Lakewood Methodist Church. She is buried in Lakewood Park Cemetery.—T.B.

The Cleveland Sorosis Club Records, WRHS.
Butler, M. M. *The Lakewood Story* (1949).
Reed, Mary M. "History of the Lakewood Public Library" (Master's thesis, Western Reserve Univ., 1958).
Borchert, Jim and Susan. *Lakewood: The First 100 Years* (1987).

**GRABER, C. LEE** (4 July 1874–23 Jan. 1954) was the founder of LAKEWOOD HOSPITAL† and a respected physician and surgeon.

Born in Justus (Stark County), OH, to Christian

and Mary G., Graber attended Ohio Northern Univ., graduating with a pharmacy degree (1895), and B.S. (1896). Graber received the Doctor of Medicine degree (1898) from the Univ. of Cincinnati and did post-graduate work at New York Univ., Harvard, Johns Hopkins, Massachusetts General Hospital, and Western Reserve Univ.

Graber practiced in Mount Eaton, OH, before settling in Lakewood around 1904. From 1905–07 he taught at the Cleveland College of Physicians and Surgeons. In 1907 Graber and his wife, BELLE TAYLOR GRABER, mortgaged their home to help obtain funds for Lakewood Hospital. Together with Dr. Wallace Benner, Lakewood's Health Commissioner, Graber opened Lakewood Hospital as a private institution, with 15 beds and 3 doctors in a double frame house on Detroit and Belle avenues. Graber created a voluntary nonprofit organization which operated the hospital until its purchase by the City of Lakewood in 1931.

In 1920 Graber built the Lakewood Medical Building on Detroit and Westwood avenues, where he maintained his offices. He was Lakewood Hospital's Chief of Staff from 1907–32, and Chief of Surgery from 1907–48. In 1953 Graber was elected emeritus of surgery.

Graber was a fellow of the American College of Physicians and Surgeons and belonged to numerous medical and surgical societies.

The Grabers were married on 11 Oct. 1899. They had no children. Graber belonged to the Lakewood Methodist Church. He is buried in Lakewood Park Cemetery.—T.B.

## GRANEY, JOHN GLADSTONE "JACK"

GRANEY, JOHN GLADSTONE "JACK" (10 June 1886–19 Apr. 1978), major league baseball player for Cleveland from 1910–22 and radio announcer of Indians games between 1932–53, was born in St. Thomas, Ontario, Canada. An excellent left-handed pitcher, he intended to attend college, but after a tryout in Buffalo, was signed, shipped to Erie, and finished the season at Wilkes-Barre with 24–4 record. His contract was purchased in 1908 by the Cleveland Naps, but in spring training he hit manager NAPOLEON LAJOIE in the head with a pitch and was sold to Portland. After hitting 6 more batters during the season, he was switched to the outfield. By 1910 he was back with Cleveland. Graney had a lifetime batting average of .250 in 1,402 games and played on the 1920 World Championship team.

In 1921 Graney became a partner in the Kane-Graney Motor Co. in Brooklyn. Selling out in 1929, Graney began his radio-announcing career in 1932. His salty voice and enthusiastic manner made him the most popular baseball announcer in Cleveland sports history. Asked the reason for his success,

Graney explained, "I tried to follow the ball, stay with the play and leave fancy words to others." Over the years, he teamed with several announcers. Graney tried television sportscasting at WEWS† in 1954 but then retired to Bowling Green, MO. He and his wife, Pauline, married in 1916, had a daughter, Margaret, and a son, Jack, Jr., killed in World War II.

## GRASSELLI, CAESAR AUGUSTIN

GRASSELLI, CAESAR AUGUSTIN (1850–28 July 1927), president and later board chairman of GRASSELLI CHEMICAL CO.,† was born in Cincinnati to Fredericka Eisenbarth and Eugene Ramiro Grasselli. His father, a chemist, taught him chemical-plant construction and operation, and he attended Mt. St. Mary's College in Emmitsburg, MD. In 1867 his father moved his chemical business to Cleveland; Caesar became a partner in 1873.

Grasselli helped develop high-explosives manufacturing; in 1885 he introduced American saltcake, or sodium sulfate, to the glass industry, which had used British supplies. After his father's death, in 1885 Grasselli became president of Grasselli Chemical Co.; in 1916 he became board chairman and his son, Thos. S., succeeded him as president. Company assets grew to $30 million, other companies were absorbed, and furnaces to manufacture zinc and plants for zinc smelting were erected. The Grasselli empire encompassed 14 plants when it merged with Du Pont in 1928.

Grasselli was also the first president of Woodland Ave. Savings & Trust Co. (1886), and president of Broadway Savings & Trust Co. (1893). In 1920 these merged with 27 other institutions to form Union Trust Co. and Grasselli remained as a director. He was a founder of the CLEVELAND MUSEUM OF ART† and CLEVELAND INSTITUTE OF MUSIC.† He gave the family home to the CLEVELAND SOCIETY FOR THE BLIND,† and in 1922 gave the Rose-Mary Home for Crippled Children to the Catholic Diocese of Cleveland, in memory of his wife, Johanna Ireland Grasselli. Grasselli had seven children: Eugene, Thomas, Josephine, Anna, Ida, Caesar, and Frederick. He was buried in Lake View Cemetery.

Grasselli Family Papers, WRHS.

## GRAUER, WILLIAM C.

GRAUER, WILLIAM C. (2 Dec. 1895–6 Apr. 1985) was a painter, muralist, and art teacher active in Cleveland for nearly 60 years. Born in Philadelphia, he graduated from the Pennsylvania Museum School of Industrial Art in 1914 and saw service in France during World War I. Coming to Cleveland as a freelance artist in 1927, he married Natalie Eynon (1888–1955), a fellow native Philadelphian and artist, with whose career his own became intertwined. Invited to contribute murals to the President's Cottage at White Sulphur Springs, WV, in 1932, they returned to found and codirect the Old White Art Colony, School and Gallery during the summers from 1934–40. During the same period, they also started the art department at Cleveland College of Western Reserve Univ. (see CASE WESTERN RESERVE UNIV.†). Grauer painted murals for the West Virginia exhibitions in both the Chicago Century of Progress (1933) and the New York World's Fair (1939). Residents of Ambleside Dr. near UNIV. CIRCLE,† the Grauers also maintained a summer home and studio in E. Claridon, Geauga County. They had 2 daughters, Blanche E. and Gretchen. Following the death of his wife, Grauer married another Cleveland College art instructor, Dorothy Turobinski, in 1964. He retired from WRU as associate professor of art in 1966 but continued to paint and to teach privately. Increasingly abstract in style in his later years, his work was exhibited in 55 MAY SHOWs† at the CLEVELAND MUSEUM OF ART.†—J.V.

**GRAUL, JACOB** (5 Nov. 1868–14 Feb. 1938), Cleveland policeman (1897–1930) and chief of police (1922–30) was born in Cleveland to John and Catherine Graul. He learned the plumbing trade, but grew bored and gained appointment to the CLEVELAND POLICE DEPT.,† joining with the intention of becoming chief and working methodically to achieve that ambition. Lacking the brawn, deep voice, and other attributes characteristic of police force members, he made his reputation as a plainclothesman at the Central Station, and later the detective bureau.

Graul's career was uneventful. Through hard work, he rose through the ranks: sergeant (1903), lieutenant (1909), captain (1912), deputy inspector (1918). He was obedient to every order, which he later demanded from those under him. He was one of few policemen to remain loyal to FRED KOHLER when Kohler was ousted as police chief in 1913. When Kohler became mayor in 1922, he installed Graul as chief. Although Graul maintained a reputation for honesty and integrity, he was often hampered by politics, as Kohler punished his opposition, rewarded his supporters, and prevented raids on slot machines and gambling spots. During the city manager years, Graul was overshadowed by Safety Director Edwin Barry, and was eased out of office by City Manager DANIEL MORGAN in 1930 with the promise of a big pension, only to see it later reduced by two-thirds. Graul married Alma Lentz on 24 Nov. 1896 and had 3 children: Alfred, Walter, and Leona (Mrs. Eldon Lewis). Graul died while serving as foreman of the grand jury and was buried in Highland Park Cemetery.

**GRAY, A. DONALD** (24 Feb. 1891–30 May 1939), landscape architect and designer in Cleveland from 1920–39, was born in Tyrone, PA, son of Charles G. and Rose (Williams) Gray. He graduated from Bucknell Univ. in Pennsylvania, and attended Harvard Univ., afterwards working briefly with Frederick Law Olmsted, Jr., in the Olmsted Bros. firm in Brookline, MA, the premier landscape architects in America. Gray came to Cleveland in 1920, establishing a practice in landscape architecture and designing many private gardens and estates in Cleveland, the Heights, and outlying suburbs. In 1925 he traveled to England, studying the gardens of great houses there. He designed the landscaping for the development of Fairhill Rd. houses in 1931, making his own home there for several years. He designed the landscape for the Cedar-Center apartments, the first federal public housing project in the nation; for FOREST HILL PARK†; and some of the designs for the Cleveland Cultural Gardens in ROCKEFELLER PARK.† Dedicated to "making a beautiful city of Cleveland," Gray worked on developing the Cleveland Garden Ctr. with Mrs. Wm. G. Mather and Mrs. Chas. A. Otis.

In 1936 Gray helped preserve DUNHAM TAVERN,† Cleveland's oldest remaining house (1842), proposing making it a museum. In the mid–1930s he contributed a regular gardening column to the *CLEVELAND PRESS.†* Gray designed the Horticultural Gardens for the GREAT LAKES EXPOSITION† of 1936–37, which remained north of CLEVELAND MUNICIPAL STADIUM† and was named for Gray after his death. On 11 Jan. 1928, Gray married Florence Ball. They had a daughter, Virginia. Gray died in Cleveland and was buried in Highland Park Cemetery.

A. Donald Gray Papers, WRHS.

**GRAY, JOSEPH WILLIAM** (5 Aug. 1813–26 May 1862), founder of the *PLAIN DEALER,†* was born in Bridgeport, VT, to Urel and Betsey (Case) Gray, emigrating with his brother, Admiral Nelson Gray, to Cleveland in 1836. After teaching in local schools, Gray read law under HENRY B. PAYNE and HIRAM V. WILLSON and was admitted to the bar. In partnership with his brother, Gray purchased the *CLEVELAND ADVERTISER,†* a faltering Democratic weekly, in Dec. 1841, resurrecting it on 7 Jan. 1842 as the Cleveland *Plain Dealer*. A. N. Gray was business manager until shortly after the weekly converted to a daily in 1845, when he left the *Plain Dealer* solely in his brother's charge.

Gray was personally involved in Democratic politics. Appointed Cleveland postmaster by Pres. Franklin Pierce in 1853, he was dismissed by Pres. Jas. Buchanan in 1858 for editorially supporting

Illinois Senator Stephen A. Douglas. Gray lost the 1858 Congressional election in the normally Republican district to Edward Wade. He went to both the Charleston and Baltimore Democratic conventions in 1860 as a delegate pledged to Douglas, maintaining his support of Douglas even through defeat, endorsing the Senator's pledge of Union loyalty after the South's secession in 1861. For 20 years, Gray kept his Democratic paper alive in the heart of a Whig, later Republican, stronghold. He married Catherine Foster in 1845 and had a daughter, Josephine, and 2 sons, Eugene and Lewis. He died after a short illness at home and was buried in the Erie St. Cemetery.

**GRDINA, ANTON** (27 Apr. 1874–1 Dec. 1957), businessman and leader in the Slovenian community, grew up in Ljubljana, Austria-Hungary, son of Luka and Marija Grdina. He arrived in Cleveland in 1897 and worked at various jobs before buying a hardware store on St. Clair Ave. in 1904. He also sold furniture and became an undertaker, incorporating Anton Grdina & Sons, home furnishers and funeral directors, in 1928, serving as its president until his death. Grdina helped organize 2 banking institutions for the Slovenian community: Slovenian Bldg. & Loan Assn.(1916), which became St. Clair Savings Assn.; and North American Bldg. & Savings Co.(1919–20), later NORTH AMERICAN BANK,† of which Grdina was president from 1939 until his death.

Grdina helped rebuild that part of the St. Clair neighborhood destroyed by the EAST OHIO GAS CO. EXPLOSION & FIRE† on 20 Oct. 1944, organizing St. Clair-Norwood Rehabilitation Corp. and giving $5,000 to the effort. The corporation bought sites of destroyed houses and built and sold 16 new homes. Grdina was also treasurer of the CLEVELAND CULTURAL GARDENS FED.† from its founding in 1926 until 1957; president of the Yugoslav Cultural Garden; organized the Grand Carnolian Slovenian Catholic Union; was a founder of the Natl. Slovene Catholic Union; and held memberships in 16 Slovenian lodges. Grdina was the first U.S. Slovenian to receive the Third Order of the Yugoslav Crown, awarded by King Peter in 1938. In 1954 he became a knight in the Order of St. Gregory by papal decree. Grdina married Antoija Bizelj in 1899; they had 6 children: Anthony, Frank, Catherine, James, Mary, and Joseph. Grdina died in Cleveland and was buried in Calvary Cemetery.

**GREEN, HOWARD WHIPPLE** (25 Apr. 1893–8 July 1959), a statistician who studied population trends in Greater Cleveland for 30 years, was born in Woonsocket, RI, to George Walter and Alice Judson Paine Whipple. He received his B.A. from Clark Univ., and attended Harvard Univ. before receiving his B.S. from MIT. Green worked for H. Koppers Co. in Lorain; as a bacteriologist for the War Dept. in the Panama Canal Zone; and with the Rockefeller Fund on malaria control in Arkansas, Louisiana, and Puerto Rico before coming to Cleveland in 1923 as director of the Bureau of Statistics & Research of the Cuyahoga County Public Health Assn., forerunner of the Cleveland Health Council. Beginning in 1925, he was secretary of that council for 34 years.

Green supervised the 1930 federal census in Cleveland, preparing, the following year, for the Plain Dealer Publishing Co., Population Characteristics by Census Tracts, Cleveland, OH, breaking down census figures into smaller units, which revealed trends that could not otherwise be discerned and allowed more efficient approaches to community health and welfare. In 1932 Green organized the nonprofit REAL PROPERTY INVENTORY OF METROPOLITAN CLEVELAND† (RPI), serving as its director until his death. RPI furnished data on family units, housing, utilities, retail stores, and industry and became the model for similar organizations throughout the country. Beginning in 1933, Green circulated "A Sheet-a-Week" among several hundred subscribers, believing businesses could profit from government information if it were abbreviated and simplified. In later years Green was a consultant.

Green, a resident of CLEVELAND HTS.,† married Leona M. Thatcher on 30 Nov. 1919. They had two children, Patricia Anne and Howard Thatcher. Green was buried in Lake View Cemetery.

**GREEN, JOHN PATTERSON** (2 Apr. 1845–1 Sept. 1940), the "Father of Labor Day," was born the son of John R. and Temperance Green, free blacks of Newberne, NC. His family moved to Cleveland in 1857. John left school in 1859 to support his family, studying on the side and publishing "Essays on Miscellaneous Subjects by a Self-Educated Colored Youth" in 1866. He attended Central High School (1866–69), and in 1870 graduated from Union Law School, moved to South Carolina, and was admitted to the bar. Green returned to Cleveland in 1872 and was elected Republican justice of the peace, the first black elected to office in Cleveland. He held the post for 9 years (1873–82). In 1881 he won election to the Ohio House of Representatives. He was elected to the Ohio legislature in 1890, there introducing the bill that established Labor Day as a state holiday; the U.S. Congress made it a national holiday in 1894.

In 1892 Green was elected to the Ohio Senate, that body's first black member. During the 1890s he became closely acquainted with leading Ohio Republicans MARCUS A. HANNA and GEO. A. MYERS, and his campaigning for the national Republican ticket earned him appointment in 1897 to the newly created position of U.S. postage stamp agent (1897–1905). He served briefly as the acting superintendent of finance in the Post Office Dept. before leaving government service in 1906, resuming his law practice in Cleveland. Green published several books and articles: *Recollections of the Carolinas* (1881); his autobiography, *Fact Stranger than Fiction* (1920); and articles for the Afro-American News Syndicate. Green was a founding member of St. Andrew's Episcopal Church. Green married Annie Walker in 1869; she died in 1912. In 1912 he married Mrs. Lottie Mitchell Richardson. Green had 4 children from his first marriage: William, Theodore, Jesse, and Clara. He died in Cleveland and was buried in Woodland Cemetery.

Green, John P. *Fact Stranger than Fiction* (1920).
John P. Green Papers, WRHS.

**GREEN, SAMUEL CLAYTON** (1872–25 Apr. 1915) was an African American businessman called "the most successful legitimate businessman" among a new generation of elite black entrepreneurs in Cleveland at the turn of the century. Born in Winterpark, VA, Green was the son of Waverly and Lilly (Lane) Green. Little biographical information is available, but city directories suggest he began with the short-lived S. C. Green Hardwood Lumber Co. in 1901. In 1902 he patented a sofa bed and, with 16 stockholders, organized the New Leonard Sofa Bed Co., owned by and employing only AFRICAN AMERICANS.† Green moved into real estate and construction in 1903, incorporating the Mohawk Realty Co. with Welcome T. Blue, building homes and erecting the Clayton Bldg. He also invested in a laundry (the Eureka Co.) and a restaurant, and in 1906 established Clayton Grocery Store and People's Drug Store. In 1907 he purchased a church building at E. 37th and Cedar, remodeling it into a skating rink and dance hall, and in 1911 purchased a motion-picture and vaudeville theater, forming the S. C. Green Amusement Co. to operate it as the Alpha Theater. Green's business ventures were designed to turn segregation and discrimination to his advantage, but the drug and grocery stores lasted less than 5 years because of insufficient support from black customers. Insufficient black patronage for the roller rink led Green to institute "white only" nights twice a week, one result of which was a 1909 lawsuit by Walter L. Brown, charging discrimination after he had been refused entry on a "white night"; Brown won the suit.

Green married Mary French in 1907; they had no children. He died in Cleveland and was buried in Woodland Cemetery.

**GREEN, VIRGINIA DARLINGTON** (16 Aug. 1850–19 April 1929) was one of the first women elected to the Board of Education of the CLEVELAND PUBLIC SCHOOLS† (1912–29). She advocated a school board bond issue to fund public school playgrounds, helped establish the first public kindergarten in connection with the CLEVELAND DAY NURSERY AND FREE KINDERGARTEN ASSN.,† and worked to increase teachers' salaries. Locally and before the Ohio legislature (supporting the Bohm bill in 1915–16), Green successfully lobbied to open schoolhouses for community uses and as polling places. An avid suffragist, Green garnered about 30,000 votes in an unsuccessful bid for the U.S. Senate (1922). She was born in Zanesville, OH, to James and Margaret Elizabeth Bowman Darlington and educated at Putnam Female Seminary, Putnam, OH. She then spent 3 years traveling and studying abroad. In 1912 she again traveled, this time promoting women's suffrage around Ohio with Judge FLORENCE ELLINWOOD ALLEN. Green also promoted world peace and opposed military training for CHILDREN AND YOUTH† in the public schools. She was a charter member of the WOMEN'S CITY CLUB OF CLEVELAND,† belonged to the CONSUMERS' LEAGUE,† and served on the Board of Directors of the local Children's Fresh Air Camp. A lifelong Episcopalian (see EPISCOPALIANS†), Green belonged to TRINITY EPISCOPAL CHURCH.†

On 15 Oct. 1876 she married Arnold Green (d. 1909), clerk of the Ohio Supreme Court. They lived in Cleveland and had 2 sons, both of whom died by 1927.—J.M.

**GREENE, DANIEL J. "DANNY"** (14 Nov. 1929–6 Oct. 1977), king of racketeering, grew up in COLLINWOOD,† the son of John and Irene (Fallon) Greene. He dropped out of high school and in 1957 became a stevedore, shortly afterwards being elected president of Local 1317 of the longshoremen's union. In 1964 Greene was indicted for taking kickbacks in return for labor assignments; he was convicted of embezzling $11,000, however the conviction was reversed on appeal because of prejudicial governmental cross-examination. In 1970 Greene pleaded guilty to violating union laws and was fined $10,000, losing his union position. He then began organizing trash haulers.

There were tales of a feud between Greene and Michael Frato, a hauler who pulled out of Greene's guild. Arthur Sneperger, Greene's associate, was killed when a bomb he was carrying toward Frato's car exploded. Police suspected Greene detonated the bomb, believing someone was leaking information to Frato. On 26 Nov. 1971, while Greene was jogging, a car pulled alongside and Frato aimed a gun at Greene. Greene pulled out his own gun and fired, killing Frato. He was acquitted on the ground of self-defense. Greene took control of running rackets and numbers in the absence of racketsman ALEX (SHONDOR) BIRNS, jailed for bribing a PARMA† policeman. After Birns's release, Greene continued in the rackets game. Greene escaped unharmed in June 1975 when a bomb destroyed his home and office on Waterloo Rd. He survived a bombing and 2 shooting attempts before he was killed by a car bomb in LYNDHURST† on 6 Oct. 1977.

Greene was married twice. His first marriage was to June Tears on 17 Dec. 1953; they were divorced on 29 Feb. 1956. The second marriage was on 27 March 1956 to Nancy Hegler; they divorced in May 1960. He had 5 children: Kelly, Daniel, Michael, Sharon, and Colleen.


**GREVE, BELL** (4 Jan. 1894–9 Jan. 1957), pioneer in relief and rehabilitation services, was born in Cleveland to Louis and Margaritha (Rummel) Greve. She entered Hiram College planning to become a missionary, but after working at HIRAM HOUSE† one summer became interested in social work and transferred to Flora Stone Mather College at Western Reserve Univ., where she received her degree. She later earned a law degree from Cleveland Law School.

In 1918 Greve became a charity visitor in Cleveland's red-light district. She spent 3 years in Europe as head of a Red Cross child-health center and director of an orphanage before becoming superintendent of the Ohio division of charities. Five years later she became director of the Community Chest in Charleston, WV. In 1933, Greve became director of the Assn. for the Crippled & Disabled, which became the Cleveland Rehabilitation Ctr. in 1943 and which she directed until 1953. Greve initiated the agency's Curative Playroom for disabled preschool children (1934), and a work treatment shop to provide light work for disabled adults (1935).

From 1937–44, Greve directed the Cuyahoga County Relief Bureau. She also established the first county nursing home. In 1953 Greve became director of Cleveland's Dept. of Health & Welfare, a position she held until her death. The first woman city cabinet member in 20 years, Greve won approval for a $2.4 million bond issue to improve the city's correctional facilities. She also worked in international relief organizations. Greve was a member of Collinwood Christian Church. Greve, never married, was buried in Knollwood Cemetery.

**GREVE, LOUIS WILLIAM** (2 Nov. 1882–2 Feb. 1942), industrial designer and pioneer in the aerospace industry, was born in Cleveland, the son of Claus and Clara (Zimmerman) Greve. Educated in public schools and CENTRAL HIGH SCHOOL,† he worked in his father's company, CLEVELAND PNEUMATIC TOOL,† beginning as an office boy and later worked as a mechanic in the shop. He was made a director and treasurer of the company in 1904 and was elected president in 1931, serving until his death. An industrial innovator, Greve was head of the company's product improvement and was instrumental in utilizing the firm's automotive shock absorber technology to cushion aircraft landings. Greve studied experimental aerols (shock absorbers) by taking motion pictures of their action from underneath an airplane as it taxied down the runway. Under his leadership, the company's design and manufacture of airplane landing gear became an industry standard.

An early promoter of the NATIONAL AIR RACES,† Greve ensured participation of the Cleveland chapter of the National Aeronautics Assn. in the first races held in Cleveland in 1929, and the following year he served as president of the event. In 1934, the Louis W. Greve trophy was first offered as a prize at the National Air Races for an international free-for-all race by planes not exceeding 550 cubic inch displacement.

Greve married Elsie Baldwin in 1906, and they had four children: Fred B., Janice, Robert, and Doris Wagenlander. He died suddenly of a heart attack at age 59 in Fort Lauderdale, FL. Internment was in Cleveland at Lake View Cemetery.—M.S.

---

The Cleveland Pneumatic Tool Co. WRHS.

**GRIES, LUCILE DAUBY** (19 Dec. 1902–5 March 1968) was a civic and social leader and philanthropist who, in 1968, founded the LUCILE DAUBY GRIES AND ROBERT HAYS GRIES CHARITY FUND,† which gives primarily to local charities. She was also an avid collector of Oriental porcelain.

Born in Cleveland to Bessie (Braham) and NATHAN L. DAUBY, MAY CO.† executive, Lucile graduated from Cleveland public schools, then attended Smith College for two years.

Lucile returned to Cleveland and became active on city boards. Among her many philanthropic activities were membership on the Board of Trustees of the Cleveland Speech and Hearing Center, her special interest, and the LOUIS D. BEAUMONT FOUNDATION† which was named for her uncle.

She was also on the Board of Directors of MT. SINAI HOSPITAL† (1954–64).

Lucile served as vice-president, director, and original board member of HILL HOUSE† (1960s until her death) and was a board member of the Cleveland Mental Health Assn.

Lucile belonged to the OAKWOOD CLUB,† was a patron of the CLEVELAND ORCHESTRA† and the Metropolitan Opera Co. and owned an important minority share in the CLEVELAND BROWNS† through her husband, who had helped found the club.

Lucile and her husband collected Oriental export porcelain, boasting the second largest collection in America. Part of the collection was donated to the WESTERN RESERVE HISTORICAL SOCIETY† and the CLEVELAND MUSEUM OF ART.†

Lucile married ROBERT HAYS GRIES on 30 June 1924. They had four children: Tom, Robert D., Betty (Dorn), and Ellen (Cole). Lucile was enurned in the Hays Mausoleum in Mayfield Cemetery.
—T.B.

Rabbi Moses Gries Family Papers, WRHS.

**GRIES, MOSES J.** (25 Jan. 1868–30 Oct. 1918), proponent of Classical Reform Judaism and spiritual leader of the TEMPLE† (1892–1917) was born in Newark, NJ, to Jacob and Kate Gries. He attended the Univ. of Cincinnati and Hebrew Union College, graduating and receiving ordination in 1889. Gries served in Chattanooga, TN, before coming to the Temple, the first native-born HUC-educated rabbi in Cleveland. Gries, believing Reformed Judaism should be Americanized, radically changed the congregation: discarding German, adopting the Union Prayer Book, moving Sabbath services to Sunday, substituting English for Hebrew, removing Hebrew from the religious school curriculum, and creating congregational groups: the Temple Women's Assn., Temple Library, Temple Alumni Assn., Educational League, Temple Orchestra, and Temple Society.

Gries was politically progressive—a founder of the CITIZENS LEAGUE OF CLEVELAND†—and active in ecumenical affairs. He helped found the COUNCIL EDUCATIONAL ALLIANCE,† a settlement house of the NATL. COUNCIL OF JEWISH WOMEN, CLEVELAND SEC.† (1899); and the Fed. for Jewish Charities (1903), to coordinate Jewish charitable activities.

Gries protested pogroms and urged help for the immigrants, yet remained removed from the largely Orthodox, Yiddish-speaking group. He denounced Zionism, believing it raised questions concerning Jewish identity and loyalty which threatened the Jewish community in America. For health reasons, Gries resigned from the Temple in 1917, dying a year later. He married Frances (Fannie) Hays on 15 June 1898, daughter of KAUFMAN HAYS.† They had two sons, Robert and Lincoln. Gries was buried in Mayfield Cemetery.

Rabbi Moses Gries Family Papers, WRHS.
Rabbi Moses J. Gries Papers, American Jewish Archives, Cincinnati, OH.

**GRIES, ROBERT HAYS** (12 Oct. 1900–14 June 1966) was a fourth-generation Clevelander (his great-grandfather was SIMSON THORMAN†) active in business, sports, cultural and civic affairs. Gries was an avid collector of Chinese porcelain, antique silver, French Impressionist lithographs and prints, and tobacco books. Gries also helped found both the CLEVELAND RAMS† and CLEVELAND BROWNS.†

Born in Cleveland to Fanny (Hays) and Rabbi MOSES GRIES, Gries attended Univ. School, Western Reserve Univ. and Yale.

Gries began his career as manager of the downtown May Co. about 1925. After 18 years, Gries left to serve two years in the U.S. Army Air Corps, then joined Morgan Steel Products Co., serving as president until 1964.

In 1936, under the leadership of Homer Marshman, Gries helped form the Cleveland Rams. In 1945 Gries teamed with Arthur (Mickey) McBride to form the Cleveland Browns, serving as vice-president and director.

Gries had one of the largest known collections of tobacco literature, which he donated to the Cleveland Public Library. A sampling of his Chinese export porcelain is found at the Western Reserve Historical Society and at the Cleveland Museum of Art.

Gries was president of the Vocational Guidance and Rehabilitation Services, served as regional vice-president of the American Council for Judaism, was a director of radio station WERE and a trustee of numerous organizations.

Gries married Lucile Dauby on June 30, 1924. They had four children: Tom, Robert, Betty (Dorn), and Ellen (Coe). Gries lived in Shaker Hts. and was enurned in the Hays Mausoleum at Mayfield Cemetery.—T.B.

Moses J. Gries Family Papers, WRHS.

**GRILL, VATROSLAV J.** (1899–21 Mar. 1976), a leader in the Cleveland Slovenian community, was born in Slovenia, son of Joseph and Anna (Hribernik) Grill. He came to the U.S. with his parents in 1914 and finished high school at Cleveland Preparatory School in 1915. In 1919 Grill became editor of the Slovenian daily newspaper ENAKOPRAVNOST† (Equality); he soon began studying law at Cleveland Law School, and in 1925 passed the bar examination.

By 1929, in addition to being an editor and practicing attorney, Grill was a teacher in the Slovenian school, director of dramatics of the IVAN CANKAR DRAMATIC SOCIETY,† a singer in the ZARJA SINGING SOCIETY,† and a member of the Board of Directors of the SLOVENIAN NATL. HOME.† In 1928 he was elected national president of the Chicago-based Slovenian Progressive Benefit Society, later editing its Napredek (Progress). Grill was active politically. In Feb. 1942 he was named asst. police prosecutor by Law Director THOS. A. BURKE, JR.; he resigned as Enakopravnost editor but remained president of the American Jugoslav Publishing Co. until 1959. By 1954 Grill was asst. prosecutor in the city's law department, but by 1956 he returned to publishing, as editor of the New Era Semi Monthly in 1958 and 1959. Grill was also a referee for the Industrial Compensation Board and asst. attorney general in Columbus before his retirement. He moved to Yugoslavia ca. 1971 and lived there 4 years before returning to the U.S. to live in Santa Clara, CA, where he died.

Grill married Anna Bergoch on 28 Dec. 1929. They had 2 children, Edwin and Raymond. Grill was buried in Santa Clara, CA.

Klancar, Anthony J., comp. Who's Who among the Yugoslavs (1940).
Grill, Vatroslav. Med Dvema Svetovoma (1979).

**GROSSMAN, F. KARL** (1886–16 May 1969), conductor, teacher, and long-time director of the CLEVELAND PHILHARMONIC ORCHESTRA,† was born in Cleveland and began formal violin training at age 11. He studied piano theory and composition in this country, and then in Paris and Berlin. Grossman's compositions were performed by various city ensembles, including the FORTNIGHTLY MUSICAL CLUB.† In 1914 he began a long association with music programs in area churches, that year establishing a professional quartet at Lakewood Christian Church, and later serving as conductor for the Lakewood Methodist Church Choir. In 1920 he became conductor and musical director of the CLEVELAND OPERA CO.,† and in 1924 he became conductor of the Hermit Club Orchestra. Grossman later conducted the Madame Butterfly Co., and orchestras at the CLEVELAND MUSIC SCHOOL SETTLEMENT† and Western Reserve Univ. He also, as a violinist, was concertmaster for the Cleveland Municipal Symphony. In 1929 Grossman joined the faculty of Cleveland College as an instructor in chamber music and music history; later he was made head of the music department. His academic career continued at WRU, serving on the faculty from 1942–57, for many years as head of the music department. He received an honorary degree in music from BALDWIN-WALLACE COLLEGE.† In 1938 the Cleveland Philharmonic Orchestra was founded to provide opportunity for instrumental students in Cleveland to acquire professional experience. Grossman directed its debut concert and remained its conductor until the 1960s. Grossman also authored A History of Music in Cleveland (1972). Grossman and his wife, Helen, had two children, Glenn and Charles F. Grossman was cremated.

**GROSSMAN, ISADOR** (13 July 1880–29 Sept. 1957), attorney and senior partner of McAfee, Grossman, Taplin, Hanning, Newcomer & Hazlett, established legal principles regarding the taxation of river boats and advocated flexible lease payments based on dollar fluctuations. Born in St. Ivan, Hungary, to Jacob and Louisa Farkasch Grossman, Grossman attended public schools in Cleveland and graduated from Central High School. He received both an A.B. (1902) and an LL.B. (1904) from Harvard Univ., where he was a member of Phi Beta Kappa. Admitted to the bar that year, Grossman first entered practice with Judge A. W. Lamson (1904–06). He then went into partnership with Henry B. Howells (Howells & Grossman, 1906–19). He spent the next 6 years with Niman, Grossman, Buss & Holliday, which became Holliday, Grossman & McAfee, the forerunner of McAfee, Grossman, Taplin, Hanning, Newcomer & Hazlett.

Grossman participated in the LEGAL AID SOCIETY† (which he helped found) and the CLEVELAND BAR ASSN.,† and served on the executive committees of the National Policy Assn. and the CLEVELAND COUNCIL ON WORLD AFFAIRS.† He was secretary and director of Chandler Motor Car (later the CHANDLER-CLEVELAND MOTORS CORP.†), and director of the Grossman Drug Co., the Merit Pharmacal Co., the Cragin Realty Co., and the Page Realty Co. Grossman also was a trustee of the TEMPLE,† the Jewish Welfare Federation (see FEDERATION OF JEWISH CHARITIES†), the Mt. Sinai Hospital Foundation (see MT. SINAI MEDICAL CENTER†), MEDICAL MUTUAL OF CLEVELAND,† the COUNCIL EDUCATIONAL ALLIANCE† and CAMP WISE,† among others. He belonged to the CLEVELAND CITY CLUB† and the Cleveland Chamber of Commerce.

On 9 Jan. 1911 Grossman married Adele

Seasongood in St. Louis, MO; they had 2 sons, James S. and Edward N.—J.M.

**GROSSMAN, MARY B.** (10 June 1879–Jan. 1977), the first woman municipal judge in the U.S., was born in Cleveland to Louis and Fannie Engle Grossman. She studied at the Euclid Ave. Business College, and from 1896–1912 worked as a stenographer and bookkeeper in her cousin's law office. She enrolled in the law school at BALDWIN-WALLACE COLLEGE† and received her law degree and passed the Ohio Bar examination in 1912. She was only the third woman lawyer in Cleveland, and in 1918 was one of the first 2 women admitted to membership in the American Bar Assn. Grossman maintained a private Cleveland practice from 1912–23. She was active in women's suffrage and was chairwoman of the League of Woman's Suffrage. Once women won the vote, Grossman decided to run for municipal judge; she lost in 1921, but in 1923 was successful and became the first woman municipal judge in the U.S., continuing until her retirement at age 80. She also served on traffic court (1925–59) and organized the morals court in 1926, serving there until her retirement. As a judge, Grossman earned a reputation as, according to her obituary, "a severe, rigidly honest jurist, sometimes irreverently referred to as Hardboiled Mary." When she took a day off to observe a Jewish holiday in 1927, 39 bail jumpers reportedly turned themselves in so they would not have to face her. Grossman was a charter member of the WOMEN'S CITY CLUB† and LEAGUE OF WOMEN VOTERS† and board chairman of ALTA HOUSE.† She never married.

Mary Grossman Papers, WRHS.

**GUILFORD, LINDA (LUCINDA) THAYER** (22 Nov. 1823–1 Mar. 1911), educator and administrator of early Cleveland PRIVATE SCHOOLS,† was born in Lanesboro, MA, and worked in a paper mill until friends enabled her to attend Mt. Holyoke Seminary, from which she graduated in 1847. In 1848 Guilford arrived in Cleveland as principal of the new Young Ladies Seminary, which soon closed due to lack of funds. From 1851–54, Guilford was principal of the first Female Academy, with over 200 students.

From 1854–60, Guilford was vice-principal of the CLEVELAND FEMALE SEMINARY,† and from 1861–66 she operated her own private day school for boys and girls. In 1865 several families organized the second Cleveland Academy, opening the school in 1866 with 90 students. Guilford, the principal, remained for 14 years, until it closed in 1881 due to declining enrollment.

After teaching, Guilford was active in the Young

Women's Temperance League, and was president of the WCTU. She volunteered at FRIENDLY INN SOCIAL SETTLEMENT,† was active in Mt. Holyoke alumnae activities, and was on the Advisory Committee of the College for Women of Western Reserve Univ. She published *The Use of Life* (1885) and *The Story of a Cleveland School from 1848–1881* (1892). In 1892 FLORA STONE MATHER presented a new girls' dormitory to the College for Women, naming it Guilford Cottage in honor of her former teacher. Guilford, who never married, was a member of Second Presbyterian Church. She died in Cleveland and was buried in Woodland Cemetery.

Linda Thayer Guilford Papers, WRHS.

**GUND, GEORGE** (13 Apr. 1888–15 Nov. 1966), head of Cleveland Trust Bank (AMERITRUST†) and philanthropist, was born to Cleveland brewery owner and real estate investor, George Frederick Gund, and his wife, Anna Louise (Metzger), in La Crosse, WI. In the first graduating class of Harvard Business School, Gund started banking in Seattle. When his father died, Gund returned to Cleveland. He acquired the Kaffee Hag Corp., makers of decaffeinated coffee and, after refining the process of extracting caffeine (which he sold to Coca-Cola), he sold the company for $10 million. He then turned to real estate and banking.

During the Depression, Gund bought good-quality stocks at bargain prices. By 1937, he was hired by Cleveland Trust, first as a director, and then, in 1941, as president. Gund expanded the bank's financial power base in Cuyahoga County through loans and investments and, to strengthen its ties to business, served on more than 30 corporate boards. In addition to being bank president until 1962 and board chairman from 1962–66, Gund was an officer, trustee, or director of 14 civic, philanthropic, and educational institutions. Two Harvard professorships were established in his honor in 1964 and 1966. Gund collected western art, notably the work of Frederic Remington. In 1936 Gund married Jessica Roesler (d. 1954) and had 6 children: George III, Agnes, Gordon, Graham, Geoffrey, and Louise. Having provided for his children before his death, he left most of his $600 million estate to his GEO. GUND FOUNDATION.† Gund died in Cleveland of acute leukemia and was buried in Lake View Cemetery.

**GUTHRIE, WARREN A.** (30 June 1911–25 Feb. 1986), used his background as a teacher of speech to set a never-surpassed standard as a pioneer local television newscaster. A native of Syracuse, NE, he earned degrees from Nebraska Wesleyan Univ., the

Univ. of Michigan, and Northwestern Univ. He came to Cleveland in 1934 to join the speech dept. of Western Reserve Univ. (see CASE WESTERN RESERVE†), serving as dept. chairperson from 1946–64. He also was the university's public relations director from 1940–42, before serving as a lt. cdr. in the U.S. Navy during World War II. Guthrie had broken into radio in 1939 as moderator of the Western Reserve Univ. Forum, a faculty roundtable, over WTAM† and WGAR.† In 1951 he began his television career as the "Sohio Reporter" over WJW-TV† (Ch. 8). He wrote the 15 min. newscast himself and delivered it with only the aid of a brief outline. Guthrie won several awards for his delivery, but after 12 years WJW dismissed him in favor of the news "team" format then gaining popularity. In protest, Sohio (see BP AMERICAN†) dropped sponsorship of the program, and a viewer asked in the *CLEVELAND PRESS,†* "Are brains taboo on TV?" Guthrie briefly returned to radio with a morning newscast over WHK† and then joined Sohio's public relations dept., becoming director in 1966. He retired in 1976 and died in Venice, FL. Married twice, to Kathleen Donaldson Guthrie, and Catherine Guthrie, he was survived by a son and 3 daughters.—J.V.

Warren A. Guthrie Biographical File, CWRU Archives.

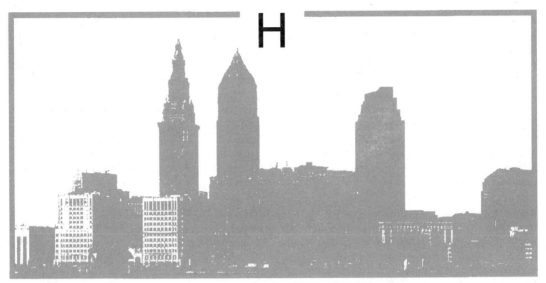

# H

**HAAS, VINCENT P.** (23 Oct. 1912–2 Apr. 1977), diocesan priest who devoted much of his ministry to working with the poor, racial minorities, and alcoholics, was born in Cleveland and educated at CATHEDRAL LATIN,† JOHN CARROLL UNIV.,† and ST. MARY SEMINARY.† He was ordained on 2 Apr. 1938, serving parishes in Akron and S. EUCLID† before being named pastor in 1946. His assignment was to organize the parish of St. Peter Claver for black Catholics. Fr. Haas spent the next dozen years successfully integrating his black parishioners into neighboring churches. He also served as a chaplain at St. Thomas Hospital, where he gave support and direction to the founders of Alcoholics Anonymous, Dr. Bob, Bill W., and SISTER IGNATIA. In 1961, Fr. Haas became the spiritual director of the St. Augustine Guild, forerunner of the Catholic Interracial Council. From 1962–66 he served as pastor of the Conversion of St. Paul Shrine. In 1963 he led a group of Clevelanders to Washington, DC, for the Freedom March. During the HOUGH RIOTS† of 1966, Fr. Haas organized a group of priests who went into the neighborhoods and urged the people to be calm and return to their homes. He also served as an unofficial advisor to the Ohio bishops on racial problems and possible solutions. In 1966 he was transferred to the pastorate of St. Colman's in Cleveland, where he encouraged and directed an outreach ministry to the poor and senior citizens. He died in Cleveland.

Archives, Diocese of Cleveland.

**HADDEN, ALEXANDER** (2 July 1850–22 Apr. 1926), Cuyahoga County probate judge, was born in Wheeling, (W)V, to Alexander and Mary Eliza Welch Hadden; the family moved to EUCLID† in 1857. Hadden graduated from Oberlin College in 1873 and began studying law. He was admitted to the bar in Oct. 1875 and practiced law until Feb. 1882, when he was appointed Cuyahoga County asst. prosecuting attorney. He was elected prosecuting attorney in 1884 and held the position until 1893. Gov. MYRON T. HERRICK appointed Hadden judge of the Probate Court of Cuyahoga County in 1905, an office he held continuously until his death. Hadden had practiced law with CARL D. FRIEBOLIN and Jas. H. Griswold, but in 1902 formed a partnership with Frank N. Wilcox—Wilcox, Collister, Hadden & Parks—principally representing a syndicate promoting development of interurban electric lines. Hadden taught the science and theory of criminal law at the Wm. T. Backus School of Law at Western Reserve Univ. from 1894 until his death. He was regarded for the clarity of his written judicial opinions and for an essay published for the PHILOSOPHICAL CLUB OF CLEVELAND† in 1918: "Why Are There No Common Law Crimes in Ohio?" During his tenure on the probate bench, Hadden was particularly concerned for the insane, who were the responsibility of the court, and argued for advanced modes of treatment and expanded treatment facilities. Hadden married Frances Hawthorne on 17 July 1883 and had 2 children, Alice (1884) and JOHN A. (1886).

**HADDEN, JOHN ALEXANDER, JR.** (3 June 1923–31 May 1994) was a distinguished child psychiatrist affiliated with many of Cleveland's medical and social service agencies. A native Clevelander, he was the son of Marianne Millikin and JOHN A. HADDEN. Upon his graduation from Harvard in 1944, he served on the staff of Gen. George S. Patton in Europe during World War II. He received his M.D. in 1954 from Western Reserve Univ. Medical School (see CASE WESTERN RESERVE†) and joined the staff of UNIV. HOSPITALS.† Hadden was also a staff psychiatrist for the CHILDREN'S AID SOCIETY† and the CUYAHOGA COUNTY JUVENILE COURT.† In 1969 he became a trustee of the Cleveland Center for Research in Child Development at the Hanna-Perkins Therapeutic Nursery School, serving as the center's president from 1979–91. He worked with the CENTER FOR HUMAN SERVICES† to have the Hanna-Perkins School established as a separate entity in 1979. Hadden also was a vice-president of the FEDERATION FOR COMMUNITY PLANNING† and a trustee for a number of other social welfare and mental health agencies. In 1986 he was given the first Distinguished Service Award of the Mental Health Assembly, an education and advocacy organization. He was married in 1955 to the former Elaine Grasselli, who later became the first woman to serve as director of a major local bank (UNION COMMERCE,† 1972) and as chairman of the Board of Overseers of CWRU (1974). Hadden died in Cleveland, survived by his wife and 2 daughters, Lucretia Weiner and Alexandra Hanna.—J.V.

**HADDEN, JOHN A., SR.** (11 July 1886–1 Jan 1979), lawyer and son of Frances (Hawthorne) and ALEXANDER HADDEN, was born in Cleveland and graduated from Harvard with his B.A. (1908) and Bachelor of Laws (1910). Returning to Cleveland, he began to practice law and joined TROOP A.† In 1912–13 Hadden was an asst. federal district attorney for the northern district of Ohio. In 1916 he served with Troop A on the Mexican border. He then went to Europe as part of the American Expeditionary Forces. When he returned to Cleveland, he took up law again as an asst. prosecuting attorney for Cuyahoga County.

Hadden was elected a Republican member of the Ohio House of Representatives in 1925 and served until 1931. His law practice consisted largely of probate and corporation reorganization. He was a trustee in the bankruptcy of the Erie Railroad Co., whose reorganization he successfully helped carry out. In the early 1930s, he was a founding partner of Andrews, Hadden & Burton, now (1995) ARTER & HADDEN.† In 1942 Hadden was appointed deputy regional director of the War Production Board for Cleveland. He was involved in the development of SEVERANCE CENTER† in CLEVELAND HTS.† in the early 1960s with Severance A. Millikin, his brother-in-law. Hadden was active in local Republican politics and was chairman of the CUYAHOGA COUNTY REPUBLICAN PARTY† finance committee. Hadden married MARIANNE ELISABETH MILLIKIN in Jan. 1922 and had 3 children: Alexander, Elisabeth, and (Dr.) JOHN A.

HADDEN. He was buried in Lake View Cemetery.—T.B.

O'Hara, Janet. *Arter & Hadden: 1843–1993, 150th Anniversary History.*

**HADDEN, MARIANNE ELISABETH MILLIKIN** (18 Dec. 1896–2 Sept. 1992) was among the early members of the Mundane Club (a women's literary society), the Maternal Health Assn., and the IN-TOWN CLUB.† Hadden was born in Cleveland to Dr. Benjamin Love Millikin and Julia Walworth Severance and grew up next door to the JOHN D. ROCKEFELLER home on EUCLID AVE.† Her father served as dean of the Western Reserve Univ. Medical School (1900–12); her uncle was JOHN LONG SEVERANCE. Educated at Froebel and LAUREL SCHOOLs,† Hadden graduated from Wells College in 1917. She returned to Cleveland and performed civilian relief work during World War I. On 7 Jan. 1922 she married lawyer JOHN ALEXANDER HADDEN; they had 3 children: JOHN, JR., Alexander H., and Elisabeth Severance. The Haddens lived on Delamere Dr. and Fairmount Blvd., CLEVELAND HTS.† She served organizations such as the Maternal Health Assn. (later PLANNED PARENTHOOD OF GREATER CLEVELAND), as trustee from 1934 until 1958, helping to instigate the Christmas Mart fundraiser. Hadden financially supported the Cleveland Center for Child Development, the MUSICAL ARTS ASSN.,† the CLEVELAND MUSEUM OF ART,† and the Medical School of CASE WESTERN RESERVE UNIV.† She died in Cleveland and was buried at Lake View Cemetery.—J.M.

Cleveland Family Oral History Collection, WRHS.
Wm. Milliken Papers, WRHS.

**HAGAN, JOHN RAPHAEL** (26 Feb. 1890–28 Sept. 1946), auxiliary bishop of Cleveland and first president of Sisters' (later St. John) College, was born in Pittsburgh to Katherine (Foley) and John Hagan. He was brought to Cleveland at age 2 and after graduation from CATHEDRAL LATIN SCHOOL,† began studies at North American College in Rome, ordained in 1914. Through study at the Univ. of Bonn (Germany) and Catholic Univ. of America, he acquired a D.S.T., a D.S.Ed., and a Ph.D. After serving as parish priest at St. Augustine (1914–16), ST. PATRICK'S† (1916–21), and St. Mary's, Bedford (1921–23), Fr. Hagan was named superintendent of schools by Bp. JOSEPH SCHREMBS,† a position he held for 23 years.

At the time, Catholic teacher education was conducted in normal schools run by religious communities with unequal resources. Hagan persuaded the communities to entrust the training to a diocese-run school, Sisters' College, which opened in 1928. Soon the institution, in response to changing state directives, switched from a normal school to a 4-year bachelor's program. With the assistance of Msgr. ROBT. NAVIN, Hagan built Sisters' College into an innovative training center. Hagan also helped found the Experimental School at Catholic Univ., aided the NEA, and founded the Catholic PTA movement. He taught at Cathedral Latin, Sisters' College, the seminary, and Catholic Univ.; and authored texts. In 1946 Hagan was named auxiliary bishop of Cleveland by Pope Pius XII. In Aug. 1946 he was taken ill with hepatitis and died following abdominal surgery. Hagan was buried in Calvary Cemetery.

**HAHN, EDGAR A.** (24 Nov. 1882–16 July 1970), a lawyer involved in many civic endeavors, was born in Cleveland to Aaron and Therese Kolb Hahn, earned his LL.B. from Western Reserve Univ. (1903), and did postgraduate work at Columbia Univ. Upon admittance to the Ohio Bar in 1904, he started practicing law with his father. In 1912 under the new state constitution, Hahn was elected to the commission responsible for forming Cleveland's home rule charter. Hahn joined the law firm of Mooney, Hahn, Loeser & Keough as senior partner in 1920. Hahn possessed an appreciation of the relationship between banking and society, and in 1933 played a major role untangling the confusion produced by the national bank holiday.

Hahn was a founder and original trustee of the NORTHERN OHIO OPERA ASSN.† (1927) and helped assure Cleveland would be a stop on the Metropolitan Opera's annual spring tour. As vice-chairman of the MUSICAL ARTS ASSN.,† Hahn helped initiate the tradition of summer concerts by the CLEVELAND ORCHESTRA† in 1938. In 1959, he was appointed a trustee of the CLEVELAND MUSEUM OF ART,† and was chiefly responsible for its acquisition of a number of fine 18th-century paintings. Hahn also served as treasurer and trustee of the LOUIS D. BEAUMONT FOUNDATION.† In Apr. 1964 Hahn was presented the Cleveland Medal for Public Service by the Cleveland Chamber of Commerce. In 1967 he was selected Sr. Citizen of the Year. Hahn married Irene Moss in 1910 and had 2 daughters, Katherine Hahn Bercovici and Mrs. Stanley Goodman.

**HALLE, MANUEL** (11 Feb. 1832–24 Nov. 1932) and **MOSES HALLE** (1834, interred 4 Dec. 1905) were Bavarian immigrants who made a fortune as wholesalers in Cleveland. Moses fathered SALMON PORTLAND CHASE HALLE (1866–1949) and Samuel Horatio Halle (1868–1954), two Cleve-land businessmen who founded HALLE BROTHERS CO.†

Born in Wilmars, Bavaria, Moses came to Cleveland in 1848 via the Erie Canal to live with his older brother, Manuel, and cousin, Aaron Halle. Moses worked alongside Manuel as a clerk at the City Mill Store.

In 1865 Manuel dissolved his partnership with William C. Schofield in Schofield Refineries and used the proceeds from the sale of his oil shares to go into business with Moses as M. Halle and Co., wholesalers of men's furnishings and notions. Their warehouse and showroom was at 145–147 Water St., 4 blocks northwest of PUBLIC SQUARE.†

Their wholesale company prospered and, in 1882, Manuel and Moses sold out to their nephews. By 1886 Moses and Manuel had each reached the age 50 and had retired from "active" business. They formed a new firm called M. & M. Halle to manage their banking, real estate holdings and develop real estate. When his sons founded the Halle Bros. Co., Moses became a director.

In 1887 Moses Halle joined a building committee to select a site at Scovill and Henry streets for a new $85,000 temple seating 1,500 persons of the ANSHE CHESED† Congregation (later Euclid Ave. Temple).

Manuel Halle married Augusta Weil in 1863 and had five children: Ida, Nora, William, Delia, and Eugene. Moses Halle married Rebecca Weil (Augusta's sister) in 1865 (d. 1871) and had sons Salmon and Samuel. He married Rosa Lowentritt in 1874 and had two daughters, Jessie and Minnie. Manuel and Moses Halle are buried in Mayfield Cemetery.—T.B.

Crooks, Edwin W., Jr. *The History of the Halle Bros. Co.* (1959).
Wood, James M. *Halle's: Memoirs of a Family Department Store, 1891–1982* (1987).

**HALLE, SALMON PORTLAND** (6 Aug. 1866–13 Sept. 1949), with his brother Samuel Horatio Halle, founded the Halle brothers company department store. In 1945 he received the Charles Eisenman Award from the Jewish Welfare Federation for his PHILANTHROPY.† Halle was born in Cleveland to Rebecca (Weil) and Moses Halle and educated in public schools. While president of Halle Brothers, he served as director of the Mutual Building & Loan Co. and the Service Recorder Co.

After Halle retired in 1921 from Halle Brothers, he maintained an office in the Hanna Building for his extensive philanthropic work. He was an early member of the CLEVELAND ADVERTISING CLUB† and helped found the Community Fund, the CLEVELAND HOSPITAL SERVICE ASSN.,† and the Jewish Welfare Federation (see JEWISH COMMUNITY FEDERATION†), serving the latter as trustee for 22 years. In other Jewish causes, he was a leader in the American-Jewish Joint Distribution Committee for overseas relief. Halle contributed between $150,000 and $200,000 to MT. SINAI MEDICAL CENTER† and served as its vice-president.

On 3 December 1893 Halle married Carrie B. Moss (d. 1965); their children were Marion (Mrs. Abraham) Strauss and S. Portland Halle. The family lived in a large French-style villa in SHAKER HTS.,† designed by JOHN WILLIAM CRESWELL COR-BUSIER. Halle traveled extensively and collected art; he helped found the PRINT CLUB OF CLEVE-LAND† (1920) and donated art works to the CLEVELAND MUSEUM OF ART.†—J.M.

**HALLORAN, WILLIAM L.** (23 July 1915–7 Dec. 1941), a young journalist who was Cleveland's first World War II casualty, was born to Lawrence and Stella (McGuire) Halloran and raised on Cleveland's west side. After graduation from CATHEDRAL LATIN SCHOOL† (1933), he worked as editor of the *Shopping News Junior* while attending JOHN CARROLL UNIV.† He transferred to OSU, graduating with a B.S. in journalism in 1938. He immediately began work as a United Press Internatl. reporter with the *Columbus Citizen*.

In early 1940, UPI transferred Halloran to Cleveland, where he worked as the UPI representative in the Cleveland Press building. With a deteriorating world situation, he left the *CLEVELAND PRESS†* to volunteer for active duty in the U.S. Naval Reserve in 1940. After attending the U.S. Naval Reserve Midshipmen's School at Northwestern Univ., Halloran received an ensign's commission in June 1941. He last visited Cleveland on 25 June 1941 and reported for duty aboard the USS *Arizona* 5 days later. Ens. Halloran perished aboard the *Arizona* on 7 Dec. 1941, when it was sunk during the surprise attack on Pearl Harbor.

Halloran became a symbol of America's loss at Pearl Harbor. Hundreds attended a memorial service at St. Ignatius Church and the Ensign William I. Halloran Club, dedicated to navy interests, was formed. The USS *Halloran* was launched in 1944, and in 1945 a Cleveland city park was named in Halloran's honor. Halloran was posthumously awarded the Purple Heart, American Defense Fleet Medal, Asiatic Pacific Campaign Medal, and World War II Freedom Medal.

**HALUPNIK, EUGENE A.** (24 Sept. 1929–7 Aug. 1993) was a civil engineer who played a major role in the construction and rehabilitation of roadway bridges throughout the Greater Cleveland area. He

was an employee of the Cuyahoga County Engineer's Office from 1968 to 1992, serving in the positions of bridge engineer, chief engineer, chief deputy engineer, and special projects engineer. Structural design plans prepared under his jurisdiction included the replacement of the Harvard-Denison Bridge (1979), Northfield Rd. Bridge (1985), and Brooklyn-Brighton Bridge (1987), plus the renovation of the HOPE MEMORIAL (Lorain-Carnegie) BRIDGE† (1983), Hilliard Rd. Bridge (1983), Lorain Rd. Bridge (1987), and Broadway (Whitehouse Crossing) Bridge (1988). He initially retired from the county in 1991 but was called back several months later to coordinate engineering plans for the reconstruction of the Burton Memorial Bridge (see MAIN AVENUE BRIDGE†), Ohio's longest roadway structure. His extensive knowledge of the project earned him the nickname "Grandfather of the Bridge."

Halupnik was born in Cleveland and grew up in the Slavic Village neighborhood. He graduated from South High School in 1946 and obtained much of his engineering expertise through self-education and on-the-job experience. His formal technical training included certificate degrees from the International Correspondence School in Scranton, PA, and the Wilson Engineering Correspondence School in Cambridge, MA.

Prior to his career with the County Engineer's Office, Halupnik worked with the Erie Railroad's Land and Engineering Departments in Corning and Sufferin, NY (1952–54); and Cleveland-based engineering design firms Turnbull Inc. (1954–62), Beiswenger, Hoch, Arnold & Assn. (1962–64), and Dalton, Dalton & Assn. (1965–68).

He married Gloria Mitchell on 12 Jan. 1952. They had 9 children: Steven, Timothy, Philip, Gregory, Gail, Cheryl, Mary, Sue, and Karen.

**HAM, THOMAS HALE** (19 July 1905–24 March 1987), pioneer in innovative medical education, was born in Oklahoma City, OK, the son of Mr. and Mrs. Thomas H. Ham, Sr. He graduated from Lincoln School of Teachers College, New York City, in 1923, received a B.S. from Dartmouth College in 1927, and an M.D. from Cornell Univ. Medical School in 1931. Before coming to Western Reserve Univ. in 1950, he worked at Thorndike Memorial Laboratory at Boston City Hospital, and taught at Harvard Medical School. From 1943–46 he served in the Army Medical Corps. During his tenure at WRU Medical School, 1950–74, he was appointed the Hanna-Payne Professor of Medicine and Director of Research in Medical Education. Although widely known for his research on the mechanisms of hemolytic anemias, Ham's major endeavor was the unique medical education curriculum he developed for WRU medical students, which was phased in over a period of 4 years, beginning in 1952. Central to the curriculum's design was the idea that medical students should be treated both as colleagues and clients. To that end, the amount of hard data students had to master was reduced, the opportunity to work with patients was offered early in the program, and students participated in and were responsible for their own education. Ham's model for medical education, considered radical at the time, was adopted nationwide. After retirement from CWRU in 1974, he moved to New Hampshire.

Ham married Fanny Curtis in 1936; they had 3 children: Thomas Caverno, Margaret Curtis, and Lola Josephine. He died in Hanover, NH, and was buried there.—M.S.

T. Hale Ham Papers, CWRU Archives.

**HAMANN, CARL AUGUST** (26 Jan. 1865–12 Jan. 1930), dean of Western Reserve Univ. Medical School (1912–19) and visiting surgeon at Charity and City hospitals (1896–1930) was born in Davenport, IA, to Claus H. and Marie Koenig Hamann. He graduated from the Univ. of Pennsylvania Medical School with an M.D. in 1890. Hamann was a resident physician at Lankenau Hospital in Philadelphia (1890–91) and asst. demonstrator of anatomy at the Univ. of Pennsylvania (1891–93) before coming to Cleveland in 1893 as professor of anatomy at WRU Medical School, additionally establishing a private practice. In 1912 he was appointed dean and professor of applied anatomy and clinical surgery, and is credited with helping build the school into one of the world's finest medical centers. As founder of the Hamann Museum of Comparative Anthropology at the medical school, he devoted much time to preparing, recording, and mounting materials he gathered for his anatomical teaching museum. Hamann was reputed to have done more charity practice than any other physician in the city. He performed over 10,000 operations, and even in his later years would perform up to 20 a day. For many years he shared the administrative burden for the department of surgery at Charity Hospital with Dr. FRANK BUNTS. With Bunts's death in 1928, Hamann shouldered the entire burden until he was struck with heart disease shortly before his own death. Hamann married Ella F. Ampt in 1900 and had 2 children, Carl A. and Elizabeth Marie.

**HAMILTON, ALEXANDER J.** (3 May 1903–26 May 1994) counted an Olympic medalist among those he trained in his lifelong hobby of speed skating. The son of Tom and Marie Hamilton, the native Clevelander was a graduate of West Techni-cal High School. He had begun skating in 1917 at EDGEWATER PARK.† He won the Ohio Olympic Skating trials in both the 5,000- and 10,000-meter races at ROCKEFELLER PARK† in 1927. Hamilton, who worked as an electrician for the M. A. HANNA CO.,† married the former Edna Senner in 1937. He started training skaters at the Edgewater Speedskating Club, which he had organized in 1935. After developing several national champions and recordholders, he formed the Town & Country Speedskating Club in STRONGS-VILLE† in 1960. One of his students there was Jenny Fish, who became the only Ohio woman to make the U.S. Olympic speed skating team. Hamilton accompanied her to the 1968 Winter Olympics in Grenoble, France, where Fish won a 2nd-place silver medal. Hamilton's awards included the J. F. Kennedy Sports Memorial Medal and selection to the Amateur Skating Union Hall of Fame. He was a director of the U.S. International Skating Assn. and a member of the U.S. Olympic Speed Skating Committee. A resident of ROCKY RIVER,† he served on the suburb's city council in 1958–59. He was buried at Sunset Memorial Park, survived by his wife and a son, James.—J.V.

**HAMILTON, JAMES MONTGOMERY** (26 June 1876–12 Jan. 1941), prominent architect active in Cleveland from 1905 until the 1930s and, in partnership with FRANK B. MEADE, responsible for designing several hundred homes in historical revival styles, was born in Ft. Wayne, IN, son of Allen and Cecilia (Frank) Hamilton. After graduating from high school in 1894, he attended MIT in Boston and moved to Cleveland in 1901. Hamilton traveled in Europe for 2 years (1903–04) to study architecture, then returned to Cleveland, where he worked for the firm of Meade & Garfield. In 1911 he formed a partnership with Meade—Meade & Hamilton—which lasted until 1941. The two architects designed many residences for industrialists living in the northeastern U.S. Among Meade & Hamilton's projects in the Greater Cleveland area were the Euclid Ave. homes of Francis E. Drury, H. G. Otis, NATHAN L. DAUBY, Kenyon V. Painter, and Henry White, and the WADE PARK† homes of Eugene R. Grasselli, A. A. Augustus, Justin Sholes, and EMIL JOSEPH. In the emerging suburbs of Euclid and AMBLER HTS.† (now CLEVELAND HTS.†), the firm designed homes for MYRON T. HERRICK, John Sherwin, and John G. W. Cowles. In SHAKER HTS.,† homes were designed for CAE-SAR A. GRASSELLI, A. H. Diebold, C. K. Chisholm, ROLLIN H. WHITE, and Ira H. Baker. In addition to residential buildings, Meade & Hamilton designed 6 clubhouses, including the SHAKER HTS. COUNTRY CLUB,† the MAY-

FIELD COUNTRY CLUB,† and the HERMIT CLUB.† Never married, Hamilton died in Cleveland and was buried in Ft. Wayne, IN.

Johannesen, Eric. *Cleveland Architecture, 1876–1976* (1979).

**HAMILTON, MARGARET** (1902–15 May 1985), a Cleveland actress best remembered as the "Wicked Witch of the West" in the film classic *The Wizard of Oz,* graduated from HATHAWAY BROWN† in 1921. Daughter of Walter J. and Jennie (Adams) Hamilton, her family wanted her to become a teacher, so she went to Wheelock Kindergarten Training School in Boston, where she acted in a production of *Little Women.* Returning to Cleveland, Hamilton taught at Hough Elementary School, then operated her own nursery for the Cleveland Hts. Presbyterian Church. She went to New York in 1922 to teach day school, but became enamored with the theater. She quit teaching, returned to Cleveland, and worked at the CLEVELAND PLAY HOUSE† from 1927–30, meeting and marrying landscape architect Paul Meserve on 13 June 1931. After the Play House, Hamilton did summer work in Massachusetts. Arthur Beckworth "discovered" Hamilton in a play entitled *The Hallems.* The Broadway version, called *Another Language,* was the surprise hit of 1932 and was made into a film with Hamilton and Helen Hayes, launching Hamilton's Hollywood career. Because of her distinctive profile, however, her roles were never very diverse; she usually played aunts and spinsters. Her role as the wicked witch came in 1939 and further typecast Hamilton. She continued making films and doing plays, appearing in more than 75 of each. She also did guest roles on television and made commercials. In her later years, Hamilton appeared several times at the Play House. She also continued to teach Sunday school and volunteer in various causes. Hamilton divorced her husband in 1938; they had a son, Hamilton. She died in Salisbury, CT.

**HAMMOND, GEORGE FRANCIS** (26 Nov. 1855–26 Apr. 1938), an important classical architect active in Cleveland from 1886–1926, was born in Roxbury, MA, the son of George and Cornelia Johnson Hammond. He attended the Massachusetts Normal Art School, and studied with Wm. R. Ware, founder of the first American curriculum based on the Beaux-Arts system of architectural training, at MIT. In 1876 Hammond worked as a draftsman in the office of Wm. G. Preston in Boston. He began independent work in 1878, setting up his own office in 1884. In 1886 Hammond moved to Cleveland, having designed the first HOLLENDEN HOTEL† in 1885, one of the first large fireproof hotels in Cleveland (see HOTELS†). Among his Ohio works were the Electric Bldg., 1900; the First Church of Christ, Scientist (Lane Metropolitan CME Church), 1904; the master campus plan and 5 original buildings of the Ohio State Normal College (Kent State Univ.), 1911–15; McKinley High School, Canton; and the U.S. Post Office in Zanesville. He designed hospitals, schools, factories, and power buildings in Chicago, Kansas City, New Orleans, Toronto, and Montreal. Hammond's own home in CLEVELAND HTS.† is a fine Colonial Revival residence. He designed a number of suburban homes, especially in the CLIFTON PARK† area of LAKEWOOD.† He published *A Treatise on Hospital and Asylum Construction* in 1891.

Hammond married Annie Borland Barstow in 1883. Following her death in 1886, he married Annie E. Butcher of Toronto in 1897; they divorced in 1922. Hammond's third wife was Dorothy Weirick, whom he divorced in 1931. Hammond had one child, Adelaid, from his first marriage. Retiring in 1926, Hammond died in Falls Village, CT.

**HAMPSON, JAMES B.** (1841–28 May 1864), a volunteer CIVIL WAR† officer killed in action during the Atlanta Campaign in Georgia, was a printer by trade, who was listed as 4th cpl. of the CLEVELAND GRAYS† in June 1860. He enlisted in Co. E, 1st Ohio Volunteer Infantry, for 3 months' service, 23 Apr. 1861. Hampson was promoted to 2nd lt. on 17 June 1861 and to 1st lt. on 2 July 1861. He was mustered out with his company on 1 Aug. 1861. Hampson enlisted in the 124th OVI as a major, dating from 1 Jan. 1863. While on staff duty with Gen. Wood, commander of the 3rd Div., 4th Army Corps, Army of the Cumberland, at the Battle of Pickett's Mills, GA, he was mortally wounded. He had stated many times that he would be killed in the line of duty. Hampson is buried in Marietta Natl. Cemetery. His bust is displayed in a medallion in the SOLDIERS & SAILORS MONUMENT† on Cleveland's PUBLIC SQUARE.† Hampson Post, No. 23, GRAND ARMY OF THE REPUBLIC,† which met at 184 Superior, was named in his honor.

Lewis, George W. *The Campaigns of the One Hundred and Twenty-fourth Regiment* (1894).

**HANDRICK, GERTRUDE M.** (FORAN) (1 May 1871–7 Sept. 1937), admitted to the bar on 21 Dec. 1911, defied tradition to become the first female lawyer in the CLEVELAND BAR ASSN.† Handrick was born in Cleveland to Judge Martin A. Foran and Kate (Kavanaugh) Foran, attended Villa Angela school and graduated in 1888 from the Georgetown

Visitation Convent in Washington, DC. On 5 April 1899, she married surgeon Franklin Aylesworth Handrick; the couple had a daughter, Martha, and a son, Martin F. After the deaths of her husband (1901) and daughter (1907), Handrick worked as a secretary in various law offices, including her father's. She began secretly studying law and, though at first opposed by her father, attended Baldwin University (see BALDWIN-WALLACE COLLEGE†). The only woman in a class of 37, she graduated in 1911. The next January she began practice and opened an office in the SOCIETY FOR SAVINGS BUILDING† that March. She served as attorney for the Home Owners' Loan Corp., among others. Handrick actively supported suffrage for women, heading the Business Woman's Suffrage League (1912). She also presided over the Catholic Ladies of Columbia, Branch No. 14, for 2 years. At her death, she lived on Detroit Ave.—J.M.

**HANDY, TRUMAN P.** (17 Jan. 1807–25 Mar. 1898), banker and financier, was born in Paris, Oneida County, NY, to William and Eunice (Parmalee) Handy. He entered banking at 18 as a clerk. In 1830 he helped organize the Bank of Buffalo and was a teller. He moved to Cleveland in Mar. 1832 at the request of historian Geo. Bancroft, who, with associates, acquired the defunct COMMERCIAL BANK OF LAKE ERIE.† Handy was cashier when the bank reopened. From 1843–45 Handy operated his own banking office, T. P. Handy & Co. In 1845, he became a director, cashier, largest stockholder, and chief executive officer of the new Commercial Branch Bank. In 1862 he became president of Merchants Branch Bank; and became president of Merchants Natl. Bank in 1865, continuing with its successor, Mercantile Natl. Bank, from 1885 until his retirement in 1892.

Handy helped organize railroads and manufacturing enterprises, including CLEVELAND & NEWBURGH RAILROAD CO.†; Cleveland, Columbus & Cincinnati Railroad Co.; Cleveland Iron Mining Co.; and Cleveland Rolling Mill Co. He was also president and executive committee member of the CLEVELAND CLEARINGHOUSE ASSN.† As a member of the first school board, Handy helped establish Cleveland public schools; he also helped organize CLEVELAND UNIV.† (1850); incorporate Case School of Applied Science and Western Reserve Univ.; and was a founder and president of CLEVELAND INDUSTRIAL SCHOOL.† He was a founding member of the Second Presbyterian Church (1844), and was also first president of the CLEVELAND MOZART SOCIETY.† Handy married Harriet N. Hall (d. 1880) in 1832. They had 2 children: a son who died in infancy, and a daughter, Helen. Handy died in Cleveland and is buried in Lake View Cemetery.

Annals of the Early Settlers Assn. (1898).

**HANKS, JARVIS FRARY** (24 Sept. 1799–27 June 1853), played a pivotal role in introducing the arts of painting and music into pioneer Cleveland. A native of Pittsfield, NY, he survived the Battle of Chippewa as a drummer boy in the U.S. Army during the War of 1812. Following the war, Hanks became an itinerant painter of everything from portraits to houses in such frontier communities as Charleston, VA (later WV), where he married Charlotte Garber. He studied portraiture with Thomas Sully in Philadelphia before working his way to Cleveland in 1825. Hanging out his shingle as a portrait, sign, and ornamental painter, Hanks stayed 2 years before going back to New York, where he exhibited at the National Academy of Design and attracted Cleveland's notice through his public renunciation of Masonry during the anti-Masonic movement. Hanks returned to Cleveland for good ca. 1836. Although he advertised his desire to concentrate his talents on portraiture, he continued through the years to solicit commissions for signs and ornamental paintings. Among his portraits were likenesses of TRUMAN P. HANDY, PETER WEDDELL, and blacksmith Abraham Hickox. An accomplished fiddler as well, Hanks began giving vocal lessons by 1840 and in 1850 was appointed music director of the newly formed CLEVELAND MENDELSSOHN SOCIETY.† He was also active civically, serving as secretary of the Cuyahoga County Total Abstinence Society (see TEMPERANCE†) and participating in anti-slavery meetings and movements. The father of 10 children, he maintained a farm at DOAN'S CORNERS† and is buried at Woodland Cemetery.—J.M.

Grant, Francis. "The Emergence of Cultural Patterns in a Great American City: Cleveland," *Fine Arts* (1971).

**HANNA, DANIEL RHODES** (26 Dec. 1866–3 Nov. 1921) was born in Cleveland, the son of Charlotte Augusta (Rhodes) and MARCUS A. HANNA. He was owner and publisher of the *CLEVELAND NEWS†* and *Sunday News-Leader,* and, as a partner in the M. A. HANNA CO.† (1891–1915), led in developing iron ore in the northwestern Great Lakes and in the bituminous coal and blast furnace industries. In 1910 Hanna purchased the *CLEVELAND LEADER,†* and in 1912 he acquired the *Cleveland News* from CHAS. A. OTIS, JR. He published the *News* and *Leader* until 1917, when the *Leader* was sold to the *PLAIN DEALER.†* The *Sunday Leader* continued to be published with the *News* as the *Sunday News-Leader*. Hanna built the Leader-News Bldg. (1912), and the Hanna Bldg. and Theater as a memorial to his father (1921). Both buildings were planned by New York architect Chas. A. Platt.

Hanna was a member of many clubs and lived at various times on Franklin Ave., Lake Ave. (LAKEWOOD†), Euclid Ave., and Bratenahl Rd., and had homes in Ravenna, OH, Lenox, MA, and Ossining, NY. He remodeled the home in Ravenna, a Rhodes-Hanna house constructed in 1817, in the early 1900s, incorporating portions of 2 rooms purportedly from the renovated Buckingham Palace. Hanna married Daisy Gordon and later May Harrington, and had 8 children: Mark A., Carl H., Dan R., Jr., Elizabeth, Natalie, Ruth, Charlotte, and Mary. He died in Ossining, NY, and was buried in Lake View Cemetery.

**HANNA, DANIEL RHODES, JR.** (28 May 1894–13 Sept. 1962), publisher and journalist, was born in Cleveland to DANIEL RHODES HANNA, SR., and May Harrington Hanna and had 2 older brothers, Marcus Alonzo Hanna II and Carl Harrington Hanna. Hanna attended CLEVELAND PUBLIC SCHOOLS,† Taft School in Watertown, CT, and Phillips Andover Academy, Andover, MA. At 19, he joined his father at the *CLEVELAND NEWS,†* which the elder Hanna owned. When his father died in 1921, Hanna took over the paper. In 1925 he became president and general manager of the Cleveland Co., which owned and operated the daily and Sunday *Cleveland News*. In 1932 FOREST CITY PUBLISHING CO.† acquired the stock of the *Cleveland News* and *PLAIN DEALER.†* By 1946 Hanna was vice-president and director of Forest City Publishing Co., but had little influence on the *News's* direction. In 1951 he became vice-president and chairman of the Hanna Bldg. Corp. and Hanna Theater Corp., replacing his brother, Carl. Hanna remained associated with the Hanna Bldg. until his death, even though it and the theater had been purchased by the T. W. Grogan Co. in 1958. Hanna was a principal founder of the Chagrin Valley Kennel Club. He married Ruth Randall in 1917 and had 4 children: Natalie, John R., Dan R., Jr., and Mary (Noss). Their marriage ended in divorce in 1935. Hanna married Lucia Otis Newell on 25 July 1936. He was buried in Knollwood Cemetery.

**HANNA, HOWARD MELVILLE** (23 Jan. 1840–8 Feb. 1921), a founder of the M. A. HANNA CO.,† was active in the shipping industry on the Great Lakes as well as in the development of the oil, steel, and tobacco businesses locally. Brother to MARCUS ALONZO HANNA and LEONARD C. HANNA, JR., he was born to Dr. Leonard and Samantha

Converse Hanna in New Lisbon, OH, where he lived until the family moved to Cleveland when he was 12. He attended public schools and graduated from Union College in Schenectady, NY. Hanna enlisted in the Union Navy at the outbreak of Civil War.

After the war, Hanna engaged briefly in shipping, then pioneered in the oil business, later selling his interest to the STANDARD OIL CO.† (OHIO). He also purchased controlling interest in the Globe Iron Works, later the AMERICAN SHIP BUILDING CO.† Hanna was one of the GLENVILLE RACE TRACK's† original stockholders and belonged to the WESTERN RESERVE HISTORICAL SOCIETY.† Interested in reform and PHILANTHROPY,† he served as the first president of the CHARITY ORGANIZATION SOCIETY.† Hanna spoke against "thoughtless giving" (see the BOLTON FOUNDATION†). His donations to Lakeside Hospital, the proposed Babies' Hospital (see UNIV. HOSPITALS†) and the medical department of Western Reserve Univ. (see CASE WESTERN RESERVE UNIV.†) were said to total over $1 million.

On 28 Dec. 1863 Hanna married Kate Smith (d. May 1919); they had 2 sons, H. M., Jr., and Leonard, who died in infancy, and 2 daughters, Mary Gertrude (Mrs. COBURN) HASKELL and Kate B. (d. 1936), who, divorced from R. Livingston Ireland, married Perry W. Harvey. Hanna died at his winter home in Thomasville, GA.—J.M.

**HANNA, LEONARD C., JR.** (5 Nov. 1889–5 Oct. 1957), a philanthropist who contributed over $90 million to cultural and charitable institutions, and a director of the M. A. HANNA & CO.,† was born in Cleveland to Leonard and Coralie (Walker) Hanna. He attended Univ. School, Hill School in Pottstown, PA, and Yale Univ. After graduation from Yale, he worked in the iron and steel industry to gain experience. He then served with the Army Signal Corps in World War I. After the war he returned to Cleveland and was admitted to the partnership of M. A. Hanna & Co. (which later became Hanna Mining) in 1917.

Hanna was an avid art collector, theatergoer, and patron of the arts, as well as a boxing and baseball fan. In 1914 he joined the Cleveland Museum of Art's advisory committee, and beginning in 1920, served on the Accessions Committee. In 1941 he incorporated the Leonard C. Hanna Jr. Fund, and as president and one of its trustees, was responsible for dispensing millions of dollars to institutions in Ohio, including KARAMU HOUSE,† the CLEVELAND PLAY HOUSE,† UNIV. HOSPITALS,† and Western Reserve Univ. From 1942–44 he served with the American Red Cross in England, establishing and directing recreational centers for American airmen stationed in England. At his death, Hanna left a bequest of over $33 million to the CLEVELAND MUSEUM OF ART.† Hanna, never married, died at his home in Kirtland; he was buried in Lake View Cemetery.

**HANNA, MARCUS ALONZO** (24 Sept. 1837–15 Feb. 1904), businessman, national Republican leader, and U.S. Senator, was born in New Lisbon, OH, to Leonard and Samantha Converse Hanna. His family came to Cleveland in 1852, where Hanna attended CENTRAL HIGH SCHOOL,† and later Western Reserve College in Hudson (1857–58). He entered his father's wholesale grocery business, and after marrying Charlotte Rhodes, joined his father-in-law's firm, Rhodes & Co., iron and coal merchants. When Rhodes died, Hanna assumed company control, and in 1885 it became the M. A. HANNA CO.† Hanna also owned West Side Railway, later WOODLAND AVE. & WEST SIDE RAILWAY.† In the late 1880s Hanna began electrifying his street railways, consolidating with Cleveland City Cable Co. to form Cleveland City Railway Co., and competing for streetcar franchises in opposition to TOM L. JOHNSON. Hanna bought the EUCLID AVE. OPERA HOUSE† in the late 1870s.

Hanna was elected to the Cleveland Board of Education ca. 1869. As a Republican, he was active at the ward level, organized a Businessman's Republican Campaign Club, and collected funds and himself donated. He became a political campaigner, managing Jas. B. Foraker's successful gubernatorial campaign (1885) and John Sherman's unsuccessful Republican presidential nominee (1888) and successful Senate (1892) campaigns. Hanna withdrew from participation in M. A. Hanna Co. in 1894 to devote himself to nominating Ohio governor Wm. McKinley for president. McKinley was nominated, and Hanna organized his successful presidential campaigns in 1896 and 1900. In 1897 Hanna was appointed U.S. Senator; the Ohio legislature elected him there in 1898 and 1904. Hanna maintained national and state Republican power, even after McKinley's death in 1901; however Cleveland politics were then dominated by Democratic mayor Tom L. Johnson. Hanna married Charlotte Augusta Rhodes in 1864 and had 2 children, Daniel Rhodes and Ruth Hanna McCormick Simms. Hanna died in Washington and was buried at Lake View Cemetery.

Beer, Thomas. *Hanna* (1929).
Croly, Herbert. *Marcus Alonzo Hanna: His Life and Work* (1912).
McCook, Henry Christopher. *The Senator: A Threnody* (1905).

**HANULYA, JOSEPH P.** (10 Aug. 1873–8 Oct. 1962) was a priest of the Byzantine Catholic Rite and a leader in preserving the cultural legacy of the Rusin (Ruthenian) people.

Born to Peter and Mary Hanulya in Nizny Repas, in what is today the Slovak Republic, he had his early schooling in his home village. Then Hanulya entered the Byzantine Rite Seminary in Presov. On 10 Nov. 1897 he was ordained to the priesthood by Bp. John Valyi of Presov.

Hanulya's first seven years as a priest were spent in his native diocese. Then in 1904 he came to the U.S., serving in several Pennsylvania parishes. In 1918 he was named pastor of HOLY GHOST BYZANTINE CATHOLIC CHURCH,† 2408 West 14th St., in Cleveland.

His Cleveland congregation was almost entirely of Rusin descent, and Hanulya soon embarked on serving not only his parishioners' spiritual needs, but also helping them preserve their cultural heritage. In the course of that commitment, Hanulya authored some twelve works, ranging from a Rusin grammar and reader to historical and catechetical works.

He also spearheaded the campaign for the Rusin cultural garden in ROCKEFELLER PARK,† cofounded the Rusin Educational Society, and sponsored *The Leader*, a monthly Rusin publication.

In 1953 Hanulya became pastor emeritus of Holy Ghost Church, but remained active in church affairs. He celebrated the sixtieth anniversary of his ordination on 10 Nov. 1957.

Hanulya married Mary Hvozdovich 23 Sept. 1897. They had five children: Joseph, Jr., Mary, Alice, Martha, and Michael. Survived by his children, Hanulya was interred in the Holy Ghost parish cemetery.—J.T.

**HARD, GEN. DUDLEY JACKSON** (4 Aug. 1873–9 Oct. 1950), military leader, was born in Wooster, OH, to Curtis V. and Adeline Jackson Hard, and graduated from the College of Wooster (1893). In 1894 he joined Cleveland Light & Power Co. which, in 1893, had bought the Williams Publishing Co.'s small steam-engine electricity business for its immediate neighbors. Hard joined the firm as treasurer, and by 1946 was president when the company's interests were purchased by CLEVELAND ELECTRIC ILLUMINATING CO.† In 1898 Hard left private business to become a serviceman, enlisting as a private in Ohio's 8th Volunteer Infantry, serving in the Spanish-American War. From 1906–10, Hard served in Troop A of the Ohio Cavalry, as a 1st lt. By 1916 he was a major, commanding a battalion from Ohio in the Mexican border campaign. During World War I, Hard was a colonel commanding the 135th Field Artillery. In 1923 he was promoted to colonel, chief of staff, of Ohio's 37th Div., and by 1928 was brigadier general of the 54th Ohio Cavalry Brigade. In 1936 Hard became major general, commanding the 37th Div. of the Ohio Natl. Guard. Retiring that year, he became the first county commander in Cleveland of the American Legion. Hard received the Cleveland Medal for Public Service in 1936. After his retirement, Hard became involved with the Cleveland Welfare Fed., Cleveland and Ohio chambers of commerce, and Cuyahoga County Boy Scouts. He married Mildred J. Hopkins in 1903 and had 2 children, Dudley J., Jr., and Mrs. Jane Russell. Hard is buried in Lake View Cemetery.

Dudley Hard Papers, WRHS.

## HARGRAVE, MASON ALEXANDER (20 Mar. 1923–12 Dec. 1988) was an African American community activist best known for his work with the UNIVERSAL NEGRO IMPROVEMENT ASSN.†

Hargrave was born in Virginia, the son of Rev. James W. and Sadie E. (Johnson) Hargrave, and raised in Buffalo, NY. He came to Cleveland in 1947, working first as a railroad waiter and then at a variety of jobs. From 1969 to 1981 he worked for HOPE Inc., an organization that developed new housing in Hough.

Hargrave joined the UNIA in 1969, at a time when membership in the organization was declining significantly. He served as the president of the Cleveland chapter, and eventually became the organization's national president. He also promoted the acceptance of the red, black, and green black nationalist flag, and was instrumental in having it flown for the first time over Cleveland City Hall in 1974. Hargrave worked for better community relations and served on the boards of several community organizations.

In the 1980s, Hargrave led efforts to restore the UNIA Building (formerly the JACOB GOLDSMITH HOUSE†). He planned to convert it into a headquarters for the UNIA as well as a museum and cultural and neighborhood center. In Nov. 1988, the house suffered a devastating fire. The following month Hargrave died, and in January, 1989, the house was demolished. After Hargrave's death, the Cleveland chapter of the UNIA went dormant.

Hargrave and his wife Mary Jane (d. 1970), had a son, Mason A. Hargrave, Jr. Hargrave, Sr. died in Cleveland and is buried in Riverside Cemetery. —D.R.

Universal Negro Improvement Association Records, WRHS.

## HARKNESS, ANNA M. (RICHARDSON) (25 Oct. 1837–27 March 1926), a philanthropist who generously supported educational and health causes in Cleveland and elsewhere, founded the Commonwealth Fund in New York City on 17 October 1918. Locally, she endowed a chair in Biblical literature at Western Reserve Univ. (WRU, later CASE WESTERN RESERVE UNIV.†), presented a $50,000 gift to Lakeside Hospital (later part of UNIV. HOSPITALS†) and, with her son-in-law, Louis Henry Severance, funded WRU's Harkness Chapel, dedicated 1902 in memory of her daughter, Florence. Harkness was born in Dalton, OH. She married Stephen V. Harkness of Monroeville, OH, in 1853 (sometimes given as 1854) (his second wife); they moved to Cleveland in 1866. The couple had 2 daughters, Jennie and Florence Harkness Severance, and 2 sons, Charles W. (d. 1916) and Edward S. In 1891, three years after her husband's death, Harkness moved to New York but continued to maintain a home in WILLOUGHBY.†

In 1917 Harkness gave $3.5 million to Yale Univ. She also donated to Fifth Ave. Presbyterian Church in New York City, as well as the national Presbyterian Church. With her son, Edward, Harkness donated 20 acres of land for the medical center of Columbia Univ. (1924).—J.M.

McGehee, A. *"For the Welfare of Mankind": The Commonwealth Fund and American Medicine* (1986).
See also PHILANTHROPY,† WOMEN.†

## HARKNESS, STEPHEN V. (18 Nov. 1818–6 Mar. 1888), financier who provided crucial support for the STANDARD OIL CO.,† was born in Fayette, NY, and apprenticed to a harnessmaker after his formal education ended at age 15. When his apprenticeship ended at 21, he moved to Bellevue, OH. Moving often in the 1850s, Harkness soon left harnessmaking for other ventures. In 1855 he established a distillery in Monroeville, OH, and by 1860 was a leading businessman, organizing a bank in 1860, and in 1864 forming a partnership with Wm. Halsey Doan to supply crude oil to refineries. His fortune made, Harkness sold his Monroeville enterprises in 1866 and moved to Cleveland. Although retired from daily involvement in business, he continued to invest, most successfully in Standard Oil. Harkness invested between $60,000 and $90,000 in the firm's forerunner, Rockefeller, Andrews & Flagler, and in 1870 became a charter member of Standard Oil Co. He was a director of the firm until his death. From 1869–72, Harkness owned one-third of the Union Elevator firm with GEO. W. GARDNER and Geo. H. Burt. In 1876 he built the Harkness Block at Euclid and Willson (E. 55th). He was a director of Euclid Ave. Natl. Bank and Ohio

River Railway Co., and president of Iron Belt Mining Co. and Cleveland Arcade Co. Harkness married twice—to Laura Osborn in 1842 and to Anna M. Richardson in 1853.

**HARNEY, HARRISON HANNIBAL** (26 June 1896–24 Sept. 1990) was an original member of the Cleveland Police Department homicide unit, organized in 1926, and the first African American promoted to detective on the Cleveland Police Force.

Born in Pulaski, TN, Harney was raised by a brother in Birmingham, AL, and attended Talladega College in Talladega, AL. Harney moved to Cleveland from Youngstown in 1918.

In 1922 Harney became a Cleveland policeman and served on the force for 36 years. He was promoted to detective in 1924 after a shootout with four robbers in a drugstore at E. 36th St. and Carnegie Ave. Harney fatally shot one robber, wounded a second, and wrestled a third to the floor as the fourth fled. Together with Horace Jenkins, his career partner, Harney investigated more than 1,000 homicides, including the assassination of Councilman William Potter in 1931, the infamous TORSO MURDERS† in KINGSBURY RUN† in the 1930s, and the SHEPPARD MURDER CASE.† They received commendations from ELIOT NESS for their work.

Harney used his free time to work in the community, sponsoring athletic teams for youths, who called him "Pops." Harney retired from the force in 1958 and worked as a bail bondsman. He deplored the changes in the police force after his retirement. He felt that the police were too quick to use their guns instead of their heads and had stopped building rapport with people on their beats.

Harney married Mary Bell in 1917. They had five children: Kenneth, Nathaniel, Alice, Barbara, and Leonard. Harney lived in Cleveland and is buried in Highland Park Cemetery.—T.B.

**HARRIS, ALFRED WILSON** (18 Aug. 1884–19 Mar. 1932), architect active in Cleveland from 1917–32, was born in Tremont, IL, to William H. and Francis F. (Fenner) Harris. He attended the Univ. of Illinois, then lived in Peoria several years, serving in the Air Force during World War I. Harris began practicing architecture in Cleveland in 1917, considered a most competent designer of English-style houses, several of which were built in SHAKER HTS.† He is best known for the design of Moreland Courts, a $30 million apartment and commercial development including MORELAND COURTS APARTMENTS,† terrace homes on Van Aken Blvd., business buildings, stores, a theater, market house, central heating plant, and parking garage. Harris spent 14 months on the preliminary planning

for the JOSIAH KIRBY development. When Kirby's plans failed in 1923, less than a year after they were announced, the VAN SWERINGEN brothers employed Harris to prepare a scheme developing Shaker Blvd. west to E. 93rd St. However, the Harris plan was never carried out, and PHILIP L. SMALL and Carl B. Rowley (see CHARLES B. ROWLEY) were engaged by the Van Sweringens to complete Moreland Courts and plan Shaker Square. Although Harris's scheme was not completely realized, the block of smaller apartments south of Shaker Square was nearly all designed by Harris, although built by different developers. Harris also painted and sculpted. Aviation was a lifelong pursuit, and he was a charter member of the Cleveland Aviation Club, founded in 1919.

Harris married Mary E. Harris and had 2 sons, Alfred, Jr., and Thomas. He died in Cleveland and was buried in Highland Park Cemetery.

**HARRIS, JOSIAH A.** (15 Jan. 1808–21 Aug. 1876), noted publisher and editor, son of Charity (Messenger) and Judge Josiah Harris, moved with his family from Becket, MA, in 1818 to N. Amherst, Lorain County. In 1832 Harris settled in Elyria, was elected sheriff, and revived Elyria's first newspaper as the weekly *Ohio Atlas & Elyria Advertiser*. He sold the paper and traveled before coming to Cleveland in 1837 and purchasing the *CLEVELAND HERALD & GAZETTE†* with Judge CHAS. WHITTLESEY, who gave up his share after 1 year. Harris solidly established the *Herald,* paying its debts and providing its own printing office. He won local support by printing marriage, death, and meeting notices, and furnishing free papers to clergymen. He refused to print ads for the more notorious quack medicines, or notices for the return of runaway slaves. Harris kept the *Herald* solidly behind the WHIG PARTY.† He was elected mayor of Cleveland in 1847. Joined by partners A. W. Fairbanks in 1849 and GEO. A. BENEDICT in 1853, Harris began loosening his ties with the *Herald.* Benedict took over as editor in 1857, when Harris moved over to EDWIN COWLES'S *Leader,* which he edited from Feb. 1857–Nov. 1860. Although Harris briefly returned thereafter to the *Herald,* he quit journalism permanently after the Civil War. His retirement was spent on a farm in ROCKY RIVER,† where he raised grapes. Harris married Esther M. Race in 1830 and had 4 children: Bryon C., Brougham E., Zacharia, and Helen (Mrs. F. X. Byerly). After suffering a series of strokes, Harris died at his daughter's home and was buried in the Erie St. Cemetery.

**HARRISON, MARVIN CLINTON** (13 July 1890– 29 Aug. 1954), labor-management and union attorney, grew up in Scribner, NE, son of Bradley and Carolina (Warner) Harrison. He graduated from Harvard Law School (1915) and considered himself a socialist. In 1916 Harrison moved to Cleveland, working briefly for a firm specializing in accident litigation. He went into partnership with Geo. Seith as a corporate attorney for General Insurance Co. During the war, Harrison served in the Naval Reserve, 1917–18.

Harrison was a partner with Homer Marshman (1934–47), then joined Harrison, Thomas, Spangenberg & Hull, which dealt primarily with accident litigation; however Harrison involved himself in cases involving labor unions and industrial accidents. In the LITTLE STEEL STRIKE OF 1937,† Harrison helped win settlements for strike victims harmed by the Republic Steel Corp.'s attacks on strikers. Harrison was also involved in labor-management disputes at Thompson Prods. and Hercules Motors, and in intra-union disputes in the Brotherhood of Railroad Trainmen and United Furniture Workers Local #450. In 1944 he helped win settlements for victims of the EAST OHIO GAS EXPLOSION.† In 1931 Harris drafted an unemployment-compensation bill for the Ohio legislature. He was an Ohio state senator from 1933–34 and worked for the ratification of the Natl. Child Labor Amendment and passage of the Ohio minimum-wage law. During the Depression, Harrison supported the New Deal and participated in a Senate investigation of defaulted banks in Cleveland. Harrison was president of the CONSUMERS LEAGUE OF OHIO† between 1934–54. Harrison married Clara Rockow in New York City on 6 June 1922. They had one child, Jean Bradley. Harrison died of a heart attack at his summer home in Canada.

Consumers League of Ohio Records, WRHS.
Marvin Clinton Harrison Papers, WRHS.

**HART, ALBERT BUSHNELL** (1 July 1854–16 June 1943) was a historian and a professor of government and history at Harvard Univ., raised in Cleveland. Hart was born in Clarksville, PA, the son of a doctor, ALBERT GAILORD HART. When the younger Hart was 10, the family moved to Cleveland, where he graduated from WEST HIGH SCHOOL† in 1871. He received his B.A. from Harvard in 1880 and proceeded to the Univ. of Freiburg in Baden, Germany, for his Ph.D. Hart returned to the U.S. and was appointed instructor at Harvard in 1883. He became full professor in 1897 and retired as professor emeritus in 1926. Hart was a member of the Massachusetts Constitutional Convention and president of the American Historical Assn. and the American Political Science Assn. He wrote and edited more than 80 volumes and contributed to numerous magazines and journals. He was editor of the 28-vol. *The American Nation*. Hart's own contribution to the series, *Slavery and Abolition* (1906), was one of his most durable works. He returned to Cleveland in April 1932 as the official historian for the U.S. Washington Bicentennial Commission to speak on Washington at SEVERANCE HALL.† Hart was honored at that time with the dedication of Albert Bushnell Hart Jr. High School by the CLEVELAND PUBLIC SCHOOLS.† Hart was married in 1889 to Mary Hurd Putnam of New Hampshire.—J.V.

**HART, ALBERT GAILORD** (17 Aug. 1821–10 Oct. 1907), physician and CIVIL WAR† army surgeon, was born in Hartford, OH (Trumbull County), son of Ambrose and Louisy (Bushnell) Hart. He graduated with a bachelor's degree from Western Reserve College in 1840, studied medicine in Mercer County, PA. (1841–43) and attended lectures at the Univ. of Pennsylvania, received his master's degree from Western Reserve College in 1844, practiced medicine in Middlesex, PA, from 1844–52, and received his medical degree from Jefferson Medical College in Philadelphia, PA, in 1852. Between 1852–60, he practiced in Clarksville (Mercer County), PA. In 1860 he moved to Hartford, OH, and invested in the oil business in Mecca, OH. When the Civil War broke out, Hart was appointed asst. surgeon, 41ST OHIO VOLUNTEER INF.† In Jan. 1864 Hart returned to Ohio, accompanying Col. AQUILA WILEY of the 41st Regiment to Cleveland, on veterans furlough, returning to the field with his regiment before resigning in Nov. 1864. Hart moved his family to Brooklyn Twp. in 1864 and served on the medical staff at the U.S. GENERAL HOSPITAL† in Univ. Hts. He became a member of the Medical Society of Cleveland in 1870, served on the Cleveland Board of Education, 1871–73, and was a member of the CLEVELAND BOARD OF HEALTH† in 1880. Hart married Mary Crosley Hornell 6 June 1844 and had 2 sons, Hastings Cornell and ALBERT BUSHNELL; and 2 daughters, Helen Marcia and Mary Jeanette. Hart is buried in Woodland Cemetery.

Albert Gailord Hart Papers, WRHS.

**HARTMAN, CHARLES A.** (1824–2 May 1863), an army surgeon in the CIVIL WAR,† served as Cuyahoga County coroner prior to his entrance into the army as surgeon of the 107TH OHIO VOLUNTEER INFANTRY† on 26 Aug. 1862. The 107th was organized and given preliminary training at Camp Cleveland, Aug.-Sept. 1862. A physician in civilian life, Hartman was listed as killed at the Battle of Chancellorsville, VA, on 2 May 1863. He was listed as being buried at Fredericksburg but is not in the register of burials at Fredericksburg Natl. Cemetery.

Hartman was married twice. His first marriage was to Sarah E. Bacon on 4 June 1850. After her death, he married Anna Magdalene Boyd on 4 Dec. 1855. Hartman had no children from either marriage. He is remembered in Cleveland by a large medallion of his bust in the SOLDIERS & SAILORS MONUMENT.†

**HARTZ, AUGUSTUS "GUS" FREDERIC** (8 Sept. 1843–22 May 1929), one of Cleveland's best-known theatrical figures, was born in Liverpool, England, apprenticed to a stage magician at 8, and studied with a tutor in the evenings. Arriving in the U.S. in 1863, he pursued a stage career until 1880, when he settled in Cleveland. He was manager of the Park Theater, which opened in 1883 as part of the 3-story Wick Block erected on PUBLIC SQUARE.† In 1884 the Park Theater was destroyed by fire; it was not reopened until 1886. During this restoration, Hartz joined the EUCLID AVE. OPERA HOUSE† as both lessee and manager from 1884 until 1920, when the lease expired. The Euclid Ave. Opera House also succumbed to flames in 1892, but reopened in 1893. Under the management skill of Hartz, the Euclid Ave. Opera House reigned as Cleveland's favorite playhouse for many years, until it was displaced by the HANNA THEATER,† the new "legitimate" favorite. In addition to his extensive theater skills and interests, Hartz displayed talents in business as president of Majestic Oil Co. and Trenton Rock Oil & Gas Co. Married in Rhode Island in 1894, Hartz and his wife, Rose, had 2 children, Clover and Fanny. Hartz was buried in Mayfield Cemetery.

**HARVEY, KATE BENEDICT HANNA** (26 Dec. 1871–15 May 1936), a philanthropist and member of one of Cleveland's most distinguished families, took a special interest in hospitals and the education of nurses and helped establish the VISITING NURSE ASSN.† Born in Cleveland to Howard Melville and Kate (Smith) Hanna, she attended Miss Porter's School in Connecticut and Miss Heloise E. Hersey's School in Boston. She was the niece of MARCUS HANNA and one of the three largest stockholders in the M. A. HANNA CO.†

In 1901 she was a founder and original trustee of the Visiting Nurse Assn. She also founded and published the *Visiting Nurses Quarterly* and served on the VNA's first lay advisory board. In 1905 she helped to establish the Cleveland chapter of the AMERICAN RED CROSS† and served on its executive committee. When a disastrous tornado hit Lorain in 1924, she was among the first to rally support for Lorain and assisted in forming the first relief expedition sent from Cleveland.

Among Harvey's chief interests were Lakeside and UNIV. HOSPITALS OF CLEVELAND.† She served on Lakeside's Board of Lady Managers (1898–1930), and as a trustee of Univ. Hospitals (1920–36) and Babies and Children's Hospital. She was also a leader in transforming the hospital's nursing program into the Western Reserve Univ. (Frances Payne Bolton) School of Nursing, Cleveland's first collegiate nursing school.

Kate Benedict married Robert Livingston Ireland on 2 May 1894 (div. 1922). They had two children, Elizabeth and ROBERT LIVINGSTON IRELAND, JR. She married Perry Harvey on 12 Feb. 1923. She is buried in Thomasville, GA.—T.B.

**HASKELL, COBURN** (31 Dec. 1868–14 Dec. 1922) was a prominent Cleveland businessman and sportsman, known as the inventor of the modern golf ball. Son of William A. and Mary Haskell, he came to Cleveland from Boston in 1892 as the result of a friendship between his father and MARCUS A. HANNA. In Cleveland, Haskell became closely associated with the Hanna family and worked for the M. A. HANNA CO.† An avid golfer, Haskell patented a ball with a rubber-wound core on 11 Apr. 1899. In 1901 he retired from M. A. Hanna to organize the Haskell Golf Ball Co. The "Haskell golf ball" replaced the universally used gutta-percha ball and revolutionized the manufacture of golf balls. Because of its greater distance, the Haskell ball reduced scores and helped considerably to increase the popularity of golf. Haskell Golf Ball was dissolved in 1917, selling its patents to other companies, including the A. G. Spalding Co. In addition to his interest in sports, Haskell was also known as a lover of music, art, and books, owning many first editions of the early illustrators.

In June 1895 Haskell married Mary Gertrude Hanna, daughter of HOWARD MELVILLE HANNA, SR. They had one son, Coburn, Jr. (d. 1900). Haskell died in Cleveland and was buried in Lake View Cemetery.

**HATTON, AUGUSTUS RAYMOND** (27 Sept. 1873–12 Nov. 1946), an author of Cleveland's City Manager Charter, member of city council, and professor of Political Science at Western Reserve Univ., was born on a farm near Vevay, IN, the son of Augustus and Mary Lavinia (Howard) Hatton. Educated in public schools there, Hatton graduated from Franklin College, Franklin, IN, with a Ph.B. in 1898, where he remained until 1901, teaching history and political science. He was an instructor, and asst. professor of political science at the Univ. of Chicago 1901–07, the year he received his Ph.D.

Hatton came to Western Reserve Univ. as associate professor of political science that year, and was appointed the Marcus A. Hanna professor of political science in 1910. During this time, Hatton was active in Cleveland's progressive reform movement. Along with NEWTON D. BAKER, he helped draft the municipal home rule amendment to the Ohio constitution. He subsequently served on Cleveland's Charter Commission, elected in 1912 (see HOME RULE†). Hatton also drafted the proportional representation section of the CITY MANAGER PLAN,† adopted in 1921. When the manager plan was implemented in 1924, Hatton was elected to the new 25-member CLEVELAND CITY COUNCIL,† where he was a foe of the political bosses. He left Cleveland in 1927 to take a teaching position at Northwestern Univ. in Evanston, IL, retiring in 1940. Hatton was a visiting professor at the Univ. of Texas in Austin 1942–43, residing there until his death.

Hatton married Nancy Mathews 11 Nov. 1903 and they had a daughter, Martha (Mrs. Edward Montague). After his wife's death in 1931, he married Esther Rutan 25 Nov. 1936.—M.S.

**HAUSER, ELIZABETH** (16 Mar. 1873–11 Nov. 1958), leader and suffragist, was born in Girard, OH, to David and Mary (Bixler) Hauser. She had over a decade of writing experience for the *Warren Tribune Chronicle* and other papers, which won her a job as secretary to TOM L. JOHNSON and editor of his autobiography, *My Story*. Hauser came to Cleveland in 1910 to organize Cuyahoga County women to win suffrage as director of the Cuyahoga County Women's Suffrage Assn. To increase the acceptability of supporting suffrage, Hauser wooed socially prominent women to attend lectures and luncheons, and allow their names to be used in conjunction with suffrage activities. The feminists collected 15,000 county signatures to present at the 1912 Ohio Constitutional Convention, which voted 76–34 in favor of submitting Amendment 23 for women's suffrage to a special election on 3 Sept. 1912. The Cuyahoga County Women's Assn., which became the Cuyahoga County Women's Suffrage party, with the organizational framework of wards and precincts, built strong grassroots support that brought out the vote in the 1912 election. Though Amendment 23 lost, the machinery was in place for further campaigns. Hauser battled antisuffragists, financial difficulties, and uninformed attitudes with lectures, debates, bake sales, rallies, whistlestops, suffrage suppers, and pageants. When suffrage passed, Hauser and other former suffrage leaders formed the LEAGUE OF WOMEN VOTERS† to continue politically educating women, in which Hauser became a national officer.

Never married and having no children, Hauser died in Girard, OH, and was buried in the Girard-Liberty Union Cemetery.

Abbott, Virginia Clark. *The History of Woman Suffrage and the League of Women Voters in Cuyahoga County, 1911–1945* (1949).

**HAWGOOD, BELLE DIBLEY** (20 July 1869–2 Feb. 1941) made an important regional contribution to botany by collecting approximately 1,000 herbarium specimens, most from northern Ohio, over a period of more than 40 years. Hawgood was born on a farm in Oak Creek, WI, now South Milwaukee, to Ebeneezer and Isabella Dibley. When she was a teenager, her mother taught her to botanize. In about 1890, her mother took ill and died, leaving Belle to take over household duties on the farmstead. She married Capt. Arthur Harrison Hawgood, who was in the shipping business, on 5 May 1892 and moved with him to Cleveland. Soon she began collecting plants in various parts of northeastern Ohio, eventually building up a large herbarium. Hawgood also traveled to various parts of the U.S. and Europe with her husband. She worked diligently on her collection over the years, using a small microscope and a copy of *Gray's Botany* and other botanical works to identify her plant specimens, which were meticulously mounted on cardboard. Hawgood was president of the WOMEN'S ART CLUB OF CLEVELAND† (1927–28) and late in her life also joined in the activities of the Cleveland Natural Science Club. Mother of Harvey Roland and Aldyth Hawgood, she died of a stroke in 1941. Her herbarium, including a large number of specimens from northern Ohio, was eventually donated to the CLEVELAND MUSEUM OF NATURAL HISTORY.†

**HAY, JOHN MILTON** (8 Oct. 1838–1 July 1905), diplomat, statesman, U.S. secretary of state, and historian, was born in Salem, IN, to Dr. Charley and Helen Leonard Hay. He graduated from Brown Univ., Providence, RI (1858), and studied law with his uncle, Milton Hay, whose offices adjoined those of Abraham Lincoln. Hay was admitted to the bar in 1861, and accompanied Lincoln to Washington as his private secretary. He was subsequently given the rank of colonel and assigned to the White House officially as a military aide, serving Lincoln until his assassination. Secretary of State Wm. H. Seward appointed Hay secretary to the legations in Paris (1865–67), Vienna (1867–68), and Madrid (1869–70). Returning to the U.S., Hay became an editorial writer for the New York Tribune. In 1874 he married Clara Louise Stone, daughter of AMASA STONE, moving to Cleveland in 1875 and remaining until 1886, working for his father-in-law and serving on various civic and cultural boards. Hay was a local celebrity, but became bored with Cleveland society, expressing his views in his anonymously authored *The Bread Winners*. Hay moved his family to Washington. In 1890 he and John Nicolay authored the 10-volume *Abraham Lincoln: A History*. In 1896 Hay campaigned for Wm. McKinley, and in 1897 was rewarded with appointment as ambassador to Great Britain. Appointed secretary of state in 1898, Hay participated in events attendant upon the Spanish-American War, enunciated the "Open Door" policy concerning China, and, under Theodore Roosevelt, aided treaty negotiations leading to construction of the Panama Canal. Hay had 4 children: Alice (Wadsworth), Helen (Whitney), Clarence, and Adelbert. He died in Newbury, NH, but was buried in Cleveland at Lake View Cemetery.

Dennett, Tyler. *John Hay* (1933).
John Hay Papers, Illinois Historical Society, Springfield, IL.

**HAYDN, HIRAM COLLINS** (11 Dec. 1831–31 July 1913), pastor of FIRST PRESBYTERIAN CHURCH (OLD STONE)† and president of Western Reserve Univ., was born in Pompey, NY, to David E. and Lucinda (Cooley) Haydn. He graduated from Amherst College in 1856, and received a D.D. from Union Theological Seminary in 1859. He served pastorates in Connecticut before coming to Ohio in 1866 as pastor of the First Congregational Church of Painesville. Haydn was called to be associate pastor of Old Stone Church in 1871 and soon after succeeded Rev. Wm. Henry Goodrich as senior pastor, remaining until 1880 when he became secretary of the Congregational Mission Board in New York. He returned to Cleveland in 1884 to resume his pastorate at Old Stone and serve 2 years as president of WRU, where he was instrumental in founding the College for Women, with the assistance and support of FLORA STONE MATHER, an influential church member and university benefactor. Mrs. Mather gave the university the building that carried Haydn's name. As pastor of Old Stone, Haydn was a visible leader in the community. He was involved in founding Goodrich House (see GOODRICH-GANNETT NEIGH. CTR.†), a settlement house sponsored by the church; the PRESBYTERIAN UNION,† which he served as president from 1907 until his death; and many Cleveland-area Presbyterian churches initially sponsored by Old Stone. His second Old Stone pastorate lasted until 1902, when he became pastor emeritus.

Haydn married twice; to Elizabeth Coit in 1851 and, following her death, to Sarah Merriman in 1864. He had four children: Charles R., Mrs. E. W. Haines, Howell M., and Mrs. Frederic Hitchings. Haydn was buried in Lake View Cemetery.

**HAYES, MAX S. (MAXIMILIAN SEBASTIAN)** (25 May 1866–11 Oct. 1945), LABOR† spokesman and editor of the *CLEVELAND CITIZEN,†* was born in Havanna, OH, to Joseph and Elizabeth (Borer) Hayes. He was educated in common schools until age 13, when he was apprenticed in printing. He completed his apprenticeship in Cleveland and was initiated as a journeyman in TYPOGRAPHICAL WORKERS UNION NO. 53† in 1884, serving the local as organizer, president, and delegate. In 1891 Hayes helped launch the *Cleveland Citizen,* editing it for almost 50 years. By 1896 he was a leading activist in the Socialist Labor party and secretary of the Central Labor Union. In 1898 he was CLU delegate to the AFL national convention, beginning his battle with Sam Gompers over demands for union democracy, solidarity, and independent political action by labor. He received one-third of the votes for president when he ran against Gompers in 1912. Yet despite his differences with national AFL policies, Hayes argued that the socialists' correct course was to fight from within, rather than divide their forces in dual organizations. Hayes campaigned as a Socialist candidate for Congress in 1900, for Ohio secretary of state in 1902, and as Farmer-Labor party candidate for vice-president in 1920. Hayes helped found the CONSUMERS LEAGUE OF OHIO† in 1900.

Hayes married Dora Schneider in 1900 and had 1 child, Maxine Elizabeth. She married A. I. Davey, Jr., who became editor of the *Citizen* when Hayes was incapacitated by a stroke in 1939. Max, Dora, and Maxine are buried in Lake View Cemetery.

Max S. Hayes Papers, Ohio Historical Society.

**HAYR, JAMES** (1 July 1838–1 Aug. 1927), a volunteer CIVIL WAR† soldier and early custodian of SOLDIERS & SAILORS MONUMENT,† was born in Hamilton, Ontario, Canada. He and his family moved to Niagara Falls, NY, in 1851. He worked as a painter in Rochester, New York City, and Cleveland. Hayr enlisted in the Zouave Light Guards, which became Co. B, 23RD OHIO VOLUNTEER INFANTRY,† in 1861. He was promoted to cpl. on 4 July 1864 and to sgt. in Sept. 1864. He was severely wounded at the battle of Cedar Creek, VA, in Oct. 1864, and was mustered out of service on 1 Aug. 1865 at Cumberland, MD. Returning to Cleveland after the war, he became active in veterans' affairs, serving as commander of the Hampson Post (Grand Army of the Republic) and as an officer on the Cuyahoga County Soldiers & Sailors Monument Commission, beginning in 1884, and as custodian of the Soldiers & Sailors Monument for a number of years. Hayr and his wife, Marth G., had a daughter, Carrie. He died in Sandusky at the Ohio Soldiers and Sailors Home and is buried in Woodland Cemetery.

**HAYS, J. BYERS** (11 Feb. 1891–26 Aug. 1968), architect active in Cleveland from 1920–63, was born in Sewickley, PA, son of Alden Farrell and Augusta (Ulrich) Hays. He graduated in architecture from Carnegie Institute of Technology in 1914. Hays came to Cleveland in 1920 to join the firm of WALKER & WEEKS,† designing the FEDERAL RESERVE BANK OF CLEVELAND† (1923), Indiana War Memorial, Indianapolis (1927), exterior of CLEVELAND MUNICIPAL STADIUM† (1926), and St. Paul Episcopal Church, Cleveland Hts. (1927–51). In 1930 Hays established a partnership with Russell Simpson, which lasted until 1950. In 1935 Hays & Simpson planned an experimental modular house for GE that was erected at NELA PARK† as a prototype for a small house specifically designed for family living, prompted by the Depression. In 1936 they designed the Hall of Progress for the GREAT LAKES EXPOSITION,† where Hays served on the architectural committee. During World War II, Hays was briefly associated with civil engineer WILBUR J. WATSON in designing war housing projects. After the war, he founded the firm of Conrad, Hays, Simpson & Ruth, which continued as Hays & Ruth from the mid–1950s until Hays's retirement in 1963. Hays drew the master plan for the Cleveland Zoo in 1948 and designed the bird and pachyderm buildings. Hays & Ruth planned the 1958 addition to the CLEVELAND MUSEUM OF ART,† and also the Lakewood High School auditorium (1960) and Riverview public-housing development (1963). Hays married Charlotte M. Hunter and had 2 children, Elizabeth (Schoenfeld) and Alden F. Hays died at his summer home in Webster, NC, and was buried in Lake View Cemetery.

**HAYS, KAUFMAN** (9 Mar. 1835–12 Apr. 1916), merchant and banker, was born to Abraham and Bentra Hexten Hays of Stormdorf, Hesse-Darmstadt, Germany. He immigrated to Cleveland in 1852, and worked in retail stores before joining SIMSON THORMAN in his hides-and-wool business in 1860, leaving to establish Hays Bros. (1864–85) clothing store. In 1868 Hays purchased stock in Citizens Savings & Loan Co., in 1875 becoming a director. He also held stock in City Natl. Bank. In 1886, he established Euclid Ave. Natl. Bank with MYRON T. HERRICK, CHAS. F. BRUSH, and SOLON L. SEVERANCE; elected vice-president in

1893, he held that position until 1905, when the bank merged with Park Natl. Bank, ultimately becoming part of Union Trust Co., of which Hays was a vice-president at his death. When Turner Mfg. Co., a textile company, failed in 1893, Hays became secretary of the reorganized company and, with Geo. H. Hodgson, built it into CLEVELAND WORSTED MILLS.† Hays was elected to CLEVELAND CITY COUNCIL† in 1886, became chairman of the finance committee, and 2 years later was elected vice-president of council. Following embezzlement of city funds by the treasurer in 1888, Hays was appointed acting treasurer and is credited with saving the city's credit. Hays was a founder of the Hebrew Benevolent Society, a member of Tifereth Israel (the TEMPLE†), and congregation president from 1867–71. He married Lizzie Thorman (d. 1907) in 1861 and had 4 daughters: Frances (Mrs. MOSES GRIES), Belle (Mrs. MARTIN MARKS), Rolinda, and Nettie. Hays was buried in the Mayfield Jewish Cemetery.

Kaufman Hays Papers, WRHS.
Joseph Hays Papers, WRHS.

**HAYWARD, NELSON** (1810–14 Apr. 1857), mayor of Cleveland (1843–44) was born in Braintree, MA, where he was locally educated. Son of William and Marjory (Thayer) Hayward, he came to Cleveland in 1825 with his 2 brothers, Joseph and John, and joined in various small enterprises with them. In 1840 he became the asst. chief of the Old Volunteer Fire Dept. Hayward's political philosophy was that of a Jacksonian Democrat. It was this new trend of thought that won him the mayoralty in 1843, after he had served as alderman in 1841 and 1842. He was never reelected to public office, however, as the political trend of the city became partisan Whig and Republican. Hayward was vice-president of the city's Temperance Society in 1842. The following year he became a member of the Cleveland Lodge of the Odd Fellows. He never married.

**HAYWARD, WILLIAM HENRY** (6 Dec. 1822–1 Mar. 1904), Cleveland printer, organizer of the CLEVELAND GRAYS,† and CIVIL WAR† army officer, was born in Lebanon, CT, to John and Maria (Whedon) Hayward. He moved to Cleveland with his family in 1825 via the Erie Canal and lake schooner. At age 15 he began work with Sanford & Lott in printing. He helped organize the Cleveland Grays in 1837, became 1st sergeant in 1852, and served as president, 1858–59. When the Civil War broke out, he was commissioned lt. colonel of the 1ST OHIO VOLUNTEER LIGHT ARTILLERY,† serving until he resigned due to illness on 1 Apr.

1863. He returned to Cleveland, where in Aug. 1863 he was elected colonel of the 29th Ohio Volunteer Militia, referred to as the City Regiment, Volunteer Militia. On 5 May 1864, Hayward was commissioned colonel of the 150th Ohio Volunteer Infantry. He led the 150th, made up largely of Clevelanders, during its period of service in the defenses of Washington, DC, until it was mustered out in Cleveland on 23 Aug. 1864. In the postwar years he was an active member of the GRAND ARMY OF THE REPUBLIC† and the Cleveland Light Artillery Assn. In 1846 he married Jane E. Willis and had 4 children: Maria, Kate, Georgiana, and William. He died at the home of his daughter and is buried in Woodland Cemetery.

Cleveland Light Artillery Assn. Records, WRHS.
Tibbits, George W. *A Brief Sketch of the Cleveland Grays* (1903).

**HEARD, CHARLES WALLACE** (1806–29 Aug. 1876), architect, was born in Onondaga, NY, the son of Enoch and Clarissa (Hopkins) Hurd. His family moved to Painesville, OH, 3 years later. In 1822 he was apprenticed to JONATHAN GOLDSMITH, marrying his daughter in 1830 and becoming Goldsmith's partner until 1847, working primarily in Cleveland beginning 1833. The Chas. M. Giddings house on Rockwell is attributed to Heard. Heard progressed from carpenter to master builder to architect, taking Warham J. Warner as his partner until 1859. They built Cleveland's first Gothic residence, the Henry B. Payne house. Heard's most important early Gothic Revival building was St. Paul's Episcopal Church (1851, demolished in 1874), for which SIMEON PORTER was master builder. Heard & Porter built the Second Presbyterian Church (1852, destroyed by fire in 1876), Old Stone Church (1855), Eagle St. School (1855), CENTRAL HIGH SCHOOL† (1856), Payne & Perry's Block (1855), the I. S. Converse Block (1859), the homes of Chas. Hickox and Hinman B. Hurlbut (1855), Lake Erie Female Seminary (Painesville, OH, 1859), and Cleveland Orphan Asylum (1859).

In 1863 Heard & Warner built CASE HALL.† By 1864 Heard was partners with his son-in-law, Walter Blythe. They designed First United Presbyterian Church (1867), Case Block (1875), EUCLID AVE. OPERA HOUSE† (1875), the Geo. Merwin house (ROWFANT CLUB†), most public schools of the 1860s, and Arlington Block (1875). Heard & Sons, as his firm was called, built the Ohio state building at the Philadelphia Centennial Exhibition in 1876, the only state building afterwards retained, and still standing for the Bicentennial.

Heard married Caroline Goldsmith and had 7 children: Regina, Imogene, Wallace, LUCAS ALLEN, Lenora, Virginia, and Dallace. He was buried in Lake View Cemetery.

Johannesen, Eric. *Cleveland Architecture, 1876–1976* (1979).

**HEARD, LUCAS ALLEN** (22 Aug. 1846–29 April 1903), architect, worked in Cleveland between 1870–81. He designed such local buildings as Ursuline Academy at Villa Angela (1878) and the Willson Ave. Baptist Church (1879, later St. Paul's AME Zion Church). Born in Cleveland, Heard was the son of Caroline James Goldsmith and CHARLES W. HEARD, a prominent architect, and the grandson of master builder JONATHAN GOLDSMITH. L. Allen Heard joined his father's firm in 1870. In 1877–78 he practiced under his own name and from 1879–81 was the partner of GEORGE HORATIO SMITH, who later designed the Cleveland Arcade. In addition to the buildings in Cleveland, L. Allen Heard designed a boarding hall at Hiram College (OH).

Heard married Hattie C. Lewis in 1873 and had 3 children: Richard B., Allen, and Clarence L. He moved to Denver in 1881. Heard drowned at Escalante, CO; his remains were not found until almost 3 months afterward, on 11 July 1903.

See also **ARCHITECTURE.**†

**HEGGS, OWEN L.** (1 Oct. 1942–17 April 1993) was a partner in the law firm of JONES, DAY, REAVIS & POGUE,† a trustee of CUYAHOGA COMMUNITY COLLEGE,† and a civic activist.

Born in Cleveland, Heggs attended Our Lady of the Blessed Sacrament and St. Cecilia Catholic schools. He graduated from Cathedral Latin High School in 1960, received his B.A. from Howard Univ. in Washington, DC, in 1964, and his J.D. from Western Reserve Univ. Law School in 1967.

After passing the Ohio Bar in 1967, Heggs began his legal career with the firm of SQUIRE, SANDERS & DEMPSEY.† In 1968 he enlisted in the U.S. Navy, serving as a military lawyer in Vietnam. Heggs served as an asst. to Congressman Louis Stokes during 1970–71 and chaired Stokes's 1972 reelection campaign. After breaking with Stokes, Heggs ran unsuccessfully against Stokes in 1976. Heggs joined CASE WESTERN RESERVE UNIV.† in 1974 as an associate professor of law and director of its clinical law programs. In 1979 he joined Jones, Day, Reavis & Pogue, becoming a member of the firm's minority hiring task force.

In 1973 Heggs joined the URBAN LEAGUE OF GREATER CLEVELAND† as president and chairman. He was cofounder and acting chairman of the Council of Affiliate Presidents of the National Urban League. Heggs was appointed a trustee of Cuyahoga Community College in 1987, serving as chairman in 1991–92.

Heggs married Sharon E. Milligan on 3 March 1984. They had 2 children, Peter and Sarah.—T.B.

Borowitz, Albert. *Jones, Day, Reavis & Pogue: The First Century* (Jones, Day, Reavis & Pogue, 1993).

**HEINZERLING, LYNN LOUIS** (23 Oct. 1906–21 Nov. 1983), broke into journalism in Cleveland and went on to win a Pulitzer Prize as a foreign correspondent for the Associated Press. He was a native of Birmingham, OH, the son of Louis and Grace Lawrence Heinzerling. Raised in Elyria, OH, he attended Akron Univ. and Ohio Wesleyan Univ. Heinzerling became a reporter for the Cleveland *PLAIN DEALER,†* 1928–33. He then joined the AP Cleveland bureau, where he covered such stories as the Ohio River floods, the LITTLE STEEL STRIKE,† and the TORSO MURDERS.† In 1938 he was assigned to Berlin, where he witnessed the outbreak of World War II. He was wounded during the war while covering the Allied campaign in Italy. Following the war he was posted to Vienna, Berlin, Geneva, Johannesburg, and London. He received the Pulitzer Prize in 1961 for his coverage of the Congo crisis and other African developments. Heinzerling returned to Ohio as chief of the AP's Columbus bureau in 1963–64, so that his son could attend Elyria High School. He rounded out his career with the AP as chief of Africa operations, until his retirement in 1971. He spent his retirement in Elyria, where he died, and was inducted posthumously into the CLEVELAND JOURNALISM HALL OF FAME.† He was survived by his wife, the former Agnes Dengate, whom he had married in 1934. His one surviving son, Larry, became an intern at the *Plain Dealer* before beginning his own career with the AP.—J.V.

**HEISE, GEORGE W.** (27 June 1888–28 Sept. 1972), chemist and researcher for Natl. Carbon Research Laboratories, was born in Milwaukee, the son of German immigrants Paul E. and Dora Tyre Heise. He earned B.S. (1909) and M.S. (1912) degrees from the Univ. of Wisconsin. He was a chemistry instructor at Grinell College (1909–10) and taught chemistry and physics at DePaul Univ. (1910–11) before returning to the Univ. of Wisconsin as assistant and later fellow in chemistry (1912–13). From 1913–17 Heise was a physical chemist in the Bureau of Science in Manila, the Philippines, performing chemical and bacteriological tests on the water. In 1917 he became a captain in the U.S. Army Reserve Corps and was assigned to the Utilities Div. at Camp Grant, IL, to work on water

softening, sanitation, and other technical problems. He was transferred to Chemical Warfare Service in 1918 before returning to civilian life in 1919. During World War II, he worked again with the Chemical Warfare Service and Natl. Defense Research Council. In 1919 Heise began working for Natl. Carbon Research Laboratories as a research chemist and engineer, first in Fremont, then in Long Island, before coming to Cleveland in 1925. In Cleveland, Heise led a group in electrochemical research and contributed to developing commercial dry batteries. He was responsible for more than 75 patents and wrote many technical papers. Heise married Margaret Armstrong in 1915 and had 3 children: Alice, Margaret, and George A.

**HEISMAN, JOHN WILLIAM** (23 Oct. 1869–3 Oct. 1936), innovative college football coach for whom the Heisman Trophy is named, was born in Cleveland to Michael and Sarah Heisman, but his family moved to Titusville, PA, during the 1870s. Heisman entered Brown Univ., playing FOOTBALL† in 1888, then transferred to Pennsylvania, playing football in 1890 and 1891 and receiving a law degree in 1892. Heisman began coaching as a player and coach at Oberlin College in 1892, with a perfect 7–0 season, twice shutting out Ohio State Univ. (40–0 and 50–0). In 1893 he coached at Buchtel College (later the Univ. of Akron), encountering faculty opposition toward his competitive approach to football. He coached at Oberlin (1894), Alabama Polytechnic Institute (later Auburn) (1895–99), Clemson (1900–03), Georgia Institute of Technology (1904–19), Pennsylvania (1920–22), Washington & Jefferson (1923), and Rice Institute (1924–27). His innovations changed football. He proposed legalizing the forward pass, used guards to lead interference on sweeps, and introduced the direct snap from center. In 1898 his teams began using audible signals to begin each offensive play. He also introduced a special shift that was the forerunner of the T and I formations. After his retirement, Heisman became an organizer and first president of the New York Touchdown Club, and director of athletics at the Downtown Athletic Club of New York which, in 1935, began awarding an annual trophy to the nation's best college football player, named in Heisman's honor after his death. Heisman married Evelyn McCollum Cox in 1903, whom he divorced in 1918. In 1924 he married Edith Maora Cole. Heisman died in New York City and was buried in Rheinlander, WI.

**HELLERSTEIN, HERMAN KOPEL** (6 June 1916–17 Aug. 1993) won recognition as a Cleveland cardiologist for his studies that made it possible for most heart patients to continue leading productive lives. Born in Dillonvale, OH, he was the son of Russian immigrants Samuel and Cecilia Zeiger Hellerstein. In 1929 the family moved to SHAKER HTS.,† allowing Hellerstein to attend Shaker Hts. High School and Western Reserve Univ. (see CASE WESTERN RESERVE UNIV.†). After graduating from the WRU School of Medicine in 1941, he served a year's internship in Philadelphia before entering the U.S. Army Medical Corps in World War II. He rose to the rank of major through 5 European campaigns, winning the Silver Star and Bronze Star and participating in the liberation of Bergen-Belsen concentration camps. Hellerstein joined the staff of UNIV. HOSPITALS† in 1947. He established the Work Classification Clinic of the Cleveland Area Heart Society (see AMERICAN HEART ASSN.† [AHA], NORTHEAST OHIO AFFILIATE, INC.†) in 1950, serving as its director until 1963. There his monitoring of 2,700 heart patients led to his advocacy of work and exercise for victims of heart attacks. Hellerstein also taught at the CWRU School of Medicine from 1950 to his death, becoming emeritus in 1986. He published 384 papers and contributed to 20 books. He was the co-author of *Healing Your Heart* (1990), and his autobiography, *A Matter of Heart* (1994), was published posthumously. He served as co-director of the National Exercise and Heart Disease Project for the U.S. Dept. of Health, Education and Welfare and on the scientific committee of the International Federation of Sports Medicine. In 1988 he was named one of 14 local pioneers in cardiology by the American Heart Assn. and the Cleveland Health Education Museum (see HEALTH MUSEUM†). He married Mary Feil Hellerstein in 1947, an asst. clinical professor in pediatrics at CWRU. He died in Cleveland, survived by his wife and 6 children: Kathryn, David, Jonathan, Daniel, Susan, and Elizabeth.—J.V.

Hellerstein, Herman K. and Snyder, Adam. *A Matter of Heart* (1994).

**HENNIG, EDWARD A.** (Oct. 1879–28 Aug. 1960) was a leading amateur athlete and the first Cleveland athlete to participate in the Olympics. Son of Fred K. E. and Johannah (Goernnes) Hennig, he was an active gymnast from age 8, when a doctor recommended he take up gymnastic exercise to build himself up. Twice a week he walked 4 mi. to a gymnasium downtown. He was a member of the Cleveland East Side Turners for 73 years and of Central YMCA for nearly 60 years. Hennig was one of 496 athletes from 10 countries to participate in the 1904 Olympic Games in St. Louis. He captured top honors in 2 events, winning the gold medal in Indian club swinging (since discontinued), and

finished in a 1st place tie in the horizontal bars with American Anton Heida. Hennig also competed in national Amateur Athletic Union competitions, winning 1st place for both Indian club swinging and the horizontal bars in the 1911 competition, and winning 10 1st-place and 3 2nd-place medals in AAU contests between 1933–50. Throughout his athletic career, Hennig won 14 national AAU championships and 3 national Turner titles. He was voted outstanding amateur athlete in northeastern Ohio in 1942, when he was 62. He was later inducted into the GREATER CLEVELAND SPORTS HALL OF FAME.† An engineer by trade, Hennig was employed by the McMeyer Interstate Corp., builders of hoist machines, and later became chief engineer for the R. A. Kaltenbach Corp., engineering consultants.

Hennig married Alma Warnke on 23 Oct. 1906. They had three children: Erla (Krueger), Lois (Curtis), and Janet (Perryman).

**HENNING, EDWARD BURK** (23 Oct. 1922–18 Apr. 1993) was an art historian and chief curator of modern art at the CLEVELAND MUSEUM OF ART† who expanded the collection by acquiring important works by modern artists.

Born in Cleveland to Marguerite and William (stepfather) Henning, Edward graduated from West Technical High School, was a stained-glass apprentice, then served in the army during World War II. Henning studied art at Western Reserve Univ. (B.S. 1949, M.S. 1952), the CLEVELAND INSTITUTE OF ART† (Certificate 1949), and Academie Julian, Paris (1949–50).

Henning was an art teacher in the CLEVELAND PUBLIC SCHOOLS† (1950–52) before joining the museum's education department as an instructor (1952–55). Henning was asst. curator of education (1955–56), associate curator (1956–59), and guest lecturer–adjunct professor in art history, Western Reserve Univ. (1958–84). In 1959 Henning was named assistant to museum director Sherman E. Lee.

Henning became the museum's first curator of contemporary art in 1962. In 1972, when modern art replaced contemporary, Henning became curator and, in 1979, chief curator. Henning acquired the works of modern masters, including Pablo Picasso, Jackson Pollock, and Isamu Noguchi. He organized exhibitions and wrote books for major shows.

Henning advised private collectors, corporations, and judged numerous art shows. He supervised the MAY SHOW† until 1973 and served on the Art Advisory Panel to the Internal Revenue Service. Retiring in 1985, Henning continued working as a research curator, cataloguing the museum's modern art collection. Henning also headed the museum's film program until 1986.

Henning married Margaret Revacko on 31 Dec. 1942. They had three children: Eric, Lisa, and Geoffrey. Henning died in CLEVELAND HTS. and was cremated.—T.B.

**HENRIETTA, SISTER, CSA** (19 July 1902–17 Oct.1983) was the director of Our Lady of Fatima Mission Center (1965–83), on E. 68th and Quimby, who worked to revitalize HOUGH† and "reclaim . . . a slum" by providing food, clothing, education, employment, health care, and housing for area residents.

Born Marie Gorris to Henry and Anna (Sulzmann) Gorris in Cleveland, she attended St. Edward Parish High School (1919), and graduated from Canton's Mercy Hospital School of Nursing (RN, 1925). She entered the SISTERS OF CHARITY OF ST. AUGUSTINE† religious order from Saint Philomena Parish in East Cleveland in 1925, taking her final vows in 1931.

Sr. Henrietta remained at Mercy Hospital as night supervisor (1928–31), surgery supervisor (1931–49), asst. administrator (1949–51), and administrator (1951–62). She came to Cleveland as director of nursing service, ST. VINCENT CHARITY HOSPITAL† (1962–65).

In 1965 Sr. Henrietta devoted herself to renewal efforts in Central (Lower) Hough. Converting an old apartment house into a convent and mission center, Sr. Henrietta moved in among the poor. She helped them achieve self-sufficiency through her neighborhood training and volunteer programs, such as Caridad and Famicos.

Sr. Henrietta received numerous awards, including the Catholic Interracial Council Award (1976), the National Urban Coalition's Distinguished Community Service Award (1980), the American Jewish Committee's Micah Award (1983), and two honorary degrees.

The Mission Center closed with Sr. Henrietta's death. She is buried in Calvary Cemetery.—T.B.

Wolff, Robert C., Rev. Msgr. *Sr. Henrietta of Hough: She Reclaimed a Cleveland Slum* (1990).

**HERBERT, THOMAS JOHN** (28 Oct. 1894–26 Oct. 1974), 56th governor of Ohio, member of the Ohio State Supreme Court, and state attorney general, was born in Cleveland to John T. and Jane A. Jones Herbert. He received his A.B. from Western Reserve Univ. in 1915, but had to drop out of law school after 1 year due to lack of money. He became a 1st lt. in the U.S. Air Service during World War I, shooting down a German plane and being himself shot down, receiving both the U.S. and British Distinguished Service Cross and the Purple Heart.

Returning to WRU's law school, Herbert graduated, was admitted to the Ohio Bar, and was appointed asst. law director in Cleveland in 1920. He served as asst. county prosecutor (1923–24); was appointed asst. state attorney general in 1928; and in 1933 became special counsel to the state attorney general in Union Trust Co.'s liquidation. In 1938 Herbert was elected Ohio attorney general for the first of 3 terms. Herbert defeated FRANK LAUSCHE for governor in 1946, but lost to Lausche in 1948, losing the Republican primary for governor in 1952. In 1953 Pres. Eisenhower appointed Herbert chairman of the Subversive Activities Control Board in Washington, DC. In 1956 Herbert won election to the Ohio Supreme Court, but a severe stroke prevented his seeking reelection. Herbert married Jeanette Judson (d. Dec. 1945) in 1919. He married Mildred Helen Stevenson in 1948. Herbert had 3 children: Metta Jane Stevers, Daniel, and John.

**HERKOMER, JOHN** (1821–1913), a woodcarver born in Waal, Bavaria, practiced his craft in Cleveland from 1851–83 and is best known for the staircases and interior decorations he carved for the homes of prominent Cleveland families. Herkomer left Bavaria in the late 1840s and traveled to New York City. In 1851, he and his brother, Lorenz, set up a woodcarving and portrait shop, first in New York City, later in Rochester, and finally in Cleveland. In 1857 Lorenz and his family moved to England. John moved his woodcarving establishment to new quarters on Erie (E. 9th) St. He married Agnes King on 17 Oct. 1857 and had three children: Bertha, Josephine, and Herman. John and his family left for England in 1883, where he was employed by his nephew, Sir Hubert Herkomer, a famous painter living in Bushey, England, to design and carve interior decorations. Herkomer died in England.

Clevelanders who had residences decorated by Herkomer included JOHN HAY, SAMUEL ANDREWS, and Amasa Stone, Jr. The stairway of the original Hay house on Euclid Ave. was removed and incorporated into the Hay house on East Blvd. (later the WESTERN RESERVE HISTORICAL SOCIETY†). Herkomer was also responsible for the lions' heads on the West Side Branch of the YMCA. Most of the homes he decorated have been torn down to make way for business and industry. Herkomer was one of the members of the original ART CLUB† with ARCHIBALD WILLARD.

Baldry, A. L. *Hubert von Herkomer R. A.: A Study and a Biography* (1901).
Herkomer, Sir Hubert von. *The Herkomers* (1911).

**HERRICK, CLAY JR.** (15 Dec. 1911–30 Jan. 1993) was an advertising executive with Carpenter, Lamb & Herrick, Inc. and Watts, Lamb, Kenyon & Herrick, a historian, author, and civic leader who worked to preserve Cleveland's historic buildings.

Born in Cleveland to Clay and Alice (Meriam) Herrick, Clay Jr. graduated from Hts. High School (1929) and received his A.B. from WRU's Adelbert College (1934).

Herrick gained public relations and management experience working with WILLIAM GANSON ROSE on the Great Lakes Expositions promotions and March of Dimes shows (1937–40). Herrick next worked in Akron as public relations director for General Tire & Rubber Co., then four years in Rochester, NY, as creative director for Eastman Kodak printing, followed by 10 years with Fuller & Smith & Ross, Inc.

In 1953 Herrick organized the Cleveland Printing Week Committee. In 1955 he organized the Graphic Arts Council of Cleveland, serving as executive secretary (1959–61) and president (1962). Herrick then became a partner in the advertising firm of Carpenter, Lamb & Herrick, Inc., serving as president until its 1973 merger into Watts, Lamb.

Grandson of Civil War veteran JOHN FRENCH HERRICK, he was president of the EARLY SETTLERS ASSN. OF THE WESTERN RESERVE† and the CLEVELAND RESTORATION SOCIETY.† Herrick also served on the 1976 Greater Cleveland Bicentennial Commission's executive committee. In 1971 Herrick was appointed to the newly created Commission on Cleveland Historical and Architectural Landmarks, serving as chairman, 1976–77.

Herrick authored *But It's So!* (1934), *Cleveland's Rich Heritage* (1974), and *Gags in Thyme* (1983). His *Cleveland Landmarks* (1986), received the Western Reserve Architectural Historians Award.

Herrick married Ruth Eleanor Penty on 27 April 1935. They had two children, Clay III and Jill. Herrick, a Presbyterian, is buried in Knollwood Cemetery.—T.B.

**HERRICK, JOHN FRENCH** (23 Feb. 1836–5 July 1909), volunteer CIVIL WAR† army officer and attorney, was born in Wellington, Lorain County, OH, to Ephraim and Chloe Wilcox Herrick. He attended Oberlin College (1856–62), and raised Co. D, 87th Ohio Volunteer Infantry, in Lorain County and was appointed captain. Unfortunately, the 87th was captured at Harper's Ferry by Confederate Gen. Thos. J. "Stonewall" Jackson on 15 Sept. 1862, 2 days before the Battle of Antietam. Paroled and out of the war, Herrick returned to Cleveland, studied law at Union and Ohio State law colleges, and graduated in 1863.

In 1863 Herrick was again eligible for military service. He raised a company for the 12TH OHIO VOLUNTEER CAVALRY,† placed on detached duty on Johnson's Island during the Nov. 1863 invasion scare at the island's Confederate prison. In the field, Herrick was promoted to lt. colonel and commanded the regiment during the last year of the war. Returning to Cleveland at the war's end, he practiced law in partnership with his brother, Gamaliel E. Herrick, until 1892. He was for a time senior partner of the firm of Herrick, Athey & Bliss, but withdrew to practice law alone. He was elected senator to the Ohio state legislature in 1901 and was noted for a bill establishing juvenile courts in Ohio. Herrick spent his last years representing E. Cleveland St. Railroad Co. and Cowell Platform & Coupler Co.

Herrick married Flora Emma Waring on 23 May 1877. They had 8 children: Clay, Flora Scott (Spelman), Pauline, Howard, Marion Gertrude (Temple), Marguerite, Francis W., and Green. He preceded his wife in death and is buried in Lake View Cemetery.

Mason, F. H. *The Twelfth Ohio Cavalry* (1871).
Grand Army of the Republic, Dept. of Ohio, Borough Post No. 359.
Collinwood, OH, Records, WRHS.

**HERRICK, MARIA M. SMITH** (1798–14 July 1895), 19th-century reformer and literary personage, active in the Female Moral Reform Society and publisher of Cleveland's earliest magazine, was born in Rensselaer County, NY, the daughter of Levi and Mary (Olmstead) Smith. In 1815 Maria married Sylvester Pierce Herrick. She came to OHIO CITY† in 1836, and became active in the Maternal Assn. of Ohio City. From 1837–40 she edited and wrote for a monthly journal, the *MOTHERS & YOUNG LADIES' GUIDE*, discussing subjects such as "Family Government," "Duties of Mothers," "Fashion," "Self Consecration," and "The Orphan's Tale." Though the magazine lasted for only a few issues, its concerns were carried on by the Female Moral Reform Society, organized in Sept. 1842 to promote family values and return runaway children to their homes. Formed by Herrick along with REBECCA ROUSE and others, the society decried "sin abroad in the land" that infiltrated homes and weakened the family, believing that because discipline and purity were not promoted in the home, children got into trouble outside the home and took to petty crime and PROSTITUTION.† Between 1842–43, the society investigated cases of women and children who had been lured into wickedness, and cared for them in members' homes until they could be returned to their families. The last recorded minutes of the society were dated Jan. 1844, when its work was taken over by the MARTHA WASHINGTON & DORCAS SOCIETY.† Maria Herrick, disabled at an early age by a fall from a carriage, remained active in social-reform causes well into her nineties.

Herrick had 4 children: John Sylvester, Mary Elizabeth, Julia Maria, and RENSSELAER RUSSEL HERRICK. She died in Cleveland.

Ingham, Mary B. *Women of Cleveland* (1893).

**HERRICK, MYRON TIMOTHY** (9 Oct. 1854–31 Mar. 1929), lawyer, businessman, politician, and diplomat, was born in Huntington, Lorain County, OH, son of Timothy and Mary (Hulbut) Herrick. He attended Ohio Wesleyan College, not completing his degree but instead coming to Cleveland to study law in 1875. He was admitted to the bar in 1878 and practiced law until 1886, when he organized Euclid Ave. Natl. Bank and began his long association with Society for Savings, serving there until 1921. He was involved in many business enterprises, such as building the ARCADE,† and also became interested in politics. He served on CLEVELAND CITY COUNCIL† from 1885–90, and as a staunch Republican, aided MARCUS HANNA in grooming Wm. McKinley for the presidency. Moving up the Republican ranks, by 1903 he was the Republican nominee for governor of Ohio and was elected by a large majority over Democrat TOM JOHNSON. He was a conservative, though controversial, governor, and was defeated for reelection in 1905.

In 1912 Herrick accepted the ambassadorship to France from Pres. Taft. Although replaced in 1914, he remained in Paris after the outbreak of World War I, evacuating stranded Americans out of Europe and providing relief to war victims. He returned to Cleveland to lead various civic committees organized for the war effort. In 1921 Pres. Harding reappointed Herrick ambassador to France, where he helped handle Chas. Lindbergh's historic Paris landing in 1927. Two years later, Herrick died in Paris. Herrick married Carolyn M. Parmely in 1880 and had a son, Parmely. He was buried in Lake View Cemetery.

Mott, Col. T. Bently. *Myron T. Herrick Friend of France* (1929).
Myron T. Herrick Papers, WRHS.

**HERRICK, RENSSELAER RUSSEL** (29 Jan. 1826–30 Jan. 1899), entrepreneur, city council member, and mayor of Cleveland (1879–82), was born in Utica, NY. One of 4 children, his father, Sylvester Pierce Herrick, died when he was 2; his mother was

MARIA MARCIA SMITH HERRICK, a successful magazine editor. In 1836 Herrick came to Cleveland and worked as a printer's apprentice but also learned carpentry. For several years he worked in carpentry, then became president of the Dover Bay Grape & Wine Co. Herrick began his public life in 1855, when he became a member of CLEVELAND CITY COUNCIL,† a post he held for 5 terms. He served on the City Board of Improvements in 1873–76 and 1877. As a Republican, he successfully ran for mayor in 1879, serving until 1882. As mayor, Herrick lowered the city's indebtedness and the levy rates. He also instituted the annual census by the police department. After his term, Herrick returned to private life and became vice-president of Society for Savings. In 1891, however, he returned to public life as director of the city's Public Works for 1 year. In 1846 Herrick married Adelaide Cushman. He later married a widow, Mrs. Laura White Hunt, on 25 Sept. 1888. Neither marriage produced any children. Herrick was buried in Lake View Cemetery.

**HERTZ, MARGUERITE ROSENBERG** (31 Aug.1899–26 June 1992), psychologist for the BRUSH FOUNDATION† (1933–37) and psychology professor at CASE WESTERN RESERVE UNIV.† (1938—70), was one of only a handful of U.S. experts on the Rorschach ink blot method of psychological testing. The author of over 70 publications, she was the first woman to receive the Great Man Award from the Society for Personality Assessment (1970). Hertz was born in New York City, the daughter of Benjamin Rosenberg. She received an A.B. from Hunter College (1918) and an M.A. and a Ph.D. from Western Reserve Univ. (WRU, 1932). Before coming to Cleveland, Hertz taught for 2 yrs in high schools in New York City. From 1930–32, she served as psychologist for CLEVELAND ASSOCIATED CHARITIES† and as a fellow in psychology with the Brush Foundation. At WRU she served as asst. professor (1938–48), assoc. clinical professor (1948–57), clinical professor (1957–64), and professor (1964–70) until she retired. In 1940 she was selected to serve on an advisory committee which presented the viewpoint of women at the Democratic National Convention.

On 27 August 1922 she married lawyer David Ralph Hertz, later a judge for the Cuyahoga County Court of Common Pleas. They had two sons, Harlan Stone and Willard Joel. Hertz was a consultant for the Veterans Administration, the Cuyahoga Council for the Retarded Child, and the Ohio Welfare Department. She headed the Ohio branch and served as national president of the Rorschach Institute (1941). Hertz served as president of the Center Women's Club, the Federation of Jewish Women's Organizations and the NATIONAL COUNCIL OF

JEWISH WOMEN, CLEVELAND SECTION.† Hertz is buried in the Mayfield Cemetery.—J.M.

---

Marguerite Rosenberg Hertz Papers, CWRU Archives.

**HERZEGH, FRANK** (11 April 1907–4 Dec. 1989) was the inventor of the first successful tubeless tire and owner of patents for over 100 inventions in the field of tire technology. Frank was born in Cleveland, the son of Zoltan and Mary Dubovan Herzegh, and graduated from West Technical High School in 1926. Four years later he received his bachelor's degree in physics from Case Institute of Applied Science. After graduation, he was employed by the B. F. Goodrich Co. in Akron as a research and development engineer. The tubeless tire, which he designed and tested himself in a Texas desert, was a significant innovation in the automotive field. He also held other patents in tire design, tire manufacturing, and testing and evaluation equipment. After 42 years at Goodrich, he retired in 1972 and worked for the company as a consultant. In 1978 he was awarded the Charles Goodyear Medal for outstanding career accomplishment in rubber technology.

Herzegh married Eleanor Pitkin Owen in 1938 and they had 3 children: the Rev. Jean E. of Juneau Alaska, and sons Frank O. of Los Alamos, NM, and Paul H. of Boulder, CO. Herzegh, who resided in Shaker Hts., was cremated.—M.S.

**HERZOG, BERTHA BEITMAN** (21 Jan. 1874–9 July 1958), the first woman president of the Jewish Welfare Federation (1927–30, later the JEWISH COMMUNITY FEDERATION†), received the Charles Eisenmann Award for outstanding community service in 1941. She helped found several local organizations, including the Cleveland Federation of Jewish Women's Organizations, the Jewish Big Sister Assn., the CLEVELAND COUNCIL ON WORLD AFFAIRS,† and the Council for the Prevention of War (1923). Herzog was born in Washington, IN, to Emanuel and Molly Beitman. She moved to Cleveland Hts. after marrying Siegmund Herzog on 1 Mar. 1900. He died in 1943.

A member of Suburban Temple, Herzog served as president of the Cleveland Council of Jewish Women (1920–24, later the NATIONAL COUNCIL OF JEWISH WOMEN, CLEVELAND SECTION†) and as Women's Co-Chair for the National Conference of Christians and Jews. In addition to her religious activities, she chaired the LEAGUE OF WOMEN VOTERS OF CLEVELAND† international relations committee, served on the board of the Maternal Health Assn. (later Planned Parenthood of Greater Cleveland) from its founding until 1941. She was one of the earliest members of the Women's Committee of the CLEVELAND OR-CHESTRA.† She also helped organize the WOMEN'S CITY CLUB† and belonged to the women's board of Western Reserve Univ. Herzog died at her home and was cremated, her remains are located at the Cleveland Temple Memorial.—J.M.

**HESSENMUELLER, EDWARD** (1811–27 Jan. 1884), lawyer, prominent German-American leader, and Democrat elected to 5 terms as justice of the peace and 2 terms as judge in police court, was born in Wolfenbuettel, Braunschweig, Germany, educated at the Univ. of Halle, and, with his wife, Minna, arrived in Cuyahoga County in 1836. He was admitted to the bar in 1839 and in 1840 moved to Cleveland. Within 3 years he was a leader in the local German-American community, organizing that community's celebration of American Independence in 1843. Later that year he was elected to his first 3-year term as justice of the peace; he became a police court judge in 1860.

Hessenmueller published *GERMANIA†* from 1846–53, the first German newspaper published in the area. In 1850 he was on a committee investigating causes and prevention of steamboat accidents, and in 1853 was appointed U.S. commissioner and pension agent for Cleveland. In 1861 he was appointed by city council to a committee visiting troops from Cuyahoga County serving in western Virginia, helping the soldiers send money home and returning with letters to their families. He also distributed relief funds for volunteers' families, and was president of the German Central military committee, which raised funds for the German 107th regiment. He was also a director of the City Infirmary. Hessenmueller was a trustee of Society for Savings and was secretary of Teutonia Insurance Co. He was president of the Cleveland Gesangverein.

Hessenmueller had 4 children: Caroline, Louisa, Andrew, and Edward. He was buried in the Erie St. Cemetery.

**HEXTER, IRVING BERNARD** (31 Oct. 1897–22 May 1960) achieved national stature both as a publisher of trade magazines and as a campaigner against heart disease. The native Clevelander was the son of Barney and Leah Heller Hexter and a graduate of East High School. After attending the Univ. of Michigan, he became president of a brother's clothing business, the Morreau Hexter Co. He left to start his own greeting card business and in 1930 diversified the seasonal trade by founding the Industrial Publishing Co. Aided by his wife, the former Eva Joseph, since 1924, he began with a single magazine, *Industry and Welding*. By 1960 the company had become the nation's 5th largest trade paper publisher, with 13 publications, an aggregate monthly circulation of 510,000, and an annual gross advertising volume of $5 million. Although he had sold the concern in 1954 to Telenews Productions, Inc., of New York, he remained as president until his death. Hexter became chairman of the Cleveland Heart Assn. (see AMERICAN HEART ASSN.† [AHA], NORTHEAST OHIO AFFILIATE, INC.†) in 1952, the same year he established the Eva and Irving Hexter Cardiopulmonary Research Laboratory at MT. SINAI MEDICAL CTR.† He was credited with originating the AHA's Heart Sunday campaign technique and in 1957 became only the 3rd layman in history to receive the association's Gold Medal Award. He was a trustee of Mt. Sinai, the FOREST CITY HOSPITAL,† and the CLEVELAND MUSEUM OF NATURAL HISTORY.† Hexter died at Mt. Sinai of a heart attack and was buried at Mayfield Cemetery. He was survived by Mrs. Hexter and 2 daughters, Barbara Kichler and Eva Broida.—J.V.

**HEYDEMANN, LILY CARTHEW** (3 Dec. 1888–8 May 1971) was active as a dramatic teacher, director, and performer in Cleveland during the 1920s. Born Lily Pelonsky in Boston, MA, she made her stage debut there at age 16 and acted professionally for 7 years, until her marriage in 1915 to a physician, Dr. Martin Heydemann. She then turned her theatrical interest toward the writing of monologues for herself and Chautauqua speakers, published through at least 5 editions as *Lily Carthew's Monologues.* Coming to Cleveland with Dr. Heydemann in 1919, she opened a dramatic studio in the Fine Arts Bldg. on EUCLID AVE.† in 1922. She acted locally at the CLEVELAND PLAY HOUSE,† gave monologues at the CITY CLUB OF CLEVELAND,† WOMEN'S CITY CLUB,† CLEVELAND WOMAN'S CLUB,† and the TEMPLE,† and did some radio broadcasting over WTAM† and WJAX. Her play "Help, Help" was produced at the METROPOLITAN THEATER† in 1925. Heydemann also directed plays at the Temple and for the Gilpin Players at KARAMU HOUSE.† Following the death of her husband in 1930, she moved to New York City. She died at the Edwin Forrest Home in Philadelphia, survived by a daughter, Betty Robins.—J.V.

**HILLIARD, RICHARD** (3 July 1800–21 Dec. 1856), entrepreneur and president of the Village of Cleveland, was born in Chatham, NY. Son of David Hilliard, he attended local schools for a few terms, but at 14, after his father's death, he left to take an apprenticeship in Albany, NY. He left the apprenticeship and became a clerk and teacher. In 1824 he went to work for the mercantile business of John Daly, quickly working his way up to partner with-

out capital. That same year, the company relocated in Cleveland, and in 1827 Hilliard bought out Daly's interest in the firm and hired a resident partner in New York, Wm. Hayes. The two men stayed together as Hilliard & Hayes until Hilliard's death. Hilliard was an active member of Trinity Church. He also helped finance Erie Railroad. In the 1830s he and Courtland Palmer of New York and Edwin Clark of Cleveland began manufacturing and waterway development in the FLATS.† Hilliard began his political career in 1830, serving 2 terms as president of the Board of Trustees of the Village of Cleveland. In the first city elections of 1836, he was elected alderman, in May serving on a select committee for the common schools of Cleveland. He joined the Board of Trade in 1849 and became a commissioner on the Board of Water Works in 1853. He was also a trustee for the Homeopathic Hospital College. In 1827 Hilliard married Sarah Katherine Hayes and had 9 children: Mary, Catherine, Julia, Richard, Newton, William, Laura, Betsey Matilda, and Charles Augustus. Hilliard died in New York City and was buried in Erie St. Cemetery.

**HIMES, CHESTER** (29 July 1909–12 Nov. 1984) overcame a criminal record acquired in Cleveland's black ghetto to become an acclaimed writer of the African American experience. He was born in Jefferson City, MO, and lived in Mississippi, Alabama, and St. Louis, MO, before coming to Cleveland as a teenager with his parents. Graduating from East High School in 1926, Himes worked as a busboy in Wade Park Manor until a fall down an elevator shaft left him with permanent spinal damage. He briefly attended Ohio State Univ. in Columbus before returning to explore the gambling clubs on Cleveland's east side, where he made the acquaintance of characters who later turned up in his detective stories. In Nov. 1928 he burglarized a home for which he received a 20–25-yr. sentence in Ohio State Penitentiary. Surviving the Easter Monday fire which killed more than 300 inmates in 1930, Himes began writing stories in prison for *Esquire* magazine. Paroled in 1936, he returned to Cleveland and secured employment on the WPA Ohio Writers' Project, where he was assigned to write a history of Cleveland for the guide to Metropolitan Cleveland. He left Cleveland during World War II to work in the shipyards of the West Coast, which furnished the background for his first novel, *If He Hollers Let Him Go* (1945). Married first to the former Jean Johnson of Cleveland, he later lived in Mexico, France, and Spain. His greatest success was the detective novel *Cotton Comes to Harlem,* which was turned into a hit movie directed by Ossie Davis. Himes died in his home at Moraira, Spain, survived by his wife, Lesley, and his brother, Joseph C. Himes, a respected sociologist and author.—J.V.

Chester Himes. *The Quality of Hurt: The Autobiography of Chester Himes,* Vol. I (1972).

**HINMAN, WILBUR F.** (1841–21 March 1905), born in BEREA,† was a volunteer Army officer in the CIVIL WAR. He enlisted in the 65th Ohio Volunteer Infantry for 3 years on 12 Oct. 1861, serving as 1st sgt. until promotion to 1st lt. of Co. E on 16 June 1861. He was wounded at the Battle of Chickamauga, GA, 19 Sept. 1863, but recovered to be promoted to captain, Co. F, June 1864. He was mustered out as captain 30 Nov. 1865. Hinman returned to Cleveland after military service, where in 1878 he was a member of the Cleveland Board of Education committee organized to set up a school library system. He served as clerk of Cuyahoga County Common Pleas Court, being elected in 1875 and reelected in 1878. Correspondence to JAS. BARNETT indicated that Hinman was either residing or employed in Washington, DC, in 1887–88.

Hinman married Sarah M. Everett in 1870 and had 3 children: Henry E., Wilbur S., and Mary S. Hinman was buried in Washington, DC.

Wilbur F. Hinman Papers, 1862–85, WRHS.

**HINSDALE, BURKE AARON** (31 Mar. 1837–29 Nov. 1900) was an educator, president of Hiram College, superintendent of CLEVELAND PUBLIC SCHOOLS,† and author of numerous books and articles on history, education, and Pres. JAMES A. GARFIELD.

Born in Wadsworth, OH, to Albert and Clarinda (Eyles) Hinsdale, Burke attended public school and, from 1853–60, the Western Reserve Eclectic Institute (Hiram College) where he befriended one of his teachers, James A. Garfield. Upon graduating, Hinsdale taught in the English Department of Hiram College until 1864.

Between 1864–68, Hinsdale was pastor of the Church of the Disciples of Christ, Solon, then of the Franklin Circle Church, Cleveland. He became associate editor of *The Christian Standard*, a religious periodical in Cleveland, authoring numerous articles.

In 1868 Hinsdale became chair of history, political economy, and governmental science at Alliance College. In 1869 he returned to Hiram as professor of philosophy, english literature, and political science. In 1870 Hinsdale became president of Hiram, serving until 1882.

After Garfield's assassination, his widow, Lucretia authorized Hinsdale to collect, edit, and publish *The Works of Garfield*. Hinsdale also wrote *President Garfield and Education, How to Study and Teach History* and *The American Government.*

From 1882–86 Hinsdale was Cleveland's superintendent of public schools. He sought to strengthen the schools and, during his administration, built 14 new buildings. Hinsdale resigned to become a professor of education at the Univ. of Michigan.

Hinsdale married Mary Turner on 24 May 1862. They had three daughters. Hinsdale died in Atlanta, GA.—T.B.

Burke Aaron Hinsdale Papers, WRHS.

**HOADLEY, GEORGE** (15 Dec. 1781–20 Feb. 1857), politician and leading legal figure in mid–19th-century Cleveland, was born in Connecticut, the son of Timothy and Rebecca Linley (Taintor) Hoadley. He graduated from Yale in 1801 and later studied law. He held various jobs as a newspaper writer and tutor at Yale before embarking on a career in law. He also served a term as mayor of New Haven. Hoadley came to Cleveland in 1830, establishing a law practice. Highly regarded for his erudition, he was often consulted on law matters. From 1832–46 he served as justice of the peace, and in 1846 was elected mayor for a 2-year term. As justice of the peace, Hoadley purportedly decided over 20,000 legal cases during his 14-year tenure, with a reputation for being firm but fair; few of his decisions were reversed. He administered the oath of office to the first city council in 1836. As mayor of Cleveland, Hoadley was largely responsible for the establishment of the city's first high school for qualified common school students. As a result of his efforts, the first high school for boys was opened in 1846; a department for girls was added the following year. The school was eventually closed because of opposition to its selective nature. Hoadley married Mary Woolsey in 1819 and had 4 children: Mary Ann, Elisabeth Dwight, George, and Laura. Mary Woolsey had a son, William, from a previous marriage. Their son, Geo. Hoadly (who dropped the e from the family name) was elected governor of Ohio in 1883. Hoadley died in Cleveland and was buried in Erie St. Cemetery.

**HOBAN, EDWARD FRANCIS** (27 June 1878–22 Sept. 1966), sixth Catholic bishop of Cleveland, was born in Chicago, IL, to William and Bridget O'Malley Hoban. He was educated at St. Mary Seminary in Baltimore, and ordained to the priesthood on 11 July 1903. Hoban graduated from Gregorian Univ. in Rome in 1906, and became professor and treasurer of the Chicago Quigley Preparatory College. He was appointed to the Chicago Diocesan Chancery staff, became chancellor in 1906, and auxiliary bishop of Chicago in 1921. In

1928 Hoban became bishop of Rockford, IL, opening many elementary and high schools, modernizing charitable institutions, and establishing a diocese newspaper. On 14 Nov. 1942, Hoban was named co-adjutor bishop of the Diocese of Cleveland, serving as administrator with the right of succession to the ailing Archbishop Schrembs. He became bishop of Cleveland when Schrembs died in 1945.

Hoban's diocesan population grew from 546,000 in 1942 to 870,000 in 1966, even though 6 counties were lost to the new Diocese of Youngstown, established in 1943. Hoban established 61 new parishes, 47 new elementary schools, and a dozen high schools. He helped rebuild and remodel ST. JOHN CATHEDRAL,† and enlarged ST. JOHN COLLEGE.† Hoban centralized the child-care facilities at PARMADALE,† constructed additional nursing homes, and opened HOLY FAMILY CANCER HOME† for terminal cancer patients. An undergraduate seminary, Borromeo, was opened in 1953. Hoban actively promoted the Lay Retreat Movement and expanded the Newman Apostolate for Catholic students attending public universities and colleges. Hoban was given the personal title of archbishop in 1951. Hoban died in Cleveland and was buried in the crypt of St. John's Cathedral.

**HODGE, JOSEPH,** also known as Black Joe, was a hunter and trapper hired in June 1796 by the surveying party of MOSES CLEAVELAND to guide the group from Buffalo across the Pennsylvania border into the Western Reserve. He has thus been called the first black American to have contact with Cleaveland, although he guided the party only as far as Conneaut Creek before returning to Buffalo in early July 1796. Little is known about Hodge's life. One recent investigator, Edith Gaines, has speculated that he was a runaway slave, escaped perhaps from a farm in the Hudson River Valley, where many slaves were owned until New York prohibited slavery in 1799. He was apparently captured by Seneca Indians in a raid during the Revolutionary War and lived with them until being returned to U.S. authorities at Ft. Stanwix in Dec. 1784. During captivity, he apparently became fluent in the Seneca tongue, for he later was a trader and storekeeper near an Indian settlement near Buffalo Creek. He was also married to an Indian woman and was reported to have had a son who was killed in the War of 1812. Hodge served as a guide and interpreter for Moses Cleaveland's surveying party from about 27 June 1796, when the party left Buffalo, until about 4 July 1796, when the surveyors crossed the Pennsylvania border. Little else is known about him, except that he died at an advanced age on the Cattaraugus Reservation.

**HODGE, ORLANDO JOHN** (25 Nov. 1828–16 Apr. 1912), politician and businessman, was born in Hamburg, NY, son of Alfred and Sophia (English) Hodge. He came to Cleveland in 1842 as a "roller boy" in a printing office. A volunteer in the Mexican American War (1847–48), wounded twice, he attended Geauga Seminary from 1849–51 with classmates Lucretia Rudolph and JAS. GARFIELD. Hodge was elected Cleveland's first police-court clerk in 1853, and in 1856 became city editor for the *PLAIN DEALER*.† In 1860 Hodge moved to Connecticut, returning to Cleveland in 1867 and being elected to the first of 4 terms on CLEVELAND CITY COUNCIL† in 1873. He was elected to 4 terms in the Ohio house. Ohio governor Foraker made Hodge a member of his staff and a colonel in the Ohio militia in 1889. In 1891 the general assembly authorized Hodge's proposal that Cleveland implement the Federal Plan of government. After Hodge was defeated for Congress in 1892, he retired from active politics. Hodge owned and edited the *Sun & Voice* from 1878–89, was president of Economy Bldg. & Loan Co. and Lion Oil Co., and was a real estate dealer with extensive holdings. In 1873 Hodge organized the Cleveland Humane Society. He published genealogies of many Cleveland families, and in 1892 Hodge published *Reminiscences,* his memoirs, which he reissued in 1910. Hodge's first wife, Lydia Doan, whom he married in 1855, died in 1879; their son, Clark R., was born in 1867 and died in 1880. In 1882 Hodge married Virginia Shedd Clark. Hodge died in Cleveland and was buried in Lake View Cemetery.

Orlando J. Hodge Papers, WRHS.

**HODGINS, AGATHA C.** (1877–24 March 1945) was a nurse who pioneered nitrous oxide anesthesia while working as chief anesthetist for DR. GEORGE CRILE. Hodgins opened Lakeside (Hospital) School of Anesthesia, the nation's first formal postgraduate program in anesthesia, and founded the American Assn. of Nurse Anesthetists (AANA).

Born in Toronto, Canada, Hodgins moved to Boston in 1898 where she graduated from Boston City Hospital's Training School for Nurses in 1900. Moving to Cleveland, Hodgins became head nurse at Lakeside Hospital's private pavilion.

At Lakeside, Hodgins became associated with Crile, a surgeon, and a dentist, Dr. Charles Teter, who were experimenting with a new method of administering nitrous oxide–oxygen anesthesia. Crile chose Hodgins, a nurse with a reputation for patience, intelligence, and diligence, as his personal, permanent anesthetist. In 1908 Hodgins was placed in charge of anesthesia for Crile's private service at Lakeside.

In 1915 Hodgins served for several months at the World War I American Ambulance Hospital in Paris, France, as part of a small volunteer team organized by Crile. Here they demonstrated the superiority of their anesthetic technique for patients in shock or who had been gassed.

Upon her return to Cleveland, Hodgins developed a course of study for a postgraduate anesthesia school at Lakeside Hospital. The school opened in 1915 to graduate nurses who had passed their state board examinations, and to qualified physicians and dentists.

In 1923 Hodgins organized the Alumnae Assn. of the Lakeside School of Anesthesia, which became the nucleus for the American Assn. of Nurse Anesthetists. Hodgins retired as director of the Lakeside School of Anesthesia in 1933.

Hodgins remained single. She died in Chatham, MA.—T.B.

**HOFFMAN, FLARRA B.** (1907–4 April 1994) played a key role in establishing a Cleveland congregation of the Church of God. Born in Snowden, WV, she moved to Cleveland in 1943. She and her husband Charles held prayer meetings in their home until their growing congregation secured the old Grace Episcopal Church building on Bolivar St. downtown, and a minister, the Rev. J. A. Lewis, head of the Church of God Home Missions Board, was sent to Cleveland. The church moved to East 55th St. in 1946 and to its current site at 12401 Cooley Ave. in 1964. Hoffman also helped establish a Church of God in North Ridgeville.

She was survived by her niece, Vivian Harmon of Olmsted Twp.; nephews, Boyd Kingery of Medina and Dewey Kingery of Nokomis, FL; grandson, Kenneth Hoffman of West Salem, OH; and brother, Arvil Elkins of Albany, OH.

**HOFFMAN (HOPFERMAN), ISAAC** (10 June 1815–26 Feb. 1890), grocer, butcher, and fur dealer, was chosen by the Israelitische Society (1839) as the city's first Jewish spiritual leader (see JEWS AND JUDAISM†). A professional mohel (circumciser), he traveled throughout Ohio and Pennsylvania. Born Isaac Hopferman in Unsleben, Bavaria, to Sara and SIMSON HOPFERMAN, he came to the U.S. with his family in 1839, and arrived in Cleveland late that summer. That fall his parents hosted the city's Jewish first religious services and the formation of the Israelitische Society. Hoffman, who apparently Americanized his name sometime after arriving in the U.S., managed the I. Hoffman & Son hide business (1861–90). He also ran a slaughterhouse with SIMSON THORMAN and others at Croton and Case Ave. Hopferman married Hannah Rosenbaum on 16 Sept. 1842.—J.M.

**HOLDEN, LIBERTY EMERY** (20 June 1833–26 Aug. 1913), owner of the *PLAIN DEALER†* and real estate investor, was born in Raymond, ME, son of Liberty and Sally Cox Stearns Holden. He began teaching at age 16, and completed 2 years at Waterville College before moving, in 1856, to finish his education at the Univ. of Michigan. While professor of literature at Kalamazoo College, he married Delia Elizabeth Bulkley on 14 Aug. 1860. After 2 years as superintendent of schools in Tiffin, OH, Holden moved to Cleveland in 1862 to study law and invest in real estate. In 1873 he began investing in mining properties, iron in the Lake Superior region and silver in Utah, and became a leading spokesman in Washington for western silver interests. Soon after Holden purchased the *Plain Dealer* from WM. W. ARMSTRONG in 1885, he launched the morning *Plain Dealer* after buying out the *Herald* in association with the *Leader*. The *Plain Dealer* supported Bryan for president while under Holden's personal direction from 1893–98, but when he subsequently leased it to CHAS. E. KENNEDY and ELBERT H. BAKER, the *Plain Dealer* withheld its support from Bryan. Holden also owned the HOLLENDEN HOTEL;† and was largely responsible, as president of the building committee, for the construction of the CLEVELAND MUSEUM OF ART† and its adjacent setting of WADE† and ROCKEFELLER PARKS.† Holden was president of the UNION CLUB,† and mayor of BRATENAHL† Village. Holden and his wife had a surviving son, Guerdon Stearns, and daughters ROBERTA BOLE, Delia White, Emery Greenough, and Gertrude McGinley. Two sons, Albert Fairchild and L. Dean, predeceased him. Holden died in Mentor, OH, and was buried in Lake View Cemetery.

**HOLLAND, JUSTIN** (1819–24 Mar. 1887), black musician and composer best known for his works on the guitar, also active in the antislavery movement and a leader in black Masonic fraternities, was born in Norfolk County, VA, to free blacks. He went to Chelsea, MA, in 1833, where he worked and studied flute and guitar, before attending Oberlin Preparatory Department (1841–42) and spending two years in Mexico learning Spanish so he could read the methods of the Spanish guitar masters. Coming to Cleveland around 1845, he established himself primarily as a guitar teacher, but is also credited with 35 original guitar works and 300 published arrangements. In 1874 Holland's *Comprehensive Method for the Guitar* was pronounced by critics as the best work of its kind in America. As a performing artist, Holland played the flute, piano, and guitar. Holland was involved in the National Negro Conventions of 1848 and 1854, the Ohio State Negro Convention in 1852, and was secretary of Colored Americans of Cleveland. Fluent in Spanish, French, and German, Holland established friendship links between black Masonic lodges in such places as Peru, Portugal, Spain, France, and Germany, thereby gaining an international reputation in that area. He and his wife, Daphine (sometimes sp. Delphine) Howard Minor, had sons Justin Minor, himself a guitarist, and Minor; and daughters Lavina, Justina, and Clara. Holland died at his son's home in New Orleans, LA.

**HOLLEY, JOHN MILTON** (7 Sept. 1777–14 Nov. 1836) was a member of General MOSES CLEAVELAND's party sent out by the CONNECTICUT LAND CO.† in 1796 to survey the lands of the Western Reserve, and kept a journal of the undertaking.

Holley was the son of Sarah and Luther Holley, a merchant in Dover, CT, and joined the Moses Cleaveland party as a surveyor in the spring of 1796, and was present at the council with Red Jacket (see RED JACKET'S SPEECH†) and the Iroquois Nation held at Buffalo Creek, which he described in his journal. As part of their surveying activities, Holley, along with AMOS STAFFORD and Theodore Shepard, laid out Cleaveland Twp. and Spafford prepared a township map, which was found among Holley's papers by his son, Governor Alexander H. Holley of Connecticut. His journal described the working life of a surveyor in the wilderness and the character of the land he traversed during the expedition. With the signs of winter approaching in mid-October, his journal entries leave no doubt that the party was anxious to leave the Reserve and return to the homes they had left in the spring. Holley returned to Connecticut and settled in Salisbury, where he remained for the rest of his life. Holley was married twice. In 1800 he married Sally Porter. After her death in 1816, he married Mary Ann Cogswell. Holley had no surviving children.

**HOLLY, JOHN OLIVER, JR.** (3 Dec. 1903–20 Dec. 1974) founded the FUTURE OUTLOOK LEAGUE† in 1935 to help secure equal employment for AFRICAN AMERICANS† in Cleveland; on 23 Oct. 1988, the General Mail Facility at 2400 Orange Ave. at Cleveland's main post office, was named for him. Holly was born in Tuscaloosa, AL. Educated at private and public schools, he quit school at 15 to work in the coal mines, after he and his family moved to Rhoda, VA. The family moved again, to Roanoke, VA; Holly resumed his studies and graduated from Roanoke Harrison High School. He worked with his father's Detroit, MI, trucking business and at other jobs there, for a time attending the Cass Technical Commercial School in Detroit.

Holly moved to Cleveland in 1926 after his marriage to Leola Lee. The couple had two sons, Arthur and Marvin. Holly worked as a porter at Halle Brothers and later for the Federal Sanitation Co., a chemical manufacturing company. As director of the Future Outlook League, he soon devoted most of his energies to controversial business boycotts and battles with unions. In Sept. 1941 Holly served a 10-day jail sentence for illegal picketing, but only a few weeks later was appointed by Mayor FRANK LAUSCHE to the city's Fair Rent Committee.

Holly, an active Democrat, unsuccessfully challenged HERMAN FINKLE for the 12th Ward council seat (1937) and attempted to secure a nomination to Congress (1954). Holly founded the state-wide Federal Democrats of Ohio, Inc., and served as a trustee of Mt. Sinai Baptist Church and on the executive board of the Cleveland Chapter of the NATIONAL ASSN. FOR THE ADVANCEMENT OF COLORED PEOPLE.† He held offices in Champion City Lodge No. 177. Holly died at Richmond General Hospital, leaving his wife, Marguerite; he was buried in Highland Park Cemetery.—J.M.

Tall, Booker T. *Biography of John O. Holly, Jr.* (n.d.).

**HOLMES, ALLEN C.** (27 May 1920–31 Oct. 1990), a national expert in antitrust law, began practicing law at JONES, DAY, REAVIS & POGUE† in 1944, and became managing partner 1 Jan. 1975. Called the most powerful man in Cleveland by *Town & Country* magazine in 1981, he received such awards as the Statesman Award from the Harvard Business School Club of Cleveland (1982), the Charles Eisenmann Award from the JEWISH COMMUNITY FEDERATION† (1983), and the Humanitarian Award from the National Conference of Christians and Jews (1987). Holmes was born in Bethel, OH, and received his A.B. from the Univ. of Cincinnati (1941) and J.D. from the Univ. of Michigan (1944). He was a member of Phi Beta Kappa. Joining Jones Day upon graduation, he was made a senior partner in 1954. Before retiring in 1985, as managing partner Holmes had expanded the firm from 170 locally based lawyers to 420 in 6 cities. Holmes belonged to the State Bar of Ohio and the District of Columbia Bar.

Holmes served on the CASE WESTERN RESERVE UNIV.† Board of Trustees from 1971 until his death, as vice-chair (1975–82), chair (1983–87), and honorary trustee (1989–90). Holmes chaired WVIZ† Channel 25 and headed the KULAS FOUNDATION,† served on the boards of the DIAMOND SHAMROCK FOUNDATION,† the SHERWIN-WILLIAMS CO.,† Kaiser Foundation Health Plans, and the NATIONAL CITY CORP.,† and participated in leadership roles with the following local organizations: CLEVELAND INSTITUTE OF MUSIC,† CLEVELAND INSTITUTE OF ART,† MUSICAL ARTS ASSN.,† Citizens Advisory Committee of the Cuyahoga Community Hospital, GREATER CLEVELAND GROWTH ASSN,† UNITED WAY SERVICES,† UNIV. CIRCLE INC.,† and the SHAKER HTS.† School Board.

He married Louise Quirk on 2 Sept. 1944; they had 4 sons: William P., Peter A., Thomas T., and Douglas Q. Holmes died in his home in Bratenahl. In his memory, CWRU set up the Allen C. and Louise Q. Holmes Endowment Fund.

**HOLTKAMP, WALTER** (1 July 1894–12 Feb. 1962), internationally known organ builder and leader in traditional techniques of organ construction, was born in St. Marys, OH. His father, Henry, moved the family to Cleveland in 1903 to become a salesman for G. F. Votteler & Co., a small, regional organ builder. Eleven years later, the firm became the Votteler-Holtkamp-Sparling Organ Co. Walter began working in the company, joined the army during World War I, and in 1919 returned to the firm, becoming artistic director in 1931, upon his father's death. He dedicated his life to organ building, divorcing his wife and residing over the shop to be nearer to his work. He was first president of the Natl. Assn. of Organ Builders in 1958, and represented America at an international convention in Amsterdam. Holtkamp could not play the organ but, with his extraordinary ear, was convinced that the tone of organs being built in the 1930s and 1940s was impaired because their pipes were being placed everywhere (roof, basement) except in the same room as the organ itself. In 1933 Holtkamp installed the innovative Rack positive organ at the CLEVELAND MUSEUM OF ART.† Holtkamp also built organs for BALDWIN-WALLACE COLLEGE,† CASE WESTERN RESERVE UNIV.,† Oberlin College, MIT, Yale Univ., the Air Force Academy, ST. JOHN CATHEDRAL,† and ST. PAUL'S EPISCOPAL CHURCH.† He married Mary McClure and had 3 children: Mary, David, and Walter, Jr. who, in 1995, still owned and operated the Holtkamp Organ Co. Holtkamp died in Cleveland and was cremated.—J.M.

**HOLTZCLAW, ROBERT FULTON** (10 April 1903–11 Nov. 1992) was an African American educator, author and publisher of historical books about African American educational and religious figures.

Born in Utica, MS, to William Henry and Mary (Patterson) Holtzclaw, Robert attended Utica Normal and Industrial School (established and operated by his father) and earned degrees at Talladega College in Talladega, AL, and Howard Univ. in Washington, DC. He also attended the Univ. of Montreal in the 1960s to study French.

Holtzclaw taught in Utica from 1925–1936, then in Talladega County schools until 1943, when he moved to Cleveland. The recipient of a MARTHA HOLDEN JENNINGS teaching fellowship, Holtzclaw taught social studies and history in several junior high schools, including Audubon, Robert H. Jamison, and Lulu Diehl.

Upon retiring from teaching in 1973, Holtzclaw wrote his first book, *Black Magnolias,* about his father's school. He also wrote *Scholars in Ebony* and two books about African American religious figures, *When the Saints Go Marching In* and *Black Citizens of Heaven.*

Holtzclaw belonged to the Assn. for the Study of African American Life and History, served on the Black Archives Committee of the WESTERN RESERVE HISTORICAL SOCIETY,† and supported the National Afro-American History Museum in Wilberforce, OH.

Holtzclaw married Tina Mosley in Dallas, TX (div. 1930). He married Laura Duncan in 1955. Holtzclaw had a son, Oscar, and stepdaughters, Anna Lewis and Jeannette Lacey. He lived in SHAKER HTS.† until July 1991 when he moved to Los Angeles, CA. Holtzclaw died in L.A. and is buried in Highland Park Cemetery.—T.B.

**HOOVER, EARL R.** (19 Nov. 1904–14 Nov. 1989) was a Cuyahoga County judge, a popular public speaker, and a historian of the local scene.

Born to John and Flora Brosier Hoover in Dayton, OH, Hoover attended local schools before going to Otterbein College, where he earned his A.B. in 1926, and then on to Harvard Law School, where he graduated in 1929.

Hoover first served as an asst. prosecutor, then in 1933 came to Cleveland and joined the law firm of Mooney, Hahn, Loeser, Keough & Friedheim. In 1946 he entered private practice, and later taught at FENN COLLEGE† and served as law director of Aurora, OH.

In 1950 he was elected to the Cuyahoga County Court of Common Pleas bench, where he served until 1969. He was much admired for his judicial work, one legal publication citing his rare "ability as a writer to combine dignity of a judicial opinion with a dashing literary style."

That style also made him a popular public speaker, and it is estimated that he delivered some 5,000 talks on historical topics. The Civil War and Cleveland history were favorite subjects of his research. In 1977 he authored *Cradle of Greatness,* a book about Cleveland area accomplishments.

Hoover served on the boards of the WESTERN RESERVE HISTORICAL SOCIETY† and the SHAKER HISTORICAL SOCIETY† and was a long-time member of the EARLY SETTLERS ASSN. OF THE WESTERN RESERVE,† which honored him in 1986 by naming him its "man of the year."

Hoover married the former Alice Propst on 18 Dec. 1931. They had one son, Richard W. Hoover was buried in West Alexandria, OH.—J.T.

Earl R. Hoover Papers, WRHS.

**HOPFERMAN (HOFFMAN), SIMSON** (1777-?), one of the first Jewish settlers in Cleveland (see JEWS AND JUDAISM†), hosted the city's first Jewish religious services in 1839 at his home at 33 Seneca St. Hopferman, his wife, Sara, son, Seckel (see ISAAC HOFFMAN), and daughters, Voegele and Zerle, left the village of Unsleben, Bavaria, in 1839 with the Moses Alsbacher party. Carrying a scroll of the Torah, the family left Germany on board the *Howard* and arrived in New York on 12 July 1839. They arrived in Cleveland in late summer. Twenty Jewish families met at the Hopferman home later that year and formed the Israelitische Society (later ANSHE CHESED†), under the religious leadership of Hopferman's son Isaac. Simson Hopferman served as the society's first chazan (cantor) and religious slaughterer.

**HOPKINS, WILLARD DEAN** (10 Nov. 1909-7 Feb. 1993) was a Cleveland lawyer and co-founder of the law firm of McDonald, Hopkins, Burke & Haber. An authority on tax law, estate planning, and professional corporations, Hopkins won a landmark federal case in 1968 against the Internal Revenue Service.

Born on a family farm near Savannah, OH, Hopkins' family moved to Wooster, where he attended Beall Ave. Grade School, graduated from Wooster High School in 1926, and from the College of Wooster in 1930. In 1933 he graduated from Harvard Law School and passed the Ohio Bar.

Hopkins' 60-year law practice began with the Cleveland firm of Fackler & Dye, which became Fackler, Dye & Hopkins in 1943. In 1946 he co-founded McDonald, Hopkins & Hood which became McDonald, Hopkins, Hood & Hardy in 1952. Hopkins specialty was tax law. In 1968 he successfully argued the case *U.S. v. O'Neill*, which allowed professionals to incorporate and be taxed as a corporation, rather than as individuals. In 1979 Hopkins relinquished ownership interest and management responsibilities in the firm. As a result of *O'Neill*, Hopkins became a registered Washington lobbyist in 1982 to protect the tax status of professional corporations.

Hopkins married Harriet Painter in 1936. They had five children: Angene, Frances, Walter, Lewis, and Giles. His "Language for the Law Office" column regularly appeared in *Ohio Lawyer* magazine. Active in community affairs, he served on the Lakewood School Board, 1957-70. Hopkins was buried in Savannah.—T.B.

**HOPKINS, WILLIAM ROWLAND** (26 July 1869-9 Feb. 1961), lawyer, industrial developer, and Cleveland's first city manager, was born in Johnstown, PA, to David J. and Mary Jeffreys Hopkins. The family came to Cleveland in 1874. At 13, Hopkins began working in the Cleveland Rolling Mills, using his earnings to attend Western Reserve Academy, graduating in 1892. He earned his A.B. (1896) and LL.B. (1899) at Western Reserve Univ., being elected to CLEVELAND CITY COUNCIL† as a Republican (1897-99) while in law school. Hopkins laid out new industrial plant developments, and in 1905 promoted construction of the Cleveland Short Line Railroad, linking Cleveland's major industrial sections. He gave up his law practice in 1906 to devote himself to business.

Hopkins became chairman of the Republican county committee and a member of the election board and, with the approval of both political parties, became Cleveland's first city manager in 1924. Removed from partisan politics, he developed parks, improved welfare institutions, began PUBLIC AUDITORIUM,† and developed Cleveland Municipal Airport. Although as city manager he was administrative head, he also took the lead in determining policy. The city council felt he acquired too much control and removed him from office in Jan. 1930. In 1931 he became a member of the council, unsuccessfully fighting for retention of the CITY MANAGER PLAN.† In 1933 he returned to private life. The airport was named in his honor in 1951 (see CLEVELAND HOPKINS INTERNATIONAL AIRPORT†). Hopkins married Ellen Louise Cozad in 1903; they had no children and divorced in 1926. He died in Cleveland and was buried in Lake View Cemetery.

**HOPKINSON, CHARLES WILLIAM** (13 Apr. 1865-13 May 1950) was an architect, designer, and builder of numerous clubs, churches, and schools in Cleveland and its suburbs.

Born in Cleveland to Alanson and Harriet (Farland) Hopkinson, Charles attended public school in Cleveland and graduated from Cornell Univ. (1887) with a B.S. in architecture.

Following graduation, Hopkinson spent three years in New York City (1887-90) working with the most prominent architects. In 1890 Hopkinson returned to Cleveland and opened his own architecture office.

Hopkinson concentrated his practice on private, rather than public, buildings and projects. Among his more notable designs are the Colonial & Clifton Club Houses in LAKEWOOD†; LAKEWOOD PUBLIC LIBRARY†; the Rockefeller Mining Building at CASE TECH†; and the Hough Ave. Congregational Church. He also built additions to Lakeside Hospital, and supervised the overhaul of the GARFIELD MONUMENT† located at LAKE VIEW CEMETERY.†

Hopkinson belonged to numerous professional organizations, including the Cleveland chapter of the American Institute of Architects, serving as president, and the Civil Engineers Club of Cleveland, also president.

Hopkinson married Franc Warren in 1889. They had a daughter, Ruth. Hopkinson was a member of the Congregational church. He is buried in Riverside Cemetery.—T.B.

**HOPWOOD, AVERY** (28 May 1882–1 July 1928) was a native Clevelander who became Broadway's leading playwright in the era immediately preceding that of Eugene O'Neill. The son of Julia (Pendergast) and James Hopwood, a west side butcher, he attended WEST HIGH SCHOOL† and briefly sampled Western Reserve Univ. before completing his education at the Univ. of Michigan. Returning to Cleveland, he worked for a few months as a reporter for the *CLEVELAND LEADER†* before leaving for New York. His first play, *Clothes,* a collaboration with Channing Pollock, established his reputation as a writer of light drawing-room comedy. According to critic Leonard Hall of the *New York Telegram,* "he was the only living man who could write French farce better than a Frenchman." His most successful play was the mystery play written in collaboration with Mary Roberts Rinehart, *The Bat,* which ran for 867 performances. At the time (1920), Hopwood had 4 simultaneous successes running on Broadway. He and other connoisseurs regarded *Fair and Warmer* as his best play. His *Getting Gertie's Garter* was opened in Cleveland, where he returned at least yearly to spend Christmas with his mother in her home on Clinton Ave. When Hopwood died in a drowning accident on the French Riviera, his mother brought the lifelong bachelor's remains back to Cleveland for burial in Riverside Cemetery. Cleveland critic ARCHIE BELL later disclosed that before his death Hopwood had substantially completed a roman a clef exposing the American "theatrical system" and its victims.—J.V.

**HOPWOOD, ERIE C.** (7 Feb. 1872–18 Mar. 1928), one of the *PLAIN DEALER's†* most honored editors, was born in N. Eaton, Lorain County, OH, to Henry Clay and Emily Clarinda (Cook) Hopwood. He grew up in Ashtabula County and attended Western Reserve Univ. from 1897–1901. After teaching a year in Middletown, OH, Hopwood returned to Cleveland as police reporter for the *Plain Dealer.* By 1907 he had worked his way up through asst. city editor and city editor to night editor, in 1912 becoming managing editor with editorial control of the paper. When ELBERT H. BAKER retired as general manager in 1920, the title of editor was revived for Hopwood. Under the slogan "Justice in the News Columns," he continued Baker's policy of unbiased news reporting. While confining himself largely to administrative duties, Hopwood continued to report on such occasions as a postwar tour of France and Belgium, and the marathon 1924 Democratic Natl. Convention. Hopwood was a founder of the American Society of Newspaper Editors in 1922, helped draft its idealistic "Canons of Journalism," adopted the following year, was the society's secretary, and had been its president for 3 years prior to his death. He was also a founding member of the CITY CLUB† and was its third president, 1914–15. Married to Ida Walter in 1903, Hopwood had 2 daughters, Eleanor and Marion, and a son, Henry. He died at his home in SHAKER HTS.,† where he practiced his prize-winning hobby of amateur photography. Hopwood was buried in Lake View Cemetery.

**HORSTMANN, IGNATIUS FREDERICK** (16 Dec. 1840–13 May 1908), third bishop of Cleveland, was born Philadelphia, PA, to Frederick and Catherine Weber Horstmann. He was educated at the Jesuit College of St. Joseph and St. Charles Borromeo Seminary in Philadelphia, became one of the first students at North American College in Rome in 1860, and was ordained a priest in 1865 in Rome. Returning to Philadelphia, he taught philosophy, German, and Hebrew at St. Charles Borromeo Seminary. In 1877 he became pastor of St. Mary Church in Philadelphia, gaining a reputation as a careful administrator and excellent preacher. In 1885 Horstmann was named chancellor of the Archdiocese of Philadelphia. He was also asst. editor of the *American Catholic Quarterly Review* and a founding member of the American Catholic Historical Society.

Horstmann was installed as bishop of Cleveland in ST. JOHN CATHEDRAL† in 1892, when European immigration was swelling Cleveland's population. Horstmann recruited priests, seminarians, and religious to serve their countrymen, starting 22 of the 30 new parishes for the benefit of various nationalities, although he faced crises with various nationalistic schismatic groups (e.g., the POLISH

NATIONAL CATHOLIC CHURCH,† and others). He expanded Catholic hospitals and orphanages, started St. Anthony Home for Working Boys and the CATHERINE HORSTMANN HOME,† and endorsed compulsory parochial schools, demanding that high standards be maintained. In 1894 he encouraged the formation of the Cleveland Apostolate, a group of missionary priests under Paulist father Walter Elliott, who spoke on Catholic doctrine and practices to non-Catholics. Horstmann died in Canton of a heart condition.

Lackner, Joseph, HSM. "Bishop Ignatius F. Horstmann and the Americanization of the Roman Catholic Church in the United States," (Ph.D. diss., St. Louis Univ., 1977).

**HORTON, WILLIAM P., SR.** (23 Oct. 1832–13 Feb. 1923), Cleveland dentist and civic leader, helped organize and served as the 3rd president of the Ohio State Dental Society, and served as president of both the Ohio College of Dental Surgery and the Northern Ohio Dental Society, secretary-treasurer of the State Board of Dental Examiners (later the Ohio State Dental Board), and secretary of section 7 of the American Dental Assn. Horton was born in Pittsfield, VT, to Nancy B. McClellan and Dennis Horton. Educated in Wallingford, VT, he taught school before coming to Cleveland in 1844; he entered Oberlin College the next year. He then attended a DENTISTRY† course in Milwaukee, WI, working for a brief time in 1851 in Oberlin as a store manager. Horton first practiced in Oberlin (1852), then in Cleveland with Dr. BENJAMIN STRICKLAND, and finally opened his own practice in Chapin's Hall. Later offices were located in the Colonial Arcade and the Osborn Building.

Horton helped organize the CUYAHOGA COUNTY REPUBLICAN PARTY† and served on CLEVELAND CITY COUNCIL† (1869–77, president for 8 years of that time) and on the Cleveland Chamber of Commerce (1883–1908). He was also active in the New England Society of Cleveland and the Presbyterian Union.

On 28 Oct. 1851 Horton married Louisa Chase of Maine; their children were William P., Jr., and Milton. He married Margaret Stroup of Pennsylvania on 21 Oct. 1897; the couple lived in EAST CLEVELAND.†

**HORVATH, HELEN** (21 Jan. 1872–15 July 1943), born Helen Zalavary, was a Hungarian immigrant who promoted sensitive Americanization as a means of combating the intolerance of more established immigrants through her "Speak United States," "See United States" philosophy. She encouraged newcomers to remember their own culture while learning enough about America to exploit its opportunities. Horvath came to Cleveland in 1897 and was politicized by an incident in a store, where a clerk mocked her accent. She studied English until her pronunciation was perfect and started language classes for other immigrants. In 1901 Horvath opened a school for Hungarian newcomers, where she imparted a working knowledge of English and American ways with the goal of making her students self-confident, hyphenated Americans. By World War I, at the height of anti-immigrant hysteria, the Cleveland Board of Education brought Horvath and her adult education program into the city system and authorized her to open new schools. Horvath also pioneered in organizing Hungarian-American exchange programs; many events were sponsored by the Pro-Hungaria Society, which she set up in Cleveland as a chapter of a worldwide organization. From 1925 onward, she took tours to Washington, DC, which, after 1928, were received at the White House by the First Lady. Tour members presented Hungarian art, needlework, and books for display in the White House. Horvath Educational Tours also visited other parts of the U.S. She was buried in Calvary Cemetery.

Papp, Susan. *Hungarian Americans and Their Communities in Cleveland* (1981).

**HORVATH, IAN (ERNIE)** (3 June 1943–5 Jan. 1990), a dancer and choreographer of national repute, was a cofounder of the CLEVELAND BALLET.† Born in LAKEWOOD,† he grew up in MAPLE HTS.† and made his local television debut at age 5, dancing on the *Gene Carroll Show*. While attending Chanel High School, he also danced during the summers at MUSICARNIVAL.† After a semester at Butler Univ. in Indianapolis, Horvath left in 1962 for New York, where by 1964 he was dancing in such Broadway musicals as *Fade Out, Fade In* and *Funny Girl*. He also made television appearances on the *Ed Sullivan Show*, the *Bell Telephone Hour*, and several Bob Hope specials. In 1965 he joined the Joffrey Ballet, where he performed as soloist and met Dennis Nahat. He and Nahat moved to the American Ballet Theater in 1967, where Horvath was a principal dancer in ballets choreographed by Geo. Ballanchine, Jerome Robbins, and Agnes DeMille. In 1972 Horvath became artistic director of the Cleveland Dance Center, a school which he had bought in association with Nahat and his former teacher, Chas. Nicoll. With the school as a nucleus, Horvath returned to Cleveland with Nahat and launched the Cleveland Ballet in 1976. Horvath served as soloist and artistic director, and also choreographed such pieces as *Ozone Hour* and *Piano Man*. Horvath and Nahat were co-winners of a Cleveland Arts Prize in 1981. Horvath left the Cleveland Ballet in 1984, returning to New York as a freelance choreographer and producing director of the Jose Limon Dance Co. from 1987–90. He choreographed his final work, *No Dominion,* before dying of AIDS.—J.V.

**HOSTETLER, JOSEPH C.** (8 Aug. 1885–2 Dec. 1958), a founding partner of the law firm of Baker, Hostetler & Sidlo (see BAKER & HOSTETLER†) was born near Canal Dover, Tuscarawas County, OH, to Joseph and Caroline Hostetler, members of the Amish community. After high school graduation, Hostetler worked at various jobs, including as a police beat reporter in Cleveland, to earn his tuition for Western Reserve Univ. and law school. After he was admitted to the Ohio Bar in 1908, Hostetler worked for 2 years in the law firm of WM. R. HOPKINS. While NEWTON D. BAKER was Cleveland mayor (1912–16), Hostetler served as his asst. city law director. When Baker left office, Hostetler joined him in the new firm of Baker, Hostetler & Sidlo, practicing law until his death.

Hostetler was an organizer of the NORTHERN OHIO FOOD TERMINALS† and chairman of its Board of Directors. He became director of Cleveland Trust Co. in 1938, succeeding Baker. He was also a director of Cleveland Welding Co. and Consolidated Iron-Steel Mfg. Co. He headed the Chamber of Commerce-sponsored Playgoers of Cleveland, an organization seeking to establish a legitimate theater season in Cleveland, presenting some of New York's best plays. He was awarded an honorary Master of Law degree by Cleveland-Marshall Law School in 1948, was elected president of the CLEVELAND BAR ASSN.† in 1947, was secretary of the Cleveland Baseball Co. for 20 years, and was counsel for the American League. Hostetler married Hazel Prior in 1917; they had no children.

**HOVORKA, FRANK** (5 Aug. 1897–9 Apr. 1984), chemistry professor and a leader in electrochemistry, was born to Frank and Anna (Pavlova) Hovorka in Cernicorvce, Bohemia, Austria-Hungary (presently the Czech Republic), where he learned barbering and attended business school at night. In 1913 he came to the U.S., settling in a Czech settlement in Amana, IA, barbering in nearby Waterloo. In 1915 Hovorka entered Waterloo public schools, then went to the subcollegiate department at the State College of Iowa (1917–19) and earned his B.A. (1922). He received his M.S. (1923), and Ph.D. (1925) from the Univ. of Illinois. His dissertation on the properties of ionic solutions is a classic study in the electrochemistry of solutions.

In 1925 Hovorka joined WRU's chemistry department, helping establish a chemistry doctorate in 1930. He became full professor and director of the chemistry labs in 1942, and chairman of the chemistry department in 1950–58 and 1962–68. In 1954 Hovorka received WRU's Hurlbut Chair in chemistry. He retired in 1968 and was granted emeritus status. In 1973 Hovorka and many former students donated over $1 million to establish the Frank Hovorka Chair in chemistry. Hovorka wrote over 100 technical papers. He perfected platinized graphite electrodes in the 1930s, facilitating the development of modern fuel cells. In 1940 he developed a technique for measuring acid concentrations of solutions using porous graphite electrodes. Hovorka married Sophie Paul Nickel in 1926; she died in July 1979. In 1982, Hovorka married concert pianist and CASE WESTERN RESERVE UNIVERSITY trustee Dorothy Humel. He had no children. Hovorka was buried in Connersville, IN.

**HOWARD, NATHANIEL RICHARDSON** (23 Apr. 1898–23 Dec. 1980), last editor of the *CLEVELAND NEWS,†* was born in Columbus, OH, to Carlos N. and Anne M. (Richardson) Howard. He began his newspaper career at 14 as a reporter for the *Conneaut News Herald* and, while a student at Oberlin College, worked for the *Oberlin Tribune* and served as campus correspondent for the Cleveland *PLAIN DEALER.†* He began working for the *Cleveland News* in 1918 but switched to the *Plain Dealer* a month later, where he rose from police reporter to managing editor. In 1937 Howard was appointed editor of the *Cleveland News* by FOREST CITY PUBLISHING CO.,† which operated both the *News* and *Plain Dealer.* He maintained the staunch Republican identity of the *News,* opposing the New Deal in the 1930s and supporting Eisenhower in the 1950s. During World War II, Howard was asst. director of the U.S. Office of Censorship, helping formulate a voluntary censorship program for the country's newspapers. Four months after the *News* ceased publication on 23 Jan. 1960, Howard rejoined the *Plain Dealer* as contributing editor until his retirement in 1963.

In retirement, Howard published *Trust for All Times,* a history of the CLEVELAND FOUNDATION† (1963), and *The First Hundred Years,* a history of the UNION CLUB† (1972). He was editor of the *Basic Papers of George M. Humphrey,* published by the WESTERN RESERVE HISTORICAL SOCIETY† in 1965. Howard married Marjorie Norton on 13 Sept. 1918. After her death in 1928, he married Edith Moriarty on 30 July 1930. He had 2 daughters, Mary Anne Amsbary and Marjorie Johnson. Howard died in Cleveland.

---

Nathaniel R. Howard Papers, WRHS.

HOWE, CHARLES SUMNER (29 Sept. 1858–18 Apr. 1939), college educator and president of the Case School of Applied Science (1902–29) was born in Nashua, NH, to William and Susan Woods Howe. In 1878 Howe received his B.S. in agriculture from both Massachusetts Agricultural College and Boston Univ. He received his Ph.D. in 1887 from Wooster Univ., doing postgraduate work at Amherst College the following year. In 1879 he accepted first a high school principalship, then a professorship at Colorado College. He entered Johns Hopkins Univ. in 1882, studying mathematics and physics. He became adjunct professor of mathematics at Buchtel College in 1883, and professor of mathematics and physics in 1884.

In 1889 Howe accepted appointment as professor of mathematics and astronomy at Case School of Applied Science. He brought the first German-made Riefler clock, then considered the world's best, to America, with his own modifications making it the most accurate timepiece in the world. Appointed acting president of Case in 1902, Howe was appointed president in 1903. He reinstituted freshman entrance examinations and maintained a class-rank status system for faculty. He was responsible for new buildings on campus, and maintained a close relationship with influential Clevelanders, including JOHN D. ROCKEFELLER, WORCESTER WARNER, and AMBROSE SWASEY. Believing engineers had an obligation to participate in civic affairs, Howe was president of the Cleveland Chamber of Commerce and chairman of the Cleveland River & Harbor Commission, and was prominent in establishing East and West Technical high schools.

Howe married Abbie A. Waite (d. 1924) on 22 May 1882; they had three children: William C., Earle W., and Francis E. He married again to Ida E. Puffer on 20 Sept. 1929. Howe was buried in the Glendale Cemetery in Akron.

HOWE, FREDERIC C. (21 Nov. 1867–3 Aug. 1940), Progressive reformer, was born in Meadville, PA, to Andrew Jackson and Jane Clemson Howe. He graduated from Allegheny College (1889) and Johns Hopkins Univ. (Ph.D., 1892), entered law school in New York, then settled in Cleveland in 1894, working for the law firm of Harry & Jas. Garfield, becoming a partner in 1896.

Howe became active in the work of Goodrich Social Settlement, the Municipal Assn. (see CITIZENS LEAGUE†), and the CHARITY ORGANIZATION SOCIETY.† He soon resigned from the latter, concerned that it was designed to keep the poor out of sight, and withdrew from the settlement, frustrated by its ineffectiveness. He then turned to politics in his efforts to reform society. The Municipal Assn. urged him to run in 1901 for city

council as a Republican. During the campaign, he was intrigued by TOM JOHNSON and cooperated closely with him after both were elected. Soon caught in the natural-gas franchise controversy, learning that even Municipal Assn. members had special interests they expected promoted, Howe ran for reelection as an independent but lost. Howe served as president of the Sinking Fund Commission (1904–05), state senator (1906–08), and member of Cleveland's Board of Quadrennial Appraisers (1909). In 1910 Howe left for New York City.

Howe published a book on taxation (1896); *The City: The Hope for Democracy* (1905); *The Confessions of a Monopolist* (1906); and *The British City: The Beginnings of Democracy* (1907) while in Cleveland. He lectured at Cleveland College of Law and Western Reserve Univ. In New York, Howe was director of the People's Institute (1911–14) and commissioner of immigration for the port (1914–19). In 1932 Howe supported Franklin D. Roosevelt and was appointed consumers' counsel in the Agricultural Adjustment Admin., resigning in 1937. In 1904 Howe married Marie H. Jenney (d. 1934), a Unitarian minister and prominent feminist. They had no children. Howe died in Martha's Vineyard, MA, and was buried in Meadville, PA.

Howe, Frederic C. *The Confessions of a Reformer* (1925).

HOYT, HARLOWE RANDALL (26 Jan. 1882–24 Oct. 1970) chronicled the Cleveland theater scene as a drama critic for more than half a century. He came by his theatrical interest by inheritance, as his grandfather had owned the local Concert Hall in his birthplace of Beaver Dam, WI. The son of Frank and Mary J. (Babcock) Hoyt, he began his career as drama critic with the *Milwaukee Free Press* in 1902. He served in the same capacity with the *Milwaukee Sentinel* and the *Evening Wisconsin*. His practical experience was rounded out as a press agent for Milwaukee's Davidson Theater and as advance man for a road show. When motion pictures made their appearance, Hoyt served as press agent for D. W. Griffith's *Birth of a Nation* in Wisconsin and Michigan and started the first syndicated movie column under the pseudonym Robert Grandon. He penned an old-fashioned melodrama, *The Defender of Cameron Dam*, and what he claimed to be the first historical movie scenario, *The Miniature*. Hoyt came to Cleveland in 1916 as movie-drama editor and Sunday editor for the CLEVELAND LEADER,† moving to the *PLAIN DEALER*† when it absorbed the *Leader* the following year. He covered drama with the *Plain Dealer* until his retirement in 1962. In 1955 he published *Town Hall Tonight*, a memoir of the "gaslight era" of the late–

19th century American theater based largely on his experiences with his grandfather's hall in Beaver Dam, which Hoyt still owned at the time. Following his retirement from the *Plain Dealer,* Hoyt continued to write drama reviews for *FINE ARTS MAGAZINE.†* He survived his first wife, Irene Thayer, and was survived by his second, Rickie Boasberg.—J.V.

**HOYT, JAMES MADISON** (16 Jan. 1815–21 Apr. 1895), lawyer and real estate developer, was born in Utica, NY, son of David P. and Mary (Barnum) Hoyt. He graduated from Hamilton College in 1884 and studied law in Cleveland in the office of Andrews & Foote. Admitted to the Ohio Bar in 1837, he became a partner in Andrews, Foote & Hoyt until 1848, when the firm became Foote & Hoyt. In 1853 Hoyt withdrew from practicing law to concentrate on real estate, developing new neighborhoods by purchasing large tracts of land, dividing them into lots, and selling them for homesteads. On his own or with other investors, he subdivided and sold almost 1,000 acres of city and suburban land. He alone was responsible for opening and naming over 100 streets, developing neighborhoods on Prospect, St. Clair, Superior, and Kinsman avenues on the east side, and Madison Ave., Colgate, Lawn, and Waverly (W. 58th St.) on the west side. Known as the "honest lawyer," Hoyt's reputation carried over to his real estate dealings. He was generous, especially to the poor and those in difficult circumstances because of unexpected illness or misfortune. In 1870 he was elected to the State Board of Equalization, and in 1873 was appointed to the Cleveland Board of Public Improvement. Closely associated with first the Baptist and later Congregational church, he was licensed to preach but was never ordained. Hoyt married Mary Ella Beebe in 1836 and had 6 children: Ella, Lydia Hoyt Farmer, Elton, Colgate, James, and Wayland. Hoyt is buried in Lake View Cemetery.

**HRUBY, FRANK, SR.** (IV) (1856–9 Dec. 1912) became one of Cleveland's foremost band leaders and patriarch of one of America's most renowned musical families. Born in Cehnice, Bohemia, the elder Hruby obtained his first musical job with the Hagenbeck Circus, beginning at the age of 9 and finishing as director of its 3 bands. For several years he then played in a band at Brighton Beach, Eng., before returning to Bohemia to organize a band that toured through parts of Europe. Hruby came to America in 1883, advised by Czech-born band leader Joseph Zamecnik of a need for experienced musicians in Cleveland. After obtaining a job through Zamecnik's intercession with the orchestra of the EUCLID AVE. OPERA HOUSE,† he brought his wife Katerina (1861–1933) and infant son Frank to Cleveland. In 1889 Hruby reorganized the Great Western Band, leading it in appearances in city parks, at the dedication of the SOLDIERS & SAILORS MONUMENT† in 1894, and at the Republican Natl. Convention in St. Louis in 1896. As a total of 8 children arrived, he taught them all to play various instruments and organized them into a family band. In 1912 he took them to Europe for a 5-month tour in which they played a repertoire of Sousa marches and the new American novelty, ragtime. Several months later, the elder Hruby died in his home on E. 51st St., survived by his wife and 8 children (see HRUBY FAMILY†).—J.V.

The **HRUBY FAMILY** has produced leading musicians in Cleveland for 3 generations, and was once known as "America's foremost musical family." It was founded by FRANK HRUBY, SR. (IV), a Czech-born musician who immigrated to Cleveland in 1883. His 8 children were taught to play various musical instruments by their father and kept to a rigid practice schedule by their mother, Katerina. They included Frank (V) (1883–1974), clarinet, piano, viola; Alois (Louie) (1886–1968), cello, trumpet, cornet; John (1887–1964), cornet, trumpet, violin; Celia (Mazanec) (1889–1936), flute and piano; Ferdinand (Fred) (1891–1978), piano and clarinet; Charles (1893–1976), cornet, trumpet, violin; Maymee (Kolda) (1897–1984), piano and cello; and William (1899–1965), percussion and trumpet. Shortly before his death in 1912, the elder Hruby took the children on a European tour. In 1916 Frank V and Fred founded the Hruby Conservatory of Music at Broadway and E. 55th St. Before it was closed in 1968, all 8 Hruby siblings taught there, as well as 3 grandchildren of Frank IV: Frank Hruby VI (b. 1918), Richard Kolda (b. 1921), and Joseph Hruby (b. 1922). There were also 3 branches of the conservatory, which in 1956 had 500 enrollees. The 5 eldest brothers from the 2nd generation formed a quintet which toured nationally. All of the siblings but Celia and Fred played for the CLEVELAND ORCHESTRA† at one time or another, 3 being on its roster for its inaugural concert in 1918. Frank Hruby VI served as music critic for the *CLEVELAND PRESS†* from 1956–82.—J.V.

**HUBBELL, BENJAMIN S.** (11 July 1867–21 Feb. 1953), architect active in Cleveland (1895–1930), who played a major role developing UNIV. CIRCLE† and who, with W. DOMINICK BENES, was responsible for designing several Cleveland landmarks, including the CLEVELAND MUSEUM OF ART† (1916) and WEST SIDE MARKET† (1912) was born in Leavenworth, KS, to Peter Hanford and Sophia (Still) Hubbell. He graduated from Cornell with an M.S. in architecture in 1894.

Within 2 years, Hubbell was a partner in Coburn, Barnum, Benes & Hubbell (1896), a year later establishing a partnership with Benes—HUBBELL & BENES (1897–1939). In 1916, when Hubbell & Benes were designing the Cleveland Museum of Art, they also exhibited drawings siting proposed cultural buildings in the Wade Park Oval along formal, symmetrical axes in an informal, parklike setting, reflecting the Beaux-Arts planning concepts utilized at the 1893 Chicago Columbian Exposition, as well as the Group Plan placing of public buildings around a formal mall in downtown Cleveland. While many portions of Hubbell & Benes's plan were not developed in detail, they established the general character for the area. Hubbell is credited with helping form the UNIV. IMPROVEMENT CO.† in 1918, to preserve the neighborhoods and open spaces in the Wade Park area, which eventually led to the construction of Univ. Circle. Hubbell married Bertha M. Tarbell on 17 June 1895 and had a son, Benjamin S., Jr., and a daughter, Virginia. They lived at their home, "Playmore," in Mentor, OH.

**HUBBELL, CHARLES HERMAN** (1 Nov. 1898–7 Oct. 1971) was one of the most recognized commercial aviation artists in the country. He created over 500 paintings, many of which are part of the WESTERN RESERVE HISTORICAL SOCIETY's† Crawford Auto-Aviation Museum collection.

Born in Lakewood to Herman and Elizabeth (Kunitz), Hubbell attended public schools, graduating from Lakewood High School in 1916. He attended Hiram College (1916–18) before joining the Naval Air Service during World War I. Stationed in Buffalo, NY, Hubbell redesigned experimental planes at the Curtiss airplane factory.

In 1919 Hubbell began painting in watercolors. He enrolled in the Cleveland School of Art, graduated in 1923, and by 1924 was exhibiting his work in group shows. Hubbell became a licensed pilot in 1927, later flying many of the aircraft he painted. In 1928 he switched to oils and, in 1930, began the first of many one-man exhibitions.

In 1934 Hubbell was commissioned by FRED CRAWFORD, chairman of Thompson Products, to paint past winners of the Thompson Trophy Air Race. Hubbell started his own freelance commercial studio in 1935 and created a calendar series published by Thompson/TRW (1937–72), with Hubbell remaining as TRW's freelance artist until 1969.

In 1939 Hubbell wrote and illustrated *Famous Planes and Pilots* and *Record Breakers of the Air.* He founded the Thompson Gallery of the Air in Euclid, and his works are represented at the Smithsonian Institution, Air Force Academy, and Truman Museum.

Hubbell was twice married. In 1923 he married Ethel Pease (div. 1951). They had two sons, Gordon and Roger. In 1954 Hubbell married Cora Kelly. He was a member of Lakewood Christian Church and is buried in Lakewood Park Cemetery.—T.B.

Charles Hubbell Papers, WRHS.

**HUDSON, CHARLES LOWELL, M.D.** (5 Aug. 1904–30 Aug. 1992) served as president of the American Medical Assn. (AMA) in 1966. Locally, Hudson taught at CASE WESTERN RESERVE UNIV.† (1935–77), advised the VISITING NURSE ASSN. OF CLEVELAND† (1957–65), presided over the Cleveland Medical Library Assn. (director, 1957–62, president 1962–63), and practiced at UNIV. HOSPITALS† (1930–62), the CLEVELAND CLINIC FOUNDATION† (1962–70), and the VETERANS ADMINISTRATION MEDICAL CENTER† (1946–62).

Hudson was born in Merrill, MI, to Sophia Dunn Hudson and James Harvey Hudson, M.D., a general practitioner. He received an A.B. from Alma College, MI, in 1924. After teaching high school in Manistique, MI, for 2 years, Hudson entered medical school. He received his M.D. from the Univ. of Michigan School of Medicine in 1930, spent his internship and residency in Cleveland at Univ. Hospitals, and then went to the Univ. of Pennsylvania for further study (1932–34). Returning to UH, Hudson became chief resident in medicine in 1934. The next year he was promoted to assistant physician, joined the faculty of Western Reserve Univ., and opened a private practice in internal medicine.

With the exception of service in the U.S. Army (1942–45), Hudson spent his entire career practicing in Cleveland HOSPITALS† and teaching at CWRU (retiring as Associate Clinical Professor Emeritus of Medicine) and the Cleveland Clinic (associate professor 1962–70). He served as a trustee of the AMA (1961–68), the National Assn. of Blue Shield Plans (1962–65), and the Regional Medical Program of Northeast Ohio (1969–73), and served on the citizens hospital study committee of the BLUE CROSS OF NORTHEAST OHIO† (1955–61), among his other extensive professional activities. On 29 Sept. 1937, Hudson married Ruth Strong; they had 2 daughters, Judith and Mary, and a son, Charles, Jr. In 1976 Hudson received an honorary Doctor of Laws from Alma College; he was also a life fellow of the American College of Physicians.—J.M.

Charles L. Hudson Papers, Dittrick Museum of Medical History.
Charles L. Hudson Papers, Medical Library Assn. Archives.

**HUDSON, JEAN ROBERTA** (6 Dec. 1919–2 July 1992), educator and expert on Cleveland history, was born in Philadelphia, the only child of J. Jones and Mary Porter Hudson. After graduation from Cleveland Hts. High School in 1938, she attended the College of Wooster, receiving a B.A. in sociology in 1942. She obtained an M.A. in education from the Graduate School of Western Reserve Univ. in 1961. In the late 1940s and early 1950s, Hudson served as an assistant to John Barden Dean of the School of General Studies at Western Reserve Univ. and project coordinator for the Adult Education Assn., U.S.A. She joined the SHAKER HTS.† school system in 1958, teaching upper level elementary classes at Sussex school for 25 years before retiring in 1983. A gifted educator, she received the distinguished teacher award from the MARTHA HOLDEN JENNINGS FOUNDATION† in 1969–70 and prepared curriculum materials for the Educational Research Council of Greater Cleveland.

Her expertise in Cleveland history grew out of her work as a writer and research assistant to William Ganson Rose, author of *Cleveland: The Making of a City,* and later when she prepared over 130 articles for the first edition of the *Encyclopedia of Cleveland History.* Her knowledge of local history was expanded as curator of the Shaker Historical Museum, 1986–92, where she created exhibits and programs, and wrote extensively on the NORTH UNION SHAKER COMMUNITY.†

Ms. Hudson died suddenly at her home in Shaker Hts. and was buried at Lake View Cemetery. She never married.—M.S.

**HUGHES, ADELLA PRENTISS** (29 Nov. 1869–23 Aug. 1950), best known as the founder of the CLEVELAND ORCHESTRA,† was born in Cleveland to Loren and Ellen Rouse Prentiss, graduated from Miss Fisher's School for Girls in 1886, and from Vassar College in 1890 with a degree in music. After a grand tour of Europe, returning to Cleveland in 1891 she became a professional accompanist. Though successful in this role, Prentiss became interested in the broader aspects of musical promotion in Cleveland, and in 1898 began bringing various performers and orchestras to the city. By 1901 she was one of Cleveland's major impresarios, regularly engaging orchestras to perform at GRAYS ARMORY.† During the next 17 years she supplied the city with a series of musical attractions, including orchestras, opera, ballet, and chamber music. Seeing the need for a permanent orchestra, Hughes created the MUSICAL ARTS ASSN.† in 1915 from a nucleus of business and professional men to furnish support for her projects. It was through her influence that NIKOLAI SOKOLOFF came to Cleveland. In 1918 she, Sokoloff, and the Musical

Arts Assn. joined forces to create the Cleveland Orchestra. She served as its first manager, holding that position for 15 years. She also held administrative positions in the Musical Arts Assn. for 30 years, retiring in 1945 only to continue her philanthropic work. Adella Prentiss married Felix Hughes in 1904. The couple divorced in 1923.

Adella Prentiss Hughes Papers, WRHS.
Hughes, Adella Prentiss. *Music Is My Life* (1947).
Musical Arts Assn. Archives, Severance Hall.

**HUGHES, (JAMES) LANGSTON** (1 Feb. 1902–22 May 1967), black poet, playwright, novelist, and lecturer, was born in Joplin, MO, to James Nathaniel and Carrie M. (Langston) Hughes. He moved to Cleveland in 1916, and began writing seriously while a student at CENTRAL HIGH SCHOOL,† where his efforts were encouraged by teachers and RUSSELL and ROWENA JELLIFFE of Playhouse Settlement (see KARAMU HOUSE†). His first stories appeared in *The Monthly* literature journal, published by Central High School. Hughes attended Columbia Univ. for a year, but dropped out to travel, working his way through Spain, France, Italy, and Africa. Hughes's first poem, "The Negro Speaks of Rivers," was published in *The Crisis,* the organ of the NAACP, in 1921. In 1922 he moved to Harlem, becoming a member of the Harlem Renaissance. Following publication of *The Weary Blues* in 1926, Hughes wrote *Fine Clothes to the Jew* in 1927. Awarded a full scholarship for his poetry by Lincoln Univ. in Pennsylvania, Hughes received his B.A. In 1930 he published his first novel, *Not without Laughter,* followed by *Scottsboro Limited* (1932) and *The Ways of White Folks* (1934). He received a Guggenheim Fellowship in 1935. In 1936–37, the Gilpin Players of Karamu House produced 6 of Hughes's plays. In 1939 he established the Negro Theater in Los Angeles and wrote a filmscript, "Way Down South." Hughes produced 8 volumes of poetry, 4 of fiction, 6 books for young people, 3 humorous works, 2 autobiographies, a number of plays and essays, and several volumes on black history. He was a noted lecturer and a foremost figure in the movement for black civil rights and the search for black identity. Unmarried, Hughes died in New York City.

Dickinson, Donald C. *A Bio-Bibliography of Langston Hughes* (1972).
Rampersad, Arnold. *The Life of Langston Hughes* (2 vol., 1986).

**HUGHES, JOHN ARTHUR** (2 Nov. 1880–25 May 1942), Congressional Medal of Honor recipient for service during the landing at Vera Cruz, Mexico, was born in New York City, enlisting in the U.S. Marines there in 1900. Captain Hughes, commanding the 15th Co. of the 2nd Provisional Regiment, was among the American marines who landed at Vera Cruz, 21–22 April 1914, in response to the failure of the Mexican government. After two days of fighting, the city was subdued and on 4 Dec. 1915 Hughes was awarded the Medal of Honor for his leadership and courage during the engagement. He retired from the service a colonel.

Hughes came to Cleveland at the end of the 1920s, working as a salesmen for Mack International Trucks. In 1933 he became director of the Ohio Repeal Council to manage the state's campaign to ratify the 21st Amendment to the Constitution, rescinding Prohibition. Later he worked for the Ohio Liquor Control Board. In 1936 he was appointed Safety Director of the GREAT LAKES EXPOSITION† in charge of the policemen, guards, watchmen, and other personnel hired to ensure the security and comfort of visitors. Hughes died in St. Petersburg, FL, and was buried at Arlington National Cemetery, Arlington, VA. He was survived by his wife, Margaret Harper Hughes.

**HULETT, GEORGE H.** (26 Sept. 1846–17 Jan. 1923), inventor of ore-loading machinery, was born in Conneaut, OH, to Erastus and Amanda Norton Hulett. Hulett came to Cleveland at age 12 and graduated from HUMISTON INSTITUTE† in 1864. He conducted a general store in Unionville, OH, until 1881, returning to Cleveland in the produce and commission business until 1890, when he began manufacturing coal- and ore-handling machinery. In 1898 he was construction engineer with Variety Iron Works of Cleveland, moving to McMyler Mfg. Co. in 1903. In 1907 he was associated with Webster Camp & Lane in Akron, which merged in 1909 with Wellman Seaver & Morgan of Cleveland (see DRAVO WELLMAN CO.†). Hulett was vice-president of the company until 1917 and a director until 1918. Hulett invented the Hulett car dumper machine and the Hulett unloader, a device with a cantilevered arm and bucket for unloading iron ore and coal from lake vessels. Whereas formerly 100 men worked 12 hours to unload 5,000 tons of ore, 4 Hulett unloaders could unload 10,000 tons in less than 5 hours, requiring only 25 men. The unloader became universally used. The car dumper unloaded entire cars of materials at ports and blast furnaces. Hulett also invented the Hulett conveyor bridge for handling coal, iron ore, and limestone. Hulett married Addie Hutchings in 1871 and had 2 children, Frank E. and Mrs. H. J. Doolittle. Hulett died in Daytona Beach, FL, and was buried in Lake View Cemetery.

**HULL, JESSIE (JESSE) REDDING** (27 July 1932– 20 Dec. 1992), author and speech therapist, wrote and published books for CHILDREN AND YOUTH† and learning-disabled adults, as well as poetry. Skilled in early American crafts, she also served the BAY VILLAGE HISTORICAL SOCIETY† as secretary-treasurer and as guide at the Rose Hill Museum. In the 1980s she demonstrated weaving at festivals statewide. Hull was born in Urbana, OH, to William and Ethel Botkin Redding, and educated at Ohio Wesleyan Univ. (B.A. 1954) and the Univ. of Missouri (A.M. 1956). She later earned teaching certification for learning disabilities at CLEVELAND STATE UNIV.† (1975–76). Hull worked as speech therapist in the Affton, MO, public schools (1956–59) and as supervisor of a speech clinic in Alabama before coming to Cleveland. She began publishing books in 1980, with 7 titles appearing that year and 1 the next, from New Readers Press and Bowmar/Noble. She also served as business manager for Bob Hull Books. Hull's articles on nature and pets appeared in magazines such as *Pets and People of the World*. She was also a puppeteer.

On 27 June 1959 Hull married writer Robert C. Hull; they lived with their children, Robert W. and Lisa Kay, in BAY VILLAGE.† She belonged to the BAY VILLAGE PRESBYTERIAN CHURCH.† Hull is buried in Lakewood Park Cemetery.—J.M.

**HUMPHREY, DUDLEY SHERMAN II** (19 May 1852–7 Sept. 1933) was owner and operator (with his family) of EUCLID BEACH PARK.† One of 5 children, Dudley Sherman II was born on the family farm in Wakeman Twp., Huron County, the son of Dudley Sherman I and Mabel Fay Humphrey. After completing his education at local schools, he attended Buchtel Univ. in Akron. He and his brothers, Harlow and David, helped operate the family farm. After their father died in 1876, the brothers were unable to make it profitable, and the property was sold in 1890 to satisfy creditors. In 1891 the family moved to GLENVILLE† where Dudley invented and patented a new type of popcorn popper which seasoned the corn as it popped. Beginning in June 1893, the family opened popcorn stands throughout the city. From 1896–99 they operated a concession stand at Euclid Beach Park amid the honkytonk atmosphere and drunkenness that prevailed. When the park failed the Humphrey family leased it in 1901. Dudley and the family set strict rules in their renovated park. The bar and beer garden were abolished and admission refused to those not properly dressed or who had been drinking. In 1908 Humphrey and his brothers also built the ELYSIUM,† an indoor ice-skating rink.

Humphrey married Effie DeEtta Shannon in

Wakeman, OH, 3 Sept. 1879, and they had 3 children: Mabel (Killaly), Harvey John, and H. Louise (Lambie). He died at his residence in Euclid Beach Park and was buried at Highland Park Cemetery. —M.S.

Euclid Beach Park Is Closed for the Season (1977).

**HUMPHREY, GEORGE MAGOFFIN** (8 Mar. 1890–20 Jan. 1970), lawyer, industrialist, president of the M. A. HANNA CO.,† and secretary of the treasury (1953–57) was born in Cheboygan, MI, to Watts Sherman and Caroline Magoffin Humphrey. He received his LL.B. degree from the Univ. of Michigan in 1912, and practiced law in Michigan, becoming a partner in his father's law firm. Attracted to corporate law, Humphrey was hired by the M. A. Hanna Co. in Cleveland as general counsel in 1918. He became a partner in 1920, in charge of iron-ore properties and operations. When Hanna incorporated in 1922, he became vice-president, and from 1929–52 was president, bringing the company to profitability after a $2 million deficit. After World War II, Humphrey was chosen to lead the Reparations Survey Committee advising the Allies on dismantling German industry. Pres. Dwight Eisenhower designated Humphrey his secretary of the treasury, the cabinet's strongest voice of fiscal conservatism, who spearheaded the administration's campaign to cut the federal budget in an effort to pare down the size of government, cut inflation, and stimulate private enterprise. He resigned in 1957, returning to private life in Cleveland and resuming chairmanships in several of the companies he had previously been associated with. His philanthropic interests were in the medical field. In 1913 he married Pamela Stark, and had 3 children: Pamela (Mrs. Royal Firman, Jr.), Gilbert Watts, and Caroline (Mrs. John G. Butler). Humphrey died in Cleveland.

George M. Humphrey Papers, WRHS.
Howard, Nathaniel R., ed. *The Basic Papers of George M. Humphrey as Secretary of the Treasury, 1953–1957* (1965).

**HUNTER, JANE EDNA (HARRIS)** (13 Dec. 1882–17 Jan. 1971), prominent African American social worker, founded the PHILLIS WHEATLEY ASSN.† The daughter of a sharecropper, she was born Jane Edna Harris at Woodburn Farm near Pendleton, SC. She acquired her last name by a brief marriage. Hunter graduated in 1905 as a trained nurse from Hampton Institute, VA, and came to Cleveland, serving in various nursing jobs. She attended Marshall Law School (later Cleveland Marshall Law School of CLEVELAND STATE UNIV.†) and

passed the Ohio Bar examination. Hunter organized the Working Girls Assn. in 1911 to provide safe living quarters for unmarried African American women and girls who needed a place of residence. Later that year, the name changed to the Phillis Wheatley Assn. The association was modeled by 9 similar institutions throughout the U.S. Hunter served as the association's executive secretary until 1948. Following retirement, she founded the Phillis Wheatley Foundation, a scholarship fund for African American high school graduates. The foundation later established the Jane Edna Hunter Scholarship Fund in her honor. Hunter held honorary degrees from Fisk Univ., Allen Univ. in Columbia, SC, and Central State Univ. in Wilberforce, OH. She founded the Women's Civic League of Cleveland (1943), belonged to the NATIONAL ASSN. FOR THE ADVANCEMENT OF COLORED PEOPLE† (NAACP), and served as vice-president and executive committee member of the National Assn. of Colored Women.—J.M.

Hunter, Jane Edna Harris. *A Nickel and a Prayer* (1940).
Jane Hunter Papers, WRHS.

**HUNTINGTON, JOHN** (8 Mar. 1832–10 Jan. 1893), industrialist, inventor, and philanthropist, was born in Preston, Lancashire, England, the son of Ann (Hewetson) and Thomas Huntington. He immigrated to Cleveland in 1854, and started his own contracting business in 1857. In 1863 he joined Clark, Payne & Co., an oil-refining business, and patented many inventions for improving furnaces, oil refining methods, and machinery used to produce barrels. In 1870 the company became part of Standard Oil Co. Huntington became part-owner of a large fleet of lake vessels in 1886, and later vice-president of Cleveland Stone Co. Serving 13 years on the city council, Huntington supported many city improvements, including a paid fire department; a municipal sewer system; deepening the river channel; reorganizing the waterworks department; and constructing the SUPERIOR VIADUCT.† In 1889 Huntington established the John Huntington Benevolent Trust with an initial gift of $200,000, which benefited over 40 charitable institutions annually. Huntington married Jane Beck in 1852 and had 4 surviving children: Margaret (Mrs. Francis P. Smith), Hannah J. (Mrs. A. C. Hord), Matilda (Mrs. Edward A. Merritt), and William B.; another son, Arthur, was killed in a train accident. After Mary died in 1882, Huntington married Mariette L. Goodwin. Huntington died in London, England, while visiting the London Polytechnic schools, prototypes of the school he envisioned for Cleveland and for which he left a substantial fortune. The JOHN HUNTINGTON POLYTECHNIC INSTI-

TUTE† existed from 1918 until 1953. Huntington's gifts also helped build and maintain the CLEVELAND MUSEUM OF ART† (1916). In 1926 Cleveland Metropolitan Park System acquired his former lakefront home, named Huntington Park in his honor. Huntington was buried in Lake View Cemetery.

**HUNTINGTON, SAMUEL, JR.** (4 Oct. 1765–7 June 1817), politician and Ohio's third governor, was born in Norwich, CT, the son of Hannah (Devotion) and Rev. Joseph Huntington. He was informally adopted by his uncle, Samuel Huntington, subsequently president of the Continental Congress and governor of Connecticut. Samuel studied at Dartmouth and Yale, graduated from Yale in 1785, and became a Connecticut lawyer, politician, and land speculator. When his stepfather died, Huntington moved in 1801 to Ohio's WESTERN RESERVE† as a land agent and hotel keeper. Already politically well known, Huntington sided with the Chillicothe Republican faction at Ohio's constitutional convention, expecting to be given a U.S. Senate seat, but he was instead shunted to the chief justiceship of the Ohio Supreme Court. Frustrated, Huntington for several years tried to win appointments in new territories.

In 1808 Huntington was elected governor during a power struggle between the legislature and judiciary. He tried to remain neutral, but won only opprobrium from both sides. In 1810 Huntington lost a Senate race to Thos. Worthington. In later years, Huntington served in the assembly, leading the anti-Chillicothe Republican faction. He was an army district paymaster in the WAR OF 1812.† Huntington married his cousin, Hannah Huntington, on 20 Dec. 1791. They had 6 children: Francis, Martha, Julian, Colbert, Samuel, and Robert G. Seriously ill for years and injured in an accident, Huntington died in 1817, survived by his widow and their children. He was buried in the Evergreen Cemetery in Painesville, OH.

Samuel Huntington Papers, WRHS.

**HURLBUT, HINMAN B.** (20 July 1819–22 Mar. 1884) was a lawyer, banker, and railroad executive, but his greatest contribution to Cleveland came from his leadership in securing a museum of art for the city.

Born to Abiram and Mary Barrett Hurlbut in St. James County, NY, Hinman received his education in the public schools there before coming to Cleveland in 1836 to work in his brother's law office. He was admitted to the bar in 1839, and one year later, on 25 May 1840, he married Jane Johnson. They lived in a stately house at 3233 Euclid Ave., which later became the site of the 1910 Carlin residence.

In 1850 he turned his attention to banking, organizing banks in Massillon, OH. In 1852 he returned to Cleveland, where he established the banking house of Hurlbut and Co. In 1871 his interest turned to railroading, and he became president of the Cleveland, Columbus, Cincinnati & Indianapolis Railroad.

Besides his business involvements, Hurlbut was also interested in health issues, and he was a major benefactor of Lakeside Hospital. He also endowed a chair of chemistry at Western Reserve Univ. (see CASE WESTERN RESERVE UNIV.†).

During two trips to Europe, Hurlbut became interested in art and soon became an ardent collector. Upon his death he earmarked both funds and his art collection toward founding an art museum for the city. Ultimately other benefactors came forward and provided money for the building, but Hurlbut's money and his art works became a cornerstone of the original collection of the CLEVELAND MUSEUM OF ART.†

Hurlbut is buried in Lake View Cemetery.—J.T.

**HYDE, GUSTAVUS ADOLPHUS** (15 Jan. 1826–26 Nov. 1912), Cleveland's first official weatherman, was born in Framingham, MA, to Henry Hovey and Keziah (Rice) Hyde. He attended Framingham Academy and apprenticed at the Boston Water Works in civil engineering and surveying. He became interested in meteorology at 17 through Dr. Jas. P. Espy, pioneer of scientific weather study in America. In 1843 Hyde became one of Espy's original 120 volunteers, forming a national network of weather observers. Hyde came to Cleveland in 1850, serving between 1859–1907 as an engineer of Cleveland Gas Light & Coke Co. Hyde enjoyed a modest scientific reputation in Cleveland, reporting local weather and explaining other natural occurrences in the newspapers. He took daily weather observations in Cleveland continuously between 1855–1906, recording observations at 7 am, 2 pm, and 9 pm, and forwarding a monthly report to Espy at the Smithsonian Institution. Espy then used data from throughout the U.S. to develop a synoptic chart, plotting the weather on a map. Hyde was the only official weather observer in Cleveland until 1870, when the signal corps established a weather station here. In 1896 Hyde wrote *The Weather in Cleveland Ohio, What It Has Been for 40 Years*, primarily factual rather than theoretical. In 1867 Hyde became curator of the CLEVELAND ACADEMY OF NATURAL SCIENCES.† Hyde sent his last report to the U.S. Weather Bureau in 1906. Of the 120 original observers, he kept the longest uninterrupted record. Hyde married Elizabeth R. Williams in 1852. They had 5 children: Edward,

Gustavus A., Florence A., Henry H., and Elizabeth R. He died in Cleveland and was buried in Lake View Cemetery.

---

Gustavus Adolphus Hyde Papers, WRHS.

**HYDE, JESSE EARL** (2 May 1884–3 July 1936) was a well-respected geologist who taught in the department of geology at Western Reserve Univ. (1915–36; see CASE WESTERN RESERVE UNIV.†) and also served as Curator of Geology (1922–36) at the CLEVELAND MUSEUM OF NATURAL HISTORY.† Hyde was born in Rushville, OH, to Eber and Flora Belle Johnson Hyde. At an early age he accompanied his father, an amateur geologist and paleontologist, into the field. Later he studied geology at Ohio State and Columbia. In 1911 he married Edna McCleery and took a job teaching at Queen's Univ., Kingston, Ontario. He joined the geology department of WRU in 1915 as an associate professor and became department chairman in 1921. Hyde's primary expertise was in stratigraphy, glacial geology, and invertebrate paleontology. At the Cleveland Museum of Natural History his work included installation of the museum's geological exhibits and supervision of the collecting of fossil fish from the Cleveland Shale. Hyde authored about 20 technical publications, including a monograph on the geology of the Camp Sherman Quadrangle, a region in southern Ohio. He also wrote non-technical articles on the collecting of fossil fish from the Cleveland Shale. Unfortunately, Hyde's perfectionism prevented him from completing what were intended to be two of his major works, a monograph on the Mississippian rock formations of central and southern Ohio, and a revision of the Cleveland Shale fishes. Hyde died at his home in CLEVELAND HTS.† and was buried in Lancaster, OH. He was survived by his wife and two sons, William and Eber. His monograph on the Mississippian was published posthumously in 1953.—J.H.

**IGNATIA, SISTER MARY, CSA** (2 Jan. 1889–1 April 1966) was one of the founders of Alcoholics Anonymous. Born Della Gavin in Shanvilly, County Mayo, Ireland, she came with her family to America at age 6. She showed proficiency in music throughout her schooling and gave lessons before entering the Sisters of Charity of St. Augustine in 1914. She earned a Bachelor of Music degree from the Univ. of Notre Dame in 1925, then taught music at St. Augustine Academy.

Believing her health too fragile for a teaching career, Sr. Ignatia's superiors named her to the less strenuous post of registrar at St. Thomas Hospital, Akron, in 1934. The next year she was approached by 2 recovering alcoholics who had created a new therapy for alcoholics who wished to quit drinking. She consented to give them space at the hospital and Alcoholics Anonymous was born. Sr. Ignatia gained the support of her community in her work with alcoholics. She did much to help spread the AA philosophy by counseling and assisting those who had come to St. Thomas for treatment. In 1952 she opened Rosary Hall, a ward dedicated to the treatment of alcoholics, at ST. VINCENT CHARITY HOSPITAL,† Cleveland. Here she put the principles of AA into action and provided spiritual counseling coupled with group therapy and medical help for thousands of alcoholics. Sr. Ignatia died at the motherhouse of the Sisters of Charity in Richfield, OH, and is buried in Calvary Cemetery in Cleveland.—T.B.

**INGALLS, DAVID SINTON JR.** (27 Aug. 1934–13 Apr. 1993) was President of the CLEVELAND MUSEUM OF NATURAL HISTORY,† Mayor of HUNTING VALLEY† and a civic and business leader.

Born in Cleveland to DAVID INGALLS and Louise (Harkness), David Jr. graduated from HAWKEN SCHOOL† in 1949, attended St. Paul's School in New Hampshire, received his A.B. from Yale Univ. (1956), was a navy fighter pilot (1956–60), and received his M.B.A. from Stanford Univ. (1962).

Following his graduation from Stanford, Ingalls returned to Cleveland and joined TRW Inc., where he gained manufacturing and sales experience in missiles and jet engines. Ingalls left TRW in 1969 to help found the Grumman American Aviation Corp., a small aircraft manufacturing company.

Ingalls served as mayor of Hunting Valley for 2 terms, 1980–87. Ingalls was a trustee of the Natural History Museum, 1970–93 and president of the board, 1979–93. Under Ingalls's leadership the museum completed two successful fundraising drives, first, $8 million for the museum's endowment, and then a $15.8 million drive to build and endow a new wing. Ingalls was elected a Life Trustee in 1988 and awarded the Harold Terry Clark medal, the museum's highest honor, in 1992.

Ingalls was active in community affairs as president of the Cleveland Eye Bank, secretary of the WESTERN RESERVE HISTORICAL SOCIETY,† and trustee of Univ. Hospitals and Hawkins School.

Ingalls married Cynthia Robinson on 16 July 1960 (div. 1973). They had five children: Rebekah, Louise, Cynthia, David III, and Fay. Ingalls later married Katharine Stewart and had two children, Nina and Redmond. Ingalls, an Episcopalian, was buried in Hot Springs, VA.—T.B.

**INGALLS, DAVID S., SR.** (28 Jan. 1899–26 Apr. 1985), the U.S. Navy's only World War I flying ace, was born in Cleveland to Albert and Jane (Taft) Ingalls. He enlisted in the 1st Yale Naval Aviation Unit when the war started. Ingalls graduated from

Yale in 1920 and from Harvard Univ. with a law degree in 1923. From 1923–27, Ingalls was a member of SQUIRE, SANDERS & DEMPSEY† in Cleveland, leaving the firm to serve as state representative. In 1932, Ingalls returned to Cleveland, where Mayor HARRY L. DAVIS appointed him welfare director; however, he resigned in 1935 when Davis refused to install x-ray equipment in the City Hospital. During the 1940s, Ingalls was involved in the military and aviation industries. In 1954 he became president and publisher of the *Cincinnati Times-Star,* resuming his law practice in Cleveland in 1958.

In World War I Ingalls flew Sopwith Camels, shooting down 4 enemy planes and 3 aerial balloons, receiving the British Distinguished Flying Cross and U.S. Distinguished Service Medal. In 1929 Pres. Hoover appointed him asst. secretary of the navy for aeronautics. He returned to active duty in World War II and in late 1942 was chief of staff for the Air Ctr. Commander Forward Area on Guadalcanal, awarded the Bronze Star and Legion of Merit. In 1983 he was inducted into the Natl. Aviation Hall of Fame. Ingalls married Louise Harkness in 1922; they had 5 children: DAVID S. INGALLS, JR., Edith (Vignos), Louise (Brown), Anne (Lawrence), and Jane (Davison). Ingalls married Frances W. Wragg in 1978. He died in his CHAGRIN FALLS† home and was buried in Hot Springs, VA.

David S. Ingalls Papers, WRHS.

**INGHAM, MARY BIGELOW (JANES)** (10 Mar. 1832–17 Nov. 1923), dedicated to teaching, missionary work, and temperance reform, was born in Mansfield, OH, to Methodist minister John Janes and Hannah Brown. She was educated at Norwalk Seminary, Baldwin Institute, and Western Reserve Seminary. Ingham arrived in Cleveland in 1846 as a primary school teacher, later leaving to become professor of French and belles lettres at Ohio Wesleyan College for Women. Later she was asst. principal at Norwalk North Grammar School and Rockwell School of Cleveland. Ingham retired from teaching in 1886. In 1870, she co-inaugurated the Women's Foreign Missionary in northern Ohio. She was also involved in the Cleveland Chap. of the Natl. Women's Christian Temperance Union, serving as national treasurer from 1874–75. She helped establish reading rooms and Friendly Inns, heading one for 7 years. In Oct. 1882, Ingham co-founded the Cleveland School of Art (later known as the CLEVELAND INSTITUTE OF ART†), serving as secretary of the board of directors from 1884–94. Ingham contributed to numerous church publications; and also wrote a 3-year series, using the pen

name Anne Hathaway, on notable Cleveland women for the *CLEVELAND LEADER.† She also authored *Notable Cleveland Women,* the story "Something to Come Home To," and the stage production "Flag Festival, a Four Hundredth Anniversary Program." She married Wm. A. Ingham, a publisher and bookseller, in 1866. After her husband's death in 1898, Ingham moved to Los Angeles in 1908 and remained active in religious and missionary work until her death.

**INGRAHAM, TIMOTHY** was born in Massachusetts in 1810. In 1832 he migrated to Cleveland. He became secretary of the Ohio Canal Packet Co. and later was a principal in the firm of Standart, Ingraham & Co., forwarding a commission merchants. He served on city council as a Whig and was secretary of the Mutual Protecting Society.

Ingraham had been a member of a volunteer militia company at New Bedford, MA. After several unofficial meetings, Ingraham gave public notice for an official meeting to organize a Cleveland company. The company was formed on 28 August 1837 and those present elected him as their captain. Initially they called themselves the Cleveland City Guards, but in June 1838 the name was changed to the CLEVELAND GRAYS.†

In 1845 Ingraham returned to New Bedford where he continued to serve in the independent militia. At the outbreak of the CIVIL WAR,† he was elected captain of the New Bedford City Guards and commanded them during three months service in 1861. Eventually he rose to the rank of colonel and commanded the 38th Massachusetts Volunteer Infantry Regiment.

Ingraham's first wife died of cholera in 1834; the following year he married Jane S. Wolverton. He had 7 children: Charles W., Robert, Alma, William Milford, Timothy, Jr., Frank, and Henry. Ingraham died in 1876.—G.V.

Vourlojianis, George N. "The Cleveland Grays: An Urban Military Co. 1837–1919" (Ph.D. diss., Kent State Univ., 1994).

**INMAN, AMIE G. STEERE** (24 May 1882–27 April 1961), among the founders and first board members of the BUSINESS AND PROFESSIONAL WOMEN OF GREATER CLEVELAND,† taught applied art and headed the department of ART† at Lincoln High School in the CLEVELAND PUBLIC SCHOOLS.† She served as first vice-president of the Cleveland Teachers' Federation and was vice-president, then president, of the Ohio League of Teachers. Inman was born in Burrillville, RI, to Augusta W. and Evelyn E. Steere, and graduated from Massillon

(OH) High School in 1899, and Harcourt Place Seminary 2 years later. Inman received a normal school diploma from the New York School of Fine and Applied Art in 1909 and later also studied at the Students League and the Teachers College (both NYC) and in Paris. Before coming to Cleveland, Inman taught drawing in the Massillon Public Schools (1908–09). Residing on Cleveland's near west side, she served on the advisory committee of the CITIZENS LEAGUE† of Cleveland. Inman died in Massillon, OH.—J.M.

**IRELAND, JAMES DUANE** (1 Dec. 1913–26 Jan. 1991) was a Cleveland industrialist and corporate leader who served on the boards of numerous institutions. He was an original trustee of the First Union Realty Co. (1961–84), a pioneer in coal mining modernization, and a developer in BRATENAHL† and UNIV. CIRCLE.†

Ireland was born in Duluth, MN, to Elizabeth Clark Ring and James D. Ireland, a partner with the M. A. HANNA CO., who died in 1921. In 1929 Elizabeth married WILLIAM G. MATHER. Raised in Cleveland, Ireland attended HAWKEN SCHOOL,† St. Paul's School and Kent School. He graduated from Cornell Univ. in 1937.

Interested in mining, Ireland joined the Hanna Coal Co. in St. Clairsville, OH, where he worked his way up the company, becoming division superintendent by 1945. In 1946 he moved to West Virginia and founded the Peters Creek Coal Co. which became the Peerless Eagle Coal Co., a leader in the field of mechanized coal mining. He sold the company in 1975. Ireland returned to Cleveland in 1950 and, in 1951, was elected to the board of Cleveland-Cliffs. He chaired the executive committee from 1980 to 1986.

Ireland was a founder and chairman of the Bratenahl Development Corp. and vice chairman of Univ. Circle Inc. He served on the boards of the Garden Center of Greater Cleveland (see CLEVELAND BOTANICAL GARDEN†), UNIV. HOSPITALS OF CLEVELAND,† the CLEVELAND MUSEUM OF ART,† the WESTERN RESERVE HISTORICAL SOCIETY,† and Society National Bank.

Ireland married Cornelia Wilmot Allen in 1946. They had four children: James III, George, Lucy, and Cornelia. Ireland was Episcopalian. He is buried in Lake View Cemetery.—T.B.

**IRELAND, JOSEPH** (17 June 1843-unknown), New York architect who practiced in Cleveland between 1865–85 before returning to New York, was trained in the design of institutional buildings and was also a specialist in fireproof construction, a goal that engaged many architects in the post-Civil War period. Ireland was born in New York to Antoinette (Ford) and Thomas Jones Ireland. His first Cleveland building was the Society for Savings on PUBLIC SQUARE† (1867), later the home of the WESTERN RESERVE HISTORICAL SOCIETY.† He also designed the Natl. Bank Bldg. (1867), whose trustees, JOSEPH PERKINS, AMASA STONE, and DANIEL EELLS, were all instrumental in securing commissions for Ireland. In 1869 Ireland designed the Geauga County Courthouse in Chardon to replace the one destroyed by fire the year before. In 1870 he planned the home of Henry B. Perkins in Warren, still in use as the city hall. His Cleveland buildings included the Retreat, a women's institution donated by Joseph Perkins (1872); the Home for Aged Gentlewomen, built for Amasa Stone (1876); Daniel Eells's home on Euclid Ave. (1876); the Second Presbyterian Church (1878); and Adelbert College of Western Reserve Univ. (1882), also built for Amasa Stone. Only the Geauga County Courthouse, the H. B. Perkins home, and Adelbert Hall remained standing in the 1990s. Ireland worked in various phases of the Victorian Italianate and Eastlake styles, but his principal contribution was the introduction and development of fireproof construction in northeastern Ohio.

Ireland married Mary DeForrest and had five children: Mary, William, Antoinette, A. Rutherford, and Cornelia. His place of burial, as his death date, remain unknown.

**IRELAND, MARGARET ALLEN** (17 Dec. 1894–22 Oct. 1961) was a leader in civic, social, and welfare causes. Her years of community service included the founding of Highland View Hospital, serving as Ohio's Director of Public Welfare (1957), and election as the first woman president of the Northern Ohio Opera Assn. (1959).

Born in Chicago, Margaret was raised in New York and graduated from Brearley School. She married ROBERT LIVINGSTON IRELAND, Jr., on 9 Feb. 1918 and later moved to Cleveland.

Ireland's interest in nursing led to her involvement with Cleveland's health-reform organizations. She was president of the Visiting Nurse Assn. and chaired its building committee and helped organize the Maternal Health Assn. She headed the Welfare Federation's committee on the chronically ill and served on its Board of Trustees. She was the first board chairman of Highland View and headed its building committee. Ireland Drive, in front of the hospital, was named in her honor. In 1951 she established the Ireland Foundation primarily to benefit nursing and hospitals.

Politically active, she helped organize the Western Reserve Women's Republican Club of Cuyahoga

County, chaired the Cuyahoga County Republican Party's Women's Committee, 1953–57, and was an alternate delegate to the 1952 and 1956 Republican National Conventions.

She received the Charles Eisenman Award for community service in 1954. The Women's City Club created the Margaret A. Ireland Citation to honor area residents exemplifying civic achievement and social devotion to community.

The Irelands had four children: Mrs. Louise Humphrey, Melville H., R. Livingston III, and Kate Ireland. An Episcopalian, she is buried in Lake View Cemetery.—T.B.

Cleveland Families Oral History Project, WRHS.

**IRELAND, ROBERT LIVINGSTON, JR.** (1 Feb. 1895–21 April 1981) was a colorful, prominent Cleveland business executive who had a long and distinguished career with the M. A. HANNA CO. and the Pittsburgh Consolidation Coal Co.

Born in Cleveland, Ireland attended Univ. School, Taft School (CT), graduating from Asheville School in North Carolina, 1914. He also attended Phillips Andover Academy (1914–15) and studied mining engineering at Yale Univ. (1915–17). During World War I Ireland left Yale to enlist in the Naval Reserve Flying Corps.

After the war he worked for Susquehanna Collieries Co., a Hanna Coal Co. subsidiary in Pennsylvania, 1920–24. Returning to Cleveland in 1924 as assistant to the general manager, Ireland rose through Hanna Coal, becoming manager in 1929, and president in 1931. With Pittsburgh Consolidation Coal's acquisition of Hanna Coal in 1946, Ireland became chairman of the executive committee, then vice-chairman of the board in 1962. Ireland retired in 1966.

Ireland was an active civic and political leader who served on the boards of numerous organizations. He financially supported all the arts, even though he disliked opera and classical music. Ireland was a prominent figure in the local and state Republican party and through his friend, Governor James Rhodes, funding was approved for the Ireland Cancer Center at Univ. Hospitals in his memory.

Ireland married twice. He married MARGARET ALLEN (d. 22 Oct. 1961) in 1918. They had four children: Mrs. Louise Humphrey, R. Livingston III, Melville H., and Kate Ireland. He married his first cousin, Mrs. Louise Ireland Grimes, in 1967. They had no children. Ireland lived in BRATENAHL† and is buried in Lake View Cemetery.—T.B.

Cleveland Families Oral History Project, WRHS.

**IRELAND, THOMAS SAXTON, JR.** (16 Dec. 1895–26 Mar. 1969), politician and writer, was born in Cleveland to Lucretia (Bailey) and Paul Francis Ireland, a manager of GRASSELLI CHEMICAL CO.† He attended Princeton and Harvard, graduated from Harvard Law School in 1927, and returned to Cleveland after passing the Ohio Bar. Following service in the army, he began a weekly column for the Cleveland Italian newspaper *Corriere di Ohio*. He worked for a time as a laborer at the Republic Steel Corp., becoming an active member of Bridge, Structural & Iron Workers Local 468. By the 1930s he was a municipal court judge, and in the mid–1930s ran unsuccessfully for the Ohio general assembly. He became a correspondent for the Cleveland *PLAIN DEALER†* in 1948 and also wrote for papers in Columbus and the Pacific Northwest. In 1959 Ireland ran for mayor in one of Cleveland's most flamboyant political campaigns. One of his great campaign issues was the transit system's inadequacies, and he garnered tremendous publicity by personally chartering transit buses and providing service to underserved areas at off-peak times. Despite his flair for public relations, he lost the election. Ireland wrote books on the St. Lawrence Seaway (1934), the politics of the Far East (*War Clouds in the Skies of the Far East*, 1935), Ireland (*Ireland, Past and Present*, 1942), and industrial relations (*Child Labor as a Relic of the Dark Ages*, 1937). In Aug. 1932 Ireland married Mildred Locke and had 7 children: Patricia, Ruth, Thos. S. III, William, John, Fred, and Pauline. He died in Hawaii and was buried in Lake View Cemetery.

Thomas S. Ireland Papers, WRHS.

**IRWIN, JOSEPHINE SAXER** (1 Mar. 1890–15 Sept. 1984), suffragist and women's-rights advocate for more than half a century, was born in LAKEWOOD,† OH, to James and E. Elizabeth (Saunderson) Saxer. She graduated from the School of Education at Western Reserve Univ. in 1910 and taught at Lincoln and McKinley elementary schools in Lakewood from 1910–19. Irwin was active in the peace movement before World War I, was one of the first members of the LEAGUE OF WOMEN VOTERS,† and was most noted for participating in a massive suffrage parade staged on Cleveland's EUCLID AVE.† in 1914. Her involvement in the women's movement also included activities in behalf of the Equal Rights Amendment during the 1970s–80s. She was also a founding member of WOMENSPACE.† From 1958–62, Irwin served as councilman-at-large in FAIRVIEW PARK,† the first woman elected to council in that city. She was a charter member of the CLEVELAND COUNCIL

241

ON WORLD AFFAIRS† and was inducted into the Ohio Women's Hall of Fame in 1983. In honor of Irwin's contributions, both the Natl. Organization for Women and WomenSpace have instituted a Josephine Irwin Award, which is conferred annually in Cleveland on women who have contributed substantially to the cause of women's rights. Josephine Saxer married J. Preston Irwin on 19 June 1919 and had 3 children: Wm. P., John P., Jr., and Elizabeth Irwin Harner. Irwin died in a Geauga County nursing home and was buried in Fairview Park Cemetery.

Josephine Irwin Papers, WRHS.

**IRWIN, ROBERT BENJAMIN** (2 June 1883–12 Dec. 1951) was an educator of the blind who organized public school classes for visually impaired children in Cleveland and throughout Ohio.

Irwin was born in Rockford, IA, to Robert and Hattie (Chappell). He was raised in Vaughn, WA. Irwin contracted inflammatory rheumatism when 5, leaving him blind. In 1890 he entered the Washington State School for the Blind, becoming its first blind graduate in 1901. Irwin graduated from the Univ. of Washington (A.B. 1906), Harvard (M.A. 1907), and received an LL.D (honorary), from Western Reserve Univ. (1943).

Irwin's work for the blind started in Cleveland where, as superintendent of public school classes for the blind (1909–23), he organized classes in Braille, placed blind students in regular classes (assisted by reader-tutors), and created "sight-saving" classes. He organized the Howe Publishing Co. to print Braille books, and the Clear Type Publishing Committee to print books in 24-point type. He was an early innovator for the CLEVELAND SOCIETY FOR THE BLIND† and, by 1913, was organizing his educational programs throughout Ohio.

Irwin's research on blindness was published in *Blind Relief Laws and Their Administration* (1919), and *Sight-Saving Classes in the Public Schools* (1920).

Irwin left Cleveland for New York to become president of the American Assn. of Workers for the Blind (1923–27) and, later, executive director of the American Foundation for the Blind (1929–49).

Irwin married Mary Blanchard on 19 June 1917. They had one son, Robert. Irwin, a Unitarian, died in Port Orchard, WA, and is buried in Pompton Lakes, NJ.—T.B.

**ISSENMANN, CLARENCE G.** (30 May 1907–27 July 1982), 7th bishop of Cleveland, was born in Hamilton, OH, to Innocent and Amelia Stricker Issenmann. He studied at St. Joseph College in Rensselaer, IN, and St. Gregory Seminary and Mt. St. Mary Seminary in Cincinnati; he was ordained on 29 June 1932. Issenmann received degrees from the Univ. of Fribourg, Switzerland, and the Angelicum, Rome. He was named to the staff of the *Denver Register* and acquired a journalism doctorate from the Register College of Journalism. In 1938 he became asst. editor of the *Catholic Telegraph Register* of Cincinnati; in 1942, professor of theology at Mt. St. Mary Seminary; in 1945, chancellor of the archdiocese; and in 1954, auxiliary bishop of Cincinnati. In 1958 he became bishop of Columbus, episcopal chairman of the Press Dept., and asst. chairman of the Dept. for Lay Organizations of the Natl. Catholic Welfare Conference in Washington. On 7 Oct. 1964, Issenmann was named coadjutor bishop of Cleveland for the ailing Archbishop Hoban, becoming bishop in 1966 when Hoban died. Issenmann restructured the school board, opened new high schools, and developed special ministries to the deaf and mentally retarded. He opened St. Augustine Manor to provide skilled short-term nursing care, established the COMMISSION ON CATHOLIC COMMUNITY ACTION,† and started the Martin de Porres Ctr. in the Glenville area. Issenmann began a priests' senate, clergy personnel board, and senate of religious women and established the Diocesan Pastoral Planning Office. Issenmann's health began deteriorating in the early 1970s, and he resigned in July 1974.

**IVANUSCH, JOHN** (30 Sept. 1879–1 Sept. 1973), Slovenian composer, music teacher, and musical director, was born in Slovenia to John and Mary (Heinrich) Ivanusch. He began his musical education at age 7 and later served in the Austro-Hungarian Navy under bandmaster Franz Lehar, composer of the opera *The Merry Widow*. Ivanusch came to Cleveland in 1919 and taught piano, strings, and brass instruments, as well as serving as director of the ZARJA SINGING SOCIETY.† In 1928 he composed the opera *Rosamund of Turjak* for the chorus. Ivanusch was married twice. His first wife, Mary, whom he wedded 19 Jan. 1920, died ca. 1927. He married again on 10 Oct. 1927 to Mary Grill, a singer and teacher at the Slovene School of the SLOVENIAN NATL. HOME.† Ivanusch had no children. He died in Chardon, OH.

**IZANT, GRACE.** See **GOULDER-IZANT, GRACE.**

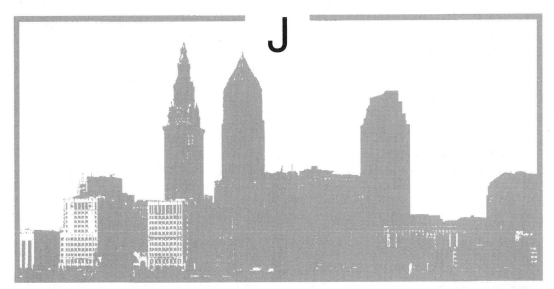

# J

**JACKSON, JAMES FREDERICK** (16 Aug. 1861–4 Jan. 1927), social worker, served ASSOCIATED CHARITIES† as general secretary for over two decades (1904–10, 1912–27) and as general superintendent of the Department of Charities and Correction of the City of Cleveland for one term (1910–12). Transforming local charity by volunteers into scientific relief administered by trained personnel, he emphasized the coordination of charitable efforts among city agencies. Jackson was born in Wabasha, MN, to Mary Pendleton Jackson and William S. Jackson, proprietor of a general store. After graduating from Carleton College (MN) in 1882, he farmed (1883–86) and worked in the lumber business (1886–92) in St. Paul before joining the fledgling St. Paul Associated Charities (1892). By the century's end he was president of that group (1899–1901) and secretary of the Minnesota State Board of Charities and Corrections (1898–1901). While serving similar organizations in New York (1901–02) and Minneapolis (1902–04) and speaking at national conferences, Jackson developed a reputation as a knowledgeable proponent and practitioner of modern methods of relief. Interested in making WELFARE/RELIEF† more efficient in Cleveland, JOHN WHITTLESEY WALTON recruited Jackson in the winter of 1903–04.

At Associated Charities Jackson quickly initiated training classes in social work and later helped organize the School of Applied Social Sciences of Western Reserve Univ. (see CASE WESTERN RESERVE UNIV.†). He also helped establish the Anti-Tuberculosis Society (see NORTHERN OHIO LUNG ASSN.†) and served as director until his death. Jackson participated in the White House Conference on Dependent Children (1909) and, as a member of the local Committee on Cooperation, helped organize the WESTERN RESERVE CONFERENCE ON NEGLECTED AND DEPENDENT CHILDREN† the next year. A member of the Cleveland Chamber of Commerce, he served as part-time secretary of the Welfare Federation (see FEDERATION FOR COMMUNITY PLANNING†), president of the PHILOSOPHICAL CLUB OF CLEVELAND† (1918), and helped coordinate disaster services for the AMERICAN RED CROSS, CLEVELAND CHAPTER.† He cultivated relationships with a group of area business and civic leaders, later informally dubbed the Society of the Friends of James F. Jackson. A Republican, Jackson also belonged to the CITY CLUB OF CLEVELAND† and served as a trustee of Carleton College (1897–1919) and president of the Ohio State Conference of Charities and Corrections (1913). Jackson married Linda C. Pomeroy in June 1885; there were no children.

James Frederick Jackson Papers, WRHS.

**JACKSON, PERRY B.** (27 Jan. 1896–20 Mar. 1986), lawyer and the first black judge in Ohio, was born in Zanesville, OH, to Brooks C. and Ida M. Jackson. He graduated from Adelbert College of Western Reserve Univ. (1919) and WRU Law School (1922), was admitted to the bar and began practicing law in Cleveland. From 1923–27 Jackson edited the *Cleveland Call*. Active in Republican politics, he was elected to the Ohio general assembly in 1928, responsible for the state's adoption of voter registration forms making no reference to race or color. From July 1934–Aug. 1941, Jackson was asst. police prosecutor; from Aug. 1941–Apr. 1942, secretary to the director of public utilities. Jackson was appointed municipal judge in Aug. 1942 but lost the election for his seat in 1943. In 1945 he won a 6-year term on the municipal court bench; he was reelected in 1951 and 1957. In 1960 he was elected to the new Domestic Relations Div. of common pleas court; and in 1964 was elected to the General Div. of common pleas court, being reelected in 1967. He retired from the bench in 1973 but remained active as a visiting judge.

Jackson was a proponent of civil rights for blacks (see AFRICAN AMERICANS†). Refused service at a bar association meeting in HOLLENDEN HOTEL† in 1935, he sued the hotel, receiving $350 in damages. He was involved in the local NAACP† and URBAN LEAGUE.† Jackson was a member of various organizations and a trustee of ST. JOHN'S AME CHURCH.† Jackson married Fern Josephine Payne (d. 1983) in 1933. They had no children. Jackson died in Cleveland and was buried at Highland Park Cemetery.

Perry B. Jackson Papers, WRHS.

**JACOBS, DAVID H.** (4 May 1921–17 Sept. 1992), real estate developer and co-owner of the CLEVELAND INDIANS,† was born in Akron, the son of Adeline (Yeiter) and V. R. Jacobs. He attended Buchtel High School in the late 1930s and served in the navy during World War II piloting blimps. Jacobs obtained a degree in Business Administration from Indiana Univ. in 1947, and by 1952 he and partner Lewis W. Mead had organized Mead-Jacobs, a real estate property management firm; his brother, Richard, soon joined the firm. Their first construction project in Cleveland was the 5-story Puritas Center at W. 150th St and Puritas Rd., built in 1954. By 1965 Meade-Jacobs had become Visconsi, Mead-Jacobs and later Jacobs, Visconsi & Jacobs Co. In 1988 the Jacobs brothers bought Dominic Visconsi's interest, forming the Richard and David Jacobs Group. As vice-chairman of the board, David acted as supervisor of their construction projects. The brothers developed a real estate conglomerate with 41 regional shopping centers, as well as major office buildings and hotels, including the Galleria and Society Center in Cleveland. Richard and David Jacobs bought control of the Cleveland Indians in 1986. David, who owned 25% of the team, was particularly interested in developing the Indians' farm system to improve the franchise.

David and his wife, Barbara, had three children: David Jr., John, and Marie Bell. A resident of Bay Village, Jacobs died in Westlake and was buried at Lakewood Park Cemetery.—M.S.

**JANICKI, HAZEL** (19 Feb. 1918–1 Jan. 1976), artist, was born in London to American parents, Joseph and Madeline Faulkner Janicki. She was raised in Paris until the family moved to Cleveland in 1929. Janicki enrolled in the Cleveland School of Art in 1937, then worked for the CLEVELAND PUBLIC LIBRARY† making posters and displays. In the 1944 Artists for Victory exhibition at the Metropolitan Museum of Art, Janicki's mural for the USO Lounge in Cleveland's Old Federal Bldg. received honorable mention. Janicki was an accomplished portraitist, but was best known for her tempera paintings of realistic figures in dreamlike settings. She exhibited nationally and locally, especially in MAY SHOWS.† She received a Tiffany Foundation grant (1949), a Univ. of Illinois prize (1948), the Clarke Prize from the Natl. Academy of Design (1951), and a grant from the Natl. Institute of Arts & Letters (1955).

Janicki combined abstraction with detailed studies of rocks, shells, nests, drawers, and draperies into the 1960s, with actual draperies and other objects beginning to emerge from her paintings, and tromp de l'oeil renderings covering wooden constructions (Children's Room Door, 1969, Akron Public Library). In the 1970s she returned to painting ("Triptych: Heaped, Stretched, Hanging," 1972, Kent State Univ.). Janicki taught design, drawing, and painting at Kent State Univ. from 1952, was active with Ten Thirty Gallery, and was president of the WOMEN'S ART CLUB.† Janicki married twice: to John Teyral in 1942, and to William Schock in 1951. Schock, Janicki, and her stepfather were killed in an automobile accident, New Year's Day, 1976, in Florida. She had no children.

Valencic, Joseph. *Hazel Janicki/William Schock: A Retrospective Exhibition* (1977).

**JELLIFFE, ROWENA WOODHAM** (23 Mar. 1892–5 Apr. 1992) became a pioneer in the field of interracial theater as an outgrowth of her career as a social worker and cofounder of KARAMU HOUSE.† Born and raised in New Albion, IL, she came to Ohio in 1910 to enter Oberlin College, where she served as president of the Oberlin Women's Suffrage League and met her future husband, RUSSELL W. JELLIFFE.† After a year spent jointly as graduate students at the Univ. of Chicago, Rowena and Russell were married and came to Cleveland to establish the east side settlement house that eventually became Karamu. To help draw their largely African American constituency into the settlement's program, Mrs. Jelliffe began producing children's plays with interracial casting. An adult dramatic group, the Gilpin Players, was organized in the couple's living room in 1920. A permanent theater was opened in 1927, after 2 summers' study by Mrs. Jelliffe at the School of Theater and Dance in New York. Besides directing 100 plays at Karamu from 1920–46, she sometimes wrote plays for the children and once completed a play by LANGSTON HUGHES† when the final act failed to arrive in time. Mrs. Jelliffe was also a campaigner for civil rights, helping to integrate the Wade Park Manor dining room in 1926 and marching with Martin Luther King, Jr., in the 1960s. Following their retirement and the death of Russell in 1980, Mrs. Jelliffe remained active in numerous civic and arts organizations, serving on the boards of the East Cleveland Theater and the Fine Arts Assn. of Willoughby. She died 2 weeks after her 100th birthday, survived by a son, Dr. Roger Jelliffe of California, and 4 grandchildren.—J.V.

Selby, John. *Beyond Civil Rights* (Cleveland: World, 1966).
Russell and Rowena Jelliffe Papers, WRHS.
Karamu House Records, WRHS.

**JELLIFFE, RUSSELL W.** (19 Nov. 1891–7 June 1980) was a social worker who, along with his wife, ROWENA WOODHAM JELLIFFE,† came to Cleveland in 1915 and established the interracial settlement house that evolved into the nationally acclaimed KARAMU HOUSE.† A native of Mansfield, OH, Russell Jelliffe entered Oberlin College, where he studied political economics and met Rowena Woodham. After their graduation in 1914, the couple received masters' degrees in sociology from the Univ. of Chicago and were married on 28 May 1915. Attracted to Cleveland by its ethnic diversity and progressive reputation, the Jelliffes established what became known as the Playhouse Settlement on E. 38th St. with the support of the Second Presbyterian Church. The settlement grew into Karamu House, renowned especially for its work in art and theater. By the time they retired as directors in 1963, the Jelliffes had built Karamu into a cultural and educational institution with 4,000 members and a $1 million plant. Russell Jelliffe was also instrumental in the development of other institutions important to Cleveland's African American community: the URBAN LEAGUE† and the CLEVELAND COMMUNITY RELATIONS BOARD.† He served on the executive committee of the local branch of the NAACP,† the board of the Cleveland Council on Human Relations, and was president of the Group Work Council of the Welfare Fed. (1938–40). Among the awards he shared with his wife were the Chas. Eisenman Civic Award in 1941 and the 1944 Human Relations Award of the Natl. Conference of Christians & Jews. Following retirement, the Jelliffes headed the Karamu Foundation and served as cultural consultants for other cities.

Russell and Rowena Jelliffe Papers, WRHS.
Karamu House Records, WRHS.

**JENNINGS, ELIZABETH (ELIZA) WALLACE** (21 Dec. 1809–25 Sept.1887), philanthropist who helped establish the CHILDREN'S AID SOCIETY† and ELIZA JENNINGS HOME,† was born in Belfast, Ireland, to James and Margaret Hannah Chambers Wallace. The family immigrated to Petersburg, OH, in 1820. In 1829 Eliza married banker Simeon Jennings (b. 7 Nov. 1791) of Salem, OH, where they lived for over 30 years, then moving to West Virginia and Cleveland. The couple had no children. Jennings acquired wealth, bought 8 acres of hilltop land on the lakeshore, and built several mansions, including an Italianate villa at 10427 Detroit Ave., where the couple lived for several years. The Jennings leased their farmland property to the newly incorporated Children's Aid Society, and after Mr. Jennings died in 1865, leaving an estate of over $1.5 million, Eliza deeded the home and additional acres to the society. The plight of an elderly, homeless, indigent, incurably ill friend, Miss Mary Love, inspired Eliza to donate property and funds to the YOUNG WOMEN'S CHRISTIAN ASSN.† to erect a home or hospital to care for indigent and incurably ill women of the city. The home, constructed at 10603 Detroit Ave., opened in 1888, a year after Mrs. Jennings' death. Renamed the Eliza Jennings Home in her honor, it severed its affiliation with the YWCA, became an independent nonprofit organization in 1922, and built an enlarged structure on the same site, which was dedicated in 1925. Mrs. Jennings also endowed the Jennings Institute, a Methodist Seminary in Aurora, IL, and the Home for Aged Women in Salem, OH.

**JENNINGS, MARTHA F. HOLDEN** (26 Dec. 1873–8 Aug. 1962) was responsible for the establishment of the MARTHA HOLDEN JENNINGS FOUNDATION† in 1959.

Born and educated in Cleveland, she was the daughter of Justice Justis and Ella Louisa Pitkin Holden. Martha Holden married Andrew R. Jennings on 14 Sept. 1897. With Andrew's promotion as the European General Manager of International Business Machine Corp. (IBM) the couple moved overseas, living in Great Britain and Europe for the next 31 years. Returning to Cleveland in 1931, Andrew Jennings died suddenly, leaving Martha a wealthy and childless widow.

Following her husband's death, Mrs. Jennings moved to Wade Park Manor, spending extensive time traveling throughout the U.S. Having no close relatives, Mrs. Jennings sought ways to distribute and use her vast wealth. She made individual bequests of $10 million to Case Institute of Technology, the Univ. Circle Development Foundation, and the CLEVELAND CLINIC FOUNDATION,† which dedicated a building to her memory. She also made a number of substantial gifts to the CLEVE-LAND MUSEUM OF ART.† Her interest in IBM stock made Mrs. Jennings's $35 million estate one of the largest ever probated in Cuyahoga County. The educational foundation bearing her name was her major gift. Mrs. Jennings is buried in Lake View Cemetery.

Martha Holden Jennings Foundation Records, WRHS.

Crail, Marc. *The Martha Holden Jennings Foundation: An Institutional History, 1959–1984.*

**JERMAN, FRED "MIKE"** (16 June 1930–30 March 1993) was a chemical technician who, during his 43 years with BRUSH WELLMAN† Technical Laboratories, helped develop high temperature, high vacuum, and nuclear reactor technology. He was also a pigeon fancier who helped found the Independence Homing Club.

Born in Cleveland to Fred and Bertha Jerman, "Mike" Jerman graduated from South High (1948) and joined Brush Wellman on 2 May 1949 as a lab technician at the Perkins Ave. Facility. Jerman first worked with scientists and engineers in developing technologies involving beryllium. Following a tour with the army in the Korean War (1952–53), Jerman returned to Brush Wellman and became instrumental in the development of electrical and electronic insulators, including synthetic mica and other materials.

In the early 1960s Jerman became involved in the emerging field of high temperature, high vacuum technology. A major interest was in the sintering and strengthening of parts made from powdered metals, including critical nuclear reactor components. Jerman would continue his technical service at the Brush St. Clair Ave. Technical Center, working on such diverse products as fuel cell components, brake systems for advanced aircraft and spacecraft, and temperature resistant intermetallic compounds. He took medical leave late in 1992.

In 1967 Jerman helped found the Independence Homing Club, serving as president in 1969–70. Jerman organized fundraising activities for ST. MALACHI CATHOLIC CHURCH.†

Jerman married Leona August on 16 July 1955. They had four sons: Michael, Fred, David, and Mitchell. Jerman is buried in Holy Cross Cemetery.—T.B.

**JICHA, JOSEPH W.** (1901–30 Aug. 1960), commercial artist and watercolorist, was born in Austria-Hungary to Rudolph and Helen (Remesch) Jicha, and came to Cleveland with his family as an infant. His father was a skilled coppersmith who worked decorations for the CLEVELAND INSTITUTE OF ART.† He apprenticed 13-year-old Jo-

seph to sculptor Walter Sinz at the institute. As a student, Jicha was a member of the KOKOON CLUB.† The Cleveland Community Fund commissioned him to design a poster for its campaign in 1928. In 1929 Jicha won the international Frank Logan Medal at the Chicago Art Institute for painting. He believed his commercial work helped him as a painter, because of the careful planning of design work. Jicha worked for Fawn Art and Creative Artists on advertisements for the Hotel Statler, SHERWIN-WILLIAMS,† and Libbey-Owens-Ford Glass Co. His work appeared in the *Saturday Evening Post* and *Life* magazine, he won the Art Director's Show in New York City in 1936, and he exhibited paintings at KORNER & WOOD BOOKSTORE† (1938) and the Hotel ALCAZAR† (1941). His paintings were described by critics as having great line strength and composition, with blazing colors. Jicha also exhibited in 1941 by invitation at the Natl. Watercolor Show in San Diego. His work is in the San Diego Museum and the Mexico Natl. Museum. He taught summer school at the Cleveland Institute of Art in 1950. Two years later, Jicha and his wife, the former Cora Smith Ingalis, whom he married in Sept. 1904, traveled across America to paint for a year. The couple had no children. Jicha died in Cleveland and was buried in Olmsted Falls.

**JIROUCH, FRANK L.** (3 Mar. 1878–2 May 1970), sculptor known mainly for his work in Cleveland's Cultural Gardens, was born of a Czech father, Austin Jirouch, and German mother, Mary (Girgur) Jirouch, in Cleveland. Little is known of his early life, but at the turn of the century he and Geo. Fischer worked together as woodcarvers on the Prudential Bldg. in New York City. In 1902 the two returned to Cleveland and started the firm of Fischer & Jirouch, mainly doing decorative architectural relief sculpture, a field the firm dominated for many years. During World War I, Jirouch attended the Philadelphia Academy of Fine Arts. Jirouch married Mary "May" Macha on 6 May 1903. In 1921 they moved to Paris, for 3 years, at which time he exhibited work at the Salon Francais and became a monitor at the Academie Julien. According to Jirouch in a 1964 interview, returning to Cleveland he found the business of decorative relief sculpture on the wane, but the Cultural Gardens were expanding. It is thought Jirouch did as many as 25 of the busts, statues, and commemorative plaques of groups sponsoring the Gardens, the greatest contribution of any single sculptor. Among his pieces were Abraham Lincoln (1950), JOHN HAY (1938), Artemus Ward (see CHARLES FARRAR BROWNE) (1948), and ERNEST BLOCH (1955).

Campen, Richard N. *Outdoor Sculpture in Ohio* (1980).

**JIRSA, FERDINAND "FERD"** (18 May 1893–29 Nov. 1971), attorney and active member of the CUYAHOGA COUNTY DEMOCRATIC PARTY,† participated in the local and national Czech Sokol movement. In May 1937, Jirsa was one of 5 Cleveland Czechs awarded the Order of the White Lion by the Czechoslovakian government in honor of contributions to Czechoslovakia and the promotion of its cultural ties with the U.S. Born in Pelec, Austria-Hungary, son of Joseph and Mary (Unk) Jirsa, he attended business school before emigrating to the U.S. in September 1913. In Cleveland he studied English and worked as a clerk, driver, and salesman while attending John Marshall Law School. He married Celia Kratochvil in 1915; they lived in SHAKER HTS.† with daughters Celia and Vera Niebuhr. After graduating (1921), Jirsa practiced law from an office in the Society for Savings Building. By 1942, with an office at 3513 E. 131 St., he was also in the real estate business. In 1946 Jirsa became a member of the Cleveland Law Department, where he battled slum landlords as assistant police prosecutor and then assistant law director. He retired in 1968.

Jirsa served as an officer in Sokol Czech-Havlicek (see SOKOL CLEVELAND†). He also served as president of the Northeast District of the American Sokol Organization and member of the financial committee of the American Sokol Organization. He belonged to the Knights of Pythias. Jirsa was buried in Highland Park Cemetery.

Ferdinand Jirsa Papers, WRHS.

**JOC-O-SOT, or WALKING BEAR** (1810–3 Sept. 1844) was a chief of the Fox (or Mesquakie) tribe which resided in the Iowa area. During 1831 Joc-O-Sot fought in the Black Hawk War against the U.S. when the Fox allied themselves with the Sauk. Following the defeat of BLACK HAWK, Joc-O-Sot, who had been wounded in the war, made his way east to Cleveland in the early 1830s. Here he began leading hunting and fishing expeditions and became a close companion of Dr. HORACE ACKLEY. Through Ackley's friends, he made the acquaintance of theater promoter Dan Marble. He joined Marble's theatrical troupe, touring various cities performing in plays which purported to represent Native American life. In March 1844, at the behest of Marble, Joc-O-Sot traveled to England in the company of Irish composer William Vincent Wallace. In June 1844 Joc-O-Sot was received in audience by Queen Victoria. Very much impressed by Joc-O-Sot, the queen commissioned a portrait of him by her royal lithographers, Day and Hague.

Joc-O-Sot fell ill (probably with tuberculosis) while in England and, on his own, made his way back to Cleveland, where he died. Ackley and his friends arranged for his burial in Erie St. Cemetery. His epitaph, bearing an incorrect date of death reads:

> Joc-O-Sot / the Walking Bear / a Distinguished Sauk Chief / Died August, 1844 / Erected by ten citizens of Cleveland and a friend / of Cincinnati.

Although the record is unclear, it is probable that Joc-O-Sot's remains were taken from his grave and used for medical experimentation, a practice that was all too common during the 1840s.

O'Neill, David. "A Cleveland Indian in Queen Victoria†s Court" (unpublished paper).

**JOHANNESEN, ERIC** (27 Oct. 1926–20 July 1990) was an art teacher, historic preservationist, and author of 5 books on architectural history. Born to Rolf T. H. and Jennie Grace (Dixon) Johannesen in Louisville, KY, Johannesen, at the age of 3, moved with his family to Detroit. Following service in the U.S. Army during World War II, he enrolled in Wayne Univ. (now Wayne State Univ.), where he graduated with a B.A. in Fine Arts in 1950 and an M.A. in the same field in 1952. His interest and talent in painting led him to the position of instructor in art at Denison Univ. in Granville, OH. In 1954 he moved to Mount Union College in Alliance, OH, where for 18 years he was professor of art and, for a time, chairman of the art department.

After 20 years of teaching, Johannesen sought a new challenge where he could apply his growing interest in architecture. In 1973 he came to the WESTERN RESERVE HISTORICAL SOCIETY,† where he headed the first regional preservation office in Ohio. In this capacity his principal goal was to identify sites and structures that qualified for inclusion in the National Register of Historic Places. Working under the aegis of the Ohio Historic Preservation Office headquartered at the Ohio Historical Society in Columbus, he traveled throughout the Western Reserve in search of historically significant places. Johannesen also undertook a detailed survey of Cleveland's historic buildings. Johannesen educated architects, builders, city planners, and the general public regarding the value of preserving historic buildings, encouraging adaptive use rather than destruction. The paucity of readily available information on Cleveland's architectural history spurred Johannesen to write his now classic *Cleveland Architecture 1876–1976* (1979). It is the indispensable work on Cleveland's architectural history. It stands as the major achievement of a scholarly career which includes 16 major journal articles and 4 other books: *Ohio College Architecture Before 1870* (1969); *Selected Landmark Architecture of*

*Alliance* (1971); *Look Again: Landmark Architecture in Downtown Toledo and Old West End* (1973); and *From Town to Tower* (1983). Johannesen's career at WRHS included being editor of publications. Johannesen was also a pianist and photographer. He died in Cleveland, survived by 2 brothers. He is buried in Arlington National Cemetery.—K.P.

Eric Johannesen Papers, WRHS.

**JOHN, HENRY J.** (5 Mar. 1885–28 Mar. 1971), an expert in diabetes, was born Jindrich Jeroslav to Czech parents, Jindrich and Filomena (Kvapilova) John, in Olomouc, Moravia. He came to the U.S. when he was 14 and graduated from the Univ. of Kansas (1911). He then received his M.A. from the Univ. of Minnesota (1912), and his M.D. from Western Reserve School of Medicine (1916), interning at ST. VINCENT CHARITY HOSPITAL.† In 1917 John joined the Army Medical Corps. and was the first doctor to administer glucose intravenously after surgery. In 1919 he joined Dr. F. M. Allen in Morristown, NJ, working on diabetes. John met Dr. JOHN PHILLIPS, a founder of the CLEVELAND CLINIC FOUNDATION,† and joined the clinic's staff. In 1924 he was the first U.S. physician to use insulin clinically. He left the clinic in 1935 and entered private practice. He served again as an army doctor in France during World War II. In 1928 John married Elizabeth (Betty) Beaman of Cincinnati. In 1930 they founded Camp Ho Mita Koda, the world's first summer vacation camp for diabetic children, donating land and their summer cabin in Newbury Ctr., OH, to the camp and directing it for 20 years. John collected Czech graphic art; as a woodcarver, made sculptures and furniture; and translated Czech literature into English. John was a founder of the American Diabetes Assn. and cofounder of the Natl. Central Society for Clinical Research. In 1937 he received the Jewish Fed.'s Chas. Eisenman Award for outstanding community work. John died in New Mexico and was buried in Arlington National Cemetery.

Henry John Papers, WRHS.

**JOHNSON, REV. CLARA LUCIL** (14 March 1900–20 Oct. 1993) was one of the first African American female ministers in Cleveland and the founder of Highlight FBH "Fire Baptized Holiness" Church in MAPLE HTS.,† which was established during the late 1950s.

Born Clara Davidson in Asheville, NC, to George and Ada (Taylor), Clara came to Cleveland in 1918 and became a day worker. She was ordained as a minister in 1920 and spent several years as a junior

pastor at Athens Fire Baptized Holiness Church in Cleveland.

Rev. Johnson spent much of her time in field work, which involved traveling around the Cleveland area and preaching at tent meetings. While on field work in Maple Hts., she decided to start a church there. For a few years Rev. Johnson conducted services out of the basement of one of the early church members' home. The Highlight FBH Church, located at 5665 Adams Ave., was built in 1959. Rev. Johnson was pastor for 35 years until failing eyesight forced her to step down.

Rev. Johnson also taught at and ran the Ruth and Esther Bible College for over 30 years out of her home in Cleveland. She taught until shortly before her death, training future ministers.

Rev. Johnson married Alex H. Johnson (d. 1978) on 21 Nov. 1923; they had two sons, Edward and Alexander (dec). Rev. Johnson is buried in Highland Park Cemetery.—T.B.

**JOHNSON, EARLE LEVAN** (29 Jan. 1895–16 Feb. 1947), developer of the national civil air defense system, was born in Great Barrington, MA, to Levan and Nellie Ann Johnson. He moved with his family to Lake County, OH, when he was 8. He graduated from Ohio State Univ. in 1917 and returned to the family farm in Lake County. He became involved in the Republican party, and beginning in 1926, served 3 terms in the Ohio House of Representatives. During the 1920s and 1930s, Johnson started his own building and real estate companies, owning and managing properties in Lake County. He also became vice-president of LEISY BREWING CO.† of Cleveland and vice-president of Northern Ohio Insurance Corp.

In the 1930s Johnson was chairman of the Come to Cleveland Committee of the CLEVELAND ADVERTISING CLUB,† drawing large conventions to Cleveland. In Lake County, he continued his father's sponsorship of Camp Levan Johnson for underprivileged children. Johnson started flying in 1929, and early in World War II urged the government to permit civilian pilots to help in the war effort. In 1941 Johnson organized pilots into a state wing of the Civil Air Defense. When the Civil Air Patrol was organized a year later, he left for Washington to become its asst. executive officer, soon becoming national commander, being awarded the Legion of Merit. After the war, he continued as national commander of CAP until a fatal airplane accident in N. ROYALTON† in 1947. He was buried in Arlington Natl. Cemetery, survived by his wife, the former Doris Doan, whom he married in 1921.

Earle L. Johnson Papers, WRHS.

JOHNSON, LEVI (25 Apr. 1786–19 Dec. 1871), who arrived in Cleveland in 1809 from Herkimer County, NY, built ships and constructed homes for the early settlers. He built Cuyahoga County's first courthouse and jail on the northwest corner of PUBLIC SQUARE† (1812), an inn (Johnson House) in 1852, and Cleveland's first lighthouse (1830). One of the jury at the trial of Indian JOHN O'MIC, Johnson also built the gallows on which the Indian was hanged. Johnson's skill as a shipbuilder contributed to the growing lake trade. In 1813 or 1814, he built the schooner *Lady's Master,* and in 1814 built the schooner *Pilot.* He also constructed the 65-ton schooner *Neptune,* launched in the spring of 1816. In 1824 Johnson and the Turhooven brothers built and launched the *Enterprise,* a 220-ton steamboat, the first in Cleveland, which carried merchandise from Buffalo to Cleveland and towns along the lake. Also interested in real estate and building, Johnson owned 96 properties by 1838. In 1843 Johnson built his permanent family home, the city's first stone house, which stood until 1909. A 65-ft. stone lighthouse was built by Johnson at Cedar Pt. in 1836. He also set the channel buoys in Sandusky Bay. In 1837 he built a 700-ft. stone pier east of the mouth of the CUYAHOGA RIVER.† He married Margaret Montier on 9 Mar. 1811. They had three children: Harriet, Perriander, and Philander. Johnson died of typhoid fever. At his death, he had continuously lived in Cleveland longer than any other person. He was buried in Woodland Cemetery.

Meakin, Alexander C. *Man of Vision: The Story of Levi Johnson and His Role in the Early History of Cleveland* (1993).

JOHNSON, TOM L. (18 July 1854–10 Apr. 1911), mayor of Cleveland and a noted American Progressive, was born in Blue Spring, KY, to Col. Albert W. and Helen Loftin Johnson. His family's Civil War Confederate support depleted their fortunes, so that Johnson earned money selling newspapers to finance his family. Johnson became an office boy in the Louisville St. Railway Co., two years later becoming company superintendent. Johnson's invention of the see-through glass fare-box realized $20,000–$30,000, which he used toward purchasing, restoring, and profitably selling the Indianapolis St. Railway. He expanded his traction holdings to St. Louis, Detroit, Brooklyn, NY, and in 1879 to Cleveland, after a battle against MARCUS A. HANNA, who operated competing lines. In 1874 Johnson married Margaret (Maggie) Johnson; they moved to Cleveland around 1883. In 1889 Johnson established Cambria Co. steel company in Johnstown, PA, and Lorain Steel Co. in Lorain, OH.

Johnson's political career was sparked by reading Henry George's books and becoming a fellow advocate of free trade and the single land tax, as well as George's personal friend. These ideas were in direct opposition to the principles that had made Johnson wealthy; this dichotomy dominated the rest of his life. In 1890 Johnson was elected as a Democrat for the U.S. House of Representatives from Cleveland's 21st district, and was reelected in 1892. In 1901 Johnson was elected Cleveland's mayor, campaigning on "home rule, 3-cent fare, and just taxation"; he was reelected for 3 terms. Using tent meetings and encouraging discussion, Johnson argued against monopolies and for MUNICIPAL OWNERSHIP† of public utilities. He initiated the Group Plan and MALL,† and with cabinet members NEWTON D. BAKER and HARRIS R. COOLEY, reformed and professionalized city hall. Reformer Lincoln Steffens stated, "Johnson is the best mayor of the best governed city in America." Dissatisfaction with some of Johnson's reforms, particularly those dealing with street railways, led to his defeat by HERMAN C. BAEHR in 1909. Johnson died less than 2 years later and was buried in Greenwood Cemetery, Brooklyn, NY, next to Henry George.

Johnson, Tom L. *My Story* (1913).
Murdock, Eugene C. "Life of Tom L. Johnson" (Ph.D. diss., Columbia Univ., 1951).
Tom L. Johnson Papers, WRHS.

JOHNSON, SIR WILLIAM (1715–11 July 1774), superintendent of Indian Affairs in North America, landed with his party on a beach "near to Cayahoga" on 26 Sept. 1761, thus becoming one of Cleveland's earliest prominent visitors. After the conclusion of the French & Indian Wars, rumors and intelligence of an impending Indian attack on Ft. Detroit prompted its commander, Capt. Donald Campbell, to seek aid. Upon request of Sir Jeffery Amherst, Johnson proceeded westward along the north shore of Lake Erie to Ft. Detroit with 140 Royal Americans and Indian scouts aboard 13 bateaux and canoes. His objective was to make treaties with the Indians and establish regulations for the fur trade. His return journey began on 19 Sept. by way of the south shore. It was on this part of the trip that he arrived, a week later, at Cleveland and encamped until departure the next morning.

JONES, CARLOS L. (18 June 1827–5 Feb. 1897) was a businessman, philanthropist, and the founder of the Jones School and Home for Friendless Children (JONES HOME OF CHILDREN'S SERVICES†) on Cleveland's west side.

Born in New Jersey, Jones came to Cleveland with his family in 1831. At about age 18 he worked as a farmhand in PARMA.† Returning to Cleveland, Jones became a successful and wealthy farm equipment manufacturer. Retiring from business in the early 1880s, Jones invested in real estate and became mayor of BROOKLYN VILLAGE.†

Jones purchased 52 acres on Pearl St. in Brooklyn Village and built a 160-acre dairy farm. Jones and his second wife, Mary Branch (d. 1898), opened their farm to 12 children to live and learn for a few weeks. Their idea of helping impoverished children through their farm gave way to a children's home.

Incorporated 5 Nov. 1886, the Jones School and Home for Friendless Children opened 15 Dec. 1887 on 7 acres of land donated by Jones at 1663 Pearl St. Carlos and Mary Jones gave the Home as a memorial to John Marvin Jones, his son from his first wife, Delia Brainard (d. 1853). It was the tragedies of the deaths of his young wife, Delia, and son, the drowning deaths of his and Mary's young son and daughter, and the poverty of his own early years that led Jones to devote his efforts and property to the care of "friendless" children.

Carlos and Mary Jones had a daughter, Daisy (Wittenmeyer). Jones belonged to the DISCIPLES OF CHRIST.† He is buried in Riverside Cemetery. —T.B.

**JONES, DAVID I.** (18 June 1818–2 June 1891) and **JOHN** (ca. 1808–1870), brothers who built the first iron mill in NEWBURGH,† were born in Monmouthshire, Wales, worked in Dowlais Mill in Glamorganshire, South Wales, and emigrated to the U.S. about 1845, working for Phoenix Iron Co. in Phoenixville, PA. Early in 1856 they joined the new Railroad Iron Mill Co. in Cleveland. The brothers joined J. W. Jones to form Jones & Co. and bought land in Newburgh in Apr. 1857 to build a rail mill. J. W. Jones, not related to the brothers, soon sold out; the company changed names as new investors joined: Chisholm, Jones & Co. after HENRY CHISHOLM invested in 1857; and Stone, Chisholm & Jones after Andros B. Stone joined in 1858. The Newburgh Mill became part of Cleveland Rolling Mill Co. when the latter was incorporated in Nov. 1863. John and David Jones were not among the incorporators of the Cleveland Rolling Mill Co., but were leading figures in its Newburgh mill. As the principal mechanic and draftsman, David was in charge of the mill until his death in 1891. John was manager of the rail mill and foreman of the puddle mill, merchant trains, and furnaces. He suffered heavy financial losses as a founder of the unsuccessful Alliance Rolling Mill Co. in Alliance, OH. In 1858 the Jones brothers were among the organizers of a Congregational church on Harvard St. which later became the JONES RD. CONGREGATIONAL CHURCH.†

John and his wife, Emma, were married on 12 May 1832 and had 3 children: Mary, William, and Catharine. David was married in 1844 and had 8 children: Susan, William, Catherine, Margaret, Sarah J., Christina, Ida, and David I. Each brother died while visiting Wales. John was buried there; David was returned to Cleveland and buried in Woodland Cemetery.

Pendry, William R. *A History of the Cleveland District* (1936).

**JONES, MYRTA L.** (ca. 1861–11 June 1954), daughter of James M. and Ermina (Barrows) Jones, was a native Cleveland social reformer dedicated to improving working conditions for women and a long-time member of the CONSUMERS LEAGUE OF OHIO.† Jones moved to New York City after attending college and worked at Rivington St. (Social) Settlement. She returned to Cleveland by Jan. 1894 and was a founding member of the FORTNIGHTLY MUSIC CLUB.† In 1901 Jones began a lifelong membership on the executive committee of the Consumers League of Ohio, serving as president from 1908–15 and 1918–20. Under her leadership, the league launched campaigns to improve working conditions for women, including shorter hours for women working in department stores during the Christmas shopping season. She also led the league from a group supporting legislation proposed by others to a more aggressive organization proposing legislation itself. Jones was also vice-president of the Natl. Consumers League in the 1910s and 1920s.

During World War I, Jones chaired 2 committees on women in industry, working to recruit women to take men's places in wartime factories while seeking to protect the health and safety of these women. In 1921 Jones came out of semiretirement to direct the Consumers League's unsuccessful campaign for a minimum-wage law in Ohio. Jones also helped organize ALTA HOUSE,† was a member of the LEAGUE OF WOMEN VOTERS,† and was active in the women's suffrage movement. In 1930 Jones married Henry W. Cannon, living in New York City from 1930 until 1952, when she returned to Cleveland. Jones had no children and is buried in Lake View Cemetery.

Consumers League of Ohio Papers, WRHS.
Harrison, Dennis Irven. "The Consumers League of Ohio Women and Reform, 1909–1937" (Ph.D. diss., CWRU, 1975).

**JONES, PAUL K.** (17 June 1904–8 Feb. 1993), instrumental in the development of SHAKER HTS.,† was born in Lonaconing, MD, the son of Joseph H. and Myrtle Geary Jones. After two years at Potomac State College in Keyser, WV, he was employed by U.S. Aluminum Co., which transferred him to Cleveland. In 1923 Jones went to work for the VAN SWERINGENS, studying architecture at JOHN HUNTINGTON POLYTECHNIC INSTITUTE† and corporate finance at Cleveland College part time. As an engineer for the brothers, he helped develop Shaker Hts., construct the Terminal Tower complex, and lay out the Shaker Hts. Rapid Transit line. When the city of Shaker Hts. bought the line in 1944, Jones, the Rapid's asst. manager, became the municipality's first director of transportation, in charge of its operation. When Shaker Hts. mayor Wilson Stapleton took a leave of absence in 1961, Jones was appointed mayor and was reelected several times, serving through 1973. As mayor, he actively opposed construction of the Clark Freeway (I-270) through the city, which would eliminate the SHAKER LAKES.† The controversy lasted until 1968 when the project was dropped due to a new federal law prohibiting freeway building in public parks. This led to the organization of the Shaker Lakes Regional Nature Center to protect them from future incursions.

Jones married Flora Lucille Fertig 3 Sept. 1926, and they had a son, Herbert, who died in 1983. A Shaker Hts. resident, Jones was buried at Lake View Cemetery.—M.S.

**JONES, ROBINSON G.** (14 Dec. 1871–18 Aug. 1938) was a prominent Cleveland educator who served as superintendent of the Cleveland City School District for 13 years.

Born in Chester, OH, Jones's early education was in the local schools. By age 15 he discovered his career as an educator, when he began teaching the farm boys of his community. Jones pursued his dream, earning a bachelor's degree at Ohio Northern Univ., and then a master's degree from Columbia Univ. In 1895 Jones moved to Illinois, and four years later he married Millie L. Gish there; they had one son, Robert Stanley.

In Illinois, Jones quickly became a school superintendent, and he occupied that position in five different Illinois districts before coming to Cleveland in 1917 to serve as asst. superintendent of the Cleveland schools.

On 1 Aug. 1920, he succeeded FRANK E. SPAULDING as Cleveland superintendent. He was twice reappointed to five-year terms, in 1923 and 1928, the first Cleveland superintendent to be honored with the legal maximum five-year appointment.

During his tenure as superintendent, the schools had their greatest growth, enrollment climbing from 105,000 to 156,000. He oversaw the construction of fourteen elementary schools, four junior highs, and five high schools.

Slowed by illness in 1931, Jones resigned the superintendency in Aug. 1933. Such was his popularity, however, that he was named asst. superintendent for secondary schools, and then, in his final year of service, he became their director of guidance.

Jones left the school system in June 1938, but before his retirement became official in Sept. he died of a heart ailment. Burial was in Lakewood Cemetery.—J.T.

**JORDAN, EDWARD STANLAW "NED"** (21 Nov. 1882–30 Dec. 1958), automotive manufacturer who changed American advertising, was born in Merrill, WI, to John and Kate (Griffin) Jordan. He worked through the Univ. of Wisconsin as a reporter, once disguising himself as a railroad yardman, boarding a presidential train, and getting an interview with Pres. Theodore Roosevelt, selling his interview for $20 to 150 newspapers. After graduating from the Univ. of Wisconsin in 1905, NEWTON D. BAKER persuaded him to come to Cleveland, where he worked for the CLEVELAND PRESS.† Jordan left Cleveland to work for Natl. Cash Register Co., then for Thos. B. Jeffrey Co., the automobile manufacturer who was the forerunner of American Motors. In June 1916 Jordan opened JORDAN MOTOR CAR CO.† in Cleveland. With insight into merchandising, manufacturing, and advertising, Jordan broke out of the mold of technological advertising and tapped into more basic desires, luxury and "snob appeal," equating automobile models with certain styles of living. Jordan's management innovations included a profit-sharing plan; most employees owned stock in the company. Years later, when asked about the company's decline (which closed in 1931), Jordan explained, "We never were automobile manufacturers. We were pioneers of new techniques in assembly production, custom style sales, and advertising." Jordan dissociated himself from the company before it closed, separated from his wife, and left for the Bahamas. Eventually he went to New York and worked in advertising–public relations for several firms. From 1950–58, *Automotive News* carried his column "Ned Jordan Speaks." Jordan was married to Charlotte E. Hannahs on 2 Feb. 1906. They had 3 children: Jack, Jane, and Joan. After leaving Cleveland, Jordan married a second time and had one other child.

Wager, Richard. *Golden Wheels* (1975).

**JOSEPH, EMIL** (5 Sept. 1857–11 June 1938), a lawyer devoting much of his life to public service and philanthropy, was born in New York to Jette Selig and MORITZ JOSEPH; his family came to

Cleveland when his father joined the clothing-manufacturing firm Goldsmith, Joseph & Feiss in 1873. Joseph graduated from Columbia Univ. with an A.B. (1879) and an LL.B. (1881). Admitted to the Ohio Bar, Joseph began practicing law in Cleveland with N. A. Gilbert. In 1883 he became partners with Gen. Edward Meyers. In 1885, he opened his own practice, performing executive as well as legal estate work. In 1936 the CLEVELAND BAR ASSN.† honored him for his 55 years in the legal profession.

In 1912 Joseph was elected to the board of the CLEVELAND PUBLIC LIBRARY.† Concerned with all the library's operations, but especially in establishing branch libraries, he was chairman of various committees. In 1932 he was elected president of the board. For many years, Joseph served as chairman of the board of the Jewish Orphan Home. In 1926 he was appointed a director of the Union Trust Co. He also was president of the Town, EXCELSIOR,† and OAKWOOD CLUBS.† In his private life, Joseph collected an extensive, 5,000-volume private library. Portions of his collections of photographs of famous people, prints, and historical mementos were displayed throughout his E. 115th St. residence. Joseph married Fannie Dreyfoss in 1891. He was survived by his son, Frank, and 2 daughters, Mrs. Louis Bing and Mrs. Adrian Ettinger.

**JOSEPH, HELEN HAIMAN** (28 Aug. 1888–15 Aug. 1978) was acknowledged as the "grandmother of American puppetry" because of her practical and scholarly knowledge of marionettes. Born in Atlanta, GA, she came to Cleveland with her family at the age of 7 and graduated from CENTRAL HIGH SCHOOL.† After attendance at Vassar, she received a degree from the College for Women at Western Reserve Univ. and married Ernest A. Joseph in 1918. Both were active in the early years of the CLEVELAND PLAY HOUSE,† he as a trustee and she as a puppeteer. Mrs. Joseph attacked her assignment seriously enough to author the first authoritative English-language history of the subject, *A Book of Marionettes*, published in 1920. Following the death of her husband in 1919, she went with her 2 daughters, Anne and Ernestine, to Europe to pursue her studies in puppetry, which were sufficiently advanced to qualify her to write the entry on puppets and marionettes for the *Encyclopedia Britannica*. Joseph returned to Cleveland in 1924 to establish a puppet theater, the Pinocchio Players, which performed both locally and nationally. She wrote many of the company's plays, some of which were published in 1927. In 1938 she became director of puppet productions at CAIN PARK,† an activity curtailed by World War II. Mrs. Joseph then became an advertising copywriter for Fuller & Smith & Ross, while maintaining her interest in puppetry as a charter member of the Puppeteers of America. Among her civic activities, she was a founder of the progressive Park School in the 1920s and a board member of the LEAGUE OF WOMEN VOTERS† and the WOMEN'S CITY CLUB.† —J.V.

**JOSEPH, MORITZ** (9 Sept. 1834–7 June 1917), responsible for making JOSEPH & FEISS CO.† one of the country's largest manufacturers of men's clothing, was born in Gauersheim, Rheinpfalz, Germany, son of Simon and Hannah Joseph. He left school at 16 to work as a clerk in a cloth business in Mainz. Joseph emigrated to the U.S. in 1853, working as a bookkeeper with a large New York mercantile house, where he eventually became a partner. In 1863 Joseph became partner in the New York company of Levi-Joseph, a subsidiary of Koch, Levi & Mayer of Cleveland. In 1867 when Levi-Joseph abandoned their New York business, Joseph visited his parents in Europe, then became a partner in Simon, Loeb & Joseph, a New Orleans wholesale dry goods firm, on his return. In 1872 Joseph sold his New Orleans interests to come to Cleveland, where in Jan. 1873 he became a partner in the wholesale clothing firm of Koch, Goldsmith, Joseph & Co. When Koch retired in 1888, and Goldsmith retired in 1907, the company became the Joseph & Feiss Co. As senior partner, Joseph was as strict with himself as he was with his subordinates. He was also known for his compassion and charity to the unfortunate. Believing that retirement meant acknowledging his usefulness was over, Joseph remained the senior partner until his retirement on 1 Jan. 1917, when he became a part-time business consultant. Joseph married Jette (Yette) Selig in 1853 and had 5 children: Issac, Siegmund, Fred, EMIL JOSEPH, and Emma, who died in infancy.

**JOSS, ADRIAN "ADDIE"** (12 Apr. 1880–14 Apr. 1911), major league baseball pitcher for Cleveland in the American League between 1902–10, whose career ERA of 1.88 is the 2nd-lowest in major league history, was born in Juneau, WI, son of Jacob and Theresa Joss. He played for the Toledo Mud Hens 2 years, then his contract was sold to the Cleveland Blues. Joss began his major league career on 26 Apr. 1902, pitching a 1-hit shutout against St. Louis. From 1905–08, Joss won over 20 games a season, topped by 27 wins in 1907. His ERA for 1908 was 1.16, and on 2 Oct. 1908 he pitched a perfect no-hit, no-run game against Chicago's Ed Walsh. On 20 Apr. 1910, he pitched another perfect game against Chicago. He completed a remarkable 90% of all games started in his career, with 160 wins and 97 losses. For several seasons, he was a sportswriter for the *Toledo News Bee*. Joss died of complications from tubercular meningitis. His funeral was one of the largest in Toledo, OH, history; noted ex-baseball player and evangelist Billy Sunday preached the funeral message. The Baseball Hall of Fame rules state a player must appear in a minimum of 10 seasons to be considered for entrance, but in 1978 the Committee on Veterans waived the rule for Joss, and the pitcher was voted into the Hall of Fame at Cooperstown, NY. Joss married Lillian Shinivar on 11 Oct. 1902. They had 2 children, Norman and Ruth.

**JURGENS, REV. WILLIAM A., H.E.D.** (3 July 1928–1 Sept. 1982) was a Catholic priest, linguist, author who translated theological and scriptural works, and Diocesan historian. An expert on Gregorian Chant and a gifted musician and composer, Jurgens was the first director of the Commission on Sacred Music.

Born in Akron to Charles and Ruth (Gardner) Jurgens, Jurgens attended Immaculate Conception School and St. Vincent High School in Akron, St. Joseph Preparatory Seminary in Westmont, IL, and St. Mary Seminary in Cleveland.

Ordained in 1954, Jurgen's first assignment was at St. Michael Parish on Scranton Rd. In 1956 Jurgens began studies in Rome at the Pontifical Music Institute, while also earning a doctorate in ecclesiastical history from Gregorian Univ.

Returning to Cleveland in 1959, Jurgens served at Blessed Sacrament Church before being named to the ST. MARY SEMINARY faculty. Jurgens was assigned to teach at Borromeo Seminary in 1961 and became Instructor of Chant at both seminaries in 1965. From 1961–68 Jurgens was diocesan director of sacred music. He served on the Diocesan Liturgical Commission and was the director of the Commission on Sacred Music. In 1974 he became Bp. CLARENCE ISSENMANN's secretary.

In 1977 Bp. James Hickey appointed Jurgens Diocesan research historian, commissioning him to write a multi-volume work on the diocese. Jurgens had completed the first volume, *A History of the Diocese of Cleveland: The Prehistory of the Diocese to Its Establishment in 1847*, and the draft of volume two at the time of his death.

Jurgens is buried in Holy Cross Cemetery.—T.B.

K

**KAIM, JAMIL (JAMES)** (1892–21 Sept. 1971), businessman and leader in Lebanese-American affairs, was born in Aitaneet, Lebanon, and graduated from American Univ. in Beirut. He served with the American Red Cross 2 years before coming to Cleveland in 1920 and opening a confectionery. Knowing nothing about sweets, he patronized a popular PUBLIC SQUARE† soda fountain, ordered a different treat each day, and wrote down the ingredients in Arabic. He later opened Kaim's Restaurant as partowner. Kaim established the AITANEET BROTHERHOOD,† a charitable club to aid residents of his birthplace, in 1929. The next year, he organized the Cleveland-Lebanese Syrian Democratic Club in Cleveland, Akron, Canton, and Toledo, and was put in charge of all such Ohio clubs by Franklin D. Roosevelt. A Cleveland correspondent for a New York Syrian paper, he also announced local Syrian radio programs. He was finance director of the Cleveland Lebanese Syrian Foundation, a member of Cleveland Cosmopolitan Group, and a trustee of ST. ELIAS MELKITE CHURCH.† During World War II, Kaim chaired a "Help Win the War" campaign that funded an entire mobile canteen for the American Red Cross and sent Christmas presents to soldiers of Lebanese and Syrian descent. Kaim and his wife, Shafiica, whom he married in 1913, had left their sons Albert and William with their grandparents in Lebanon, sending money for their passage; but the grandparents, desiring company in their old age, sent William but kept Albert. Albert was not able to enter the country until 1949. Kaim and his wife had 6 children: William, Caroline, Albert, Victor, Elizabeth, and Robert. Kaim was buried in Calvary Cemetery.

**KALISCH, ISIDOR** (15 Nov. 1816–11 May 1886), the first rabbi serving the Cleveland Jewish community, was born in Krotoschin, the Duchy of Posen. He was the son of Burnham and Sarah Tobias Kalisch. He studied in the yeshivot of Posen and attended universities in Berlin, Breslau, and Prague before becoming a journalist and taking an active part in the Revolution of 1848 in Germany; in 1849 he was forced to emigrate to the U.S. Kalisch entered the rabbinate and assumed a post at Cleveland's ANSHE CHESED† Congregation early in 1850. Probably too liberal for the then-Orthodox congregation, after a few months the congregation dismissed him. Kalisch and 20 supporters established a new congregation, TIFERETH ISRAEL,† on 26 May 1850, with Kalisch as rabbi, chazan, preacher, and teacher.

Kalisch was a representative to the CLEVELAND ASSEMBLY† in 1855, the first general conference of Jewish religious leaders ever held in America; he was appointed, with Rabbis Isaac Mayer Wise and Wolf Rothenheim, to prepare a new Jewish prayerbook. In 1857 they issued *Minhag America,* the most popular prayerbook of moderate Reform congregations in the 1860s and 1870s. On 4 Jan. 1856, Kalisch dedicated Tifereth Israel's newly erected Huron St. Synagogue, but because the congregation could not afford both to maintain the building and pay a rabbi, Kalisch was relieved of his duties. After leaving Cleveland, Kalisch served congregations throughout the U.S. In 1875 he settled in Newark and returned to writing, dying there in 1886. Kalisch married twice. His first wife, Charlotte Bankman, whom he married in 1843, died in 1856; he then married his second wife, Adelaide. Kalisch had 6 children: Albert, Leonard, Samuel, Abner, Burnham, and Hannah.

Kalisch, Samuel. "Rabbi Isidor Kalisch, a Memoir," in *Studies in Ancient and Modern Judaism . . . Selected Writings of Rabbi Isidor Kalisch* (1928).

KALISH, MAX (1 Mar. 1891–18 Mar. 1945), sculptor, was born Max Kalichik in Valozin, Lithuania, son of Joel and Hannah (Levinson) Kalichik. He immigrated with his family to Cleveland in 1898 and was given an Orthodox Jewish education. He won a scholarship to the CLEVELAND INSTITUTE OF ART,† graduating at 19 and winning 1st prize for life modeling. Kalish created *Rebecca and Judas Maccabeus,* judged the best piece of sculpture ever exhibited in the annual student show, a copy of which was purchased by Rabbi LOUIS WOLSEY. In 1910 Kalish studied at the Natl. Academy of Design in New York with roommate ALEX WARSHAWSKY. In 1912 he went to Europe to study, exhibiting at the Paris Salon of 1913. Kalish returned to the U.S. via San Francisco, where he was a sculptor for the Pan-Pacific Exposition. Returning to Cleveland in 1915, he tried and abandoned dental school, yet there gained a mastery of body structure. From 1916–19 he was in the army, assisting reconstructive work on war-mutilated soldiers.

Kalish traveled to Europe, exhibited at Korner & Wood Gallery, won 1st prizes at MAY SHOWS,† and received excellent press for his labor figures. In 1923 Cleveland schoolchildren funded a statue of Abraham Lincoln which Kalish executed, and which was installed at the School Admin. Bldg. Commissions came from across the country for statues of famous personalities. Upon his death, CLEVELAND CITY COUNCIL† enacted a tribute and the CLEVELAND MUSEUM OF ART† gave a memorial exhibition of his work jointly with the paintings of Alex Warshawsky.

Married to Alice Neuman on 20 Nov. 1927, Kalish had two children, Richard and James. Kalish died in New York City and was buried in Cleveland's Mayfield Cemetery.

Kalish, Alice. *Max Kalish—As I Knew Him* (1969).

**KAPPANADZE, JASON R.** (1874–15 Apr. 1962), pastor of ST. THEODOSIUS RUSSIAN ORTHODOX CATHEDRAL,† was born in Sviry, Georgia, Russia, son of Roman Kappanadze. He graduated from Tiflis Seminary in 1894, and was sent by the Russian government and church to Kodiak, Alaska, to run a parochial school in 1895. He married Mary Kashevaroff in 1896. Consecrated into the priesthood in 1898, Kappanadze worked in Alaska and Pennsylvania before coming to Cleveland in 1902 to St. Theodosius Russian Orthodox Cathedral, where he directed the acquisition of St. John's Convent property. In 1908 he returned to Russia as professor of theology at Kutais seminary. During World War I, he was regimental pastor in the Imperial Russian Army. In 1918 he went to Tiflis to Slonsky Sobor, an ancient 5th century cathedral. With help from the American Near East Relief and passports from a Communist official who was his son's former classmate, Kappanadze and his family escaped from Russia in 1921.

Kappanadze returned to St. Theodosius in 1922, remaining until his retirement in 1957, establishing social centers and developing an a capella choir, while also helping form Russian Orthodox parishes in Detroit, Akron, and Lorain. Kappanadze advanced to protopresbyter, the highest office open to a married priest. After retiring and becoming pastor emeritus at St. Theodosius, he was chaplin at the Brotherhood of St. John Home for the Aged near Hiram. Kappanadze and his wife were killed in an automobile accident. They were buried in St. Theodosius Cemetery. The Kappanadzes had 2 children: Roman and Nicholas. Kappanadze's likeness is on a mural at St. Theodosius painted by Andrei Bicenko in the 1950s.

**KATAN, ANNY ROSENBERG, M.D.** (1 May 1898–24 Dec. 1992), child psychoanalyst, established the HANNA PERKINS SCHOOL† (1951) in Cleveland and pioneered the use of psychoanalysis with emotionally disturbed CHILDREN AND YOUTH.† Dr. Katan, who taught child analysis at the School of Medicine of Western Reserve Univ. (1946–64), also helped establish the Cleveland Psychoanalytic Institute (1960) and, with Robert A. Furman and Eleanor Hosley, organized the CLEVELAND CENTER FOR RESEARCH IN CHILD DEVELOPMENT† (1966). Katan was born in Vienna, Austria, and grew up with close family ties to pioneer psychoanalyst Sigmund Freud and his daughter, Anna. A nurse during World War I, Katan graduated from the Medical College of the Univ. of Vienna (1923) and studied under Anna Freud at Vienna's Psychoanalytic Institute. She was among the first child analysts in that city.

In the mid–1930s Katan married psychoanalyst MAURITS KATAN.† They had one child, Annemarie Angrist. Anny Katan also had a son, Klaus Angel, by a previous marriage. The Katans moved from Austria to the Netherlands just prior to World War II. As Jews, they went into hiding in 1939 to avoid Nazi persecution. Using false papers to survive, Anny Katan worked in Anti-Fascist movements and helped others flee. After the war, she served as chief psychoanalyst of the Child Guidance Clinic of the Hague in the Netherlands before coming with her family to Cleveland in 1946, at the suggestion of Anna Freud and through the efforts of Dr. DOUGLAS BOND. Bond was building a department of psychiatry at WRU. The weekly meetings of Cleveland-area child analysts, begun by Katan in her CLEVELAND HTS.† home, continued in 1995. In 1993 the Katans' library was donated to

255

the Cleveland Center for Research in Child Development as the KATAN ARCHIVES.†—J.M.

---

Katan Archives, Center for Research in Child Development.

See also MEDICINE† and WOMEN.†

**KATAN, MAURITS, M.D.** (25 Nov. 1897–3 April 1977), a psychoanalyst known for his work on schizophrenia, taught analysis at the School of Medicine of Western Reserve Univ. (see CASE WESTERN RESERVE UNIV.†) (1946–64) and with his wife Dr. ANNY KATAN and others, developed the Cleveland Psychoanalytic Institute (1960). Some call him the father of adult psychoanalysis in Cleveland. Born in Vlaarndingan, the Netherlands, Katan trained at the Univ. of Leyden, where he assisted at the psychiatric clinic. He then went to Vienna for further study under Anna Freud (daughter of Sigmund Freud). In the mid–1930s he married child analyst Anny Katan. With his wife, young daughter Annemarie (later Annemarie Angrist), and stepson Klaus Angel, Katan returned to the Netherlands just prior to World War II. After the war, the Katans remained in the Netherlands for a brief time and worked at the Hague. At the suggestion of Anna Freud and through the efforts of Dr. DOUGLAS BOND, who was building a department of psychiatry at WRU, both doctors accepted positions there and moved to CLEVELAND HTS.† Anny and Maurits Katan helped establish the Detroit Psychoanalytic Institute before setting up a training center in Cleveland (1954), the forerunner of the Cleveland Psychoanalytic Institute. Maurits Katan, unusual among adult analysts in recognizing the contributions of child psychoanalysis, served as a trustee of the CLEVELAND CENTER FOR RESEARCH IN CHILD DEVELOPMENT.† Katan died in Fort Myers, FL. After his wife's death, their library, the KATAN ARCHIVES,† was donated to the Cleveland Center for Research in Child Development.—J.M.

---

Katan Archives, Center for Research in Child Development.

See also MEDICINE.†

**KATZ, MEYER MYRON "MICKEY"** (15 June 1909–30 April 1985) was a well-known American-Yiddish parodist and dialect performer who brought bilingual humor to English-speaking Jewish communities throughout the U.S.

One of four children, Meyer Katz was born in Cleveland, the son of Menachem and Johanna (Herzberg) Katz. While at CENTRAL HIGH SCHOOL,† he helped support his family by playing the saxophone and clarinet in local bands. After graduation, Katz toured with PHIL SPITALNY's orchestra and worked for Phil's brother, MAURICE, in the early 1930s as a pit musician at the State and Palace Theaters. In the summer he led his own orchestra on the *Goodtime*, entertaining passengers on Lake Erie excursions. He later organized a novelty band, "Mickey Katz and His Kittens." During World War II, he toured the European Theater of Operations with actress Betty Hutton. When the family moved to Los Angeles in 1946, Katz played briefly with the Spike Jones band, then recorded his first hit record, "Haim Afen Range" (Home on the Range), the first of many English-Yiddish parodies of popular songs. He also developed the highly successful "Borschtcapades," an American-Jewish variety show which attracted a wide audience by presenting Jewish humor and culture in a modern format. It toured the country for two decades. Through the 1970s, Katz continued to perform in the theater and on records.

In 1930 Meyer (Mickey) Katz married Goldie (Grace) Epstein, and they had 2 children, Joel (Grey), who became a noted actor, and Ronald. Katz died in Los Angeles.—M.S.

**KATZ, MORRIS L.** (8 Aug. 1915–14 April 1994) was a well-known Cleveland artist. Born in Cleveland to Louis and Becky Brinn Katz, Morris attended local schools and graduated from East Technical High School.

In 1938 he went to work for Brown & Gage, Inc. in Cleveland, the start of a 53-year career with the commercial printing company. There he learned how to cut film and mix colors, soon becoming a master in all the elements of the silk-screen process.

His work for Brown & Gage was interrupted in 1943 when Katz entered the military. He served in the army's 3rd Photo Reconnaissance Unit and held the rank of staff sergeant.

During the war he found the opportunity to exercise his artistic talents, and in particular he enjoyed adding art to the nose cones of airplanes. Perhaps his most remembered contribution was to the plane of Admiral Chester Nimitz.

After the war he returned to Cleveland and to Brown & Gage, where he soon became head of the company's art department. He continued with the company until 1991, when he retired. Besides commercial art work, he was also a dedicated watercolorist. He favored outdoor scenes and a realistic style. His works were shown in the MAY SHOW† of the CLEVELAND MUSEUM OF ART† and in shows in GATES MILLS† and CHAGRIN FALLS.† Katz was also a member of the Jewish War Veterans.

Katz married Helen Stern 1 Nov. 1947, and they had two children, Leslie and Paula. He is buried in Mt. Olive Cemetery in Solon, OH.—J.T.

**KAYE, SAMMY** (13 March 1910–2 June 1987), well-known local and national bandleader, was born Samuel Zarnocay, Jr., in LAKEWOOD, the son of Samuel and Mary Sukenik Zarnocay. He attended local schools, graduating from Rocky River High School in 1928. While in high school, he organized a band known as Sammy's Hot Peppers and played semi-professional baseball to earn extra money. By the time he enrolled in Ohio Univ., he had changed his name to "Kaye," and his band was known as "Kaye's Ohioans." He and his band played engagements at college and performed at the nickel-a-dance Roxy Ballroom in Lakewood during summer vacations. Although he earned a university degree, Kaye elected to stay in the music business. While playing at Cleveland's Cabin Club in the mid–1930s, he adopted the slogan, "Swing and Sway with Sammy Kaye," which described his smooth danceable music.

Kaye, who played the clarinet and saxophone, took his band to New York in 1938, where he was featured on the NBC radio show "Sunday Serenade" for 12 years. Kaye's hits include "Remember Pearl Harbor," "Harbor Lights," and "It Isn't Fair." In the 1950s he hosted several musical shows on network television. Although Kaye invested in publishing and other business ventures successfully, he and his band continued to play into the mid–1980s.

Kaye married Ruth Knox Elden in 1940. They divorced in 1956 and had no children. A resident of New York City, Kaye died in Ridgewood, NJ, and was buried here in Lakewood Park Cemetery.—M.S.

Lamparski, Richard. *Whatever Became of..? Ninth Series* (1985).

**KEELER, HARRIET LOUISE** (ca. 1846–12 Feb. 1921) capped a career of more than 4 decades in the CLEVELAND PUBLIC SCHOOLS† with a brief term as the city's first woman superintendent of schools. A native of South Kortright, NY, she entered the Cleveland School System following her graduation from Oberlin College in 1870. Among her assignments were teacher and principal at CENTRAL HIGH SCHOOL† and superintendent of the system's primary grades. She published numerous English textbooks, nature studies, and other works both during and after her career, including *The Wild Flowers of Early Spring* (1894), *Our Northern Shrubs and How to Identify Them* (1903), and *The Life of Adelia A. Field Johnson* (1912). Although she retired in 1909, she was recalled to succeed Wm. H. Elson as superintendent of schools from Jan.-Aug. 1912. She was a charter member of the FORTNIGHTLY MUSICAL CLUB† and president of the Cuyahoga County Suffrage Assn. As a tribute to her

interest in nature, the 300-acre Harriet L. Keeler Memorial Woods was dedicated in Brecksville Reservation of METROPARKS.† Unmarried, Keeler died at Clifton Springs, NY, and is buried at Oberlin.

**KELLER, HENRY GEORGE** (3 Apr. 1869–3 Aug. 1949), painter and teacher, was born at sea as his parents, Jacob and Barbara (Karcher) Keller, came to Cleveland. In 1887 Keller entered the Cleveland School of Art, studying for 3 years, then studying at Karlsruhe in Germany 2 years before returning to complete his Cleveland education. He studied in Dusseldorf, then at Munich from 1899–1902, and also attended the Art Students' League in New York and the Cincinnati School of Art, working as a lithographer to finance his schooling. He joined the teaching staff at Cleveland School of Art (see CLEVELAND INSTITUTE OF ART†), serving until 1945.

Keller had little sympathy with modernism, seeing his function as expressing nature as he saw it. In 1928 Keller won the Davis Purchase Prize at Witte Memorial Museum in San Antonio; in 1929, the Blair Purchase Prize at the Art Institute Internatl. Exhibition of Water Colors in Chicago. He made 11 Carnegie shows in Pittsburgh, and had 1-man shows throughout the country. In 1919 he won the Special Award for sustained excellence for entries in the first MAY SHOW† at the CLEVELAND MUSEUM OF ART.† Keller's themes were American, and he felt the Midwest was the great reservoir of the American Idea. He started a summer school at Berlin Hts., OH, ca. 1908. Keller married Imogene Leslie on 2 Jan. 1893 and had 2 sons, Henry Leslie and Albert Fay. Following his wife's death in 1948, Keller moved to San Diego, CA. Both Keller and his wife are buried in the old burying ground at Berlin Hts. Village.

**KELLER, WILLIAM G.** (19 April 1876–20 Sept. 1963), a recipient of the Congressional Medal of Honor for service during the Spanish-American War, was born in Buffalo, NY, where he enlisted in the U.S. Army. While serving in Cuba, Private Keller, a member of the 10th U.S. Infantry Regiment, participated in the general advance on the city of Santiago, beginning 1 July 1898 with an attack on San Juan Hill to gain the heights overlooking the city. During the engagement Keller aided in the rescue of wounded men under fire on the hill, carrying them a mile to the aid station. He was officially awarded the Medal of Honor for his action on 22 June 1899.

After military service, in 1918 Keller moved to Cleveland, where he worked for the Ohio Bell Telephone Co. for 28 years, retiring in 1941. As a Medal of Honor recipient, he was invited to join a special guard of honor for Pres. Franklin Roosevelt at his 1937 inaugural ceremonies in Washington, DC. Keller married Emma Baker and they had two children, Edna Colburn and Harold. In 1943 he and his wife moved to Sarasota, FL, where he died. His remains were returned to Cleveland for burial in Lake View Cemetery.—M.S.

**KELLEY, ALFRED** (7 Nov. 1789–2 Dec. 1859), "Father of the Ohio-Erie Canal," was born in Middlefield, CT, son of DANIEL KELLEY and Jemima (Stow) Kelley. He came to Ohio in 1810, where he was admitted to the bar and appointed prosecuting attorney for Cuyahoga County, after education at Fairfield Academy and in the law offices of Judge Jonas Platt (Supreme Court of New York). Kelley was the first president of the village of Cleveland (1815), member of the Ohio House of Representatives, state senator, president of the COMMERCIAL BANK OF LAKE ERIE† (1816), and president of several railroad companies. As a member of the State Canal Commission, once he took up canal campaigning in 1823 the OHIO & ERIE CANAL† dominated his life for several years. His leadership resulted in the canal's having the lowest cost per mile of any canal of comparable length in Europe or America. Kelley first fought to get the canal bill passed. Studying voting records on previous bills, Kelley realized the legislators voting for Nathaniel Guilford's education bill voted against canal bills, and vice versa. Kelley eventually convinced Guilford to piggyback the two issues so that both bills passed. Canal construction began in 1825, with Kelley personally supervising the work. In 1844 Kelley was elected to the state senate, originating the bill organizing the State Bank of Ohio and other banking companies. This bill eventually became the basis of the Natl. Bank Act of 1863. Kelley married Mary Seymour Welles in 1817 and had 11 children: Maria, Jane, Anna, Alfred, Helen, and Katherine survived into adulthood, five others died in infancy. Kelley died and was buried in Columbus, OH.

**KELLEY, DANIEL** (27 Nov. 1755–7 Aug. 1831), who, with his family of 6 sons were early settlers of Cleveland, was born in Norwich, CT, to Daniel and Abigail Reynolds Kelley. He moved to Middletown, CT, and in 1787 he married Jemima Stow, sister of a member of Moses Cleaveland's survey party that founded Cleveland in 1796, and one of the 35 original members of the CONNECTICUT LAND CO.† In 1787 Kelley moved to Lowville, NY, acquiring considerable real estate and personal property.

In 1810 Kelley's oldest son, DATUS KELLEY, left

for Cleveland. Later that year, Joshua Stow and Jared Kirtland persuaded Kelley's son, Alfred, to move there with them. Sons Irad and Reynolds soon followed, leaving only sons Thomas and Daniel at home. Jemima's yearning for her sons resulted in the family's moving to Cleveland in 1814. The Kelleys were in better financial condition than almost any other settler in Cleveland. They gave $1,000 to each son to invest in land or business. In Mar. 1816 Kelley was elected to succeed his son Alfred as president of the village of Cleveland; he was re-elected in 1817, 1818, and 1819. In October 1816 Kelley succeeded his son Irad as postmaster, serving until 1817. In 1816 Kelley and his sons Alfred, Datus, and Irad were among the incorporators of a company that built the first pier at the mouth of the CUYAHOGA RIVER.† Upon his death, Kelley was interred in Erie St. Cemetery.

**KELLEY, DATUS** (24 April 1788–24 Jan. 1866) and his family were the first permanent settlers in the part of Rockport Twp. that became ROCKY RIVER.† The first of the early settler Kelley family to move to the Western Reserve, Datus, together with his brother, IRAD, purchased and developed Cunningham (Kelley's) Island.

Born in Middlefield, CT, to Jemima (Stow) and DANIEL KELLEY, Datus attended elementary schools in Middlefield and Lowville, NY. In 1810 Datus visited his uncle, JOSHUA STOW, in Cleveland. Impressed with the settlement, Kelley purchased land one mile west of Rocky River in 1811. A surveyor by trade, Kelley was active in the social and political life of the community. He introduced the first industry in Rockport by erecting a sawmill next to the creek on Detroit Rd. at Elmwood in Rocky River, and supervised the construction of a log schoolhouse near the mouth of the Rocky River.

In 1813 Cuyahoga County Commissioners appointed Kelley to head a committee to cut a road between the Cuyahoga and Rocky Rivers. In 1815 the commissioners appointed him to open the road to Black River in Lorain. In 1816 Kelley became a member of the Cleveland Pier Co. and a trustee of Dover Village.

In 1833 Datus and Irad Kelley began buying parcels of land on Cunningham Island in Lake Erie which was renamed Kelley's Island. In 1836 Kelley moved to the island and spent the rest of his life developing the island.

Kelley married Sara Dean on 21 Aug. 1811. They had nine children. Datus is buried in Kelley's Island municipal cemetery.—T.B.

**KELLEY, HORACE** (18 July 1819–4 Dec. 1890) was a wealthy real estate investor who bequeathed in excess of $500,000 from his estate for the purpose of building and maintaining an art museum.

Born in Cleveland, Kelley was the only child of Betsey (Gould) and Joseph Reynolds Kelley, a successful businessman. Joseph's death in 1823 left Horace heir to his father's fortune, and in the care of his uncles who raised him on Kelley's Island. Horace later acquired ownership of much of the island.

In 1845 Kelley sold his island interests and returned to Cleveland. Like his father, Kelley multiplied his wealth through real estate investments in Cleveland and off Lake Erie's shore.

Kelley's introduction to art museums came with his first trip to Europe in 1868. Influenced by his wife's art interests, Kelley made four subsequent trips abroad and accumulated a fine collection of paintings and other art works which would become the core of Cleveland's art museum.

In 1899 trustees of Kelley's will incorporated the funds under the name the Cleveland Museum of Art. In 1913, after overcoming several legal obstacles, the Kelly interests agreed to surrender that corporate title in favor of the Horace Kelley Art Foundation. Three-tenths of the monies needed for the art museum were provided by the foundation, and the remaining seven-tenths was provided by the museum's second major benefactor, the John Huntington estate.

Kelley married Fanny (Fannie) Miles of Elyria (ca. 1859). They remained childless. Kelley lived in Cleveland and is buried in Lake View Cemetery. —T.B.

KELLEY, IRAD (24 Oct. 1791–21 Jan. 1875), one of Cleveland's first merchants, postmaster, real-estate investor, and co-owner of Kelley's Island, was born in Middletown, CT, to Jemima Stow and DANIEL KELLEY.† He moved to the Cleveland area ca. 1812, and opened his first store in Cleveland's first brick building (1814). When he became postmaster on 31 Dec. 1817, the post office moved into his store. Annual receipts were $500, of which Kelley got 25% as compensation for rent, fuel, and hiring of a clerk. Kelley replaced his building in 1850 with the brick Kelley Block, with the store on the 1st floor, and Kelley's Hall, where concerts, lectures, and balls were held, on the upper floor. In 1863 the building was renamed Athenaeum after the theater located therein.

Kelley also worked as a sailor, and while commanding the ship *Merchant,* became acquainted with the Lake Erie Islands. In 1833 he and his brother, Datus, began purchasing land on Cunningham's Island at $1.50/acre, until they owned the whole island, changing its name to Kelley's Island (1840). They opened stone quarries

and made Kelley's Island famous for limestone, red cedar, peach orchards, and vineyards. In 1833 Irad helped establish the CLEVELAND LYCEUM.† Kelley ran unsuccessfully against JOSHUA GIDDINGS for U.S. Congress in 1850. He also wrote about a number of political issues, including women's rights and railroad routes. He produced political songs for 1840 presidential candidate Wm. Henry Harrison. Kelley married Harriet Pease in 1819 and had 10 children: Gustavas, George, Edwin, Charles, Franklin, Martha, Laura, William Henry, Mary Louisa, and Norman. Kelley was buried in Lake View Cemetery.

Irad Kelley Papers, WRHS.
Kelley, Irad. "A Sketch of Irad Kelley," WRHS (1871).

KELLEY, SAMUEL WALTER, M.D. (15 Sept. 1855–20 Apr. 1929), a pediatrician and pioneer in the study of diseases of children and youth, published "The Surgical Diseases of Children" (1909), the first such treatise by an American surgeon. He chaired the American Medical Assn.'s section on the diseases of children (1900–01) and was the first president of the American Assn. of Teachers of Diseases of Children (1907–08). He was born in Adamsville, OH, to Walter and Selina Kaemmerer Kelley. Educated in public schools in Zanesville, OH, and St. Joseph, MI, Kelley worked as a farmer, sailor, cowboy and other jobs before turning to medicine. He graduated from Western Reserve Univ. (see CASE WESTERN RESERVE UNIV.†) Medical School in 1884 and did postgraduate work in London, England.

Kelley spent his entire career in Cleveland. He served as: chief of the Department of Diseases of Children in the "polyclinic" of Western Reserve Univ. (1886–93); professor at the Cleveland College of Physicians and Surgeon (1893–1910); pediatrician at Cleveland City Hospital (1893–1910), where he was both secretary (1891–99) and president of the medical staff (1899–1902); chief surgeon at ST. LUKE'S MEDICAL CENTER† (1927–29) and surgeon for Holy Cross Home for Crippled and Invalid Children. He was commissioned a brigade surgeon, as a major, in the Spanish-American War and served with French forces and the American Red Cross in World War I.

Kelley edited the *Cleveland Medical Gazette* (1885–1901) and was president of both the CLEVELAND MEDICAL LIBRARY ASSN.† (1929) and the Ohio State Pediatric Society (1896–97). In addition to medical articles, Kelley published two volumes of poetry and a historical novel about MEDICINE,† *In the Year 1800* (1904).

Kelley married Amelia Kemmerlein in Wooster, OH, on 2 July 1884; they had two children, Walter, who died in infancy, and Katherine Mildred (Mrs. William) Taylor.

Samuel Walter Kelley, M.D. Papers, Dittrick Museum of Medical History.

**KELLY, GRACE VERONICA** (31 Jan. 1877–10 Jan. 1950), parlayed her experience as a painter to achieve a second career as art critic for the Cleveland *PLAIN DEALER.†* The daughter of Irish immigrants, Thomas and Mary Hart Kelly, she was born in Cleveland and received her first art lessons at St. Joseph's Convent on Starkweather Ave. Entering the Cleveland School of Art (see CLEVELAND INSTITUTE OF ART†), she studied under HENRY G. KELLER there and in Keller's popular summer school in Berlin Hts. While still a student, she began teaching watercolor classes at the School of Art, where she continued to teach for several years after her graduation in 1896. In 1904 she opened a commercial art studio on Prospect Ave. She was invited to become the *Plain Dealer*'s art critic by Editor ERIE C. HOPWOOD in 1926, on the strength of a series of sketches she had written on Cleveland landmarks, which were also a favorite painting subject of hers. She soon gathered further subjects from several trips to Ireland in the late 1920s and in the following decade to Guatemala, where her friend, Dr. Frank P. Corrigan of ST. ALEXIS HOSPITAL,† had been appointed ambassador. As art critic, Kelly's stories on the Guelph Treasure in 1931 were credited with helping to draw record crowds to view those objects at the CLEVELAND MUSEUM OF ART.† A noted raconteur, she exhibited regularly in the MAY SHOW† and at the WOMEN'S CITY CLUB.† Never married, she was survived by a brother, John, and 3 sisters, Mary, Julia, and Maria.—J.V.

**KELSEY, LORENZO A.** (22 Feb. 1803–13 Feb. 1890), steamboat captain and mayor of Cleveland from 1848–49, was born in Port Leyden, NY, the son of shipowner Eber Kelsey and Lucy Ann Leete Kelsey. He was educated in his local district and moved to Youngstown to work in lumber. Kelsey moved to Cleveland in 1837 with his wife and became manager of the Cleveland House Hotel for 1 year. He then became captain of the steamship *Chesapeake*, and later captain of the *General Harrison*. He also served as proprietor (1818–19) of the New England Hotel. With no political experience, Kelsey ran as a dark-horse mayoral candidate for the Democratic party in 1848, defeating 2 other opponents, Chas. Bradburn and Milo Hickox. As mayor, Kelsey supported civic improvements and worked frequently with top members of the Democratic party. Throughout his career, he served as a

delegate to Democratic conventions. In 1849 he returned to the hotel business, until his retirement in the late 1850s. Kelsey married Sophia Smith (1806–93) of Windsor, CT, in 1825. They had 7 children: Edgar A. (b. 1832 and died in infancy), Eugene, Antoinette, Theodore, Ada Helen, Josephine H., and Edgar A. (b. 1840). Kelsey died in Cleveland and was buried in Erie St. Cemetery; in 1903 his remains were moved to Lake View Cemetery.

**KENNEDY, CHARLES E.** (17 May 1856–12 June 1929), prominent journalist born in W. Farmington, OH, to James C. and Sarah (Curry) Kennedy, began his long career in Cleveland journalism as a reporter for the *Leader* in 1876. He moved to the *Herald* in 1880, serving as city editor and then advertising manager, and joined the *PLAIN DEALER†* as advertising manager following the *Herald*'s demise in 1885. After 2 years of advertising work in New York, Kennedy rejoined the *Plain Dealer* in 1893 as general manager and small stockholder. Hired away by Joseph Pulitzer in 1897 to be business manager of the *St. Louis Post-Dispatch,* he returned the following year to assume direction of the *Plain Dealer* in conjunction with ELBERT H. BAKER, under an agreement signed with publisher LIBERTY E. HOLDEN. This arrangement lasted from 1898–1907, when Kennedy withdrew, leaving Baker in sole control as general manager. Since he had been editorial manager in the partnership, while Baker was business manager, Kennedy later claimed he deserved a share of the credit accrued to Baker as "founder of the modern *Plain Dealer.*" Following his departure from the *Plain Dealer,* Kennedy became general manager of the *CLEVELAND LEADER,†* then retired from journalism to devote himself to advertising. He served as a member of the Cleveland Public Library board from 1903–20, and in 1925 published a memoir entitled *Fifty Years of Cleveland.* He married Harriet L. Pratt of Warren in 1880, with whom he had a daughter, Winifred. Kennedy died in his home and was buried in Lake View Cemetery.

Kennedy, Charles E. *Fifty Years of Cleveland* (1925).

**KENNEDY, JAMES HENRY** (17 Jan. 1849–22 Jan. 1934) made distinguished contributions to the fields of local journalism and history. A native of Farmington, Trumbull Co., OH, and son of James C. and Sarah (Curry) Kennedy, he was the older brother of CHARLES E. KENNEDY, who also became a Cleveland journalist. The elder Kennedy joined the staff of the *CLEVELAND LEADER†* in 1872 after attending the Western Reserve Seminary. As the *Leader*'s city editor, Kennedy was the first newspaperman to reach the scene of the Ashtabula railroad disaster of 1876 (see AMASA STONE†). He moved over to the *CLEVELAND HERALD†* as managing editor in 1880, after MARCUS A. HANNA purchased the paper and hired away most of the *Leader*'s staff. When the *Herald* folded in 1885, Kennedy became part owner of the *SUNDAY VOICE,†* where he served as managing editor until 1889. Kennedy published a history of the *Early Days of Mormonism* in 1888, which was followed by his *A History of the City of Cleveland* in 1896 (see HISTORIES OF CLEVELAND†). He also served as editor of the *Magazine of Western History,* following it to New York when its offices were shifted there from Cleveland. In New York, Kennedy also served as a correspondent for the Cleveland *PLAIN DEALER†* and wrote the *History of the Ohio Society of New York* (1906). He changed his middle name from Henry to Harrison in 1915. Kennedy married Mary G. Pierce on 24 Dec. 1874. The final decade of his life was spent in California; he died in Pasadena, survived by a daughter, the writer Louise Kennedy Mabie.

**KERN, FRANK J.** (18 Mar. 1887–4 Oct. 1979), physician and leader in the Slovenian community, was born Frank Jauh near Skofja Loka in Slovenia to parents Francis and Mary Jauh. He studied for the priesthood, going to St. Paul Seminary in Minnesota in 1903, but moved to Cleveland in 1906 before completing his education to work for *Nova Domovina.* He moved to Calumet, MI, briefly to edit a newspaper, but returned to Cleveland, teaching English and penmanship. Kern entered Western Reserve Medical College in 1908, added the surname Kern in 1911, and, after an internship at ST. VINCENT CHARITY HOSPITAL,† began 50 years work as a physician. He was medical counsel for several fraternal insurance societies, including AMERICAN MUTUAL LIFE ASSN.† and Serbian Beneficial Fed., "Unity." He also wrote medical columns for Slovenian newspapers in Cleveland and Chicago.

Kern was the first Slovenian-American candidate for councilman, running unsuccessfully in 1913. In 1916 he helped what became the St. Clair Savings Assn. He was the first president of the SLOVENIAN NATL. HOME† Committee. During World War I, he promoted creation of Yugoslavia, and represented the Slovenian Natl. Union to the Jugoslav Natl. Council in Washington. He was also an executive board member of the SLOVENIAN AMERICAN NATL. COUNCIL† formed to assist the homeland during World War II. Kern's English-Slovenian dictionary (1919) was followed by an English reader featuring penmanship lessons (1926). Kern married Agnes Wertin on 19 Nov.

1912. They had 3 children: Ella, Frank, and Edward. Kern died in Cleveland and was buried in All Soul's Cemetery. An autobiography of his early life was published in Ljubljana in 1937.

Kern, Frank Jauh. *Spomini ob Tridesetletnici Prihoda v Ameriko* (1937).

**KETTERINGHAM, GEORGE H.** (11 Feb. 1876–29 Dec. 1954) was a developer of technical instruments manufactured by Cleveland industry. His innovations included the harvesting of spider web for use as cross hairs in optical equipment and perfection of electro-pezioid crystal for electrical devices.

Ketteringham was born in Crowland, England, and came to Cleveland with his family in 1881. On 11 Aug. 1905, he was married to Rose L. Wise. They had twin girls, Rose and Ruth.

Ketteringham began his career as an apprentice at the J. C. Ulmer Co. in 1896. There he became an expert in the manufacturing of surveying and other precision instruments. During World War I, Ketteringham played a major role in the development of periscopes used in submarine warfare. His technical knowledge also led to special projects with Dr. GEORGE CRILE, founder of the CLEVELAND CLINIC FOUNDATION,† who requested assistance with the development of surgical tools.

During construction projects such as the DETROIT-SUPERIOR BRIDGE,† the HOPE MEMORIAL (Lorain-Carnegie) BRIDGE,† and the CLEVELAND UNION TERMINAL† complex, Ketteringham was often called upon to make immediate repairs to surveying equipment. An interest in construction led to his photographing many buildings and other civic improvements. These photos are part of the George H. Ketteringham Collection housed at the CLEVELAND PUBLIC LIBRARY.†

In 1933 Ketteringham joined the Bonnar-Vawter Fanform Co. His mechanical expertise was utilized for the care and maintenance of large-scale printing presses.

At the start of World War II, Ketteringham joined the BRUSH DEVELOPMENT CO.† He was a member of several research and development projects charged with harnessing the use of electro-pezioid crystals and the production of underwater sonar, electrocardiograph devices, and the modern dictograph machine. He remained associated with Brush until his death in 1954.

In April 1993 the Smithsonian Institute accepted Ruth Ketteringham's submission of her father's professional papers, spider web harvesting tools and webbing samples to their permanent collection.

View Rd., adjacent to the METROHEALTH MEDICAL HOSPITAL,† was dedicated as Ketteringham Drive in honor of George on 10 Sept. 1993. It was the longtime site of the family residence.

**KIDD, ISAAC CAMPBELL** (26 Mar. 1884–7 Dec. 1941), senior officer on board the battleship U.S.S. *Arizona* when it was attacked and sunk during the Japanese attack on Pearl Harbor, was born in Cleveland, the son of Isaac and Jemima (Campbell) Kidd. He graduated from West High School in 1902, then from the U.S. Naval Academy in 1906. Kidd's first service was aboard the U.S.S. *Columbia* during the Panama Expedition in 1906. Further assignments took him on 6 other ships until 1925, when he served as executive officer of the U.S.S. *Utah*. His first command came the following year aboard the U.S.S. *Vega*. Kidd was named commanding officer of the *Arizona* in 1936. When the *Arizona* was attacked, Kidd, as commander, Battleship Div. I, went to the bridge, taking charge until the ship was hit and sunk. He and much of his crew were killed. He was posthumously awarded the Congressional Medal of Honor; a destroyer, the U.S.S. *Kidd,* and the Navy's Rear Admiral Isaac C. Kidd Computer Ctr. in BRATENAHL† were named in his honor.

In 1911 Kidd married Inez Nellie Gillmore of LAKEWOOD.† They had 2 children, Nereide and Isaac.

**KILBANE, JOHN PATRICK "JOHNNY"** (18 Apr. 1889–31 May 1957), world featherweight boxing champion (1912–23) was born in Cleveland to John and Mary (Gallagher) Kilbane. He trained with Jimmy Dunn and had his first fight in 1907, a 3-round decision, which paid him $1.50 and carfare. Kilbane fought featherweight champion Abe Attell on 22 Feb. 1912, winning a 20-round decision. The 5' 5" 120 lb. champion retained the crown 11 years, the longest reign in featherweight-division history.

After retaining his title with a disputed 20-round draw with Johnny Dundee on 29 Apr. 1913, Kilbane fought mostly no-decision contests. During World War I, he was a physical training instructor at Camp Sherman and Camp Gordon, GA. On 17 Sept. 1921 at Cleveland's LEAGUE PARK,† he knocked out contender Danny Frush in the 7th round, for which a crowd of 17,235 paid a record $97,239. Kilbane received $60,000. He did not box again until 1923, when he lost the title to Eugene Criqui in 6 rounds, ending his career 142–4. Although Kilbane received $75,000 for his last fight, he was almost broke by the time of the Depression. He worked for CLEVELAND PUBLIC SCHOOLS† as a physical education instructor in 1934–35, but by the 1940s served in the Ohio senate and house of representatives. In 1951 he was elected clerk of the municipal court, a post he held at his death. He married Irene McDonald in 1910 and had 2 daughters, Helen,

who died at age 6, and Mary. Kilbane died in Cleveland and was buried in Calvary Cemetery.

**KILGORE, JAMES C.** (2 May 1928–16 Dec. 1988) was an English professor at CUYAHOGA COMMUNITY COLLEGE† who gained wide recognition as an African American poet. He was born in Jackson Parish, LA, the son of James W. and Ruth (Armstrong) Kilgore. He received his bachelor's degree in 1952 from Wiley College in Marshall, TX. Kilgore earned advanced degrees at the Univ. of Missouri and Columbia Pacific Univ., and saw overseas duty with the U.S. Army. Inspired to write poetry by the civil-rights movement, he cited LANGSTON HUGHES and Gwendolyn Brooks as 2 of his models and published his first poem in 1962. Coming to Cleveland, he joined the CCC English Dept. in 1966 and continued to publish poems in such periodicals as *Phylon* and *Negro Digest*. Eventually 9 volumes of poetry were issued under his own name, including *A Time of Black Devotion, A Black Bicentennial,* and *Let It Pass*. Kilgore won an Ohio Arts Council Award in 1978, and in 1982 he was named Ohio Poet of the Year by the Ohio Poetry Assn. Always eager to encourage other writers, he founded the Cuyahoga Writers Conference in 1974 and helped organize an Urban Writers Workshop Series in Cleveland. In a voice likened to that of actor James Earl Jones, the 6' 5" Kilgore gave readings of his work in venues ranging from the CLEVELAND MUSEUM OF ART† to the Mansfield Reformatory. Not long after his retirement from full-time teaching in 1986, he died in a fire that destroyed his BEACHWOOD† home and also took the lives of his daughter and grandson. He was survived by his wife, Alberta, and 2 sons.

**KING, WOODS** (31 Jan. 1900–15 Jan. 1947), real estate dealer, patron of the mounted police, and World War II hero promoted to brigadier general in 1945, was born in Cleveland to Ralph and Fannie T. King. He enlisted in the military while a student at Williams College. After World War I, King's interest in horses led him to volunteer in developing the Cleveland Div. of Mounted Police. As a member of TROOP A,† 107th Ohio Cavalry, King was awarded a gold badge as a special city officer when, on Memorial Day, 1926, when all the police horses were ill, King and his brother lent the department 22 mounts from their private stables for the parade.

Resuming active duty in 1940, King commanded the 107th Cavalry Regiment, a reconnaissance regiment. In 1944 King was sent to China to advise and train native troops. On 23 Feb. 1946, he received the Distinguished Service Medal for his work retraining, reorganizing, and inspiring Chinese troops in South China. He was twice awarded the Legion of

Merit for his liaison work in the Chinese Theater. In 1946 King was discharged because of a heart ailment he contracted during his strenuous service in China. In private life, King was vice-president and treasurer of the Ventura Corp., a real estate firm. He was also on the board of officers of the Realty Investment Co. He was in many Cleveland sporting circles. King was survived by his wife, Louise Baldwin, and 3 children: Woods, Jr., Arthur, and Sally.

**KINGSBURY, JAMES** (29 Dec. 1757–12 Dec. 1847), son of Absalom and Martha (Smith) Kingsbury was, at 29, the first settler in the WESTERN RESERVE.† He came to Conneaut, OH, from Alsted, NH, with his wife, Eunice Waldo Kingsbury, and 3 children. In 1797 he and his family accompanied the surveyors of the CONNECTICUT LAND CO.† and relocated in Cleveland in a log cabin near the CUYAHOGA RIVER.† Later they moved to higher ground away from the swamps, to a ridge southeast of Cleveland (Woodhill Rd.), beginning the Newburgh settlement. The Kingsburys became the parents of the first white child born in the Western Reserve. The birth occurred when supplies were dwindling, game was absent, and Kingsbury had traveled east for supplies and was away on his return trip. The child survived only a short while after Mrs. Kingsbury became ill and the cow died, cutting off the baby's supply of milk. Kingsbury's appointment as judge by Gen. St. Clair in 1800 was part of the formation of the first governmental agency in the Reserve. Kingsbury was elected in 1803 to serve in various positions for the township: trustee, overseer of the poor, lister, and supervisor of the highways. In 1805 he was elected a member of the legislature of the State of Ohio.

The Kingsburys had 12 children: Amos, Almon, Abigail, Nancy, Elmina, Calista, Diana, Albert, James, Alfred, Sylvester, and Nabby. The child who starved never received a name. Kingsbury died in his Newburgh home five days after his wife, and was buried in Erie St. Cemetery.

**KINZER, GERTRUDE C.** (19 Jan. 1878–22 Dec. 1946), a pioneer in the field of industrial nursing, was born in Tiffin, OH, the daughter of Gottlieb and Matilda Thol Kinzer. One of the first to graduate from the HURON RD. HOSPITAL† School of Nursing, Kinzer completed the program in 1907 and launched her career in public nursing, which included service with the VISITING NURSE ASSN. OF CLEVELAND† and the CLEVELAND PUBLIC SCHOOLS.† During World War I, Kinzer served with the American Red Cross, and when she returned in 1919 she was among the first to be employed as an industrial nurse. At that time, compa-

nies were hiring medical personnel as a cost-containment measure with the advent of workman's compensation.

As an industrial nurse (probably at National Carbon) Kinzer assisted the company physician in treating accident victims and carried out his standing orders when he was not there. With the doctor often employed part time, the industrial nurse was the company's only full-time health care giver, providing first aid and referring individual employees to appropriate agencies for their health problems. As such, she was isolated from other members of her profession, and to rectify this Kinzer organized the Industrial Nurses Club in the early 1920s to provide a meeting place for the exchange ideas about this new field. By 1936 she had left industrial nursing to specialize in private duty cases.

Kinzer, who was unmarried, resided in EAST CLEVELAND,† where she died. Her body was cremated.—M.S.

**KIRBY, JOSIAH** (16 May 1883–4 Feb. 1964), controversial businessman, was born in Wyoming, OH, came to Cleveland in 1911 following a business failure, and formed Cleveland Discount Co., a $10 million mortgage company, which by 1921 was the largest company of its kind in the U.S., with capital of $37 million. But Kirby's company was taken over by receivers in 1923 with huge losses. Kirby also headed the CLEVELAND YACHT CLUB† (1918–20), taking over when the club was in receivership, yet constructing new buildings and making improvements. However, when Kirby's finances collapsed the club went into bankruptcy. Following several trials during the mid–1920s, in which he was acquitted or released by failure of juries to agree, Kirby was sentenced to prison, convicted of using the mails to defraud and of jury tampering. Kirby was released in 1932, returned to Cleveland, but by 1940 was living in New York, indicted by a federal grand jury on 14 counts, including conspiracy, mail fraud, and market rigging. He was permanently enjoined from selling securities in 1949, served 10 months in prison, and returned to Cleveland upon his release. In 1962 the Securities & Exchange Commission charged Kirby had been selling and buying stocks since 1954, and he was placed on 5 years' probation. Little is recorded about Kirby's family life other than in the 1962 trial he lived with his second wife, Ruth, after "tragedy had deprived him of his [first] wife and all but one of his children."

**KIRTLAND, JARED POTTER** (10 Nov. 1793–10 Dec. 1877), naturalist, physician, and a founder of the CLEVELAND ACADEMY OF NATURAL SCIENCES† (forerunner of the CLEVELAND MU-

SEUM OF NATURAL HISTORY†) and the Western Reserve Univ. School of Medicine, was born in Connecticut, the son of Turhand and Polly (Potter) Kirtland. In 1815 he graduated from Yale Univ.'s medical department and practiced medicine in Durham, CT, before coming to Poland, OH, in 1823. Kirtland was elected to the Ohio House of Representatives in 1828, serving 6 years, chairing the Penitentiary Committee, advocating prison reform, and becoming known as the "Father of the New Penitentiary." In 1837 he became professor of the theory of medicine at the Medical College of Ohio and moved to Cleveland. In 1840–41 he taught at Willoughby Medical School. In 1844, along with JOHN DELAMATER, HORACE ACKLEY, and JOHN CASSELS, he founded Cleveland Medical College—the medical department of Western Reserve College. As professor, he taught medicine there from 1844 until his retirement in 1864. In 1851 Kirtland served on a committee to secure safe drinking water for Cleveland. Kirtland was one of America's leading naturalists, with a great interest in horticulture and sea shells. He published numerous natural history articles, was elected to the American Philosophical Society, and was a founder and president of the Kirtland Society of Natural History and the Cleveland Academy of Natural Science. After 1843 he lived in Rockport (LAKEWOOD†). Kirtland married twice, first to Caroline Atwater in 1815, then to Hannah Taucey in 1825. He had three children: Mary E., Carolyn A., and Jared P., Jr.

Kirtland and Morse Family Papers, WRHS.

**KLAIMAN, RALPH** (6 Dec. 1913–29 May 1993) was the founder of Bilt-Rite Fabrics and an avowed Socialist and civic activist.

Born in Cleveland to Manuel and Yetta (Bogen) Klaiman, Ralph graduated from Glenville High School in 1929. His first job was servicing penny peanut machines, followed by a number of odd jobs. During World War II Klaiman worked for Eaton Axle in production of military parts.

After the war Klaiman went to work in his father's business, Built-Rite Upholstery at Euclid Ave. and Noble Rd. In the 1960s Klaiman opened his own business, Bilt-Rite Fabrics, at the same location. He created a new business by being the first in the area to develop the idea of selling fabrics for a variety of uses in interior design (instead of just upholstery) at discount prices. Bilt-Rite's success made Klaiman wealthy. In 1985 Klaiman sold the business to his daughter, Patricia. It is now located on Northfield Rd.

Klaiman and his wife, Lillian, belonged to the WORKMAN'S CIRCLE,† a secular Jewish fraternal organization which included Socialists in its membership. The Klaiman's published the Workman's Circle Newsletter which had Socialist leanings.

Klaiman donated much time and money to the community. He volunteered many hours visiting Alzheimer's patients at Menorah Park and volunteered for Cleveland Hts. Meals on Wheels and the Cleveland Hts. Hunger Center.

Klaiman married Lillian Revitch on 8 October 1935. They had three children: Kenneth, Conrad, and Patricia. After Lillian's death, he married Virginia Chambers in 1991. Klaiman is buried in Workman's Circle Cemetery in PARMA.†—T.B.

**KLEMENTOWICZ, BRONIS J.** (22 Oct. 1915–7 April 1993) was a councilman, utilities director, and law director who worked under mayors Lausche, Celebrezze, and Locher. Influential in the Polish-American community, Klementowicz, during his political prime, was one of the powers at CLEVELAND CITY HALL.†

Born and raised in Cleveland's Warszawa (see SLAVIC VILLAGE†), Klementowicz attended St. Stanislaus Elementary School and graduated from South High School in 1934. He received his A.B. degree from Western Reserve Univ. in 1938. He then worked for the U.S. Department of Commerce and served in the U.S. Navy from 1943–46. In 1950 he received his LL.B. from the WRU Law School and passed the Ohio Bar.

In 1948 Klementowicz was elected to the first of six terms as councilman for Ward 14 on the southeast side, two terms of which he served as Democratic majority floor leader. In 1948 he staged the first filibuster in council history when his ward was denied a streetcar turnaround.

In 1958 Mayor Anthony Celebrezze appointed Klementowicz as utilities director. Klementowicz conceived the city's "no sewers, no water" policy, which prohibited water tappings by communities lacking adequate sewage, and directed construction on the Lake Erie water crib. In 1959 he successfully led administration forces against the proposed county charter. From 1962–67 he was law director under Mayor Ralph Locher, when he was appointed an asst. state attorney general supervising legal acquisitions in Northeast Ohio. In 1967 Klementowicz retired from politics, returning to his law practice.

Klementowicz married Dorothy Seamans in 1941. They had no children. He is buried in Harvard Grove Cemetery.—T.B.

**KLONOWSKI, STANLEY J.** (29 May 1883–3 Feb. 1973), prominent businessman and banker, was born in Poland, graduated from the Univ. of Poland at Warsaw, and was fluent in Russian, French, and

English as well as Polish. After working as a postal clerk, telegraph operator, and serving in the Russian army, he came to the U.S. in 1904, working in several cities before settling in Cleveland in 1912. Klonowski worked for Polish businessman MICHAEL KNIOLA before opening his own private bank and foreign exchange, selling real estate, insurance, and steamship tickets as well. Klonowski incorporated in 1920 as Klonowski Savings Bank; the institution was reorganized in 1921 as the Bank of Cleveland, located on Broadway. Klonowski was bank president until 1957, then becoming chairman of the board.

Klonowski made headlines in 1931 when he wrote to Pres. Herbert Hoover suggesting the government create an agency separate from the Federal Reserve to provide credit for banks and businesses on the brink of collapse during the Depression. When Hoover later announced a $500 million credit plan for banks, the *PLAIN DEALER†* hailed Klonowski as father of the plan, but Klonowski wisely refused the credit. In 1933 Klonowski used $280,000 of his own money to pay his depositors and creditors all the money his bank owed them, rather than pay a percentage. Klonowski served on the board of the CLEVELAND PUBLIC LIBRARY† for 25 years. He was active in Polish and Catholic affairs, serving CATHOLIC CHARITIES CORP.† and helping establish MARYMOUNT HOSPITAL.† In 1912 he married Stella Akuszewski; they had five children: Eva, Joseph, Leonard, Bernard, and Stanley, Jr. Klonowski died in Cleveland and was buried in Calvary Cemetery.

**KLUMPH, ARCHIBALD (ARCH) C.** (6 June 1869–3 June 1951), successful businessman, musician, and pioneer in the Rotary Club movement, contributed to the economic and cultural life of the city. Arch was born in Conneautville, PA, the son of Mortimer and Emma Cooper Klumph. Coming to Cleveland as a youth, he went to work for a small lumber company as a boy of 14. The company was the nucleus of the Cuyahoga Lumber Co. at 1848 Carter Rd., where Klumph served as president beginning in 1898; he became sole owner of the firm in 1912. Klumph organized the Security Savings & Loan Co. in 1916 and served as president for 35 years.

An expert flutist, Klumph was a member of the PHILHARMONIC ORCHESTRA.† He helped organize and manage the Cleveland Symphony Orchestra, in which he played flute. Klumph was one of the founders of the ROTARY CLUB OF CLEVELAND† in December 1910 and was elected president of Rotary International in 1916. He conceived the idea of a Rotary Club Foundation and convinced Rotarians to begin an endowment during World War I. By 21 Oct. 1992, when Rotary officials dedicated a granite monument to Klumph in Cleveland's lakefront park, rotary clubs had raised $500 million to provide scholarships, food, and medicine for the needy, began a global program to inoculate children against polio as part of their worldwide program.

Klumph, a Shaker Hts. resident, married Eva M. Weideman of Cleveland 23 July 1898 and they had 2 daughters, Mrs. Mary Watson and Mrs. Kathryn McGuire. He died in Cleveland and was buried in Lake View Cemetery.—M.S.

**KLUNDER, BRUCE W.** (12 July 1937–7 April 1964) was a martyr in the campaign to desegregate the Cleveland public schools. Born in Greeley, CO, son of Everett and Beatrice Klunder, he moved with his family to Oregon where he was educated. Klunder earned his bachelor's degree from Oregon State Univ. (1958) and there met his future wife, Joanne Lehman. The couple wed 22 Dec. 1956, and had two children, Janice and Douglas.

Klunder and his wife moved to New Haven, CT, where he enrolled in the Yale Divinity School. He graduated with a B.D. in 1961. In Sept. 1961 Klunder came to Cleveland as executive director of the Student Christian Union of the YMCA. He was ordained to the Presbyterian presbyterate in Cleveland at the Church of the Covenant on 4 March 1962. In April 1962 Klunder was a founding member of the Cleveland area CORE (Congress for Racial Equality).

Klunder believed his calling demanded social activism and was soon a leader in the civil-rights movement. He frequently did picket duty, demonstrating for fair housing, and against segregated public facilities and discrimination in hiring.

When the Cleveland City School District decided to build new schools which would have reinforced the pattern of segregated neighborhood enrollment, Klunder took the lead in attempting to stop construction. On 7 April 1964, he and four other protesters gathered at the construction site for Stephen E. Howe Elementary School on Lakeview Rd. He lay down behind a bulldozer while four other pickets blocked its forward path. The operator, seeking to avoid the protesters in front of him, unknowingly backed over Klunder, instantly killing him. His death was ruled an accident.

The next day 150 people marched in silent memorial in front of the Board of Education Building downtown. Funeral services were held at the Church of the Covenant with Eugene Carson Blake, head of the United Presbyterian Church, delivering the eulogy, and 1,500 attending.

Klunder's ashes were interred in the columbarium of the CHURCH OF THE COVENANT.†—J.T.

Bruce Klunder Papers, WRHS.

**KNAPP, HAROLD JENNINGS** (15 July 1887–25 Jan. 1955), public health advocate and Cleveland health commissioner, was born in Elyria, the son of William Pitcher and Mary Ann (Churchill) Knapp. Educated at Elyria public schools, Knapp received an A.M. degree from Western Reserve Univ. in 1911 and an M.D. from its Medical School in 1919. After working briefly for the U.S. Public Health Service, he began his long career in Cleveland's Department of Health, becoming health commissioner in 1930. During his tenure, death rates for many types of life-menacing diseases reached new lows in the city. In collaboration with the CLEVELAND DENTAL SOCIETY,† the Cleveland Welfare Federation, and the Board of Education, Knapp established free dental clinics for all indigent grade school children as well as immunization programs for diphtheria, smallpox, whooping cough, and tetanus. He organized the Newton D. Baker Health Center in 1949, the first of five such projects and instituted a city chest X-ray survey and a blood testing project which attracted national interest. An active proponent of community water fluoridation, the health commissioner initiated legislation to permit the addition of fluoride to city water, which began in 1956. Through his efforts, Cleveland had one of the best health records in the nation.

Knapp married Hannah Gray 24 July 1913, and they had a daughter, Helen Maurine. A resident of Cleveland, he died in the city and was buried at Lakewood Park Cemetery.—M.S.

**KNIGHT, THOMAS A.** (24 Feb. 1876–17 June 1946) was a journalist, real estate dealer, and author. He was born in Toronto, Canada, where his parents had repaired following the Great Chicago Fire, but brought to Cleveland by them during his first year. At age 12 he became a newsboy for the *CLEVELAND LEADER,†* where he worked his way up to star reporter and covered the political campaigns of Wm. McKinley. During this period he wrote 2 short works, *Beautiful Lakewood* and *Country Estates of Cleveland Men*. He resigned from the *Leader* in 1914 to devote his time to writing, publishing *Country Estates of the Blue Grass* and *The Kentucky Horse*. In 1912 Knight entered the field of industrial real estate in Cleveland under the appellation of "Tom Knight, the Factory Man." He continued his interest in history, writing *The Strange Disappearance of William Morgan* and *Tippecanoe*. Knight was also active as a field secretary of the WESTERN RESERVE HIS-

TORICAL SOC.† and long-time secretary of the EARLY SETTLERS ASSN. OF THE WESTERN RESERVE.† Working with the latter group, he was instrumental in preserving the Erie St. Cemetery from downtown encroachment and historic cannon on PUBLIC SQ.† from being melted as scrap metal during World War II. A resident of BRECKS-VILLE,† Knight served the suburb as councilman and published a newspaper called the *West County Advocate*. He died a year after his wife, the former Leora Squire, whom he had married in 1896. They were survived by 2 married daughters, Edith Dean and Dorothy Sykes.—J.V.

**KNIOLA, MICHAEL P.** (16 Sept. 1859–17 Sept. 1944), prominent businessman in Cleveland's Polish community, was born in Samostrzel, Poland, to Peter and Anna Nowakowski Kniola. He immigrated to Spotswood, NJ, in 1873 and moved to Cleveland in 1880, working at Cleveland Rolling Mill Co. He continued his education at Broadway Night School, and eventually became a mill foreman. In 1886 Kniola opened a grocery store and, using the store as a base, provided other services to the Polish community: advancing credit, renting lodgings, selling insurance and real estate, and, working as a labor broker, finding jobs for immigrants. He sold money orders and arranged steamship passages, organizing Kniola Travel Bureau in 1890, which was so successful by 1900 that he sold his grocery and concentrated on the travel business until the late 1920s, when he turned it over to his son, Raymond.

Kniola helped organize Cleveland's first Polish newspaper, *Polonia w Ameryce*, in 1892. In 1893 he began the Polish Republican Club; he also was a director of the Polish-American Chamber of Commerce, an administrator of probate court, and ran for city council in 1909. Kniola helped organize the Knights of St. Casimir, and was a director of both the Polish Alliance of America and the Polish Roman Catholic Union of the U.S. He was a purchaser, incorporator, and president of Polish Falcon Hall and was director and treasurer of Polish Falcon Nest 141 (see SOKOL POLSKI†). Kniola was also an organizer and trustee of ST. STANISLAUS CHURCH.† In 1880 he married Mary Skarupski and they had 7 children: Caroline, Benjamin, John B., Raymond J., Celia, Casimer, and Joseph M. Kniola died in Cleveland and was buried in St. Joseph's Cemetery.

Coulter, Charles W. *The Poles of Cleveland* (1919).
Kniola Travel Bureau Records, WRHS.

**KNOWLTON, DONALD SNOW** (22 Nov. 1892–27 July 1976) attained success in his field of public relations and his avocation as a freelance writer. Born in Cleveland, he was the son of Fanny Snow Knowlton (13 June 1859–11 Nov. 1926), a distinguished local composer and one of the founders of the CLEVELAND MUSIC SCHOOL SETTLEMENT.† Educated at Lincoln High School and Western Reserve Univ., Donald Knowlton went into advertising and became advertising manager of the Union Trust Co. (see HUNTINGTON NATIONAL BANK†). His job included managing radio station WJAX during the period when it was operated by the bank. He authored the book *These Bankers* (1925) and articles for such periodicals as *Atlantic Monthly, American Mercury,* and *Saturday Evening Post.* Drawing upon his experience as banjoist in a jazz band, he wrote one of the first serious discussions of jazz as an American art form in a 1926 article in *Harper's,* "What is Jazz?". After the closing of the Union Trust during the Depression, Knowlton teamed with John W. Hill to form the public relations firm of Hill & Knowlton, where he remained until his retirement in 1962. A member of the HERMIT CLUB,† ROWFANT CLUB,† and CITY CLUB,† Knowlton frequently collaborated with JOSEPH NEWMAN and CARL D. FRIEBOLIN in the latter organization's annual ANVIL REVUE.† He also wrote mystery stories for *Ellery Queen's Mystery Magazine.* The privately printed *Brick House Stories* (1936), containing recollections of his mother's home in BRECKSVILLE,† was written for his daughter, Patricia Stange, who became a reporter for *Life* magazine and the *CLEVELAND PRESS.†* Knowlton died 4 years after the death of his wife, Beatrice.—J.V.

**KOBRAK, HERBERT L.** (16 Dec. 1890–22 July 1943), became involved in Cleveland's extensive foreign-language publishing field between the 2 world wars, until financial reverses led to his murder of the publisher of the *PLAIN DEALER.†* He was born and educated in Hungary, emigrating to the U.S. in 1908. After various newspaper experience in other cities, notably with the *Chicago Tribune,* he came to Cleveland in 1917 and soon became general manager of the Hungarian-language daily, *SZABADSAG.†* Apparently prosperous at first, he married Erna Clara Botschen of Chicago in 1919, resided on Clifton Blvd., and belonged to such organizations as the Cleveland Chamber of Commerce, the CITY CLUB,† and the Northeastern Ohio Gun and Country Club. When *Szabadsag* became linked with the German-language *WAECHTER UND ANZEIGER†* in 1928, Kobrak became general manager of the resultant Consolidated Press & Printing Co. Ten years later Consolidated went bankrupt, however, and Kobrak lost not only his job but a claimed investment of $40,000.

His wife died in 1940, and he became obsessed with starting a new publishing venture, importuning not only his old associates for funds but the publisher of the *Plain Dealer,* John S. McCarrens, as well. Making an appointment to see McCarrens on 22 July, 1943, Kobrak entered the publisher's office and, during the course of his interview, fatally shot McCarrens before committing suicide with the same weapon.—J.V.

**KOHANYI, TIHAMER** (1863–10 March 1913), founder of *SZABADSAG†* (Liberty), the largest Hungarian daily newspaper in the U.S., was born in Saros, Hungary, and came to America at age 27 after an unsuccessful attempt to practice law in Hungary. Kohanyi had jobs as a coal shoveler, traveling book salesman, janitor, and clerk before settling in Cleveland in 1891, immediately beginning organizing the Hungarian community, starting with the Cleveland Hungarian Young Mens' & Ladies' Society, which presented the first Hungarian drama presentation in Cleveland. Kohanyi founded *Szabadsag* in Nov. 1891, securing $600 contributions from 2 Hungarian industrialists, Joseph Black and THEODOR KUNDTZ; and $15 pledges from 117 countrymen, although, afraid the effort would fail, only 50 pledges were paid. Kohanyi managed, edited, and typeset the paper, and wrote many of the articles. *Szabadsag* became an important influence for Hungarian-Americans, offering them news from their native land as well as useful information, such as how to address letters and function in American society. *Szabadsag* promoted projects such as the KOSSUTH MONUMENT† in Cleveland in 1902 and the Washington Monument in 1906 in Budapest. Despite his generosity to immigrants through his paper, Kohanyi sustained himself on a meager income, after 20 years writing that if one is truly cursed by fate, he will become a Hungarian journalist. Kohanyi married Rose Molnar on 19 May 1896. He helped found the Catholic Hungarian Insurance Assn. in 1897 and the American Hungarian Fund in 1906. Kohanyi was buried in St. Joseph's Cemetery.

**KOHLER, FREDERICK** (2 May 1864–30 Jan. 1934), police chief, Cuyahoga County commissioner, mayor of Cleveland, and sheriff, was born in Cleveland to Christian and Fredericka Kohler. He left school in the 6th grade to help his father in Kohler Stone Works. After his father's death, the business failed, and Kohler worked several laboring jobs. In 1887 he was appointed superintendent of WOODLAND CEMETERY. He married Josephine (Josie) Modroch in 1888. The couple had no children.

Kohler joined the police force in 1889, rose rapidly, became a captain in 1900, and in 1903 was appointed chief of police by Mayor TOM L. JOHNSON. Kohler was a strict disciplinarian, demanding a neat appearance and full day's work from all policemen. He became involved in a scandal growing out of a divorce suit brought by a traveling salesman against his wife, and in Feb. 1913 the Civil Service Commission removed him as police chief on charges of neglect of duty and gross immorality. Kohler was elected county commissioner as a Republican in 1918, serving 2 terms. He was mayor in 1922–24, emphasizing economy in city government, cutting payrolls and city services, and persuading private agencies to care for families on relief. In 1924 Kohler was elected sheriff. He was accused of underfeeding the prisoners in jail, found at fault by the legal board of jail governors, and ordered to improve prison meals and return any unused money to the county. He left office in 1926. He died in Cleveland.

**KOKLOWSKY, ALBERT, S. T.** (23 Feb. 1916–1 Apr. 1983), called "the slum priest," advocated for AFRICAN AMERICANS† in the community and in the diocese, as pastor of OUR LADY OF FATIMA CHURCH† (1963–69) during the HOUGH RIOTS.† Koklowsky was born in Newark, NJ, to Kasper and Mary Comski Bajol. He attended parochial schools, St. Joseph Minor Seminary in Alabama (1929) and the Catholic Univ. of America (1930s), interrupting his studies for mission work in Pensacola, FL (1937). In Washington, DC, Koklowsky was ordained 18 May 1944 into the Order of the Missionary Servants of the Most Holy Trinity. His first charge was Holy Rosary Parish, Newark, NJ (1944). From 1946–53 the priest did missionary work among rural residents around Maysville, NC, and served as auxiliary military chaplain to a nearby U.S. Marine base, then continued mission work in Philadelphia, MI (1953–58), and Puerto Rico. While in HOUGH,† Fr. Koklowsky purchased and rehabilitated homes for needy residents. The activist fasted for 7 days in 1967, supporting striking nonprofessional employees of ST. LUKE'S HOSPITAL MEDICAL CENTER.† Koklowsky also founded the ecumenical HOPE, Inc. to acquire low-income housing.

After his tenure at Our Lady of Fatima, Koklowsky was assigned to Sacred Heart Chapel, Lorain, OH, primarily an Hispanic parish. He left in 1972, serving in Puerto Rico, Mexico, and at Our Lady of Victory Parish, East Los Angeles, CA (1981). Koklowsky died in Orange, CA.

**KOLASZEWSKI, ANTON FRANCIS** (5 Sept. 1851–2 Dec. 1910), dynamic priest, was born in Russian Poland to John and Catherine Gergens Kolaszewski. His family emigrated to America, and

Kolaszewski studied for the priesthood at Franciscan College at Teutopolis, IL, and St. Mary Seminary in Cleveland, being ordained in 1883 and becoming pastor of ST. STANISLAUS CHURCH.† His congregation grew as Polish immigrants arrived seeking steel mill jobs. With their religion alone familiar in the new land, Kolaszewski was not only their pastor but also their community leader. As his congregation grew, Kolaszewski envisioned a soaring brick Gothic church and, counting on the generosity of his poorly paid parishioners, let out contracts and began the work in 1886. When completed in 1891, St. Stanislaus Church cost $250,000. Earlier Kolaszewski established Sacred Heart of Jesus church for Poles living in the southern part of the district. By 1889 he built a church for that congregation.

St. Stanislaus parish developed factions. Kolaszewski's appraisal of his congregation's financial resources proved false, and Kolaszewski had unwisely concealed both the church cost and resulting debt from diocesan authorities. Bp. IGNATIUS HORSTMANN demanded Kolaszewski's resignation in 1892. Kolaszewski went to Syracuse, NY, beginning an association with a Polish nationalistic movement of dissident Roman Catholics. In 1894 Kolaszewski returned to Cleveland. Popular with many former parishioners, a number joined IMMACULATE HEART OF MARY,† which Kolaszewski organized, emphasizing both the congregation's orthodoxy yet its independence from diocesan control. Kolaszewski refused to concede and was excommunicated. He reconciled with the church in 1908 but resigned the pastorate.

**KOLLER, JOHN JOSEPH** (2 July 1863–6 Oct. 1923), a noted physician and surgeon of Cleveland, was born in Funfkirchen (Pecs), Hungary, the son of Adolph and Theresa (Mandell or Mautal) Koller. He attended the High School and the Univ. at Budapest. In 1887 he graduated from the Univ. of Vienna with an M.D. Koller served 1 year as a lt. in the Medical Corps of the Austrian Army while a resident of Vienna. He opened his medical practice in that city, working there until 1890, when he came to Baltimore, MD, at the urging of his friend, Dr. Howard Kelly. After a short stay in Baltimore, Koller moved to Cleveland.

Koller practiced medicine for over 30 years in the Broadway neighborhood and was affiliated with St. Alexis Hospital for many years. He was known as an authority on eye, ear, nose, and throat problems, rheumatism, and cataract surgery; his highly successful work in these areas attracted patients from all parts of the U.S. Koller also invented and patented several surgical devices.

Koller was married 3 times. His first marriage

was to Annie Smith in July 1893. He married Emily Rees in February, 1900 (div. 1914). On 16 June 1917 he married Emma R. Kohler. Koller died in Cleveland and was cremated; his ashes were interred in Lake View Cemetery.—D.R.

**KOLLIN (KOLINSKY), ABRAHAM** (1879–4 Apr. 1968), attorney and community leader, was born in Lithuania to David and Hannah Rose (Wolf) Kolinsky. He came to the U.S. when a boy and studied at Cleveland and Western Reserve Univ. law schools. Admitted to the Ohio Bar in 1902, Kollin practiced law until his retirement in 1959. An ardent Zionist, Kollin was the first local writer to defend political Zionism in the Cleveland Jewish press, arguing that there had to be a territorial basis in a person's belief in Judaism, an argument that put him in direct conflict with the Reform community leaders. He was president of the Cleveland Zionist District during the 1920s. Kollin was a leader of 2 unsuccessful attempts to organize the East European Jewish immigrants' organizations into a single representative body. In 1906 he was a founder of the UNION OF JEWISH ORGANIZATIONS,† and in 1913 helped organize the KEHILLAH,† another umbrella organization. Kollin was a charter member of the American Jewish Committee and was president of the Cleveland Lodge No. 16 of B'NAI B'RITH† in 1910. He was also a member of ANSHE EMETH† congregation. He was a charter member of the Cleveland CITY CLUB.† In June 1917 Kollin was one of 5 men elected in a community-wide vote to represent Cleveland at the first American Jewish Congress, an attempt to create a democratically elected national Jewish organization with representatives from all sectors of the American Jewish community. Kollin died at his sister's home in CLEVELAND HTS.† and was buried in the PARK SYNAGOGUE† Cemetery.

**KOUDELKA, JOSEPH MARY** (8 Dec. 1852–24 June 1921), first auxiliary bishop of Cleveland, was born in Chilstova (Bohemia), to Markus and Anna Jazousshek Koudelka. He began his studies at the Imperial College in Klattan, Bohemia. In 1869 his family immigrated to Wisconsin. Koudelka studied for the priesthood at Mt. Calvary and St. Francis Seminary in Milwaukee, transferring in 1874 to St. Mary Seminary in Cleveland. After his ordination as deacon, he became administrator of St. Procop Church in Cleveland. He was ordained to the priesthood in 1875, and became pastor of St. Procop's. Koudelka, in addition to his pastoral duties, published a set of Bohemian readers, a church history, and several prayerbooks. In May 1882 Bp. RICHARD GILMOUR allowed Koudelka to go to St. Louis, MO, to take charge of *Hlas*, an influential

Bohemian publication. In 1883 Koudelka was called back to Cleveland, taking charge of the German parish of St. Mary, which, under Koudelka's direction, became the parish of St. Michael. During his 28-year pastorate, Koudelka established a school and built a Gothic Cathedral–style church, which became a national landmark. Bp. IGNATIUS HORSTMANN, Gilmour's successor, sent Koudelka to Europe to recruit priests and seminarians to work with the East European immigrants. Koudelka was a diocesan consuler from 1904–10. On 25 Feb. 1908 he was consecrated the first auxiliary bishop of Cleveland. In 1911 Koudelka was named auxiliary bishop of Milwaukee; in 1913 he became the second bishop of Superior in Wisconsin. Koudelka is buried in St. Mary Cemetery in Cleveland.

Houck, George F. *A History of Catholicity in Northern Ohio* (1903).
Hynes, Michael J. *The History of the Diocese of Cleveland* (1953).

**KOVELL, MARGARET N.** (1893–3 Oct. 1992), composer and poet, founded the Lakewood Four Arts Society (1950s), an acting group. Her original works include an operetta, *Tonight is the Night*, presented in the Lakewood Civic Auditorium (1960s). Kovell was born in Austria-Hungary and came to Cleveland in 1905. Interested in music as a child, she studied voice before her marriage to Frank Kovell. The couple lived in LAKEWOOD† and had no children. In 1958 Kovell translated the long Hungarian opera *Janos Vitez* into English, helped shorten it, and recruited performers. It was sung in English for the first time at the WHK† studio on EUCLID AVE.†

Kovell belonged to the WOMEN'S CITY CLUB,† the Lakewood League of Women Voters, and the Cleveland chapter of the Composers, Authors, and Artists of America. She was also a collector of and authority on antiques. Kovell was a member of the St. Luke Catholic Church in Lakewood.

**KRAFT, EDWIN ARTHUR** (1883–15 July 1962), musician and organist-choirmaster of TRINITY CATHEDRAL† for over 50 years, was born in New Haven, CT, to John J. and Marie F. (Kohne) Kraft. He began his musical training early, becoming a church organist in New Haven at 14. Kraft studied at Yale and became the organist at St. Thomas Church (Episcopal) in Brooklyn, NY. He continued studying in Berlin and Paris, returning to become organist-choirmaster of St. Matthew's Church (Episcopal) in Wheeling, WV. In 1907 Kraft was appointed organist-choirmaster of Trinity Cathedral. He played extensively in Cleveland and gave recitals around the country. In addition to playing the organ, he directed the choir of men and boys. In 1914 Kraft left Cleveland to become municipal organist in Atlanta, GA, but he returned to Cleveland and the cathedral the following year. In 1922 he played before an audience of 12,000 at the dedication of the Cleveland Municipal Organ at the PUBLIC AUDITORIUM.†

Kraft participated in founding 2 chapters of the American Guild of Organists, in Cleveland (1909) and Atlanta (1914). He transcribed a large number of orchestral and piano works for the organ and composed over 60 choral works. Kraft married Nancy Lovis in Dec. 1909 and had 3 children: Nanetta, Margaret, and Edwin Arthur, Jr. Mrs. Kraft died 1925, and the following year Kraft married Marie Simmelink. Kraft retired from Trinity Cathedral in 1959. He died only minutes after playing one of his own organ transcriptions informally before a group of friends and former students. Kraft was cremated and interred in the Mausoleum of Knollwood Cemetery.

Edwin A. Kraft Papers, WRHS.

**KUBINYI, KALMAN** (29 June 1906–3 Sept. 1973) excelled in 2 artistic fields, moving from a reputation as Cleveland's preeminent printmaker to launch, in conjunction with his artist wife, Doris Hall (b. 5 Feb. 1907), a second career in enameling. A product of the Hungarian neighborhood around Buckeye Rd., Kubinyi graduated from South High School and the Cleveland School of Art (see CLEVELAND INSTITUTE OF ART†). In the early 1930s he taught printmaking at CSA, the JOHN HUNTINGTON POLYTECHNIC INSTITUTE,† and the CLEVELAND MUSEUM OF ART.† As founder of the Cleveland Print Makers Club (1930), he instituted the Print-a-Month Club to raise money for Depression-struck artists by selling limited-edition prints to subscribers. Together with Doris Hall, whom he married in 1933, Kubinyi also became involved in liberal politics, joining the COMMUNIST PARTY† and the American Artists' Congress. In 1935 Kubinyi joined the WPA Federal Art Project in Cleveland as Print Supervisor, becoming the project's fourth and last general supervisor in 1939. According to the historian of the local FAP, his tenure was "the most productive and memorable in project annals." During World War II, while employed as a war worker at S. K. WELLMAN CO.,† Kubinyi installed a kiln in the basement of their LAKEWOOD† home on West Clifton Blvd. Doris Hall used it to experiment with enamels, winning a 1st prize in the 1948 MAY SHOW.† Kubinyi joined her in the venture, which prospered after they were

discovered by gift shop owner H. George Caspari. The pair also contributed illustrations to the Labor Calendar sponsored by the CIO in 1946. Moving from Cleveland in 1950, they settled in Gloucester, MA, where they became Art Directors for the Bettinger Corp. Kubinyi died in Stockbridge, MA, survived by Hall and 2 children, Moisha Blechman and Laszlo Kubinyi.—J.V.

Dancyger, Ruth. *Kubinyi and Hall: Cleveland's Partners in Art* (1988).

**KUEKES, EDWARD DANIEL** (2 Feb. 1901–13 Jan. 1987) won Cleveland journalism's only unshared Pulitzer Prize for his work as cartoonist for the Cleveland *PLAIN DEALER*.† Ed Kuekes moved with his family from his native Pittsburgh, PA, to BEREA† in 1913. There he graduated from Berea High School before pursuing art studies at the Cleveland School of Art (see CLEVELAND INSTITUTE OF ART†) and the Chicago Academy of Fine Art. In 1922 he married Clare Gray of Berea and began his career at the *Plain Dealer* as understudy for cartoonist JAMES H. DONAHEY. Two weeks after Donahey's death, Kuekes was named editorial cartoonist of the *Plain Dealer,* on 13 June 1949. His Pulitzer Prize came in 1953 for a cartoon which had appeared in the *Plain Dealer* on 9 Nov. 1952. Entitled "Aftermath," it depicted 2 stretcher-bearers carrying a fallen soldier from a Korean battlefield. One informed the other that the victim wasn't old enough to have voted in the recent election. By the time of his retirement on 28 Feb. 1966, Kuekes had produced more than 5,000 cartoons, the originals of which he donated to the Newhouse School of Communications at Syracuse Univ. Several of his etchings had been exhibited at the Cleveland MAY SHOW.† Kuekes also performed publicly as an amateur magician, which gave him his cartoonist's trademark of a magician's rabbit dubbed the "Kernel." Kuekes and his wife, Clara, had 2 sons, Edward and George. They resided in Berea, NORTH OLMSTED,† and ROCKY RIVER.† He died at the Baptist Retirement Home in Oklahoma City, OK. —J.V.

**KULAS, ELROY JOHN** (21 Mar. 1880–13 May 1952), prominent in the steel and railroad industries, founded the Midland Steel Products Co. and was a director of several railroads. He cofounded, with his wife, Fynette Hill Kulas, The KULAS FOUNDATION† and was an active supporter of and contributor to area music interests and higher education. Kulas was also a recognized expert in the field of business mergers.

Born in Cleveland to Frank and Margaret (Hoeffer), Kulas attended public schools, quitting

Central High School in 1898 to work for the B & O Railroad. Around 1901 he joined National Electric Lamp Co. (absorbed by General Electric, 1912) and helped reorganize various divisions. During World War I Kulas helped organize the Cuyahoga Stamping & Machine Co., becoming president and general manager.

Kulas accumulated his wealth in steel. As president of Parish & Bingham Co., 1923, he organized the merger with Detroit Pressed Steel Co. to form Midland Steel, serving as president and director. In 1925 Kulas became president of Otis Steel Co. until it merged with Jones & Laughlin Steel Corp. in 1942. Kulas served J&L as vice-chairman until 1946, and director until 1948.

Kulas was a director of the WHEELING & LAKE ERIE RAILROAD† and the Pittsburgh & West Virginia Railroad.

In 1937 the Kulases established the Kulas Foundation and, in 1938, donated $50,000 to BALDWIN-WALLACE COLLEGE† for construction of the Kulas Musical Arts Building. Kulas was elected a trustee and received an honorary doctorate degree.

The Kulases married on 5 June 1901 and had no children. Kulas, a 32nd Mason, is buried in Lake View Cemetery.—T.B.

**KUNDTZ, THEODOR** (1 July 1852–14 Sept. 1937) was an inventor, manufacturer, financier, philanthropist, and patriarch of the Hungarian community.

Kundtz was born in Metzenseifen, Hungary, to Joseph and Theresia (Kesselbauer) Kundtz. He learned woodworking from his father and after immigrating to Cleveland in 1873, Kundtz found a job with the Whitworth Co., a small cabinet shop at 28 St. Clair Ave. Kundtz and several co-workers purchased the company in 1875 after a fire seriously damaged the business, reorganizing as the Cleveland Cabinet Co. In 1878 Kundtz split from his partners and opened the THEODOR KUNDTZ CO.† at 122 Elm St. in the FLATS.†

Among his early customers was THOMAS WHITE of the White Sewing Machine Co. (see WHITE CONSOLIDATED INDUSTRIES†), for whom Kundtz made what became his chief product, sewing machine cabinets. Kundtz patented 44 inventions, most of which were mechanisms enabling sewing machines to fold up into fine cabinetry of his own design.

Over the years Kundtz employed a significant portion of his home town of Metzenseifen. When his business peaked around 1900, 92% of his 2500 employees were from Hungary. Kundtz helped thousands immigrate to Cleveland, acquire homes, and start their own businesses. He founded the Hungar-

ian Savings and Loan Co. and built Hungaria Hall on Clark Ave. in 1890.

At the turn of the century, Kundtz built a magnificent mansion in LAKEWOOD† overlooking Lake Erie. The Kundtz Castle, as it was called, was torn down in 1961.

Kundtz served on the Mayor's Advisory War Committee during World War I. He was an officer and director of the United Banking and Savings Co., the Forest City Savings and Loan, and the Lorain St. Bank. In 1884 Kundtz married Maria Ballasch of Cleveland and they had ten children: Theodore, Jr., William, Ewald, Leo R., Joseph E., Merie (Mrs. Wm. Tubman), Irene (Mrs. A. C. Weizer), Angela (Mrs. A. T. Hueffed), Dorothy (Mrs. W. J. O'Neil), and Joseph P.

Theodor Kundtz was knighted by Emperor Franz Joseph of Austria-Hungary in 1902. In 1994 the American-Hungarian Foundation posthumously awarded Kundtz the George Washington Medal. He died in Cleveland and was buried in Lakewood Park Cemetery.—C.E.

Eiben, Christopher J. *Tori in Amerika* (1994).

**KURDZIEL, AUGUST JOSEPH "GUS"** (2 Aug. 1902–30 April 1993) was active in Cleveland's Polish-American Community as publisher of the *POLISH DAILY NEWS†* (*Wiadomosci Codzienne*). He was also the youngest person to serve as Cleveland's director of public parks and properties.

Born in Cleveland to Paul and Mary (Dedo) Kurdziel, August attended school in Cleveland, Alliance School in Cambridge Springs, PA, and Adelbert College at Western Reserve Univ.

Kurdziel left WRU in 1921 to become a writer at the *Polish Daily News,* and by 1933, its advertising manager. The *News* was founded by his father as a weekly in 1912, and in 1915 had become Cleveland's only Polish language daily. Kurdziel became general manager and publisher after his father's death in 1940.

Under Kurdziel the *Polish Daily News* was a full-service daily sold in shops and stores. Its largest circulation was in the Broadway–E. 55th St. area, Garfield Hts., Brooklyn, Parma and Lakewood. Kurdziel was forced to close the paper in 1966 due to costs and difficulty in recruiting a bilingual staff.

In 1933 Mayor HARRY DAVIS appointed Kurdziel director of parks and public properties, which included Public Auditorium, Public Hall, Municipal Stadium, and Hopkins Airport. Throughout his career Kurdziel remained active in Cleveland's Polish-American community. He was friend and mentor to many judges and politicians, including Blanche Krupansky and former Cleveland

Mayor Ralph Perk. Kurdziel belonged to the Polish National Alliance and the Cleveland Society of Poles.

Kurdziel married Pauline Lacki in 1924. They had a son, Henry. Kurdziel, a Roman Catholic, is buried in Holy Cross Cemetery.—T.B.

**KUSCH, POLYCARP** (26 Jan. 1911–20 Mar. 1993) was co-winner of the 1955 Nobel Prize for physics. Born in Blankenburg, Germany, to Henrietta (van der Haas) and John Mathias K., Kusch and family emigrated to America in 1912, eventually settling in Cleveland where Kusch was naturalized. In 1926 he graduated from CENTRAL HIGH SCHOOL† and got his first job as a CLEVELAND PUBLIC LIBRARY† page. (Kusch would later credit CPL for his love of books). He received his B.S. (1931) from Case School of Applied Science, his M.S. (1933) and his Ph.D. (1936) from the Univ. of Illinois.

Kusch was an asst. physics instructor at the Univ. of Illinois (1931–36), a research assistant at the Univ. of Minnesota (1936), and a physics instructor at Columbia Univ. (1937).

During World War II Kusch was a development engineer at Westinghouse Electric Corp. (1941–42), on the staff of Columbia's Division of War Research (1942–44), and Bell Telephone Laboratories (1944–46).

In 1946 Kusch returned to Columbia as associate professor, becoming full professor (1949), vice-president and dean of faculties (1969–70), and executive vice-president and provost (1970–71). In 1955 Kusch shared the Nobel Prize with Willis E. Lamb, Jr. Their independent research in determining the magnetic moment of the electron laid the foundation for quantum electrodynamics.

In 1972 Kusch became Eugene McDermott Professor of Physics at the Univ. of Texas in Dallas, regental professor in 1980, and professor emeritus in 1982.

Kusch married Edith Starr McRoberts on 12 Aug. 1935 (dec. 1959). They had three children: Kathryn, Judith, and Sara. He married Betty Jane Pezzoni in 1960. They had two children, Diana and Maria. Kusch died in Dallas, TX.—T.B.

**KUTH, BYRON D.** (ca. 1895–18 July 1965) was a prominent lawyer and owner of one of the country's finest harness racing stables. His horses toured the Grand Circuit and were world record holders, winning numerous trotting championships and taking top purses at leading tracks.

Born in New Paris, OH, to James and Mae (Potts) K., Kuth received his A.B. from Earlham College (IN) in 1917 and his LL.B. from Western Reserve Univ. Law School in 1921.

Kuth began practicing in Cleveland. He was special counsel for the Ohio Delinquent Tax Commission and instrumental in preparing Ohio's 1936 "Gallagher Act," which aided cities facing bankruptcy.

Kuth was solicitor for several Cuyahoga County suburbs and succeeded in voiding millions of dollars in unpaid assessments and penalties imposed on residential lots during wholesale foreclosure actions of the Depression.

During the 1940s Kuth began developing his 60-acre Merrie Meadows farm in Chesterland into a racing establishment with facilities for training stables, a small track, and a breeding stable. At one time Kuth had 22 racing trotters and pacers, with the prize horse being Merrie Annabelle, called the fastest two-year-old trotting filly that ever lived, and valued at $150,000.

Kuth was an official and general counsel of the U.S. Trotting Assn.

Kuth married Florence Porter on 26 Aug. 1919 (div. 1939). They had two children, James and Mrs. Joanne Patterson. On 10 Oct. 1939 Kuth married Vivian Carney. They had no children. Kuth is buried in New Paris.—T.B.

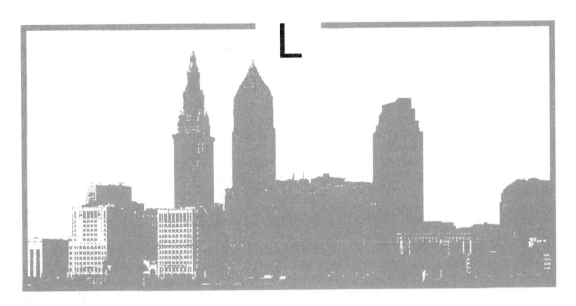

LAJOIE, NAPOLEON "NAP" (5 Sept. 1875–7 Feb. 1959), baseball player with Cleveland (1902–14), was born in Woonsocket, RI, to John and Celina Guerton Lajoie. He worked in cotton mills and completed his education to the 9th grade. Playing semipro baseball in 1895, Lajoie signed with the Fall River team in the New England League. After 80 games his contract was purchased by the Philadelphia Phillies. When the AL was founded in 1901, Lajoie signed with the Athletics, batting .422, the highest average in AL history. In 1902 he joined the Cleveland Blues, and in 1905 was named the playing manager of the team soon called the "Naps" in his honor. He led the team in 1908 to a 2nd-place finish but resigned as manager the next year with the team in 6th place. He played for Cleveland until 1914, when he signed with the Philadelphia Athletics. In 1917 Lajoie managed Toronto, and in 1918, Indianapolis.

Lajoie was voted into the Hall of Fame in 1937. With a lifetime batting average of .339, he had 3,251 hits in his 21-year major league career. Lajoie led the AL in hitting 3 of its first 4 years. On the last day of the 1910 batting season, he had 7 bunt singles and 1 triple in 8 times at bat in a doubleheader against St. Louis. A graceful second baseman, he led the league in fielding 6 times. He served briefly as commissioner of the Ohio & Pennsylvania League before moving to Florida in 1925. Lajoie married Myrtle Everturf in 1907. They had no children. Lajoie is buried in Cedar Hills Cemetery, Daytona Beach, FL.

LAKE, CHARLES H. (2 Jan. 1879–14 Dec. 1958), nationally known in EDUCATION,† was an administrator in the CLEVELAND PUBLIC SCHOOLS† for 21 years and superintendent from 1933–47. During his tenure, the schools initiated a radio station, school safety programs, and classes for the disabled, among other changes. Born in Granville, OH, Lake graduated from Ohio State Univ. (M.A., 1910) and studied at the Univ. of Chicago. At 19 he served in the Spanish-American War. He taught and served as an administrator in schools in Columbus, Alexandria, and Hamilton, OH, before coming to Cleveland in 1916 as principal of EAST TECHNICAL HIGH SCHOOL.† Lake was appointed asst. superintendent of the Cleveland schools (1919), asst. superintendent in charge of senior high schools (1921), and acting superintendent in May 1933. He became superintendent in September that year. The author of textbooks in science and mathematics, Lake advocated creative financing of schools. He kept the Board of Education apprised of both sides of controversial issues. After leaving the superintendency, Lake served as consultant to the Cleveland Board of Education for a year and a half.

In 1910 Lake married Edna Thornton; they lived in SHAKER HTS.† with son Thornton and daughter Elizabeth. Lake served as president of the CITY CLUB OF CLEVELAND† in 1926 and was appointed trustee of Kent State Univ. (OH) in 1936. President of the American Assn. of School Administrators (1946), he was awarded a life membership by that group in 1950. Lake is buried in Lake View Cemetery.—J.M.

LAMBRIGHT, MIDDLETON HUGHER, SR., M.D. (3 Aug. 1865–21 March 1959) was a physician and obstetrician and, at one time, the oldest practicing African American doctor in Ohio.

Born to former slaves in Summerville, SC, Dr. Lambright's surname was adopted by his grandmother from her master so named. (His mother's owner was named Gelzer and his father's Crawford.) Lambright graduated from Claflin Univ. in Orangeburg, SC. Teaching school to earn his way through medical school, he earned his M.D. in 1898 from Meharry Medical College in Nashville, TN.

Dr. Lambright began practicing medicine in Aug. 1898 in Kansas City, MO. He rose to chief of the Obstetrical Division of Kansas City General Hospital No. 2, the only African American in the department at the time and the first in the U.S. to head a hospital department.

In 1923 Dr. Lambright came to Cleveland and continued his practice for over 35 years. His office was at 5424 Woodland Ave. S.E. and for many years he was associated in practice with his physician son, Middleton, Jr. During his 60-year career Lambright delivered over 5,000 babies.

Dr. Lambright was one of the founders in 1939 of FOREST CITY HOSPITAL,† Cleveland's first interracial hospital, and served as a trustee and a member of the executive committee at the time of his death. He belonged to the Cleveland Medical Assn.

Lambright married Bartley Oliver and had 2 children, Middleton, Jr., and Elizabeth (Carr). Dr. Lambright belonged to the Shiloh Baptist Church. He is buried in Lake View Cemetery.—T.B.

**LANDY, RACHEL (RAE) D.** (27 June 1885–5 Mar. 1952) was a nationally recognized military nurse who served around the globe in service to the U.S. Army and the medical profession. Landy was born to Rabbi Jacob Landy and Eva Gross Landy in Lithuania. Her family emigrated to Cleveland in 1890. Landy's father established Hebrew Books, the first Jewish bookstore in Cleveland, and her mother was instrumental in the founding of MENORAH PARK.† Landy attended CENTRAL HIGH SCHOOL.†

Following her 1904 graduation as a member of the first nurses training class from Jewish Women's Hospital (MT. SINAI HOSPITAL†), Landy worked with Dr. GEORGE W. CRILE, SR. as a private duty nurse and surgical nurse. From 1913–15, working under the auspices of the Hadassah organization and the Hebrew Medical System, Landy initiated the first public health and sanitation systems in Palestine. Landy later joined the U.S. Army in 1918, serving in France and Belgium during World War I. During her 37 years of foreign and domestic service, Landy was stationed in occupied Germany (1919–20) and several other overseas locations, including a tour of duty in the Philippines as chief of nurses at the Sternberg Hospital in Manila (1936–38). During WORLD WAR II,† Landy served as chief of nurses of the Second Command at Governor's Island, NY, and achieved the rank of lt. col. Landy

returned to Cleveland in January 1944 to serve as chief of the nursing staff at CRILE HOSPITAL.† She retired in June 1945 but remained active in the recruitment of nurses for army service.

Landy never married. She died in CLEVELAND HTS.† and is buried in Arlington National Cemetery.

**LANGLEY, JOHN W.** (21 Oct. 1841–10 May 1918), chemist, electrical engineer, and teacher, was born in Boston, the son of Samuel and Mary Summer Langley. He received a B.S. degree from Harvard Univ. in 1861, and joined the Univ. of Michigan as a medical student and asst. instructor in chemistry. His brief medical training qualified him as an asst. surgeon in the U.S. Navy during the Civil War. He resigned in 1864 and spent the several years studying in Europe. Langley taught in 1866–67 as asst. professor of chemistry and natural science at Antioch College; resigning for further travel and study. He became asst. professor of physics and mathematics at the U.S. Naval Academy from 1868–70, resigning to begin a career as a consulting chemist and metallurgist for steel manufacturers. Langley's knowledge of steel was greatly enhanced between 1871–75 while he was professor of chemistry and metallurgy at Western Univ. of Pennsylvania at Pittsburgh. He was professor of chemistry at the Univ. of Michigan from 1875–90, when he returned to Pittsburgh as a steel-industry consultant. In 1888–89 he organized the Internatl. Committee for Standards of Analysis of Iron & Steel. Langley moved to Cleveland in 1892 to accept the chairmanship of the new electrical engineering department of Case School of Applied Science, serving as department head until 1905 and as a professor until his retirement in 1907. He directed the planning and equipping of the new department building and developed the curriculum. In 1871 Langley married Martica Irene Carret (d. 1955). Langley died in Ann Arbor, MI, and was buried in Lake View Cemetery.

**LAUSCHE, FRANK JOHN** (14 Nov. 1895–21 Apr. 1990), a politician known for his independence and integrity, was born in Cleveland, the son of Slovenian immigrants Louis and Frances (Milavec) Lausche. He attended the Central Institute Preparatory School 1915–16, completing his high school education by correspondence. Lausche graduated from John Marshall Law School, passing the bar in 1925, and worked at the firm of Locher, Green, and Woods, where Cyrus Locher encouraged him to go into politics. Lausche was appointed and then elected judge in Cleveland Municipal Court, 1932–35, and served in Common Pleas Court 1936–41, where he helped close down the Harvard and Thomas gambling houses in NEWBURGH HTS.† As a

Democrat, Lausche was elected Mayor of Cleveland in 1941, the first mayor of Eastern European descent. During his mayoralty, negotiations for the city to take over the Cleveland Railway system were finalized, and in 1942 the Cleveland Transit System was organized. Concerned about postwar development, Lausche organized the Post War Planning Council in 1944 to coordinate future planning in the areas of labor, health, transportation, and racial toleration. Noted for a clean and frugal government, he served 2 terms as mayor, and then was elected Governor of Ohio, 1945–46, and again 1948–56. Lausche was elected to the U.S. Senate in 1956, defeating GEORGE BENDER, and served there until he lost to John Gilligan in the 1968 Democratic primary. He remained in the Washington, DC, area practicing law. While nominally a Democrat, Lausche operated outside the party throughout his career, often refusing to campaign for other Democratic party candidates.

Lausche married Jane O. Sheal of Cleveland in May 1928; they had no children. After her death in 1981, he remained in Washington until 1990, when he returned to Cleveland and moved into the Slovene Home for the Aged.—M.S.

Frank Lausche Papers, Ohio Historical Society.

**LAWRENCE, WASHINGTON H.** (17 Jan. 1840–23 Nov. 1900) was a pioneer in the manufacture of electricity who organized and served as president of the National Carbon Co., forerunner of Union Carbide & Carbon Corp.

Born in Olmsted to Joel and Catherine (Harris) L., Lawrence attended Olmsted common schools and Baldwin Univ. In 1864 he moved to Cleveland and became involved in the manufacturing and sale of sewing machines and, later, the manufacturing of bolts in Elyria. In 1874 Lawrence sold these business interests and turned his attention to electricity. Recognizing its commercial value, Lawrence invested as a stockholder in the Telegraph Supply Co., which later merged into the Brush Electric Co.

Lawrence associated himself with CHARLES F. BRUSH and provided a significant portion of the original capital for establishing the Brush Electric Co. Lawrence served as general manager until he retired in 1882 and sold his company interests. Lawrence briefly turned his attention to real estate investments.

In 1886 Lawrence returned to the electrical manufacturing business when, with associates MYRON T. HERRICK, James Parmlee, and Webb C. Hayes, he purchased an interest in the Boulton Carbon Co., took over the Boulton plant, and organized the NATIONAL CARBON CO.† In 1891 Lawrence purchased the carbon department from Brush Elec-

tric. After fire destroyed the Boulton plant in 1893, Lawrence moved National Carbon to W. 117th & Madison Ave. in Lakewood.

Lawrence married Harriet Collister on 29 June 1863. They had seven daughters. Lawrence is buried in Lake View Cemetery.—T.B.

Borchert, Jim & Susan. *Lakewood: The First 100 Years* (1989).

**LAWRENCE, WILHEMINA PRICE** (24 Oct. 1919–11 June 1991), administrative secretary of the ST. JAMES AFRICAN METHODIST EPISCOPAL CHURCH,† held state and national offices in missionary societies and organizations for women, such as Church Women United of Ohio (vice-president) and the National Council of Negro Women (nominating committee chair and vice-president). She was also vice-president for the World Federation of Women's United Nations office. Lawrence was born in Point Pleasant, WV, to Hazel M. Williams and William H. Price. She married William Lawrence; they had one child, Patricia M. Harris. Lawrence came to Cleveland from Pittsburgh, PA, in 1949 to accept the position at St. James AME. In 1985 Wilberforce Univ. granted Lawrence an honorary doctorate. Lawrence died in Washington, DC, where she had lived since 1987, and is buried in Lake View Cemetery.—J.M.

**LAZAR, ALMA TREBEC** (13 July 1911–11 April 1993) was an original trustee member who helped found the Slovene Home for the Aged and served as either board secretary or treasurer from when the nursing home opened in 1962 until her death.

Born in Austria-Hungary, she emigrated to the U.S. with her parents at the age of 2, settling initially in Cleveland. The family then moved to a farm in LeRoy, OH, where she graduated from Westfield High School in 1929. She then moved to Cleveland and worked as a bookkeeper. Alma married Walter Lazar on 12 February 1932. During World War II she began working as an assembler at the Coit Rd. Fisher Body Plant, retiring after 30 years in 1972.

During the late 1950s, Alma Lazar volunteered to help organize the Slovene Home for the Aged at 18621 Neff Rd. When it opened it was only the second nursing home in the country built to serve Slovenian-Americans. In 1971 Mrs. Lazar helped plan an addition that tripled the home's capacity and provided facilities for occupational and physical therapy.

In 1980 Mrs. Lazar was twice honored: first, by the Greater Cleveland Hospital Assn. as an outstanding trustee and, second, by the United Slovene Society for outstanding service to the Slovenian community.

Mrs. Lazar belonged to Progressive Slovenian Women, serving as secretary from 1965–85, and worked 20 years on the farm board of the Slovenian National Benefit Society, which operates a campground in Kirtland.

The Lazars had three children: Joanne Zupancic, Walter Jr., and Robert. Mrs. Lazar is buried in Highland Park Cemetery.—T.B.

**LEACH, ROBERT BOYD** (1822–29 July 1863), the first black physician in Cleveland and one of the first AFRICAN AMERICANS† in Cleveland to advocate full citizen rights for blacks, was originally from Virginia, moving to southern Ohio, and then to Cleveland in 1844. As a young man, he worked as a nurse on the lake steamers during navigation season. His preliminary knowledge of medicine came entirely from books. He entered the Western Homeopathic College in 1856 and in 2 years received a degree in homeopathic medicine. In 1858, after obtaining his medical degree, Leach established a practice in Cleveland, its black population then less than 800. He was a spokesman for blacks, and his name was frequently mentioned in news items relating to the struggle of blacks in Cleveland and Ohio. As a doctor, Leach had both white and black patients. He is credited with a specific remedy for the treatment of cholera, successfully used throughout the Great Lakes region. During the Civil War, Leach helped recruit black soldiers for the Union Army but was refused service himself; the army would not accept doctors trained in homeopathic medicine. Leach then began to study allopathic medicine, but within several months died of a liver ailment in Philadelphia while en route to Washington, DC. He was buried in the Columbian Harmony Cemetery in New York City.

**LEATHEM, BARCLAY SPENCER** (10 Mar. 1900–2 Feb. 1981) was an educator at CASE WESTERN RESERVE UNIV.† who formed CWRU's Department of Drama and Theater, secured a Rockefeller Foundation Grant to build its Eldred Theater, and promoted working relationships between CWRU, the CLEVELAND PLAY HOUSE,† and KARAMU HOUSE† Theater.

Barclay was born in Philadelphia, PA, to Thomas and Matilda (Smith) Leathem. Following army service in World War I, he received his A.B. from Pennsylvania State Univ. (1922), his LL.B. from WRU (1924), and attended the Academy of Music & Dramatic Art, and the Univ. of Vienna, Austria (1929–30).

Leathem joined WRU's English Department as a teaching assistant in 1921. He rose to instructor in 1924, asst. professor in 1927, associate professor in 1931, and professor in 1942. Leathem helped form

the Department of Speech in 1927 and the Department of Drama & Theater in 1931. He served as the Department's first chair until 1970 and retired from teaching in 1971, the first CWRU faculty member to serve 50 years.

Leathem established working relationships with the Cleveland Play House and Karamu that provided students practical experience in working with actors and technicians in professional productions. His pioneering campus productions introduced students and local audiences to Nobel Prize-winning playwrights. Through Leathem's foresight, CWRU offered one of the country's first TV courses.

Leathem served as a consultant to television station WEWS,† Channel 5, during its startup. He directed the first dramas produced on Cleveland TV, and conducted an interview show for 15 years. Leathem also directed the CITY CLUB's† Anvil Revues.

Barclay married Ruth Elton on 13 June 1922. They had a daughter, Patricia. Leathem is buried in Hillcrest Cemetery.—T.B.

**LEBLOND, CHARLES HUBERT** (21 Nov. 1883–30 Dec. 1958), organized and directed the CATHOLIC CHARITIES CORP.† (1919–33) in Cleveland. LeBlond was born in Celina, OH, to Ann Brennan and Charles LeBlond. When he was 5 the family moved to Cleveland, where he attended ST. JOHN CATHEDRAL† School, St. Ignatius High School and College, and ST. MARY SEMINARY.† He was ordained in 1909. After 2 years as assistant at St. John Cathedral, LeBlond served for 2 months as director of St. Anthony Home (1911). At this time, Bp. JOHN PATRICK FARRELLY selected him as the first director of the charitable institutions of the Diocese of Cleveland. After 8 years of frustrating fundraising, LeBlond organized Catholic Charities to support diocesan charitable efforts. Its first appeal raised $79,000. Under his direction, the corporation laid a base for the many Catholic institutions which developed to serve the needy, ill, and dependent of the diocese.

Pope Pius XI appointed LeBlond as bishop of St. Joseph, MO, on 21 September 1933. On a train returning to Cleveland from a conference, LeBlond was informed of his elevation by fellow passengers, who included Cleveland mayor RAYMOND T. MILLER. Also director of Catholic Charities in St. Joseph, LeBlond retired 24 Aug. 1956. He died in St. Joseph.—J.M.

Diocese of Cleveland, Archives.

**LECHOWICK, MARGARET (TROUGHTON)** (1907–10 Apr. 1992), basketball champion, child welfare advocate, lawyer, and mother of 10, presided over the Cleveland Women Lawyers Assn. (1971–73). Born in Cleveland, Lechowick's parents, Edward J. and Katherine Troughton, owned a candy store. She attended Ursuline Academy, where in 1925 she was the nation's top scorer in women's basketball, with 400 points in 20 games. Lechowick graduated from URSULINE COLLEGE† with a B.A. in 1925 and then earned a master's in child welfare from Western Reserve Univ.'s School of Applied Social Sciences. She worked for the Cleveland Humane Society, the Child Welfare Board, and the CUYAHOGA COUNTY JUVENILE COURT† while attending night school. Lechowick received her Bachelor of Laws from John Marshall Law School at CLEVELAND STATE UNIV.† in 1935. Admitted to the bar in 1935, Lechowick practiced in Sylvester V. McMahon's office before marrying Stanley J. Lechowick, asst. director of the Cleveland Community Relations Board, in 1937.

The family lived in Mentor. At least 3 children attended law school, Vincent, Paul, and Monica (Mrs. William) Donahue. Lechowick helped found the Lake County Center on Alcoholism and belonged to the National Assn. of Social Workers, the Cuyahoga County Bar Assn., and the Lake County Mental Health Board. In 1990 she moved to Austin, TX, where she died.—J.M.

**LEDBETTER, ELEANOR EDWARDS** (6 May 1870–19 July 1954), librarian known for her pioneering work with immigrant groups and ethnic literature, was born in Holley, NY, daughter of Ira Edwards. She was educated at Brockport State Normal College, Syracuse Univ., and New York State Library School in Albany. Ledbetter began her career as a cataloguer at Worcester, MA, in 1896, then working in Buffalo, South Bend, IN, the Univ. of Texas, and in Newark, NY, before coming to Cleveland in 1909 as asst. organizer for the Ohio State Library Commission. She was appointed a professional librarian at the Broadway Branch of the CLEVELAND PUBLIC LIBRARY† in 1909, and the following year assumed the position of branch librarian until her retirement in July 1938.

Reflecting the surrounding communities of CZECHS† and POLES,† the Broadway Branch housed Bohemian and Polish collections. Ledbetter developed both an extensive knowledge of the literature and an understanding of these immigrant groups. During the AMERICANIZATION† campaign during World War I, Ledbetter ran citizenship classes and authored 3 books, *The Jugoslavs of Cleveland* (1918), *The Slovaks of Cleveland* (1918), and *The Czechs of Cleveland* (1919), under the auspices of the Americanization Committee of the MAYOR'S ADVISORY WAR COMMITTEE,† which remain primary sources for the history of

these communities in Cleveland. Following the war, Ledbetter prepared three volumes, *Polish Literature in English Translation* (1932), *The Polish Immigrant and His Reading* (1924), and a translation of the Czech work *The Shepherd and the Dragon* (1930), as well as articles for professional and ethnic journals. She was elected chairman of the American Library Assn.'s Committee on Work with Foreign Born. Ledbetter was honored for her work by both the Polish and Czechoslovak governments. She married Dancy Ledbetter in 1903 and had a son, Dancy E. Ledbetter was buried at Crown Hill Cemetery in Twinsburg, OH.

**LEE, WILLIAM GRANVILLE** (29 Nov. 1860–1 Nov. 1929), leader of the Brotherhood of Railroad Trainmen for more than a quarter of a century, was born in La Prairie, IL, the son of James and Sylvesta (Tracey) Lee. He began his railroading career as a telegraph operator in 1877 and worked on several railroads as a brakeman and conductor 1879–95, including the Santa Fe, Wabash, and Union Pacific roads. Lee joined the Brotherhood in 1889, was elected vice-grandmaster in 1895, and president in Jan. 1909, relocating to Cleveland, the brotherhood's headquarters. He maintained a disciplined organization which included both roadmen and yardmen in its membership, leading successful strikes on the Southern Pacific, the Delaware and Hudson, and the Chicago Belt railroads in 1913 and 1914. Lee and representatives from the other railway brotherhoods successfully fought to extend the 8-hour day to employees on interstate railroads, which became part of the 1916 Adamson Law. During the 1919–20 negotiations to return the railroads to private ownership, Lee, seeking to preserve labor's wartime gains, broke a wildcat strike by the Switchmen's Union of North America by putting loyal membership into yard service and arranging to reroute trains around important strikebound yards. A conservative unionist, Lee took the lead in persuading the brotherhoods to accept the Railway Labor Board's disappointing wage decision in 1921. He remained president of the Brotherhood of Railroad Trainmen until 1928.

Lee married Mary Rice of Chicago in 1901; they had no children. He died at his home in Lakewood and was buried in Lake View Cemetery.—M.S.

**LEGGETT, MORTIMER DORMER** (19 Apr. 1821–6 Jan. 1896) promoted free, graded, public education in Ohio and has been credited with creating the public school system in Akron (1845). In Cleveland, with CHARLES FRANCIS BRUSH and George W. Stockley, he founded the BRUSH ELECTRIC CO.† (1880), precursor to the GENERAL ELECTRIC CO.,† and was elected a permanent commissioner of the Cuyahoga County SOLDIERS AND SAILORS MONUMENT† (1888). Leggett was born near Ithaca, NY, to Isaac and Mary (Strong) Leggett; the family moved to a farm near Montville, OH (Geauga Cty.) in 1836. He entered Teachers' Seminary in Kirtland, OH, in 1839. Admitted to the bar in 1844, he also graduated from Willoughby Medical College in 1845. In the 1850s, Leggett served as school superintendent in the Ohio cities of Akron, Warren, and Zanesville, and also practiced law for a time with JACOB D. COX. In 1855 his law firm, which included Judge Chester Hayden and Marcus King, created the Poland Law College, forerunner of the OHIO STATE AND UNION LAW COLLEGE.† Leggett taught at the college from 1856–57.

In the CIVIL WAR,† Leggett first served on the staff of Gen. George B. McClellan in Virginia. He led the 78th Ohio at the battle of Ft. Donelson, TN (12–16 Feb. 1862) and was wounded at both Champion's Hill (16 May 1863) and Vicksburg, MS. After his command (3rd Div., 17th Army Corps) captured Bald Hill, Atlanta, GA (21 July 1864), the hill was renamed in his honor. Leggett resigned on 28 Sept. 1865 as Major General, U.S. Volunteers. He served as Pres. Ulysses S. Grant's commissioner of patents (1871–74) before coming to Cleveland. Leggett established the law firm of M. D. Leggett & Co., with partners Albert Lynett, Charles H. Dorer, and William E. Donnelly.

On 9 July 1844, Leggett married Marilla Wells (d. 1876); they had 5 children, 4 of whom lived to adulthood: Wells, Leverett L., Mrs. H. A. Seymour, and another son. In 1879 Leggett married Weltha Post of Sandusky. Leggett is buried in Lake View Cemetery.

Mortimer D. Leggett Papers, WRHS.

**LEHMAN, ISRAEL J.** (29 Oct. 1859–2 Apr. 1914), architect, was a senior partner in the firm of LEHMAN & SCHMITT,† which designed many religious, public, and commercial buildings in Cleveland. Lehman was born in St. Joseph, MO, the second child of Joseph (d. 1883) and Hannah Schwarz Lehman (d. 1869). The family moved to Cleveland in 1862, where Lehman's father worked in dry goods. Lehman attended public schools and was apprenticed to an architect at 14. In 1880 he worked for Cuyahoga County as a draftsman, drawing county maps. Lehman was employed in the office of George H. Smith from 1880–84, and with Theodore Schmitt (1860–1935). Schmitt and Lehman began their long-lived partnership in July 1884. In 1899 Lehman spent 4 months designing schools in Mexico. He belonged to the AMERICAN INSTITUTE OF ARCHITECTS, CLEVELAND CHAPTER,† and to the CLEVELAND ARCHITECTURAL CLUB.†

On 27 May 1885 Lehman married Nannie Scheuer of Cleveland. They lived on EUCLID AVE.† with children Joseph, Irene, Nina, and Edgar. Lehman served on the Cleveland Chamber of Commerce. He was a member, trustee, and chair of the Temple committee of Willson Ave. Temple (see TIFERETH ISRAEL†). Lehman is buried in Mayfield Cemetery.—J.M.

**LEIMKUEHLER, PAUL ELMER** (22 Aug. 1918–27 Aug. 1993), turned the loss of a leg during World War II into a successful prosthetics business and the pioneering hobby of 3-track skiing. The son of Clevelanders Elmer and Clara Leimkuehler, he graduated from West Tech High School and attended Ohio State Univ. Employed as a research engineer for the Tinnerman Products Co., he married Catherine Cowley in 1940. He lost his left leg as the result of a shrapnel wound received during the Battle of the Bulge as a 1st lt. in the U.S. Army's 84th Div. Leimkuehler helped fashion his own artificial limb and, after a brief return to Tinnerman Products following the war, started the Leimkuehler Limb Co. on W. 3rd St. in 1948. He became an acknowledged leader in the field, serving as president of the Ohio Rehabilitation Assn., the American Orthotics and Prosthetics Assn., and the American Board of Certification. In 1957 he was appointed to the Prosthetics Research Board of the National Academy of Sciences. Moving his business to Detroit Ave. and W. 46th, he organized a subsidiary supply distributorship, PEL Supply Co., in 1960. Always an avid athlete, Leimkuehler was inspired to take up skiing after watching a film of amputee skiers in Europe. Working with another World War II amputee, Clevelander Stan Zakas, he developed a 1-legged technique with the use of outrigger skis attached to elbow crutches in place of the usual skiers' poles. As the "Father of 3-Track Skiing," he was inducted into the U.S. Ski Hall of Fame in 1981. Leimkuehler retired from business in 1978, selling the prosthetics company to his sons. Survived by his wife, sons Jon, Robert, and William, and daughter Paulette Vaughn, he is buried in Lakewood Park Cemetery.—J.V.

**LELAND, JACKSON MILLER** (1818–20 Feb. 1896), music teacher and brass-band leader, was born in Holliston, MA, to John and Sylvia Leland. With a proficiency in violin, bugle, and clarinet playing, he arrived in Cleveland in 1843 and shortly thereafter organized Leland's Band, which played on lakeboats sailing between Buffalo and Chicago. Leland also toured the South with a theatrical group in 1846.

When the CIVIL WAR† broke out, Leland and many band members enlisted in the 41ST OHIO VOLUNTEER INFANTRY.† The band of the 41st Ohio was mustered out on 6 June 1862 after the War Dept. phased out regimental bands. Leland's Band returned to Cleveland, where it played at local army camps, and daily at the NORTHERN OHIO SANITARY FAIR† on PUBLIC SQUARE† between 22 Feb.–10 Mar. 1864. The band was without a leader when Leland again enlisted, as a private in Co. D, 150th OVI, on 2 May 1864. He was promoted to principal musician and mustered out with the 150th in Cleveland on 23 Aug. 1864. In Apr. 1865 the band participated in Pres. Abraham Lincoln's funeral procession in Cleveland. As troops returned from Civil War service, Leland's Band greeted them at UNION DEPOT† and marched to Public Square for official welcoming ceremonies. The band serenaded Gen. Wm. T. Sherman on 29 July 1866 at the Kennard House. Leland's Band continued to participate in most major parades, events, and funerals until Leland's death.

Leland was married twice. He and his first wife, Elizabeth Pinkney (d. 1855), had 3 children: Andrew, Joseph, and Fred. Leland's second wife was Mary J. Brainard. Together they had 3 children: Clara, Delia, and Hattie. Leland, who died in Cleveland, was survived by his second wife and 4 of his children.

Kimberly, Robert, and Ephraim S. Holloway. *The Forty-first Ohio Veteran Volunteer Infantry in the War of the Rebellion, 1861–1865* (1897).

**LEMMERS, A. EUGENE** (7 July 1907–2 June 1992), inventor in the field of lighting, was born in Cleveland the son of Maurice and Florence V. (Beerbrier) Lemmers. After graduation from Glenville High School in 1926, he began working for General Electric at Nela Park and took college courses but did not earn a degree. While at GE he developed the first flash bulbs that photographers could safely use and actively participated in fluorescent lighting development, designing a shock-proof socket for fluorescent lamps and a control to extend their useful life. Lemmers also devised an airtight exhaust system for the Army Air Corps P-61 nightfighter planes, eliminating fumes which were dangerous to the pilots. During World War II, he also invented the first battery-operated fluorescent light for use on the airplane instrument panels. Lemmers, who held 68 patents, received the Cleveland Technical Society's Distinguished Service Award in 1981. After 66 years with GE, he retired in Feb. 1992.

Lemmers married M. Eloise Nuhn 12 Mar. 1932, and they had three children: Robert E. of Cleveland Hts., Richard E. of Gettysburg, PA, and Mary Jane Harvey of Farmington, MI. A Resident of CLEVELAND HTS.,† he died at age 84 and was buried at Whitehaven Cemetery.—M.S.

**LENHART, CARL H.** (1 Sept. 1880–8 Apr. 1955), surgeon and medical researcher in shock, hemorrhaging, kidney studies, and endemic goiter treatment, was born to country doctor Peter J. Lenhart and Ida I. (Pfeifer) Lenhart in Wauseon, OH. He graduated with an A.B. from Adelbert College (1901) and an M.D. from Western Reserve Univ. Medical School (1904). During his residency and internship between 1904–06 at Lakeside Hospital, he did research with Dr. GEO. W. CRILE into the problems of shock and hemorrhaging. Between 1915–20, Lenhart worked closely with Dr. DAVID MARINE in investigating the etiology of simple goiters. As a teacher, he worked in the physiological laboratories of Dr. JOHN J. R. MACLEOD, the codiscoverer of insulin. In 1918 Lenhart became demonstrator of surgery at WRU Medical School. He was appointed instructor later in 1918, professor of clinical surgery in 1930, and head of the school's department of surgery in 1932. In 1921 he was appointed head of the department of surgery at St. Luke's Hospital. Later he was chief of surgery (1930–32) at City Hospital and director of surgery (1932–50) at Lakeside Hospital.

Lenhart, with SAMUEL O. FREEDLANDER, worked out the physiology of the pneumothorax and helped pave the way for open-heart surgery. He worked with Dr. TORALD SOLLMAN on studies of the kidney. He retired from practicing medicine in 1950. In 1952 he was named a trustee of WRU and established the Lenhart Memorial Lecture Fund. Lenhart was survived by his wife, Ora, whom he married on 12 April 1909. They had no children. Lenhart was buried in Lake View Cemetery.

**LEONARD, WILLIAM ANDREW** (15 July 1848–21 Sept. 1930), bishop coadjutor of the Episcopal Diocese of Ohio (1889) and 4th bishop (1889–1930), was born in Southport, CT, to William B. and Louise D. (Bulkley) Leonard. He graduated from St. Stephen's College (1866) and received his B.D. from Berkeley Divinity School (1871). Ordained a deacon in 1871 and priest in 1872, Leonard began a long career in the Anglican church with a rectorship in Brooklyn, NY (1872–80). His popularity with national leaders such as JOHN HAY,† made while a rector in Washington, DC (1880–89), helped overcome a Tractarian-versus-evangelical dispute that caused the Diocese of Ohio to vote 5 times before electing him bishop coadjutor. Although an evangelical himself, Leonard used his personal wealth to adopt the lifestyle of his neighbors on Euclid Ave.'s Millionaires' Row, as he cajoled them to financially support the diocese.

Leonard founded the Free Library in Brooklyn, NY; was a trustee of Kenyon College; and helped St. John's Home for Girls in Painesville. Diocesan clergy doubled and membership quadrupled during Leonard's episcopacy. He supervised the building of Trinity Cathedral and saved Kenyon College and Bexley Hall from enrollment disasters caused by the high church–low church dispute. He was first president of Mid-West (1914–24) and presiding bishop of the church (1929, 1930). He supervised the American Episcopal churches in Europe (1897–1906).

Leonard married Sara Louisa Sullivan in 1873. The couple had no children. Leonard died and was buried in Gambier, OH.

**LEONARDS, JACK R.** (25 Feb. 1919–15 July 1978), internationally known for his biochemical research and a world expert on aspirin, was born in Montreal, Canada, son of David and Sara R. Leonards. He graduated from McGill Univ. in 1939, and 2 years later received master's degrees in chemistry and nutrition from Virginia Polytechnic Institute. He became associated with Western Reserve Univ. in 1941 as a research fellow and received his doctorate there 2 years later. In 1957 he received a medical degree from the university. In 1943 Leonards joined Ben Venue Laboratories, Inc., as a researcher. The BEDFORD† firm was an early manufacturer of penicillin; Leonards did some of the original research on its production. From 1948 he was associated with Miles Laboratories as a consultant; he later operated his own laboratory, the Dr. Jack R. Leonards Medical Laboratory, in the Lakeland Medical Bldg. in EUCLID.† From 1953 he was also associate professor of clinical biochemistry at Western Reserve School of Medicine. In the last 10 years of Leonards's life, most of his research was concerned with aspirin. He testified as a leading expert at the FDA hearings on aspirin. During his career he had other notable achievements, including the development of glucola, a test for diabetes, and instant glucose as emergency treatment for persons in a diabetic coma. He also codeveloped one of the first mechanical kidneys. Leonards authored over 125 articles published in professional journals throughout the world.

Leonards was married twice. With his first wife, Alice E. Sizer, whom he married on 21 July 1941, he had five children: Alice, Ruth, William, Ralph, and George. After divorcing in 1958, Leonards married Margaret C. Degar on 10 Aug. 1961. They had no children. Leonards died in CLEVELAND HTS.† and was cremated.

**LETTER, BEN I.** (25 Dec. 1907–27 June 1983), spent nearly half a century as a technician and stage manager at the CLEVELAND PLAY HOUSE.† A native Clevelander, he acquired his first taste for the theater at Glenville High School, where his drama instructor was Katherine Wick Kelly, wife of Play House director FREDERIC McCONNELL. After 2 years of study at the Cleveland Law School (see CLEVELAND STATE UNIV.†), Letter joined the Play House staff in 1928 as an apprentice technician. In 1940 he became a technical director and in 1958 associate scenic director, building scenery and handling the lighting for 200 shows. After 1946 he increasingly served as stage manager, handling a total of 500 plays in that capacity. Whenever necessary, he also appeared on stage as an actor in bit parts or walk-on roles. He also worked during the Play House's summer seasons in Chautauqua, NY, continuing his visits there even after his retirement from the theater in 1976. Letter died at MT. SINAI MEDICAL CENTER;† never married, he was survived by a brother and a sister.—J.V.

**LEUTNER, WINFRED G.** (1 Mar. 1879–25 Dec. 1961), classical scholar, educator, and administrator, was born in Cleveland to Frederick M. and Mary Ernst Leutner. He graduated from Adelbert College in 1901. He was an instructor in Greek at Flora Stone Mather College and Adelbert College (1904), and attended Johns Hopkins Univ., receiving a master's degree (1903) and Ph.D. (1905). He was asst. professor of Greek at Wittenberg College (1905–06) and instructor of Latin and Greek at Adelbert (1906–09). From 1907–08 he studied at the American School of Classical Studies at Rome and Athens. He was instructor of Greek and Latin at Adelbert (1909–15), becoming a full professor in 1915. In 1912 he became dean of Adelbert College, and in 1925 dean of university administration. Leutner helped establish Cleveland College, the downtown adult education college, and was its acting director (1925–26). In 1934 he was inaugurated WRU's 8th president. During his tenure (1934–49), Adelbert College, the School of Architecture, Case Reference Library, and Cleveland College were absorbed into the university corporation. Leutner received LL.D.s from the College of Wooster (1935); Wittenberg College (1935); and Oberlin College (1937); and an L.H.D. from Case Institute of Technology (1948). Leutner retired as president emeritus in 1949 and was named an honorary trustee of WRU. He married Emily Payne Smith in 1910 and had a son, Frederick S., and 2 daughters, Mrs. Mary (John L.) Willett and Mrs. Ruth (Geo. M.) Gantz.

**LEVIN, ALBERT ARTHUR** (2 March 1899–2 Feb. 1969) was a Cleveland attorney and commercial real estate developer whose one-man multimillion dollar property renewal program helped revitalize downtown Cleveland.

Born in Philadelphia, PA, to Morris and Mina (Kaufman) L., Levin and family moved to Lorain in 1908, where his father opened a men's clothing store. When Morris died in 1918, Albert took over the family business. In 1934 Levin graduated from Ohio State Univ. Law School and passed the Ohio Bar.

Practicing in Cleveland, Levin entered the real estate investment area by liquidating insolvent lending institutions. Recognizing the investment potential in Cleveland, particularly Euclid Ave., Levin worked to preserve and rejuvenate the city. His restorations included the former Taylor Department Store (666 Euclid Ave. Building), the Number One Public Square Building (former Marshall Building), and the modernized 1021 Euclid Ave. Building.

Levin also constructed a $1.5 million parking garage at E. 6th and Prospect Ave. and proposed a nonprofit organization of community leaders to buy and repair old houses in the Hough area. In 1966 Levin was recognized by the Federation of Realty Interests as an outstanding example of private renewal.

Levin was a board member of the Jewish Community Federation and honorary chairman of the United Jewish Appeal. In 1969 the Albert A. Levin Chair of Urban Studies and Public Service was established at CLEVELAND STATE UNIV.†

Levin married Maxine Goodman on 30 Mar. 1946. They had no children. Levin died while visiting Brazil and is buried in Mayfield Cemetery.—T.B.

**LEVINE, MANUEL V.** (25 May 1881–6 May 1939), lawyer and judge, was born in Vilna, Russia, to David J. and Michelle (Corban) Levine. He immigrated to Cleveland in 1897 and was a star alumnus of the English-language and naturalization classes at HIRAM HOUSE.† Levine graduated from Western Reserve Univ. Law School with an LL.B. degree and was admitted to the Ohio Bar in June 1902. Appointed asst. police prosecutor and asst. solicitor to NEWTON D. BAKER in May 1903, Levine targeted employment offices that bled foreigners seeking their first jobs of a large portion of their wages. Very much aware of the necessity for immigrants to learn English, he taught evening naturalization and English classes at Hiram House. Levine was elected police judge in 1908, municipal judge in 1911, and common pleas court judge in 1914, with reelection in 1920. In 1923 he became a judge on the Ohio Court of Appeals, twice selected as chief justice. As a judge, Levine displayed understanding, great sympathy, and empathy for those in distress. His philosophy was to place human rights above property rights, and he sought to guard the individual against any unlawful intrusions. Levine seldom hesitated to strike out against social conditions he saw as breeding grounds for crime. He instituted the Domestic Relations Bureau in common pleas court, established the state's first probation department, and pioneered court-sponsored domestic conciliation efforts. Levine married Jessie Bialosky in Mar. 1910 and had 3 children: Robt. M., Alfred D., and Mitzi. Levine was buried in the Mayfield Jewish Cemetery.

Manuel Levine Papers, WRHS.

**LEVY, DARRYL ALLEN [d.a. levy]** (29 Oct. 1942–24 Nov. 1968) was a native Cleveland poet well known within the national counterculture of the 1960s for his publications celebrating free expression and attacking social injustice and repression. Son of Joseph J. and Carolyn Levy, d.a. levy was also a painter and publisher; he published Cleveland's first underground newspaper, the *Buddhist Third Class Junkmail Oracle* (see UNDERGROUND PRESS†). Locally, Levy gained notoriety for bringing the counterculture to Cleveland and his subsequent confrontations with police. His journal, *Marijuana Quarterly,* advocated the legalization of marijuana and was one reason narcotics agents raided Jas. Lowell's Asphodel Bookstore, which sold the journal, on 1 Dec. 1966. In Nov. 1966 a grand jury indicted Levy on charges of obscenity. On 28 Mar. 1967 he was arrested and charged with contributing to the delinquency of a minor during a poetry reading on 15 Nov. 1966. His arrest attracted much local publicity, and his supporters distributed "legalize levy" buttons and stickers. Afraid of going to jail, Levy pleaded no contest to the latter charge in return for probation and dismissal of the obscenity charge. The legal battle left him angry, increasingly paranoid, and despondent. His arrest made him a media star but deepened his disillusionment with society, which he attacked as fascist. After arguing with his companion, Dagmar Ferek, and burning much of his poetry, Levy committed suicide on 24 Nov. 1968. Stunned by his death, Levy's friends paid tribute to him by continuing his newspaper and publishing his remaining poetry periodically through 1976. d.a. levy was buried in Whitehaven Cemetery.

d. a. levy Papers, WRHS.

**LEWIS, FRANKLIN ALLAN "WHITEY"** (18 Jan. 1904–12 Mar. 1958), sports editor of the *CLEVELAND PRESS†* from 1939–58, was born in

Lafayette, IN, to John R. and Mae (Armacost) Lewis and grew up on Cleveland's east side. Lewis was an All-Senate football halfback at Glenville High School and the catcher for the Edelweiss Cream Cheese sandlot baseball team. After 1 year at Purdue Univ., Lewis moved to Florida, writing for several newspapers. In 1929 he returned to Cleveland as the boxing writer and asst. sports editor of the *Press*. Lewis left the *Press* in 1937 and worked for 2 years as a sportscaster at radio station WGAR,† but returned to the *Press* as sports columnist and editor. He wrote in the language of the typical fans, whom he called "Joes and Josephines." Two of his campaigns were to build a baseball fence in Municipal Stadium to make more home runs possible, and to clean up the lakefront for more public recreational use. Lewis worked to keep boxing and horse racing honest to protect betting fans.

To find out what average fans thought, Lewis watched games from the bleachers. In 1945 he toured the Pacific war zones to inform servicemen what was going on in the sports world. His book, *The Cleveland Indians* (1949), was a bestseller. In the 1930s he wrote and published several popular songs. He was at Tucson, AZ, covering the Indians' spring training in 1958 when he died of a heart attack. He married Helen Virginia Palmer in 1939. The couple had no children.

**LEWIS, ROBERT ELLSWORTH** (29 Sept. 1869–23 Oct. 1969), general secretary of the Cleveland YMCA and advisor to the Minister of Foreign Affairs of China, was born in Berkshire, VT, the son of C. P. VanNess and Ellen E. (Haynes) Lewis. Educated at the Univ. of Vermont, he received a Ph.B., M.A., and an L.H.D in 1892. He worked for the YMCA in Vermont, spent five years as a traveling YMCA secretary for students, and went to Shanghai as an international YMCA representative in 1898. Lewis came to Cleveland in 1909 and served as general secretary of the Cleveland YMCA 1909–29. Under his stewardship, the Y worked with the city's social settlements and welfare agencies, increasing its efforts to work with young boys, and conducted a successful fundraising campaign to erect a new YMCA building at E. 22nd and Prospect in 1913. Lewis also helped arbitrate Cleveland's building trades strike in 1921. Throughout his stay in the city, Lewis retained his connection with China, serving as secretary of the International Committee YMCA, Shanghai for 10 years. Lewis left Cleveland to become advisor to China's foreign minister, 1930–35, the crucial time when Japan invaded Manchuria and installed the puppet Emperor Henry P'u-i. He retired in 1936 and moved to California in 1943.

Lewis married Grace Brackett in Newton MA, 24

Aug. 1893, and they had five sons: Brackett, Neil, Philip, Charles, and Arthur, and three daughters, Miriam Frick, Alice Turcotte, and Sarah Lowe. He died in Los Angeles and was buried at Forest Lawn Cemetery in Glendale, CA.—M.S.

Lewis, Robert Ellsworth. *The Educational Conquest of the Far East* (1903).

**LINCOLN, JAMES F.** (14 May 1883–23 June 1965), head of LINCOLN ELECTRIC CO.† from 1914 until his death, was born near Painesville, OH, the son of William Ellerby and Frances Louise (Marshall) Lincoln. He studied electrical engineering at Ohio State Univ., leaving without his degree in 1907 due to typhoid fever; he was awarded his degree in 1926. In 1907 Lincoln joined his brother John's Lincoln Electric Co. as a salesman, becoming general manager in 1914, and president from 1928–54, when he became chairman of the board. An inventor, Lincoln received 20 patents; his engineering enabled him to make the technological improvements necessary to make arc welding a dependable and commercially viable process of joining metals.

Lincoln was a defender of individualism and critic of the New Deal. During World War II, Lincoln Electric Co.'s incentive bonus payments from government war contracts raised the suspicions of government officials; in May 1942, the company was investigated by the House Naval Affairs Committee, and in 1943 the Price Adjustment Board ordered Lincoln to return $3.25 million, which it claimed was excessive profit. Lincoln fought the charge and defended the incentive payments. The Treasury Dept. later charged the company with tax evasion; Lincoln was acquitted of all charges, however. Lincoln was a prolific author, writing letters to the editor, pamphlets on political and social issues, and 3 books on industrial economics and the Lincoln incentive plan. He was also active in Republican politics. In 1908 Lincoln married Alice Patterson, who died in 1954. In 1961 he married Jane White. Lincoln had 4 children: Alice J., Frances P., Mary M., and James F.

James F. Lincoln Papers, WRHS.

**LINDSTROM, E(CHEL) GEORGE** (24 Feb. 1879–2 July 1968) was an author and historian and the founder of Lindstrom Typesetting Co.

Born in Sweden to Gustaf and Matilda Lindstrom, George came to America with his family in 1881. He attended public school in Oil City, PA. He started working in the composing room of the *Oil City Derrick* in 1901, and graduated from International Correspondence School, Scranton, PA, in 1903.

Lindstrom went to New York in 1905 and took a course in the Mergenthaler Instruction School. On 16 Aug. 1905 Lindstrom married Marion Spears in Cleveland. Shortly after his marriage he moved to Jamestown, NY, and entered local politics. He returned to Cleveland in 1914 and worked briefly for the Cleveland *PLAIN DEALER.†*

Lindstrom founded Lindstrom's Linotype Service (changed later to Lindstrom Typesetting Co.) in 1919 in Cleveland, and headed the company for 30 years before retiring in 1950. He then returned to the *Plain Dealer* to work part-time as a typesetter and proofreader from 1954–60.

Lindstrom wrote *The Story of Lakewood* (1936). His other works included *Oil Creek Tales* (1935) and a novel, *Out of the Sand* (1943). In 1954 he completed a 10-volume work, *History of the Presidents and Their Wives.*

Lindstrom was a member of the Clifton Masonic Lodge and other Masonic organizations, and also editor and publisher of the *Masonic High Twelve,* which he started in 1924.

The Lindstroms had one daughter, Ruth (Spieth). Lindstrom lived in Lakewood and is buried in Lakewood Park Cemetery.—T.B.

**LIPSCOMB, JAMES SAMUEL** (15 Dec. 1923–5 June 1987) was the first executive director of the GEORGE GUND FOUNDATION.† Under his leadership the foundation achieved national and international acclaim through its support of educational, artistic, social, economic, civic, and environmental programs.

Born in Jersey City, NJ, Lipscomb attended the Peddie School, graduated from Princeton Univ. (1944), then served in the navy until 1946. After receiving his M.B.A. from Harvard Univ. (1948), Lipscomb remained as the dean's administrative assistant until 1951.

From 1951–55 Lipscomb worked for Wachovia Bank and Rich Plan Corp. From 1955–58 he was a partner in Amundsen-Lipscomb, an investment management company. Lipscomb was a business professor at the Univ. of Ghana, 1958–61, then returned to Harvard in 1961 as director of the International Teachers Program.

In 1963 Lipscomb became the Ford Foundation's representative philanthropoid in Egypt, spending 5 years planning, initiating, and implementing foundation grants. In 1969 Lipscomb was hired as the Gund Foundation's first paid employee. Lipscomb remained executive director until his death.

Lipscomb's experience abroad helped the foundation evolve from giving grants to higher institutions to initiating and supporting community projects, including innovative teaching methods through Project Perform, child and drug abuse prevention, juvenile justice, and inner city housing. Lipscomb moved the foundation to finance the initial study leading to the creation of CLEVELAND TOMORROW,† a private economic development organization.

Lipscomb married Barbara Apostolacus in 1955. They had three children: William S. II, Joseph, and Anne (Jewitt). Lipscomb lived in SHAKER HTS.† and is buried in Lake View Cemetery.—T.B.

George Gund Foundation Records, WRHS.

**LODZIESKI, STEFAN (STEPHEN)** (27 Nov.1882–24 April 1951) was a Polish immigrant who founded the Lakewood Bakery Co. and achieved national prominence as a leader in Polish-American political and cultural circles. Lodzieski helped found the National Committee of Americans of Polish Descent and was president of the Joseph Pilsudski Institute of Modern History.

Born in Wierzbno, Russia (Poland), Lodzieski emigrated to America in 1902, becoming a naturalized citizen in 1910. Settling in LAKEWOOD,† Lodzieski learned the baker's trade and opened his first shop in 1911 when he bought Puritan Bakery. Around 1920 he sold Puritan and bought Lakewood Bakery at 11717 Detroit Ave. As president and director, Lodzieski expanded the Lakewood Bakery Co. into a successful chain employing over one hundred workers. By 1952 Lakewood Bakery operated fifteen stores in Lakewood and neighboring west side communities, including Rocky River and Parma. The family sold the business in 1960.

Lodzieski's work with Polish-American organizations involved helping to organize and serving as vice-president of the National Committee of Americans of Polish Descent, an anti-communist organization, and serving as president of the Joseph Pilsudski Institute of Modern History, a New York information library.

Lodzieski was a member of the Polish National Alliance Lodge and the Polish National Council.

Lodzieski married Victoria Twarogowska (d. 1950) on 6 Sept. 1909. They had three children: Edward, Edwin, and Elizabeth (Sliwinski). Lodzieski lived in Lakewood, belonged to St. Hedwig Catholic Church, and is buried in Calvary Cemetery.—T.B.

Stefan Lodzieski Family Papers, WRHS.

**LOEB, CHARLES HAROLD** (2 April 1905–21 Aug. 1978), earned the title of "dean of black newsmen" during his 35-year career on the *CLEVELAND CALL AND POST.†* Born in Baton Rouge, LA, the son of Leon and Lillian Loeb, he was educated in the New Orleans public schools and attended Howard Univ. Returning to New Orleans, Loeb had a hand in the establishment of 2 black newspapers, the *Louisiana Weekly* and the *Southern News Weekly*. During the next few years he also sold advertising for the *Amsterdam News* in New York and the *Atlanta World*. He came to Cleveland and in 1933 joined the recently merged *Call and Post,* where he filled the positions of advertising salesman, reporter, city editor, and finally, managing editor. He married Beulah Franklin in 1943 and left the following year to cover the Southwest Pacific Theater as a war correspondent for the National Newspaper Publishers Assn. He was 1 of only 2 African American newsmen to cover the surrender of Japan aboard the USS *Missouri*. Loeb served several terms as chairman of the Editorial Society of the NNPA and in 1975 received the Community Service Award of the URBAN LEAGUE OF CLEVELAND.† He wrote a history of the FUTURE OUTLOOK LEAGUE† entitled *The Future Is Yours*. In 1956 he conducted an unsuccessful campaign as Republican candidate for Congress, and in 1970 he was appointed to the Cleveland Boxing and Wrestling Commission by Mayor Carl B. Stokes. Loeb was survived by his wife and 2 daughters, Jennie Elbert and Stella Loeb-Munson.—J.V.

**LOEBELL, ERNST** (23 Oct. 1902–19 Sept. 1979) was an engineer whose extracurricular interest in rocketry made Cleveland an early center for research in that field. A native of Germany, he received degrees from Breslau and Oldenburg Universities and became a member of the pioneering German Interplanetary Society of Berlin. Brought to New York by the Otis Elevator Co., he moved on to Cleveland in 1929 to work for the WHITE MOTOR CORP.† In 1933 Loebell and Charles W. St. Clair organized the CLEVELAND ROCKET SOCIETY,† the only group of its type in America outside of the American Rocket Society of New York. Using the Waite Hill estate of Carl H. Hanna as a proving ground, the society designed a liquid oxygen-cooled engine which attracted favorable attention when displayed in model at the 1937 Paris Exposition. Having lost his job in the meantime, Loebell worked for a time in Grand Rapids, MI. When he returned to Cleveland he worked for LEAR SIEGLER, INC.,† until his retirement in 1968. Though he maintained an interest in postwar aerospace developments, he apparently made no effort to resume active involvement in the field. As late as 1966, he hadn't even visited the NASA LEWIS RESEARCH CTR.† in Cleveland. A member of the CLEVELAND ENGINEERING SOCIETY,† he last lived in Bainbridge Twp. in Geauga County. He died in WARRENS-

VILLE HTS.,† survived by his wife, the former Lucile Markel, and a daughter, Hildegarde.—J.V.

**LOESER, NATHAN** (8 Aug. 1869–30 June 1953), a founder of one of the city's most prestigious law firms and prime mover creating MT. SINAI HOSPITAL,† was born in Cleveland to Moses and Marianna (Loeb) Loeser. Loeser was raised in Buffalo and studied law and journalism at Cornell Univ. He worked as a writer for the *Buffalo Express, Buffalo Courier, New York Herald,* and Associated Press. Loeser returned to Cleveland in 1892 and took a position in the law office of Louis Grossman. He was admitted to the bar in 1896. Loeser and Grossman published the *American Lawyers Quarterly* for several years. In 1920 Loeser established Mooney, Hahn, Loeser & Keough, which in 1985 was Hahn, Loeser, Freedheim, Dean & Wellman. Loeser was president of Mt. Sinai Hospital from the late 1890s until 1910. With JOHN ANISFIELD, he was instrumental in obtaining support from the Fed. of Jewish Charities for the hospital's construction in 1916. Loeser was a long-time trustee of the federation. In 1901 he was president of the Baron deHirsch Lodge of B'NAI B'RITH.† As his father before him, Loeser was president of Euclid Ave. Temple. A close friend of LOUIS BEAUMONT, principal owner of MAY CO.,† Loeser was chosen by Beaumont to be a trustee of the LOUIS D. BEAUMONT FOUNDATION,† a charitable trust providing money for social welfare projects. For his leadership in citywide and Jewish community activities, Loeser received the Eisenman Award by the JEWISH COMMUNITY FED.† in 1949. In 1913 Loeser married Beatrice Moss and had 2 children, Mary Ann and Dr. Chas. N. Loeser.

**LOESSER, ARTHUR** (26 Aug. 1894–4 Jan. 1969), internationally known pianist and head of the piano faculty at the CLEVELAND INSTITUTE OF MUSIC,† was born in New York City, the son of Henry and Bertha Loesser. He studied at New York College, Columbia Univ., and with Stojowski at the Institute of Musical Art (later part of the Julliard School). He began his concert career in 1913 and toured Europe, Australia, and the Far East. He joined the piano faculty of the Cleveland Institute of Music in 1926, becoming its head in 1953. In 1943 he was commissioned as an officer in the U.S. Army and became a Japanese interpreter. He later became the first American musician to appear in Japan, with the Nippon Symphony, following World War II. In Cleveland, Loesser not only taught but also was a writer on music. He was program editor and annotator for the CLEVELAND ORCHESTRA† from 1937–42, and music critic for the *CLEVELAND*

PRESS† from 1938–56. His popular books, *Humor in American Song*, and *Men, Women, and Pianos*, were published in 1943 and 1954 respectively. Loesser's later concert career included appearances with the New York Philharmonic, Minneapolis Symphony, Cincinnati Symphony, and Cleveland Orchestra. Loesser married Jean Bassett; they had a daughter, Anne. He was the brother of Frank Loesser, well-known popular composer. Loesser died in Cleveland and was cremated.

**LOGAN, WALTER** (19 June 1876–11 Mar. 1940) was a violinist who helped organize the CLEVELAND ORCHESTRA† and, as a pioneer musical director, was the first to produce operas for radio broadcast.

Logan was born in Montreal, Canada, to James and Grace McIlvried Logan. He came to Cleveland as a boy and studied music under violinist Sol MARCOSSON. Logan gave his first professional engagement at age 12 and at 14 became the city's youngest conductor, leading the YMCA Orchestra. Logan pursued music studies at Oberlin College, graduating from the Conservatory of Music in 1899.

Moving to Chicago, Logan studied under Max Bendix, concert master of the Chicago Symphony, and violinist Emile Sauret. Logan studied further at Northwestern Univ., later joining the faculty, teaching violin, and was a violin soloist for the Chicago Symphony. Logan remained in Chicago for 15 years, where he taught, conducted, and composed.

Returning to Cleveland in 1912, Logan identified himself with almost every local event of musical importance. He became dean and head of the CLEVELAND MUSIC SCHOOL SETTLEMENT† violin department and composed the comic opera "Nearly a Duchess," produced in Cleveland in 1916. In 1918 Logan conducted the Cleveland Young Peoples Symphony Orchestra and became an original violinist with the Cleveland Orchestra, whose nucleus he had helped gather. Logan also helped organize the Cleveland Concert Band, the city's official band. Logan was a radio music director (1922–40) for stations WTAM†/WEAR and WHK.†

Logan married Vida Cotabish on 24 Dec. 1919. They had one child, Nelson Logan. Logan was buried in Woodland Cemetery.—T.B.

**LONG, DAVID** (29 Sept. 1787–1 Sept. 1851), Cleveland's first physician, was born in Hebron, NY, to David and Margaret (Harkness) Long. He attended medical school in New York City, received his medical degree in 1810, and moved to Cleveland, the first permanently settled physician and the only doctor until 1814. During the War of 1812,

Long was a surgeon in the Western Army. In 1824 Long became first president of the Society of the State of Ohio's 19TH MEDICAL DISTRICT,† forerunner of the ACADEMY OF MEDICINE† of Cleveland.

Long was also involved in business. He operated a dry goods and notions store; in 1816 he was an incorporator of the COMMERCIAL BANK OF LAKE ERIE†; helped organize the Cleveland Pier Co.; and with LEVI JOHNSON erected the first warehouse on the CUYAHOGA RIVER† in 1817. Later, Long concentrated more on business than on medicine. When Cleveland was incorporated as a village in 1814, Long was elected a trustee, serving off and on until 1836; in 1829 he was village president. In 1832 Long was appointed to Cleveland's first board of health, and in 1835 to the committee framing Cleveland's first city charter. In 1811 Long became the first librarian of the Library Society of Cleveland, which he helped organize. He helped establish Cleveland's first church, Trinity Episcopal, in 1817; and in 1820, with his family, became members of Cleveland's first Sunday school. In 1833 he was president of the CLEVELAND ANTI-SLAVERY SOCIETY.†

Long married Julianna Walworth (see JULIANA WALWORTH LONG†) on 7 April 1811 and had 2 children: Mary and Horace. He died in Cleveland and was buried in Erie St. Cemetery.

**LONG, JULIANA (JULIA) WALWORTH** (19 Sept. 1794–2 July 1866), an advocate of TEMPERANCE,† helped organize both FIRST PRESBYTERIAN (OLD STONE) CHURCH† and SECOND PRESBYTERIAN CHURCH† and devoted much time to social service in Cleveland. Born in Aurora, NY, to Julianna Morgan and Judge JOHN WALWORTH, Long came to Ohio with her family in 1800 and settled east of Cleveland in Painesville, then sparsely populated. The family moved to Cleveland in 1806. On 7 Apr. 1811 Long married surgeon DAVID LONG. From their second home on Water (W. 9th) St. (the later site of the city lighthouse), they moved in 1813 to the large log cabin built by SAMUEL HUNTINGTON. In the 1830s, the Longs lived on a farm in Kinsman, the later site of ST. ANN HOSPITAL†; in 1845 they moved to a brick home at Longwood and Kinsman. With her husband, Long gave medical care to the poor, the sick, and soldiers. During the War of 1812, Long served as a nurse and her husband as a surgeon for wounded brought to Cleveland. She also worked among the homeless. In addition to raising her own children, Mary H. (Mrs. SOLOMON LEWIS SEVERANCE†) and Horace Long (who died as a child), she took orphans into her home. After Dr. Lyman

Beecher convinced her of the rightness of temperance, she joined area reform work.

Severance Family Papers, WRHS.

**LONG, WILLIAM FREW** (28 Apr. 1880–7 Jan. 1984), businessman, officer, and mayor of Macedonia, OH, was born in Allegheny, PA, to Edward and Ella Edgar Long. He spent his early days in affluence until his father lost his fortune. Long left school at 11, sold newspapers, did clerical work, bought a laundry, and became president of the Pittsburgh Laundry Assn., and subsequently manager of the Pittsburgh, PA, Mfrs. Assn. (1913–20). Long joined the Signal Corps in 1917, was commissioned a captain, and transferred to the Army Air Corps—flying early Jenny planes and commanding the 414 Pursuit Squadron. After the war, he became manager (1920–49) of the American Plan Assn. of Cleveland, which became ASSOCIATED INDUSTRIES OF CLEVELAND.† Long stood against trade unionism, especially the closed shop and compulsory union membership, and often debated labor relations with union leaders and appeared before congressional committees.

In 1931 Long was promoted to colonel in the Army Reserve. He was recalled to active service in 1941, serving as civilian personnel relations officer, and in 1944 becoming general manager of the Natl. War Labor Board. At 69, Long was appointed to the Macedonia Twp. Board of Zoning, and in 1962 was elected mayor, serving for 13 years and helping it incorporate as a city.

Long and his first wife, Martha Ertzman, were divorced in 1923; they had one son. His second wife, Isabel Elizabeth (Patterson), whom he married in 1936, died in 1956. Survived by his son, Wm. Frew, Jr., Long died in Hudson, OH, and was buried in Northfield-Macedonia Cemetery. Long donated his Longwood Farm to Macedonia for a park.

William Frew Long Papers, WRHS.

**LORD, RICHARD** (13 Aug. 1780–24 Jan. 1857), prominent early citizen and mayor of OHIO CITY,† was, with JOSIAH BARBER, one of the earliest property owners on record. Born in Connecticut, Lord was the son of Samuel Phillips and Rachel White Lord. In 1807 he and Barber undertook to develop land extending along the west border of the CUYAHOGA RIVER† in Brooklyn Twp. With his brother, Samuel, Lord settled permanently in the area in 1818; his 320-acre farm included much of the lakeshore to what is now W. 117th St. In 1834 Lord became one of the 3 chief stockholders in the CUYAHOGA STEAM FURNACE CO.,† the first manufacturing concern in Cleveland. In 1840 he

and Barber dedicated a parcel of land for a public square at the corner of Pearl and Lorain streets. It later became known as Market Square (now the WEST SIDE MARKET†). Lord was mayor of Ohio City in 1843; earlier he served in various local government offices.

On 29 Sept. 1811 Lord married Anna Attwood; they had one daughter, Hope Hird.

**LORENZ, CARL** (31 March 1858–30 April 1924) was for 37 years a key staff member of Cleveland's German-language daily, the *WAECHTER UND ANZEIGER.†* The son of an architect or builder, Lorenz was born in Stuttgart, Germany, and studied languages in the Univ. of Genf, Switzerland, and later in England. Emigrating to the U.S. in 1880, he first settled in Portsmouth, OH, where he taught school and married a German girl named Riemenschneider. Coming to Cleveland in 1887, he joined the staff of the *Waechter am Erie* and remained after the paper's merger into the *Waechter und Anzeiger* in 1893. He filled the positions of Sunday editor and, after 1920, city editor. Locally, he was also a member of the Cleveland Art Club (see CLEVELAND SOCIETY OF ARTISTS†) and secretary of the Cleveland library board (see CLEVELAND PUBLIC LIBRARY†). Lorenz authored a considerable number of works, including a German-language dramatization of Hawthorne's *The Scarlet Letter* under the title *Das Schandmal* (Mark of Infamy). Among several German novels he penned was *Ein Deutscher Stromer* (A German Tramp). His major English-language work was *The Life and Character of Tom L. Johnson* (1911). Lorenz was survived only by his wife.—J.V.

**LOVELAND, ROELIF** (31 Aug. 1899–20 Feb. 1978), with CHAS. F. BROWNE and HERMAN FETZER, was one of Cleveland's greatest feature writers, spending 42 years with the Cleveland *PLAIN DEALER.†* He was born in Oberlin, OH, to Arthur M. and Gertrude (Smith) Loveland. He saw combat in France as a U.S. Marine in World War I, and following attendance at Oberlin College, worked briefly for the *CLEVELAND PRESS†* before joining the *Plain Dealer* in 1922. During the 1920s and 1930s, Loveland became a specialist in writing "color" pieces, as well as occasional verse. In 1944 he was sent to Europe to cover the coming invasion of France, observing the invasion from a bomber piloted by a fellow Clevelander. His eyewitness account of the D-Day bombardment was later reprinted by Louis Snyder and Richard Morris in their anthology, *A Treasury of Great Reporting.* Subsequently, Loveland landed at Normandy to cover Patton's 3rd Army in its breakthrough across northern France. He was one of the first correspondents in liberated Paris, and followed the 3rd Army to the borders of Germany before being recalled by the *Plain Dealer*. After covering the CLEVELAND INDIANS† in 1948, Loveland was made associate editor, and editorial writer the following year. A year before his retirement in 1965, he was assigned to write a regular column. Following the death of his wife, Mildred, in 1951, whom he married on 23 May 1925, Loveland married Wanda Arndt in 1953. After a long fight against bone cancer, he died of a stroke at UNIV. HOSPITALS OF CLEVELAND.† He was survived by 2 sons, Peter and David, from his first marriage.

**LOWE, K. ELMO** (27 Aug. 1899–26 Jan. 1971), capped 48 years as an actor and director with the CLEVELAND PLAY HOUSE† by serving as its second managing director in the 1960s. He was born in San Antonio, TX, but raised in Los Angeles, CA, where one of his boyhood friends was future baritone Lawrence Tibbett. He studied acting at the Carnegie Institute of Technology in Pittsburgh, PA, where he worked with FREDERIC MCCONNELL and married fellow student Dorothy Paxton (1900–3 July 1982) of Greenville, MS. When McConnell was named first managing director of the Cleveland Play House in 1921, he brought the Lowes with him. Lowe achieved a reputation as a matinee idol in the 1920s, one Play House legend holding that they couldn't display his picture in the lobby without its being stolen by female admirers. No one at the Play House seemed to know what the K stood for in his name; even his wife called him "K," and he always called her "Paxton." They often appeared together on the same stage, sometimes playing husband and wife. Lowe appeared in an estimated 300 roles and also began directing, exerting a formative influence on the careers of such Play House alumni as Russell Collins, MARGARET HAMILTON, and Joel Grey. Serving as assistant to McConnell, he also organized the local Federal Theatre Project of the WPA in 1935–36. Following McConnell's retirement in 1958, Lowe succeeded to the post of managing director of the Play House, which he held until his own retirement in 1969. He died at UNIV. HOSPITALS,† survived by Paxton and an actress daughter, Stanja.—J.V.

**LOWER, WILLIAM EDGAR** (6 May 1867–17 June 1948), a founder of the CLEVELAND CLINIC FOUNDATION† and pioneer in genito-urinary surgery, was born in Canton, OH, to Henry and Mary (Deeds) Lower. He received his medical degree from Wooster Univ. Medical School in 1891 and entered medical practice with his cousin, GEO. W. CRILE, SR., and FRANK E. BUNTS. He was on the staffs of ST. ALEXIS HOSPITAL† and Lakeside Hospital,

and was chief of surgery at both Lutheran General (1914–38) and Mt. Sinai hospitals (1916–24). He served during the Spanish-American War and became commanding officer (1918) of the famed LAKESIDE UNIT† during World War I. In 1921 Lower joined Crile, Bunts, and JOHN PHILLIPS in establishing the Cleveland Clinic Foundation, patterned after the group medical practice model of the Mayo brothers in Rochester, MN. Lower was president of the American Urological Assn. and a member of numerous prestigious and specialized medical societies in the U.S. He wrote 2 books in collaboration with Crile and numerous papers on genito-urinary surgery. Lower married Mabel Freeman in Sept. 1910; they had a daughter, Mary. He died in Cleveland and was buried in Arlington National Cemetery.

Bunts, Alexander T., and George W. Crile, Jr., eds. *To Act as a Unit* (1971).

**LUCAS, CHARLES P., SR.** (18 April 1911–14 Sept. 1989) began his career as an educator, became a real estate broker, and served many years in a variety of public offices. Above all, he was a dedicated advocate for civil rights.

Born in Cadiz, OH, Lucas earned a bachelor's degree from Wilberforce Univ. in 1933 and a master's degree in education from the Univ. of Kansas in 1936. He then returned to his home town where he served as both a teacher and then as a principal. He married Hazel Jones in 1939 and had one child, Charles P., Jr. In 1945 Lucas came to Cleveland where he became the executive director of the local chapter of the NAACP (see NATIONAL ASSN. FOR THE ADVANCEMENT OF COLORED PEOPLE†). He served that organization until 1952, more than doubling its membership, and helping organize protests against segregated facilities at EUCLID BEACH PARK.† In 1955 he became a member of the first State Board of Education. In 1956 he opened his own real estate office and was active in efforts to promote fair housing practices. From 1958 to 1968 he served two terms on the Cleveland Transit System board. A Republican, in November 1968 he was his party's candidate for the Congressional seat in the 21st District. He was defeated by Louis Stokes. In 1971 he was appointed deputy director of the Cleveland office of the Federal Housing Administration, and director two years later. His tenure, however, was marred by federal charges that he had benefited personally in office, and he was forced to stand trial in 1978. Although the jury found him innocent, his career was nevertheless damaged. He returned to work for the Department of Housing and Urban Development as an office specialist, continuing until illness forced his retirement in 1989. He is buried in Cleveland's Highland Park Cemetery.—J.T.

**LUCKIESH, MATTHEW** (14 Sept. 1883–2 Nov. 1967), renowned authority in the study of light and color application, was born in Maquoketa, IA, the son of John and Frances Root Luckiesh. He graduated from Purdue Univ. with a B.S. in electrical engineering in 1909, an E.E. degree from Iowa State College in 1911, and an M.S. in 1912 from the State Univ. of Iowa. He began work for the General Electric Lamp Division at NELA PARK† in 1910, becoming director of applied science in 1919 and director of the Research Laboratory in 1924, a position he held until his retirement in 1949. He was a pioneer in the study of the visible spectrum of light, developing the first accurate glass filters for the production of artificial daylight and meters for measuring it. His work demonstrated the need for higher levels of illumination and the benefits of using indirect lighting with separate specific lighting for a seeing task. He held numerous patents, including a no-glare device for vehicle headlights and an apparatus for measuring visual efficiency. He also made important contributions in the fields of camouflage and airplane visibility during both world wars.

Luckiesh married Frances Clark in Maquoketa in 1913. After her death in 1925, he married Helen C. Pitts in Cleveland in 1928 and they had two daughters, Nancy L. Tobin and Peggy Kundtz. A resident of SHAKER HTS.,† he died at his home and was buried at Calvary Cemetery.—M.S.

Luckiesh, Matthew. *Torch of Civilization: The Story of Man's Conquest of Darkness* (1940).
Covington, Edward J. *A Man from Maquoketa: A Biography of Matthew Luckiesh* (1992).

**LUDLOW, ARTHUR CLYDE** (4 June 1861–16 Apr. 1927), pastor of Miles Park Presbyterian Church (1887–1923) and author of several works on Presbyterian history in Cleveland, was born in Chardon, OH, son of Linnaeus C. and Helen A. (Stafford) Ludlow. He graduated from Adelbert College of Western Reserve Univ. with a bachelor's degree (1884) and master's degree (1887) before studying at Lane Theological Seminary (1884–85) and Union Theological Seminary (1885–87), where he received his divinity degree (1887). Ludlow's ministerial career was confined to Miles Park Presbyterian Church; much of the church's history for almost 40 years was a reflection of his activities and interests. While he was its pastor, Miles Park became recognized as a Presbyterian leader in northern Ohio. Ludlow coauthored a *History of Cleveland Presbyterianism* (1896) with his second wife,

Rosa Elizabeth Roeder. He also wrote *The Old Stone Church: The Story of a Hundred Years, 1820–1920* (1920). At his death, he was working on a centennial history of WRU, to which he was devoted and where he had a retirement office in AMASA STONE CHAPEL.† Service on the Cleveland School Board (1904–10) and support for the then unusual idea of manual education characterized Ludlow's civic contributions. He served as stated clerk of the Cleveland Presbytery (1900–27) and also held the denominational offices of permanent clerk and moderator of the Synod of Ohio. Ludlow married 3 times. First on 17 May 1888 to Jennie Gould (d. 1888); then on 28 Mar. 1898 to Rosa Roeder (d. 1918), with whom he had a son, Carroll G. He married Lillian S. Prall in 1923; she died in 1935. Ludlow was buried at Lake View Cemetery.

**LYBARGER, DONALD FISHER** (19 Dec. 1896–6 Nov. 1970), lawyer, served as recorder of Cuyahoga County (1933–50) and judge in the Court of Common Pleas from 1950–69 (chief justice from 1967–69, then chief justice emeritus). A man of liberal views, he asked in 1963 that his name be removed from the rolls of the Sons of the American Revolution, after a 42-year membership, due to the national group's "totalitarianism" and racism. Lybarger was born in Harrisburg, PA, to Jesse J. Lybarger and his second wife, Margaret Schuler Fisher. He attended the Friends' School and public schools in Wilmington, DE, graduated from Gettysburg Academy in 1915, and completed a degree at Pennsylvania College with first honors in 1919. Lybarger served in U.S. Navy during World War I. He came to Cleveland in 1920 to attend law school at Western Reserve Univ. (see CASE WESTERN RESERVE UNIV.†). The year he graduated, 1923, Lybarger was admitted to the bar; he joined the CLEVELAND BAR ASSN.† in 1925. He served with the firm of Horn, Weisell, McLaughlin & Lybarger until 1945.

In 1932 Lybarger was elected recorder of Cuyahoga County (see CUYAHOGA COUNTY GOVERNMENT†), succeeding Lyman Newell; during his tenure, he initiated cost-saving measures. He was elected to the Court of Common Pleas in 1949. As county recorder, Lybarger was instrumental in WPA work relief during the New Deal years in Cleveland. Lybarger served as official sponsor of the HISTORICAL RECORDS SURVEY† (HRS) *ANNALS OF CLEVELAND*†project, which produced the Cleveland Newspaper Digest (covering years 1819–75), the Cleveland Court Records Series (1837–77), the Register of Cleveland Office Holders (1802–52), as well as the Foreign Language Newspaper Digest (1937–38) and Index to Cleveland Periodicals.

Lybarger married Cornelia Marjorie Hartshorne on 16 Sept 1924; they had four children: Cornelia (Mrs. Henry) Neuswanger, Virginia (Mrs. James R.) Patterson, Lee, and Leonard. Cornelia Lybarger died on 4 Nov 1953. Lybarger married Helen Baldwin Dean on 7 Aug 1956 in Harrisburg. Both he and his new wife were active members of Lakewood Presbyterian Church. A lifelong stamp collector, Lybarger served as president of the American Philatelic Society. He belonged to the WESTERN RESERVE HISTORICAL SOCIETY† and presided over the EARLY SETTLERS ASSN. OF THE WESTERN RESERVE.†—J.M.

---

Donald F. Lybarger Papers, WRHS.

**LYNCH, FRANK** (5 Nov. 1836–27 Feb. 1889), volunteer army officer in the CIVIL WAR,† was born in Canada but had moved to Cleveland by the outbreak of the war. On 14 Aug. 1861, he was commissioned captain, Co. G, 27th Ohio Volunteer Infantry. In late Oct. 1862, he was ordered to open a recruiting office in Cleveland, which he established on Superior St. He later returned to the 27th Ohio, of Fuller's Ohio Brigade, which was heavily engaged throughout the Atlanta Campaign as part of the 4th Div., 16th Army Corps. During the Battle of Atlanta, 22 July 1864, Lynch was severely wounded during a charge; he never regained full use of his arms. He was promoted to lt. col. on 3 Mar. 1864 but never was mustered as such, being mustered out 20 May 1865. Lynch returned to Cleveland and became involved in Republican politics in the 9th Ward. His war wounds had debilitated his general strength, which plagued him for the rest of his life. In 1869 he was elected treasurer of Cuyahoga County; he was reelected in 1871. Lynch served on the committee for Decoration Day (now Memorial Day) ceremonies in 1871, chaired the Cleveland delegation to the Reunion of the Army of the Tennessee in Cincinnati, 6–7 Apr. 1872, and was a member of Creighton Post No. 69, Grand Army of the Republic. Lynch died from an apparent heart problem coupled with his war wounds.

Married on 10 Feb. 1864 to Rebecca Nevins, they had 2 children: Augusta K. and Frank W. Lynch was buried in Lake View Cemetery.

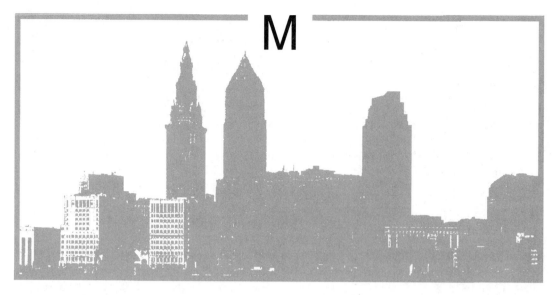

# M

**MABERY, CHARLES F.** (13 Jan. 1850–26 June 1927), chemist, professor, and researcher, was born in New Gloucester, ME, to Henry and Elizabeth Mabery and received a public school education. In 1876 he earned a bachelor's degree from Lawrence Scientific School at Harvard Univ., and in 1881 received a Ph.D. from Harvard Graduate School. From 1874–83 he was an assistant in chemistry at Harvard and director of Harvard Summer School in Chemistry for Teachers. Mabery came to Case School of Applied Science in Cleveland in 1883, becoming a professor in 1884 and heading the chemistry department until he retired in 1911. Among his students were ALBERT W. SMITH and HERBERT DOW, founder of Dow Chemical Co.

As an organic chemistry researcher, Mabery was most interested in the composition of petroleum and published more than 60 papers on the substance. He was also interested in electrochemistry and helped develop an electric furnace for smelting. He studied the metallurgy of aluminum, the extraction of bromine from brine, and the atmosphere of Cleveland. He was concerned about contemporary urban conditions and wrote papers on municipal water supplies and sanitation. Mabery was an art connoisseur and helped develop the CLEVELAND MUSEUM OF ART† and Cleveland School of Art. Upon his death, he left $65,000 to Case School of Applied Science, stipulating that the money be held until it accumulated enough annual interest to endow a professorship. The first Chas. F. Mabery Professorship was awarded in 1969. Mabery married Frances A. Lewis in 1872; they had no children. He died in Portland, ME, and was buried in Gorham, ME.

**MACAULEY, CHARLES RAYMOND** (29 March 1871–24 Nov. 1934), drew cartoons for several Cleveland newspapers before moving on to New York and a Pulitzer Prize. A native of Canton, OH, he contributed his first cartoons to the *Canton Repository* before being lured to Cleveland in 1892 by winning a $50 prize for best cartoon from the *CLEVELAND PRESS.†* During the 1890s Macauley's work also appeared in the *CLEVELAND WORLD,†* the *PLAIN DEALER,†* and the *CLEVELAND LEADER.†* In 1899 he became cartoonist for the *Philadelphia Inquirer,* and he also did freelance work for *Puck, Judge,* and the old *Life.* Macauley also wrote and illustrated novels such as *Fantasmaland* (1904) and a number of early screenplays for the moving pictures. From 1904–14 he was editorial cartoonist for Joseph Pulitzer's *New York World,* followed by a stint with the *New York Globe.* Among his symbolic inventions were the "Big Stick" of Teddy Roosevelt and the camel and hippopotamus representative of drys and wets, respectively, on the Prohibition issue. He joined the staff of the *Brooklyn Eagle* in 1929, winning the Pulitzer Prize for a cartoon he did that year on the subject of World War I reparations, entitled "Paying for a Dead Horse." He was working for the *New York Daily Mirror* when he died in New York. Married 3 times, to (1) Clara Hatter, (2) Emma Worms, and (3) Edythe Belmont Lott, he was survived by his third wife and a daughter, Clara, from the first marriage.—J.V.

Spencer, Dick III. *Pulitzer Prize Cartoons: The Men and Their Masterpieces* (1951).

**MCAULEY, EDWARD J. "ED"** (24 Aug. 1903–25 Oct. 1961), sportswriter and columnist for the *CLEVELAND NEWS†* (1925–59) was born in Hazelwood, PA, to Charles E. and Anna Logan. He grew up in Cleveland and graduated from JOHN CARROLL UNIV.† in 1925. McAuley played football and baseball in high school but worked on the school newspaper in college, leading to a job at the *Cleveland News* in 1925. McAuley covered the Cleveland Rosenblums basketball team and area college football, but was best known for covering the sport he loved best: baseball. From 1934–48 he covered the CLEVELAND INDIANS,† and in 1939 began writing a daily column in addition to his daily articles and features. He was also the local correspondent for the *Sporting News,* later becoming its chief editorial writer. According to his *PLAIN DEALER†* obituary, McAuley's baseball writings "ignored statistics and play-by-play to reflect the warmth of the human side of the game," and he became "one of baseball's foremost authorities." In the 1930s he led a successful campaign to have hits and errors displayed on the scoreboard. He was president of the Baseball Writers Assn. of America (1954), and the official scorer at Indians games (1960–61). In 1952 the *News* editors added a daily column on general and world affairs for the paper's first page to McAuley's duties; he continued it about a year. McAuley won 3 awards from the CLEVELAND NEWSPAPER GUILD†; also the 1958 Community Service Award of the Greater Cleveland Knights of Columbus.

McAuley married Genevieve Quinn in 1929. They had seven children: Ann, Mary Kay, Rita, Donald, Noreen, Jean, and Joan. McAuley died in Cleveland and was buried in Sharon, PA.

**MCBRIDE, ARTHUR B. "MICKEY"** (20 Mar. 1888–10 Nov. 1972), founder of the CLEVELAND BROWNS,† was born in Chicago and moved to Cleveland in 1913 as circulation manager of the *CLEVELAND NEWS.†* In 1930 McBride went into business for himself, in 1931 buying a majority of Zone Cab Co., which later merged with Yellow Cab Co. McBride also owned taxicab companies in Akron and Canton, and real estate in Chicago and Florida.

McBride founded the Cleveland Browns in 1944 after unsuccessfully trying to purchase the CLEVELAND RAMS† in 1942, helping organize the All-American Football Conference and holding the Cleveland franchise when the league was announced in 1944. McBride spent 1945 organizing and promoting his team, hiring PAUL BROWN as head coach, and building fan support with a team-naming contest and advertisements. When the AAFC collapsed in 1949, McBride arranged for the Browns to join the NFL. He introduced the "cab" or "taxi" squad for reserve players, so named because they drove cabs for McBride when not needed for actual play. In June 1953 McBride sold the team for about $600,000.

Not everyone believed all of McBride's ventures were entirely legal. In Jan. 1951, McBride testified before the Senate Crime Investigating Committee, which questioned his Continental Press Service, a nationwide distributor of racing news, and his alleged ties to organized crime. McBride denied connections and claimed he never broke the law. He was never charged. Congress later passed legislation making such wire services illegal. McBride married Mary Jane Kane. They had 3 children: Arthur B., Jr., Edward, and Jane. McBride died in Cleveland and was buried in Holy Cross Cemetery.

**MCBRIDE, LUCIA MCCURDY** (21 July 1880–18 Jan. 1970) spoke and organized for suffrage for WOMEN,† holding offices in local (founder and director, Cleveland Woman Suffrage party), state (founder, financial secretary and director, Ohio Woman Suffrage Assn., 1911–20) and national (finance committee) in suffrage organizations. She was an organizer of the LEAGUE OF WOMEN VOTERS OF CLEVELAND† (LWV, local president 1933, 1943) and the state LWV and worked on the national LWV committee for governmental reform (1934). She served on the Board of Education of the CLEVELAND PUBLIC SCHOOLS† (1933–35) and as the only female member of the City Planning Commission (1946). McBride was born in Cleveland to William Henry and Fannie S. Rhodes McCurdy. McBride attended Shaw Academy and graduated from HATHAWAY BROWN SCHOOL† (1899) and Miss Hersey's School in Boston (1901). On 6 June 1905, she married Malcolm Lee McBride. They had three children: Lucia, John Harris, and Malcolm Rhodes.

McBride played an active role in causes such as health, peace, LABOR,† GOVERNMENT,† and FAMILY PLANNING.† She was an early board member of the VISITING NURSE ASSN.† (1904–11). McBride was vice-chair of the women's committee of the Ohio Council for National Defense during World War I, and later, reversing her stance, served on the executive board of the Cleveland Council for the Prevention of War. In 1923 she took 2 women to Columbus, OH, to testify in favor of minimum wage laws; she condemned the labor of CHILDREN AND YOUTH† as a member of the National Child Labor Commission. McBride took a leave from organizations such as the CITIZENS LEAGUE† (vice-president), the JUNIOR LEAGUE OF CLEVELAND, INC.† (founder), and the WOMEN'S CITY CLUB† (charter member) in 1929 to promote the proposed city manager system for Cleveland. She helped lay the groundwork for and was a founding trustee of Cleveland's first birth control clinic, the Maternal Health Assn. (est. 1928, later PLANNED PARENTHOOD OF GREATER CLEVELAND†). McBride was a board member of the Cleveland School of Art (later the CLEVELAND INSTITUTE OF ART†) and the CLEVELAND PLAY HOUSE,† served on the Cleveland Commission on Public Works of Art and on the advisory committee of the CLEVELAND MUSEUM OF ART† (CMA). A collector of contemporary art (which she displayed in a gallery in her Cleveland home and loaned to museums), McBride helped initiate the forerunner of Patrons' Previews for the CMA's MAY SHOW† (1930s). She is buried in Lake View Cemetery.—J.M.

"A Short History of Lucia McCurdy McBride (Mrs. Malcolm L. McBride)," Typescript (n.d.), CWRU Archives.

**MCCARTHY, SARA VARLEY** (2 Dec. 1891–19 Mar. 1987), reporter and social welfare volunteer who helped organize the Cleveland Diocesan Council of the NATIONAL COUNCIL of CATHOLIC WOMEN† (NCCW) in 1923, received a papal medal for distinguished service by a layperson to the Catholic Church in 1936. She continued to serve religious and secular organizations locally and nationally for 50 more years. McCarthy served NCCW as local president (1935–38) and as national board member and committee chair, and chaired the women's committee for the SEVENTH NATIONAL EUCHARISTIC CONGRESS† (1935).

McCarthy was born in Youngstown to John and Mary Cavanaugh Varley, one of 9 children, and educated there by Ursuline nuns. She married Cleveland journalist Eugene McCarthy in 1931; they resided in EAST CLEVELAND.† After her husband died (1956), McCarthy moved to a SHAKER HTS.† apartment. She was a reporter for the Youngstown *Telegram,* the *PLAIN DEALER,†* and the *CATHOLIC UNIVERSE BULLETIN†* and assisted at the Diocesan Bureau of Information. Both URSULINE COLLEGE† and the Catholic Youth Organization honored McCarthy for her extensive social service involvement. McCarthy died in Cleveland and is buried in Calvary Cemetery in Youngstown, OH. —J.M.

**MCCLELLAND, JAMES M.** (12 Aug. 1831–10 April 1915), Congressional Medal of Honor recipient for service during the Civil War, was born in Hickory, PA, moved to Ohio, and settled in Harrison County where he enlisted in the 30th Ohio Volunteer Infantry 30 July 1861. During General Grant's campaign to capture Vicksburg, MS, Private McClelland and 149 others volunteered to storm the Confederate earthworks north of the city, 22 May 1863. Although they failed to capture the enemy position in two attempts, all members of the storm-

ing party were recommended to receive the Medal of Honor for their heroic action. McClelland was mustered out of service at Little Rock, AR, on 13 August 1865 and returned to Harrison County where he farmed and worked as a blacksmith. McClelland married his fourth wife, Lydia, in 1910 and moved to Cleveland, receiving an army invalid pension because of injuries sustained during military service. He died in Cleveland and was buried in Riverside Cemetery.—M.S.

**MCCONNELL, FREDERIC** (18 Sept. 1890–10 Aug. 1968), transformed the CLEVELAND PLAY HOUSE† from an amateur company into the nation's oldest resident professional theater during his 37 years as its managing director. A native of Omaha, NE, McConnell earned a law degree from the Univ. of Nebraska before enrolling in the Carnegie Institute of Technology Drama School in Pittsburgh, PA, where he received his bachelor's and master's degrees. Called to service during World War I, he spent 5 mos. as a German prisoner of war. He was asst. director of the Greek Theater of the Univ. of California and codirector of the Pittsburgh Guild Players, before coming to the Play House as its first professional employee in 1921. As the nucleus of a resident professional company, he brought K. ELMO LOWE and Max Eisenstat with him from Pittsburgh. During his Cleveland tenure, the diminutive McConnell produced and directed 800 plays, acting in 75 of them himself. He helped design the theaters in the Play House's first permanent plant on E. 86th St. as well as the innovative open stage in the old E. 77th St. theater in 1949, which was later named the Frederic McConnell Space Stage in his honor. In 1936 he took a leave of absence to direct Robt. Turney's *Daughters of Atreus* on Broadway. His first wife, Katherine Wick Kelly, having died in 1926, McConnell married Play House actress Harriet Brazier in 1943. Both marriages were childless. Retiring as managing director in 1958, McConnell served the Play House as a consultant and stage director for 4 years before moving to South Laguna, CA. He was consulting architect for the Laguna Playhouse before his death in Santa Ana.—J.V.

**MCCORD, GRACE BERNARDINA DOERING** (16 June 1890–31 Jan. 1983) became one of the first Cleveland women to achieve prominence in the legal profession. The daughter of Anton and Frances Langer Doering, she was born in downtown Cleveland and graduated from CENTRAL HIGH SCHOOL.† She taught for several years in Ohio high schools after receiving a bachelor's degree from Western Reserve Univ. (see CASE WESTERN RESERVE†) in 1911. She graduated from Cleveland

Law School (see CLEVELAND STATE UNIV.†) in 1925 with the highest scholastic average in the school's history and acquired a master's degree 2 years later from the John Marshall Law School (see also CLEVELAND STATE†). In 1933, the same year she began private practice with her brothers, Milan and Roy, she became Ohio's first woman law professor with a class on appellate practice and procedure at the Marshall Law School. From 1935–42 McCord served as Cleveland's assistant law director. During World War II she was named a regional attorney for the Office of Price Administration. She had been a founding member in 1919 of the BUSINESS & PROFESSIONAL WOMEN'S CLUB OF GREATER CLEVELAND,† and in 1957 she became president of the National Assn. of Women Lawyers. In 1957 she married John W. McCord, an Alaskan mining entrepreneur who died in 1969. Mrs. McCord was a frequent lecturer on the status of women and a supporter of the Equal Rights Amendment. Besides numerous articles in professional journals, she wrote a sketch in 1935 on 2 controversial Ohio Supreme Court cases, entitled "Alice in Lawyerland." Childless, she died in EAST CLEVELAND.†—J.V.

Grace Doering McCord Papers, WRHS.

**MCCORMICK, ANNE (O'HARE)** (16 May 1880–29 May 1954), the first woman on the editorial board of the *New York Times* (1936–54) and the first woman to receive the Pulitzer Prize for foreign correspondence (1937), began her writing career in Cleveland.

Of Irish heritage, Anne Elizabeth was the oldest of three daughters of Teresa (Berry) and Thomas J. O'Hare. Born in Wakefield, Yorkshire, England, she and her family soon came to the U.S., first to Massachusetts, then to Columbus, OH, where O'Hare graduated from St. Mary of the Springs Academy (1898). After her father's desertion, McCormick's family moved to Cleveland. Both she and her mother, a published poet, worked for the *Universe* (later the *Catholic Universe Bulletin*), McCormick as associate editor and her mother as column author and women's section editor. Anne O'Hare married engineer Francis J. McCormick 14 Sept. 1910 and moved to join him in Dayton. She began freelance writing, publishing articles in *Catholic World, Reader Magazine,* and the *New York Times Magazine,* and poetry in magazines such as *Smart Set* and *Bookman.* McCormick's strong Catholic faith always influenced her work; in 1920 she completed a history of her former parish, entitled *St. Agnes Church, Cleveland, Ohio.*

During travels abroad with her husband, McCormick sent dispatches to the NYT concerning post-World War I Europe. She became a NYT correspondent in 1922 and by 1936 had a thrice-weekly column, "In Europe," and was "freedom editor" on the paper's editorial board. She interviewed Mussolini, Hitler, Roosevelt, and Stalin. McCormick received many honorary degrees and awards in addition to the Pulitzer. She published one book, *The Hammer and the Scythe: Communist Russia Enters the Second Decade* (1928). In 1946 and 1948 she served as a UNESCO delegate. McCormick died in New York City, where she and her husband had lived since 1936, and is buried in the Gate of Heaven Cemetery, Mt. Pleasant, NY.—J.M.

McCormick, Anne O. *The World at Home: Selections from the Writings of Anne O'Hare McCormick,* ed. Marion Turner Sheehan (1956).

**MCCORNACK, WALTER ROY** (2 Mar. 1877–6 Nov. 1961) was an architect best known for his work with schools and public housing. His work in these areas is credited with changing the face of Cleveland.

McCornack, the son of Andrew Fletcher and Ella Carruthers (Brown) McCornack, was born near Oneida, IL. He attended Knox College and MIT, graduating in 1903. He worked in the office of Edmund M. Wheelwright in Boston from 1909 to 1913 before moving to Cleveland.

He served as the official architect for the Cleveland School Board from 1914 to 1925, and most of the new schools built during this time were designed by him. He established, in 1915, a "comprehensive research laboratory" for the board to assist in such areas as school planning and design. Thereafter, McCornack entered private practice. He continued to design school buildings, including ones for SHAKER HTS.,† EAST CLEVELAND,† and CLEVELAND HTS.†

McCornack was also an advocate of public housing projects as a remedy for both substandard housing and joblessness. He was considered a pioneer in the area of slum clearance and was a founder of Cleveland Homes, Inc., which organized slum clearance programs under public works agencies. He was the architect of the Cedar-Central Apartments (1937), one of the first three public housing projects in the nation. In 1939 he returned to Boston to become dean of the School of Architecture and Regional and City Planning at MIT. He retired from MIT in 1945. During his career he also worked on the Boston and Minneapolis Museums of Fine Art.

McCornack married Lillian Hutchins Amsden on 6 June 1906; they had a son, Donald. McCornack died in Littleton, NH.—D.R.

**MCCULLOUGH, W. THOMAS** (4 Sept. 1907–7 June 1992), social administrator and head of the FEDERATION FOR COMMUNITY PLANNING† (1958–72), helped build Cleveland's network of social service agencies. McCullough was born in Orrville, OH. He graduated from Wooster College (1929) and received a master's degree from the School of Applied and Social Sciences of Western Reserve Univ. (1933, see CASE WESTERN RESERVE UNIV.†). McCullough worked at ALTA HOUSE† before joining the Federation in 1934 as asst. to the secretary. After serving the Federation as field worker in TREMONT,† executive secretary of the group work council, research secretary, and associate executive secretary, McCullough left the city in 1947 and held offices at both the Philadelphia, PA, Community Chest and United Fund. When he was appointed executive director of the Federation of Community Planning, he returned to area, living in LAKEWOOD.†

After retirement, McCullough served on the board of the CLEVELAND METROPOLITAN HOUSING AUTHORITY† (1973–80), as a trustee of LAKEWOOD HOSPITAL† (1980–88), and as an elder of Lakewood Presbyterian Church. He consulted for the Federation and others on budgetary matters, human services trends, and PHILANTHROPY.†

McCullough married Elizabeth Bunn (d. May 1992) in 1932. They had 2 sons, Thomas B. and William G., and a daughter, Nancy Saborio. McCullough died at Lakewood Hospital.—J.M.

W.T. McCullough Papers, WRHS.

**MCDERMOTT, WILLIAM F.** (17 Feb. 1891–16 Nov. 1958), drama critic for nearly 40 years, was born in Indianapolis, IN, to John and Elizabeth (McCarthy) McDermott. He attended Butler College and began a newspaper career on the *Indianapolis News* in 1914, and in 3 years became its drama critic. Acting on the advice of numerous New York theatrical personalities, editor ERIE C. HOPWOOD brought McDermott to Cleveland as drama critic of the *PLAIN DEALER†* in 1921. In addition to his customary critical jaunts to New York, McDermott persuaded the *Plain Dealer* to send him on annual tours of the European theatrical capitals, where he sent back interviews with such luminaries as Somerset Maugham and Ferenc Molnar, and accounts of visits to Max Reinhardt's castle and a Russian production of Hamlet.

With the decline of the legitimate stage in Cleveland after the 1930s, McDermott began writing columns on general topics. He covered the Detroit sit-down strikes of 1937, the Spanish Civil War, and during World War II, the Italian front and subsequently the formation of the United Nations. Following the war, McDermott took a strong stand against local censorship, which won the notice of *Newsweek,* and voiced tentative concerns over the postwar growth of presidential power. Probably the high point of his critical career occurred during an illness in Dec. 1950, when Katherine Cornell brought the entire cast of her latest offering at the HANNA THEATER† to his Bratenahl living room for a private performance.

McDermott was married twice. First, in May 1910, to Georgie Richards; they had a daughter, Louise (Corcoran). After divorcing in 1921, McDermott married his second wife, Eva Pace, in 1938.

**MACDONALD, CALVINA** (12 April 1874–21 Nov. 1944) was a nurse and administrator who was a leader in bringing modern maternity care and obstetrical nursing methods to Cleveland.

MacDonald was born in Nova Scotia, the daughter of Archibald and Jane MacDonald. She began her career as a school teacher in Chatham, Ontario. She switched to a nursing career and practiced for 5 years in Boston, where she specialized in maternity cases.

In 1908 she came to Cleveland and worked with Dr. Edward Cushing, who convinced her to remain in the city. When MacDonald joined Maternity Hospital she was shocked at the conditions she found; the mortality rate for both mothers and infants was high. Upon becoming superintendent of nurses she instituted new methods, new equipment, new standards of cleanliness, strict discipline, and a new attitude toward patients. These improvements were credited with saving hundreds of lives. MacDonald also helped improve conditions at the hospital's 7 city-wide dispensaries. She continued her work when the new Maternity Hospital was built in 1925 as part of the Univ. Hospitals (see UNIV. HOSPITALS OF CLEVELAND†) group. She later served as an asst. director of Univ. Hospitals in direct charge of Maternity Hospital.

She retired in 1933, and three years later Maternity Hospital was rededicated as MacDonald Hospital for Women in recognition of her work as a nurse and administrator. Her work helped bring Cleveland's infant mortality rate to the lowest among the nation's 10 largest cities.

MacDonald never married. She died in Cleveland and was cremated.—D.R.

**MCFADDEN, JAMES A.** (24 Dec. 1880–16 Nov. 1952), auxiliary bishop of the Diocese of Cleveland (1932–43) and first bishop of Youngstown, was born in the Newburgh section of Cleveland to Edward and Mary Cavanaugh McFadden. He studied at Cathedral and Holy Name grade schools and ST. IGNATIUS HIGH SCHOOL† and College before entering ST. MARY SEMINARY† to study for the priesthood. He was ordained in 1905 by Bp. IGNATIUS F. HORSTMANN, and from 1905–14 was assoc. pastor of St. Agnes Church in Cleveland. In 1914 he was named the founding pastor of St. Agnes Church in Elyria. He was called back to Cleveland in 1917 to serve as rector of St. Mary Seminary. In 1923 Bp. JOSEPH SCHREMBS named him the first diocesan director of the Society of the Propagation of the Faith, the diocesan mission office. Two years later, McFadden was named a domestic prelate, became chancellor of the diocese, and was given the title of monsignor. On 13 May 1932 he was named auxiliary bishop of Cleveland. His episcopal consecration took place on 8 Sept. 1932. On 15 May 1943, the formation of the Youngstown Diocese was announced and McFadden was appointed its head in July, serving until ill health forced him to ask for the appointment of a co-adjutor bishop in Nov. 1949. His co-adjutor bishop, Emmet Walsh, succeeded McFadden as bishop when McFadden died. McFadden was buried in the Cathedral of St. Columba in Youngstown.

---

Archives, Diocese of Cleveland.

**MCGANNON, WILLIAM HENRY** (5 Oct. 1870– 17 Nov. 1928) was a chief justice of Cleveland Municipal Court twice acquitted of murder but convicted of perjury. He was born in Willoughby to James and Mary (Coyle) McGannon. He attended Western Reserve Law School (1894–97), passed the bar in 1898, and appointed Cuyahoga County examiner. He was asst. county prosecutor (1906–07), police court judge (1907–11), and elected chief justice of municipal court in 1911, reelected to a 6-year term in 1915. McGannon was favored for the 1921 Democratic mayoral nomination until 8 May 1920, when he hired mechanic Harold Kagy to fix his Cadillac. That afternoon, they test-drove the car to a speakeasy, met bondsman and saloon keeper John W. Joyce, and returned with him downtown. Around midnight, Kagy was shot. Kagy stated on his deathbed that Joyce had shot him, charges which Joyce denied.

Joyce was indicted for murder but acquitted; the judge disallowed Kagy's claims. McGannon then was indicted. The first jury deadlocked despite the testimony of May Neely, who had followed McGannon's car and stated McGannon had shot Kagy. At the second trial, Neely refused to testify on 5th Amendment grounds, and McGannon was acquitted. Neely had known McGannon for years, and rumors of an affair between them circulated. In a grand jury investigation, 15 people were indicted

for perjury, including McGannon, who was sentenced to 1 to 10 years but served only 19 months because of diabetes. McGannon moved to Chicago in 1928, where he clerked for a law firm, and died there. He married Anna O'Donnell on 18 Oct. 1900; they had no children.

**MCGHEE, NORMAN L. SR.** (20 Nov. 1897–20 July 1979) was the first African American licensed stock dealer in the Midwest and founded the first black-owned brokerage firm in the nation. He was born in Austell, GA, to college-trained parents, schoolteacher Maidee (Haywood) and AME minister Daniel McGhee. McGhee worked as a railway porter to earn his way to Howard Univ. He completed high school (1916), college (1920), and law school (1922) there. McGhee came to Cleveland in 1925 to practice law. His association with HERBERT S. CHAUNCEY, a local black entrepreneur, led to his involvement as a legal consultant and shareholder in EMPIRE SAVINGS & LOAN CO.† and Peoples Realty Co. He also became editor of the *Cleveland Post*, a weekly newspaper for Chauncey's insurance societies. When the *Post* merged with the *Call* to form the *CALL & POST*,† McGhee became the paper's first editor.

McGhee became increasingly active in real estate. He organized McGhee & Co. in 1952 to encourage blacks to gain a stronger foothold in the economy through stock investment. He established a mutual investment fund, Everyman's Fund, primarily for the black community. A Democrat, McGhee was appointed to the City Planning Commission 1942–46 and served as a ward leader in 1956. McGhee was involved in many civic organizations, and was a trustee of ST. JAMES AME CHURCH† and Wilberforce Univ.

McGhee was married 3 times: first to Margery Vashon (d. 1933) in 1925; then to Dorothy Cook (d. 1966) in 1934; and last, to Rosalind Bulcher Lewis in 1967. McGhee had four children: Marjorie M. Baker, Alice Bell, Norman McGhee, Jr., and Ronald.

**MCGINTY, JAMES J.** (1882–27 Nov. 1937), son of James and Mary (McCriddon) McGinty, was a councilman (1912–21) who represented the HAYMARKET district. A native of Cleveland, he quit school at 14 to be a messenger for Western Union, then turned to real estate, and by 1911 to politics. McGinty also ran a bar below his Commercial St. home. Elected councilman in 1911, he built support through backslapping and entertainment that sometimes masked his concern for his constituents' well being. He turned the annual ball of the Peerless Club, an organization of Haymarket youth, into the 9th Ward Ball, bringing in truckloads of sandwiches and beer for the annual event until Prohibition, after which the balls failed; but McGinty recouped by introducing ragtime concerts attracting over 20,000 people. On 11 Dec. 1902, McGinty married Mary (Lukacsko) who was known as the "Angel of the Haymarket" for her work among the poor. She died in 1921 and their only son died in infancy. In city council, McGinty was known as a hard worker who became the favorite of mayors and political leaders because of his affable nature and ability to get things done, sponsoring legislation for dock building on the lakefront; central heating plant ordinances to eliminate smoke and soot downtown; White Way downtown lighting; and zoning for orderly development. An ally of the VAN SWERINGENS, he also promoted development of the Terminal Tower nearby Ohio Food Terminal. In 1931 McGinty announced his resignation, becoming a land and tax agent for the CLEVELAND RAILWAY CO.,† later (1936) its vice-president. He died of a heart attack and was buried in Calvary Cemetery.

**MACHOL, MICHAELIS** (13 Nov. 1845–26 Aug. 1912) advanced moderate Reform Judaism in Cleveland as rabbi of ANSHE CHESED† (1876–1906); during his tenure the temple, then Eagle St. Synagogue, instituted occasional English sermons, installed an organ, and moved to uncovered heads. However, Machol demonstrated personal Conservative leanings in sermons and published articles, e.g., deploring the destruction of "every ceremony." He was born in Germany, one of 4 children of Zadek and Esther Machol. After graduating from the Theological Seminary of Breslau, Germany, and obtaining a doctorate from the university in the same city (both in 1869), he traveled to America. He settled first in Leavenworth, KS, then became rabbi at Kehillath Anshe Maariv, Chicago, IL. As rabbi of Anshe Chesed, he oversaw the congregation's growth in the 1880s and the building of a new temple (1886). Active in advocacy for the Jewish community, Machol joined other rabbis and lay leaders in protesting the 1901 decision of the board of the CLEVELAND PUBLIC SCHOOLS† to begin each school day with the Lord's Prayer, the Ten Commandments, and the 23rd Psalm. Anshe Chesed designated Machol rabbi emeritus in 1907.

In Sept. 1871 Machol married Minnie Rosenthal; they had 5 children: Jacob, Henry, Bernhard, Gertrude, and Ernest. Machol belonged to the MASONS.† He died in Denver, CO, and funeral services were held in Cleveland.—J.M.

Anshe Chesed Congregation Records, WRHS.

**MCILVAINE, CHARLES PETTIT** (18 Jan. 1799–14 Mar. 1873), second bishop of the Episcopal Diocese of Ohio (1832–73) and president of Kenyon College (1833–40), was born in Burlington, NJ, the son of Joseph and Maria (Reed) McIlvaine. He graduated from the College of New Jersey (1816), and studied theology privately (1816–17) and in a Presbyterian seminary (1817–19). Ordained a deacon (1820) and priest (1823), he preferred society and power, and advocated religious freedom while warning about Catholic intrusion into Protestant America. He received honorary doctorates from Princeton, Brown (1832), Oxford (1853), and Cambridge (1858). McIlvaine joined a deputation in 1871 to Czar Alexander II, protesting Russian religious persecution in the Baltic area. Of his many writings, his most popular book, *Evidences of Christianity* (1832), went into 30 editions.

McIlvaine organized one of the nation's first Sunday schools and was chaplain to the U.S. Senate (1822–25). He was chaplain and professor of ethics (1825–27) at West Point, where he influenced many students who became prominent in the Civil War. As professor of religion at the Univ. of the City of New York (1831–32), he inaugurated a series of popular lectures. In Ohio, McIlvaine traveled, confirming members and consecrating churches, including Cleveland's ST. JOHN'S† (1836), Trinity (1854), and ST. PAUL'S† (1858). He redeemed Kenyon from bankruptcy and instituted its rebuilding. Pres. Lincoln appointed McIlvaine special envoy to England to salvage Anglo-American relations after the Trent Affair (1861). McIlvaine married Emily Coxe in 1822. They had 7 children: Margaret, Maria, Emily, Anne, Sarah, Joseph, and Charles. McIlvaine died in Italy, and his funeral was held in Westminster Abbey. He was buried in Clifton, OH.

Bishops of Ohio Records, Episcopal Diocese of Ohio Archives.

**MACK, CLARENCE** (29 Apr. 1888–6 Jan. 1982) was an architect, master builder, designer, and developer best known for his work done 1925–32, which included designing suburban Georgian Revival-style houses in LAKEWOOD† and SHAKER HTS.†

Mack was born 29 April 1888 and grew up on Cleveland's west side and in Lakewood. His grandfather, father, and uncle were all builders. Though he did not study architecture in college, he spent 10 years studying the subject in Europe and the Cleveland area. With THEODORE KUNDTZ's help, Mack built a development in the 13800 block of Lake Ave. and Edgewater Blvd. in Lakewood in 1922–27. From 1928–30, with the help of the VAN SWERINGENS, he developed an area in Shaker Hts. on Courtland and South Park Blvds. Mack's houses were all apparently built for speculation; he is said to have bought the property, designed each house, acted as contractor, and then furnished and lived in many of them before they were sold. He was also the architect of "Kingwood" (1926) in Mansfield for industrialist Charles King.

Mack's business slowed with the advent of the Stock Market Crash of 1929. He spent 5 years traveling around the world before settling in Palm Beach, FL, in 1935. He continued to design and build in this area until his retirement in 1962. Never married, Mack died in Palm Beach, FL.—D.R.

**MCKAY, GEORGE PERRY** (13 Jan. 1838–5 Aug. 1918), a pioneer Great Lakes captain credited with playing a significant role in the development of the Great Lakes merchant marine and shipping trade, had a career that spanned the era of the small schooners to that of the great ore freighters.

McKay, born aboard the steamer *Commodore Perry* in Toledo, was the son of John McKay. The senior McKay captained some of the first vessels operating on Lake Superior after the batteaux of the early explorers; trade at that time included carrying supplies to trading posts and returning with such goods as furs, wild rice, maple sugar, and salt fish, as well as prospecting for copper and iron ore. John McKay settled his family in Cleveland about 1857.

George McKay began sailing as a boy on his father's ships. He himself commanded, from 1861 to 1882, some of the finest steamers on the Great Lakes. McKay came ashore in 1883 to become general manager of the Cleveland Transportation Co.'s fleet. He served as secretary and treasurer of the Cleveland Vesselowners Assn., and later as treasurer of the LAKE CARRIER'S ASSN.† He also served as chairman of the Lake Carrier's Committee on Aids to Navigation, and is credited with inventing the lighted buoy.

George McKay married Mary Ann Swaffield in 1858. Both were Roman Catholic. They had one child, Georgana Florence McKay (Mrs. Samuel Hiram Crowl, Jr.). McKay died in LAKEWOOD† and is buried in St. John's Cemetery.—D.R.

**MCKEE, ARTHUR GLENN** (12 Jan. 1871–19 Feb. 1956), engineer and designer of iron and steel mills, was born in State College, PA, the son of Professor James Y. and Margaret Anne (Glenn) McKee. He attended public schools in the college town and Pennsylvania State Univ., receiving a B.S. in 1891 and later an M.S. in Mechanical Engineering. After holding a series of responsible positions in the iron and steel industry, McKee came to Cleveland in 1901 to work at the American Steel & Wire Co., becoming district engineer by 1905. That year he left and founded his own consulting engineering firm; and in 1906 electrical engineer, Robert E. Baker, and construction engineer, Donald Herr,

joined as partners in the firm. McKee developed blastfurnace specialties, including the revolving distributor, stock bins, and test rods and held many patents in the field. The Blast Furnace Appliance Co. was organized to hold the patents and license their use in the iron and steel industry. The Arthur G. McKee Co., which incorporated in 1915, expanded and gained a reputation for sound engineering. McKee himself became one of the top engineers in the country.

McKee married Marion Fairbanks Deane 20 April 1899, and they had 2 daughters, Mary Katherine (Mrs. Paul O. Semon, Jr.) and Marion Glenn (Mrs. John Latta). After his wife's death, 4 June 1948, he married Mrs. Bennetta Heath Alexander, who survived him. McKee died at his Cleveland home and was buried at Lake View Cemetery.—M.S.

---

Arthur G. McKee Co. *The McKee Organization* (1961).
Mills, Charles E. *Fifty Years of Engineering* (1955).

**MCKELVEY, DOROTHY MARKS** (24 Oct. 1902– 14 July 1993) was the founder, president, and trustee of the Berea Area Historical Society (BAHS). She was the caretaker of Berea history and historian of BALDWIN-WALLACE COLLEGE.†

Born in Berea to Thomas and Mary (Benton) Marks, Dorothy was a fourth-generation descendant of Berea pioneers. She graduated from Baldwin-Wallace College in 1924, then taught drama and public speaking at Maple Hts. High School for five years before leaving to marry and raise her family.

In 1950 McKelvey became the full-time historian and college archivist at Baldwin-Wallace College, remaining in that position until 9 April 1993. In 1959 she helped found the Berea Area Historical Society, serving as its first president from 1959 to the 1970s, and as a director until her death.

In 1980 McKelvey was designated the official Historian of Berea (a non-paying position) by Mayor Jack Kafer and the city council. She gave illustrated lectures on Berea for groups and schools and became the person newspapers called to verify facts about Berea's past.

Dorothy was enamored of the life of Queen Victoria. She began a collection of Victorian furniture and glassware and gave lectures on the Victorian Period and its influence. In 1979 the BAHS dedicated an exhibit room in her name in its Mahler Museum. In 1984 Berea honored her by placing her name on a park in the center of the city.

Dorothy married Wilfred McKelvey in 1929. They had two sons, Thomas and Wilfred. Dorothy belonged to the United Methodist Church of Berea. She is buried in Woodvale Cemetery.—T.B.

**MCKENNEY, RUTH** (18 Nov. 1911–15 July 1972) immortalized the nostalgia felt for her Cleveland upbringing in the stories she wrote under the collective title *My Sister Eileen*. Born in Mishawaka, IN, to John Sidney and Marguerite (Flynn) McKenney, she was brought by her family as a child to East Cleveland, where she became valedictorian at Shaw High School. After attending Ohio State Univ., she became a reporter for the *Akron Beacon Journal* and the *New York Post*. Her "Eileen" stories, based on the experiences of her and her sister, first appeared in *The New Yorker* in the 1930s, becoming the basis for a play of the same title and a later musical, *Wonderful Town*. She also wrote a nonfiction account of the Goodyear rubber strike in Akron under the title *Industrial Valley*. Married in 1937 to the writer Richard Bransten (aka Bruce Minton), she and her husband were expelled from the Communist party in 1946 for questioning party tactics. They became expatriates, but she returned to Cleveland following his suicide in 1955 while her daughter Eileen attended Griswold Institute in 1958–59. She died in New York, survived by the daughter, a stepson, and an adopted son of her sister Eileen, who had been killed in an automobile accident with her husband, the novelist Nathaneal West.

**MCKENNEY, THOMAS E.** (22 Oct. 1889–27 May 1945) served as the founding pastor of OUR LADY OF THE BLESSED SACRAMENT CHURCH† (1922–34), the first Roman Catholic church in the Diocese of Cleveland established for AFRICAN AMERICANS.† He also served as the second priest of St. Thomas Aquinas Church (1940–45), then the largest Catholic parish on Cleveland's east side. McKenney was born in Cleveland, one of 6 children of John P. and Theresa Riley McKenney. He was educated at Immaculate Conception School and St. Ignatius College (later JOHN CARROLL UNIV.†). A graduate of ST. MARY SEMINARY† in 1914, he was ordained 6 June 1914 by Bp. JOHN PATRICK FARRELLY. His first charge was asst. pastor at St. Agnes Church. During World War I, McKenney served as a U.S. Army chaplain in France (1918–19). Before being appointed to Our Lady of the Blessed Sacrament, he was priest of churches in Maximo and Harrisburg, OH (1919–21), and EAST CLEVELAND† (St. Philomena Church, 1921). From 1934–40 he was pastor of ST. MALACHI'S CHURCH.† McKenney is buried in Calvary Cemetery.—J.M.

**MCKINNEY, WADE HAMPTON** (19 July 1892–18 Jan. 1963), and **RUTH BERRY** (24 Sept. 1900–4 Dec. 1966), were religious and civic leaders in Cleveland. As pastor of ANTIOCH BAPTIST CHURCH,† McKinney was a powerful figure among the city's black population. Ruth McKinney, an activist in church circles, was also an important speaker and leader. Wade was born in Cleveland, GA, to Wade and Mary Brown McKinney. He attended Atlanta Baptist College Academy, Morehouse College, and Colgate Rochester Theological Seminary. He served in the U.S. Army in World War I. In 1924, while serving as pastor of Mt. Olive Baptist Church in Flint, MI, he married Annie Ruth Berry, born in Birmingham, AL, daughter of Rev. Samuel and Ada Virginia Berry. Ruth Berry was educated at Spelman College and Columbia Univ. The couple moved to Cleveland in 1928 to lead the fast-growing Antioch Church.

Rev. McKinney was president of the CLEVELAND BAPTIST ASSN.† and Cuyahoga Interdenominational Ministerial Alliance. An outstanding orator, Rev. McKinney was frequently spokesman for Cleveland's black community and was the first black foreman of the Cuyahoga County Grand Jury. Rev. McKinney was an organizer of Quincy Savings & Loan Co. and of FOREST CITY HOSPITAL,† and he led many voter-registration campaigns. He also helped to establish the FUTURE OUTLOOK LEAGUE† and the Cleveland Business League.

Annie Ruth Berry McKinney was a college teacher when she married. As the wife of Antioch's minister, she became active in the affairs of religious organizations in Cleveland and across the nation and was in great demand as a speaker. Beginning in 1952, she broadcast 1-minute radio "Thot-O-Grams" under the auspices of the United Church Women of Cleveland.

The McKinneys had 4 children: Wade H., III, Samuel B. (Rev.), Virginia Ruth (Henderson), and Mary Louise (Miles).

———

Wade Hampton McKinney Papers, WRHS.

**MCKISSON, ROBERT ERASTUS** (30 Jan. 1863–14 Oct. 1915), mayor of Cleveland (1895–99), was born in Northfield, OH, to Martin Van Buren and Finette Adeline Eldridge McKisson. He came with his family to Cleveland in the early 1870s, and moved to LaGrange, OH, in 1879. He enrolled in Oberlin Preparatory School in 1885 and came to Cleveland in 1887 to study law in the offices of THEODORE E. BURTON. Admitted to the bar in 1889, he practiced law with John Webster and Elgin Angell in 1891.

McKisson was elected to Cleveland City Council in 1894 and became an active critic of the Democratic administration of Mayor ROBT. BLEE, succeeding Blee as mayor in 1895. During his 2 terms, construction was begun on a new city water and sewer system, the CUYAHOGA RIVER† was widened and straightened to facilitate steamer traffic, and 5 new bridges were built across the river. McKisson built a local political machine loyal to him and challenged MARCUS A. HANNA for control of the Republican party. In 1898 he and Hanna were rival candidates for the U.S. Senate, and McKisson came very close to defeating Hanna. McKisson was defeated for reelection as mayor in 1899, after which he retired from politics, returned to law practice, and became a partner in the firm of McKisson & Minshall in 1905. He married Celia Launette Watring in 1891 (div. 1900). He married Mamie Marie Langenau in 1901 (div. 1912). He married Pauline E. Reed of Buffalo 3 weeks before his death in Cleveland. McKisson had no children from any of these marriages. He died in Cleveland and was buried in Lake View Cemetery.

Campbell, Thomas F. "Background for Progressivism" (Master's thesis, Dept. of History, WRU, 1960).

**MCLAUGHLIN, RICHARD JAMES** (14 Aug. 1913–28 Oct. 1986), spent his entire journalistic career with the CLEVELAND PRESS.† A native of Elyria, OH, he was brought to the Cleveland area at the age of 2 by his parents, James and Cleo McLaughlin. He was a graduate of Lakewood High School and the Medill School of Journalism at Northwestern Univ. Hired by LOUIS B. SELTZER,† he joined the Press in 1936 as a police reporter. He became book editor in 1942, shortly before induction into the U.S. Army during World War II. He saw combat as an infantry sergeant in Europe, winning a Bronze Star. As a general assignment reporter and rewrite man at the Press, McLaughlin covered such stories as the TORSO MURDERS,† the SHEPPARD MURDER CASE,† and the Kent State shootings. To most Press readers, however, he was probably best known for such offbeat stunts as camping in a tent outside CLEVELAND MUNICIPAL STADIUM† for 3 days in 1948, waiting for a ticket to the World Series. In the pursuit of enlightening readers, he had a Fenn College chemistry professor process his shirt into a compound that would allow him to eat it, and emptied a tube of toothpaste on his kitchen table to determine how many inches of paste it contained. He retired from the Press only 3 weeks before the paper's final edition in 1982 and was inducted into the CLEVELAND JOURNALISM HALL OF FAME† the following year. McLaughlin was also a past president of the CLEVELAND NEWSPAPER GUILD.† He died in Sarasota, FL, survived by Beatrice, his wife since 1939, and 2 children, Richard J., Jr., and Jamie Lawrence.—J.V.

**MCLAUGHLIN, ROBERT H.** (16 Nov. 1877–16 Jan. 1939), dominated the legitimate stage in Cleveland as a playwright and theatrical manager from 1912–32. Born in St. Petersburgh, PA, he was raised in Fostoria, OH. After studying at Ohio State Univ. and Rush Medical College in Chicago, he became editor of the News-Democrat in Canton, OH. Coming to Cleveland in 1905, he worked for the PLAIN DEALER† 5 years before breaking into show business as a press agent. Among the local theaters he managed during the following decade were the Duchess, METROPOLITAN,† and COLONIAL.† In 1915, prompted by the closing by police of Cleveland's vice zone on Hamilton Ave. (see PROSTITUTION†), McLaughlin wrote the dream play The Eternal Magdalene. Following its premiere in the Colonial Theater (30 Aug. 1915), it became a successful vehicle for the return of actress Julia Arthur to the Broadway stage. Other plays written by McLaughlin include The Sixth Commandment, Demi-Tasse, Pearl of Great Price, and Decameron Nights, which in 1922 became the first play by an American to be produced in London's Theater Royal. In 1919 McLaughlin promoted the construction of the OHIO THEATER,† which he managed during the 1920s. When the theater wasn't booked by Broadway touring companies, he organized and directed a summer stock company to fill out the season. After a brief appointment as manager of PUBLIC AUDITORIUM† in 1933, he went to Hollywood to work as a screenwriter and casting director, returning to Cleveland a few months before his death. Survived by his wife, Myrtle, McLaughlin was buried in Fostoria.—J.V.

McLaughlin, Robert. The Eternal Magdalene: A Modern Play in Three Acts (1918).

**MCLEAN, PHIL** (4 May 1923–28 May 1993) was one of the nation's leading disc jockeys from the 1950s through the 1970s.

He was born in Detroit, MI, the son of Joseph and Phyllis (Hopkins) McLean. He started working as a disc jockey while still in high school. After serving as a navy fighter pilot during World War II, he attended the Univ. of Michigan, graduating in 1948.

In 1951 he was hired by WERE-AM/1300 in Cleveland, where he and colleague Bill Randle formed a unique partnership among on-air talent. The popularity of their show is said to have been responsible for helping to launch the careers of many national recording artists. McLean made a recording that reached the charts. It was "Small Sad Sam," a parody of "Big Bad John." He also conducted an American Bandstand-type television show in Cleveland for teen-age rock 'n' roll dancers during the 1950s, and hosted a daily late-night movie program.

With a change in the program format at WERE, he left for New York City in 1961, where he had an overnight show for many years. In 1971 he returned to Cleveland to work at WHK-AM/1420.† He later worked for WWWE-AM/1100 in Cleveland and for WHHR in Hilton Head, SC.

McLean was married twice. He married his first wife, Patty, on 19 July 1952 (div. 1963). His second wife was Donna Fisher; they married in 1972 and divorced in 1982. McLean died in Hilton Head, SC, survived by a son, Paul J. McLean.—R.W.

**MACLEOD, JOHN JAMES** (6 Sept. 1876–17 Mar. 1935), head of the Physiology Dept. at Western Reserve Univ. and later awarded a Nobel Prize as a codiscoverer of insulin, was born in Cluny, Scotland, to Rev. Robert and Jane (McWalter) MacLeod. He received a medical degree with honors from Marischal College in Aberdeen in 1898. After further study in Leipzig, he returned to England, where from 1900–03 he taught physiology and biochemistry at London Hospital Medical School. In 1903 he was appointed professor of physiology at WRU. While at WRU, MacLeod began research on the pathology of diabetes. His research and publications on diabetes and other subjects helped establish the reputation of the medical school. In 1918 MacLeod became professor of physiology at the Univ. of Toronto, where he continued his work on diabetes. His collaboration with Dr. F. G. Banting led within a few years to the discovery of insulin. As a result, the two men were awarded the Nobel Prize in Medicine in 1922. MacLeod returned to Scotland in 1928 to become Regius Professor of Physiology at Marischal College. His last visit to Cleveland was in 1926.

MacLeod married Mary Watson McWalter in July 1903. They had no children. He died in Aberdeen, Scotland, and was buried there.

**MCQUIGG, JOHN REA** (5 Dec. 1865–26 Oct. 1928), banker, lawyer, military officer, and mayor of E. CLEVELAND† (1907–13), was born near Hudson, OH, to Samuel and Jane McKinley McQuigg. He graduated from Wooster College in 1888, and after 1 year at Cornell Law School, transferred to the Natl. Law School in Washington, DC, receiving his law degree, being admitted to the Ohio Bar, and joining the Ohio Natl. Guard Infantry in 1890. From 1892–98, McQuigg was a member of the CLEVELAND GRAYS.† During the Spanish-American War, he was captain of the 10th Ohio Volunteer Infantry, and from 1899–1916, was lt. colonel of engineers of the Ohio Natl. Guard. During World War I, McQuigg was commander of the 112th Engineers of the 37th Div. in France, being discharged in 1919. In 1920 McQuigg was recommissioned colonel of engineers. Devoting considerable time, money, and energy to developing the

American Legion, McQuigg was commander of its Ohio Dept. from 1920–21 and was also an active member of the finance and executive committees, becoming Legion national commander 1925.

McQuigg helped organize the E. Cleveland office of Windermere Savings & Loan Co. (1915), moving from director to vice-president, then to president and general counsel. In addition, McQuigg and former classmate Geo. B. Riley established the law firm of Riley & McQuigg. McQuigg's special interest in municipal law aided his successful bid for the office of mayor of E. Cleveland. McQuigg married Gertrude W. Imgard in 1892, and had 2 children, Pauline and Donald.

**MCVEY, WILLIAM MOZART** (12 July 1905–31 May 1995) became Cleveland's most visible artist largely through his numerous local commissions for public sculpture. He was born in Boston, MA, the son of Silas and Cornelia Mozart McVey, who brought him to Cleveland in 1919. Graduating from Shaw High School in 1922, he studied architecture at Rice Institute in Texas before returning to graduate from the Cleveland School of Art (see CLEVELAND INSTITUTE OF ART†) in 1928. He furthered his studies during 2 years in Paris, where he was a pupil of Charles Despiau and attended the Colarossi and Scaninave academies. In 1932 he returned to Cleveland and married Leza Marie Sullivan. Working for the New Deal art projects, he sculpted a grizzly bear now at the CLEVELAND MUSEUM OF NATURAL HISTORY† and a bas-relief of Paul Bunyan for the community center at LAKEVIEW TERRACE.† His allegorical statue of "Dawn" was a centerpiece of the horticultural gardens at the GREAT LAKES EXPOSITION.† During the late 1930s, while teaching in Texas, he executed monuments to Jim Bowie and Davy Crockett and a stone frieze at the base of the San Jacinto Monument near Houston. After service in the Army Air Force during World War II and postwar teaching in Michigan, McVey returned to Cleveland as head of the sculpture department at CIA from 1953–67. He subsequently worked as a full-time sculptor in his studio in PEPPER PIKE.† Local commissions in his later period included bronzes of George Washington at the Anthony J. Celebreeze Federal Bldg., JESSE OWENS at HUNTINGTON PARK,† Archbishop John Carroll at JOHN CARROLL UNIV.,† HART CRANE and TOM L. JOHNSON at CASE WESTERN RESERVE UNIV.,† and a 7'-high B clef at Blossom Music Ctr. In Washington, DC, he is represented by bronze doors in the Federal Trade Commission Bldg., 5 stone statues in the National Cathedral, and, possibly his masterpiece, the 9' heroic bronze of Winston Churchill standing outside the British Embassy with one foot within British jurisdiction and the other on American soil. He died in Chardon, OH, leaving no survivors.—J.V.

William McVey Papers, WRHS.

**MAGEE, ELIZABETH STEWART** (29 June 1889–14 May 1972), active securing labor reform legislation, especially child- and female-labor laws, was born in Des Moines, IA, to William A. and Lizzie Dysart. She graduated from Oberlin College in 1911, and taught in Altoona, PA, public schools before moving to Denver, CO, in 1916 as YWCA secretary. In 1918 she went to Detroit, MI, as industrial secretary of the YWCA, responsible for planning and directing recreational and educational programs for women industrial workers. From 1922–24 she was the YWCA national industrial secretary in New York City, organizing national concerns of female industrial workers. While in New York, Magee attended Columbia Univ., receiving a master's degree in economics in 1925.

From 1925 until she retired in 1965, Magee was executive secretary of the CONSUMERS' LEAGUE OF OHIO.† She immediately became active in the labor movement and developed a close relationship with labor leaders in state and federal government. Her study of unemployment in 1928 and her work as secretary for Ohio Gov. George White's Ohio Commission on Unemployment Insurance (1931–32) led to the Ohio Plan of unemployment compensation, which, as a form of unemployment insurance, stressed more secure funding and larger benefits and was influential in the formation of the Social Security Act of 1935. Magee was instrumental in the Consumers League's campaign for passage of a minimum-wage law for women in 1933 and for Ohio's ratification of the federal child-labor amendment. Magee worked to prevent child labor; for a shorter work week for women; to improve the status of Ohio's migrant workers; and for other social welfare issues. From 1943–58, Magee also served as general secretary for the Natl. Consumers' League.

Consumers' League of Ohio Records, WRHS.
Elizabeth Stewart Magee Papers, WRHS.

**MAJERUS, LAWRENCE (LARRY MADGE)** (19 May 1908–13 Dec. 1993), outstanding local boxer, was born in Cleveland, the son of Henry and Gusta Grabowski Majerus. After graduation from Lincoln High School he worked as a machinist, joining Thompson Products in 1933, where he remained for 38 years. Using the name Larry Madge, he boxed professionally as a welterweight (147 pounds) in the 1920s and 1930s. A solid puncher, Madge had many bouts in Cleveland, Akron, Youngstown, and in western Pennsylvania, where he narrowly lost to welterweight title contender Thaddeus (Teddy) Yarosz. Majerus also promoted local boxing matches at the Navy Gym in Cleveland and taught the elements of boxing to disadvantaged children at the Old Angle gym. He was inducted into the Cleveland Boxing Hall of Fame in 1984.

Majerus married Alice Yager in Cleveland 20 Aug. 1931. Apparently there were no children. He died in Cleveland and was buried at Holy Cross Cemetery.—M.S.

**MAJESKE, DANIEL HAROLD** (17 Sept. 1932–28 Nov. 1993) was concertmaster of the CLEVELAND ORCHESTRA† for a record 24 years. A native of Detroit, he was the son of Daniel and Esther Ebert Majeske, both of whom were ardent amateur musicians. After graduating from Dearborn High School, the younger Majeske studied violin at Philadelphia's Curtis Institute of Music. He married Marilyn Jeup in 1950 and joined the armed services to become a member of the U.S. Navy Band. He left the navy in 1955 to join the first violin section of the Cleveland Orchestra, becoming asst. concertmaster in 1959 and associate concertmaster in 1967. He was appointed the orchestra's 11th concertmaster by GEORGE SZELL 2 years later, following the sudden resignation of Rafael Druian. During his long tenure he worked under Szell and his 2 successors, Lorin Maazel and Christoph von Dohnanyi. He performed on his 1718 Stradivarius as soloist with the orchestra on more than 100 occasions and in many of the ensemble's recordings. Majeske also taught at the CLEVELAND MUSIC SCHOOL SETTLEMENT† from 1965–86 and gave frequent master classes at the CLEVELAND INSTITUTE OF MUSIC.† He also taught Sunday school and preached at many area churches. He died at his home in EUCLID,† survived by his wife, daughter Sharon Chari, and son Stephen, a member of the Cleveland Orchestra's violin section since 1979.

**MALONE, EMMA BROWN** (30 Jan. 1859–12 May 1924), with her husband J. WALTER MALONE, organized the Christian Workers' Training School for Bible Study and Practical Methods of Work (opened 17 March 1892) in Cleveland, the precursor of Malone College, Canton, OH. (It was also known as the Bible Institute or Cleveland Friends Bible Institute.) The school trained more women ministers than anywhere else in the country, at least 14 in 1892–93 alone. Malone was born in OHIO CITY† to Charles W. and Margaret Haight Brown. After graduating valedictorian of Cleveland's West High School, she began attending the Friends Meeting in Cleveland and was soon serving the Sunday school, led by J. Walter Malone. The two married on 19 January 1886; they had 6 children: Carroll B., J. Walter, Jr., Franklin, Margaret Crobaugh Day, Esther M. Waterbury, and Ruth M. Osborne.

Discouraged by secular influences in denominational colleges, the devout Malones opened a training school, serving as co-principals and teachers. Under their auspices, students attended services and performed mission work first at the ACADEMY OF MUSIC† and then at the Whosoever Will Mission, at an old Free Methodist church. The couple wrote for local and national publications and participated in national conferences of Friends. In 1892 Emma Malone served as clerk of the national meeting. —J.V.

J. Walter Malone Papers, Malone College, Canton, Ohio.
Oliver, John W., ed. *J. Walter Malone: The Autobiography of an Evangelical Quaker* (1993).
Osborne, John W. *The Malone Story: The Dream of Two Quaker Young People* (1970).

**MALONE, J. WALTER** (11 Aug. 1857–30 Dec. 1935), and his wife, EMMA BROWN MALONE, Evangelical Quakers, founded the Christian Workers' Training School for Bible Study and Practical Methods of Work in March 1892 in Cleveland. Also known as the Bible Institute or Cleveland Friends Bible Institute, the facility later developed into Malone College of Canton, OH. Walter Malone was born in Clermont County, near Cincinnati, OH, the 7th of 8 children of Quakers Mary Ann Pennington Malone (a preacher) and John Carl Malone. The family later moved to New Vienna, OH, then a state center for Quakerism. Malone was educated first at public schools, then at the preparatory department of Earlham College (1874), and graduated from Chickering Institute in Cincinnati in 1877. In 1880 he came to Cleveland to work in his brother's stone quarry firm, Malone and Co. Malone taught Sunday school at the Euclid Ave. Congregational Church before taking leadership of the Sunday school of the CLEVELAND MEETING OF FRIENDS† (begun in 1871 by JAMES and MERBIAH BUTLER FARMER ). In March 1882 he organized the first local Quaker revival, which added enough new members to set up the Cleveland Monthly Meeting the next spring.

Malone married Emma Brown on 19 Jan. 1886; they had 6 children: Carroll B., J. Walter, Jr., Franklin, Margaret Crobaugh Day, Esther M. Waterbury, and Ruth M. Osborne. The couple concentrated on urban ministry to people of all races and social classes, holding evangelistic meetings in the ACADEMY OF MUSIC† until it burned in 1892, then opening the Whosoever Will Mission,

which served meals to the poor in a former Free Methodist church. Malone was elected to the Board of Directors of the Publishing Assn. of Friends in 1890 and cofounded *The American Friend*. He and Emma published *The Christian Worker, The Bible Student, The Soul-Winner, The Evangelical Friend,* and *The Young People*.—J.M.

J. Walter Malone Papers, Malone College, Canton, Ohio.
Oliver, John W., ed. *J. Walter Malone: The Autobiography of an Evangelical Quaker* (1993).
Osborne, John W. *The Malone Story: The Dream of Two Quaker Young People* (1970).

**MALVIN, JOHN** (1795–30 July 1880), a leader of Cleveland's black community, worked at various times as a cook, sawmill operator, carpenter and joiner, and canal-boat captain, and was a licensed and ordained Baptist preacher. He was born in Dumfries, Prince William County, VA, to a slave father and free mother, making him free under the Slave Code. He was apprenticed as a carpenter, secretly taught to read, and arrived in Cleveland in 1831 after a short stay in Cincinnati.

Malvin organized a black school committee in Cleveland (1832) and a statewide committee (1835) to finance black education; the resulting School Fund Society opened schools for black children in Cleveland, Columbus, Springfield, and Cincinnati. The committees also worked to change Ohio laws prohibiting municipalities from even establishing segregated schools for blacks. Efforts of black citizens in Cleveland resulted in a limited subsidy from city council for the privately supported black school and abolishment of the state law clause limiting public school access to white children in 1848.

Malvin and his wife, Harriet (married 8 Mar. 1829), were charter members of FIRST BAPTIST CHURCH† in 1833 and prevented the church from segregating its members. At the onset of the Civil War, Malvin organized a black military company that joined the 54th and 55th Massachusetts regiments. Malvin lectured for the Ohio State Anti-Slavery Society and was reportedly active in the Underground Railroad. Malvin vigorously opposed Ohio's BLACK LAWS.†

Known to many as "Father John," Malvin died at his Cleveland home and was buried in Erie St. Cemetery.

Peskin, Allen. *North Into Freedom: The Autobiography of John Malvin, Free Negro, 1795–1880* (1966).

**MANDELBAUM, MAURICE J. (MOSES)** (1863–16 July 1938), philanthropist, Jewish community leader, banker, and a powerful interurban-railway magnate, was born in Cleveland to Jacob and Mary (Schwab) Mandelbaum. After graduating from CENTRAL HIGH SCHOOL† (1880), he worked for his father, a wealthy retail clothier. Mandelbaum was involved in several businesses. He founded Fisher Book Typewriter Co., which later became the Underwood Elliot Fisher Co., and was a founder of Western Reserve Trust Co., which merged with Cleveland Trust Co., where Mandelbaum was on the Board of Directors. In 1896 Mandelbaum began in the interurban railway business when he and his brother-in-law, Leopold Wolf, formed the Western Ohio lines. They also were interested in the Aurora-Chicago-Elgin line. Mandelbaum later became the principal owner of Southern Ohio Traction Co.

Mandelbaum was a consummate fundraiser and active in community-wide organizations, as well as being a leader in Jewish communal affairs. He chaired the Cleveland chapter of the Red Cross for 2 years, and was on the Board of Directors of the CITIZENS LEAGUE.† Following his father's death in 1916, Mandelbaum became president of the board of the MONTEFIORE HOME,† serving as director, treasurer, or president for 25 years. He was also on the Board of Trustees of the TEMPLE† and was vice-president of the Educational League, an organization established by Rabbi MOSES GRIES to ensure that alumni of the Jewish Orphan Home had the opportunity to receive college educations. Mandelbaum married three times. His first marriage was on 22 March 1893 to Amanda Mayer. After divorcing, he married Florence S. Levy on 10 Oct. 1905 (d. 13 Feb. 1920). His third marriage was to Florence Burnet Beck, 9 Dec. 1922. Mandelbaum had no children. He was buried in Mayfield Cemetery.

**MANNING, THOMAS EDWARD "RED"** (27 Sept. 1899–4 Sept. 1969), a radio sportscaster, was born in Cleveland to John and Catherine (Cahill) Manning. Winning a Euclid Beach contest for the newsboy with the loudest voice led to Manning's career as an announcer. An outfielder with the Telling team in Class AAA, Manning was hired by the CLEVELAND INDIANS† as field announcer at Dunn Field (LEAGUE PARK†). Using a 4' megaphone, Manning shouted the lineups to the press box and the batteries to the fans, with "the second loudest noise in Cleveland, the first being the foghorn off WHISKEY ISLAND."†

Manning's first radio job came in 1926 when WJAY hired him to give baseball scores. Manning moved to WTAM† in 1928, and the Tribe hired him as the first radio voice of the Indians. In 1931 another radio station got the baseball contract, and Manning's connection with the Indians ended. Years later, in 1956, he joined Jimmy Dudley to announce Cleveland baseball over station WERE, but had to resign in 1957 because an ear infection made it painful to fly. For 6 years, beginning in 1929, Manning joined Graham McNamee to do network baseball and World Series broadcasting. He was the radio voice of the Ohio State Univ. football team for 30 years. He announced for WERE, KYW, and WHK† before retiring in 1967. Manning married his first wife, Amelia, in 1924; they divorced in 1939. His second wife, Hazel, whom he married on 30 Sept. 1939, survived him.

**MANNIX, JOHN R.** (4 June 1902–9 Feb. 1990), a national consultant in health care, was inducted into the National Health Care Hall of Fame in Philadelphia (1989) for, among other contributions, pioneering prepaid health service in the U.S. Mannix conceived the idea of prepaid hospital insurance, a program which later developed into Blue Cross and Blue Shield (see BLUE CROSS OF NORTHEAST OHIO, BLUE CROSS AND BLUE SHIELD MUTUAL OF NORTHERN OHIO†). Mannix, raised in Cleveland, was born to Henry H. and Cecelia Mannix, the oldest of 7 children. Family medical bills led to financial troubles, which triggered Mannix to create a different payment system. While working at MT. SINAI MEDICAL CENTER† as a youth, Mannix suggested the idea of prepaid medical insurance. He initiated the idea at Elyria Memorial Hospital, where he became administrator in 1926, at age 24. Appointed asst. director of UNIV. HOSPITALS† in 1930, 2 years later Mannix convinced the Cleveland Hospital Council to study prepaid hospital care. The study resulted in the creation of the CLEVELAND HOSPITAL SERVICE ASSN.† (1934), modeled across the U.S. Mannix later created a statewide Blue Cross plan in both Michigan (1939), enhancing national enrollment by wooing auto manufacturers, and Illinois (1944); he founded and directed the John Marshall Insurance Co. (1946).

In 1948 Mannix returned to Cleveland as chief executive officer of the Cleveland Hospital Service Assn., later Blue Cross of Northeast Ohio. He lived in LAKEWOOD.† He retired in 1965 and became a research consultant at Blue Cross. Mannix, who was divorced, had 3 children, Rose Ann Post, Frank, and John, Jr. He is buried in Calvary Cemetery. —J.M.

John Mannix Papers, Stanley Ferguson Archives, Univ. Hospitals.
John Mannix Papers, Center for Hospital and Health Care Administration History, AHA, Chicago, IL.

**MANRY, ROBERT N.** (3 June 1918–21 Feb. 1971), who sailed the 13½ ft. sloop *Tinkerbelle* across the Atlantic, was born in Landour, India, to Presbyterian missionary Dr. James C. and Margaret Manry. He left India in 1936, studied briefly in China, and enrolled at Antioch College in 1937, receiving an A.B. in 1948 after service during World War II. Manry worked as a newspaper reporter Washington Court House, OH, and Pittsburgh and Erie, PA, before coming to Cleveland in 1953 to work at the *PLAIN DEALER†* as a copyeditor.

Manry's enthusiasm for boating began on the Jumna River in India, but he could not afford his own secondhand boat until 1958. Manry first sailed *Tinkerbelle* on Lake Erie in 1959, improved his sailing skills, and modified his boat. Taking vacation time and a leave from the *Plain Dealer* in 1965, he left Falmouth, MA, on 1 June for Falmouth, England, 3,200 miles away. The voyage took 2½ months, during which time Manry was knocked overboard 6 times and had to repair a broken rudder. His progress was covered by news services, and the *Plain Dealer* flew his wife and 2 children to England to meet him. Manry landed at Falmouth on 17 Aug. 1965, completing a 78-day voyage. Manry wrote a book about his adventure, *Tinkerbelle,* and donated the sailboat to the WESTERN RESERVE HISTORICAL SOCIETY.†

Manry married Virginia Place in 1950 (d. 1969); they had two children, Robin and Douglas. He then married Jean Flaherty. Manry died of a heart attack in Willowick and was buried in Mt. Lebanon Cemetery in Mt. Lebanon, PA.

Robert Manry Papers, WRHS.

**MARCOSSON, SOL** (10 June 1869–10 Jan. 1940) was Cleveland's premiere violinist for several decades and a key performer in some of the city's leading musical organizations. Born in Louisville, KY, he received his early training there before going to Europe to study at the Berlin Hochschule under violinist Joseph Joachim. He toured Europe before returning to the U.S., where he played first violin in Boston's Mendelssohn Quintet and in the quartet of the New York Philharmonic Club. Brought to Cleveland in 1895 by the FORTNIGHTLY MUSICAL CLUB,† Marcosson added his 1730 Cremona violin to the city's PHILHARMONIC STRING QUARTET† in 1897, filling the group's first violin chair for the next 30 years. He also served as concertmaster for the Chicago Symphony, for JOHANN BECK's Cleveland Symphony Orchestra of 1900–01, and for the inaugural season of the present CLEVELAND ORCHESTRA† in 1918–19. As a teacher, he directed the violin dept. at the Chautauqua Institute in Chautauqua, NY, and at Lake Erie College in

Painesville. In the 1920s he opened the Marcosson Music School in the Fine Arts Bldg., and later maintained a studio in Cleveland's Carnegie Hall. Married since 1902 to the former Dorothy Frew of Youngstown, OH, he had 4 children: Fred, John, June, and Ruth. He was also survived by his brother, Isaac Marcosson, a nationally known magazine writer. He was buried in Lake View Cemetery.—J.V.

**MARCUS, SARAH, M.D.** (22 Aug. 1894–11 May 1985) served WOMAN'S GENERAL HOSPITAL† as head of the department of obstetrics and gynecology (1933–50) and as vice-president (1932–58) and president of the hospital board (1958–71). Among the first physicians at the Maternal Health Assn. (MHA) clinic (later PLANNED PARENTHOOD OF GREATER CLEVELAND†), Marcus served on the MHA Medical Advisory Board and later initiated marriage counseling and a fertility clinic there. Marcus was born in Sommerville, SC, one of 7 children of Aaron and Etta Horovitz Marcus (spelled Marcu in their native Romania). She attended public schools in the south and after moving to Cleveland, graduated from CENTRAL HIGH SCHOOL† (1912) and Phi Beta Kappa from Women's (later Flora Stone Mather) College of Western Reserve Univ. (WRU, 1916, see CASE WESTERN RESERVE UNIV.†). Denied admission to WRU's School of Medicine on the basis of sex, Marcus attended medical school at the Univ. of Michigan, graduating in 1920. She interned at Women's Hospital in Detroit, MI (1920–21) and looked in vain for a residency in Cleveland. Marcus worked at Ohio City Hospital in Akron, OH, for only 1 year before becoming Chief Resident. In 1923 Cleveland's Mt. Sinai Hospital (see MT. SINAI MEDICAL CENTER†) hired her in the outpatient clinic. She joined Woman's General in 1925. Marcus, who studied with a disciple of Sigmund Freud in Vienna (1928), maintained a large general private practice, located first on the west side and then in the Republic Building, into her 80s.

Marcus joined the Board of Trustees of Woman's General Hospital in 1931. A champion of the special contributions of women to medicine, she helped found the WOMEN'S MEDICAL SOCIETY OF CLEVELAND,† served as vice-president of the American Medical Women's Assn., and contributed to the *Medical Women's Journal.* In 1971 Marcus received the distinguished alumna award from the Univ. of Michigan.

Marcus married twice. Her first marriage was on 17 Aug. 1924 to William Schwartz; they had a son, Joseph. After divorcing in 1939, Marcus married Dr. Samuel B. Cowen on 25 Oct. 1942. She died in Chicago.—J.M.

Marcus, Sarah. Oral History (with Ellen Chesler, *Women and Family Planning in America* Series, Schlesinger Library, Radcliffe College, 1977), WRHS.

Sarah Marcus Papers, Dittrick Museum of Medical History, Cleveland Health Sciences Library.

Woman's General Hospital Records, Dittrick Museum of Medical History.

**MARGOLIES, SAMUEL** (April 1879–6 July 1917), educator, Zionist, and rabbi of ANSHE EMETH CONGREGATION† (1904–16) was brought to America from his native Russia by his parents, Moses Zebulon and Nellie Margolies in 1882. In 1890 he returned to Russia to study at Telshe Yeshiva, coming to the U.S. 8 years later, graduating from Harvard Univ. in 1902. Margolies accepted the pulpit at Anshe Emeth in 1904 and made it the most important Orthodox congregation in the city. Margolies introduced a modern element into Orthodoxy, preaching not only in Yiddish, the vernacular of immigrant Jews, but also in English, encouraging his listeners to Americanize. In 1912 he encouraged the creation of Congregation Beth Tifilah for Orthodox Jews in GLENVILLE,† and helped arrange its merger with Anshe Emeth in 1916.

Margolies was a founder of the UNION OF JEWISH ORGANIZATIONS† (1906); president of the Cleveland KEHILLAH† (1913–14); a leader in revitalizing Cleveland's Talmud Torahs; and founder of the Hebrew School & Institute. He spearheaded the drive ensuring that Mt. Sinai Hospital's kitchen would be kosher, although the kitchen remained kosher only 1 year. An ardent Zionist, Margolies was president of the Ohio Fed. of Zionists, and in 1917 received the largest number of votes to represent Cleveland Jewry at the first American Jewish Congress, but died before the convention convened from injuries suffered in an automobile accident. Margolies resigned from Anshe Emeth in 1917 and entered the insurance business. He was also manager and an editor of *YIDDISHE VELT,†* a local Yiddish newspaper.

Margolies married Rena Franks in 1904. They had two children, Asher F. and Daniel F. Margolies died in Geneva, OH, and was buried in New York, NY.

**MARINE, DAVID** (20 Sept. 1880–26 Nov. 1976), whose research on thyroid disorders led to salt iodation to prevent goiter, was born in Whitleysburg, MD, and attended Western Maryland College and Johns Hopkins School of Medicine, receiving his medical degree in 1905 and coming to Cleveland as resident pathologist at Lakeside Hospital. He was also demonstrator of pathology (1905–06), then associate professor of experimental medicine (1915–20) at Western Reserve Univ. School of Medicine.

Marine studied thyroid disorders at WRU's Cushing Laboratory for Experimental Medicine. Cleveland was in the nation's "goiter belt," and Marine noticed dogs' swollen necks walking to his first day of work. He studied animals, investigating the thyroid gland; his first study of goiter in humans involved pediatric patients at Lakeside Hospital Dispensary. In 1917 Marine and his student, O. P. Kimball, published "The Prevention of Simple Goiter in Man," describing the goiter-prevention program they had established in Akron, OH, involving 4,500 schoolgirls. The final results, published in 1920, demonstrated the efficacy of sodium iodine. Despite some opposition, the prevention of goiter through iodized salt eventually became standard public health practice.

During and immediately after World War I, Marine was a medical officer with the U.S. Army in Europe. He returned briefly to Cleveland, then moved to Montefiore Hospital in New York City, where he spent the rest of his career until retiring in 1945 and moving to Sussex County, DE. He married Mary Elizabeth Nuttle and had a son, David. Marine died in Lewes, DE, and was buried in the Hillcrest Cemetery in Federalsburg, Maryland.

David Marine Papers, Univ. Hospitals Archives.

**MARKEY, SANFORD** (22 May 1914–2 June 1995) was accorded the title of "Renaissance Man" for his experience in all facets of communications. The son of Morris and Fannie Grossman Markey, he was born in Cleveland and graduated from Glenville High School. He earned a bachelor's degree from Western Reserve Univ. (see CASE WESTERN RESERVE†) and a master's in journalism from Columbia. Markey entered journalism with the International News Service before joining the *CLEVELAND NEWS†* from 1941–44. He then broke into radio as news director for WTAM† and subsequently filled the same position for television station WNBK (see WKYC†). Among the innovations he brought to local news broadcasting were the area's first helicopter traffic reports, live City Hall broadcasts, and computerized election returns based on exit polls. In 1951 he organized Cleveland's first AFTRA awards, which eventually evolved into the local Emmy awards for outstanding work in broadcasting. Markey then moved into the publicity field, becoming director of public relations for JOHN CARROLL UNIV.† in 1966 and for the JEWISH COMMUNITY FEDERATION† the following year. He became director of university-community relations for CLEVELAND STATE UNIV.† in 1975, retiring as the university's vice-president for special projects in 1984. Even in retirement, he continued to work as the Cleveland stringer for *Variety,* the national show business weekly. A former president of the PRESS CLUB OF CLEVELAND,† Markey was inducted into the CLEVELAND JOURNALISM HALL OF FAME† in 1990. Unmarried, he died in Hudson, OH.—J.V.

**MARKS, MARTIN A.** (6 Feb. 1853–31 Aug. 1916), businessman and community leader, was born in Madison, WI, the son of Aaron and Sarah (August) Marks. He quit school at age 13, and as a young man became active in B'NAI B'RITH.† He was appointed to the Board of Trustees of the Jewish Orphan Home in 1885. While traveling to Cleveland on business, Marks met Belle Hays, daughter of KAUFMAN HAYS; he married her in 1885 and a year later moved to Cleveland. Marks purchased an interest in a wholesale clothing firm, in 1890 worked for Northwest Life Insurance Co., and a year later became northern Ohio manager for Equitable Life Assurance Co. of New York, remaining there 14 years. In 1902 Marks became a director of CLEVELAND WORSTED MILLS†; in 1906 he became secretary-treasurer, a position he held until his death. He also was on the Board of Directors of First Natl. Bank and GUARDIAN SAVINGS & TRUST CO.†

Marks was president of the TEMPLE† (1890–1904, 1906–15), serving when Rabbi MOSES GRIES was hired. When Gries suggested the creation of the Educational League to ensure higher education opportunities for orphans, Marks became the first president of the B'nai B'rith-sponsored organization. Marks helped establish the Fed. of Jewish Charities (1903), and was appointed to an FJC committee to review and report on all immigration bills proposed in Congress. Marks was a founder in 1913 of the Fed. for Charity & Philanthropy, and chaired the Committee on Benevolent Associations of the Chamber of Commerce.

Marks had 2 children, Florence and Ethyl. He died in Cleveland and was buried in Mayfield Cemetery.

**MARSH, W. WARD** (12 Aug. 1893–23 June 1971), *PLAIN DEALER†* movie critic for half a century, was born in MacLean, PA, to Elmer W. and Emma (Davis) Ward. He attended Edinboro State Teachers College, Erie Business College, and Adelbert College at Western Reserve Univ. (see CASE WESTERN RESERVE UNIV.†) before joining the *Plain Dealer* in 1915 as police reporter, religion editor, and copyeditor. He married coworker Mabel Boyes on 22 Jan. 1920. He served in France during World War I. In 1919 Marsh wrote his first of 23,000 movie reviews for the *Plain Dealer.* Marsh numbered Joan

Crawford and Ross Hunter among his friends, and made a cameo appearance in Clark Gable's film, *Teacher's Pet,* in 1957. As the area's movie trivia authority, Marsh wrote and produced a local television movie quiz program in the 1950s called "Lights, Camera, Question." He also taught "The History, Enjoyment, and Criticism of the Movie" course at Western Reserve's Cleveland College. In the 1960s Marsh fought a losing battle against the screen's increasing sexual permissiveness. His scathing review of a film called *The Lovers* in 1959 contributed to the prosecution of its exhibitor, Nico Jacobellis of the Hts. Art Theatre, for obscenity. In a landmark censorship ruling in 1964, the U.S. Supreme Court declared the film was not obscene. Marsh died less than a year after his retirement, survived by his wife. Roger Marsh, their only child, died in 1967. Marsh's collection of movie memorabilia, including 3 personally bound copies of scripts presented to him by Cecil B. DeMille, was donated to the CLEVELAND PUBLIC LIBRARY.† He was buried in Markillie Cemetery in Hudson.

**MARSHALL, JOHN D.** (14 Mar. 1885–17 May 1961), city councilman for 12 years and, as president of the council, mayor of Cleveland under the CITY MANAGER PLAN† (1925–33) was born in Bucyrus, OH, to Daniel and Mary Gerster Marshall. He received an A.B. degree from Ohio Wesleyan Univ. and an LL.B. degree from Western Reserve Univ. in 1914. Marshall became asst. law director of the city in 1917 and 3 years later was appointed commissioner of franchises. He was elected to city council as a Republican in 1921. As president of the council, he succeeded CLAYTON TOWNES as mayor in 1925 and remained until 1933, when the City Manager Plan was abolished. At that time, he retired from politics, resuming his law practice and serving as secretary of the Ohio Brewers Assn. Marshall married Susan Ridell (d. 1944) on 17 Nov. 1917. They had a daughter, Susan Marshall McDonald. Marshall died in Cleveland. He was survived by his second wife, Irene Morash, whom he married on 26 Oct. 1945.

**MARSHALL, LYCURGUS LUTHER** (9 July 1888–12 Jan. 1958), lawyer and brother and law partner of Cleveland mayor JOHN D. MARSHALL, was born in Bucyrus, OH, to Daniel and Mary (Gerster) Marshall. He graduated from Ohio Wesleyan Univ. (1909) and taught while attending law school at Western Reserve Univ. He graduated and was admitted to the bar in 1915. A Republican, Marshall was elected state representative (1921–22), and state senator (1923–35). He was also president of the Euclid Board of Education (1923–31). As state senator, Marshall was chairman of the Senate Judiciary Committee and noted for introducing the bill eliminating legal restrictions against the presentation of motion pictures on Sundays. In 1931 he successfully supported a new corporation code and a new probate code. Marshall also authored the bill allowing the issuance of tax-anticipation warrants, or "scrip money," to pay county employees during the Depression. In 1933 Marshall chaired the banking committee, investigating banks closed by the Depression. This resulted in the conviction of 2 bank presidents and several bank officers. In 1934 and 1936 Marshall ran unsuccessfully as the Republican nominee for congressional representative-at-large, winning in 1938. He was defeated in 1940 for reelection, as well as for a common pleas court vacancy. He returned to his law practice, but in 1950 ran for Ohio secretary of state; however he was ruled off the ballot because of invalid petitions and a resulting lack of signatures in enough counties. Marshall married Minnie Martin on 14 Aug. 1911 and had 2 sons, Hubert and Edward. He died in Cleveland and was buried in Lake View Cemetery.

**MARSHALL, WENTWORTH GOODSON** (13 Dec. 1864–24 Feb. 1936), pioneer Cleveland druggist and experimental botanist, was born in Mount Forest, Ontario, the son of John Jacob and Sarah Ellen (Langton) Marshall. He was educated in Toronto and worked for a chemist in Canada before he came to Cleveland in 1884, buying an interest in Arthur F. May's drug store, located where the Terminal Tower now stands. A few years later, Marshall and May bought a second store in the Rouse Block on the northwest corner of Superior and PUBLIC SQUARE,† and the W. G. Marshall Co. was formed. The name was shortened to the Marshall Drug Co. when he bought Mr. May out. Early drugstores such as Marshall's were meeting places for the medical men of the time, and where people sent messages when they needed a physician. Marshall gradually began to stock proprietary medicines manufactured by pharmaceutical houses and installed a soda fountain. He built the Marshall Bldg. on the Superior site in 1913. By 1946 he owned a chain of 46 stores. Marshall also owned the 1,000-acre Rocky Run arboretum in Summit County, where he conducted botanical experiments in conjunction with the U.S. government and Western Reserve Univ. experts, in order to determine what trees, shrubs, and flowers could thrive in this climate.

Marshall married Louise Marie Gehring 14 Sept. 1888; they had 2 sons, George G. and Wentworth J., who entered the business. He died at his home in Shaker Hts. and was buried at Northfield Cemetery in Northfield, OH.—M.S.

**MARTIN, ALEXANDER H.** (8 Dec. 1872–13 or 14 Nov. 1962), well known black lawyer and a leader among the city's black Republicans, was born in Ironton, OH, to Jake and Lydia (Calloway) Martin. He graduated from high school in Geneva at 16 and learned the barber trade. In 1891 he entered Adelbert College of Western Reserve Univ., graduating Phi Beta Kappa in 1895 and receiving a scholarship to WRU law school. He qualified to take the state bar exam after only his second year, and was admitted to the bar a year before graduating from law school. Martin practiced law in Cleveland for 65 years. For many years he was a perennial candidate for judge in various courts, but was never elected. He also attempted to gain the Republican nomination for Congress in 1936. Martin helped organize the Attucks Republican Club of Cleveland and was its president. In 1900 he was instrumental in shifting black support in Cleveland to the Democratic nominee for president, Wm. Jennings Bryan. He later returned to the Republican party. Among his many civic involvements, Martin served on the executive committee for the CLEVELAND ASSN. OF COLORED MEN† and, in 1922, was one of the chief organizers of the Cedar Ave. Branch of the YMCA.

Martin married Mary Brown (see MARY BROWN MARTIN) in 1905. They had four children: Lydia J., Alexander H., Jr., Stuart B., and Sarah M. (Pereira). He was buried at Highland Park Cemetery.

**MARTIN, MARY BROWN** (1877–19 Nov. 1939), the first black woman elected to the Cleveland Board of Education, was born in Raleigh, NC, to M. Scott and Jane (Curtis) Brown, both former slaves. She came to Cleveland in 1886 and attended Rockwell School and CENTRAL HIGH SCHOOL,† graduating in 1900 as the class vocalist. She graduated from Cleveland Normal Training School in 1903. Brown taught school for 2 years in Alabama and Arkansas, then returned to Cleveland. In the 1920s, Martin became a teacher in the CLEVELAND PUBLIC SCHOOLS,† and in 1930 she was elected to the Board of Education. She served 2 terms, declining to run for a third term in 1937. In 1939, however, she was elected again. Martin was also one of the few black women in Cleveland active in the women's suffrage movement. Mary B. Martin Elementary School at 8200 Brookline Ave. was named in her honor.

Martin married ALEXANDER H. MARTIN in 1905. They had four children: Lydia J., Alexander H., Jr., Stuart B., and Sarah M. (Pereira). Martin was buried in Highland Park Cemetery.

Mary B. Martin Scrapbook, WRHS.

**MARTINEK, JOSEPH** (23 Mar. 1889–21 Mar. 1980), Czech socialist and nationalist, was born in Podebrady, near Prague, to John and Anna (Borecka) Martinek. He trained as a metalworker, and worked in Germany 3 years before coming to Cleveland in 1909, working as a lathe operator while taking courses in sociology at Western Reserve Univ. Martinek was a member and gym instructor of the WORKERS GYMNASTIC UNION,† a socialist gymnastic and Czech nationalist organization. He was a valued speaker at labor meetings, speaking German, Slovak, Russian, Spanish, Czech, and English. In 1912 he became editor of *AMERICKY DELNICKY LISTY*,† and edited Czech-American publications until 1934. From 1918–34 he was president of the Workingman's Cooperative, a chain of 7 co-op grocery stores, also serving as a director of the Cooperative League of America. Martinek helped carry Cuyahoga County for Sen. Robt. M. La Follette in the 1924 presidential primary, and ran unsuccessfully as a Socialist for county commissioner (1926), state representative (1928), and city council (1929, 1933).

Martinek fought with the Czechoslovakian Foreign Legion in Siberia in World War I, and in 1934 returned to Czechoslovakia as editor of the labor paper *Pravo Lidu*. An active anti-Nazi, Martinek fled to escape Hitler's forces in 1938, returning to the U.S. as executive secretary of the Czechoslovak Natl. Council in Chicago from 1939–45. In 1947 Martinek moved to Tucson, AZ, writing scripts for Radio Free Europe and the Voice of America, as well as poetry, publishing 5 books between 1944–68. Martinek married Marie Fiserova on 1 Dec. 1914. They had no children. Martinek died in Arizona and was buried there.

Frank Bardoun Papers, WRHS.

**MASCHKE, MAURICE** (16 Oct. 1868–19 Nov. 1936), leader of the CUYAHOGA COUNTY REPUBLICAN PARTY† for 35 years, was born in Cleveland to Joseph and Rosa Salinger Maschke. He received his A.B. from Harvard Univ. in 1890, returned to Cleveland, studied law, and was admitted to the Ohio Bar in 1891. While reading law, he worked searching titles at the CUYAHOGA COUNTY COURTHOUSE,† and eventually became an authority on title law. In 1914 he became a partner in the law firm of Mathews, Orgill & Maschke.

In 1897 Maschke was a precinct worker for Republican Mayor Robt. E. McKisson, being appointed deputy county recorder after McKisson's reelection. Maschke formed a political alliance with ALBERT "STARLIGHT" BOYD and worked with Republican congressman THEODORE BURTON.

He served briefly as county recorder in 1910. In 1911 he was appointed collector of customs by Pres. Wm. Taft, serving until 1914, when he became the head of the county Republican party organization, the peak of his power being 1914–28. He was elected Republican national committeeman 1924–32. Maschke initially supported the appointment of WM. R. HOPKINS for city manager; however, as Hopkins's influence over city council grew, Maschke's support turned into opposition and he was instrumental in persuading the council to remove Hopkins in 1930. With the ascendancy of the Democratic party in the 1930s, his influence began to wane, and he retired as county Republican chairman in 1933. Maschke married Minnie Rice in 1903 and had 2 children, Maurice, Jr., and Helen Lamping Hanna. He died in Cleveland.

Maurice Maschke Papers, Ohio Historical Society.

**MASTERS, IRVINE U.** (1823–13 Nov. 1865), OHIO CITY† politician, shipbuilder, and Cleveland mayor, was born in New York and moved to Ohio in 1851 with his first wife, Naomi. He became a trustee of Ohio City and helped WM. B. CASTLE negotiate the merger between Cleveland and Ohio City. Masters served on CLEVELAND CITY COUNCIL† (1854–63), 3 times as council president (1859–61, 1862–63), officially welcoming Abraham Lincoln to Cleveland when he visited in Feb. 1861. In 1863 Masters, a Republican, defeated incumbent mayor EDWARD S. FLINT, supporting measures to improve business and showing support for the war effort, holding public meetings and ceremonies for soldiers. Masters had tuberculosis and resigned because of poor health in May 1864. Masters was also a businessman, as a partner with E. M. PECK in Peck & Masters shipbuilding company: the firm's ships were among the larger on the Great Lakes. After resigning his mayoral office, Masters tried to maintain his business interests, but his declining health overwhelmed him, and he sold his interest in the business in 1865. Masters's first wife, Naomi, died in 1863, leaving him with 3 children: Willis, Harriet, and Main. He then married M. Augusta Prull on 27 Oct. 1863. After resigning from office, Masters went to New England and Nova Scotia in the summer of 1864 in hope of regaining his health; however, it did not improve. In 1865 Masters relocated to Pine Island, MN, with his family, however his health continued to decline and he died several months later.

**MATHER, ELIZABETH RING IRELAND** (3 April 1891–10 Nov. 1957) was a leader in civic and cultural activities and dedicated to making Cleveland a more beautiful city. She founded the Garden

Center of Greater Cleveland (see CLEVELAND BOTANICAL GARDEN†), funded the development of a master plan for rebuilding the UNIV. CIRCLE† area into a cultural center, supervised beautification of the grounds surrounding the CLEVELAND INSTITUTE OF ART,† and organized relief projects and work programs during the Great Depression.

Born in Saginaw, MI, to Clark and Lizzie Palmer Ring, Elizabeth left Saginaw at age 14 and traveled extensively with her family. She was educated at Miss Masters School in Dobbs Ferry, NY. On 8 Jan. 1913 she married James Duane Ireland and had one child, James Jr. They left Duluth in 1918 for Cleveland, where Ireland became a partner in the M. A. Hanna Co. He died in 1921. In 1929 she married industrialist WILLIAM GWINN MATHER. They had no children. He died in 1951.

As the first president of the Garden Center of Greater Cleveland in 1930, Mather guided the center into becoming one of the nation's leading horticulture institutions. In 1931 she was named the Cuyahoga County Grand Jury's first woman foreman. Seeking to improve the well-being of others, Mrs. Mather promoted a vegetable relief garden project during the Depression, which benefitted over 40,000 people.

She worked as a social worker at Rainbow Hospital for Crippled Children and made generous contributions to Western Reserve Univ., the CLEVELAND MUSEUM OF ART,† and TRINITY CATHEDRAL.† In 1954 she established the ELIZABETH RING AND WILLIAM GWINN MATHER FUND† to promote Cleveland interests. In 1957 she provided the monies needed to create the Univ. Circle Development Foundation and to hire an urban-planning firm to design the Circle area. An Episcopalian, she is buried in Lake View Cemetery.—T.B.

## MATHER, FLORA STONE

**MATHER, FLORA STONE** (6 Apr. 1852–19 Jan. 1909) was a philanthropist dedicated to Cleveland religious, educational, and social reform activities. Flora Amelia Stone, youngest daughter of AMASA STONE and Julia Gleason Stone, was born in the family mansion on Superior Ave. and graduated with honors from CLEVELAND ACADEMY.† In 1875 her sister, Clara, married JOHN HAY; in 1881 Flora married SAMUEL MATHER. Their children were SAMUEL LIVINGSTON MATHER, Amasa Stone, Philip Richard, and Constance (later Mrs. Robt. Bishop).

In 1896 Mrs. Mather founded Goodrich House in honor of her childhood pastor, Rev. Wm. H. Goodrich, also supporting its outgrowth activities, including the LEGAL AID SOCIETY† and CONSUMERS LEAGUE OF OHIO.† Mrs. Mather supported many activities of Western Reserve Univ., including the Advisory Council, College for Women (renamed Mather College in her honor in 1931), and Adelbert College. In 1892 she constructed Guilford Cottage (later Guilford House), a dormitory on campus named in honor of her former teacher, LINDA T. GUILFORD. She gave funds in 1902 to construct Haydn Hall, in honor of Dr. HIRAM C. HAYDN of Old Stone Church, to which Mrs. Mather belonged for her entire lifetime. Mrs. Mather died in 1909 at Shoreby, the family's lakeshore home in BRATENAHL.† Her will included bequests to over 30 religious, educational, and charitable institutions, including funds to complete AMASA STONE CHAPEL† on the WRU campus, which she and her sister, Mrs. John Hay, gave in memory of their father. In 1913 a women's dormitory, named Mather House in her honor, was given to the university by alumnae and friends.

Univ. Archives, CWRU.
Mather Family Papers, WRHS.

## MATHER, SAMUEL

**MATHER, SAMUEL** (13 July 1851–18 Oct. 1931), industrialist and philanthropist, son of Samuel and Georgiana Woolson Mather, was born and educated in Cleveland. He planned attending Harvard, then working at his father's business, Cleveland Iron Co., but had a mining accident requiring lengthy recuperation. In 1882 Mather joined Jas. Pickands and Jay C. Morse to form PICKANDS, MATHER & CO.,† a rival to Cleveland Iron. After 2 years, the company leased a mine in the Gogebic Range, later acquiring interests in the Minnesota Mesabi and Michigan Marquette Ranges. Mather allied Pickands-Mather with the steel industry, providing resources and transportation; and facilitating the U.S. Steel merger in 1902. Success compounded his inherited wealth.

Mather was senior warden and vestryman of TRINITY CATHEDRAL,† president of Federated Churches of Cleveland, and a trustee and benefactor of HIRAM HOUSE.† During World War I he organized the War Chest, donating over $.75 million, and receiving the Cross of the Legion of Honor from the French government. He helped establish the Community Chest, contributing $100,000 annually, and in 1930 establishing a $1.6 million trust fund to ensure its prosperity. Mather married FLORA STONE in 1881 and fathered 4 children: S. Livingston (see SAMUEL LIVINGSTON MATHER), Phillip, Constance, and Amasa Stone. When Mather died, he was the richest man in Ohio. His estate was divided among his children, grandchildren, and daughter-in-law, and various charitable causes. Major benefactors included Western Reserve Univ. and Univ. Hospitals, JOHN

CARROLL UNIV.,† Kenyon College, the Episcopal Church, St. Luke's Hospital of Tokyo, Japan, and the Community Chest. Because of declining stock values in the Depression, the bequests could not be paid. As the value of the estate increased with market improvements, heirs contested the will, since Mather had changed the terms within a year of his death, and some bequests (notably one to WRU) were invalidated.

Mather Family Papers, WRHS.

**MATHER, SAMUEL LIVINGSTON** (22 Aug. 1882–10 Sept. 1960) was an industrialist and a member of one of Cleveland's most prominent families. Principally associated with the CLEVELAND-CLIFFS IRON CO.,† he also served on the boards of many companies, including Otis Steel, and Bessemer Limestone & Cement Co., and was active in philanthropy.

Born in Cleveland to SAMUEL and FLORA STONE MATHER, he graduated from UNIV. SCHOOL† in 1901, and received his A.B. from Yale in 1905. Mather immediately went to work for Cleveland-Cliffs at the iron ore mining department in Ishpeming, MI. Mather returned to Cleveland to work in the main office, becoming asst. secretary of mining operations (1908), secretary (1914), and vice-president in charge of operations (1926), the office he held until his retirement in 1947.

An active philanthropist, Mather contributed heavily to his alma mater and to the Holden Arboretum in Geauga County, OH. He was a trustee of Western Reserve Univ., the Home for Aged Women, and the HORACE KELLEY ART FOUNDATION.†

In 1953 he founded the S. LIVINGSTON MATHER CHARITABLE TRUST† to support educational, health, and welfare programs. In 1955 he was the principal donor to the State of Ohio of over 400 wooded acres north of Chardon, known as Big Creek Reservation.

Mather lived in Mentor. In 1906 he married Grace Fleming Harman, with whom he had four children: Samuel Harman, Grace Flora Hosmer, Elizabeth Harman McMillan, and Samuel Livingston. Grace died in 1931. In 1932 he married Alice Nightengale Keith. They had no children. An Episcopalian, he is buried in Lake View Cemetery. —T.B.

S. Livingston Mather Family Papers, WRHS.

**MATHER, WILLIAM GWINN** (22 Sept. 1857–5 April 1951) was a civic, cultural, and philanthropic leader. Known as Cleveland's "first citizen", Mather headed CLEVELAND-CLIFFS IRON CO.,† was

the first president of the Cleveland Stock Exchange, and president of the CLEVELAND MUSEUM OF ART† from 1933–49.

Born in Cleveland to Elizabeth (Gwinn) and Samuel Livingston Mather, he attended Cheshire Academy in Connecticut, and received his A.B. in 1877 from Trinity College.

Mather entered the family business, the Cleveland Iron Mining Co., as a clerk and worked his way up to vice-president in 1885. He succeeded his father as president in 1890. In 1891 the business merged with the Iron Cliffs Co. to form the Cleveland-Cliffs Iron Co. and Mather remained president until 1933. Under Mather's command the company grew and diversified into ore-related industries by acquiring coal mines in Pennsylvania and West Virginia. In 1933 Mather became chairman of the board and, in 1947, he was named honorary chairman.

Mather was the first chairman of the Chamber of Commerce-City Planning Committee, 1899–1911. In 1930 he helped form the REPUBLIC STEEL CORP.† and served as a director. Mather was also director of the Kelley Island Lime & Transport Co., and chairman of the Lake Superior & Ishpeming Railroad Co.

In 1933 the Cleveland Chamber of Commerce awarded Mather the medal for distinguished public service. He was a trustee of many institutions, including the CLEVELAND MUSEUM OF ART,† UNIV. HOSPITALS OF CLEVELAND,† Western Reserve Univ. (see CASE WESTERN RESERVE UNIV.†), and the WESTERN RESERVE HISTORICAL SOCIETY.†

Mather married Elizabeth Ring Ireland (see ELIZABETH RING IRELAND MATHER) on 18 May 1929. He had no children of his own and was survived by his wife and her son from a previous marriage, James Duane Ireland. Mather is buried in Lake View Cemetery.—T.B.

William Gwinn Mather Family Papers, WRHS.

**MATHEWS, ALFRED** (15 Sept. 1852–15 Oct. 1904), moved from a background in local journalism to become a prolific writer of regional histories. Born in Painesville, OH, he was the son of Dr. Samuel Mathews and former Clevelander Huldah Ford Mathews, and a great-grandson of former governor SAMUEL HUNTINGTON, JR. Graduating from high school in Painesville in 1871, Mathews began his writing career on the staff of the *Painesville Telegraph*. He soon left for Cleveland, where he worked for the *CLEVELAND LEADER†* and published his first book, *History of Washington County, Ohio* (1880). Moving to the East, he became a freelance contributor to such publications as the *New York Times, Philadelphia Press,* and *Scribner's Magazine.* He joined the Philadelphia publishing house of L. A. Evarts, for whom he wrote several Pennsylvania county histories himself and edited more of the same. His last book, *Ohio and Her Western Reserve,* was published by the New York firm of Appleton in 1902. His thesis that Puritan Connecticut stock had laid the basis for Ohio's prosperity was received more favorably in Cleveland than elsewhere in the state. Mathews never married. Survived by his mother, he died in Philadelphia and was returned to Painesville for burial. —J.V.

**MATZEN, HERMAN N.** (15 July 1861–22 April 1938), left a rich legacy of public sculpture in Cleveland and elsewhere. Born in Denmark, he came to America as a boy and was educated in Detroit, MI, before returning to Europe for art studies. After graduation from the Royal Academy of Fine Arts in Berlin, he returned to begin teaching design and sculpture at the Cleveland School of Art (see CLEVELAND INSTITUTE OF ART†) in 1885. Among his students over the following 40 years were MAX KALISH, FRANK WILCOX, and stage designer Norman Bel Geddes. Matzen's own works include the Moses and Pope Gregory IX statues on the exterior of the CUYAHOGA COUNTY COURTHOUSE,† the Richard Wagner monument in EDGEWATER PARK,† and the Collinwood Fire Memorial (see COLLINWOOD SCHOOL FIRE†) in Lake View Cemetery. Easily his most familiar local monument is the statue of Mayor TOM L. JOHNSON dedicated in PUBLIC SQUARE† in 1916. His choice of Cain and Abel to adorn the Painesville County Courthouse also attracted widespread notice. Matzen prided himself on the fact that most of his work was done in open competition. In other cities, it included the Schiller Monument in Detroit and the War and Peace Group for the Indianapolis, IN, Soldiers and Sailors Monument. He retired as head of the Sculpture Dept. from the CSA in 1926. After the death of his first wife, the former Emma Hale of Cleveland, he was married in 1908 to Blanche Dissette Matzen (1880–3 Oct. 1964), who in a long career of civic leadership became the first woman foreman of a Cuyahoga County grand jury in 1934. Survived by her and 3 children (Madeline, Mrs. Dorothy Coleman, and Herman N., Jr.), Matzen was buried in LAKE VIEW CEMETERY,† amid such examples of his art as the Burke Chapel and White memorial.—J.V.

**MAYER, REV. DR. JACOB** (d. 1890) was a German orator and Rabbi at the Temple (see TEMPLE-TIFERETH ISRAEL†), 1867–74. Liberal, outspoken, and controversial, he sought to end antipathy between Jews and Germans, and promote the study of Hebrew and religious literature. In 1871 Mayer was president of the committee organizing the FRANCO-PRUSSIAN WAR PEACE JUBILEE.†

Born in Prussia, Mayer came to the U.S. in 1866 and was naturalized in 1872. Mayer came to Cleveland from Cincinnati in 1867, when he was elected rabbi of Tifereth Israel on the recommendation of Rabbi Wise, who believed Mayer would strengthen the congregation's Reform affiliation. The congregation initially favored Mayer's liberal views regarding Judaism. A brilliant orator, Mayer gained the reputation as "the best preacher in Cleveland".

In 1870 Mayer was re-engaged as rabbi for 10 more years, although his term actually ended in 1872. Although he elevated Judaism in the eyes of many Christians, critics claimed that his sermons lacked substance and accuracy, and that he alienated both traditionalist Jews and Christians.

The Franco-Prussian War Peace Jubilee celebrating the German victory ending the Franco-Prussian War was held 10 April 1871. Cleveland's German societies began planning the celebration in March 1871, electing Mayer to head the organizing committee.

Mayer resigned as rabbi of Tifereth Israel in 1874 to become rabbi of Baltimore's Har Sinai Congregation. In 1876 it was revealed that before coming to America Mayer had converted to Christianity and was a missionary in Glasgow. Mayer denied the allegations, yet their persistence eventually forced Mayer to admit their truth. Mayer left Baltimore for St. Louis, where he died.—T.B.

**MAYO, LEONARD WITHINGTON** (4 Sept. 1899–1 Sept. 1992) advised 4 presidents (Truman, Eisenhower, Kennedy, and Johnson) on mental retardation and physical disabilities and advocated for children, serving on the Federal Commission on Children in Wartime and the U.S. Children's Bureau Commission; four White House Conferences on Children and Youth; as director of the Assn. for the Aid of Crippled Children (1949–65); and as president of both the Child Welfare League (1935–45) and the International Union for Child Welfare (1957–73). Mayo was dean of Western Reserve Univ.'s School of Applied Sciences (SAS, 1941–48); vice-president of the university (1948–49), and as a member the visiting committee at SAS (1982–92).

Mayo was born in Canaan, NY, to William Withington and Myra Dooley Mayo. After graduating from high school in Oxford, MA (1918), he attended Colby College in Maine, receiving an A.B. (1922) and the New York School of Social Work (1929–35). He later served on the faculties of both institutions and, before coming to Cleveland, worked in social services in Maine, Maryland, and New York; Mayo worked in Washington, DC, New York and Maine between 1949 and his return to the city in 1982.

Mayo was president of the National Conference of Social Work (1948). Locally, he served on the board of the Cleveland Welfare Federation, as asst. director of civilian defense (1942), and chaired a SASS panel which developed the CLEVELAND COMMUNITY RELATIONS BOARD† (1945), among other contributions. Mayo received a citation for distinguished service from Pres. John F. Kennedy, the Albert Lasker Award in World Rehabilitation, and other honorary doctorates from Colby College (1942) and CWRU (1992).

Mayo married Lena Cooly of Harmony, ME, in 1924; they had two children, Margaret Louise Tippit and Thelma Kathryn Loomis. He belonged first to the CHURCH OF THE COVENANT† and then to the Federated Church, CHAGRIN FALLS VILLAGE.† He died at his Chagrin Falls home. —J.M.

**MEADE, FRANK B.** (6 Jan. 1867–Mar. 1947), architect active in Cleveland from 1895 until the 1930s, designing more than 800 homes, was born in Norwalk, OH, to Alfred N. and Mattie Morse Meade. His grandfather was an architect-builder for 25 years in Huron County, and his father ran a lumber company in Cleveland. Meade graduated from MIT in 1888, moved to Chicago as a draftsman in the firm of Jenney & Mundie (1889–93), and in 1894 returned to Cleveland, forming partnerships with Alfred H. Granger (Meade & Granger, 1896–97) and ABRAM GARFIELD (Meade & Garfield, 1898–1904). Meade ran his own firm until 1911, then formed a partnership with JAS. M. HAMILTON (Meade & Hamilton, 1911–41), together designing the great majority of residences for Cleveland industrialists and professional men on EUCLID AVE.,† in WADE PARK,† and in the suburbs and villages.

In addition to their residential practice, Meade & Hamilton completed 6 club buildings. Meade, an active club member (Union, Roadside, Euclid, and Century clubs in Cleveland) was also an organizer and first president of the HERMIT CLUB† and designed that group's clubhouse. Meade also played a leading role in developing the Group Plan in Cleveland, appointed secretary of the Group Plan Commission in 1911. Meade's colleagues on the commission were prominent landscape architect Frederick Law Olmstead of Boston and sculptor Arnold Brunner of New York City. Meade was a member and president of the AMERICAN INSTITUTE OF ARCHITECTS, CLEVELAND CHAP-

TER† and a member of the Cleveland Chamber of Commerce.

Meade married Dora Rucker in 1898; they had no children. He died in Cleveland and was buried in Lake View Cemetery.

Johannesen, Eric. *Cleveland Architecture, 1876–1976* (1979).

**MELLEN, EDWARD J., JR.** (31 Dec. 1909–6 Sept. 1982) was an investment banker who helped organize nearly 20 Cleveland companies and a philanthropist who cofounded the Mellen Foundation with his wife, Louise Shepler Mellen (d. 1977), and who provided a bequest which helped establish the Mellen Center for Multiple Sclerosis Treatment and Research.

Born in Lakewood to Edward and Jane (Scheel), Mellen attended Lakewood High School and Cleveland College, then joined the Cleveland Stock Exchange. Following World War II army service, Mellen joined the investment securities firm H. L. Emerson Co. as vice-president, then worked for Skall, Joseph & Miller, becoming executive vice-president.

In 1949 Mellen cofounded the investment securities firm of Joseph, Mellen & Miller, Inc., retiring as chairman in 1974. In 1954 Mellen formed Basic Ceramics Co., which became a leader in making precision ceramic cores for jet engines, rockets and missiles. Mellen was president and CEO when he sold Basic in 1974.

In 1957 Mellen purchased the failing Sherwood Drug Store, a downtown Cleveland landmark, and turned it into a successful chain of drugstores under H. J. Sherwood, Inc., a holding company, with Mellen as president and CEO.

In 1963 the MELLEN FOUNDATION† was established to award the Louise Mellen Fellowship (Mrs. Mellen had MS) for nursing education and critical-care nursing. Mellen was president and chairman. In 1985 the CLEVELAND CLINIC FOUNDATION† opened the Mellen Center with the help of his $2 million gift.

The Mellens were married on 10 Jan. 1942. They had no children. Mellen lived in LYNDHURST† and is buried in Ft. Lauderdale, FL.—T.B.

**MELLEN, LOWELL O.** (18 Dec. 1897–16 Jan. 1993), pioneer in the successful application of Training Within Industry (TWI) programs, was born in Streetsboro, OH, the son of Ottis and Gertrude (Cannon) Mellen. After attending Ravenna High School for 2 years, the family moved to Cleveland in 1910, where he specialized in shop courses at West Technical High School, graduating in 1912. Mellen began his career in industrial training and instruction at the Goodyear Tire & Rubber Co. in Akron. After returning to Cleveland in 1921, he taught drawing and math at local industrial plants and opened his own automobile agency. He moved to Buffalo, NY, in 1924, serving as district sales supervisor for B. F. Goodrich until 1941. Returning to Cleveland, he became the Northern Ohio district representative for the new Training Within Industry programs set up by the U.S. government to improve productivity and production of critical war-related industries. Mellen organized courses in job instruction, work methods, and worker-supervision relations. After World War II, he formed a company to market TWI programs to peacetime industries. His company attracted the attention of General Douglas McArthur who, fearful of mass starvation and unrest in occupied Japan, was anxious to revive industry there. In 1951 Mellen took the TWI program to Japan, where his efforts did much to shape the postwar Japanese management style. Back in this country, he continued to teach TWI techniques until he retired in 1985.

On 31 Aug. 1929 Mellen married Mildred Manthey (d. 1965); they had no children. A resident of BAY VILLAGE,† he was buried at Lakewood Park Cemetery.—M.S.

---

Lowell Mellen Papers, WRHS.

**MENOMPSY (NOBSY)** (d. 1802 or 1803), a Chippewa or Ottawa medicine man, was the victim of the first murder in Cleveland. Menompsy was treating the wife of Big Son, who was the brother of the Seneca chief STIGWANISH, or "Chief Seneca." Despite all his efforts, Big Son's wife died. Big Son, believing that Menompsy was responsible for his wife's death, sought retribution. According to Indian justice, Big Son had the right to retaliate, and he threatened Menompsy's life. Menompsy, who was a sacred priest as well as a medicine man, asserted he was a charmed man and no bullet could harm him. While walking together one day, Big Son extended his hand as if to make amends and shake hands, but instead drew a knife and stabbed Menompsy in the side. Despite all efforts, Menompsy died. The murder threatened the peace of Cleveland with Indian tribal warfare. Maj. LORENZO CARTER, friend to the Indians, negotiated a peace treaty between the two sides. The price for peace was 2 gallons of whiskey.

**MERCHANT, AHAZ** (21 Mar. 1794–28 Mar. 1862), surveyor, builder, and civil engineer, was born in western Connecticut, son of Silas and Huldah (Platt) Merchant. He was raised near Morristown, NJ, and taught himself surveying. After moving to Cleveland in 1818, Merchant acquired

military experience in the state militia, attaining the rank of general. Like many early pioneers, Merchant applied himself to several occupations, but was mainly distinguished as a surveyor. He was county surveyor from 1833–35 and 1845–50. He was also Cleveland's first surveyor and street commissioner, from 1834–36. Merchant St. (W. 11th) was named after him. Merchant, as a surveyor, laid out most of the important allotments in OHIO CITY,† supervised the first improvements to the old river bed, and graded many of Cleveland's major streets. In 1831 he resurveyed many of the city's existing streets, and in 1835 published a "Map of Cleveland and Its Environs," showing the city's entire street plan. He also built several new roads, including Prospect Ave. and the road from Cleveland to Aurora (Rt. 43).

While county surveyor, Merchant constructed the first horse-drawn railroad in the county (the CLEVELAND & NEWBURGH RAILROAD CO.†) in 1834. Merchant's son, Silas, was in charge of its operation. Merchant later constructed another horse railroad, which ran out Euclid Ave. to E. Cleveland. As a builder, Merchant built several structures in Cleveland, including the Angier House, a fashionable 5-story hotel that opened in 1854 and was later known as the Kennard House. Merchant married Catherine Stewart in 1819. They had 5 children: Aaron, Martha, Harriet, Mary, and Silas. Merchant died in Cleveland.

---

Merchant Family Papers, WRHS.

**MERRICK, MYRA KING** (1825–11 Nov. 1899), the first female physician in Ohio and one of the first in the U.S., was born in Hinkley, Leicestershire, England, the daughter of Richard and Elizabeth (King) Merrick. She immigrated to Boston with her parents, worked in cotton mills, and moved to Cleveland in 1841. After marrying Chas. H. Merrick in 1848, they moved to Connecticut. When her husband became ill, Merrick entered medicine to support her family and care for her husband. As far as can be determined, she attended lectures at Hyatt's Academy, New York; studied with Levi Ives, New Haven, CT; was trained at Nichol's Hydropathic Institute; and received her M.D. from Central Medical College, Rochester, NY, in 1852.

Returning to Cleveland in the 1850s, Merrick developed a thriving medical practice, especially among the rich and influential, such as JOHN D. ROCKEFELLER's family. During the Civil War, while her husband served in the Union Army, she also ran the family lumber business. Since the Western Homeopathic College was closed to females, Merrick helped establish Cleveland Homeopathic Hospital College for Women in 1867, serving as president and professor of obstetrics and diseases of women and children. In 1878 Merrick and former student, Kate Parsons, founded Women's & Children's Free Medical & Surgical Dispensary, forerunner of WOMAN'S GENERAL HOSPITAL.† Merrick was president until her death. Merrick, who divorced her husband in 1881, had 2 children, Richard L. and Arthur (d. 1864). Her daughter-in-law, Eliza K. Merrick, practiced medicine with her. Merrick was a member of the Unity Church and the Homeopathic Society. She is buried in Elyria, OH.

Chas. H. Merrick Papers, WRHS.

Gibbons, Marion N. "A Woman Carries the Caduceus— Myra K. Merrick." In *Pioneer Women in the Western Reserve*, ed. Howard Dittrick (1932).

Brown, Kent L. ed. *Medicine in Cleveland and Cuyahoga County, 1810–1976* (1977).

**METZENBAUM, MYRON, M.D.** (1 April 1876– 25 Jan. 1944), ear, nose, and throat specialist at Mt. Sinai Hospital (see MT. SINAI MEDICAL CENTER†), designed the surgical scissors which bear his name. He was a national authority in reconstructive surgery. Metzenbaum was born in Cleveland to Joseph and Fanny Firth Metzenbaum, and educated in the public schools. He attended Adelbert College and Case School of Applied Sciences (see CASE WESTERN RESERVE UNIV.†) and received a B.S. from Ada Univ. In 1900 he received a medical degree from the School of Medicine of Western Reserve Univ.; he did postgraduate work in Vienna, Austria, and London, England. Metzenbaum did his internship and residency at St. Alexis Hospital (1899–1901, see ST. ALEXIS HOSPITAL MEDICAL CENTER†) under Dr. GEORGE WASHINGTON CRILE, SR. He lectured in anatomy at the Cleveland College of Physicians and Surgeons (1903–05). In addition to Mt. Sinai, Metzenbaum was on the courtesy staff of St. Luke's Hospital (see ST. LUKE'S MEDICAL CENTER†). Active in the CLEVELAND ACADEMY OF MEDICINE,† Metzenbaum belonged to other local, state, and national medical societies.

Metzenbaum married Elsa Puldheim on 20 March 1912; their children were Louise Feldman and Jane Cukor. A CLEVELAND HTS.† resident, his interests included travel and MUSIC.†—J.M.

**MEYER, EDWARD S.** (10 Aug. 1843–26 Sept. 1920), volunteer army officer in the CIVIL WAR† and U.S. attorney, was born in Canton, OH, son of Seraphim and Ellenora (Schuchard) Meyer. He graduated from St. Vincent's College, and enlisted as a private when the Civil War started. He became a sgt. 20 Apr. 1861; 1st lt., 1 Nov. 1861; capt., 11 Nov. 1862; and major, 16 Feb. 1865. Meyer re-

ceived brevets for war service at the Battles of Shiloh (6–7 Apr. 1862) and Chancellorsville (1–4 May 1863), and was awarded the rank of brevet brig. gen., U.S. Volunteers, on 13 Mar. 1865. After the Civil War, Meyer transferred to the Regular Army cavalry, served on the frontier, and retired 24 Aug. 1875 as a result of physical disability from wounds received in the service. He returned to Canton, studying law under his father, and was appointed asst. U.S. attorney, Northern District of Ohio, in Apr. 1877, apparently moving to Cleveland. He received an appointment as U.S. attorney from Pres. JAS. A. GARFIELD in 1881. After leaving the U.S. attorney's office in 1883, he worked to stop the manufacture and sale of alcoholic beverages, supporting the proposed 2nd Amendment to the Ohio constitution, serving on the advisory board of the *Second Amendment Herald*. The amendment never passed. He returned to private law practice in Cleveland, also serving as 1st lt. in the 1st Cleveland Troop, 1877–78, and 2 terms as president of the CLEVELAND GRAYS,† 1885–87.

Meyer married Jennie Houser and had 4 children: Oren B., Edward S., Albert W., and John H. He died in Cleveland and was buried in Lake View Cemetery.

**MEYETTE, GRACE E.** (ca. 1890–9 Apr. 1967) was born in Vermont to Joseph and Katherine Daly and came to Cleveland in 1927 as industrial secretary of the YWCA. She was educated at the London School of Economics, Columbia Univ., and the New York School of Social Work. Previously working for the Philadelphia YWCA, Meyette was fired from her post in 1931, having allegedly tried to exert too much authority in other departments. The CONSUMERS LEAGUE OF OHIO† objected to her dismissal, and Meyette remained active in the league for many years. She served on Mayor THOS. A. BURKE's race relations committee and in 1931 was named local executive secretary to the Natl. Women's Trade Union League. Dedicated to defending the rights of women in industry, Meyette was appointed inspector for fair wages in the Cleveland district under the Natl. Recovery Act in 1934. She was fired from this post in 1935 in a move criticized by the press as a political maneuver by Gov. Martin L. Davey. In 1935 Meyette was chosen executive secretary of the LEAGUE FOR HUMAN RIGHTS,† a Cleveland group founded to combat the influence of Nazism in America and expose Nazi propaganda, serving until the league's dissolution in the 1940s. Meyette died in CLEVELAND HTS.† after a long illness.

**MICHELSON, ALBERT ABRAHAM** (19 Dec. 1852–9 May 1931), the first American to win a

Nobel Prize in the sciences (physics, 1907), was born in Strelno, Prussia (Strzelno, Poland), the son of Rosalie (Przylubska) and Samuel Michelson. He came to America with his parents in 1855. Michelson was educated in San Francisco and Virginia City, NV, and attended the U.S. Naval Academy (1869–73) where he ranked first in his class in optics.

Michelson began measurements of the speed of light while an instructor in physics and chemistry at the Academy. After a leave of absence in 1880 to study in Europe, he secured appointment as chair of the Dept. of Physics at the Case School of Applied Science and resigned his naval commission. He assumed his position in Cleveland in 1882 and resumed his measurements of the speed of light, arriving at a figure of 186,320 miles per second. This figure remained the accepted standard for 45 years, until Michelson further refined this determination while at Mt. Wilson in California. In 1886, with Professor EDWARD E. MORLEY of Western Reserve Univ., he undertook the MICHELSON-MORLEY EXPERIMENT† to measure the motion of the earth through the "luminiferous aether."

In 1889 Michelson left Case for Clark Univ., where he remained briefly until accepting the chairmanship of the Department of Physics at the Univ. of Chicago. In the years which followed, he developed various optical measuring methods and refined his measurements of the speed of light. He published more than 70 scientific papers and books. Among his awards were the Rumford Premium Medal of the American Academy of Arts and Sciences, the Copley Medal of the Royal Society of London and the Royal Astronomical Society medal.

He married Margaret Hemingway in 1877. They had three children and were divorced in 1898. A year later he married Edna Standon; they had three daughters.

Livingston, Dorothy Michelson. *The Master of Light: A Biography of Albert A. Michelson* (1973).

**MIHALIK, EMIL J.** (6 Feb. 1920–27 Jan. 1984) was the founding bishop of the Byzantine-Ruthenian Rite Catholic Eparchy of PARMA.†

Born to William and Mary Jubic Mihalik in Pittsburgh, PA, Emil attended public school in his hometown before entering St. Procopius Seminary in Lisle, IL. Following studies he was ordained in Trenton, NJ, 21 September 1945, by Bp. Emil Takach.

After ordination, Mihalik served as a parish priest in Ohio, Pennsylvania, New York, and New Jersey. In 1968 he was appointed chancellor of the Eparchy of Passaic.

On 21 February 1969 the Vatican announced formation of the Eparchy of Parma, carved from the western portion of the Archeparchy of Pittsburgh. The new diocese encompassed most of Ohio and included 24 other states, west to California, Hawaii, and Alaska. Mihalik was named founding bishop. He was ordained bishop and installed 12 June 1969, in the diocese's new Cathedral of St. John the Baptist, Snow and Broadview roads in Parma.

Organizing and providing new churches and priests for the far-flung diocese was Mihalik's first priority. As bishop he added eighteen new parishes, relocated several others, ordained 23 priests, and granted bi-ritual faculties to 20 others, and brought the Byzantine Nuns of St. Clare to the diocese.

In 1982, because of the eparchy's growth, the Vatican split off the 13 westernmost states into a new Eparchy of Van Nuys, CA. That same year architectural reconstruction of the cathedral church was begun.

Funeral services for the bishop were held in the partially renovated cathedral on 1 March 1984. His body was then transported to Calvary Cemetery at Mt. St. Macrina, Uniontown, PA, where he was buried next to the bishop who had ordained him. —J.T.

**MILLER, DAYTON CLARENCE** (13 Mar. 1866–22 Feb. 1941) was a pioneer user of X-rays. Born in STRONGSVILLE,† OH, to Charles Webster Dewey and Vienna Pomeroy Miller, he was raised in BEREA† and graduated from Baldwin Univ. (BALDWIN-WALLACE COLLEGE†) in 1886. He received a doctorate from Princeton in 1890, and became professor of mathematics and physics at Case School of Applied Science (CASE WESTERN RESERVE UNIV.†). From 1895–1936, he headed the Physics Dept.

After Konrad von Roentgen's discovery of X-rays in 1895 was reported in the *PLAIN DEALER,†* Miller, who worked in surgical X-rays, built an X-ray apparatus with a Crookes Tube and 12 wet-cell batteries. In 1896, he X-rayed his entire body, section by section, producing the first full X-ray of the human body. The value of these X-rays became partially realized when Miller used the process to detect an improperly set broken arm of a patient of Dr. GEO. CRILE. Miller's other interests included sound; he developed a "phonodeik" (forerunner of the oscilloscope) and worked on architectural acoustics for many buildings, including SEVERANCE HALL.† He also performed and composed music; built a pipe organ; made a golden flute; and collected 1,500 flutes, which were left to the Library of Congress. As a consultant for the Aeolian Co., he was instrumental in developing the Webber piano. In 1921 Miller met with Albert Einstein regarding his recreation of the Michelson-Morley experiments that had led to the development of the Theory of Relativity.

Miller married Edith Easton in 1893. He died in Cleveland and was buried in Lake View Cemetery.

**MILLER, RAYMOND THOMAS** (10 Jan. 1893–13 July 1966), head of the CUYAHOGA COUNTY DEMOCRATIC PARTY† for over 20 years, was born in Defiance, OH, to Martin E. and Anne Riley Miller. He received his LL.B. degree from Notre Dame Univ. (1914), and moved to Cleveland to practice law. In the Ohio Natl. Guard, he served on the Mexican border in 1916 and in France during World War I. Miller was elected county prosecutor in 1928, actively helped defeat the CITY MANAGER PLAN† of government, and was elected mayor in 1932. During his term he reduced expenditures to cope with the growing Depression, and persuaded the utilities to lower their rates. HARRY L. DAVIS defeated him in 1933.

In 1938, after a power struggle with W. BURR GONGWER, Miller was made chairman of the Cuyahoga County Democratic party. Lawsuits and countersuits followed until 1940, when the state central committee declared his appointment official. He helped the party attract black voters which, combined with its ethnic base, allowed the Democrats to elect mayors for 30 years and obtain a Democratic majority in council. Miller resigned his chairmanship in 1964. Miller also established a successful law practice, serving as counsel for the BROTHERHOOD OF LOCOMOTIVE ENGINEERS† and Brotherhood of Railway Trainmen. In business, he helped organize radio station WERE and was active in forming the CLEVELAND BROWNS.† He married Ruth Hamilton in 1926 and had 6 children: Mrs. Roseanne Perme, Ray T., Jr., Mrs. Ruth Mary Galvin, Richard, Robert, and Riley. Miller died in Cleveland.

Ray T. Miller Papers, WRHS.

**MILLIKEN, WILLIAM M.** (1889–14 Mar. 1978), second director of the CLEVELAND MUSEUM OF ART,† was born in Stamford, CT, to Thomas Kennedy and Mary S. Mathewson Milliken. He graduated from Princeton Univ. (1911), and was asst. curator of the Dept. of Decorative Art in New York City's Metropolitan Museum of Art before serving in the U.S. Army during World War I. Following his discharge, he became curator of decorative arts at CMA, a post he held until his retirement from the museum in 1958. Milliken served briefly as curator of painting (1925–30) before his appointment as director† in 1930, serving in that capacity until 1958. The purchase of the Guelph Treasure in 1930, which gave the museum international stature, and the annual MAY SHOW,† exhibiting local art and crafts and under Milliken's guidance from 1919–58, are generally considered his major accomplishments. After leaving CMA, Milliken was advisor to the Natl. Gallery in Australia, presented lectures, organized the "Masterpieces of Art Exhibition" at the Seattle World's Fair in 1963, held the post of regent professor at the Univ. of California in Berkeley, and authored 3 books. He was a trustee of the American Fed. of Arts (1929–62), board member of the American Assn. of Museums and president of that organization from 1953–55, and president of the Assn. of Art Museum Directors (1946–49). He also served on numerous international museum councils and was presented many awards and honors by the European art world. Milliken is buried at Bridgeport, CT.

Wm. M. Milliken Papers, WRHS.
Milliken, Wm. *Born under the Sign of Libra: An Autobiography* (1977).

**MILLIS, JOHN SCHOFF** (22 Nov. 1903–1 Jan. 1988), president of Western Reserve Univ. (1949–67), strengthened its teaching of sciences and centralized university services and faculty.

Millis was born in Palo Alto, CA, the son of Alice Schoff and Harry Alvin Millis, an economics professor. Millis attended Hyde Park High School (1917–18) and graduated from Univ. High School (1920), both in Chicago. He received three degrees from the Univ. of Chicago: B.S. (1924), M.S. (1927), and a Ph.D. in physics (1931). Before coming to Cleveland, among other positions, Millis served as dean of Lawrence College in WI (1936–41), and as president of the Univ. of Vermont and State Agricultural College (1941–49).

In Cleveland, Millis helped organize the Univ. Circle Development Foundation, predecessor to UNIV. CIRCLE, INC.,† Case Institute of Technology, and Western Reserve Univ. federated during his last year as WRU president (1967). Millis served as chancellor of the new CASE WESTERN RESERVE UNIV.† He retired on 30 June 1969, becoming chancellor emeritus. Millis served on the boards of the National League for Nursing (1958–63) and the Carnegie Endowment for the Advancement of Teaching (executive committee, 1952–58; chair, 1962). Locally, Millis belonged to the ACADEMY OF MEDICINE OF CLEVELAND† and served on the board of UNIV. HOSPITALS† and the Advisory Council of the CLEVELAND MUSEUM OF ART,† among other activities.

On 13 June 1929, Millis married Katherine Roseberry Wisner of Baltimore, MD; they had three children: Jean Ann (Mrs. Robert G.) Gilpin, Alice G.

Vest, and Harry Ward Millis. Millis won the prestigious Frank H. Lahey Memorial Award (1973) from the National Fund for Medical Education, in recognition for his work with the Citizen's Commission on Graduate Medical Education of the American Medical Assn. (chair, 1966) and the National Fund for Medical Education (president, 1971–77, vice-president, 1969–71). Millis held 14 honorary degrees. A Republican and a pianist, he was a also licensed lay reader and preacher at ST. PAUL'S EPISCOPAL CHURCH.† He died in his CLEVELAND HTS.† home.—J.M.

**MILLS, JOSHUA** (1797–29 Apr. 1843), pioneer physician and mayor of Cleveland (1838–39, 1842) was born in New England. After an education in medicine, he came to Cleveland as a physician in 1827. Once established, Mills opened what was to be the most successful pharmacy in the city. Mills became a public figure in 1832 when his assistance in that year's CHOLERA EPIDEMIC† made him a member of the city's first Board of Health. In the first city elections of 1836, he became a Whig alderman. He soon became a member of city council and its president in 1837. He ran unopposed for mayor in 1838, and was elected again in 1839. He was defeated for reelection by NICHOLAS DOCKSTADTER in 1840 and by JOHN W. ALLEN in 1841. In 1842 he finally succeeded in being reelected to another term in office. Mills married Phoebe Stafford Higby in 1826. The Mills's had four children: Harriet and John Willey (both died of scarlet fever in 1835) and Sylvester and Minerva. Mills died in Cleveland and was buried in the Erie St. Cemetery.

**MINOR, NORMAN SELBY** (19 July 1901–15 May 1968), noted criminal trial attorney, under whom a number of Cleveland's prominent black attorneys, including Merle McCurdy and Louis and Carl Stokes, trained, was born in Oak Park, IL, to Arthur and Rebecca Walden Minor. He came to Cleveland when he was 4. After 2 years at the Univ. of Michigan, he graduated with an LL.B. degree from John Marshall Law School in 1927, and was admitted to the Ohio Bar in 1928. From 1928–30, Minor was associated with the firm of Payne, Green, Minor & Perry, taking cases of men in jail who needed a free lawyer, in order to gain trial experience. Appointed asst. Cuyahoga County prosecutor in 1930, he was assigned to cases in which the defendants were black, since the discriminatory system at the time limited general use of his skills. He worked effectively to change the policy for subsequent black prosecutors and, despite discrimination, became one of Cleveland's best criminal trial lawyers. He prosecuted more than 5,000 felony cases, including 13 successful prosecutions for 1st-degree murder, his most famous case being that of Willie "The Mad Butcher" Johnson, convicted of murdering 12 women during the 1930s and 1940s. Involved in Democratic party politics, Minor polled the largest vote of any black candidate to that time in a 1937 election defeat for a municipal court judgeship. In 1948 Minor returned to private practice as a criminal defense lawyer specializing in homicide cases.

Minor married three times and had two children: Harold Craig (Green) Minor (1921–1992), and Valena (Williams) from the Feb. 1922 marriage to Grace C. Jones, which ended in divorce in 1926. Minor married Norvell Major (d. 1937) in 1928; and in 1938, Minor married Mary Christian. He is buried in Lake View Cemetery.

**MINTZ, LEO** (1911–4 Nov. 1976) was instrumental, with ALAN FREED, in the development of ROCK 'N' ROLL† and making Cleveland the "capital of Rock 'n' Roll." Mintz founded Record Rendezvous in 1938 at 214 Prospect Ave. and moved to 300 Prospect Ave. in 1945.

He was the first record merchant in the country to bring records out from behind the counter into bins so his customers could browse through them. His store was also the first site of record store listening booths and in-store promotional appearances by recording artists. In the late 1940s, Mintz saw the decrease in sales of JAZZ† and big band records. He realized that his young customers would dance around his store when a rhythm & blues record was played. To break the taboo of white people listening to black music, he called it "rock 'n' roll," borrowing a term from old blues lyrics. He convinced a young WAKR-AM disc jockey, Alan Freed, to play a rock 'n' roll record as a novelty song on his program in 1949.

Mintz was Freed's supporter, helping him to get jobs in Cleveland at WXEL-TV and WJW-AM† in 1951. Record Rendezvous sponsored all of Freed's concerts, including the Moondog Coronation Ball at the CLEVELAND ARENA† on 21 Mar. 1952, the first rock concert. Freed left Cleveland for New York City in 1954, taking with him the credit for starting rock 'n' roll. Mintz operated his popular record store until 6 months before his death. In those years he regaled his customers with tales of inventing rock 'n' roll.

Mintz married Betty Kulkin in 1936. They were survived by 3 children: Stuart, Leslie Trattner, and Sherri Kowit. Mintz was a member of the Men's Club and B'NAI B'RITH at the Temple on the Heights (see B'NAI JESHURUN CONGREGATION†), and the Hawthorne Valley Country Club. He is buried in the Mount Olive Cemetery.—J.H.

**MITCHELL, L. PEARL** (June 1883–6 Sept. 1974), civil-rights activist, was born in Wilberforce, OH, to Amanda M. and Dr. Samuel F. Mitchell, president of Wilberforce College, from which she received a bachelor's degree. Mitchell briefly studied music at Oberlin Conservatory of Music and sociology at Kalamazoo College before turning to war-camp community service during World War I. After her father's death, she worked as a typist to finance her siblings' education, coming to Cleveland in the early 1920s. In 1926 Mitchell became a probation officer in juvenile court, a position held until ill health prompted her resignation in the 1940s. In 1923 she joined the Cleveland branch of the NAACP, eventually serving as president (1936–37), executive secretary (1945), national vice-president (1959), and national director of membership campaigns. Locally, Mitchell led protests against the school system's discriminatory operation of special-activity schools and against segregated public housing projects. She mobilized newspaper support for the employment of black nurses at City Hospital, and also organized the NAACP's youth council.

After her retirement, Mitchell continued her civic involvement. She served on the board of the Ohio Soldiers' & Sailors' Orphans' Home, integrating the Columbus facility; and was on the Women & Manpower Commission, Greater Cleveland Fair Employment Practices Commission, and Commission on the Aged. Mitchell, interested in drama, was a member of the Gilpin Players and appeared in performances at the Play House Settlement, including JO SINCLAIR's *The Long Moment*, the first interracial play performed at the CLEVELAND PLAY HOUSE.†

Mitchell, never married, lived in EAST CLEVELAND.† She was buried at Lake View Cemetery.

L. Pearl Mitchell Papers, WRHS.
NAACP Cleveland Branch Records, WRHS.
Salem, Dorothy C., ed. *African-American Women: A Biographical Dictionary* (1994).

**MITCHELL, THEODORE** (5 May 1835–2 March 1910), Congressional Medal of Honor recipient for service during the CIVIL WAR,† was born in Tarentum, PA, and enlisted in the 61st Pennsylvania Volunteer Infantry in Pittsburgh 1 Aug. 1861. Priv. Mitchell remained with the 61st throughout the war, participating in the final assault on Confederate troops at Petersburg, VA, 2 April 1865. At some point during the day, Mitchell captured the flag of the Confederate Tennessee Brigade and received recognition in an official report. Promoted to cpl. for his deed, Mitchell also was recommended to receive the Medal of Honor on 18 April 1865. He was mustered out of the army 28 June 1865 and

returned to Pittsburgh, where he worked as a plasterer. In 1883 Mitchell moved to Cleveland with his wife, Mary E. (Quinn) Mitchell, and they lived there on his army invalid pension. He died in Cleveland and was buried in Woodland Cemetery.—M.S.

**MITERMILER, ANDREW ROBERT** (27 Jan. 1840–10 Sept. 1896), architect who practiced in Cleveland from 1871–96 designing business blocks, social halls, breweries, and churches for CZECHS† and GERMANS,† was born in Chocen, Austria-Hungary to Antonin and Maria Theresa (Minaronk) Muttermiller. He was educated at the Univ. of Vienna as a civil engineer, and worked on the Innsbruck Tunnel in Austria. When about to be conscripted into the Austrian army, he escaped to Baltimore, MD, in 1861 where he practiced engineering before coming to Cleveland ca. 1871, working as foreman in the office of architect J. M. Blackburn before setting up his own office in 1873.

By 1886 Mitermiler advertised numerous churches, breweries, halls, commercial blocks, and residences among his complete works. Among his buildings still standing in the 1980s were the Lohmann Block (1885), A. Zverina Block (1889), Rauch & Lang Carriage Works (1889), Czech Sokol Hall (1891), and Pilsner Brewery (1894). He designed the first building for ST. ELIZABETH CHURCH,† the first Hungarian Catholic parish in the U.S.; worked on the church of St. Mary of the Assumption, a German Evangelical church on Scranton Ave.; and did the decoration of St. Michael Catholic Church. Mitermiler was associated with another Bohemian architect, John W. Hradek, on some commissions, especially the preliminary design for the BOHEMIAN NATL. HALL.† DOMINICK BENES worked as an apprentice in Mitermiler's office from 1872–75. Mitermiler married Elizabeth Staral on 23 May 1869 and had 5 children: Mrs. Rose Zverina, Mrs. Elizabeth Kennedy, Andrew S., John A., and Anton.

**MIZER, CONRAD** (12 Jan. 1857–28 May 1904) was a tailor whose chief contribution to Cleveland was his promotion of summer band concerts in public parks. Mizer asked the city for $5,000 to finance a season of music, and met with resistance not only from the city, but also from ministers who wished to keep the Sabbath free from nonreligious activities. Nevertheless summer band concerts began in 1898 with band members paid $3 per concert. Among the performing bands were the Great Western, Natl. Military, and Cleveland Elks bands. In Sept. 1903, an all-Wagner program in ROCKEFELLER PARK† was presented, with the Great Western Band and a German chorus performing.

After the collapse of the CLEVELAND SYMPHONY ORCHESTRA† in 1902, Mizer attempted to revive it with a winter concert series, seeking financial support from prominent citizens and chairing an executive committee to handle business arrangements. Mizer had JOHANN BECK and EMIL RING alternate as conductors. On 4 Jan. 1903, at GRAYS ARMORY,† the Cleveland Symphony Orchestra gave a well-attended production featuring the music of Bizet, Liszt, and Weber. These Sunday afternoon programs continued for 10 years with great success. They also gave local composers an opportunity for their works to be performed. Mizer's funeral was held in Grays Armory and he was buried in Lake View Cemetery. A monument in his honor was erected in EDGEWATER PARK.† Mizer, born in Orwell, OH, to John and Margaret Mizer, was unmarried.

**MOELLMAN, CARL FREDERICK** (19 Aug. 1879–3 July 1950), combined an artistic temperament with business acumen to become one of the area's foremost lithographers. Born in Cincinnati, he was the son of Charles and Mary Frey Moellman. His father was associated with the U.S. Lithograph and Playing Card Co., headed by an uncle, John H. Frey. Young Moellman studied art with Frank Duveneck at the Cincinnati Art Academy and proceeded to New York, where he worked for the Ottomann Lithograph Co. and became a follower of the avant-garde group of artists known as "The Eight." He came to Cleveland in 1905 to become superintendent for the Otis Lithograph Co. in the CAXTON BLDG.† Continuing to paint, he joined with WM. SOMMER in 1911 to establish the KOKOON ARTS CLUB.† He became the first president of the group. When Otis Lithograph was sold in 1926, Moellman founded the Continental Lithograph Corp. on E. 72nd St. with $121,000 capital. It grew from a volume of $250,000 its first year to $4 million during World War II. By the 1950s it employed 250 skilled artisans in the production of outdoor billboards, movie lobby posters, and sales displays. Moellman was active in several local clubs and a director of the Lithographers National Assn. In 1912 he married the former Laura Conkey, who predeceased him. They had 4 children: Albert, Laura, Thomas, and Gwendolyn.—J.V.

**MOLEY, RAYMOND** (27 Sept. 1886–18 Feb. 1975), professor, presidential advisor, and director of the CLEVELAND FOUNDATION,† was born in Berea, OH, to Felix James and Agnes Fairchild Moley. He attended Baldwin Univ. (1902–06) and received an A.M. (1913) from Oberlin College and a Ph.D. (1918) from Columbia Univ. in political science. In 1916 Western Reserve Univ. hired Moley to teach political science. During World War I Moley also served as head of the local and state Americanization boards. In 1919 Moley resigned from WRU to become director of the Cleveland Foundation, which became noted for its surveys of city social problems. Moley accepted a teaching position at Columbia's Barnard College in 1923, remaining until 1954. In Jan. 1932, Franklin D. Roosevelt asked Moley to assemble advisors to develop programs for his presidential campaign; Moley selected mainly Columbia professors, who became the "Brain Trust."

Moley wrote speeches and advised FDR in 1932–33. He resigned in Aug. 1933 over conflicts with Secretary of State Cordell Hull, but continued to advise and write speeches for FDR on a part-time, non-paid basis until 1936, when he grew disillusioned with New Deal hostility to business and FDR's increasing involvement in foreign affairs. In 1933 Moley became editor of *Today* magazine, remaining after the 1937 merger with *Newsweek*, until 1967. In 1941 he began a nationally syndicated tri-weekly newspaper column. He wrote 19 books.

Moley was a senior advisor to Republican presidential aspirants Wendell Willkie, Barry Goldwater, and Richard Nixon. In 1970 he received the Medal of Freedom. Moley married Eva Dall in 1916 and had 2 sons, Malcolm and Raymond, Jr. They divorced in 1948, and Moley married Frances Hebard in 1949. Moley is buried in Phoenix, AZ.

Moley, Raymond. *Realities and Illusions, 1886–1931,* ed. Frank Freidel (1980).
Raymond Moley Papers, Hoover Institution on War, Revolution, and Peace, Stanford, CA.

**MOLYNEAUX, JOSEPH B.** (1 Jan. 1840–23 Apr. 1925), volunteer Civil War officer and secretary of the Cuyahoga County Soldiers & Sailors Monument Commission, was born in Ann Arbor, MI, son of Thomas and Margaret (Twamley) Molyneaux. He came to Cleveland before the Civil War and became a printer. He enlisted as a private in the 7TH OHIO VOLUNTEER INFANTRY† in the spring of 1861 for 3 month's service. He reenlisted with the 7th OVI for 3 year's service and was promoted to captain on 1 Sept. 1862. At the Battle of Cedar Mountain, he was twice wounded and had 2 horses shot out from under him (9 Aug. 1862), taking command of the regiment after all senior officers were either wounded or killed. He was mustered out as a lieutenant because of disability on 31 Dec. 1863.

Once recovered from his wounds, Molyneaux accepted a commission as captain of Co. E, 150th OVI in May 1864. He served in the defenses of

Washington, DC, in the summer of 1864 and was mustered out in Cleveland in August of that year. After the war, he returned to the printing business and served as deputy Cuyahoga County recorder, as asst. postmaster, and on the Board of Equalization & Assessment. He served on the Cuyahoga County Soldiers & Sailors Monument Commission from 1894–1925. Molyneaux married Henrietta A. Lyon in 1863. He was survived by her and 3 sons: Wm. V., Robt. T., and Raymond L. Molyneaux is buried in Woodland Cemetery.

**MONCOL, ANDREW JOHN** (3 Dec. 1877–16 March 1974), pastor of St. Cyril Congregational Church (1922–39), wrote and published articles in local and national Czech newspapers. An active participant in ethnic affairs among CZECHS,† he was supreme trustee of the Slovak National Society of America and Canada (1910–12). Moncol was born in Klenovec, Austria-Hungary, to Matey and Emilia Figuli Moncol. He came to the U.S. around 1900. After graduating from Oberlin College (1905), he traveled abroad and returned for postgraduate work at Oberlin Theological Seminary (1906). Ordained to the ministry in 1906, Moncol served as pastor of the Congregational church of Braddock, PA, and then as missionary to the Slavic community there (1906–09). During World War I, he worked with the YOUNG MEN'S CHRISTIAN ASSN.† in Siberia among Czech soldiers (1919). Just before and after the war, Moncol served a church in South Elmdale, MN. He came to Cleveland in 1922. Moncol retired in 1939 after suffering a stroke but then worked as a translator and a missionary to Slavic immigrants.

On 29 May 1906 Moncol married Mary Zoltak (d. 1951); they lived in Cleveland with their children, Helen M. and Emilie C. (Mrs. Milan) Siebert. He later married Edna Arnold on 16 June 1954; the couple lived on Cleveland's west side. Moncol is buried in West Park Cemetery.—J.M.

Andrew John Moncol Papers, Oberlin College Archives.

**MONTGOMERY, REV. ANZO** (13 July 1918–8 Aug. 1991), worked in Cleveland to help gain civil rights for AFRICAN AMERICANS,† while serving first as pastor of the Lane Metropolitan Christian Methodist Episcopal Church (1965–78) and then as general secretary of evangelism for the denomination (1978–82). He helped register voters in Cleveland with Dr. Martin Luther King, Jr. Before coming to Cleveland, Montgomery had been among the group of Topeka, KS, clergy whose challenges of segregation eventually resulted in the landmark U.S. Supreme Court case, *Brown v. Board of Education* (1954). The oldest of 10 children, Montgomery was born in Jackson, TN, to Roy and Lucille Ross Montgomery. He was ordained in 1938, having graduated from Henderson Business College, Memphis, TN, and Washburn Univ., Topeka, KS. Following a series of pastorates in Memphis, Montgomery ministered to churches in Topeka (1946–51) and Wichita, KS (1951–65). He participated in the URBAN LEAGUE OF CLEVELAND,† was an officer of the Cleveland Council of Churches (see INTERCHURCH COUNCIL OF GREATER CLEVELAND†), and presided over both the ecumenical Ministerial Alliance and the local chapter of the Opportunities Industrialization Center. He left Cleveland in 1982 for a church in Winston-Salem, NC, but returned to Ohio in 1986, where he served churches in Columbus and Springfield before retiring in 1990.

Montgomery married Saphronia Gooden (d. 1980). The couple had no children. On 24 Nov. 1982 he married Daisy Horne, who had two sons (Preston and Gilbert) by a previous marriage. While in Cleveland, Montgomery lived first in SHAKER HTS.,† then BEDFORD HTS.† Montgomery died in Columbus, OH.—J.M.

**MONTRESOR, JOHN** (22 Apr. 1736–26 June 1799), an engineer in the British Army in North America between 1754–78 and a member of Bradstreet's Expedition into the Lake Erie region, conducted the first preliminary survey of the CUYAHOGA RIVER.† Montresor was born in Gibraltar, served as asst. engineer under his father in the Engineer Corps of the British Army, and came to America in 1754 with Maj. Gen. Edward Braddock. After the French & Indian War, he conducted a partial survey of the St. Lawrence River and built redoubts around British forts in Canada. In 1764 Montresor accompanied Col. John Bradstreet's expedition to Detroit as chief engineering officer and commander of a detachment of Canadian volunteers. On the expedition's return, most of its ships were wrecked in a storm near Rocky River. Montresor, using one of the few remaining boats, engaged in minor exploration of some of Lake Erie's tributaries. According to his journal, one of the rivers he apparently visited was the "Cayahuga." Montresor went approximately 5 mi. up the river, measuring the depth and width of the channel in order to learn its potential for navigation. He then returned to Canada and later worked on British fortifications in the present northeastern U.S., and helped establish the long-disputed boundary between New York and New Jersey. During the Revolutionary War, until his retirement due to poor health in 1778, he was the principal engineer of the British.

Journals of Capt. John Montresor, Collections of the New York Historical Society (1881).
Webster, John. *Life of John Montresor* (1928).

**MOONEY, MICHAEL PATRICK** (22 Oct. 1866–6 Sept. 1936), an attorney known as "M. P.," served the city of Cleveland in various legal capacities and participated in the statewide charter movement. He advocated greater representation in CLEVELAND CITY GOVERNMENT† for immigrant residents (see IMMIGRATION AND MIGRATION). Mooney was born and educated in Ireland, the son of Thomas and Anne McHugh Mooney. Admitted to the U.S. Bar in 1891, for the next 2 years he served as asst. corporation counsel to the city of Cleveland. From 1910–11 Mooney was president of the Civil Service Commission of Cleveland. He was a member of both the city Charter Commission and the State Board of Charters in 1913. Four years later he was chosen for the MAYOR'S ADVISORY WAR COMMITTEE.† Mooney was director and general counsel to the Cleveland Life Insurance Co. (est. 1907) and the Mutual Building & Investment Co., director and president of the Realty & Rental Co., and director of the Gund Brewing Co. and the D. C. Griese & Walker Co. He belonged to the Chamber of Commerce and the Catholic Mutual Benefit Assn., among other groups.

Mooney married Mary Slowey (d. 1935) in Cleveland on 19 Sept. 1891; they lived in SHAKER HTS.† with children Francis G., Robert E., Mary C., Agnes M., Charles A., and Eleanor E. He is buried in Calvary Cemetery.—J.M.

**MOORE, EDWARD W.** (1 July 1864–8 May 1928) was a Cleveland businessman with interests in regional traction companies and public utilities. The son of Philip and Abbie Moore, he was a native of Canal Dover in Tuscarawas County, OH. He came to Cleveland in 1880 with only a common-school education and began as an office boy in the banking house of Everett, Weddell & Co. In 1891 he married Louise Chamberlin of Cleveland and helped organize the Dime Savings & Banking Co., where he eventually rose to vice-president by 1899–1901. He also helped to found and served as vice-president of the Western Reserve Trust Co. Meanwhile, Moore began investing in street and suburban electric railways. In 1894 he joined forces with Clevelander HENRY A. EVERETT to form the Everett-Moore syndicate, which built the Akron, Bedford & Cleveland line and then consolidated it into the Northern Ohio Traction Co., the first interurban in the nation operated by electric power. They constructed the CLEVELAND, PAINESVILLE & EASTERN† in 1895 and extended it in 1901 with the CLEVELAND, PAINESVILLE & ASHTABULA.† In 1901

they merged 4 interurbans between Cleveland and Toledo into the LAKE SHORE ELECTRIC.† With its control of street railways in Cleveland and Detroit and 15 interurbans in 3 states, the syndicate formed the country's first great trolley system. It also organized the Cuyahoga Telephone Co. and the U.S. Telephone Co., both of which were later merged into the Bell System. Moore died in his home on EUCLID AVE.† and was buried in Lake View Cemetery. Surviving were his wife and 4 children: Margaret, Franklin, Kathryn, and Elisabeth.—J.V.

**MORAN, REV. FRANCIS T.** (16 Feb. 1865–19 Oct. 1929), Roman Catholic priest and civic leader, was a nationally known writer and lecturer. He served as pastor of ST. PATRICK'S PARISH† (1901–28) and rector of ST. MARY SEMINARY† (1928–29). Moran was born in Valparaiso, IN, to Katherine Kelleher and Peter Moran. Educated in parochial schools in Indiana, he graduated from St. Francis Seminary (Milwaukee, WI), St. Charles College (Baltimore, MD), and Cleveland's St. Mary Seminary. He was ordained 19 December 1888.

Before coming to Cleveland, Fr. Moran served churches in the Toledo, OH, area (1889–96) and St. Mary Church in Akron (1896–1901). He served as treasurer of the Catholic Education Assn. of the U.S. and, locally, as a member of the Chamber of Commerce, the Civic League, Associated Charities, and the CLEVELAND HUMANE SOCIETY.† He belonged to the school board of the Diocese of Cleveland and worked on the parish level for integration of AFRICAN AMERICANS† into diocesan schools (see PAROCHIAL EDUCATION (CATHOLIC)†).—J.M.

Archives, Diocese of Cleveland.

**MORGAN, DANIEL EDGAR** (7 Aug. 1877–1 May 1949), councilman, state senator, city manager, and judge, was born in Oak Hill, OH, to Elias and Elizabeth Jones Morgan. He received his B.A. from Oberlin College (1897) and LL.B. from Harvard Law School (1901). While practicing law in Cleveland, he was elected as a Republican to CLEVELAND CITY COUNCIL† (1909–11), supported HOME RULE,† and helped write Cleveland's new charter, supporting a large council with small wards, believing people should have neighborhood representation. In 1928 he was elected Ohio state senator, earning a reputation for improving pending legislation to make it more effective.

Cleveland adopted the CITY MANAGER PLAN† in 1923; city council elected Morgan city manager in 1930. He negotiated settlements over utility rates; opened all staff positions at City Hospital to Negroes; and persuaded county officials to put a $31 million bond issue on the ballot to pay for public works to provide jobs during the Depression. However, mounting unemployment outstripped the means available to alleviate the problems, and in Nov. 1931 the plan was abolished, the city returned to mayor-ward government, and Morgan ran unsuccessfully for mayor in 1932. Morgan became judge on the Court of Appeals in 1939, serving until his death. Morgan supported Goodrich House, the CONSUMERS LEAGUE,† and LEGAL AID SOCIETY,† and was also a founder and first president of the CITY CLUB.† He married Ella A. Matthews (d. 1923), a women's suffragist, in 1915, and had a daughter, Nancy Olwen (Mrs. Armand B. Leavelle). In 1926 he married Wilma Ball.

Campbell, Thomas F. *Daniel E. Morgan, 1877–1949, The Good Citizen in Politics* (1966).
Daniel Edgar Morgan Papers, WRHS.

**MORGAN, GARRETT A.** (4 Mar. 1877 [sometimes given as 1879]–27 July 1963) was an important inventor and businessman active in the affairs of Cleveland's black community. Among his inventions were a gas mask and a traffic light. Born in Paris, KY, to Sydney, a former slave and son of Confederate Col. John H. Morgan, and Eliza Reed, also a former slave, Morgan received 6 years of education before leaving home at age 14 for Cincinnati, where he worked and hired a tutor to continue his education. He came to Cleveland on 17 June 1895. After various positions as a sewing-machine adjuster for clothing manufacturers, Morgan went into business for himself in 1907, establishing a shop on W. 6th St. to repair and sell sewing machines. In 1909 he opened a tailoring shop; with 32 employees, he manufactured suits, dresses, and coats. In 1913 he organized the G. A. Morgan Hair Refining Co. to market a hair-straightening solution he had discovered by accident in 1905. This company soon offered a complete line of hair-care products.

Morgan invented a safety helmet to protect the wearer from smoke and ammonia, introducing his "Breathing Device" in 1912, patenting it in 1914, and using it to descend into the gas-filled tunnel beneath Lake Erie to rescue workers and retrieve bodies after the Cleveland Waterworks explosion on 25 July 1916. Morgan established the Natl. Safety Device Co. in 1914. Morgan's other major invention, a traffic light (1923), was unique in using a third, cautionary signal between "stop" and "go." Morgan sold his traffic light to General Electric Co. for $40,000 in 1923.

Morgan in 1920 founded the *Cleveland Call*, a weekly newspaper, and in 1908 helped found the CLEVELAND ASSN. OF COLORED MEN.† In 1923 he bought a farm near Wakeman, OH, establishing the black Wakeman Country Club. Morgan married Madge Nelson in 1896; they were divorced in 1898. In 1908 he married Mary Hasek. He had three children: John P., Garrett A., Jr., and Cosmo H. Morgan died in Cleveland and was buried in Lake View Cemetery.

Garrett Augustus Morgan Papers, WRHS.

**MORIARTY, ELAINE M.** (11 Dec. 1899–25 Apr. 1994) was a noted community volunteer who worked with numerous social service organizations. She was born Elaine McElroy in Port Huron, MI, the daughter of William P. and Mabel (Chambers) McElroy. She was a descendant of Great Lakes ship captains. Her family moved to Lakewood when her father became superintendent of the Pittsburgh Steamship fleet. She graduated from Lakewood High School, the Univ. of Michigan (in 1923), and then Western Reserve Univ. At the latter she earned a master's degree at the School of Applied and Social Sciences in 1925. Afterwards she worked as a counselor at the FAMILY SERVICE ASSN.†

On 21 April 1926 in Cuyahoga County, she married Wilson Harold Moriarty, who later served as a vice-president and director of the National Castings Co.

Mrs. Moriarty was known for devoting a great deal of her time to community volunteer work, especially with social service organizations. She headed numerous organizations over the years, including the Neighborhood Settlement Assn., the FRIENDLY INN SOCIAL SETTLEMENT,† the Shaker Hts. Community Council, the Cleveland USO, the Cleveland Welfare Federation, the Cleveland YWCA, and the Hudson Boy's Farm. She also served on boards of many other organizations.

Her husband died in 1981. She died in Cleveland and was buried at Hillcrest Cemetery. Moriarty was survived by a daughter, Jane M. Breckling, and a son, Wilson P. Moriarty.—D.R.

**MORITZ, ALAN RICHARDS** (25 Dec. 1899–12 May 1986), forensic pathologist, was born in Hastings, NE, son of Richard Daniel and Genevieve Richards Moritz. He received his B.S., A.M., and M.D. (1923) degrees from the Univ. of Nebraska and came to Cleveland as a house officer at Lakeside Hospital (1923–24) and research fellow, then instructor in pathology at Western Reserve Univ. School of Medicine (1924–26). After a year in Vienna, Moritz returned as resident in pathology at Lakeside Hospital (1927–31), then pathologist in charge at UNIV. HOSPITALS OF CLEVELAND† (1931–37). At WRU he was assistant, then associate professor of pathology from 1930–37. In 1937 he left for Harvard as professor of legal medicine. During the 1940s Moritz was consulting pathologist to the Massachusetts State Police Force and Department of Mental Health, and chief pathologist at Boston's Peter Bent Brigham Hospital.

In 1949 Moritz returned to Cleveland as professor of pathology at the School of Medicine, director of the Institute of Pathology of WRU and Univ. Hospitals, and chairman of the Hospitals' Department of Pathology. He became provost of WRU in 1965, and subsequently of CASE WESTERN RESERVE UNIV.,† through 1968. He became Director of Professional Affairs (1969), then chief of staff (1970–1971), at Univ. Hospitals. Moritz wrote books on forensic pathology and provided expert testimony in many cases, including Cleveland's SHEPPARD MURDER CASE† and Pres. Kennedy's autopsy investigation. In 1970 the American Assn. of Pathologists and Bacteriologists recognized his great achievements. Moritz married Velma Lucina Boardman in 1927 and had 3 children: John Alan, Richard Boardman, and Anne Boardman.


**MORLEY, EDWARD WILLIAMS** (29 Jan. 1838–24 Feb. 1923), scientist and professor at Western Reserve Univ. whose work with ALBERT MICHELSON laid a foundation for Albert Einstein's later work, was born in Newark, NJ, to Sardis Brewster and Anna Clarissa Treat Morley. He graduated from Williams College (1860), received his master's degree from Andover Theological Seminary (1863), and worked for the Sanitary Commission during the Civil War. In 1868 Morley received 2 job offers: first as clergyman in Twinsburg, and then as chair of natural history and chemistry at Western Reserve College in Hudson, which he chose. From 1873–88 he was professor of toxicology in WRC's Medical Department in Cleveland.

From 1878–82 Morley studied the concentration of oxygen in the atmosphere, and from 1882–93 worked to determine the relative atomic weights of hydrogen and oxygen. In 1884 Morley began work with Albert A. Michelson, first building an accurate interferometer (1885), then conducting the experiment (1887) which found that the supposed all-pervasive ether had no apparent effect on the speed of light, contributing significantly to the upheaval in late–19th-century physics that was essentially resolved by Einstein's Special Theory of Relativity. Morley was president of the American Assn. for the Advancement of Science (1895) and the American Chemical Society (1899). In 1902 he finished second in balloting for the Nobel Prize in chemistry. In 1907 he received the Rumford Medal from the Royal Society (London). Morley retired as professor

emeritus to West Hartford, CT, in 1906, with his wife, Isabella Birdsall Morley, whom he married in 1868. They were childless.

Univ. Archives, CWRU.

**MORRIS, CHARLES** (13 Aug. 1869–27 Jan. 1930), a classical architect active in Cleveland from 1902–05 and 1923–30, was the son of Charles E. Morris. Born, educated, and trained in New York, Morris studied at the Ecole des Beaux-Arts in Paris for 2 years. Returning to New York, he became associated with Richard Walker, whose firm designed a number of Carnegie Library buildings. In 1902 Morris was invited to Cleveland to assist architects LEHMAN & SCHMITT† in designing the CUYAHOGA COUNTY COURTHOUSE,† becoming its principal designer. In 1905 he planned Cleveland's Broadway Free Library, a Carnegie library, then returned to Walker & Morris in New York, helping design the 22nd Regimental Armory, Municipal Ferry Houses, and bridge and pavilions on Riverside Dr. After Walker & Morris broke up, Morris became chief designer in the office of the supervising architect of the U.S. Treasury, designing post offices throughout the country during the 1910s. At the end of World War I he moved to Cleveland, in 1923 joining JOSEPH WEINBERG to form Morris & Weinberg. They designed successful commercial buildings, but their major work may be BELLEFAIRE† (the Jewish Orphan Asylum) in UNIV. HTS.† Opened in 1929, it is a model residential campus based on the "cottage" plan. Morris was a fellow of the American Institute of Architects and president of the Cleveland Chap. (1925–26). He was a founder of the Cleveland School of Architecture in 1992 and its secretary until its affiliation with Western Reserve Univ. in 1929. Morris married Jean Walker in 1903 and had 2 children, Jean and Robert. He died in Cleveland and was buried in Knollwood Cemetery.


**MOSIER, HAROLD GERARD** (24 July 1889–7 Aug. 1971), Ohio senator, U.S. Congressman, and Ohio lt. governor, was born in Cincinnati to Moody G. and Anna Hogsett Mosier. He moved to Cleveland to attend East High School, and earned his A.B. degree from Dartmouth (1912) and LL.B. degree from Harvard Univ. (1915). Admitted to the Ohio Bar in 1915, Mosier practiced law with the firm of TOLLES, HOGSETT, GINN & MORLEY until 1920, serving 1 year during World War I with the U.S. Ordnance Dept. In 1921 Mosier helped form the firm of Christopher, Mosier & Dover, leaving in 1930 to form Minshall & Mosier with Wm. Minshall.

Elected to the Ohio Senate in 1932, Mosier

authored the Ohio Liquor Control Bill and legislation ratifying the constitutional amendment repealing Prohibition, and served as chairman of the Judiciary Committee and headed the Cuyahoga County legislative delegation. Elected lt. governor in 1934, he withdrew his candidacy for governor in 1936 to run for the U.S. House of Representatives, serving as a member of the Dies Committee investigating "un-American" activities. Fighting to rid the country of Communist influence, he became known as the "Dies Red-Hunter." Defeated in the 1938 primary, Mosier ran for Ohio governor in 1940 but was defeated. Admitted to the Maryland Bar in 1943, he served as counsel to Glenn L. Martin Co. in Baltimore, 1942–52, and as legislative advisor to Aircraft Industries Assn. in Washington, DC, from 1952–60, when he retired. He married Grace Hoyt Jones in 1918. Mosier died in Washington, DC, and was buried in the Fort Lincoln Cemetery in Maryland.

**MUELLER, ERNST W.** (13 Oct. 1851–15 Jan. 1931) was a prominent local German-American civic leader and one of Cleveland's leading brewers.

Mueller was born in Alsenz, Rhineland-Palatinate, Germany. His father, Peter, took the family to America in 1856, settling in Cleveland, where 3 of Peter's brothers (including JACOB MUELLER) already lived.

In 1887 Mueller established the Cleveland Brewing Co. which produced what became recognized as "the best Cleveland beer." In 1897 his firm merged with 10 other breweries to form the CLEVELAND-SANDUSKY BREWING CORP.† Ernst became president of this "syndicate" in 1898. After leading this company on to success, he left in 1907 to found the CLEVELAND HOME BREWING CO.†

Mueller was a founder and leader of the Turnverein Vorwaerts, a German-American cultural and gymnastic group. He was captain of the prize Turnverein gymnastic team at the Philadelphia Centennial in 1876.

Mueller married Agathe Leick in 1879. He was survived by 3 sons: OMAR EUGENE, Curt, and Lynn. Mueller is buried in Lake View Cemetery. —D.R.

Mueller, Werner D. and Gardiner, Duncan B. *To Cleveland and Away: Of Muellers, Reids, and Others* (1993).

**MUELLER, JACOB** (9 Mar. 1822–31 Aug. 1905) was a German emigre who became a civic leader in Cleveland's German-American community, active in local, state, and national politics. He was elected lt. governor of Ohio, serving 1 term, 1872–74. Born in Alsenz, Rhineland-Palatinate, Germany, the son of manufacturer Wilhelm Muller and Anna Elisabetha (Geib) Muller, Mueller received a common-school education, studied law, and worked as a lawyer after 1845. He was active in the Revolution of 1848 and served as a civil commissioner under the revolutionary government; when that government was overturned in 1849, he fled to the U.S., where he joined his 2 brothers in Cleveland in Sept. 1849. He studied law and English in the law offices of Geo. Willey and J. E. Carey. After being admitted to the bar in 1854, he practiced in partnership with Benjamin R. Beavis and Louis Ritter, which dissolved in 1859. Mueller then established the German Insurance Co. and served as its director and secretary until 1869, when he resigned to travel in Europe.

Mueller became active in politics and in the civic affairs of the local German-American community in the 1850s. Along with Louis Ritter, he formed a stock company in 1852 to establish a new German newspaper, *Waechter am Erie,* and was later an editor of *WAECHTER UND ANZEIGER.†* He served on CLEVELAND CITY COUNCIL† in 1857–58 as the representative from the 6th Ward, and in addition to his election as lt. governor in 1871, he was elected as a representative from Cuyahoga County to the 1873–74 state constitutional convention. He was a delegate to the Free-Soil party's national convention in 1885 and to the Republican national conventions in 1860 and 1872. In 1873 he broke with the Republican party; joining the Democrats, he attended that party's national convention in 1876. In 1885 Pres. Grover Cleveland appointed him consul-general at Frankfurt am Main; he served there for 4 years. In 1896 Mueller published a book of his writings concerning German life in Cleveland, entitled *Memoirs of a '48er.*

Mueller was married twice. His first wife, Charlotte Finger, died in 1858. He married Laura Schmidt in 1860; she died in 1886. Mueller died in Cleveland and was buried in Woodland Cemetery. He was survived by 4 daughters: Emma (Mrs. Frank Cudell) from his first marriage, and Minna (Mrs. Odo Portmann), Paulina (Mrs. Jean Baptiste Hepp), and Elsie (Mrs. Richard Writh) from his second marriage.

Mueller, Werner D. and Gardiner, Duncan B. *To Cleveland and Away: Of Muellers, Reids, and Others* (1993).

**MUELLER, OMAR EUGENE** (27 July 1880–22 June 1946) was a prominent Cleveland brewer and businessman. Born in Cleveland, Mueller was the son of ERNST W. and Agathe Leick MUELLER.

Mueller was educated at UNIV. SCHOOL,† Harvard Univ., and Washington Univ. His early career included service as U.S. Consul in Bahia, Brazil, from 1911 to 1914; and later, in the 1920s, employment as vice-president of Packless Valve Co. and Packless Quick Closing Valve Co.

In 1932 Mueller became president of the CLEVELAND HOME BREWING CO.,† which had been founded by his father in 1907, and headed the company until his death.

Eulogized by the Cleveland *PLAIN DEALER†* as a "man of unusual attainments," Mueller was also recognized as a nationally ranked tournament bridge player.

Mueller married Elsa Weideman (daughter of JOHN CHRISTIAN WEIDEMAN) in 1914. He was survived by 4 children: Ernst W., Erna L. Berry, Jay C., and Werner D. Mueller. A son, Omar John, died at the age of six. Mueller lived in CLEVELAND HTS. He is buried in Riverside Cemetery.—D.R.

Mueller, Werner D. and Gardiner, Duncan B. *To Cleveland and Away: Of Muellers, Reids, and Others* (1993).

**MURAL, KATHERINE** (12 July 1904–2 June 1993) was a Ukrainian immigrant-rights activist, serving as secretary for 20 years of Cleveland Branch 358 of the Ukrainian National Assn., a fraternal insurance organization, and president of Cleveland Branch 30 of the UKRAINIAN NATIONAL WOMEN'S LEAGUE OF AMERICA.†

Born Katherine Mural in Cassandra, PA, to John and Anna (Prunchak) Mural, Katherine moved from Johnstown, PA, to Cleveland with her family at age 16. Katherine worked as a waitress, becoming involved in Ukrainian organizations through her church. Together with her husband, Katherine would sponsor Ukrainian immigrant families, then help these displaced people find homes and a job in the Cleveland area, particularly after World War II. Katherine would introduce them to life in America and teach them such basics as riding buses, shopping and banking.

From the 1930s until her death, Katherine was active in Soyuz-Ukrainok—the Ukrainian National Women's League of America, serving as president during the 1940s and 1950s. In the early 1960s, Katherine chaired the committee of the Ukrainian National Assn., which raised funds for and purchased the statue of Ukrainian poetess Lesya Ukrainka for the Cleveland Cultural Gardens.

Katherine was honored many times for her lifelong work in and commitment to the Ukrainian community of Cleveland by the Ukrainian National Assn. and the Ukrainian National Women's League of America.

Katherine married Frank Mural on 7 Feb. 1920 (d. 1981). They had two children, William and Helen (Shipka). She lived in PARMA† and belonged to St. Josaphat Ukrainian Catholic Cathedral. Katherine is buried in St. Andrews Cemetery.—T.B.

**MURCH, MAYNARD HALE** (3 Nov. 1874–28 Feb. 1966) founded the Maynard H. Murch Co. and was called the dean of area investment bankers. He was a conservationist, philanthropist, and promoter of the natural sciences.

Born in Chardon, OH, to Maynard Hale and Lucy (Stephenson), Murch received his A.B. from Western Reserve Univ. in 1898, then worked as a reporter for the *Plain Dealer* until 1903, when he entered the investment field as a bond salesman.

In 1911 he organized the Maynard H. Murch Co., an investment brokerage firm, and served as president and senior partner. In 1920 he transferred the investment part of the business to Maynard H. Murch & Co., a brokerage partnership, with the original firm continuing as a holding company. Murch is credited with putting together the company known as the Whirlpool Corp. In 1950 the investment company became Fulton, Reid & Co., incorporating in 1956 with Murch as a special partner.

Nature and conservationism interested Murch, resulting in a long association as a trustee of the Cleveland Zoo (he donated two Kodiak bears in 1946), Holden Arboretum, and the CLEVELAND MUSEUM OF NATURAL HISTORY.† Murch became a museum trustee in 1938; president, 1949–52; and life trustee in 1952. He helped provide funding for joint programs with Western Reserve Univ. and Case Institute of Technology (see CASE WESTERN RESERVE UNIV.†). In 1960 the museum honored him with the Harold T. Clark Medal. In 1956 he established the MURCH FOUNDATION† to promote educational, cultural, and hospital programs.

Murch married Leah Daggett in 1905. They had two sons, Maynard Jr. and Boynton. Murch was Episcopalian, lived in Kirtland, and is buried in Lake View Cemetery.—T.B.

**MURDOCH, MARIAN E.** (9 Oct. 1848–28 Jan. 1943) served with FLORENCE BUCK as joint ministers of the First Unitarian Society of Cleveland, 1893–99.

Born in Garnavillo, IA, to Judge Samuel and Louisa (Patch) Murdoch, Marian attended Evanston College for Women, Fayette College (Iowa), the Univ. of Wisconsin (1868–69), and Boston Univ.'s School of Oratory and Literature (1875). Murdoch taught in Dubuque, IA, and Omaha, NE, before entering the Meadville Theological School in 1882. When Murdoch received a B.D. degree in 1885, she became the first woman to earn this degree from Meadville. She returned to do postgraduate work in 1891, then studied for a year in England at Manchester College and Oxford Univ.

Murdoch was ordained on 1 Sept. 1885 in Humboldt, IA, where she performed her first duties as a minister over the next five years. In 1893 Buck and Murdoch were called by the First Unitarian Society of Cleveland to serve as joint ministers of the First Unitarian Church (Unity Church). During their tenure the church prospered, growing to 80 members.

In 1899 Buck and Murdoch resigned in order to travel and study in Europe. Returning to the U.S., Murdoch lived in Geneva, IL, from 1904–06, joined Florence Buck in Kenosha, WI, in 1906, then moved to California in 1911, where she was actively involved with All Soul's Unitarian Church.

Murdoch was a published poet and author of *The Hermit Thrush*, as well as a teacher of art, literature, and public speaking. She died in Santa Monica, CA.—T.B.

Morton, Marian. *Women in Cleveland: An Illustrated History* (1995).

**MURPHY, EDWARD F.** (15 July 1891–7 Mar. 1950), president of Teamsters Local 407 and policymaker in the CLEVELAND FED. OF LABOR,† was born in Cleveland to Patrick and Margaret (Sullivan) Murphy. He was a horsecart driver and then a drayman. His experience with long hours and low pay led him to join Teamsters Local 407 when it was organized in 1911. By 1916 he was vice-president, and by 1924, president. In 1929 he began working full time for the union.

Murphy helped found Teamsters Joint Council 41 to coordinate the 7 Teamster locals in the area. He also became general organizer for the International (1931). Under Murphy, the TEAMSTERS UNION† became powerful enough to stop deliveries at struck plants, allowing Murphy to negotiate contracts guaranteeing better service to employers in return for fair wages. Murphy believed strikes were only a last resort, and was regarded by employers as trustworthy, fair, and tough. Murphy kept area locals free of racketeering and strong-arm tactics.

Because of his integrity and union power, Murphy was important in the Cleveland Fed. of Labor. Seeing that the dominance of the building trades in the federation threatened its stability, he challenged their leadership. A truce was executed, and in 1939 Murphy resigned his Teamster duties to work full-time for the CFL, holding the balance of power. Injured in an auto accident, Murphy cut back his activities.

Murphy married Mae O'Connel on 27 Nov. 1913. They had three children: Mary, Edward, and Joseph. When he died, his local erected a monument for him at Calvary Cemetery and donated a floor at ST. VINCENT CHARITY HOSPITAL† in his memory.

**MURPHY, JOHN PATRICK** (25 April 1887–15 July 1969) was a lawyer and businessman whose railroad expertise led to his association with the Van Sweringens and the Higbee Co., a Van Sweringen interest acquired in 1929. He established the JOHN P. MURPHY FOUNDATION† to promote his interest in Catholic education, hospitals, and music.

Born in Westboro, MA, Murphy attended Holy Cross College, 1906–08, and received his law degree from Notre Dame Univ. in 1912. Admitted to the Minnesota Bar in 1913, he practiced in Minneapolis until 1915, when he moved to Montana and focused on railroad law. In 1917 he enlisted in the U.S. Army Air Corp. In 1918 Murphy became senior counsel for the U.S. Spruce Products Corp. in Portland, OR.

His work with railroads attracted the attention of the Van Sweringens, who brought Murphy to Cleveland. Between 1920–37, he helped develop the Van Sweringens' real estate and railroad interests and served as director of several of their companies.

Murphy's association with Higbees began in 1937 when he was named an executor of O. P. Van Sweringen's will. Together with Charles Bradley, they took control of the company, with Bradley as president and Murphy as secretary. Murphy served as president and director of Higbee's from 1944–62, chairman, 1962–68, and honorary chairman, 1968–69. Murphy continued his law practice as partner in the firm of Morley, Stickle & Murphy in 1941, and Morley, Stickle, Keeley & Murphy in 1944.

Murphy married Gladys Tate on 30 June 1924. They had no children. Murphy is buried in St. Luke's Cemetery, Westboro, MA.—T.B.

**MURRAY, J. D. BAIN** (26 Dec. 1926–16 Jan. 1993) was a composer, music critic and professor of music at CLEVELAND STATE UNIV.† Born in Evanston, IL, son of Donald Bain and Frances Lewis (Langworthy) Murray, he graduated from North Shore County Day School in Winnetka, IL, in 1945. He was a World War II veteran, having served in the U.S. Army (1945–46).

He received an A.B. Degree in Music from Oberlin College in 1951 and a master's degree from Harvard Univ. in 1952. He conducted research at the Univ. of Liege and studied composition and counterpoint with Nadia Boulanger in Paris in 1953–54.

Murray taught at the Oberlin College Conservatory from 1955–57, and came to Cleveland in 1959. He held teaching positions at the CLEVELAND MUSIC SCHOOL SETTLEMENT,† Fenn College, and Cleveland State Univ., where he became head of the Composition Division in the Music Department. Among his many compositions are two operas: "The Legend" (1987) and "Mary Stuart: A Queen

Betrayed" (1991), both of which were premiered by the CLEVELAND CHAMBER SYMPHONY.† Among his most remembered songs are "Now Close the Windows" (1949), based on the poetry of Robert Frost, and "Flame and Shadow," based on the poetry of Sara Teasdale.

Murray created the music column for the Sun Newspapers and published widely on musical subjects, especially the new music of Poland. He was also a *PLAIN DEALER†* music critic in the late 1950s.

He was the recipient of a Fulbright grant, two Harvard Prizes, the Polish Medal of Distinction, annual ASCAP awards, grants from the Ohio Arts Council, and the Ohio Joint Council of Arts and Humanities, among others.

Murray married Laurie Jean Wolfe on 3 Feb. 1951; they had one daughter, Ruth Elizabeth. Murray died in UNIV. HTS.† and was cremated; his ashes were buried in Riverton, WV.—R.W.

J. D. Bain Murray Papers, Oberlin College Archives.

**MYERS, GEORGE A.** (5 Mar. 1859–17 Jan. 1930), an African American politician and leader, was born in Baltimore, MD, to Isaac and Emma V. (Morgan) Meyers. He became a barber, arrived in Cleveland in 1879, and worked at Weddell House Barber Shop. In 1888 he opened shop in the new HOLLENDEN HOTEL,† financed by white friends LIBERTY E. HOLDEN and JAS. FORD RHODES. By 1920 Myers's shop had 17 barbers, 6 manicurists, 5 porters, 3 ladies' hairdressers, 2 cashiers, and 2 podiatrists.

The shop brought Myers into contact with politicians, and he became a close ally to MARCUS HANNA,† even bribing a state legislator in 1897 to ensure Hanna's election to the U.S. Senate. In 1892, 1896, and 1900 he was a delegate to the Republican Natl. Convention. His support for Wm. McKinley earned him offers of political appointments; Myers refused appointment himself but gained positions for 4 other AFRICAN AMERICANS.†

After the deaths of McKinley (1901) and Hanna (1904), Myers retired from national politics. During the 1920s, Myers became more militant in racial matters, possibly because of the Hollenden's decision in 1923 that after Myers retired, all black barbers would be replaced by whites. In the 1920s Myers successfully campaigned to have newspapers capitalize Negro and stop using offensive words, and persuaded authorities to guard Woodland Hill municipal swimming pool to prevent threatened violence to blacks. In 1930 Myers sold his barbershop to the hotel management and died in the train ticket office while preparing for a vacation. Survived by his first wife, Sarah, and his second wife, Maude E. Stewart, whom he married in 1896, Myers had two children, Dorothy and Herbert P. He was buried in Lake View Cemetery.

Garraty, John A. *The Barber and the Historian* (1956). George Myers Papers, Ohio Historical Society.

**MYERS, PIERRE (PETE, "MAD DADDY")** (1928–4 Oct. 1968) served a brief but trend-setting stint as a Cleveland radio disc jockey at the beginning of the rock 'n' roll era in the late 1950s. Born in San Francisco to Pierre and Gayle Myers, he trained as an actor at the Royal Academy of Dramatic Art in London and moved into the field of radio announcing in San Diego. Seeking to break into the Cleveland market, he found work first in Akron and then (Jan. 1958) with WJW† in Cleveland as the nighttime disc jockey. He drew upon his acting experience to develop the persona of the crazy DJ, affecting a flowing black cape and such signature phrases as "mellow as Jello" and "Hang loose, Mother Goose." "Once he got into a character, it really took him over," said Bill Randle, one of his contemporaries on another station. Taken off the air by WJW for signing on with WHK† before giving his contractual 90-day notice, Myers stayed in the public eye by parachuting 2,200 feet into Lake Erie from an airplane on 14 June 1958. He remained with WHK for about a year before moving to WNEW in New York. There he was given one test evening in his "Mad Daddy" role, but adverse reaction forced him to play it straight thereafter. Frustrated in his efforts to recapture his Cleveland fame, Myers shot himself to death a decade later. His first marriage to Sylvia Crane in 1955 ended in divorce. He then married in Cleveland to Ann Boyce Myers on 29 Mar. 1958; he was survived by a later wife, Lisa Jordan Myers. —J.V.

N

**NADAS, JOHN B.** (28 Jan. 1903–25 Aug. 1992) won honors from Cleveland mayors George Voinovich and Ralph Perk for his international contributions in ethnic affairs. He founded the Hungarian Assn. to preserve native culture among HUNGARIANS† in Cleveland, the ARPAD ACADEMY OF ARTS AND SCIENCES† (1966, which later spread to 50 countries) to recognize authors, scientists and artists of Hungarian descent, and the Arpad Federation. Nadas also organized what was reportedly the first Hungarian Meeting in the Free World (1961), later the annual Hungarian Congress. Nadas was born in Kecskemet, Hungary, son of Janos and Rozsa Boka Papp Nadas. He was president of the Hungarian Assn. of Student Organizations as a youth and part of a delegation representing Hungary at the dedication of New York City's Kossuth Memorial (1928). Having worked in political and cultural organizations in Hungary, after World War II, Nadas immigrated first to Austria (1944) and then to the U.S. (1950). Moving to Cleveland in 1951, he worked for GENERAL ELECTRIC† at NELA PARK† for 10 years before retiring. Mayor Voinovich presented Nadas with the key to the city and designated him honorary mayor in 1989.

Nadas served as an officer in the American Hungarian Federation, the National Federation of American Hungarians, the U.S. Chapter of the Transylvanian World Federation, and the Free Hungarian World Council. A single man, he lived in LAKEWOOD† and is buried in West Park Cemetery.—J.M.

**NASH, HELEN MILLIKIN** (21 Feb. 1893–31 Aug. 1990) was an original trustee of the Shaker Lakes Regional Nature Center whose interest in the preservation of open space contributed to local efforts to create the center.

Born in Cleveland to Benjamin and Julia Severance Millikin, Helen attended Froebel School, graduated from HATHAWAY BROWN† in 1910, and Wells College in 1914.

Interested in horticulture and conservation, Nash became a member of the Shaker Lakes Garden Club and served as president, 1934–38. She later joined the Garden Center of Greater Cleveland (see CLEVELAND BOTANICAL GARDEN†), serving as first vice-president, 1947–48, and president, 1949–51. Under her leadership, the Garden Center increased its membership and added responsibilities in community development. In 1957 she received the Frances McIntosh Sherwin Award for outstanding service to the Garden Center.

When the SHAKER LAKES† area was threatened in the mid–1960s by the proposed Clark Freeway, Nash anonymously contributed one-half the cost of a National Audubon Society Study which concluded that the Lakes area should be preserved (Audubon paid the other half). This led to the creation of the Shaker Lakes Regional Nature Center in 1966 and later designation of the area as a national environmental education landmark.

Nash served on the boards of numerous institutions, including the Beech Brook Children's Home (see BEECH BROOK INC.†), 1929–32; Lyndhurst-South Euclid Board of Education, 1935–44; VISITING NURSE ASSN. OF CLEVELAND,† board president 1943–46; and CLEVELAND ORCHESTRA,† 1944–90.

She married Richard Preston Nash on 10 July 1923 and lived in SOUTH EUCLID.† They had three children: Julia, Louise, and Richard Jr. A Presbyterian, she is buried in Lake View Cemetery.—T.B.

Interview, Cleveland Families Oral History Project, WRHS.

NASSAU, JASON J. (29 Mar. 1893–11 May 1965), astronomer and skillful popularizer, was born in Smyrna, Turkey, to Greek parents, John and Maria Christie Nassau. He earned a Ph.D. from Syracuse Univ., and did graduate study at Columbia, Cambridge, and Edinburgh Universities. In 1921 he became assoc. professor of mathematics and astronomy at Case Institute of Technology; in 1928 he became director of the Warner & Swasey Observatory on the Case campus, holding that position until he retired as chairman of the Astronomy Dept. and director of the observatory in 1959, when he became professor emeritus.

Nassau installed a 35" Schmidt telescope in Warner & Swasey Observatory. Interested in public education, Nassau made "public nights" a monthly feature at the observatory. When the smog and lights of Cleveland made it necessary to move the telescope to Chardon, the new observatory was named the Nassau Astronomical Station in his honor. Nassau's research on the structure of the Milky Way brought him international acclaim. He developed a technique to study the distribution of red stars that was adopted all over the world, and in 1957 discovered a new cluster of 9,000 stars in the galaxy. With Chas. Stephenson, he also discovered 2 novae in 1961.

Nassau spoke at international conferences and was equally effective with area high school audiences. Nassau published more than 80 papers, was president of the Cleveland Astronomical Society and a fellow of the American and Royal astronomical societies. Nassau married Laura Johnson in 1920 and had 2 sons, Sherwood and James.

NAVIN, ROBERT B. (27 Apr. 1895–13 Feb. 1970), sociologist, dean, and president of ST. JOHN COLLEGE† for 30 years, was born in Youngstown, OH, the son of John and Bridget (Kenney) Navin. He studied for the priesthood in Rochester, NY, was ordained in 1923, and received a doctorate in Sacred Theology in Rome. He pursued graduate studies in education and sociology at Catholic Univ. His dissertation, "The Analysis of a Slum Area," was a study of Cleveland's E. 21st-E. 55th-Central-Woodland area, and became a pattern for studies in 34 other U.S. cities.

When Navin came to Sisters' College in 1929, the school was a newly formed college to train nuns for teaching in diocesan schools. Within a decade, he won its accreditation from the American Assn. of Teachers' Colleges and developed a masters of education program. The school moved into a new building, becoming St. John College in 1946, and Navin became its president. The school developed an accredited nursing program, offered adult-education classes, and opened the auditorium and classrooms to community groups. Interested in the Catholic trade-union movement, Navin encouraged labor-management and collective-bargaining workshops at the college.

In World War II Navin was chairman of the Cleveland Area Rent Control Board and Cleveland Area Rent Committee. Later, he was president of Better Homes & Neighborhoods Assn. and on the mayor's advisory boards of housing and urban renewal. He retired from St. John in 1960, becoming president emeritus. As his health failed, he moved to an apartment at ST. VINCENT CHARITY HOSPITAL.†

NEARON, JOSEPH R. (4 Dec. 1928–7 June 1984) was a priest of the Congregation of the Blessed Sacrament. During his priestly years, he was both a professor of religious studies and a leader in the Catholic African American community.

Born in Yonkers, NY, son of Roy and Josephine Nearon, Joseph earned his B.A. from Manhattan College, and then in 1951 entered the novitiate of the Blessed Sacrament Fathers in Barre, MA. In 1952 he came to Cleveland where he continued his studies at the order's St. Joseph Seminary, 17608 Euclid Ave. He then was sent to Rome to complete his studies at the Gregorian Univ. He was ordained there 10 Oct. 1955. He later returned to the Gregorian, earning a doctorate in sacred theology.

In 1959 Nearon was assigned to Cleveland to teach at St. Joseph Seminary. In 1967 he joined the religious studies faculty at JOHN CARROLL UNIV.,† and from 1969 through 1976 served as its chairman. In 1978 he became superior of the Cleveland Blessed Sacrament community.

In 1980–81 Nearon was assigned to teach at St. Paul Inter-territorial Seminary at Gbanga, Liberia. His stay shortened by illness, he returned to the U.S. in 1981 and joined the faculty of Xavier Univ., New Orleans. There he helped found the Institute of Black Catholic Studies. The last three years of his life were devoted to issues concerning African American Catholics.

In 1984, while on a trip back to Cleveland, Nearon took ill. Hospitalized in Fort Oglethorpe, GA, he succumbed to encephalitis and pneumonia. Funeral services were held at St. Paschal Baylon Church in HIGHLAND HTS.†; burial was in St. Paul's Cemetery in EUCLID.†—J.T.

NEFF, EARL J. (4 April 1902–12 March 1993), moved from a career in commercial art to an avocation as Cleveland's acknowledged authority on "ufology"—the study of UFOs, or "Unidentified Flying Objects." Born in Cleveland, the son of Albert and Bertha Beutel Neff, he graduated from Lakewood High School and the Cleveland School of

Art (see CLEVELAND INSTITUTE OF ART†). He also studied at the JOHN HUNTINGTON POLYTECHNIC INSTITUTE† and in 1928 married the former Vivian Uhl. During the Depression, Neff completed a mural at LAKEVIEW TERRACE† as part of the New Deal's Treasury Relief Art Project. He joined TRAP's successor, the Federal Art Project, becoming 3rd director of the Cleveland unit for a few months in 1938–39 and completing another mural for the community cabin in FAIRVIEW PARK.† As a commercial artist, he maintained his own studio and served as art editor for several local businesses, including 10 years at Sohio (see STANDARD OIL CO./B.P. AMERICA†). He also served as a counselor for the Vocational Guidance and Rehabilitation Service before retiring in 1966. Neff's interest in UFOs had begun in 1958 with the first of an alleged 8 personal sightings by 1973. He was elected chairman of the Cleveland Ufology Project (CUP) in 1958 and served as U.S. representative of the Intercontinental UFO Observer and Analytical Network (ICUFON). He gained a national forum through lecturing and talk radio programs. Though personally convinced that UFOs were genuine phenomena emanating from outer space, Neff included the exposure of "frauds in ufology." A resident of PARMA,† he was buried in Sunset Memorial Park, survived by a son, Roger J., and daughter, Joann Conner.—J.V.

**NESS, ELIOT** (19 Apr. 1903–16 May 1957), nationally known for leading the Chicago "Untouchables," was Cleveland's safety director. Born in Chicago, son of Peter and Emma (King) Ness, he graduated from the Univ. of Chicago (1925) before joining the U.S. Prohibition Bureau in 1929, forming the "Untouchables," who obtained the conviction of Al Capone. Following Prohibition's repeal, Ness was transferred to the Treasury Dept.'s Alcohol Tax Unit in Cincinnati, arriving in Cleveland in 1934 as the head of the alcohol tax unit for the northern district of Ohio. His reputation as honest and capable led Mayor HAROLD H. BURTON to appoint Ness city safety director in 1935 to clean up the scandal-ridden police department. Ness formed his own Cleveland "Untouchables," funded by an anonymous group of businessmen known as the "Secret 6," and quickly reformed, reorganized, and upgraded the department, motorizing the patrol and using car radios to enhance communication. He established a separate traffic section, hired a traffic engineer, and enabled Cleveland, which had the worst U.S. traffic-fatality record, to twice win awards for reducing traffic deaths. Ness also modernized the fire department, created the Police Academy and Welfare Bureau, and helped found the local chapter of BOYSTOWN.†

Ness cracked down on labor-union protection rackets, illegal liquor suppliers, and gambling. He closed down the HARVARD CLUB,† a notorious gambling house located just outside the city limits in NEWBURGH HTS.† Critics called for Ness's removal, citing his social drinking, divorce, work with the federal government, and a traffic accident that looked suspiciously like a hit-skip incident. Mayor FRANK LAUSCHE retained Ness; however, Ness left Cleveland in 1942 to direct the Div. of Social Protection of the Federal Security Agency. After the war Ness returned to Cleveland, ran unsuccessfully as Republican candidate for mayor in 1947, then devoted himself to business, finally leaving for Coudersport, PA, in 1956. Shortly before his death, suffering financial reverses, Ness collaborated with journalist Oscar Fraley to produce the book *The Untouchables*. Ness, however, died before the book was published.

Ness was married 3 times. His first marriage was in 1929 to Edna Staley; they divorced in 1938. On 14 Oct. 1939 Ness married Evaline McAndrew; they divorced in 1945. His third marriage was to Elizabeth Anderson Seaver on 31 Jan. 1946; in 1947 he adopted a son, Robert Warner.

Eliot Ness Scrapbooks, WRHS.
Nickel, Steven. *Torso: The Story of Eliot Ness and the Search for a Psychopathic Killer* (1989).

**NEWBERRY, JOHN STRONG** (22 Dec. 1822–7 Dec. 1892), is best known for his work in vertebrate paleontology and paleobotany and as head of the 2nd Ohio Geological Survey. He was born in Windsor, CT, the son of Henry and Elizabeth Strong Newberry, and came to the Western Reserve with his family in 1824, graduating from Western Reserve College in 1846 and Western Reserve Medical School in 1848. Newberry married Sarah Brownell Gaylord in 1849. He practiced medicine in Cleveland in the early 1850s and was recording secretary of the Cleveland Academy of Natural Science (1845) and first president of the Cleveland YMCA (see YOUNG MEN'S CHRISTIAN ASSN.†) (1854). In the second half of the 1850s, he participated in three major western expeditions, making a number of important geological observations and discoveries. Newberry joined the Sanitary Commission during the Civil War. Afterward (1866) he was appointed to the faculty of the School of Mines at Columbia Univ., where he remained for 24 years. During this time he maintained a Cleveland residence, where his family lived, and from 1869 to 1882, he headed the 2nd Ohio Geological Survey. In 1867 he was president of the American Assn. for the Advancement of Science. In 1884 Newberry joined the U.S. Geological Survey and in 1888 helped to found the Geological Society of America. He died in New Haven, CT, and was buried in Lake View Cemetery. Among things named in his honor are various fossils, a preglacial Ohio river, a glacial lake in New York, both a point and a butte in the Grand Canyon, and a volcano in Oregon. Three of Newberry's seven children founded what was to become the MEDUSA CORP.†—M.S.

Fairchild, H. L. "A Memoir of Professor John Strong Newberry," *Proceedings of the Second Joint Meeting, Scientific Alliance of New York* (1893).
John S. Newberry Files, Cleveland Museum of Natural History.

**NEWBORN, ISSAC (ISI) MANDELL** (July 1908–7 Aug. 1972) enjoyed national repute as the horse racing handicapper of the *CLEVELAND PRESS.†* A native of New York City, he came to Cleveland as a boy and graduated from Glenville High School. After earning his college degree from Miami Univ. of Ohio, he joined the staff of the *CLEVELAND NEWS†* in 1929 but moved over to the *Press* sports dept. within a year. Although he also covered professional hockey for much of his career, his reputation was firmly rooted on his accuracy in predicting winners at the racetrack. In 1953 he was the only newspaper handicapper to pick the longshot Dark Star to beat favored Native Dancer in the Kentucky Derby. After repeating the feat with his selection of Venetian Way in 1960, he was awarded a silver tray as a "Champion Derby Picker." Newborn disseminated his expertise in 3 books: *Common Sense at the Races* (1945), *If You're Going to Play the Races* (1949), and *Helpful Hints for Horseplayers* (1961). "Play the horses only for fun and recreation," and "Never bet more than you can afford to lose," was the essence of his advice. Newborn was a competitive tennis player and collected old streetcar transfers as a hobby. Stricken with a fatal heart attack while on the job at THISTLEDOWN RACE TRACK,† he was memorialized by the annual Isi Newborn Memorial Handicap race at that track beginning in 1976. He was survived by his wife, the former Norma Clapp (married 1937), and 2 sons, Monroe and Norton.—J.V.

**NEWMAN, AARON W.** (1881–22 Dec. 1963), moved from a career in newspapers and advertising to inaugurate and promote Cleveland's annual Sportsman's Show. A native Clevelander, the son of Simon and Hanna Cohn Newman, he left Western Reserve Univ. (see CASE WESTERN RESERVE UNIV.†) after a semester because of poor eyesight and went to Colorado to work as a ranchhand, surveyor, and newspaperman. Returning to Cleveland, he became a reporter for the *CLEVELAND*

*WORLD†* and in 1906 the first business manager of the *Jewish Independent* (see *CLEVELAND JEWISH NEWS†*). Newman then spent several years in advertising, working among others for the NEWMAN-STERN CO.,† a sporting goods store run by his brothers, Arthur and JOSEPH S. NEWMAN. In 1927 he opened the Little Theater of the Movies on E. 9th St., reputedly the city's first foreign movie house. Newman teamed with Morris Ackerman, outdoors editor of the *CLEVELAND PRESS,†* that same year to launch the first Sportsman's and Outdoors Show in PUBLIC AUDITORIUM.† After 3 years the pair sold the enterprise, which then fell victim to the Depression. Newman revived it alone in 1938, promoting it annually as president of Expositions, Inc., until his death (see AMERICAN AND CANADIAN SPORT, TRAVEL AND OUTDOOR SHOW†). A charter member of the CITY CLUB OF CLEVELAND,† Newman wrote several satirical political pamphlets during the 1930s. Married twice, his 1st wife Rita died in 1933, and his 2nd wife Lucille succeeded him as promoter of the Sportsman's Show. He was also survived by 4 children: Edward S., William S., Marian H., and David.—J.V.

**NEWMAN, JOSEPH SIMON** (6 Dec. 1891–10 Nov. 1960) earned his living as a founder of the NEWMAN-STERN CO.† and gained renown as a writer of light verse. Born in New London, OH, he was the son of Simon and Hanna Cohn Newman, who soon brought him to Cleveland. A graduate of CENTRAL HIGH SCHOOL,† Newman attended Case Institute of Technology (see CASE WESTERN RESERVE†) before withdrawing to go into business. He married Babette Weidenthal, daughter of Cleveland journalist Maurice Weidenthal, in 1913. Two years later, with brother Arthur S. Newman and partner Arnold Stern, he founded the Electro-Set Co. to manufacture educational toys, some being of his own invention. The firm soon added sporting goods to its line and became the Newman-Stern Co. Newman meanwhile began writing columns on electricity for the *PLAIN DEALER†* and contributing humorous rhymes to TED ROBINSON's "Philosopher of Folly" column under the pseudonym, "Prof. Cy N. Tific." A member of the CITY CLUB OF CLEVELAND,† from 1925–58 he teamed with CARL D. FRIEBOLIN to write lyrics (775 in all) for the club's annual ANVIL REVUE.† His first volume of verse, *Poems for Penguins*, was published in 1941, followed by *It Could Be Verse* (1948), *Perishable Poems* (1952), and *Verse Yet* (1960). Following his retirement from business, he began a weekly column for the *CLEVELAND PRESS†* in 1952 under the heading "It Could Be Verse." A daily counterpart, "Joe

Newman's Frying Pan," was added in 1957. Among many other activities, Newman taught at Cleveland College and served as trustee of the CLEVELAND PLAY HOUSE.† Survived by his wife and 2 sons, James M. and Robert W., he was buried in Mayfield Cemetery.—J.V.

Joseph Simon Newman Papers, WRHS.

**NEWMARKER, HOWARD L.** (15 June 1928–23 Jan. 1993), a commercial photographer who specialized in pictures of Cleveland, was born here, the son of Albert and Esther Rosenbaum Newmarker. He graduated from Cleveland Hts. High School, attended Ohio Univ., and then served in the Marine Corps 1946–48. In 1951 Newmarker founded the Howard Studio's commercial photography business in Cleveland, and for 25 years he provided photographic services for advertising agencies and industrial concerns. He began Ohio Natural Color Card Co. as a division of Howard in 1957, taking pictures of Cleveland area scenes, including colleges, museums and public buildings, for color postcards, which were distributed in department stores, drugstores, and gift shops. He produced similar cards for Lorain, Akron, Youngstown, Ashtabula, and other local communities. Newmarker received the degree of master of photography from the Professional Photographers of America in 1959. In 1977 he moved to Santa Fe, NM, to begin a new career in videotaping travelogues for use by hotels and travel agents in the area. Utilizing his earlier experience in photographing Cleveland landmarks, Newmarker provided information about local attractions that would appeal to tourists.

Newmarker married Mary Ann Morris 20 Dec. 1951 in Youngstown, and they had three children, Joan Marsh of Bath, OH, Judy Winnegar of Santa Fe, and David of LYNDHURST.† He died in Santa Fe and was returned to Cleveland to be buried in Hillcrest Memorial Park.—M.S.

**NICOLA, BENJAMIN (BENEDETTO) D.** (17 March 1879–21 March 1970) prominent Cleveland jurist, was born in Monterero Val Cocchiara, Italy, the son of Vincenzo and Pasqua Miraldi Nicola. The family came to the U.S. in 1881 and settled in Uhrichsville, OH, where Benjamin graduated from Uhrichsville high school in 1897. He attended Ohio State Univ., receiving his LL.B. in 1900. After passing the bar in 1904, Nicola came to Cleveland to open a law office, the first practicing attorney of Italian ancestry in the city. During his long career he was an officer and counsel for several local companies, including the Euclid Railroad Co. and South Euclid Concrete. Associated with several law firms over the years, he was the senior partner in Nicola

and Horn by the 1930s. In addition, Nicola served as U.S. Commissioner for the northern district 1930–1964. As commissioner, he ruled on legal issues such as the acquisition and retention of evidence for use in Federal cases. Nicola was appointed to the Common Pleas Court in 1948, where he served until the end of 1964.

Nicola married Harriet Stuckey in Midvale, OH, 29 June 1905; they had 4 children: Kenneth, Esther, Margaret, and Samuel. He died in Aurora, OH, and was buried in Lake View Cemetery.—M.S.

**NORTON, DAVID Z.** (1 June 1851–6 Jan. 1928), banker, partner in OGLEBAY NORTON CO.,† and philanthropist, was born in Cleveland to Washington Adams and Caroline Harper Norton. He began in banking as a messenger for Commercial Natl. Bank in 1868, becoming cashier at 21. In 1890, at the urging of his friend JOHN D. ROCKEFELLER, SR., Norton resigned from the bank to join Earl W. Oglebay in organizing Oglebay, Norton & Co., from which he retired in 1924, although remaining a director until his death.

Norton supported the CLEVELAND ORCHESTRA† and CLEVELAND MUSEUM OF ART.† He was a trustee of the Cleveland School of Art, Western Reserve Univ., Adelbert College, Kenyon College, UNIV. SCHOOL,† WESTERN RESERVE HISTORICAL SOCIETY,† HURON RD. HOSPITAL,† Lake View Cemetery, and Society for Savings. He was a director of Natl. Commercial Bank, Bank of Commerce, Woodland Ave. Savings & Trust Co., Bankers Surety Co., and American Ship Building Co. He was involved with Commonwealth Iron Co., Montreal Mining Co., Castile Mining Co., and several lake-shipping companies. In 1910 Norton became president of Citizens Savings & Trust Co., becoming a director upon its merger into Union Trust Co.

Norton collected Napoleana, left to the Western Reserve Historical Society, and Japanese art, given to the Cleveland Museum of Art. His historic family homestead in Unionville, OH, Shandy Hall, is a property of the Western Reserve Historical Society. Norton married Mary Castle, daughter of WM. B. CASTLE, in 1876 and had 3 children: Miriam (Mrs. Frederick R. White), Robt. Castle, and Laurence Harper. Norton and his wife are buried in Lake View Cemetery.

Corporate Records, Columbia Steamship Co. *Memorial to David Z. Norton, Jan. 1928.*
*Oglebay Norton Co.—125 Years, 1854–1979* (1979).
Taylor, Harrie S. *Oglebay, Norton: 100 Years on the Great Lakes* (1954).

**NORTON, GEORGIE LEIGHTON** (29 Nov. 1864–18 Aug. 1923) headed the Cleveland School of Art (see CLEVELAND INSTITUTE OF ART†) for 3 decades during the critical period of its development. A native of Newton, MA, she was the daughter of George and Emily Leighton Norton and a relative of Harvard art historian, Charles Eliot Norton. After graduating from the Massachusetts Normal Art School, she became supervisor of drawing in the Medford, MA, public schools. She was brought to Cleveland as director of the Cleveland School of Art in 1891, shortly after the termination of its unsuccessful affiliation with Western Reserve Univ. (see CASE WESTERN RESERVE†). Under her tenure, the school twice moved into larger quarters, first from the Case Block into the old Horace Kelley mansion on Willson Ave. (E. 55th St.), then in 1905 into a new building on Juniper at Magnolia Dr. Norton also took several initiatives to make the school's graduates more employable. She introduced a teacher training department in 1906, added ceramics to the curriculum in 1909, and set up a department of commercial art under the instruction of HENRY KELLER. She became an aggressive fundraiser in order to realize her goal of providing an endowment for the school, which was done in 1913. In failing health, she handpicked Henry Turner Bailey as her successor and turned over the directorship in 1919. She continued as associate director until her death after a lingering illness. Unmarried, she was survived by a brother, Charles W. Norton, who had been associated with CSA as an asst. treasurer.—J.V.

Wixom, Nancy Coe. *Cleveland Institute of Art: The First Hundred Years, 1881–1982* (1983).

**NORTON, LAURENCE HARPER** (8 May 1888–11 June 1960), director (1927–60) and treasurer (1957–60) of OGLEBAY NORTON CO.,† and president of the WESTERN RESERVE HISTORICAL SOCIETY,† was born in Cleveland to Mary Castle and DAVID Z. NORTON. He graduated from Yale Univ. in 1910, and received his M.A. from Harvard Univ. in 1912. He was secretary to the U.S. ambassador to France, MYRON HERRICK, between 1912–14. Returning to Cleveland in 1915, he started at City Savings & Trust as a teller in order to learn the business.

A member of TROOP A,† Ohio National Guard, Norton served on the Mexican border campaign, and later in Europe during World War I. After discharge in 1919, he returned to France as secretary to reappointed U.S. Ambassador Herrick, returning to Cleveland to assume family business interests when his father's health began to fail. Elected to 3 terms as state representative (1925–31), and 1 term as state senator (1931–33), Norton coauthored the Norton-Edwards Highway Bill

recodifying the highway laws, and helped create the Ohio Battle Monument Commission. He served 2 terms on the Cleveland School Board, and in 1935 was appointed to the Cleveland Ports & Harbor Commission, and was director of the Cleveland Crime Commission.

Norton was president of the Western Reserve Historical Society for over 25 years. During his tenure, the society erected a new wing to the East Blvd. building, part of it becoming the Napoleon Room, housing his father's collection. Norton was on the board of the CLEVELAND PLAY HOUSE† (1925–60), and its president from 1934–38. Norton never married.

Laurence H. Norton Papers, WRHS.

**NORWEB, EMERY MAY HOLDEN** (30 Nov. 1895–27 Mar. 1984), benefactress, officer, and trustee of the CLEVELAND MUSEUM OF ART,† was born to Albert Fairchild and Katherine Davis Holden. Norweb was also the granddaughter of LIBERTY E. HOLDEN, an early benefactor of the CMA and founder of the *PLAIN DEALER.†* In 1917 she married R. HENRY NORWEB, who had joined the U.S. diplomatic service in 1916. Over the next 30 years, Norweb's diplomatic career took them to Japan, the Netherlands, Chile, Mexico, the Dominican Republic, Peru, and several other countries. During this period, Mrs. Norweb furthered her study of art and languages. While in Japan in the 1920s, she became interested in Oriental art and began acquiring pieces, which she eventually donated to the Cleveland Museum of Art. While living in South America during the 1930s, she began collecting pre-Columbian art when there was little interest in that genre. Her acquisitions later formed the nucleus of the museum's pre-Columbian collection. When the Norwebs returned to Cleveland in 1948, Mrs. Norweb became an active member of the museum's accessions committee. In 1949 she joined the museum's Board of Trustees. In 1962 she became the first woman president of the art museum; one of 2 women holding such a position at that time in the U.S. Norweb was a trustee of the Garden Ctr. and a chairperson of the American Numismatic Society of London. She donated many valuable English coins to the art museum.

Norweb had three children: R. Henry, Jeanne Katherine, and Albert. She was buried in Lake View Cemetery.

**NORWEB, RAYMOND HENRY** (31 May 1894–1 Oct. 1983), a diplomat who held posts around the world, was born in England to Henry H. and Jeannie Norweb. The family moved to Elyria, OH, in 1907. Norweb received his B.A. from Harvard in 1916 and entered the diplomatic service that same year, taking the post of 2nd secretary to France in Paris. He was recalled to Washington in 1921, and between 1923–48 was assigned to posts covering much of the globe: Japan, the Dutch East Indies, the Hague, Chile, Mexico, Bolivia, the Dominican Republic, Peru, Portugal, and Cuba. He retired in 1948. Throughout his assignments, Norweb's home remained Cleveland, and it was to his house in BRATENAHL† that he retired. He served as Bratenahl City Councilman from 1950–69. Norweb was considered an authority on coins and coin collecting. He served as a trustee of Kenyon College and the WESTERN RESERVE HISTORICAL SOCIETY.†

Norweb married EMERY MAY HOLDEN, granddaughter of the founder of Cleveland's *PLAIN DEALER,†* LIBERTY E. HOLDEN, in 1917 in Paris and had 3 children: Jeanne, Albert, and R. Henry, Jr. He was buried in Lake View Cemetery.


**NOWAK, ABRAHAM** (28 Aug. 1890–22 Jan. 1977) was a leader in the Jewish community and served as rabbi of two conservative Cleveland congregations.

Born in New York to Harris and Jennie (Yarzumbek) Nowak, Abraham was educated in the New York schools, earning his bachelor's from the City College of New York and his master's degree from Columbia Univ. He then went on to the Jewish Theological Seminary for his rabbinical studies. He was ordained in 1913.

During World War I, Nowak served as a military chaplain. Following the war he moved to Hartford, where he married Ann Segal (d. 1943) on 22 June 1921. They raised two sons, Wellville and Peter.

In April 1923 Nowak was called from Hartford to Cleveland to serve as rabbi for the B'NAI JESHURUN† Temple, then located at Scovill Ave. and East 55th St. Under his leadership, in 1926 the congregation moved to a new temple on Mayfield Rd., just east of Lee Rd., which became commonly known as the Temple on the Hts.

In 1931 the congregation elected him to a new term, but soon thereafter he found himself at odds with the temple board. The dispute between the board and members of the congregation who supported Nowak escalated, and eventually became public. In 1933 Nowak decided to resign.

He then helped organize a new congregation, known as the Community Temple (Temple Beth Am), with temporary headquarters in Coventry School. He stayed with the new congregation until 1936, when he accepted a call to Beth El Synagogue in New Rochelle, NY (1936–43). During World War II, Nowak again served as a military chaplain. Nowak died in Brooklyn, NY.—J.T.


**NUTT, JOSEPH RANDOLPH** (9 March 1869–18 Dec. 1945), president and board chairman of the Union Trust Co. and treasurer of the Republican National Committee, was born in Uniontown, PA, the son of Adam C. and Charlotte Frances Wells Nutt. He was educated in public schools and Madison Academy. Coming to Akron, OH, in 1893, he operated a jewelry store and four years later organized his first bank. Nutt came to Cleveland in 1901 as secretary of the Savings & Trust Co. of Cleveland, which was superseded by the Citizens Savings & Trust Co., of which he became president in 1918. Citizens merged into the Union Trust in Dec. 1920, and Nutt became president of the new bank. The Union Trust prospered under his leadership as president, and later chairman, accumulating resources of $375 million. A close friend of O. P. VAN SWERINGEN, Nutt was credited with introducing the Vans to Thomas J. Lamont of J. P. Morgan & Co., which lent the brothers millions for their railroad empire. Nutt resigned as president of Union Trust in 1930 and as chairman in 1932; he was absolved of any wrongdoing in the subsequent demise of the bank. He also was a personal friend and supporter of Republican Pres. Herbert Hoover and served as treasurer of the Republican National Committee from 1928–33.

Nutt married Elizabeth Hasbronck 27 Nov. 1907 and they had 3 children: Joseph R. Jr. and Davis C., and daughter Frances. He also had a son, Robert H., from a previous marriage to Leora Hay. He died at his home in CLEVELAND HTS.†—M.S.

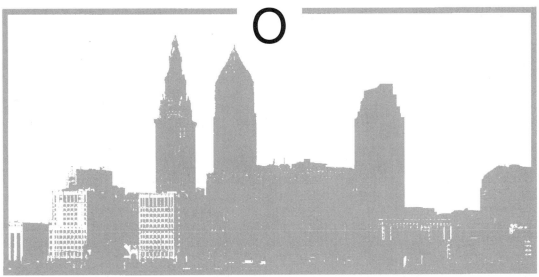

# O

**O'BRIEN, MATTHEW J.** (17 Nov. 1894–21 Aug. 1992), founded the O'Brien and Nye Cartage Co. in 1929, one of the first Cleveland companies to use refrigerated trucks to transport meat and groceries. He helped establish the Cleveland Draymen Employers' Assn. and was a founder and trustee of the Health and Welfare Fund, a union benefits plan. For his PHILANTHROPY,† URSULINE COLLEGE† awarded him the Ursula Laurus Medal and named the campus student center after him. O'Brien was born in Cleveland, one of 9 children of Edward P. and Mary Jane Kelly O'Brien. During World War I, he was awarded the Purple Heart for his service with the American Expeditionary Forces in France.

On 20 July 1920 O'Brien married Anna G. Driscoll; they had 6 children: Raymond F., Norma M. (Mrs. Martin J.) Carney, Sister Margaret, O.S.U., Jane (Mrs. Donald J.) O'Connor, and Norman J. and John M., both deceased by 1992. O'Brien served on the advisory board of Ursuline College and helped organize the Father's Club at BEAUMONT SCHOOL† to assist fatherless girls with tuition. A world traveler, he revelled in leading his children and grandchildren on crosscountry trips. O'Brien is buried in Calvary Cemetery.—J.M.

**ODENBACH, FREDERICK L., SJ** (21 Oct. 1857–15 Mar. 1933), priest, meteorologist, and professor at JOHN CARROLL UNIV.† for 40 years, was born in Rochester, NY, the son of John and Elizabeth Minges Odenbach. He received his bachelor's degree from Canisius College in Buffalo in 1881, joined the Society of Jesus in Sept. 1881, and was sent to the Netherlands for training. Although he taught at Canisius for two years (1885–87), he spent much of the decade studying in Europe. He was ordained into the Catholic priesthood in England in 1891.

Odenbach returned to the U.S. in 1892 to become professor of physics and chemistry at St. Ignatius College (later John Carroll Univ.) in Cleveland, where he remained until his death. In 1902 he became professor of astronomy and meteorology at the college. In 1895 Odenbach, with the assistance of Geo. E. Rueppel, established a meteorological observatory; on 6 Dec. 1901 becoming the sixth person to observe the rare Helvetian Halo. He was skilled in mechanics as well as science; in 1898 he took only 3 days to reassemble the 1,001-piece Secchi meteorograph offered to him by the Smithsonian Institution. He made many of his own scientific instruments. In 1899 he invented the ceraunograph, an instrument recording the occurrence of thunder and lightning. He also developed an electrical seismograph after he established a seismological observatory in 1900. In 1909 he proposed a plan for a cooperative seismological program involving Jesuit schools throughout the U.S. and Canada, and later became director of the Jesuit Seismological Service.

**O'DONNELL, JAMES M.** (3 Nov. 1872–1 Oct. 1946), owner of the first Cleveland franchise in what became the National Football League (NFL), was the son of Mary Murray O'Donnell. O'Donnell served as a deputy sheriff, was associated with Dann Spring Insert Co., and worked for the Bailey Co. as personnel manager, 1914–34, after which he established a real estate business on Cleveland's west side. Active in local Democratic politics, O'Donnell was the party's nominee for state representative when he died, shortly before the 1946 election. As a sports promoter, he and pro football player Stanley Cofall established the CLEVELAND TIGERS† in 1919, playing in the loosely organized Ohio League. They both attended the 17 September 1920 meeting in Canton where 10 team leaders created the American Professional Football Assn., forerunner of the

NFL. At the end of the APFA's first season, the Cleveland Tigers finished 9th in the 14-team league. In 1921 the association had 21 teams, and the Tigers finished in 11th place. APFA was reorganized as the NFL at the beginning of 1922, and to ensure its financial viability, the league voted to have each team post a $1000 guarantee against forfeiture during the season. O'Donnell was unable to provide the money and sold the defunct Cleveland franchise to jeweler Samuel Deutsch in 1923.

O'Donnell and his wife, Nora Mitchell O'Donnell, had three children: William M., Mrs. John Joyce, and James E. He died at his home in Cleveland and was buried at St. John's Cemetery. —M.S.

**OGLEBAY, EARL W.** (4 March 1849–22 June 1926), developer of iron mines in Michigan and Wisconsin, cofounder of OGLEBAY NORTON† and Central National Bank, was born in Bridgeport, OH, the son of Crispin and Charlotte Scott Oglebay. Brought up in Wheeling, WV, he graduated from Bethany College in Bethany, WV, in 1871 and worked for his father in Wheeling. After his father's death, Earl inherited his interests in the Benwood Iron Works and became president of Wheeling's National Bank of West Virginia, which his grandfather had founded in 1817. Oglebay came to Cleveland in 1881 through his bank's interest in mining and, together with Horace A. Tuttle, established the partnership Tuttle, Oglebay & Co. in 1884 to mine iron ore in Michigan and Wisconsin, where Oglebay had already purchased a mining interest. When Tuttle died in 1889, Oglebay bought the interests of his heirs and acted as sales agent for mines in the Gogebic, Menominee, and Marquette Ranges. Backed by JOHN D. ROCKEFELLER and DAVID Z. NORTON, he organized Oglebay Norton in 1890 to mine iron ore on the lands that Rockefeller owned. That same year, Oglebay was one of the founders of the Central National Bank, and remained a director of the institution throughout his life.

Oglebay divided his time between Cleveland and Wheeling, where he owned the 1200-acre Waddington farm, practicing scientific farming to improve methods of soil and crop adaptation. He married Sallie Howell 27 Oct. 1881; they had a daughter, Sarita. He died in Cleveland, survived by brothers James and Frank of Kansas City, Sarita Burton Russell (Mrs. Albert), and grandson Courtney Burton. He was buried in Wheeling.—M.S.

**OGONTZ (OGANTZ)** was the leader of a band of Ottawa Indians encamped near the mouth of the CUYAHOGA RIVER† during the first few years of Cleveland's settlement. The Ottawas usually spent the winter months on the west side of the river, migrating in the spring to the Sandusky area. Ogontz, although not known for his friendliness, was nonetheless tolerant of the white settlers and encouraged trade with them. As white settlement increased in the first years of the 1800s, the Ottawas resettled further west, mainly in the Sandusky area. Ogontz, by white accounts, was last seen there in 1811.

**OLLENDORFF, HENRY B.** (14 Mar. 1907–10 Feb. 1979), lawyer and founder of the Council of Internatl. Programs, was born in Esslingen, Germany, to George and Alice Ollendorff. He received a law doctorate from the Univ. of Heidelberg in 1929, and was imprisoned by the Nazis in 1937, spending 13 months in solitary confinement. Ollendorff married Martha Agnes Burge in 1934 and in 1938 they came to the U.S. Ollendorff graduated from the New York School of Social Work at Columbia Univ. in 1940, moving to Cleveland in Sept. 1940 to work at the FRIENDLY INN SOCIAL SETTLEMENT.† He became head worker there in 1943, and in 1948 executive director of the Neighborhood Settlement Assn., a position he held until 1963. Ollendorff returned to Germany in 1954 at the request of the U.S. State Dept. to teach a 5-month seminar for German youth leaders. While there, he conceived the idea for an exchange program to bring German social leaders to the U.S. for study. The Council of Internatl. Programs was formally established in 1956, in the next 22 years bringing representatives from 105 countries to the U.S. Ollendorff's efforts earned him many honors, including the 1959 Internatl. Services Award from the ROTARY CLUB,† the 1971 Golden Door Award from INTERNATIONAL SERVICES CTR.,† a bronze plaque from the State Dept. in 1976, West Germany's Order of Merit, and France's Order of Merite Social. In 1978 trustees of the Council of Internatl. Programs established the Henry B. Ollendorff Foundation to continue his efforts toward world peace and friendship. Ollendorff and his wife had one child, Monika.

Henry B. Ollendorff Papers, WRHS.

**OLMSTED, GEORGE HENRY** (21 Sept. 1843–8 April 1925), a leading representative of insurance interests and founder of two major agencies in Cleveland, was born on a farm near La Grange, OH, the son of Jonathan and Harriet (Sheldon) Olmsted. After attending local public schools and Elyria High School, he graduated from Eastman's Business College at Poughkeepsie, NY, and taught school for 3 years. He was a traveling salesman in Michigan and Wisconsin before coming to Cleveland in 1867.

Olmsted entered the insurance business, successfully representing Atlantic Mutual Life, and 8 years later was made superintendent of its agencies in the U.S. and Canada. He left the firm in 1879 to represent National Life Insurance Co. of Vermont in Ohio and Indiana, an affiliation for the duration of his business career. In the early 1880s he and S. S. Coe became partners in an insurance agency which evolved into the George H. Olmsted & Co. in 1889. The general insurance agency specialized in writing fire insurance for some of the largest insurers in the country. At the same time, George and his brother, Oscar, organized Olmsted Brothers & Co., representing National Life Insurance of Vermont in Ohio and Indiana. In Cleveland's highly competitive insurance business, Olmsted Brothers doubled their business by 1909. In recognition of George Olmsted's contribution to National Life, he was elected a director of the company.

Olmsted married Ella L. Kelley 24 Oct. 1872 in Saybrook, OH. They had 2 children, Howard and Grace (Mrs. Alexander P. Grigor). He died in Cleveland and was buried at Lake View Cemetery.—M.S.

**OLNEY, CHARLES FAYETTE** (1832–18 July 1903), provided Cleveland with its principal art gallery in the pre-CLEVELAND MUSEUM OF ART† era and was a leading proponent of the Group Plan of public architecture. A native of Southington, CT, he was the son of Jesse Olney, author of a widely used series of standard school textbooks. After graduating from the Southington Academy, the younger Olney made a career in the public schools of New York City, where he rose to a supervisory position prior to his retirement. Following the death of his first wife, the former Louisa Brown, he came to Cleveland ca. 1885 and married Abigail Bradley Lamson, widow of the cofounder of the LAMSON AND SESSIONS CO.† Olney headed the Loan Assn., which secured art objects for the first of Cleveland's ART LOAN EXHIBITIONS† in 1893–94. Its success led to the building of the OLNEY ART GALLERY† adjoining the couple's home on Jennings Ave. (W. 14th St.). Olney also taught fine arts in the educational program of the neighboring PILGRIM CONGREGATIONAL CHURCH.† As a member of the Chamber of Commerce, he introduced the resolution in 1899 which resulted in the creation 3 years later of the Group Plan Commission (see MALL†). He then represented the Public Library Board (see CLEVELAND PUBLIC LIBRARY†) on the commission's consulting board. Olney was also active in the Sons of the American Revolution (see PATRIOTIC SOCIETIES†) and founding president of the Society for the Promotion of Atmospheric Purity. He died in New Haven, CT, stricken during a visit to relatives of Mrs. Olney, who was his only immediate survivor. He was buried in New York's Woodlawn Cemetery.—J.V.

**O'MALLEY, PATRICK** (1903–14 June 1983), leader of the UNITED AUTO WORKERS† and AFL-CIO, was born in County Mayo, Ireland, to Charles and Anna (McGinty) O'Malley. He emigrated to Cleveland in 1924, and joined WHITE MOTOR CO.† in 1928 as an inventory checker and timekeeper, a position he held for 21 years. When the CIO organized White in 1932, he became a member; he eventually held every position in the local. The CIO turned its efforts toward ridding itself of Communists in the late 1940s; as president of the CLEVELAND INDUSTRIAL UNION COUNCIL† after 1948, O'Malley helped purge the regional body, as well as individual unions, of leftists. When he became a UAW regional director in 1949, O'Malley quit his job at White. He was reelected until he reached 65, a mandatory retirement age he had pressed for years before. As the AFL and CIO tried to amalgamate on a national level, O'Malley forged the merger locally, becoming part-time president from 1958–68 and full-time president from 1968–70. Ironically, O'Malley became CLEVELAND FED. OF LABOR† president when the UAW was suspended over nonpayment of dues, so O'Malley secured membership in the Internatl. Assn. of Machinists. He resigned in 1970 to serve as foreman of the Cuyahoga County Grand Jury, later serving on the Cuyahoga County Commission on Aging. Sensitive to struggles in Ireland, he led Freedom for Ireland supporters who confronted Prince Charles when he dedicated the Cleveland State Univ. Law School in 1977. O'Malley married Mary Masterson on 12 Apr. 1928; they had 2 children, Patricia (Rattay) and Nancy (McNamara).

**O'MEARA, JAMES E., JR.** (5 May 1908–14 Nov. 1988) earned an international reputation in education, law, and labor. Born in Cleveland to James and Anna (Freidel) O'Meara, he graduated from the CLEVELAND PUBLIC SCHOOLS† and received an M.A. and Ph.D. from JOHN CARROLL UNIV.† In 1933 he began a 39-year teaching career in the Cleveland Public Schools. He also served as an instructor at John Carroll Univ. and Telshe Yeshiva. He was admitted to the bar in 1941, and earned his J.D. in 1968 from Marshall Law School. Sioux Empire College also honored him with the Doctor of Humane Letters degree.

In 1934 he became a charter member of the CLEVELAND TEACHERS UNION.† Over the course of his career, O'Meara held leadership positions in the Cleveland Teachers Union, the Ohio

Federation of Teachers, and the American Federation of Teachers. He also served the U.S. government as a delegate to the U.S. Department of State Conference on Foreign Affairs for Education. He was also director of the National Organization on Legal Problems in Education, and one of the trustees of the Militancy Fund of the American Federation of Teachers for six years.

His involvement in civil rights activities led to service on the Civil Rights Committee of the Cleveland AFL-CIO, the Ohio Civil Rights Commission, the United Negro College Fund Committee, and the Urban League (see URBAN LEAGUE OF CLEVELAND†).

He married Margaret Riester in June 1935 and was the father of four children: James, Thomas, Mary Catherine, and Terrence. He died in Cleveland and is buried in Calvary Cemetery.—R.W.


**O'MIC, JOHN** (ca. 1790–26 June 1812), the first person executed in northern Ohio, belonged to the Massasauga band of Chippewas that resided near Pymatuning Creek, Jefferson County, until 1811 when they moved to the west bank of the Cuyahoga. On 3 Apr. 1812, 2 trappers named Buel and Gibbs were murdered in Sandusky. O'Mic and 2 other Indians were arrested. One committed suicide; the other was released because of his extreme youth. O'Mic was sent to Cleveland for prosecution.

The trial took place on 29 Apr. 1812, and O'Mic was sentenced to death for the murder of Daniel Buel. Execution was set for 26 June. A large crowd gathered at PUBLIC SQUARE† to watch. Sheriff Baldwin tried to cover O'Mic's face, but he lunged for a platform post and clung to it, telling Lorenzo Carter he would die courageously if he could have some whiskey. After several drinks, O'Mic was executed. The day after they witnessed the execution, a group of physicians, led by Dr. DAVID LONG, reportedly took the body to use it for medical studies. The skeleton was reportedly later taken to Hudson, OH, then to Pittsburgh. O'Mic's death coincided with the outbreak of the War of 1812. Many Indians fought on the side of the British, partly in anger over O'Mic's hanging. When Gen. Hull surrendered Detroit to the British shortly after the hanging, settlers in the Sandusky area headed east for fear that Indians would avenge O'Mic's death. But the marauding bands never came.

Anonymous, "Partial Narrative of Murder Trial & Execution in the Public Square, Cleveland, June 24, 1812," WRHS.

Wright, Morgan, Ashtabula County, OH, "eyewitness" account of O'Mic's hanging, 17 Sept. 1908, WRHS.

**O'NEILL, CORDELIA L.** (7 Feb. 1866–29 May 1928), elementary school principal in the CLEVELAND PUBLIC SCHOOLS,† pioneered in the AMERICANIZATION† of immigrant CHILDREN AND YOUTH† and helped organize the WESTERN RESERVE CHILD WELFARE COUNCIL† (1911). Her introduction of preventive dental care (see DENTISTRY†) into the schools reportedly led to the creation of the National Mouth Hygiene Assn. She served as vice-president and trustee of the Cleveland Mouth Hygiene Assn. and participated actively in religious and civic causes, helping to organize both the Roman Catholic CATHERINE HORSTMANN HOME† and the SAFE AND SANE FOURTH OF JULY† celebration. O'Neill was born in Cleveland to Michael and Margaret Nagle O'Neill. She attended public school and graduated from West High School and the Cleveland Normal School. During World War I, she worked with the AMERICAN RED CROSS, CLEVELAND CHAPTER.† O'Neill taught at Scranton School and served as asst. principal at Brownell School (1900–04), then principal at Marion, Kennard, Gilbert, and Kinsman (1925–28) schools.

A member of St. Agnes Roman Catholic Church, O'Neill's religious activities included serving as president of the Cleveland Diocesan Council of the NATIONAL COUNCIL OF CATHOLIC WOMEN† and organizing the St. Joseph's Guild. She was a charter member of the WOMEN'S CITY CLUB OF CLEVELAND† and the Women's Club House Assn., and belonged to the BUSINESS & PROFESSIONAL WOMEN'S CLUB OF GREATER CLEVELAND.† O'Neill was a life member of CLEVELAND ASSOCIATED CHARITIES† and a trustee of the CLEVELAND HUMANE SOCIETY.† O'Neill, a single woman, lived in Cleveland with her sister, Margaret.—J.M.

Western Reserve Child Welfare Council Records, WRHS.

**O'NEILL, FRANCIS JOSEPH "STEVE"** (18 Sept. 1899–29 Aug. 1983), businessman and CLEVELAND INDIANS† owner, was born in Cleveland, the son of Louisa and Hugh O'Neill. He attended Campion College and Notre Dame Univ. O'Neill's father had started a cartage business which developed into several transportation companies; Steve, like his brothers, worked for several of his family's companies. In 1961 79 O'Neill family companies merged to form LEASEWAY TRANSPORTATION†; O'Neill was chairman of the board until 1969, remaining afterwards on the Board of Directors. He was also part of the group that bought Sheraton Cleveland Hotel on PUBLIC SQUARE† and leased it to Stouffer Corp., which renamed the hotel STOUFFER'S INN ON THE SQUARE.†

O'Neill played football, basketball, and baseball in high school and basketball in college. O'Neill was commonly called Steve after his hero, Steve O'Neill, Cleveland Indians catcher of the 1920 championship season. O'Neill became an Indians owner in 1961 as part of the group led by VERNON STOUFFER. In 1973 he had to sell his Indians stock when he joined the Geo. Steinbrenner syndicate that bought the New York Yankees. In 1978 O'Neill sold his Yankees stock and put together a new ownership to buy the Indians; he was principal owner and chairman, holding approximately 63% of the stock. Although he lost $10–12 million on the team, O'Neill refused many offers by groups wishing to move it elsewhere. O'Neill married Anne Henry in 1926; she died in 1971. They had 3 children: Francis, Jr., Mary, and Elizabeth. O'Neill married Nancy Marsteller in 1974. O'Neill was buried in Calvary Cemetery.

**ORLIKOWSKI, BERNARD E.** (10 Jan. 1876–5 Dec. 1957), a key political figure in the Polish community, was born in Meisterwald, Germany, the son of Michael and Julia Slawinski Orlikowski. He came to Cleveland at an early age, completing his education at South High School and Canton's Business College. An independent businessman, Orlikowski headed the Polish-American Realty and Trust Co. for many years and was associated with his uncle, Frank Orlikowski, in the liquor business until Prohibition. Active in local democratic politics, he was appointed superintendent of paving by Cleveland Mayor John Farley at the turn of the century, remaining there until 1910, and served in the 80th Ohio General Assembly 1913–14. Orlikowski represented Cleveland's Ward 14 area in city council, 1920–27, where he was attentive to the needs of his largely Polish constituents. After service in the council, he was appointed to various city posts, including Director of Real Estate Purchases in 1928, Commissioner of Streets under Mayor Ray T. Miller in 1932, and in 1940 was made superintendent of the 1940 U.S. Census in the 21st Congressional District. During his lifetime, Orlikowski took an active role in the neighborhood associations of his community

Orlikowski married Apolonia Sczyglenski 9 Sept. 1903; they had 8 children: Edward A., Theodore C., Lloyd M., Leona, Frank, Sylvia Watling, Bernard F., and Dolores. He died at his home in Cleveland and was buried at Calvary Cemetery.—M.S.

**ORNDORF, HARRY WESTLEY** (9 Nov. 1892–14 July 1938), recipient of the Congressional Medal of Honor for service during the Boxer Rebellion, was born in Sandusky, OH, the son of John and Julia Clark Orndorf. He enlisted in the U.S. Marine Corps. 17 Oct. 1896 at Mare Island, CA. After serving in the Philippines during the Spanish-American War and the insurrection which followed, Private Orndorf was assigned to the USS *Newark*, operating off the China coast between May and August of 1900. The *Newark*, part of an international relief expedition, helped put down the Boxers, a secret Chinese society angered by foreign commercial exploitation, and rescued personnel in U.S. legations in Peiking and Tientsen. Orndorf was wounded 23 June and received a medical discharge 21 Jan. 1901. On 19 July 1901, he was one of three marines receiving the Medal of Honor for heroism "In action with the Allied forces in China 13, 20, 21, and 22 June 1900." Orndorf married Louise E. Touhey in Cleveland 23 May 1906. After working as a machinist for some time, he opened his own company, Emergency Rd. Service, Inc., operating it for many years. During the last five years of his life, he and his wife owned and operated Orndorf's Cafe in Lakewood. He died at U.S. Marine Hospital and was buried 16 July 1938 at Highland Park Cemetery in Cleveland. The couple had no children.—M.S.

**ORTH, SAMUEL PETER** (1 Aug. 1873–26 Feb. 1922), attorney, educator, lecturer, author, and historian, was born in Capiac, MI, the son of German Evangelical clergyman Rev. John and Katharine Troeller Orth. He accompanied Frederick A. Cook on his expedition to Greenland in 1894, graduated from Oberlin College with a B.S. in 1896, and studied law and political science at the Univ. of Michigan from 1896–97. He held the chair of political science and public law at Buchtel College, Akron, from 1897–1902, was appointed honorary university fellow in political science at Columbia Univ., and received his Ph.D. degree in public law from Columbia in 1903, coming then to Cleveland to practice law. He was elected a member of the Board of Education in 1904 and became president in 1905, appointing an "Educational Commission" to investigate the CLEVELAND PUBLIC SCHOOLS,† whose findings led to the establishment of a technical high school, a high school of commerce, a comprehensive plan for playgrounds, a reorganized school curriculum, and a normal school for teacher training.

While in Cleveland, Orth was also asst. U.S. attorney (1905–06) and lectured on political science at Case School of Applied Science, Western Reserve Univ., and Oberlin College. He left Cleveland in 1912 to teach at Cornell Univ. Orth wrote several books, including *Centralization of Administration in Ohio* (1903), and *A History of Cleveland* (3 vols.) (1910). Orth married Jane Davis on 17 Aug. 1899.

The couple was en route to Egypt as part of a sabbatical leave when Orth died in Nice, France. They had no children.

**OSIKA, CHARLOTTE "LOTTIE"** (3 Dec. 1916–1 Dec. 1993) was an officer for the UNION OF POLES IN AMERICA† and secretary of Branch #71 who, during her 50-year association, helped the organization prosper and increased membership.

Born to Anthony and Valerie Osika, Lottie sold U.S. War Bonds during World War II and raised money for the American Red Cross and Polish-American aid for Poland. Osika was active in the Ohio Division of the Polish American Congress, serving as a delegate to several state conventions. Osika was elected to the union's Board of Directors in 1939. In 1942 she became its youngest elected national vice president, a post she held until her 1990 retirement, when the National Convention named her an Honorary Vice-President.

For many years Osika chaired the Cleveland-based Booster Committee and served as its coordinator and tour director for the entire union. She was very active in the Polonia and served the Ohio Division of the Polish American Congress. During the early 1970s Osika raised money for the Institute of Blind Children of Laski, Poland, and also helped raise money for the National Shrine of Our Lady of Czestochowa in Doylestown, PA. Osika was honored by the Union of Poles in 1974, 1978, and 1982 for her years of service.

Osika organized Cleveland Chapter 25 of the Ladies Auxiliary of Orchard Lake Seminary, Orchard Lake, MI, and served as its first and only president. Osika remained single, lived in GARFIELD HTS.† and is buried in Calvary Cemetery. —T.B.

**OSTENDARP, CAROL ANNE** (12 May 1941–14 July 1992) was head nurse in a special kidney unit of MT. SINAI MEDICAL CENTER† and then instructor in nursing there (1965–83). With Francine Hekelman, she edited a textbook on her specialty, *Nephrology Nursing* (1979). Ostendarp was born in Cincinnati, OH, to Anne S. and Harold E. Ostendarp, and graduated from Norwood High School in Norwood, OH. She completed her studies in NURSING† at Cincinnati's Jewish Hospital School of Nursing (1961), studied at Western Reserve Univ. (see CASE WESTERN RESERVE UNIV.†) and the Univ. of Cincinnati, and CLEVELAND STATE UNIV.† After she moved to Cleveland in the 1960s, Ostendarp joined the Young Republicans of LAKEWOOD† and quickly became very active in politics, serving as president of that group and holding various offices in the Young Republicans of Greater Cleveland. Also a member of the Young Republi-

cans of Ohio, Ostendarp campaigned for Paul Matia (Ohio senate) and Jim Betts (Ohio house). In 1972 she was elected committeewoman of precinct 4B. She also served as trustee of the ELIZA JENNINGS HOME,† chaired the board of the Eliza Jennings Group, and was utilization management coordinator of the Community Mutual Assn. A resident of ROCKY RIVER,† Ostendarp belonged to the American Nephrology Nurses and the American Assn. of Homes for the Aging.—J.M.

**OTIS, CHARLES AUGUSTUS, JR.** (9 July 1868–9 Dec. 1953), industrialist who played a brief but pivotal role in the evolution of Cleveland newspapers, son of Mary Shepard and CHAS. A. OTIS, SR., graduated from Yale's Sheffield Scientific School and in 1893 returned to Cleveland as a steel broker with Otis, Hough & Co. In 1899 Otis purchased the first seat held on the New York Stock Exchange by a Clevelander and formed the banking firm Otis & Hough to market steel securities. He helped organize and became president of the Cleveland Stock Exchange.

During the administration of Mayor TOM L. JOHNSON, Republican Otis acquired the *CLEVELAND WORLD†* in 1904, the *CLEVELAND LEADER†* and *News & Herald* in 1905, merged the latter with the *World,* then added the *Evening Plain Dealer* to the consolidated afternoon paper which he renamed the *CLEVELAND NEWS.†* Within a few years, Otis disposed of both the *News* and *Leader* to DAN R. HANNA.

In 1912 Otis reorganized Otis & Hough as Otis & Co. and became president of both Wm. Edwards & Co. and Otis Terminal Warehouse Co. During World War I, he served with the War Industries Board. He sold his brokerage business in 1931 and largely retired. Otis helped organize the TAVERN,† CLEVELAND ATHLETIC,† and CHAGRIN VALLEY HUNT† clubs, was president of the Cleveland Chamber of Commerce, and cochairman of the Cleveland Sesquicentennial Commission. In 1894 Otis married Lucia Edwards. He was survived by his daughter, Lucia Otis Hanna, and son, Wm. E. Otis.

Chas. A. Otis Papers, WRHS.
Otis, Charles. *Here I Am: A Rambling Account of the Exciting Times of Yesteryear* (1951).

**OTIS, CHARLES AUGUSTUS, SR.** (30 Jan. 1827–28 June 1905), businessman and Cleveland mayor (1873–74) was born in Bloomfield, OH, to Eliza Proctor and WILLIAM A. OTIS. He attended local schools until his family moved to Cleveland in 1836, worked in his father's ironworks until 1848, then became a steamboat purser. In 1852 Otis founded the Lake Erie Iron Co.; he sold out his interest after the Civil War. He then spent a few months in Prussia (1866), studying that country's iron and steel mills, and upon his return founded the Otis Iron & Steel Co., the first company in America formed solely to make acid open-hearth steel. He remained as president until 1899.

Otis ran on the Democratic ticket for mayor and defeated Republican JOHN HUNTINGTON. Although business interests prevented him from seeking a second term, he served on several boards, including the Board of Imprisonments (1878–79) and House of Correction Board (1882–84). He established Cleveland's first Board of Fire Commissioners and BOARD OF POLICE COMMISSIONERS.† Otis's later business pursuits included establishment of American Wire Co., American Steel Screw Co., and CLEVELAND ELECTRIC RAILWAY CO.† In 1894 he became president of New Commercial Natl. Bank, from which he retired in 1904.

Otis married Mary Shepard (d. 1860) in 1853, and had 2 daughters, Anna (Mrs. Wm. B. Sanders) and Nelly (Mrs. J. Kent Sanders). In 1863 he married his sister-in-law, Anna Elizabeth Shepard; they had 3 sons: CHARLES A., JR., Harrison G., and William A. Otis died in Cleveland and is buried in Lake View Cemetery.

**OTIS, WILLIAM A.** (2 Feb. 1794–11 May 1868), merchant, industrialist, banker, and civic leader instrumental in developing the WESTERN RESERVE† as a trading partner with eastern markets, was born in Massachusetts to William and Philina Shaw Otis. He moved to Pittsburgh about 1818, working in ironworks. Two years later he moved to Bloomfield, Trumbull County, OH, opening a tavern and mercantile business, furnishing settlers with goods in exchange for wheat, produce, and ash.

Otis is credited with shipping the first Ohio wheat to New York City via Buffalo and the Erie Canal (1825), becoming a primary factor utilizing the waterways to open the Western Reserve to eastern markets. He later began shipping wool and pork, becoming a leading shipper for 20 years. Recognizing Cleveland's advantages as a port, Otis moved his mercantile operations in 1836 to the city, quickly becoming one of Cleveland's leading dealers in pork, flour, and potash. His business gave him cause to study the area's transportation problems. With the waterways opened to eastern markets, the major problem confronting trade involved getting inland goods to port, so he supported the development of good HIGHWAYS† and the building of railroads, including the Cleveland, Columbus & Cincinnati and Cleveland & Pittsburgh railroads.

Otis concentrated on iron manufacturing and was involved with the banking firms of Wick, Otis & Brownell, Commercial Branch Bank of Cleveland, Commercial Natl. Bank, and Society for Savings, serving all as president. He was a founder of the Board of Trade. Otis married Eliza Proctor in 1825, and had 3 children: CHARLES, Eliza, and William. He died in Cleveland and was buried in Woodland Cemetery.

**OWEN, JAMES ALEXANDER, M.D.** (6 Sept. 1891–19??), physician and member of the executive committee of the CUYAHOGA COUNTY DEMOCRATIC PARTY,† ran unsuccessfully for the seat vacated by THOMAS W. FLEMING (third district) on CLEVELAND CITY COUNCIL† (1929). He was an unsuccessful candidate again in 1933 (18th Ward). His platforms included better SANITATION† and increased access to medical care.

Owen was born in Natchez, MS, to Sarah J. (Mazigue) and Samuel Henry Clay Owen, president of Natchez College. He received an A.B. from Natchez College (1912) and an M.D. from the Meharry Medical College (TN) in 1916. One of 4 medical professionals in his family, Owen interned at Kansas City General Hospital and served overseas in the Medical Corps during World War I, holding the rank of capt. upon his discharge in 1919. On 27 July 1921 he married Marie E. Thomas and began a private medical practice in Cleveland, maintaining an office on Cedar Ave. by 1933. In POLITICS,† Owen was asst. ward leader of Cleveland's 18th Ward and a charter member of the Conservative Republican Voters League, formed in the late 1920s by AFRICAN AMERICANS.† He served as president of the Board of Trustees of the combined normal and industrial department, Wilberforce Univ. (OH), and as vice-president of the Ohio Medical Assn. Owen also belonged to the American Legion. By 1940 he lived in Detroit, MI.—J.M.

**OWENS, JESSE (JAMES CLEVELAND)** (9 Sept. 1913–30 Mar. 1980), track and field athlete, was born in northern Alabama to Henry and Emma Alexander Owens. He moved to Cleveland as a child. His athletic talent was first noted at Fairmount Jr. High School. His track coach, Chas. Riley, was amazed when he ran the 100-yd. dash in 10 seconds flat, a new junior high school record. As a high school senior at E. Technical, he equaled the world's record of 9.4 in the 100-yd. dash.

At Ohio State Univ., on 25 May 1935, Owens equaled or bettered 6 world records within 1 hour in Ann Arbor, MI, the only athlete to establish new track and field world records on the same day. His long jump record of 26' 8⅛" stood for 33 years. The Cleveland track star gained his greatest fame at the Berlin Olympic Games in 1936, where he won 4 gold medals. In the 100- and 200-meter sprints, he set records of 10.3 and 20.7 seconds. In the long jump he set an Olympic record of 26' 5 5/16". Owens then joined with Ralph Metcalfe, Floyd Draper, and Frank Wycoff to set a new world record of 39.8 seconds in the 400-meter relay.

After graduating from Ohio State Univ. in 1937, Owens became a "professional entertainer," tap dancing with Bill "Bojangles" Robinson. After trying several occupations, Owens's drycleaning business failed. From 1940–42, the office of Civilian Defense employed Owens as national director of physical education for Negroes. From 1942–46, Owens was director of Negro personnel for the Ford Motor Co. in Detroit. In 1946 he moved to Chicago as a sales executive. Noted for his inspirational addresses, Owens served on the Illinois Athletic and Illinois Youth commissions, and was on the board of directors of Up with People, centered at Tucson, AZ, where he lived at the time of his death. He married Ruth Solomon in 1931 and had 3 daughters: Gloria, Beverly, and Marlene.

Baker, William J. *Jesse Owens* (1986).

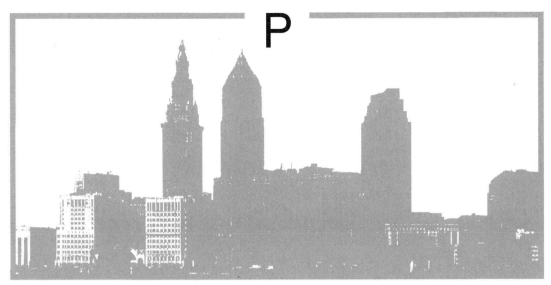

P

PAGE, IRVINE HEINLY (7 Jan. 1901–10 June 1991), clinician and director of research at the CLEVELAND CLINIC FOUNDATION† (1945–66), pioneered the scientific study of blood pressure and hypertension, promoted the development of hypertensive drugs, and raised national awareness about hypertension and atherosclerosis. His research isolated the hormones serotonin and angiotensin, the basis of much modern brain chemistry research and treatment. Page was born in Indianapolis, IN, to LaFayette and Marian Page. He began a lifelong membership in the American Chemical Society at age 14. Page graduated from Cornell Univ. (B.A., 1921) and its medical school (1926). He interned at Presbyterian Hospital in New York and then worked as a brain chemist at the Kaiser Wilhelm Institute for Psychiatry in Munich, Germany (1928–31). Page returned to America to work at the Rockefeller Institute for Medical Research, NY; Indianapolis City Hospital, a clinical branch of the Eli Lilly Co.; and, finally, in 1945, at the Cleveland Clinic Foundation, where he, Arthur Corcoran, and Robert Taylor began a new research division. Page proposed the "mosaic theory" of hypertension, emphasizing multiple causation rather than a single cause.

On 28 Oct. 1930 Page married Beatrice Allen; they had two children, Nicholas and Christopher. Author of over 300 articles, Page edited *Modern Medicine*. He participated in the formation of: the Council for High Blood Pressure Research (founded in 1947 in Cleveland as the American Foundation for High Blood Pressure); the American Society for the Study of Atherosclerosis; and the International Society of Hypertension (1960s). Page, having isolated a variety of cholesterol in the 1920s, helped instigate the massive National Diet-Heart Study in 1960. He and industrialist U. A. Whitaker, both

heart attack victims, created the Coronary Club in the late 1960s. In retirement Page moved to Hyannis Port, MA (1978), and continued to publish and serve actively in professional associations, including the Council for High Blood Pressure Research (vice-chair, 1987–89).—J.M.

Irvine H. Page Papers, Cleveland Clinic Foundation Archives.
Irvine H. Page Papers, National Library of Medicine, Washington, DC.
Page, Irvine H. *Hypertension Research: A Memoir 1920–1960* (1988).
———. *Chemistry of the Brain* (1937).
———. *Speaking to the Doctor* (1972).
———. *Hypertension Mechanisms* (1987).

PAIGE, LEROY ROBERT "SATCHEL" (7 July 1906–8 June 1982), legendary BASEBALL† pitcher, was born in Mobile, AL, the son of John and Lula (Coleman) Page. He earned the nickname "Satchel" as a child carrying bags at the railroad station: using a rope, carrying more bags and increasing his tips, he looked like a "walking satchel tree." Paige went to industrial school at 12 after truancy problems and became a semi-pro ballplayer at 17. Pitching in the Negro Professional Leagues from 1926–50, he could not play in the majors because of the unwritten agreement barring blacks (see AFRICAN AMERICANS†). Paige was a drawing card, known for his trick pitches, often calling in his outfield while pitching and giving up no runs, and announcing he would strike out a certain number of batters and succeeding. Paige's teams often played and won exhibition games against white major-leaguers. Hall of Fame pitcher Dizzy Dean called Paige the best pitcher he ever saw.

Paige first pitched for a Cleveland team, the Negro Natl. League's Cleveland Cubs, in 1931. The team disbanded at midseason. With the elimination of baseball's color line in 1946, Paige signed with the Cleveland Indians at midseason in 1948, becoming the oldest rookie in major league history at age 42. Paige was 6–1, helping the Indians to their pennant. He was 4–7 in 1949, and released. He pitched with the St. Louis Browns from 1951–53. Paige estimated that he pitched over 2,500 games and won about 2,000. He was elected to the Baseball Hall of Fame in 1971. Paige married Janet Howard in 1934; they divorced in 1943. He then married Lahoma Brown in 1947. Paige had 4 children: Carolyn, Linda, Pamela, and Robert Leroy. He died in Kansas City, MO, and was buried in Forest Hill Cemetery there.

Paige, LeRoy (Satchel), as told to David Lipman. *Maybe I'll Pitch Forever* (1962).
Paige, LeRoy (Satchel), as told to Hal Lebovitz. *Pitchin' Man* (1948).
Holway, John B. *Josh and Satch* (1991).
Ribowsky, Mark. *Don't Look Back* (1994).

**PAINE, SETH** (died 1815) was a land surveyor who surveyed what is now BRECKSVILLE† and the first permanent white settler in the township. Paine came to the Western Reserve in 1811 as an assistant to Alfred Wolcott, a surveyor from Boston employed by John Breck, the person for whom Brecksville was named. Paine and Wolcott surveyed Brecksville Twp. and returned to Northampton with their report. Paine liked the area so well that he returned in June 1811 from Williamsburgh, MA, with his wife and children, Oliver, Spencer, Almira, and Lorina, and a young unmarried man named Melzer Clark. Paine settled in the southwest corner of Brecksville Twp. on lot 64 at what became known as Carter's Corners. Soon afterwards Clark and Almira Paine were married, this being the first marriage in Brecksville.

As land agent for John Breck, Paine had power of attorney to grant title to land sold. Paine's compensation for services rendered was to choose 200 acres anywhere in the township, with the exception that it should not be bottom land and should not include a mill site. Paine chose the southwest part. He left his family at a settlement in Newburgh, near the corner of Walker and Broadway in Cleveland, during the winter of 1810–1811, while he proceeded to Brecksville to build a log house. Paine died in 1815, four years after his arrival.—T.B.

**PALMER, WILLIAM PENDLETON** (17 June 1861–17 Dec. 1927), steel industrialist who worked from apprentice to president of American Steel & Wire Co. (1899–1927), and president of the WEST-ERN RESERVE HISTORICAL SOCIETY† (1913–27) was born in Pittsburgh, PA, to James Stewart and Eleanor Pendelton Mason Palmer. He graduated from high school in 1878 and entered the steel industry as an apprentice with Lewis, Oliver & Phillips. In 1881 he went to work for Carnegie, Phipps & Co., becoming company secretary in 1887 and general sales agent in 1888. He was appointed asst. to the president of Carnegie Steel Co. in 1894, and in 1896 became 2nd vice-president of Illinois Steel Co. He became general manager and president of American Steel & Wire, a subsidiary of U.S. Steel Corp. in Cleveland, in 1899, serving until 1927. He also was president of American's subsidiaries, NEWBURGH & SOUTH SHORE RAILROAD† and Trenton Iron Co.; and a director of Cleveland Trust Co., H. C. Frick Coke Co., and the Bank of Commerce. Palmer was elected president of the WRHS in 1913, serving until 1927. During his tenure, the society acquired the Wm. Palmer Collection, an extensive collection of books, manuscripts, and photographs relating to the Civil War which he had amassed. Palmer married Mary Boleyn Adams in 1898 and had 2 children, Jane and William, Jr. Palmer is buried in Lake View Cemetery.

**PANKUCH, JAN "JOHN"** (1869–28 Feb. 1952), newspaper editor and publisher active in Slovak organizations, was born in Saris County, Slovakia, came to the U.S. in 1886, and worked as a laborer, grocer, and coal dealer in Cleveland while trying to establish a publishing business. In the beginning he tried to establish newspapers that would appeal to Slovaks throughout the U.S. First was *Americky Slovak* (1892–94), which failed because of Pankuch's inability to manage the paper's business affairs. In 1894 he established a Lutheran weekly, *Cirkevne Listy* (Church Letters), which he published for 5 years, finally selling it in 1899 to a competitor, who moved it out of Cleveland. He then founded the *Lutheran* in 1900, publishing it until 1902; in 1904 the *Lutheran* was one of several papers that merged to form *Slovensky Hlasnik* (Slovak Herald), the official organ of the Slovak Evangelical Union. Pankuch was more successful publishing for the Cleveland Slovak community. He published *Hlas* (Voice) from 1907–47 and *Denny Hlas* (Daily Voice) between 1915–25. Pankuch was also treasurer of the Slovak League of America during World War I, a member of the American branch of the Czecho-Slovak Natl. Council, and in 1937 became president of the Natl. Slovak Society. A Republican, Pankuch was praised for his Americanism and patriotism. He married Rozalia Gasgeben in 1889 and they had eleven children: Cyril,

Ann, Rose, Margaret, Pauline, John, George, Mildred, Jewel, Irene, and Theresa. Pankuch lived in LAKEWOOD† from 1917 until he died.

Ledbetter, Eleanor E. *The Slovaks of Cleveland* (1918).
Megles, Susi, Mark Stolarik, and Martina Tybor. *Slovak Americans and Their Communities of Cleveland* (1978).
Pankuch, Jan. *Dejiny Clevelandskych a Lakewood Slovakov: Sosbieral, pod tlac pripravil Jan Pankuch* (1930).

**PARSONS, KATE** (11 June 1832–3 Sept. 1907) was the second woman physician in Cleveland and a cofounder of what became WOMAN'S GENERAL HOSPITAL.† Parsons was born in 1832 in Southampton, England, the child of John and Ann Parsons. She came to Cleveland with her family in 1849. After the death of her parents she began to study medicine. She was a student of Dr. MYRA MERRICK. In 1872 Parson graduated from the Cleveland Homeopathic College and opened her practice in the city, on Prospect Ave., a year later. Her practice grew to be large and successful and included some of the city's wealthiest families.

In 1878 Parsons and Merrick set aside one morning a week from their regular practice to provide free medical service for needy woman and children. This evolved into the Women's and Children's Free Medical and Surgical Dispensary, which was the first charitable institution of its kind established in Cleveland. The dispensary was staffed by women physicians who were often denied clinical experience in the city's hospitals and dispensaries. Thus it was a pioneering center for the practice of medicine by women in Cleveland. The dispensary also allowed women to receive medical treatment from members of their own sex. In 1894 the dispensary was incorporated as the Women's and Children's Medical and Surgical Dispensary, of which Parsons later became treasurer. She continued to work with the Dispensary until November 1906, when she retired due to failing health. She died in Cleveland and was buried in Lake View Cemetery. The Dispensary evolved into Woman's General Hospital. —D.R.

**PARSONS, RICHARD C.** (10 Oct. 1826–8 Jan. 1899), prominent lawyer and politician, was born in New London, CT, to Thomas and Frances Catherine (Chappel) Parsons. He moved with his family to New York City and came to Cleveland in 1849 to study law with Chas. Stetson. Parsons was admitted to the Ohio Bar in 1851. His political career spanned the years 1852–77; after which he was editor-in-chief of the *CLEVELAND HERALD,†* a paper he co-owned, for 3 years. Not until 1880 did he establish a full-time law practice. In

1852 Parsons was elected to CLEVELAND CITY COUNCIL,† the next year becoming council president. He was elected to the Ohio legislature in 1857, was reelected in 1859, and the following year became speaker of the house of representatives, perhaps the youngest person to ever hold that position. Pres. Lincoln appointed him consul at Rio de Janeiro. Parsons returned to Cleveland in 1862 as collector of internal revenue, being removed from office 4 years later for refusing to support Pres. Johnson. In 1866 he procured federal appointment as marshal of the Supreme Court, and in 1872 was elected to Congress as a Republican. As a congressman, he brought major improvements to Cleveland's harbor, securing the first appropriation for a breakwater to aid the commercial value of the city, and securing a lifesaving service and lighthouse. Later in life, Parsons was president of the EARLY SETTLERS ASSN.,† and in 1896 was active in the city's centennial celebration.

Parsons married Sarah Starkweather in 1851; they had two children, Julia and Richard. He died in Cleveland and was buried in Lake View Cemetery.

**PAYER, HARRY FRANKLIN** (3 July 1875–12 Oct. 1952), lawyer, government official, and linguist, was born in Cleveland to Frantisek and Mary Kris Payer. He graduated from Western Reserve Univ. in 1897 and from Cleveland Law School in 1899, and was admitted to the Ohio Bar in 1899. In 1900 he managed TOM L. JOHNSON's first mayoral campaign, from 1901–07 serving as asst. city solicitor under NEWTON D. BAKER. In 1907 he became the senior member of the law firm of Payer, Winch, Minshall & Karch. Nicknamed "Demosthenes" because of his oratorical abilities, Payer became one of the area's top criminal lawyers and won renown for the huge awards he gained in personal-injury cases.

In June 1933 Pres. Franklin D. Roosevelt appointed Payer asst. secretary of state. In December, Payer was made special counsel of the Reconstruction Finance Corp, resigning in Apr. 1934 to return to private practice. Payer was a founder of the CUYAHOGA COUNTY BAR ASSN.† and its president from 1929–31. As chairman of the association's Committee on Judicial & Legal Reforms, he supported common pleas courts' psychiatric clinic, bail-bond reform, and the three-fourths jury laws. Payer spoke Czech, Polish, Italian, French, and German and read classical Greek and Latin. During World War I, Payer, of Czech background, served on the Czechoslovakian Relief Commission. Payer owned a home in CLEVELAND HTS.† with a 10,000 book library, carved furniture, and oil paintings. Payer married Florence L. Graves on 24 June 1902 and had 2 children, Franklin Lee and Dorothea. He was buried in Lake View Cemetery.

Harry F. Payer Papers, WRHS.

**PAYNE, HENRY B.** (30 Nov. 1810–9 Sept. 1896), lawyer and politician, was born in Hamilton, NY, to Elisha and Esther Douglass Payne. He graduated from Hamilton College (1832), moved to Cleveland in 1833, studied law with SHERLOCK ANDREWS, and was admitted to the Ohio Bar in 1834. After 12 years of practice with HIRAM WILLSON, Payne had to retire from legal practice because of a lung hemorrhage.

Payne was Cleveland's first solicitor under its municipal charter, and was elected to city council in 1847. In 1856, 1860, and 1872 he was a delegate to the Democratic national conventions. In 1849 he was elected to the state senate. In 1857 he joined Sen. Steven Douglas in opposing the Lecompton constitution, and assisted Douglas in his 1858 campaign against Abraham Lincoln. In 1849 Payne, with others, worked for completion of the Cleveland & Columbus Railroad, serving as its president from 1851–54. During the Civil War, Payne encouraged army enlistments and advanced monies as a guaranty for the advance of county funds to equip new regiments. In 1862 he became head of the Board of Sinking Funds Commissioners.

Payne was elected to Congress in 1874, serving on the committees on banking and currency, civil service reform, and on the Electoral Commission determining the electoral votes. A candidate for the presidential nomination in 1880, Payne served 1 term, 1885–91, in the U.S. Senate. Payne married Mary Perry in 1836 and had 6 children: Flora, OLIVER, Henry, Howard, Mary, and NATHAN. He is buried in Lake View Cemetery.

**PAYNE, LAWRENCE O.** (11 Oct. 1892–26 Sept. 1959), black lawyer and politician who moved from traditional Republican support to an independent stance, was born in Columbus, OH, son of Robert and Madaline (Wittington) Payne. During World War I he served in the army in France and came to Cleveland after the war. Graduating from Cleveland Preparatory School (1922) he received a LL.B. from John Marshall Law School in 1923. Payne was admitted to the Ohio Bar and appointed Cleveland's first African American asst. police prosecutor.

Payne's election to city council in 1929 came when the old black leadership was waning. Ward leaders as councilmen, the black "Triumvirate" of LEROY BUNDY, CLAYBORNE GEORGE, and Payne significantly increased their power and political patronage by holding the balance of power. In return for supporting DANIEL MORGAN as city manager in 1930, the councilmen won the admission of blacks to the School of Nursing and as interns at City Hospital, as well as black appointments to city offices. In 1932 the councilmen withheld support for the Republican candidate for council president until all three were given committee chairmanships.

In council, Payne was chair of the welfare committee and supported a larger police force, a permanent policewomen's bureau, the separation of first-time and habitual offenders, and enlargement of the correction farms. Payne was appointed to the State Parole Board in 1938; and in 1940, with WILLIAM O. WALKER, formed P. W. Publishing Co., publishing the *CLEVELAND CALL & POST.†* Payne resigned from the Parole Board in 1945 and returned to private practice. In 1924 he married Maybelle Cross. They had no children. Payne died in Cleveland and was buried in Lake View Cemetery.

**PAYNE, NATHAN PERRY** (13 Aug. 1837–11 May 1885), Cleveland mayor, was born in Cleveland, the eldest son of Mary Perry and HENRY B. PAYNE, and attended CLEVELAND PUBLIC SCHOOLS† and Pierce Academy in Middleborough, MA, before returning to Cleveland as an accountant in a coal firm. In 1860 he helped form a coal company, Cross, Payne & Co., which later became Payne, Newton & Co. Late in the Civil War he became a "100 day" volunteer, although he had enlisted at war's outbreak in the CLEVELAND GRAYS.† He served 2 terms on the local board of education and 6 years on city council at several times between 1862–72. He was elected mayor of Cleveland on the Democratic ticket in 1875 but served only 1 term, declining renomination for the sake of his business activities. He was, at various times, park commissioner, vigorously promoting the development of public PARKS.† Payne never married. He lived in his later years with his grandmother, Mrs. Nathan Perry, Jr. (Paulina Skinner Perry).

**PAYNE, OLIVER HAZARD** (21 July 1839–27 June 1917), businessman and philanthropist, was born in Cleveland to Mary Perry and HENRY B. PAYNE. He was educated at Phillips Academy and Yale, leaving the latter in 1861 to serve in the Civil War, earning the brevet of brigadier general. In Nov. 1864 he resigned his commission and returned to Cleveland, organizing Clark, Payne & Co., the largest Cleveland competitor of Rockefeller, Andrews & Flagler and largest single oil refiner in the city. In 1872 it merged into STANDARD OIL CO., of which Payne became treasurer until 1884, when he moved to New York. Payne's holdings in Standard

Oil were exceeded only by those of Rockefeller, the Chas. Pratt estate, and the Harkness Family. In New York, Payne invested in American Tobacco Co. Active in politics, Payne contributed to the Democratic party. A philanthropist, Payne established Cornell Medical College, anonymously donating more than $8 million to that institution in his lifetime. Other gifts and bequests were made to Lakeside Hospital, Yale, the Jewish Orphan Asylum, Hamilton College, Western Reserve Univ., ST. VINCENT CHARITY HOSPITAL,† and the Univ. of Virginia. A bachelor, Payne was a noted yachtsman; his ship, *Aphrodite,* a 300' steam yacht, was the largest such ship in the country when completed in 1898. When Payne died in New York his estate, estimated at $190 million, was distributed, after bequests, among nieces and nephews, including Wm. Bingham II, Elizabeth Bingham Blossom, FRANCES PAYNE BOLTON, and Harry Payne Bingham of Cleveland. He is buried in Lake View Cemetery.

**PEAKE, GEORGE** (sometimes Peek or Peak) (1722-Sep. 1827) was the first African American to settle permanently in Cleveland and something of an inventor, developing a new hand mill for grinding grain. He was a native of Maryland and former resident of Pennsylvania. Peake came to Cleveland with his wife and 2 sons in Apr. 1809. They were apparently well off financially when they arrived; Peake's wife reportedly possessed half a bushel of silver dollars, a remarkable sum at a time when most commercial activity involved barter and trade. Peake himself was also rather wealthy; on 31 Dec. 1811 (sometimes cited as 1812), he purchased 103 acres of land in Rockport. Peake's initial wealth was apparently ill-gotten; as a British soldier in the French & Indian War, he had served under Gen. Jas. Wolfe in the battle of Quebec, but later was reported to have deserted the army, taking with him the money he had been given to pay the other soldiers. Peake endeared himself to his Cleveland neighbors by inventing a new hand mill, which was easier to use than the crude "stamp mortar and spring pestle" they had adapted from the Indians' process for grinding grain. Peake's mill used stones that were 18–20" in diameter, which produced a much better quality of ground meal. Geo. Peake was reportedly "a highly respected citizen." He had 4 children: George, Joseph, James, and Henry. His burial place is unknown.

**PEASE, SETH** (9 Jan. 1764–12 Sept. 1819), early surveyor in the WESTERN RESERVE,† was born in Suffield, CT, to Joseph and Mindwell Pease. He first came to the Western Reserve as an astronomer and surveyor for MOSES CLEAVELAND's 1796 expedition for the CONNECTICUT LAND CO.† Under the direction of Augustus Porter and with fellow surveyor AMOS SPAFFORD, he began surveying the area around Cleveland in Sept. 1796. Both Pease and Spafford produced maps of the town. Although the cabin the surveyors lived in was known as "Pease's Hotel," Pease was a resident of the area only long enough to complete his work, then returned to his Connecticut home. In the spring of 1797, he again returned to the Western Reserve as an employee of the Connecticut Land Co., principal surveyor in a 9-member party that laid out all the townships east of the CUYAHOGA RIVER.† In 1797 Pease produced the first published map of the Western Reserve. His field notes, journals, and letters provide a detailed description of his experiences in the Reserve. Pease also carried out surveys of a township in present-day Maine in 1795, and of the Holland Purchase in New York in 1798–99. In 1806–07 he was U.S. surveyor general in the Mississippi & Orleans Territory and ran the government survey of the southern boundary of Western Reserve lands west of the Cuyahoga River. He was named asst. postmaster general in 1814. He married Bathsheba Kent in 1785; they had no children. Pease died in Philadelphia, PA.

Seth Pease Papers, WRHS.

**PECK, ELIHU M.** (14 Sept. 1822–8 May 1896), with his partner IRVINE U. MASTERS, an important shipbuilder, was born in Butternuts, Oneida County, NY. He came to Ohio by the fall of 1845, when he married Susan Ettling Rogers, and worked as a ship carpenter until the mid–1850s. By 1854 he and Masters had formed a partnership, in a decade building about 50 steam and sail vessels as a leading Cleveland shipbuilding firm. By 1865 the partnership dissolved because of Masters's poor health. Peck continued in business alone, designing and building about another 50 ships in the next 7 years. He increasingly devoted his time to other matters, however, and around 1872 withdrew from shipbuilding, leaving Cleveland for Detroit in the mid–1870s. He was a delegate to the county Republican convention in 1855 and was elected a waterworks commissioner in 1867. His other business ventures included Citizens Savings & Loan Assn. (vice-president, 1868–71), Peoples Savings & Loan Assn. (vice-president, 1872), and Peoples Gas Co. (president, 1872). Peck was reportedly the first to employ a tow boat in the ore-carrying business, using a steamer to tow a schooner filled with ore from the upper to the lower lakes, thus revolutionizing the ore trade. He also organized Northwestern Transportation Co. and built the *Amazon,* then the largest steamer on the lakes. Peck died in Detroit. At his death, he was the principal stockholder in Northwestern and was president of Swain Wrecking Co. Peck was buried in Lake View Cemetery.

**PECKHAM, GEORGE GRANT GUY** (1 Aug. 1874–8 Aug. 1945) was a pioneer in automobile sales in Cleveland, building one of the largest car dealerships in the state. Peckham was born in Troy, OH, the son of George Washington and Lavine Jane (Shilling) Peckham and was educated in public schools until age 18, when he entered commercial school in Dayton to study bookkeeping. He organized his own carriage sales company in Dayton and began to sell electric cars as the automotive industry developed, founding Peckham Motor Car Co. in 1903. When his business was destroyed by the Dayton flood in 1913, leaving him $40,000 in debt, he was able to buy the Cleveland Buick factory distributorship, pay off his debt with help from JEREMIAH J. SULLIVAN, founder of Central National Bank, and organize Ohio Buick Co. The automobile was becoming a necessity rather than a luxury, and under Peckham's leadership Ohio Buick became the largest in the state. He also headed Motors Realty Co. and Peckham Estates Co.

In addition to his automotive activities, Peckham was actively involved in the war effort during World War II, as president of the Canadian-American Truck Co. and treasurer of the National Munitions Corp., both with offices in New York.

Peckham married Elizabeth Finch of Dayton 5 Jan. 1898, and they had a daughter, Phyllis. A resident of SHAKER HTS.,† he died suddenly of a heart attack in New York City and was buried at Knollwood Cemetery.—M.S.

**PEIXOTTO, BENJAMIN FRANKLIN** (13 Nov. 1834–18 Sept. 1890), journalist, lawyer, and diplomat, was born in New York City, son of Rachel (Seixas) and DANIEL LEVY PEIXOTTO. He was brought to Cleveland at age 2 when his father accepted a position at Willoughby Univ. Medical School, left with his family in 1841, but returned at 13. Peixotto entered the retail clothing business in the mid–1850s with Geo. A. Davis, and became an editorial writer for the *PLAIN DEALER*† in 1856, quitting the paper in 1862 when it sympathized with Copperheads.

In 1855 Peixotto and Davis founded the Hebrew Benevolent Society; Peixotto was its secretary. In 1863 Peixotto helped found the first Cleveland lodge of B'NAI B'RITH.† In 1860 he founded the Young Men's Hebrew Literary Society, four years later convincing it to affiliate with B'nai B'rith as Montefiore Lodge. At age 29 Peixotto was elected leader (Grand Saar) of the national B'nai B'rith for

4 years. He helped B'nai B'rith District #2 decide to establish the Jewish Orphan Asylum in Cleveland, pushed for a $1 capitation tax on members, and organized women's groups in 9 cities to raise funds for the orphanage. Peixotto was a member of Tifereth Israel, serving as its treasurer and trustee, and establishing and superintending its Sunday school in 1858. Peixotto left Cleveland in 1866 for New York City, where he established a law firm. In 1870 he became American consul to Romania, and in 1877, to Lyon, France, until 1885 when he returned to New York. He married Hannah Strauss in 1858 and had one child, George. Peixotto died in New York and was buried there.

**PEIXOTTO, DANIEL LEVY** (18 July 1800–13 May 1843), the first Jewish doctor to teach medicine in Ohio and one of the first to establish a practice, was born in Amsterdam to Moses Levy Maduro and Judith Lopez Salzedo Peixotto. He received his medical degree from Columbia Univ. in 1819. He later became secretary of the New York Academy of Medicine and president of the *New York Medical & Physical Journal,* to which he contributed many scientific articles. In 1835 he moved his family to Cleveland in order to accept a position at the new Willoughby Medical College. In 1836 he gave the introductory address for the college. Also that year, he was elected to the newly established Chair of the Theory & Practice of Medicine & Obstetrics. Peixotto resigned from the troubled college in 1838, continued his practice in Cleveland, and occasionally lectured on hygiene at the CLEVELAND LYCEUM.† In 1839 he appeared on the science program at the Ohio Medical Convention meeting in Cleveland. He returned to New York in 1841, where 2 years later he died of consumption. Peixotto married Rachel Seixas in 1823. They had 8 children: Judith, Zipporah, Sarah, Moses Levy Maduro II, Rebecca, Benjamin Franklin, Raphael, and Miriam. His son, BENJAMIN FRANKLIN PEIXOTTO, returned to Cleveland as a young man and became prominent in the Jewish community.

Nebel, Abraham Lincoln. *Cleveland Jewish Miscellany, 1831–1971,* WRHS.

**PELTON, FREDERICK W.** (24 Mar. 1827–15 Mar. 1902), banker, soldier, and Cleveland mayor (1871–73), was born in Chester, CT, to Russel and Amelia Abbey Pelton. He came with his father to BROOKLYN† in 1835 and attended Brooklyn Academy. He then worked with Wheeler, Chamberlain & Co. in Akron, which later relocated to Cleveland, bringing Pelton back to the city. From 1858–67, he worked in the ship chandler business, serving as an artillery captain during the Civil War. After the war, he became secretary of Buckeye Insurance Co., and also joined the Halcyon lodge, becoming a 33rd-degree Mason. In 1865 Pelton was elected to city council, serving as its president from 1866–69. He was also county treasurer. In 1871 Pelton was elected mayor and as such headed a committee to find a bridge site for the SUPERIOR VIADUCT.†

After his term, Pelton became president of Citizen's Savings & Loan Assn., which he founded in 1868. He also was a founder of Riverside Cemetery Assn., becoming its director in 1876. He was later a director of People's Savings & Loan Co., as well as president of Masonic Mutual Life Insurance Co. Pelton served on the board of the House of Correction (1886–89) and as a director on the board of the city's workhouse (1889–91). Pelton married Susan Dennison in 1848 and had 7 children: Lucy, Elizabeth, Susie, Emily, and three others who died young. Pelton was buried in Riverside Cemetery.

**PENFOUND, RONALD A. (CAPTAIN PENNY)** (28 Jan. 1927–16 Sept. 1974), who worked in television and radio, entertained Cleveland children on the Captain Penny Show on WEWS† from 2 March 1955 through 4 Sept. 1971. Penfound was born in Elyria, OH, to Archie and Marjorie (Saywell) Penfound. He first entered Kenyon College (OH), planning to become an Episcopal priest, but then transferred to study broadcasting at the Univ. of Denver. He worked as a radio announcer in Lamar, CO, while attending school (1950). Penfound announced for KVOD in Denver before returning to Elyria as news and sports director at WEOL radio. He also worked at Cleveland radio station WERE as an announcer and salesman before beginning his long affiliation with WEWS-TV on 26 April 1953 as a sports announcer and floorman. The Captain Penny Show appeared at various times over the years—in the morning, at noon, and in the late afternoon. Dressed as a railroad engineer, Captain Penny featured cartoons, "Little Rascals" and "Three Stooges" shorts, and live features. At a show's end, Captain Penny's closing advice was, "You can fool some of the people some of the time, and some of the people all of the time, but you can't fool Mom." After 1971, Penfound served as weekend weatherman and staff announcer at WEWS. He also announced for the Cleveland Indians (1969–72). Penfound left Cleveland in 1972, moving first to New Hampshire, then to Florida (1973), continuing in broadcasting. Penfound married Gail Gilmore in 1951 and had one child, Amy. Their marriage ended in divorce in 1959. He then married Phyllis Yoder Hunter (d. 1964) in 1960. They had two children, Tracy and Matthew. In 1967 Penfound

married Jo Ann Dudas and had two children, Julie and Samantha. He died in Naples, FL.

**PEPPERCORN, BERYL** (25 Apr. 1887–28 May 1969) was a founder and longtime head of the Amalgamated Clothing Workers of America (ACWA) in Cleveland and one of the city's most influential labor leaders.

Born in Austria, Peppercorn began working as a tailor's apprentice at age 9 and came to the U.S. with his parents in 1899. When his family settled in Cleveland in 1902, Peppercorn worked at the Douglas Tailoring Co., where he became union steward and was a founder, with Frank Rosenblum, of the ACWA in 1914. At that time, the work day was often 19 hours and weekly pay ranged from $1.25 to $14 per week. In recognition of his organizing efforts, Peppercorn was elected manager of the Cleveland Joint Board of the Union in 1922. Under his leadership, contracts had been negotiated between the ACWA and most of the local men's clothing companies by 1935, making it one of the area's largest industrial unions. In the mid–1930s, Peppercorn, who endorsed the concept of unions organized by industry rather than craft, became involved in the local wars to recruit members for the Committee for Industrial Organization (CIO). In 1937 he was one of the organizers and first president of the CLEVELAND INDUSTRIAL UNION COUNCIL,† the CIO's local affiliate. An honest and dedicated unionist, Peppercorn opposed the radical socialists and communists infiltrating the CIO and worked for their exclusion. He also encouraged CIO unions to enter politics by forming Labor's League for Political Action. In 1958 he resigned as manager of the ACWA's Cleveland Joint Board.

He and his wife Margaret had two sons, Leonard and Howard, and a stepson, Bernard Matthesen. Peppercorn died in Cleveland.—M.S.

Beryl Peppercorn Papers, WRHS.

**PERK, RALPH.** See **MAYORAL ADMINISTRATION OF RALPH PERK.**†

**PERKINS, ANNA "NEWSPAPER ANNIE"** (ca. 1849–1 Feb. 1900), a fixture on PUBLIC SQUARE† in the 1890s who acquired the sobriquet "Newspaper Annie" from selling the *CLEVELAND PRESS,†* was also conspicuous for advocating women's dress reform, exemplified in her self-devised costume of tennis cap, cropped hair, men's jacket, knee-length white duck trousers, and cotton stockings. Born to Alvah and Cynthia Perkins in Green Springs, OH, in the late 1840s and growing up in Berlin Hts., Perkins found her unconventional feminism and poetry vocation incompatible with small-town life. She came to Cleveland in the late 1880s and brought privately printed copies of her self-explanatory poem, "What Is It?", apparently the only surviving example of her work outside of occasional newspaper contributions. She lived by selling the *Press* on Public Square. Among her other idiosyncrasies were vegetarianism, hydrotherapy, and spelling reform, to which she conformed by spelling her name "Ana Purkin."

After an initial period of ridicule and harassment, Perkins seems to have earned the tolerant respect of Clevelanders, becoming a kind of elder statesman among the city's newsboys and a frequent speaker at the Franklin and Sorosis clubs. A favorite Cleveland folklore relates how grocer W. P. Southworth, seeing her shivering in the winter cold in front of his store, escorted her to Hull & Dutton's to outfit her with a man's overcoat. Anna Perkins died of typhoid fever in St. Alexis Hospital. After a simple service arranged by local clubwomen, her body was returned to Berlin Hts. for burial in accordance with her wishes.

**PERKINS, EDNA BRUSH** (25 Mar. 1880–11 Oct. 1930), social reformer and painter, organized and lectured for women's suffrage (1912–20), chaired the Woman's Suffrage Party of Greater Cleveland (1916–18), helped found the WOMEN'S CITY CLUB† (WCC) of Cleveland (1917), and exhibited at the CLEVELAND MUSEUM OF ART† (CMA) MAY SHOWS† (1927–30). Perkins was also a poet, published travel writer, and pianist.

Born in Cleveland, the oldest daughter of Mary Morris and CHAS. FRANCIS BRUSH and sister of Helene and Chas. F. Brush, Jr., Perkins attended HATHAWAY BROWN† and Miss Hersey's school in Boston and took courses at the Women's College of Western Reserve Univ. On 14 Nov. 1905, she married ROGER GRISWOLD PERKINS, M.D.; the couple lived on E. 46th St. before settling at 1481 East Blvd. They resided in Mantunuck, RI, in the summers. Perkins promoted local Liberty Loan and food conservation drives during World War I. She worked for the Anti-Tuberculosis League and served on the founding boards of the BRUSH FOUNDATION† and the Maternal Health Assn. (1928–30) as well as the boards of the CLEVELAND PLAYHOUSE† (1927–30) and the Welfare Federation of Cleveland, and the advisory committee of the Cleveland School of Art.

Perkins began her art career in mid-life. She studied painting at the Cleveland School of Art and in Provincetown, MA, and maintained studios in Provincetown and New York City. Her work, also exhibited in Wichita, KS, Provincetown, and Akron, OH, received honorable mention in the 1928 and 1929 CMA May shows. She was buried in Lake

View Cemetery. She left three children: Maurice, Roger G., and Chas. Brush Perkins; another son, John, died in 1927.—J.M.

---

Perkins, Charles Brush. *Ancestors of Charles Brush Perkins and Maurice Perkins* (1976).

**PERKINS, JOSEPH** (5 July 1819–26 Aug. 1885), businessman, philanthropist, and congressman in the U.S. House of Representatives the last two years of his life, was born in Warren, OH, to Simon and Nancy Bishop Perkins. He graduated from Marietta College in 1839, and returned to Warren to work for his father in the railroad business. He came to Cleveland in 1852 as president of the Bank of Commerce, serving until 1872. He was also president of the Cleveland & Mahoning Railroad and had interests in several other companies and banks. Perkins was a founder of the WESTERN RESERVE HISTORICAL SOCIETY†; first president of Cleveland City Hospital (later Lakeside); and contributed $5,000 toward purchase of the Holden property for the Case and Western Reserve campuses. He was a trustee for Western Reserve College from 1846–85. A founder of LAKE VIEW CEMETERY,† he served on the public committee raising funds for the GARFIELD MONUMENT.† As a philanthropist, Perkins gave extensively to city charities, particularly homes for orphans and the aged. He gave large amounts to the convent of the Good Shepherd (a Catholic home for girls) and to the Protestant Orphan Asylum. In 1869 he donated a house to be used as a retreat for "unfortunate" women. A few years later, he built a house for aged women. While on the Ohio Board of Charities, Perkins devised a system for classifying prisoners and developed a plan for controlling the state's infirmary system. He married Martha Steele in 1840. They had six children: Douglas, Joseph, Ellen, Lawrence Lewis, Charles, and Olive. Perkins died in Sarasota Springs, NY, and was buried in Lake View Cemetery.

**PERKINS, MAURICE** (ca. 1850–16 Oct. 1895), journalist, wrote for Cleveland's major newspapers before leaving for New York and Indiana. Perkins was probably born on a Michigan farm, although one account gives his birthplace as Cleveland. He graduated from Hillsdale College (MI) and got a job reporting for the *Detroit News,* where he may have met the owner's brother, EDWARD WYLLIS SCRIPPS. Perkins then moved to Toledo and worked for the *Blade.* He married Jessie Davis there in 1879. After E. W. Scripps founded the *CLEVELAND PRESS,†* Perkins became its star reporter at an unequalled salary of $25 a week. He became the pivot in a feud between Scripps and Cleveland ironmaster HENRY CHISHOLM. Chisholm allegedly had his employees cover Perkins from head to toe with black paint for mistakenly identifying his son as the instigator of a street brawl. Scripps exploited the resultant threat to Perkins's life to defeat libel and criminal suits pressed by Chisholm. Perkins became known locally for his shabby appearance and numerous idiosyncrasies, including a penchant for collecting pencils and pads and an addiction to coffee—consuming perhaps as many as 40 cups per day. Though considered an indifferent reporter by some, all rated his writing skills as unsurpassed.

Quitting the *Press,* Perkins worked for the *CLEVELAND HERALD*† and the *PLAIN DEALER*† before leaving Cleveland. In New York City, he won a position on the *Evening Sun.* He later worked for the *Indianapolis Sun* (1888) and the *Evening Telegram* (New York City, 1894). Back in Indiana, he wrote for the *Indianapolis News* before being hospitalized. He died from injuries received after he jumped from the hospital's third floor while delerious.

**PERKINS, ROBERT KENNETH** (ca. 1936–11 Jan. 1993) was the founder of PERKINS SCHOOL OF PIANO TUNING AND TECHNOLOGY,† the only such institution in Ohio and one of only a handful of its kind in the U.S. Born in Clarksburg, WV, to Frank and Irene (Lawman) Perkins, Robert grew up on a small farm. As a youth he took voice lessons and sang in operas. (He never played the piano.) After a brief career with the Clarksburg Opera Guild, Perkins moved to Cleveland in 1960 and joined his brother in the piano-moving business. In 1961 he started Bob's Piano Co. on Lorain Ave., providing tuning and off-site renovations.

The Perkins School opened in Cleveland in 1962 in the old Cleveland Trust building on Lorain and W. 98th St. Perkins started his school when a blind person asked him to teach him piano tuning and repair. Shunning anything technical, Perkins preferred to tune a piano by ear. He taught students how to tune and how to completely take apart and put together a piano. The school attracted 500–600 students for the year-long program. Perkins moved the school to Elyria in 1977.

Perkins had a daughter, Theresa JoAnne, by his first marriage. He married Angela LaCanci in 1982. He married Dora Massaro in 1985 and had a stepdaughter, Cheryl Ryder. Perkins was a Methodist and is buried in Bridgeport, WV. His school closed following his death.—T.B.

**PERKINS, ROGER GRISWOLD** (17 May 1874–28 Mar. 1936), responsible for filtrating and chlorinating Cleveland's water, was born in Schenectady, NY, to Maurice and Anna D. (Potts) Perkins. He gradu-

ated from Union College (1893), Harvard, with an A.B. (1894), and Johns Hopkins with a medical degree (1898), and came to Cleveland in 1898. He began teaching in 1899 at Western Reserve Univ., remaining until 1930, becoming head of the Department of Hygiene and Bacteriology in 1914.

Perkins began investigating the city's water supply in order to eradicate typhoid in 1901. Appointed city bacteriologist in 1906 and 1913, he established and became chief of the Bureau of Laboratories of Cleveland's Div. of Health from 1914–23. His studies isolated and identified streptococcus mucosus, and established filtration of Lake Erie water. Perkins experimented to determine the possibility of chlorinating the city's water in 1910–11. Chlorine treatments began in 1911, but when citizens complained that the water tasted bad, erroneously blaming the chlorine, treatments were reduced and typhoid escalated. Full chlorination and filtration was achieved in 1925.

Perkins served in World War I as scientific attache at the U.S. embassy in Paris and worked with the Red Cross in the Balkans, being awarded the Order of the Crown of Romania and the Order of the Serbian Red Cross. Perkins, also interested in milk and food purification, introduced efficient food inspection. He formed the Cleveland Health Council in 1925.

Perkins married Edna Brush on 14 Nov. 1905. They had four children: Charles Brush, Roger Griswold, Jr., Maurice, and John. Perkins retired to Providence, RI, in 1930, where he died and was buried.

Roger Griswold Perkins Papers, Allen Memorial Medical Library Archives.
Perkins, Charles Brush. *Ancestors of Charles Brush Perkins and Maurice Perkins* (1976).

**PERRY, ELEANOR (ROSENFELD-BAYER-PERRY)** (13 Oct. 1914–14 March 1981) went from writing whodunits with her first husband in Cleveland to writing screenplays for her second husband in New York and Hollywood. A Cleveland native, daughter of Anna (Nybes) and Max Rosenfeld, she earned a B.A. (1935) and M.S. (1950) from Western Reserve Univ. and married local attorney Leo G. Bayer on 3 July 1937. With him supplying the plots and her doing the actual development, they coauthored several crime novels under the pseudonym Oliver Weld Bayer. They also had a thriller entitled *The Left Hook* produced at the CLEVELAND PLAY HOUSE† in 1952 and co-edited the nonfiction collection *Cleveland Murders* in 1947. In 1960 her career entered a new phase with her marriage to film director Frank Perry. Their first collaboration was on *David and Lisa,* for which her screenplay received an Academy Award nomination. Other films produced by the pair included *Ladybug, Ladybug, The Swimmer,* and *Diary of a Mad Housewife.* Following her divorce from Perry in 1971, she continued to do screenplays and co-produced *The Man Who Loved Cat Dancing.* She also won two Emmys for television screenplays. Perry was one of the movie industry's most outspoken critics for its habitual depiction of women as victims. She died in Manhattan from cancer, survived by two children, William and Ann, from her first marriage.

**PERRY, SAMUEL V.** (10 June 1895–14 May 1968), Cleveland lawyer, safety expert, and private investigator, was appointed as Ohio's first African American parole officer, in charge of Cuyahoga County parolees (1930–32). From 1932–48, Perry worked in various municipal offices, including the Streets Department (1933–47), and Municipal Court, first as clerk (1951–53), then information consultant (1953–64). Perry was born in Jamestown, NY, but came to Cleveland as a child; he attended the CLEVELAND PUBLIC SCHOOLS.† He worked at HALLE BROTHERS† (1912–17, 1919–21), moving from shining shoes to inspecting "floor boys." Perry joined the U.S. Army during World War I. In 1923 he received a Bachelor of Law degree from the Blackstone College of Law in Chicago, after apprenticing under Cleveland attorney Frank W. Stanton. He later attended the Marshall School of Law and FENN COLLEGE.† Interested in traffic safety, Perry led programs such as an anti-jaywalking effort and traffic surveys, which reduced neighborhood traffic deaths dramatically.

Perry once managed the advertising for the *Cleveland Call & Post* (1927) and edited a newspaper of his own, the *Searchlight* (between 1948 and 1951). During the last two decades of his life, Perry worked ardently to remove the word "Negro" from the American vocabulary, periodically publishing an "Open Letter to the Citizens of Cleveland" in local newspapers.

In August 1919 Perry married Willette A. Strode (d.1935); they had four sons: Herbert L., A. William, Charles B., and Samuel S. Perry, who served as first black mayor of WOODMERE† from 1966–69. Perry married again in 1941, to Ellen B. Wilson. Perry belonged to the ANTIOCH BAPTIST CHURCH.†—J.M.

Samuel V. Perry Papers, WRHS.
Perry, Samuel V. "Rhymes of Life" (1966).

**PETERS, HARRY ALFRED** (4 Aug. 1879–15 May 1961), doubled the enrollment, solidified the finances, and created a new campus for UNIV. SCHOOL† during his term as headmaster (1908–47, afterwards, headmaster emeritus). Under his administration, the school established its reputation as one of the area's top private schools. Peters was born in Mauch Chunk, PA, to Harry Alfred and Abigail (Horn) Peters. After a brief stint in the paymaster's office of the Lehigh Valley Railroad, he attended Phillips Academy in MA (1896–98), and Yale Univ. (1898–1902), where he was a member of Phi Beta Kappa. Peters first taught history, physical geography, French, Latin, and German at Univ. School (1902–07) and coached baseball (1903–07). Just prior to his appointment as headmaster, Peters was considering trading teaching for gold mining.

Among other professional activities, Peters chaired the committee on education of the Chamber of Commerce (see GREATER CLEVELAND GROWTH ASSN.†) and presided over the North Central Academic Assn., the Headmasters' Assn. of the U.S., and the Country Day School Headmasters' Assn. He also served as the first president of the PROFESSIONAL MEN'S CLUB OF CLEVELAND† (1930–31). On 1 Jan. 1908 Peters married Rosamund Zuck; they had a son, RICHARD D., a former chief editorial writer for the *CLEVELAND PRESS.†* After divorcing his first wife, Peters married Ruth Miller (d. 1950) in Oct. 1929. Peters, a member of the CHURCH OF THE COVENANT (PRESBYTERIAN)†, lived in SHAKER HTS.† and, after retirement, in CLEVELAND HTS.† In 1933 he received honorary degrees from both Kenyon College and Yale Univ. Peters is buried in Lake View Cemetery.—J.M.

**PETERS, RICHARD DORLAND** (29 May 1910–27 Oct. 1984), spent a major part of his journalistic career with the Scripps-Howard organization in his hometown of Cleveland. The son of Dr. HARRY A. PETERS, longtime headmaster of UNIV. SCHOOL, "Dick" Peters graduated from Yale in 1932 and broke into journalism with the *Washington Daily News.* He then worked for the *Knoxville News-Sentinel* before returning home in 1936 to become a reporter, then drama critic, for the *CLEVELAND PRESS.†* During World War II he served as press officer on the staff of Gen. Douglas MacArthur. Returning to the *Press,* Peters served as the paper's chief editorial writer from 1947–57. Scripps-Howard then made him public service director for the entire chain, followed by appointments as editor of the *Indianapolis Times* in 1960 and the *New York World Telegram and Sun* in 1962. When the *World Telegram* was merged in 1966, Peters resigned and helped design the op-ed page of the *New York Times* in 1967. He returned to Cleveland to join the MAYORAL ADMINISTRATION OF CARL B. STOKES,† where he served as executive assistant in charge of the CLEVELAND NOW!† program. He resigned in 1970 to teach at Univ. School and in the Living Room Learning Program of CASE WESTERN RESERVE UNIV.† His special interest in the settlement house movement led to the presidencies of the GOODRICH-GANNETT NEIGHBORHOOD CTR.† and the National Federation of Settlements and Neighborhood Centers. A bachelor, Peters provided in his will for a $500,000 bequest to the CLEVELAND PUBLIC LIBRARY† and a cocktail party for his friends.—J.V.

**PETRARCA, FRANK J.** (31 July 1918–31 July 1943), Congressional Medal of Honor winner for service during World War II, was the son of Dominic and Bettina (Tondia) Petrarca. One of 10 children, Frank grew up in Cleveland, attending St. Marian's parochial school and graduating from East High School in 1938. After working for his father as a carpenter, he joined the 145th Ohio National Guard Regiment in 1939.

On active duty with the Medical Detachment, 145th Infantry Regiment, 37th Infantry Division on New Georgia in the Solomon Islands, Pfc. Petrarca gave aid to 3 wounded solders in direct line of fire (27 July 1943) and rescued a wounded sergeant also in direct line of fire (29 July 1943). He was mortally wounded by enemy mortar fire while trying to rescue another wounded soldier under the same circumstances on his 25th birthday. The Medal of Honor was awarded to Petrarca posthumously, 23 Dec. 1943, and his body was buried at Calvary Cemetery in Cleveland 26 June 1948.

A number of local sites and organizations were named after him, including a classroom at St. Marian's School, Petrarca Rd. in Cleveland, the Petrarca Ohio National Guard Armory in Brookpark, and the Petrarca Post, American Legion, organized in 1947.

**PETRASH, LOUIS** (1 Jan. 1891–13 Oct. 1967), lawyer and municipal judge, was a member of CLEVELAND CITY COUNCIL† from 1921–31, the first native-born Clevelander of Hungarian descent to be elected to public office. Petrash was born in Cleveland to Michael and Mary (Fesco) Petrash and attended St. Ignatius High School. He graduated with an A.B. and an A.M. from JOHN CARROLL UNIV.† and received his law degree in 1914 from the law school of Western Reserve Univ. (see CASE WESTERN RESERVE UNIV.†). Petrash was admitted to the bar in 1915 and became associated with the firm of Locher, Green & Woods. He served as deputy clerk for the Board of Elections (1917), as license commissioner for the city (1932–33), and was a member of the Cuyahoga County Charter Commission. He was a representative to the International Bar Convention in London in 1924.

Appointed to the municipal bench in 1934, Petrash was reelected in 1935 and served until his death.

Petrash chaired and served on various war relief committees after World War I and was active in the Hungarian community, as the first president of the Magyar Club (1920s), for example. He also served the EAST END NEIGHBORHOOD HOUSE† (campaign director), the CITIZENS BUREAU† (trustee), the Community Fund (vice-president), the Cleveland Cultural Garden Federation, and was a director of Third Federal Savings and Loan Assn.

Petrash married Zelder Weizer in 1928 (d. 1966); they had a daughter, Jean M. (Mrs. Robert) Henley. Petrash died at ST. LUKE'S HOSPITAL.†—J.M.

**PHILLIPS, (BISHOP) CHARLES HENRY** (17 Jan. 1858–11 Apr. 1951) served as bishop of the Colored Methodist Episcopal (CME) Church (1902–46, see METHODISTS†), founded and served the California-New Mexico-Arizona CME Conference (1902–40), and organized many CME districts and churches, sometimes called "Phillips Chapels." Between 1910 and 1932 his efforts helped raise the number of CME members in Ohio from 250 to 2100. Born a slave in Milledgeville, GA, he was the 10th of 12 children of Nancy and George Washington Phillips, a minister and farmer after the Civil War. First schooled at home, Phillips then attended Atlanta Univ. (GA). In 1878 he was licensed to preach. He received a B.A. (1880), M.A. (1885), and a degree in medicine (1882) from Central Tennessee College in Nashville. Wilberforce and Wiley universities, among others, awarded him honorary degrees. Rev. Phillips taught school, served churches, and headed CME conferences in Tennessee, Washington, DC, Ohio, Texas, and Kentucky before being elected to the bishopric. He was a delegate to many general CME meetings (including one in Cleveland in 1896) and Ecumenical Conferences in the U.S. and abroad, at times the only CME representative or African American on the program (see AFRICAN AMERICANS†). He was editor of the *Christian Index,* the church's official publication (1894–1902). Phillips spoke for TEMPERANCE† and against segregation, claiming, "There is no color line in Christianity."

Phillips married Lucy Ellis Tappan of Tennessee (d. 1913) on 16 December 1880. His second marriage, to Ella Cheeks of Virginia, took place on 28 August 1918. Phillips moved to Cleveland in 1921. He had 6 children, 5 by his first wife (Charles H., Jr., Jasper, Carlotta James, Lucy Stewart, Lady Emma Conway) and 1 by his second wife (Laura Stokes). Phillips is buried in Lake View Cemetery.—J.M.

Phillips, C. H. *From the Farm to the Bishopric: An Autobiography* (1932).

**PHILLIPS, JOHN** (19 Feb. 1879–15 May 1929), physician, faculty member of Western Reserve Univ. School of Medicine, and a founder of the CLEVELAND CLINIC FOUNDATION,† was born in Welland, Ontario, Canada, the son of Robert and Ann Jane (McCullough) Phillips. He received his medical degree from the Univ. of Toronto in 1903, then moved to Cleveland as an intern at Lakeside Hospital until 1905 and as resident in medicine until 1906. He joined the WRU faculty in 1906 as asst. professor of therapeutics. In 1917–18 he served as a captain in the medical corps of the U.S. Army. As a practicing physician, Phillips was mainly concerned with internal medicine and diseases of children. He was one of the founders, with Drs. GEO. W. CRILE, FRANK E. BUNTS, and WM. E. LOWER, of the Cleveland Clinic Foundation, under whose auspices the Cleveland Clinic was opened in 1921, and the Cleveland Clinic Hospital in 1924. With the other founders, Phillips established an endowment, enlarged by public donations, for care of the sick and for medical research. Although he continued at WRU, he relinquished his duties as a practicing physician to direct both the Cleveland Clinic and the Cleveland Clinic Hospital. As a physician, Phillips was variously associated with Lakeside Hospital, Babies Dispensary & Hospital, and St. John's Hospital. He contributed about 70 articles to medical journals and was a member of many medical societies. He was also a trustee of the CLEVELAND MEDICAL LIBRARY ASSN.† Phillips married Cordelia Sudderth on 18 Sept. 1907 and they had a son, John E.; Phillips was killed in the CLEVELAND CLINIC DISASTER† and was buried in Lake View Cemetery.

John Phillips Papers, WRHS.

**PICKANDS, JAMES S.** (15 Dec. 1839–14 July 1896), cofounder of PICKANDS MATHER & CO.,† was born in Akron, OH, the son of Rev. James D. and Louisa Pickands. He moved to Cleveland and left his cashier job to enlist in the 1st Ohio Volunteer Infantry in 1861, eventually becoming 1st sergeant before being mustered out in Aug. 1861. Pickands became a major in the 124TH OVI in 1862, was seriously wounded at the Battle of New Hope Church, GA (May 1864), recovered in time to be present at the battle of Nashville, TN (Dec. 1864), and was promoted to colonel in June 1865.

In 1867 Pickands moved to Marquette, MI, where, with Clevelander Jay C. Morse, he opened a hardware store, supplying iron ore-mining companies. In 1870 he added a coal-fuel business. By 1875 Pickands was mayor of Marquette, and in 1880 formed Taylor Iron Co. with Jay Morse. His wife,

Caroline Martha Outhwaite, whom he married in 1870, died in 1882 at Marquette, and Pickands moved back to Cleveland, forming Pickands Mather & Co. with SAMUEL MATHER in 1883. He became president of Western Reserve Natl. Bank, the Cleveland Chamber of Commerce, and the Military Committee in charge of dedicating SOLDIERS & SAILORS MONUMENT† (1894). Pickands married Seville Hanna, MARCUS HANNA's sister, in 1887. His health began failing in 1895 and he died at home a year later. He raised 3 sons with his first wife: Joseph, Henry S., and Jay M. Henry took over his father's partnership; Jay worked for the company until his death in 1913. Pickands died in Cleveland and was buried in Lake View Cemetery.

Havinghurst, Walter. *Vein of Iron* (1958).
Lewis, George W. *The Campaigns of the One Hundred and Twenty-fourth Regiment* (1894).

**PICKUS, ABE** (16 Oct. 1891–28 March 1980), a Cleveland businessman, attracted national renown for his efforts to promote peace through personal contacts with world leaders in the period before World War II. Born in Russia, he came to Cleveland in 1910 and saw service with the AEF in France during World War I. Returning to Cleveland, he married Etta Friedman in 1922 and operated the A. Pickus Lumber Co. before setting up an oil distributorship, the Majestic Oil Co. Keenly interested in international affairs, he was sufficiently disturbed by a news item from Manchuria in April 1936 to place a long-distance telephone call to the Japanese ambassador in Washington, D.C. During the next few years, Adolf Hitler and Mussolini's son-in-law, Count Ciano, were among those on the receiving end of calls from A. Pickus. By 1940, he revealed on a national radio program that his telephone and cablegram messages on behalf of peace had cost him $10,000. Having made an unsuccessful bid for a Democratic nomination to Congress in 1944, Pickus obtained his only political position in 1959 with an appointment to the State Fire Marshall's Advisory Council. He continued to campaign publicly for his political views, which included improved Soviet-American relations, tougher laws against drug dealers and drunk drivers, and the benefits of physical fitness. He was survived by his wife and 2 children, Sheldon Pickus and Elaine Marks.—J.V.

Vacha, J. E. "The Man Who Put Hitler on Hold," *Ohio Magazine* (1992).

**PIERCE, LUCY ANN BOYLE** (28 Mar. 1905–30 July 1993), received the Meritorious Public Service Citation from the U.S. Navy in 1965 and a citation from the U.S. Army the same year for her volunteer work with the USO (United Service Organizations) in Cleveland and abroad. Pierce began working with Cleveland's USO in 1941 and became director in 1951; she also helped organize USO branches overseas. Pierce was born in Oil City, PA, to Edward E. and Marquerita (Weber) Boyle, and moved to Cleveland in 1918. She graduated from West High School and Marshall College and received a master's degree in social work from Western Reserve Univ. (see CASE WESTERN RESERVE UNIV.†). On 10 Sept. 1924 she married Gar Pierce (d. 1971), later the mayor of Willoughby. They had a daughter, Jettielee McCormick. Pierce worked for ASSOCIATED CHARITIES† (1930–42). At Cleveland's USO, located in the TERMINAL TOWER† and later in the Federal Building and at the CLEVELAND-HOPKINS INTERNATIONAL AIRPORT,† she organized volunteers and solicited donations of food and entertainment tickets for soldiers. Cleveland's chapter was reportedly the only one (among 273 in the world) headed by a volunteer. As a member of the National USO Council, Pierce made goodwill trips to military bases abroad. Locally, she worked with the West Lake County United Appeal, among other Lake County organizations, and served on the board of the Cleveland Community Fund (see UNITED WAY SERVICES†). She belonged to the WOMEN'S CITY CLUB OF CLEVELAND,† the Daughters of the Nile, and the Presbyterian Church in Willoughby. Pierce died in Coral Springs, FL, where she had moved in 1990.—J.M.

PIRC, LOUIS J. (4 July 1888–29 June 1939) became a leader in Cleveland's ethnic community through the means of teaching citizenship classes and editing a Slovenian newspaper. A native of Ljubljana, Slovenia, he came to Cleveland in 1906 and immediately became involved in the affairs of the Slovenian neighborhood. By 1908 he had reorganized a moribund Slovenian newspaper as the weekly *Amerika*, which he nurtured as editor into the daily *AMERIŠKA DOMOVINA*.† During World War I he served on the MAYOR'S ADVISORY WAR COMMITTEE† as well as in the Intelligence Bureau of the Department of War. Pirc had begun teaching citizenship classes shortly after his arrival in Cleveland, originally in Knaus' Hall on St. Clair Ave. After 1923, under the auspices of the Citizens Bureau, he continued his classes in the St. Clair Branch of the CLEVELAND PUBLIC LIBRARY.† Over the course of 28 years he gave instruction to an estimated 18,000 immigrants from 22 nationality groups. He was also influential in the establishment of the Yugoslav Cultural Gardens (see CLEVELAND CULTURAL GARDEN FEDERATION†).

Predeceased by his wife, Constance, he died in his home on E. 108th St. and was buried in Calvary Cemetery. He was survived by a son, Louis Jr., and a daughter, Mildred Gray.—J.V.

PLANK, EMMA NUSCHI (11 Nov. 1905–13 Mar. 1990) was an educator, author, and associate professor of child development at CASE WESTERN RESERVE UNIV.† For Cleveland's City Hospital she created a "child life" program that became renowned internationally and served as the impetus for founding the Assn. for the Care of Children's Health. Emma Plank was born in Vienna, Austria, where she studied under Maria Montessori and Anna Freud. In 1938 she emigrated to the U.S. and earned a master's degree in child development from Mills College in San Francisco. She came to Cleveland in 1951 to direct the school of the Children's House (later Hanna Perkins School) of Univ. Hospital. In 1955 Dr. Frederick C. Robbins asked Plank to come to the Department of Pediatrics of City Hospital (later MetroHealth Medical Center) to address the educational, social, and psychological needs of children receiving long-term care. Plank seized this opportunity to found the Child Life and Education Division of the Department of Pediatrics at City Hospital and directed it until 1972. She was a cofounder of the interdisciplinary Assn. for the Care of Children's Health in 1965. Her 1962 book, *Working with Children in Hospitals*, has been translated into several languages; it endures as both a philosophical guide and a practical manual for those providing health-care to children worldwide. Plank received an honorary degree from Wheelock College in Boston (1988) and many awards, including the Medal of the City of Vienna (1970), the Gold Medal from the Montessori Centennial (1970), and the Early Childhood Award from the Ohio Assn. for the Education of Young Children (1979).

Plank married psychiatric social worker Robert Plank in 1932; there were no children. The couple lived in CLEVELAND HTS.† In 1983, after her husband died, Plank returned to Vienna.—J.M.

Plank, Emma. *Working with Children in Hospitals* (1971, 1962).
Dittrick Museum of Medical History.

POLK, FRANKLIN A. (26 April 1911–30 Oct. 1991), attorney and journalist, was the youngest president of the CUYAHOGA COUNTY BAR ASSN.† (1948) and its first delegate to the American Bar Assn. House of Delegates for 12 years. In 1984, for "'improving the administration of justice,'" he received the American Judicature Society's highest honor, the Herbert Haley Citation. For his efforts in maintaining impartial federal juries, the National

Assn. of Criminal Defense Lawyers also honored him.

Polk was born in Cleveland to John and Mary (Cerny) Polk, natives of Czechoslovakia, and graduated from South High School in 1928. Polk graduated from JOHN CARROLL UNIV.† (1934) and from Cleveland Law School (1939). He worked as a claims attorney for the Travellers Insurance Co. while in law school and in 1944 was associated with the firm of Walter & Haverfield. The youngest member of the Cleveland Board of Education (1944), the outspoken Polk ran unsuccessfully as a Republican for mayor against Mayor THOMAS A. BURKE in 1949. Remaining active in politics, Polk managed the campaign of Ralph Perk for Cuyahoga County Auditor (1958). He edited the *Buckeye Rd. and Luna Park News* and corporate house organs and belonged to the CITY CLUB OF CLEVELAND.† A delegate to the Ohio Bar Assn. House of Delegates for 40 years (the longest tenure in its history), he founded and presided over the Cleveland Academy of Trial Attorneys. Polk retired in August 1991.

On 20 June 1939 he married Julia Gabriel and the couple lived on Cleveland's east side with their 2 children, Loretta Gainor and Franklin G. At his death, Polk lived in INDEPENDENCE.† He attended St. Michael Catholic Church there and is buried in All Saints Cemetery.—J.M.

**POLLOCK, SAMUEL** (21 June 1909–4 Mar. 1983), labor union activist and pioneer in securing health care and retirement benefits for union members, was born in Cleveland, the son of Isadore and Sonia Gordon Pollock. The family moved to Toledo in 1914 where he attended school, graduating from Woodward High School in 1926. He also took courses at the Univ. of Toledo and Bowling Green State.

Pollock, following in his father's footsteps, became involved in a bitter strike at Toledo Auto-Lite in 1934, lost his job, and was blacklisted for his activities on behalf of Federal Union 18384 of the UAW. Labeled a radical for his socialist views, Pollock remained outside labor's mainstream until 1938, when he was hired by the Amalgamated Meat Cutters and Butcher Workmen of North America (the Amalgamated) to organize Local 372 in Akron, OH. His skills were recognized in 1941 when he became Amalgamated's general organizer. Pollock came to Cleveland in 1950 when Local 372 merged with Amalgamated District 427 and was appointed interim district president in 1952. His aggressive leadership secured a 2-year contract establishing a 5-day, 40-hour work week, substantial wage increases, and an employer-paid Health and Welfare Fund, one of the first in the nation. Pollock was

elected district president in 1953. Under his stewardship the Health & Welfare Fund established dental and eye care programs for its membership. The district also organized a Community Health Foundation in 1964, the first prepaid, direct-service medical care program in Northeastern Ohio, and the following year it established a portable national pension plan funded by employers for all Amalgamated members. Pollock retired from the union in 1973, moving to Chatsworth, CA, where he taught courses in Health Science at California State Univ. at Northridge.

Pollock married Sally (Sarah) DeVera Kooperman 23 April 1934, and they had a daughter, Frances Packard, who died in 1968. He died in Chatsworth and his remains were cremated.—M.S.

United Food & Commercial Workers International Union, Direct 427, Records, 1937–73, WRHS.
Hansen, Roger Hall. *Sam Pollock, Labor Activist: From Radical to Reformer, 1932–1972* (Ph.D. diss., Bowling Green State Univ., Aug. 1993).
Sam Pollock Papers, 1932–1982, Center for Archival Collections, Bowling Green State Univ., Bowling Green, OH.

**POMERENE, ATLEE** (6 Dec. 1863–12 Nov. 1937), a Democrat, served as lt. governor of Ohio (1910–11) and U.S. Senator (1911–23) before joining the Cleveland law firm of SQUIRE, SANDERS & DEMPSEY† in 1923. He was selected by 2 Republican presidents, first to prosecute (with Owen J. Roberts) cases arising from the Teapot Dome scandal, and then to chair the Reconstruction Finance Corp. Board (1932–33). Pomerene was born in Berlin, OH, to Peter P. and Elizabeth (Wise) Pomerene and educated at Vermilion Institute in Hayesville, OH. He received both an A.B. (1884) and an A.M. (1887) from Princeton Univ., and a law degree from the Cincinnati Law School (1886). Admitted to the bar that year, Pomerene began practice in Canton, OH, and soon became involved in politics, as city solicitor (1887–91), county prosecutor (1897–1900), and a member of the Ohio Tax Commission (1906).

Called the "gloomy senator," the serious Pomerene was known for his integrity and a lack of dependence on the political machine. He helped create the Federal Tariff Commission and supported the League of Nations, but not women's suffrage. He defied both the railroad unions and the Anti-Saloon League, which some said cost him a third senatorial term. He lost to Simeon D. Fess.

On 29 June 1882, Pomerene married Mary H. Bockius of Canton; they lived in Wade Park Manor after he moved to Cleveland in 1923. There were no children. Pomerene received honorary degrees from Mount Union College, the College of Wooster, Miami Univ., and Kenyon College. He died at his home and was buried in Canton.—J.M.

Pomerene, Atlee. *America's Position in the Two World Wars* (1917).
———. *Economy? Yes* (1921).
Shriver, Phillip R. "The Making of a Moderate Progressive: Atlee Pomerene," Ph.D. diss. (1954).

**POMEROY, ALSON HORATIO** (7 March 1836–1 April 1906) was a BEREA† banker who became involved in the organization of interurban railroad lines. The son of farmer Alanson Pomeroy, he was born and received his common school education in STRONGSVILLE.† He entered business as an assistant in his father's general store, until 1866, when he moved to Elyria to operate his own dry goods business. In 1876 Pomeroy moved to Berea and became president of the Bank of Berea, a position he held for the remainder of his life. In association with W. D. Miller, he acquired a small horsecar railway in Berea in 1890. Reorganizing it as the CLEVELAND & BEREA ST. RAILWAY CO.,† they converted it to electric power and extended it to Cleveland. Pomeroy then formed a syndicate in 1895 with Cleveland banker M. J. MANDELBAUM to extend the line to Elyria. By 1903 they had merged it with several other lines between Norwalk and Wooster to form the Cleveland & Southwestern Traction Co. As the CLEVELAND, SOUTHWESTERN & COLUMBUS RAILWAY† it went on after Pomeroy's death to become one of Ohio's largest interurban lines. Pomeroy also served 2 terms as mayor of Berea, where he died from an attack of apoplexy. Survived by his wife, the former Ellen Tillinghast of Berlin Hts., OH, he was buried at Lake View Cemetery. He also left 2 sons, F. T. Pomeroy and J. B. Pomeroy, and a daughter, Mrs. J. O. Wilson.—J.V.

**PORATH, ISRAEL** (3 July 1886–11 Apr. 1974), "dean" of Cleveland's Orthodox rabbis for almost 5 decades, was born in Jerusalem, Palestine, received a traditional Talmudic education, and graduated from Jerusalem's Etz Chaim Yeshiva. In Palestine, Porath was responsible for negotiating with Turkish rulers regarding school affairs, and administered relief efforts for Jews during and after World War I. In 1923 he emigrated, accepting a pulpit in Plainfield, NJ. Two years later he became the rabbi at Cleveland's Congregation OHEB ZEDEK,† a position he held for 14 years, afterwards serving Congregation Neveh Zedek for 6 years. In 1945 Porath became dean of Salanter Yeshiva in New York City, however he returned to Cleveland within a year to become rabbi of the HEIGHTS JEWISH CTR.,† remaining there until his retirement in 1972.

Porath represented the Orthodox in Cleveland's Jewish community, serving as a trustee of the ORTHODOX JEWISH CHILDRENS HOME† and Orthodox Old Home, and as chairman of the education committee of YESHIVATH ADATH B'NAI ISRAEL.† He was a founder and chairman of Cleveland's Orthodox Rabbinical Council, and also served on councils and boards of the Jewish Community Council, Jewish Welfare Fed., and B'NAI B'RITH.† In 1960 he became an honorary life trustee of the JEWISH COMMUNITY FED.† and honorary president of Cleveland Histadrut Ivrit. He received the A. H. Friedland Award of the BUREAU OF JEWISH EDUCATION† in 1968. Porath wrote an 8-volume outline of the Talmud. He married Miriam Tiktin in 1905 and had 7 children: Shoshana, Samuel, Tzve, Benjamin, Ben Zion, Joseph, and David. Porath was buried in Israel.

Rabbi Israel Porath Papers, WRHS.

**PORTER, ALBERT S.** (29 Nov. 1904–7 Jan. 1979), Cuyahoga County engineer for 29 years and county Democratic party chairman for 6 years, was born in Portsmouth, VA, to Albert S. and Lena Edmonds Porter. He moved with his family to LAKEWOOD† in 1913, graduated from Lakewood High School in 1922, and from Ohio State Univ. with a B.S. in civil engineering in 1928. In 1929 he joined the Cleveland Highway Research Bureau, becoming chief asst. to county engineer John O. McWilliams in 1933, where he remained until 1947, with time out for 5 years of navy service during World War II. After McWilliams's resignation in 1947, Porter became county engineer, serving in that capacity for almost 30 years. During his tenure, much of the freeway system linking Cleveland to its suburbs was built. Porter was active in Democratic politics, becoming county chairman of the Democratic party in 1963 upon the resignation of RAY T. MILLER, serving until 1969. He was defeated for reelection as county engineer in 1976. As a result of a grand jury investigation in 1977, he pleaded guilty to 19 counts of theft in office, was fined $10,000, and was placed on probation for 2 years. Porter married Genevieve Shaveyco in 1949 and had 2 sons, Lee and Alan, and a daughter, Carol.

**PORTER, PHILIP WYLIE** (7 Aug. 1900–20 May 1985), reporter, columnist, and editor at the *PLAIN DEALER†* for 44 years, was born in Portsmouth, VA, to Albert S. and Lena Edmonds Porter. He moved with his family to LAKEWOOD† in 1913. As a high school junior, he got a summer job at the *CLEVELAND LEADER†* and after graduation attended Ohio State Univ., majoring in journalism, working as the campus correspondent for the *Plain Dealer* during the academic year and as staff police reporter during the summer. He joined the *Plain Dealer* after graduation in 1922 as a general-assignment reporter, was promoted to city editor, began his "Inside the News in Cleveland" column in 1929, and was made news editor in 1936. After military service during World War II, he became *Plain Dealer* Sunday editor, managing editor, and, in 1963, executive editor. He retired in 1966 but continued writing a column for the SUN NEWSPAPERS† until 1983.

Porter authored 2 books, *The Reporter and the News* (1935) and *Cleveland: Confused City on a Seesaw* (1976). In 1979 he edited *The Best of Loveland*, a compilation of pieces by his *Plain Dealer* colleague, ROELIF LOVELAND. Porter helped found the City Club Forum Foundation (1941) and became a charter member of the City Club Hall of Fame in 1985. He married 3 times, to Annanette Blue in 1922, Helene Betschart in 1945, and Dorothy Rutka Kennon in 1960. He had 3 daughters: Phoebe Ann, Susan Wood, and Molly Schaeffer. He and his third wife were victims of a double homicide in 1985.

Porter, Philip. *Cleveland: Confused City on a Seesaw* (1976).

**PORTER, SIMEON C.** (23 April 1807–6 May 1871), architect active in Cleveland between 1848–71, was born in Waterbury, CT, to Lemuel and Margatana Welton Porter. His father was a woodworker and joiner. The family moved to Tallmadge, OH, in 1818, and later to Hudson. Porter erected several buildings of Western Reserve College (now Western Reserve Academy) and many Hudson houses before moving to Cleveland in 1848. From 1849–59, Porter was a partner of CHAS. W. HEARD, and their firm of Heard & Porter was the leading architectural company of the decade in Cleveland. They planned the Second Presbyterian Church (1852), Old Stone Church (1855), CENTRAL HIGH SCHOOL† (1856), several commercial blocks, and numerous other schools and residences, including those of HINMAN B. HURLBUT and Chas. Hickox. Porter separated from Heard in 1859 and continued practicing independently. He designed Cleveland's West Side High School in 1861, but he was most active outside of Cleveland, erecting buildings in Akron, Brecksville, Kent, Hudson, and Alliance. When Porter died in 1871, he was buried in the new Lake View Cemetery.

**POST, CHARLES ASA** (28 Oct. 1848–2 May 1943) spent most of his life in business but earned the honorific of "Dean of Doan's Corners" for local historical recollections written after his retirement. He was born at EUCLID AVE.† and what later became E. 101st St., just a few blocks from DOAN'S CORNERS.† He left Doan School at 16 to enter business, becoming a bookkeeper for the Everett Weddell Co. in the WEDDELL HOUSE.† In 1883 Post briefly left Cleveland to enter the electrical supply business in New York, returning 4 years later to head the East End Bank, followed in 1905 by the presidency of the Dime Savings Bank. He was an organizer and director of the Cleveland Stock Exchange and the first secretary and treasurer of the Dow Chemical Co. (see HERBERT H. DOW), which was organized in his office. He was a member of the ROWFANT CLUB† and the EARLY SETTLERS ASSN.† From 1910–25 Post conducted banking and brokerage activities on the Pacific Coast and in New York. When he returned, he took a room in the Hotel Haddam at E. 105th and Euclid and published his first book, *Doan's Corners and the City Four Miles West*, in 1930. It was followed by *Those Were the Days* (1935), an account of Euclid Ave.'s "Millionaires Row" days, and *The Cuyahoga: The Crooked River that Made a City Great* (completed 1942 but unpublished). Distinguished by a white, spadelike beard, the octogenarian bachelor was often mistaken for Chief Justice Charles Evans Hughes of the Supreme Court. He died in a convalescent home on Crawford Rd.—J.V.

**POUTNEY, RICHARD IRVING** (28 Feb. 1927–24 Jan. 1993) was the founder of the West Side Institute of Technology and a leader in vocational training. He was also president and chairman of the board of the Stella Maris Home (see STELLA MARIS DETOX CENTER†) where he counseled recovering alcoholics.

Born in Cleveland to Clifford and Mary Poutney, Richard graduated from St. Boniface High School and joined the maritime service as a marine engineer (1944–1953). Leaving the maritime service, Poutney worked at Republic Steel as a turbine engineer until 1960.

In 1957 Poutney founded the West Side Institute as an adult occupational training school at his home on 3812 W. 132 St. For five years he taught classes in the basement, which housed his laboratory. In 1963 Poutney purchased a 3-story former bakery building on Denison Ave. In 1968 he leased two administration buildings of the former Industrial Rayon Co. plant on Walford Ave. Poutney offered two-year associate's degrees in power plant operation, stationary engineering, environmental technology, steam technology, electrical refrigeration, air conditioning, instrumentation, water chemistry, combustion control, and domestic and commercial heating. He continued as consultant for the school after retiring in 1988.

For more than 30 years Poutney volunteered as a

counselor for recovering alcoholics through the alcohol and drug treatment facility at the Stella Maris Home, where he served as president and chairman of the board from the mid–1980s until his death.

Poutney married Betty Nally on 22 April 1949. They had 3 children: Richard, Peter, and Patricia (Tehorek). Poutney is buried in Holy Cross Cemetery.—T.B.

**POWER, EFFIE LOUISE** (12 Feb. 1873–8 Oct. 1969) was the first children's librarian at the CLEVELAND PUBLIC LIBRARY† (CPL), and taught courses in library science and literature for CHILDREN AND YOUTH.† At the request of the American Library Assn., she wrote one of the first major textbooks on children's library work (1928). Power was born in Conneautville, PA, to Frances Billings and William Ellis Power. She graduated from Cleveland's CENTRAL HIGH SCHOOL† (1892) and the Carnegie Library School, Pittsburgh, PA (1904). During World War I she served with the Red Cross. Before leaving for positions in Pittsburgh and St. Louis, Power worked in Cleveland for about a decade. She was children's librarian for CPL (1898–1903), library science instructor in library science and children's literature for the Cleveland Normal School (1903–08), and lecturer at Western Reserve Univ.'s Library School (WRU, 1904–11, see CASE WESTERN RESERVE UNIV.†). During this first tenure at CPL, Power and vice-librarian LINDA EASTMAN created the Children's Library League, which emphasized the responsibilities of readership to young library users.

Power returned to Cleveland for a brief stint as librarian of Central High School. In 1920 she came back to CPL as director of work with children. Under her direction, CPL's training program developed into a graduate program in library science. She then became as asst. professor of library science at WRU. In 1926 she took children's books to the streets with the Book Caravan, a precursor of the bookmobile. Power retired from CPL in 1937. In "retirement" she taught at Columbia Univ., served as librarian in Pompano Beach, FL, and continued her avocation, writing fiction for children. In addition to local and national professional associations, Power belonged to the WOMEN'S CITY CLUB† of Cleveland. An authority on children's literature, she collected rare children's books and enjoyed golf.
—J.M.

**PRENTICE, WALTER M.** (1824–2 June 1864), physician and army surgeon in the CIVIL WAR,† was born to Athalia and Noyes B. Prentice, a saddler, in Unionville, Lake County, OH. In 1850–51 Prentice was practicing medicine in Canfield, OH, with his younger brother, Noyes Billings Prentice, studying medicine under him. By the time of the Civil War, the brothers had formed a partnership and were practicing medicine in Cleveland with an office on Pearl St. on the west side. Walter entered the army "on the staff of General Frye and became recognized as a surgeon of rare ability." He died of disease at Stanford, KY, while serving as commandant, Medical Corps, at the hospital at Pt. Burnside, TN. Noyes Billings Prentice served on the medical staff at the U.S. GENERAL HOSPITAL† at Cleveland on Univ. Hts. during the Civil War.

Married in 1847, Walter and his wife, Sarah, had two children, Frank and Thalia. His brother, Noyes B., married in 1852. Noyes and his wife, Georgia, had two children also, Charles and Mary. Walter was buried in Monroe St. Cemetery.

**PRENTISS, ELISABETH SEVERANCE ALLEN** (16 Nov. 1865–4 Jan. 1944) was a generous benefactress of educational, art, and medical causes. Recipients of her gifts included St. Luke's Hospital, the Cleveland Health Museum (see HEALTH MUSEUM†), Western Reserve Univ. (see CASE WESTERN RESERVE UNIV.†), and the CLEVELAND MUSEUM OF ART.†

Born in Titusville, PA, to Louis H. and Fanny Benedict Severance, Elisabeth was educated in Cleveland and graduated from Wellesley College in 1887. Elisabeth was twice widowed. On 4 Aug. 1892 she married Cleveland surgeon DUDLEY P. ALLEN; he died in 1915. On 19 Sept. 1917 she married industrialist FRANCIS F. PRENTISS; he died in 1937. Neither marriage produced children.

Continuing a family tradition of philanthropy, Elisabeth and her husbands provided building and/or operating funds for many institutions. She established the Allen Memorial Library in 1926 in honor of her first husband. She received the Cleveland Chamber of Commerce distinguished public service medal in 1928, the first woman so honored. In 1937 she succeeded her second husband as president of St. Luke's Hospital and continued his work in its expansion.

In 1939 she helped establish the ELISABETH SEVERANCE PRENTISS FOUNDATION† to promote medical/surgical care and research in Cleveland. She was a trustee of the Cleveland Art Museum and made gifts to its art collection and its endowment fund. In 1944 the Cleveland Health Museum established the Elisabeth Severance Prentiss National Award in Health Education honoring Mrs. Prentiss who, in 1936, donated a building on Euclid Ave. as the museum's first home, and contributed to its operating fund. She is buried in Lake View Cemetery.—T.B.

---

Severance Family Papers, WRHS.

**PRENTISS, FRANCIS FLEURY** (22 Aug. 1858–1 Apr. 1937), founder of Cleveland Twist Drill Co. (see ACME-CLEVELAND†) and philanthropist, was born in Montpelier, VT, son of Joseph Addison and Rebecca Loomis Prentiss. Growing up in Winona, MN, Prentiss worked as a bank clerk before moving to Cleveland in 1879. In 1880 he formed a partnership with JACOB D. COX, the forerunner of Cleveland Twist Drill Co. Prentiss was president of the company from 1904–11, then chairman of the Board of Directors until his death. He was also a director of Lake Shore Savings & Trust Co., Cleveland Life Insurance Co., Superior Steamship Co., Cleveland Graphite Bronze Co., OSBORN MFG.,† and Youngstown Steel Co.

Prentiss was president of the Chamber of Commerce (1906) and chairman of the Cleveland INDUSTRIAL EXPOSITION† (1909), Cleveland Committee of the Natl. Education Assn. Convention (1908), and the City Planning Commission (1915). Between 1901–19, Prentiss backed the visiting orchestra series, forerunner of the CLEVELAND ORCHESTRA.† He helped form the MUSICAL ARTS ASSN.† and was a trustee of the CLEVELAND MUSEUM OF ART,† WESTERN RESERVE HISTORICAL SOCIETY,† Western Reserve Univ., Case School of Applied Science, and Andrews School for Girls in Willoughby. Prentiss was president and chairman of the board of HIRAM HOUSE,† and president of ST. LUKE'S HOSPITAL† beginning in 1906, giving it an estimated $6 million during his lifetime and leaving 70% of his estate to the hospital. Prentiss married Delight Sweetser in 1900; she died in 1903. In 1917 he married Elisabeth Severance Allen, widow of Dr. DUDLEY P. ALLEN, who succeeded Prentiss as St. Luke's president in 1937. Prentiss died in Pasadena, CA, and was buried in Winona, MN.

**PRESCOTT, JAMES SULLIVAN** (26 Jan. 1803–3 Apr. 1888), stonemason, educator, and historian of the NORTH UNION SHAKER COMMUNITY,† was born in Lancaster, MA, the son of Levi and Mary (Townsend) Prescott. He moved at age 16 to Springfield, MA, then to Hartford, CT, and apprenticed as a stonemason. He joined the Baptist revival movement, in 1821 becoming a teacher in the African Sunday School. While serving his apprenticeship, he attended high school and in 1824 entered Westfield Academy (MA).

After a year (1825) teaching the Oneida Indians for the Baptist Missionary Convention of New York, Prescott moved to Cleveland, working as a journeyman stonemason. That summer Elisha Russell, an elder in the N. Union Colony of Shakers, persuaded Prescott to come to N. Union to assist in building a dwelling house. After working for several

months in the colony, Prescott was admitted to the Shaker Society. In 1827 he was appointed an elder, and the following year became a teacher in the colony. He served as a farmer, educator, headmaster, stonemason, and craftsman (especially furniture), and in positions of leadership, including presiding elder, deacon, and legal trustee. He was the spokesman for the Shakers at national spiritualist conventions held in Cleveland in 1852 and 1871. In 1870 Prescott wrote the history of N. Union for the WESTERN RESERVE HISTORICAL SOCIETY† which was published as a series in the *CLEVELAND HERALD.†* Subsequently Prescott revised his manuscript, dedicating it to the EARLY SETTLERS ASSN.† in 1881. Prescott died about a year before the dissolution of the N. Union Colony. He was buried in an unmarked grave in the N. Union Colony Cemetery.

———————

MacClean, John P. *Shakers of Ohio* (1907).
Piercy, Caroline P. *The Valley of God's Pleasure* (1951).
Shaker Manuscript Collection, WRHS.

**PRESSER, JACK (JACKIE)** (6 Aug. 1926–9 July 1988), son of labor leader WILLIAM PRESSER, was head of the 1.6 million-member Teamsters Union and served as labor advisor to Pres. Ronald Reagan.

Jackie was born in Cleveland, the son of William and Faye (Friedman) Presser and attended local schools. Although his early jobs with the Teamsters Union ended badly, Presser's father made him secretary-treasurer of Local 507, newly chartered in the mid–1960s to organize warehouse workers. By 1971 Local 507 had grown to 4,430 members scattered across northern Ohio in 121 different bargaining units, and Presser acquired more salaried positions, including president and general manager of Teamster Local 10, Hotel and Restaurant Employees; financial secretary of Local 19, Bakery and Confectionery Workers, and vice-president of Joint Council 41. In 1976 he was elected International Vice-President for Communications, where he planned innovative programs for Teamsters which attracted positive media attention. Court records show that Presser and his father were informants for the FBI in the late 1970s and transcripts of wiretaps linked both of them to organized crime figures. Despite this, Presser was elected president of the International Union in April 1983, and was appointed labor advisor to Pres. Ronald Reagan in return for the union's support of his presidential campaign.

Presser married Pauline Walls 31 May 1947; they had a daughter, Suzanne. After their divorce in 1949, Presser was briefly married to Elaine Goeble. He and his third wife, Patricia, whom he married in

1952, had a daughter, Bari Lynn (Joseph) and a son (Gary). They divorced in 1971 and Presser married Carmen DeLaportilla. He divorced his fourth wife in 1986 in order to marry Cynthia Jarabek. Presser died in Cleveland at age 61.—M.S.

James Neff. *Mobbed Up: Jackie Presser's High-Wire Life in the Teamsters, the Mafia and the F.B.I.* (1989).

**PRESSER, WILLIAM E.** (14 July 1907–18 July 1981) was a labor organizer and an influential Teamsters Union official who played a key role in the union's growth. The oldest of 6 children of Benjamin and Yetta Presser, William was born in Cleveland, where he attended local schools until he was 16. Presser had numerous jobs during the depression, and by 1939 was employed by several local unions to recruit members. Through intimidation and threats, Presser gained control of the Cleveland area's jukebox and vending machine operations in the 1940s, organizing its distributors into associations where prices were fixed, and exclusive territories were allocated to the members in order to eliminate competition. He completed his monopoly by establishing a union for the workers who serviced the jukeboxes and vending machines and negotiated their wage increases with the same association members he controlled. Assn. and union dues gave Presser a sizeable income, which increased as he expanded his operations. He joined the growing Teamsters Union in 1951, bringing his unions with him, and two years later, with the support of James Hoffa, was elected president of the Ohio Conference of Teamsters and Joint Council 41. Under his leadership membership grew from 23,000 to 100,000. The subject of several federal investigations for labor racketeering, Presser served a brief term in prison in 1961 for destroying evidence and was fined $12,000 in 1971 for illegal shakedowns of local businesses. Presser's growing influence in the Teamsters culminated in his election as vice-president for the International Union in 1967, a position he held for the rest of his life.

On 15 Jan. 1928 Presser married Faye Friedman, and they had 4 children: Jack (see JACKIE PRESSER), Marvin, Toby (Mrs. Bernard Bader), and Ronald. William Presser died in Cleveland. —M.S.

James Neff. *Mobbed Up: Jackie Presser's High-Wire Life in the Teamsters, the Mafia and the F.B.I.* (1989).

**PRICE, GRACE FINLEY "MOMMA GRACE"** (30 April 1896–2 July 1992) was, with her husband, Rodgers, a pioneer African American entrepreneur. Born in Paulding, OH, to Ida Stuart, Grace attended Paulding public schools. She met Rodgers in Toledo, and they lived in Detroit before coming to Cleveland in 1927.

The Prices' first business was the Log Cabin Grille, an African American restaurant and nightclub at E. 55th & Central. In the 1940s they purchased Shauter's Drug Store (see SHAUTER DRUG CO.†) at E. 55th & Woodland, the first drugstore in Cleveland to employ African American pharmacists. They also opened the first medical-professional building for African Americans at East 55th & Woodland, and built United Recreation Center at E. 85th & Cedar, the only place in Cleveland where African Americans could bowl.

An avid 50-year plus golfer, Grace and her husband golfed at Cedar and Warrensville Center Rd. on the only golf course where African Americans were allowed. They introduced golf to Cleveland's African American community when they founded the Six City Golf Assn. in the early 1930s.

Grace married Oscar A. Scott on 9 Mar. 1914 and had a daughter, Helen Marie (Ellis). Grace married Rodgers Price (d. 1989) on 28 Oct. 1929 and had a daughter, Allistine. Grace received an honorary nursing diploma from MERIDIA HURON† Hospital for her exemplary nursing care of Rodgers during his battle against cancer. Grace belonged to MT. ZION CONGREGATIONAL CHURCH.† She is buried in Lake View Cemetery.—T.B.

**PRIDGEON, LOUISE JOHNSON** (27 Jan. 1891–13 July 1932) was the first practicing African American woman lawyer in Cleveland who was also active in welfare work and politics.

Born in Gallipolis, OH, to Joseph and Mary (Ferguson) Johnson, Louise attended public school in Springfield, graduating from Springfield High School in 1907. Louise came to Cleveland in 1913 and found work as a bookkeeper.

In 1917 Louise took a special course in social science at Wester Rerserve Univ. and also studied at Ohio Univ. and Northwestern Univ. She worked at the Goodrich Settlement House (see GOODRICH-GANNETT NEIGHBORHOOD CTR.†) and the Playhouse Settlement (see KARAMU HOUSE†), and later as a volunteer social worker with the WOMEN'S PROTECTIVE ASSN.† and as a probation officer at the Central Police Station. During World War I she was a field worker in the U.S. Interdepartmental Social Hygiene Board.

Pridgeon graduated from Cleveland Law School in 1922 and was admitted to the Ohio Bar. As a partner in the firm of Frey & Pridgeon, she practiced during the 1920s and 1930s in courts of the Northern District of Ohio and specialized in Federal Court practice.

Pridgeon was president of the Women's Civic

Organization of the East Side, the Harlan Law Club, a member of the Cleveland Federation of Colored Women's Clubs, and a contributor and supporter of the PHILLIS WHEATLEY ASSN.† She ran for City Council in the Fourth District in 1931.

Louise married Frank Pridgeon. They had no children. She belonged to St. Andrew's Episcopal Church and is buried in Highland Park Cemetery. —T.B.

**PROSSER, DILLON** (2 July 1813–11 Apr. 1897), a Methodist leader and pioneer in social work as founder of the "Ragged School," was born in Otsego County, NY. At age 17 was licensed to "exhort," and after 2 years at Western Reserve Seminary, received a license to preach in 1833. Prosser worked in churches in Pittsburgh, 1834–36, was ordained a deacon in 1836, and moved to Erie, at 25 becoming an elder, the highest office he would achieve.

Prosser came to Cleveland in 1850, in 1853 opening a mission school for poor children. The "Ragged School" was an outreach effort of a young men's prayer group, forerunner of the YMCA; relief work was directed toward "the rescue of destitute children." With the assistance of women volunteers, Prosser visited homes reported to have malnourished, abused, or "idle" children. At school these children received instruction, clothes, food, and shelter. The school was reorganized in 1856 as the City Industrial School and in later years changed names several times as it was managed by different charities. Prosser was responsible for organizing 9 Methodist Episcopal churches in Cleveland and several others outside the city. He made money from real estate investments and contributed a considerable part of it, including land, to religious and charitable work. Prosser married 3 times. In 1840 he married Caroline Blakeslee. After her death in 1849, he married May Holloway in 1850. She died a few years later, and he married Cornelia McFarlane of CHAGRIN FALLS† in 1856. Prosser was buried in Lake View Cemetery.

**PRUSHECK, HARVEY GREGORY** (11 March 1888–7 June 1940), son of Jerney and Maria Prusheck, was a Slovenian artist and art teacher who came to Cleveland from Austria-Hungary at age 14. Several of his paintings won prizes at art shows in Chicago in 1930 and 1932, and his Slovene Village is in the permanent collection at the CLEVELAND MUSEUM OF ART.† In Cleveland, Prusheck founded the Yugoslav School of Art and served as its director and instructor. He also became director of the city's Crafts & Art Ctr. Showings of Prusheck's and his students' work were held at the SLOVENIAN NATL. HOME† in the 1930s. Prusheck and his wife, May, had a daughter, Mariann.

He died in Cleveland and was buried in Highland Park Cemetery.

**PRUTTON, CARL F.** (30 July 1898–15 July 1970), chemical engineer and educator, was born in Cleveland to Daniel and Julia Seelbach Prutton. He attended Purdue Univ. (1915–16) before serving in Mexico with the Natl. Guard., graduated from Case School of Applied Science in 1920, and joined the school's faculty as an instructor in chemistry. He received a master's in chemical engineering from Case in 1923, and a doctorate in physical chemistry from Western Reserve Univ. in 1928.

Prutton became an asst. professor in 1925, associate professor in 1929, and full professor and chairman of the Dept. of Chemistry & Chemical Engineering in 1936. He developed new courses and laboratory programs, oversaw the construction of a new laboratory in 1938, and created a program in graduate study in chemistry. Prutton also served as a consultant to several companies, among them Dow Chemical (1921, 1928–41) and LUBRIZOL CORP.† (1929–51). In 1944–45, he took a leave of absence from Case to serve full-time as the director of research. Working both on his own and with ALBERT KELVIN SMITH, Prutton was responsible for more than 100 patents, known in the oil and chemical industries as "the Prutton patents."

Prutton resigned from Case in 1948 to join Olin Mathieson Chemical Corp. in Baltimore as director of research, becoming a vice-president in 1949. In 1954 he joined Food Machinery & Chemical Corp. in San Jose, CA, as vice-president and director of the chemical division. He retired in 1960 and lived in Florida.

Prutton married Marie Agatha Saunders in 1919. They had six children: Helen (Mrs. George C. Conrad), Mary (Mrs. Robt. L. Sutherland), Carolyn (Mrs. J. Robinsmall), Dorothy (Mrs. Jose Castillo), Carl, and John. He died in New York City and was buried in Calvary Cemetery.

**PUCKETT, NEWBELL NILES** (8 July 1898–21 Feb. 1967), educator, sociologist, and folklorist, was born in Columbus, MS, to Willis Newbell and Matilda (Boyd) Puckett. He received his B.S. (1918) from Mississippi College at Clinton, and his Ph.B. (1920), A.M. (1921), and Ph.D. (1925) from Yale Univ. In 1919 he was a hospital apprentice in the navy, joining the sociology faculty of Western Reserve Univ. in 1922. He was appointed professor in 1938, and was chairman of the Sociology Dept. from 1954–62.

Puckett's life was devoted to traditional folk cultures, from black studies to ethnic traditions, rural and urban. He studied naming practices, superstitions, folk beliefs, wit and humor, and religious beliefs on field trips to the deep South, throughout Ohio, and into the Canadian wilderness. He was president of the Ohio and Cleveland folklore societies and elected a fellow of the American Folklore Society (1959). Puckett wrote *Folk Beliefs of the Southern Negro* (1926) and *Names of American Negro Slaves* (1937), and offered a pioneering course in black studies at WRU. He compiled detailed, extensive collections of data on "Black Names," "Religious Life of the Southern Negro," "Canadian Lumberjack Songs," and "Ohio Superstitions and Popular Beliefs." His papers, tapes, transcripts, and photographs are part of the Newbell Niles Puckett Memorial Gift deposited in the John G. White Collection of CLEVELAND PUBLIC LIBRARY.†

Puckett was married twice. His first wife was Marion A. Randall (d. 1959) whom he married in 1923. He then married Ruth Neuer in 1960. Puckett had three children: Randy W., Robert K., and Sally N. He is buried in Knollwood Mausoleum.

**PUEHRINGER, FERDINAND** (2 Nov. 1841–15 Sept. 1930), impresario, conductor, composer, and teacher, came to America in 1863 from Vilma, Austria, after having studied music with Franz Von Suppe. He became a professor of music at Wittenberg College in Springfield, OH, and came to Cleveland in 1872. As an impresario, Puehringer put the GERMANIA ORCHESTRA† on a sound financial basis by beginning subscription concerts. He organized and directed many of his own groups, including the Boys Band; a singing and orchestra school; and the PHILHARMONIC ORCHESTRA,† 30 amateur, then later professional musicians, which gave its first performance on 31 Oct. 1881 to benefit the Society for Organizing Charities. He also produced many operas, including Lortzing's *Der Waffenschmied* (1874), and *The Czar and Zimmerman, The Bohemian Girl* with EFFIE ELLSLER, and Offenbach's *Orpheus in the Underworld* (1876). Puehringer later became director of the Park Theatre Orchestra. In 1887 his light opera *Captain Cupid,* with libretto by Wm. R. Rose of the *PLAIN DEALER†* and Wm. E. Sage of the *CLEVELAND LEADER,†* was produced. His other works include *The Hero of Erie* (about Oliver Hazard Perry's battle on Lake Erie in 1813), and *Anna Liese.*

Puehringer married Mary Emich (d. 1938) and had 1 child, Ritta (Caldwell). He was buried in Highland Park Cemetery.

**PURNELL, EDWARD WARD, M.D.** (21 Feb. 1928–8 Oct. 1993) was a physician, surgeon, researcher, and director of Ophthalmology at CASE WESTERN RESERVE UNIV.† School of Medicine and UNIV. HOSPITALS† of Cleveland. During the 1960s and 1970s Dr. Purnell pioneered the application of ultrasound to the study of the eye and the diagnosis of eye diseases, and developed new techniques in eye surgery using sound waves.

Born in Youngstown, Purnell attended Rayen School and graduated from Mercersburg (PA) Academy (1946). He received his A.B. from Princeton Univ. (1950), M.D. from WESTERN RESERVE UNIV.† School of Medicine (1957), and studied ophthalmology (1958–59) at Harvard Medical School. He served in the U.S. Navy (1950–53) during the Korean War.

Purnell completed his internship and residency at Univ. Hospitals (1957–61). He joined CWRU as an Instructor of Ophthalmology (1961–62), advancing to senior instructor (1962–64), asst. professor (1964–68), assoc. professor (1968) and full professor. He was appointed director of the Division of Ophthalmology (1973) and Charles I. Thomas Professor Emeritus of Ophthalmology (1976).

In 1961 Purnell obtained a National Institutes of Health grant to use ultrasound to study ocular disease and physiology. Assisted by Dr. Adnan Sokullo, Purnell pioneered the use of high-frequency sound waves to push back into place a detached retina, and of even higher frequencies to weld it into place. Purnell and associates then designed an ultrasound scanner enabling ophthalmologists to identify which patients may benefit from certain types of eye surgery.

Purnell married Marjorie Eynon and had 4 children: Edward, Laura, Jennie, and Frank. Purnell lived in EUCLID† and is enurned in Lake View Cemetery.—T.B.

**PUTNAM, MILDRED OLIVE ANDREWS** (19 June 1890 or 1892–13 April 1984) and **PETER ANDREWS PUTNAM** (1925–1987) were art benefactors and philanthropists who funded numerous notable causes, including 3 projects in Sandusky, Ashtabula, Franklin, and Pickaway counties. They left a $37 million bequest in their wills to the Nature Conservancy, the largest nonprofit land preservation group in the world. Mildred's benevolence was through various family foundations and funds bearing her own name, and that of her husband, John B. Putnam, a prominent Cleveland lawyer.

Born in Norwalk, OH, to Horace and Laura (Dempsey) Andrews, Mildred graduated from HATHAWAY BROWN SCHOOL† in 1909. After her husband's death, Mildred assumed control of the family real estate and investment holdings. She kept an office in the Point Building, and owned the Winous Building on PLAYHOUSE SQUARE.† She spent millions on sculptures and paintings by such artists as Picasso, Henry Moore, Jacques Lipchitz, and George Segal, which she presented to Princeton

Univ., CASE WESTERN RESERVE UNIV.† and the CLEVELAND MUSEUM OF ART.† In 1978 Mildred commissioned Segal to sculpt a memorial to the Kent State Univ. students killed by Ohio National Guard troops in 1970. KSU officials rejected the proposed sculpture of Abraham ready to sacrifice his son, Isaac, as "inappropriate" and "too violent." She then gave it to Princeton Univ.

Mildred was a member of the vestry of TRINITY CATHEDRAL† from 1970–74. She endowed a special music program which included the series of free concerts at noon for people who want to eat a brown-bag lunch while listening to music.

Mildred and John Berman Putnam married on 29 Dec. 1917. They had two sons, John Jr. (died in World War II) and Peter. An Episcopalian, Mildred lived in BRATENAHL† and died in Houma, LA. She is buried in Lake View Cemetery.

Born in Cleveland to John and Mildred Putnam, Peter earned a doctoral degree in physics at Princeton Univ., where he apprenticed under Albert Einstein. Peter eventually moved to Houma, LA, where he lived a spartan existence with a friend in a modest apartment. He worked as a night watchman and janitor while writing philosophical essays and monitoring the family's stock portfolio. He was killed by a drunken driver while riding his bicycle at night. Although eccentric, Peter tripled his family's fortune by successfully investing in stock ventures. His will left the bulk of his estate to the Nature Conservancy.—T.B.

**PYKE, BERNICE SECREST** (22 Mar. 1880–10 May 1964), the first woman ever elected a delegate to a national political convention and the first woman to serve in a Cleveland mayor's cabinet, was born Bernice Secrest in Frankfort, Ross County, OH. After high school graduation in Chillicothe, OH, in 1898, she attended Ohio Wesleyan Univ. and received her A.B. degree from Smith College in 1902. She taught mathematics in Illinois schools until her marriage in 1905, when she and her husband came to Cleveland. Pyke was active in the women's suffrage movement in Cuyahoga County and in 1920 was elected a delegate to the Democratic Natl. Convention, where she was in charge of the women's effort to promote the candidacy of Gov. Jas. M. Cox of Ohio for president. She was elected a delegate to 4 more national Democratic conventions. Mayor RAY T. MILLER appointed her director of public welfare in 1932; she served through 1933. In 1934 Pres. Franklin Roosevelt appointed her collector of customs for the Cleveland district, a position she held until 1953. She had married Arthur B. Pyke on 4 Jan. 1905, and had a son, John Secrest Pyke. She died at her home.

# Q

**QUAYLE, THOMAS** (9 May 1811–31 Jan. 1895), with his partner, John S. Martin, an important Cleveland shipbuilder and Democratic city councilman, was born on the Isle of Man, where he learned ship carpentry. Coming to the U.S. with his parents in 1827, he became an apprentice ship carpenter and entered into his first shipbuilding partnership in 1847 with John Cody. In 1850 he took on a new partner, Luther Moses, and the business prospered, with sometimes 7 ships under construction at once. But it was the partnership of Quayle and Martin (1854–74), that enjoyed the greatest success, building as many as 12 or 13 ships a year and by 1865 turning business away. Quayle continued building ships after Martin's death, taking on 2 of his sons, Thos. E. and Geo. L., as partners in Quayle & Sons. Quayle's firms built some of the largest wooden ships on the lakes, such as the 2,082-ton *Commodore* in 1875, reportedly the largest ship on the lakes at the time. They were considered pioneers in the development of large wooden propellers. When the elder Quayle retired from shipbuilding in the early 1880s, a third son, William, joined the firm and the business continued as Thos. Quayle's Sons for the next decade, until steel vessels replaced wooden ships on the lakes. Quayle married twice. His first marriage was to Eleanor Cannon (d. 1860) in 1835; they had 11 children, 8 of whom survived to adulthood: Thomas, William, George, Charles, Matilda, Kate, Mary, and Caroline. In 1867 he married Mary Proudfoot. Quayle died in Cleveland and was buried in Woodland Cemetery.

**QUINTRELL, MARY CORINNE** (8 Jan. 1839–18 July 1918) was an educator in Cleveland public schools who introduced the phonic method of teaching reading, and a founder of the CLEVELAND SOROSIS SOCIETY.†

Born in St. Austell, Cornwall, England, Quintrell came to Cleveland with her parents, Thomas and Emma Brewer Quintrell. Quintrell attended Cleveland (West) High School where she edited the high school paper, the first school publication west of the Cuyahoga River, and was its first female graduate in 1857.

Quintrell resided in Cleveland while devoting herself to teaching, becoming the first graduate of Cleveland (West) High School to teach in public schools. For nearly 25 years she taught reading using the phonic method and trained fellow teachers to use the system. She authored large portions of the chart used in teaching reading in the schools and worked to restore Bible reading in the classroom.

For nearly 30 years Quintrell supplied area hospitals with reading materials. She frequented Lakeside Hospital conducting the singing for religious services for the patients and distributing literature.

As a leader in women's activities, Quintrell became the first woman to run in the Republican primaries as a candidate for the Cleveland School Council in 1895.

Quintrell wrote many papers and poems for Cleveland clubs, several of which had been published. She was an original trustee and charter member of the Cleveland Sorosis Society, founded on 7 Oct. 1891. She chaired both the parliamentary law and art departments for the society and contributed numerous writings. Quintrell never married. A Presbyterian, she is buried in Lake View Cemetery. —T.B.

R

**RADDATZ, WILLIAM JOSEPH** (25 Feb. 1880–29 July 1940), printing executive and Shakespeare scholar, was born in Cleveland, the son of Herman and Mary Ann (Peters) Raddatz. After graduating from St. Ignatius High School, he attended St. Ignatius College, receiving an A.B. degree in 1901 and an M.A. degree in 1912. He was a Cleveland *PLAIN DEALER†* reporter before entering the advertising and lithograph business in 1903, and founded Stratford Press in 1911. In the mid–1920s he incorporated his printing business as W. J. Raddatz & Co. and later served as vice-president of A. S. Gilman, another printing concern. A recognized authority on Shakespeare, Raddatz was interested in confirming that Shakespeare wrote the works attributed to him. As a result, he penned "Shakespeare Wrote Shakespeare" and "Bacon and Shakespeare Paralleled." He also wrote "Golden Texts from Shakespeare" and served as a visiting lecturer at Ursuline College for Women. Involved in diverse activities, Raddatz was a delegate to the first World Court Congress in 1915 and served as chairman of publicity for Liberty Loans in the 4th Federal Reserve District during World War I. Active as a trustee and board member of many local charities, he made a substantial contribution to the betterment of the Cleveland community.

Raddatz married Mary Eleanor (Mollie) Leslie 25 April 1906, and they had 2 children, William Leslie and Edward Dustin. He died in Cleveland at age 60 and was buried at Calvary Cemetery.—M.S.

**RAINEY, SHERLIE HEREFORD** (3 Feb. 1939–7 Aug. 1992), mayor of WOODMERE† (1985–89) was the first African American woman to hold a mayoral position in Cuyahoga County. In 1991 she received the highest number of votes in the Woodmere Village Council race. Also an athlete, Rainey set an American record for the standing long jump (1958) and was National Amateur Athletic Union champion of that event for 3 years. She was elected to the Greater Cleveland Sports Hall of Fame in 1991. Rainey was born in Cleveland to Jessie and Beatrice (Smith) Hereford. She graduated from EAST TECHNICAL HIGH SCHOOL† (1956) and studied at Talladega College in Alabama before graduating from CLEVELAND STATE UNIV.† She later attended CASE WESTERN RESERVE UNIV.'s† School of Applied Social Sciences. Rainey taught at East Tech (1960s), worked with underprivileged minorities for the U.S. Department of Labor, and later became an independent insurance agent. On 24 Oct. 1969 Rainey married William F. Rainey, Jr.; they had 2 sons, William F. III and Charles E. She played the trumpet at the Evangelical Community Church in EUCLID,† where she was a member.

Rainey won a position on the Woodmere City Council in 1977 and later served 2 terms as council president. Despite charges raised against her in 1988 for obstruction and in 1991 for financial mismanagement during her mayoral term, she was elected to the council again in 1991. Rainey died in Cleveland and was buried in Hillcrest Cemetery.—J.M.

**RAMMELKAMP, CHARLES HENRY, JR.** (24 May 1911–5 Dec. 1981), scientist and teaching physician who discovered that streptococcus bacteria causes rheumatic fever, was born in Jacksonville, IL, to Charles Henry and Jeanette Capps Rammelkamp. He graduated from Illinois College with an A.B. (1933) and from the Univ. of Chicago with an M.D. (1937). He was an assistant in medicine at Washington Univ. in St. Louis (1939); research fellow in medicine at Harvard Univ. (1939–40); and instructor of medicine at Boston Univ. (1940–46). During World War II he was a member of the army's commission on acute respiratory diseases. In 1946 Rammelkamp became asst. professor of medicine and preventive medicine at Western Reserve Univ. Medical School. He was assoc. professor of preventive medicine (1947–60); professor of medicine (1950–60); and professor of preventive medicine (1960–80). In 1950 he became research director at City Hospital, and was director of medicine from 1957–80. At his retirement he was named professor emeritus.

In 1948 Rammelkamp became a member of the army's streptococcal disease commission and field director of its laboratory in Cheyenne, WY. There he and his research team studied men with sore throats and discovered that streptococcal bacteria throat infection can lead to rheumatic fever; therefore, adequate penicillin at the time of strep throat prevents rheumatic fever. In 1952 Rammelkamp and Dr. John Dingle identified the specific strain of streptococcus bacteria that causes the kidney disease acute nephritis. In 1954 Rammelkamp was awarded the Lasker Award for his discoveries.

Rammelkamp married Helen Chisholm and had 3 children: Charles H., III, Colin C., and Anne R. (Davies). He died in Cleveland.

**RANKIN, ALFRED M.** (19 July 1913–23 Jan. 1994), a corporate and estate lawyer by profession, was best known for his extensive commitments to community service, and especially for his work on behalf of the CLEVELAND ORCHESTRA.†

Son of Henry P. and Anne Marshall Rankin, Alfred was born in Beaver, PA. When he was a child, the family moved to Cleveland, where he attended UNIV. SCHOOL.† He then earned his baccalaureate and professional degrees from Yale College and Yale Law School.

Back in Cleveland, he joined the firm of THOMPSON, HINE & FLORY,† eventually becoming senior partner. On 30 Mar. 1940, he married Clara L. Taplin, and they raised five sons: Alfred M., Jr., Thomas, Clairborne, Roger, and Bruce.

During World War II he served as a naval intelligence officer aboard the carrier USS *Tripoli.*

Returning to Cleveland, Rankin began a distinguished career of service to Cleveland institutions. His commitments included: WESTERN RESERVE HISTORICAL SOCIETY,† UNIV. CIRCLE, INC.,† the YMCA, Cleveland Zoological Society (see CLEVELAND METROPARKS ZOO†), the SHAKER LAKES† Nature Center, HAWKEN SCHOOL,† the Boy Scouts, and the CLEVELAND SOCIETY FOR THE BLIND,† to which he was

particularly devoted. He also served as president of Cleveland's MUSICARNIVAL† and trustee of the American Museum of Natural History in New York City.

He is probably best remembered, however, for his long service to the MUSICAL ARTS ASSN.,† parent organization of the Cleveland Orchestra. He joined its board in 1948, became its president in 1968, and chairman in 1983. He guided the efforts to hire music directors Loren Maazel and Christoph von Dohnanyi and was a key figure in the planning and development of Blossom Music Center. Rankin was buried in Lake View Cemetery.—J.T.

**RANNEY, RUFUS P.** (30 Oct. 1813–6 Dec. 1891), lawyer and jurist, was born in Blandford, MA, to Rufus and Dollie (Blair) Ranney. He moved to Freedom, Portage County, OH, in 1824, and enrolled in Nelson Academy and later Western Reserve College, but was unable to finish because of lack of means. In 1835 Ranney began studying law with JOSHUA GIDDINGS and Benjamin Wade in Jefferson, and was admitted to the bar in 1836. When Giddings entered Congress in 1838, Wade and Ranney formed a law partnership. In 1845 Ranney opened a law office in Warren, in 1846 and 1848 making unsuccessful bids for that district's congressional seat. In 1850 Ranney was a delegate to the convention revising Ohio's constitution, gaining recognition as one of the convention's leading figures while serving in the judicial department and on the revision, enrollment, and arrangement committees.

In 1851 Ranney became a judge on the Ohio Supreme Court. In 1856 he resigned from the court and moved to Cleveland, where he resumed practicing law as senior member of Ranney, Backus & Noble. In 1857 he was appointed U.S. attorney for northern Ohio, but resigned after 2 months. In 1858 Ranney made an unsuccessful bid to become governor. Against his express desire, Ranney was nominated and elected for the state supreme court again in 1862; he resigned in 1865 and resumed his Cleveland law practice. In 1881 he was unanimously elected the first president of the Ohio Bar Assn.

Ranney married Adeline W. Warner on 1 May 1839. They had 7 children: Rufus P., Jr., John R., Charles, Richard, Howard, Cornelia, and Harriet. Ranney died in Cleveland and was buried in Lake View Cemetery.

**RANSOM, CAROLINE L. ORMES** (1838–18 Feb. 1910) was a portrait painter born in Newark, OH, daughter of John and Elizabeth Ransom. She began her art education in New York, taught by A. B. Durand, Thos. Hicks, and Donald Huntington in landscapes, figure painting, and portraits. She then studied 2 years with Wilhelm von Kaulkoch in Munich. Ransom returned to America in 1860, setting up a studio in Cleveland. Her specialty was portraits, and her subjects included Col. CHAS. W. WHITTLESEY, first president of the WESTERN RESERVE HISTORICAL SOCIETY†; Gen. Jas. B. McPherson; Benjamin Franklin Wade, lawyer and statesman; and Gen. JAS A. GARFIELD in military dress. Ransom was paid an extraordinary amount of money for the time for her portraits. In 1867 Congress allowed $1,000 for a portrait of JOSHUA R. GIDDINGS, and in 1875, $15,000 for one of Gen. Geo. H. Thomas. Both likenesses were hung in the Capitol in Washington. In 1876 Ransom was unanimously elected an honorary member of the Army of the Cumberland, the only woman so honored. She was a founder of the Daughters of the American Revolution. She moved to Washington, DC, in 1884, combining her studio and living quarters so she could paint constantly. The walls were covered with copies of the masters' works and her own work in progress. Ransom also founded the Classical Society and was its leader for 15 years. Never married, Ransom died in Washington DC, and was buried in Lake View Cemetery.

**RAPER, JOHN W. "JACK"** (20 Feb. 1870–12 Dec. 1950), journalist, was born in McArthur, Vinton County, OH, son of John T. and Sarah Frances (Wolfe) Raper. He was raised in Chillicothe, where his father edited the *Scioto Gazette*. He began newspaper work at 19 and worked in several cities before joining the *CLEVELAND PRESS†* in 1899. Beginning as drama critic, he caused a 2-year boycott of *Press* advertising by theater managers for such barbed reviews as his 3-word classic "Burn a rag." Raper began his daily column, "Most Anything," in 1900. It usually started with a down-to-earth philosophical observation by Raper's rustic alter ego, "Josh Wise." Once a week, events in an imaginary small town were chronicled in "All the News from Hicksville." The column's most popular feature was the "bullpen," first appearing in 1907, where the most pompous pronouncements by public figures were simply reprinted verbatim, alongside a bold cut of a bull, which ultimately came in 3 sizes, according to the egregiousness of the offense.

Raper was a frequent speaker and a member of the leftist "Soviet Table" at the CITY CLUB.† Raper supported Franklin Roosevelt long after the *Press* had abandoned him. During World War II, Raper published a detailed description of the army's "Forbidden City" of Los Alamos, more than a year before the bombing of Hiroshima. In 1945 he compiled a book from his "Josh Wise" sayings titled *What This World Needs*. Raper married Marie A.

Delahunt in 1899 and had a daughter, Dorothy (Mrs. Wick R. Miller). Retiring in 1947, he died in Pueblo, CO, but was buried in Lake View Cemetery.

**RAPPE, LOUIS AMADEUS** (2 Feb. 1801–8 Sept. 1877), first bishop of the Diocese of Cleveland, was born in Audrehem, France, to Eloi and Marie-Antoinette Noel Rappe. He studied at the college of Boulogne-sur-Mer and the seminary at Arras, and was ordained in 1829. Rappe was a parish priest before becoming chaplain of the Ursuline nuns at Boulogne-sur-Mer, where he met Cincinnati bishop John B. Purcell, who was recruiting priests for Ohio. Rappe arrived in America in 1840, and Purcell named him pastor of St. Francis de Sales Parish in Toledo. Rappe established a school and academy and became an advocate of the Total Abstinence Movement (see FATHER MATHEW TOTAL ABSTINENCE SOCIETY†). On 23 Apr. 1847, Pope Pius IX established the new Diocese of Cleveland, and Rappe was consecrated bishop of the diocese on 10 Oct. 1847 in Cincinnati.

In Cleveland, Rappe began work on ST. JOHN CATHEDRAL,† created new congregations for Irish and German groups, and made trips to Europe to recruit priests and nuns. The Ursulines from Boulogne-sur-Mer came to teach, and the Daughters of the Immaculate Heart of Mary opened 2 orphanages for girls: ST. MARY'S† (1851) and ST. JOSEPH'S† (1863). Rappe organized the SISTERS OF CHARITY OF ST. AUGUSTINE,† who opened the first general hospital in Cleveland, ST. VINCENT CHARITY,† in 1857. Concerned about priestly training, Rappe began St. Francis de Sales Seminary, which became ST. MARY SEMINARY.† Rappe resigned in 1870 and spent his last years as a missionary in Vermont and Canada, dying at St. Albans, VT. He was buried in St. John Cathedral in Cleveland.

**RATNER, LEONARD** (1896–30 Dec. 1974), businessman, Jewish community leader, and philanthropist, was born Leiser Ratowczer in Bialystok, Russia, son of Moishe and Pesha (Koppelman) Ratowczer. He received a Jewish education and entered the weaving trade. He emigrated to the U.S. in 1920 and settled in Cleveland in 1921, first working as a weaver, but soon quitting to open first one, then a second creamery with his sister, Dora, and brother, Max. They sold the creameries in 1926 to concentrate on the lumber and building business. Chas. Ratner, another brother, established Forest City Lumberyard in 1922 and in 1924 helped Leonard open Buckeye Lumber. In 1929, Leonard turned the lumberyard over to his brother Max and established the B. & F. Bldg. Co. He specialized in constructing 3-bedroom homes, erecting houses primarily in E. CLEVELAND,† EUCLID,† and along Lake Shore Blvd. In 1934 Leonard joined Forest City Lumber (see FOREST CITY ENTERPRISES†).

Leonard was active in Jewish communal affairs. In 1931 he began volunteer work with the Jewish Welfare Fed., serving as treasurer and vice-president during the 1960s, and elected honorary life trustee in 1966. In 1961 he was elected honorary trustee for life of MT. SINAI HOSPITAL† after serving on the Board of Trustees for 2 decades. The Ratner family helped build PARK SYNAGOGUE† in CLEVELAND HTS.†; Leonard was its president from 1952–55. Ratner also served a number of national Jewish organizations. In 1924 he married Lillian Bernstein, founder of the Lillian Ratner Montessori School at Park Synagogue. They had 2 children, Albert and Ruth. Ratner died in Florida and was buried in Park Synagogue Cemetery.

Tanzer, Shirley Blum. *The Ratner House* (1988).

**RATNER, MAX** (26 Dec. 1907–31 May 1995), business executive, Jewish community leader, and philanthropist, was born Meyer Ratowczer, the son of Moishe and Pesha (Koppelman) Ratowczer in Bialystok, Russia (now Poland). He attended German- and Hebrew-sponsored schools in Bialystok. In 1920 he and his family emigrated to America, following the lead of his brother, Charles. The family arrived in Cleveland in 1921 and adopted the Ratner surname.

The family settled on Cleveland's east side, where Max Ratner attended and graduated from Glenville High School. In 1925 he began working at the family's lumber business. He graduated from CLEVELAND-MARSHALL LAW SCHOOL† in 1929 and began working as an attorney. Along with his brothers, Charles and LEONARD RATNER, he was one of the founders of Forest City Materials (later FOREST CITY ENTERPRISES†), which he incorporated in 1929. He served as president of the company from 1929 until 1975, and as chairman of the board from 1975 until his death.

Ratner was also widely known for his work in the Jewish and Cleveland civic communities, as well as for his efforts on behalf of Israel, especially through building that nation's economy. Locally he served as president of PARK SYNAGOGUE† in the late 1960s. He was a founder (1978) and later president of the New York-based American-Israeli Chamber of Commerce and Industry, and one of the organizers of Israel's Electro-Chemical Industries, Ltd., also serving as president.

Ratner married Betty Wohlvert on 7 May 1939. They had four sons: Charles (Chuck), Mark, James, and Ronald. Ratner died in SHAKER HTS.† and was buried in Park Synagogue Cemetery, BEACHWOOD.†—D.R.

Tanzer, Shirley Blum. *The Ratner House* (1988).

**RAUSCHKOLB, RUTH (ROBISHAW), M.D.** (24 Nov. 1900–13 Jan. 1981), dermatologist, was the first (and, as of 1994, the only) woman president of the CLEVELAND MEDICAL LIBRARY ASSN.† (1968), the first woman president of the Cleveland Dermatologic Society, and among the first women to teach at CASE WESTERN RESERVE UNIV.† Medical School and intern at City Hospital (later Cleveland Metropolitan General Hospital). Rauschkolb was born in Cleveland to Elizabeth (Williams) and William Robishaw; her father, a steelworker, died when she was a child. She graduated valedictorian from East High School, received a B.A. from Ohio State Univ. (1921) as a member of Phi Beta Kappa, and graduated at the top of her class from the medical school of Western Reserve Univ. (WRU, 1923). She later studied dermatology at the CLEVELAND CLINIC FOUNDATION,† at Bellevue Hospital in New York, and elsewhere. After a brief internship at City Hospital, Rauschkolb could not obtain a residency due to her age and gender. She opened her own practice and after her marriage entered into dermatology practice with her husband. (She practiced under both her married and maiden names.) After his death in 1954, Rauschkolb continued the practice. She began her teaching career as a demonstrator in pediatrics at WRU (1924–29) and taught there continuously from 1943 until retiring as Associate Clinical Professor of Dermatology in 1978. She headed both the dermatology division (1956–65) and the diabetes clinic (1952–54) at Cleveland Metropolitan General Hospital, served as staff physician (1954–64) and trustee of FOREST CITY HOSPITAL,† and was clinical physician and a member of the Medical Advisory Board of the Maternal Health Assn. (later PLANNED PARENTHOOD OF GREATER CLEVELAND†) at its inception (1928). She also helped organize and was a charter member of the Cleveland Diabetes Assn.

Rauschkolb lived in SHAKER HTS.† after her marriage in 1926 to John E. Rauschkolb, M.D.; their two daughters, Elizabeth (Mrs. Gordon) Farrell and Diana Bogdonoff, both practiced dermatology. Rauschkolb is buried in Lake View Cemetery.—J.M.

Dittrick Museum of Medical History.

**RAWSON, BARBARA HAAS** (28 Dec. 1918–21 Sept. 1990) was a prominent woman executive long active in civic and political affairs. She helped establish the Greater Cleveland Associated Foundation, which later merged with the CLEVELAND FOUNDATION.† She was also the first woman appointed to the newly created Ohio Ethics Commission.

Born in Cleveland, she graduated from Shaker Hts. High School in 1936, and received her bachelor's degree from Bennington College in 1940. After college she worked in the U.S. Department of Agriculture in Washington, DC, and then at the Office of War Information during World War II.

In 1961 the Greater Cleveland Associated Foundation was formed with financing from the Ford Foundation and the Leonard C. Hanna Fund. The foundation sought to address urban problems through philanthropy. In 1967 the Greater Cleveland Associated Foundation merged with the Cleveland Foundation. Rawson served as its asst. director and, in 1973 and 1974, was interim director.

In 1973 Rawson was appointed by Gov. John Gilligan to serve a 4-year term on the Ohio Ethics Commission. She was a member of the Cuyahoga County League of Women Voters and Citizens League of Cleveland. Rawson received the Distinguished Citizen Award from the National Civic League and, in 1989, shared the Citizen of the Year Award by the Citizens League of Greater Cleveland with her husband, Robert H. Rawson, president of Empire Plow Co.

The Rawsons married on 20 Sept. 1941 and had two children, Robert H., Jr., and Susan R. Driscoll. They attended the First Unitarian Church of Cleveland. Rawson was cremated.—T.B.

**RAWSON, LOUISE R. BARRON** (31 Jan. 1843–24 June 1920) spurred the kindergarten movement in Cleveland as the third president of the CLEVELAND DAY NURSERY AND FREE KINDERGARTEN ASSN.† (1885–1908). She directed efforts to establish a nursery for Italian mothers, which evolved into ALTA HOUSE† and served on its first Board of Trustees. Rawson also presided over the local WOMAN'S CHRISTIAN TEMPERANCE UNION, NONPARTISAN† (1880). Born in Vermont to Eliza (Carpenter) and William Barron, Rawson was raised by grandparents after her mother's death. She studied education and accepted a teaching position at Cleveland's CENTRAL HIGH SCHOOL† (1866). Within the next few years, LINDA (LUCINDA THAYER) GUILFORD hired her to teach at the second Cleveland Academy. One of her students was FLORA STONE MATHER, later Rawson's close friend and associate. Rawson and fellow teacher Mary Ingersoll took an administrative role at the academy in 1871 while Guilford was overseas, after the accidental drowning of acting principal Julia Hopkins.

In 1872 Rawson left teaching to marry civil engineer Marius E. Rawson (d. 1919); the couple lived near what later became UNIV. CIRCLE† with one child, Willie. Rawson then became active in TEMPERANCE† and education reform and worked to better conditions for CHILDREN AND YOUTH.† During her tenure, the Day Nursery Assn. named one of its nurseries (formerly the Case Nursery) for her (the Louise Nursery); it also opened a pioneering kindergarten training school (1894) which drew prospective teachers from throughout the Midwest. Rawson was president of the Young Ladies' Branch of the Women's Christian Assn. (see YOUNG WOMEN'S CHRISTIAN ASSN.†) and served as vice-president of the War Emergency Relief Board (1898) of the Daughters of the American Revolution during the Spanish-American War. She died in Yankton, SD, and is buried in Lake View Cemetery.—J.M.

Cleveland Day Nursery and Free Kindergarten Assn. Records, WRHS.

**REASON, PATRICK HENRY** (1816–12 Aug. 1898), an African American engraver and lithographer, was born in New York City to Michel and Elizabeth Melville Rison and was baptized Patrice Rison. He was educated at the New York African Free School, where he made an engraving of the school that was used as the frontispiece of Chas. C. Andrew's *History of the New York African Free Schools* (1830). In 1833 he was apprenticed to an engraver; in 1835 he became interested in portraiture; and over the next 15 years he became a widely published artist whose works appeared in periodicals and as frontispieces in books, especially slave narratives. Reason was an abolitionist; he worked for Harper's and other New York publishers and did some engraving for the government, but firms often refused to hire him because their engravers would not work with him because of his race.

Reason received several employment offers from firms in Cleveland, and by 1869 moved there with his family. By 1872 he was working for jeweler Sylvester Hogan; by 1886 he had his own shop. While in New York, Reason was a founding member of the Philomatheon Society in 1830; in 1842 the society became the first lodge of the Negro Grand United Order of Odd Fellows. Reason became a prominent member of the Odd Fellows and was active in lodge affairs into the 1860s. He also lectured on the educational, social, and economic condition of black Americans.

Reason married Esther Cunningham of Leeds, England, in 1862. They had a son, Charles L. Reason died in Cleveland and was buried in Lake View Cemetery.

**REAVIS, JOHN WALLACE "JACK"** (13 Nov. 1899–27 July 1984) was a preeminent business lawyer, tax specialist, and managing partner of the law firm of JONES, DAY, REAVIS & POGUE† from 1948–75. Active in civil rights, Reavis used his influence to help promote better race relations. He received the NAACP's Human Rights Award for his work in 1969. Born in Falls City, NE, Reavis attended the public schools in Washington, DC, and received the LL.B. degree from Cornell Univ. in 1921, following service in the U.S. Navy during World War I. Reavis began his career in 1921 as an associate in the law firm of TOLLES, HOGSETT, GINN & MORLEY,† predecessor to Jones, Day, Reavis & Pogue. As a tax specialist, he was mainly responsible for developing the firm's tax practice. On 1 Jan. 1928 Reavis was made a partner in the firm, which bore his name as Jones, Day, Cockley & Reavis on 1 Jan. 1939. Reavis became managing partner in 1948 and led the firm's national expansion.

Reavis served on the Board of Directors for eleven major corporations including National City Bank and Diamond Shamrock Corp. In 1964, while Chairman of the Cleveland Chamber of Commerce (see GREATER CLEVELAND GROWTH ASSN.†) Reavis created and chaired the Interracial Business Men's Committee. Composed of business and civic leaders, the group worked to diffuse inner-city tensions and discuss grievances concerning housing, employment, and education.

Reavis married Helen H. Lincoln on 23 May 1924. They had two sons, John W. and Lincoln. Reavis, an Episcopalian, is buried in Lake View Cemetery.—T.B.

Borowitz, Albert. *Jones, Day, Reavis & Pogue: The First Century* (1993).
Peirce, Neal R. *The Megastates of America: People, Politics, and Power in the Ten Great States* (ca. 1972).

**REDINGER, RUBY VIRGINIA** (3 April 1915–9 Feb. 1981) was a Cleveland novelist and college educator whose most famous works were *The Golden Net* (1948) and *George Eliot: The Emergent Self* (1975), each of which received critical praise and established Redinger's reputation as an author.

Born in Cleveland to Elber and Maude Redinger, Ruby graduated from John Adams High School in 1932. She received her A.B. from Fenn College in 1936; an M.A. in 1937, and a Ph.D. in 1940 from Western Reserve Univ. She taught English at Cleveland College, then joined Fenn as an instructor in 1941.

Her first book, *The Golden Net*, was acclaimed as a superb novel exploring the physical, intellectual, and moral aspects of university life. The *Saturday Review of Literature* named her one of the year's outstanding new authors.

One of the most popular professors at FENN COLLEGE,† Redinger became chairman of the Philosophy Dept. in 1948. She resigned in 1951, citing administrative intimidation and restriction of faculty free speech. She joined the BALDWIN-WALLACE COLLEGE† faculty in 1951 where she taught English until her retirement in 1980.

Redinger's biographical study, *George Eliot: The Emergent Self,* was critiqued as the most insightful work yet of this literary giant. In 1976 she received the Ohioana Award for biography, and in 1977 the literary award from the Cleveland WOMEN'S CITY CLUB† and Women's Art Council. Redinger published numerous shorter works in the *American Scholar* and *Encyclopedia Americana*.

Baldwin-Wallace College established the Ruby V. Redinger Memorial Award to recognize outstanding English students. Never married, she is buried in Sunset Memorial Park.—T.B.

Fenn College President's Papers, CSU Archives.

**REED, J. ELMER** (6 May 1903–27 Dec. 1983), instrumental in integrating the sport of bowling on the local and national level, was born in Cleveland, the son of James E. and Harriet Brown Reed. He went to work for the U.S. Postal Service in 1922 and remained there for 36 years, retiring in 1958. In 1932 Reed established the Cleveland Bowlers group, which was formally organized as the Cleveland Bowling Senate in 1940 to govern local black leagues. Reed also built the United Recreation Center at 8217 Cedar Ave. in 1941, the first black-owned bowling alley in the country. A tireless promoter, Reed helped found the National Bowling Assn. in 1940 to promote blacks in bowling, serving as its secretary, and fought the caucasian clause in the American Bowling Congress (ABC) constitution which prohibited blacks from joining their ranks. The clause was removed in 1950 and as a result, Reed was admitted to the Bowling Proprietors Committee of the ABC in the early 1950s and named to its Board of Directors. Reed's achievements were recognized in March 1978 when he was the first black elected to the ABC National Hall of Fame for his contributions to the sport. He also gained membership in the GREATER CLEVELAND SPORTS HALL OF FAME† that year.

Reed married Ruth Stanard Lockhart 18 June 1938. After her death in May 1964, he married Margaret E. Jordan, 29 Oct. 1966, who survived him. There apparently were no children. Reed died in Aurora, OH, and was buried in Cleveland.

**REED, JACOB E.** (1852–9 Oct. 1935), called by one historian "the black version of the Horatio Alger myth," came to Cleveland with very little but became a wealthy businessman. He was born in Harrisburg, PA, son of Adam and Mary (Evans) Reed. He came to Cleveland in the late 1880s and worked as a waiter, streetcar conductor, and janitor before forming a partnership with Mathias Reitz to open a fish market in 1893. Located at the SHERIFF ST. MARKET† and specializing in fish, oysters, and other seafood, their business did very well, supplying some of the city's leading hotels, restaurants, and families. About 1914, Reed bought out his partner, and Reitz & Reed became the Jacob E. Reed Co. Reed's extremely successful business made him a member of the small black elite at the turn of the century; he owned a Peerless touring car and was a member of the Cleveland Automobile Club. He also owned his own home. Reed was active in civic and fraternal affairs in the black community. He was the first vice-president of the CLEVELAND ASSN. OF COLORED MEN,† a founding member of ST. ANDREWS EPISCOPAL CHURCH,† a 33rd-degree Mason, a member of the Elks, and an officer in the Odd Fellows. Reed was married three times. With his first wife, Rebecca, Reed had a daughter, Birdie. His second marriage was in 1918 to Emma Cleague (d. 1921). Reed's third wife, Rena Stowers, whom he married in 1928, survived him. Reed died in Cleveland and was buried in Woodland Cemetery.—M.S.

**REGNATZ, CAROLINA/CAROLINE OBELZ** (1879–19 Jan. 1936) was one of Cleveland's best known caterers and restaurant proprietors.

Born Carolina Obelz in Belli-Kikinda, Austria-Hungary, she was the daughter of French parents, Mr. & Mrs. Joseph Obelz. Receiving no formal education, Carolina applied herself in the catering business. She married Anton Regnatz in 1901 and they came to America in 1906.

Regnatz began catering in 1917 for churches and organizations. She operated a soup kitchen for World War I Doughboys, ran a kitchen at JOHN CARROLL Univ.,† served dinners at the Cleveland Air Races at Hopkins Airport, operated the cafeteria for *CLEVELAND NEWS†* employees, and taught a cooking school for girls attending area Catholic high schools.

In 1920 she opened her first Regnatz's restaurant, the Roseland Dining Hall, on 3218 Warren Rd. Seating 40, Regnatz expanded the Hall in 1922 to 3242 Warren, sat 400 and served nearly 1000 meals daily. Totaling 9 acres, Regnatz's Hall also included 3 baseball diamonds, swings and slides, umbrella tables for outdoor fashion shows and card parties, an outdoor stage for theatrical productions and a

winter skating rink. There also was a delicatessen offering her famous foods.

Regnatz provided limousine service from East Cleveland to her west side establishment. She opened two more restaurants, one at Fairmount and Cedar and, in 1931, Regnatz's at 3618 Euclid Ave. Caroline adopted two nephews, Joseph and Anthony, and raised them as her own. She is buried in St. Mary's Cemetery at W. 41st & Clark Ave.—T.B.

**REID, JAMES SIMS** (22 Nov. 1894–29 Nov. 1981), inventor, manufacturer, and physician, was born in Yazoo County, MS. He received an M.D. degree from the Univ. of Louisville in 1916 and then served as a medical captain in Europe during World War I. He came to Cleveland about 1920 where he worked for two years with the Cleveland Board of Health.

His entrepreneurial career began in 1920 when he invented a much-improved gas cap and radiator cap for automobiles and founded the Easy-On Cap Co. to manufacture and market his inventions. That company was sold to a forerunner of the EATON CORP.† in 1928.

"Doc" Reid then acquired the STANDARD PRODUCTS CO.† in 1930 to manufacture and market his other inventions, including a greatly improved, flexible window channel, within which automobile windows moved up and down, as well as a revolutionary rotary automobile lock. By 1954, from one to 50 parts developed by Reid could be found on every car. He also made several significant improvements to the M–1 Carbine rile, of which Standard Products was a major producer in World War II.

Standard Products early became, and still is, a world leader in the manufacture and production of automotive window channel and weather-strip. By 1981, the year of Reid's death, the company had 21 plants, 4,000 employees, and sales of $228,984,000.

Reid and his wife, Felice Marjorie Crowl (1896–1967), had three children: James Sims, George McKay, and Margaret Crowl (Mrs. Werner D. Mueller). Reid died in Sarasota, FL, and is buried in Crown Hill Cemetery, Twinsburg, OH.—D.R.

**REINBERGER, CLARENCE THOMPSON** (29 Nov. 1894–2 Dec. 1968) was a prominent businessman and philanthropist who chaired the Board of Directors of Genuine Parts Co., parent organization of NAPA auto parts stores. In 1968 he established the REINBERGER FOUNDATION† to fund and support Cleveland and Columbus area hospitals, colleges, schools, museums, and the arts.

Born in Cleveland to Nicholas and Sarah (Thompson), Reinberger was raised in Cleveland and educated in the public school system. In the 1920s,

Reinberger started work as a clerk for Automotive Parts Co. in Cleveland, which was part of the NAPA network of automotive stores and warehouses. He was then promoted to manager of the company's Akron store.

Reinberger remained with Automotive Parts, where he became president in 1947. From his office in Columbus, Reinberger oversaw the NAPA warehouses in Cleveland, Columbus, and Charleston, WV. When Genuine Parts purchased the NAPA warehouses in 1950, Reinberger was named a director and board chairman of Genuine Parts.

While attending a NAPA meeting in Chicago, Reinberger suddenly collapsed and died. According to his will, his widow gave one-half of his estate, or $6 million, to the Reinberger Foundation, which he had established shortly before his death.

Reinberger married Louise V. Fischer (d. 1984) on 5 Oct. 1918. They had no children. Reinberger lived in Cleveland, moved to Florida, and is buried in St. Petersburg Beach.—T.B.

**REINTHAL, DAVID F.** (28 April 1915–17 Nov. 1992), businessman and educator, was born in Cleveland, the son of Manuel and Cora Fuld Reinthal. He graduated from UNIV. SCHOOL† in 1932 and attended Yale Univ., receiving his B.A. degree 4 years later. Reinthal joined the family business, Bamberger-Reinthal Co., manufacturers of knitted outerwear, and eventually became plant manager and vice-president/treasurer of the company. He also conducted local industry negotiations with the International Ladies' Garment Workers Union for 15 years. During World War II, he was an intelligence officer with the Army Air Corps, returning to Bamberger-Reinthal after the war. Always interested in education, Reinthal left the business in 1965 to become a teacher, beginning his new career at Univ. School, where he taught seventh and eighth grade social studies. In the classroom he utilized his past experience to develop activities in economics, business, careers, and current and historic events as teaching tools to enhance his students learning. He was still working as a substitute teacher when he died.

Reinthal married Jean H. Kaynes 23 Aug. 1949. After their 1951 divorce, he married Dorothea J. Nicholson, 23 June 1953, and they had three children, Peter, Douglas, and Susan Jennings. He died at his home in PEPPER PIKE† and was cremated. —M.S.

**REMENYI, JOSEPH** (1 Dec. 1892–25 Sept. 1956) was a widely recognized Hungarian-American writer who served as professor of comparative literature at Western Reserve Univ. (see CASE WESTERN RESERVE†) for a quarter-century. Born in Pozsony, Hungary, he was educated at Francis Joseph Royal Univ. in Szeged, and also studied at the Universities of Budapest and Vienna. He worked for several European newspapers before emigrating to Cleveland in 1914 to become an editorial writer for the Hungarian-language daily, SZABADSAG.† In 1918 he married Margaret Papolczy (1892–1975), a Hungarian-born actress who gave up the stage, except for an appearance later that year in a one-act play written by her husband for the CLEVELAND PLAY HOUSE.† Entitled *30 Jefferson Arcade,* its setting was reminiscent of LAUKHUFF'S BOOKSTORE† in the Taylor Arcade. Remenyi also began writing novels about the Hungarian-American immigrant experience, which were published in Hungarian back in Budapest. Some of them, such as *Szerelmesek Voitak (They Were in Love),* had a Cleveland background. He was hired by RAYMOND MOLEY† in 1922 to conduct social surveys for the CLEVELAND FOUNDATION† and also was an immigration consultant for Cleveland Trust (see AMERITRUST†). He began teaching in 1929 at WRU's Cleveland College, where his lectures on European writers often earned spontaneous applause from his classes. In 1935 he published an anthology of American authors, *Modern American Fiction,* in Budapest, while a collection of his own writings, *Hungarian Writers and Literature,* was published posthumously in this country under the direction of his widow in 1964. He died childless.—J.V.

Joseph Remenyi Papers, WRHS.
Flory, Julia McCune. *The Cleveland Play House: How It Began* (1965).

**REVELT, RICHARD D.** (27 Apr. 1932–7 Nov. 1992), though a photographer by trade, was better known as "The Deaf Advocate" because of his lifelong commitment to the hearing impaired.

Born and raised in Cleveland, Revelt contracted spinal meningitis when he was 3, and the disease left him deaf. He attended Alexander Graham Bell School in Cleveland, and then St. Mary's School for the Deaf in Buffalo, NY.

He met his future wife, Gladys Hemstreet, at a club for the deaf. They were married 15 May 1954. They had 3 daughters: Gloria, Roseanne, and Joan, and a son, Bill.

Long a photography enthusiast, in 1966 Revelt made it his profession. Specializing in portraits, he opened a studio at 11848 Lorain Rd. A member of Professional Photographers of America, in 1976 he won 1st prize in the International Wedding Photography Awards Program.

Revelt was indefatigable on behalf of the deaf. In 1973 he co-chaired Ohio's first deaf exposition.

Held at the Higbee Auditorium, the 3-day exhibit drew some 30,000 attendees.

A member of St. Augustine Catholic Church on West 14th St., Revelt was both secretary and president of the Catholic Deaf Center headquartered there. A member of the International Catholic Deaf Assn., his efforts brought that group to Cleveland for its conventions in 1959, 1982, and 1991. He belonged to both the Cleveland and Ohio associations of the deaf, and was a trustee of FAIRMOUNT THEATRE FOR THE DEAF† and president of the Flying Fingers Club. Revelt led the campaign for local television stations to close-caption their newscasts.

Following funeral services at St. Augustine Church, Revelt was buried in Riverside Cemetery. —J.T.

**REYNOLDS, JAMES A.** (6 Dec. 1871–15 April 1951) was a lifelong member of the INTERNATIONAL ASSN. OF MACHINISTS AND AEROSPACE WORKERS† and a progressive era politician. Reynolds was born in Wiltshire, England. He quit school at age 9 to work in the coal mines of South Wales. In 1885 he came to the U.S. with his parents.

Reynolds learned the machinist trade at Alliance, OH, at the Morgan Engineering Co. In 1890 he moved to Cleveland and became a member of Cuyahoga Local 83 of the Machinists Union. In 1892 he assisted in organizing Local 233 and Local 238 in the city and continued organizing work in the West with headquarters in Milwaukee. In 1899 he returned to Cleveland and was elected the union's business agent for the city. In 1901 he was elected a member of the General Executive Board of the International Assn. of Machinists.

Reynolds became part of TOM L. JOHNSON's progressive administration when he was appointed machine inspector for the city water works in 1901. In 1906 he began his career in the Ohio legislature, serving 3 terms in the house and 2 in the senate. In 1908 he initiated and passed the Reynolds' Child Labor Law. Reynolds championed the nonpartisan judiciary bill in 1912, and Ohio women's suffrage bill in 1918, and a workmen's compensation bill. In 1920 he was the only Democrat to survive the Harding Republican landslide in the Senate. Reynolds was elected a Cuyahoga County Commissioner in 1932 and was president of the Board of County Commissioners when he suffered a stroke in 1943.

In 1909 Mayor Johnson appointed Reynolds superintendent of the Warrensville Farm. In this capacity he was able to expand his hobby of raising pedigreed cattle. Between 1916 and 1924 he worked for the Van Sweringen brothers on their DAISY

HILL† Farm and produced one of the outstanding dairy herds in the nation.

Reynolds married Florence Greenman in 1902. They had one daughter, Nina.

**RHODES, DANIEL POMEROY** (22 Nov. 1813–5 Aug. 1875) was a pioneer in the Cleveland coal mining business, contributed to the development of railroads in northern Ohio, and heavily promoted the development of Cleveland's west side.

Rhodes was born and raised in Brandon, County of Rutland, VT. He worked on the family farm, receiving little formal education. At age 21 he moved west, settling in Cleveland by 1844.

Rhodes met David Tod and formed Rhodes & Tod to mine coal near Youngstown and in Wayne county between 1845–55. In 1857 Rhodes and I. F. Card formed Rhodes & Card to mine coal in Tuscarawas County, expanding to Stark County in 1860, and into the manufacture of pig iron in 1864. In 1867 Rhodes & Card dissolved and was succeeded by Rhodes & Co., predecessor firm of M. A. Hanna & Co.

Rhodes helped construct several railroads, including the northern division of the Cleveland & Toledo Railroad, the Massillon & Cleveland, and Lake Shore & Tuscarawas Valley Railroads, and the West Side St. Railroad Co. (becoming president in 1863). He helped organize the Rocky River "Dummy" Railroad, running from Bridge Ave. and W. 58 St. to the Cliff House resort overlooking Rocky River Valley. This line helped promote Lakewood's development. To further develop the area Rhodes helped establish the Clifton Park Assn.

Rhodes was president of the People's Savings & Loan Assn. (1873), a member of the first Cleveland Board of Education and promoter the West Side Gas Works.

Rhodes married Sophia Lord Russell on October 22, 1839. They had three children: Charlotte Augusta (Mrs. Marcus) Hanna, Robert R., and JAMES FORD. Rhodes lived in Franklin Circle and is buried in Riverside Cemetery.—T.B.

**RHODES, JAMES FORD** (1 May 1848–22 Jan. 1927), historian and businessman, was born in Cleveland to Sophia Lord Russell and DANIEL POMEROY RHODES. He attended the Univ. of the City of New York (1865–66) and Univ. of Chicago (1866–67), but never graduated. Rhodes studied history and French literature in Paris and iron metallurgy at the Berlin School of Mines, before joining his father's business in 1870. He founded Rhodes & Co., producers and commission merchants in iron, iron-ore, and coal, in 1874, with his brother Robert, his brother-in-law MARCUS A. HANNA, and others. In 1881 he began writing monthly trade circulars for his company; they circulated widely and were well received. In 1884 Rhodes retired from business to devote his life to studying and writing history. The firm was dissolved in 1885, later reorganized as M. A. Hanna & Co.

Rhodes published articles in the *Magazine of Western History* (1885–86), and wrote the first 2 volumes of his 7-volume *History of the United States from the Compromise of 1850* before moving to Cambridge, MA, in 1891, and to Boston in 1895. By 1906 he had completed vol. 7 of the history. He published many books, in 1918 receiving the Pulitzer Prize in history for his *History of the Civil War, 1861–1865*. Rhodes received many honors and honorary degrees. In 1898–99 he was president of the American Historical Assn.

Rhodes married Ann Card in 1872 and had a son, Daniel Pomeroy Rhodes II. Rhodes died in Brookline, MA. His ashes are buried in Riverside Cemetery.

Cruden, Robert. *James Ford Rhodes* (1851).

RICE, HARVEY (11 June 1800–7 Nov. 1891), reorganizer of Ohio schools, was born in Conway, MA, to Stephen and Lucy (Baker) Rice. He graduated from Williams College (1824) and came to Cleveland as a teacher. In 1826 he studied law, and eventually entered into partnership with REUBEN WOOD.† Rice became justice of the peace in 1829, and was Democratic representative to the Ohio legislature in 1830. In 1831 he was appointed agent for the school land sales of the Connecticut Western Reserve, with the $150,000 received being deposited into a fund for educating the children of the WESTERN RESERVE.†

From 1834–41 Rice was clerk of the common pleas and supreme courts. He was elected in 1851 to the Ohio senate, introducing a bill reorganizing the common schools of Ohio, creating a uniform district structure and establishing an equitable system of taxation to benefit all schools. He also introduced a bill establishing reform farms for criminal youth. Both bills passed in 1853. As a member of Cleveland City Council in 1857, Rice secured passage of a resolution consolidating the INDUSTRIAL SCHOOL† and CHILDREN'S AID SOCIETY,† and introduced a resolution resulting in the erection of the PERRY MONUMENT.† From 1861–63 Rice was president of the Cleveland Board of Education. He became director of the CLEVELAND WORKHOUSE† in 1871. From 1879 until his death, he was president of the EARLY SETTLERS ASSN.† Rice wrote *Pioneers of the Western Reserve, Nature and Culture,* and *Mount Vernon and Other Poems.*

Rice married twice. He and his first wife, Fanny (d. 1837), had four children: Percy and Fanny, two others died in infancy. In 1840 Rice married Emma Marie Wood. They had five children: Henrietta, Emma, Mary, James, and Harvey. Rice died in Cleveland and was buried in Lake View Cemetery.

Akers, William J. *Cleveland Schools in the Nineteenth Century* (1901).
Freese, Andrew. *Early History of the Cleveland Public Schools* (1876).
Harvey Rice Papers, WRHS.
Rice, Harvey. *Leaflets of a Lifetime* (1895).

RICE, WALTER PERCIVAL (2 Sept. 1855–21 Aug. 1941) exerted a formative influence on Cleveland's water, harbor, and sewage systems during his career as a civil engineer. A native Clevelander, he was the son of Percival and Mary Cutter Rice and the grandson of educator HARVEY RICE. Upon graduating from Lehigh Univ. in 1876, he joined the office of the Cleveland city engineer, succeeding into that position himself from 1887–90 and 1893–95. During his tenure Rice made a study of Lake Erie currents in order to determine the best locations for the city's water intake and sewage outfall. He also designed a unique bridge over the CUYAHOGA RIVER† at Columbus Ave., consisting of 2 revolving spans operated by electricity and compressed air. Built in 1895, it was dismantled in 1940. He formed the Walter P. Rice Engineering Co. in 1895, serving until his retirement in 1930 as a consulting engineer specializing in foundation construction and shore protection. Among the projects he supervised was construction of a sewage purification plant for EAST CLEVELAND.† As Cleveland director of public works from 1899–1901, he instituted the idea of white wings to clean city streets. Rice was a founding member in 1880 of the CLEVELAND ENGINEERING SOCIETY† and its president in 1892–93. In retirement he served 10 years as president of the EARLY SETTLERS ASSN. OF THE WESTERN RESERVE.† In 1903 he married Margaret Barteau of St. Paul, MN, who survived him. He died in Cleveland and was buried at Lake View Cemetery.—J.V.

RICHARDSON, JOHN NEWTON (Feb. 1837–5 May 1902) was an architect and engineer who, with FRANK (FRANZ) E. CUDELL, formed Cudell & Richardson, one of the most important and innovative architectural firms in Cleveland during the 1870s and 1880s. Born, raised, and educated in Scotland, Richardson came to the U.S. in Nov. 1863 and was naturalized on 27 June 1871. In 1867 Richardson started in the architectural office of J. M. Blackburn. In 1870 Richardson joined Cudell and formed Cudell & Richardson.

During the 1870s Cudell & Richardson designed churches in the Victorian-Gothic style, including St.

Stephen's Church at W. 54th St. and Courtland, the FRANKLIN CIRCLE CHRISTIAN CHURCH,† and St. Joseph's Church at E. 23rd St. and Woodland. Cudell & Richardson's commercial buildings, designed during the 1880s, included George Worthington Hardware (Geo. Worthington Co.) on St. Clair Ave., the Root McBride Building (Bradley Building) on W. 6th St., and the PERRY-PAINE BUILDING† on Superior Ave. Cudell and Richardson dissolved their partnership around 1890.

Richardson helped construct numerous power plants in Cleveland and other cities. In 1892 MARCUS HANNA commissioned Richardson to design the powerhouse at Elm and Riverbed St. in the FLATS† to generate power for Hanna's Woodland & West Side St. Railway Co. Richardson designed the 6-story Jennings Apartments (1898) on Jennings Ave. (W. 14th St.), one of Cleveland's first high-rise apartments having an elevator.

Richardson married Martha Ann Wood on 15 Sept. 1870. They had 2 sons, Francis and Edward A. Richardson is buried in Riverside Cemetery.—T.B.

Johannesen, Eric. *Cleveland Architecture 1786–1976*, WRHS.

**RICHARDSON, LYON NORMAN** (20 July 1898–16 Aug. 1980), found time to run the university libraries while serving as a distinguished professor of American literature at CASE WESTERN RESERVE UNIV.† Born in Andover, OH, he returned following his graduation from Western Reserve Univ. to edit the *Kinsman Journal* and then assume the principalship of Andover High School. In 1923, the year he married the former Helen Hartman, he returned to WRU as an English instructor, earning his master's there, then a doctorate in 1931 from Columbia Univ. His books included *A History of Early American Magazines* (1931) and *Henry James* (1941). He was also coauthor of a 2-vol. textbook, *The Heritage of American Literature* (1951). At WRU he served as faculty adviser to the *Reserve Tribune*, asst. dean of Adelbert College, and head of the university press. Though lacking a library degree, he was named director of the university libraries from 1946–67. Under his tenure the Mather and Cleveland College libraries, together with parts of the Case Library, were consolidated into the university system, easing the path to the federation of Case and WRU in 1967. As full professor of English since 1946, Richardson helped to establish and became head of the university's Program of American Culture until his retirement in 1969. He was on the executive council of the American Studies Assn. from 1959–61 and chaired the American literature section of the American Language Assn. in 1965. Before moving in 1974 to Laguna Hills, CA, he

spent a year as visiting professor at Duquesne Univ. He was survived by his wife and a daughter, Cora Ella Scott.—J.V.

**RICHARDSON, WILLIAM R.** (1840–24 Oct. 1873), Congressional Medal of Honor recipient for service during the CIVIL WAR,† was born in Cleveland. However, he enlisted in the 2nd Ohio Volunteer Cavalry at Akron, OH, on 16 Aug. 1861. The company was mustered on 27 Aug. 1861 at Camp Wade on Univ. Hts. (the Tremont area), just south of the Cleveland boundary at that time. Priv. Richardson, with the Army of the Potomac in Virginia 1864–65, was captured by the Confederate Army at Sayler's Creek, VA, on 6 April 1865. He escaped and returned to Union lines with important information on southern troop positions and approaches, and for this action he was awarded the Medal of Honor 7 April 1866.

He married Clara M. (last name unknown) 3 Oct. 1865 in Dover Canal, OH, and after leaving the service they lived in NEWBURGH† for a time before moving to Massillon, OH, where he and his wife raised four children. Richardson died of army-related consumption and was buried in Massillon City Cemetery.—M.S.

**RICHMAN, SAMUEL** (ca. 1845- ), Congressional Medal of Honor recipient for service during the Indian Wars, was a native of Cleveland, enlisting in the U.S. Army 24 Oct. 1866 at age 21. Assigned to the 8th U.S. Cavalry, Priv. Richman served in the Arizona Territory on patrols and scouts from Camp Whipple (near Prescott) which extended during 1868 into the Juniper Mountains to the northwest. Richman was cited for bravery in skirmishes with hostile Indians residing there. Beginning 24 July 1868, however, he was listed as a deserter, and his Medal of Honor was not officially issued until 6 Sept. 1869.

**RICKOFF, ANDREW JACKSON** (23 Aug. 1824–29 March 1899), reorganized the CLEVELAND PUBLIC SCHOOLS† as superintendent during the formative period following the Civil War. Born in New Hope, NJ, he graduated from Woodward College in Cincinnati and later received a master's degree from Ohio Univ. After conducting his own private school, he became a teacher and school superintendent in Portsmouth, OH. In 1864 he became superintendent of schools in Cincinnati, and came to Cleveland in the same capacity in 1867. During his 15-yr. Cleveland tenure he abolished separate education by sex and reorganized all grades into 3 divisions: primary, grammar, and high schools. He was aided in some of his reforms by his wife, Rebecca Davis Rickoff, an authority on primary education. Rickoff also undertook to improve teacher training, inaugurating a week-long preschool institute in fall 1868, and opening the Cleveland City Normal School (see TEACHER EDUCATION†) in 1874. He introduced the study of German in order to attract the children of the city's GERMANS† from their own private schools into the public system. By the time of his replacement by a new school board in 1882, the school system had grown from 9,643 students and 123 teachers to 26,990 students and 473 teachers. Rickoff had served on the first executive committee of the NORTHEASTERN OHIO TEACHERS ASSN.,† formed in 1869, and was made a life director of the National Council of Education in 1881. He later became superintendent of schools in Yonkers, NY, and headed Felix Adler's Workingmen's School. He authored numerous readers and arithmetic textbooks, as well as *Past and Present of Our Common School Education* (1877). Dying in Berkeley, CA, he was returned to Cleveland for burial in Lake View Cemetery. His daughter, Bertha M. Rickoff, a Cleveland public school teacher, survived him.—J.V.

**RIDDLE, ALBERT G.** (28 May 1816–16 May 1902), lawyer, politician, and promoter of equal rights for AFRICAN AMERICANS,† was born in Monson, MA, to Thomas and Minerva (Merrick) Riddle. He moved with his family to Newbury in 1817, began studying laws under Seabury Ford in 1838, and was admitted to the Ohio Bar in 1840, establishing a practice in Chardon and Painesville and being elected Geauga County prosecuting attorney within a year. In 1848 he was elected to the state legislature with the FREE SOIL PARTY,† and in 1850 he moved to Cleveland, resuming his law practice with SAMUEL WILLIAMSON. Riddle was the principal defending lawyer in the 1859 OBERLIN-WELLINGTON RESCUE† case, and was asked to defend John Brown, but received the message late so did not arrive until the trial had already begun.

In 1861 Riddle was elected to Congress, the first to support arming the slaves when the Civil War broke out. The war ended Riddle's political career. He viewed the first battle at Bull Run, and after the confused retreat, wrote a letter to his wife which was published in the *CLEVELAND LEADER†* without Riddle's knowledge. The *CLEVELAND HERALD,†* the *Leader*'s rival, published another account depicting Riddle as a coward, which caused Riddle's reelection defeat in 1863. After the war Riddle moved to Washington, becoming a lawyer in military cases and attorney for the District of Columbia. In 1873 Riddle wrote the novel *Bart Rigby*, and in the 1880s a series on the Civil War and American leaders of the time. Riddle married

Caroline Avery on 22 Jan. 1845. They had 7 children: Florence, Mary, Caroline, Henrietta, Albert, Alice, and Frederick. Riddle died in Washington, DC, and was buried in the Rock Creek Cemetery there.

———

Albert G. Riddle Papers, WRHS.

**RIEMENSCHNEIDER, ALBERT** (31 Aug. 1878–20 July 1950), became a world renowned authority on the music of Johann Sebastian Bach and founder of the BACH FESTIVAL† in BEREA.† A native of Berea, he was the son of Dr. Karl Riemenschneider, president of German Wallace College, a forerunner of BALDWIN-WALLACE COLLEGE.† The younger Riemenschneider was appointed head of the music dept. during his junior year at the college, in 1898. He held that position for 49 years, overseeing the establishment of a full-fledged Conservatory of Music in 1912. In 1904 he married Selma Marting, daughter of the college's treasurer and one of his own music students. Riemenschneider furthered his musical education by studying organ in Paris under Alexandre Guilmant and Charles Marie Widor. He inaugurated the Bach Festival at Baldwin-Wallace in 1933, sustaining it annually for the rest of his life with the aid of his wife, who helped to maintain the series after his death. Riemenschneider also collected an extensive library on Bach, including rare editions of the master's music. He edited 2 collections of Bach organ works, *The Liturgical Year* and *Liturgy for Organ*. Upon occasion, he would also use a large Bach manuscript to mask the paperback mysteries and westerns to which he was addicted. Resisting offers from the Library of Congress for the collection, valued during his lifetime at $83,000, Riemenschneider left it to Baldwin-Wallace, where it became the nucleus of the Bach Memorial Library of the Riemenschneider Bach Institute. Dying in Akron, Riemenschneider was survived by his wife, 2 sons (Edwin and Paul), and a daughter, Mrs. Wilma Powell of California. —J.V.

**RILEY, JOHN FRANCIS** (1 July 1924–25 Aug. 1992) played a key role in the development and manufacture of superior wind velocity gauges. Born in Cleveland, the son of Frank J. and Mary Connor Riiey, he was a product of ST. IGNATIUS HIGH SCHOOL.† He attended JOHN CARROLL UNIV.† for 2 years before enlisting in the army during World War II. He was with the infantry in Europe, participating in the liberation of Dachau concentration camp, and was sent to the Philippines as the war ended. He remained in the Army Reserves for 26 years. In collaboration with his father and James V. Malone, Riley helped to develop a stainless steel cupwheel capable of measuring wind speeds of up to 200 mph. He and his father founded the Electric Speed Indicator Co. on Triskett Rd. to produce the device, which was utilized by the Federal Aviation Administration, the National Weather Service, and the Department of Defense. Rival indicators often broke down at velocities of 140 mph., but Riley's products proved even more resistant than the towers supporting them. The younger Riley remained as a partner in the concern until his retirement in the early 1980s. His hobbies included membership in the R.C. Model Airplane Club and operation of a ham radio for 41 years. He was also active in several singles social groups, serving as president at various times of the West Side Singles Club, the Big Five Plus, and West Shore Units. Unmarried, he died in Cleveland.—J.V.

**RING, EMIL** (21 Nov. 1863–1 Feb. 1922), oboe player, pianist, teacher, conductor, and composer, was born in Fetchen, Czechoslovakia, son of Alvin and Anna (Roth) Ring. He trained at the Prague Conservatory of Music, and played in orchestras in Leipzig, Berlin, Vienna, Holland, and England. He met Cleveland soprano Rita Elandi at a royal command performance for Queen Victoria and they became friends. Ring came to Cleveland in 1888 as conductor of the PHILHARMONIC ORCHES-TRA† after playing in the Boston Symphony Orchestra for a year. Ring immediately demonstrated his conducting ability through his knowledge of a range of music, including works by Liszt, Grieg, Berlioz, Wagner, Hartman, Massenet, and Volkman, in the orchestra's summer concerts in HALT-NORTH'S GARDENS† and 14 regular programs. From 1888–95, Ring was a piano instructor at the Cleveland Conservatory of Music. In 1898 the FORTNIGHTLY CLUB† under Ring united with the SINGERS CLUB† in a performance of Rossini's Stabat Mater at TRINITY CATHEDRAL.† In 1902 Ring and JOHANN BECK were selected to lead the Cleveland Grand Orchestra, with the two men alternating as conductor for 10 years. Ring was also a long-time director of the Gesangverein and festival conductor of the 27th Saengerfest in July 1893 (see SAENGERFESTS†). The Gesangverein premiered his An die Tonkrenst, a short oratorio work that was published in 1900. Ring left the Emil Ring Memorial Collection to the CLEVELAND PUBLIC LIBRARY†; it is one of the largest collections of music in the area. Ring was a member of the Musicians' Club from its inception.

Ring was married twice. In 1897 he married Edith Bohm. His second marriage was to Elsbeth Pluemer on 1 July 1903. Ring had no children. He died in Cleveland and was cremated.

**RINGWALL, RUDOLPH** (19 Mar. 1891–26 Jan. 1978), violinist and conductor, was born in Bangor, ME, son of Knute and Teckla Ringwall. He graduated from the New England Conservatory in 1913 and from 1913–15 and 1917–20 was a violinist with the Boston Symphony Orchestra under the direction of Karl Muck. In 1914–17 Ringwall played in a string quartet in San Mateo, CA, with NIKOLAI SOKOLOFF. He also taught at the New England Conservatory from 1916–20, and from 1920–21 played with the Natl. Symphony Orchestra in New York City under Willem Mengelberg. He took a year off to study with Arnold Rose in Vienna in 1924. Ringwall began with the CLEVELAND ORCHESTRA† as asst. conductor from 1926–34, and assoc. conductor from 1934–1956. He performed as either asst. or assoc. conductor with Sokoloff, ARTUR RODZINSKI, Erich Leinsdorf, and GEO. SZELL. Ringwall also started and directed the twilight and summer pops concerts with the Cleveland Orchestra. In addition to his orchestra duties, Ringwall played in the CLEVELAND STRING QUARTET† with Joseph Fuchs and others until 1936. He also hosted a radio program of classical and semiclassical records on WHK† and WJW† before and after his retirement. A witty and articulate speaker, he was often on the podium at local musical events. He married Lucy Adams in 1915 and had two children, Rudolph, Jr. and Rosamond (Humel).

**RINI, MARTIN** (29 Mar. 1901–24 Aug. 1994) was the founder and head of Rini Supermarkets and the Stop-N-Shop Assn. who introduced and pioneered numerous concepts to the Cleveland supermarket industry.

Born in Cleveland to Charles and Rose (Capodice) Rini, Martin attended Cleveland schools and learned the grocery business from his Italian immigrant father, who opened Charles Rini & Sons on the west side in 1923.

After attending a West Coast grocers' convention, where he saw prepackaged meats displayed in refrigerated cases, Rini returned home and pushed to have the family's Kamm's Corners Foodtown store remodeled to introduce the self-service concept locally.

In 1948 Rini joined with several independent Cleveland grocers to form Foodtown Inc., a voluntary co-op which operated supermarkets. In 1957 brothers Anthony, Michael, and Martin Rini formed Rini Supermarkets, opening their first modern supermarket in Southland Shopping Center. Faced with the difficulties of promoting a single store, Rini met with other independent supermarket operators to form the Stop-N-Shop Assn.

Rini was chairman of Stop-N-Shop and president

of the company operating supermarkets under the name of Rini's Stop-N-Shop. When Rini enterprises merged with American Seaway Foods and Rego supermarkets in 1988 to form Riser Foods Inc., the Rinis owned 11 Stop-N-Shop stores. Rini retired from the food industry in 1988, but remained active in the development and management firm, Rini Realty Co., until his death.

Rini married Grace Provenzano on 30 Sept. 1930 (d. 1990). They had no children. A Roman Catholic, Rini is buried in Sunset Memorial Park.—T.B.

**RISKO, JOHN "JOHNNY"** (18 Dec. 1902–13 Jan. 1953), heavyweight boxer who gained fame between 1925–34 as a "spoiler" of aspiring heavyweight champions' dreams, was born in Austria-Hungary in what is now the Slovak Republic. Son of John and Susan Risko, he arrived in Cleveland at age 6 and attended school until he was 8, at which time he began working at a bakery. A friend introduced "Baker Boy" to "Dapper Danny" Dunn (see DANIEL A. DUNN), who became his trainer and manager. Risko soon became a local hero, fighting 59 amateur bouts and scoring 39 knockouts.

After turning pro in 1925, Risko injured his right shoulder in his fourth professional bout, and from then on counted on his aggressive style, competitiveness, and devastating left hook to win fights. He was nicknamed "Cleveland's rubber man" because of his ability to absorb opponents' blows. Risko fought Gene Tunney in Cleveland on 18 Nov. 1925, losing a close 12-round decision. He defeated both Jack Sharkey and Max Baer, later world heavyweight champions. Only Max Schmeling knocked him out, in an important fight in 1929. In 17 years as a professional fighter, Risko fought 137 times, won 44 decisions, scored 22 knockouts, lost 36 decisions, and was knocked out 3 times. Risko was a big spender of his prize-fight earnings. His manager, Dunn, forced him to invest part of his income in a $100,000 trust fund. Risko joined the army in 1942. He married Margaret E. Yoder in 1930. They divorced, and Risko married Mildred Weber. He had no children. Risko died while vacationing in Miami, FL. He was buried in Brooklyn Hts. Cemetery.

**ROBB, HUNTER** (30 Sept. 1863–15 May 1940), the first Cleveland physician with special training in gynecology and a proponent of aseptic surgical techniques, was born in Burlington, NJ, to Thomas and Caroline Woolman Robb. He was educated at Burlington College and the Univ. of Pennsylvania, received his medical degree in 1884, and was a resident in Philadelphia between 1884–86. In 1886 he became the assistant of Dr. Howard A. Kelly, founder of the Kensington Hospital for Women.

When Kelly moved to Johns Hopkins in 1889, Robb joined him as an associate and began investigating wound contamination in the new field of aseptic surgical techniques, publishing a book on the subject in 1894. One of Robb's associates, Dr. Wm. Steward Halsted, had introduced rubber gloves, manufactured by Goodyear Co., for his surgical assistants as protection from harsh sterilizing solutions. Halsted did not consider them a preventive device, but Robb saw those possibilities as he studied infection.

Robb came to Cleveland in 1894 as professor of gynecology at WRU and visiting gynecologist at Lakeside Hospital. He continued his studies in abdominal surgery and infection, advocating the use of rubber gloves and being the first physician in Cleveland to use them. He was also the first Cleveland surgeon to use a gas-ether combination in anesthesia. Retiring in 1914, Robb was a major in the Medical Corps during World War I.

Robb married ISABEL HAMPTON ROBB (d. 1910) in 1894, and had 3 children: Hampton, Phillip, and Hunter. Robb married Marion Wilson in 1929. He died in Philadelphia and was buried there.

**ROBB, ISABEL ADAMS HAMPTON** (Aug. 1860–15 April 1910), nurse and textbook author, helped standardize education for NURSING† in the U.S. and abroad. She played a key role in founding the forerunner of the Frances Payne Bolton School for Nursing in Cleveland. Robb was born in Welland, Ontario, Canada, to Sara M. (Lay) and Samuel James Hampton. She graduated from the New York Training School for Nurses at Bellevue Hospital in New York City in 1883. After 18 months at St. Paul's House in Rome, Italy, and a stint as superintendent of nurses at the Illinois Training School in Chicago (1886–89), Robb organized and was the principal of the Johns Hopkins School for Nurses in Baltimore (1889). She chaired the subsection for nursing for the 1893 World's Fair and helped form the Society of Superintendents of Training Schools (later the National League for Nursing Education). On 12 June 1894 she married HUNTER ROBB, M.D., in London, England; Robb carried flowers sent by another nursing pioneer, Forence Nightingale. In November the couple came to Cleveland.

In 1895 Robb gave the first series of formal lectures on nursing at Lakeside Hospital, as a new member of the hospital's Board of Lady Managers (see UNIV. HOSPITALS). Chair of Lakeside's Training School Committee (1896–1910), she spoke at the dedication of the new Lakeside Hospital (1898). She helped organize and was first president of the national Nurses' Associated Alumnae Assn. (1897, later the American Nurses Assn.), belonged to the local Graduate Nurses Assn. (see GREATER CLEVELAND NURSES ASSN.†), and helped found the *American Journal of Nursing*. Robb was an Honorary Member of the Matrons' Council of London, England, and in 1909 chaired the education committee of the International Council of Nurses. The mother of 3 children, Hampton, Phillip H., and Hunter, Robb died in a streetcar accident in Cleveland. Friends created the Isabel Robb Memorial Fund, which supported the Graduate Nurses' Assn. and, later, nursing school scholarships. Robb was buried in Welland, Ontario.—J.M.

Stanley A. Ferguson Archives, Univ. Hospitals of Cleveland.
Lakeside School of Nursing Records, CWRU Archives.
Robb, Isabel H. *Nursing Ethics* (1907).
———. *Educational Standards for Nurses* (1907).
———. *Nursing: Its Principle and Practice* (1906).
Faddis, Margene O. *The History of the Francis Payne Bolton School of Nursing* (1948).

**ROBERTS, NARLIE** (14 April 1931–18 Dec. 1987), prominent businessman who purchased the first black-owned McDonald's franchise in Cleveland, was born in Allendale, SC, the son of George and Mary Goodman Roberts. Roberts, who came to Cleveland in 1952, organized the R & B Lath and Plastering Co. in partnership with his brother-in-law, Eugene Bush, and the business prospered. Picketing for a black-owned McDonalds franchise by a coalition of civil-rights groups in 1970 gave Roberts the opportunity to establish a McDonalds restaurant at 13705 Euclid Ave. in EAST CLEVELAND.† By the end of 1972 he had sold his interest in R & B in order to increase his fastfood business and eventually operated seven McDonald's restaurants through his Royal Ridge Management Co., which grossed over $10 million annually. Expanding into the motel business, Roberts bought the North Shore Inn located at I–90 and Euclid Ave., refurbished it, and obtained a Best Western Franchise in September 1987. Instrumental in paving the way for blacks, he also invested in minority-owned businesses such as the Advertising Connection, a full-service ad agency, and Capital for Minority Business Enterprises, Inc., and established the Royal Ridge Foundation, which provided scholarships and support for educational institutions.

Roberts married Ann Bush 30 April 1951. He died at his Best Western Motel in EUCLID† and was interred at Evergreen Cemetery at BEDFORD HTS.† His wife and five children, Yvonne, Michael, Turan, Julie, and Mary survived him.

**ROBERTS, WILLIAM (BILL) E.** (17 Oct. 1914–18 Nov. 1978), spent his entire working life in the art department of the *CLEVELAND PRESS,†* culmi-nating in a 16-year reign as the paper's editorial cartoonist. A native Clevelander, he joined the *Press* upon graduation from WEST HIGH SCHOOL† in 1932, pursuing art lessons at night at the JOHN HUNTINGTON POLYTECHNIC INST.,† where his instructors included PAUL TRAVIS and WILLARD COMBES. Much of his early work on the *Press* was done for the sports page, but he attracted general notice for the creation of the "Week's Wash," a humorous cartoon review of local and national news which appeared at the bottom of the front page every Saturday from 1948–62. Memorable characters invented by Roberts for the series included hockey fan Julius P. Bodychec, chuckhole expert Foxhole Freddy, and members of the Jolly Set from Cleveland's nightlife strip along SHORT VINCENT† Ave. Roberts himself executed a 70' mural for Kornman's Restaurant on Short Vincent, as well as other murals for Cavoli's Restaurant and the Artists and Writers Club. He was appointed editorial-page cartoonist for the *Press,* succeeding Combes in 1962. For several summers he sat in for cartoonist Gene Bassett in the Scripps-Howard Washington bureau, from where his work was syndicated nationally. Pres. Lyndon Johnson requested 5 of Roberts's originals during the summer of 1965. Locally, Roberts won numerous "Best Cartoon" awards from the CLEVELAND NEWSPAPER GUILD† and the PRESS CLUB OF CLEVELAND.† Married since 1938 to the former Marguerite MacGillis, he was survived by her and their 7 children.—J.V.

William Roberts Collection, Cleveland State Univ. and WRHS.
Feingold, Rachel G. (ed.). *Provocative Pens: Four Cleveland Cartoonists, 1900–1975* (1992).

**ROBERTSON, CARL TROWBRIDGE** (31 Jan. 1876–2 June 1935), journalist and son of Georgia Trowbridge and George A. Robertson, founder of the *Cleveland Morning Recorder,* was born in N. Bloomfield, Trumbull County, OH. He graduated from Harvard in 1898, and after a year teaching returned to Cleveland. Following a short apprenticeship on the *Morning Recorder,* Robertson moved to the *PLAIN DEALER†* in 1901, covering city hall during the TOM L. JOHNSON era before being promoted to editorial writer and associate editor.

Robertson was an authority on contract bridge, joining the Cleveland Whist Club and playing on its national championship teams in 1902 and 1903. He was also an explorer, in 1920 directing an expedition which discovered a previously unknown section of Mammoth Cave, KY, subsequently named Robertson Ave. Three years later he crossed the

Atlantic in a 3-masted schooner with the CLEVE-LAND MUSEUM OF NATURAL HISTORY's† Blossom expedition to Cape Verde. Robertson's travel led to many *Plain Dealer* articles. From 1920 until his death, Robertson also contributed a widely followed "Outdoors Diary" to the paper. Married twice, Robertson had a daughter, Jane, from his first marriage, on 12 June 1912, to Martha Bushea, whom he divorced in 1924. Later that year he married JOSEPHINE WUEBBEN, a *Plain Dealer* medical reporter, on 14 July 1925. Their son, Donald (Don) Robertson, was a reporter for the *Plain Dealer,* a columnist for the CLEVELAND PRESS,† and a novelist best known for his fictional account of the East Ohio Gas disaster, *The Greatest Thing since Sliced Bread.* Robertson is buried near Rabat, Morocco, where he died suddenly while traveling.

Shaw, Archer H. *The Plain Dealer* (1942).

**ROBERTSON, GEORGE A.** (14 Jan. 1850–20 Feb. 1908), reporter, editor and publisher, founded and edited the *CLEVELAND RECORDER†* (1895–97). He also acquired and ran the *DAILY LEGAL NEWS†* as a morning edition of the *Recorder.* Robertson's birth place was Hampden, OH (Geauga County). Graduating from Hiram College in 1874, he became secretary to Congressman JAMES A. GARFIELD. After this service and a year as principal of Bloomfield Academy in North Bloomfield, OH, Robertson came to Cleveland as a reporter for the *CLEVELAND LEADER,†* which he also served as city editor and editorial writer. From the Republican *Leader,* Robertson went to work for the Democratic *PLAIN DEALER†* as managing editor and Washington correspondent. Upon his return from Washington, he purchased the *SUNDAY VOICE†* with William R. Rose; in 1889 Robertson founded the *Evening Sun.*

With B. F. Bower, Robertson acquired the newly established *CLEVELAND WORLD†* (ca. 1889) and merged it with the *Evening Sun.* In April 1895 Bower and Robertson sold the *World* to Robert P. Porter; Robertson founded the *Cleveland Recorder.* Mayor TOM L. JOHNSON appointed Robertson to one term on the Cuyahoga County Board of Elections. Robertson was regarded as an authority on the history of Mormonism in Ohio as well as on the early career of James A. Garfield. His son, CARL TROWBRIDGE ROBERTSON, was an associate editor at the *Plain Dealer.*

**ROBERTSON, JOSEPHINE (JO) WUEBBEN** (1900–19 Oct. 6. 1990), pioneered first as a woman reporter in daily journalism and later as a reporter in the field of medical journalism. The daughter of a Lutheran minister, she was born in Napoleon, OH, raised in Logan, and received degrees from Ohio Univ. and Ohio State Univ. After a year as an asst. principal in an Indiana high school, she visited Cleveland in 1923 and on an impulse secured a job as the only woman reporter on the staff of the *PLAIN DEALER.†* She retired 2 years later to marry the *Plain Dealer*'s associate editor, CARL TROWBRIDGE ROBERTSON, but returned following Robertson's death in 1935. Mrs. Robertson continued her husband's editorial-page column, "Outdoors Diary," for 20 years, but also began filing stories in the field of medical reporting. As Cleveland's first full-time medical reporter, she was given membership in the National Science Writers Assn. A series she wrote in 1963 on the shortage of general practitioners in Ohio's small towns received a citation from the Ohio Academy of General Practice, while a 1965 series on cancer won a National Headliner award from the national women's journalism sorority, Theta Sigma Psi. Robertson's hobbies included bridge, gardening, and the piano, on which she received instruction from ARTHUR LOESSER. Having retired from the *Plain Dealer* in 1967, she published the history *St. Luke's Hospital, 1894–1980,* in 1981. She died in a nursing home near Chardon after several years' affliction with Alzheimer's disease, survived by her son, the novelist Don Robertson.—J.V.

**ROBESON, LILA PAULINE** (4 April 1880–7 Dec. 1960) was an international opera star and the first Cleveland-born artist to sing with the Metropolitan Opera (1912–22) in New York.

Born in Cleveland to William and Sarah McIlrath Robeson, she attended Central High School and graduated from Western Reserve Univ. in 1902. Robeson studied voice in New York with Isidore Luckstone and received opera training from Oscar Saenger.

A contralto, Robeson was one of the first Americans to succeed in opera theater without European training or experience. She made her operatic debut with the Aborn Opera Co. in Boston on 4 April 1911 as Ortrud in Lohengrin. The protege of Johanna Gadski, Robeson was a favorite with Gatti Casazza, the Metropolitan Opera impresario who signed her.

Robeson made her debut with the Metropolitan Opera in 1912 as the Witch in Koenigskinder. She possessed the phenomenal ability to step onstage at a moment's notice and sing any of 60 operatic parts without rehearsal. Robeson specialized in Wagnerian opera and sang all the leading roles. She appeared opposite Caruso, Schumann-Heink, Alda, and other stars of the Metropolitan Opera's "Golden Era."

In 1922, following a decade with the Metropolitan Opera, Robeson returned to Cleveland. She taught voice at Adelbert, Mather, and Cleveland colleges and had her own music studios in Carnegie Hall and the WHK† Auditorium. Robeson was credited with bringing the first taste of musical appreciation to Clevelanders during her long career as a voice teacher.

Robeson never married. She lived in SHAKER HTS.† and is buried in Lake View Cemetery.—T.B.

**ROBINSON, EDWIN "TED" MEADE** (1 Nov. 1878–20 Sept. 1946), conductor of Cleveland's most prestigious contributors' column in the *PLAIN DEALER,†* was born in Lima, IN, son of William E. and Alice Drake Meade Robinson. He graduated from Wabash College in 1900 and worked briefly for papers in Indianapolis before joining the *CLEVELAND LEADER†* in 1905, beginning a column called "Just by the Way." He moved to the *Plain Dealer* in 1910, and under the heading "Philosopher of Folly," combined his own light verse and wry commentary with similar fare from regular contributors writing under such noms de plume as "Prof. Si N. Tific," "Homo Seidel," "N. Deavor," and "Sue Burbanite." Eventually more than 600 volunteer writers saw their contributions printed in Robinson's column, their only other reward being an invitation to an annual contributors' dinner hosted by Robinson from ca. 1912–38.

Robinson's poetry included 2 volumes of verse, *Mere Melodies* (1918) and *Pipings and Pannings* (1921). He also wrote the novel *Enter Jerry* (1922). At the *Plain Dealer*, Robinson became an associate editor, as well as the literary editor after 1922. Throughout the 1930s, he lectured on language and philology at Cleveland College. Robinson married Martha Coon in 1909. Their only child, Ted Robinson, Jr., later was a contributing editor for *Time* magazine. Robinson died on vacation at Provincetown, MA. A poem he had written to appear in his column the following morning bore the recurring refrain, "The Autumn comes—and I must go!" He was buried with his parents in Brooklyn, CT.

Edwin Robinson Papers, WRHS.

**ROBISON, FRANK DE HAAS** (1852–25 Sept. 1908), pioneer in street railway lines and owner of the CLEVELAND SPIDERS,† was born in Pittsburgh, the son of Martin Stanford and Mariah Allison Robison. After spending his boyhood in Dubuque, IA, he attended Delaware Univ. briefly. In 1877 Robison and his father-in-law, Charles Hatha-

way, organized Hathaway & Robison to build and operate street railway systems. Located at 611 Superior St. in Cleveland, the company established street railway systems throughout the U.S. and Canada. Robison personally organized the Cleveland City Cable Railway Co. in 1889 and built 24 miles of cable lines on Payne and Superior Ave.'s. In 1893 he merged with MARCUS A. HANNA's Woodland Ave. and West Side St. Railway to form the Cleveland City Railway Co. In the transaction, Robison lost his railway stock, control of the system, and $1 million when broker John Shipherd fraudulently sold the stock to Hanna and kept the proceeds. In a court settlement Robison acquired a substantial interest in the new railway co.

Robison organized the Cleveland Forest Citys (see FOREST CITY BASEBALL CLUB†) in 1887, affiliated with the American Assn., and renamed his club the Cleveland Spiders in 1889 when he entered the National League. Two years later Robison built LEAGUE PARK† on his Payne Ave. cable line at E. 66th St. and Lexington Ave. to increase ridership and baseball attendance. The Spiders were successful until 1898, when Robison, angered by poor attendance, transferred its best players to the St. Louis team he had just purchased. He sold the Cleveland team to Charles Somers and John Kilfoyle in 1900.

Robison married Sarah P. Hathaway of Philadelphia in 1875, and they had a daughter, Mrs. Schuyler P. Britton. He died at his BRATENAHL† home and was buried at Lake View Cemetery. —M.S.

**ROCK, FREDERICK** (15 Feb. 1840–8 Nov. 1924), Congressional Medal of Honor recipient for service during the Civil War, was born in Meisenheim, Hessen-Darmstadt, Germany, emigrated to the U.S. with his parents in 1846, and settled in Cleveland. Rock moved to Canada prior to 1860 to farm but returned to Cleveland where he enlisted in the 37th Ohio Volunteer Infantry 18 Aug. 1861. During General Grant's campaign to capture Vicksburg, MS, Private Rock volunteered with 149 others on 22 May 1863 to storm an enemy position at Fort Pemberton outside the city. Although the attack failed, Rock along with the others were recommended to receive the Medal of Honor by the divisional commander. Subsequently, he left his regiment without authorization and was carried as a deserter from 28 April 1864 until his discharge at Camp Cleveland 7 August 1865.

Rock remained in Cleveland working as a laborer and watchman until 1875. He was living in Tampa, FL, 14 Aug. 1894 when the Medal of Honor was given to all members of the Vicksburg Storming

Party. Rock received his medal although, as a deserter, he was denied an invalid pension by the War Department. He died at age 84 and was buried at Woodlawn Cemetery in Tampa with his wife, Mary, who had preceded him in death.

**ROCKEFELLER, JOHN D.** (8 July 1839–23 May 1937), industrialist and philanthropist, rose from his position as an asst. bookkeeper for a Cleveland commission merchant to become one of the wealthiest men in the U.S. through his efforts in developing the STANDARD OIL CO.† Born on a farm near Richfield, NY, Rockefeller was the son of Wm. A. and Eliza Davison Rockefeller. He came to the Cleveland area with his family in 1853, settling in STRONGSVILLE.† Boarding in Cleveland, he attended CENTRAL HIGH SCHOOL† from 1853–55. After additional courses at a business college, he became asst. bookkeeper for commission merchants Henry B. Tuttle and Isaac L. Hewitt in Sept. 1855. In Mar. 1859, Rockefeller and Maurice B. Clark established their own commission business, which prospered during the Civil War.

In 1863 Rockefeller entered the oil business, and in 1865 left the commission business to work full-time in oil. He organized Standard Oil Co. as its largest stockholder in 1870, directing the company until he retired in 1896, but retaining the title of president until 1911. By 1880 Rockefeller was worth about $18 million. He was also involved in other business ventures, holding stock in the Cleveland Arcade Co., and in 1905 building the ROCKEFELLER BLDG.† Rockefeller's business dealings necessitated increasingly more time in New York; he bought a home there in 1884 and eventually made that his legal residence. Nevertheless, he maintained 2 homes in Cleveland and until 1915 continued to summer at Forest Hill.

Rockefeller's charity, as well as business, began in Cleveland. In 1856 he donated $19.31 to local charities; his donations grew to $250,000 in 1887 and $1.35 million in 1892. Many institutions to which he belonged received donations, including Erie St. Baptist Church (later EUCLID AVE. BAPTIST CHURCH†), the WESTERN RESERVE HISTORICAL SOCIETY,† EARLY SETTLERS ASSN.,† and YMCA. Rockefeller also supported the Ragged School (later Industrial School and CHILDREN'S AID SOCIETY†), BETHEL UNION,† the WOMEN'S CHRISTIAN TEMPERANCE UNION,† ALTA HOUSE,† the VISITING NURSE ASSN. OF CLEVELAND,† the DORCAS† Invalids' Home, and Children's Fresh Air Camp. He donated more than $865,000 worth of land to the city for use as PARKS.† Rockefeller established several organizations to handle his giving: the

Rockefeller Institute for Medical Research (1901), the General Education Board (1902), the Rockefeller Foundation (1913), and the Laura Spelman Rockefeller Memorial (1918).

Rockefeller married Laura Celestia Spelman in 1864. They had four children: John D., Jr., Elizabeth, Edith, and Alta. Rockefeller died in Ormond Beach, FL. He is buried in Lake View Cemetery.

---

Goulder-Izant, Grace. *John D. Rockefeller* (1972).

**ROCKER, SAMUEL** (Feb. 1864–18 March 1936) founded and served as editor in chief of *Die YIDDISHE VELT* (Jewish World). He also contributed to other papers and was a correspondent for the *Jewish Daily News* of New York. Rocker was born in Galicia, Austria, to Faigela and Ephraim Fishel Rocker. He studied for the rabbinate at Talmudic College in Lisko, Hungary, before coming to the U.S. in 1891. He first settled in Bridgeport, CT, then came to Cleveland, where he began the city's first Yiddish weekly, the *Jewish Star,* from a small print shop. He next printed the *Jewish Banner,* part Yiddish and part English. In 1908 he founded the *Yiddishe Tegliche Presse* (Jewish Daily Press), the Midwest's only such paper. In 1913 Rocker consolidated the *Jewish World* and the *Jewish Daily Press,* creating the new *Jewish World.* According to a speech in his honor, Rocker mediated between Orthodox and Reform Judaism and advocated Zionism in his publications. Rocker, a director of the COUNCIL EDUCATIONAL ALLIANCE† participated in the founding and/or expansion of institutions such as MT. SINAI MEDICAL CENTER,† the HEBREW FREE LOAN ASSN.,† and CLEVELAND HEBREW SCHOOLS.†

After a previous marriage Rocker married Hannah Friedman in 1890. They lived in CLEVELAND HTS.† with their children, Henry A., Phillip, Lee, Myrtle (Mrs. Stephen G.) Newman, Rose (Mrs. Morris) Rapport, and Mollie (Mrs. David) Schonberg. Rocker is buried in the ANSHE EMETH† Cemetery in WARRENSVILLE HTS.†—J.M.

**RODZINSKI, ARTUR** (2 Jan. 1892–27 Nov. 1958), second conductor of the CLEVELAND ORCHESTRA,† was born of Polish parents in Dalmatia, Yugoslavia, graduated from the Univ. of Vienna as a Doctor of Law to please his father, while studying music at the Vienna Academy of Music. When World War I started and his father, a general, was separated from Rodzinski, he began to pursue his first love, music. He continued at the Vienna Academy, studying piano with Saur and Lalewicz. When the war ended, Rodzinski became conductor of the Lemberg Opera. In 1925 he accepted a position as asst. conductor of the Philadelphia Orchestra. He also directed the Los Angeles Philharmonic Orchestra before coming to Cleveland as conductor for the Cleveland Orchestra in 1933. Under his direction the orchestra flourished, impressing a national audience. Rodzinski initiated opera productions; helped select and train the NBC Symphony Orchestra, conducting it with Arturo Toscanini; and was the first American conductor selected for the Salzburg Festival. He conducted the Cleveland Orchestra from 1933–43, leaving because of strained relations with the management. He conducted the New York Philharmonic Orchestra but spent the rest of his life guest-conducting. He received an honorary Doctor of Music degree from Oberlin College. Rodzinski was married twice. His first marriage in 1917, to Mme Ilse, a concert pianist, ended in divorce in 1934; they had one child, Witold. In July 1934 he married Halina Lilpop Wieniawski and had a son, Richard. Rodzinski was buried in Boston, MA.

Marsh, Robert C. *The Cleveland Orchestra* (1967).
Musical Arts Assn. Archives.

**ROGERS, JAMES HOTCHKISS** (7 Feb. 1857–28 Nov. 1940), composer, music critic, organist, and teacher, was born in Fair Haven, CT, son of Martin L. and Harriett Hotchkiss. He began piano lessons at age 12 and organ lessons later, and studied in Europe from 1875–80. In 1883 Rogers moved to Cleveland, becoming organist at Euclid Ave. Temple (see ANSHE CHESED†), playing until his retirement in 1932. He was also organist for Shaker Hts. Neighborhood Church and FIRST UNITARIAN CHURCH.† Rogers was music critic for the *PLAIN DEALER†* from 1915–32. It was said Rogers was never harsh; even when Isadora Duncan danced in an outrageous red costume in 1922, Rogers simply wrote, "all things considered, the orchestra did very well." Rogers explained his role was not to discourage but rather to encourage and advise.

Rogers composed over 550 works: over 50 compositions for the organ, 5 cantatas, over 130 songs, and instruction books for both piano and organ. His composing style was Late Romantic and tended toward the sentimental. "In Memoriam," a 6-song cycle centering on Walt Whitman's poems, was written for his son, Henry, who was killed in World War I. In 1946 the CLEVELAND ORCHESTRA† dedicated a program to Rogers, and a portrait, painted by Mary Seymour Brooks, was presented to the WESTERN RESERVE HISTORICAL SOCIETY.† Rogers taught at the Cleveland School of Music. Upon his retirement, he was honored by 500 musicians and friends at a farewell dinner. He

moved to Pasadena, CA, where he died. Rogers married Alice Abigail Hall on 20 Oct. 1891 and had 2 other children, Stewart and Marian. He was buried in Lake View Cemetery.

Alexander, J. Heywood. *It Must Be Heard* (1981).

**ROGERS, MARGARET MARIE HARDEN** (30 March 1914–26 April 1993) was a Cuyahoga County welfare administrator who in 1965 became the first African American in the department to become a caseworker supervisor.

Born Margaret M. Harden in Tallahassee, FL, to Grover and Rev. Evelena (Baker) Harden, Margaret received her B.A. from FENN COLLEGE† (1945) and her M.S. in sociology from WESTERN RESERVE UNIV.† (1962). She also attended Ohio State and Wilberforce Universities. Rogers was a legal secretary before working as an administrative assistant in the Cleveland branch of the NATIONAL ASSN. FOR THE ADVANCEMENT OF COLORED PEOPLE,† 1945 to 1948.

Rogers joined the Cuyahoga County Welfare Department in 1948 as a caseworker and became an intake interviewer in 1958. She took 2 years off to earn her master's degree and returned in 1962 as a field work supervisor. In 1965 Rogers became the first African American in the welfare department to become a caseworker supervisor. She later became administrator of the HOUGH† District Office and a special administrator to EAST CLEVELAND.† She also assisted in the development of the East Cleveland Human Services Center. Rogers retired in 1981.

Rogers was a member of the National Assn. of Social Workers. She served on the Citizens Advisory Board of the Fairhill Mental Health Center, Community Service of Mount Pleasant, and the boards of the Helen S. Brown Center and the Murtis H. Taylor Multi-Services Center.

Margaret married Olmstead B. Evans and had two sons, John and Everett. Her second husband was Edward Rogers. Margaret Rogers belonged to ST. JAMES AME CHURCH.† She was cremated. —T.B.

**ROGERS, WARREN LINCOLN** (14 Nov. 1877–6 Nov. 1938), bishop coadjutor of the Episcopal Diocese of Ohio (1925–30) and fifth bishop (1930–38), was born in Allentown, NJ, son of Samuel Hartshorne and Josephine (Lincoln) Rogers. He converted to Episcopalianism while at the Univ. of Michigan, from which he graduated in 1907. He received Bachelor of Divinity degrees from Union Seminary (1911) and General Theological Seminary (1912). After being ordained deacon and priest in 1911, he was a rector in Detroit (1911–13), Pittsburgh (1913–16), and Jersey City (1916–20) before becoming dean of Detroit's St. Paul's Cathedral (1920–25). Assuming the episcopacy, Rogers faced problems caused by the reduced circumstances of the Depression. He cut his salary by half and subjected all other diocesan salaries to 3-month reviews and adjustment. He raised $400,000 for a capital fund and gave up the bishop's home, which was converted into a crippled-children's shelter. He published his official activities in *Church Life,* presenting an active leadership to keep up morale. Rogers was a member of the Cleveland YMCA board and on the boards of trustees of Kenyon College, Western Reserve Univ., and Lake Erie College, and was president of Harcourt School for Girls in Gambier, Ohio. He was also a member of the American Peace Society. Rogers's Detroit radio sermons were the first in the country; he was known as the Radio Dean, with a popular nationwide hookup. Rogers married Helen Clingen Speakman (d. 1919) in 1911; they had no children.

Bishops of Ohio Records, Episcopal Diocese of Ohio Archives.

**RORIMER, LOUIS** (12 Sept. 1872–30 Nov. 1939) was born in Cleveland, the son of Minnie (Iglauer) and Jacob Rorimer, a wealthy tobacco dealer. He was educated under sculptor HENRY MATZEN at Manual Training School, and at 16 went to Europe to study, attending the Kunstsgewer in Munich and Academie Julien in Paris for decorative arts. Returning to Cleveland in 1893, Rorimer established a studio in the ARCADE,† later merging with Brooks Household Arts Co., a consultant firm in interior design, becoming nationally known as Rorimer Brooks Co. Their clientele included the Statler Hotels, Chamber of Commerce Clubs, and Van Sweringen offices.

Rorimer stated he was an artist first, a teacher second, and a businessman third, believing art was an essential ingredient in daily life. With this philosophy, he vigorously promoted and used the cleaner, more utilitarian designs of modern art, as opposed to Victorian styles. From 1918–36 Rorimer taught architectural design at Cleveland School of Art. He exhibited drawings, sculpture, and furniture at the CLEVELAND MUSEUM OF ART.† His studios were stocked with treasures from Spain, Britain, and France. Rorimer was a vice-president and on the Board of Directors of the American Institute of Decorators. He was president of the CLEVELAND PLAY HOUSE† from 1932–34. He was a member of the 1925 Hoover Commission from the U.S. to the Paris Industrial Arts Exposition. Rorimer married Edith Joseph in 1903 and had 2 children, Louise and James J. James became a curator at the New York Metropolitan Museum of Art.

Pina, Leslie Ann. *Louis Rorimer: A Man of Style* (1990).

**ROSA, STORM** (18 July 1791–3 May 1867), doctor and an advocate of homeopathic medicine, was born in Coxsackie, NY, to Isaac and Agnes Storm. He attended and later taught at the village school; at age 22 began studying medicine under local doctors; and in 1816 received a license to practice from the Medical Society of Seneca County, NY. Soon after, he established a practice in Madison, OH, and 2 years later moved to Painesville. Between 1834–35 he taught at the Medical College of Willoughby Univ. as adjunct professor of materia medica, receiving an honorary degree at the college's first commencement.

Rosa was also associate judge of the Court of Common Pleas in Geauga County, secretary for the Geauga County Agricultural Society, and from 1838–39 edited the *Painesville Telegraph.* In 1843 Rosa turned to homeopathic medicine, helping found the Homeopathic Society, which met in Burton in 1847. In 1840 the faculty of the Eclectic Medical Institute in Cincinnati established a chair of HOMEOPATHY†; Rosa filled the position, but the chair was abolished after the first semester because Rosa had converted too many students and professors to homeopathic medicine. He returned to Painesville and in 1850 became professor of gynecology and obstetrics at Cleveland Homeopathic Medical College. In 1852, Rosa, with Dr. Horatio Gatchell, built a stone bath house at Little Mountain for water cures and a gymnasium to provide the benefits of exercise. The experiment faltered, lasting only a few years. Rosa married Sophia Kimball in 1818 and had 2 children, Catherine and Lemuel. He was buried in the Evergreen Cemetery in Painesville, Oh.

Biographical File, Howard Dittrick Museum of Historical Medicine.

**ROSE, BENJAMIN** (13 Mar 1828–28 June 1908), businessman noted particularly for his philanthropic interest in the care of the aged, was born in Warwickshire, England, son of George and Mary Rose. He came to the U.S. at age 10 and settled in Cincinnati with his family. At 12 he got his first job as a laborer in a Cincinnati slaughterhouse. The following year he moved to Cleveland and went into the provision business with his brother. After a partnership with Chauncey Prentiss, Rose organized the CLEVELAND PROVISION CO.† in 1877, which became the largest meat packer in Cleveland, its success based largely on Rose's innovative practices, centering on his use of refrigeration in his packinghouse and in rail and ocean shipping of his products. In 1908 Rose used some of his capital to build the Rose Bldg. at E. 9th St. and Prospect Ave., the largest office building in Ohio at that time.

Rose was married on 16 Dec. 1855 to Julia Still. They had 2 children, who both died in infancy. Rose's death occurred while on a trip to England; he left a permanent memorial to Cleveland by bequeathing his fortune of $3 million to charity, making possible the establishment of the BENJAMIN ROSE INSTITUTE,† which provides relief and assistance to the needy aged and to curable crippled children. Rose was buried in Lake View Cemetery.

**ROSE, H. (HORACE) CHAPMAN** (11 Feb. 1907–17 Feb. 1990), attorney and civic leader, clerked to U.S. Supreme Court Justice Oliver Wendell Holmes and served as asst. undersecretary of the U.S. Treasury (1953–55) and undersecretary of the Treasury (1955–56) under Pres. Eisenhower. A staunch Republican, he represented Pres. Nixon in income tax matters during the Watergate era. Rose (known as "Chappie"), was a partner in JONES, DAY, REAVIS & POGUE.† He was born in Columbus, OH, to Henry N. and Grace Chapman Rose. He was educated at Columbus Academy and Princeton Univ. (1928), and received a law degree from Harvard Univ. (1931). After passing the Ohio Bar (1932), Rose was first associate, then partner at Tolles Hogsett & Ginn in Cleveland, forerunner of Jones Day. Commissioned by the U.S. Army, Rose served in World War II in the office of the undersecretary of War, the Army Service Forces, and with the 24 other lawyers known as the Army Legal Branch. He was discharged as a col. and awarded the Legion of Merit.

Appointed by Pres. Truman, Rose directed the Office of Contract Settlement in the U.S. Dept. of War (1946–47) and then joined the Washington office of Jones Day Cockley & Reavis as partner. He was a partner in the firm's Cleveland office from 1949–53, when he was appointed to the office of the Treasury. Rose served as Jones Day partner in Cleveland again from 1956–74. From 1974–76, he served as the firm's national managing partner and then returned to the Washington office (1977–83).

In addition to professional activities (president of the CLEVELAND BAR ASSN.,† 1970), Rose was a corporate director of such firms as Gould, Inc., the Brush Beryllium Co. (see BRUSH WELLMAN CORP.†), and Cleveland Trust (see AMERITRUST†). He was trustee of the AMERICAN HEART ASSN., NORTHEAST OHIO AFFILIATE,† the CLEVELAND ORCHESTRA,† the

CLEVELAND COUNCIL ON WORLD AFFAIRS,† and the CLEVELAND PLAY HOUSE.†

Rose married Cleveland Play House actress Katherine Cast on 1 Oct. 1938; they had a son, Jonathan C. Rose died in Washington, DC.—J.M.

**ROSE, IRVING S. "NIG"** (7 Feb. 1893–6 Aug. 1972), a leader in promoting amateur baseball, was born in Cleveland, the son of Morris and Ida Melowitz Rose. While attending St. Edward High School he won medals as a sprinter in 1910. After high school, Rose went to work for clothier MAX ROSENBLUM in 1916, retiring as vice-president of the firm in 1967. When Rosenblum organized the Cleveland Rosenblums in 1925 to compete in the newly formed American Basketball League, Rose managed the team which won the league championship in 1925–26, 1928–29, and 1929–30. Although he collaborated with Rosenblum in promoting local sports enterprises, he was most closely associated with the Cleveland Baseball Federation, beginning in 1919. As treasurer of the Federation for over 50 years, he was responsible for raising hundreds of thousands of dollars to equip Cleveland youngsters playing sandlot baseball and set up a fund to cover medical expenses for injuries incurred during the games. The cornerstone of his successful fundraising was the Sandlot Day exhibition baseball game played annually by the CLEVELAND INDIANS† beginning in 1948. For many years Rose also was chairman of the Muny Softball Assn., which named a softball field in Brookside Park after him in 1970. In 1978 he was elected to the GREATER CLEVELAND SPORTS HALL OF FAME.†

Rose married Tillie Weiss in 1917 and they had 3 children: Norton, Earl, and Florence Kesselman. A resident of SHAKER HTS.,† Rose died in Cleveland and was buried in Mayfield Cemetery.—M.S.

**ROSE, WILLIAM GANSON** (29 Oct. 1878–16 Aug. 1957), author, advertising executive, and civic promoter, was born in Cleveland to William R. and Eliza F. Ganson Rose. He graduated from Adelbert College of Western Reserve Univ. in 1901, and was dramatic editor of the *PLAIN DEALER†* from 1902–07. He became an advertising and business counsel to several banks and private industries, and in 1915 formed an advertising and public relations firm, Wm. G. Rose, Inc. During his career, Rose managed fairs and expositions, including Cleveland's INDUSTRIAL EXPOSITION† (1909); ART LOAN EXPOSITION† (1913); and first Electrical Exposition (1914). In 1930 he managed the Internatl. Gordon Bennett Races, and in 1936–37 directed the GREAT LAKES EXPOSITION.† He directed 5 4th of July FESTIVALS OF FREEDOM,† and the cultural, educational, and entertainment features of the Cleveland Sesquicentennial in 1946.

Rose served on the City Planning Commission in 1915, and in 1916–17 chaired the Committee of 100 Organizations, securing passage of the $2.5 million Public Hall Bond Issue. He was president of the CLEVELAND ADVERTISING CLUB† from 1914–16 and program chairman of the Cleveland Chamber of Commerce from 1927–57. Rose wrote articles for newspapers and magazines, as well as several books: *The Comic History of Cleveland* (1901); *The Radium Book* (1905); *The Ginger Cure* (1911); *Putting Marshville on the Map* (1912); *Success in Business* (1913); and *Cleveland, The Making of a City* (1950). Rose married Julia Miller in 1927 and had a daughter, Mrs. Walter R. (Nancy) Jones. Rose died in Cleveland and was buried in Lake View Cemetery.

---

Wm. Ganson Rose Papers, WRHS.

**ROSE, WILLIAM GREY** (23 Sept. 1829–15 Sept. 1899), businessman, real estate developer, and Republican mayor of Cleveland (1877–78, 1891–92) was born in Mercer County, PA, to James and Martha McKinley Rose. He attended Austinburg Grand River Institute in Ohio and Beaver Academy, studied law in Mercer, and was admitted to the Pennsylvania Bar in 1855, practicing law there. He served in the Pennsylvania legislature, 1857–58. Rose came to Cleveland in 1865 and became a member of the Cuyahoga County bar. He helped found CLEVELAND PROVISION CO.,† prospered in the oil-refining business, and developed real estate subdivisions east and south of the city. By 45 he was independently wealthy.

Elected mayor during a depression resulting from the Panic of 1873, Rose cut the administrative expenses of the city government. He also helped prevent violence during the strike against the Lake Shore & Michigan Southern Railway in 1877 and the coopers' strike that same year. His second term as mayor was the first under a new charter granted by the state known as the federal plan of government. He was an able administrator, providing the city with cleaner streets and better enforcement of city contracts. He supported lower gas rates to consumers. Rose married Martha E. Parmelee in 1858, and they had 4 children: Alice Evelyn (Mrs. Chas. R. Miller), Hudson, Frederick Holland, and Wm. Kent. Rose died in Cleveland.

**ROSENBLUM, MAX** (5 Dec. 1877–5 Sept. 1953), owner of the Rosenblum-Celtics professional basketball team, was born in Austria-Hungary to Adolph and Esther Rosenblum. He came with his family to the U.S. when he was 6, and settled in Cleveland ca. 1885. Rosenblum left school after the 6th grade, but later enrolled in Canton Business College to study bookkeeping. At 17 he was an errand boy for a clothier, by 1902 was manager of Enterprise Credit Clothing Co., and in 1910 opened his own clothing store, selling clothes on credit.

As owner of the Cleveland Rosenblums, he helped establish the American Basketball League in 1925. His team won the league championship in 1925–26, averaging 10,000 attendance in the 2 playoff games at Public Hall, with seats ranging in price from $.75-$1.65. When the championship New York Celtics broke up, Rosenblum signed Joe Lapchick, Dutch Dehnert, and Pete Barry, and regained the championship in 1928–29 and 1929–30. With the Depression, attendance at games dwindled, and the team folded in Dec. 1930.

In 1917 Rosenblum organized a softball team, and later helped organize the Cleveland Amateur Baseball Assn., backing numerous sandlot teams. He promoted amateur baseball, basketball, football, bowling, and soccer. He was also president of the Welfare Assn. for Jewish Children for 15 years. Rosenblum married Sallie Weiss in 1900 and had a son, Harvey, and 2 daughters, Mrs. Thelma Sobel and Mrs. Pearl Hartman. After her death in 1938, he married Ann Whitney in 1943. He died in Cleveland.

**ROSENTHAL, RUDOLPH M.** (7 May 1906–19 June 1979), rabbi and rabbi emeritus at Temple on the Heights for 46 years, was born in Cleveland, the son of Harry and Dora (Kober) Rosenthal. He studied at Hebrew Union College and the Univ. of Cincinnati, where he received a B.A. in 1928, and moved to New York City, receiving a Master of Hebrew Letters from the Jewish Institute of Religion and a Master of Arts from Columbia Univ.'s Teachers College in 1932. Rosenthal was ordained in 1932, marrying Bertha Becker that same day, and accepting a position in Louisiana serving several small congregations. In 1933 he accepted a call to Congregation B'NAI JESHURUN,† the Temple on the Heights, in Cleveland. During his tenure, Rosenthal was active in Jewish affairs. An ardent Zionist, Rosenthal established the Hts. Temple Zionist District, making the congregation the first in America to affiliate with the Zionist Organization of America. In 1936 he was a delegate to the first World Jewish Congress. He was also president of the local chapter of the American Jewish Congress.

Rosenthal, active in civil rights, was cochairman of the NAACP Membership Campaign in 1960 and received the NAACP's Freedom Plaque in 1975. He worked on behalf of the United Negro College Fund and was a board member of Wilberforce Univ., as well as treasurer of the Wilberforce Univ. Foundation. Rosenthal served on several civic commissions, and in 1952 was appointed the first Jewish chaplain of the CLEVELAND FIRE DEPT.† He received a dozen honorary doctoral degrees and several citations for his humanitarian work.

Rosenthal had 2 children, Susannah and Jonathan. He was buried in Chesterland Memorial Park.

Rabbi Rudolph M. Rosenthal Papers, WRHS.

**ROSENTHAL, SAMUEL** (15 Mar. 1885–11 May 1957), founded and presided over the Cleveland Overall Co. (1915, see the WORK WEAR CORP.†) and created the Buckeye Garment Rental Co. in 1941. His unique approach to work clothes—renting standardized uniforms to INDUSTRY†—permanently altered the market. Active in many local and national Jewish organizations, Rosenthal was a founder and honorary trustee of PARK SYNAGOGUE† in CLEVELAND HTS.† Born in Austria, son of Marcus and Chana (Weisbrot) Rosenthal, he came to the U.S. in 1901, settling first in Rochester, NY, then moving to Cleveland in 1914. He was a life trustee of the CLEVELAND HEBREW SCHOOLS† and the BUREAU OF JEWISH EDUCATION† and belonged to the Jewish Welfare Federation (see JEWISH COMMUNITY FEDERATION†). In the national arena, he helped found and served as vice-president of the American Assn. for Jewish Education.

In 1912 Rosenthal married Sadie Dosberg; they lived in SHAKER HTS.† with their children, Leighton A. and Charlotte R. Kramer. Rosenthal is buried in Warrensville Cemetery.—J.M.

**ROSENWASSER, MARCUS** (4 Oct. 1846–4 Sept. 1910), physician and teacher, was born in Bohemia, son of Herman and Rosalia Rosenwasser. He came to Cleveland with his family in 1852, graduated from CENTRAL HIGH SCHOOL† in 1864, then returned to Europe to study medicine at the universities of Prague and Wurzburg. He worked in European hospitals and completed postgraduate work at Wurzburg and the Univ. of Vienna before returning to Cleveland in 1868. Rosenwasser specialized in obstetrics and gynecology, serving for many years as an obstetrician at St. Ann's Maternity Hospital in Woodland, in great demand by the immigrant community. He was also a resident gynecologist at MT. SINAI HOSPITAL,† consulting gynecologist at ST. JOHN HOSPITAL† and City Hospital, and visiting surgeon at Cleveland General Hospital. Rosenwasser was professor of gynecology at Cleveland College for Physicians & Surgeons and professor of obstetrics at Wooster Univ. Medical School. He served as dean at both institutions.

In 1901 Mayor TOM L. JOHNSON appointed Rosenwasser president of the CLEVELAND BOARD OF HEALTH,† a position he held 2 years. Rosenwasser belonged to several medical societies and was president for 1 term of the CUYAHOGA COUNTY MEDICAL SOCIETY.† Although not an active Jewish communal leader, Rosenwasser rendered service to the community as volunteer physician for the Jewish Orphan Home for 42 years. He was also a board member of the TEMPLE† and was a member of B'NAI B'RITH† and the EXCELSIOR CLUB.†

Rosenwasser married Ida Rohrheimer in 1877. They had 4 children: Paul, Herman, Alice, and an unnamed son who died in infancy. Rosenwasser was buried in Mayfield Cemetery.

Marcus Rosenwasser Diary, WRHS.

**ROUDEBUSH, GEORGE MILTON** (25 Jan. 1894–29 Feb. 1992), athlete and Cleveland lawyer for 73 years, was born in Newtonville, OH, the son of George Milton and Rose Patchel Roudebush. He attended Denison Univ., where he was all-Ohio Conference in football and lettered in basketball, baseball, and tennis. He graduated in 1915 with a B.Ph. degree, followed by an LL.B. degree from the Univ. of Cincinnati. During World War I, he served as an army captain in France for 18 months. Coming to Cleveland, Roudebush began his law practice in 1919 with Snyder, Henry Thomsen, Ford & Seagrave, becoming a specialist in public finance and taxation. Later he was senior partner in Roudebush, Brown, Corlett & Ulrich which merged with ARTER & HADDEN† in 1986. As chairman of the Chamber of Commerce committee on taxation in the 1930s, he favored repealing the enabling act, which allowed cities to vote taxes for relief purposes. Roudebush successfully combined his law career with athletics, playing professional football and basketball in Dayton during the 1920s and officiating at college football and baseball games. In 1929 he and Harold Lowe won Cleveland's tennis doubles championship. In 1975 he was inducted into the Athletic Hall of Fame at Denison Univ.

Roudebush married Harriette McCann in Dayton 28 June 1924; they had three children: Jane Daganhardt of Dayton, George M. III of Chardon, and Thomas of Overland Park, KS. A resident of SHAKER HTS.,† he died in Chardon and was buried at Maple Grove Cemetery, Licking County, OH.—M.S.

**ROUSE, BENJAMIN** (23 Mar. 1795–5 July 1871), a pioneer philanthropist, was born in Boston, MA, son of Joseph and Mahitable Corbet Rouse. He lost both parents at age 6, and, unable to secure a formal education, compensated through common sense and fanatical determination. At 17 he served in the War of 1812, after the war becoming a building contractor. On 12 Aug. 1821, he married Rebecca Elliott Cromwell (see REBECCA ROUSE); they moved to New York in 1824. A strong devotion to Christianity characterized Rouse's new career as a real estate developer, and he became deeply interested in the establishment of Sunday schools for the city's poor. He was so successful in this task that the American Sunday School Union asked him to become their agent in Cleveland, commissioning him to open a depository and organize Sunday schools in the Western Reserve. Rouse accepted this appointment and moved to Cleveland with his wife in Oct. 1830.

In the village of about 1,000, Rouse opened a depository of Sunday school books in his home at the corner of PUBLIC SQUARE,† and spent many years spreading the Gospel both literally and figuratively throughout northern Ohio. In addition, he founded a Tract Society, a Seamen's Friend Society, and several other organizations. He was active in organizing FIRST BAPTIST CHURCH† of Cleveland in 1833, and for nearly 40 years was a leading member and deacon. In 1852 he erected the Rouse Bldg. at the corner of Public Square.

Rouse had four children: Benjamin Franklin, Edwin Cooleridge, Ellen Rebecca, and George W. He and his wife were buried in Lake View Cemetery.

Adella Hughes Family Papers, WRHS.

**ROUSE, REBECCA CROMWELL** (30 Oct. 1799–23 Dec. 1887), leading social-services organizer and reformer, was born in Salem, MA, to John and Rebecca Elliot Cromwell. Rouse was educated in religion and the classics and acquired worldly knowledge through her extensive travels abroad. In 1821 she married BENJAMIN ROUSE; they lived in Boston and New York before moving to Cleveland in 1830. As a member of the LADIES TRACT SOCIETY,† Rouse made personal visits to every home in the village. She was an original member of the FIRST BAPTIST† Society. In 1842 she founded and became president of the MARTHA WASHINGTON & DORCAS SOCIETY,† one of the first benevolent organizations in the city, which originated the Protestant Orphan Asylum, where she served for many years as director. Dedicated to reforming the baneful effects of alcohol, she helped organize the CLEVELAND LADIES TEMPERANCE UNION† in June 1850.

Rouse organized the Ladies' Aid Society on 20 Apr. 1861, 5 days after Pres. Lincoln's first call for troops. Later to become the SOLDIERS' AID SOCIETY† of Cleveland, U.S. Sanitary Commission, a precursor to the AMERICAN RED CROSS,† Rouse served as its president and was personally respon-

sible for raising vast amounts of money through sanitary fairs. The society collected and distributed supplies of inestimable value and offered nursing to military men and their families throughout northern Ohio during the Civil War. In her honor, Rouse's figure is reproduced in one of the bronze panels on the SOLDIERS & SAILORS MONUMENT† in Cleveland's PUBLIC SQUARE.†

Rouse outlived her husband, Benjamin, by 16 years. They had four children: Benjamin Franklin, Edwin Cooleridge, Ellen Rebecca, and George W. Three other children died in infancy. Rouse, along with her husband, was buried in Lake View Cemetery.

Adella Hughes Family Papers, WRHS.

**ROWLAND, AMY FARLEY** (30 May 1872–10 March 1953), editor and teacher, served with the LAKESIDE UNIT,† World War I, edited a number of publications by Dr. GEORGE W. CRILE, SR., and was an advocate for women and girls. She was born in Saratoga Springs, NY, to Tace Wardwell Rowland and Rev. Lyman S. Rowland. The family soon moved to Lee, MA, where Rowland attended public schools. She graduated from Mount Holyoke College (B.S. 1893) and did 1 year of postgraduate study at Columbia Univ. Rowland taught school in New York and Washington, DC, for the next decade, and for 3 years, represented the U.S. at the International Institute for Girls in Spain. She became editorial secretary and assistant in surgical research to Dr. Crile of Cleveland in 1914. In the winter of 1914–15 she worked with the American Ambulance in France, as part of the Western Reserve Univ. Unit. After America entered World War I, she again traveled to France, this time with the Lakeside Hospital Unit as assistant registrar (May–October 1917). After Crile and others founded the CLEVELAND CLINIC FOUNDATION,† Rowland took charge of its editorial department (1921–26) and then became executive secretary.

Rowland was a charter member of the WOMEN'S CITY CLUB† of Cleveland and its director (1919–25) and president (1923–24); a founder of the Women's Council for the Promotion of Peace; a founder, officer and trustee of the Cleveland Girls' Council, a trustee of ALTA HOUSE† and WOMAN'S GENERAL HOSPITAL† and president (1919–22) of the Mt. Holyoke Alumnae Assn. of Cleveland. From 1928–35 she served as trustee of Mt. Holyoke College, which awarded her an honorary Master of Science degree in 1921. Rowland is buried in Ipswich, MA.—J.M.

**ROWLEY, CHARLES BACON "CARL"** (2 Apr. 1890–17 Dec. 1984) was an architect best known for his work with Philip Small in the 1920s. Rowley was born in Springfield, OH, and attended high school in Jackson, MI. He continued his education at MIT, where he graduated in 1912. He moved to Cleveland in 1920 and established the architectural firm of SMALL & ROWLEY† in 1921. Small and Rowley's projects for the VAN SWERINGENS included numerous homes, SHAKER SQUARE,† and the MORELAND COURTS† apartments. The firm was dissolved in 1928.

Rowley formed the firm of Chas. Bacon Rowley & Assoc that same year. From 1957–72 he worked with Ernst Payer, the firm becoming Rowley, Payer, Huffman & Leithold (1962–69), then Rowley, Payer, Huffman & Caldwall (1969–72).

Rowley designed public schools for several suburbs, the SHAKER HTS.† Public Library, the MAYFIELD COUNTRY CLUB,† and the CLIFTON CLUB,† as well as structures in the Cape Cod, MA, area. He designed many homes in Cleveland's east side suburbs, including an experimental house of steel sheathed with porcelain enamel shingles (1932).

Rowley retired in 1961 and then served as a consulting architect, including work for TRUE TEMPER.† In 1976 he moved to his former summer home in Harwich Port, MA. His wife, Elizabeth, whom he married in 1914, died in 1983. Rowley died in Hyannis, MA, on 17 Dec. 1984. He was survived by a son, Charles B. Jr., and two daughters, Hazel Collord and Elizabeth Tittman.—D.R.

**RUBINSTEIN, BERYL** (26 Oct. 1898–29 Dec. 1952), pianist, composer, teacher, and director of the CLEVELAND INSTITUTE OF MUSIC† from 1932–52, was born in Athens, GA, son of Isaac and Matilda (Abrahams) Rubinstein. He began his pianist career as a child performer touring the U.S. from 1905–11, making his debut with the Metropolitan Opera Orchestra in 1911. He went to Europe to study with Jose Vianna De Motta and Ferrucio Busoni, making his professional debut in New York in 1916 and appearing with the New York Philharmonic, Cleveland, Detroit, Philadelphia, San Francisco Symphony, and London Symphony orchestras. In 1921 Rubinstein joined the piano faculty of the Cleveland Institute of Music; he became head of the piano department in 1925, dean of faculty in 1929, and director in 1932, where he remained until his death. During his tenure at the institute, he brought world-renowned musicians to the faculty. He continued his active concert and recital career. As a composer, he produced works for orchestra, piano, violin, string quartet, and voice, and an opera, *The Sleeping Beauty,* premiered in New York in 1938. He served in the U.S. Army 1942–44 and gave over 75 concerts for servicemen.

On 29 Dec. 1925 Rubinstein married Elsa Landesman. They had two children, Ellen and Beryl David. Rubinstein died in CLEVELAND HTS.† and was buried in the Mayfield Cemetery.

**RUETENIK, HERMAN J.** (20 Sept. 1826–22 Feb. 1914), leader in the local German Reformed church, was born in Demerthin, Brandenburg, Germany, to Karl A. and Charlotte Woldman Ruetenik. He graduated from Joachimsthal Gymnasium, Berlin, and studied divinity at the Univ. of Halle (1846–48). After the 1848 revolution failed, he came to the U.S. as a political refugee. In 1852 Ruetenik entered the ministry, was ordained in 1853, and later that year came to Ohio. After serving in Toledo and as a professor at Heidelberg Univ. in Tiffin, Ruetenik came to Cleveland in 1859 as pastor of the independent Congregation of Brethren, which eventually became the First Reformed Church. He later established the Second and Third Reformed Churches, and the German Sunday School Mission (1886), which became the Eighth Reformed Church in 1889. He also helped establish the deaconess's home on Scranton Rd., and in 1913 organized an Italian mission in the HAYMARKET† district.

Soon after his arrival in Cleveland, Ruetenik began publishing religious periodicals; this evolved into Central Publishing Co. of the Reformed Church. He also founded Calvin College in 1866 with $600 raised in Germany. The school was to give instruction in German and teach Greek and Latin, but Ruetenik's plans apparently received little support from church officials, and the college's goals were revised to more closely follow American educational practices.

Ruetenik authored 7 published works, including *German Grammar* (1900) and *Pioneers of the Reformed Church in America* (1902). Ruetenik married Amelia Clara Martin in 1853 and had 6 sons and 4 daughters: Martin, Gustave, Otto, Calvin, Fred, John, Ruth, Clara, Natalie, and Charlotte. Ruetenik was buried in Riverside Cemetery.

**RUMBOLD, CHARLOTTE MARGARET** (28 Dec. 1869–2 July 1960) was active in urban planning in 2 cities, St. Louis, MO, and Cleveland. Daughter of Thomas Frazier and Charlotte Rumbold, she was born in Belleville, IL, graduated from Columbia Univ. and studied social work in Europe. Rumbold worked in St. Louis as superintendent of playgrounds and recreation (1906–15) and through her time there was involved in the national Playground Assn. of America (1906). She became acquainted with FRANCIS F. PRENTISS and others who championed the "city efficient." Holding to the principle of equal pay, Rumbold left

St. Louis in 1915 when the Board of Aldermen refused to raise her salary.

Rumbold, at the request of the CLEVELAND FOUNDATION,† undertook a social survey in 1916 on commercial recreation. She worked for the Chamber of Commerce (1917–38) as asst. secretary and secretary of its City Plan Committee until her retirement. Nationally and locally, as a member of the WOMEN'S CITY CLUB,† Rumbold argued for the planned city: land-use ZONING† (see *VILLAGE OF EUCLID v. AMBLER REALTY CO.†*); the Group Plan; PUBLIC HOUSING,† PARKS,† and HIGHWAYS.† She was secretary and board member for several chamber-initiated groups, such as the Euclid Ave. Assn. (1920). WM. HOPKINS appointed her to the Cleveland City Plan Commission (1924–42). Rumbold sparked the Ohio Planning Conference (1919), serving as its president, secretary, treasurer, and statehouse lobbyist. In 1933, as secretary of Cleveland Homes, Inc., she secured New Deal funds for the Cedar-Central housing project. Rumbold was described in 1945 by LOUIS B. SELTZER: "Tiny Woman Never Shrinks from Storms." A Catholic, Rumbold died in Cleveland and was buried in Belleville, IL. She never married.

**RUSSELL, JACK PAUL** (2 Feb. 1915–7 June 1979), 16th Ward councilman from 1943–71, was born Paul Ruschak in the Buckeye Rd. area of Cleveland to Stephen and Mary Ruschak, immigrants from Austria-Hungary. He began in politics by managing Joseph Stearns's council campaign in 1933, and built his influence in the neighborhood by publishing newspapers, including the *Buckeye Press*. In the late 1930s, he changed his name to Jack Paul Russell, and in 1943 he was elected to city council. He was Democratic majority leader from 1944–52 and council president from 1955–63. After losing the council presidency to Jas. V. Stanton, he continued representing the 16th Ward until 1971. Russell, with his trademark white Stetson hat, Cuban cigar, and Cadillac, was an influential ward politician who used his Buckeye area political base to rise to power in city government. He supported projects aimed at improving the city and was noted for keeping his word. In 1957 he lectured at Harvard on municipal government; a year later, he was the subject of a national CBS television documentary dealing with urban machine politics. During his years in council, he operated several businesses, including the Ohio Fire Protective Systems. In 1935 he married Irene Maguary; they had 3 children: Richard, Marilyn Richards, and Elaine Thomas. He died in Cleveland.

Jack P. Russell Papers, WRHS.

**RUSSELL, RALPH** (1789–28 Dec. 1866), founder of the North Union Shaker colony, was born in Windsor Locks, CT, the son of Jacob and Esther Dunham Russell. In 1811 Ralph and his brother, Elijah, traveled to the Warrensville area to inspect land their father had bought from the Connecticut Land Co. Favorably impressed, they returned in 1812, bringing 20 members of the Russell family to settle here. Ralph married Laura Elsworth 8 Jan. 1818 in Chester MA, and they returned to Warrensville. On a trip to Union Village, a Shaker community (near Lebanon, OH) in 1821, Ralph was enthused by the good deeds and right living of the society in which property was held in common and celibacy was practiced as part of their faith. He returned home and began to proselytize the large, closeknit Warrensville families to adopt Shaker ways, aided by biannual visits from Union Village elders. Ralph founded the NORTH UNION SHAKER COMMUNITY† of believers, only to be superseded by Elder Ashbel Kitchell, who arrived in 1826 to prepare converts for the transition to a celibate life where men and women lived separately. When the final covenant was signed by those who committed themselves to Shaker beliefs in 1828, Ralph Russell did not sign. He and his family left North Union, moving to BENTLEYVILLE,† where he continued to farm until he died and was buried in the village churchyard. Among his survivors were sons Ralph Elsworth, Jacob Huffman, Hezikiah Loomis, Andrew Jackson, and Joseph Pelton Russell.—M.S.

Piercy, Caroline B. *The Valley of God's Pleasure* (1951).

**RUTHENBERG, CHARLES** (9 July 1882–3 Mar. 1927), prominent in the Cleveland Socialist and, later, Communist parties, was born in Cleveland to August and Wilhelmenia (Lau) Ruthenberg. He was educated at DYKE COLLEGE,† and worked as a salesman and bookkeeper for the Cleveland office of Selmer Hess Publishing Co. of New York. Ruthenberg first considered himself a Progressive, backing TOM L. JOHNSON; however, after reading Marx's *Das Kapital* he became committed to the Socialists, and by 1912 was a militant party member. As leader of the local Socialist party, Ruthenberg was an effective organizer and perennial political candidate. He ran for mayor 4 times (1911, 1915, 1917, 1919); for Ohio governor in 1912; for the U.S. Senate in 1914; and for the U.S. House of Representatives in 1916 and 1918. By 1917 Ruthenberg had given up his job to devote himself more to political work, and had also moved to the radical left of the party. After the Bolshevik Revolution, he switched to the COMMUNIST PARTY,† becoming executive secretary of the Communist Party of America.

Ruthenberg's last major political action in Cleveland was leading the May Day Parade of 1919, which resulted in a riot and his arrest on a charge of assault with intent to kill (see MAY DAY RIOTS†).

Ruthenberg married Rosaline Nickel and they had one son, Daniel. Ruthenberg died suddenly in 1927 of a ruptured appendix. His body was cremated in Chicago, and his ashes sent to Moscow and interred in the Kremlin Wall. Ruthenberg and John Reed were the only American Communists so honored by the Soviet Union.

Johnson, Oakley C. *The Day Is Coming: The Life and Work of Charles E. Ruthenberg, 1882–1927* (1957).

RYCHLIK, CHARLES VACLAV (26 June 1875–6 Dec. 1962), Cleveland-born composer and violinist, son of Vaclav and Karoline Cermack Rychlik, was, at 14, the youngest member of the Cleveland Musicians Union. In 1891 he began studies at the Prague Conservatory, joining the Bohemian String Quartet, performing throughout Europe and meeting Brahms and Bruckner in Vienna. Brahms, in fact, played viola with the group on a piece he had written. Rychlik boarded at the home of Antonin Dvorak, graduated from the conservatory in 1895, and in 1897 joined the Chicago Symphony Orchestra. In 1901 Rychlik's father died and he came back to Cleveland. He played violin in the forerunner of the CLEVELAND ORCHESTRA† under JOHANN BECK and then EMIL RING. In 1908 he replaced Carl Dueringer as 2nd violinist in the PHILHARMONIC STRING QUARTET,† playing with the group until its demise in 1928. Rychlik also played with the Cleveland Orchestra from its inception in 1918 for 2 years. During this time, Rychlik began teaching and composing. He wrote numerous works for violin. His *Rhapsody* in 4 contrasting movements (1923) was premiered in 1933 by the Detroit Orchestra. He composed and taught at his home/studio; his students included F. KARL GROSSMAN and child prodigy Erni Valasek. Forty of his pupils became members of the Cleveland Orchestra. In 1940 400 pupils, friends, and colleagues gathered in the Hotel Cleveland ballroom to pay him tribute. Rychlik was internationally known through his 25-volume *Encyclopedia of Violin Technique,* which took 20 years to complete. Rychlik was unmarried and buried in Lake View Cemetery.

RYDER, JAMES F. (7 Apr. 1826–2 June 1904), photographer locally best known for encouraging ARCHIBALD WILLARD to paint *THE SPIRIT OF '76* and popularizing it through chromolithography, was born in Ithaca, NY. Inspired by the local daguerreotypist to purchase a camera, Ryder joined his establishment in 1847. In 1849 Chas. E. Johnson, a daguerreotypist from Cleveland, invited him to visit his studio. Ryder left Ithaca and became a traveling daguerreotypist, working in Kirtland, Painesville, CHAGRIN FALLS,† and BEDFORD† before settling in Elyria in 1850. Johnson asked Ryder to become manager-operator of his Cleveland studio, so for 2 years Ryder divided his time between Cleveland and Elyria.

In 1868 Ryder introduced negative retouching to the U.S., paying the passage for Prof. Karl Leutgib from the Munich Academy to teach him the new process. As a result, Ryder received an award at a photography show in Boston in 1869. In 1872 Archibald Willard sent 2 paintings to Ryder's shop to be framed. Ryder displayed the paintings, and they became so popular he decided to make chromolithograph copies of the works, which became bestsellers across the country. Ryder encouraged Willard to paint *The Spirit of '76* for the Centennial Exhibition. Ryder also photographed several U.S. presidents, most notably Pres. Garfield. Retiring in 1894, he produced his autobiography, *Voightlander and I,* in 1902. This was one of few autobiographical accounts produced by a 19th-century photographer. Ryder married Susan Park in 1852; they had no children. Ryder died in Cleveland and was buried in Lake View Cemetery.

Ryder, James F. *Voightlander and I* (1902).

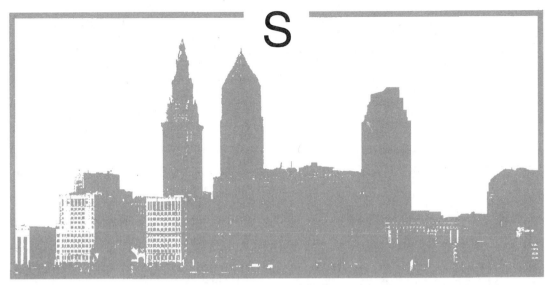

# S

**SADATAKI, MARY HATA** (13 Nov. 1916–24 Aug. 1993) was a teacher at a Japanese relocation camp, a founding member in 1965 of the Cleveland Japanese-American Foundation, and together with her husband, William, helped develop the Cleveland Chapter of the Japanese American Citizens League.

Born in San Francisco, CA, to Reverend and Katsura Hata, Mary attended San Francisco public schools and Westminster junior college. Mary then studied in Japan prior to World War II. In 1942 Mary and her family were placed in the Rowher Relocation Camp in Arkansas. She taught elementary school at the camp. Mary gained release from the camp to attend Macalaster College in St. Paul, MN, on a scholarship. She graduated from Macalaster College in 1944 with a degree in social work and took a job working with juvenile delinquent children in Chicago.

Mary moved to the Cleveland area in 1953. She helped to negotiate a rental program allowing elderly first-generation Japanese to live together at Euclid Villa Apartments and hosted regular parties for senior citizens at her home. As president in 1973 of the Japanese American Citizens League, Mary helped to initiate scholarship programs for college-bound seniors, and started an annual holiday fair of Japanese crafts in EUCLID.† She served on the board of the Cleveland Japanese-American Foundation until her death.

Mary Hata married William Sadataki in 1953 and had a son, William, Jr. A Methodist, she was buried in Northfield Macedonia Cemetery in Northfield.—T.B.

**SAGUIN, SIEUR DE** (variations Seguin, Seguein, Shaguin; no given name is known), a French trader, was the first recorded resident of Cuyahoga County to construct a permanent residence. During his stay, the locality was under the control of France, to whom the Indians gave their allegiance. A trader such as Saguin was needed to trade with and maintain the good will of the Indians, as well as to relay intelligence of Indian attitudes and English influence and deployments. That Saguin stayed near Cleveland is affirmed in the memoirs of Robt. Navarre, intendant of Detroit from 1730–60, who in 1743 was sent to visit the trading post that had been established on the CUYAHOGA RIVER† by Saguin; and is also confirmed by reference to the Cuyahoga as Riviere á Seguin (de Lery, 1754) and River de Saguin (Montresor, 1764), and by Lewis Evans's 1755 map notation of the "French House." Estimates of Saguin's location on the Cuyahoga River range from the junction of TINKER'S CREEK† to BROOKLYN HTS.† The exact length of Saguin's short tenure, beginning by 1742, is uncertain, but he constructed at least 2 buildings and apparently cultivated corn before being instructed by Sieur Pierre Joseph Celoron De Blainville in 1743 to depart his post, when Detroit authorities became afraid of losing their Ottawa fur trade to Saguin and refused to send him the gunpowder the Indians needed and requested in trade, making his position increasingly untenable.

**ST. ANDREWS, HELENE** (20 Apr. 1912–29 Mar. 1993), during her 55 years with the Higbee Co. (see DILLARD DEPARTMENT STORE†), influenced the tastes and styles of thousands of women in Greater Cleveland.

Born in Cleveland to Henry and Rose St. Andrews, she graduated from CENTRAL HIGH SCHOOL,† and attended Ohio State Univ. and JOHN CARROLL UNIV.† She studied at the Darvas School of Fashion and appeared in musical comedy for 3 years in New York City before she returned to Cleveland in 1937.

St. Andrews began her career with the Higbee Co. in 1938 as an in-house fashion model, advanced to asst. fashion director, and later, fashion director. As fashion coordinator, a position created for her at Higbee's in 1958, she worked with national and international designers during Higbee's Import Fairs. She also produced departmental fashion shows in Higbee's auditorium, on television, at private clubs, and other institutions. Higbee's Stag Shop for men was one of her innovations. By 1975 she had become Higbee's Personal Fashion Consultant and advised many Cleveland women.

St. Andrews organized the first teen and college boards for students interested in fashion. In 1962 she created the Fashion Therapy Clinic for Patients of Fairhill Psychiatric Clinic (see FAIRHILL MENTAL HEALTH CENTER†). She was a founding member and past regional director of the Fashion Group of Cleveland, Inc. and wrote and lectured on fashion.

She married Charles Varga on 2 Jan. 1945. They had two children, Gregory and Maureen. A Roman Catholic, St. Andrews is buried in Holy Cross Cemetery.

The Helene St. Andrews Fund for Costume Exhibition was established in her honor in 1992 to benefit the Chisholm Halle Costume Wing at the WESTERN RESERVE HISTORICAL SOCIETY.†

**ST. JOHN, SAMUEL** (29 Mar. 1813–9 Sept. 1876), science professor, proponent of natural history, and newspaper publisher during his short time in the Cleveland area in the mid–1800s, was born in New Canaan, CT, son of Samuel and Hannah Benedict Richards St. John. He graduated as valedictorian from Yale in 1834, and in 1839 became professor of chemistry, geology, and mineralogy at Western Reserve College in Hudson, teaching biology as well. When the college established its Medical Dept. in Cleveland in 1843, St. John was appointed to oversee the awarding of degrees by the medical faculty, becoming professor of chemistry, natural history, and medical jurisprudence at the Medical College. St. John was an original curator and secretary of the CLEVELAND ACADEMY OF NATURAL SCIENCES† when it was organized in 1845, and also was secretary of the publication committee for the 1853 meeting in Cleveland of the American Assn. for the Advancement of Science. In 1851 he and Prof. Jehu Brainard published a geology text, *Elements of Geology*. St. John tried his hand at newspaper editing, joining Dr. JARED P. KIRTLAND and O. H. Knapp in 1850 as coeditor of the weekly *Family Visitor*, which was published until around 1858. In 1852 St. John resigned from Western Reserve College in a dispute with the administration over back salary owed him. He stayed in Cleveland, reportedly becoming principal of the CLEVELAND FEMALE SEMINARY† in 1854. In 1856 he accepted a chair in chemistry at the College of Physicians & Surgeons in New York.

St. John married Amelia Parkinson Curtis ca. 1840. They had 3 children: Eliza, Samuel Benedict, and George. He died in New Canaan, CT.—T.B.

**SALEN, CHARLES P.** (5 Dec. 1860–23 June 1924), CUYAHOGA COUNTY DEMOCRATIC PARTY† leader, was born in Portsmouth, NH, to Peter and Fredericka Wyx Salen, came with his family to Cleveland around 1866, and attended 1 year at Concordia College in Ft. Wayne, IN, before returning to Cleveland to work for the *West Side Sentinel*. Attracted to politics, he established a weekly Democratic newspaper, as well as the Young Men's Democratic League of Cleveland.

Salen was elected city clerk, serving from 1883–85 and 1887–89. In 1890 he became secretary of the Board of Elections, initiating the use of metal election booths to insure voting secrecy. He managed TOM L. JOHNSON's successful campaigns for Congress in 1890 and 1892, and his mayoral campaigns in 1901, 1903, and 1905. He was director of accounts from 1899–1901, with his investigation of the previous McKisson administration returning $20,000 to the city. He was director of public works under Mayor Johnson for 1 year, and was elected county clerk in 1902, serving until 1910. He was also a member of the State Executive Committee of the Democratic party and its chairman in 1903.

A promoter of amateur sports, Salen supported Sunday baseball, organized the Ohio Skating Assn., and maintained a free skating rink at West Blvd. and Detroit known as Salen's Rink. He operated refreshment stands at PUBLIC SQUARE,† LUNA PARK,† and Gordon Gardens in association with Jacob Mintz.

Salen married Mamie Schwab and had 2 daughters, Aimee (Lowensohn) and Lorna (Giffin). He died in LAKEWOOD† and was buried in Lakewood Park Cemetery.

Chas. P. Salen Papers, WRHS.

**SALISBURY, JAMES HENRY** (13 Oct. 1823–23 Aug. 1905), a physician and medical researcher who investigated the germ-causation theory of disease, was born in Scott, NY, to Nathan and Lucretia Babcock Salisbury. He graduated with a Bachelor of Natural Science from Rensselaer Polytechnic Inst. in 1846; an M.D. from Albany Medical College in 1850; and an M.A. from Union College in 1852. In

1844 he was appointed asst. chemist with the Geological Survey of the State of New York. Promoted in 1849 to principal chemist, he served until 1852 and afterwards applied himself to private practice and research. After serving as a physician during the Civil War, Salisbury came to Cleveland to help start Charity Hospital College, where he lectured on physiology, histology, and microscopic anatomy between 1864–66. He had a private practice in Cleveland until around 1880, when he moved to New York City. He specialized in the treatment of chronic diseases, especially those previously considered fatal. Salisbury began studying germs as the cause of diseases as early as 1849. Severely criticized in Europe and America, not until 1865 was he proved correct. In 1860 Salisbury began studying the origin and functions of blood, later turning to the relation of food and drink to the occurrence of disease, advocating dietary measures, including Salisbury steak, as cures. He also studied the chemical analysis of plants, spores, fungi, and parasites as causes of diseases; other interests led him to study ancient rocks and earth writings.

Salisbury married Clara Brassee in 1860 and had 2 children, Minnie and Trafford. He died in Cleveland and was buried in Lake View Cemetery.

**SALTZMAN, MAURICE** (25 May 1918–21 Jan. 1990), businessman, civic leader, and philanthropist in Cleveland and Israel, received the Human Relations Award from the National Conference of Christians and Jews (1966) and the Charles Eisenman Award from the JEWISH COMMUNITY FEDERATION† (1974). A "zillionaire" by age 48, Saltzman, born in Cleveland, was orphaned at age 4 and lived at the Jewish Orphan Home (BELLEFAIRE†) until he graduated from Cleveland Hts. High School at 16. He worked in the shipping room of Lampl Fashions, Inc. for 5 years, when he and Max Reiter founded Ritmore Sportswear, which later became BOBBIE BROOKS, INC.† His philanthropy soon reflected his business success: between 1941 and 1966, he and his wife donated more than $2.5 million to institutions such as MT. SINAI MEDICAL CENTER† and the Univ. of Notre Dame. Saltzman led the dress company until 1987. He maintained a lifelong relationship with Bellefaire, serving as benefactor and honorary trustee and hiring student employees. Among many community activities, he was founder trustee for life of the *CLEVELAND JEWISH NEWS*,† vice-president of TEMPLE EMANU EL,† president of both the Jewish Community Federation and Mt. Sinai Medical Center (1976–79), and a trustee of the Univ. Circle Development Foundation, Inc. (predecessor of UNIV. CIRCLE, INC.†), Brandeis Univ., and CASE WESTERN RESERVE UNIV.,† among other institutions. In Israel, he established a senior citizen center, a library, and a museum.

Saltzman married his secretary, Shirley Rosenberg, in 1944; they had three daughters: Lorrie Fromson, Judith Bea-Taylor, and Terry Saltzman. Saltzman died in Palm Beach, FL.—J.M.

**SAMPLINER, HERMAN** (8 Nov. 1835–5 Dec. 1899) was an activist in the Cleveland Jewish community and the founding president of the B'NAI JESHURUN† congregation, the third oldest Jewish congregation in Greater Cleveland.

Son of Joseph and Lena Sampliner, he was born in Lemes, Hungary, and along with two brothers came to Cleveland in 1864. In Cleveland, he tried his hand as a merchant, selling liquor, then shoes, then appliances. His most enduring involvement was as a tavern keeper, his establishment located downtown on Ontario St. Sampliner's greatest interest, however, was his support of Jewish causes. Cleveland's Hungarian Jewish population had been too small to have its own congregation, but Sampliner organized those interested, and his home on California Alley became the site for B'Nai Jeshurun's first worship service, with 16 in attendance. He was also a member of Sons of Benjamin, Sons of Israel, Knights of Joseph, Kesher Shel Barzel, Knights of Pythias, and B'NAI B'RITH.† He served as treasurer of the Hungarian Aid Society and was president of the Ladies Legal Aid Society.

In 1892 he founded the Young Ladies' Hebrew Assn. and served as its president. The association was committed to alleviating the suffering of the sick, and among its aims was establishing a Jewish hospital in the city. The efforts of the association led to the 1902 founding of a small hospital which became the forerunner of today's MT. SINAI MEDICAL CENTER.†

Sampliner married twice. His first wife, Sallie Klein, bore him four children: Adele, Joseph, Lena, and Armand. After her death in 1887, Sampliner married Rebecca Stern on 13 May 1888. Sampliner is buried in Fir St. Cemetery in Cleveland.—J.T.

**SANCHEZ, GENEVIEVE** (9 Oct. 1918–9 Aug. 1993) was one of Cleveland's greatest sandlot stars. Born in Cleveland to John and Mary Shnel Peck, Genevieve grew up in the SLAVIC VILLAGE† neighborhood and graduated from South High School. In high school she lettered three times in track. Following graduation in 1934 she switched from track to softball and joined a team in the industrial fast pitch league and began an outstanding pitching career. Her team won the city championship.

In 1936 her prowess on the mound led her National Screw and Manufacturing Co. team to the national softball championships and she was named the Most Valuable Player in the national tournament in Chicago. In 1937 the team again won the national championship. In 1939 she switched teams and began commuting between Cleveland and New Orleans, where she pitched for the Jax Brewery team, leading it to world championships in 1942 and 1943. Her last year as a softball pitcher came in 1946 when, joined by 2 of her sisters, she helped capture the Greater Cleveland metropolitan title for her Puritas Springs Park team. Altogether in her 13-year mound career, she hurled 6 no-hit games and 24 1-hitters. Seldom did opposing batters garner more than 3 hits. Her best record was 27–3, and she achieved several 20-win seasons.

Genevieve married John Penkowski on 22 Feb. 1941, and they had a son, John. The first marriage ended in divorce. On 19 Sept. 1969, she married Daniel Sanchez. Sanchez is buried in Calvary Cemetery in Cleveland.—J.T.

**SANDERS, WILLIAM BROWNELL** (21 Sept. 1854–25 Jan. 1929), corporate lawyer and founding partner of the law firm of SQUIRE, SANDERS & DEMPSEY,† was born in Cleveland to William and Cornelia Smith Sanders. He grew up in Jacksonville, IL, and graduated from Illinois College with A.B. and A.M. degrees, and from Albany (N.Y.) Law School with an LL.B. degree in 1875. Sanders joined the Cleveland law firm of Burke, Ingersoll & Sanders. In Feb. 1888 he became a Cuyahoga County Common Pleas Court judge, resigning in 1890 to form Squire, Sanders & Dempsey, of which he was a partner until his death. Sanders directed the opposition in a 7-year legal and political battle against Mayor TOM L. JOHNSON concerning municipal control of Cleveland's street railroads. The resulting Tayler Grant, formulated by Sanders and Federal Judge ROBT. W. TAYLER, gave an exclusive street railway franchise to CLEVELAND RAILWAY CO.† while stipulating low fares and municipal oversight of the system. The strain of battle was disastrous to Sanders, whose health was ruined. Thereafter Sanders devoted less time to law, instead traveling and summering at his New England home. Sanders helped establish the financial foundation for the CLEVELAND MUSEUM OF ART† by incorporating the 3 separate trust funds established for the museum into one. Sanders was the museum's first president (1913–20) and a trustee. He was also a trustee for Society for Savings and a director of Guardian Trust Co. and Kelly Island Line & Transport Co. Sanders married Annie Otis in 1884 and had a daughter, Mary Ermina.

**SANFORD [or SANDFORD], ALFRED S.** (5 Mar. 1805–23 Dec. 1888), born in Milford, CT, was the antebellum captain of the CLEVELAND GRAYS† and Cleveland fire chief in 1845. In 1863 he became an incorporator of St. Clair St. Railroad Co. At Pres. ABRAHAM LINCOLN'S FUNERAL† in Cleveland, Sanford served on the General Committee, the Sub-committee on Location of Remains, and the Sub-committee on the Military. By the time of the 1865 funeral, Sanford was referred to as "General Sanford."

Sanford married Maria Hayward in 1833, taking her son, W. H. Hayward, as his step-son. He and Maria had a son, JULIUS R. Sanford is buried in Lake View Cemetery.

**SANFORD, JULIUS R.** (1835–16 May 1904), son of Maria Hayward and ALFRED S. SANFORD, was active in the Ohio Militia before the Civil War as a 3rd sergeant in the CLEVELAND GRAYS† in 1856, and a lt. colonel in the Cleveland Battalion. He was elected lt. colonel, Cleveland Battalion, Ohio Militia, 15 June 1858. After the Civil War broke out, Sanford served as adjutant, 41ST OHIO VOLUNTEER INFANTRY† Regiment, beginning on 23 Aug. 1861, being promoted to 1st lt. on 25 Aug. He resigned 5 Jan. 1862. Apparently returning to Cleveland, he taught military tactics at Cleveland Institute (formerly CLEVELAND UNIV.†) on Univ. Hts., across the street from Camp Cleveland, between 1862–65. Sanford reentered military service as captain of Co. E, 128TH OHIO VOLUNTEER INFANTRY, beginning in Nov. 1863. He was later appointed acting asst. inspecting general on the staff of Gen. Samuel P. Heintzelman, commander of the Northern Dept. On 25 Mar. 1865, he was promoted to major; he was mustered out on 13 July 1865. Sanford died suddenly at his Cleveland home. He worked as a clerk during the latter part of his life. He is buried in Lake View Cemetery.

**SANSOM, ARTHUR B. (ART) JR.** (20 Sept. 1920–4 July 1991) launched a winner when he developed his "Born Loser" comic strip in 1965. The son of Arthur B. and Elizabeth Seurig Sansom, Art was born and educated in Cleveland, graduating from Shaw High School. He then attended Ohio Wesleyan Univ., where he earned his bachelor's degree in art and where he also met Isabel Henry, his future wife. They were married in Youngstown 3 Oct. 1941, and they raised one son, Arthur B., III (Chip).

During World War II, he worked as a draftsman for General Electric (see GENERAL ELECTRIC CO.†) in NELA PARK,† before joining the Newspaper Enterprises Assn. (NEA) syndicate as a staff artist. It was for NEA in 1965 that he began to draw the "Born Loser" comic strip featuring Brutus Thornapple. The strip grew very popular, becoming one of the 10 most widely syndicated comics in the world. In 1995 it appeared in nine languages, in over 1,300 newspapers, in 26 countries. Four paperback editions of the strip have also been published.

In 1977, after working on "Born Loser" alone for 12 years, Sansom was joined by his son, Chip. The father-son team also collaborated on another strip named "Dusty Chaps." The "Born Loser" was nominated six times for the National Cartoonists Society's Reuben Award, as the best humor strip of the year, and it came away with the prize in 1988 and again in 1991.

Following the death of his first wife in 1984, Sansom married Angelyn Mancuso on 3 Dec. 1987. Sansom is interred in Lakewood Cemetery.—J.T.

**SAPIRSTEIN, JACOB J.** (30 Oct. 1884–24 June 1987), founder of AMERICAN GREETINGS CORP.† and Jewish philanthropist, was born in Wasosz, Poland, the son of Rabbi Isaac and Molly Sapirstein and grew up in Grajeyvo, Poland. He came to Cleveland in 1906 and obtained a job selling postcards at a stand in the HOLLENDEN HOTEL.† He soon went out on his own, buying German-made cards and distributing them to drug and candy stores and novelty shops. When the World War I embargo on the importation of German-made cards heightened the demand for cards in the U.S., Sapirstein expanded his business, foregoing his horse-drawn wagon for a Ford automobile, which became his traveling office. He also pioneered the use of wall racks and rotating floor stands for card displays. By 1932 his sons had joined the firm, and the Sapirstein Card Company began to design and print its own line of cards. For business reasons, his sons changed their name to Stone in 1940. American Greetings thrived and Sapirstein retired as president in 1960, succeeded by his eldest son, Irving.

Sapirstein was vitally interested in the furtherance of Jewish education in the Cleveland area as a way to maintain Jewish values. He was a long-time benefactor of the Rabbinical College of Telshe and the HEBREW ACADEMY.† He married Jennie Kantor in 1906; they had 3 sons: Irving I., MORRIS S., and Harry H., and daughter Bernice M. Davis. Sapirstein died at his home in Univ. Hts. and was buried in Zion Memorial Park.—M.S.

Sapirstein Family Book, WRHS.
Sapirstein Family Papers, WRHS.

**SAUER, AUGUSTA "GUSTIE" VCELA** (8 Sept. 1893–3 Nov. 1985) was a licensed funeral director and cofounder, with her husband, Carl Henry Sauer, of Sauer funeral homes on Cleveland's West Side.

Born in Vienna, Austria, she came with her 3 siblings to Cleveland about 1904, following their mother, Anna's, death. They settled on W. 46th St. with their father, Josef Vcela, who had immigrated two years earlier. After his death (ca. 1906) all 4 children entered an orphanage.

Sauer received an eighth grade education. At age 14 she left the orphanage to board with a couple and do housework. At 16 she joined JOSEPH & FEISS CO.,† clothing manufacturers, as a seamstress. She married Carl Sauer in 1916. In 1922 Carl became a licensed embalmer and funeral director. In 1924 they opened Sauer's Funeral Home at 5303 Storer Ave. (now closed), where Gustie Sauer did the hair, make-up, and clothing for the deceased and chauffeured the hearse.

In 1934 Gustie Sauer became a licensed funeral director. In 1938 the Sauers opened a second funeral home at 4801 Memphis Ave. (Sauer-Good Funeral Home, their second location, is at 4438 Pearl Rd.) In 1946 the Sauer sons joined the business. Gustie Sauer retired in 1965, yet continued as consultant to the family business. She belonged to the Cuyahoga, OH, and National Funeral Directors Assns. A skilled horsewoman and instructor, she operated Sauer's Riding Academy on Tiedeman Rd. in Brooklyn Village with her husband during the 1930s.

The Sauers had 3 children: Charles, Donald, and Janice (Szilagyi). Gustie Sauer belonged to the Bethany United Church of Christ. She is buried in Riverside Cemetery.

**SAWICKI, JOSEPH F.** (18 Mar. 1881–30 Oct. 1969), lawyer, politician, and judge, was born in Gorzno, Poland, to Peter and Bogumila Jurkowska Sawicki, emigrated with his family to Cleveland when he was 5, and worked his way through St. Ignatius College, BALDWIN-WALLACE,† Western Reserve Univ. Law School, and Cleveland Law School, receiving the LL.B. degree, being admitted to the Ohio Bar, and beginning to practice law in 1904.

Sawicki served in the Ohio legislature from 1905–08 and 1911–12. He was appointed judge of municipal court on 1 Jan. 1919 and won his first election to the post that November. In 1932 Sawicki was forced into involuntary bankruptcy, with over $200,000 debt from real estate investments and campaign expenses. When court records made public the numerous loans made to Sawicki from practicing lawyers, the executive committee of the CLEVELAND BAR ASSN.† demanded his resignation, so Sawicki retired from the bench in 1933 and returned to private practice. In 1953 Sawicki served as a member of the Cleveland Charter Commission, and in 1959 was appointed special counsel for the Ohio attorney general.

Active in the Polish-American community, Sawicki was honored by the Cleveland Society of

Poles as "Good Joe of 1967" for his work in numerous Polish relief groups and the Polish-American Chamber of Commerce. An avid coin collector, he was president of the Western Reserve Numismatic Assn. Sawicki married Elizabeth Veronica Sadowska in 1908 and had 2 daughters, Mrs. Edward Gilbert and Mrs. Jas. Wager, and 2 sons, Eugene and Edwin.

**SCHANDLER, HYMAN** (11 Aug. 1900–3 Sept. 1990) was called by one local music critic, "Cleveland's most universally beloved living musician." His long career encompassed 48 years with the CLEVELAND ORCHESTRA,† 55 years as founding conductor of the CLEVELAND WOMEN'S ORCHESTRA,† and 65 years as violin teacher at the CLEVELAND MUSIC SCHOOL SETTLEMENT.† Born in Riga, Latvia, he was brought to Cleveland at the age of 3 and educated at Central and West high schools. He took violin lessons at Bailey's music school and later at the Cleveland Music School Settlement, where he began teaching at 18. In 1926 he married Rebecca White (d. 1955), a pianist and fellow faculty member at the Settlement. The following year Schlander joined the second violin section of the Cleveland Orchestra, where he occupied the first chair for 35 years. He also began to hone his conducting prowess, working under Herbert von Karajan and Bernhard Paumgartner at Salzburg in 1931. Concerned about the number of women musicians whose talents at that time were almost totally ignored by symphony orchestras, Schandler formed the Cleveland Women's Orchestra in 1935. He led the organization for the rest of his life, yielding the baton to another only 2 years before his death. When not teaching, playing, or conducting, he pursued such hobbies as fishing, drawing, and rock collecting, presenting a large part of his extensive rock collection to the CLEVELAND MUSEUM OF NATURAL HISTORY.† He was survived by 2 daughters, Dorothy Williams of Washington State and Linda Porter of California.—J.V.

**SCHAUFFLER, HENRY A.** (7 April 1837–15 Feb. 1905), missionary to CZECHS† in Cleveland, founded the Slavic Bible Readers' Home (School) (see SCHAUFFLER COLLEGE OF RELIGIOUS AND SOCIAL WORK†) for Slavic women in 1886. Schauffler was born in Constantinople, Turkey, to missionaries Mary Reynolds and Dr. William G. Schauffler. Before coming to Cleveland, he served missions in Turkey and Bohemia. He married Clara Gray in November 1862; the couple had 9 children: William Gray, Eleanor (Hawkes), Lilian (Boswell), Charles Edward, Mary, Henry Park, Frederick Herrick, Rachel (Capen), and Robert Haven. At the request of Rev. Charles T. Collins, pastor of Ply-

mouth Congregational Church, Schauffler arrived in Cleveland in 1882 to minister to the Olivet Chapel, a mission of Plymouth. In October 1883 the Congregational Home Missionary Society appointed him superintendent of Slavic missions in the U.S. under the auspices of the Bohemian Mission Board of Cleveland. His first wife died on 3 Sept. 1883, shortly after the move. Schauffler became the pastor of the newly erected BOHEMIAN CONGREGATIONAL CHURCH† in 1885. On 28 July 1892 Schauffler married Schauffler College's first teacher, Clara Hobart, of Cleveland. They had 3 children: Lawrence, Grace (Leavitt), and Margaret. Schauffler was buried in Riverside Cemetery.—J.M.

**SCHMIDT, LEO WALTER** (10 Dec. 1896–17 June 1993) forged a second career as a banker after more than 30 years as a successful builder. A native Clevelander, he was the son of Walter and Martha Schmidt. He left school at 13 to fill a variety of jobs before starting his own plumbing business at 19. The following year he formed the Leo W. Schmidt Construction Co., which built the CUYAHOGA HTS.† city hall and high school as well as hundreds of homes on the city's southeast side. Schmidt married the former Salomea Nowak in 1917, and in 1928 they moved to GARFIELD HTS.,† where they lived for nearly 50 years. Elected a director of the old Warsaw Savings & Loan Assn. in 1925, Schmidt turned his construction business over to his sons after assuming the bank's presidency in 1949. Under his guidance Warsaw Savings became United Savings in 1952, increased its assets from $5.5 million to $334 million, and opened 10 branch offices. Schmidt later served as chairman of the institution until its merger into the TRANSOHIO SAVINGS BANK† in 1980. He had also served as president of the Northeastern Ohio Savings & Loan League. Though largely self-educated, he received an honorary doctorate from Alliance College. Schmidt moved to INDEPENDENCE† in 1974 and died in ST. ALEXIS HOSPITAL MEDICAL CTR.† Buried in All Souls Cemetery, he was survived by 2 sons, Ernest and Arnold.—J.V.

**SCHMITT, DOROTHY PRENTISS** (24 June 1897–29 Dec. 1985) served on the Board of Trustees of Western Reserve Univ. (1953–67), was the only woman charter member of the board of the federated CASE WESTERN RESERVE UNIV.† (CWRU, 1967), and was made honorary board member in 1969. She was also president of many reform and cultural groups, including the EAST END NEIGHBORHOOD HOUSE,† the Garden Center of Greater Cleveland, and the Friends of the CLEVELAND PUBLIC LIBRARY.† Schmitt established the Andrew E. Schmitt Auditorium at CWRU in memory of her son, and the Alice Chalifoux harpist chair in the CLEVELAND ORCHESTRA† in her husband's memory. The niece of FRANCIS FLEURY PRENTISS, she was born in Winona, MN, to Samuel and Maude Lewis Prentiss. She graduated from Rosemary Hall in CT (1916), Vassar College (1920), and received a library science degree from WRU (1925). She worked at the Cleveland Public Library until her marriage, 24 June 1927, to Ralph S. Schmitt (d. 1974).

Schmitt then devoted her energies to her family (Rebecca, Richardson, and Andrew) and community efforts. She was a member of the advisory council for the CLEVELAND MUSEUM OF ART,† a chair of the Junior Board of ST. LUKE'S HOSPITAL,† and served on the boards of the CLEVELAND INSTITUTE OF MUSIC,† UNIV. CIRCLE, INC.,† the Cleveland Welfare Federation, and the Cleveland Center on Alcoholism, among others. She received many local awards, including the Margaret Ireland Award from the WOMEN'S CITY CLUB,† of which she was a member, and an honorary doctorate from CWRU (1970). The Cleveland Chamber of Commerce (see the GREATER CLEVELAND GROWTH ASSN.†) gave Schmitt and her husband its Public Service Medal in 1962. Schmitt belonged to the CHURCH OF THE COVENANT (PRESBYTERIAN).†—J.M.

**SCHMITT, JACOB W.** (29 Jan. 1829–16 Dec. 1893), pioneer in urban police work, was born in Mannheim, Baden, Germany, the son of Joseph Schmitt. He grew up in Germany and came to the U.S. after the 1848 revolution. Arriving in Cleveland during the early 1850s, Schmitt was appointed constable in 1857, city marshal in 1865, and chief of detectives the following year, when a metropolitan police system was introduced. Schmitt's 1871 appointment as superintendent of police was followed by the organization of a new Board of Police Commissioners, which established seven precincts, five on the east side and two on the west side, to protect the city's 318 miles of streets with day and night patrols. During his 22-year tenure, Schmitt was largely responsible for the successful operation of Cleveland's metropolitan police force. He improved police coverage of the growing city by expanding the number of patrol officers, installing call boxes to connect them with the stationhouse, and introducing patrol wagons to take lawbreakers to jail. In 1886 competitive civil service examinations for police applicants were implemented. Schmitt resigned 1 July 1893.

Schmitt married Antonetta Reutlinger in Germany; they had five children: Conrad P., Theodore, Carl F., Mrs. Phillip Decumbe, and Mrs. William

Boehmke. He died at his home in Cleveland and was buried at Lake View Cemetery.—M.S.

**SCHMITT, RALPH S.** (1894–1 Sept. 1974), with his wife DOROTHY PRENTISS SCHMITT, received both the Charles Eisenman Award (1951) and the Public Service Medal from the Cleveland Chamber of Commerce (1962) for their PHILANTHROPY† and community service. A business and civic leader, Schmitt became a partner in the Hayden, Miller & Co. investment firm (1942) and served as: treasurer, vice-president, and director of Cleveland Twist Drill (see ACME-CLEVELAND CORP.†); president of Laird Norton Co.; board chair of Northwest Paper Co.; and a director of Potlatch Forests. Schmitt was born in Knoxville, TN, graduated from the Univ. of Tennessee (1914), and worked for a time at a Knoxville bank. During World War I, he served as a lt. and pilot in the U.S. Army Signal Corps. On 24 June 1927 Schmitt married Dorothy Prentiss, niece of FRANCIS FLEURY PRENTISS and ELISABETH SEVERANCE PRENTISS. The couple lived in SHAKER HTS.† with 2 children, Andrew E. and Rebecca Richardson. They belonged to the CHURCH OF THE COVENANT (PRESBYTERIAN).†

Both Schmitt and his wife served as officers in local cultural and educational organizations. He presided over the CLEVELAND HOSPITAL SERVICE ASSN.,† BLUE CROSS OF NORTHEAST OHIO,† the CLEVELAND INSTITUTE OF MUSIC† (1938–44), ST. LUKE'S MEDICAL CENTER,† and the CUYAHOGA COUNTY HOSPITAL SYSTEM.† He retired from Cleveland Twist Drill in 1969. Schmitt is buried in Winona, MN. Dorothy Schmitt endowed the Alice Chalifoux harpist chair at the CLEVELAND ORCHESTRA† in her husband's memory.—J.M.

**SCHMUNK, WALTER GEORGE** (10 Aug. 1877–9 Oct. 1947), pioneer in the automobile industry, was born in Cleveland, the son of Capt. John and Minnie D. (Arndt) Schmunk, and attended public school. His association with the automobile industry dated from 1901, when he joined the automobile department of the White Sewing Machine Co., forerunner of the WHITE MOTOR CO.† and stayed there until 1911. He opened a company branch in London in 1902–03 and participated in hill climbing contests in England, Scotland, and France to demonstrate the new automobiles. He then returned to Boston to sell them. From 1911–14 Schmunk was a salesman at Peerless Motor Car Co. While there he designed and built the first fire apparatus for the Automobile Chemical Flying Squadrons of Cleveland Fire Department. Schmunk then moved to the Brown Auto Body Co. as vice-president and developed a motor bus which became a company specialty. He returned to auto sales in the 1930s, marketing the Hudson and Cadillac in his brother Robert's car dealership. During World War II he served as an executive assistant in the Cleveland ordnance district.

Schmunk married Helen Gallagher in Boston 28 Feb. 1905. They had 3 sons: John Robert, Walter G., and William G. Although a resident of Cleveland Hts., he also maintained a farm on River Rd. in GATES MILLS.† Schmunk was buried at Lake View Cemetery.—M.S.

**SCHNEIDER, CHARLES SUMNER** (1874–10 Mar. 1932), a brilliant eclectic architect from 1901–32, was born in Cleveland, son of Rev. William F. and Amanda (Esslinger) Schneider. He received his first architectural training in the office of Meade & Garfield, and afterward studied at the Ecole des Beaux-Arts in Paris. Returning to Cleveland, he joined the office of Wm. Watterson in 1901, designing the ornate Italian Renaissance-style Rockefeller Physics Bldg. at Case School of Applied Science (1905) and the office building of the Cleveland Baseball Co. at LEAGUE PARK.†

Schneider began an independent practice in 1908. In 1912 he was associate architect with Geo. B. Post in the Hotel Statler. In the 1920s, Schneider was associated with architects Edward J. Maier and Francis Hirschfeld. Working in both the classical and medieval idioms, he designed private residences in CLEVELAND HTS.,† SHAKER HTS.,† LAKEWOOD,† and other cities, including homes for Ernest S. Barkwill and Mrs. Sophia S. Taylor, president and chairman of WM. TAYLOR SON & CO.†; and a classic revival residence for Edwin Motch. Schneider's residential masterpiece was the Tudor mansion Stan Hywet (1915), based on several great English country houses, for the estate of F. A. Seiberling in Akron.

Schneider also designed Plymouth Church in Shaker Hts. (1923) in the Georgian Colonial-style, Shaker Hts. City Hall (1930), and several public schools. He designed Quad Hall on Euclid Ave. (1925), Austin Hall at Ohio Wesleyan Univ. in Delaware, OH, and the classical Brotherhood of Railroad Trainmen Bldg. (1921). Schneider married Georgia P. Leighton on 14 Sept. 1904 and had 4 children: Margery, George, Leighton, and Charles S. Schneider died in Cleveland and was buried in Lake View Cemetery.

**SCHOENFELD, FRANK K.** (7 Dec. 1904–29 Dec. 1984), chemical engineer and director of the research center of the B. F. Goodrich Co. in the 1960s (see B. F. GOODRICH CO. RESEARCH & DEVELOPMENT†), was born in Pittsburgh to George and Rose Koch Schoenfeld. He graduated in chemical engineering (1927) and received his master's (1933) and doctorate degrees (1937) from Western Reserve Univ. He joined B. F. Goodrich as a chemist in 1927, working on vinyl resins. In 1939 he became manager of Koroseal Research & Development, in 1942 becoming director of this group, developing manufacturing processes for vinyl chloride and polyvinyl chlorides. In 1943 he became a technical superintendent in the newly formed B. F. Goodrich Chemical Co., a division of B. F. Goodrich, advancing to vice-president of technology in 1946, to vice-president of research for the parent firm in 1954, and to vice-president of research and development in 1959, holding that position until he retired in 1968. Schoenfeld earned patents in the fields of pigments, adhesives, rubber derivatives, polymerization, manmade rubbers, and plastics. He received the medal from the Industrial Research Institute (1959) and Cleveland Technical Societies Council's Annual Distinguished Service Award (1966). Schoenfeld was also a director of British Geon, Ltd. In 1957 he became a member of the Board of Governors of WRU, and its chairman in 1963. Schoenfeld married Helen Mars Wood in 1930; they had no children. He died in Crystal River, FL.

**SCHOTT, HAROLD C.** (6 Jan. 1907–28 Feb. 1977) was an industrialist and financier who, along with his brothers, created a business empire of companies in Cleveland and throughout the Midwest.

Born in Cincinnati, Harold joined his brother Walter's Willys-Overland automobile distributorship after graduating from high school in Cincinnati. In 1940 the Schott brothers moved into the industrial field, purchasing the Columbia Axle Co. with Harold becoming president. At the height of their partnership, the brothers owned 31 companies throughout the Midwest worth almost $20 million, including Cleveland Pneumatic Tool, U.S. Air Compressor Co., and Champion Machine & Forging Co.

In 1952 Harold and Walter split their assets and amicably dissolved their partnership over the policy of buying businesses and liquidating or reselling them for a quick profit. In 1953 Harold and another brother, Joseph, were involved in the merger of Ohio Bearings with several bearing companies to form BEARINGS, INC.† Headquartered in Cleveland, Bearings, Inc. became the largest bearing distributing company in the U.S. Schott also owned American National Corp. and HCS Corp. in Cleveland, Van Lock Co. and Lennox Trucking in Cincinnati, and Progress Tool & Engineering Co. in Indianapolis.

In 1959 Schott established the HCS FOUNDA-

TION,† with gifts limited to Ohio and having benefitted primarily the Roman Catholic Church, hospitals and secondary education. Schott was active in CATHOLIC CHARITIES CORP.† of Cleveland.

Schott never married. He lived in Cleveland and LAKEWOOD† and had a home in Golden Beach, FL, where he died. Schott, a Roman Catholic, is buried in St. Joseph's New Mausoleum in Cincinnati.—T.B.

**SCHREMBS, JOSEPH** (12 Mar. 1866–2 Nov. 1945), fifth bishop of the Diocese of Cleveland, was born in Wurzelhozen (Regensburg), Germany, to Geo. and Mary Gess Schrembs. He came to America at age 11 and studied at St. Vincent Archabbey in Latrobe, PA, before teaching in Louisville, KY. He studied for the priesthood in Quebec and Montreal, was ordained in 1889, and served parishes in Michigan before becoming vicar general of Grand Rapids Diocese in 1903, consecrated auxiliary bishop in 1911. Schrembs was named first bishop of the new Diocese of Toledo in 1911. He was one of 4 bishops on the administrative committee of the Natl. Catholic War Council during World War I, after the war successfully lobbying Rome for its continuance and becoming a member of the Natl. Catholic Welfare Council's permanent committee. Schrembs also helped organize the Natl. Council of Catholic Men and the Natl. Council of Catholic Women.

Schrembs became bishop of Cleveland on 8 Sept. 1921. He expanded the Board of Catholic Charities; consolidated the boys' orphanage, opening a model institution on the Parmadale site; began ROSEMARY HOME†; and relocated ST. MARY SEMINARY.† In 1931 he began Sisters' College to provide standardized preparation for teachers in diocesan schools (see ST. JOHN COLLEGE†). Schrembs actively supported the trade union movement, and used radio to evangelize and instruct. Schrembs hosted the SEVENTH NATL. EUCHARISTIC CONGRESS† in Cleveland in 1935, and was given the honorary title of archbishop in 1939. As a diabetic condition increasingly disabled him, a coadjutor bishop, EDWARD F. HOBAN, was appointed in 1942. Schrembs died in Cleveland and was buried in a crypt beneath the altar of St. John's Cathedral.

**SCHUBERT, ORLANDO V.** (1844–11 Dec. 1927) was an early Cleveland artist especially noted for his marine paintings. Born on Erie (E. 9th) St., he was the son of early settlers Mary and Balthasar Schubert (see GERMANS†), a nephew of Austrian composer Franz Schubert, and founder of the CLEVELAND GRAYS† band. Orlando Schubert acquired a proficiency on many musical instruments

before leaving home to work on a Great Lakes boat. By 1873 he had returned with enough knowledge of art to render a well-regarded watercolor of Cleveland's lakefront. He joined the group of local artists in the old City Hall known as the "Old Bohemians" and was a charter member of the BRUSH AND PALETTE CLUB.† Schubert then left Cleveland to study and paint in Munich for 4 years. Upon his return he ran a print shop on Detroit Ave. to support his painting, which he pursued at his lakefront home in BAY VILLAGE.† In 1913 he painted his magnum opus, *The Battle of Lake Erie*, on the centenary of that event. Some of his paintings were destroyed 2 years later by a fire that consumed the next-door home of his brother and threatened his own. The lifelong bachelor died in St. Petersburg, FL, where he bequeathed many of his paintings to form the nucleus of an art museum. His remains were returned for interment in Lakewood Park Cemetery. *The Battle of Lake Erie*, which he had once unsuccessfully tried to sell to Cuyahoga County, was presented to the county in 1961 by a former Clevelander in St. Petersburg.—J.V.

**SCHULTE, LAURETTA (OBERLE)** (24 Jan. 1902–3 Jan. 1993), licensed funeral director for half a century, was born in Cleveland, the daughter of John and Mary O'Hearn Oberle. After attending Western Reserve Univ., she worked in the legal and engineering departments at General Electric's NELA PARK† complex. Interested in politics, Oberle was executive secretary to LEONARD HANNA, JR. who actively campaigned for Republican Herbert Hoover during his 1928 presidential campaign, and she later helped DAVID INGALLS, SR., who supported Ohio Senator Robert Taft in his quest for the 1952 Republican presidential nomination. Nine years after her marriage to Joseph C. Schulte, 30 Nov. 1933, she and her husband established the Joseph C. Schulte Funeral Home at 4090 Mayfield Rd., SOUTH EUCLID† and by 1957 they had a second operation at 5244 Mayfield Rd. in LYNDHURST.† In the meantime, she obtained her funeral director license from the Pittsburgh Institute of Mortuary Science and became vice-president of the company. Lauretta Schulte died at her home in Chester Twp. and was buried at All Souls Cemetery. She was survived by her husband and three brothers; there apparently were no children.—M.S.

**SCHWAN, HEINRICH CHRISTIAN** (5 April 1819–29 May 1905) presided over the growth of local Lutheranism (see LUTHERANS†) as a Cleveland pastor and later as a synod official. The son of Pastor G. H. C. and Charlotte Wyneken Schwan, he was born in Horneburg, Germany, and in 1842 graduated from Jena Univ. Upon his ordination the following year, Schwan went to Brazil as a missionary. In 1849 he married Emma Blum, daughter of a German plantation owner. The couple emigrated to the U.S. in 1850, and Schwan became pastor of a Lutheran congregation in Missouri. They came to Cleveland in 1851, when Schwan was installed as pastor of ZION EVANGELICAL LUTHERAN CHURCH.† He attracted considerable local attention during his first Christmas in Cleveland by introducing a lighted Christmas tree into his church service. Though originally criticized from some quarters as an idolatrous act, the event was later celebrated as one of the country's first public Christmas tree displays. Schwan remained as Zion's pastor for 30 years, performing 2,793 baptisms and 1,034 confirmations. Schwan also played an active role in the Evangelical Lutheran Synod of Missouri, Ohio, and other states, becoming president of that church council in 1878. He filled that office for 21 years, resigning the pastorate of Zion when the synod presidency was made a full-time position in 1881. He maintained his residence in Cleveland, serving as an asst. preacher at Zion and 2 other local congregations while performing his synod duties. He was buried in Lake View Cemetery, survived by his wife and 8 children: Paul, Manuel, Ernst, Carl, George, Frederick, Johanna, and Emma.—J.V.

**SCHWEINFURTH, CHARLES F.** (3 Sept. 1856–8 Nov. 1919), architect of many of Cleveland's finest residences, churches, and educational buildings, was born in Auburn, NY, son of Charles J. and Katharine (Ammon) Schweinfurth. After graduating from high school (1872), Schweinfurth worked at architectural offices in New York City (1872–74) and Washington, DC (1874–80) before coming to Cleveland as the architect of SYLVESTER T. EVERETT's Euclid Ave. mansion. By 1910 Schweinfurth had completed at least 15 residential designs for prominent Clevelanders on EUCLID AVE.'s† "Millionaires Row," one of which, the SAMUEL MATHER house (1910) at 2605 Euclid Ave., is now used as a conference center by CLEVELAND STATE UNIV.† Schweinfurth also designed Samuel Mather's residence, "Shoreby" (1890), in BRATENAHL†; the MARCUS A. HANNA house (1890); his own home; and the Gordon Morrill residence (1915) in UNIV. CIRCLE.† He remodeled the interior of the Old Stone Church (1884) and designed CALVARY PRESBYTERIAN† (1890), the Ursuline Convent (1893), and TRINITY CATHEDRAL† & Parish House (1907). Schweinfurth's relationship with SAMUEL and FLORA STONE MATHER led to designs for the UNION CLUB† (1905) and several buildings on the early Adelbert and Mather college grounds, three of which are still on the CASE WESTERN RESERVE UNIV.† campus: Florence Harkness Chapel (1902), Haydn Hall (1902), and the former Backus Law School (1896). Four landmark stone bridges (1896–1900) crossing Martin Luther King Blvd. are Schweinfurth designs.

Schweinfurth married twice. His first marriage was to Mary Ella Griggs (d. 1903) in 1879; his second was to Anna Jopling in 1910. He had no children from either marriage. Schweinfurth died in Cleveland and was buried in Auburn, NY.

Johannessen, Eric. *Cleveland Architecture, 1876–1976* (1979).
Perry, Regenia. "The Life and Works of Charles Frederick Schweinfurth" (Ph.D. diss., WRU, 1967).

**SCOFIELD, LEVI T.** (9 Nov. 1842–25 Feb. 1917) was an architect specializing in institutional structures and public monuments. Born in Cleveland, son of William and Mary (Coon) Scofield, he served in the Civil War from 1861–65, and was chief engineer on the staff of Gen. Jacob Cox. After the war he designed several large state institutions, including the asylums for the insane at Athens (1868) and Columbus (1869), North Carolina State Penitentiary at Raleigh (1870), and the reformatory at Mansfield (1884). Because of his war service, he was a chief proponent of the Cuyahoga County SOLDIERS & SAILORS MONUMENT,† which he designed and supervised between 1886–94. Scofield designed many private residences, of which the R. K. Winslow house (1878) on Euclid Ave. was representative, and Cleveland public schools, such as Central High (1878) and Broadway (1881). In 1893 he received the commission for the Ohio Monument at the 1893 World's Columbian Exposition, a standing figure symbolic of the state surrounded by bronze sculptures of her most distinguished sons. In 1901 he designed the Schofield [*sic*] Bldg., a 14-story office building on the southwest corner of Euclid and E. 9th St. Most of Scofield's architectural designs were in the massive, picturesque, Late Victorian manner, with Gothic or Romanesque details.

Scofield married Elizabeth Clark Wright, president of the YWCA, and first president of the board of the PHILLIS WHEATLEY ASSN.,† in 1867. They had two children, William M. and Sherman W. Scofield died in Cleveland and was buried in Lake View Cemetery. The Scofield residence (1898) stands at 2438 Mapleside, Cleveland.

Gleason, William J. *Soldiers and Sailors Monument* (1894).
Levi T. Scofield Papers, WRHS.

**SCOTT, FRANK A.** (22 Mar. 1873–15 Apr. 1949), businessman and civic leader, was born in Cleveland to Robert Crozier and Sarah Ann Warr Scott. At 18 he began working for a railroad company, moving into increasingly responsible positions. From 1899–1905 he was secretary of the Cleveland Chamber of Commerce, and from 1905–09, secretary and treasurer of Superior Savings & Trust Co. In 1909 he joined WARNER & SWASEY CO.,† within a few years rising from secretary to vice-president, serving as president and chairman of the board from 1920–28. Prior to U.S. involvement in World War I, Scott advocated military preparedness, in 1916 becoming a member of the U.S. Naval Consulting Board. When the U.S. entered the war, Scott was appointed chairman of the Munitions Standards Board by the Council of Natl. Defense. He had to resign later that year because of poor health, but maintained his rank of colonel and was honorary advisor to the Army Industrial College, receiving the Distinguished Service Medal in 1919. Scott was vice-president of ASSOCIATED CHARITIES,† and treasurer and vice-president of Lakeside Hospital. He played a leading role in the building fund drive for UNIV. HOSPITALS,† becoming hospital president in 1928. As a trustee of WRU and member of the Corp. of Case Institute of Technology, Scott attempted to merge the two institutions.

Scott married Bertha B. Dynes in 1886 (d. 1909); they had three children: Katherine (Ridley), Chester, and Eleanor (Neally). He then married Faith Alice Fraser in 1911 (d. 1936); they had two children, Faith Elizabeth (Taylor) and Malcom Fraser. His last marriage was to Dulcie Schiflet in 1938. Scott died in Mentor.

Frank A. Scott Papers, WRHS.

**SCOVILL, PHILO** (30 Nov. 1791–5 June 1875), pioneer, contractor, and merchant, was born in Salisbury, CT, to Timothy and Chloe (Kelsey) Scovill. The family moved several times during his youth, and in 1816 came to Cleveland. Scovill established himself as a merchant in the drug and grocery business. Disenchanted with this line of work, he moved into a lumber venture with Thos. O. Young. Once a local sawmill was completed, Scovill & Young began building and house contracting. At that time their only competition was LEVI JOHNSON, and because the town was growing rapidly both businesses prospered. In 1825 Scovill built Franklin House, a popular tavern, which he managed until 1848. In 1938 the tavern was torn down, and the site became a parking lot. During his career, Scovill purchased over 110 acres of land in and around Cleveland. The popularity achieved through his entrepreneurial developments gained him seats as county commissioner, 1827; Whig representative to the state legislature, 1835–36; and on CLEVELAND CITY COUNCIL,† 1841–42. Scovill was

content to serve only single terms in office. During his later career, he became director of the Cleveland & Pittsburgh Railroad Co. and a founder of First Natl. Bank (1863), later its president. Scovill married Jemima Bixby in 1819; she was the founder of the Old Women's Home of Cleveland. The Scovills had 2 sons, Edward and Oliver, and a daughter, Caroline. Scovill died in Cleveland and was buried in Erie St. Cemetery.

**SCRANTON, IRENE HICKOX** (1800–15 Mar. 1858), educator, churchwoman, and benefactor, was born in Durham, NY, daughter of David and Phebe (Post) Hickox. She came to Kinsman, Trumbull County, OH, in 1817, and taught school there for 3 successive summers. She returned East in 1820 to attend Female Academy in Litchfield, CT, subsequently returning to Kinsman and opening a boarding school for young ladies. After coming to Cleveland she became principal of a school for girls. She was a founder of the FIRST PRESBYTERIAN (OLD STONE) CHURCH.† On 27 June 1828 she married JOEL SCRANTON, a leather and dry goods merchant whose store was located at the corner of Superior and Water (W. 9th) streets. In 1833 they moved to a farm known as Scranton's Flats. Mrs. Scranton was considered one of the most benevolent of Cleveland women at the time, caring for many poor and ill people in the city. The couple had 6 children: Helen Maria, Mary J., George H., Emily Louise, Charles H., and an adopted daughter, Jenny. Mary (Scranton) Bradford was one of the founders and main benefactors of the Cleveland School of Art. She became second president (1885–1904) and was later named a trustee of the CLEVELAND INSTITUTE OF ART.† Irene Scranton was buried in Woodland Cemetery.

**SCRANTON, JOEL** (5 Apr. 1793–9 Apr. 1858), an early Cleveland resident, merchant, and landowner, was born in Belchertown, MA, to Stephen and Asenath Scranton. He spent his childhood in Otsego County, NY, and settled in Cleveland in 1819, with most accounts reporting he arrived with "a schooner load of leather" to sell. Primarily a leather merchant in the early 1820s, Scranton opened a store in 1827 selling leather, dry goods, groceries, crockery, and machine cards. In the early 1830s, J. Scranton & Co. also advertised its interest in buying corn and rye. By Jan. 1833 Scranton had sold the store. With the proceeds from his retail enterprises, Scranton bought land at low cost, including the flats on the west side of the CUYAHOGA RIVER,† along what became Scranton Ave., where he operated a farm. That area was known by 1847 as "Scranton's Flats"; in the 1840s and 1850s it became a business and sporting center, with everything from railroads to shooting contests to circuses located there. As more businesses located next to his property, Scranton's land grew in value and he left a large estate upon his sudden death from apoplexy in 1858. In 1838 Scranton was elected a director of the Bank of Cleveland. He was a member of the Presbyterian church and was a Mason.

Scranton married IRENE HICKOX SCRANTON on 27 June 1828. They had 6 children: Helen Maria, Mary J., George H., Emily Louise, Charles H., and Jenny, an adopted daughter.

**SCRIPPS, EDWARD WILLIS** (18 June 1854–12 Mar. 1926), founder of the *CLEVELAND PRESS,†* was born near Rushville, IL, son of James M. and Julia Osborne Scripps. He helped his brother, James, start the *Detroit News* in 1873. Scripps came to Cleveland in 1878, starting the *Penny Press* on 2 Nov. with his cousin, John Scripps Sweeney, as business manager; 60% of the $10,000 capital was provided by his brothers, James and George, in Detroit. Scripps was editor for 16 months, when he left Cleveland to start the *St. Louis Evening Chronicle*. A year later he returned to Cleveland for 6 months before leaving for Europe. Scripps's brief Cleveland residence was marked by a major confrontation with HENRY CHISHOLM. When a *Press* reporter mistakenly identified Chisholm's son as a participant in a street brawl, Chisholm instigated an attack on the reporter by his employees and started civil and criminal proceedings against Scripps and the *Press*. Scripps retaliated, preparing a special edition of the *Press* headed "Chisholm's Infamy" (referring to the attack on his reporter), running a condensed version of the same daily until he won the criminal libel suit and Chisholm dropped the civil suit and paid $5,000 damages to the reporter. Chisholm's subsequent death was attributed partly to the *Press*'s attacks.

After 1881, Scripps spent only about 30 total days in Cleveland while founding and running the other papers that eventually merged into the Scripps-Howard organization. Scripps married Nackie Holtsinger on 5 Oct. 1885. They had 6 children: James George, John Paul, Edward Willis, Jr., Robert Paine, Dolla Blair, and Nackey. Scripps retired from active business to San Diego in 1890. He died on his yacht "Ohio" in Monrovia Bay, Liberia.

Gardner, Gilson. *Lusty Scripps: The Life of E. W. Scripps* (1932).
Cochran, N. D. *E. W. Scripps* (1933).

**SEARS, LESTER MERRIAM** (13 May 1888–20 Feb. 1967) was an engineer who invented the gasoline-powered industrial tractor, the forklift industrial truck, and founded the Towmotor Corp. of Cleveland.

Sears was born to Frederick Wayland and Anna (Merriam) Sears in Ravenna, NE, where he attended grade school. He attended high school in Minneapolis and graduated from the Univ. of Minnesota in 1912.

Sears was an associate consulting engineer in Minneapolis from 1912–15. In 1916 he came to Cleveland as an asst. factory manager for the Peerless Motor Car Co. In 1918 the Secretary of War assigned Sears to a special mission as valuator of public utilities in New Orleans.

After the war Sears returned to Cleveland. In 1919 Sears organized the Towmotor Co. with his father to manufacture the gasoline propelled tractors he had spent a year designing and developing. Called the "towmotor," this tractor was the company's mainstay until 1933, when Sears invented the forklift to carry and stack heavy loads. It helped make Towmotor an industrial truck leader by 1944. Sears was Towmotor's director of operations, 1919–34; president, 1934–51; and chairman of the board, 1951–65. When the Caterpillar Tractor Co. purchased Towmotor in 1965, Sears remained as honorary chairman until his death.

In 1949 Sears established the Lester M. Sears Foundation to support local health, education, and environmental research. In 1966 Sears donated $1 million each to Case Tech for a humanities center, and to Western Reserve Univ. for a medical center.

Sears married Ruth Parker in 1914. They had one daughter, Mary Ann (Swetland). Sears is buried in Lake View Cemetery.—T.B.

**SEAVER, JOHN WRIGHT** (8 Jan. 1855–14 Jan. 1911), designer and builder of large industrial and transportation structures, was born in Madison, WI, the son of Daniel M. and Charlotte Ann (Cook) Seaver. Educated in the public schools of Buffalo, NY, he also studied practical mathematics and mechanics with inventor Robert Stevenson. In 1869–80, Seaver was employed by the Shepherd Iron Works, the Howard Iron Works, and the Kellogg Bridge Co. as draftsman and later asst. engineer. Relocating to Pittsburgh in 1880, he worked at the Iron City Bridge Works for 4 years and spent 12 years with Riter-Conley Manufacturing as chief engineer, designing and contracting for a diverse line of industrial installations, including oil refineries and steel plants. In 1896 he joined Charles H. and Samuel T. Wellman to form the Wellman-Seaver Engineering Co. in Cleveland (later Wellman-Seaver-Morgan). The firm became well known as consulting and contracting engineers, and Seaver achieved a worldwide reputation for his work. Among his accomplishments was the construction of a steel bridge across the Mississippi River—the longest steel bridge in the world at that time. He was the first designer of Gantry cranes and other materials handling and steel manufacturing machinery, compiling the first standard steel railroad bridge specification for major railroad companies.

Seaver married Mary Tassey Patterson 19 Feb. 1891; they had 4 children: John Tassey, Charlotte deBeaumont, Hugh Davis, and William Patterson. He died at his home in CLEVELAND HTS.† and was buried in Lake View Cemetery.—M.S.

**SEBIAN, MONSIGNOR THOMAS B.** (22 July 1921–11 Oct. 1986), a pioneer in ministry to Cleveland's HISPANIC COMMUNITY,† founded and directed the Spanish Catholic Mission Center of the Diocese of Cleveland (see CATHOLICS, ROMAN†) at the Conversion of St. Paul Parish (1953) and later directed the revived Spanish Catholic Mission Office (1970–73) at St. Stephen's. He also began the Ecos Latinos program on radio (1957–64) and was superior of the Cleveland Latin American Mission in San Salvador, Central America (1964–70). Sebian was born in Painesville, OH, to Joseph and Elizabeth Pecery Sebian and graduated from CATHEDRAL LATIN SCHOOL† (1939) and ST. MARY SEMINARY† (1946). He was ordained on 18 May 1946. Sebian began learning Spanish while assigned to the Conversion of St. Paul Parish in 1952. In 1958 he was named asst. pastor at ST. JOHN CATHEDRAL,† and 3 years later, to the same position at St. Augustine Church. Pope Paul IV named him monsignor in 1968.

From 1973–78 Sebian served as pastor of St. Mary Catholic Church in Wooster, OH. After recovering from a heart attack, he worked as pro tem administrator at St. Victor Catholic Church (Richfield, OH), and senior assoc. at St. Thomas More Catholic Church in Brooklyn. Monsignor Sebian was appointed senior assoc. pastor at Cleveland's St. Francis Catholic Church in charge of Spanish ministry in 1983 but retired the next year. Despite poor health, he received a master's degree from JOHN CARROLL UNIV.† in 1984.—J.M.

**SEID, RUTH. See SINCLAIR, JO.**

**SELDEN, GEORGE G.** (13 Oct. 1915–18 Dec. 1993) was a chemical company executive, an industrial chemist, an internationally recognized authority in mortar and ceramic technology, and the inventor of both an anti-icing propeller coating used by the Army Air Corps, Alaska, during World War II to keep planes operating in severe winter weather, and all-climate concentrated paints for military use.

Born in Cleveland to Franz and Lucia (Golay) Selden, George graduated from East High School

(1932) and received a B.S. chemical engineering (1936), M.S. (1939), and Ph.D. (1942) in organic chemistry from CASE WESTERN RESERVE UNIV.†

Selden started as a chemist at the family-owned Upco Co., 1936–39. From 1941–47 he was resin chemist and head of the resin and varnish lab at the Finishes Division of Interchem Corp. in Cincinnati. Selden returned to Cleveland and Upco in 1947 as factory manager and became company president upon his father's death in 1949.

After USM Corp. purchased Upco Co. in 1965, Selden continued as president of the Upco subsidiary until 1979 when he became group business director of USM's Bostile Division through 1981. After retirement, Selden formed Selden Chemical Consulting Inc., serving as president, 1981–90.

Selden was a past commodore and trustee of the Forest City Yacht Club, helped to found Bratenahl Community Foundation and raise funding for the BCF Community Center's Children's Room.

Selden married Frances Knight on 9 Sept. 1941 (div. 1975; remarried 1991). They had two children, Philip and Barbara. He married Josephine Hershey on 7 July 1977 (d. 1990). Selden lived in BRATENAHL.† He was cremated.—T.B.

**SELTZER, LOUIS B.** (19 Sept. 1897–2 Apr. 1980), long-time editor of the CLEVELAND PRESS,† was born in Cleveland to Chas. Alden and Ella Albers Seltzer, and quit school to work as an office boy at the CLEVELAND LEADER† at age 12, quickly becoming a reporter and writer of a Sunday column, but being fired 2 years later. A year later, Seltzer was a police reporter for the Cleveland Press, in 1916 being named city editor but, feeling his lack of experience, voluntarily resigned after 3 months, becoming political editor. Appointed editor in 1928, Seltzer held that position 38 years. Stressing the public-service role of the newspaper, Seltzer established close ties with the city's neighborhoods by personal involvement in civic and charitable endeavors. He became "kingmaker" in Ohio politics, notably through the Press's successful sponsorship of FRANK J. LAUSCHE and Anthony J. Celebrezze. In the last years of his tenure, Seltzer was editor-in-chief of Scripps-Howard Newspapers of Ohio.

Seltzer's autobiography, *The Years Were Good* (1956), was in the classic Horatio Alger mold, emphasizing Seltzer's rise through application and industry to professional preeminence. Stepping down as editor of the *Press* in 1966, Seltzer wrote occasional columns for suburban newspapers. He also published a short collection of character sketches, *Six and God* (1966). He was affiliated with more than 50 organizations, including the Pulitzer Prize Advisory Board from 1956–68. He married Mary Elizabeth Champlin in 1915. Seltzer died in the Medina County home of his daughter, Mrs. Shirley Cooper. His son, Chester E. Seltzer, was also a newspaperman and writer.

Seltzer, Louis. *The Years Were Good* (1956).
Louis Seltzer Papers, WRHS.

**SEMENOFF, NIKOLAI PROKOFIEVITCH** (12 Mar. 1881–7 July 1932), once ballet master of the Imperial Moscow Theater, conducted a dance studio in Cleveland in the years prior to his suicide in protest of "the slander and persecution of the ballet." A native of Moscow, he graduated from the Imperial Russian school in 1899 with the title of "artiste." After working as ballet master with the Moscow Art Theater, he joined Serge Diaghileff's Ballet Russe, serving as *regisseur*, or administrator, for choreographer Michel Fokine. Prior to the Russian Revolution in 1917, he was ballet master at the Imperial Moscow Theater. Semenoff, who claimed that his entire family was killed by the Bolsheviks, fled from Russia in 1921. He walked across Poland and eventually reached Paris, where he remained 2 years. He arrived in the U.S. in 1923 as a member of Nikita Bialeff's *Chauve-Souris*, a touring Russian vaudeville show. Semenoff came to Cleveland in the mid–1920s to conduct the Martha Lee dancing school. Within 2 years he opened his own studio, the Imperial Russian School of the Dance, in Carnegie Hall on Huron Rd. He faithfully patronized local cultural events and placed ads in concert programs. By the early 1930s, however, his livelihood was threatened by the Depression and the vogue of modern dance. Semenoff was dismayed by the opening of a modern dance department at the CLEVELAND INSTITUTE OF MUSIC† and the commissioning of modern dance choreography by the STADIUM OPERA CO.† After closing his dance studio, he poured out his frustrations in a letter to Fokine and threw himself over Niagara Falls in Canada. He left no survivors, nor was the body recovered.—J.V.

**SEMON, JOHN** (22 Feb. 1852–14 Dec. 1917) was a landscape painter associated with the group of 19th-century local artists known as the "Old Bohemians." Although he was born in Cleveland, little is known of his early life, including his artistic education. Influenced by the style of the French Barbizon School, he specialized in the painting of atmospheric woodland interiors, depicting the interplay of sunlight and shadow. From 1884–88 he taught at the Western Reserve School of Design for Women (see CLEVELAND INSTITUTE OF ART†), located in the old City Hall. Semon also maintained a studio there, where his private pupils included the young

Marsden Hartley from 1896–98. He exhibited regularly and was a founding member of the Society of Cleveland Artists, the BRUSH AND PALETTE CLUB,† and the Artists Painters Club. By 1901, however, Semon had abandoned his studio and gone to live and paint in the woods of BEDFORD,† where he acquired the reputation of a recluse. "Commercialism and sensationalism had no habitat in his makeup," wrote *CLEVELAND PRESS†* critic Wilson G. Smith in an appreciation. Apparently never married, Semon died without survivors after a year's illness.—J.V.

Haskell, Barbara. *Marsden Hartley* (1980).
Sackerlotzky, Rotraud. *F. C. Gottwald and the Old Bohemians* (1993).

**SENTER, GEORGE B.** (1827–16 Jan. 1870), councilman, mayor, and military leader during the Civil War, was elected to Cleveland City Council from the 1st Ward in 1858, and served as mayor from 1859–60. Senter, born in Potsdam, NY, was the son of David K. and Susan Senter. When the Civil War broke out, Senter, for whom no military record can be found, probably served in an honorary capacity as asst. commissary-subsistence officer at Camp Taylor (see CIVIL WAR CAMPS†) on Woodland Ave. during Apr.-May 1861. He was elevated to commandant of Camp Cleveland on 16 July 1862, a post at which he served until 20 Apr. 1864. In 1864 the Cleveland City Council elected Senter to serve the remainder of the mayoral term of IRVINE MASTERS,† who had died in office. Senter, a staunch supporter of the Union cause, had, in 1861, invited president-elect Abraham Lincoln to visit Cleveland (see ABRAHAM LINCOLN'S VISIT†). In 1865, as mayor, Senter performed the sad task of proclaiming a day of mourning on 15 Apr. to honor the assassinated president. Senter apparently spent the period after the war practicing law and holding part-interest in a wholesale wine and liquor business. He died at his home on Euclid Ave and is buried in Woodland Cemetery. His 2-story brick mansion, built in 1842, was purchased for $60,000 in 1872 by the UNION CLUB† and converted into its first headquarters. Senter married Delia Wheaton in 1851; they had three children: George B., Jr., Cornelia E., and J. Augusta.

Geo. B. Senter Papers, WRHS.

**SETTLE, REV. DR. GLENN THOMAS** (10 Oct. 1894–16 July 1967) was the pastor of Gethsemane Baptist Church who organized and directed the famed African American WINGS OVER JORDAN CHOIR.† Born in Reidsville, NC, to Rubin and Mary Settle, he moved with his family to Uniontown, PA, and attended public school. Settle then moved to Elyria, beginning his pastorate as assistant pastor of Mount Haven Church.

Settle moved to Cleveland about 1920, worked as a city clerk, and joined Gethsemane, becoming pastor in 1935. He founded Wings Over Jordan in 1935. It aired locally in July 1937 on WGAR's† "Negro Hour." On 9 Jan. 1938 it debuted nationally over the CBS network as the Wings Over Jordan Choir. In 1939 the choir earned national recognition for outstanding radio series rendered by AFRICAN AMERICANS.† In 1940 the choir toured America. Settle was honored for distinguished achievement in improving race relations by the Assn. for the Study of Negro Life and History. In 1941 Settle received a plaque from the National Negro Insurance Assn. for his outstanding contribution as a builder of interracial and international goodwill.

In 1946 Settle legally changed his name from "Glenn" to "Glynn" in order to inherit an islet in the Dan River near Reidsville. He earned his doctor of divinity in the late 1940s. He had moved back to Uniontown by the 1950s. Settle married Mary Elizabeth Carter in 1917 (d. 1955). They had 3 children: Elizabeth, Glenn H., and Gwendolyn. Settle then married Mildred Ridley in California, ca. 1960. He died and was buried in Los Angeles.—T.B.

**SEVERANCE, CAROLINE M.** (12 Jan. 1820–10 Nov. 1914), early feminist activist in Cleveland and known as America's first clubwoman, was born Caroline M. Seymour in Canandaigua, NY. Daughter of Orson and Caroline M. (Clarke) Seymour, she came to Cleveland with her family and at age 20 married Theodoric C. Severance, a banker. While raising 5 children, Orson, James, Julia, Mark, and Pierre, she pondered the inferior legal status of women and became the first woman to lecture in Cleveland on women's suffrage. In 1851 she heard Sojourner Truth at a women's-rights convention in Akron and helped found the Ohio Women's Suffrage Assn. When Antoinette Brown from Oberlin, later the first ordained female minister, was refused entrance to a New York City temperance convention where she was a delegate, Severance retorted with "Humanity," a speech voicing the sentiments of the infant women's movement that was repeated at other gatherings. In 1854 Severance addressed the Ohio legislature on women's rights to hold inherited property and their own earnings. When her husband's career led him to Boston in the mid–1850s, Severance directed her growing awareness of women's rights toward club work. With Julia Ward Howe she organized the New England's Women's Club, whose interests ranged from infant mortality to the admission of women to higher education.

Severance resided in Boston until 1875, then moved to Los Angeles, CA, where she formed the first kindergarten and continued her suffrage work. She lectured on suffrage, abolition, peace, birth control, and morality, and in 1869 was a signer of the first national suffrage convention in Cleveland. Severance died in Los Angeles and was buried there.

**SEVERANCE, JOHN LONG** (8 May 1863–16 Jan. 1936), industrialist, was born in Cleveland to Fannie Benedict and LOUIS HENRY SEVERANCE. He graduated from Oberlin College in 1885 and returned to Cleveland to work for STANDARD OIL CO.† In 1892 Severance left Standard Oil to work with the Cleveland Linseed Oil Co., a paint and varnish industry. In 1899 he was instrumental in founding American Linseed Co., into which Cleveland Linseed was merged. In 1901 he organized and became president of Colonial Salt Co., and about the same time helped form Linde Air Products. His other business connections included serving as chairman of the board of Cleveland Arcade Co. and Youngstown Steel Door Co., and as director of Cleveland Trust Co. and Youngstown Sheet & Tube Co. Philanthropically, he was president of the CLEVELAND MUSEUM OF ART† and MUSICAL ARTS ASSN.† Besides being a liberal benefactor to the art museum during his life, at his death he left it a collection valued at over $3 million. In 1929 he gave the city $1.5 million to build SEVERANCE HALL† for the CLEVELAND ORCHESTRA†; in 1930 increasing his donation to $2.5 million in memory of his wife. Severance was an initial member of the Cleveland Community Fund, a trustee of Oberlin College, Western Reserve Univ., and Nanking Univ. in China. He sponsored Severance Medical School & Hospital at Seoul, Korea, an institution founded by his father. Severance married Elizabeth Huntington DeWitt in 1891; she died in 1929. They had no children. Severance died in Cleveland and is buried in Lake View Cemetery.

Severance Family Papers, WRHS.

**SEVERANCE, LOUIS HENRY** (1 Aug. 1838–25 June 1913), treasurer of Standard Oil (1876–94), began his business career at the Commercial National Bank in Cleveland. Severance was the younger son of Mary Long and SOLOMON LEWIS SEVERANCE. He attended Cleveland public schools. After service in the Civil War (1863) he returned to his position at the Commercial National Bank. He left the city in 1864 to pursue the oil business, first in Titusville, PA, and later in New York City. Severance resided in Cleveland again from 1874–76 and split his time between New York and his hometown thereafter, serving as church elder and Sunday School Superintendent (1897) of Cleveland's Woodland Ave. Presbyterian Church. He served as president of the Cleveland Presbyterian Union (1893–1903) (see PRESBYTERIAN UNION†). Severance also invested in salt, sulphur, and steel. In the 1890s, with HERMAN FRASCH, F. B. Squire, and Frank Rockefeller, he established the Union Sulphur Co. Severance retired in 1894.

Severance was the benefactor of the Severance Hospital and the Severance Medical College in Seoul, Korea. Severance married Fannie Buckingham Benedict (d. 1874) of Norwalk, OH, on 13 August 1862. The couple's children were JOHN LONG SEVERANCE, ELISABETH SEVERANCE ALLEN PRENTISS, and Anne Belle Severance. In 1894 Severance married Florence Harkness (d. 1895), daughter of STEPHEN V. HARKNESS.

Severance Family Papers, WRHS.

**SEVERANCE, SOLOMON LEWIS** (9 April 1812–13 July 1838) was the progenitor of one of Cleveland's most prominent families and, also, one of Cleveland's earliest dry goods merchants. He helped found and served as an officer of both the CLEVELAND ANTI-SLAVERY SOCIETY† and the CUYAHOGA COUNTY ANTI-SLAVERY SOCIETY.†

Born in Shelburne, MA, to Dr. Robert Bruce and Diana (Long) Severance, Solomon came to Cleveland in 1830 and established himself as a dry goods merchant, opening a store at No. 57 Superior St. In 1833 Severance went into a business partnership as Cutter & Severance, doing business at the Brick Corner.

When the Cleveland Anti-Slavery Society was founded as an auxiliary of the Western Reserve Anti-Slavery Society in 1833, Severance served as secretary. He also served as treasurer of the CUYAHOGA COUNTY ANTI-SLAVERY SOCIETY† when it was founded on 4 July 1837.

Severance married Mary Helen Long (d. 1902), the daughter of Dr. DAVID LONG, Cleveland's pioneer physician, on 12 Nov. 1833. The Severances had two sons, SOLON LEWIS and LOUIS HENRY SEVERANCE who would shape the social and business interests of Cleveland's future. Severance died of tuberculosis at Red Sulphur Springs, VA, and is buried in Erie St. Cemetery.—T.B.

Severance Family Papers, WRHS.

**SEVERANCE, SOLON LEWIS** (8 Sept. 1834–8 May 1915), banker and philanthropist, was born in Cleveland, the son of Mary Long and SOLOMON LEWIS SEVERANCE, and grandson of Dr. DAVID LONG. He was educated in district and private Cleveland schools and became an office boy in a banking firm at age 14. He rose in the firm and later organized Euclid Ave. Natl. Bank with several other investors. That bank merged with Euclid Park Bank, and later became part of First Natl. Bank. He was a director of the latter bank and also of First Trust & Savings Bank. Severance's great interests were in religion and philanthropic work and in travel. He was a charter member of Woodland Ave. Presbyterian Church and one of the first directors of the Fresh Air Camp. He married Emily Allen, the younger sister of Dr. DUDLEY P. ALLEN, on 10 Oct. 1860. Their daughter, Julia Severance, married Dr. Benjamin L. Millikin. Like his brother, Louis, Solon Severance tried to encourage sympathy for foreign missions. A world traveler, he made illustrated lectures of his journeys and presented them to friends and groups in Cleveland. Severance died in Cleveland and was buried in Lake View Cemetery.

Severance Family Papers, WRHS.

**SEWELL, JOSEPH WHEELER** (9 Oct. 1898–6 Mar. 1990), outstanding CLEVELAND INDIANS† baseball player for 11 years, was born in Wetumpka, AL, the son of Jabez Wesley and Susan Hannon Sewell, one of three brothers to play professional baseball. After attending public schools, he enrolled at the Univ. of Alabama, playing college football and baseball with his brother, James Luther (Luke) Sewell, and contributing to the school's four Southern Intercollegiate baseball championships. After graduation in 1920, he signed with the New Orleans baseball club, but the Cleveland Indians purchased his contract to replace shortstop RAY CHAPMAN, who died when hit by a pitched ball. Sewell batted .329 in the final 22 games of the 1920 season, as the Indians won the American League title and the World Series. He played shortstop and third base for the Indians through 1930, moving to the New York Yankees for the 1931–33 seasons. During his 14-year career, he compiled a batting average of .312 and set five major league records, including fewest strikeouts in a season (3) and fewest total strikeouts in a career by an everyday player (114). After Sewell retired in 1933, he coached for the Yankees and scouted for the Indians. As head baseball coach at the Univ. of Alabama, 1964–71, Sewell compiled a 114–99 won/loss record. He was elected to the National Baseball Hall of Fame in 1977.

Sewell married Willie Veal 31 Dec. 1921; they had three children: Joseph, Jr., James, and Mary Sue. He died at the home of his son in Mobile, AL.—M.S.

**SHANKLAND, ROBERT SHERWOOD** (11 Jan. 1908–5 Mar. 1982), physicist-educator and noted acoustical designer, was born in Willoughby, OH, to Frank N. and Margaret Jane Wedlock Shankland. After graduating from Willoughby High School, he attended Case School of Applied Science, receiving a B.S. in 1929 and an M.S. in 1933. He then went to the Univ. of Chicago, teaching there until 1935, when he received his Ph.D. in physics.

Shankland returned to Case in 1937 and rose rapidly through the academic ranks, becoming chairman of the Physics Department in 1940 and the Ambrose Swasey Professor of Physics in 1941. He resigned as chairman in 1958 but continued to teach until he retired in 1976. During World War II he was director of the Underwater Sound Reference Laboratory at Columbia Univ., charged with calibration and testing underwater sound equipment. During his career as a scientist and teacher, Shankland's interest centered on nuclear and reactor physics and architectural acoustics. He worked in nuclear physics research at the Univ. of California at Berkeley for several summers and served as acting technical director of the Materials Testing Reactor operated by the Atomic Energy Commission in Idaho Falls. Shankland published extensively on architectural acoustics and acted as consultant for many churches and concert halls, including SEVERANCE HALL.†

Shankland married Hilda C. Kinnison in Philadelphia 15 June 1931. They had 5 children: Sherwood, Ruth (Fielder), Dorothy (Eisenhour), and twins Lois (McIntyre) and Ava (Prebys). After his wife's death in Sept. 1970, Shankland married Eleanor Newlin. Shankland is buried in Willoughby Cemetery.—M.S.

**SHAPIRO, EZRA ZELIG** (7 May 1903–14 May 1977), attorney, Jewish community leader, and international Zionist figure, was born in Volozhin, Poland, to Esther (Brudno) and Rabbi Osias Shapiro. He was brought to Cleveland by his parents in 1906 and received his Jewish education in CLEVELAND HEBREW SCHOOLS.† He earned a law degree from Northern Univ. in 1925 and established a practice in Cleveland that year. He was Cleveland city law director from 1933–35. Shapiro was elected president of the Cleveland Zionist District in 1924. Ten years later he became chairman of the Natl. Executive Committee of the Zionist Organization of America. He was national vice-president of United Israel Appeal (1955–70) and a founder and first president (1957–60) of the American League for Israel, becoming honorary president in 1960. Shapiro was a delegate to several World Zionist Congresses beginning in 1937, and was instrumental in drafting the Jerusalem Platform that defined the direction for Zionism following the creation of the state of Israel.

Interested in Jewish education, Shapiro was president of Cleveland Hebrew Schools (1939–43) and the BUREAU OF JEWISH EDUCATION† (1953–56). From 1959–66, he was vice-president of the American Assn. for Jewish Education. Shapiro was on the board of the JEWISH COMMUNITY FED.† (1934–70), PARK SYNAGOGUE† (1950–70), and CLEVELAND COMMUNITY RELATIONS BOARD† (1963–70); and president of the Jewish Community Council (1942–45). In 1971 Shapiro emigrated to Israel, becoming the world chairman of Keren Hayesod–United Israel Appeal.

Shapiro married Sylvia Lamport in 1932 and had 2 children, Daniel and Rena (Mrs. Michael Blumberg). He died in Jerusalem and was buried there.

———

Ezra Z. Shapiro Papers, WRHS.

**SHAUTER, ROBERT HARRIS** (8 Oct. 1903–27 Dec. 1944), a successful black druggist and professional man, was born in Saybrook, OH, the son of Thomas J. and Florence L. Richardson Shauter. He attended Cleveland public schools and graduated from the School of Pharmacy at Western Reserve Univ. in 1923. After working as a prescription pharmacist for several drug stores in the Central Ave. area, Shauter purchased the Fox Pharmacy at 9208 Cedar Ave. 16 April 1936. Backed by entrepreneurs William Pierson and Roger Price, Shauter soon expanded his store, and two years later he established a prescription center at 2315 E. 55th St. In 1943 Shauter acquired the Leiken Drug Store in the Reserve Building at E. 55th and Woodland, where he set up the Shauter drug chain offices, operated by his wife, Frances. He was the only black member of the Ohio Northern Druggists Assn. and the Cleveland Academy of Pharmacy at that time.

Shauter married Frances Johnson in Cleveland 3 July 1930. They had no children. He died at his home in Cleveland and was buried in the family plot at Saybrook.—M.S.

**SHAW, ELSA VICK** (28 Jan. 1891–28 March 1974) was a Cleveland artist especially noted for her work in design. A native Clevelander, she and future husband GLENN M. SHAW both received their education at WEST HIGH SCHOOL† and the Cleveland School of Art (see CLEVELAND INSTITUTE OF ART†). Married in 1917, she taught design at the CSA for 15 years alongside her husband, who headed the mural department. They had joint exhibits at the Old White Gallery at White Sulphur Springs, WV, in 1933 and at the CLEVELAND SOCIETY OF ARTISTS† in 1942. Mrs. Shaw won numerous prizes in painting and weaving in the MAY SHOW† and painted a series of panels representing the origins of music, which were installed in the foyer of SEVERANCE HALL.† In 1941 she won a national competition to design a mural for the passenger ship S.S. *President Polk* of the President Lines. Entitled "Oceania," her design was carved in plate glass by the Rose Iron Works of Cleveland. A past president of the WOMEN'S ART CLUB OF CLEVELAND,† Elsa Shaw lived in LAKEWOOD,† then Moreland Hills. She concentrated on designing wallpaper for several Cleveland firms before moving to Arizona with her husband in 1968. He was her sole survivor upon her death in Sun City.—J.V.

**SHAW, GLENN MOORE** (6 Feb. 1891–22 Aug. 1981) achieved his reputation as a painter primarily on the strength of his murals. Born to Arthur B. and Grace Moore in OLMSTED FALLS,† he graduated from WEST HIGH SCHOOL† and the Cleveland School of Art (see CLEVELAND INSTITUTE OF ART†). In 1917 he married ELSA VICK SHAW, a schoolmate from both institutions. He taught at the art institute from 1922–57, serving as head of the mural painting section for the last 20 years. The first of Shaw's more than 60 murals was an Italian market scene he executed for the United Bank Bldg. across from the WEST SIDE MARKET† on W. 25th St. Other mural commissions included scenes for the Federal Reserve Bank in Pittsburgh, the Canton, OH, post office, the Lakewood High School auditorium, the Chicago Century of Progress exhibition, and the liner S.S. *America*. During World War II he taught classes at CSA in camouflage. Shaw was also an easel painter, winning numerous prizes in the annual MAY SHOW.† He was first president of the Lakewood Art Club and also served as president of the Cleveland Fine Arts Advisory Committee, the CLEVELAND SOCIETY OF ARTISTS,† and the Ohio Water Color Society. Moving with Mrs. Shaw to Arizona in 1968, he became a frequent writer of letters to the editor prior to his death in Sun City. He left no survivors.—J.V.

**SHEPHERD, ARTHUR** (19 Feb. 1880–12 Jan. 1958), prominent in Cleveland's musical community for nearly 30 years, was born to Mormon parents, William Nathaniel B. and Emily Mary (Phips) Shepherd, in Paris, ID. He graduated from the New England Conservatory of Music by 1897, and returned to Salt Lake City to organize and conduct the Salt Lake City Symphony Orchestra. His composition, *Overture Joyeuse,* won the Paderewski Prize in 1902. Beginning in 1910, Shepherd taught at the New England Conservatory and conducted at the St. Cecilia Society. In World War I he went overseas as bandmaster of the 303rd Field Artillery.

Called to Cleveland in 1920 by NIKOLAI SOKO-

LOFF, Shepherd became asst. conductor and program annotator for the CLEVELAND ORCHESTRA,† primarily responsible for the "pops" and children's concerts. Shepherd resigned in 1927 to become lecturer in music at Western Reserve Univ., remaining, however, as the orchestra's annotator until 1930. He was also music critic for the *CLEVELAND PRESS†* from 1928–31. When music was raised to departmental status at WRU in 1928, Shepherd was appointed chairman, inaugurating a 20-year program of experimental opera.

Shepherd's music was traditional and strongly flavored with the folk idiom of his native West. Eight of his orchestral compositions, including his 2 symphonies, were programmed by the Cleveland Orchestra. His over 100 works included a violin concerto, 4 string quartets, 2 piano sonatas, and numerous songs and choral pieces. After retiring from teaching in 1950, he continued composing until his death in Cleveland.

Shepherd married Hattie Jennings on 5 Mar. 1913; they had four children: Wm. Jennings, Arthur Phipps, Richard Jennings, and Mary Anne. After divorcing Hattie, he married Grazella Puliver on 27 May 1922. They had one son, Peter. Shepherd died in Cleveland and was buried in Salt Lake City, UT.

Koch, Frederick. *Reflections on Composing* (1983).
Marsh, Robert C. *The Cleveland Orchestra* (1967).

**SHEPHERD, DOROTHY G. PAYER** (15 Aug. 1916–13 Aug. 1992), curator of textiles and Near Eastern art for the CLEVELAND MUSEUM OF ART† (CMA, 1954–81), was one of only a few women museum curators in the U.S. in the 1960s and was internationally known for her scholarship in medieval textiles and ancient Near Eastern and Islamic art. She was born in Welland, Ontario, Canada, to English parents, George P. and Ethel Shepherd. When she was 2, the family moved to Fenton, MI, where Shepherd attended public schools. A graduate of the Univ. of Michigan (A.B., 1939, M.A. 1940), she worked toward a Ph.D. at the Institute of Fine Arts (NYC) and New York Univ. From 1942–44, Shepherd was asst. curator in decoration for the Cooper Union Museum of Arts (NYC), and during World War II worked for the Office of War Information in London, Luxembourg, Frankfurt, and Berlin.

Shepherd came to Cleveland in 1947 as asst. curator of textiles at the CMA. In 1954 the museum designated her as official curator of textiles and Near Eastern Art. She became chief curator of textiles and Islamic Art in 1979, a position she held until retiring. She taught Near Eastern art as adjunct professor at CASE WESTERN RESERVE UNIV.† Shepherd was a member of the Directing Council of

*Centre International d'Etudes des Textiles Anciens,* in France, of the Board of Governors of the American Research Center, in Egypt, and of the Board of Trustees of the American Institute of Iranian Studies.

Shepherd married architect Ernst Payer on 22 March 1951; he had 2 children by a previous marriage, Peter and Mark. After her husband's death in 1981, Shepherd moved first to Florida, then to Asheville, NC, where she died.

**SHERA, JESSE HAUK** (8 Dec. 1903–8 Mar. 1982), internationally respected librarian and library educator and dean of the School of Library Science at Western Reserve Univ. (subsequently CASE WESTERN RESERVE UNIV.†), was born in Oxford, OH, the son of Charles H. and Jessie (Hauk) Shera. He received an A.B. from Miami Univ. (Ohio) in 1925, an A.M. from Yale in 1927, and a Ph.D. from the Univ. of Chicago in Library Science in 1944. He became dean of the Library School at WRU in 1952, having worked for the Scripps Foundation for Research in Population Problems (1928–40), Library of Congress (1940–41), Office of Strategic Services (1941–44), and as assoc. director of the library and assoc. professor of library science at the Univ. of Chicago. As dean of WRU Library School, Shera helped found the Center for Documentation & Communication Research, which did pioneering research in automated information storage and retrieval and machine literature searching, and of which Shera became director in 1959.

Shera was president of the Ohio Library Assn. and on advisory commissions to the Census Bureau, Education Office, and Natl. Science Foundation. He represented the U.S. government in Europe and Latin America at international conferences on documentation and librarianship, served on Pres. Lyndon Johnson's Commission on Employment of the Handicapped, and the Cleveland Mayor's Commission on Employment of the Handicapped. Shera was dean of the Library School until 1970; in 1972 he was appointed dean and professor emeritus. Shera married Helen M. Bickham and had 2 children, Mary (Baum) and Edgar B.

**SHERWIN, BELLE** (20 Mar. 1868–9 July 1955), noted reform and feminist leader, was born in Cleveland to Frances Mary Smith and Henry Alden Sherwin, a founder of SHERWIN-WILLIAMS CO.† She received a B.S. degree from Wellesley College in 1890, Phi Beta Kappa, and studied history for a year at Oxford Univ. from 1894–95. Returning to the U.S., she taught 4 years in Boston at St. Margaret's and Miss Hersey's School for Girls. In 1900 she returned to Cleveland, serving as the first president of the CONSUMERS LEAGUE OF OHIO.† During

the period before World War I, Sherwin was active in numerous Cleveland welfare organizations, serving as director of the Public Health Nursing Assn. and a member of the Fed. for Charity & Philanthropy and the Council for Social Agencies. Following World War I, she was director of the Cleveland Welfare Fed., and from 1921–24 was vice-president of the Natl. League of Women Voters, serving as league president from 1924–34. Sherwin was a founder of the WOMEN'S CITY CLUB† in Cleveland. She received honorary degrees from Western Reserve Univ. (1930), Denison Univ. (1931), and Oberlin College (1937). Sherwin never married. —J.M.

Belle Sherwin Papers, Radcliffe College.

**SHERWIN, FRANCIS MCINTOSH** (7 March 1906–16 Dec. 1969) was a prominent banker, corporate director, and philanthropist, as well as mayor of the Village of Waite Hill.

Sherwin was born in Cleveland to Frances (McIntosh) and John Sherwin. He graduated from Hotchkiss School (CT), 1925, and received his B.S. degree from Yale Univ., 1929. Sherwin started as a banker with Midland Bank in Cleveland, 1929–32, then became asst. treasurer of Cleveland Trust Co., 1932–42. He joined Mid-Continent Securities Co. as secretary in 1934, later becoming treasurer and a director. From 1942–45 Sherwin was a major in the Army Air Corps.

In 1946 Sherwin joined Lake Erie Management Co., serving as president and a director. He was elected a director of Brush Beryllium Co. (Brush-Wellman Corp.) in 1946, serving until his death. He also chaired the executive committee, and served as board chairman from Dec. 1964 to May 1965.

In 1954 Sherwin was elected a director of the Halle Bros. Co., and in 1955 he joined the newly created executive committee and was a trustee of the Cleveland Health Education Museum (see HEALTH MUSEUM†) from 1950–63.

Sherwin served alternately as councilman (1948–51, 1958–62) and mayor (1952–57, 1962–65) of Waite Hill.

In 1953 Sherwin and his wife established the SOUTH WAITE FOUNDATION†, which provides grants to organizations in the arts, secondary education, and medical research.

Sherwin married Margaret Halle on 30 Jan. 1931; they had three sons: Peter, Brian, and Dennis. Sherwin lived in Waite Hill and is buried in Lake View Cemetery.—T.B.

**SHIELDS, JOSEPH C.** (10 May 1827–21 Dec. 1898), Civil War artillery officer, businessman, and politician, was born in New Alexandria, Westmoreland County, PA, son of John Shields. He was a tanner and furrier by trade, but between 1845–52 worked as a mechanic in Pittsburgh before moving to Cleveland in 1852. Shields was employed by Cleveland Transfer Co. (1852–53) and Cleveland & Toledo Railroad (1853–58). For 2 years, working for future Confederate leader Judah Benjamin, he superintended the building of a stage line across the Isthmus of Tehuantepec in Nicaragua. In 1860 he worked for Adams Express Co. in New Orleans, LA. By Apr. 1861, he was back in Cleveland with the Cleveland & Toledo Railroad. During the first 3 months of the Civil War, Shields served in Battery D, 1ST OHIO VOLUNTEER LIGHT ARTILLERY.† In July 1862 he recruited the 19TH OHIO INDEPENDENT BATTERY,† achieving the rank of captain on 28 July 1862. Shields resigned his commission on 15 Sept. 1864 to attend to business matters in Cleveland, becoming a passenger conductor on the Lake Shore & Michigan Southern Railroad, owning a grocery store, and running a paving contracting business. He was Cleveland city councilman (1867–68), deputy treasurer, Cuyahoga County (1886), and county treasurer (1889–94). Shields married Ellen S. Crawford in 1862. They had no children. Shields is buried in Lake View Cemetery.

**SHURTLEFF, GLEN KASSIMER** (21 Nov. 1860–5 Jan. 1909), secretary of the YOUNG MEN'S CHRISTIAN ASSN.† (YMCA) of Cleveland (1 Sept. 1893–1909), promoted the extension of YMCA religious work locally and nationally. An active member of the Cleveland Chamber of Commerce, he advocated a city-wide sanitary code (see SANITATION†) and creating the CUYAHOGA COUNTY JUVENILE COURT.† Born in Watkins Glen, NY, to Julia M. Finney and the Rev. Alonzo H. Shurtleff, he was educated at the Monroe Collegiate Institute, the Phoenix Academy, the Syracuse Classical School, and Syracuse Univ. He was secretary of the YMCA in Utica, NY (1883), and Denver, CO (1889). Shurtleff entered YMCA work in Cleveland in 1892 as president, and became secretary the next year. During his superintendency, the local YMCA acquired new staff and 5 new buildings—the Erie St. Annex, at Broadway, in Linndale, the West Side Boys' Club, and the Central Boys' Dept. Annex. During his tenure the Cleveland YMCA's religious work department had the most attendees at Bible study of any in North America, though it was only the continent's 7th largest YMCA. Shurtleff promoted the association's expansion of religious work nationally, organizing and directing the Niagara Falls Conference (1897) to study and discuss the matter. Founder and president of the Society for the Promotion of Social Service, he worked for social betterment, especially of CHILDREN AND YOUTH,† promoting improved playgrounds, among other causes. His friends and advisees included NEWTON D. BAKER, then city solicitor. Shurtleff married Gertrude E. Packard on 8 Oct. 1884. They had no children. He is buried in Lake View Cemetery.—J.M.

———

YMCA. *Glen K. Shurtleff Memorial* (1909).

**SIDLO, THOMAS L.** (10 Mar. 1888–27 May 1955), lawyer and founding partner of the law firm of Baker, Hostetler, Sidlo & Patterson (see BAKER & HOSTETLER†) was born in Cleveland to Thomas and Anna Sidlo, started as a freshman at Western Reserve Univ. but transferred to the Univ. of Wisconsin at Madison for 2 years, returning to WRU in 1908 and graduating in 1909, receiving his M.A. (1910) and LL.B. (1912) from WRU. He was admitted to the Ohio Bar in 1912. Sidlo supported NEWTON D. BAKER for Cleveland mayor, and when Baker took office Sidlo was made chief deputy under PETER WITT, the street railway commissioner. In 1913 Sidlo became commissioner of franchises, shortly thereafter commissioner of information and publicity, and in 1914 director of public service. When Baker left office in 1916, Sidlo joined him in forming Baker, Hostetler, Sidlo & Patterson. Sidlo was the financial director, controller, and general counsel for Scripps-Howard Newspapers, United Press Assn., and the Newspaper Enterprise Assn. from 1924–36. After Sidlo resigned, he devoted his time to his numerous outside interests, which encompassed more than 200 organizations, chiefly in music, theater, foreign affairs, and science. He was chairman of the NORTHERN OHIO OPERA ASSN.†; president of the MUSICAL ARTS ASSN.,† CLEVELAND PLAY HOUSE,† CLEVELAND MUSEUM OF NATURAL HISTORY,† and the Foreign Affairs Council in Cleveland; chairman of the Cleveland Committee for Relief in Czechoslovakia; and a trustee of Science Service, Inc. Sidlo married Winifred Morgan in 1914. She died in 1932. He later married Elizabeth Avery in 1935. Sidlo was buried in Lake View Cemetery.

**SIEDEL, FRANK** (5 Sept. 1914–9 May 1988), popularized aspects of state history in radio, television, and print under the title of "The Ohio Story." The son of Frank and Mary Ann Junglas Siedel, he was born in STRONGSVILLE,† where his father operated a general store. He went from CATHEDRAL LATIN SCHOOL† to Ohio State Univ., where he graduated with a degree in journalism. After marrying Clevelander Alyce Louise Van den Mooter in 1936, he worked as a radio writer in Pittsburgh and New York City before returning to

Ohio in 1941. In 1947 he sold a script about Ohio sharpshooter Annie Oakley to the Ohio Bell Telephone Co. (see AMERITECH†) as a pilot for a proposed radio series. "The Ohio Story" made its debut that year, broadcast from Cleveland 3 times weekly to a statewide network. Including a later television version, it ran for 20 years over 20 stations. Siedel published some of the scripts in *The Ohio Story* (1950) and *Out of the Midwest* (1953). He founded Storycraft, Inc., in 1947 to produce radio and television scripts for education as well as industry. Located in LAKEWOOD,† it numbered the WESTINGHOUSE CORP.† among its major clients. A longtime resident of ROCKY RIVER,† Siedel served as president of that suburb's Board of Education and in 1955 was elected to the first State Board of Education. During the 1980s he moved to Catawba, OH, where he died and is buried. Following the death of his first wife, he had married Mardith Jacobson in 1982. He was survived by her, sons James and Jonathan, and a daughter, Jeri Audiano.—J.V.

**SIEGEL, RICHARD H.** (21 Dec. 1935–31 Aug. 1993) was a Cleveland attorney whose civic activism included the establishment of the alternative newspaper, the *CLEVELAND FREE TIMES.†* A native Clevelander, son of Dr. Samuel and Kathleen Marshall Siegel, he graduated from Cleveland Hts. High School and took a degree from Western Reserve Univ. (see CASE WESTERN RESERVE†) in 1957. He earned his law degree from the Univ. of Chicago in 1960, the year he married the former Madeleine (Mimsy) Ross, and established a successful Cleveland law practice specializing in labor arbitration. During the 1960s Siegal helped organize several Cleveland visits by Rev. Martin Luther King, Jr., and became active as a fundraiser for presidential candidates. He helped direct the Ohio presidential campaign for Sen. Eugene McCarthy in 1968 and attended the 1980 Democratic convention as a supporter of Sen. Ted Kennedy. A resident of PEPPER PIKE,† he ran an unsuccessful campaign for that suburb's council in 1967 on a platform challenging discriminatory housing patterns. Siegel was elected president of the CITIZENS LEAGUE† in 1976. He opposed tax abatement for the Gateway sports complex as harmful for the CLEVELAND PUBLIC SCHOOLS.† After the demise of the *CLEVELAND EDITION,†* Siegel started the weekly *Free Times* in Sept. 1992, primarily to provide a forum for points of view that otherwise might have gone unheard. The paper continued, after his death in New Mexico, under the direction of his wife and 4 surviving sons: Randy, Peter, Michael, and William.—J.V.

**SIFLEET, WILLIAM J.** (1860–8 May 1932) is remembered as "the father of Brook Park" for his pivotal role in the formation of that Cleveland suburb. The son of Thomas and Elizabeth Sifleet, he was born on their farm on Smith Rd., in what was then Middleburg Twp. Sifleet inherited and worked the family farm, marrying his wife Alice ca. 1887. He became a leader in the movement by residents in the northern part of the township to incorporate their own municipality, which was accomplished in 1914. Credited with naming the resultant village of BROOK PARK† after the nature of its terrain, Sifleet served as its first mayor from 1914–21. After an interim of one term, he was elected a second time, 1924–27. He was also a member of the Brook Park Grange and the Cuyahoga County Health Board, as well as a trustee of Berea Community Hospital. He died in the same house in which he had been born and had lived all his life. Having been predeceased by a daughter, Hazel, Sifleet was survived by his wife and a son, A. Corwin. He was buried in Berea's Woodvale Cemetery.—J.V.

**SIHLER, CHRISTIAN, M.D.** (2 Oct. 1848–22 Aug. 1919), physician, researcher and writer, and founder of WINDSOR HOSPITAL† and Lutheran Hospital (1896) (see LUTHERAN MEDICAL CENTER†), was among the first physicians in Cleveland to promote HYDROTHERAPY.† While studying biology at Johns Hopkins Univ., he developed pioneering techniques to trace nerve endings. Sihler was born in Fort Wayne, IN, to Wilhelm and Susanna Kern Sihler. He attended Lutheran schools and Concordia College, IN (later Concordia Theological Seminary), where his father, a Lutheran minister, was president. After graduating from the Univ. of Michigan Medical School (1871), he studied abroad, at the Univ. of Berlin, for 2 years. Sihler then opened a practice in Cleveland, leaving in 1877 to study for his Ph.D. at Johns Hopkins Univ. In Baltimore he married Rosa Horn; the couple returned to Cleveland after Sihler's graduation (1881). He wrote 2 books (one in German), which he published himself, and several brochures. In addition to serving the Windsor Hydriatic Institute and as chief of staff of Lutheran Hospital, Sihler taught at the Cleveland Medical College and at the Medical School of Western Reserve Univ. (see CASE WESTERN RESERVE UNIV.†). Sihler retired from his practice in 1909 and died in Cleveland. His family presented Dr. Sihler's Gundlach microscope to the CLEVELAND MEDICAL LIBRARY ASSN.† for the museum collection (see DITTRICK MUSEUM OF MEDICAL HISTORY†).—J.M.

**SILBERT, SAMUEL H.** (15 Apr. 1883–18 Feb. 1976), lawyer and long-time Common Pleas Court judge, was born in Kiev, Ukraine, to Joseph and Nurious (Brook) Silbert. He came to Newark, NJ, at age 6 with his widowed mother, and worked selling newspapers and in an ink factory. By 16, Silbert was a state champion amateur boxer. Moving to Denver, he worked as a train news butcher before coming to Cleveland in 1902. He worked days, attending school at night. Silbert graduated from Cleveland Law School and was admitted to the Ohio Bar in 1907. In 1912 he was appointed asst. police prosecutor by Mayor NEWTON D. BAKER, serving until 1915. He established a conciliation system credited with settling over 29,000 disputes. In 1915 Silbert won election to the municipal court bench, where he introduced several judicial novelties, including a water cure for alcoholics by which defendants could avoid the workhouse by downing 10 glasses of water each day. In 1923 he was defeated for chief justice of the municipal court. Elected to the Common Pleas Court in 1924, Silbert continued serving at that post, also serving as chief justice (1955–63), until his retirement on 1 Jan. 1969. Most of the time he served in divorce court, handling almost 100,000 cases in his career. As a nationally recognized authority on domestic relations, divorce, and marital problems, Silbert reconciled thousands of couples. His popularity was so great and his vote-getting ability so formidable, that he often ran for reelection unopposed.

Silbert married Anna Weinstein in 1909 in Steubenville, OH. The couple had no children. Silbert died in Cleveland and was buried in Mayfield Cemetery.

Samuel Silbert Papers, WRHS.
Silbert, Samuel. *Judge Sam* (1963).

**SILVER, ABBA HILLEL** (28 Jan. 1893–28 Nov. 1963), religious leader, Zionist, and social-welfare activist, was born Abraham Silver in Neinstadt, Schirwindt, Lithuania, to Moses and Dinah Seaman Silver. His father, grandfather, and great-grandfather had all been rabbis. Silver and his family emigrated to America and settled in New York City in 1902. In 1904 Silver and his brother, Maxwell, founded the Hebrew-speaking Herzl-Zion Club. In 1907, at age 16, Silver addressed the 10th annual convention of the Federation of American Zionists. Silver attended Hebrew Union College and the Univ. of Cincinnati, during which time he changed his name to Abba Hillel. He graduated from both institutions in 1915. Ordained as a Reform rabbi, Silver served the Congregation Leshem Shomayim (the Eoff St. Temple), in Wheeling, WV, from 1915–17. Silver was awarded a Doctor of Divinity degree from Hebrew Union College in 1927.

Coming to Cleveland in 1917, Silver succeeded

MOSES GRIES as rabbi of TEMPLE-TIFERETH ISRAEL,† turning it from an "institutional synagogue" to one more religiously and culturally centered. He reinstituted Hebrew in religious education and openly espoused political Zionism, for which he was a vocal advocate throughout his career. The congregation became the largest Reform congregation in the country by 1927. While affiliated with the Zionist Organization of America from the 1920s to the 1940s, he also was president of the United Palestine Appeal and co-chair of the United Jewish Appeal (1938). In 1943 Silver became co-chair with Rabbi Stephen S. Wise of the American Zionist Emergency Council (AZEC). In 1944 Silver lobbied for passage of a Palestinian Resolution by the U.S. Congress, which did so in December of 1945. That year Silver was elected president of the ZOA. Silver was appointed chairman of the American section of the Jewish Agency, on whose behalf he addressed the United Nations General Assembly 8 May 1947, advocating creation of the State of Israel. Following the establishment of Israel in 1948, control of the Zionist movement slowly transferred to Israeli officials. The resulting power struggle and controversies about fundraising led Silver to resign his positions at the ZOA, AZEC, and the Jewish Agency in 1948–49. However, Silver's support for Israel remained strong. In 1956 an Israeli agricultural school, Kfar Silver, was named in his honor.

Locally, Silver was the first president of the BUREAU OF JEWISH EDUCATION† (1924–32), and in 1933 helped create the LEAGUE FOR HUMAN RIGHTS,† as well as the non-sectarian Anti-Nazi League to Champion Human Rights in 1938. Silver also supported trade unionism and worked for the Ohio Commission on Unemployment Insurance, which helped to pass the state's unemployment insurance law in 1936. Silver was a prolific rabbinic scholar, publishing 7 major works, including *The Democratic Impulse in Jewish History* (1928), *The World Crisis and Jewish Survival* (1941), *Where Judaism Differed* (1956), and *Moses and the Original Torah* (1961). Silver married Virginia Horkheimer in Wheeling in 1923. They had two children, Daniel Jeremy and Raphael David. When Silver died his son, Daniel, succeeded him as rabbi at the Temple.

Papers of Rabbi Abba Hillel Silver, The Temple-Tifereth Israel, WRHS.
Silver, Rabbi Daniel J., ed. *In the Time of Harvest* (1963).

**SINCLAIR, JO** (1 July 1913–3 April 1995) was the pen name Ruth B. Seid used to write award-winning fiction. Sinclair won the biennial Harper publishing prize of $10,000 in 1946 for *Wasteland,* her first novel. Sinclair was born in Brooklyn, NY, the fifth child and third daughter of Ida Kravetsky Seid and Nathan Seid, Russian-Jewish immigrants. The family moved to Cleveland when Sinclair was 3. Sinclair graduated from John Hay High School as valedictorian (1930). She lived in CLEVELAND HTS.,† SHAKER HTS.,† and finally, on a farm on Fairmount Blvd. in Novelty, OH, at times sharing residences with Mr. and Mrs. Mort Buchman. In the early 1970s Sinclair moved to Philadelphia, PA.

During the 1930s and 1940s, Sinclair wrote and edited for the WPA and its Foreign Language Newspaper Digest project, and worked for a bookbindery and the AMERICAN RED CROSS, CLEVELAND CHAPTER.† She published her first story in *Esquire* (Jan. 1938), using her new pen name to sidestep that magazine's policy of using only male writers. Later that year three other magazines (*New Masses, Ken, Coronet*) published her work. Sinclair wrote and published stories, novels, and plays about discrimination, diversity, and prejudice against immigrants and minorities. Her story "The Red Necktie," published in *Common Ground* (spring, 1941), was included in a 1942 anthology, *This Way to Unity,* and was dramatized by Radio Stuttgart in Germany. Many of Sinclair's works were reprinted in foreign editions. In addition to the Harper prize, Sinclair won local and state awards: the Ohioana Award (1956) for *The Changelings* (1955), her 3rd novel; the Harry and Ethel Daroff Memorial fiction award from the Jewish Book Council (1956), and the first annual Cleveland Arts Prize from the WOMEN'S CITY CLUB† of Cleveland (1961). The CLEVELAND PLAY HOUSE† produced *The Long Moment,* a play by Sinclair, in 1951. Sinclair died in Jenkintown, PA.—J.M.

**SISSLE, NOBLE** (10 Aug. 1889–17 Dec. 1975), black composer, bandleader, and vocalist, was born in Indianapolis, son of Rev. George A. and Martha (Scott) Sissle. He moved with his family to Cleveland in 1909, graduated from CENTRAL HIGH SCHOOL† in 1911, and studied at DePauw Univ. (1913), and Butler Univ. (1914–15). Sissle began singing professionally in 1908, in 1915 organizing his own short-lived group in Indianapolis. He also sang in Baltimore, where he met Eubie Blake and formed a songwriting team, with Sissle as lyricist. Sissle joined a New York society dance orchestra in 1916. In 1917 he joined the 369th Infantry Regimental Band and served overseas until 1919. Sissle and Blake toured the vaudeville circuit—in 1921 their production of "Shuffle Along" opened an 18-month Broadway run, followed by another 2 years on tour. Sissle and Blake toured Europe in 1926. After dissolving the partnership, Sissle performed as a soloist and with his own band in Europe before returning to New York in 1931. From the mid-1930s to mid–1950s, Sissle led his own Noble Sissle Orchestra, touring the U.S. In 1937 he helped found the Negro Actors' Guild, serving as its first president. During World War II he toured with a USO troop. Throughout the 1940s, Sissle wrote columns for the *New York Age* and *Amsterdam News*. During the 1960s, he continued managing his own publishing company and nightclub, as well as leading his own orchestra.

Sissle married Harriet Toye; they had three children: Noble, Cynthia, and Helen (Toye). Sissle retired to Florida in the 1970s and died there. He was buried in New York City.

Kimball, Robert. *Reminiscing with Sissle and Blake* (1973).

**SKEEL, ARTHUR J.** (1874–7 Dec. 1942) was nationally known for advancing obstetrics and serving as director of the Obstetric Div. of ST. LUKE'S HOSPITAL† from 1910–38. Born in Augusta, MI, son of Frances Adelbert and Hettie (Butler) Skeel, he attended Cleveland schools and studied medicine at the Univ. of Michigan. He began practicing medicine in 1897 under an older brother who was an obstetrician and gynecologist. From 1907 he specialized in obstetrics and diseases of women. During his 40 years of practice, great strides were made in obstetrics. Skeel himself was especially concerned with new ideas in prenatal and postnatal care that minimized the mortality rate among mothers and newborns. He founded the St. Luke's Obstetric Dispensary for out-patient services, one of the earliest such organizations in Cleveland. He also founded Cleveland Hospital Obstetric Society and was active in similar organizations in Ohio and other states. He was made a fellow of the American Assn. of Obstetricians. In addition to his work at St. Luke's, Skeel was professor of obstetrics at the Cleveland College of Physicians & Surgeons, which later merged with Western Reserve Univ.

Skeel married Blandina Kern on 15 April 1908; they had 3 children: Marguerite Julia, Roland Alexander, and Arthur Edward. Skeel died in Cleveland and was buried in Lake View Cemetery.

**SLAUGHTER, HOWARD SILAS, SR.** (19 Oct. 1890–15 June 1936) was a funeral director, embalmer, and founder and president of Slaughter Funeral Home, Inc., one of the earliest African American funeral businesses established in Cleveland.

Born in Urbana, OH, to Hugh Campbell and Clara (Wills) Slaughter, Howard attended public school in Urbana. He first entered the funeral business in 1911 when he went to work as a manager for J. WALTER WILLS, SR. in the undertaking firm of

J. Walter Wills & Sons in Cleveland. Slaughter graduated from the Cleveland Training School for Embalmers on 17 Jan. 1914. He was licensed by the Ohio State Board of Embalming Examiners on 26 Feb. 1914.

In 1915 Slaughter and his two brothers opened their first funeral home under the name Slaughter Bros., Funeral Directors and Embalmers, at 3839 Central Ave. Howard Slaughter was a member of the board and president of the Slaughter Bros. firm. Slaughter eventually assumed control of the entire Slaughter Bros. firm and in 1926 purchased and remodelled property at 2165 East 89th St. to accommodate his new business, Slaughter Funeral Home, Inc., of which he served as president. It was the Slaughter Funeral Home that E. F. Boyd purchased following Slaughter's death, becoming the E. F. BOYD & SON FUNERAL HOME.†

Slaughter was a member of the National Funeral Directors and Embalmers Assn. He married Ruby A. Yates on 3 June 1913. They had 2 children, Howard Jr. and Ruby C. Slaughter belonged to the MT. ZION CONGREGATIONAL CHURCH† and is buried in Highland Park Cemetery.—T.B.

**SMALL, PHILIP LINDSLEY** (18 July 1890–16 May 1963) was a Cleveland-based architect best known for his work with CHARLES ROWLEY. Small was born in Washington DC, and was the son of Charles Herbert and Cora Lindsley Small. He was raised in Springfield, OH, and moved to Cleveland in 1904. His education included Adelbert College of Western Reserve Univ. and MIT, where he graduated in 1915. He began practicing architecture in Cleveland in 1920. In 1921 he teamed up with a childhood friend, Charles Rowley, to form the firm of SMALL AND ROWLEY.† Small and Rowley were best known for their work for the VAN SWER-INGENS,† including SHAKER SQUARE,† the MORELAND COURT APARTMENTS,† and DAISY HILL.† The partnership dissolved in 1928 and Small formed a new firm, Philip Small & Associates. Small thereafter worked almost exclusively for the Van Sweringens, designing interiors for Higbee's Dept. Store, the Country Club of Pepper Pike, and railroad projects. Small later did the planning and design for JOHN CARROLL UNIV.† In 1936 the firm became Small, Smith & Reeb, and in 1956, Small, Smith, Reeb & Draz. The firm designed the KARAMU HOUSE† Theater and Community Service Building (1949–59) and several buildings for Western Reserve Univ. and Case School, including the science center, 2 dormitories, the physics building, and Freiberger Library. Small retired in Dec. 1960.

Small married Grace Hatch in 1920. They had two children, Philip L. Small, Jr., and Martha (Mrs.

Elliott E. Stearns, Jr.). Philip Small died in Cleveland.—D.R.

**SMEAD, TIMOTHY** (1811–3 Jan. 1890), one of Cleveland's pioneer printers, brought the first newspaper to what later became the city's west side. The son of a printer, he was born in Bennington, VT, and raised in Bath, NY. Moving to Cleveland in 1835, he initially settled in the west side community then known as OHIO CITY,† where he established the *OHIO CITY ARGUS†* with Lyman W. Hall on 16 May 1836. After Hall's withdrawal, Smead replaced the *Argus* in 1838 with the *Ohio Transcript and Farmers' Register.* Having married Mary E. Herrick in 1836, he also started a monthly magazine called *MOTHERS' AND YOUNG LADIES' GUIDE†* under the editorship of his new mother-in-law, Mrs. MARIA M. HERRICK. Begun in June 1837, it was probably the first magazine published in Cleveland, east or west. Both the newspaper and magazine, however, as well as the abolitionist weekly *Palladium of Liberty,* which he had printed for the Liberty party, were suspended by 1841. Smead then moved to Cleveland, where he formed a partnership with another antislavery printer, EDWIN W. COWLES. They printed both the *Cleveland American* and the *DAILY TRUE DEMOCRAT,†* which was converted by Cowles into the *CLEVELAND LEADER†* in 1855. Thereafter Smead concentrated on the printing business, although he also wrote poetry for private distribution to friends. Smead was credited by some with the coinage of Cleveland's nickname of "FOREST CITY,"† but former Mayor WM. CASE is more commonly regarded as its originator. Blind during his last 8 years, Smead was survived by his wife and 4 children: Franklin, Sylvester, Maria, and Mary.—J.V.

**SMETONA, ANTANAS** (10 Aug. 1874–9 Jan. 1944), who came to Cleveland in Apr. 1942 as the exiled president of Lithuania, was born of peasant parents in Uzulenents. He became an ardent promoter of Lithuanian nationalism as a youth and as a result was expelled from college and later from law school in St. Petersburg, where he was also jailed. Upon his release from prison he settled in Vilna, where he worked in a bank and later edited a small periodical.

Persisting in supporting Lithuanian freedom, Smetona was one of 3 ministers chosen to head the provisional government after Russia renounced its claim to the country in 1918. He served as president of the country from 1919–22, and was reelected in 1926 and 1930. He and his wife were forced to flee the country on 15 June 1940, during the Soviet invasion. They escaped first to Germany, then to Switzerland, and traveled to other countries before arriving in the U.S. in Mar. 1941, greeted by Pres. Franklin D. Roosevelt. In Cleveland Smetona and his wife, Sophie, lived in an attic suite above the apartment of their son, Julius, a grinder for Standard Tool Co. Smetona traveled to Lithuanian communities throughout the U.S. and wrote and spoke on behalf of his Soviet-controlled homeland, using the home at Ablewhite Ave. as his base, until his death in a house fire. Smetona was buried in Knollwood Cemetery and then reinterred in a family crypt in All Soul's Cemetery.

Cadzow, John F. *Lithuanian Americans and Their Communities of Cleveland* (1978).

**SMITH, ALBERT KELVIN** (5 Jan. 1899–15 Nov. 1984), a founder of LUBRIZOL CORP.† and philanthropist, was born in Cleveland to Mary Wilkinson and ALBERT W. SMITH, who with HERBERT DOW founded Dow Chemical Co. Kelvin shared his father's interest in chemistry, graduating from Dartmouth College with a bachelor's in physics in 1920, and with a bachelor's in chemical engineering from Case School of Applied Science in 1922. He worked 4 years as a chemist for Dow before becoming research director of France Mfg., and later chemical engineer for McGean Chemical Co.

In 1928, Smith and his brothers, KENT H. and Vincent K. (4 June 1896–9 Mar. 1980) joined Alex Nason to form Graphite Oil Prods. Co., Lubrizol's predecessor. Smith was a leading stockholder and director of research. He founded Cleveland Industrial Research, Inc. in 1935, serving as its president until 1945. He was president of Lubrizol from 1951–62, establishing manufacturing subsidiaries in 5 foreign nations, expanding domestic operations, becoming a publicly owned company, and more than doubling its sales and earnings. Smith was chairman of the Board of Directors from 1964–66 and director of the company until 1971.

Smith amassed a fortune, much of which he donated to institutions and agencies in whose works he had an interest. He endowed a chair for the music director of the CLEVELAND ORCHESTRA,† was a major contributor to the development and construction of Blossom Music Ctr., and was also a trustee of the MUSICAL ARTS ASSN.† He was a trustee of Case Institute of Technology, where he funded the Albert W. Smith Merit Scholarships, and of Lake Erie College, where he helped establish an equestrian program. He endowed a professorship in physics at Dartmouth and, with his brothers, established a professorship in chemistry there. Smith College, his wife's alma mater, also received his support. Smith gave to the CLEVELAND SOCIETY FOR THE BLIND† Sight Ctr., the CLEVELAND CLINIC FOUNDATION,† and the Garden Center of Greater Cleveland (see CLEVELAND BOTANICAL GARDEN†), and served as a trustee of UNIV. HOSPITALS† and the Cleveland HEALTH MUSEUM.† Smith served as an officer in the Ohio Mfrs. Assn. and the Chemical Industrial Council of Ohio, and held memberships in the American Chemical Society and the Franklin Institute.

Smith married Eleanor Armstrong in 1923 and had two children, Cara and Lucia.

Smalheer, Calvin V. *The Story of Lubrizol* (1972).

**SMITH, ALBERT W.** (4 Oct. 1862–4 Mar. 1927), chemist, professor, and a founder of Dow Chemical Co., was born in Newark, OH, to Geo. H. and Mary Smith, graduated from the Univ. of Michigan in chemistry (1885), received a B.S. from Case School of Applied Science (1887), and his Ph.D. from the Univ. of Zurich (1891). Smith was professor of metallurgy and chemistry at Case from 1891–1907, when he became head of the metallurgical engineering department, serving there until 1911, when he succeeded CHAS. F. MABERY as head of the chemistry department. Smith headed that department until his death. He had a reputation as an informal but dedicated teacher.

As a student at Case, Smith became friends with HERBERT DOW, with whom he established Dow Chemical Co., providing not only his knowledge but also part of the initial funding. He was an original director and chemical consultant for the firm. Smith also helped establish Midland Corp., a subsidiary of Dow, to develop products from the deep-well brines from which Dow produced bromine. At Midland, Smith developed processes to manufacture chloroform and carbon tetrachloride. Midland was eventually absorbed by Dow. During World War I, Smith helped Dow and the war effort by developing machinery to produce mustard gas in large quantities. Smith served on Cleveland's water purification commission under mayor NEWTON D. BAKER and was influential in having the west side water-filtration plant built. Smith married Mary Wilkinson in 1890. Their 3 sons, ALBERT K., KENT H., and Vincent K., were among the founders of LUBRIZOL CORP.† Smith is buried at Lake View Cemetery.

Smalheer, Calvin V. *The Story of Lubrizol* (1972).

**SMITH, ALLEN, JR.** (1810–11 Sept. 1890), portrait and landscape painter, was born in Dighton, MA, to Allen and Lydia (Wardwell) Smith. He worked in Detroit for 6 years before moving to Cleveland in 1841, where he practiced for over 40 years. Smith embarked on his artistic career as a youth by copying prints and drawings. His first practical experience as a painter was working in the scene-painting department of the Bowery Theater. His formal academic training came while he was a student at the Natl. Academy. In 1835 Smith moved to Detroit; in 1841 he moved to Cleveland. While there he painted some of his most famous portraits: Gov. Tod of Ohio, Gov. Fairchild of Wisconsin, and the presidents of Western Reserve and Kenyon colleges. He also painted Leonard Case, Jr.'s, formal portrait. In 1848 he won an Art Union Prize for his portrait, *Young Mechanic*.

Smith married twice. He married Harriet Hosmer on 19 Apr. 1830, and Josephine Stevenson on 31 Dec. 1864. He had 8 children: Frances, Elizabeth, Benjamin W., George, Alice, Charles, Adrian, and Ida. In 1883 Smith moved to Painesville and then to Concord, OH, where he died. He is buried in Woodland Cemetery in Cleveland.

**SMITH, CHARLES HENRY** (23 Nov. 1837–13 Aug. 1912), attorney, merchant, banker, and volunteer Civil War officer, was born in Taunton, MA, to Thomas and Ann Clark Smith. He lived in Fall River, MA (1845–50), and Jamestown, NY (1850–56), before moving to Cleveland in 1856 and going into the furniture business. When the Civil War broke out, he enlisted in Co. A, 7TH OHIO VOLUNTEER INFANTRY, composed of the Cleveland Light Guard Zouave Co., of which he was a member. After 3 month's service, Smith returned to Cleveland to recruit a company for 3 year's service, Co. G, 27th OVI. He was appointed sergeant on 27 July 1861, orderly sergeant on 12 May 1862, and 2nd lt. on 2 Nov. 1862 for meritorious conduct at the Battle of Corinth, MS, in which he led a charge against the 9th Texas Infantry, capturing its flag and color guard.

Smith was commissioned 1st lt. on 9 May 1864, captain on 3 Nov. 1864, and major on 3 May 1865. He was mustered out and discharged in July 1865. Smith received a law degree from Ohio State Univ. in 1871, but did not practice. Instead, he spent 33 years in the grain trade, also serving as a director and treasurer of Equity Savings & Loan Co. He married Louisa M. Johnson in 1868 and had 3 daughters: Mildred, Nina, and Edith, and a son. He participated in several military organizations and was a Mason. Smith died at his residence in Cleveland, and was buried in Lake View Cemetery.

Chas. H. Smith Papers, WRHS.
Smith, Charles H. *The History of Fuller's Ohio Brigade, 1861–1865* (1909).

**SMITH, DOROTHY** (26 Apr. 1892–30 Dec. 1976) was a prominent social worker born in Springfield,

MO, to James H. and Emily G. (Russell) Smith. She attended Vassar College, and entered social work upon her graduation in 1914, assuming a position with the YWCA in Pawtucket, RI. Named general secretary of the Pawtucket YWCA in 1916, she established vocational programs in nursing and child care, placing her organization in the forefront of the local war effort. Smith came to Cleveland in 1921, a year later becoming general secretary of the Cleveland YOUNG WOMEN'S CHRISTIAN ASSN.† Under her guidance, the YWCA built a new headquarters, established a program to aid senior citizens, added recreation programs, and strongly supported Prohibition. Smith resigned on the eve of the Depression to enter the insurance business, while also acting as an advisor to many programs assisting people crippled by the Depression. World War II and the resulting shortage of skilled administrators brought her back to social work. In 1943 she became an adult worker at EAST END NEIGHBORHOOD HOUSE,† becoming director in 1944, instituting volunteer programs allowing the settlement to cut its administrative costs by 40% and constructing a new recreation building in 1947. Smith resigned in 1955 but continued serving as an advisor for 10 more years. During this period she also became active with the Mentor Community Fund, serving on its board of trustees from 1957–64. Smith spent her last 10 years in quiet retirement in Mentor. She was unmarried.

East End Neighborhood House Records, WRHS.

**SMITH, ELMER JOHN** (21 Sept. 1892–3 Aug. 1984), who hit the first grand slam home run in World Series history, was born in Sandusky, OH, the son of George C. and Mary Lentz Smith. His baseball career began in Cleveland, playing with the Naps in 1914. He continued with the newly renamed CLEVELAND INDIANS† until 1921, with the exception of the 1916–17 season, when his playing time was divided between the Indians and the Washington Senators. Smith's history-making grand slam occurred at Dunn Field 10 Oct. 1920 during the fifth game of the World Series. In the first inning of the game of the BASEBALL WORLD SERIES† against the Brooklyn Dodgers, Smith hit his home run with Charlie Jameson, BILL WAMBSGANSS, and player-manager TRIS SPEAKER on base, enabling the Indians to win 8–1 and take the series lead 3 games to 2. The Indians went on to win the world championship. Smith later played with Boston and New York in the American League, and Cincinnati in the National League. During his 10-year major league career as an outfielder, 1914–25, he compiled a .276 batting average. However, his best years were with Cleveland when he hit .321 in

1914 and .316 in 1920. After he retired from baseball in 1925, Smith lived in Cleveland, working as a salesman for the Leisy Brewing Co. in the 1930s and 1940s. In 1974 he moved to Kentucky.

Smith married Ruth E. Hanrath in Cleveland 28 Dec. 1920. He died in Columbia, KY, and was survived by four grandchildren.—M.S.

**SMITH, FRANK A.** (1 May 1894–8 Aug. 1992) was a long-time pastor in the Christian Methodist Episcopal Church and a charter member of Lane C.M.E. Church in Cleveland.

One of eight children of Rev. Anthony T. and Caroline Smith, Frank was born in Monticello, GA, where early on he learned the role of the circuit preacher.

In 1902 his family came to Cleveland, where together with seven other families which had moved from Georgia, they became charter members of Lane Christian Methodist Episcopal Church, the denomination's first church in Cleveland.

Smith completed elementary school in Cleveland before attending Lane College in Jackson, TN. He then attended Payne Theological Seminary in Wilberforce, OH, and Toledo Univ. He completed his B.A. degree at the Univ. of Akron, then earned bachelor's and master's degrees in divinity at Northern Baptist Theological Seminary in Chicago.

Following his studies, he served as pastor in several churches in Ohio, Pennsylvania, Kentucky, Illinois, and Kansas. During World War II he spent just over two years in the army's chaplain corps.

Retiring from full-time ministry in 1966, Smith returned to Cleveland and to Lane C.M.E. Church as an asst. pastor. In 1984 he wrote *A Pilgrimage of Faith*, a history of the congregation. In 1969 he also became active in civil rights efforts, and became joint coordinator of a United Methodist Church leadership program for the local African American community.

Smith married twice. His first wife, Helen, died in 1966. His second wife was Marie. Smith was buried at White Haven Park.

**SMITH, GEORGE HORATIO** (July 1848–8 Apr. 1924) was a Cleveland architect best known as a collaborator in designing the ARCADE.† Little is known of Smith's upbringing, training, family, and early career. He began his architecture practice in Ohio between 1879 and 1880 with LUCAS ALLEN HEARD under the name Heard & Smith. He appeared on the Cleveland scene in 1882 with the design for Samuel Andrews's great Victorian Gothic baronial mansion (see ANDREWS'S FOLLY†). He then designed the Euclid Ave. mansion of CHAS. F. BRUSH (1884), nearly as pretentious. Both houses already showed a complete confidence in handling European styles. In 1890 Smith's Hickox Bldg. and the Arcade were both completed. From the similarities in the facade composition of the two buildings, it is assumed Smith's responsibility in the Arcade was designing the Superior and Euclid Ave. office buildings, and that JOHN EISENMANN planned the structural engineering for the interior. Smith also designed the Colonial Arcade between Euclid and Prospect in 1898.

Smith was chosen as architect of Lakeside Hospital, which opened in 1898. Consisting of a group of separate administrative, ward, nurses' residence, and dispensary buildings, it was used until the hospital moved to UNIV. CIRCLE† in 1931. In 1900 Smith designed the Rose Bldg. on Prospect and E. 9th St.; in 1906–10 the new plant of White Sewing Machine Co. (later WHITE MOTOR†) on St. Clair; and in 1908–11 the new Plain Dealer Bldg. on Superior (Cleveland Public Library Business & Science Annex) to harmonize with the Group Plan buildings. Smith retired in 1918.

Smith married Ruhamah Henkle in the early 1870s. They had 4 children: Eugene, Dudley, Ruhamah G., and Dorothy. He died in Bethlehem, PA, and was buried there.

**SMITH, HARRY CLAY** (28 Jan. 1863–10 Dec. 1941), a pioneer of the black press, was brought to Cleveland at age 2 after his birth in Clarksburg, WV, to John and Sarah Smith. Shortly after graduating from CENTRAL HIGH SCHOOL,† he and 3 associates founded the *CLEVELAND GAZETTE†* in 1883. Beginning as managing editor, Smith soon became the sole proprietor of the weekly newspaper, which he published for 58 years. A disciple of MARCUS A. HANNA, Smith was a deputy state oil inspector from 1885–89, and was elected as a Republican to 3 terms in the Ohio general assembly, where he sponsored the Ohio Civil Rights Law of 1894, establishing penalties against discrimination in public accommodations, and the Mob Violence Act of 1896, an antilynching law. Smith for years crusaded to block the showing in Ohio of the classic but racist film *The Birth of a Nation*; and when a miscegenation bill was proposed, personally led a delegation to Columbus to lobby for its defeat. Running for the Republican nomination for secretary of state in 1920, he defeated an attempt to remove his name from the ballot because of its similarity to that of another candidate, but lost the nomination nonetheless. Though he lost bids for the Republican nomination for governor in 1926 and 1928, he felt he broke ground as the first black candidate for that position. Smith died suddenly in his office. He had no wife or children; his property was left for the benefit of the Negro blind.

**SMITH, HERALD LEONYDUS** (20 April 1909–20 July 1992), printer, pastor, and organist, edited and published *The Herald* (1959–80) for members of the African Methodist Episcopal denomination and served as asst. minister at ST. JOHN'S AME (AFRICAN METHODIST EPISCOPAL) CHURCH† (1957–62) and pastor of Quinn Chapel AME Church, Cleveland (1962–67). Smith and his wife attended the 1977 inauguration of Pres. Jimmy Carter, after receiving a VIP invitation. The enterprising editor seized the opportunity to interview King Hussein of Jordan while the monarch was a patient at the CLEVELAND CLINIC FOUNDATION.†

Smith was born in Smithville, OH, and graduated from Smithfield High School. He earned a bachelor's degree in theology from Wilberforce Univ. in 1945, and a decade later received a doctor of divinity degree in Monrovia, West Africa. In addition, he studied at Payne Theological Seminary and at Akron and Ohio State universities. Smith served churches in Ironton and Cincinnati, OH, before coming to St. John's. He headed building campaigns for 2 churches, Quinn and the Greater St. Matthew AME Church, Lorain (1967–71), his last pastorate. Smith presided over the AME Ministers Fellowship (1971–80) and served as chief secretary for state and regional AME conferences. From 1978–80 he played the organ at the Cleveland Clinic's chapel. Smith also served as eulogist for both the BOYD† and the HOUSE OF WILLS† funeral homes.

Smith married Dorothy I. McClinton; they lived in Cleveland with sons Herald, Verl, and David, and daughter Rosalie Jackson.—J.M.

**SMITH, KENT H.** (9 Apr. 1894–26 Mar. 1980), a founder of LUBRIZOL CORP.,† was born in Cleveland to Mary Wilkinson and ALBERT W. SMITH. He graduated from Dartmouth College in 1915, then earned a degree in chemical engineering from Case Institute of Technology in 1917. After serving in France during World War I, he worked for Dow Chemical Co. (1919–21), then became president of Ce-Fair Development Co. (1921–28). In 1928 Smith joined his brothers, ALBERT KELVIN and Vincent, in founding Graphite Oil Prods. Corp., which became Lubrizol Corp. Smith was the first president (1928–29), then vice-president (1929–32), before resuming the presidency (1932–51). During his presidency, the company grew from 5 employees to 590, and sales increased from $8,000 to $26 million. He was chairman of the board (1951–59) and a director until his retirement in 1967. Smith had other business interests as well.

Smith was active in charitable and educational institutions, especially Case Institute of Technology, becoming a trustee in 1949 and acting president from 1958–61. Smith promoted a merger between Case and Western Reserve Univ., becoming an honorary trustee of the institution in 1967. He donated large sums of money to Case and other universities, helped establish the Corporate 1% Program for Higher Education, Inc., and cofounded the Greater Cleveland Assn. Foundation, serving as the chairman of its board (1961–69). He served as a trustee for many institutions and received numerous awards, including the 1962 public-service award from the Cleveland Chamber of Commerce and the 1969 Chas. Eisenman Award from the Jewish Community Fed. Smith married Thelma Gertrude Sampson in 1946. He was buried at Lake View Cemetery.

---

Smalheer, Calvin V. *The Story of Lubrizol* (1972).

**SMITH, WILLIAM T. (WEE WILLIE)** (22 Apr. 1911–14 Mar. 1992), outstanding professional basketball player in the 1930s and member of the National Basketball Hall of Fame, was born in Montgomery, AL, the son of Isaac and Mary Wheeler Smith. His family moved to Cleveland, and as a youth he learned to play basketball at HIRAM HOUSE. Smith, big for his age, played on adult amateur teams at night while attending EAST TECHNICAL HIGH SCHOOL,† joining the Slaughter Bros. Funeral Home basketball team, one of the best Class A teams in the city. While playing for Slaughter Bros in 1931, he caught the eye of Robert Douglas, owner of the New York Renaissance, a successful all-black professional team, and 6' 5" "Wee Willie" Smith joined the team in 1932. The "Rens" took on all comers, playing one-night stands, and from 1932–36 Smith and his 6 teammates were considered the best team in the world, compiling a record of 473–49. In 1963 the entire team was elected to the Basketball Hall of Fame. Smith was a regular with the Renaissance until World War II, when he returned to Cleveland permanently, working for the Cleveland Transit System during the week and playing with the Rens and other teams on weekends. After the war he became a custodian for the Cleveland Public School System and also operated the Renaissance Beverage Store at Cedar Ave. & E. 79th St. In 1977 he was elected to the Harlem Hall of Fame and the GREATER CLEVELAND SPORTS HALL OF FAME.

Smith married Estelle Taylor 7 Aug. 1937; they had 3 children: June Stallworth, Faith Foster, and James Taylor Smith. Smith was a resident of Cleveland Hts.—M.S.

**SMITH, WILSON G.** (19 Aug. 1856–27 Feb. 1929), composer, writer, and music critic, was born in Elyria to George T. and Calista M. Smith. He graduated from West High School but health problems prevented him from attending college until 1876. He graduated from the Univ. of Cincinnati and went directly to Berlin in 1880, where he studied music under Scharwenka, Kiel, Moszkonski, and Oscar Raif. Upon returning to Cleveland, Smith opened a studio and taught organ, piano, voice, and composition. He joined the CLEVELAND PRESS† in 1902, known and admired for his honest music critique, which was both intelligent and laced with humor.

The author of many musical texts used in the U.S. and Europe, Smith's most popular work was *Thematic Octave Studies: In the Form of Variations on Original Theme: Opus 68*, published in 1902. Smith wrote over 1,000 compositions, including piano solos and suites, songs and technical studies for the piano, dances, and waltzes. His piano suites, such as the Bal Masque, have been orchestrated and played by the CLEVELAND ORCHESTRA.† Smith's compositions also include the popular songs "If I But Knew," "Heart Sorrow," "Humoresque," and "Mazurka." His major work was *Homage to Edward Grieg*, a 5-part piece dedicated to the Scandinavian music master. Grieg himself commended Smith on this work. Smith married Mez Brett, a writer and artist, in Apr. 1883. They had a daughter, Edna. Smith died in Cleveland and is buried in Lakewood Cemetery.

**SMITHKNIGHT, LOUIS** (16 Dec. 1834–27 Mar. 1915), volunteer artillery officer during the Civil War and a postwar militia artillery officer, was born in Saxony to Frederick and Auralia Smithknight. He came to the U.S. in 1845 and lived in Columbus, OH, before arriving in Cleveland in 1850. After an unsuccessful gold-hunting journey to Colorado in 1858, he returned to Cleveland and opened a drugstore.

When the Civil War broke out, Smithknight enlisted as a private in the 1ST OHIO VOLUNTEER LIGHT ARTILLERY† for 3 month's service. Returning to Cleveland, he was appointed captain, 20TH OHIO INDEPENDENT BATTERY,† which organized in Cleveland in 1862. The battery spent the winter of 1863 at Murfreesboro, TN, where Smithknight was forced to resign on 23 Apr. 1863 from disability after falling from a horse. Returning to his drugstore, he reorganized the CLEVELAND LIGHT ARTILLERY† in 1872, and remained its captain until 1887. Smithknight also served as colonel of a battery of statewide artillery. He was active in Republican politics and a member of the Grand Army of the Republic. He served on 3 committees for the dedication of the SOLDIERS & SAILORS MONUMENT. He married Nettie Kingsley (d. 1906) in 1865 and had a daughter, Julia, and a son,

Albert. Smithknight died of bronchitis and was buried next to his wife in Woodland Cemetery.

Cleveland Light Artillery Assn. Records, WRHS.

**SMYTH, ANSON** (1 Jan. 1812–2 May 1887), "the Father of the Cleveland Public Library" and an educator and Presbyterian minister, was born in Franklin, PA. He attended Milan Academy and Williams College, and after teaching a few years, graduated from Yale Theological Seminary. Smyth's early pastorates included a home missionary assignment on the "frontier" of Michigan; and the Congregational Church of Toledo, where he became interested in the public schools, serving successively as superintendent of the Toledo public schools and state commissioner of the Common Schools of Ohio (1856–62). He was given broad powers to reform the school system, visited schools in every county of the state, and along with HARVEY RICE and other professional educators, worked on restructuring Ohio's public schools. He came to Cleveland in 1863 to become superintendent of the CLEVELAND PUBLIC SCHOOLS† (1863–66), emphasizing strict classification by age and ability, which led to overcrowding in some grades and many objections, but also led to the creation of 10 new primary and secondary schools within 2 years. Smyth declined reelection in 1866. In 1867 Smyth was the key figure in creating the CLEVELAND PUBLIC LIBRARY.† Largely through his efforts, the legislature passed an act authorizing the support of libraries through taxation. In 1872 he became pastor at NORTH PRESBYTERIAN CHURCH,† remaining until the loss of his voice forced his retirement. Smyth and his wife, Caroline, has 3 children: George, William, and Sarah. He died in Cleveland and was buried in Lake View Cemetery.

**SNAJDR, VACLAV** (26 Sept.1847–4 Sept. 1920) was a prominent Czech-American journalist and publisher who was active in Cleveland business and politics. Snajdr was born in Ceska Budejovice, Bohemia , the son of John and Appolonice Snajdr. Educated at the Gymnasium School at Mlada and the College of Neuhaus in Prague, Snajdr was forced to flee to Berlin during student demonstrations in 1867–68. In Berlin, he used his journalistic skills by contributing articles to local Czech newspapers.

Snajdr was sent to America in 1869 to solicit funds to support the Berlin-based newspapers, but stayed in America instead to edit Czech newspapers in Racine, WI, and Omaha, NE. In 1873 he came to Cleveland as editor of *Pokrok* (Progress), and when it failed in 1877 he established a new weekly, *Dennice Novoveku* (Star of the New Era). In his several newspapers, Snajdr expressed his anti-clerical views, as well as championing Czech immigrant literature and art, and his editorials gained national attention from the Czech intelligentsia. Drawn to free thinkers and rationalists, Snajdr wrote "For a Better Understanding of Robert Ingersoll" in 1904 and "Ladislav Klacil, His Life and Teachings" in 1908. He sold his newspaper and publishing business to Svet (World) Publishing in 1910.

Snajdr was one of the original organizers of the Pilsner Brewing Co. and served as its president from 1903 until 1919, when he moved to Pasadena, CA. He also was a member of the Board of Directors of the Broadway Bank and served on the Cleveland School Board.

He married Cecelia Korizek in 1873; they had 6 children: Slava, Mila, Robert, Celia, Ladimir, and Charles. He died in Pasadena at age 72.—M.S.

The Vaclav Snajdr Papers, WRHS.
Ledbetter, Eleanor. *The Czechs of Cleveland* (1919).

**SNOW, DORCAS LAVINA** (27 July 1902–13 April 1994) was a nationally known piano and music teacher as well as a local historian of the BRECKS-VILLE† area. Snow was born in Brecksville into a family that was among the first residents of the area. She was the daughter of Harry W. and Alice P. (Noble) Snow. Snow studied piano at the Cleveland School of Music, graduating in 1923. She briefly played piano for radio stations WJAY and WHK† before rejecting that career for teaching. In 1923 she began teaching piano, and her students gave their first recital the following year. Over the years she taught piano to a number of Brecksville area residents and was known for her high standards of teaching.

In the mid–1970s she began her composing and writing career. The first of her works came out in 1980. Over the next decade she produced such titles as "To the City of Brecksville" (1980), "Dear Brecksville" (1981), "Prelude" (1990), and "Opus 1" (1992). Her publications, which numbered a dozen in all, featured such topics as the history of Brecksville and neighboring communities as well as music and Christmas. Brecksville's mayor, Jerry Hruby, dubbed her the "City Historian" and credited her with instilling an interest in the community's history.

Snow presided over her 69th student piano recital in 1993 and continued to teach and write until shortly before her death. She never married. She is buried at Highland Drive (Center) Cemetery, Brecksville.—D.R.

**SNOW, JANE ELLIOT** (14 June 1837–27 Aug. 1922), Cleveland lecturer, editor, and writer, pro-moted woman's suffrage, dress reform, and the accomplishments of other women. At age 84, she was the editor-in-chief of the women's section of the *Cleveland Enterprise* and special correspondent to publications such as the *Cuyahogan*. Snow was born in Cleveland's Royalton Twp. to Elizabeth Coates and Richard S. Elliot. She attended Brooklyn Academy and LINDA THAYER GUILFORD's School. On 31 Dec. 1854 she married W. C. Snow, farmer and holder of various township offices in PARMA.† The couple had four children: Frank H., Albert M., Abbie May, and Bertha L. Brainerd. By 1892 Snow had published short articles in local papers on history, travel, domesticity, and other topics. Books written by her include *Women of Tennyson* (1901) and *The Life of William McKinley* (1908). Beginning in 1895, Snow served on the Woman's Department of the Cleveland Centennial Commission, planning the Centennial's Woman's Day, 28 July 1896. (The department later evolved into the Women's Centennial Commission.) Snow helped organize both the Woman's Club (1909) and the Snow Monday Club (1904), study groups affiliated with the FEDERATION OF WOMEN'S CLUBS OF GREATER CLEVELAND†; she was the Snow Monday Club's namesake and primary lecturer. Snow belonged to the CLEVELAND SORO-SIS SOCIETY,† the WOMAN'S CHRISTIAN TEMPERANCE UNION,† NON-PARTISAN,† the CONSUMERS' LEAGUE,† the Woman Suffrage Party of Greater Cleveland, the Women's Press Club, and the Municipal School League. She died at her daughter's home in LAKEWOOD.†—J.M.

**SOCKALEXIS, LOUIS FRANCIS, "CHIEF"** (24 Oct. 1871–24 Dec. 1913), a Penobscot Indian who played professional baseball with the CLEVELAND SPIDERS† from 1897–99, is said to be the person for whom the CLEVELAND INDIANS† team is named, making him the only individual to have a major league baseball team named after him. Sockalexis was born on the Penobscot Indian Reservation in Old Town, ME, to Francis P. and Frances Sockabeson Sockalexis. He excelled in track, gymnastics, polo, skating, and baseball and attended Holy Cross College in Worcester, MA, playing on its baseball team, hitting .436 in 1895 and .444 in 1896. He also played amateur baseball in Maine's Knox County League.

Sockalexis turned professional in 1897, joining the Cleveland Spiders as an outfielder. He hit home runs in his first 2 at bats and hit .338 over 66 games. The team was frequently referred to as the "Indians" when he played for it. Unfortunately, he became addicted to alcohol. He appeared in only 21 games in 1898, hitting just .224, finishing his major league career after only 7 games in 1899, released by the team and unwanted by any other. In 1915, the Cleveland American League team needed a new nickname, having been known since 1905 as the Naps, in honor of player-manager NAPOLEON "NAP" LAJOIE. Local sportswriters selected a new name, "Indians," which may have harkened back to the old Spider's nickname. Sockalexis lived as a drifter after leaving baseball. Unmarried, he died in Burlington, ME.

**SOKOLOFF, NIKOLAI** (28 May 1886–25 Sept. 1965), first conductor of the CLEVELAND ORCHESTRA,† was born in Kiev, Russia, to Grigori and Marie Sokoloff. At 13 Sokoloff moved with his family to New Haven, CT, where he enrolled at Yale Univ.'s music school. After graduation, he studied music with Chas. Martin Loeffler in Boston, later studying with Vincent d'Indy in Paris. At 17 he became a violinist in the Boston Symphony Orchestra. He left Boston and, after studying in Paris, became the conductor of the Manchester Orchestra in England. In 1918 he returned to America, where in Cincinnati he met ADELLA PRENTISS HUGHES and was persuaded to accept a position from the MUSICAL ARTS ASSN.† to make a survey in Cleveland's public schools and outline an instrumental music program. He accepted the position on the condition that he would be able to organize and conduct his own orchestra.

Sokoloff conducted the Cleveland Orchestra for 14 years (1918–32), initiating highly acclaimed national and international tours. He established a unique series of educational concerts for schoolchildren, and introduced recording and broadcasting concerts. Upon leaving Cleveland, Sokoloff became director of the Federal Music Project in 1935, channeling money into Cleveland for unemployed musicians through this organization, providing the city with more opera and orchestral music than it had in many years. When he left the Federal Music Project in 1937, he became the conductor for the Seattle Orchestra. Later he organized an orchestra in La Jolla, CA, where he remained until his death.

Sokoloff was married three times. He and his first wife, Lyda, were married in 1911; they had three children: Boris, Martin, and Noel. He married Ruth Ottaway in 1937, and was survived by his 3rd wife, Emma, whom he married in 1957.

Marsh, Robert C. *The Cleveland Orchestra* (1967).
Musical Arts Assn. Archives.

**SOLLMAN, TORALD HERMAN** (10 Feb. 1874–11 Feb. 1965), dean of American pharmacology, was born in Colberg, Germany, to August and Adelhaid Eckhardt Sollman, and came to America at age 13 to live with his brother, a druggist in Canton, working in his store and studying medicine in his spare time. At 17 he became the youngest person to receive a pharmacist's license from the state of Ohio. He studied pharmacology at the Val de Grace Military Hospital in Paris (1893–94), graduated from Western Reserve Univ. Medical School with an M.D. degree in 1896, and did additional studies in Strasbourg in 1899.

Sollman was a demonstrator in physiology at WRU (1895–99); lecturer in pharmacology (1898–1901); asst. professor of pharmacology and materia medica (1901–04); and professor (1904–44), responsible for building up the pharmacology department. During World War I, he was a consultant to the U.S. Army on poison gas and treating mustard-gas burns. In 1917 he authored *Laboratory Experiments in Pharmacology*, the first laboratory manual in pharmacology written in English. In 1928 Sollman was appointed dean of the WRU Medical School, instituting higher standards for selecting students and insisting on a balance of students desiring to be practitioners with those wishing to enter research. Upon his retirement in 1944, he was named professor and dean emeritus. Sollman married Alice Sersall in 1902 and had a daughter, Mary Alice. Sollman was honored when Wyeth Laboratories in Philadelphia established the Torald Sollman Award in Pharmacology, international in scope and comparable to the Nobel Prize.

**SOMERS, CHARLES W.** (13 Oct. 1868–28 June 1934) was a founder of the CLEVELAND INDIANS† baseball team and financier of the American League in the early 20th century. Born in Newark, OH, to Joseph Hook and Philenia McCrum Somers, he came with his family to Cleveland in 1884 and attended business school before working for the J.H. Somers Co., his father's bituminous coal operation. Somers established his own coal business and by age 31 was worth $1,000,000 before selling out and rejoining his father's company as general manager. Along with John F. Kilfoyle (1863–1913), Somers purchased LEAGUE PARK† from FRANK DE HAAS ROBISON in 1900 and founded a team in the newly established American League. Kilfoyle became president of the Cleveland franchise and Somers vice president, with Somers succeeding to the presidency upon Kilfoyle's retirement in 1908. Somers also invested his money to start teams in Philadelphia and Boston, and loaned money to the owners in Chicago and Baltimore-New York. During his years as the owner of the Cleveland Baseball Co., he acquired NAPOLEON LAJOIE, the team's first superstar player, modernized League Park, and organized a farm system to develop young players. Because of declining attendance, growing competition from the Federal League, and bad business investments, Somers was forced to sell the team in late 1915. He continued to own the New Orleans Pelicans in the Southern Assn., but spent most of his time rebuilding his business investments.

Somers was married twice. He had a daughter, Dorothy (Mrs. W. W. Clark) from his first marriage. His second wife, Mary Alice Gilbert, survived him. Somers died at Put-in-Bay, OH, and is buried at Lake View Cemetery.

**SOMMER, WILLIAM** (18 Jan. 1867–20 June 1949), Cleveland artist, was born in Detroit and from age 11 to 16 studied drawing with a church woodcarver and trainer for Detroit Calvert Lithograph Co, where he served an apprenticeship from 1881–88. He studied a year in Europe (1890–91), then worked for lithograph companies in New York before moving to Cleveland in 1907. Sommer worked for W. J. Morgan Lithograph Co. until 1929, when he was laid off as they adopted the offset press. He then painted full-time, doing the murals in Public Hall; Brett Hall, CLEVELAND PUBLIC LIBRARY†; the post office, Geneva, OH; and the Board of Education Bldg., Akron, with the WPA Federal Art Project, an assignment he secured through the assistance of WM. MILLIKEN. In the 1920s and 1930s, he regularly won prizes in drawing and watercolor at the MAY SHOWS.† Sommer helped found the KOKOON CLUB† in 1912.

Sommer purchased a house and old school at Brandywine, OH, for a studio, which was a meeting place for local artists, including ABEL and ALEX WARSHAWSKY, and poet HART CRANE. When Crane moved to New York, he took Sommer's paintings and drawings with him. Some were bought; however, only after Sommer's death did the Metropolitan Museum of Art, the Whitney in New York, the Smithsonian Institution in Washington, and the Nelson-Adkins Gallery in Kansas City purchase his work, and films, books, and articles began recognizing his art. Sommer married Martha Obermeyer in 1894. They had 3 children: William L., Jr., Edward, and Ray.

Cleveland Museum of Art. *The William Sommer Memorial Exhibition Catalogue* (1950).

**SONES, F. MASON, JR., M.D.** (28 Oct. 1918–28 Aug. 1985) was a medical science pioneer in cardiac cinematography whose work was instrumental in the development of coronary bypass and cardiac surgery. Born in Noxapeter, MS, to Frank Mason and Myrtle (Bryan) Sones, Sones graduated from Western Maryland College in 1940. He received his M.D. from the Univ. of Maryland School of Medicine in 1943, and from 1944 to 1946 served in the Army Air Corps in the Pacific. Sones later interned

at Univ. Hospital in Baltimore and was a resident at Henry Ford Hospital in Detroit.

In 1950 Sones joined the CLEVELAND CLINIC FOUNDATION† as the Director of Pediatric Cardiology and the Cardiac Laboratory. Sones's first major contribution was the introduction of cardiac catheterization of neonatal patients in 1954. His 1958 discovery that human coronary arteries could safely be invaded with catheters and dyes to photograph their configurations initiated a new era for cardiology. Sones was also the first to combine cardiac catheterization, angiography, and high speed x-ray motion picture photography as a single procedure. Sones's subsequent work in video engineering (with Eastman Kodak), the chemistry of dye compounds, design of arteriography equipment, and optical image amplification allowed for improved cardiovascular diagnosis and treatment. From 1966 to 1975 Sones was the director of the Clinic's Department of Cardiovascular Disease, and later served as senior physician of the Department of Cardiology.

Sones was honored with numerous awards during his career, including the American Medical Assn.'s 1978 Scientific Achievement Award and the Cumming Humanitarian Award in 1966 and 1967. He founded the Society for Cardiac Angiography and was its first president. Sones also served as the national consultant to the Air Force Surgeon General, and worked with the National Institute of Health in the study of cardiovascular disease. In 1942 Sones married Geraldine Newton. The couple had 4 children, Frank Mason III, Geraldine Patricia, Steven, and David. Sones died in Cleveland. He is buried in Evergreen Cemetery.—M.M.

**SOUTHGATE, ROBERT L.** (24 Oct. 1921–6 Sept. 1988), librarian, teacher, writer and publisher, pioneered the local study of the history of AFRICAN AMERICANS.† He worked as librarian in the CLEVELAND PUBLIC SCHOOLS,† taught history and literature at CLEVELAND STATE UNIV.† (CSU) and BALDWIN WALLACE COLLEGE,† and formed and operated Tish's Press (1984). He authored several books, including *Black Plots and Black Characters: A Handbook for Afro-American Literature* (1979). Southgate was born in Cincinnati to William and Martha (Buchanan) Southgate. He graduated from the Univ. of Cincinnati in 1955. In 1969 he earned a master's degree in library science from CASE WESTERN RESERVE UNIV.† Southgate served as librarian for Central intermediate school, then Lincoln intermediate before retiring in June 1987. A civic leader, he helped found and taught in the freedom schools sponsored by the NATIONAL ASSN. FOR THE ADVANCEMENT OF COLORED PEOPLE† (NAACP) (1963) and later volunteered with the Senior Citizens Coalition. While at CSU he advised both the Black Studies Program and the Organization for African American Unity, and was among the founders of a literary club.

On 22 June 1957 Southgate married Joan E. Harris; they lived in Cleveland with children Letitia, Martha, Robert, and Daniel. Southgate died in Cleveland.—J.M.

**SPAFFORD, AMOS** (11 Apr. 1753–5 Aug. 1816), surveyor for the CONNECTICUT LAND CO.† who performed one of the earlist surveys of Cleveland, and made the first map detailing its original plan ("Original plan of the town and village of Cleaveland, Ohio, October 1, 1796"), was born in Sharon, Litchfield County, CT. Spafford was known as "Major" because of the service he performed in the War of 1812.

Spafford was a surveyor in both parties sent to the WESTERN RESERVE† between 1796–97. During Cleveland's initial years of settlement, Spafford was given authority for fixing lot and street lines and determining land titles. He was also active as a public official: township trustee in 1802, and township chairman in 1803. In 1802 he applied for and received a license to keep a tavern in Cleveland. Spafford himself was one of the original lot owners in Cleveland. He was partly responsible for persuading the Connecticut Land Co. to reduce the higher price it had attached to city lots, threatening in 1801 to leave the Western Reserve altogether if the price was not lowered. He reportedly had problems with real estate, acquiring more land than he could pay for or resell. In 1809 he was elected to the lower house of the state legislature from Geauga County. Soon afterward he was appointed collector for the new port of entry on the Maumee River, in 1810 leaving Cleveland to assume that post near Perrysburg, OH.

Spafford married Olive Barlow on 3 July 1773; they had 7 children: Samuel, Anna, Chloe, Gay, Adolphus, Aurora, and Jarvis. Spafford was buried in Waynesfield, OH.

**SPALDING (SPAULDING), RUFUS** (3 May 1798–29 Aug. 1886), lawyer, judge, congressman and a vocal opponent of slavery and the Fugitive Slave Law, was born on Martha's Vineyard, MA, son of Rufus and Lydia Paine Spalding. He was educated in Presbyterian schools and studied at Yale, 1813–17. He moved to Cincinnati in 1818, and the following year to Little Rock, AR, to practice law. In 1821 he returned to Ohio, settling in Warren, then Ravenna and Akron. He originally visited Cleveland in Mar. 1823, moving there permanently to practice law in 1852. Spalding led Cleveland lawyers against southern slaveowners who came North to claim fugitive slaves throughout the mid–1800s. In 1859 he defended Underground Railroad supporter Simeon Bushnell from charges he had tried obstructing a slaveowner from returning a captured runaway to the South. Bushnell was found guilty, but public opinion was moved by the abolitionists' efforts (see ABOLITIONISM†). Politically, Spalding had been a Democrat until the party turned proslavery, then joined the Free-Soilers and later became an organizer for the Republican party. On this ticket he was elected Ohio congressman in 1863, after having served as state representative from Portage (1839) and Summit (1841) counties. He also served as Ohio Supreme Court judge (1852). Spalding assisted building the collection of the Cleveland Law Library and in 1883 was named to a committee to erect a monument to Gen. MOSES CLEAVELAND. Spalding married Lucretia Swift in 1822; they had 7 children: Zephediah, George, Lucretia, William, Philura, Emily, and Lucretia (one of the daughters named Lucretia died four years before the other was born). Spalding married Nancy Sargeant Pierson in Jan. 1859. He died in Cleveland and was buried in Lake View Cemetery.

**SPANGLER, BASIL L.** (1822–19 Jan. 1876), dry goods merchant who served as asst. quartermaster in the U.S. Army during the Civil War, was the son of Michael and Elizabeth Miller Spangler, who came to Cleveland from Stark County in 1816 and entered the tavern, hotel, and real estate business. Another son, Miller M. Spangler (1813–5 May 1897), served as Cleveland fire chief (1842, 1844, 1847, 1850–55) and county sheriff. Basil served on the Cleveland Board of Water Works in 1853. He began his military service as quartermaster, with the rank of captain, at Camp Cleveland (see CIVIL WAR CAMPS†) in July 1862. In Sept. 1863 he was in charge of the commissary at Camp Cuyahoga, a militia drill and training camp located at Willson's Grove in Cleveland for the 7th Military District, Ohio Militia. Spangler served as quartermaster at Cleveland until July 1865. Spangler married twice: Julia Stedman, ca. 1845, and Matilda McCarg (n.d.). He had no children from either marriage. Spangler was buried in Lake View Cemetery.

**SPAULDING, FRANK ELLSWORTH** (30 Nov. 1866–6 June 1960), an educator of national stature, left an indelible imprint on the CLEVELAND PUBLIC SCHOOLS† despite a relatively brief tenure as superintendent. The son of William and Abby Stearns Spaulding, he was a native of Dublin, NH. After receiving his bachelor's degree from Amherst College and advanced degrees from the Univ. of Leipzig, Dr. Spaulding married Mary Elizabeth

Trow of Massachusetts in 1895. He served successively as superintendent of public school systems in Ware, MA, Passaic, NJ, Newton, MA, and Minneapolis, MN, before being lured to Cleveland in 1917 by a nationally unprecedented salary of $12,000. With a mandate to implement recommendations of the CLEVELAND FOUNDATION's† public school survey, he combined both educational and business functions of the system under his control. Other reforms included the institution of junior high and vocational programs (see EDUCATION†). With the coming of World War I, he presided over the schools' AMERICANIZATION† program until obtaining a leave of absence to head the Army Education Commission in France. He never returned to Cleveland, resigning his position in 1920 to organize and chair the Education Dept. of the Yale Graduate School. He retired in 1935 as professor emeritus, having also lectured at Harvard and served on numerous boards and commissions. One of the many books and readers to his credit was *The Individual Child and His Education* (1904). He died in La Jolla, CA, survived by 2 unmarried daughters, Mary and Catherine, and a son, William E., president of Houghton Mifflin publishers. Another son, the late Dr. Francis T., had been dean of the Harvard Graduate School of Education.—J.V.

**SPEAKER, TRISTRAM "TRIS"** (4 Apr. 1888–8 Dec. 1958), "The Gray Eagle," centerfielder for the CLEVELAND INDIANS† (1916–26) was born in Hubbard City, TX, to Archie and Nancy Peer Speaker. By 1909 he was centerfielder for the Boston Red Sox, and the AL's Most Valuable Player when Boston won the 1912 World Championship. After a salary dispute, Speaker's contract was traded to Cleveland in 1916 for $50,000. In his first year with Cleveland, Speaker hit .386 to win the AL batting championship. His salary of $40,000 was the highest in baseball. In 1919 Speaker became manager; the team finished 2nd that year. In 1920 Speaker hit .388 and set a record of 11 consecutive hits as Cleveland won the league and world championships. Unjustly accused of fixing a game with Ty Cobb, Speaker resigned from the Indians in 1926. He was cleared of the charge and played his last 2 years with Washington and Philadelphia.

Speaker holds the AL outfield record for the most lifetime putouts of 6,706, and 449 assists (also a major league record). Speaker had a lifetime batting average of .345, and his 3,515 hits in 22 seasons rank him in the top 10 hitters of all time. He was elected to the Baseball Hall of Fame in 1937.

Speaker helped found the SOCIETY FOR CRIPPLED CHILDREN† and Camp Cheerful. During the 1930s, he was in the wholesale liquor business and for a time chairman of the Cleveland

Boxing Commission. From 1947 to his death, Speaker was an advisor, coach, and scout for the Indians. He married Mary Frances Cudahy in 1925. Speaker is buried in Hubbard, TX.

**SPENZER, JOHN GEORGE** (6 Sept. 1864–28 July 1932), an expert in forensic medicine who introduced the latest European toxicological techniques to Cleveland, was born in Cleveland to Peter Ignatius and Mary Theresa (Molloy) Spenzer. In 1880 he entered Western Reserve Univ., studying chemistry and toxicology under Dr. EDWARD MORLEY. He received his medical degree in 1884 but continued studying under Morley until 1887. After 5 years of additional study at the Univ. of Strassburg and in Paris, Spenzer returned to Cleveland to teach at the College of Pharmacy, and later at the Cleveland College of Physicians & Surgeons. In 1910 he joined the faculty at WRU to teach legal chemistry and medical jurisprudence, covering topics such as medical evidence and testimony and criminal acts determined by medical knowledge. He became a regional expert on blood and poison analysis and was often called upon for blood identification. He also testified in numerous court cases requiring medical evidence, such as whether or not a person was poisoned, or if certain spots were human blood. In 1917 Spenzer became director of the Medical Chemistry Laboratory. Much of his research was devoted to vitamins and vitamin treatment for malnutrition. Because of his work in toxicology, in 1926 Spenzer was called upon to analyze the CUYAHOGA RIVER† to determine how harmful the discharge of acids and alkalines was to the water supply. Spenzer married Minnie Elizabeth Kittelberger in 1898 and had two children, John Calvin and Caroline.

Biographical Files, CWRU Archives.

**SPERO, HERMAN ISRAEL** (24 Aug. 1924–7 Sept. 1979) was an independent television producer who specialized in music programs as disparate as polkas and rock 'n' roll. The son of Phillip and Rebecca Saperstein Spero, he was born in Cleveland and graduated from Glenville High School. He had already appeared on radio and with the Curtain Pullers at the CLEVELAND PLAY HOUSE.† After working in USO shows while in the army during World War II, he did a radio show for WJMO† in Cleveland before going to Raleigh, NC, and Richmond, VA. Returning to Ohio, he broke into television in Akron and then began producing shows for Cleveland's WEWS,† including "Old Dutch Polka Review" and "Souvenir Showtime." A long-time feature was his "Polka Varieties," which began in 1956 and ran into the 1970s. He began a rock 'n' roll dance program called "The Big Five Show" in

1964, bringing Don Webster from Canada as host. It went into national syndication as "The Upbeat Show" in 1966, appearing in more than 100 cities weekly, with such acts as Sonny and Cher, the Supremes, and Steppenwolf, through 1971. Spero also booked big band acts in Cleveland and produced special events such as the "World Series of Accordions" in 1971 at THISTLEDOWN RACE TRACK.† He was married twice, to Joy Kiefer in 1948 and, following a divorce, to Shirley Hessel in 1974. He died in New York City, survived by both wives, and children Harry, David, Ted, and Sheri, and stepdaughter Deborah Lyman.—J.V.

**SPIRA, HENRY** (21 June 1862–10 Apr. 1941) was a banker whose principal customers were the immigrants settling in Cleveland during the first 3 decades of the century. Spira, son of Bernath and Esther (Deutsch) Spira, was born and educated in Richwald, Hungary, emigrating to the U.S. in 1879. He worked as a laborer for a steamship company before migrating to central Ohio, where he worked as a peddler and shopkeeper. In 1885 he returned to Hungary for 5 years, where he established a liquor business. He returned to America in 1890, settled in Cleveland, and opened a saloon in the Woodland neighborhood.

In 1891 Spira became involved in a foreign-exchange and steamship ticket sales business, catering to the immigrant community in Woodland. By 1916 he had expanded into general banking, creating the Bank of Henry Spira, later the Spira Savings & Loan Assn. He maintained the foreign-exchange business through a new company, Spira Internatl. Express Co., which was also an investment firm. In 1932 Spira retired from banking and Spira Savings & Loan was taken over by Guardian Trust Co. Spira was president of the Temple on the Heights for 12 years. Beyond that, his involvement in Jewish community organizations seldom included a leadership role. However, at his death a large portion of his estate was willed to Jewish institutions, including the HEBREW FREE LOAN ASSN.,† the Temple on the Heights, the Jewish Orthodox Home for the Aged, MONTEFIORE HOME,† MT. SINAI HOSPITAL,† the JEWISH ORPHAN HOME,† and the Jewish Welfare Federation.

Spira married Mathilda Ehrlich on 13 June 1886. They had six children: Ethel, Sigmund, Philip, Rolla, Sylvia, and Violet.

Henry Spira Papers, WRHS.

**SPITALNY, MAURICE** (27 Feb. 1893–28 Oct. 1986), musician and director of Cleveland's theater orchestras, was born in Odessa, Russia, the son of Jacob and Rachel (Burstein) Spitalny. He and his family came to Cleveland in 1905, where he attended public schools. Like his brothers, PHIL, Leopold, and Hyman, Maurice became a musician, pursuing his musical studies at the American Conservatory of Music in Chicago and later at the Royal Conservatory of Berlin as a scholarship student. An accomplished violinist, Spitalny gave music lessons in the city and was asst. concertmaster of the CLEVELAND ORCHESTRA† during its first season, 1918–19. He led the orchestra at the METROPOLITAN THEATRE† on Euclid Ave. at E. 49th St. and was musical director of the Stillman and State theaters in the 1920s and 1930s. Spitalny moved to Pittsburgh in 1938 and became supervisor of music at radio station KDKA, where he directed many musical shows, including "A Festival of Music," which was carried nationally by NBC. He also served as bandleader on Pittsburgh stations KQV-AM, WJAS-AM, and KDKA-TV. Retired in Florida by the late 1960s, he remained active in the music world.

Spitalny married Dorothy E. Kahn 1 June 1915: they had three children: Jean, Iris, and stepson James Roy. He died in Hollywood, FL.—M.S.

**SPITALNY, PHIL** (7 Nov. 1890–11 Oct. 1970), composer, conductor, and clarinetist, was born in Odessa, Russia, to Jacob and Rachel Spitalny. He attended the Odessa Conservatory, and toured Russia as a child clarinet prodigy. His family emigrated to Cleveland in 1905, and Spitalny played in and directed local bands in Cleveland and Boston, including a 50-piece symphony orchestra in one of Boston's larger movie houses. He conducted his own orchestra on radio, in hotels, and on recordings and made a successful New York debut in 1930. In 1934 Spitalny organized an all-girl orchestra, which made its debut at the Capital Theater in New York and performed on the radio program "The Hour of Charm" beginning in Jan. 1935. It continued performing on the radio, in concerts, and eventually on television; and received the Achievement Award of 1937 from the radio committee of the Woman's National Exposition of Arts and Industries for the most distinguished work of women in radio that year. Spitalny composed such songs as "Madelaine," "Enchanted Forest," "It's You, No One But You," "Save the Last Dance for Me," "The Kiss I Can't Forget," and "Pining for You." In June 1946 he married Evelyn Kaye Klein, a member of the all-girl orchestra. They had one child, Norma (Rein). Spitalny died in Miami Beach, FL, and was buried in the Ridge Rd. Cemetery of Cleveland.

**SQUIRE, ANDREW** (21 Oct. 1850–5 Jan. 1934), corporation lawyer who planned the organizational structure of numerous companies, was born in Mantua, OH, to Andrew Jackson and Martha Wilmot Squire, graduated from Hiram College in 1872 with an LL.B. degree, and came to Cleveland with a letter of introduction from Congressman JAS. GARFIELD. Squire worked in the law office of Caldwell & Marvin while reading the law, and was admitted to the Ohio Bar in 1873, becoming a member of the firm of Hart & Squire in 1876, and Estep, Dickey & Squire in 1878. In 1890 Squire and JAS. DEMPSEY, a junior partner in the firm, united with WM. SANDERS to form SQUIRE, SANDERS & DEMPSEY.†

Because of Squire's specialization in corporation law, he handled the affairs of many of Cleveland's largest businesses. In the courtroom, Squire presented facts with such conviction that juries were generally convinced. With his courtesy, candor, and kindness, Squire became the close friend and advisor to many business and political leaders, including MARCUS HANNA, Wm. McKinley, SAMUEL MATHER, and MYRON HERRICK. He also advised young and upcoming lawyers on their problems. Squire served as a trustee or officer of numerous Cleveland businesses, including Union Carbide & Carbon, CLEVELAND QUARRIES,† Corrigan-McKinney Steel, CLEVELAND UNION STOCKYARDS,† and Cleveland & Pittsburgh Railroad. During his later years, Squire spent considerable time at Valleevue, his Chagrin Valley estate, growing rare plants and herbs. In June 1873 Squire married Ella Mott, who died in 1895. In 1896 he married Eleanor Seymour Sea. Squire had two children, Carl and May (d. 1891). He is buried in Lake View Cemetery.

White, Jack, Esq. "Biography on Andrew Squire," undated.

**STAGE, CHARLES WILLARD** (26 Nov. 1868–17 May 1946) was a lawyer active in civic affairs and politics who became Cleveland's first utilities director under the Home Rule charter.

Born in Painesville to Stephen and Sarah (Knight) S., Stage graduated from Painesville High School (1888). He received his A.B. from Western Reserve Univ. (1892), an A.M. in 1893, and graduated in the first class of WRU's Law School (1895). Stage was captain of WRU's first football team, and was a National League umpire. He was admitted to the Ohio Bar in 1895 and entered into private practice in Cleveland.

Stage served in the Ohio House of Representatives, 1902–03, and was Cuyahoga County Solicitor from 1903–08. He was secretary for the Municipal Traction Co., 1906–08, and secretary of the City Sinking Fund Committee, 1910–12. Under Mayor NEWTON D. BAKER, Stage was public safety

director, 1912–14, and the city's first utilities director, 1914–16.

From 1916–22 Stage was general counsel for the VAN SWERINGENS. When Stage retired in 1938 he was vice-president, director, and general counsel for the Cleveland Union Terminal Co., and had been secretary and a director of the Cleveland Interurban Road. Co., Cleveland Traction Terminals Co., Cleveland Terminal Co., Terminal Buildings Co., Terminal Hotels Co., Traction Stores Co., and Van Ess Co.

On 29 Aug. 1903 Stage married Dr. Miriam Gertrude Kerruish, who died in the 1929 CLEVELAND CLINIC DISASTER.† They had four children: Charles Jr., William, Miriam, and Edward. Stage, an Episcopalian, was cremated.—T.B.

**STAGER, ANSON** (20 Apr. 1825–26 Mar. 1885), a pioneer in telegraphy, was born in Ontario County, NY, son of Joseph and Elmira Stager. At age 16 he worked on the *Rochester Daily Advertiser,* owned by Henry O'Reilley, who also had a contract to construct a line of Morse's electromagnetic telegraph from Philadelphia to the Midwest. Stager learned telegraphy and in 1846 became an operator on, and later manager of, the first line between Harrisburg and Philadelphia. In 1847 he became general superintendent of the Pittsburgh, Cincinnati, & Louisville Telegraph Co. In 1852 he was appointed general superintendent of the New York & Mississippi Valley Printing Telegraph Co. Stager came to Cleveland as general superintendent of Western Union Telegraph Co. in 1856, after helping JEPTHA H. WADE consolidate various lines into that company earlier that year.

Following the outbreak of the CIVIL WAR,† Stager entered military service as asst. quartermaster of volunteers. In Feb. 1862 he was appointed col. on the staff of Gen. Henry Halleck, Pres. Lincoln's chief military advisor and general-in-chief at the War Dept. In this position, Stager served as chief of the U.S. Military Telegraph, devising and implementing the military cipher system used throughout the war. Stager was general superintendent of Western Union until 1869, when he became vice-president of its Central Div. and moved to Chicago, where he remained until his death.

Stager married Rebecca Sprague in 1847 and had 3 children: Emma, Anna, and Charles. His Euclid Ave. mansion later became the headquarters of the UNIV. CLUB.† Stager is buried at Lake View Cemetery.

Thompson, Robert Luther. *Wiring a Continent* (1948).

**STAIR, PATTY** (12 Nov. 1869–26 April 1926) was a distinguished figure in Cleveland music circles during the first quarter of the 20th century. She was a Cleveland native and niece of Edwin Stair, a well-known tenor. Her education was received from the CLEVELAND PUBLIC SCHOOLS,† HATHAWAY BROWN, and private musical instructors such as Franklin Bassett. From ca. 1889–1921 she taught organ at the Cleveland Conservatory of Music, which was affiliated with Western Reserve Univ. through the College for Women. Among the churches she served as organist were FIRST UNITED METHODIST,† FIRST BAPTIST,† Windermere Methodist, and Wade Park Methodist. She was the first woman member of the Ohio Chapter (org. 1908) of the American Guild of Organists, which she later served as dean. Stair was also active in the FORTNIGHTLY MUSICAL CLUB,† where she directed the chorus and contributed other talents to its programs. She also served as president of the Women's Music Teachers Club of Cleveland. A prolific composer, Stair wrote an Intermezzo for Orchestra, a light opera, and numerous partsongs and anthems. Her works were performed by the CLEVELAND GRAND ORCHESTRA,† the SINGERS CLUB,† the Pittsburgh Male Chorus, and the Rubinstein Club of New York. Never married, Stair died of pneumonia at her home in EAST CLEVELAND.†—J.V.

**STANDART, NEEDHAM M.** (1797–4 Dec. 1874), shipbuilder and banker, was also engaged in the beef packing industry. He served as mayor of OHIO CITY† (1840–41) and was one of the 3 Ohio City commissioners who negotiated the union with Cleveland (1850s). Born in Oneida County, NY, Standart moved to Ohio in 1818, entering the shipbuilding and the forwarding and commissioning business in Huron. He built steamers such as the *Washington,* the *Sheldon Thompson,* and the *Cleveland.* In 1836 Standart moved his business to Cleveland, operating first as Standart, Griffith & Co. and later as Standart, Ingraham & Co. He and his wife, Naomi Wilbur, raised 5 children in their Detroit Ave. home. Standart retired about 1870, having built a reputation, according to his *Leader* obituary, as "one of the ablest of the pioneers who built up the magnificent commerce of the Great Lakes."

**STANDIFORD-MEHLING, ETHEL** (?-?) won prizes for her photographs of Cleveland's elite of the 1920s and 1930s at the CLEVELAND MUSEUM OF ART's† MAY SHOWs†; a collection of her work is held by the WESTERN RESERVE HISTORICAL SOCIETY.† Born in Jackson County, KY, Standiford was educated to teach school but apprenticed to a local photographer instead. She opened her own studio in Louisville, KY, in 1901. Standiford moved the Standiford Photographic Stu-

dio to Cleveland in 1919, first locating in the GAGE GALLERY OF FINE ARTS,† then in the Chilcote building (1925), and finally in the Hickox Bldg. at 1030 Euclid Ave. (1930s). Plagued by debts, Standiford filed bankruptcy and closed the studio in 1936, presenting 500 autographed photographs of prominent Cleveland residents to the CLEVELAND PUBLIC LIBRARY.† The first woman to be elected president of Cleveland Photographers Assn., Standiford was noted especially for her portraits of men and her innovative methods of photographing children.—J.M.

**STANTON (DAY SESSIONS), LUCY ANN** (16 Oct. 1831–18 Feb. 1910), became the first black American woman to complete a four-year college course when, in 1850, she graduated with a Literary Degree from the Ladies' Literary Course of Oberlin College.

Born free in Cleveland to Samuel and Margaret Stanton, Lucy attended her stepfather John Brown's school and entered Oberlin in the mid–1840s. She became president of the Oberlin Ladies Literary Society and delivered the graduation address, "A Plea for the Oppressed," an antislavery speech published in the "Oberlin Evangelist."

After graduation Stanton taught in a black school in Columbus. She married WILLIAM HOWARD DAY on 25 Nov. 1852 (div. 1872) and returned to Cleveland. In 1854 Stanton wrote a short story on slavery for her husband's newspaper, the *ALIENED AMERICAN,*† the first time a black woman had published a fictional story.

In 1856 the Days moved to Buxton, Canada. In 1858 Stanton had a daughter, Florence. In 1859 William Day left for England, abandoning his family. Stanton returned to Cleveland and worked as a seamstress. Committed to aiding freedmen, Stanton was sent by the Cleveland Freedmen's Assn. in 1866 to teach in Georgia. During the 1870s she taught in Mississippi, where she met and, in 1878, married Levi Sessions.

Stanton moved to Tennessee and, in the 1880s and 1890s, was an officer in the Women's Relief Corps, a grand matron of the Order of Eastern Star, and president of a local chapter of the Women's Christian Temperance Union. Stanton belonged to the African Methodist Episcopal Church and died in Los Angeles, CA.—T.B.

Lawson, Ellen N. *The Three Sarahs: Documents of Antebellum Black College Women* (1984).

**STARKWEATHER, SAMUEL** (27 Dec. 1799–5 July 1876), lawyer, judge, and mayor of Cleveland, was born in Pawtucket, RI, son of Oliver and Miriam (Clay) Starkweather. He worked on a farm, graduated from Brown College in 1822, and tutored at Brown until 1824, when he left to study law with Judge Swift in Windham, CT. Starkweather was admitted to the Ohio Bar in Columbus in the winter of 1826–27, soon afterwards moving to Cleveland, joining the CLEVELAND GRAYS† in 1837 and assuming a prominent position in Cleveland politics. He was a staunch Democrat and supporter of presidents Jackson and Van Buren, during their administrations serving as collector of customs for the Cleveland district and superintendent of lighthouses.

In 1844 Starkweather was elected mayor of Cleveland, winning reelection in 1845, and again in 1857 for a 2-year term. In 1852 he was the first judge of the Court of Common Pleas for Cuyahoga County elected under the new state constitution, serving for 5 years. Starkweather took a special interest in CLEVELAND PUBLIC SCHOOLS,† helping establish, along with ANDREW FREESE and Chas. Bradburn, the first high school in Cleveland and the first in the West established in connection with common schools. He was active in promoting the development of RAILROADS† in Cleveland, helping establish the Cleveland, Columbus & Cincinnati Railroad. Starkweather married Julia Judd on 25 June 1828. They had 4 children: Sarah, Samuel, William, and Julia. Starkweather is buried in Lake View Cemetery.

**STASHOWER, FRED P.** (29 Oct. 1902–10 Jan. 1994), combined during his lifetime careers in journalism, advertising, and public office. Born in Cleveland to Max D. and Sarah Polansky Stashower, Fred attended local schools and graduated from Glenville High School. He then entered the Wharton School of Business at the Univ. of Pennsylvania, where he earned his bachelor's degree in economics in 1924.

He began his working career in journalism; he was a reporter for both the *CLEVELAND LEADER†* and the *CLEVELAND NEWS.†* Then in 1927 he joined the WILLIAM TAYLOR SON & CO.† department store as its director of publicity. After ten years there, in 1937 he joined the Lang, Fisher & Kirk advertising agency. In 1942, when he became partner and vice-president, the firm was renamed Lang, Fisher & Stashower (it became LIGGETT-STASHOWER† in 1987).

In 1952 he ran for and was elected to the city council of CLEVELAND HTS.† He continued as a district councilman until 1968, when he was chosen council president and mayor. Deteriorating health prompted him to resign public office in Jan. 1972.

Stashower also devoted many hours to public service. He served as a trustee of the Cleveland Convention Bureau, the MONTEFIORE HOME† for the Aged, the REAL PROPERTY INVEN-

TORY,† the Community Chest, the CITIZENS LEAGUE,† and the Cleveland Automobile Club.

He married Hildegarde Darmstadter (see STASHOWER, HILDEGARDE) on 24 Nov. 1926. The couple raised two children, David L. and Deborah. In 1976 Stashower was honored by being named to the Cleveland Advertising Club's Hall of Fame. Stashower is buried in Lake View Cemetery.—J.T.

**STASHOWER, HILDEGARDE DARMSTADTER** (23 Dec. 1902–30 Apr. 1994) was a leading figure in the early growth and continuing development of the CLEVELAND PLAY HOUSE.†

Born to Ludwig and Freida Freundlich Darmstadter in Cleveland, Hildegarde attended Cleveland public schools, graduating from Glenville High School. She then began her college studies in Cleveland at Western Reserve College (see CASE WESTERN RESERVE UNIV.†), but later transferred to Barnard College in New York, where she received her bachelor's degree in 1924.

After returning to Cleveland, she married FRED P. STASHOWER on 24 Nov.1926; they had 2 children, David L. and Deborah.

Her professional life began in journalism, working for the short-lived *CLEVELAND TIMES,†* but she soon left the newspaper to join the public relations firm of Farnham & Moriarty, one of the first such enterprises to be owned and managed by women.

In 1929 she began the long association with the Cleveland Play House for which she is best remembered. She began as the theater's publicity manager, but her role soon broadened to include not only marketing but promotions and development. In 1950 she retired from full-time employment at the Play House, but continued to actively serve the theater as honorary life member of its Women's Committee. She was involved in the project to write the theater's history, *Leaps of Faith*, which was published in 1985. She was also a member of the Play House's advisory council, retaining that post until the time of her death.

Stashower survived her husband of 65 years by only three months. She is buried with him in Lake View Cemetery.—J.T.

**STEFANSKI, BEN S.** (26 Jan. 1902–8 Oct. 1991) was the founder and long-time leader of THIRD FEDERAL SAVINGS AND LOAN ASSN. OF CLEVELAND,† one of Cleveland's most successful savings institutions. Born in the Broadway neighborhood of Cleveland to William and Anna (Czarniak) Stefanski, his early life was rooted in the Polish-American traditions which characterized the area. He attended Fullerton School and South and

East Technical high schools. Later he attended Cleveland Business College and took additional coursework from the American Savings and Loan Institute.

On 24 Aug. 1937 he married Gerome Rita Rutkowski. The couple honeymooned in Washington, DC, where they applied for a federal charter for a new savings and loan company. Third Federal Savings and Loan came into existence on 3 May 1938. Stefanski's aim for the fledgling organization was straightforward: "helping the working man attain a home of his own." Third Federal prospered, always adhering to its original purposes. In the 1980s some other Cleveland savings and loan officials remarked that Stefanski's approach had become old-fashioned. He was not deterred, however, and Third Federal emerged from the decade stronger than ever, while his critics' institutions foundered. In 1995 Third Federal had 21 offices, and assets topping $4.5 billion. Stefanski served as Third Federal president and then chairman until his retirement in 1987.

Active in the Polish-American community, he was honored by the Polish American Congress and the Polish Legion. Devoted to the Catholic Church, in 1965 he pledged $1 million dollars to its high school building fund.

Stefanski was father to five children: Ben S. II, Hermine, Abigail, Floyd, and Marc, who succeeded his father as Third Federal chairman. Stefanski is buried in Cleveland's Calvary Cemetery.—J.T.

**STEMPUZIS, JOSEPH** (24 June 1921–24 April 1992) was a leader in the cultural and political affairs of Cleveland's Lithuanian-American community. A native of Kaisiadorys, Lithuania, he graduated from the Vilnius Pedagogical Institute in 1944 and was a family friend of Vytautas Landsbergis, who would become Lithuania's first president after independence. Stempuzis participated in both the anti-Nazi and anti-Soviet resistance movements before escaping to the West in 1945. He toured Europe with the CIURLIONIS LITHUANIAN NATIONAL ART ENSEMBLE,† marrying fellow member Aldona Butkis in Germany in 1948. They came with the ensemble when it made Cleveland its headquarters in 1949 and were both naturalized here in 1956. Aldona Stempuzis pursued a career in music, touring in the U.S. and Europe, in between raising 2 sons and maintaining a home. A contralto, she made her Cleveland recital debut in 1967 and taught at the CLEVELAND MUSIC SCHOOL SETTLEMENT.† Joseph Stempuzis became head of the personal property tax dept. in the Cuyahoga County auditor's office and active in the affairs of Cleveland LITHUANIANS.† Having produced and announced the Lithuanian Voice radio program since 1949, he became a founder and chairman of the Nationalities Broadcasters Assn. He was also a board member of the Lithuanian Village, which played a major role in the construction of the Lithuanian American Community Ctr. in 1973. A member of the GREATER CLEVELAND ROUNDTABLE,† he worked with Mayor Ralph J. Perk to organize the American Nationalities Mvt. Dying at his SOUTH EUCLID† home, he was survived by his wife and sons, Almis and Linas.—J.V.

Joseph Stempuzis Papers, WRHS.

**STEWART, JOHN HALL** (20 April 1904–31 Oct. 1991) occupied the Henry E. Bourne chair of history at CASE WESTERN RESERVE UNIV.† as an authority on the era of the French Revolution. Born near Springfield in Ontario, Canada, he earned his bachelor's degree from the Univ. of Ontario and advanced degrees at Cornell. Joining the History Dept. at Western Reserve Univ. in 1930, he became a full professor in 1951. He became a naturalized U.S. citizen in 1944, and 2 years later married Helen F. Doolittle (b. July 1906), then asst. university registrar at WRU. Stewart published *France, 1715–1815: A Guide to Materials in Cleveland* in 1942, which was followed in 1951 by his magnum opus, *A Documentary Survey of the French Revolution*. Working in collaboration with James Friguglietti, a former student and later colleague in the History Dept., he also prepared an English translation of Georges Lefebvre's *The French Revolution from 1793 to 1799*, which appeared in 1964. Possessed of a convivial personality, Stewart was well known at conventions of the American Historical Assn. for the parties hosted by him and Mrs. Stewart. An accomplished tuba player, he performed with several Dixieland bands including Dr. Stewart's Dixielanders and an Akron group known as the Rubber City Retreads. During the manpower shortage of World War II, he also served with enthusiasm as director of the university band. Named Henry E. Bourne professor of history in 1954, Stewart occupied the chair emeritus following his retirement in 1969. He died in Naples, FL, survived by his wife.—J.V.

Siney, Marion C. *Ups and Downs: The History Department, Western Reserve Univ.-Case Western Reserve Univ.* (1980).

**STEWART, N. COE** ( 1838–28 Feb. 1921), conductor, composer, and instructor, as director of music in the CLEVELAND PUBLIC SCHOOLS,† was responsible for implementing a highly successful music program in the 1870s. Born in Pennsylvania, Stewart studied music under Lowell Mason, a nationally recognized expert from Boston who, like

Stewart, was a pioneer in emphasizing the value of music education in public schools. Stewart took charge of music in the Cleveland schools in 1869 and instructed the system's 160 teachers on how to teach music, himself teaching choral music in Cleveland high schools. He was later president of the Music Teachers Assn., an organization that was his idea. Stewart was active in other areas of the city's music life. In 1881 he organized the Central Musical Assn., a large choral group, and for 7 years was its conductor. In the 1890s, he became director of the Star Course concert series, which included, in 1892, the New York Symphony's first performance in Cleveland. Stewart conducted a combined chorus from the Cleveland schools on many occasions, in 1874 directing a chorus of 1,600 children at SAENGERFEST,† and directing 4,000 schoolchildren in 1893's Saengerfest. He presented a similar performance the following year for the dedication of the SOLDIERS & SAILORS MONUMENT.† He published widely circulated songbooks for children and systematic courses of elementary instruction in music. Stewart and his wife, Gabriella, who organized series of winter concerts at the Music Hall, had 3 children: Gabriella, Esther, and William G. His daughter, Gabriella, assisted him in managing the Star Course series.

**STIGWANISH**, also known as Stigwandish, Stigonish, or Seneca, a prominent Indian chief in the early years of Cleveland's settlement, whose name translates Standing Stone, was chief of the Seneca Indians remaining in Ohio after "Mad" Anthony Wayne's 1794 victory at Fallen Timbers. He helped the first survey party of the WESTERN RESERVE† in 1796, and remained in the settlement, helping JOB STILES and his wife, Tabitha Cumi, and others survive the winter of 1796–97. Edward Paine, Jr., whose family settled Painesville, wrote, "Seneca has the dignity of a Roman Senator, the honesty of Aristides, and the philanthropy of William Penn." Stigwanish continually traveled to Cleveland, Painesville, Ashtabula, and his wintering residence near the CUYAHOGA RIVER† in Streetsboro Twp.

Stigwanish moved to Seneca County (named after him), in 1809. Before the start of the War of 1812, most Indians in northeast Ohio left for Canada to aid the British and plan raids along Lake Erie's south shore. Stigwanish warned that the British were inciting the Indians. When the British finalized their plans, Stigwanish warned settlers, so that most women and children were evacuated from lakeshore settlements. However, spies alerted the British, who canceled their plans. Stigwanish died in 1816. Three versions of his death exist; in all three, a white man whose family had been murdered and scalped by

Indians killed him. The Northeast Ohio Council of the BOY SCOUTS OF AMERICA† named their camp in Madison Stigwandish in the chief's honor.

**STILES, JOB PHELPS** (ca. 1769-ca. 1849), and his wife, Tabitha, were the first settlers of Cleveland. They accompanied MOSES CLEAVELAND's party to the WESTERN RESERVE† in 1796. Stiles was born in Granville, MA, son of Job and Lydia Phelps Stiles. He and his wife, purportedly schoolteachers, lived in Vermont. Stiles was never officially listed as a member of the surveying party; it is probable, however, he had some arrangement with the CONNECTICUT LAND CO.† or Cleaveland. Before leaving in the autumn of 1796, the surveying party erected a cabin for Stiles on Lot 53, the present corner of Superior and W. 3rd St., and left him in charge of their supplies.

The Stiles were joined for a short time by boarder Jacob Landon, then by Edward Paine, who traded with the Indians. On 23 Jan. 1797, 17-year-old Tabitha gave birth to Chas. Phelps Stiles, the first white child born in Cleveland, attended, according to tradition, by Indian women. The Stileses remained in the cabin until 1798, when they moved to higher ground southeast of the city in NEWBURGH† to escape the unhealthy stagnant water at the Cuyahoga's mouth. They lived there until 1800, when for unknown reasons they returned to Vermont. Stiles's wife, formerly Tabitha Cumi Elderkin of Hartford, CT, was given a city lot (2 acres), a 10-acre lot, and a 100-acre lot for being the first white woman to settle in Cleveland. Stiles died in Branford, VT; Tabitha survived him several years. Their son, Charles, died in Beaver, IL, in 1882.

**STINCHCOMB, WILLIAM ALBERT** (5 June 1878–17 Jan. 1959), father of the CLEVELAND METROPARKS SYSTEM,† was born in Cleveland, to William and Julia Stinchcomb. He was educated in CLEVELAND PUBLIC SCHOOLS,† and in 1895 began as a surveyor for the city engineer. Appointed chief engineer of the City Parks Dept. in 1902, he laid out detailed plans for developing the park system. Stinchcomb became county engineer in 1912 for 3 terms, responsible for the DETROIT-SUPERIOR BRIDGE† construction and Lorain-Carnegie Bridge planning, drafting the first comprehensive plan for lakefront public development, and convincing the Ohio legislature to block a city deal turning over $30 million worth of shoreland to railroads. In 1913 Stinchcomb got the Ohio legislature to revise the state constitution to permit legislation authorizing natural resource conservation. When the Ohio Supreme Court ruled Cuyahoga

County's park law unconstitutional in 1913, Stinchcomb drafted and lobbied through new legislation establishing the Metropolitan Park System, of which he was appointed first engineer. Stinchcomb mapped out a great circle, "emerald necklace," around Cleveland, and used proceeds from a levy to buy land. During the Depression, he employed Civilian Conservation Corps and Public Works Admin. grants to put thousands to work making roads; building shelterhouses, parking lots, bridges, nature trails, ball fields, playgrounds, and museums; and reforesting thousands of acres. Stinchcomb retired in 1957; a park on Rocky River's east bank, designed by Ernst Payer, has a 30'-high carillon tower designed by WM. MCVEY, that honors him. Stinchcomb married Annie M. Long in Aug. 1905 and had 2 children, Thomas and Betty. He was buried at West Park Cemetery.

## STOKES, CARL B. See MAYORAL ADMINIS-TRATION OF CARL B. STOKES.†

STONE, AMASA (27 Apr. 1818–11 May 1883) was a contractor, railroad manager, financier, and philanthropist, born in Charlton, MA, to Amasa and Esther (Boyden) Stone. He apprenticed in construction, and worked with his brother-in-law, Wm. Howe, to perfect the Howe truss bridge, buying the patent rights in 1842 and eventually constructing hundreds of bridges using his own improved design.

After building the Cleveland-to-Columbus spur of the Cleveland, Columbus & Cincinnati Railroad, in 1851 Stone came to Cleveland to superintend the road and build the Cleveland, Painesville & Ashtabula. By 1852 he was a director of both roads; by 1857, he was president of the CP&A. He built or directed other railroads, including the Lake Shore and Michigan Southern Rd., taking part of his pay in stock, then investing his wealth as a major stockholder in Cleveland Rolling Mill and related mills throughout the country, as well as in several banks.

On 29 Dec. 1876, a Lake Shore Rd. Howe truss bridge collapsed at Ashtabula, plunging a train into a ravine, killing 92. An investigation implicated Stone who, ignoring engineers, had used an overly long span. The road's chief engineer, Chas. Collins, committed suicide. He was also vexed by William H. Vanderbilt's 1883 plan to consolidate the Lake Shore Rd. with the NICKEL PLATE ROAD.† On 11 May 1883, after several steel mills he controlled failed, Stone committed suicide, leaving a wife, Julia Gleason Stone, 2 daughters, Clara Stone Hay and FLORA STONE MATHER. His multimillion-dollar estate included a $100,000 bequest to Western Reserve Univ. In 1881 Stone donated $500,000 to WRU to establish Adelbert College in memory of his son, who had died in a swimming accident at Yale in 1866. He was buried in Lake View Cemetery.

Dow, Burton Smith, III. "Amasa Stone, Jr.: His Triumph and Tragedy" (Master's thesis, WRU, 1956).

STONE, MORRIS SAMUEL (15 March 1911–23 June 1989) was an executive at the AMERICAN GREETINGS CORP.† who, along with his father (company founder, 1906) and two brothers, helped build American Greetings into the world's largest manufacturer of greeting cards and related products.

Born in Cleveland to Jennie (Kantor) and JACOB SAPIRSTEIN, Stone attended Glenville High School. At age 7 Stone helped make postcard deliveries for his father. By 1929 Stone was a full-time salesman for the Sapirstein Greeting Card Co. In 1939 the company began operating as American Greetings.

Stone's commitment helped push sales of American Greetings cards and other products from card shops to department, discount and drug stores. By the 1940s American Greetings counted every major American drugstore chain as a customer. Stone's contacts with retail customers gave American Greetings insight for innovations that became industry standards, such as printing retail price coding on the backs of cards and displaying cards in open cabinets. Stone remained with American Greetings until 1989, retiring as vice-chairman.

In addition to his contributions to American Greetings, Stone supported religious and community organizations. He was a board member of PARK SYNAGOGUE,† the JEWISH COMMUNITY CENTER,† and the Jewish Welfare Fund. Stone contributed to the Crawford Auto-Aviation Museum with financing and gifts of a 1934 Chrysler Air Flow and a 1920 Jordan Playboy.

Stone married Evelyn Weiss on 29 July 1934 (div. 1959). They had a son, Robert. Stone married Maxeen Myerson on 14 May 1960. They had five children, Steven, Jon, James, Susan, and Patricia. Stone lived in SHAKER HTS.† and is buried in Park Synagogue Cemetery.—T.B.

STONE, SILAS SAFFORD (13 Feb. 1815–18 Feb. 1884), real estate dealer, leased property to the U.S. government for military use during the Civil War. He engineered what was then the largest real estate sale in the history of the city when he sold one block of property valued at one-half million dollars to the Cleveland, Columbus, Cincinnati & Indianapolis Railroad (see RAILROADS†). Born in Charlotte, VT, Stone came to Cleveland in 1832 and entered the forwarding and commissioning business. He became associated with Dennison and Foster and the Troy and Erie Transportation Co. By 1848 he was a member of the City of Cleveland Board of Trade. In the 1850s Stone began buying up large parcels of land in and around Cleveland. In Aug. 1861 he leased property on Univ. Hts. in Brooklyn Township to the U.S. government. Camp Wade was built here for the 2nd Ohio Volunteer Calvary (see CIVIL WAR CAMPS IN CLEVELAND†). In the summer of 1862 the U.S. GENERAL HOSPITAL† was also built on this property, directly across from Camp Cleveland. Stone died at his Prospect Ave. home.

**STOUFFER, ABRAHAM E.** (7 July 1875–16 Oct. 1936) and **STOUFFER, LENA MAHALA (BIGELOW)** (June 1880–8 Oct. 1953), were founders of the Stouffer restaurant chain. Abraham was born on a farm in Columbiana County, the son of James B. and Sarah Busbey Stouffer, and received his education in public grade schools. Lena, the daughter of Orrin and Della M. (Gordon) Bigelow, married Abraham in Cleveland 12 Sept. 1900. They were living in Medina in 1914 when Abraham and his father organized the Medina County Creamery and also opened a dairy stand at Cleveland's SHER-IFF STREET MARKET.† The Stouffers moved to Lakewood in 1916 to manage the Creamery business. Abraham resigned as president of the company in 1922 to operate one of the creamery's milk stands located in the lower level of the ARCADE.† Stouffer and his wife converted the stand-up dairy bar to a restaurant where they began serving buttermilk, toasted sandwiches, and Lena's homemade dutch apple pie. Working together, they opened another Stouffer restaurant at 2030 E. 9th St. the following year, and Abraham incorporated Stouffer Lunch Systems with $15,000 capital in 1924. As the firm expanded he and Lena increasingly left the business in the hands of their sons, VERNON and Gordon, who organized the Stouffer Corp. in 1929. Abraham served as chairman of the firm's board until he died in 1936. At that time, the family controlled a chain of 10 restaurants.

A resident of West Richfield, Abraham died in Cleveland and was buried at Lakewood Park Cemetery. Lena Stouffer married again in 1939 to Roy H. Southworth. She died in Akron, OH, and is buried with Abraham in Lakewood Park Cemetery.—M.S.

**STOUFFER, VERNON BIGELOW** (22 Aug. 1901–26 July 1974), president of Stouffer Corp., a national chain of restaurants, motor inns, and food-service operations, was born in Cleveland to ABRAHAM AND LENA MAHALA BIGELOW STOUFFER, and graduated with a B.S. in 1923 from Wharton School of Business, Univ. of Pennsyl-

vania. In 1922 Abraham Stouffer opened a dairy counter in the ARCADE† featuring buttermilk, cheese sandwiches, and Lena Stouffer's Dutch apple pies. Vernon joined his father in 1924, opening Stouffer's Lunch, a restaurant serving quick, tasty meals at moderate prices, the first of a chain. In 1929 the Stouffers went public, founding STOUFFER CORP.,† which eventually became part of Litton Industries. Stouffer personally tested new products, and while traveling, secretly checked food and service quality at his restaurants and inns.

In 1966 Stouffer purchased controlling interest in the CLEVELAND INDIANS,† selling the franchise in 1972 to a group headed by Nick Mileti, after what he said was the longest 5 years of his life, as the club suffered from poor teams, low attendance, and a poor economy. He was a trustee for Litton Industries, United Airlines, REPUBLIC STEEL,† and Society Natl. Bank. Stouffer established the Vernon Stouffer Corp. to support activities in medicine, education, and public welfare. In 1966 he established the Stouffer Prize, recognizing research in hypertension and arteriosclerosis. He was president of the Zoological Society and a founder of the Natl. Recreation & Park Assn. Stouffer married Gertrude Dean in 1928 and had 3 children: Marjorie, Deanette, and James.

**STOW, JOSHUA** (22 Apr. 1762–1842), an original shareholder in the CONNECTICUT LAND CO.,† accompanied MOSES CLEAVELAND and later helped develop land in Summit County. He was born in Middlefield, CT, to Elihu and Jemima Stow and, although associated with the WESTERN RESERVE,† never settled there himself, remaining in Connecticut. As commissary manager for Cleaveland's surveying party, Stow was given charge of the company's provisions. After returning to Connecticut, he encouraged development of his land grants, trading Western Reserve land he was unable to use for land in Connecticut. Stow was involved in Connecticut government, primarily responsible for including the freedom-of-religion clause he authored in that state's constitution. He was also postmaster of Middletown and judge of the county court.

When Cleaveland's surveying party set out from Schenectady in the spring of 1796, Stow, with several men, was to transport the supplies by water and meet the main party in Buffalo. At Oswego, the British detained Stow and for a while prevented him from entering Lake Ontario. He was eventually allowed to pass, only to lose 1 of 4 boats in a storm. When the surveying party reached Conneaut Creek, a crude structure was erected to house supplies, referred to as "Stow's Castle." In his lifetime, Stow purportedly made 13 trips between Connecticut and the Western Reserve. He managed his Ohio affairs through his business partner, Wm. Wetmore. In 1809 these two men, with Henry Newberry, founded Cuyahoga Falls. Stow Twp. in Summit County was named after Stow. Several of his relations did eventually settle there. Stow married Samantha Griffin in 1838. He had no children.

**STREIBLER, MARTIN** (10 Feb. 1825–14 May 1864), a sergeant in Co. E, 103RD OHIO VOLUNTEER INFANTRY† during the CIVIL WAR,† and one of 2 local men depicted by name on the sculpture titled the Color Guard on SOLDIERS & SAILORS MONUMENT,† was born in France to Mary and Geo. Streibler. After his father died in 1844, Streibler reportedly served with the French dragoons for 6 years. Sometime before 1862, he, his mother, and a younger brother, Joseph, immigrated to the U.S., settling in Cleveland. Streibler was enlisted in the 103rd regiment on 11 Aug. 1862 by Capt. LEVI T. SCOFIELD, who would eventually sculpt his figure for Soldiers & Sailors Monument. Streibler was a "thoroughly disciplined" soldier who was much admired by his comrades. After being promoted to cpl., he was made sgt. on 9 Feb. 1863. On 14 May 1864, Streibler was killed while leading the 9-man color guard at the battle of Resaca, GA. Scofield, an engineer for the regiment, viewed this action from his position in the rear and later used it as his inspiration for the monument sculpture.

**STRICKLAND, BENJAMIN** (27 July 1810–21 Feb. 1889), Cleveland's first permanent dentist, was born in Montpelier, VT, son of Benjamin Strickland. He received an M.D. degree from an eastern school and practiced medicine for a short time before coming to Cleveland in 1835. He opened an office in the Central Bldg. and advertised his services as a dentist; in the morning he made house calls, and in the afternoon received patients in his office. In 1841 Strickland was admitted to the American Society of Dental Surgeons; two years later he received an honorary D.D.S. degree from the Baltimore College of Dental Surgery. Strickland was later quite active in developing state and local dental associations, as a charter member of the Ohio State Dental Society, and president (1858–65) of the Ohio Northern Dental Assn. He also organized the Forest City Society of Dental Surgery, which later became the CLEVELAND DENTAL SOC.† Strickland advertised through the newspapers the painless extraction of teeth with the use of cold application; he also, for this purpose, was one of the first dentists in the state to use Morton's Letheon. A source for dental supplies, Strickland manufactured porcelain teeth and sold gold, tin, foil, and various instruments. Regionally, he was considered an authority

on pulp treatment, fillings, and root-canal work. In 1875 Strickland retired. He died 14 years later of pneumonia.

Strickland married Hannah Walworth in 1841. He was buried in Lake View Cemetery.

Gellin, Milton E. *Cleveland Dentists before 1856* (1946).

**STRIEBINGER, FREDERIC WILLIAM** (22 Apr. 1870–30 Sept. 1941), an architect active in Cleveland from 1898–1940, was born in Cleveland to Martin and Anna Raparlie Striebinger, attended Cleveland public schools until 1888, studied painting for 1 year with Wm. Merritt Chase in New York (1889), and is said to have been the first Clevelander to study at the Ecole des Beaux-Arts in Paris (1891–96). Striebinger was an accomplished classical architect. His major buildings include the Second Church of Christ, Scientist, 1916 (later the 77th St. Cleveland Play House); the Harry Coulby residence, 1912 (Wickliffe City Hall); Cleveland Gesangverein Hall, 1900 (HOUSE OF WILLS† Funeral Home); Woodward Masonic Temple, 1907 (Call & Post Bldg.); the Heights Masonic Temple, 1915; the Third Church of Christ, Scientist, 1906; and the Tremaine-Gallagher House in Cleveland Hts., 1914. Striebinger was known among his peers as the epitome of the eclectic architect, with the broad knowledge necessary for the appropriate handling of historical sources, but without great creative originality. This judgment is refuted by the buildings themselves, especially the Coulby and Tremaine mansions, which are superb examples of the Renaissance Revival of the early 20th century. Striebinger married twice. He and his first wife, Elizabeth Maude Smythe (d. 1938) were married on 25 Aug. 1918. Striebinger married Alice M. Rabensdorf in June 1939. He had no children from either marriage.

**STRONG, ELEANOR PAINTER** (12 Sept. 1891–3 Nov. 1947), singer, actress and author, settled in Cleveland after a 19-year career as an operetta star. Strong was born in Walkerville, IA. She spent part of her childhood in Colorado and later went to New York City to become a singer. She studied singing in Berlin, Germany (1912), and sang at Covent Garden in London the next year. Her career took off: she was offered a 5-year contract at the Charlottenburg Opera in Berlin and hired to sing in *The Lilac Domino*, an operetta produced in New York City in 1914. Later composer Victor Herbert wrote the operetta *Princess Pat* for her. Between 1914 and 1931 Painter starred in dramatic productions as well as musicals and operas, including *Madame Butterfly* and *Carmen,* in New York City, Philadelphia, PA, and Berlin.

After the dissolution of an earlier marriage to Louis Graveure (Wilfred Douthitt), Painter married Major Charles H. Strong, president of WILLIAM TAYLOR SON AND CO.† in 1931. She gave up her professional career but not her interest in music. The couple lived in BRATENAHL†; there were no children. Strong supported the musical arts and theater in Cleveland, performed locally, and wrote a novel about music, *Spring Symphony* (1941). Her local performances included the leading role in Wolf-Ferrari's *Secret of Suzanne* (1935) and a presentation of *Peter and the Wolf* (1941), both in conjunction with the CLEVELAND ORCHESTRA.† Strong died in Cleveland.—J.M.

**STUPKA, LADDIE** (4 March 1878–20 Feb. 1946), a peacetime recipient of the Congressional Medal of Honor for service in the U.S. Navy, was a native of Cleveland, originally enlisting in the U.S. Navy in 1899 at New York. Stupka was serving as a Fireman, 1st Class aboard the USS *Leyden* when the Civil War–vintage vessel foundered in a heavy fog off the coast of Rhode Island and sank 21 Jan. 1903. Stupka survived and received the Medal of Honor for "seaman-like" qualities in times of emergency on 26 Dec. 1903. He was buried in the Maryland National Cemetery in Baltimore.

**SULLIVAN, JEREMIAH J.** (16 Nov. 1844–2 Feb. 1922), businessman and banker, was born in Ireland to Jeremiah and Mary (Moylan) Sullivan. Coming to the U.S. in the 1850s, Sullivan attended local schools, and in 1879 and 1885 was elected state senator representing Wayne, Knox, Holmes, and Morrow counties. He helped establish the Soldiers Home in Sandusky and was a trustee. In 1887 Pres. Grover Cleveland appointed him national bank examiner for Ohio. He came to Cleveland and in 1890 helped organize Central Natl. Bank of Cleveland, in 1900 becoming its president. In 1905 he organized Superior Savings & Trust, and was also its president. The two banks merged in 1921 into Central Natl. Bank Savings & Trust Co.; Sullivan became chairman of the Board of Directors. Sullivan was involved in local and national banking organizations. In 1899 he became the Cleveland Assn. of Credit Men's first president; he was also the first president of the Bankers' Club of Cleveland and president of the Ohio Bankers' Assn. In 1905–06 he was president of the Natl. Board of Trade, and in 1914 president of the CLEVELAND CLEARING-HOUSE ASSN.† Sullivan was among a few prominent bankers favoring the Federal Reserve Act of 1913, and helped bring the 4th FEDERAL RESERVE BANK† to Cleveland. He was Cleveland Chamber of Commerce president in 1905, and was active in the Ohio Democratic party. The Ohio Natl.

Guards' 5th Ohio Regiment elected him colonel in 1893. Sullivan married Selina J. Brown in 1873. They had three children: Selma, Corliss, and Helen.

**SUNDQUIST, GUSTAF ADOLF** (4 June 1879–25 August 1918), recipient of the Congressional Medal of Honor for service during the Spanish-American War, was one of nine children born to Anders Gustaf and Eva Sofia (Kullgren) Sundquist in Irsta, Sweden. Gustaf Adolf arrived in New York about 1895 and enlisted in the U.S. Navy 30 July 1897. On board the USS *Nashville* in the Caribbean, Seaman Sundquist participated in the attempt 11 May 1898 to cut the underwater telegraph cables, linking Cuba with Spain, which were located offshore near the Cuban city of Cienfuegos. Under fire from Spanish riflemen, the party was able to cut only two of the three telegraph lines and had to return to their ships. On 2 Nov. 1899 the Medal of Honor for bravery and coolness under fire was authorized for Sundquist and the other members of the cable-cutting party. Sundquist was discharged from the navy 26 Sept. 1900. In 1905 he married Matilda E. Pearson in Brooklyn, NY, and the couple had five children. They came to Cleveland about 1915, where he was employed as a structural ironworker until 4 May 1918 when he reenlisted in the U.S. Naval Reserve to serve in World War I. Assigned to Ft. Lafayette Naval Air Station at Crois D'Hins, France, Sundquist drowned 25 August while swimming off shore. His body was never recovered.—M.S.

**SUTLER, ELEANORE MARGUERITE YOUNG** (27 Jan. 1915–16 Dec. 1992) served the YOUNG WOMEN'S CHRISTIAN ASSN.† (YWCA) in Cleveland, Chicago, and Indianapolis. Beginning part-time at Cleveland's YWCA in 1966, she later became Metropolitan Program Director for area branches, holding that position until 1978. Sutler was born in Evanston, IL, to James Walter Young and Ethel Avendorph Young; she attended public schools there. In 1938 she received a degree in social work from Howard Univ. Before coming to Cleveland in the 1940s, she worked at the Phillis Wheatley Assn. in Chicago as well as the various YWCAs.

Sutler married Dr. MARTIN RANDOLPH DELANEY SUTLER, JR. The couple lived in UNIV. CIRCLE† with children Marguerite Gray, Sheryl Darden, and Susan E. Committed to the area, they maintained that residence even after other African American professionals (see AFRICAN AMERICANS†) had begun moving into nearby suburbs. Sutler belonged to the Presbyterian CHURCH OF THE COVENANT† and taught Sunday school there. She died in Washington, DC, where she had moved in 1990, and is buried in Lake View Cemetery.—J.M.

**SUTLER, MARTIN RANDOLPH DELANEY, JR., M.D.** (4 Nov. 1913–1 June 1981), surgeon, was president of FOREST CITY HOSPITAL† (1956), taught at the School of Medicine of CASE WESTERN RESERVE UNIV.† (1951–81), and was surgeon consultant to the Veterans Administration. Active in civic affairs, he served as a trustee of the CLEVELAND PUBLIC LIBRARY† (1970–74) and the HOUGH DEVELOPMENT CORP.,† and presided over League Park Settlement House (1970) (see SETTLEMENT HOUSES†). Sutler was born in Newport, RI, to Martin R. and Mary Jeter Sutler. He graduated from Howard Univ. (1935) and the School of Medicine of the Univ. of Michigan (1941), where he served as a teaching fellow (1944) and a research fellow in surgery (1945–47). Opening a practice in Cleveland, Sutler maintained an office on EUCLID AVE.† He also held appointments in surgery at City Hospital (1951–73) and at ST. VINCENT CHARITY MEDICAL CENTER† (1960–63). Less than a year before Sutler's library board term expired he resigned, along with the only other African American trustee at the time, George Livingston. They charged racial and sexual discrimination in hiring and claimed to have been ostracized by other trustees.

Sutler married ELEANORE MARGUERITE YOUNG; they lived in UNIV. CIRCLE† with their children, Marguerite Gray, Sheryl Darden, and Susan E. Sutler is buried in Lake View Cemetery.—J.M.

---

Forest City Hospital Records, Dittrick Museum of Medical History.
Case Western Reserve Univ. Archives.

---

**SUTPHEN, REV. PAUL FREDERICK** (15 Jan. 1856–11 Aug. 1929) guided 3 significant local congregations during his career as a Presbyterian clergyman. A native of Brooklyn, NY, he was the son of Ten Eyck and Harriet White Sutphen. After graduating from Rutgers Univ., he studied for the ministry at Union Theological Seminary. He married Bertha Davies of New Jersey in 1878 and became pastor of a Presbyterian congregation in Valatia, NY. Following further assignments in Minnesota and Elizabeth, NJ, Sutphen became pastor of Cleveland's Woodland Ave. Presbyterian Church (see WOODLAND HILLS COMMUNITY CHURCH†) from 1886–93. He spent a brief period behind pulpits in Newark and Philadelphia before returning to Cleveland as pastor of Second Presbyterian Church at Prospect Ave. and E. 30th St. Noted for his eloquence in the pulpit, Sutphen, in the words of one historian, "wrote a sermon as an artist paints a picture." More important, however, was his support for the work of RUSSELL and ROWENA JELLIFFE, which resulted in the establishment of the Playhouse Settlement (see KARAMU HOUSE†). Sutphen was also a trustee of HIRAM HOUSE.† When Second Presbyterian merged with the Euclid Ave. Presbyterian Church in 1920 to form the CHURCH OF THE COVENANT,† Sutphen was named assoc. pastor, along with Dr. Alexander McGaffin of the Euclid Ave. church. He resigned for reasons of health in 1926 and died in Cleveland, survived by his wife and 4 children: J. Walworth, Helen, Ruth Farnsworth, and Dorothy Bullard.—J.V.

**SUTPHIN, ALBERT C. (AL)** (11 Apr. 1895–25 June 1974), sports promoter and businessman, was born in Franklin, OH, the son of Carleton Ernest and Elizabeth Thayer Sutphin. About 1912 the family came to Cleveland, and Albert attended CENTRAL HIGH SCHOOL,† playing hockey on the school team until he left to work for the Braden Ink Co. By the mid–1920s, he was vice-president of the Braden-Sutphin Ink Co. and later president of the firm, which produced graphic arts equipment, inks, printing materials and supplies. A sports enthusiast, Sutphin played semipro football and baseball, and was Cleveland's boxing commissioner in the early 1930s. In 1934 he bought the faltering Cleveland Indians hockey team, changed their name to the Cleveland Falcons, and entered the newly formed American Hockey League. The team played at the ELYSIUM† until Sutphin organized a syndicate of investors in 1936 to build the CLEVELAND ARENA,† which opened in 1937 with the Ice Follies show. Although the hockey team, now named the CLEVELAND BARONS,† was its primary tenant, Sutphin tirelessly promoted the Arena as the site for a variety of indoor events, and its mortgage was paid off in 12 years. In 1949 he sold the arena and the Barons to a group of Minneapolis businessmen, but continued to support sports in Cleveland. He retired to Florida in 1967.

Sutphin married Mary A. Hoynes 14 Aug. 1922; they had six children: James H., Albert C., Mary Elizabeth, Jane, Caroline Leitch, and Alberta Stoney. He died at his home in Fort Myers, FL, and was buried there.—M.S.

**SVOBODA, FRANK J.** (28 Nov. 1873–1 Mar. 1965), Czech newspaper publisher (1899–1939) and state legislator (1943–60), was born in Bohemia, and came to the U.S. in 1884 with his parents, John and Mary (Marova) Svoboda. He left school at 14 to become a printer's helper, by 1894 opened his own printing office, and in 1899 began publishing a Czech daily newspaper, the *American,* especially popular among Czech Catholics. In 1908 the *American* absorbed the weekly *Volnost* (Freedom). Svoboda was sole owner until the Depression forced him to take on partners in 1932, when he became president and general manager of the American-Bohemian Publishing Co. Svoboda continued publishing the *American* until June 1939, when the paper was bought by the *Svet* (World) (see SVET-AMERICAN†).

Svoboda served on the City Planning Commission for 10 years and was also a leader in the local and state Townsend movement for an old-age pension (see TOWNSEND PLAN†), including serving as president of the Fleet Ave. Townsend Club, resigning his positions in Feb. 1936 to run for U.S. Congress against incumbent ROBT. CROSSER in the May primary. In 1942 Democrat Svoboda won election to the Ohio House of Representatives, serving 2 terms (1943–44, 1945–46); then was elected to 6 terms in the Ohio Senate. When he retired in 1960, he was the oldest person to serve in the senate and had served the longest of any legislator elected from Cleveland. Svoboda married Julia Holpuch in 1896. They had 5 children: Josephine, Elsie, Frank J., Marie, and Robert. Svoboda was buried in Calvary Cemetery.

**SWASEY, AMBROSE** (19 Dec. 1846–15 June 1937), mechanical engineer, manufacturer, and philanthropist, was born in Exeter, NH, to Nathaniel and Abigail C. (Peavey) Swasey. He served as apprentice machinist (1865–69) and met WORCESTER WARNER, with whom he formed a partnership in 1880 to build and sell machine tools. The business eventually became the WARNER & SWASEY CO.† of Cleveland. Swasey held several patents on gear-cutting machinery and, influenced by his partner, became a designer of astronomical instruments, for which their company became world famous. He was a founding member of the American Society of Mechanical Engineers in 1880 and served on several government agencies, including the Natl. Research Council during World War I. A generous benefactor of higher education and Baptist missionary work, between 1914–31 Swasey gave a total of $890,000 to the United Engineering Society in New York to establish an "Engineering Foundation" to promote research. In 1900 he was decorated by France for his work on astronomical instruments. Swasey was president of the Cleveland Chamber of Commerce in 1905. On 19 Dec. 1936 he received the Hoover Medal of the Engineering Societies of America, and in 1930 the Cleveland Medal of Service from the Chamber of Commerce. On 14 Nov. 1923, Dr. Otto Struve named a newly discovered asteroid Swasey in his honor. In 1871 Swasey married Lavinia Marston of Exeter; they had no children. The Swaseys moved to Cleveland when the company relocated there from Chicago in 1881. Swasey died at Exeter.

**SWEENEY, MARTIN L.** (15 Apr. 1885–1 May 1960), congressman and politician, was born in Cleveland to Dominic and Anna Cleary Sweeney, at age 12 found work to support himself while attending St. Bridget's Parochial School, and later worked as a longshoreman and construction worker while attending Cleveland Law School part-time, graduating and being admitted to the Ohio Bar in 1914. After 1 term (1913–14) in the Ohio legislature, Sweeney entered private practice, until 1923 when he became a Municipal Court judge. On the bench, he vocally opposed Prohibition.

In 1931 Sweeney won election to Congress. Attending the 1932 Democratic Natl. Convention pledged to Al Smith, Sweeney instead supported Franklin Roosevelt, splitting with county party chairman BURR GONGWER; the split widened when Sweeney supported the Republican candidate after losing the 1933 Democratic mayoral primary. In mid-1936, he turned against Pres. Roosevelt, supporting the Catholic priest, Chas. Coughlin. Reelected in 1934 and 1936 without Democratic party support, Sweeney considered his victories as mandates for independent action. During the late 1930s, he became increasingly isolationist. Sweeney reconciled with Gongwer in 1937, but RAY T. MILLER broke with Sweeney and Gongwer and won the county party leadership. Sweeney failed to oust Miller as party chairman in 1940, but successfully defended his congressional seat against Miller-supported Michael Feighan, losing to him in 1942. After failing to win the governor's nomination in 1944, Sweeney returned to private practice with his son, Robert. Sweeney married Marie Carlin in 1921 and had 4 children: Martin, Jr., Anne Marie, Robert, and Eileen.

**SZELL, GEORGE** (7 June 1897–30 July 1970), internationally renowned conductor and music director of the CLEVELAND ORCHESTRA,† was born in Budapest to George Charles and Margarite Harmat Szell, and grew up in Vienna, studying with Mandyczewski (theory), J. B. Foerster and Max Reger (composition), and Richard Robert (piano). He made his debut as a pianist at age 10, playing his own music. His conducting debut came at 16 with the Vienna State Opera Orchestra. Two years later, Szell was engaged by Richard Strauss for the staff of the Berlin State Opera House. He subsequently held other conducting posts, and was general musical director of the German Opera and Philharmonic of Prague and director of the Scottish Natl. Orchestra. He became music director of the Cleveland Orchestra in 1946, continuing in that position until his death. With the orchestra, he toured the U.S. and Canada, Europe (1957, 1959), and the Far East just before his death in 1970. He was known as a stern taskmaster, bordering at times on the tyrannical, but was greatly respected by fellow musicians. At the time of his death, the Cleveland Orchestra had gained its stature as one of the finest in the world. Szell held honorary degrees from Western Reserve Univ. and Oberlin College, and was a Chevalier of the French Legion of Honor. His recordings with the Cleveland Orchestra are among the best symphonic documents of their era. Szell was married twice: Olga Band was his first wife; he married Helene (Schulz) Teltsch in 1938 and was step-father to her sons, Thomas and John Teltsch.

Grossman, F. Karl. *A History of Music in Cleveland* (1972).

# T

**TAFT, KINGSLEY ARTER** (19 July 1903–28 March 1970) was a justice on the Ohio Supreme Court between 1948–62, and chief justice, between 1963–70. An astute student of the law, Taft's judicial career was marked by the establishment of the Ohio Judicial Conference, and the adoption of the Ohio Rules of Civil Procedure in 1970.

Born in Cleveland to Frederick and Mary Arter Taft, Taft attended Bolton School and Cleveland Hts. High School, graduating in 1921. He received the A.B. degree from Amherst College in 1925. In 1928 he received the LL.B. from Harvard Law School and was admitted to the Ohio Bar.

Taft began his career in 1928 when he joined the firm of Dustin, McKeehan, Merrick, Arter & Stewart (ARTER & HADDEN†). He became a partner in 1940 and continued with the firm until 1948, interrupting practice from 1942–46 to serve as a major in the U.S. Army's Cleveland Ordnance Department.

Taft was elected to the Ohio House of Representatives, serving from 1933–34. Taft served on the Shaker Hts. School Board from 1940–42, serving as president in 1942. In 1946 Taft was elected to the U.S. Senate to fill the unexpired term of Harold Burton.

Taft won election to the Ohio Supreme Court in 1948, winning reelection in 1954 and 1960. Taft became the first Ohio associate justice to challenge an incumbent chief justice, defeating Carl Weygandt in 1962. While on the court Taft wrote 609 opinions.

Taft married Louise Dakin on 14 Sept. 1927. They had four sons: Charles, Kingsley, Sheldon, and David. A Methodist, Taft is buried in Lake View Cemetery.—T.B.

*In Memoriam: Kingsley A. Taft 1903–1970.* Memorial Committee, the Supreme Court of Ohio. Arter & Hadden archive.

O'Hara, Janet. *Arter & Hadden: 1843–1993 150th Anniversary History,* 1993.

**TALL, BOOKER T.** (12 Dec. 1928–13 Feb. 1994) had a varied career—teacher, businessman, politician—but he is best remembered for a lifetime of work on behalf of the African American community.

Born to sharecropper Booker T. (Sr.) and Julia MacFulton Tall in Hooker Bend, TN, Tall early learned the virtue of industry. His family relocated to Akron, OH, in 1943 where he held a variety of jobs to help support his family while continuing his high school education.

He worked full-time while attending the Univ. of Akron, where Tall earned his bachelor's degree in 1952, and while there, he also found time to establish an NAACP branch on campus. He spent 1953 as a Fulbright scholar at Oxford Univ. in England. He completed his master's degree at Western Reserve Univ. in 1956 and later did other graduate work at both Harvard and Case Western Reserve universities.

Tall moved to Cleveland in 1952 and began a teaching career in the CLEVELAND PUBLIC SCHOOLS.† In 1968 he joined the CUYAHOGA COMMUNITY COLLEGE† faculty and organized that school's first African American studies program. He later worked for the City of Cleveland, helping promote minority-owned businesses, and as an assistant to U.S. Rep. Louis Stokes.

In 1969 as a member of Operation Black Unity, Tall helped to organize a boycott of MacDonald's that helped open the door for AFRICAN AMERICANS† to own their own franchises in the chain. Tall was also involved in the founding of the Cleveland Chapter (est. 1970) of the Assn. for the Study of African American Life and History, and was a member of the Black History Archives Project Advisory Committee (later the African American Archive Auxiliary) of the WESTERN RESERVE HISTORICAL SOCIETY.† During the MAYORAL ADMINISTRATION OF GEORGE VOINOVICH,† Tall served as director of the City Minority Enterprise Center and Cleveland's Equal Employment Opportunity Office.

Tall married Carolyn Smith on 25 Aug. 1956. They raised five sons: Reginald, Bruce, Victor, Christopher, and Michael. He died in Cleveland and is buried in Highland Park Cemetery.—J.T.

Booker Tall Papers, WRHS.

**TAMAS, ISTVAN** (8 Aug. 1897–5 May 1974) was a Hungarian-born writer and inventor who lived in Cleveland after World War II. He was born of Hungarian parents in Pecsvarad, Hungary (some accounts indicate the city of Subotica, which became part of Yugoslavia). After studying literature and chemistry at the Univ. of Budapest and the Sorbonne, he became editor of *Magyar Magazin* in Budapest. During the next 12 years, he wrote more than a dozen novels and children's books and 4 movie scenarios. His story "Moscow-Paris and Return" became the basis of the 1939 Greta Garbo film, *Ninotchka*. Shortly after his marriage to Ilona Farkas, a Hungarian heiress, he came to the U.S. in 1940 at the invitation of the DuPont Corp., which was interested in his formula for a cigarette paper made from cellophane. Though the war curtailed the commercial development of his invention, his novel about the Chetnik brigades in Yugoslavia, *Sergeant Nikola*, was a Book of the Month Club selection. In 1943 Tamas was persuaded to settle in Cleveland by ZOLTAN GOMBOS, publisher of the Hungarian-language daily, *SZABADSAG.†* He became an associate editor of the paper. Another novel of guerrilla warfare in Yugoslavia, *The Students of Spalato* (1944), proved to be his last. During the Cold War, four of his books were banned by the Communist government of Hungary. Tamas concentrated his attention on invention, coming up with a coating for sharper razor blades that was marketed in 1960 as the Gillette Super Blue blade. He lived in LYNDHURST† until 1967 when he moved to St. Petersburg, FL. He died there, survived by his wife and a son, Paul Farkas.

**TAMBO TAMBO** (ca. 1863–24 Feb. 1884) was an Australian aborigine whose misplaced, mummified remains were returned to his homeland for burial 109 years after his death with a traveling circus troupe in Cleveland. His real name was Dianarah or Wangong, according to Australian anthropologist Roslyn Poignant, and he was probably kidnapped from Queensland in 1883 by Robert A. Cunningham, an agent for P. T. Barnum. Opening in San Francisco and then touring the East Coast, the company of 9 "Australian Boomerang Throwers" was booked by Frank Drew's Dime Museum at 189 Superior St. for the week of 25 Feb. 1884. Advertised as "ferocious, treacherous and uncivilized savages," they checked into the New England House at 6 p.m. on Sunday night. Tambo Tambo, however, described as a "mulatto of light color," had come down with a severe cold 3 weeks earlier in Baltimore and had to be carried to his room. By 11 p.m. he was dead of pneumonia. The *Cleveland Herald* saw him as "a victim to the mania for curiosity exhibitions which has raged in this country and Europe for the past ten years." His companions apparently were in the process of preparing his body for burial when they were interrupted by Cunningham, who had the corpse taken to the funeral establishment of Hogan & Harris. There it was embalmed but forgotten, as Hogan & Harris over the years was succeeded by C. J. Smith & Son on St. Clair Ave. Tambo turned up in 1993, when the C. J. Smith home was sold and his remains were turned over to the Cuyahoga County Coroner. Two of his descendants came to Cleveland to claim the body, which was returned to Australia for burial on 8 Dec. 1993.—J.V.

**TAPLIN, FRANK E.** (28 Oct. 1875–7 June 1938), coal and railroad financier, was born in Cleveland, the son of Charles G. and Frances Smith Taplin. After graduating from CENTRAL HIGH SCHOOL† in 1893, he worked as a clerk in the tank wagon department of Standard Oil until 1900, when he joined the Pittsburgh Coal Co. as a salesman. Later he became sales manager for the Youghiogheny & Ohio Coal Co. Taplin organized the Cleveland & Western Coal Co. in 1913 to sell coal mined in Belmont County, OH, and expanded his operation by leasing additional coal acreage and dock facilities, making his company the largest coal shipper on the Great Lakes. He reorganized the firm as NORTH AMERICAN COAL CORP.† in 1926.

Taplin's career as a railroad financier began in 1923 when he headed a syndicate to purchase control of the Pittsburgh & West Virginia Railway as the first step in establishing a lakes-to-sea trunk line from Cleveland to Baltimore. To acquire the Cleveland connection, he tried unsuccessfully to gain control of the WHEELING & LAKE ERIE RAILROAD† line dominated by the VAN SWERINGENS—a struggle that made him a national figure in the late 1920s. Stymied, he sold his stock in the Pittsburgh & West Virginia for a profit a month before the stock market crash in 1929.

Taplin married Edith R. Smith 1 Feb. 1912; they

had three children: Frank E. Jr., Clara Louise, and Thomas E. A resident of CLEVELAND HTS.,† he died at home and was buried at Lake View Cemetery.—M.S.

**TAYLER, ROBERT WALKER** (26 Nov. 1852–26 Nov. 1910), U.S. federal judge and author of the Tayler Grant ending Cleveland's traction war and regulating the reorganized street railways, was born in Youngstown, OH, to Robt. Walker and Louisa Maria Woodbridge Tayler, and spent 3 years at Georgetown Univ. before entering Western Reserve Univ. Law School, earning an LL.D. degree in 1872. He taught 1 year at Lisbon (OH) High School, for 2 years superintended the schools, and from 1875–76 edited the Buckeye State while continuing to study law. Admitted to the Ohio Bar in 1877, he practiced in E. Liverpool until 1880, when he became prosecuting attorney of Columbiana County. In 1894 he won election to Congress for the first of 4 terms, retiring from Congress in 1903 to join the law firm of Arrel, McVey & Tayler in Youngstown. In 1905 Pres. Theodore Roosevelt appointed Tayler to the federal judgeship of northern Ohio with courts at Cleveland and Toledo. Tayler heard the trial of CASSIE CHADWICK and the reorganization actions arising from the "traction war" and Mayor TOM L. JOHNSON's attempt to take public control of Cleveland's railway systems. The resulting court action, authored by the judge and known as the Tayler Grant, became effective on 18 Dec. 1909 and provided a sliding scale limiting trolley lines' profits to 6% and giving jurisdiction over railway operations to the CLEVELAND CITY COUNCIL,† thereby returning peace and stability to Cleveland's streetcar operations. Tayler married Helen Vance in 1876; they had no children. He died in Cleveland and was buried in Lisbon, OH.

**TAYLOR, ALBERT DAVIS** (8 July 1883–8 Jan. 1951), landscape architect active in Cleveland from 1914–51, was raised in Carlisle, MA, son of Nathaniel and Ellen F. Davis. He studied 1 year at Cornell Univ., and received his A.B. from Massachusetts College in 1905. He began his career in the office of Warren Manning in Boston, while there preparing the topographic survey for the new campus of Ohio State Normal College (Kent State Univ.) in 1911. He accompanied Manning to Cleveland in 1914 and established his own office. Taylor is credited with introducing many principles of European landscape design to the U.S. His projects included residential, institutional, and public properties, in which he used both formal and informal planning principles. Taylor designed the garden of Trinity Cathedral House in 1930 and planned some of the

later additions to LAKE VIEW CEMETERY† in the 1930s.

Taylor's public works included the site plan for the Baldwin Filtration Plant in 1920, plans for developing Ambler Park from the Baldwin plant to Coventry Rd. in the 1930s, the retaining walls along Cedar Glen in CLEVELAND HTS.,† a plan for the completion of the Mall in 1931, and a development plan for FOREST HILLS PARK† in 1938. Taylor was the landscape architect for the Pentagon, completed in 1943. Taylor found inspiration in European precedents such as the Ecole des Beaux-Arts and English estates and gardens. He wrote numerous pamphlets and articles on landscape design and home gardening. Taylor married Genevieve Brainerd in 1917 and had a son, Chas. B. Taylor. He died in Cleveland and was buried in Riverside Cemetery.

**TAYLOR, DANIEL RICHARDSON** (28 Mar. 1838–19 Aug. 1924) was a pioneer real estate agent, businessman, and Cleveland developer who recognized an existing relationship between community welfare and municipal development, a concept known today as "city planning." He led in transforming the real estate business into a profession and, in 1892, was a founder and first president of the Cleveland Real Estate Board (CLEVELAND AREA BOARD OF REALTORS†).

Born in Twinsburg, OH, to Col. Royal and Sarah Ann (Richardson) Taylor, Daniel was educated in Twinsburg and CHAGRIN FALLS.† He was a schoolteacher, then, in 1856, a Cleveland & Mahoning Railroad station agent. In 1862 he joined the 84th Ohio Volunteer Infantry as quartermaster and was Ohio State Military Agent at Louisville and Nashville from 1863–65.

In 1867 Taylor came to Cleveland and began investing in residential property on EUCLID AVE.† He was among the first to foresee Euclid's importance as a business district rather than residential street. In 1874 he and his brother, William, opened a real estate office. Taylor heavily invested in real estate, owning wholly or in part about 500 acres of land in Cleveland, including several miles of railroad frontage which he purchased for manufacturing purposes.

Taylor was an original member of the UNION CLUB OF CLEVELAND,† president of the Manufacturers Realty Co., and the Harbor View Co., and a director of several manufacturing and business enterprises.

Taylor lived in Cleveland and never married. He is buried in Lake View Cemetery.—T.B.

**TAYLOR, (HOWARD) LESTER** (18 Aug. 1884–11 Apr. 1950) was a well-known physician of Cleveland who devoted a great deal of his time to health education. He was also a founder of the CLEVELAND HEALTH EDUCATION MUSEUM.†

Taylor was born in Verona, NY, the son of William Cullen and Irene (Mather) Taylor. He attended school in Ilion, NY, received an A.B. from Oberlin College in 1906, and a medical degree from Johns Hopkins Univ. in 1910. He came to Cleveland that year and interned at Lakeside Hospital for 3 years. He served in World War I in Langeres, France, eventually becoming a major in the Army Medical Corps. He returned to Cleveland and set up his practice, specializing in internal medicine. He was appointed to St. Luke's Hospital in 1929, beginning a long partnership with that institution.

He conceived the idea of the Cleveland Health Education Museum and took a leading role its establishment. The museum was incorporated in 1936 and opened in 1940, and Taylor served as its president until his death. He also became director of medicine at St. Luke's Hospital in 1945. Taylor served on the editorial staff of the *Cleveland Medical Journal* in 1916.

Taylor married Marion Kuykendall on 6 July 1917 in Washington, DC; they were divorced in 1933. On 2 Feb. 1934 in Erie, PA, he married Hilda Leisy Warner, a divorcee, the daughter of brewer Otto Leisy. Taylor died in Pinehurst, NC, while on vacation, and was buried in Lake View Cemetery. He was survived by his wife.—D.R.


**TAYLOR, RICHARD S.** (21 Sept. 1934–29 May 1993), union leader and community activist, was born in Maybeury, WV, the son of Ralph and Ruby Taylor. He attended Elkhorn High School and served in the army before moving to Cleveland in the 1950s. Employed by WHITE MOTOR CORP.,† Taylor worked there until it closed in 1981, becoming a supervisor and also elected to the Executive Board of UAW Local 32 at the 79th St. plant. As a union leader, Taylor was vocal in his opposition to the last-minute changes in White's pension fund rules in 1982, which postponed workers' eligibility for the retirement benefits they had earned for as long as 20 years. In the 1980s he worked for Nationwise Auto Parts and later in the Division of Clerks at Cleveland Municipal Court. Taylor also was a neighborhood activist serving as a spokesman for Citizens Opposing Prison Site (COPS) which helped persuade the state to drop its plan to build a prison at the former Fisher Body plant on Coit Rd.

Taylor married Margie Collins in the 1950s; they had 3 children: Kenneth, Marilyn, and Aleta. A resident of Cleveland, he died at MERIDIA HURON† hospital and was buried at Highland Park Cemetery.—M.S.

**TAYLOR, SOPHIA ELIZABETH STRONG** (5 May 1861–25 Sept. 1936) was principal owner of the WILLIAM TAYLOR SON & CO.† department store from 1892 until her death. She was also known for her philanthropies, including St. Luke's Convalescent Home and missionary activities of the Presbyterian church.

Born in Mexico, MO, to Charles and Elizabeth Roe Strong, Mrs. Taylor moved to Cleveland as a child, being educated through private schools and tutors. She married John Livingstone Taylor, president of Taylor's department store, on 30 April 1890. When Taylor died in 1892, Sophia inherited the business.

In 1902 William Taylor Son & Co. was incorporated, with Mrs. Taylor serving as president until 1935, when she became chairwoman of the board. In business, Mrs. Taylor was considered a progressive who modernized operations. Under her leadership Taylor's moved to 630 Euclid Ave. and expanded greatly.

Choosing not to remarry and having no children, Mrs. Taylor divided her time between the store and her philanthropic interests. Deeply religious, her charitable instincts led to the creation of St. Luke's Convalescent Home, a private children's hospital located on her Bratenahl estate in 1924.

Viewing her employees as "family," she spent many hours out in the store getting to know them. She turned over one of her homes as an employees' summer retreat and often lent money in times of need. They returned her generosity with unswerving loyalty and commitment to maintain the store's high quality. The store observed her death by closing its doors the day she was buried in Lake View Cemetery.—T.B.

**TEBELAK, JOHN MICHAEL** (17 Sept. 1949–2 Apr. 1985), composer of the musical *Godspell,* was born in Berea to John and Genevieve Tebelak. At age 9 he was active in the Berea Summer Theater. A choirboy at TRINITY CATHEDRAL,† he was fascinated with the pageantry and drama of religion. At 21, he directed productions of *Macbeth* and *Cabaret.* He later attended Carnegie-Mellon Univ. in Pittsburgh, where he wrote *Godspell,* a musical based upon the Gospel according to St. Matthew. With music by Stephen Schwartz, *Godspell* was first produced in 1971 by the Cafe La Mama in New York City. The show moved to off-Broadway and won the Natl. Theater Conference Award for best production and several honors from *Variety*'s 2nd annual poll of New York drama critics. Leonard Bernstein later consulted with Tebelak for a presentation of the musical mass *Godspell,* and it opened at the John F. Kennedy Ctr. for the Performing Arts in Washington, DC. Tebelak conducted its opening at Cleveland's Great Lakes Shakespeare Festival, then the show moved to Broadway and thereafter became the basis of a movie. Even though Tebelak stated he loathed organized religion because it "missed the point," he became a postulant in the Episcopal church in 1978. He was also dramatist in residence at the Cathedral of St. John the Divine in New York City and staged several plays, including his own about the American hostages in Iran in 1979–81. In 1981 Tebelak dropped out of seminary and began full-time theater work again. He never married.

**TELLO, MANLY** (25 Feb. 1842–4 Apr. 1905), lawyer and editor of the *Catholic Universe,* was born to Don John and Jane (Manly) Tello in Porto Santo, Madeira, Spain. He was educated at Holy Cross College in Worcester, MA, and St. Charles Seminary in Maryland, and served in the Confederate Army until his capture by Union forces while carrying secret dispatches. He later escaped from Rock Island prison camp and fled to Canada. After the war Tello practiced law in Louisville, KY, until offered the editorship of the *North West Chronicle,* a Catholic newspaper in St. Paul, MN. His work attracted the attention of Bp. RICHARD GILMOUR, who brought him to Cleveland in 1877 to assume the editorial management of the *Catholic Universe* (see CATHOLIC UNIVERSE BULLETIN†), which he managed until after Gilmour's death in 1892. As a mouthpiece of the church hierarchy, Tello enlarged the *Universe* and it became one of the most influential Catholic papers in the country. The *Universe* was not a financial success under Tello, who was known more for his literary sense than for his business acumen. He was also criticized, even by Bishop Gilmour, for occasionally using the paper to promote Southern interests. In an attempt to broaden the paper's appeal, Tello introduced baseball coverage, which caused some controversy. For his outspoken views, Tello, even within the diocese, attracted as much negative attention as positive. Tello spent the remaining 13 years of his life practicing law in Cleveland.

Tello married twice. His first marriage was in 1866 to Rowena Scales. They had 5 children: John, Hortense, Albert, Rosemary, and Agnes. After Scales's death, Tello married Anna Boylan in 1890; they had a daughter, Eulalia. Tello died in Cleveland and was buried in Calvary Cemetery.

**TENESY, ROSE L. GERAK** (19 June 1890–16 Aug. 1992), who claimed to have voted in every election since women gained the franchise in 1920, was the first woman ward leader for the CUYAHOGA COUNTY DEMOCRATIC PARTY† (1920–40). As state committeewoman from the 21st District, she helped form the Federated Democratic Women of Ohio (1932), presided over the organization for 18 years and was honored by it in February 1992 for her continuous service. Tenesy was born in Cleveland to John and Julia Matowitz Gerak. Her father, a manager of the Landisman-Hersheimer factory, did not believe in educating women and forced Tenesy to quit school and work in the factory after the third grade.

Tenesy married George S. Tenesy (d. 1948) on 3 July 1907 and managed a store to help him through law school. He later became a Cleveland Municipal Court judge. The couple lived in Cleveland with their son, George W. Tenesy ran unsuccessfully for state representative in 1948 and again in 1950. Her campaign platform included the elimination of sales tax. In other activities, she was district leader of the AMERICAN RED CROSS, CLEVELAND CHAPTER,† worked with the Community Fund, served as president of the Women's Slovak Club for 27 years, and belonged to FIRST CATHOLIC SLOVAK LADIES ASSN. OF THE USA AND CANADA† and St. Benedict Catholic Church, Cleveland. She helped raise the funds to build the VILLA SANCTA ANNA HOME,† where she died. Tenesy is buried in Calvary Cemetery.—J.M.

**THAYER, LYMAN C.** (11 June 1821–23 Dec. 1863), attorney and volunteer cavalry officer, was born in Berkshire, MA, son of Daniel and Mary Thayer. He was admitted to the bar in 1845, and became a well-known attorney in Boston. Moving to Cleveland in 1853, he formed a partnership in law with Geo. H. Wyman, with whom he was affiliated until 1856, when he formed a partnership with David Kellogg Cartter. After the outbreak of the Civil War, Thayer enlisted in the 2ND OHIO VOLUNTEER CAVALRY on 19 Aug. 1861. He served as regimental quartermaster during campaigns in Missouri, Kansas, and the Indian Territory before resigning because of ill health on 22 Mar. 1862. Once recuperated, he was commissioned a major in the 10TH OHIO VOLUNTEER CAVALRY† on 10 Nov. 1862 at Camp Cleveland. Ill health again beset Thayer while he was campaigning in Tennessee. After a medical furlough, he returned to Tennessee, only to resign because of ill health on 6 Oct. 1863, returned to Cleveland, and succumbed to pleurisy at his residence. On 26 Dec. 1863, the Cleveland Bar held a meeting at which appropriate resolutions were passed and speeches read in Thayer's honor. Thayer and his wife, Elisa, had 4 children: James L., Daniel R., Joseph L., and

Nelly A. Thayer died in Cleveland and was buried in Woodland Cemetery.

---

Proctor Thayer Papers, WRHS.

**THAYER, RICHARD N.** (5 June 1907–27 March 1992), leading engineer in the development of fluorescent lighting, was born in Pittsburgh, the son of Horace and Abbie Lincoln Thayer. He attended high school in Scranton, PA, and graduated from the Univ. of Pittsburgh in 1928. After graduation, he came to Cleveland to work for General Electric Lamp Division at NELA PARK.† Thayer participated in the research and development of a tubular electric lamp with a synthetic fluorescent coating on its inner surface. The lamp depended on mercury vapor to generate ultraviolet energy, which was converted into white or colored light by the fluorescent coating. An experimental lamp was first shown to the public in 1935, and commercial fluorescent lighting was introduced in 1938. The long-lasting, low voltage lamp adapted easily to existing electrical wiring and was widely used in factories, offices, stores, public buildings, and homes. Thayer held seven patents on the lamps as further improvements continued to be made, and he was the author of several articles on their development. He retired as manager of fluorescent engineering in 1969.

Thayer married Leona Falce 14 Feb. 1931; they had 3 daughters: June Murany, Marilyn Warber, and Nancy Preston. A resident of MAYFIELD HTS.,† he was buried at Lake View Cemetery. —M.S.

**THIEME, AUGUST** (1823–15 Dec. 1879) edited Cleveland's principal German-language newspaper, the *Waechter am Erie* (see *WAECHTER UND ANZEIGER†*) for more than a quarter of a century. Born in Saxony, he received a doctorate from a German university and participated in the abortive Revolution of 1848 as a member of a rump parliament in Stuttgart. Forced into exile upon the suppression of the revolution, he spent a year writing for German newspapers in Switzerland before emigrating in 1849 to the U.S. After 2 years in Buffalo, he was invited to Cleveland in 1852 to edit the newly founded *Waechter am Erie*. Within a year Thieme purchased the weekly himself and over the years nurtured it into a prosperous daily. As a confirmed liberal, he supported the Republican cause before the Civil War but turned against the regular party during the Grant era. He was an accomplished speaker, recognized as a leader of the city's progressive German element. Thieme's love of music was manifested in his enthusiastic support of the CLEVELAND VOCAL SOCIETY.† He was elected in 1871 to serve on the first Board of Managers of the Public School Library (see CLEVELAND PUBLIC LIBRARY†). Partially incapacitated from a stroke during the last 3 years of his life, Thieme was survived by his wife, Pauline (Schmidt), whom he married on 17 Nov. 1853, and 2 children, Bertha and Walter.—J.V.

**THOME, JAMES A.** (20 Jan. 1813–4 Mar. 1873), Presbyterian minister and antislavery activist, was born in Augusta, KY, son of Arthur and Mary Armstrong Thome. His father was a slaveowner and when Thome attended college in Augusta, in 1833 and entered into Lane Seminary in Cincinnati, he was influenced by abolitionists and ousted from the seminary for his extreme views. From 1835–36 he studied at Oberlin, received a degree in theology, and in 1836 became involved with the American Anti-Slavery Society, sent by its officers on a 6-month tour of the West Indies to report on emancipation there. The society published an account of his travels in 1838. In 1840 Thome jointly authored a paper, "Slavery and the Internal Trade in the United States," submitted to the General Anti-Slavery Convention in London. From 1838–48 Thome filled the chair of rhetoric and belles lettres at Oberlin College.

Thome was minister of First Presbyterian Church of Brooklyn (Ohio City) from 1848–71, where he continued in the antislavery movement and raised funds for black education. In 1867 he took a year-long sabbatical to go to England to seek aid from benevolent societies to help freed slaves. Thome's church united with Congregationalists in 1857 and became First Congregational Church of Cleveland. He resigned as minister in 1871, a few years later dying of pneumonia in Chattanooga, TN, where he had gone to continue his ministry. He married Anna S. Allen in 1838; they had three daughters: Mary Elizabeth, Anna Bradford, and Maria Ellen.

**THOMPSON, CHARLES EDWIN** (16 July 1870–4 Oct. 1933), automotive pioneer whose Thompson Valve made high-powered automobile and aircraft engines possible, was born in McIndoe Falls, VT, to Thomas and Mary Ann Young Thompson, attended Boston Preparatory School, and came to Cleveland in 1892 as inspector and branch manager for Cleveland Telephone Co. In 1898 he became district manager with Bell Co. in Dallas, but returned to Cleveland in 1900. In 1901 Thompson helped organize Cleveland Cap Screw Co., becoming general manager in 1905 when it became Electric Welding Prods. Co., welding automobile chassis and bicycle parts. In 1916 Electric Welding merged with 2 Detroit firms to form Steel Prods. Co. Thompson helped solve a major problem with early automobile engines, creating valves that could withstand tremendous stress by electrically welding the head to the stem. In 1917 he developed a solid 1-piece valve from steel alloy; and in 1920 he fabricated a high-resistance valve from a chromium, nickel, and silicon alloy, so that soon almost all American cars used Thompson Valves. In 1926 the company name changed to Thompson Prods. (see TRW INC.†). In 1929 Thompson began sponsoring the Thompson Trophy Race at the NATL. AIR RACES.† Thompson married Maora Hubbard (d. 1900) in 1889, Alberta Brown in 1919 (div. 1927), and Gloria Hayes Hopkins in 1927. He had 6 children: Edwin, Howard, Kenneth, Thomas, LaRene, and Mrs. Philip Farley. Thompson's body was cremated and his ashes released over PUBLIC SQUARE† from a plane piloted by Jas. Doolittle.

TRW Records, WRHS.

**THOMPSON, DONALD SCOUGALL** (27 March 1899–16 May 1994) achieved national repute in both the field of statistics and the sport of fencing. The son of Fred and Marion Scougall Thompson, he was born in Kansas City, MO, and reared in the Philippines, where his father was working with the U.S. Army. After service in the U.S. Navy during World War I, he earned bachelor's and master's degrees in business and foreign trade at the Univ. of California and married the former Esther Gilkey. He worked as a statistician for the Federal Reserve Bank of San Francisco and the Silberlingt Research Corp. in California. During the 1930s he was an economist for the Federal Reserve Board and the Federal Deposit Insurance Corp. in Washington. From 1944–46 he was director of the Urban Real Estate Finance Project of the National Bureau of Economic Research in New York. Thompson came to Cleveland in 1946 as a vice-president and general economist for the FEDERAL RESERVE BANK OF CLEVELAND† and became the district bank's first vice-president in 1953. The author of numerous articles on statistics and economics, he was elected a fellow of the American Statistical Assn. in 1950. He was also a trustee of the REAL PROPERTY INVENTORY OF METROPOLITAN CLEVELAND† and the CLEVELAND COUNCIL ON WORLD AFFAIRS.†

A former college fencer, Thompson returned to the sport when his son made the American Olympic fencing team in 1948. The elder Thompson became part of a northern Ohio epee team that won the national dueling sword championship in 1952, marking the first time in 47 years that the trophy had left New York or Boston. He was elected president of the Amateur Fencers' League of America in 1957 and inducted into the CLEVELAND SPORTS HALL OF FAME.† Thompson retired from the Federal Reserve in the 1960s and moved from his home in SHAKER HTS.† to Illinois in 1987. He died in Glenview, IL, survived by his son, Donald, and a daughter, Abigail Sbarge.—J.V.

**THORMAN, SIMSON** (1811–12 June 1881), businessman and the first permanent Jewish resident of Cleveland, was born in Unsleben, Bavaria, emigrated to the U.S. by the late 1820s, passed through Cleveland in 1832, purchasing land at Erie (E. 9th) and Woodland, then went to Donaphin, MO, where he was a trapper and purchased land. Thorman returned to Cleveland in 1837, settling in the FLATS† and continuing in the hide and fur business, making periodic trips to St. Louis to purchase pelts from trappers and Indians. Although he remained in this business until his retirement, he also owned a grocery for a time, and in the late 1850s owned a cattleyard and slaughterhouse. In 1839 several friends and acquaintances from Unsleben settled in Cleveland and Thorman and his cousins Aaron Lowentritt and Isaac Hoffman established the Israelitic Society of Cleveland, the city's first Jewish congregation. The following year, Thorman was an incorporator of WILLETT ST. CEMETERY,† the city's first Jewish burial ground, which he gave to the city. He was a founder and first president (1853–59) of the Solomon Lodge No. 6 of B'NAI B'RITH,† the first chapter of B'nai B'rith in Cleveland. In 1867 he served 1 term on CLEVELAND CITY COUNCIL.† Thorman married Regina Klein (1816–85) in 1840, the first Jewish marriage in the city. That same year a son, Samuel, was born, the first Jewish child born in Cleveland. In all, the Thormans had 11 children: Samuel, Esther, Elizabeth, Laura, Rebecca, Fanny, Abraham, Judy, Frank, Simon, and a son who died in infancy.

Simson Thorman Family Papers, WRHS.

**THORNTON, WILLIS** (10 March 1900–20 May 1965) experienced a varied career as a journalist, historian, and editor. A native Clevelander, he was raised in Akron, where his father, Willis, was business manager of the *Akron Press*, a Scripps-McRae newspaper (see EDWARD WILLIS SCRIPPS†). After graduating from Adelbert College (see CASE WESTERN RESERVE UNIV.†) in 1921, the younger Thornton himself joined what had become Scripps-Howard, working for the *CLEVELAND PRESS†* and then the *Washington Daily News*, where he became city editor. In 1930 he moved to the Scripps-Howard feature service, Newspaper Enterprise Assn., working both in the New York office as bureau manager and in the Cleveland office as writer and editor. During World War II he enlisted in the army as a private, serving with a prisoner of war interrogation unit in Europe and returning as a captain. From 1945–58 he worked as an associate editor based in Cleveland for Greenburg: Publisher of New York. In the meantime he earned a master's in history from WRU and lectured there in journalism and American history. Among Thornton's books were *The Third Term Issue* (1939), *Almanac for Americans* (1941), *Fable, Fact and History* (1957), and *The Liberation of Paris* (1962). In 1959 he was appointed director of the newly reorganized Press of Western Reserve Univ., a position he held until his death from a heart attack in his SHAKER HTS.† home. He was survived by his wife (see EUGENIA THORNTON-SILVER†), a fellow book lover whom he had married in 1935.—J.V.

**THORNTON-SILVER, EUGENIA** (31 July 1916–10 March 1992) was a well known Cleveland book reviewer and lecturer. Born in Chicago to Eugenia (Huestin) and Thomas MacKrennan, she was raised in Kinsman, OH, and attended Lake Erie and Hiram colleges. After experience as a substitute English teacher, she conducted a Cleveland radio show called "People and Places in the News" during World War II. She began writing book reviews for a newspaper syndicate and for the Cleveland *PLAIN DEALER.†* When public television came to Cleveland, she hosted a book program entitled "Eugenia" over WVIZ.† Her reviews were also a regular radio feature over WCLV-FM† for several decades ending in the 1980s. She appeared as a book lecturer under the auspices of the Friends of the CLEVELAND PUBLIC LIBRARY.† She was known professionally as Eugenia Thornton from her first marriage to WILLIS THORNTON, a writer and director of the Press of Western Reserve Univ. Following Thornton's death she married Dr. Francis F. Silver, a former Cuyahoga County health commissioner, on 10 Sept. 1966. The owner of an estimated 10,000 books, she could read up to two of them a day. A 1993 auction of ca. 4,000 of Thornton-Silver's books raised an estimated $55,000 for the Cleveland Public Library. She died in her BRATENAHL† home, survived by 3 stepchildren, Michael, Deborah, and Timothy. —J.V.

**THROCHMORTON, ARCHIBALD HALL** (28 Mar. 1876–20 May 1938), legal scholar and educator, was born in Loudon County, VA, to Mason and Annie Humphrey Throchmorton, spent much time in his father's justice of the peace courtroom, received an A.B. from Roanoke College (1896), an A.M. from Princeton Univ. (1897), and an LL.B. from Washington & Lee Univ. (1900), admitted to the Virginia Bar in 1900. From 1900–02 Throchmorton practiced law in Leesburg, VA; from 1902–

11 he was dean of Central Univ. of Kentucky in Danville; and from 1911–14 he was professor of law at Indiana Univ. From 1914 until his death, he was professor of law at Western Reserve Univ. Law School, teaching torts, constitutional law, and pleadings. Throchmorton's *Ohio General Code* (1921) became an authoritative text. As editor of *Cooley on Torts*, Throchmorton rewrote the original text of the legal classic. His other works included *Cases on Contracts* (1913), *Cases on Evidence* (1913), *Cases on Equity Jurisprudence* (1923), and *Cases on Code Pleadings* (1926). A strong advocate of individual liberties, Throchmorton frequently denounced what he saw as efforts to establish state socialism, feeling America needed more common sense, less legislative and bureaucratic interference, and more encouragement of individual initiative. Throchmorton was a member of the Cleveland Hts. Charter Commission in 1921, and served on the Cleveland Hts. Board of Health, as president of the Cleveland CITY CLUB† (1926), and as a director of Cleveland Hts. Savings & Loan Co. Throchmorton married Julia Elizabeth Painter in 1899. They had no children.

**THUNDERWATER, CHIEF. See CHIEF THUNDERWATER.**

**THWING, CHARLES FRANKLIN** (9 Nov. 1853–29 Aug. 1937), author, educator, and clergyman, was born in New Sharon, ME, to Joseph Perkins and Hanna Morse Hopkins Thwing, graduated from Harvard College (1876) and Andover Theological Seminary (1879), was ordained in 1879, and served as Congregationalist pastor of churches in Massachusetts (1879–86) and Minnesota (1886–90) before becoming president of Adelbert College and Western Reserve Univ. (see CASE WESTERN RESERVE UNIVERSITY†), inaugurated in 1891. During Thwing's 31-year administration, the schools of Library Science (1904), Applied Social Sciences (1916), Law, Dentistry, Pharmacy (1919), Education, the Graduate School (1892), and the Dept. of Religious Education became part of WRU; over 26 new buildings were erected; and instructors increased from 37 to 415. Thwing received many honorary degrees as well as the Cleveland Chamber of Commerce Medal for Distinguished Public Service (1925). He was a life senator of United Chapters of Phi Beta Kappa (national president 1922–28); and a trustee of CLEVELAND CLINIC,† HIRAM HOUSE,† and the Carnegie Foundation for the Advancement of Teaching (1905–21). Thwing resigned in 1921, becoming president emeritus. He published over 400 articles and 50 books. Thwing married Carrie F. Butler in 1879 and had 3 children: Mary Butler (Mrs. Jas. M.) Shallenberger, Francis Wendell Butler-Thwing, and Apphia (Mrs. Roy K.) Hack. Carrie died in 1898. In 1906 Thwing married Mary Gardiner Dunning, who became the first president of the WOMEN'S CITY CLUB† and a founder of the School of Nursing. Thwing died in Cleveland and was buried in Lake View Cemetery.

Cramer, Clarence H. *Case Western Reserve* (1976).

**TILLEY, MADISON** (1809–30 Oct. 1887), black political leader and businessman, was born in slavery, escaped to Ohio as a young man, and came to Cleveland ca. 1837, working as a boatman and teamster. According to his *PLAIN DEALER†* obituary, Tilley "obtained a fair education and accumulated considerable property" in Cleveland. By 1840 he was one of only 5 AFRICAN AMERICANS† in the city owning taxable property. He worked as an excavating contractor with 20 wagons, 40 horses, and an integrated workforce at times numbering 100 men. He acquired property in the Haymarket district and left an estate estimated at $25,000–$30,000. Although reportedly illiterate, Tilley became an aggressive leader in the city's black community, using his forceful personality and public-speaking ability to promote the value of the ballot to blacks. He changed political views several times during his career, beginning as a Whig, later becoming a Republican, and finally switching to the Democratic party. He was one of the local delegates to the 1854 NATL. EMIGRATION CONVENTION† held in Cleveland.

By the time Tilley died at his Hill St. home after a long bout with dropsy, he had gained the respect of both blacks and whites. The *CLEVELAND GAZETTE†* noted the "vast attendance of both white and colored" at his funeral, while the *Plain Dealer* praised him as "a man of unusual force of character, of rare judgement, and of great moral courage." Tilley and his wife, Rachel (d. 1879), had 6 children: Alexander, Hattie, Alice, Thomas, Mary, and Josephine. Tilley was buried in the Erie St. Cemetery.

**TITUS, SIGMUND ALEXANDER** (30 Jan. 1884– ca. 30 July 1936) was a lawyer involved in the affairs of Cleveland's Polish community. Born near Grodzisk, Poland, he was the son of Joseph and Leokadia Balczynska Titus. A product of the Berlin public schools, he graduated from Friedrich Werder College and studied at the Oriental Seminary in Berlin. He saw military service in Germany and served as editor of the *Berliner Lokal Anzeiger* and the *Hamburger Woehe* before emigrating to Cleveland in 1910. Joining Cleveland's flourishing ethnic journalism field, Titus edited the *Narodowiec Polish Weekly* from 1910–11 and *The Mediator,* a magazine on industrial efficiency, from 1911–18. Meanwhile he studied law at the CLEVELAND LAW SCHOOL,† the John Marshall Law School (see CLEVELAND STATE UNIV.†) and Northern Ohio Univ., being admitted to the bar in 1918. Titus married Elizabeth Landphair in Akron in 1921 and began a general law practice, becoming the senior member of Titus, Lombardo & Kovachy. He served as president of the Polish Educational Society and as attorney and director of the White Eagle Savings and Loan Assn. In 1931 he was appointed consular agent for Poland in Cleveland. He died apparently by suicide, of a gunshot wound, in his automobile near Van Wert, OH, being buried at Highland Park Cemetery and survived his wife and a brother, T. Paul Titus.—J.V.

**TOD, DAVID** (21 Feb. 1805–13 Nov. 1868), businessman and governor of Ohio, was born near Youngstown, OH, to George and Sarah (Isaacs) Tod. He attended Burton Academy in Geauga County, and after studying law in Warren, was admitted to the Ohio Bar in 1827, entering private practice. Tod was appointed postmaster in Warren in 1832; elected to the state senate in 1838; returned to private practice in 1840; and after being defeated for governor in 1844, started developing the coal and iron-ore deposits in the Mahoning Valley, shipping coal to Cleveland and other lake markets. In 1847 Tod became ambassador to Brazil, helping restore normal relations between the two countries and recovering American citizens' claims amounting to $300,000. In 1852 he returned home to Youngstown and his coal and iron interests, meanwhile serving as president of the Cleveland & Mahoning Railroad. Although a delegate to the 1860 Democratic Natl. Convention, Tod later supported Abraham Lincoln. With the Union party, Democrats and Republicans supporting the war effort, Tod won the Ohio governorship in 1862, when he moved his family to Cleveland. Tod spent most of his term dealing with problems of the Civil War. After leaving office in 1864, he returned to Youngstown to tend his business interests. Poor health forced him to decline Lincoln's offer of secretary of the treasury. Chosen a presidential elector in 1868, Tod died before the Electoral College selected the new president. He married Maria Smith in 1832 and had 7 children: John, Charlotte, Henry, George, William, Grace, and Sally. Tod died in Brier Hill, OH, and was buried there.

**TODD, THOMAS WINGATE** (15 Jan. 1885–28 Dec. 1938), professor of anatomy at Western Reserve Univ. Medical School, was born in Sheffield, England, to James and Katharine Wingate Todd,

448

and graduated with M.B. and Ch.B. degrees from Manchester Univ. and London Hospital in 1907. He served at Manchester as a junior and senior demonstrator of anatomy (1907–08), and lecturer on anatomy and clinical anatomy (1910–12); and at the Royal Infirmary as house surgeon and lecturer (1909). During World War I, Capt. Todd was surgical medical officer with the 110th Canadian Regiment base hospital in London, Ontario. Appointed Henry Wilson Payne Professor of Anatomy at WRU, Todd came to America in 1912. In 1920 he became director of the Hamann Museum of Comparative Anthropology & Anatomy. In teaching, Todd was an innovator, using roentgenology and fluoroscopy extensively, and devising a stereoscopic slide projector for his lectures. With the opening of new School of Medicine facilities in 1924, he created a modern anatomy department, including a medical librarian, statistician, medical illustrator, machinist, photographic staff, animal facilities, and embalmer. To the Hamann Museum, he added a curator and assembled a comprehensive osteologic collection, including the world's largest collections of anthropoid and documented human skeletons. He authored *The Atlas of Skeletal Maturation,* enabling doctors to determine the health and maturation of children by examining the bones of their hands. Todd married Eleanor Pearson in 1912 and had 3 children: Arthur, Donald, and Eleanor.

**TOOMEY, JOHN A.** (28 May 1889–1 Jan. 1950), physician and professor at Western Reserve Univ. Medical School, was born in Cleveland to Hugh and Mary Jane Burr Toomey, graduated from JOHN CARROLL UNIV.† with a B.A. in 1910 and M.A. in 1912, and from Cleveland Law School with an LL.B. in 1913. While in school he worked as asst. superintendent at MT. SINAI HOSPITAL† and steward at City Hospital. Admitted to the Ohio Bar in 1913, Toomey entered private practice but soon returned to school, graduating from WRU Medical School with an M.D. in 1919. While interning at City Hospital, he was appointed medical superintendent; when the hospital opened a ward for contagious diseases in 1924, he was placed in charge. At WRU, Toomey was demonstrator of anatomy and medicine (1920–22); instructor of pediatrics (1922–24); senior instructor in contagious diseases (1924–28); asst. professor of contagious diseases (1928–31) and pediatrics (1931–33); associate professor of pediatrics (1933–40); and professor of clinical pediatrics (1940–50). For poliomyelitis and the treatment of infantile paralysis, Toomey disliked using plaster casts, arguing that in polio treatment early detection and vigorous massage were vital. He was among the first to realize polio entered the body not

through the respiratory system but rather through the gastrointestinal tract. Toomey married Mary Louise Baget in 1918. After her death in 1947, he married Helen Katharine Toomey in 1949. Toomey had 4 children: Charles, John, Mary, and Francis.

**TORBENSEN, VIGGO V.** (28 Sept. 1858–4 Jan. 1947), pioneer in the automotive industry and founder of the Torbensen Axle Co. was born in Copenhagen, Denmark, the son of Hans W. and Marian (Peterson) Torbensen. He was educated in Danish public schools and studied engineering at the Naval Technical School, graduating in 1879. After 2 years as a machinist's apprentice and a year working in England, he came to America where he was employed by a succession of firms. In 1892 Torbensen traveled to Germany for further training. Returning to the U.S. in 1899, he designed and produced the first internal automobile gear drive used in this country while managing the DeDion-Bouton Motorette Co. of Brooklyn, NY. In 1912 he founded the Torbensen Gear & Axle Co. at Newark, NJ, and moved it to Cleveland in 1915, reincorporating it as the Torbensen Axle Co. with a capital of $1.75 million. By 1917 the company was generating an annual income of $6 million from the sales of 30,000 axles, most of them produced at its 4-acre plant on E. 152nd St. Torbensen axles equipped 1 out of every 3 trucks made in the U.S. The founder retired in the early 1920s, when the company was absorbed by the Eaton Axle Co.

He married Evelyn L. Smith of Philadelphia; they had 3 children: Allen, Clara U. (Mrs Charles J. Long), and Mrs. Margaret Rauchmiller. Torbensen's second wife was Gertrude Stritmater, whom he married 5 Aug. 1922. He died in Cleveland and was buried in Lake View Cemetery.—M.S.

**TOTH, JOHN, JR.** (7 Nov. 1897–8 Sept. 1960) was, for more than 23 years, a business representative of the International Assn. of Machinists. He held positions at the Chicago Pneumatic Tool Co. and the WARNER AND SWASEY CO.,† where he learned the machinist trade. As a member of the International Assn. of Machinists, he served on the policy committee of the national organization, was second in command in the local unit, District 54, and served as secretary-treasurer of the Ohio State Council of Machinists. During World War II, he served on the Labor Relations and Rationing Boards in Cleveland.

Toth was born in the village of St. Jakab in Abaj County, Hungary, to John Toth, Sr., and Katalin Abosi. He emigrated to the U.S. on 1 May 1912, settled in Cleveland and acquired his citizenship on 1 Dec. 1921. He attended Dubuque College in Iowa, and eventually returned to Cleveland where he earned a degree in Electrical Engineering at FENN COLLEGE.†

He married Julia Galambos on 14 Sept. 1919; they had four daughters: Edith, Dorothy, Eleanor, and Charlotte. Toth was a member of the Christian Reformed Church in Cleveland. He is buried in Fairview Cemetery in Boston Hts., OH.—M.S.

**TOWLE, JOHN R.** (19 Oct. 1924–21 Sept. 1944), Congressional Medal of Honor winner for service in World War II, was the son of William J. and Mary Simpkins Towle. One of 4 children, he grew up on E. 73rd St. in Cleveland, and as a boy attended St. Agnes school. He joined the army in March 1943, becoming a member of the 504th Parachute Infantry Regiment, of the 82nd Airborne Division and served in North Africa, Italy, and the European Theater of Operations. Pvt. Towle single-handedly defeated a tank-supported German infantry counterattack at Osterhout, Holland, 21 Sept. 1944, and was posthumously awarded the Medal of Honor. He was 19 years old.

Major General C. L. Scott presented the medal to Towle's parents at a ceremony at Ft. Knox, KY, in March 1945 and his body was buried in Calvary Cemetery in Cleveland 23 Jan. 1949; Major General James A. Gavin, wartime commander of the 82nd Airborne spoke at the interment. Several facilities at Ft. Bragg, NC, were named in his honor. Towle was survived by his parents, a brother, Thomas R., and sisters Edith Ryan and Joanne Chessar.

**TOWNES, CLAYTON C.** (30 Jan. 1888 [1887?]–24 Feb. 1970), president of city council and first mayor of Cleveland under the CITY MANAGER PLAN,† was born in Cleveland to Wm. C. and Kate Hoyt Townes, received his LL.D. degree from Western Reserve Univ. Law School in 1911, and that same year took over his father's seat in city council when his father died. Although he lost the seat in the next election, Townes was elected to council as a Republican 2 years later and served 6 terms, 4 of them as its president. When the City Manager Plan went into effect in Jan. 1924, Townes, as council president, became mayor. He resigned as mayor in 1925 and resumed his law practice as a partner in Townes & Portmann. He married Grace Dix in 1917 and had 3 children: Betsy Townes Abbey, Jean Townes Weaver, and Rachel Townes Hale. After his wife's death in 1932, he married Rose Bud. He moved to Florida in the 1930s, where he died.

**TOWNSEND, AMOS** (1819–17 Mar. 1895), businessman and politician, was born in Brownsville, PA, and attended school until age 15, when he became a clerk in a Pittsburgh retail establishment. At 19 he moved to Mansfield, forming the mercan-

tile business partnership of A. Townsend & Co. with N. D. Hogg, which lasted 5 years, until the partnership dissolved and the business closed. When violence over slavery erupted in Kansas, the U.S. House of Representatives appointed a special committee to visit the area, investigate, and report. Townsend accompanied the committee as marshal, a position he filled in a manner that gained him the respect of all parties.

Townsend arrived in Cleveland in 1858, accepting a position with Gordon, McMillan & Co., wholesale grocers, where he remained until 1861, when he became a junior partner in the wholesale grocery firm of Edwards, Iddings & Co. When Iddings died in 1862, the firm became Edwards, Townsend & Co., establishing an extensive business and reputation for stability and enterprise. During the Civil War, Townsend served with the 1ST OHIO VOLUNTEER LIGHT ARTILLERY.† Elected to CLEVELAND CITY COUNCIL† in 1866, Townsend served 10 years, the last 7 as president. In 1873 he was a member of the state constitutional convention; in 1876, 1878, and 1880 he won election to Congress, serving on the Post Offices & Post Rds., and Commerce Committees, and securing passage of large appropriations to build the Cleveland breakwater. Unmarried and childless, Townsend died in St. Augustine, FL, and was buried in Lake View Cemetery.

Amos Townsend Papers, WRHS.

**TOWSLEE, LILLIAN GERTRUDE, M.D.** (4 Dec. 1859–22 April 1918), lectured, published, and designed and invested in real estate while maintaining an active medical practice. She helped found Woman's Hospital (see WOMAN'S GENERAL HOSPITAL†), and, as its second president (1916–18), succeeded MARTHA CANFIELD. Towslee was born in Lodi, OH, to Maria Pollock Towslee and George Washington Towslee. She attended Lodi Academy and graduated from Oberlin College Conservatory of Music (1882). She taught music while studying medicine at Wooster Univ. (Cleveland); she graduated in 1888. After postgraduate work in New York City, Towslee opened a general practice in Cleveland. She specialized in gynecology, which she taught first at Wooster Medical School (beginning in 1889) and later at the College of Physicians and Surgeons of Ohio Wesleyan Univ. Towslee, gynecology editor of the *Woman's Medical Journal* (1897–1903), also lectured on hygiene at the forerunner of Flora Stone Mather College of Western Reserve Univ. (later CASE WESTERN RESERVE UNIV.†) and at the Schauffler Missionary Training School (see SCHAUFFLER COLLEGE OF RELIGIOUS AND SOCIAL WORK†). She served on the staff of

Cleveland General Hospital and chaired the advisory board of the Training School for Nurses of City Hospital.

Towslee was a charter member of the ACADEMY OF MEDICINE OF CLEVELAND,† a trustee of the CLEVELAND MEDICAL LIBRARY ASSN.† (1898–1900), and an active member of CALVARY PRESBYTERIAN CHURCH.† She served as president of the women's league of the CUYAHOGA COUNTY REPUBLICAN PARTY† and of the Health Protective Assn. Towslee, a single woman, lived with companion Mrs. Katherine D. Arthur and an adopted son, George Arthur Towslee, in a home on Carnegie Ave. which she designed and had built in 1895.—J.M.

**TRACY, FLORENCE COMEY** (20 Dec. 1886–13 June 1974), welfare volunteer, received a citation from the Friends of UNIV. HOSPITALS† for her voluntary service. Born to Nancy Gill and George Preston Comey of Cleveland, Tracy graduated from HATHAWAY BROWN SCHOOL† and attended the CLEVELAND INSTITUTE OF ART.† Tracy concentrated her volunteer activities in health and welfare (see WELFARE/RELIEF†). She served on the board of MacDonald House of Univ. Hospitals, as a director of the CLEVELAND SOCIETY FOR THE BLIND,† and was a life member of the Family Services Assn. Tracy was an early member of the JUNIOR LEAGUE OF CLEVELAND, INC.† An avid gardener, she served as treasurer of the Garden Center of Greater Cleveland (see CLEVELAND BOTANICAL GARDENS†) and was active in other local gardening associations.

On 8 June 1912 Tracy married JAMES JARED TRACY, JR. The couple lived in SHAKER HTS.† with son James J. and daughters Barbara (Mrs. Webster) Sandford, Clara (Mrs. David R.) Upson, and Ann (Mrs. Frank) Carvell. Tracy is buried in Lake View Cemetery.—J.M.

**TRACY, JAMES JARED, JR.** (27 Feb. 1884–16 May 1950), machine designer and manufacturer, held at least 28 U.S. patents for engines, hat production machinery, and carburetors and other accessories for the AUTOMOTIVE INDUSTRY,† among other inventions. Born in Cleveland to JANE ALLYN FOOTE TRACY and JAMES JARED TRACY, SR., Tracy attended Rockwell public school and summered with his family in New London, NH. After graduating from UNIV. SCHOOL† (1903) and Harvard Univ. (B.A. 1907), he worked for WHITE MOTOR CORP.† before entering the field of machine design full-time. He did postgraduate study in mechanical engineering at Harvard. After 1923 Tracy also managed his father's extensive real estate holdings. In this capacity he presided

over the Apartment House and Home Owners Assn. He also served as director of the F. H. Hill Co. (later the Hill Casket Co.) and trustee of the Euclid Ave. Assn.

On 8 June 1912 Tracy married FLORENCE COMEY TRACY of Cleveland. The couple lived in SHAKER HTS.† with son James J. and daughters Barbara (Mrs. Webster) Sandford, Clara (Mrs. David R.) Upson, and Ann (Mrs. Frank) Carvell. Active in civic affairs, Tracy was a life member of the FAMILY SERVICES ASSN.,† a trustee of UNIV. HOSPITALS,† and a member of the Chamber of Commerce of EAST CLEVELAND.† A Republican and a Presbyterian, he belonged to the CHURCH OF THE COVENANT† and the Mayflower and New England societies. Tracy is buried in Lake View Cemetery.—J.M.

**TRACY, JAMES JARED, SR.** (3 Dec. 1819–4 Jan. 1910), banker and civic leader, was born in Lansingburg, NY, and came to Cleveland in 1836, where he was employed by the COMMERCIAL BANK OF LAKE ERIE.† After it collapsed in 1842, Tracy became teller of the Commercial Branch Bank (org. 1845) and remained there for 15 years. Over time he acquired substantial property, including business blocks in the heart of the city. Tracy was an original member of the "Arkites," an informal group organized by William and his brother, Leonard, Case, who were interested in natural science, whist, chess, and the promotion of Cleveland's cultural institutions. He also was an incorporator of Case School of Applied Science in March 1880 and served on its first Board of Trustees.

Tracy married JANE ALLYN FOOTE 25 April 1883; they had two children, JAMES JARED, JR. and Catherine Wallace Tracy. He died after a fall at his home in Cleveland and was buried in Lake View Cemetery.—M.S.

**TRACY, JANE ALLYN FOOTE** (8 Nov. 1857–5 Aug. 1944), founded and served as a trustee for educational, medical, and arts organizations in Cleveland and elsewhere. Born in Detroit, MI, to Phoebe Dwight and George Foote, she moved to Cleveland with her sister and brother-in-law, Mr. and Mrs. George A. Stanley, and attended the CLEVELAND FEMALE SEMINARY.† Tracy married JAMES J. TRACY 25 April 1883; they lived at 309 Euclid Ave., later the site of Sterling & Welch Co., and on Harcourt Dr.

Tracy served as one of the original members of the advisory committee of the College for Women, West. Reserve Univ. (1890), helped found the CLEVELAND DAY NURSERY AND FREE KINDERGARTEN ASSN.† (1894), and served as trustee of the Cleveland School of Art. She traveled extensively, including an around-the-world venture in 1911, and wrote and lectured on her experiences. Tracy became a Life Member of the CLEVELAND MUSEUM OF ART† in 1919 and a Fellow for Life in 1923.

Tracy summered in New London, NH, after 1890. There she served as the founding president of the New London Hospital and donated a community library, the Tracy Memorial Library (opened in 1926), in her husband's memory. Tracy died at her SHAKER HTS.† home and was buried in Lake View Cemetery. She was survived by two children, JAMES JARED, JR., and Catherine Tracy Wallace, 10 grandchildren, and 5 great-grandchildren.—J.M.

CWRU Archives, Flora Stone Mather College Advisory Committee papers.

**TRAVIS, PAUL B.** (2 Jan. 1891–23 Nov. 1975), artist and teacher, was born on a farm in Wellsville, Columbiana County, OH, to William M. and Elizabeth Bough Travis. He won an engineering scholarship to Washington & Jefferson College, but instead taught in the country school. He came to Cleveland and entered the Cleveland School of Art in 1913, graduating in 1917. He served a year with the American Expeditionary Forces in France, after the armistice spending 6 months teaching life drawing at the AEF Univ. in Beaune, France. Travis began teaching full-time at the Art Institute in 1920, continuing until his retirement in 1957; also teaching at John Huntington Polytechnic Institute. In 1927–28, Travis made a much-celebrated and widely publicized African expedition. The Gilpin Players (at KARAMU HOUSE†) and the African Art Sponsors, a group of black citizens interested in African art, financed his 7-month collecting and painting trip. The art and artifacts he collected were received by the CLEVELAND MUSEUM OF ART,† the CLEVELAND MUSEUM OF NATURAL HISTORY,† and Karamu House. This trip motivated Travis to prolific production. Travis was equally at ease with oil, watercolor, the etcher's needle, and the lithographer's crayon. He lectured at museums and universities and was a trustee of Goodrich House, Karamu, and the Cleveland Council on Human Relations. When the Museum of Art held its 52nd MAY SHOW† in 1971, Travis had exhibited and won regularly in every show. Travis married Marjorie Penfield on 4 Oct. 1925 and had a son, William P., and 2 daughters, Jane (Spangler) and Elizabeth (Dreyfuss).

Paul B. Travis Papers, WRHS.

**TRENKAMP, HERMAN J.** (27 Feb. 1865–27 May 1943), business leader, helped found the CATHO-

LIC CHARITIES CORP.† of Cleveland (1918) with Roman Catholic Bp. CHARLES LEBLOND and served as its vice-president and on its executive committee. He became honorary trustee for life in 1936. Trenkamp was born in Cleveland to Elizabeth Sutkamp and Henry Trenkamp, Sr., founder of the Trenkamp Stove Co. (est. as the Schneider and Trenkamp Co.). He followed his father's business path, organizing the American Stove Co. and running Trenkamp Stove with his brothers. Herman Trenkamp also served as director and secretary of another family company, the Ohio Foundry Co. (est. 1842).

Trenkamp married Catherine G. Miller; the couple lived in CLEVELAND HTS.† with children Henry J., Robert, Olga, and Gertrude (Mrs. George) Byrider. He is buried in Lake View Cemetery.—J.M.

**TREUHAFT, WILLIAM C.** (21 Oct. 1892–24 Dec. 1981), industrialist and civic leader, was born in Cleveland to Morris and Bertha Treuhaft. From 1910–14 he attended both Case Institute of Technology and Adelbert College in a 5-year engineering and humanities course, but left after 4 years to go into business. In 1916 he became president of Sterling Prods. Co., which consolidated with Arco Co. in 1927; Treuhaft was a vice-president. In 1928 Treuhaft formed his own company, Tremco Mfg. (see TREMCO, INC.†), where he was president until 1966, then chairman of the board until 1973.

Treuhaft's career of service began early. He played piano for teenage dances at ALTA HOUSE,† and in college worked at Camp Wise. He was president of Community Chest (1956, 1957) and United Appeal (see UNITED WAY†) campaigns (1966, 1967); was an officer in BLUE CROSS OF NORTHEAST OHIO,† MT. SINAI HOSPITAL,† and the JEWISH COMMUNITY FED.†; a trustee of CLEVELAND HEALTH MUSEUM† and president of the CLEVELAND MUSEUM OF ART.† He was also chairman of the board and an executive committee member of UNIV. CIRCLE, INC.† Treuhaft was a trustee of BALDWIN-WALLACE† and URSULINE† colleges and CASE WESTERN RESERVE UNIV.†; at CWRU in 1968 he endowed 2 chairs, 1 in the humanities and another in the school of management. In 1914 Treuhaft married Elizabeth Marting. They shared the 1950 Chas. Eisenman Award of the Jewish Welfare Fed. and the 1972 Natl. Human Relations Award of the Natl. Conference of Christians & Jews. They had no children.

**TROSKY (TROJOVSKY), HAROLD ARTHUR "HAL"** (11 Nov. 1912–18 June 1979), firstbaseman with over 200 home runs for the CLEVELAND INDIANS† (1933–41) was born in Mansay, IA, and signed to play baseball with the Cleveland Indians farm team at Cedar Rapids in 1931, after completing high school. By the fall of 1933, Trosky was a member of the Indians, hitting 33 home runs for Toledo that season. In a newspaper interview he remarked, "Out here [LEAGUE PARK†] I figure I can hit the wall at least once in a while." From 1934–39, Trosky hit on and over the wall as he averaged over 100 RBIs each season. His greatest year was 1936, when he hit safely in 28 consecutive games, drove in a team-record 162 runs, slugged 42 home runs, and had a batting average of .343. In games played on 30 May 1934 and 5 July 1937, Trosky hit 3 consecutive home runs. During the late 1930s, Trosky began suffering from migraine headaches; he did not play for the Indians after the 1941 season. He returned to baseball in 1944 with the Chicago White Sox, remained out of the game in 1945, and finally retired after playing 88 games for Chicago in 1946. In retirement, Trosky became a successful hog and dairy farmer. He married Lorraine Glenn in 1933 and had 4 children: Hal, Jr., James, Lynn, and Mary Kay. Hal, Jr., pitched during the 1958 season for the Chicago White Sox. Inducted into the Iowa Sports Hall of Fame, Trosky died in Cedar Rapids, IA.

TRUEMAN, JAMES R. (25 April 1935–11 June 1986) was the founder of the Red Roof motel chain as well as one of the nation's leading race car drivers, owners, and sponsors. A native of Cleveland, the son of George and Alma Trueman was raised in EUCLID.† He was a 1953 graduate of Benedictine High School, where he became an outstanding runner in cross country and track. His engineering studies at Ohio State Univ. were interrupted by service in the U.S. Army. He married Barbara Colucci of Dayton in 1961 and entered the construction business in Columbus. He also began driving race cars, winning 125 victories, including 2 Sports Car of America championships. Traveling the race car circuit demonstrated to Trueman the need for inexpensive lodgings, and he opened his first Red Roof Inn near Columbus in 1973. The chain grew to more than 100 units within a decade, and Trueman began to sponsor his own race cars and promising young drivers. He purchased the Mid-Ohio Sports Car Course in Lexington, Oh, and formed the TrueSports Indy Car team with driver Bobby Rahal. It won the first BUDWEISER-CLEVELAND 500† in 1982 and the Indianapolis 500 in 1986, only 11 days before Trueman's death from cancer in Columbus. Trueman was survived by his wife, son Colin, and daughters Michelle and Megan. He was the first inductee into the Benedictine High School Hall of Honors, and in 1994 the school

dedicated its renovated gym as the Trueman Memorial Fieldhouse in honor of him and his brother, Bill.—J.V.

TUCKER, BEVERLEY DANDRIDGE (4 Feb. 1882–4 July 1969), sixth bishop of the Episcopal Diocese of Ohio (1938–52) was born in Warsaw, VA, to Anna Maria (Washington) and Beverley Dandridge, an Episcopal clergyman. He received a B.A. from the Univ. of Virginia (1902); graduated from Virginia Theological Seminary (1905); and earned a B.A. (1908) and M.A. (1912) at Oxford Univ. as a Rhodes Scholar. Ordained a deacon (1908) and priest (1909), Tucker assumed rectorships in Virginia (1908–20, 1923–38) and a professorship at Virginia Theological Seminary (1920–23). In Virginia, and after becoming bishop in Cleveland, Tucker worked to improve interracial harmony and ecumenicalism, also fostering the interests of small churches while encouraging the development of schools, colleges, and welfare organizations. Tucker was on the Board of Trustees of Kenyon College, Lake Erie College, and Western Reserve Univ.

Tucker reversed a tradition allowing only Ohio rectors who had graduated from Bexley Hall seminary in Gambier, OH, thus allowing the recruitment of rectors with different backgrounds. He also made sure churches were established in the suburbs, to accommodate movement there from the city. He was president of the Cleveland Church Fed. (1947). His fundraising resulted in increasing diocesan giving to missions from $13,000 to $150,000 annually. He also helped achieve Bexley Hall's first accreditation by the American Assn. of Theological Seminaries. In July 1963, Tucker introduced Martin Luther King, Jr., to a Cleveland audience, comparing him favorably with Pope John XXIII.

Tucker married Eleanor Carson Lile in 1915; they had five children: Maud, (Rev.) Beverley D., Jr., Eleanor, Maria, and Louisa. He died in Cleveland and was buried in Charlottesville, VA.

Baker, Wallace J. *Bishops of Ohio, 1819–1968* (1968).

TUCKERMAN, JACOB E. (1876–27 Feb. 1967) was born in Austinburg, OH, son of Mary Ellen (Hopkins) and Dr. LOUIS B. TUCKERMAN, social reformer and an eminent physician. He received his medical degree in 1902 from the Cleveland College of Physicians & Surgeons, and interned at ST. ALEXIS.† While managing a growing private practice, he served many civic causes, including the 1913 Cleveland City Charter Commission, the CLEVELAND MEDICAL LIBRARY ASSN.,† and the Negro Welfare Assn. He was also active in local and national medical academies, president of the American Academy of Medicine (1917–18) and the Cleveland ACADEMY OF MEDICINE† after its incorporation in 1924. Eventually joining the staff of Euclid-Glenville Hospital, he was chief of surgery and chief of surgery emeritus for many years. Tuckerman, whose father, uncles, and brothers were doctors, raised a family of doctors and nurses, with interning at St. Alexis and working at Euclid-Glenville becoming a family tradition. He and his wife, Katherine (Barton), had six children: Jacob B., William D., Betty, Margaret, Warren, and Robert. Tuckerman, an accomplished figure skater to within 2 years of his death, was buried in Lake View Cemetery.

**TUCKERMAN, LOUIS BRYANT** (15 Feb. 1850–5 Mar. 1902), reformer dubbed the "Father of Cleveland Liberalism" by TOM L. JOHNSON, was born in Rome, Ashtabula County, OH, to Elizabeth Ellinwood and Jacob Tuckerman. He graduated from Amherst College, attended Yale Theological Seminary, and received his medical degree from Long Island in 1877. He organized the FRANKLIN CLUB,† where municipal affairs, public ownership of utilities, and public health were discussed. Tuckerman claimed the club, through its petitions and delegations to city officials, was responsible for progressive reforms; while their weekly discussions, reported in the *Citizen* and conservative dailies, spread their progressive message far beyond the club.

An idealist and moderate, Tuckerman promoted third-party campaigns of various working-class parties before supporting the Populist party in the 1890s (see POPULIST POLITICAL PARTIES†). In 1885 and 1889 he ran for local office, campaigning for better hospital facilities, more adequate health services, labor representation on the Police Board, public ownership of utilities, and an improved school system. Though he received few votes, he generated public interest in the issues.

Beginning in 1885, Tuckerman edited the *Workman*, a $.01 labor journal discussing important issues before the state legislature relating to labor, selling the paper after 3 years to devote more time to his medical practice; the paper collapsed a few months later. As a pioneer member of the Cleveland ACADEMY OF MEDICINE,† Tuckerman stirred up his colleagues on urban public-health issues, heading the organization's committee on legislation and lobbying in Columbus for public-health laws.

Tuckerman married Mary Ellen Hopkins and had four sons: Louis B., JACOB E., Warren H., and William C. He died of malaria and was buried in Lake View Cemetery.

**TURNBULL, RUPERT B., JR.** (3 Oct. 1913–18 Feb. 1981), surgeon, was born in Pasadena, CA, to Irene Archibald and Judge Rupert Turnbull. He received his undergraduate degree from Claremont College (1936), his medical degree from McGill Univ., Canada (1941), served at hospitals in San Francisco and the Panama Canal Zone, and was a field surgeon with the 1st Marine Div. in the Pacific. He came to Cleveland to complete his surgical training at CLEVELAND CLINIC,† and developed a surgical technique to make a stomach opening for the intestines (ileostomy/colostomy). Turnbull became the world's authority on ulcerative colitis and recognized the importance of postsurgical therapy for colostomy and ileostomy patients. As the "father of enterostomal therapy," Turnbull, along with Norman Gill, founded the world's first school of enterostomal therapy and the Internatl. Assn. of Enterostomal Therapists.

Turnbull published over 185 scientific articles, and along with Frank L. Weakey wrote the standard *Atlas of Intestinal Stomas*. He served on the editorial boards of various publications, including *Disease of the Colon and Rectum*. In 1976 the Rupert B. Turnbull Surgical Society was formed by former residents and fellows who had trained under him. Turnbull was head of the Dept. of Colon & Rectal Surgery at Cleveland Clinic until 1976, when he became senior surgeon. In 1978 he left Cleveland to take a position at Santa Barbara Medical Foundation in California. He was an active member of Christ Episcopal Church. Rupert married Dougal Isabel Fisher in 1938. The Turnbulls had 2 sons, Robert and John, and a daughter, Dae. Turnbull died while vacationing in Honolulu.

Rupert B. Turnbull Papers, Archives, Cleveland Clinic Foundation.

Cleveland Medical Society Bulletin (1976).

**TURNER, CARRIE STARK** (1 July 1901–14 Oct. 1992), social worker and lecturer, was the first Clevelander to be named Handicapped Citizen of the Year by the U.S. Department of Human Services (1980). She served as a social worker for the CLEVELAND SOCIETY FOR THE BLIND† (1941–67) and originated the Book Review Club of CLEVELAND PUBLIC LIBRARY.† Turner was born to Mary L. Perkins and Anderson Stark in Atlanta, GA, where she attended public school. She graduated from Tuskegee Institute in Alabama. A fall in 1928 damaged Turner's optic nerve; she was blind by 1930. Turner held positions with the Urban League in Pittsburgh, PA, and the PHILLIS WHEATLEY ASSN.† in Cleveland and volunteered for the Cleveland Society for the Blind for 9 years before joining its staff. She continued as part-time consultant after her retirement (1967). The American Assn. of Workers for the Blind awarded Turner the Distinguished Service Award in 1974; other organizations, such as the Urban League, the Phillis Wheatley Assn., and the United Appeal, also honored her.

Divorced, Turner lived independently in Cleveland. Despite her lack of sight, she traveled widely and pursued photography, publishing some photographs in *Ebony* magazine and the Cleveland *PLAIN DEALER.†* Turner died at the MARGARET WAGNER HOME† and is buried in Lake View Cemetery.—J.M.

**TURNER, JAMES K.** (6 May 1864–27 Sept. 1916), expert on industrial mediation and the labor questions of his time, was born in Chicago, son of James K. and Ellen (Brady) Turner. He received his early education in Athens, NY. In 1899 he came to Cleveland to continue his writing on the need for mediation and education to promote cooperation between capital and labor on a basis of equality and justice. Turner was a frequent contributor to *The Mediator,* a magazine founded in 1909 by C. B. Bartlett and H. G. Evans, owners of the Mediator Printery, and by 1911 Turner was both its editor and publisher. Topics discussed in the magazine included the divergent interests of financial and production people in industry, the need for old age pensions, and women's economic freedom. A forum section contained letters from its readers, presenting a variety of issues related to labor and capital. In addition, Turner published *Turner's Digest*—a summary of industrial progress throughout the world, aimed at businessmen—and translated *The Mediator* into Polish, Hungarian, and Italian to reach labor men in the growing ethnic communities. He also established the Mediator Lecture Lyceum. Although he resided in Cleveland, Turner maintained a country house and farm near Chardon, arranging outings where those interested in his ideas could discuss important industrial problems in a setting close to nature.

Turner married May Grace Schiffman of Milwaukee 22 Jan. 1896; they had two daughters, Norine Ellen and Nona May. He died at his home in Cleveland.—M.S.

**TURNER, RACHEL WALKER** (1868–12 Nov. 1943) was a black soprano who began her career in Cleveland and later toured the U.S. and Europe singing classical selections, as well as songs such as "The Last Rose of Summer" and "Swanee River." Rachel Walker, daughter to T. W. and M. L. (Lenyar) Walker, graduated from Cleveland's CENTRAL HIGH SCHOOL,† entered Cleveland Normal Training School, and became a teacher in 1889.

She taught in the city schools until sometime in the mid–1890s, when she went to study in New York, apparently after JOHN P. GREEN secured her financial assistance from JOHN D. ROCKEFELLER. In late 1895 or early 1896, she toured California as the prima donna of the Henry Wolfsohn Musical Bureau, and in July 1896 she made her debut as "the creole nightingale" in New York City at the Olympia Roof Garden, where the "unusual compass and excellent quality" of her voice made her "an extraordinary hit." A correspondent for the *CLEVELAND GAZETTE†* who saw her New York performance complained about her "palm[ing herself] off as a 'creole'" rather than stressing "the Afro-American connection." She later sang in Washington, DC, as a member of the Robt. Downing Co., then went to London to study and made frequent appearances in Europe. She remained in Europe until the outbreak of World War I, when she returned to Cleveland. On 27 June 1916 she married Robt. Turner. Although she made a few concert appearances, opportunities were few and her singing career came to an end.

**TUSSEY, RICHARD B.** (7 Nov. 1918–5 June 1981) was an ardent campaigner for liberal causes. A dedicated unionist, his motto was "to make life better for working people." Born to Jesse and Romaine Berlin Tussey in Pittsburgh, PA, Richard completed elementary and high school there, then pursued courses with various labor organizations. In 1938, inspired by the ideals of Eugene Debs, he became a member of the Socialist Labor Party.

In 1941 he married Viola Bencsis, with whom he had two daughters, Bonnie L. and Romaine. They were divorced and on 1 Aug. 1952, Tussey married Jean Yatrovsky Simon.

In 1941 Tussey came to Cleveland and joined the Industrial Workers of the World (IWW). After its dissolution, he joined the MECHANICS EDUCATIONAL SOCIETY OF AMERICA,† and then the Meat Cutters Union, which eventually merged to form the UNITED FOOD AND COMMERCIAL WORKERS† Union.

Tussey's life was unreservedly for the ideals of the political left. He was granted a deferment in World War II because he "could not fight a capitalist war." Arrested for challenging a Cleveland ban on public speaking in the city's parks, he won the case and the limitations were rescinded. In 1960 he traveled to Cuba with the Fair Play for Cuba committee, a visit that later saw him hauled before the U.S. Senate's Internal Security Committee. He fought for disarmament, an end to nuclear weapons, the equal rights amendment, and an end to discrimination in employment and housing. Stricken by cancer, Tussey willed his body to the CLEVELAND CLINIC

FOUNDATION.† His ashes were interred in his family's burial plot in Saltsburg, PA.—J.T.

Richard Tussey Papers, Wayne State University.

**TUTTLE, BLOODGOOD** (23 Jan.1889–23 Feb. 1936) made his reputation as an architect on the residences he designed for suburban SHAKER HTS.† in the 1920s. The son of Chicagoans Wiley F. and Frances Tuttle, he graduated from the Univ. of Chicago and studied architecture at the Beaux Arts in Paris. After launching his career in Detroit, he came to Cleveland in 1920. He designed 2 groups of demonstration homes for the VAN SWERINGEN brothers' planned suburb of Shaker Hts. Predominantly English and French revival in style, the 9 homes were built on Van Aken Blvd. in 1924. Tuttle eventually designed a total of 36 homes located in all sections of the suburb. Active in affairs of the AMERICAN INSTITUTE OF ARCHITECTS, CLEVELAND CHAPTER,† he devoted much of his efforts in the 1930s to writing and speaking in favor of home "renovization" as a means of promoting economic recovery. He died of a cerebral hemorrhage at MT. SINAI MEDICAL CTR.,† survived by his wife, Marie, son, Arthur B., and daughter, Marian Robinson. A display and walking tour of his work was organized by Shaker Hts. in 1984, to mark the bestowal of landmark status upon his Van Aken demonstration homes.—J.V.

**TYLER, ALICE S.** (27 Apr. 1859–18 Apr. 1944), librarian, began her career as the first professionally trained assistant at the CLEVELAND PUBLIC LIBRARY† (CPL), hired by WILLIAM HOWARD BRETT. She later served as the second director of the School of Library Science at Western Reserve Univ. (1913–29) and dean from 1925–29. She was also the third woman president of the American Library Assn. (ALA, 1920–21).

Descended from presidents James Monroe and John Tyler, Tyler was born in Decatur, IL, to John W. and Sarah Roney Tyler. She graduated from the Armour Institute of Technology (predecessor of the Illinois Library School) in Chicago in 1894 and was hired as head of CPL's Catalog Division the next year. In 1900 she left Ohio to serve as secretary of the Iowa State Library Commission (1900–13), director of the Iowa Summer Library School, State Univ. of Iowa (1901–12), and editor of the *Iowa Library Quarterly* (1901–13). She visited Cleveland regularly as lecturer at WRU and elsewhere.

Returning to Cleveland in 1913, first as director of WRU's Library School, then as dean, Tyler maintained her professional involvement, serving as president of the Assn. of American Library Schools (1918–19), the Ohio Library Assn., and the Cleveland Library Club (1922–23). Tyler actively supported suffrage for women, belonged to the local league of women voters and CITIZENS' LEAGUE,† and served as charter member and president of the WOMEN'S CITY CLUB.† The library school appointed her dean emeritus after her retirement on 13 June 1929. Unmarried, Tyler shared an apartment in the ALCAZAR HOTEL† with colleague Bessie Sargeant-Smith.—J.M.

Cramer, Clarence H. *The School of Library Science at WRU, 1904–1979* (1979).
Klyver, Richard D. *They Also Serve: 12 Biographies of Notable Cleveland Women* (1986).

**U**

URBAN, HELEN E. WILLIAMS (8 Nov. 1904–19 Dec. 1988), fundraiser for health causes, helped establish the HEALTH FUND OF GREATER CLEVELAND† (1959) and the SOUTH EUCLID HISTORICAL SOCIETY† (1966). Urban was born in Oil City, PA, to Dora Keltner and James B. Williams. She studied botany at Ohio Wesleyan Univ. Urban moved to SOUTH EUCLID† after her marriage on 14 Sept. 1929 to George Urban (mayor of his hometown, South Euclid, 1948–71); they had 5 children: Mark A., Alice Glady, James J., Joann Taylor, and Thomas. Urban was a life member of the South Euclid Historical Society, the Garden Club, the Women's Club, and the League of Women Voters in South Euclid. She also belonged to the City Hall Wives and served on many committees at the United Methodist Church of South Euclid. The couple moved to Clarion, PA, in 1971, following George Urban's retirement from public service and from the Northern Ohio Food Terminal. Helen Urban died in Franklin, PA, and is buried in Knollwood Cemetery in MAYFIELD HTS.†—J.M.

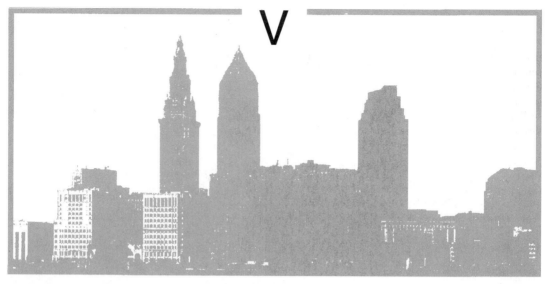

**VADNAL, FRANK L.** (24 July 1921–29 May 1995) belonged to a family quartet which became a leading exponent of Cleveland-style polka music (see POLKAS†). The native Clevelander, son of Anthony and Anna Kappus Vadnal, was a graduate of Collinwood High School. A banjo and guitar player as well as vocalist, he performed with the Vadnal Reveliers at the GREAT LAKES EXPOSITION† in 1937. Under the leadership of his brother, Johnny, he and his brother Tony and their sister Valeria formed the Vadnal Quartet, which was based at the Slovenian Workmen's Home. They toured regularly through Ohio, Michigan, and Illinois and broadcast over the Mutual radio network in the 1950s. From 1949–61 they also appeared on local television station WEWS† with "Vadnal's Polka Parade," "Polka Varieties," and "Old Dutch Polka Review." The family also toured in Europe, Mexico, and Hawaii. In addition to Anglicizing original Slovenian lyrics, Frank Vadnal composed such songs as "String-a-Ling" and "Happy Guitar." An Army Air Force veteran from World War II, he married the former Mary Volk in 1950 and worked most of his life at Addressograph-Multigraph (see AM INTERNATIONAL, INC.†). Inducted into the Cleveland-Style Polka Hall of Fame in 1993, he died in Seven Springs, PA, while appearing in the Seven Springs Polka Festival. He was survived by his wife and 2 sons, Frank L., Jr., and Carey.—J.V.

**VAIL, HARRY LORENZO** (11 Oct. 1860–27 Feb. 1935), journalist, lawyer, and politician, was born in Cleveland to Judge I. C. and Clara Van Husen Vail. At 19, Vail received his B.A. from Ohio Wesleyan and over the next 5 years studied law at intervals, being admitted to the bar in 1884, although he did not begin practicing until 1888. Following college, Vail worked for the *Cleveland Herald, Cincinnati*

*Enquirer,* and *Cincinnati Times,* where he was managing editor. In Cleveland, he was also city editor of the *SUNDAY VOICE,*† which, as the first Sunday paper in Cleveland, drew criticism from clergymen. In 1894 Vail became clerk of the Court of Common Pleas and circuit courts, a position he held until 1900. He was then a county commissioner (1904–13), helping initiate some of the city's largest public building projects, including the new courthouse and DETROIT-SUPERIOR BRIDGE.† In 1917 Mayor HARRY L. DAVIS appointed Vail secretary of the War Advisory Board, and in 1921 the governor appointed him to an advisory committee for the state's Div. of Americanization. Vail devoted his later life to real estate interests, as director of Lawmer Land Co. and vice-president of Warner Land Co. He continued to be active in the Republican party. Vail married Sarah Wickham, organizer of the Cleveland YWCA and a founder and president of the Cleveland Art Assn., on 18 Sept. 1894. They had one child, HERMAN LANSING VAIL.

Herman Lansing Vail Family Papers, WRHS.

**VAIL, HERMAN LANSING** (6 July 1895–7 Jan. 1981), lawyer and newspaper publisher, was born in Cleveland to Sarah A. Wickham and HARRY L. VAIL, earned an A.B. from Princeton Univ. in 1917 and an LL.B. from Harvard Univ. Law School in 1922, being admitted to the Ohio Bar in 1922. Vail was a partner in the law firm of Sayre, Vail, Steele & Renkert, and later senior partner in the firm of Vail, Steele, Howland & Olson. A lifelong Republican, Vail served 2 terms (1929–33) in the Ohio legislature, where he was chairman of the House Tax Committee; and in 1934 and 1935 was a member of the Ohio Special Joint Taxation Commission. He served on the BRATENAHL† Village Council from

1933–51, as president from 1940. Vail became involved in FOREST CITY PUBLISHING CO.,† publisher of the *PLAIN DEALER*,† as a trustee representing the Holden family. His first wife, Delia, was a granddaughter of LIBERTY E. HOLDEN, owner of the newspaper. In 1941 Vail was named a director of Forest City, and in 1962 he succeeded Stanley E. Graham as president, serving until 1970. He was also president of Art Gravure Corp. of Ohio. Vail was chairman of the NORTHERN OHIO OPERA ASSN.,† president of WESTERN RESERVE HISTORICAL SOCIETY,† the CITIZENS LEAGUE,† and the CLEVELAND COUNCIL ON WORLD AFFAIRS.† Vail married Delia B. White in 1922 and had 2 sons, Herman, Jr., and Thomas. Delia died in 1952. In 1965 Vail married Mary Louise Gleason.

Herman Lansing Vail Family Papers, WRHS.

**VAN AKEN, WILLIAM J.** (29 Oct. 1884–28 Dec. 1950), prominent real estate magnate and mayor of SHAKER HTS.† (1915–30, 1931–50) was born in E. Cleveland Twp. to John and Mary Dier Van Aken. He graduated from CENTRAL HIGH SCHOOL† in 1903, and immediately became an office boy for Natl. Malleable Castings Co, later rising to the position of accountant. In 1916 he entered the real estate profession, joining the firm of Green, Cadwallader & Long. Within the year, he left that firm and became an independent broker. In 1915 Van Aken, a Republican, became mayor of what was then the village of Shaker Hts., where he had previously served as trustee (1911) and councilman (1912). When the village became a chartered city in 1930, Van Aken became the first mayor of the city in the 1931, serving in that position until his death. Van Aken was active in many community organizations, including the Cleveland Chamber of Commerce and Knights of Columbus. He was also the director of the Cooperative Investment Co. Van Aken married Florence Swallow in 1911. The couple had 6 children: WILLIAM R., Florence M., Marion L., Jean M., Margaret L., and Ruth.

**VAN AKEN, WILLIAM RUSSELL** (1 Dec. 1912–28 Sept. 1993) was a lawyer and politician, president and trustee of the Ohio State Bar Foundation, cofounder of the National Conference of Bar Foundations, and author of books on Real Estate law and the history of the Ohio Bar.

Born in Cleveland to Florence (Swallow) and WILLIAM J. VAN AKEN, former mayor and head of one of Shaker Hts.' most influential political families, William graduated from Shaker Hts. High School (1930), and received his B.S. from LaFayette College (1934), and his LL.B. from WESTERN RESERVE UNIV.† Law College (1937). He passed

the Ohio Bar in 1937 and opened the law office of Van Aken & Bond from which he retired in 1987.

Van Aken, a conservative, served in the Ohio House of Representatives (1943–44, 1947–48), Shaker Hts. City Council (1951–55), and on the Ohio Republican Party central and executive committees. He was also general counsel for the Cleveland Real Estate Board (1964) and president of his father's real estate company.

As a 50-year member of the Ohio Bar Assn., Van Aken held several positions in the association. before becoming president (1958–59). He was cofounder of the National Conference of Bar Foundations.

Van Aken wrote two books, *Ohio Real Estate Law and Practice* with Robert Hauser, and *Buckeye Barristers*, a history of the Ohio Bar Assn.'s first 100 years.

Van Aken married Dorothy Harrison on 27 April 1940. They had four children: Nancy, Mary Alice, Louise, and William. Van Aken belonged to the Church of the Western Reserve. He is buried in Lake View Cemetery.—T.B.

**VAN HORN, FRANK R.** (7 Feb. 1872–1 Aug. 1933), mineralogist, geologist, and head of Case School of Applied Science's athletic association for 26 years, was born in Johnsonburg, NJ, to Geo. W. and Ellen Robertson Van Horn, and graduated from Rutgers with a B.S. (1892) and master's degree in mineralogy (1893) before earning his Ph.D. at the Univ. of Heidelberg (1897). In 1897 Van Horn became an instructor in geology and mineralogy at Case School of Applied Science, advancing to asst. professor in 1899 and professor in 1902. He traveled widely, studying and collecting minerals, making trips to Europe, Alaska, Africa, and the Pacific Coast; his collection included 10,000 specimens. Van Horn lectured on his travels and authored 2 textbooks, 26 technical papers, and coauthored a U.S. Geological Survey report, Geology and Mineral Resources of the Cleveland District (1931).

Van Horn helped develop Case's athletic program. Made head of the athletic association in 1900, he structured its finances and paid off its debt, built a new athletic field, and increased its athletic assets to $155,000. Called "the father of Case athletics," Van Horn saved the football program and encouraged other athletic endeavors. Van Horn was a member of several professional organizations, including a charter fellow and later secretary of the Mineralogical Society of America. In 1898 Van Horn married Myra Van Horn, his first cousin. Part of their wedding trip was a mineral-collecting expedition to Wyoming. The couple had two children, Kent Robinson and Hilda Lucile.

VAN SWERINGEN, ORIS PAXTON (24 Apr. 1879–22 Nov. 1936), and **MANTIS JAMES** (8 July 1881–12 Dec. 1935), real estate developers of SHAKER HTS.,† SHAKER SQUARE,† the SHAKER RAPID,† and the Terminal Tower complex, were born near Wooster, OH, to Jas. T. and Jennie Curtis Van Sweringen. About 1890 the family moved to Cleveland, and by 1897 both brothers were working for Bradley Fertilizer Co. They soon entered real estate on their own; a LAKEWOOD† venture failed, but by 1905 they were buying the old Shaker property (see NORTH UNION SHAKER COMMUNITY†) and developing Shaker Hts. Needing transportation between the suburb and downtown, in 1909 they began acquiring property along KINGSBURY RUN† to build their own interurban line. The New York Central's Nickel Plate owned lands the brothers needed, so in 1916 they bought the railroad. The Van Sweringens then acquired other railroads; by 1929 they owned a $3 billion, 30,000-mi. railroad empire and also had holdings in Midland Steel, Goodyear Tire & Rubber, and WHITE MOTOR.† In 1920 they began operating the Shaker Rapid. To provide a new central rail terminal downtown, the Van Sweringens won government and voter approval for a massive development near PUBLIC SQUARE†; construction began in 1923, and the Terminal Tower officially opened on 28 June 1930. In 1926 the brothers received the Cleveland Chamber of Commerce's Medal for Public Service. The brothers' finances were dependent on stock values, and after the stock market crash in 1929, they could not cover their debts. On 1 May 1935, the Van Sweringens defaulted on $48 million in loans from J. P. Morgan & Co., which ordered the collateral sold at auction in September. The brothers arranged backing and bought back their holdings for just over $3 million, but neither brother lived to rebuild the empire. The Van Sweringens were very private men. Neither married, and they avoided Cleveland society, living at their HUNTING VALLEY† estate, DAISY HILL.†

Haberman, Ian S. *The Van Sweringens of Cleveland* (1979).

**VICKERY, WILLIS** (26 Nov. 1857–26 Sept. 1932) was a judge of Cuyahoga County Common Pleas Court and Ohio 8th District Court of Appeals, and an organizer of Baldwin Univ. Law School.

Born on a farm in Bellevue, OH, Vickery received little formal schooling until he entered high school in Clyde, OH, at age 19, graduating in 1880. He began studying law with the firm of Everett & Fowler in Fremont. To finance college he taught school while continuing his studies. In 1882 he

entered Boston Univ. to study law, graduating in 1884. He was admitted to the Ohio Bar in 1885.

Vickery opened a practice in Bellevue with his brother, Jesse. In 1896 he moved his practice to Cleveland. In 1897 he helped found Baldwin Univ. Law School, with Arthur Rowley and Charles Bentley, serving as secretary and managing officer. When the Cleveland Law School was formed he combined his duties as dean with teaching. Vickery partnered briefly with Bentley in the firm Bentley & Vickery, then formed Vickery, Fleharty & Corlett shortly before his election to the Common Pleas Court in 1908. One of his first judicial decisions concerned Cleveland's fight against railroad interests for control of the lake front. Vickery's opinion favored the city, opening the way for later court rulings upholding Cleveland's title claim. He was elected to the Court of Appeals in 1918 where he served until his death.

Vickery outlived his first two wives, Anna Snyder, with whom he had three children: Lucille, Melville, and Howard; and Eleanor Grant. His third wife, Rosalie Griggs Mayberry, survived him. Vickery was buried in Bellevue.—T.B.

**VLCHEK, FRANK J.** (4 Jan. 1871–10 June 1947), industrialist, master tool maker, and author, was born in Budyn, Bohemia, the son of John and Anna Hladek Vlchek. One of 8 children, Frank was an apprentice blacksmith at age 12 and later learned to produce fine surgical instruments in Stryra, Austria. In 1889 he came to Cleveland and worked as a blacksmith, opening his own shop in 1895. Beginning with 6 employees, he organized the VLCHEK TOOL CO.,† which was incorporated in 1909. It became one of the largest automobile tool manufacturing concerns in the country.

As a successful industrialist and community leader, Vlchek served as a link between the immigrants in Cleveland's Czech Community and their native country through his writings. His first book, *Povidko Meho Zivota: Historie Americkeho Cecha,* which told of his early life and struggles as an immigrant in America, was popular in Czechoslovakia and went through 3 printings. His volume of poems *Cesky Vystehovalec* (Czech Emigrant) and *Nas Lid v Americe* (Our People in America) also dealt with the difficulties of life in a new country. In addition, he wrote *Prace a Odmena* (Labor and Reward) which discussed his experience as a factory owner and the industrial creed he formulated. In 1937 the Czech government decorated him for his cultural contributions to his people in Cleveland, and in 1947 Pope Pius XI recognized his contributions to the Catholic Church.

Vlchek married Mary Birhanzl 3 July 1893. They had 3 children: sons Henry F. and Valerian Frank, and a daughter, Mary (Mrs. Edwin C. Koster). A resident of Shaker Hts., Vlchek died at age 76 and was buried in Calvary Cemetery.—M.S.

---

Vlchek, Frank. *Povidko Meho Zivota: Historie Americkeho Cecha* (1928).

Frank Vlchek Papers, WRHS.

**VOINOVICH, GEORGE.** See **MAYORAL ADMINISTRATION OF GEORGE VOINOVICH.**†

**VON BAEYER, ERIC** (1909–2 Feb. 1990) was a prominent physician who helped establish the department of radiology at Fairview Park Hospital. Born in Munich, Germany, he studied medicine there, in Heidelberg and in Frankfurt. He immigrated to the U.S. in 1938 and worked for some time as a portrait painter. He resumed his medical career in 1941.

Von Baeyer, an accomplished cellist, was one of the founding members of the CLEVELAND CHAMBER MUSIC SOCIETY† in 1949. He was married to Ruth Hirschman; they had three children: Barbara, Matthew, and Christopher.—R.W.

**VORCE, MYRON BOND** (14 Aug. 1871–?) was president of the Vorce Engineering Co. and responsible for the design of much of the present park and boulevard system in Cleveland.

Vorce was a native of the city of Cleveland and was educated in the CLEVELAND PUBLIC SCHOOLS.† His father was Charles M. Vorce, and his mother was Evelyn Cornelia Marshall. After securing a position with a surveying company, Vorce began to study engineering and held various positions in that field. While employed by E. W. Bowdich of Boston, he was sent to Cleveland to develop Euclid Hts., Clifton Park, and other local projects. He worked as an assistant engineer with the park board and in 1898 joined the city engineering department as asst. engineer in the work of intercepting sewers and led reorganization efforts within the sewer maintenance department. He also served as pavement engineer of Cleveland and inspector of buildings before deciding to organize the Vorce Engineering Co. in 1907.

In 1903 Vorce married Ethel Ridgley Stearns of Detroit. He was at one time commodore of the Lakewood Yacht Club.—R.W.

**VORMELKER, ROSE L.** (11 June 1895–3 Nov. 1994), though not 5' tall, was regarded as a towering figure in the field of library science. A native Clevelander, she was the daughter of Julius and Amy Hippler Vormelker and went to East High School. She entered library work at 16 as a page in the Superior branch of the CLEVELAND PUBLIC LIBRARY† and received her library science certificate from Western Reserve Univ. (see CASE WESTERN RESERVE†) in 1919. After experience with the Detroit Public Library and the research library of the WHITE MOTOR CORP.,† she returned to the Cleveland Public Library in 1928. At the request of Director LINDA EASTMAN, she organized and ran a Business Information Bureau, which gained international respect for the accuracy and thoroughness of its resources. During World War II she was asked by the federal government to install war and defense information centers in 4,000 libraries across the country. She published a 2-vol. reference on *Special Library Resources* (1941–6) and a pamphlet on "The Company Library" (1951). Vormelker became asst. director of the CPL in 1955 but left the following year to become library director for the Cleveland *PLAIN DEALER†* and the *CLEVELAND NEWS,†* combining 2 formerly separate libraries into a unified system. She retired in 1962 to become an asst. professor at Kent State Univ. There she taught possibly the only course in the country on newspaper libraries and continued teaching until 1984. Among many honors, she was inducted into the Special Libraries Assn. Hall of Fame and the Ohio Library Assn. Hall of Fame. Never married, she died at home in SHAKER HTS.†—J.V.

**VOSMIK, JOSEPH FRANKLIN "JOE"** (4 Apr. 1910–27 Jan. 1962), baseball player for the CLEVELAND INDIANS† (1930–36) was considered by baseball experts the best hitter to come from the Cleveland sandlots—he averaged over .300 in his major league career. Vosmik was born in Cleveland to Anna and Josef Vosmik. A local idol of the fans in the Broadway-E. 55th St. neighborhood, he was befriended by Bill Kuchta, a Harvard and E. 71st St. druggist, who kept him supplied with bats and baseballs. Signed by the Indians after an All-Star Class A game at LEAGUE PARK† in 1928, Vosmik began his professional career in 1929 with Frederick of the Blue Ridge League. He reported to the Indians in Sept. 1930, after batting .397 with Terre Haute of the Three-I League. In Vosmik's debut in 1931 against the White Sox, he went 5 for 5, including 3 doubles off the right-field wall. His greatest season was 1935, when he lost the batting title to Buddy Meyer of Washington, who hit .3490 to Vosmik's .3483. In 1935 Vosmik led the league in base hits (216), doubles (47), and triples (20), driving in 110 runs. Vosmik was traded to St. Louis in Jan. 1937. In 1938 he was sent to Boston and led the league with 201 base hits. Finishing his career with Brooklyn in 1942 and Washington in 1944, Vosmik compiled a lifetime batting average of .307. During the late 1940s and early 1950s, he managed teams at Tucson, Dayton, Oklahoma City, and Batavia and scouted for the Cleveland Indians (1951, 1952). Later he was an automobile and appliance salesman. Vosmik married Sally Joanne Okla in 1936 and had 3 children: Joseph, Larry, and Karen. He died in Cleveland and was buried at Highland Park Cemetery.

**VOTIPKA, THELMA** (20 Dec. 1898–24 Oct. 1972), opera singer with the Metropolitan Opera Co., was born in Cleveland to Emil and Jessie Votipka, and studied at Oberlin Conservatory and with LILA ROBESON in Cleveland, and Anna Schoen Rene in New York City. Her operatic debut was as the singing countess in the *Marriage of Figaro* for the American Opera Co. in 1927. She sang with the Chicago Opera from 1929–31, the STADIUM OPERA CO. in 1930, and the Philadelphia Opera in 1932. In 1935 Votipka joined the Metropolitan Opera Co., remaining with the Met 28 years. She specialized in small roles, never wanting to become a prima donna. Her most notable roles were Marianne in *Der Rosenkavalier,* Mamma Lucia in *Cavalleria Rusticana,* Flora in *La Traviata,* and Marthe in *Faust.* Her favorite role was that of the witch in *Hansel and Gretel.* After retiring in 1961, she made a brief return to the stage of the Met for the 1962–63 season. During her years with the Metropolitan, she also sang in San Francisco, Hartford, CT, Cincinnati, and Puerto Rico. She married John C. Groth on 24 Dec. 1947. They had no children. Votipka died in New York City.

# W

**WADE, EDWARD** (22 Nov. 1802–13 Aug. 1866), lawyer and member of the U.S. House of Representatives (1853–61), was born in W. Springfield, MA, son of James and Mary Upham Wade. He was educated locally and admitted to the bar in 1827. Wade practiced in Jefferson, Ashtabula County, OH, and in 1831 became Justice of the Peace for the county for 1 year. He moved to Unionville in 1832 and worked as a prosecuting attorney. In 1837 Wade came to Cleveland, continuing his law practice and becoming one of the area's leading abolitionists. In 1837 he became president of the CUYAHOGA COUNTY ANTI-SLAVERY SOCIETY,† often defending fugitive slaves in court. In 1842 he organized the Liberty party. Wade's reputation as an abolitionist gained him a seat in Congress as a Free-Soiler in 1853, a position he held until 1855, when he was again elected, but on the Republican ticket. He remained a congressman until 1861. Wade was on the first boards of trustees of the Homeopathic Hospital College (1849) and CLEVELAND UNIV.† Wade married twice. His first wife, Sarah Louise Atkins, died shortly after their marriage in 1832. His second marriage was to Mary P. Hall. Wade had no children from either marriage. He died in East Cleveland and was buried in Woodland Cemetery.

**WADE, JEPTHA HOMER I** (11 Aug. 1811–9 Aug. 1890), financier and telegraph pioneer, was born in Romulus, Seneca County, NY, the son of Jeptha and Sarah (Allen) Wade. He operated a factory and worked as portrait painter before becoming interested in the telegraph. In 1847, as a subcontractor for J. J. Speedy, he began constructing a telegraph line from Detroit to Jackson, MI. Wade soon added lines from Detroit to Milwaukee, and to Buffalo by way of Cleveland. In 1849–50 he built lines from

Cleveland to Cincinnati and St. Louis. In 1854 he consolidated his lines with those of Royal E. House to create a network of lines across the Old Northwest, and in Apr. 1856 their network was part of the 13-company consolidation of telegraph lines that created the Western Union Telegraph Co. Wade served as the general agent for Western Union and he continued to develop new lines and telegraph companies in the West, forming the California State Telegraph Co. and the Pacific Telegraph Co.; the latter was connected to St. Louis and San Francisco by wire in Aug. 1861. Wade became president of Western Union in 1866, but poor health forced him to resign the following year.

Wade moved to Cleveland in 1856. He was a director of 8 railroad companies; helped organize Citizens Savings & Loan Assn. (1867), becoming its first president (1868); was president of Natl. Bank of Commerce and an incorporator of Cleveland Rolling Mill Co. (1863); became a sinking-fund commissioner in 1870 (serving 20 years); was an organizer and first president of LAKE VIEW CEMETERY† Assn.; and was an incorporator of Case School of Applied Science (1880). In 1881 Wade offered the city 75 acres of land along Doan Brook as a park (See WADE PARK†). He also donated land to Western Reserve Univ.

Wade married Rebecca Loueza Facer in 1832 (d. 1836). He married Susan M. Fleming in 1837. Wade had one natural child, Randall P., and 4 adopted children: Delia (Moore), Eusebra (Bates), Myra (Huggins), and Bessie (Reynolds).

Jeptha Homer Wade Family Papers, WRHS.

**WADE, JEPTHA HOMER II** (15 Oct. 1857–6 Mar. 1926), the grandson of JEPTHA HOMER WADE, was a financier and philanthropist who helped develop the CLEVELAND MUSEUM OF ART.† He was born in Cleveland to Randall P. and Anna R. (McGaw) Wade. Randall Wade (26 Aug. 1835–24 June 1876) went into the telegraph business before becoming a bank executive in 1857. Jeptha Wade II was educated by tutors and in private schools, graduating from Mt. Pleasant Academy in Ossining, NY, and earning a master's degree from Western Reserve Univ. Wade developed a close relationship with his grandfather after his father's early death. He served as an executive in 45 companies, including railways, mining companies, manufacturing firms, and banking institutions; and was a trustee and supporter of Cleveland Art School, the Protestant Orphan Asylum, WESTERN RESERVE HISTORICAL SOCIETY,† and WRU. He also contributed to the Children's Fresh Air Camp, Lakeside Hospital, and CLEVELAND MUSEUM OF NATURAL HISTORY.† Wade shared his grandfather's interest in art, was one of the incorporators of the Cleveland Museum of Art in 1913, and served as its first vice-president, becoming president in 1920. His many contributions to the museum included a collection of rare lace, textiles, jewels, enamels, and a number of paintings. He also established a purchasing fund, which grew to more than $1 million. In 1878 Wade married Ellen Garretson. Upon her death in 1917, Wade established a memorial fund in her name to aid charities in which they were interested. Wade had 3 children: Jeptha H., Jr., George G., and Helen W. (Mrs. E. B. Brown).

Jeptha Homer Wade Family Papers, WRHS.

**WADSWORTH, HOMER C.** (3 Apr. 1913–13 Apr. 1994), spent most of his career in community planning and trust work, including ten years as the director of the CLEVELAND FOUNDATION.† Born to Leon K. and Ethel Raynor Wadsworth in Pittsburgh, PA, Homer attended local schools and earned his bachelor's degree from the Univ. of Pittsburgh in 1935, with graduate work at a number of other schools, including the Univ. of Chicago, Univ. of Minnesota, and Univ. of Missouri.

He worked for the City of Pittsburgh in a variety of positions from 1937–46. After a stint at the New School for Social Research in New York City, in 1949 he moved to Kansas City, MO, where he served as executive director and president of the Kansas City Assn. of Trusts and Foundations. He held that post for 25 years. Wadsworth became director of the Cleveland Foundation in Jan. 1974, accepting a 10-year contract for the position. During his term as director, he played a major role in the city's downtown renaissance. Cleveland Foundation supported the forming of the CLEVELAND BALLET† and CLEVELAND OPERA† companies,

and played a pivotal role in the preservation and revitalization of the PLAYHOUSE SQUARE† Theater District.

Besides his foundation work, Wadsworth was involved in many other civic projects. Among them, locally he served on the boards of the Metrohealth Foundation and NORTH COAST HARBOR,† and nationally for the Council for Foundations, the National Endowment for the Arts and Humanities, and the National Institutes of Health. In Cleveland the GREATER CLEVELAND GROWTH ASSN.† honored his achievements, and nationally he was named the 1986 Distinguished Grant Maker.

On 11 Nov. 1939 Wadsworth married Alice Crutchfield; she served as director of the Vocational Guidance Rehabilitation Services until her death on 29 Jan. 1995. They had seven children: Robert, Harriet (Orlock), Alice, Homer, Ethel (Mirviss), Marjorie (De Leo), and James.—J.T.

Cleveland Family Oral History Collection, WRHS.

**WAGNER, MARGARET W.** (19 Oct. 1892–19 Aug. 1984), innovative director of the BENJAMIN ROSE INSTITUTE† for 29 years, was born in Cleveland to financier Frank B. and May Warnock Wagner. She graduated from HATHAWAY BROWN SCHOOL† in 1910 and studied at Miss Spence's School in New York, Finch College, and the School of Applied Social Sciences at Western Reserve Univ. Her career in social work began in 1912, volunteering in the children's division of Lakeside Hospital as a member of the JR. LEAGUE OF CLEVELAND.† She became interested in working with handicapped children, was the first social worker hired by the Assn. for the Crippled & Disabled, and urged the city's director of public welfare, DUDLEY S. BLOSSOM, to establish a social-service department at City Hospital, joining the hospital to administer the new program in 1924.

In 1930 Wagner became executive secretary of the Benjamin Rose Institute, making it an advocate for seniors and expanding its services. She studied the needs of the elderly in the community and established new institutions to meet those needs, such as Benjamin Rose Hospital for the elderly (1953). The institute also operated residential and nursing homes to house senior citizens. After her retirement in 1959, Wagner helped design the institute's modern nursing home, built and named for her in 1961 (See MARGARET WAGNER HOME†). Wagner was active in social-work organizations locally and nationally, initiated Cleveland Welfare Fed.'s first committee on the elderly, and received many awards. She was unmarried and was buried in Lake View Cemetery.

WAITE, FREDERICK CLAYTON (24 May 1870–30 Mar. 1956), founder of the Dept. of Histology & Embryology at Western Reserve Univ. Medical & Dental Schools, was born in Hudson, OH, to Nelson and Cynthia Post Waite, graduated from Western Reserve Academy in 1888, and from WRU with the B.Litt. degree in 1892 and A.M. in 1894. From 1892–95, he worked at WRU as an assistant in biology; then earned his A.M. (1896) and Ph.D. (1899) from Harvard. Waite taught at Peter Cooper High School in New York (1898–1900), at New York Univ. (1899–1900), and spent 1900–01 as an assistant in anatomy at Rush Medical College in Chicago. In 1901 Waite was appointed asst. professor of histology and embryology at Reserve's Medical & Dental Schools, promoted to associate professor in 1904, and to professor in 1906. He remained chairman of the department until his retirement in 1940, when he was appointed professor emeritus. Before World War I, Waite devoted much time working with the American Medical Assn., inspecting virtually every U.S. medical school several times. During World War I he was a captain in the U.S. Surgeon General's Office. After the war, working for the Natl. Dental Education Conference, he inspected and raised standards at both medical and dental schools throughout the country. Waite was a prolific author, after retirement writing books on the history of WRU Medical & Dental Schools and the Hudson Academy years. Waite married Emily Fisher Bacon in 1916. They had no children. Waite died in Dover, NH, and was buried there in the Pine Hill Cemetery.

WAITT, MAUDE COMSTOCK (11 Aug. 1875–13 Dec. 1935), the first woman elected to the Ohio senate, where she served 4 terms, was born in Middlebury, VT, to Orvis and Mary Comstock, graduated from the Normal School at Vermont College, and afterwards taught school in Rockland, MA. Shortly after her marriage to Walter G. Waitt around 1901, she and her husband came to Cleveland, living here from 1902–04, and then moving to Fremont, OH. They returned to Cleveland in 1916. Waitt became active in the woman's suffrage movement and served as a member of Lakewood City Council in 1921 and 1922. In 1922 she was elected to represent the 25th Ohio senatorial district as a Republican. After being reelected 3 times, she retired from the senate in 1930 due to poor health. She died in Lakewood. She and her husband had a daughter, Doris Ida.

Maude C. Waitt Scrapbook, WRHS.

WALKER, FRANK RAY (29 Sept. 1877–9 July 1949), with HARRY E. WEEKS, founded the architectural firm Walker & Weeks. He was born in Pittsfield, MA, son of Frank and Helen Theresa (Ranous) Walker, and graduated from MIT in 1900. He studied at the Atelier of Monsieur Redon in Paris and lived a year in Italy. Walker then practiced architecture in Boston, New York, and Pittsburgh before moving to Cleveland in 1905 to join the firm of J. MILTON DYER, which had been commissioned to design a city hall for Cleveland as part of the Group Plan. Both Walker and Weeks worked for Dyer; they established their own practice in 1911. They completed 60 bank buildings throughout Ohio. In Cleveland, they designed major commercial, public, and religious structures in classical revival styles, including Bingham Co. Warehouse (1915); Guardian Bldg. renovation (1915); PUBLIC AUDITORIUM† (1922); FEDERAL RESERVE BANK† (1923); CLEVELAND PUBLIC LIBRARY† (1925); EPWORTH-EUCLID METHODIST CHURCH,† with architect Bertram Goodhue (1928); First Baptist Church in Shaker Hts. (1929); ST. PAUL'S EPISCOPAL CHURCH† in Cleveland Hts. (1929); Pearl St. Savings & Trust; and CLEVELAND MUNICIPAL STADIUM† with OSBORN ENGINEERING CO.† (1931). Walker also played a major role establishing design and planning standards for Cleveland as the first professional advisor to the City Planning Commission and a member of that body 10 years. He assisted the development of GATES MILLS† as president of the Gates Mills Improvement Society (1917–19) and the village's first mayor (1920–24). He was a trustee of St. Christopher's Episcopal Church of Gates Mills.

Walker married Katharine Tollett Stone in 1915. They had two children, Richard Stone and Joan. He died in Cleveland and was buried in Lake View Cemetery.

Walker & Weeks Records, WRHS.

WALKER, HAZEL MOUNTAIN (16 Feb. 1889–16 May 1980), the first black Cleveland school principal and among the first black women admitted to practice law in Ohio, was born in Warren, OH, daughter of Charles and Alice (Bronson) Mountain. She graduated from Cleveland Normal Training School, received bachelor's and master's degrees (1909) in education from Western Reserve Univ., and from 1909–36 taught at Mayflower Elementary School, known for teaching reading to children whose families either could not read or spoke no English. During the summers, Walker studied law at BALDWIN-WALLACE COLLEGE,† receiving her degree and passing the bar examination in 1919. She had no intention of practicing law, but wanted to prove black women could become lawyers. She worked with juvenile court, tutoring black children from the South having problems adjusting to Cleveland schools. In 1936 Walker became principal of Rutherford B. Hayes Elementary School; then of Geo. Washington Carver Elementary School in 1954, serving until retiring in 1958. She was elected to the Ohio State Board of Education in 1961 but resigned in 1963 when she moved out of state. Walker was an early member of and actress at KARAMU HOUSE† and is credited with choosing the theater's name in 1924. She was also active in politics, serving on the CUYAHOGA COUNTY REPUBLICAN PARTY† executive committee in the 1930s. She was one of the first AFRICAN AMERICANS† to become a member of the WOMEN'S CITY CLUB.† Walker married twice. Her first husband, Geo. Herbert Walker, whom she married on 28 June 1922, died in 1956; in 1961 she married Joseph R. Walker of Massachusetts. Walker had no children. She died in Cleveland.

**WALKER, WILLIAM OTIS** (19 Sept. 1896–29 Oct. 1981), black Republican publisher, was born in Selma, AL, son of Alex and Annie Lee (Jones) Walker. He worked for the Pittsburgh Urban League after studying at Wilberforce Univ. and Oberlin Business College, and entered journalism, first reporting for the *Pittsburgh Courier,* then as city editor of the *Norfolk Journal & Guide,* cofounding the *Washington (DC) Tribune* in 1921. Walker came to Cleveland in 1932 to manage the *CALL & POST,†* within a few years acquiring majority ownership. Walker helped found the FUTURE OUTLOOK LEAGUE,† but, a loyal Republican, was conservative in politics. He was councilman from 1940–47; and as Ohio's director of industrial relations from 1963–71, was the first black to hold a cabinet-level position in state government. In his *Call & Post* column, Walker criticized relief expenditures, calling instead for policies creating more private sector jobs.

Despite his conservatism, Walker took radical stands when he thought blacks would benefit. He supported Democrat Carl Stokes for mayor in 1967, and when several black councilmen were accused of taking kickbacks, he organized a fund for their defense. In the 1960s, he boycotted McDonald's Restaurant, forcing it to grant franchises to blacks. He helped organize black self-help groups such as Operation Alert and the Surrogates.

Walker married Theresa Brooks on 2 July 1919; they divorced in 1955. Walker was survived by his second wife, Naomi (Russell). He had no children from either marriage. Walker died of a heart attack in the Call & Post Bldg. and was buried in Lake View Cemetery. He was elected posthumously to the Gallery of Distinguished Newspaper Publishers at Howard Univ.

**WALLACE, GEORGE ALEXANDER LEROY** (22 Feb. 1848–3 Aug. 1940), CLEVELAND FIRE DEPT.† member 62 years, and chief from 1901–31, was born in Erie, PA, to Geo. A. and Margaret Hendrickson Wallace, came to Cleveland with his family in 1854, and at 14 left school to work as a railroad brakeman. Wallace joined the Cleveland Fire Dept. as a 2nd-class fireman in June 1869, acquired a reputation as a fine horseman and troubleshooter, rising through the ranks to horseman, then horsecart driver, then captain of Hook & Ladder Co. No. 4 in 1873. In 1883 Wallace was appointed 5th asst. chief, and in 1901, after rising to 4th, then 3rd asst., he was appointed chief by Mayor JOHN FARLEY, commanding 1,040 officers and men at 63 engine houses and stations. Throughout his tenure, Wallace fought to keep out politics and make the department's operations a matter of fitness and faithfulness. He displayed executive and leadership ability, maintaining discipline and inspiring respect. At the scene of a fire, Wallace was the boss, demanding strict obedience from his men and any crowds standing by. Many times he risked his life entering burning buildings to save victims, family pets, or heirlooms. Among the memorable fires at which Wallace directed firefighting efforts were the COLLINWOOD SCHOOL FIRE† of 1908 and the CLEVELAND CLINIC FIRE† of 1929. Wallace married Emma Stanhope in 1874 and had 2 sons, George and Stanhope.

**WALSH, EDWARD JOHN** (28 June 1920–18 Feb. 1993) was executive director from 1953–85 of the Foundry Educational Foundation (FEF) which represented the cast metal industry at 35 leading engineering colleges nationwide. Born in Chicago to Edward and Loretta Walsh, he attended Catholic school and graduated from St. Mary's College in Winona, MN. Walsh studied at Georgetown Univ. until he was called to serve as a navy officer during World War II. After the war he worked for the Pure Oil Co., then as executive secretary of the National Foundry Assn. in Chicago.

In 1953 Walsh came to Cleveland as executive director of FEF. Under his leadership, FEF's educational program steadily grew, involving more than 15,000 graduate and undergraduate engineering students who benefited from its scholarship and summer work programs. In 1982 FEF and Walsh moved to Chicago. In 1983 Walsh returned to operate FEF's Cleveland office.

Walsh received numerous honors, including a special service citation by the Gray and Ductile Iron Founders' Society, 1965, and the American Foundrymen's Society's Board of Directors Award, 1968. The National Foundry Assn. bestowed an honorary membership on Walsh in 1971. Walsh received the university of Missouri-Rolla's Centennial Medal in 1971 and received the first gold medal of the Iron Castings Society. In 1983 Walsh was named Foundryman of the Year by the Northeastern Ohio chapter of the American Foundrymen's Society. An E. J. Walsh annual service award was established by FEF in 1985.

Walsh married Kathryn Sprague on 29 May 1963. He had 3 children: Barbara, Patricia, and James. Walsh lived in North Olmsted and is buried in Sunset Memorial Park.—T.B.

**WALSH (WALASIEWICZ), STELLA (STANISLAWA)** (3 Apr. 1911–4 Dec. 1980), named the greatest woman athlete of the first half of the 20th century by the Helm Athletic Foundation (1951), was born in Wierzchownin, Poland, daughter of Julian and Veronica (Uninski) Walasiewicz. Brought to Cleveland when she was 10, Walsh attended South and Notre Dame high schools. In 1926 she tied the women's record of 6 seconds for the 50-yd. dash; and by 1928 was prepared to represent the U.S. in the Olympics, when it was discovered she had never become an American citizen. With naturalization nearly completed, Walsh was laid off from her job, but then offered employment by the Polish consulate if she would represent Poland in the Los Angeles Olympics in 1932. She did not become an American citizen until Dec. 1947. Representing Poland, Walsh won the 100-meter dash at the 1932 Olympic games, setting a world record. In 1936, she finished 2nd. Still competing in her 50s, in 1967 Walsh won a 60-yd. dash in 7.7 seconds, less than .5 second slower then her 7.3 world record time in 1934. She won over 5,000 track and field events during her career. In 1948 she founded the San Fernando Valley Women's Athletic Club. In the 1970s she coached the Polish Falcons (see SOKOL POLSKI†) track club in Cleveland. Married for a short time to Harry Olson during the 1950s, Walsh used Walsh-Olson as her legal name thereafter. Walsh was shot to death in a parking lot during an attempted robbery; she was buried in Calvary Cemetery.

**WALTER, PAUL WILLIAM** (18 April 1907–4 Nov. 1992), arbitration lawyer, served on the National War Labor Board and chaired the regional Steel Inequity Panel during World War II. He was a Republican candidate for the Ohio House of Representatives (1930s) and for the U.S. Congress (1953). Walter was born in Cleveland to Carl Frederick and Leda A. (Schneidemantel) Walter. He graduated from West High School (1924), Western Reserve Univ. (WRU, 1928), and WRU School of Law (1932). That year, with D. Rusk Haverfield, he formed the Walter, Haverfield & Poe law firm, which by 1992 had become Walter, Haverfield, Buescher & Chockley. He later served as solicitor for both CUYAHOGA HTS.† and SOLON.†

An activist, Walter organized the Municipal Light Plant Assn., a citizens' group (1937), and the Friends of the Car Riders (late 1930s) to fight for buses in addition to streetcars. He worked in Robert A. Taft's senatorial campaigns (1938, 1944, 1950) and managed his bid for the Republican presidential nomination in 1952. Walter's business interests included the local Manners Big Boy restaurant chain and Sheet Metal Products of Willoughby. While a student, Walter began volunteering at HIRAM HOUSE,† where he met both his law partner and his wife. He chaired the settlement from 1940 until his death. In 1961, in recognition of 25 years of board service, the local YMCA named its North Woods Camp lodge for Walter. Among many other activities, Walter chaired the WESTERN RESERVE HISTORICAL SOCIETY† (1980–89), served as a trustee for the CLEVELAND METROPARKS ZOO,† helped found the Cleveland International Program (1962–64), and advocated international peace as president of the United World Federalists (1961–64).

In 1938 Walter married Susan E. Hamilton (d. 1983). The couple had 2 children, Susan E. and Paul W., Jr. (Timmy).—J.M.

Paul W. Walter Papers, WRHS.

**WALTERS, CLAIRE A.** (21 Aug. 1872–18 Nov. 1937) was for 41 years a teacher and psychologist in the Cleveland public school system whose life work was the rehabilitation of underprivileged children.

Born in Cleveland to Phillip and Mary (Whelan) Walters, Claire graduated from Central High School in 1893 and Cleveland Normal School in 1897. She began her career by teaching at Fowler, Barkwill, Brownell, and Eagle public schools. Continuing her own education, Walters graduated from the Vineland (NJ) Training School in 1912.

In 1922 Walters was appointed psychologist in the bureau of attendance for the Cleveland School Board and was responsible for examining difficult children. Never married, Walters devoted herself to her students and was often successful in helping them overcome such hardships as broken homes and poverty. For 25 years she taught at the Boys School, originally located at Clinton and W. 29th St., and was renowned for her ability to handle truants and antisocial boys.

Walters was also a psychologist and child study and placement worker for the Cuyahoga County Juvenile Court from its founding in 1902. In 1912 she began work in Juvenile Delinquency child study. She served on the Board of Education for 30 years, doing special work with problem children.

Walters helped organize the first detention home and school which opened in Cleveland in 1908. She also helped establish a playground at Forest and Woodland avenues.

Walters lived in Cleveland. Services were held at the Wade Memorial Chapel in Lake View Cemetery.—T.B.

**WALTERS, REUBEN W.** (22 Aug. 1838–19 Apr. 1918), CIVIL WAR† soldier, physician, and Cuyahoga County Soldiers & Sailors Monument Commission member, was born in Russell, OH (Geauga County), son of Reuben and Emily W. Walters. He began studying medicine in 1861, but halted his education to enlist as a private in Co. D, 7TH OHIO VOLUNTEER INFANTRY,† on 15 Aug. 1864. When the 7th was mustered out in the summer of 1864, Walters was transferred to the 5th OVI to complete his enlistment. Appointed hospital steward on 16 Mar. 1864, he was mustered out of the army 17 Mar. 1865. After the war, Walters studied at and graduated from Jefferson Medical College in Philadelphia, Cleveland Medical College, and Cleveland Homeopathic Hospital College. Gov. Bishop of Ohio appointed him surgeon of the 15TH OHIO NATL. GUARD REGIMENT† on 17 July 1878. Walters practiced medicine in Chagrin Falls beginning in 1867. He also served on the original building commission of the Cuyahoga County SOLDIERS & SAILORS MONUMENT,† dating from 20 June 1884. Walters married Sarah F. White and had 2 children, Wilson and Franklin. He was buried in Evergreen Hills Cemetery, Chagrin Falls, OH.

**WALTON, JOHN WHITTLESEY** (15 Jan. 1845–19 Nov. 1926), prominent businessman and philanthropist, son of Lucius Clark and Mary (Vesta) Whittlesey Walton, formed a partnership with J. E. Upson in 1871 and started a business as ship chandlers and grocers in the Winslow Bldg. The ship chandlery business grew, leading to the incorporation of the Upson-Walton Co. in 1893, with Walton as the second president of the company after Upson. Upson-Walton eventually achieved worldwide distribution and was the only U.S. company to combine the manufacturing of wire rope, tackle blocks, and rope fittings. It also operated the only rope mill in Ohio. Walton used his wealth and influence to aid various civic and charitable causes in Cleveland. In 1867 he helped revive the Cleveland YMCA. From 1874–1926, Walton was actively involved in charity, serving as treasurer of Bethel Associated Charities. He also headed the section on philanthropy for the city's Centennial Commission. Throughout his life, Walton was keenly interested in the emerging scientific approach to social work. He donated many books to CLEVELAND PUBLIC LIBRARY†

relating to this field and sociology, and other books of educational value. Walton married twice. His first marriage, on 6 Oct. 1869, was to Lemira Augusta Lyman (d. 1879). They had 3 children: Edwin Augustus, Ethel (Osborn), and Florence (Dorr). His second marriage was on 6 Aug. 1885 to Gertrude L. Hutchinson. They had 3 children also: Gertrude (Holt), Margaret (DeWitt), and Gladys (Jennings). Walton was buried in Lake View Cemetery.

John Whittlesey Walton Papers, WRHS.

**WALWORTH, ASHBEL W.** (1790–24 Aug. 1844), responsible for improving Cleveland's harbor, was born in Croton, CT, to Julianna Morgan and JOHN W. WALWORTH. He moved with his family to New York State, then to Painesville in 1800, coming to Cleveland in 1806. After his father's death in 1812, Walworth assumed his duties as Cleveland postmaster, and collector of the District of Erie (i.e., the port of Cuyahoga), an office he held until 1829. Walworth was elected township clerk (1815–17), treasurer (1821–26), and justice of the peace (1823–26). In 1835 he was treasurer of the Tippecanoe Club of Cuyahoga County, and was also a member of the First Presbyterian Society of Cleveland, which purchased land for FIRST PRESBYTERIAN CHURCH† (Old Stone Church).

Walworth wanted to improve Cleveland's commercial possibilities as a port. The sandbar continuously forming over the mouth of the CUYAHOGA RIVER† needed to be rectified, so Walworth helped form Cleveland Pier Co. in 1815 to construct a pier into the lake, which was later wrecked in a storm. Walworth received $5,000 from Congress in 1824 to construct another pier, which did not keep the river mouth clear. Cleveland only received 30–40 ships a year, so Congress would not grant additional funds; therefore Clevelanders raised $150 to send Walworth to Washington to promote Cleveland, where he secured $10,000 and help form the U.S. Engineer Corps.

In 1820 Walworth married Mary Ann Dunlop. They had five children: John, Anne, Sarah, William, and Mary. Walworth and his wife are buried in Erie St. Cemetery.

John and Ashbel Walworth Papers, WRHS.

**WALWORTH, JOHN W.** (1765–10 Sept. 1812), early settler and government official, was born in Groton, CT, son of Samuel and Hannah (Woodbridge) Walworth. He left Connecticut in 1792 to settle near Lake Cayuga, NY. Spending the winter of 1799 near Painesville, OH, he purchased 2,000 acres of land and settled his family there in 1800. In

1802 Gov. St. Clair appointed Walworth justice of the peace for Trumbull County. Two years later he became postmaster of Painesville. When the CUYA-HOGA RIVER† was made a port of entry into the U.S. in 1805, Pres. Jefferson appointed Walworth inspector of revenue (collector of the District of Erie), so Walworth resettled in Cleveland in 1806. He received 2 other appointments in 1806, as Cleveland postmaster and associate judge of Geauga County. When Cuyahoga County was organized in 1810, he became county clerk and recorder, as well as clerk of the Supreme Court of Ohio. Walworth was a farmer, having exchanged his Painesville land for 300 acres in Cleveland. Walworth was a founder of the first Masonic Lodge in northern Ohio, established in Warren in 1803. He was also a member of the Board of Commissioners for the Improvement of the Cuyahoga & Tuscarawas Rivers, a project conceived to provide an improved connection between Lake Erie and the Ohio River. Walworth married Julianna Morgan on 22 Mar. 1789. She was one of 3 women who refused to leave Cleveland when war broke out in 1812. She chose to remain with her husband, who was dying of tuberculosis. They had 6 children: ASHBEL, Juliana, John P., Horace, Hannah, and John A. Walworth died in Cleveland and was buried in Woodland Cemetery.

John and Ashbel Walworth Papers, WRHS.

**WAMBSGANSS, WILLIAM (BILL WAMBY)** (19 Mar. 1894–8 Dec. 1985), played second base for the CLEVELAND INDIANS† (1914–23) and enjoyed lifelong fame for making an unassisted triple play in the 1920 World Series. Wambsganss was born in what is now Garfield Hts., OH, but grew up in Fort Wayne, IN, son of Philip and Carrie (Shellman) Wambsganss. He graduated from Concordia College (IN) and attended a Lutheran seminary in St. Louis but soon signed with a Class B baseball team in Cedar Rapids. Cleveland Indians scouts recruited him in 1914. Called Wamby in Cleveland (to fit on the LEAGUE PARK† scoreboard and program), Wambsganss was known as a strong fielder, a steady hitter and a fine bunter.

Wambsganss's triple play moment came in the 5th game of the 1920 World Series (see BASEBALL WORLD SERIES†). Brooklyn batters Otto Miller and Pete Kilduff singled to begin the 5th inning, with the Indians leading 7–0. With Miller on second and Kilduff on first, the next batter, Clarence Smith, lined a ball toward right field. Wambsganss made a brilliant catch for one out, caught Miller off second base for the second out, and tagged Kilduff, for the third out. In 1923 Wambsganss was traded to Boston; he finished his career in Philadelphia in 1926

with a .259 batting average. He managed minor-league teams in Springfield, IL, Fort Wayne, and professional women's teams in Muskegon, MI, and Fort Wayne until 1931. Wamby returned to Cleveland to manage the Class A teams of Lyon Tailors and Fisher Foods. In 1948 he took a sales position with the Tru-Fit Screw Products Corp. and managed its ball team. He lived in LAKEWOOD† the remainder of his life.

On 30 June 1917 Wambsganss married Effie L. Mulholland (d. 1977); they had 3 children: Mary Brandes, Lois Hauer, and Bill Wamby, Jr.

**WARNER, WORCESTER REED** (6 May 1846–25 June 1929), a founder of WARNER & SWASEY CO.† and developer of telescopes, was born in Cunningham, MA, to Vesta Wales (Reed) and farmer Franklin John Warner. He apprenticed as a machinist, and by 1869 was a foreman with Pratt & Whitney in Hartford, CT, where he met AMBROSE SWASEY. In 1880 Warner and Swasey opened their own machine-tool business, first in Chicago, but relocated in 1881 to Cleveland, which had more skilled mechanics. The firm became a leader in designing and building turret lathes, used to make brass plumbing parts, but its early reputation was built on telescopes. Fascinated by astronomy, Warner was sent by Pratt & Whitney to handle their exhibition at the Centennial Exhibition in Philadelphia in 1876. He continued experimenting with new telescopes. In 1880 the purchase of a telescope built at their Chicago plant by Beloit College put the company in the telescope business, and soon they were a major builder of equatorial mounts, known for their accurate and reliable drive mechanisms, and refractor telescopes. After 1900 the company concentrated on producing machine tools, but still built telescopes until 1970. In 1918 Warner donated a 9' refractor telescope to Case School. Later, he and Swasey donated money for an observatory to house this telescope and other scientific instruments. Warner was active in many scientific and professional societies. He died while on a trip to Germany, survived by his wife, Cornelia Blakemore, whom he married on 26 June 1890, and a daughter, Helen Blakemore Warner. Warner was buried in Tarrytown, NY.

**WARREN, DANIEL** (1786–13 Oct. 1862), the first settler in WARRENSVILLE TWP.,† was born in New Hampshire, the son of Moses and Priscilla (Nourse) Warren. In 1808 he left Acworth, NH, for Painesville and eventually settled in Jefferson. The following year he moved to NEWBURGH† to claim property, sight unseen, he had received in exchange for $300 owed to him for making bricks for the first courthouse at Jefferson. In the spring of 1810, Warren bought a farm in the western part of Twp. 7, Range 11, built a cabin and cleared the land for a small farm. He was both a farmer and brickmaker and as a brickmaker was often away from his family for several days at a time. His wife, Margaret Prentiss, whom he married in 1807, purportedly gave the township her husband's name at a housewarming party held in their first cabin. In the first township election, Warren was elected chairman. In 1817 he was elected justice of the peace; later he served in various township offices, including trustee 1827–28. As another form of public service, he established a tavern in Warrensville, on the northeast corner of Milverton and Kinsman roads.

Warren had 6 children: William H., Moses N., Pauline, Julia, James M., and Othello. He was buried in Woodland Cemetery.

**WARSHAWSKY, ABEL "BUCK"** (28 Dec. 1883– 30 May 1962) and **ALEXANDER "XANDER"** (29 Mar. 1887–28 May 1945), artists, were 2 of 9 children of Ezekiel and Ida Warshawsky, Jewish immigrants from Poland who came to Cleveland from Sharon, PA. Both brothers attended Cleveland School of Art and the Natl. Academy of Design in New York, then went to Europe. Abel went to France in 1908, with the help of LOUIS RORIMER, his Cleveland Art School sculpting instructor, and until 1938 divided his time between Paris and Brittany. Abel described himself as a classic Impressionist. Alexander went to Paris in 1916. He painted Breton peasants and landscapes using flat surfaces and clear outlines, smoothly brushed surfaces, and highly keyed colors. Both brothers were pacifists, serving together behind the French lines in World War I, decorating soldiers' huts with murals and organizing sports events. In recognition for this work, the French government asked them to exhibit in the Luxembourg Gallery. They returned at least once a year to Cleveland. Several times they exhibited jointly.

The threat of World War II forced Abel to leave France and settle in Monterey, CA. His works were shown in many galleries and acquired by the French government and 13 American art museums. He was named Chevalier of the Legion of Honor by the French government. He married 3 times: to Vantine Laudell (div. 1926), Minny (died), and Ruth Tate, whom he married in 1939.

Alex organized an exhibition in Cleveland of Postimpressionism in 1914, a controversial show but giving Cleveland the opportunity to view modern art. Alex lived in Paris over a 25-year period, exhibiting his paintings during his frequent jour-

neys to the U.S. He lived in Los Angeles for 12 years before his death. He married Berthe, a designer of children's clothes, and had a son, Ivan.

Warshawsky Family Papers, WRHS.
Bassham, Ben L., ed. *The Memories of an American Impressionist: Abel G. Warshawsky* (1980).

**WATERFIELD, ROBERT "BOB"** (26 July 1920– 25 Mar. 1983), football player with the Cleveland and Los Angeles Rams (see CLEVELAND RAMS†), in his rookie season led the Cleveland Rams to the 1945 Natl. Football League championship and was unanimously elected the league's Most Valuable Player. Born in Elmira, NY, to Jack and Frances Waterfield, he played football for UCLA (1941, 1942, 1944), then spent his entire professional career with the Rams. In 1945, the 6'2" 200-lb. quarterback completed 51% of his passes, threw 16 touchdowns, and scored 5 touchdowns himself. He was also the punter and placekicker, making 31 of 34 field goals in 1945. During his first 4 years, he also played defense, intercepting 20 passes. Waterfield led the NFL in passing (1945, 1951) and field goals (1949, 1951), during his career completing 813 of 1,617 attempted passes (50.3%) for 11,849 yards and 98 touchdowns. Waterfield himself scored 573 points on 13 touchdowns, 315 points after touchdowns, and 60 field goals. As a punter he kicked for a 42.4-yard average. He led the Los Angeles Rams to 3 Western Div. crowns and the NFL championship (1951). After retiring, Waterfield coached the Rams (1960–62), then became a team scout and a rancher near Van Nuys, CA. During his 1 season in Cleveland, Waterfield attracted special attention because his wife, actress Jane Russell, spent the football season with him. Married in 1943, the couple divorced in 1968. They had three adopted children: Thomas, Tracy, and Robert. Waterfield married again in 1970 to Ann Mangus. Waterfield was inducted into the Pro Football Hall of Fame in 1965.

**WATKINS, SAMUEL "SAMMY"** (ca. 1904–26 July 1969) was a well-known dance orchestra leader and songwriter in Cleveland whose style, quality, and good taste brought pleasure to Greater Clevelanders for over 40 years.

Born in a small Russian village, the son of Joseph Watkovitz, Sammy was brought to Cleveland by his parents when he was a year old. He learned to play the violin and saxophone and went into the music business after attending Glenville High School. The music of Watkins and his orchestra made dining and dancing a memorable occasion for guests at the Vogue Room at the old Hollenden Hotel for 13 years and at the Terrace Room of the Statler Hilton for 12 years. Watkins was generally credited with the discovery of singer Dino Crocetti, who sang with his orchestra at the Vogue Room as Dean Martin from 1940 to 1943. He also played for the annual Ribs 'n' Roast show for 20 years and numerous private gatherings throughout the area. Among his many songs, Watkins composed an all-purpose number entitled "Greatest Location in the Nation" which he could adapt for any local occasion, from a charity drive to a civic celebration. He also wrote jingles for the post office and the Cleveland Indians baseball team. In later years he operated a music booking agency for orchestras and combos, playing under the Watkins name at parties, dances, and nightclubs. He was a businessman as well, serving as president of a steel company, Seaway Warehouses.

Watkins and his wife, Lee Curry, had a daughter, Mrs. Stephanie Feldman, and a son, Jon. He died in Cleveland.—M.S.

**WATSON, WILBUR J.** (5 Apr. 1871–22 May 1939), a civil engineer especially eminent in bridge design, was born in BEREA† to David R. and Maria (Parker) Watson. Receiving his B.S. from the Case School of Engineering, Watson developed a carefully stated philosophy of the relationship between engineering and aesthetics and used structural and reinforced concrete to produce some of the most beautiful BRIDGES† in northern Ohio. He helped set standards for bridge construction across the country. While employed by OSBORN ENGINEERING CO.† in Cleveland, Watson was designing bridges as early as 1898. Marrying Harriett Martha Barnes in 1900, Watson founded his own firm, Wilbur J. Watson & Associates, in 1907. His achievements include recognizing the possibility of using precast concrete beams for bridges (1908); the pioneer design of steel centering for erecting concrete bridges (Rocky River Bridge, 1910); early experiments with mushroom-and-slab floor construction (1911); the design of the Howard St. Bridge in Akron, highest bridge of its kind in 1912; concrete bridges for the Cleveland & Youngstown Railroad (SHAKER RAPID TRANSIT LINE†) (1916); construction of the unique Akron Goodyear Zeppelin Airdock (1929) covering 8½ acres, the largest uninterrupted interior space in the world; engineering the Lorain-Carnegie (1932) and Main Ave. (1939) bridges in Cleveland; and the bascule bridge in Lorain (1940). His publications included *Bridge Architecture* (1927), *A Decade of Bridges: 1926–1936* (1937), and *Bridges in History and Legend* (1937), the latter written with his daughters, Sara Ruth and Emily.

**WEARN, JOSEPH T.** (15 Feb. 1893–26 Sept. 1984), dean of Western Reserve Univ. School of Medicine, was born in Charlotte, NC, the son of Joseph H. and Ann (Treloar) Wearn. He received his B.A. from Davidson College (1913) and medical degree from Harvard Medical School (1917); served as a resident in Boston, then as an instructor at the Univ. of Pennsylvania before joining the faculty of Harvard Medical School. He joined WRU in 1929, serving as dean of the School of Medicine from 1945–59. He was an officer in the Medical Corps of the U.S. Army briefly in World War I. Prior to 1929, Wearn published articles on the kidney and heart, performing experiments making possible much of the present understanding of renal function. During World War II, he was medical consultant to the secretary of war, and was awarded the Medal of Freedom.

Wearn strengthened the faculty and financial position of WRU School of Medicine. In 1952 he changed the medical school curriculum, teaching medicine as a whole concept rather than as a series of unrelated disciplines, teaching subject areas by committees of faculty members rather than strictly by department. After retiring in 1960, Wearn served both CASE WESTERN RESERVE UNIV.† and Harvard Medical School as a consultant. He was a member of many medical societies. CWRU honored Wearn in 1973, giving him the first Univ. Medal for outstanding service. In 1961 the $5.3 million Joseph Treloar Wearn Laboratory for Medical Research was dedicated to him. Wearn married Susan Lyman; they had a daughter, Susan. Wearn died at his summer home in Brooklin, ME, and was buried there.

Personal Papers of Joseph T. Wearn, M.D. CWRU Archives.

**WEBB, ELLA STURTEVANT** (15 Dec.1856–6 Sept. 1931), writer, helped compile the 3-volume *Memorial to the Pioneer Women of the Western Reserve (1896–1924)* and served as recording secretary of the Women's Department of the Cleveland Centennial Commission (1896). She wrote for publications such as *Leisure Hours* (Philadelphia). Webb was born in Cleveland at the present site of the Terminal Tower to Ezra and Louisa Park Sturtevant, pioneer settlers of the WESTERN RESERVE.† She was educated in public schools and took an extension course at Columbia Univ. Webb was active in professional organizations, as treasurer of the Ohio Women's Press Club and later secretary to the Cleveland Writers Club. She also belonged to the New England Society of Cleveland and the Western Reserve, the CLEVELAND MU-

SEUM OF ART,† and the WOMEN'S CITY CLUB OF CLEVELAND.†

On 4 April 1876 she married Chandler L. Webb, who worked for the Lake Shore Railroad. They lived in Cleveland with their daughter, Louise (Mrs. Charles Lester) Bryant.—J.M.

**WEBER, GUSTAV C. E.** (26 May 1828–21 Mar. 1912), surgeon, professor, and a founder of ST. VINCENT CHARITY HOSPITAL,† was born in Bonn, Germany, to anatomy professor Moritz Ignaz Weber and Josephine Philippina (Von Podowilz) Weber. He immigrated to St. Louis in 1848, received his degree from St. Louis Medical College (1851), then returned to Europe to study and intern in Amsterdam. He began practicing in New York City in 1853; in 1856 he became professor of surgery and of principles and practices of medicine at Cleveland Medical College, remaining until 1863, when he joined Bp. AMADEUS RAPPE to found Charity Hospital, becoming chief of staff in 1864. He also founded the associated medical school and was professor of surgery, dean, and treasurer of the faculty. When Charity Medical College was absorbed into the Univ. of Wooster in 1870, Weber continued as dean of the faculty until 1881, when he returned to Cleveland Medical College. When Western Reserve Univ. was incorporated in 1884, he became a trustee and dean of the Medical Dept. until 1893. In the Civil War, Weber was surgeon of Ohio. In 1859 he established the *Cleveland Medical Gazette,* the city's first medical journal, editing it for 2 years. Weber's library and armamentarium were donated to CLEVELAND MEDICAL LIBRARY ASSN.† In 1896 he was appointed U.S. consul in Nurnberg, Germany. Upon his return 4 years later, Weber suffered a stroke at a welcome dinner. He spent his remaining years in Willoughby. Weber married Ruth Elizabeth Chaney in 1854 and had 2 children, Carl and Ida. He was buried in Lake View Cemetery.

Gustav Weber Papers, Allen Memorial Medical Library Archives.

**WEDDELL, PETER MARTIN** (1788–1847) was the prominent merchant and owner of WEDDELL HOUSE,† Cleveland's most fashionable hotel during the mid–1800s. Son of Peter M. and Sarah Weddell, he was born in Westmoreland County, PA. Weddell moved to Paris, KY, when he was 14, working in a general store and becoming a partner within 5 years. Moving to Newark, OH, he opened his own general store. He came to Cleveland in 1820 and opened a store which soon became one of the largest in Ohio. Through the 1830s, Peter M. Weddell & Co. was one of Cleveland's leading merchandising firms, offering dry goods, carpets and rugs, and groceries. In 1827 Weddell joined Edmund Clark and Geo. Stanton in organizing the Cleveland & New York Line, a commission storage and transportation firm. He was a director for the COMMERCIAL BANK OF LAKE ERIE† from 1832 and later headed its successor, Merchants Bank. He was also an incorporator of Ohio Railroad Co., which collapsed in 1843. Weddell was on the board of Cleveland Medical College, contributed funds to Western Reserve Univ. in Hudson, and also helped purchase land on PUBLIC SQUARE† for the Old Stone Church. In 1845 Weddell tore down the store that had made him wealthy to begin construction of a hotel, two years later laying the cornerstone of the "Astor House of the Lakes" (later Weddell House), intending to make it the finest hotel in Cleveland, purchasing lavish furnishings in the East. He died shortly before its opening.

Weddell married Sophia Perry (d. 1823) in 1815; they had four children: Laura, Caroline, Peter P., and Horace. In 1824 Weddell married Eliza Owen Bell. Weddell died in Cleveland and was buried in the Erie St. Cemetery.

Weddell Family Papers, WRHS.

**WEEDEN, JOHN T.** (2 Aug. 1901–17 Sept. 1988), a Baptist minister for 65 years, served 41 years at St. Timothy Baptist Church in Cleveland. He demonstrated for civil rights for AFRICAN AMERICANS† locally and in Atlanta, GA, and Selma, AL; was community liaison for Rep. Louis Stokes (D–21), and managed the 1967 mayoral campaign for Carl Stokes (see MAYORAL ADMINISTRATION OF CARL B. STOKES†). Weeden was born in Watertown, TN, to Dovie and Will Weeden. He was educated at Butler Univ. in Indianapolis, IN, and received an honorary doctorate from Monrovia College in Liberia, Africa. He came to Cleveland in 1947 from a pastorate in Indianapolis.

Activist Martin Luther King, Jr., often spoke at Weeden's church (see MARTIN LUTHER KING, JR.'S VISITS TO CLEVELAND†). Weeden presided over the Baptist Ministers Conference of Cleveland and Vicinity and held offices in his denomination, the National Baptist Convention USA (see BAPTISTS†). He served on the boards of the CONVENTIONS AND VISITORS BUREAU OF GREATER CLEVELAND† and the local KIWANIS CLUB.† In 1966 he traveled to Nicaragua as a member of the International Brothers Foundation, which provided medical service to Third World nations.

Weeden and Gladys May Evans (d. 1979) were married 2 Aug. 1922. They had 4 daughters: Sara

472

Richardson, Katherine, Evelyn Jackson, and Phyllis Oliver, and 4 sons: Paul, Lawrence, Kenneth, and John P. Some family members belonged to the 38-person Weeden Family Singers, gospel recording artists, led by Rev. Weeden.—J.M.

Rev. John T. Weeden Papers, WRHS.

**WEEKS, HARRY ELLIS** (2 Oct. 1871–21 Dec. 1935), architect who, with FRANK R. WALKER, founded WALKER & WEEKS,† Cleveland's foremost architectural firm during the 1920s. The son of Charles F. and Clarissa Allen Weeks, he was born in W. Springfield, MA, graduated from MIT in 1893, and worked for several prominent Massachusetts architectural firms before owning his own firm in Pittsfield, MA, for 3 years. In Pittsfield, Walker's birthplace, Weeks met his future business partner. At the suggestion of John M. Carrere, a member of the Cleveland Group Plan Commission, Weeks moved to Cleveland in 1905, the same year as Walker. Both men joined the firm of J. MILTON DYER.† In 1911 Walker and Weeks left Dyer's office to establish their own practice. Their firm was known as a specialist in financial buildings, completing 60 banks throughout Ohio. In Cleveland, however, Walker & Weeks were best known for designing major commercial, public, and religious structures, most of them in classical revival styles, including Bingham Co. Warehouse (1915); Guardian Bldg. renovation (1915); PUBLIC AUDITORIUM† (1922); FEDERAL RESERVE BANK† (1923); CLEVELAND PUBLIC LIBRARY† (1925); EPWORTH-EUCLID METHODIST CHURCH,† with architect Bertram Goodhue (1928); First Baptist Church in Shaker Hts. (1929); ST. PAUL'S EPISCOPAL CHURCH† in Cleveland Hts. (1929); Pearl St. Savings & Trust; and CLEVELAND MUNICIPAL STADIUM† with OSBORN ENGINEERING CO.† (1931). Weeks was a member of Euclid Ave. Baptist Church and president of its Board of Trustees in 1926. He married Alice B. Tuggey in 1896. They had two children, Ellis and Donald. Weeks was buried in Lake View Cemetery.

**WEIDEMAN, JOHN CHRISTIAN** (14 Oct. 1829–9 Dec. 1900) was a leading wholesale grocer, prominent businessman, and an early German settler of Cleveland. He was born in Lehrensteinsfeld, Wurttemberg, Germany. His family emigrated to America in 1833, first residing in Philadelphia before moving to Medina County, OH, in 1836. "J. C." moved to Cleveland at age 17, where he apprenticed himself in the grocery business.

In 1861 he began his independent business career by establishing the WEIDEMAN CO.,† a wine and liquor firm. Within a decade, partners were brought into the firm, and its line expanded to include groceries. The firm, which grew rapidly, was incorporated as the Weideman Co. in 1889. By the 1890s, it was one of Cleveland's largest firms and one of the largest wholesale grocery companies in the U.S.

Weideman was also a founder and original director of the Union National Bank (1884), the Savings and Trust Co. (1883), the Forest City Savings Bank (1890), and the Ohio Abstract Co. He also served as president of the latter two firms.

Weideman, prominent in the local Republican party, was Cleveland's first elected police commissioner (1876). He declined to consider a second term, as well as offers to run for mayor.

Weideman married Laura Muntz in 1853 (1834–77), and from this marriage was survived by one son, Henry W. (1855–1930), who married Dorothy Burke. In 1879 J. C. married Louise Diebolt (1847–1931). From this marriage a daughter was born, Elsa L., who married OMAR E. MUELLER. Weideman died in Cleveland and was buried in Riverside Cemetery.

**WEIDENTHAL, LEO** (23 Apr. 1878–8 May 1967), editor of the *Jewish Independent* and founder of CLEVELAND CULTURAL GARDENS FED.,† was born in Cleveland to Emanuel and Julia (Kretch) Weidenthal. He began his newspaper career as a reporter for the *CLEVELAND WORLD†*; then for the *CLEVELAND LEADER†*; then, in 1906, for the *PLAIN DEALER,†* assigned to the city hall beat. In 1917 he became editor of the *Jewish Independent*, a weekly founded in 1906 by his brother, Maurice, a former *Plain Dealer* and *Press* reporter. Leo's brother Henry was also a journalist, once managing editor of the *Press* and *News*.

Weidenthal spent much time cataloguing his large collection of books, autographs, and letters marking the history of the theater since the early 19th century. He was also an amateur painter and authored *From Dis Waggon*. Weidenthal was a founder of the Cleveland Chap. of the Natl. Conference of Christians & Jews (1933) was vice-president of the EARLY SETTLERS ASSN.,† and is credited with suggesting a mounted police patrol. He was a critic of the modern freeway and worked to establish more parks and playgrounds. Until his retirement from the *Jewish Independent* in 1964, Weidenthal supposedly never took a vacation and worked 6 days a week, his only diversion being occasional weekends in New York City to attend plays. He received many honors, including a resolution passed by city council on 24 Sept. 1917 praising his service to the city during his 10 years as city hall reporter for the *Plain Dealer*. Weidenthal died a bachelor and was buried in Mayfield Cemetery.

**WEIL, HELEN KAHN** (3 Jan. 1902–20 Aug. 1992), pioneer in gerontology, introduced innovations at the MONTEFIORE HOME† for the aged with her husband Julius (see WEIL, JULIUS), such as the sheltered workshop, which were later modeled nationwide. The couple founded the Schnurmann House (1968) in Shaker Hts., an independent living facility for the elderly, which Helen Weil served as president from 1969 until her death. Weil was born in Germany but received her professional education in the U.S., studying at Columbia Univ. and graduating with an undergraduate degree from JOHN CARROLL UNIV.† (1943) and a master's in social work from Western Reserve Univ.'s School of Applied Social Sciences (1945). She then became Montefiore's social director (her husband served as president from 1941–68), beginning programs such as day care and foster care. Weil also published articles in gerontological journals and taught at WRU (later CASE WESTERN RESERVE UNIV.†) as adjunct professor, among the first social workers to teach gerontology. The local chapter of the National Conference of Christians and Jews honored Helen and Julius Weil for outstanding community service; among other awards, the couple was inducted into the Ohio Senior Citizens Hall of Fame.

Weil married Julius Weil in Germany, where they directed a home for delinquent boys. They emigrated to the U.S. in 1936, fleeing Nazi Germany, and worked in New York City before moving to Cleveland in 1940. The Weils lived in Shaker Hts. and had 2 daughters, Naomi Feil and Gabriele Hays. Weil died in MT. SINAI MEDICAL CENTER.†—J.M.

Montefiore Home Records, WRHS.
Julius & Helen Weil Papers, WRHS.

**WEIL, JULIUS** (6 Oct. 1902–9 April 1989), spent 45 years of his life working with senior citizens in Greater Cleveland. His contributions earned him national and international recognition. Born in Steifurt, Germany, to Gustav and Matilda Weil, Julius was educated in Germany, eventually earning his Ph.D in clinical psychology from the Univ. of Munich. On 20 Nov. 1924, he married Helen Kahn (see WEIL, HELEN KAHN), and the couple had two daughters, Naomi and Gabriele. Forced to flee the Nazis, the Weils left their native land in 1936, making their way to Cleveland in 1940.

Weil came to Cleveland at the invitation of the MONTEFIORE HOME† for senior citizens in CLEVELAND HTS.† Under his leadership, the home grew in capacity from 60 to 200 residents. He also instituted a program of occupational therapy there, and through a sheltered workshop gave resi-

dents the opportunity of earning some income and augmenting their sense of independence.

He was close friend of another immigrant, Cornelia Schnurmann, and when she died her will directed him to undertake another chapter in serving the elderly. Leaving Montefiore Home at the end of 1968, Weil established the Cornelia Schnurmann Foundation, and through it built Schnurmann House in MAYFIELD HTS.,† a residential compound serving 198 golden-agers. It is located on Julius Weil Drive. He led the home from 1969 to 1985, when he retired.

Besides his leadership of the Cleveland homes for the aged, Weil wrote for the *Geriatrics* and *Jewish Social Service Quarterly* journals, and went around the country giving talks on the needs of seniors. Weil is buried in Mt. Olive Cemetery in Solon, OH.—J.T.

Montefiore Home Records, WRHS.
Julius & Helen Weil Papers, WRHS.

**WEINBERG, JOSEPH LEWIS** (12 Nov. 1890–14 Jan. 1977), architect who pioneered urban-renewal and slum-clearance efforts with his design of LAKEVIEW TERRACE† (1934), was born in Omaha, NE, to Lewis and Mollie Lazar Weinberg and at age 10 came to Cleveland to live at the JEWISH ORPHAN HOME† after his father's death. When he was 15, he brought his mother to Cleveland and attended CENTRAL HIGH SCHOOL,† while working as a lamplighter. After graduation from Harvard Univ. in 1912, he trained in architects' offices in New York, Detroit, and Cleveland, where he worked for WALKER & WEEKS† and J. MILTON DYER. After a year in the Army Signal Corps during World War I, Weinberg entered private practice in Cleveland in 1919. He was a partner from 1923–30 in Morris & Weinberg. From 1928–41 he taught architecture at Western Reserve Univ. and John Huntington Polytechnic Institute. During World War II, he was the chief architect in the 5th construction zone for the U.S. Quartermaster Corp, 1941–42, and chief engineer at Holston Ordnance Works for the Kingsport Tennessee District Engineer Office, 1942–44. He was a planning consultant to the Cleveland Neighborhood Constr. Project, 1945–46. Weinberg was a partner in firms from 1946–77. His designs included portions of the interior of CLEVELAND CITY HALL† and Lakeside Courthouse; Lakeview Terrace, 1934; Lakeview Towers, 1975; BELLEFAIRE,† 1929; and the Community Chest Headquarters Bldg., 1957. Weinberg married Edith Lazarus in 1933 and had 2 children, Judith and Daniel.

Joseph Weinberg Papers, WRHS.

**WEINBERGER, ADOLPH** (5 Jan. 1891–16 Dec. 1977), founder of a nationwide chain of drug stores, was born in Hungary, the son of Nathan N. and Tillie Hocheiser Weinberger. Arriving in Cleveland as a youth, he combined work with study, attending CENTRAL HIGH SCHOOL† at night and enrolling as special student at the School of Pharmacy at Western Reserve Univ. 1910–12. After opening his first drug store at E. 30th and Scovill Ave. in 1912, Weinberger acquired other stores and incorporated the Weinberger Drug Co. in 1921 with $20,000 capital. Adopting cut-rate prices, Weinberger was successful, operating 21 stores throughout Cleveland, and in Mansfield, Sandusky, Youngstown, and Pittsburgh by 1934. He acquired two other chains in Ohio and Pennsylvania in 1946 and changed the name to GRAY DRUG STORES, INC.,† which became one of the largest in the nation. As president of the Ohio State Pharmacy Board, Weinberger led the fight to tighten controls on barbiturates in 1950. He also was chairman of the committee which raised $500,000 to establish the School of Pharmacy at Hebrew Univ. in Jerusalem which was named in his honor.

Weinberger married Minnie Jacobs 10 Sept. 1916; they had four children: Carl, Jerome, Ruth Herman, and Elaine Berwitt. After his wife's death in 1964, Weinberger married Lillian Abrams 16 June 1965. A resident of SHAKER HTS.,† he died at Gates Mills Manor nursing home and was buried at Glenville Cemetery.—M.S.

**WELTER, KATHERINE J. KESSLER** (1901–14 June 1992), opened and managed an all-woman real estate office, Katherine J. Welter Real Estate, Inc., in Cleveland before World War II, and helped secure mortgage loans for single professional women. Welter was born in Transylvania, then a part of Austria-Hungary, to Martin and Katie Zaker Kessler. While her father fought in World War I, she helped care for her ill mother and siblings. Welter worked as a governess following the war, when she came to Cleveland at age 19. She was employed as a housekeeper and in a knitting mill before marrying cabinetmaker and singing waiter Rudolph Welter on 17 Dec. 1921. They had two daughters, Kay Everson and Ruth Mistretta. The couple restored an estate on Chardon Rd., ran a butcher shop and a beauty shop and sold corsets before Welter went into real estate.

In 1956 Welter represented the CLEVELAND AREA BOARD OF REALTORS† at an international conference in Vienna, Austria. An avid dancer who won local and national competitions, Welter belonged to the Arthur Murray Dance Studio. After her husband's death in 1972, Welter moved to BRATENAHL.† She died in a nursing home in Willowbrook, IL.—J.M.

**WEMBRIDGE, ELEANOR HARRIS ROWLAND** (1882–19 Feb. 1944), psychologist and nationally known author on juvenile delinquency, served as girls' referee for the CUYAHOGA COUNTY JUVENILE COURT† (1926–35). Wembridge (half-sister of AMY ROWLAND) was born in Lee, MA, to Rev. Lyman Sibley and Elizabeth McClellan Gould Rowland. She attended Oberlin College and graduated Phi Beta Kappa from Radcliffe College (A.B., 1903; A.M. 1904; and Ph.D., 1905). Wembridge taught psychology at Mt. Holyoke (1910) and Reed (1915) colleges and, during World War I, served with the American Red Cross in New York City. She worked as head aide at the Walter Reed Hospital (1918) and supervised military aides in the U.S. Surgeon General's office in Washington, DC, before coming to Cleveland in 1922 as a clinical psychologist. Before Judge HARRY LLOYD EASTMAN appointed her to the Juvenile Court, Wembridge served as psychologist for the Women's Protective Assn. She promoted better health and dental care, more recreational facilities, and advocated the improvement of institutions such as BLOSSOM HILL SCHOOL FOR GIRLS† (see CHILD CARE†).

Wembridge was a fellow of the American Assn. for the Advancement of Science. In addition to books and prize-winning plays, she published numerous articles in popular magazines such as *American Mercury* and *McCall's,* and in scientific journals. On 1 June 1917, Wembridge married Harry A. Wembridge, later president of Cleveland's Independent Neon Sign Co. They had a daughter, Mary Althea. The Wembridges moved to California in 1935. Wembridge died in Santa Monica, CA, and is buried in Lee, MA.—J.M.

**WENHAM, FREDERICK L.** (21 Dec. 1916–22 Sept. 1965) built one of the region's largest trucking firms and sponsored one of the city's most successful amateur baseball teams. He was born in Willoughby, OH, the son of Percival and Catherine Burmeister Wenham. After attending Cleveland College (see CASE WESTERN RESERVE UNIV.†), he went to work for his father's Willoughby Express Co., becoming president upon the elder Wenham's death in 1940. In 1942 he reorganized the company as Wenham, Inc. and moved it to Cleveland. He then purchased the Great Lakes Motor Dispatch Co., which was reorganized in 1948 as Wenham Transportation, Inc. When the terminal serving both companies was displaced by the INNERBELT FREEWAY,† Wenham moved them into a new trucking terminal he built on E. 79th St. By the time of his death he was operating 460 tractor-trailer rigs over an 8-state area.

For 22 years he had sponsored a Class A baseball team, Wenham Truckers, which won several championships. He also sponsored Little League and Pony League teams in several cities and was a member of the Cleveland Baseball Federation. In addition to his trucking companies, he was also president of the Wenham Supply Co., the Ridler Tank and Welding Corp., and the Contract Carrier Corp. Wenham married the former Lois Solomon of Cleveland in 1946 and was survived by her and 4 sons: Frederick L. III, Jeffrey, Christopher, and Timothy. He died at his home in SHAKER HTS.†
—J.V.

**WEST, THOMAS DYSON** (31 Aug. 1851–18 June 1915), pioneer in factory safety and authority on foundry practice, was born in Manchester, England, the son of William H. and Sara (Faraday) West, who came to America when he was an infant. After receiving a grammar school education, he began work in a foundry at age 12. By 1872 he and his family resided in Cleveland, where Thomas worked as a molder for the Eclipse Foundry. Later he served as foreman at the CUYAHOGA STEAM FURNACE CO.† In 1887 West, Samuel Landsdown, and Charles Neracher organized the Thomas West Foundry. Five years later the company moved to Sharpesville, PA. After the turn of the century, West divided his time between Cleveland and Sharpesville, until he returned to Cleveland permanently in 1909. In 1906 he incorporated the West Steel Casting Co. in Cleveland with himself as chairman and his son, Ralph H., as president and general manager. West wrote *American Foundry Practice* (1882), which became a standard in the field. He originated the use of "direct metal" to make ingot molds for steel works and patented processes for hardening and obtaining an even depth of chill in railroad car wheels. From 1907 until his death he was active in factory safety, publishing *Accidents, Their Cause and Remedies* in 1908. He also originated Cleveland's "Sane Fourth" celebrations to prevent accidents from the use of fireworks.

West married Emma Robison and they had 3 children: sons Thomas J., Ralph H., and daughter, Mrs. William E. Ward. He married his second wife, Clara G. Gerblick, 7 March 1900. West is buried at Lake View Cemetery.—M.S.

**WESTROPP, CLARA E.** (7 July 1886–25 June 1965), cofounder of WOMEN'S FEDERAL SAVINGS BANK† and a leading supporter of Roman Catholic missions, was born in Cleveland to Thos. P. and Clara Stoeckel Westropp, graduated from West High School and Dyke School of Commerce, and

later studied at the Savings & Loan Institute in Mercersburg, PA. Convinced women could bring to the business world an appreciation of home ownership, and recognizing the value of regular saving, Westropp and her sister, LILLIAN M. WESTROPP, began a savings and loan association directed and run by women in 1922, the first such institution in the country. Originally organized under a state charter, it was reorganized under a federal charter in 1935, renamed Women's Federal Savings & Loan Assn. of Cleveland. Clara personally sold over half the initial stock capitalization of $85,000. By 1954 the association was the 3rd-largest savings and loan in Cuyahoga County, with assets exceeding $38 million. In 1952 the Cuyahoga Savings & Loan League chose Westropp as its president, the first woman holding that office. She was the founder and for 20 years chairman of St. Xavier Mission Assn. of the Cleveland Diocese, and was also diocesan mission chairman of the Natl. Council of Catholic Women. In 1965 she was awarded posthumously the Mission Secretarial Award from Washington, DC, making her Catholic Woman of the Year. Also posthumously, Clara E. Westropp Jr. High School was named in her honor. Westropp died in Cleveland. She was unmarried.

**WESTROPP, LILLIAN MARY** (9 May 1884–15 Aug. 1968), Cleveland Municipal Court judge and cofounder of WOMEN'S FEDERAL SAVINGS BANK,† was born in Cleveland to Thos. P. and Clara Stoeckel Westropp. She graduated from West High School and Dyke School of Commerce, and after a brief theatrical career enrolled in BALDWIN-WALLACE COLLEGE's† law school, graduating in 1915 with an LL.B. Entering private practice, emphasizing real estate and finance, Westropp was one of the first women admitted to the CLEVELAND BAR ASSN.† and the first woman elected to its executive committee. In 1929 she became asst. county prosecutor, instituting a bail-bond system ensuring 100% collection. In 1931 she was appointed to fill a municipal judgeship; she was continually reelected until she retired in 1957. She initiated a court psychiatric clinic in 1937.

With her sister, CLARA E. WESTROPP, Westropp organized Women's Federal Savings & Loan Assn. of Cleveland, serving as president from 1936–57 and as chairman of the Board of Directors until her death. Her objective was to give women confidence in their own financial ability and prove they could succeed. Westropp was an active Democrat, organizing Democratic Women, State of Ohio (1920), and chosen a member of the executive committee of the CUYAHOGA COUNTY DEMOCRATIC PARTY† (1923). She was an organizer of the Women Lawyers' Club of Cleveland;

WOMEN'S CITY CLUB†; LEAGUE OF WOMEN VOTERS†; Catholic Daughters of America; Cleveland Diocesan Council of Catholic Women; BUSINESS & PROFESSIONAL WOMEN'S CLUB†; and Woman's Hospital. She was unmarried.

**WEY, ALEXANDER JOSEPH** (12 Dec. 1896–17 Nov. 1981) was an influential Catholic layman who devoted half a century to the service of the religious press. The son of John and Barbara Wey of Cleveland, he attended St. Mary High School and in 1917 began working for the *Catholic Bulletin*, a weekly founded in 1911 by his brother, Linus G. Wey. At the request of Bp. JOSEPH SCHREMBS, A. J. Wey merged the *Bulletin* with the older *Catholic Universe* in 1926 to form the *CATHOLIC UNIVERSE BULLETIN.†* As general manager of the Catholic Press Union, publisher of the *Universe Bulletin*, Wey helped establish diocesan newspapers in Toledo and Youngstown. He originated the Student Press Crusade, whereby subscriptions to the *Universe Bulletin* were sold by parochial students. He also participated in organizing the Catholic Press Assn. of the U.S. and Canada, which he served 2 terms each as president and vice-president. His retirement from the Catholic Press Union on 1 Feb. 1967 occurred 50 years to the day after his entrance into Catholic journalism. He was named a Knight Commander of the Order of St. Gregory by Pope Pius XII in 1940, and elected honorary president for life after 3 terms as president of the ST. VINCENT DePAUL SOC.† of Cleveland. A lifelong resident of LAKEWOOD,† he married Matilda Wirtz in 1921. He was survived by her, their son, Matthew, and daughter, Sister Maretta, a former asst. dir. for curriculum for the Diocesan Education Office.—J.V.

**WEYGANDT, CARL** (14 June 1888–4 Sept. 1964), lawyer and chief justice of the Supreme Court of Ohio for 30 years, was born near Wooster, OH, to Cora (Mock) and Common Pleas Judge Wm. E. Weygandt. He graduated from Wooster College in 1912. After teaching for 3 years, he entered Western Reserve Univ. Law School, graduated and was admitted to the bar in 1918. Weygandt practiced with THOMPSON, HINE & FLORY in Cleveland. In 1920 he was elected to the Ohio general assembly, introducing bills to reform the state judiciary and fighting for a minimum wage for women. He returned to practice in 1923 as counsel for the Cleveland Automobile Club. An outstanding college athlete, until 1932 Weygandt officiated as a football referee in games from Massachusetts to Nebraska.

In 1924 Weygandt was appointed to the common pleas court bench to replace a retiring judge. In 1930 he was elected judge of the Court of Appeals of Ohio, and in 1933 was elected chief justice of the

Supreme Court of Ohio. During his first term, Weygandt quelled personal feuds within the Ohio Supreme Court and improved its efficiency. He was reelected to 5 more terms. Weygandt often advocated higher salaries and a better retirement plan for judges in order to keep competent men on the bench. During his 30 years as chief justice, Weygandt heard over 20,000 cases and swore in more Ohio governors than any of his predecessors. He was defeated for reelection by Kingsley A. Taft in 1962.

Weygandt married Jessie M. Silver on 14 June 1915. They lived in LAKEWOOD† with children Richard S., Clark W., and Mary C. Weygandt died in Lakewood and was buried in Wooster.

**WHITAKER, MAY TARBELL CANNON** (15 Oct. 1858–14 July 1944), writer and civic leader, was elected to the Cleveland School Council (1900–04), served on the executive committees of both the state and the CUYAHOGA COUNTY DEMOCRATIC PARTY,† and was an associate editor for the Cleveland *PRESS†* in 1915. Whitaker was born in BEDFORD,† OH, to Leverett and May Helen Tinker Tarbell. She attended Willoughby College and Ohio Wesleyan Univ., graduating in 1879. She married salesman Grover Gordon Cannon (d. 1888) on 30 September 1879. They lived first in Marion, OH, then in Bedford, and had 3 children: Tom Tarbell, Herbert Grove, and Dana Alonzo Cannon. Whitaker married Brooks Oil Co. founder Alfred Whitaker on 15 Oct. 1894; he died less than 2 years later. They had one son, Alfred Andrew, Jr. Twice widowed, she then moved with her children from Bedford to Cleveland.

Whitaker took over her husband's business (serving as president of Brooks Oil for 3 years), and plunged into political, civic, and social leadership. In about 1904 she began writing, first published in *Suburban Life*. Other magazines later published her work and she joined the Cleveland Women's Press Club (later the Cleveland Writers' Club), which she served as president, and Ohio Newspaper Women. Whitaker served on the executive committee of the women's department of the Centennial Commission (see CLEVELAND ANNIVERSARY CELEBRATIONS†) and helped to publish *The Memorial to the Pioneer Women of the Western Reserve*. She was a member and state and local president of the WOMAN'S CHRISTIAN TEMPERANCE UNION, NON-PARTISAN, OF CLEVELAND,† serving projects such as the FRIENDLY INN SOCIAL SETTLEMENT† and the RAINEY INSTITUTE.† Whitaker belonged to the Epworth Memorial Church (later EPWORTH EUCLID UNITED METHODIST CHURCH,† the Daughters of the American Revolution, and the Society of New England Women. She died in Sacramento, CA, and is buried in Bedford, OH.—J.M.

**WHITE, CHARLES MCELROY** (13 June 1891–10 Jan. 1977) was chairman and chief executive officer of REPUBLIC STEEL CORP.,† with a reputation as a tough labor negotiator opposing any intervention in collective bargaining.

Born in Oakland, MD, to Charles and Estella (Jarboe), White attended grammar school in Hutton, MD, and received a B.S. (mechanical engineering) from the Univ. of Maryland, 1913.

White's introduction to the steel industry came in 1913 as a machinist's helper with the American Bridge Co. (PA). Later that year he joined Jones & Laughlin Steel Co. in Pittsburgh as a millwright helper, working up to general superintendent in 1919. White became superintendent of J&L's subsidiary, Monongahela Connecting Railroad, 1920–27, and Aliquippa Railroad, 1927–29.

In 1930 White came to Cleveland as asst. vice-president of operations at Republic Steel. He served as vice-president of operations, 1935–45; president, 1945–56; CEO, 1955–60; and chairman, 1956–60. Retiring as chairman in 1960, White remained a director until 1966, and honorary chairman until his death.

As Republic's leader, White spent millions to improve and expand production facilities, making Republic one of the nation's leading steel producers. His expertise on blast furnaces helped make Republic a leader in developing an electric model. White's reputation in the steel industry earned him numerous honors and awards.

White helped found the Cleveland Development Foundation, Boys Club of Cleveland, and raised millions for area charities and institutions. In 1955 he received the Cleveland Chamber of Commerce medal for distinguished public service.

White married Helen Bradley in 1918. They had one daughter, Jean. An Episcopalian, White is buried in Lake View Cemetery.—T.B.

**WHITE, CHARLES W.** (26 Dec. 1897–21 Aug. 1970), lawyer and civic servant, was the first African American common pleas judge in Ohio, appointed 16 Jan. 1955 by Democratic governor FRANK J. LAUSCHE to fill an unexpired term, and the first African American appellate judge (1966, chief justice, 1969–70). White was born in Nashville, TN, to Nellie Allen and Dr. Robert S. White, Sr., a medical school graduate who served as an elementary school principal. White attended school in Nashville and Evanston, IL. After serving in World War I, he received a B.A. from Fisk Univ. in 1921 and graduated from Harvard Univ. Law School in 1924. He came to Cleveland but, after

passing the bar in 1925, could find no law firm to hire him. He worked as a social worker and waited tables at the UNION CLUB† until beginning practice with Charles R. Chandler, a Fisk classmate. He later went into practice with CLAYBORNE GEORGE and entered politics as leader of the 18th Ward. Mayor HARRY LYMAN DAVIS appointed White asst. city law director (1933–55), and Mayor HAROLD HITZ BURTON named him to the Metropolitan Housing Authority (1940–55, later the CUYAHOGA METROPOLITAN HOUSING AUTHORITY†). White was elected to a full term on the Court of Appeals in Nov. 1956 and named chair of the Rules Committee in Oct 1957.

White helped found and served as vice-president of Forest City Hospital. He served as president of the Council of Human Relations (1961) and the KARAMU HOUSE† Board of Trustees, as well as on the boards of the YOUNG MEN'S CHRISTIAN ASSN.† (YMCA) and the Welfare Federation. With his wife, Elizabeth (d. 1947, two years after they divorced), White had one daughter, Lillian A. In 1951 White married Stella Godfrey. He belonged to the St. Andrew's Episcopal Church.—J.M.

---

Charles W. White Papers, WRHS.

**WHITE, JOHN GRISWOLD** (10 Aug. 1845–26 Aug. 1928), lawyer and bibliophile, was born in Cleveland to lawyer Bushnell White and Elizabeth Brainard (Clark) White. In 1865 White graduated from Western Reserve College and was admitted to the bar in 1868. He went into partnership with Robt. E. Mix and Judge Conway W. Noble in 1870. The firm subsequently became White & Mix and was still active in 1995 as SPIETH, BELL, MCCURDY & NEWELL CO. White practiced largely in real estate, but was also well versed in maritime, church, and municipal law. He was special counsel for CLEVELAND RAILWAY CO.† in its fight with TOM L. JOHNSON over Municipal Railway; attorney for the Catholic Diocese of Northern Ohio; and participated in litigation between 2 factions of the Evangelical church.

White was a charter member of the UNION CLUB,† and with Mix, founded the CLEVELAND YACHT CLUB.† He served on the CLEVELAND PUBLIC LIBRARY† Board of Trustees (1884–86, 1910–28), as president for 15 years (1913–28), and was instrumental in selecting WM. H. BRETT and LINDA EASTMAN to head the library. Largely through his efforts, CPL grew to national prominence, established a branch library system, introduced the open-shelf policy, and implemented an employee retirement plan. White personally selected and donated over 60,000 books on Orientalia, folklore, and related subjects to the library; upon his death he bequeathed his 12,000-volume chess and checker collection to it. He left the bulk of his estate as an endowment to maintain and develop its John G. White Collection of Folklore, Orientalia and Chess. Never married, White died in Jackson, WY, and was buried in Lake View Cemetery.

Cleveland Public Library. *The Open Shelf. Memorial Number: John Griswold White, Citizen of Cleveland, Lawyer, Scholar, Bookman, Donor of the White Collection* (ca. 1929).

Cleveland Public Library Round Table. *Tribute Presented to Mr. White by the Round Table on the Occasion of his Eightieth Birthday* (1925).

Reece, Motoko B. Yatabe. "John Griswold White, Trustee, and the White Collection in the Cleveland Public Library" (Ph.D. diss., Univ. of Michigan, 1979).

**WHITE, MOSES** (25 Feb. 1791–1 Sept. 1881), early settler and very active in Cleveland's early religious life, though a layman, was born in Warwick, MA, son of Jacob and Catherine (Penniman) White. He trained as a tailor and with his wife, Mary (Andrews), came to Cleveland in 1816 and operated a tailor shop for several decades. Discouraged by the absence of organized religion in Cleveland, White, with ALFRED KELLEY and Noble H. Merwin, worked to promote Christianity in the early settlement. White himself publicly professed his faith in Christ in 1816. The three men retained visiting ministers or, in the absence of clergy, conducted their own services. As part of the Sunday school movement, in 1819 White helped organize the first religious school in Cleveland, serving as its secretary. In 1833 he was a charter member of FIRST BAPTIST CHURCH† of Cleveland, serving as a deacon for almost 50 years. White had 8 children, only two of which survived to adulthood: Eliza, Charles, Edna, Sarah, Annie, George, Judson, and Minerva. White died in Cleveland and was buried in Erie St. Cemetery.

**WHITE, ROLLIN CHARLES** (3 June 1837–5 July 1920) was a businessman with connections in several leading local industries. The son of Hiram and Abagail Harris White, he was born in Putney, VT. In 1865 he married Lizzie T. Warren of Hubbardston, MA, and moved to Cleveland. When the family sewing machine business (see WHITE CONSOLIDATED INDUSTRIES†) was relocated the following year from Massachusetts to Cleveland, Rollin C. White became its vice-president. He was later admitted to partnership. In 1895 White joined his son-in-law, WALTER C. BAKER, in organizing the American Ball Bearing Co. He was also a founder of the Baker Motor Vehicle Co. 3 years later, disposing of his interest in the White concerns about the same time. He also served as president of the Cleveland

Machine Screw Co., another Baker venture, and as officer or director of several banks. A resident of EUCLID AVE.,† he was a real estate broker at the time of his death. Buried in Lake View Cemetery, he was survived by his daughter, Frances "Fannie" Baker, and a son, Fred C.—J.V.

**WHITE, ROLLIN HENRY** (11 July 1872–10 Sept. 1962), a founder of WHITE MOTOR CORP.† and Cleveland Tractor Co., was born in Cleveland to Almira Greenleaf White and THOMAS H. WHITE. He graduated from Cornell Univ. in 1894 and worked in Cleveland for his father's White Sewing Machine Co. during the 1890s, when the company added roller skates, kerosene lamps, bicycles, automatic lathes, and screw machines to its production. Thomas left the automobile-manufacturing business to his sons, Windsor, Walter, and Rollin. In 1899 Rollin invented a flash boiler that could safely be used on steam automobiles. In 1900 the Stanhope model, the first White Steamer, was introduced. To demonstrate White automobiles were safe, Rollin raced them; in 1901 he set a world land speed record for steam carriages. In 1906 White became vice-president of the newly formed White Co., continuing production of White Steamers until 1909. In 1910 the first gasoline White trucks were produced. In 1914 Rollin left White Co. and in 1916 organized Cleveland Motor Plow Co. to produce tractors. In 1917 the company became Cleveland Tractor Co., or CLETRAC,† with White as its president. From 1921–23, Cletrac produced the Rollin automobile. In 1930 White became the company's chairman of the board; his son, W. King White, became president. White retired in 1944 when Cletrac merged with Oliver Farm Equipment Co. He married Katharine King in 1896 and had 3 children: Rollin Henry, Jr., Wm. King, and Elizabeth King. White died in Hobe Sound, FL, and was buried in Lake View Cemetery.

White Family Papers, WRHS.

**WHITE, THOMAS H.** (26 Apr. 1836–22 June 1914), founder of White Sewing Machine Corp., parent company of WHITE MOTOR CO.† and Cleveland Automatic Screw Machine Co., was born in Phillipston, MA, to Betsey Pierce and manufacturer Windsor White. After a common-school education, he devoted himself to mechanical studies. By 1857 he had invented a small hand-operated single-thread sewing machine, starting his own business with partner Wm. Grothe and $500 initial capital, making "The New England Sewing Machine," which retailed for $10. Seeking a central location near markets and materials, in 1866 White moved his company, White Mfg. Co., from Templeton,

MA, to Cleveland. In 1876 White Sewing Machine Corp. was formed, with White as president and treasurer. Within 10 years production had increased from 25 to 2,000 units per week, making Cleveland the center for sewing machine production. Branch dealers were opened across the country and in England. Civically active in Cleveland, White gave generously to charities and educational institutions, including, in 1908, financing the building of a separate studio for sculpture at the Cleveland School of Art. He also served on CLEVELAND CITY COUNCIL,† 1875–76. White married Almira L. Greenleaf of Boston on 2 Nov. 1858 and had 8 children: Windsor, Clarence, ROLLIN H., Walter, Ella, Alice, Alice Maud, and Mabel. He is buried at Lake View Cemetery.

**WHITE, WILLIAM J.** (7 Oct. 1850–16 Feb. 1923), chewing-gum manufacturer, was born in Rice Lake, Ontario, moved to Cleveland with his parents, John and Laura (Brooks) White, at age 6. He entered business operating a candy store and in 1884 mistakenly bought a barrel of Yucatan chicle. White, after discovering it could be softened and made chewable, added mint, and sold the product as "Yucatan." In 1890 he established and became president of AMERICAN CHICLE CO.† White put Dr. EDWIN E. BEEMAN's pepsin into his gum to create Beeman's Pepsin Gum. By 1893 the company had sold over 150 million sticks of gum.

White moved to W. Cleveland and was elected its mayor in 1889. In 1892 he was elected as a Republican to the U.S. House of Representatives. White's personal tastes were extravagant. In 1889 he purchased 455 acres for a stock farm and racetrack. Thornwood, his 52-room mansion, showcased paintings, tapestries, Oriental rugs, and antique furnishings. White divorced his first wife, Ellen, in 1906, the next day marrying divorcee Helen Sheldon. They moved to New York. Probably in 1916, White became penniless after business difficulties and was removed as president of American Chicle. Four years later, White was running Wm. J. White Chicle Co. in Niagara Falls. He lost this fortune because of litigation with his original company. He returned to Cleveland in 1922, penniless, but built a new factory. In Jan. 1923 White slipped on a sidewalk and died a few weeks later.

White, buried in Lake View Cemetery, had seven children: Miles A., Harry W., Pearl M., Arthur M., Ada M., Ralph, and Brook.

**WHITEHEAD, REV. EATON** (30 Sept. 1933–8 April 1993) was the founder and pastor of Pine Grove Baptist Church, and pastor of several Baptist churches on Cleveland's East Side. He was also involved in the civil-rights movement. Born in

Bolizee, AL, Rev. Whitehead grew up in Tishabee, AL, and moved to Cleveland in 1952, where he worked for several years for the National Terminal Corp. Whitehead also worked for BOBBIE BROOKS, INC.† for 2 decades and was a steward in the INTERNATIONAL LADIES GARMENT WORKERS UNION.†

Whitehead graduated from the Ohio branch of the American Baptist Theological Seminary of Nashville, TN, and was ordained in 1958. Whitehead helped found Pine Grove Baptist Church in 1959 and served as its pastor for 5 years. He became asst. minister of Second New Hope Baptist Church, pastor of Second St. John Baptist Church, and treasurer and trustee of Fidelity Baptist Church. He was also affiliated with Treidstone, Love Devine, and Avon Ave. Baptist churches. Whitehead resumed the pastorate at Pine Grove only a year before his death.

Whitehead helped establish Operation Breakfast in Cleveland during the late 1960s. The organization was the job advocacy arm of the Southern Christian Leadership Conference (SCLC). He worked with the Rev. E. Randall Osborn, executive director of the SCLC, at its Atlanta headquarters.

Whitehead married Arvetta Burton on 14 Dec. 1991. Whitehead's children are Eaton Jr., Benjamin, Chester, Jo-Ann Ferris, and step-children Samuel, Thomas, Paul, Audrey, Brenda Burton, Ruth Mitchell and Theresa Morton. Whitehead is buried in Highland Park Cemetery.—T.B.

**WHITING, FREDERIC ALLEN** (26 Jan. 1873–20 Dec. 1959), established the CLEVELAND MUSEUM OF ART† as an accessible community asset during his 17-year term as its first director. He was born in Oakdale, TN, but reared in his ancestral state of Massachusetts, where he was educated by public schools and private tutors. After a period in business, in 1900 he became secretary of the Society of Arts and Crafts in Boston. His interest in skilled craftsmen also led him to organize the National League of Handicraft Societies and establish the journal *Handicraft*. In 1904 he had charge of the handicraft exhibition at the Louisiana Purchase Exhibition at St. Louis in conjunction with his wife, Olive Cook Whiting, whom he had married the previous year. Named director of the John Herron Art Institute in Indianapolis in 1912, Whiting left after only 1 year to assume the directorship on 1 May 1913 of the yet unbuilt Cleveland Museum of Art. His first task was to supervise construction of the museum, which opened in 1916. Whiting developed a collection of handicrafts to aid the city's craftsmen and an educational program for both adults and children. He promoted local artists through the annual MAY SHOW† and the development of UNIV. CIRCLE† through organization of the Cleveland Conference for Educational Cooperation. From 1921–23 he served as president of the American Assn. of Museums. Whiting resigned the CMA directorship in 1930 to assume the presidency of the American Federation of Arts in Washington, DC. After 6 years there, he retired to Framingham, MA, where he died survived by a son, Frederic A. Whiting, Jr.

Witchey, Holly Rarick. *The Fine Arts in Cleveland* (1994).
Wittke, Carl. *The First Fifty Years: The Cleveland Museum of Art, 1916–1966* (1966).

**WHITLEY, R. (ROUSARA) JOYCE** (20 May 1930–22 Dec. 1992), architect, city planner, and writer, served as chief planner for the U.S. Department of Housing and Urban Development (1967–68). She received awards for her architectural designs in Chicago and St. Louis. With a Rockefeller Fellowship in the Humanities at Brown Univ. (1980), she wrote a play, *Dreams of Callahan* (produced at KARAMU HOUSE† in 1990), about the effects of urban policies on neighborhoods. Whitley was born in Monroe, NC, to Beatryce Mae Nivens and Moses James Whitley. Her family moved to Warren, OH, where Whitley attended high school, and then to Cleveland. She attended Flora Stone Mather College and received a B.A. from Fisk Univ. (1950), an M.A. in sociology from Western Reserve Univ. (1953), and an M.A. in city and regional planning from the Univ. of Chicago (1956). She later attended the Harvard Univ. Graduate School of Design. In 1968 Whitley joined her brothers, James M. and William, in forming the WHITLEY-WHITLEY, INC.† architectural firm in SHAKER HTS.† By 1976 she was the firm's vice-president.

With her firm, Whitley designed projects across the country, including master plans for the North Side Preservation Group in St. Louis, the Civic Center in Atlanta, GA, the Cleveland Clinic Hotel, and the NASA LEWIS RESEARCH CENTER.† She served on the executive committee of the American Institute of Planners (1972–73), the boards of the Harvard School of Design and the Black Economic Union, and belonged to the National Assn. of Housing and Redevelopment Officials and the National Organization of Minority Architects. She was a trustee of Karamu House (1973–75), an officer for United Torch Cleveland (1974–75), on the executive committee of UNIV. CIRCLE, INC.,† and a member of the Cleveland Planning Commission. Whitley was buried in Lake View Cemetery.—J.M.

**WHITTAKER, (LOUIS) HOWARD** (19 Dec. 1922–30 May 1989) served as a catalyst in Cleveland cultural circles during his 36 years as director of the CLEVELAND MUSIC SCHOOL SETTLEMENT.† A LAKEWOOD† native, he studied at Lakewood High School and the CLEVELAND INSTITUTE OF MUSIC† before taking a master's degree in composition from Oberlin College in 1947. He served as a chaplain's assistant during World War II and married the former Donna Moorhead in 1945. Named acting director of the Music School Settlement in 1947, he became director the following year. Under his tenure (1948–84), the school grew from an enrollment of 400 to 3,000 students and its budget from $40,000 to more than $1 million a year. Whittaker was also a noted composer, having a piano concerto performed at the 1959 World's Fair in Brussels and 2 orchestral pieces played by the CLEVELAND ORCHESTRA† in Mexico in 1960. According to music critic Robert Finn, "He played the political and artistic bureaucracy the way Horowitz plays the piano keyboard." With Cleveland Orchestra associate conductor Louis Lane, he founded the LAKE ERIE OPERA THEATER† in 1964, serving as its producer from 1964–70. Prompted by the urban unrest of the 1960s, he established the Cleveland Summer Arts Festival in 1967 and directed it for 3 years. He also served as chairman of the Cleveland Society of Aesthetics and president of the National Guild of Community Schools of the Arts. Among his many awards was a Cleveland Fine Arts Award in 1963. Besides his wife, he was survived by a daughter, Katherine, and 2 sons, Dwight and John.—J.V.

Cleveland Music School Settlement Records, WRHS.

**WHITTLESEY, CHARLES W.** (4 Oct. 1808–17 Oct. 1886), geologist and historian, was born in Southington, CT, to Asaph and Vesta Hart Whittlesey, moved to Tallmadge, OH, in 1813, graduated from West Point in 1831, and was stationed in Wisconsin as a 2nd lt. before serving in the Black Hawk War (1833). Whittlesey resigned his commission and came to Cleveland, practicing law until 1837 and owning and editing the *CLEVELAND DAILY GAZETTE†* and *CLEVELAND HERALD & GAZETTE.†* He was then appointed asst. geologist of Ohio and helped conduct the first geological survey in the state. For 20 years, Whittlesey participated in or led surveys, including those of iron and copper ranges in Michigan (1845), the Whitney Survey of Lake Superior and the Upper Mississippi (1847–51), and the Hall Survey of Wisconsin (1858–61). He also investigated ancient Indian earthworks throughout the state.

With the outbreak of the Civil War, Whittlesey was appointed asst. quartermaster general by Gov. Dennison. Later, as colonel in the 20th Ohio Volunteer Infantry, he planned and constructed fortifications at Covington, KY, defending Cincinnati. He commanded a brigade at Ft. Donelson and participated in the Battle of Shiloh (1862). Whittlesey resigned his commission in Apr. 1862 because of ill health. After the war he became active as a historian. In 1867 he published *Early History of Cleveland* and helped found the WESTERN RESERVE HISTORICAL SOCIETY,† serving as its president until 1885. Whittlesey married Mary E. Morgan in 1858. He died in Cleveland and was buried in Lake View Cemetery.

Charles Whittlesey Papers, WRHS.

**WHITTLESEY, ELISHA** (19 Oct. 1783–7 Jan. 1863), lawyer and politician, was born in Litchfield County, CT, son of John and Mary Beale Whittlesey. He studied in Danbury, where his older brother, Matthew, practiced law; moved to Canfield, OH; and was soon appointed prosecuting attorney for the WESTERN RESERVE,† serving from 1807–23, except during the WAR OF 1812† when he was private secretary to Gen. Wm. Henry Harrison. As a lawyer, Whittlesey was the senior partner with Eben Newton in the area's best-known partnership, the proprietor of a 1-room law school, and an early leader of the Ohio Bar. He was a circuit lawyer specializing in land cases. As a businessman, Whittlesey earned a small fortune by slow, steady work, basically handling eastern capital invested in Ohio lands and holding stock in Ohio banks. He lost a considerable sum in the Panic of 1837. Whittlesey's elective career began in 1820 with 2 terms in the Ohio general assembly. He served in Congress, first as a Natl. Republican, then as a Whig, from 1823–38, nicknamed "watchdog of the Treasury," a recognized example of official integrity in government. As a party leader, Whittlesey was a conciliator in party rivalries. Active in the American Colonization Society, he believed expatriation was the answer to slavery. After 1848 Whittlesey served the Taylor, Fillmore, Pierce, and Lincoln administrations as comptroller of the Treasury. He married Polly Mygatt on 5 Jan. 1806. They had 10 children: Royal F. Lewis, John, Harriet, Anna Maria, George Beale, Lucy, William Wallace, Elisha Mygatt, Comfort Starr, and Granville. Whittlesey died in Washington, DC, and was buried in Canfield, OH.

Elisha Whittlesey Papers, WRHS.

**WICAL, NOEL** (29 Jan. 1910–18 April 1993), copyeditor at the *CLEVELAND PRESS*† and leader of the Cleveland Newspaper Guild, was born in Wilmington, OH, the son of Frank W. and Clara B. Morris Wical. After graduation from Bethany College in 1932, he taught high school English at Tiltonville, OH, and in 1934 began teaching at Mentor High School. In a gradual shift of interest from education to journalism, Wical briefly took a job with the *Painesville Telegraph* before joining the *Cleveland Press* as a reporter in 1942. Continuing his interest in education, Wical began covering schools for the *Press* in 1946, and his perceptive articles won him awards from education organizations. He also was active in the Cleveland Newspaper Guild for nearly 20 years. During the Guild's 126-day strike against the *PLAIN DEALER*† and the *Press*, the issue of union security was debated by Wical, head of the Press Newspaper Guild Unit and Editor LOUIS SELTZER at a televised meeting held at the City Club, 6 Feb. 1963. *Plain Dealer* columnist PHILIP PORTER reported that Wical was more convincing in his arguments for the union than Seltzer was in opposition. After the strike, he retained his position at the *Press* and continued as a Guild officer. He retired after 37 years as a writer and copyeditor.

Wical married Dorothy Morris in 1933 and they had two children, Susan Vanessa Baker of Columbus, and son Lee of Kaneohe, HI. A resident of Mentor during his years with the *Press*, Wical was living in Columbus when he died. He was cremated.—M.S.

**WICKENDEN, WILLIAM E.** (24 Dec. 1882–1 Sept. 1947) was president of the Case School of Applied Science (later Case Institute of Technology; see CASE WESTERN RESERVE UNIV.†) and was active in the civic life of Cleveland.

Born to Thomas R. and Ida Consaul Wickenden in Toledo, OH, William's early education took place in his home town. He then went to Denison Univ., where he earned his B.S. degree in 1904.

Following graduation he began a teaching career in higher education, first at Rochester Athenaeum & Mechanics Institute, then at the Univ. of Wisconsin, and later at the Massachusetts Institute of Technology. He left academia for a career with Bell Telephone and AT&T. Between 1924 and 1929, he served as director of a national program to bolster engineering education standards in the U.S.

In 1929 he came to Cleveland as president of Case, a position he held through the end of the 1946–47 academic year. His administration coincided with the onset of the Depression, and Wickenden exerted considerable energy in keeping the school solvent.

Shortly after coming to Case, he made the suggestion that an alliance with neighboring Western Reserve Univ. made sense. The idea was discussed, but shelved until the 1960s. Despite financial constraints, he worked to add formal graduate programs to the Case curriculum, and during his tenure the first master's and doctoral degrees were conferred.

Wickenden married Marion Lamb in Toledo, 2 Sept. 1908. They had two children, William and Elizabeth. Wickenden retired to Peterboro, NH, where he died.—J.T.

**WICKHAM, GERTRUDE VAN RENSSELAER** (18 Mar 1844–20 May 1930), journalist and local historian, was born in Huron, daughter of Sanders and Malinda Woodruff (Hayward) Van Rensselaer. She attended public schools and married Capt. Samuel Wickham on 1 Aug. 1864, with whom she had a daughter, Katherine. After his death in 1869, Wickham for a few years was a principal of the lower grades at Huron High School. Wickham entered journalism when a letter she wrote to the *SUNDAY POST†* was published and drew a positive public response, so that she was asked to contribute weekly. When the paper folded in 1878, she joined the *CLEVELAND HERALD,†* persuading the editors to hire her by suggesting she write a fashion column which, she pointed out, would bring more women into Cleveland to shop, subsequently attracting more advertisers.

In 1881 Wickham joined the editorial staff of the *CLEVELAND LEADER†* when the *Herald* merged with that paper. Her columns grew increasingly oriented toward women and children, especially the needy, using letters from indigent women and underprivileged children. She established the Woman's Repository, where destitute women could sell handicrafts. Wickham left the *Leader* in 1884 because of poor health, although she continued occasional newspaper writing. In 1886 she was a charter member of the Women's Press Club (later CLEVELAND WRITERS' CLUB†). In the 1890s her interests turned to the history of the WESTERN RESERVE.† In 1896 she was chosen historian of the women's department by the Cleveland Centennial Commission; she published *Pioneer Women of the Western Reserve* and *Pioneer Families of the Western Reserve.*

---

Gertrude Van Rensselaer Wickham Papers, WRHS.

**WIDDER, MILTON "MILT"** (20 Nov. 1907–15 Dec. 1985), the paragon of Cleveland's gossip columnists, was born in Berlin, Germany, raised in Hungary, and came to the U.S. with his parents, Adolph and Rosa (Habermann) in 1920. He graduated from Adelbert College. Although he briefly studied law, he began work as a copyboy for the *CLEVELAND PRESS†* in 1926, working various beats for 20 years. In 1946 Widder was assigned to do the *Press's* gossip column, making his "Sights

and Sounds" column into a local institution. Competition among press agents for a "mention" became so intense that Widder needed 2 telephones. A "Halo of the Week" award from Widder was one of the community's highest accolades for meritorious public service. Widder's diet tips were in such demand that the *Press* reprinted them as the "Milt Widder Diet" and distributed more than a million copies. Widder could find news as well as make it. He was the first in the nation to report the marriage breakup of Howard Hughes and actress Jean Peters. *Press* editors often killed items from his column because they "scooped" stories planned for the front page. A member of the CITY CLUB OF CLEVELAND† for over 40 years, Widder was its president in 1969 and a veteran performer in its ANVIL REVUE.† On 20 Nov. 1932 he married Dorothy Louise Stone, who died in 1980. They had 4 children: James, John, Robt. Andrew, and Mrs. Barbara Beazle. Failing vision and health problems forced his retirement in 1972. He died in Cleveland.

**WIEBER, CHARLES L. F.** (15 Feb. 1861–28 Aug. 1931) was a successful businessman identified primarily with the Rauch & Lang Carriage Co. who also skillfully managed many businesses in the tailoring, real estate, and investment fields.

Born in Cleveland to Jacob and Salome (Zipf), Wieber attended private schools and enrolled in the Spencerian Business College to prepare for a business career. After his father's death Wieber helped his mother manage the family tailoring business on Detroit Ave. In 1902 Wieber incorporated the business as the Wieber Co., Merchant Tailors, naming himself president and treasurer and relocating downtown in the Lennox building on Euclid Ave. The Wieber Co. became the largest, most exclusive men's tailoring shop west of New York City.

In 1910 Wieber sold his interest in the Wieber Co. to focus his attention on Rauch & Lang, electric auto manufacturers, which he had joined in 1907. Wieber was vice-president and general manager of the company, remaining so after it merged with the Baker Motor Vehicle Co. to form Baker-R&L in 1915.

During his later years Wieber worked in real estate, serving as president of the Lakewood Realty Co. and the Wieber Realty Co. Wieber helped organize the Forest City Savings & Trust Co. and, at the time of his death, was president of the Detroit St. Investment Co.

Wieber married Martha Dietz on 8 Jan. 1889. They had four children: Charles Jr., Alvina, Martha, and Walter. Wieber lived in Lakewood, belonged to the First Unitarian Church and is buried in Lake View Cemetery.—T.B.

WIEDER, JUDITH MARX (4 Aug. 1916–19 Dec. 1992) served as president (1970s) and chair of the Board of Trustees (1950s–1960s) of Mill Distributors, Inc., a textile company founded in 1926 in Cleveland by her mother, Beatrice S. Marx. Wieder was born in Cleveland to Beatrice Sacheroff and Herbert Marx. She graduated from Cleveland Hts. High School and Cornell Univ. (1937). Wieder opened and operated the Judy Shoppe, her own dry goods store, in the 1940s before returning to her mother's company, where she had begun working after college. On 27 Jan. 1947 Wieder married Ira J. Wieder (d. 1988). The couple lived in SHAKER HTS.† and raised three sons: Thomas, Douglas, and Bruce. Wieder was active in many organizations, such as the NATIONAL COUNCIL OF JEWISH WOMEN, CLEVELAND SECTION,† CLEVELAND HADASSAH,† the auxiliary of MT. SINAI MEDICAL CENTER,† Women's American ORT (Organization for Rehabilitation Through Training), and the Cornell Club of Northeastern Ohio. She also presided over the Women's Committee of Suburban Temple. Wieder is buried in Lake View Cemetery.—J.M.

WIESENFELD, LEON (7 Feb. 1885–1 March 1971), wielded considerable influence in Cleveland's Jewish community as editor of various Yiddish and English-language newspapers. He was born in Rzeszow, Poland, and worked for various Polish and German publications before emigrating to America. Married in 1912 to Esther Wiesenfeld, he worked in New York for Abraham Cahan's famous *Jewish Daily Forward* before coming to Cleveland in 1924. For 10 years Wiesenfeld served as associate editor of the *YIDDISHE VELT†* *(Jewish World)*, Cleveland's principal Yiddish-language newspaper, before succeeding owner Samuel Rocker as editor in 1934. In 1938 he left the *World* to establish an English-Yiddish weekly, *Die Yiddishe Stimme (Jewish Voice)*, which failed after about a year. He then began publishing an English-language annual called the *Jewish Voice Pictorial*, which endured into the 1950s. His extra-journalistic writing included a novel, *The Rabbi's Daughter,* 2 plays performed in Yiddish theaters of Cleveland and other cities, and an account of Jewish life in Cleveland in the 1920s and 1930s. Wiesenfeld was also active in Jewish affairs, notably as an organizer of the Cleveland Zionist Society and a director of the Jewish Orphan Home (see ORTHODOX JEWISH CHILDREN'S HOME†). A resident of CLEVELAND HTS.,† he was survived by his wife.—J.V.

Leon Wiesenfeld Papers, WRHS.

WIGGERS, CARL JOHN (28 May 1883–28 Apr. 1963), famous for his heart and blood pressure research, was born in Davenport, IA, to George and Margret Kuendal Wiggers, graduated from the Univ. of Michigan with an M.D. in 1906, and attended the Institute of Physiology at the Univ. of Munich. He was an instructor of physiology at the Univ. of Michigan (1906–11), and asst. professor at Cornell Univ. Medical School (1911–18). From 1918–53, he was professor and chairman of the Dept. of Physiology at Western Reserve Univ. Medical School. Wiggers achieved world recognition for developing a new method of registering heart and blood pressure; finding the effects of low oxygen pressure on circulation; discovering the effects of valve defects on the heart; studying the effects of shock; and his pioneering efforts along with Dr. CLAUDE BECK and others in techniques of resuscitation from death in the operating room. After retiring as professor emeritus in 1953, Wiggers joined the Frank Bunts Institute of the CLEVELAND CLINIC FOUNDATION,† taking part in postgraduate training for student doctors and in medical and scientific seminars. Wiggers was the first editor of the medical journal *Circulation Research* and authored 7 books and over 300 articles. In 1952 he received the Gold Heart Award from the American Heart Assn. In 1954 he received the Modern Medicine Award, and in 1955 the Albert Lasker Award for distinguished research in cardiovascular research. Wiggers married Minnie E. Berry in 1907 and had 2 sons, Harold and Raymond.

WIGMAN, JOHN B. (1806–1 Feb. 1890), building contractor, was actively involved in local politics as a member of CLEVELAND CITY COUNCIL† and an unsuccessful candidate for other offices. Local structures built by Wigman include the first brick warehouse on the CUYAHOGA RIVER,† the ACADEMY OF MUSIC† building, ST. JOHN CATHEDRAL† at the corner of Superior and Erie (E. 9th) streets, and many business blocks. Born in Germany, Wigman received a common-school education there before leaving for the U.S. at age 14. He became an apprentice bricklayer in Cleveland and by 1843 had developed his own construction business. That year the Cleveland City Council authorized him to build a wooden bridge across Johnson's Run at Lake St. (Lakeside Ave.). Wigman was elected to city council from the 1st Ward in 1842, serving a 2-year term. He helped organize the German celebration of American independence the next year. After a year as an alderman (1852–53), he was returned to city council. A Democrat (see CUYAHOGA COUNTY DEMOCRATIC PARTY†) who strongly opposed Prohibition,

Wigman ran unsuccessfully for state representative in 1853. In 1843 he married Catharine Hackman (d. Sept. 1901), also a native of Germany. Wigman had 3 children: Augustus, Henry, and Catharine. He is buried in St. Joseph's Cemetery.

**WILCOX, FRANK NELSON** (3 Oct. 1887–17 Apr. 1964), painter, printmaker, and teacher, was born in Cleveland, the son of Frank N. and Jessie F. (Snow) Wilcox. He studied at the Cleveland School of Art with HENRY G. KELLER and FREDERICK C. GOTTWALD, graduating in 1910 and going to Europe for more training. In 1913 he began a 40-year teaching career at the CLEVELAND INSTITUTE OF ART.† He also taught briefly at JOHN HUNTINGTON POLYTECHNIC INSTITUTE† and BALDWIN-WALLACE COLLEGE.† He was founder and president of the CLEVELAND SOCIETY OF ARTISTS,† a member of the American Watercolor Society, and an honorary member of the Artists & Craftsmen Assn. of Cleveland. Besides garnering 35 awards from the MAY SHOW,† Wilcox received the 1920 Penton Medal for sustained excellence. His many other medals were awarded for work in etching, industrial paintings, and oil landscapes. His work can be found in the CLEVELAND MUSEUM OF ART† and in museums in Toledo and San Diego. Wilcox was a traditional watercolor painter; his works were a wet blending of restful, romantic moods. He enjoyed working with rural Ohio scenery, the Rocky Mts., and Indian subjects. Wilcox was also a student of Ohio history, writing and illustrating *Ohio Indian Trails* in 1933. *Weather Wisdom*, a 1949 limited edition of 24 silk-screen prints, was a portfolio illustrating the seasonal moods of nature. He contributed technical notes to *Seascapes and Landscapes in Watercolor* by Watson Guptill. Wilcox married artist Florence Bard on 24 June 1916; they had a daughter, Mary. Wilcox was buried in EAST CLEVELAND.†

**WILDE, JOSEPH** (28 Feb. 1857–29 March 1923) provided music for the residents of Cleveland's "Little Bohemia" (see CZECHS†) both as a performer and as a dealer in musical instruments. A native of Prague, Bohemia, he served his apprenticeship as a maker and repairer of instruments in the old country. Emigrating to America at 17, he came to Cleveland and married Marie Trnka in 1883. After working as an instrument maker for Joseph Fischer Musical Instruments downtown, by 1885 he had opened his own establishment in the Broadway-E. 55th neighborhood. There he made, sold, and repaired violins, violas, and button-box accordions. As a performer on the latter, he was a fixture at weddings, dances, and excursions via the old OHIO AND ERIE CANAL† to picnic grounds on Rockside Rd. Wilde eventually had his own shop built at 4043 Broadway, a storefront structure with attached living quarters and workshop. His 4 oldest sons saw service in World War I; Alexander was killed in action. Wilde died in Cleveland and was buried in Highland Park Cemetery. He was survived by his wife and 7 children: John, Joseph, Mary, Rose, Yaro, William, and Christine Wintle.—J.V.

**WILEY, AQUILA** (20 Feb. 1835–5 June 1913), volunteer army officer during the CIVIL WAR,† was born in Mechanicsburg, PA, son of William and Susan (Spahr) Wiley. He settled in Wooster, OH, in 1852, and was commissioned a 1st lt. in the 16th Ohio Volunteer Infantry in Apr. 1861, promoted to capt. in May, and assigned to the 41st OVI in Sept. Wiley trained at Camp Wood in Cleveland. At the Battle of Shiloh, 7 Apr. 1862, he was seriously wounded in the left leg. He recovered and was promoted to major on 22 June and to lt. col. on 6 Dec. Advancing to col. of the 41st, he led the regiment at the Battle of Missionary Ridge on 25 Nov. 1863 and was wounded again in the left leg, necessitating amputation above the knee. He was appointed commandant of Camp Cleveland, assuming his responsibilities on 20 Apr. 1864, successfully overseeing the rendezvous and training of several new infantry regiments. He received a medical discharge on 7 June and left Camp Cleveland to return to Wooster. Appointed capt. in the 8th Regiment, Veteran Reserve Corps, in Mar. 1865, Wiley rose to major in Apr.; assigned chief mustering officer at Camp Cleveland, he discharged approximately 11,654 Union troops. After discharge, he was awarded a brevet brigadier generalship, U.S. Volunteers, for his service. Returning to Wooster, Wiley practiced law and served 1 term as probate judge in Wayne County. A Baptist, he married Emma Power in 1870 and had 2 children, Walter and Ada. Wiley died in Wooster and was buried in the Wooster Cemetery.

**WILLARD, ARCHIBALD MACNEAL** (22 Aug. 1836–11 Oct. 1918), artist best remembered for his *SPIRIT OF '76*, was born in BEDFORD,† OH, to Rev. Samuel R. and Catherine Willard. In 1855 he settled in Wellington, OH, and taught himself to draw. In the early 1860s he apprenticed himself to a local decorative artist and wagonmaker, where he painted vignettes on wagons and carriages. He also painted portraits. In 1863 Willard enlisted in the 86th Ohio Volunteer Infantry, serving until Feb. 1864, when he married Nellie S. Challacombe (d. ca. 1912) and contacted Cleveland photographer and art dealer JAS. F. RYDER, who photographed and printed several of Willard's Civil War sketches.

After serving briefly again in the army in 1865, Willard returned to Wellington. He sent a comical painting he did of 3 of his children and the family dog, entitled *Pluck,* to Ryder in Cleveland, who displayed it and a similar work, *Pluck II,* in his display window. The paintings were so popular that Ryder made 10,000 chromolithograph pairs, selling them for $10 a set. In 1873 Willard went to New York for a few weeks of formal painting training with J. O. Eaton. Willard moved to Cleveland and in 1875 began painting a 4th of July subject to be made into chromolithographs and sold at the centennial celebration in Philadelphia the following year, producing the *Spirit of '76.* Willard was prominent in the Cleveland artists' colony, was a founding member and principal director of the ART CLUB,† and instructed students in portraiture, landscape, oil painting, and life drawing classes. Willard had 4 children: Byron, Charles, Maude, and Harry. He died in Cleveland and was buried in Greenwood Cemetery, Wellington, OH.

---

Gordon, Willard F. *America's Best Known Painting, Least Known Artist: Archibald Willard and the Story of "The Spirit of '76"* (1975).

**WILLEY, JOHN WHEELOCK** (1797–9 July 1841), Cleveland's first mayor, was born in New Hampshire, son of Allen and Chloe (Frink) Willey. He was educated at Dartmouth, studied law in New York, was admitted to the bar, and came to Cleveland in 1822. He became known as a witty, sharp debater, winning 3 years in the state house of representatives (1827–30) and 3 in the state senate (1830–32) as a Jacksonian Democrat. When Cleveland was chartered as a city in 1836, Willey became its first mayor (1836–38), responsible for writing the municipal charter as well as many of the original ordinances. He was also on the first Board of School Managers. Willey speculated in real estate in OHIO CITY.† With Jas. Clark and others, he bought a section of the FLATS† on the east side, planning to transform it into Cleveland Centre, a business and residential district. Next they bought land in Ohio City, named it WILLEYVILLE,† and built a bridge connecting the 2 sections of Columbus St., diverting Cleveland-bound traffic that previously traveled through the WEST SIDE MARKET† to Willeyville, Cleveland Centre and CENTRAL MARKET.† CLEVELAND CITY COUNCIL† legislated removal of the Cleveland section of the Detroit St. Bridge, aggravating Ohio City residents and leading to the "Bridge War" (see COLUMBUS ST. BRIDGE†). Willey was also involved in the proposed construction of railroad lines. In 1840 he was appointed to serve as presiding judge of the 14th Judicial District. Willey married Laura Maria Higby in 1829 and had no children. He died in Cleveland and was buried in Erie St. Cemetery.

**WILLIAMS, ARTHUR BALDWIN** (11 Apr. 1874–18 Aug. 1951) was an ecologist, Curator of Education for the CLEVELAND MUSEUM OF NATURAL HISTORY,† park naturalist for the Cleveland Metropolitan Park District and author of many writings on nature subjects.

Born in Glen Ridge, NJ, to Arthur Williams, Sr., and Ida Lydia (Harrison), the family moved to Scranton, PA, where Williams attended public school and the School of the Lackawanna. He received his A.B. from Yale Univ. (1898), and his M.A. (1932) and Ph.D. (1935) in ecology from Western Reserve Univ.

In 1905 Williams came to Cleveland and worked as a general agent for the Cleveland Humane Society. In 1909 he entered Cleveland Law School, and later worked in real estate.

Williams joined the Natural History Museum in 1930 as naturalist and ecologist with a special assignment as naturalist for the Cleveland Metropolitan Park Board. In 1931 he opened the Trailside Museum in North Chagrin Park, the first of its kind in America. In 1932 he organized bird walks in the parks. In 1939 Williams became Curator of Education at the Museum (retired 1950) and served on the managing board until 1946.

He served on the managing board and executive committee of Holden Arboretum (1936–50), was Cleveland's naturalist (1943–50), and chaired the Cleveland Sesquicentennial Committee on Moses Cleaveland trees (1945–46).

In 1943 Williams began weekly nature columns for the *CLEVELAND PRESS.†* In 1946 the museum published his illustrated volume, *The Native Forests of Cuyahoga County, Ohio.* In 1950 he published *Birds in Cleveland.*

Williams married Emma Maude Hanley in 1901. They had a daughter, Barbara. Williams is buried in Lake View Cemetery.—T.B.

**WILLIAMS, EDWARD CHRISTOPHER** (11 Feb. 1871–24 Dec. 1929), an African American librarian, teacher, and scholar who laid the foundation for library collections at Western Reserve Univ. and Howard Univ., was born in Cleveland of mixed racial parentage to Daniel P. and Mary Kilkary Williams. He graduated from Adelbert College of WRU in 1892, and after a brief stint as a stenographer, was appointed first asst. librarian of Adelbert College, head librarian in 1894, and university librarian in 1898. Williams took a leave of absence in 1899 to study library science at New York Library

School in Albany, completing the 2-year course in 1 year. Williams more than doubled WRU's library collection and increased its quality, becoming a recognized expert on library organization and bibliography. Williams was on a committee recommending formation of a school of library science at WRU, and taught courses in reference work, bibliography, public documents, criticism, and selection of books when it opened in 1904. He was a charter member of the Ohio Library Assn. and chairman of the committee drafting its constitution. Williams left Cleveland in 1909 to become principal of M Street High School in Washington, DC. In 1916 he became university librarian at Howard Univ., also directing Howard's library training class, teaching German, and later heading the Dept. of Romance Languages. In 1929 he took a sabbatical to study for his Ph.D. at Columbia Univ.; however he died shortly after beginning his studies. Williams married Ethel P. Chesnutt in 1902 and had a son, Charles.

**WILLIAMS, EDWARD MASON** (9 Nov. 1871–25 July 1936) withdrew from an active business career in midlife in order to increase his involvement in civic affairs, notably as a member of the Cleveland Board of Education. Born in Cleveland, he was the son of Edward P. and Mary Mason Williams. After graduating from Yale in 1893, he began working for the paint firm cofounded by his father, the SHERWIN-WILLIAMS CO.† He married Clevelander Mary Raymond in 1899 and began his civic involvement as a director of the Children's Fresh Air Camp from 1900–12 (president, 1905–12). As vice-chairman of the CHAMBER OF COMMERCE† Committee on Benevolent Associations in 1911–12, he helped organize the Federation of Charity & Philanthropy, which led to the innovative United Way fundraising technique (see UNITED WAY SERVICES†). Though retaining a seat on the company's executive committee, Williams ceased his day-to-day involvement at Sherwin-Williams upon his election to the Board of Education (see CLEVELAND PUBLIC SCHOOLS†) in 1914. Serving as board president from 1919–32, he was praised for his executive ability to delegate authority as well as follow up. Under his tenure the system raised teacher salaries, introduced junior high schools, and worked with the CLEVELAND PUBLIC LIBRARY† to establish libraries in all secondary and some elementary schools. Williams used his own funds to campaign, against the opposition of the CITIZENS LEAGUE,† for construction of the Board of Education administration building on the MALL.† Mounting opposition to school costs in the face of the Depression, however, led to the election of an independent slate which successfully challenged Williams's control of the board and led to his

resignation. Buried in Lake View Cemetery, he was survived by his wife and 4 children: Hilda, Madeline, Mary, and Edward.—J.V.

**WILLIAMS, GERALDINE** (1915–30 Aug. 1993), civic activist and strategist in POLITICS,† planned and worked with other AFRICAN AMERICANS† to draft and elect Carl Stokes as mayor of Cleveland (see MAYORAL ADMINISTRATION OF CARL B. STOKES†). Williams was born in St. Louis, MO. A Fisk Univ. graduate, she also studied at Kansas City Teachers College and the Univ. of Colorado. As a teacher in Kansas City for a decade, Williams had extraordinary success in raising the test scores of underachievers. During World War II, Williams volunteered with the USO (United Service Organization) at Fort Riley, KS, and there met Elliott S. Pogue, Jr., of Cleveland, whom she married in 1943. After the war they returned to Cleveland and operated the private 32nd-Cedar Club in the Park-Lang Hotel. Williams helped manage the club after the couple divorced (1949). She was later employed by the URBAN LEAGUE OF CLEVELAND,† the HOUGH AREA DEVELOPMENT CORP.,† and Community Action Against Addiction.

In early 1965 Williams met with former City Council member (later judge) Jean Murrell Capers to draft a mayoral candidate. After Stokes was elected in 1967, she worked as executive assistant in the mayor's office for a few months in 1968. A Democrat, Williams herself made unsuccessful bids for CLEVELAND CITY COUNCIL† (1961) and the U.S. Congress (1968). She presided over MADONNA HALL† and served on the boards of the NATIONAL ASSN. FOR THE ADVANCEMENT OF COLORED PEOPLE, CLEVELAND CHAPTER,† and the National Council of Negro Women, among other agencies. Williams died in the MARGARET WAGNER HOME.†—J.M.

**WILLIAMS, KATHERINE WITHROW** (12 Aug. 1904–23 Feb. 1994) a leading patron of Cleveland's arts community, was born in Shepardstown, WV, the daughter of Tully and Lalla Reynolds Biays. She and her husband, Alfred, who helped found the BRUSH DEVELOPMENT CORP.,† came to Cleveland in 1928. Her ability to recognize talent and secure the cooperation of administrators, benefactors, and artists made her invaluable in the promotion of the city's cultural organizations. Williams saw to it that Ray Shepardson was introduced to the people who could assist him in reviving the theatre complex at PLAYHOUSE SQUARE.† Recognizing the talent of novelist Les Roberts, she invited him to the salon she maintained in her home where authors, artists, and visiting musicians could meet with one another. Williams helped dancers Dennis

Nahat and IAN HORVATH organize the Cleveland Ballet School in 1972, and in 1988 she funded an endowment which annually awarded a student scholarship in her name for study there. She was also a founding board member of the CLEVELAND BALLET† and was a trustee of the CLEVELAND MUSIC SCHOOL SETTLEMENT,† the CLEVELAND INSTITUTE OF MUSIC,† and DANCE-CLEVELAND.†

Katherine Biays married Alfred L. Williams in 1926, and they had two children, Clurie Williams Bennis and Leslie Williams Mills. A resident of Cleveland, she died at her home and was cremated.—M.S.

**WILLIAMS, LE ROY W.** (18 Aug. 1844–14 Feb. 1930), recipient of the Congressional Medal of Honor for service during the CIVIL WAR,† was born in Oswego, NY, and enlisted in the 129th New York Volunteer Infantry 29 July 1862. The 129th, redesignated the 8th New York Heavy Artillery, participated in the 3 June 1864 attack against the Confederate Army at Cold Harbor, VA, where Sgt. Williams and four others volunteered to recover the body of Col. Peter A. Porter, killed close to enemy lines. The mission was successfully conducted under the cover of darkness to evade nearby confederate sharpshooters, and all volunteers received the Medal of Honor for the action. Williams, who was mustered out as a 1st lt. 30 June 1865, received his medal 1 April 1898.

Williams moved to Cleveland in 1900 with his family and was employed by the White and Standard Sewing Machine Co. He died in Cleveland and was buried at Oakwood Cemetery, Niagara Falls, NY.—M.S.

**WILLIAMS, WHITING** (11 Mar. 1878–14 Apr. 1975), author and lecturer on labor and management problems, was born in Shelby, OH, to Benjamin J. and Ida Whiting Williams, graduated from Oberlin College (1899) and studied at the Univ. of Berlin (1899–1900) and Univ. of Chicago (1900–01) before managing the Bureau of Univ. Travel (1901–04). He became the asst. to the president at Oberlin College (1904–12) while earning a master's degree in 1909. In 1913 Williams moved to Cleveland as executive secretary of the Fed. for Charity & Philanthropy, pioneer of more than 2,400 United Appeals. He left in 1918 to become vice-president and personnel director of Hydraulic Pressed Steel Co.

In 1920 Williams took a leave of absence to study firsthand the working conditions in various countries and workers' attitudes. Speaking French, German, Spanish, and Italian, he worked as a laborer in coal mines, railroad shops, shipyards, and oil refineries under an assumed name in the U.S., Europe, and Central and South America. He lectured and wrote books such as *What's on the Worker's Mind, By One Who Put On Coveralls to Find Out* (1920), *Full Up and Fed Up* (1921), *Horny Hands and Hampered Elbows* (1922), and *Mainsprings of Men* (1925). Williams became a consultant on labor relations, personnel management, and public relations for several large businesses and lectured, until he retired at age 90, about his experiences for such graduate schools as Harvard, Dartmouth, and CASE WESTERN RESERVE UNIV.† In 1940 he became a member of the Natl. Panel of Arbitrators. He was a member of the Cosmos Club in Washington, DC, and the UNION CLUB† of Cleveland. In Cleveland, he was a trustee of both HIRAM HOUSE† and the School of Art (see CLEVELAND INSTITUTE OF ART†). Williams married Caroline Harter in 1906 (d. 1938); they had two children, Carol R. and Harter Whiting. In 1941 he married Dorothy Rogers. Williams was buried in Shelby, OH.

Whiting Williams Papers, WRHS.
Wren, Daniel A. *White Collar Hobo: The Travels of Whiting Williams* (1987).

**WILLIAMSON, SAMUEL** (1772–8 Sept. 1834), businessman; **SAMUEL WILLIAMSON, JR.** (1808–14 Jan. 1884), lawyer, public official, and railroad director; and **SAMUEL E. WILLIAMSON** (1844–21 Feb. 1903), lawyer, judge, and railroad counsel, comprise 3 generations of a distinguished Cleveland family. Samuel Williamson arrived in Cleveland from Crawford County, PA, the son of Samuel and Sarah (Miller) Williamson, in 1810, built a tannery, was a trustee of the Village of Cleveland upon its formation in 1815, and became assoc. judge of the Court of Common Pleas. In 1816 he was an incorporator of the Bank of Lake Erie, becoming a director in 1832. Williamson's wife, Isabella McQueen, whom he married in 1807, was a charter member of FIRST PRESBYTERIAN CHURCH† (Old Stone); he was also a member. They had 3 children: Mary, Samuel, and Sarah. Williamson was buried in ERIE ST. CEMETERY.†

Samuel Williamson, Jr., graduated from Jefferson College, Washington, PA (1829), read law with SHERLOCK J. ANDREWS, and was admitted to the bar in 1832, practicing with LEONARD CASE 2 years, then with ALBERT G. RIDDLE for nearly 30 years. He was county auditor, city councilman, member of the Board of Education and the Ohio legislature, and prosecuting attorney. Williamson retired from law in 1866 and was president of Society for Savings until his death. He was a director and attorney for the Cleveland, Columbus, Cincinnati & Indianapolis Railroad, an incorporator of Case School of Applied Science, and a member of Old Stone Church. Williamson and his wife, Mary E. Tisdale, whom he married in 1843, had 3 sons, Samuel E., Geo. T., and Jas. D. Mary was prominent in the Cleveland Ladies Temperance Union. Samuel Williamson, Jr. was buried in Lake View Cemetery.

Samuel E. Williamson graduated from Western Reserve College (1864), studied law with his father, and completed a course at Harvard Law School. Samuel E. was judge of the Court of Common Pleas (1880–82), and legal counsel for the NICKEL PLATE ROAD,† heading the legal department of New York Central Railroad from 1898 until his death. Samuel E. was a founder of UNIV. SCHOOL† and trustee of the Old Stone Church. The first Williamson Block was built on the corner of Euclid and Public Square in 1889–90. It suffered a serious fire in 1895, and the second WILLIAMSON BLDG. was erected in 1899–1900, demolished in 1982 for the construction of the BP Bldg. (see BP AMERICA†). Samuel E. was married twice. His first marriage was to Mary P. Marsh on 4 June 1878 (d. 1881). They had 2 children, Mary P. and Ethel. His second marriage was to Harriet W. Brown in 1884. They had a son, Samuel B. Samuel E. Williamson is buried in Lake View Cemetery.

**WILLS, J. WALTER, SR.** (3 June 1874–23 Apr. 1971), founder and director of the state's largest black-owned funeral business, HOUSE OF WILLS,† was born to Silas and Anna (Wilson) Wills and educated in Yellow Springs, OH. He graduated from Antioch College, and came to Cleveland in 1899, working as a streetcar conductor and insurance salesman while attending law school at night. In 1904 he became a partner with William W. Gee in the Gee & Wills Funeral Co. When the partnership dissolved in 1907, Wills formed J. W. Wills & Sons Co. An ardent believer that economic self-help was the key to black progress, Wills helped organize the city's first black business organization in 1905, the Cleveland Board of Trade. In 1908 an organization that grew out of the board, the CLEVELAND ASSN. OF COLORED MEN,† affiliated with Booker T. Washington's Natl. Business League. Wills broke with more traditional integrationists to advocate black solidarity in trying to find a way to end racial discrimination and improve the lives of AFRICAN AMERICANS.† Among numerous organizational activities, he was a founder of the local branch of the NAACP, the Negro Welfare Assn. (URBAN LEAGUE OF CLEVELAND† affiliate), and the PHILLIS WHEATLEY ASSN.† Wills was often called upon to aid the needy as the city's black population expanded, and also donated to MT. ZION CONGREGATIONAL CHURCH,† of

which he was a member. Wills was a conductor and trainer of choral groups. In 1969 the Community Ctr. at the King-Kennedy Apts. in the Central area was named in his honor.

Wills was married twice. His first marriage, on 29 Mar. 1900, was to Alberta L. Gamblee; they had a son, J. Walter, Jr. Divorced in 1915, Wills's second marriage was to Blanche Gilmere on 24 June 1916. He adopted her son, Harry A. Wills died in Cleveland and was buried in Lake View Cemetery.

**WILLSON, HIRAM V.** (Apr. 1808–11 Nov. 1866), lawyer and first judge of the Northern District Court of Ohio, was born in Madison County, NY, graduated from Hamilton College in 1832, studied law with Jared Willson in Canandaigua, NY, and Francis Scott Key in Washington, DC, and initially supported himself as a teacher. He moved to Painesville, then came to Cleveland, where he opened a law practice with HENRY B. PAYNE in 1833. Payne later retired, and the firm became Willson, Wade & Hitchcock, later Willson, Wade & Wade. In 1854 Willson and a group of commissioners from Cleveland and OHIO CITY† worked out the details annexing Ohio City to Cleveland. Also in 1854, Willson lobbied for a bill that would divide Ohio into 2 federal court districts. He succeeded, and the U.S. Court for the Northern District of Ohio was formed. Pres. Franklin Pierce appointed Willson the first judge of the Northern District Court in 1855, where he presided over a number of civil and admiralty cases. In 1859 he presided over the trial of 37 leaders in the OBERLIN-WELLINGTON RESCUE† incident who had violated the Fugitive Slave Law. Willson was a director of the CLEVELAND FEMALE SEMINARY† in 1854; an officer of the Univ. Hts. Congregational Church in 1859; and a contributor to the Cleveland Law Library Assn. He married Martha Ten Eyck in 1835; they had 2 children, Jennie and Mary. Willson died in Cleveland and was buried in Lake View Cemetery. Willson Ave. (E. 55th St.) was named after him.

**WILSON, ELLA GRANT** (7 Sept. 1854–16 Dec. 1939), florist and author who wrote about EUCLID AVE.'s† "Millionaires Row," was born Ella Lawton Grant in Jersey City, NJ, to Gilbert W. and Susan Lawton Grant and came to Cleveland at age 6. With $10 savings and $100 borrowed, she started a business of floral decorations. Wilson arranged over 300 weddings and 1,000 funerals, including JAS. A. GARFIELD's† funeral in Cleveland. Her position as a florist gained her entry into the homes of Cleveland's wealthiest and most prominent citizens. Wilson designed floral arrangements for 18 years for the Chamber of Commerce and HOLLENDEN

HOTEL.† When a cyclone destroyed her greenhouse on 22 Apr. 1909 and nearly buried her son, she got out of the business. She went to work again in 1918, as garden editor for the *PLAIN DEALER,†* remaining in that position 6 years. In 1929 Wilson began a new career. She had collected and maintained a huge series of scrapbooks of the history of Cleveland, and with them began a series of articles in Sunday magazine of the *Plain Dealer* dealing with Cleveland and Euclid Ave. The articles became the basis of the first of 2 volumes on Millionaires Row entitled *Famous Old Euclid Ave.* The first volume contained anecdotes, history, biographies, and geography of Euclid Ave. from E. 30th to E. 79th streets. Her second volume, published in 1937, continued the story to E. 105th St. Wilson married twice. Her first marriage was on 25 Dec. 1880 to Jas. A. Campbell; they divorced in 1888. Her second marriage was to Chas. H. Wilson on 29 July 1891. Wilson had 5 children from her second marriage: Pansy, Helen, Carl, Fern, and Earnest.

Ella Grant Wilson Scrapbooks, WRHS.

**WILSON, JOHN** (28 Nov. 1893–2 Jan. 1993), a master marble setter who helped create some of the outstanding buildings in the area, was born in Milngavie, Scotland, the son of John and Mary (Smith) Wilson and came to the Cleveland area when he was 19. After service with the 70th Engineers during World War I, he returned to Cleveland to pursue his trade as a marble setter, installing slabs of marble for the CLEVELAND MUSEUM OF ART† and the Terminal Tower complex in the 1920s. During the 1930s he was hired full time by the FEDERAL RESERVE BANK OF CLEVELAND† to maintain and repair the extensive Sienna and Etowah Georgia marble, part of the imposing building designed by WALKER & WEEKS.† He retired in 1958.

Wilson married Mary W. Dyson in 1923; they had a son, John Dyson. A longtime resident of CLEVELAND HTS.,† he moved to Willoughby in the late 1980s and died there. He was buried in Knollwood Cemetery.—M.S.

**WING, MARIE REMINGTON** (5 Nov. 1885–27 Dec. 1982), lawyer, feminist, and reformer, was born in Cleveland to federal judge Francis J. Wing and Mary Brackett Remington, prepared for college at MISS MITTLEBERGER'S SCHOOL† for Young Ladies, and attending Bryn Mawr until her father's financial reverses forced her to return to Cleveland, working with the YWCA as both industrial and financial secretary. She also served as its general secretary in New York and sat on the Board of Trustees. In 1922 Wing left the YWCA and enrolled

in Cleveland Law School, which her father had helped found. She was elected to CLEVELAND CITY COUNCIL† for 2 terms (1923, 1925), having previously sat on the charter review instituting the city manager system in Cleveland. As one of the first 2 women on council, Wing worked to establish a women's bureau in the police department. She was admitted to the Ohio Bar in 1926. Wing served on the executive board of the Cleveland Fed. of Women's Clubs, and as executive secretary of the CONSUMERS LEAGUE OF OHIO,† where she worked to pass legislation protecting women and children in industry and providing a minimum wage. In 1934 Wing was appointed to the Women's Advisory Committee of the Cleveland Regional Labor Board, heading a special works program committee appointed by the Cuyahoga County Relief Commission. She was the first regional attorney for the Cleveland Social Security office from 1937–53, afterwards opening a private law practice. In 1956, Wing, unmarried, retired to live in Mentor, OH.

Marie Wing Papers, WRHS.

**WINTER, HAROLD EDWARD** (14 Oct. 1908–22 July 1976), a writer, and his wife, **THELMA FRAZIER** (17 Dec. 1908–24 June 1977), a sculptor, were both enamelists who studied at the CLEVELAND INSTITUTE OF ART† and married on 21 Dec. 1939. In 1930 Thelma, born in Gnadenhutten, OH, daughter of Robert and Ester (Eggenberg) Frazier, went to Ohio State Univ. to study ceramics, then to OSU Medical School to study anatomy. She received her B.C. in education in 1935 from Western Reserve Univ. Edward, born in Pasadena, CA, to John Edward and Lila (Deveny) Winter, studied in Vienna, Austria. Although both taught, Edward at the Institute of Art (1935–37) and Old White Art Colony in West Virginia, and Thelma at LAUREL SCHOOL,† the Institute of Art, and CLEVELAND MUSEUM OF ART,† the Winters were primarily artists. Edward wrote *Enamel Art on Metals, Enameling for Beginners,* and *Enamel Painting Techniques* as well as many articles. His style and technique were decorative and abstract expressionism in flora and fauna, using foil inlay or transparent and opaque surface copper, steel, silver, and aluminum in his enameling. His work is in the Cleveland and Butler museums of art and New York State's Ceramics Gallery. In 1933 Edward was commissioned by FERRO CO.† to do a series of murals, designing large blue angelfish in porcelain enamel. Edward also drew a special commission in 1944 from the U.S. Army to do educational posters for GIs while serving as a technical sergeant. Thelma's media were stylized sculpture, decorative enamels, and ceramics that were also semiabstract; her work is in the

Cleveland and Butler museums of art, the Everson Museum, and WESTERN RESERVE HISTORICAL SOCIETY.† Her commissions include the Arisen Christ for ST. MARY'S ROMANIAN CHURCH† and the Annunciation and Last Supper for the Catholic Diocese. The Winters are buried in Lake View Cemetery.

H. Edward and Thelma Frazier Winter Papers, WRHS.

**WINTON, ALEXANDER** (20 June 1860–21 June 1932), automobile developer and popularizer, was born in Grangemouth, Scotland, to Alexander and Helen Fea Winton. He came to the U.S. at age 19, and worked in Delameter Iron Works and a marine engine shop before arriving in Cleveland in 1884. In 1891 he organized Winton Bicycle Co., manufacturing a bicycle design he patented that year. The business flourished, but within 10 years Winton left it to manufacture automobiles, completing his first motor car in 1896, incorporating WINTON MOTOR CARRIAGE CO.† in 1897, and on 28 July beginning America's first reliability run, a 9-day drive to New York, stimulating investment and permitting construction of 4 more cars. The sale of one of these on 24 Mar. 1898 was the first of an American-made standard-model gasoline automobile. In 1899 Winton made a better-publicized 5-day drive to New York, boosting interest and expanding sales.

Winton continued developing new automobile models, including racing cars, but a decline in sales in the 1920s prompted Winton to liquidate the company and concentrate on Winton Gas Engine & Mfg. Co., formed in 1912 to produce marine engines (see CLEVELAND DIESEL ENGINE DIV. OF GENERAL MOTORS CORP.†). In 1913 the company produced the first American diesel engine. Winton retired after selling the firm to GM in 1930.

Married 4 times, his first was in 1883 to Jeanie Muir McGlashan (d. 1903) with whom he had six children: Helen F., James M., Agnes M., Jeanie, Cathrine, and Alexander. In 1906 he married LaBelle McGlashan (d. 1924) and they had two children: LaBelle and Clarice. In 1927 Winton married Marion Campbell (div. 1930); and in 1930, Mary Ellen Avery. Winton died in Cleveland and was buried in Lake View Cemetery.

Wager, Richard. *Golden Wheels* (1975).

**WIRTZ, JOHN J.** (1 Nov. 1914–20 Aug. 1992), outstanding football and basketball coach for many years at St. Ignatius High School, was born in Columbus, the son of Frederick and Barbara (Greene) Wirtz. He played football, basketball, and baseball at Columbus St. Mary high school and at the Univ. of Dayton, where he received his degree in business administration in 1938. He worked for the Pennsylvania Railroad and coached grade school sports in Columbus until 1940, when St. Mary's asked him to coach the school's football team. He left to enter the Army Air Corps during World War II, attaining the rank of captain and returned to St. Mary in 1946. In 1948 he accepted a job at St. Ignatius high school in Cleveland as the football line coach and track coach. Three years later he was appointed head football and basketball coach and later became the school's athletic director. During his 28-year tenure at St. Ignatius, his football teams won 13 West Senate titles and 3 city titles and a co-championship; his basketball teams were champions of the West Senate 8 times and won the city title once. Wirtz retired in 1976 with many honors and was inducted into the Ohio High School Football Coaches Hall of Fame.

Wirtz met and married Joan Smith while serving in England during the war; they had two children, Carol Wessel of PARMA† and Joan of Cleveland. He died in Parma and was buried at Brooklyn Hts. Cemetery.—M.S.

**WISE, SAMUEL D.** (28 Nov. 1875–25 Mar. 1953), Jewish industrialist and philanthropist, was born to Daniel and Leah (Florshim) Wise. He was educated in Cleveland and began work in 1889 as an office boy and bookkeeper for Atlantic Refining Co., which produced roof coating, lubricating oils, axle grease, and industrial paints. Wise and some associates acquired all the company's stock when owner Geo. C. Haskell retired in 1901. They changed the company's name to Arco Co. in 1914. With Wise as its president, Arco became the 3rd-largest company in its field after GLIDDEN† and SHERWIN-WILLIAMS CO.† Wise retired in 1936. Before he left Cleveland for Katonah, NY, in 1951, Wise contributed to many causes and organizations. He is best remembered for founding CAMPE WISE† and the Camp Wise Assn. for children, begun on a once-fashionable 20-acre resort in EUCLID† in 1906 as a summer camp for indigent children and their mothers. Its success led to selection of another camp site at Painesville-on-the-Lake, occupying 70 acres east of Painesville. Wise was an organizer of MT. SINAI MEDICAL CTR.,† giving the principal donation to build its nurses' home and training school. He was also a founder of the Jewish Welfare Fund in 1931, and a trustee and supporter of the Jewish Welfare Fed. Wise donated several art treasures to the CLEVELAND MUSEUM OF ART.† Cultural and needy members of the community still benefit from the Samuel D. & May W. Wise Fund. Wise was honored as Cleveland's Distinguished Citizen on 27 May 1931.

Wise married May Weil on 15 Jan. 1903. They had three children: Howard E., Margaret, and Francis. Wise died in Katonah, NY, and was cremated.

**WISH, HARVEY** (4 Sept. 1909–7 March 1968) was named Elbert J. Benton Distinguished Professor of History at Western Reserve Univ. in recognition of his renown in the field of American social and intellectual history. A Chicagoan by birth, he earned a baccalaureate from the Illinois Institute of Technology, a master's from the Univ. of Chicago, and the doctorate from Northwestern. After marrying Anne Kruger in 1932, he taught at DePaul Univ. (1936–43) and Smith College (1944–45) before becoming the first Jew to be appointed to the Faculty of Arts and Sciences at Western Reserve Univ. in 1945. Having previously published *George Fitzhugh, Propagandist of the Old South* (1943), Wish soon added *Contemporary America* (1945) and *Society and Thought in America* (2 vols., 1950–52) to his catalogue. Named a Fulbright Professor in 1954, he lectured in American history in Munich, Vienna, and Scandinavia. He was also a Carnegie Visiting Professor at the Univ. of Hawaii (1956) and John G. Winant Distinguished Professor in American Institutions in London (1961). At Western Reserve, Wish was a cofounder of the graduate program in American Studies. His editing of classic works on the history of American slavery placed him on the cutting edge of the Black Studies movement of the 1960s. After the publication of his *The American Historian* (1960), Wish was elected president of the Ohio Academy of History in 1965. He died in Denver of a heart attack suffered on a train returning from California to Cleveland, survived by his wife and a daughter, Mrs. Dorothy Braroe.—J.V.

Siney, Marion C. *Ups and Downs: The History Department, Western Reserve University–Case Western Reserve University* (1980).

**WITT, PETER** (24 July 1869–20 Oct. 1948), politician and transit expert, was born in Cleveland to Christian and Anna Witt. He attended school through the 5th grade and then worked in a basket factory. He later worked as an iron molder and foundryman. Rebellious and outspoken, Witt took part in union activities and was blacklisted in 1896. A follower of the single-tax philosophy of Henry George, Witt wrote *Cleveland before St. Peter,* about tax dodging by wealthy Clevelanders. In 1900 Witt became Cleveland's decennial appraiser; in 1903, city clerk, serving TOM L. JOHNSON. After Johnson's defeat in 1909, Witt worked with Forest City Investment Co. From 1911–15 he was commissioner of street railways under NEWTON D.

BAKER, introducing the "pay-leave" system on streetcars and eliminating many stops, reducing running time (see URBAN TRANSPORTATION†).

In 1915 Witt ran unsuccessfully for mayor. From 1916–23, he was a consultant on mass transit for other cities. He helped establish a city manager form of government for Cleveland in 1921 (see CITY MANAGER PLAN†). In 1923 Witt was elected to CLEVELAND CITY COUNCIL† as an independent, serving until 1927. In 1924 he supported Robert La Follette for president, later supporting Al Smith and Franklin D. Roosevelt. In 1928 Witt ran unsuccessfully for Ohio governor; in 1932, for Cleveland mayor. From 1932 until his death, Witt lived in semiretirement, spending time on N. Bass Island. He died following a heart attack, survived by his wife, Sadie James, whom he married in 1892, and 3 daughters: Hazel, Norma, and Helen.

Peter Witt Papers, WRHS.

**WITT, STILLMAN** (4 Jan. 1808–29 Apr. 1875), railroad president and philanthropist, was born in Worcester, MA, to John and Hannah (Foster) Witt. At 13 he moved to Troy, NY, and apprenticed with Canvass White of the U.S. Engineer Corps, then was sent by White to administer Cohoes Mfg. Co., employed to build a bridge at Cohoes Falls and on other building projects. Then, still connected with White, he became an agent of the Hudson River Steamboat Assn. in Albany. With the emergence of railroads in the 1840s, Witt became manager of Albany & Boston Railroad Co. In the late 1840s, Witt moved to Cleveland, forming the firm of Harbach, Stone & Witt which built the Cleveland, Columbus & Cincinnati Railroad, completed in 1851. The firm then constructed the Cleveland, Painesville & Ashtabula Railroad, and the Chicago & Milwaukee Railroad. Witt managed the large interests he had acquired in railroads and other properties, becoming director of the above railroads and others. In 1863 Witt was an incorporator of Cleveland Rolling Mill Co. He also helped build the CLEVELAND & NEWBURGH RAILROAD† in 1868.

In 1869, Witt bought and donated a boarding home for the Women's Christian Assn. (later YWCA); in 1873, he donated money for a second home, later known as the Stillman Witt Boarding House. Witt was active in many other Cleveland charitable and educational organizations, especially those for women. In the 1850s he served on the first directorate of the CLEVELAND FEMALE SEMINARY.† Witt married Eliza A. Douglass in 1834. They had 4 children: Emma, Eugenia, Giles, and Mary (Mrs. Daniel Eells), who was actively involved in the Women's Christian Assn. Witt died while at sea on the steamship *Suevia*, a trip he took for restorative purposes.

**WITTKE, CARL FREDERICK** (13 Nov. 1892–24 May 1971), historian, was born in Columbus, OH, to Carl William Oswald and Caroline Kropp Wittke, received his A.B. from Ohio State Univ. (1913), and M.A. (1914) and Ph.D. (1921) from Harvard Univ. before becoming a history instructor (1916–21), asst. professor (1921–25), and full professor and chairman of the department at OSU (1925–37). He was professor of history and dean of Oberlin College (1937–48) before joining Western Reserve Univ. as professor of history and dean of the Graduate School in 1948, becoming department chairman in 1952, Elbert Jay Benton Distinguished Professor of History in 1959, and vice-president of the university in 1961. He retired in 1963 as dean emeritus of the Graduate School and professor and history department chairman emeritus of the university.

Wittke presented many speeches, wrote over 80 articles, edited historical reviews, and authored over 14 books, including *History of Canada* (1928); *We Who Built America: The Saga of the Immigrant* (1939); *Against the Current: The Life of Karl Heinzen* (1945); and *Refugees of Revolution: The German Forty-eighters in America* (1952). He edited the 6-volume *History of the State of Ohio*, and in 1966 wrote *The First Fifty Years: The Cleveland Museum of Art, 1916–1966*. He received many honorary degrees and civic awards. In 1916 Wittke married Lillian Bowshans; they had a son, Carl Francis. After Lillian's death in 1918, Wittke married Lillian Nippert in 1921.

Cramer, Clarence H. *Carl Frederick Wittke* (1971).

**WOLDMAN, ALBERT A.** (1 Jan. 1897–30 Dec. 1971), lawyer and CUYAHOGA COUNTY JUVENILE COURT† judge, was born in Russia to Isadore and Gertrude (Kudish) Woldman. He came to Cleveland with his family at age 18 months. Woldman graduated with an A.B. from Adelbert College in 1917, and attended Western Reserve and Ohio Northern law schools, graduating with an LL.B. in 1919. In 1914 he became the youngest probation officer in juvenile court's history. While in college, he worked as a reporter for the *CLEVELAND PRESS†* and asst. state editor for the *PLAIN DEALER.†* Between 1919–41, Woldman maintained his private practice and taught at John Marshall Law School. In 1941 he became Cleveland's asst. law director; in 1945, chairman of the Ohio Bureau of Unemployment Compensation's Board of Review; in 1949, director of Ohio's Dept. of Industrial Relations. He was appointed to the Cuyahoga County Juvenile Court in Aug. 1953. Winning a 2-year term in 1954, Woldman was twice reelected to 6-year terms. As the court's administrative judge, viewing juvenile delinquency as the number-one social problem, he was also responsible for the county juvenile detention home. During his later years on the bench, he had to deal with discontent and poor morale among court employees because of low pay. Woldman was an avid student of Abraham Lincoln, writing *Lawyer Lincoln,* a study of Lincoln's career as a lawyer and the constitutional problems of the Civil War. Woldman was president of B'NAI B'RITH† of Cleveland. He married Lydia Levin on 3 July 1921 and had 3 children, Robert, Phyllis, and Stuart. Woldman died at his home in BEACHWOOD† and was buried in the Warrensville Cemetery.

Albert A. Woldman Papers, WRHS.

**WOLF, EDITH ANISFIELD** (1889–23 Jan. 1963), poet, businesswoman, and philanthropist, was born in Cleveland to Doniella (Guttenberg) and JOHN ANISFIELD and graduated from Women's College (later Flora Stone Mather College). On 7 Aug. 1918, she married attorney Eugene E. Wolf. Able to read French, German, and Spanish, Wolf was devoted to literature and charitable work; she managed her family's estate and wrote poetry from her downtown office. She published several books of poetry, including *Snacks* (1938) and *Balance* (1942), as well as magazine articles. In 1934 she established an annual $1,000 prize for the outstanding book in race relations in honor of her father. In 1941, in honor of her husband, she added a second prize of $1,000 for a creative book that performs "an outstanding service in clarifying the problems of racial relations," and the first award was then designated for the best work of a scientific nature on racial relations. Among the winners of the Anisfield-Wolf awards have been Dr. Martin Luther King, Jr., and LANGSTON HUGHES. In 1943 Wolf was elected by the school board to serve on the board of the CLEVELAND PUBLIC LIBRARY.† Upon her death she left all her books to the library; willed her family home on East Blvd. to the Cleveland Welfare Fed.; and left funds to the CLEVELAND FOUNDATION,† which were used to establish the $5,000 Anisfield-Wolf Award for community service. Wolf, who had no children, died in Cleveland. Her remains are in the Knollwood Mausoleum.

**WOLF, FREDERICK C.** (22 April 1902–23 Sept. 1972) became noted in Cleveland RADIO† as a pioneer in nationality and classical music programming. A native of Prague, he was the son of Vaclav and Magdalena Rosmanova Wolf. After attending the Prague Commercial Academy, he worked for the Krupp Munition Works before emigrating to Cleveland in 1927. He became an editor for the Czech daily *American* (see *SVET-AMERICAN†*) and in 1928 married Clevelander Lillian Cervenka. He began broadcasting a Czech program in 1929 over WHK,† moving it to WJAY the following year and to WGAR† in 1936. In 1934 he founded the Cleveland Recording Co. for the production of spot commercials, nationality music, and auditions. He also formed the Nationalities Broadcasting Assn., an organization for all foreign radio programs, the same year. On 30 April 1950 Wolf and several partners started their own station, WDOK. By 1957 it was the radio home for 18 different nationality programs, most of them broadcast on Sundays. It also bucked contemporary music trends by broadcasting 2 hours of classical music each night. Wolf sold WDOK to Transcontinent Television Corp. of New York in 1962. He also sold Cleveland Broadcasting Co., though continuing as a director. Because of his influence in ethnic affairs, Wolf was an important voice in local Republican politics. He was a member of the Sokol Nova Vlast and the Czech Cultural Garden Assn. Predeceased by his wife, he died childless in PARMA HTS.† and was buried in Calvary Cemetery.—J.V.

**WOLFENSTEIN, MARTHA** (1869–16 Mar. 1906) was perhaps the first Jewish woman author to write Jewish stories for the secular press. She was born in Insterburg, Prussia, to Samuel and Bertha (Briger) Wolfenstein and brought to the U.S. as an infant when her father became rabbi of Congregation B'nai El in St. Louis. The family moved to Cleveland in 1878 when Samuel became superintendent of the JEWISH ORPHAN HOME,† living at the home. Following her mother's death from tuberculosis in 1885, Martha became her father's housekeeper and child-rearer, and also served as matron of the orphan home for a time. Martha's earliest literary endeavor was as a translator of German poetry and stories. She soon began writing short fiction based on her father's reminiscences about his childhood in a Central European ghetto. She published widely in the secular literary press and also in the local Anglo-Jewish press and *Jewish Orphan Asylum Magazine*. In 1901 the Jewish Publication Society of America published a collection of short fiction that had appeared in *Lippincott's* and *Outlook* under the title *Idylls of the Gass*. Four years later, they published a collection of stories, *The Renegade and Other Stories*, all of which had appeared in the *Jewish Review & Observer*. Martha was working on a play, which was never published or performed, when she died from tuberculosis. A year later the Council of Jewish Women established a residence

for homeless girls, naming it Martha House, after Martha Wolfenstein. Unmarried, she was buried in Willett St. Cemetery.

**WOLFRAM, CHARLES J.** (5 Nov. 1871–8 June 1951) played an influential role in the political, cultural, and fraternal affairs of Cleveland's German population (see GERMANS†). Born in Connersville, IN, he was the son of Claus and Margaret Baumgartner Wolfram and came with the family to Cleveland. In 1898 he was one of the founders of Gilmour Council, the first unit of the Knights of Columbus in Ohio, and became an insurance agent for the lodge. In the aftermath of World War I, he became involved in the organization of the national Von Steuben Society to counteract the anti-German sentiments engendered during the war. Locally, Wolfram became the first president of the CLEVELAND CULTURAL GARDEN FEDERATION,† a post he held for 25 years. He also helped establish the German Cultural Garden, which was dedicated in 1929. As an ally of City Manager WILLIAM R. HOPKINS, Wolfram made an unsuccessful campaign for CLEVELAND CITY COUNCIL† in 1931. He later swung his influence among west side Germans behind Mayor RAY T. MILLER and was rewarded with an appointment as secretary of the City Plan Commission. In 1941 he was appointed chairman of the Board of Zoning Appeals, a position he held until his death. Wolfram married the former Mary E. Patterson in 1898 and was survived by 2 children, Carl and Josephine Sheehy. He died in ST. ALEXIS HOSPITAL MEDICAL CTR.†—J.V.

**WOLSEY, LOUIS** (8 Jan. 1877–4 Mar. 1953), the first American-born and trained rabbi to serve ANSHE CHESED CONGREGATION,† was born in Midland, MI, to William and Frances (Krueger) Wolsey. He graduated from Hebrew Union College and was ordained in 1899. He served at Congregation B'nai Israel in Little Rock, AR, before being hired by Anshe Chesed in 1907 when its membership was 150; by 1925 it was 1,300 and the congregation had moved to their new Euclid Ave. Temple. Wolsey embraced a conservative view of Reform Judaism, countering the Classical Reform in vogue and engaging in a bitter public debate with Rabbi MOSES J. GRIES of the TEMPLE.† Following Gries's death in 1918, Wolsey moved into the mainstream of Classical Reform. Wolsey was interested in Jewish education, revitalizing the Anshe Chesed Sunday school from 135 pupils in 1908 to 650 in 1916 and supporting CLEVELAND HEBREW SCHOOLS.† By 1918 Wolsey was an outspoken critic of political Zionism, in 1943 founding the

American Council for Judaism, an organization of Reform rabbis and lay leaders opposed to the perceived pro-Zionist stance taken by the Central Conference of American Rabbis. Three years later he renounced his membership in the ACJ, in 1948 calling for support for the state of Israel. Wolsey was treasurer, corresponding secretary, vice-president, and president of the Central Conference of American Rabbis. He left Cleveland in 1925 to be the rabbi at Rodeph Shalom in Philadelphia, where he remained until his retirement in 1947. He married Florence Wiener on 12 June 1912. They had two children, Allon and Jonathan.

Anshe Chesed Records, WRHS.

**WOOD, HARLAN GOFF** (2 Sept. 1907–12 Sept. 1991), internationally known scientist and the first director of the Department of Biochemistry at the School of Medicine, CASE WESTERN RESERVE UNIV.† (CWRU, 1946–67), proved in 1935 that animals (including humans) and bacteria utilized carbon dioxide. His lifelong research into this revolutionary discovery changed traditional understanding of cell biology and improved the treatment of diseases such as diabetes, which involve the metabolism. Wood was elected to the National Academy of Sciences (1953) and received the National Medal of Science (1989), among numerous other honors. Nobel prize winners gathered in Cleveland for his 77th and 80th birthdays. Wood was born in Delavan, MN, to Inez Goff and William Clark Wood and was educated at Macalester College in St. Paul (B.S., 1931) and Northwestern Univ. (Ph.D., 1935). Before coming to CWRU, he taught at Iowa State Univ. (1936–43) and the Univ. of Minnesota (1943–46).

Among the first scientists to use radioisotopes in cell biology, Wood ingeniously isolated them in an elevator shaft. He took his research to various parts of the world on Fulbright fellowships and published copiously, serving as editor of the *Journal of Biological Chemistry* (1949–54). At CWRU, after leaving the chair of biochemistry, Wood was Dean of Sciences (1967–69), the first Univ. Professor (1970–78), and professor emeritus (1978–91). He served on the advisory board of the AMERICAN CANCER SOCIETY† (1965–69), on the President's Science Advisory Committee (1967–71), and as a council member of the International Union of Biochemistry and Molecular Biology (1967–76, secretary general, 1970–73).

Wood married Mildred L. Davis in Minnesota in 1929; they had 3 daughters: Louise Lake, Beverly Abram, and Donna McCutcheon Pleasants. Wood was an avid hunter and learned to ski at age 55. Wood is buried in Minnesota. In Wood's honor, CWRU's School of Medicine established an annual memorial lecture.—J.M.

**WOOD, REUBEN** (1792–1 Oct. 1864), 16th governor of Ohio (1850–53) was born in Middletown, VT, son of Nathaniel and Lucretia Wood. He moved to Canada at age 15 and studied law, was conscripted into the Royalist Militia during the War of 1812, but fled to the U.S. and served briefly in the U.S. Army. He arrived in Cleveland in 1818, bringing his family in 1819 aboard the first steamship to visit the city, *WALK-IN-THE-WATER.†* Wood was elected president of the village of Cleveland in 1821. In 1825 he was elected to his first of 3 terms in the Ohio senate; in 1830 he was elected judge of the Common Pleas Court; in 1832 he was elected to his first of 2 terms as judge of the Ohio Supreme Court (1833–47), serving the last 3 years as chief justice. Wood was elected governor in 1850, however in June 1851 voters approved the new Ohio constitution requiring the election of officials in odd-numbered years; Wood was again elected governor in 1851. In his 1851 inaugural address, he expressed his abhorrence of the Fugitive Slave Law and urged its repeal. Wood narrowly missed being nominated for president at the 1852 Democratic Natl. Convention, losing to Franklin Pierce. He resigned the governorship in 1853 to become consul in Valparaiso, Chile. A year later he returned to Cleveland and resumed his law practice. Wood married Mary Rice in 1816 and had 2 daughters, Loretta and Mary. Wood and his wife are buried in Woodland Cemetery.

**WOODRUFF, MABEL ALICE** (30 Dec. 1893–30 Aug. 1963) was one of Cleveland's first psychiatric social workers and the founder of Ingleside Hospital. She was born in Windsor, OH, the daughter of Ulrich and Florence (Pond) Woodruff. She grew up in Niles and Oberlin, OH, and graduated from Oberlin College. Afterwards she worked as a rehabilitation worker in the Army Medical Corps during World War I.

In 1922 she came to Cleveland and worked for Lakeside and City Hospitals. Woodruff soon became aware of the inadequate conditions in many private mental health hospitals and spearheaded an investigation into Cleveland's private sanitariums. In response to the need for quality private mental health care she founded Ingleside Hospital in 1935. She began the hospital with $1,300 in borrowed money and housed it in a rented house on Ingleside Ave. In 1936 Woodruff gained the assistance of George Holmes, and later his wife Dorothy. She continued to work at City Hospital during the day and used some of her income to pay the hospital's bills out of her own pocket. In 1937 Ingleside was incorporated as a nonprofit institution with Woodruff as director. By the early 1960s, Ingleside, located at 8811–21 Euclid, and its Eldercare Center near Chardon, OH, were rated among the top 12 private mental hospitals in the U.S.

Woodruff's health began to fail late in 1962. She died in Cleveland and was buried at Westwood Cemetery, Oberlin. She never married, and was survived by a brother, A. Byrne Woodruff.—D.R.

**WOOLSON, CONSTANCE FENIMORE** (Mar. 1840–24 Jan. 1894), author, was born in Claremont, NH, to Chas. Jarvis and Hannah Pomeroy Woolson. The family moved to Cleveland later that year after scarlet fever killed 3 of her siblings in 3 weeks. While living in Cleveland, Constance came to know the Lake County region and Tuscarawas Valley, which would later appear in her books. She graduated from Mme Chegary's School in New York City in 1858. "Two Women," was Woolson's first published poem (1862). It was her father's death in 1869 that prompted Woolson to discover her roots from her father, who was interested in literature, and her great-uncle, James Fenimore Cooper. In 1871 the family moved South, to the Carolinas and Florida. Eight years later, Woolson and her sister went to England. Woolson eventually settled in Venice, where she met Henry James and Wm. Dean Howells. Woolson began publishing descriptive articles in magazines (*Harpers, Atlantic Monthly, Galaxy*) a year after her father's death. She wrote a children's book, *The Old Stone House,* under the name Anne March in 1873; published her first book of short stories, *Castle Nowhere: Lake County Sketches,* in 1875; and a second collection, *Rodman the Keeper: Southern Sketches,* in 1880. Woolson's first novel, *Anne* (1883), was a great success and might well be considered a feminist statement. Woolson wrote 4 more novels, *For the Major, East Angel, Jupiter Lights,* and *Horace Chase* (1894). Woolson never married and died in Venice, Italy. She was buried in the Protestant Cemetery in Rome.

Kern, John. *Constance Fenimore Woolson, Literary Pioneer* (1934).
Moore, Rayburn S. *Constance Fenimore Woolson* (1963).
Tornsey, Cheryl B. *Constance Fenimore Woolson: The Grief of Artistry* (1989).
Tornsey, Cheryl B., ed. *Critical Essays on Constance Fenimore Woolson* (1992).

**WORTHINGTON, GEORGE** (21 Sept. 1813–9 Nov. 1871), founder of Cleveland Iron & Nail Works, Cleveland Iron Mining Co., and GEO. WORTHINGTON CO.,† was born in Cooperstown, NY, to Ralph and Clarissa Clarke Worthington, completed a common-school educa-

tion, and started his career in 1830 as a hardware store clerk in Utica. After 4 years he moved to Cleveland, where with $500 borrowed from his brother he started his own hardware business. Almost all of Worthington's early business was conducted by barter. At first his goods were carted to him in oxen-drawn wagons; later they were shipped by lake schooner from Buffalo. He associated himself with WM. BINGHAM in 1835, and they bought out the stock of Cleveland Sterling & Co. In 1841 Bingham sold his interests in the company to Worthington. A few years later, Worthington associated with JAS. BARNETT and Edward Bingham. By establishing new markets in neighboring towns, their company soon became the largest hardware business in the region, with annual sales of over $1 million. Worthington started Cleveland Iron & Nail Works with Wm. Bingham in 1863. Worthington helped organize and was president of First Natl. Bank of Cleveland, director of Ohio Savings & Loan Bank and Hahneman Life, and vice-president of Sun Insurance Co. He was president of Cleveland Iron Mining Co. and a director of the Cleveland, Columbus & Cincinnati Railroad. Worthington married Maria Blackmar in 1840 and had 8 children, 6 of whom survived to adulthood: Abigail, May, Clarissa, Alice, Ralph, and George. Worthington is buried in Lake View Cemetery.

**WRIGHT, ALONZO G.** (30 Apr. 1898–17 Aug. 1976), a black southern migrant who became a millionaire, was born in Fayetteville, TN, son of Alonzo and Joyce Kelso Wright. He worked as a shoeshine boy and a messenger and moved to Cleveland in the early 1910s. Alonzo earned his high school diploma at night while working as a teamster, foundry hand, mail-truck driver, and garage attendant at Auditorium Hotel for 8 years, there meeting Sohio executive Wallace T. Holliday. Impressed by his work, Holliday arranged for Wright to become the first African American to lease a Sohio station, at E. 93rd and Cedar, the first Standard Oil station in a predominantly black neighborhood. Customers were attracted by new services Wright offered: cleaning windshields regularly and offering free tire and radiator checks. By 1937 Wright operated 6 stations; he operated 11 stations before leaving the business in the mid–1940s.

Wright created job opportunities for young blacks, credited by 1940 with having hired more black youths than any other businessman in the U.S. As gas rationing slowed sales, Wright left the service station business, in 1943 establishing Wright's Enterprises, a real estate investment firm. He bought Carnegie Hotel (1947), Ritzwood Hotel, and established Dunbar Nursing Home. In the 1960s Wright concentrated on industrial and residential construction. Even as a successful businessman, when he moved into an all-white section of CLEVELAND HTS.† in the 1930s, his home was bombed; in 1947 he moved to Chesterland. Wright married Henrietta Cheeks in 1929 (d. 1963), and Helen Keith in 1964. Wright died at his home in BRATENAHL† and was buried in Lake View Cemetery. He had one son, A. Gordon, Jr.

**WRIGHT, WALTER BENJAMIN** (1852–1939) advanced from railroad porter to secretary for the industry's top administrators. He was born in Harrisonburg, WV, and moved to Columbus, OH, at age 12. Wright started out as a porter on the Lake Shore and Michigan Southern Railroad and then became porter on the private car of Daniel W. Caldwell, general superintendent of the Panhandle Railroad (1873). Wright followed him to Pittsburgh and, in 1882, to the NICKEL PLATE RAILROAD† in Cleveland. In 1892 Wright became private secretary to Caldwell, president of the Lake Shore Line (1894–97). He also served two successors (Samuel R. Calaway and W. H. Caniffin) in the same capacity before retiring in 1922.

On 21 April 1891, Wright married Sarah Marie Johnson; their children were Harry B., Woodworth M., Lloyd L., and Beatrice Wright Fox. The family lived in Cleveland and owned property in Zanesville, OH. Wright helped sponsor local cultural events featuring AFRICAN AMERICANS.† He belonged to the Veteran Assn. and the Round Table Club, both of the Nickel Plate Railroad, and was a trustee of ST. JOHN'S AME (AFRICAN METHODIST EPISCOPAL) CHURCH.†—J.M.

Walter B. Wright Scrapbooks, WRHS

# Y

**YOUNG, AGNES BROOKS** (18 Nov. 1898–6 Feb. 1974), turned her talents to the writing of novels after achieving wide recognition as an authority on fashion and costuming. The daughter of Edward and Agnes Chapin Brooks, she was born in Cleveland and educated at the Cleveland School of Art (see CLEVELAND INSTITUTE OF ART†), the School of Arts and Design and Columbia Univ. in New York, and L'Ecole Francais in Paris. Following her marriage in 1920 to Cleveland lawyer George Benham Young (1894–1957), she served as costume director at the CLEVELAND PLAY HOUSE† from 1923–27 and filled the same function at Yale Univ.'s School of the Theater in 1928–9. A faculty member at Western Reserve Univ. (see CASE WESTERN RESERVE†) from 1930–32, she published studies on *Stage Costuming* and *Recurring Cycles in Fashion, 1760–1937*. She and her husband later lived in SHAKER HTS.† and in her family homestead in CHAGRIN FALLS,† which had an English garden planned by her and A. DONALD GRAY. During World War II, Mrs. Young served as statistical consultant for the War Dept. and the War Manpower Commission. Published under the pen name of Agatha Young, her first novel, *Light in the Sky* (1948), featured a Cleveland setting during the 1870s. Another novel, *Clown of the Gods,* won the 1955 fiction award of the Martha Kinney Cooper Ohioans Library Assn. She and Brooks later lived in Vermont and New York City. She died in the latter city, leaving no survivors.—J.V.

**YOUNG, DALLAS M.** (15 Jan. 1914–23 July 1990), professor of labor relations and a national figure in the field, was born in Christopher, IL, the son of Arvel and Jennie Jordan Young. He graduated from Southern Illinois Teachers College in 1936 with a B.Ed. degree and attended the Univ. of Illinois, receiving an A.M. in 1936 and a Ph.D. in 1941. During World War II, Young was an industrial relations analyst for the National War Labor Board, 1941–45. Appointed to the Regional Wage Stabilization Board in 1951, he mediated wage disputes in Ohio and Kentucky during the Korean War. From 1948–84 Young was a professor of economics and labor relations at Western Reserve Univ., where he became a widely known expert on urban transportation and the use of arbitration to resolve labor disputes. He umpired disputes between the Cleveland Transit System and the local Amalgamated Transit Union for 5 years and also served on the CTS Board of Trustees 1968–70, during which time he tried unsuccessfully to find alternate sources of revenue for the failing system to prevent a succession of transit fare increases.

Young and his wife, Christina, were married 13 August 1939; they had a son, Dallas Jr. After their divorce, he married Evelyn Stiles 1 March 1974. He died at his Cleveland residence and was buried in Mulkeytown, IL.—M.S.

**YOUNG, DENTON TRUE "CY"** (29 Mar. 1867–4 Nov. 1955), baseball pitcher (1890–11) for the Natl. League CLEVELAND SPIDERS† (1890–98) and for Cleveland in the American League (1909–11), winning a major-league record 511 games in his career, was born at Gilmore, OH, son of MacKenzie and Nancy Mot Miller Young. He farmed full-time, playing baseball locally, until he was 23. After pitching for Canton in the Tri-State League, his contract was sold to the Cleveland Spiders. For 16 seasons he won 20 or more games, averaging 8 innings a game for 22 years. In 1899 Young was switched from Cleveland to St. Louis by FRANK DE HAAS ROBISON, who owned both franchises. After 2 years he signed with the Boston Red Sox in the new AL, receiving a $600 raise over his $2,400 NL salary. Young pitched in the first World Series, winning 2 games as Boston defeated Pittsburgh in 1903. After the 1908 season his contract was sold to Cleveland. Released by the Naps in Aug. 1911, he ended his career that year with Boston. Young pitched 3 no-hit, no-run games during his career, including a perfect game on 5 May 1904 against Philadelphia. He appeared in 906 games, a major league record until 1968. Young was a farmer in Tuscarawas County until well past 80. He was inducted into the Baseball Hall of Fame in Cooperstown in 1939, and further recognized when baseball commissioner Ford Frick established the Cy Young Award in 1956 to honor the outstanding pitcher in both leagues. Young married Robba Miller in 1892. They had no children. He was buried in Newcomerstown, OH.

**YOUNG, MERRILL A.** (15 Aug. 1905–5 Jan. 1993), labor relations expert, was born in Lulu, MI, the son of Charles and Sophia Solwich Young. After graduation from Windham, OH, high school, he came to Cleveland in the 1920s and began working as a shipping clerk at Cleveland Graphite Bronze, eventually mastering all aspects of bearing manufacture. To develop his managerial skills, Young attended classes at Case School of Applied Science and JOHN CARROLL UNIV.† During World War II, he was manager of CGB's Cleveland plant, which manufactured automotive and aircraft bearings, when a strike by the MECHANICS EDUCATION SOCIETY† of America erupted over employee discipline in 1944, and the plant was put under control of the army to maintain production (see the CLEVELAND GRAPHITE BRONZE SEIZURE†). By 1947 Young was the company's director of personnel and later was promoted to vice-president in charge of training and labor negotiations for 4,500 employees in the midwest and Canada. He developed a program of economic education for employees and also sought to increase understanding between industry and the public, teaching adult education courses on worker supervision and vocational guidance. After Young left CGB during the

1950s, he was works manager at Marquette Metal Products Division of the Curtiss Wright Corp. for 9 years.

Young married Henrietta Harris and they had a daughter, Wanda (Will). After his wife's death in 1964, he married Hilda R. Warnment 29 May 1965. He died at his home in GATES MILLS† and was buried at Gates Mill South Cemetery.—M.S.

**YOUNGLOVE, MOSES C.** (13 Dec. 1811–13 Apr. 1892), innovative businessman, was born in Cambridge, NY, son of Moses and Hannah (Wells) Younglove. He entered college to study law, but abandoned his studies to go into business. Younglove arrived in Cleveland in 1836, in 1837 joining Edward P. Wetmore in establishing a book and stationery store. In 1838 Younglove bought his partner's share, beginning a job-printing and publishing business in addition to selling books and paper. He sold his book business in 1852.

Younglove brought several steam-powered machines to Cleveland. In Aug. 1845 he set up a steam-powered printing press in the offices of the *CLEVELAND HERALD*,† using it to print the city's papers and his publishing. In 1848 Younglove and John Hoyt established Cleveland Paper Mill, the first paper mill west of the Alleghenies powered by steam. They later merged their company with Lake Erie Paper Co. forming Cleveland Paper Co., of which Younglove was president until he sold his interest in 1867. Younglove gained control of Cleveland Gas Light & Coke Co. (see EAST OHIO GAS CO.†) in 1848 and mortgaged everything he owned to finance construction of the gas works. He was a company director for years and its president in the 1860s. Younglove was a founder of Younglove & Massie Agricultural Works, helped organize Society for Savings, and was president of Kelley Island Lime & Transport Co. and Lakeside & Marblehead Railroad Co. He retired from daily business in 1865. He was a member of the CLEVELAND ANTI-SLAVERY SOCIETY.†

Younglove married Maria Day in 1839 and had 5 children: Caroline, Albert, Cornelia, Gertrude, and Lucy. Younglove was buried in Lake View Cemetery.

Z

**ZABOLY, BELA (BILL)** (4 May 1910–11 April 1985), made Cleveland the home port of "Popeye the Sailor Man" for 2 decades as artist for the syndicated cartoon strip. Born to Hungarian immigrant parents on Cleveland's west side, Zaboly attended WEST HIGH SCHOOL,† where he contributed cartoons to the school newspaper, *The West Higher.* His art education came from Saturday morning classes under Louise Dunn at the CLEVELAND MUSEUM OF ART† and special classes at the Cleveland School of Art (see CLEVELAND INSTITUTE OF ART†). He turned down a scholarship to the CSA to continue his studies at night at the JOHN HUNTINGTON POLYTECHNIC INSTITUTE.† After winning an honorable mention in the MAY SHOW† with an oil painting in 1932, he began working for the Scripps-Howard Newspaper Enterprise Assn. in Cleveland in 1934, drawing the "Major Hoople" cartoons among others. Following the death of its creator, Elzie C. Segar, Zaboly took over Popeye and the "Thimble Theater" cartoon for the King Features syndicate in 1939. Working in his homes in CLEVELAND HTS.† and later MORELAND HILLS,† he prepared the finished strips from written texts mailed from writers in other cities. His distinctive signature featured the picture of a bee (for Bela or Bill) in front of his last name. After giving up the Popeye assignment ca. 1960, he formed his own syndicate and did freelance work. He was survived by his wife, the former Irene Elizabeth Chandas, and 3 children: Alwyn Zaboly, Irene Z. Church, and Marianne Z. Dodds.—J.V.

**ZAMECNIK, JOHN S.** (1872–13 June 1953), utilized his experience as a Cleveland theater musician to become a pioneer in the scoring of Hollywood film music. A native Clevelander, he was the son of Bohemian immigrants Joseph and Katherine Zamecnik. The elder Zamecnik was a bandleader, and young Zamecnik had already shown compositional and conducting talent before going to study music under Antonin Dvorak at the Prague Conservatory, where he graduated in 1897. He then took a post as violinist in the Pittsburgh Symphony under Victor Herbert. Zamecnik returned to Cleveland in 1907 to assume a post as composer-director at the new HIPPODROME THEATER.† His duties included providing music to the lyrics of William J. Wilson for the theater's opening stage attraction of *Coaching Days* in 1908. Zamecnik also married Mary Barbara Heodons in 1908 and in 1911 joined the Sam Fox Publishing Co. in the ARCADE,† where he served as musical editor-in-chief after 1914. Among his compositions, he provided musical numbers for the early shows of the HERMIT CLUB† and won a contest against 900 competitors to compose the California state song in 1915. In 1925 he went to Hollywood, where he contributed the scores to such films as *Abie's Irish Rose, Old Ironsides, Wings,* and *Betrayal.* By the time of his death in Los Angeles, he was credited with nearly 2,000 compositions. He was survived by his wife and 2 sons, Edwin H. and Walter J.—J.V.

**ZANGERLE, JOHN A.** (12 Apr. 1866–1 Oct. 1956), Cuyahoga County auditor (1913–51) and the last surviving public official of the TOM L. JOHNSON era, was born in Cleveland to Adam and Maria Reisterer Zangerle, graduated from West High School in 1884, read law, and was admitted to the Ohio Bar in 1890 before studying economics at the Univ. of Berlin. Zangerle practiced law with the firm of Zangerle, Higley & Maurer, while also consolidating several breweries into Cleveland & Sandusky Brewing Co. He was elected to the Cleveland School Board in 1890 and to the Quadrennial Board of Assessors in 1910. In 1912 Zangerle first won election as county auditor. Never aspiring a higher office, Zangerle became so strong politically that Republicans often made only token efforts to defeat him. The county auditor's office became responsible for property assessments for taxation purposes in 1917, and Zangerle established a system of uniform tax appraisals. In the 1930s he replaced antiquated equipment in the tax division with efficient mechanical equipment and a new accounting and records system. Zangerle was not afraid to confront prominent individuals or corporations on assessments, securing additional revenues from STANDARD OIL CO.,† REPUBLIC STEEL,† Society for Savings, and Sears. He championed a more equitable method of taxation based solely on land values and executed by the state rather than the 88 individual county auditors. From 1951 until his death, Zangerle returned to practicing law. Zangerle married Blanche Norton in 1912 and had 3 children Willis, Hildegard, and Jane Elisabeth.

**ZAPF, NORMAN F.** (14 July 1911–23 June 1974), a mechanical engineer whose research in streamlining led to the design and construction of streamlined locomotives, was born in Cleveland to Herman R. and Mabel (McNess) Zapf. He entered Case School of Applied Science, studying aerodynamics under Dr. Paul Hemke. As an undergraduate, Zapf used the recirculating-type wind tunnel at Case and scale models of steam locomotives to achieve a practical streamlined design that reduced drag 90–100%. At 75 mph his version required 350 hp less than the unstreamlined form. The findings were part of his senior thesis, "The Streamlining of a Steam Locomotive." He graduated in 1934 with a B.S. degree in mechanical engineering and took a job with New York Central Lines, but eventually resigned when he failed to procure an engineering position. He returned to Case as a graduate student but soon left to work for a Boston firm that produced hardware for locomotives. In the 1930s, railroads were searching for ways to improve their image while reducing costs in view of competition from airplanes and automobiles. New streamlined diesel-electric locomotives were introduced, but most railroads already had enormous investments in their steam locomotives. Conclusions from Zapf's thesis were used by New York Central Lines in the design for their *Commodore Vanderbilt,* the company's first streamlined steam locomotive. Zapf served in the Coast Guard during World War II and afterward moved to Florida, where he and his family developed Zapf Groves, Inc.

Zapf married Mildred Anderson in 1935; they had four children: Frederick, Douglas S., Shirley, and Laura. He died in Vero Beach, FL, and was buried there.

**ZEVIN, BEN D.** (16 May 1901–27 Dec. 1984), built the WORLD PUBLISHING CO.† into one of the country's leading book publishers in the period during and after World War II. Born in the Ukraine, he came to America with his family and settled in New York City early in the 20th century. He had his own advertising agency by the age of 21 and became manager of a trade paper. After a childless marriage to Susan Zevin, in 1933 he married Lillian Cahen (1908–93) of Cleveland, daughter of the founder of the Commercial Bookbinding Co., Alfred Cahen. Zevin came to Cleveland in 1934 to become advertising manager of the firm, which became World Publishing the following year. Working alongside his wife, who became World's editor-in-chief, Zevin took the company from sales of $600,000 in 1935 to an estimated $17 million in 1965, when he retired as chairman of the board. Building on the company's reputation as a publisher of Bibles, he made it a leader in dictionary publishing with the introduction of *Webster's New World Dictionary* in 1953. For the publisher Houghton Mifflin of Boston, Zevin edited *Nothing to Fear: The Selected Addresses of Franklin Delano Roosevelt* (1946). A cofounder and president of the Cleveland Council on Human Relations, he also served as president of the CITIZENS LEAGUE† and the CITY CLUB OF CLEVELAND.† He and his wife Lillian raised 4 children: Bernice (Eaton), Rima (Parkhust), Jacquelyn, and Robert B. Following their divorce in 1966, he married Sonia Grau. Zevin died in Miami, FL, survived by his last 2 wives and the 4 children of his 2nd marriage.—J.V.

**ZHUN, ELLEN MARIE STEMPIEN** (17 Aug. 1922–5 Jan. 1993) was a real estate broker and one of the first female land developers in the Cleveland area; she created Foxcroft Estates in Russell Twp. in the early 1970s. She was also an interior designer.

Born in Cleveland to John and Antoinette (Brozyna) Stempien, Ellen graduated from South High School in 1940. She studied drafting at Cleveland College while working in the drafting department of the Weatherhead Co. During World War II Zhun was hired as the first woman draftsman at the Gabriel Co., later becoming the senior member of engineering department.

She moved with her husband to Philadelphia in 1956. Returning to Cleveland in 1963, Zhun obtained her real estate broker's license and started her career with the W. I. White firm in Cleveland, becoming one of their most successful realtors. She then established her own brokerage, Ellen M. Zhun & Associates, operating in LYNDHURST† and SHAKER HTS.,† for 10 years. Zhun sold the firm to Edward Rybka in 1979. Suffering from lymphoma, Zhun moved to Florida in 1980.

Zhun advocated the rights of women and minorities. She was one of the first realtors to hire minorities and open housing opportunities for them. Zhun served as a trustee of the CLEVELAND AREA BOARD OF REALTORS† during late 1970s.

Ellen married Peter Zhun on 20 Sept. 1945 and had 6 children: Mary Ellen (Russell), Janet (Nasif), Peter, Paul, William, and Robert. She died in Clearwater Beach, FL. A Roman Catholic, she is buried in All Souls Cemetery.—T.B.

**ZIMMERMAN, CHARLES X.** (18 Jan. 1865–14 Nov. 1926), military commander, businessman, civic activist, and sportsman, was born in Cleveland, the son of Charles X. and Theresa Reis Zimmerman. After receiving his education in Cleveland public schools, he joined the Ohio National Guard 8 May 1884 and rose through the ranks to become a captain. He served in the Spanish American War 1898–99 and was promoted to colonel. After duty on the Mexican border in 1916–17, Zimmerman was appointed Brigadier General and commanded the 73rd Infantry Brigade during World War I. As a civilian, he worked as the asst. auditor of Cleveland 1910–11, and later was president of the Amiesite Asphalt Co. of Ohio. Zimmerman was elected mayor of Euclid Village in 1921 and during his four years in office the village improved their waste disposal. In 1926 he obtained a Cleveland franchise in the newly organized American Football League, and his CLEVELAND PANTHERS,† co-owned with M. Fred Bramley, played their games at LUNA PARK† at Woodland Ave. at Woodhill, posting a won-loss record of 3–2 before disbanding at the end of October of that year.

Zimmerman married Ethel M. Vogt 5 June 1900; they had a son and daughter. A resident of Euclid Village, Zimmerman died suddenly in New York and was returned here for burial at Knollwood Cemetery.—M.S.

**ZLAMAL, OLDRICH** (4 Apr. 1879–24 Mar. 1955), pastor of Our Lady of Lourdes Parish and a leader in Bohemian affairs in both Cleveland and Czechoslovakia, was born in Kokory, Moravia, to Anthony and Antoinette Roussila Zlamal. He was educated at Olmutz and Prerov, and came to Cleveland to complete his studies at St. Mary Seminary. Bp. IGNATIUS HORSTMANN ordained him on 3 Nov. 1904. Zlamal's first assignment was as pastor of St. Wendelin Church (see ST. WENDELIN PARISH†); during his pastorate he built a school and purchased property for expansion. In 1905 he organized the parish of SS. CYRIL & METHODIUS† for SLOVAKS† living in eastern LAKEWOOD.† In 1908 he was transferred to Youngstown as pastor of SS. Cyril & Methodius Church. In 1915 succeeded the

late Fr. STEPHAN FURDEK as pastor of Our Lady of Lourdes Church, one of the largest Bohemian congregations in Cleveland. Fr. Zlamal was also very active in Czech affairs. In 1919 he went to Czechoslovakia at the request of the Natl. Catholic Ward Council, traveling for 6 months, lecturing on democracy and religious topics. In 1938 he organized a war relief committee for CZECHS.† In recognition of his accomplishments, Fr. Zlamal was named a domestic prelate by the Vatican on 1 Dec. 1934 and given the title of monsignor. He was buried in Calvary Cemetery in Cleveland.

Archives, Diocese of Cleveland.
Zlamal, Oldrich. *Povidka Meho Zivota* (1954).

**ZORACH, WILLIAM** (28 Feb. 1887–15 Nov. 1966) was one of America's foremost sculptors. He was born Zorach Finklestein in Euberick, Lithuania. His family emigrated to America when he was 4, settling first in Port Clinton, OH, and 3 years later on Cleveland's Woodland Ave. While his father supported them as a junk dealer, Zorach sold papers, shined shoes, and attended school through the 7th grade. A teacher helped him get a job with the Morgan Lithograph Co., where he developed his artistic skills by watching such local artists as ARCHIBALD WILLARD and WM. SOMMER. At 18 he went to New York to study for 2 terms at the National Acad. of Design, returning to Cleveland to work during the summers. With the encouragement of ABEL WARSHAWSKY he went in 1909 for further study in Paris, where he met California artist Marguerite Thompson, whom he married in New York in 1912. Both had paintings accepted in the 1913 New York Armory Show, and the CLEVELAND PLAY HOUSE† gave them a combined exhibition in 1919. Zorach gave up painting in the 1920s for sculpture, in which he carved his realistic figures directly into the stone or wood. His most renowned work, *Mother and Child*, is in the Metropolitan Museum of Art. *Spirit of the Dance*, done for Radio City Music Hall, was first removed by the management as "too modern" but later restored after protests from the artistic community. One of his bronze sculptures was done for Cleveland's FAIRMOUNT TEMPLE.† He died in Bath, ME, survived by his wife, son Tessim, and daughter Dahlov Ipcar.—J.V.

Zorach, Wm. *Art Is My Life* (1967).

**ZORMAN, IVAN** (Apr. 1885–7 Aug. 1957), poet and composer, was born in Austria-Hungary to John and Marie Pucichar Zorman. The family moved to the U.S. when Zorman was 4. He returned to his homeland only once, at age 10, staying for a year. When he came back to the U.S., he began studying the Slovene language, attending Central Institute and St. John's College in Minnesota. He graduated from Western Reserve Univ. with degrees in language, literature, and music. For 40 years Zorman was organist at St. Lawrence's Catholic Church. He taught organ, piano, and voice, and directed and composed for many Slovene singing societies in the Slovene language. His first 2 books of poetry went largely unnoticed in his homeland, but in 1933 Zorman became acknowledged as a legitimate writer, and his poems Slovene school-room classics. In 1938 his 5th book of poetry, *From the New World*, received honorable mention in the Jugoslav Univ. Club at HOLLENDEN HOTEL.† Zorman eventually wrote 6 volumes of poetry and translated many others. Zorman was honored in May 1941 at a banquet in the Slovene Society Home in EUCLID† as an outstanding poet and composer in America. Zorman married Josephine Meznarsic (d. 1936) on 22 June 1910. They had 1 child. Two years after Zorman's death his daughter, Carmen, dedicated a memorial bust to him in the Yugoslav Cultural Garden. Zorman was buried in Calvary Cemetery.

---

Ivan Zorman Papers, WRHS.

# Subject Guide to Entries

## AFRICAN AMERICAN HISTORY

Albritton, David
Alexander, William Harry
Ali-Bey, Omar
Bailey, Horace Charles
Beard, Charles Augustine
Bell, Myrtle Johnson
Bell, Nolan D.
Ben
Benn, Luther
Boyd, Albert Duncan "Starlight"
Boyd, Elmer F.
Brown, Anna V.
Brown, Jere A.
Brown, John
Brown, Lloyd Odom
Brown, Russel S.
Bryant, Eliza
Bundy, Leroy N.
Burten, Lonnie L., Jr.
Carr, Charles Velmon
Carter, Wilfred Carlyle "Whiz Bang"
Chauncey, Herbert S.
Chesnutt, Charles Waddell
Clarke, Melchisedech Clarence
Clement, Kenneth W.
Clifford, Carrie Williams
Clifford, William H.
Cole, Allen E.
Conners, William Randall
Dandridge, Dorothy
Davis, Harry Edward
Davis, Russell Howard
Davis, Sylvester Sanford, Jr.
Day, William Howard
Dearing, Ulysses S.
Dixon, Ardelia Bradley
Dorr, David
Drimmer, Melvin
Durden, Edward
Easter, Lucious "Luke"
Fairfax, Florence Bundy
Felton, Monroe H.
Ferrell, Frederic Leonard
Fleming, Thomas Wallace (Tom)
Fleming, Lethia Cousins
Ford, Leonard "Lenny"
Forte, Ormond Adolphus
Fox, Beatrice Wright
Freeman, Ernest (Ernie)
Freeman, Harry Lawrence
Garvin, Charles H.
Gassaway, Harold T.
Gayle, James Franklin
Gentry, Minnie Lee Watson
George, Clayborne
George, Zelma Watson
Gillespie, Chester K.
Green, John Patterson
Green, Samuel Clayton
Hargrave, Mason Alexander
Harney, Harrison Hannibal
Heggs, Owen L.
Himes, Chester
Hodge, Joseph
Holland, Justin
Holly, John Oliver, Jr.
Holtzclaw, Robert Fulton
Hughes, (James) Langston
Hunter, Jane Edna (Harris)
Jackson, Perry B.
Jelliffe, Rowena Woodham
Jelliffe, Russell W.
Johnson, Clara Lucil
Kilgore, James C.
Lambright, Middleton Hugher, Sr.
Lawrence, Wilhelmina Price
Leach, Robert Boyd
Loeb, Charles Harold
Lucas, Charles P., Sr.
McGhee, Norman L., Sr.
McKinney, Ruth Berry

McKinney, Wade Hampton
Malvin, John
Martin, Alexander H.
Martin, Mary Brown
Minor, Norman Selby
Mitchell, L. Pearl
Montgomery, Anzo
Morgan, Garrett A.
Myers, George A.
Nearon, Joseph R.
Owen, James Alexander
Owens, Jesse (James Cleveland)
Paige, Leroy Robert "Satchel"
Payne, Lawrence O.
Peake, George
Perry, Samuel V.
Phillips, Charles Henry
Price, Grace Finley
Pridgeon, Louise Johnson
Rainey, Sherlie Hereford
Reason, Patrick Henry
Reed, J. Elmer
Roberts, Narlie
Rogers, Margaret Marie Harden
Settle, Glenn Thomas
Shauter, Robert Harris
Sissle, Noble
Slaughter, Howard Silas, Sr.
Smith, Frank A.
Smith, Harry Clay
Smith, Herald Leonydus
Smith, William T. (Wee Willie)
Southgate, Robert L.
Stanton (Day Sessions), Lucy Ann
Sutler, Eleanore Marguerite Young
Sutler, Martin Randolph Delaney, Jr.
Tall, Booker T.
Tilley, Madison
Turner, Rachel Walker
Walker, Hazel Mountain
Walker, William Otis
Weeden, John T.
White, Charles W.
Whitehead, Eaton
Whitley, R. (Rousara) Joyce
Williams, Edward Christopher
Williams, Geraldine
Wills, J. Walter, Sr.
Wright, Alonzo G.
Wright, Walter Benjamin

## ARCHITECTURE

Austin, Samuel
Badgley, Sidney R.
Barnum, Frank Seymour
Benes, W. Dominick
Braverman, Sigmund
Brown, Wendell Phillips
Burdick, Harold Bennett
Burrows, George Howard
Ceruti, Joseph
Chapman, Edmund
Colman, Charles Cecil
Corbusier, John William Creswell
Cudell, Frank (Franz) E.
Dall, Andrew (Jr.)
DiNardo, Antonio
Dyer, J. Milton
Eisenmann, John
Eldredge, Hezekiah
Frary, Ihna Thayer
Garfield, Abram
Goldsmith, Jonathan
Gray, A. Donald
Hamilton, James Montgomery
Hammond, George Francis
Harris, Alfred Wilson
Hays, J. Byers
Heard, Charles Wallace
Heard, Lucas Allen
Hopkinson, Charles William
Hubbell, Benjamin S.
Ireland, Joseph

Johanneson, Eric
Johnson, Levi
Lehman, Israel J.
McCornack, Walter Roy
Mack, Clarence
Meade, Frank B.
Mitermiler, Andrew Robert
Morris, Charles
Porter, Simeon C.
Richardson, John Newton
Rowley, Charles Bacon "Carl"
Schneider, Charles Sumner
Schweinfurth, Charles F.
Scofield, Levi T.
Small, Phillip Lindsley
Smith, George Horatio
Striebinger, Frederic William
Taylor, Albert Davis
Tuttle, Bloodgood
Walker, Frank Ray
Watson, Wilbur J.
Weeks, Harry Ellis
Weinberg, Joseph Lewis
Whitley, R. (Rousara) Joyce

## BUSINESS, INDUSTRY AND TECHNOLOGY

Adomeit, George S.
Allyne, Edmund E.
Ambler, Nathan Hardy
Andrews, Samuel
Anisfield, John
Armington, Raymond Q.
Austin, Samuel
Ayers, Leonard Porter
Baehr, Herman C.
Baer, Alice Dorothy
Bage, Helen
Baker, Edward Mose (Max)
Baker, Walter C.
Baldwin, John
Baldwin, Norman C.
Ball, Webb C.
Barber, Josiah
Barnett, James
Battista, Joseph
Bayless, William Neville
Beaumont, Louis D.
Beckwith, C.G.
Beeman, Edwin E.
Beidler, Jacob A.
Benade, Arthur H.
Benjamin, Charles H.
Bertman, Joseph
Bicknell, Warren (Jr.)
Bingham, Charles W.
Bingham, William
Black, Louis
Black, Morris Alfred
Blossom, Dudley S.
Blossom, Henry S.
Bolton, Charles Chester
Bolton, Chester Castle
Boyd, Elmer F.
Boyer, Willis Booth
Bradley, Alva
Brainard, Silas
Bramley, Matthew Fredrick
Britton, Brigham
Britton, Charles Schuyler II
Brooks, Oliver Kingsley
Brown, Alexander Ephaim
Brown, Fayette
Brown, John
Brush, Charles Francis
Bulkley, Robert Johns
Burke, Edmund Stevenson Jr.
Burnham, Thomas
Burton, Courtney (Jr.)
Butkin, Noah L.

Campanaro, Dorothy M.
Cannon, Austin Victor
Carabelli, Joseph
Case, Leonard (Sr.)
Case, William
Celeste, Frank Palm
Chamberlain, Selah
Chapin, Herman M.
Chauncey, Herbert S.
Chisholm, Henry (Jr.)
Clark, Maurice B.
Clarke, Melchisedech Clarence
Coach, Richard J.
Coakley, John Aloysius
Cole, Allen E.
Corcoran, Charles Leslie
Corrigan, James W. Jr.
Cowan, R. (Reginal) Guy
Cowgill, Lewis
Cox, Jacob D. (Jr.)
Cox, Jacob D. (Sr.)
Crawford, Frederick Coolidge
Creech, Harris
Cunin, John R.
Dall, Andrew (Jr.)
Dall, Andrew (Sr.)
Dalton, Henry George
Dauby, Nathan L.
Dearing, Ulysses S.
Demaioribus, Alessandro Louis "Sonny"
DePaolo, Louis
Deutsch, Samuel H.
Devereux, John H.
Dietz, David
Dively, George Samuel
Dockstader, Nicholas
Dow, Herbert H.
Drury, Francis Edson
Dunkle, David A.
Dyball, Adelaide
Eaton, Cyrus Stephen
Eells, Dan Parmelee
Eisenman, Charles
Elliot, Henry Wood
Elliott, Campbell W.
Elliott, Franklin Reuben
Everett, Morris (Sr.)
Everett, Sylvester T.
Everrett, Henry A.
Farmer, James
Fawick, Thomas
Feather, William A.
Feikert, William Frederick
Feiss, Paul Louis
Felton, Monroe H.
Fenn, Sereno Peck
Flagler, Henry M.
Ford, David Knight
Ford, Horatio
Ford, Horatio Clark
Foster, Claud Hanscomb
France, Mervin Bair
Frasch, Herman
Freiberger, Isadore Fred
Friedman, Max R.
Fritzsche, Alfred
Gammeter, Harry C.
Gardner, George W.
Gates, Holsey or Halsey
Gaylor, Verna Frances
Getz, Hester Adelia
Girdler, Tom Mercer
Glasser, Otto
Glass, Myron E.
Glennan, Thomas K.
Goff, Frederick H.
Gonzalez, Louis A.
Gordon, Helen
Gordon, William J.
Grasselli, Caesar Augustin
Grdina, Anton
Green, Howard Whipple
Green, Samuel Clayton
Greve, Louis William

Gries, Robert Hays
Gund, George
Halle, Moses & Manuel
Halle, Salmon Portland
Halupnik, Eugene A.
Handy, Truman P.
Hanna, Daniel Rhodes
Hanna, Daniel Rhodes (Jr.)
Hanna, Howard Melville
Hanna, Marcus Alonzo
Harkness, Stephen V.
Haskell, Coburn
Hawgood, Belle Dibley
Hays, Kaufman
Heise, George W.
Herrick, Clay, Jr.
Herrick, Myron Timothy
Herzegh, Frank
Hexter, Irving Bernard
Hodge, Orlando J.
Holden, Liberty Emery
Holtkamp, Walter
Hopkins, William Rowland
Hovorka, Frank
Hoyt, James Madison
Hulett, George H.
Humphrey, Dudley Sherman II
Humphrey, George Magoffin
Hurlbut, Hinman B.
Hyde, Gustavus Adolphus
Hyde, Jesse Earl
Ireland, James Duane
Ireland, Robert Livingston, Jr.
Jacobs, David H.
Jerman, Fred "Mike"
Johnson, Tom L.
Jones, David I. and John
Jordan, Edward Stanlaw "Ned"
Joseph, Moritz
Kaim, Jamil (James)
Kelley, Horace
Kelley, Irad
Kelsey, Lorenzo A.
Ketteringham, George H.
King, Woods
Kirby, Josiah
Klaiman, Ralph
Klonowski, Stanley J.
Klumph, Archibald (Arch) C.
Kniola, Michael P.
Kulas, Elroy John
Kundtz, Theodor
Kusch, Polycarp
Langley, John W.
Lawrence, Washington H.
Leimkuehler, Paul Elmer
Lemmers, A. Eugene
Lincoln, James F.
Lindstrom, E(chel) George
Lodzieski, Stefan (Stephen)
Loebell, Ernst
Long, William Frew
Luckiesh, Matthew
McBride, Arthur B. "Mickey"
McGhee, Norman L. (Sr.)
McKee, Arthur Glenn
Mabery, Charles F.
Mandelbaum, Maurice J. (Moses)
Markey, Sanford
Marks, Martin A.
Marshall, Wentworth Goodson
Mather, Samuel
Mather, Samuel Livingston
Mather, William Gwinn
Mellen, Edward J., Jr.
Mellen, Lowell O.
Michelson, Albert Abraham
Miller, Dayton Clarence
Mintz, Leo
Moore, Edward W.
Morgan, Garrett A.
Morley, Edward Williams
Mueller, Ernst W.
Mueller, Omar Eugene
Murch, Maynard Hale
Murphy, John Patrick
Myers, George A.
Nassau, Jason J.
Newberry, John Strong
Newman, Aaron W.
Newman, Joseph Simon
Norton, David Z.
Norton, Laurence Harper
Nutt, Joseph Randolph
O'Brien, Matthew J.
Odenbach, Frederick L., S.J.
Oglebay, Earl W.
Olmsted, George Henry
O'Neill, Francis Joseph "Steve"
Otis, Charles Augustus, Sr.
Otis, Charles Augustus (Jr.)
Otis, William A.
Palmer, William Pendleton
Payne, Oliver Hazard

Peck, Elihu M.
Peckham, George Grant Guy
Pelton, Frederick W.
Perkins, Joseph
Perkins, Robert Kenneth
Pickands, James S.
Prentiss, Francis Fleury
Price, Grace Finley
Prutton, Carl F.
Raddatz, William Joseph
Ratner, Leonard
Ratner, Max
Reason, Patrick Henry
Reed, J. Elmer
Regnatz, Caroline/Caroline Obelz
Reid, James Sims
Reinberger, Clarence Thompson
Reinthal, David F.
Rhodes, Daniel Pomeroy
Rhodes, James Ford
Rice, Walter Percival
Riley, John Francis
Rini, Martin
Roberts, Narlie
Rockefeller, John D.
Rose, Benjamin
Rosenblum, Max
Rosenthal, Samuel
St. Andrews, Helene
Saltzman, Maurice
Sapirstein, Jacob J.
Sauer, Augusta "Gustie" Veera
Schmidt, Leo Walter
Schmunk, Walter George
Schoenfeld, Frank K.
Schott, Harold C.
Schulte, Lauretta (Oberle)
Scott, Frank A.
Sears, Lester M.
Seaver, John Wright
Selden, George G.
Severance, John Long
Severance, Louis Henry
Severance, Solomon Lewis
Severance, Solon Lewis
Shankland, Robert Sherwood
Shauter, Robert Harris
Sherwin, Francis McIntosh
Slaughter, Howard Silas, Sr.
Smith, Albert Kelvin
Smith, Albert W.
Smith, Kent H.
Spira, Henry
Stager, Anson
Stashower, Fred P.
Stefanski, Ben S.
Stone, Amasa
Stone, Morris Samuel
Stone, Silas Safford
Stouffer, Abraham E.
Stouffer, Vernon Bigelow
Sullivan, Jeremiah J.
Sutphin, Albert C. (Al)
Swasey, Ambrose
Taplin, Frank E.
Taylor, Daniel Richardson
Taylor, Sophia Elizabeth Strong
Thayer, Richard N.
Thompson, Charles Edwin
Thorman, Simson
Tilley, Madison
Torbenson, Viggo V.
Towslee, Lillian Gertrude
Tracy, James Jared
Tracy, James J., Jr.
Trenkamp, Herman J.
Treuhaft, William C.
Trueman, James R.
Van Sweringen, Oris Paxton & Mantis James
Vlchek, Frank J.
Vorce, Myron Bond
Wade, Jeptha Homer I
Wade, Jeptha Homer II
Walsh, Edward John
Walton, John Whittlesey
Warner, Worcester Reed
Weddell, Peter Martin
Weideman, John Christain
Weinberger, Adolph
Welter, Katherine I.
Wenham, Frederick L.
West, Thomas Dyson
Westropp, Clara E.
Westropp, Lillian Mary
White, Charles McElroy
White, Rollin Charles
White, Rollin Henry
White, Thomas H.
White, William J.
Whittlesey, Charles W.
Wieber, Charles L.F.
Wieder, Judith Marx
Wigman, John B.

Williamson, Samuel
Wills, J. Walter, Sr.
Wilson, Ella Grant
Wilson, John
Winton, Alexander
Wise, Samuel D.
Witt, Stillman
Worthington, George
Wright, Alonzo G.
Younglove, Moses C.
Zapf, Norman F.
Zevin, Ben D.
Zhun, Ellen Marie Stempien

# COMMUNICATIONS

Addison, Hiram M.
Alexander, William Harry
Andorn, Sidney Ignatius
Andrica, Theodore
Armstrong, William W.
Ashmun, George Coates
Alburn, Wilfred Henry
Baker, Elbert H.
Baldwin, Samuel Prentiss
Bandlow, Robert
Bang, Edward F. "Ed"
Beaufait, Howard G.
Bell, Archie
Bellamy, Paul
Bellamy, Peter
Benedict, George A.
Bergener, Albert Edward Myrne
Black, Hilbert Norman
Blodgett, Walter
Bohm, Edward H.
Bone, John Herbert Aloysius (J.H.A.)
Briggs, Joseph W.
Browne, Charles Farrar (aka Artemus Ward)
Carroll, Gene
Catton, Bruce
Chandler, Neville (Nev) Albert Jr.
Clifford, Louis L.
Clowser, Jack
Cobbledick, Gordon
Collins, James Walter
Combes, Willard Wetmore
Covert, John Cutler
Cowgill, Lewis
Cowles, Edwin W.
Davy, William McKinley
Day, William Howard
Dietz, David
Donahey, James Harrison "Hal"
Elwell, Herbert
Faist, Russell
Fetzer, Herman
Fisher, E. Burke
Fisher, Edward Floyd
Forte, Ormond Adolphus
Freed, Alan
French, Winsor
Fuldheim, Dorothy
Gayle, James Franklin
Gombos, Zoltan
Graney, John Gladstone "Jack"
Gray, Joseph William
Grill, Vatroslav J.
Guthrie, Warren A.
Halloran, William L.
Hanna, Daniel Rhodes
Hanna, Daniel Rhodes, Jr.
Harris, Josiah A.
Hayes, Max S. (Maximilian Sebastian)
Heinzerling, Lynn Louise
Herrick, Maria M. Smith
Hexter, Irving Bernard
Holden, Liberty Emery
Hopwood, Avery
Hopwood, Erie C.
Hovorka, Frank
Howard, Nathaniel Richardson
Hoyt, James Madison
Kelly, Grace V.
Kennedy, Charles E.
Kennedy, James Henry
Kobrack, Herbert L.
Kohanyi, Tihamer
Kuekes, Edward Daniel
Kurdziel, August Joseph "Gus"
Lewis, Franklin Allan "Whitey"
Loeb, Charles Harold
Lorenz, Carl
Loveland, Roelif
McCarthy, Sara Varley
McAuley, Edward J. "Ed"
McCormick, Anne (O'Hare)
McDermott, William E.
McLaughlin, Richard James
McLean, Phil

MacAuley, Charles Raymond
Manning, Thomas Edward "Red"
Manry, Robert N.
Markey, Sanford
Marsh, W. Ward
Mueller, Jacob
Myers, Pierre (Pete,"Mad Daddy")
Newborn, Isaac (Isi) Mandell
Newman, Aaron W.
Otis, Charles Augustus, Jr.
Pankuch, Jan "John"
Peixotto, Benjamin Franklin
Penfound, Ronald A. (Captain Penny)
Perkins, Anna "Newspaper Annie"
Perkins, Maurice
Peters, Richard Dorland
Porter, Philip Wylie
Raper, John W. "Jack"
Roberts, William (Bill) E.
Robertson, Carl Trowbridge
Robertson, George A.
Robertson, Josephine (Jo) Wubben
Robinson, Edwin "Ted" Meade
Rocker, Samuel
Rogers, James Hotchkiss
Scripps, Edward Willis
Seltzer, Louis B.
Siedel, Frank
Siegel, Richard H.
Smead, Timothy H.
Smith, Harry Clay
Smith, Herald Leonydus
Snajdr, Vaclav
Spero, Herman Israel
Stager, Anson
Stashower, Fred P.
Stempuzis, Joseph
Svoboda, Frank J.
Tello, Manly
Thieme, August
Thornton, Willis
Vail, Harry Lorenzo
Vail, Herman Lansing
Walker, William Otis
Weidenthal, Leo
Wey, Alexander Joseph
Wical, Noel
Wickham, Gertrude Van Rensselaer
Widder, Milton "Milt"
Wiesenfeld, Leon
Wolf, Frederick C.

# EDUCATION

Ackley, Horace A.
Addison, Hiram M.
Arbuthnot, May Hill
Arthur, Alfred F.
Babin, Victor
Babin, Victoria (Vitya) Vronsky
Baldwin, Lillian Luverne
Bates, Kenneth F.
Beckwith, Ada Bel
Bell, Myrtle Johnson
Benesch, Alfred Abraham
Benjamin, Charles H.
Benton, Elbert Jay
Binkley, Robert Cedric
Bloch, Ernest
Bolton, Frances Payne
Bond, Douglas Danford
Bourne, Henry E.
Bradburn, Charles
Braverman, Libbie Levin
Briggs, Paul Warren
Brillant, Nathan
Cadwallader, Starr
Case, Leonard, Jr.
Cassels, John Lang
Casto, Frank M.
Chapman, Edmund
Clemens, Charles Edwin
Cowgill, Lewis
Coyle, Grace Longwell
Cramer, Clarence Henley
Cushing, Harvey W.
Cushing, Henry Platt
Cutler, Carroll
Cutler, Elliot Carr
Cutler, James Elbert
Davis, Russell Howard
Delamater, John
DeSauze, Emile Bials
Drimmer, Melvin
Dunmore, Walter T.
Dupertis, C. Wesley
Earnest, G. (George) Brooks
Elson, William H.
Emeny, Brooks
Emerson, Oliver Farrar
Evans, Dina Rees (Doc)
Fox, Beatrice Wright

505

Freese, Andrew J.
Friedland, Abraham Hayyim
Gehring, Albert
Gerber, Samuel R.
Gerfen, Elizabeth H.
Glennan, Thomas K.
Goldman, Solomon
Goodman, Lester
Green, Virginia Darlington
Grossman, F. Karl
Guilford, Linda (Lucinda) Thayer
Guthrie, Warren A.
Hagan, John Raphael
Ham, Thomas Hale
Hamann, Carl August
Hart, Albert Bushnell
Hatton, Augustus Raymond
Haydn, Hiram Collins
Hertz, Marguerite Rosenberg
Hinsdale, Burke Aaron
Holtzclaw, Robert Fulton
Howe, Charles Sumner
Hudson, Jean Roberta
Hull, Jessie (Jesse) Redding
Huntington, John
Hyde, Jesse Earl
Ingham, Mary Bigelow (Janes)
Inman, Amie G. Steere
Irwin, Robert Benjamin
Jones, Robinson G.
Keeler, Harriet Louise
Kilgore, James C.
Kusch, Polycarp
Lake, Charles H.
Langley, John W.
Leathem, Barclay Spencer
Leggett, Mortimer Dormer
Leonards, Jack R.
Leutner, Winfred G.
Loesser, Arthur
Mabery, Charles F.
MacLeod, John James
Martin, Mary Brown
Michelson, Albert Abraham
Miller, Dayton Clarence
Millis, John Schoff
Moley, Raymond
Moritz, Alan Richards
Morley, Edward Williams
Murray, J.D. Bain
Navin, Robert B.
O'Neill, Cordelia L.
Orth, Samuel Peter
Peters, Harry Alfred
Plank, Emma Nuschi
Prutton, Carl F.
Puckett, Newbell Niles
Quintrell, Mary Corinne
Rawson, Louise R. Barron
Reinthal, David F.
Remenyi, Joseph
Rice, Harvey
Richardson, Lyon Norman
Rickoff, Andrew Jackson
Riemenschneider, Albert
Rubinstein, Beryl
Sadataki, Mary Hata
St. John, Samuel
Scranton, Irene Hickox
Shankland, Robert Sherwood
Shepherd, Arthur
Shera, Jesse Hauk
Smyth, Anson
Sollman, Torald Herman
Southgate, Robert L.
Spaulding, Frank Ellsworth
Spenzer, John George
Stewart, John Hall
Stewart, N. Coe
Tall, Booker T.
Thwing, Charles Franklin
Todd, Thomas Wingate
Toomey, John A.
Van Horn, Frank R.
Walker, Hazel Mountain
Walters, Claire A.
Wearn, Joseph T.
Whiting, Frederic Allen
Whittaker, (Louis) Howard
Wickenden, William E.
Wirtz, John J.
Wish, Harvey
Wittke, Carl Frederick
Wood, Harlan Goff
Young, Dallas M.

## EXPLORATION AND EARLY SETTLEMENT

Alger, Henry
Allen, Peter

Atwater, Amzi
Ayers, Leonard Porter
Benedict, Daniel
Bentley, Adamson
Black Hawk
Cahoon, Joseph
Carter, Lorenzo
Cleaveland, Moses
Cozad, Samuel
Croghan, George
DeLery, Joseph Gaspard Chaussegros
Doan, Nathaniel
DuShattar, Joseph
Fitch, Zalmon
Gates, Holsey (Halsey)
Goldsmith, Jonathan
Hilliard, Richard
Hodge, Joseph
Holley, John Milton
Huntington, Samuel, Jr.
Joc-O-Sot, Walking Bear
Johnson, Levi
Johnson, Sir William
Kelley, Daniel
Kelley, Datus
Kelley, Irad
Kingsbury, James
Long, David
Long, Juliana (Julia) Walworth
Lord, Richard
Menompsy (Nobsy)
Merchant, Ahaz
Montresor, John
Ogontz or Ogantz
O'Mic, John
Paine, Seth
Peake, George
Pease, Seth
Prescott, James Sullivan
Russell, Ralph
Scovill, Philo
Scranton, Irene Hickox
Scranton, Joel
Saguin, Sieur De
Spafford, Amos
Stigwanish
Stiles, Job Phelps
Stow, Joshua
Tebelak, John Michael
Walworth, Ashbel
Walworth, John W.
Warren, Daniel
White, Moses
Williamson, Samuel

## FINE ARTS & LITERATURE

Adams, Almeda
Adomeit, George Gustav
Ames, Lydia May
Arbuthnot, May Hill
Arthur, Alfred F.
Alburn, Wilfred Henry
Avery, Elroy McKendree
Babin, Victor
Babin, Victoria (Vitya) Vronsky
Bacher, Otto Henry
Ball, Ernest R.
Barnard, Maxwell ("Max") Vosper
Bates, Kenneth F.
Beck, Johann Heinrich
Beckwith, Ada Bel
Bell, Archie
Bell, Nolan
Benade, Arthur H.
Benton, Elbert Jay
Bernardi, Giacomo
Bickford, Clara L. Gehring
Bickford, George P.
Biehle, August Fredrick, Jr.
Biehle Family
Binkley, Robert Cedric
Birinyi, Louis Kossuth
Bloch, Ernest
Blodgett, Walter
Blossom, Emily Elkins
Bock, Joseph Courtney
Bolton, Sarah Knowles
Bourke-White, Margaret
Bourne, Henry E.
Brainard, Silas
Braverman, Libbie Levin
Brett, William Howard
Brillant, Nathan
Broemel, Carl William
Brooks, Charles Stephen
Brooks, Minerva Kline
Browne, Mary Kendale "Brownie"
Browne, Charles Farrar (aka Artemus Ward)

Brudno, Ezra
Burchfield, Charles Ephriam
Butler, Margaret Manor
Cafarelli, Carmela E.
Cahill, Vaughn Dabney
Campbell, Marion Winton Strongheart
Carabelli, Joseph
Catton, Bruce
Champa, Frank A.
Chapman, Edmund
Chesnutt, Charles Waddell
Church, Henry, Jr.
Clemens, Charles Edwin
Clifford, Carrie Williams
Coates, William R.
Cohen, Gustave M.
Cole, Allen E.
Cowan, R. (Reginal) Guy
Cramer, Clarence Henley
Crane, Hart
Cutler, Carroll
Dandridge, Dorothy
DaSilva, Howard
Davis, Russell Howard
Dawe, Charles Davis
DeCapite, Michael
Decker, Edgar
Deharrack, Charles Peretz
Deike, Clara L.
Demmy, Olean Wells
Dick, Marcel
Dorr, David
Drury, Francis Edson
Edmondson, George Mountain
Elliot, Henry Wood
Ellsler, Effie
Ellser, John Adam
Elwell, Herbert
Emerson, Oliver Farrar
Evans, Dina Rees (Doc)
Feather, William A.
Feder, Mark
Fetzer, Herman
Fogg, William Perry
Forsyth (Myers), Josephine
Foster, Leonard Gurley
Frary, Ihna Thayer
Freeman, Ernest (Ernie)
Freeman, Harry Lawrence
Gaertner, Carl Frederick
Garlick, Theodatus A.
Gayle, James Franklin
Gehring, Albert
Gentry, Minnie Lee Watson
George, Zelma Watson
Gilchrist, Marie Emilie
Ginn, Frank Hadley
Gittelson, Benjamin
Gollman, Julius
Goodman, Alfred Thomas
Gottwald, Frederick Carl
Goulder, Grace Izant
Grauer, William
Grossman, F. Karl
Hahn, Edgar A.
Hamilton, Margaret
Hanks, Jarvis Frary
Hanna, Leonard C.
Hart, Albert Bushnell
Hartz, Augustus "Gus" Frederic
Hauser, Elizabeth
Hay, John Milton
Henning, Edward Burk
Herkomer, John
Herrick, Clay, Jr.
Heydemann, Lily Carthew
Himes, Chester
Hinsdale, Burke Aaron
Holland, Justin
Holtkamp, Walter
Holtzclaw, Robert Fulton
Hoover, Earl R.
Hopwood, Avery
Horvath, Ian (Ernie)
Howard, Nathaniel Richardson
Hoyt, Harlowe Randall
Hruby, Frank, Sr (IV)
Hruby Family
Hubbell, Charles H.
Hughes, Adella Prentiss
Hughes, (James) Langston
Ingham, Mary Bigelow (Janes)
Ireland, Thomas Saxton, Jr.
Ivanusch, John
Janicki, Hazel
Jelliffe, Rowena Woodham
Jelliffe, Russell W.
Jicha, Joseph W.
Johanneson, Eric
Joseph, Helen Haiman
Jurgens, William A.
Kalish, Max
Katz, Morris L.

Keller, Henry George
Kelly, Grace V.
Kelley, Samuel Walter
Kennedy, Charles E.
Kennedy, James Henry
Kilgore, James C.
Klumph, Archibald (Arch) C.
Knight, Thomas A.
Knowlton, Donald Snow
Kovell, Margaret N.
Kraft, Edwin Arthur
Kubinyi, Kalman
Leathem, Barclay Spencer
Leland, Jackson Miller
Letter, Ben I.
Levy, Darryl Allen (d.a. levy)
Loesser, Arthur
Logan, Walter
Lorenz, Carl
Lowe, K. Elmo
Ludlow, Arthur Clyde
McConnell, Frederic
McDermott, William E.
McKenney, Ruth
McLaughlin, Robert
McVey, William Mozart
Majeske, Donald Harold
Marcosson, Sol
Mathews, Alfred
Matzen, Herman N.
Milliken, William M.
Mizer, Conrad
Moellman, Carl Frederick
Murray, J.D. Bain
Newmarker, Howard L.
Norton, Georgie Leighton
Olney, Charles Fayette
Orth, Samuel Peter
Perkins, Edna Brush
Perkins, Robert Kenneth
Perry, Eleanor (Rosenfeld-Bayer-Perry)
Post, Charles Asa
Prusheck, Harvey Gregory
Puehringer, Ferdinand
Putnam, Mildred Olive Andrews
Putnam, Peter Andrews
Raddatz, William Joseph
Ransom, Caroline L. Ormes
Redinger, Ruby Virginia
Remenyi, Joseph
Rhodes, James Ford
Rice, Harvey
Riemenschneider, Albert
Ring, Emil
Ringwall, Rudolph
Robeson, Lila Pauline
Rodzinski, Artur
Rogers, James Hotchkiss
Rorimer, Louis
Rose, William Ganson
Rubinstein, Beryl
Rychlik, Charles Vaclav
Ryder, James F.
Schandler, Hyman
Schubert, Orlando V.
Semenoff, Nikolai Prokofievitch
Semon, John
Settle, Glenn Thomas
Shaw, Elsa Vick
Shaw, Glenn
Shepherd, Arthur
Sinclair, Jo
Smith, Allen, Jr.
Smith, Wilson G.
Snow, Dorcas Lavina
Snow, Jane Elliot
Sokoloff, Nikolai
Sommer, William
Standiford-Mehling, Ethel
Stashower, Hildegarde Darmstadter
Stewart, John Hall
Stewart, N. Coe
Strong, Eleanor Painter
Szell, George
Tamas, Istvan
Tebelak, John Michael
Thornton- Silver, Eugenia
Thornton, Willis
Travis, Paul B.
Turner, Rachel Walker
Von Baeyer, Eric
Votipka, Thelma
Warshawsky, Abel "Buck" & Alexander "Xander"
Webb, Ella Sturtevant
Weber, Gustav C.E.
Weidenthal, Leo
Whitaker, May Tarbell Cannon
Whiting, Frederic Allen
Whittaker, (Louis) Howard
Wilcox, Frank Nelson
Wilde, Joseph
Willard, Archibald MacNeal

Williams, Katherine Withrow
Wilson, Ella Grant
Winter, Harold Edward
Winter, Thelma Frazier
Wish, Harvey
Wittke, Carl Frederick
Woldman, Albert A.
Wolf, Edith Anisfield
Wolfenstein, Martha
Woolson, Constance Fenimore
Young, Agnes Brooks
Zamecnik, John S.
Zorach, William
Zorman, Ivan

## IMMIGRATION AND ETHNICITY

Albl, Michael Albert
Andrews, Samuel
Andrica, Theodore
Anisfield, John
Artl, Joseph A.
Austin, Samuel
Babka, John Joseph
Baldwin, Lillian Luverne
Bandlow, Robert
Bardoun, Frank J.
Barricelli, Giovanni Alfonso
Battista, Joseph
Bernardi, Giacomo
Bernon, (Bernstein) Maurice
Bernstein, Harry
Bertman, Joseph
Bielen, Casimir
Birns, Alex "Shondor"
Birinyi, Louis Kossuth
Black, Louis
Blythin, Edward
Boehm, Charles
Bohm, Edward H.
Boiardi, Hector
Bone, John Herbert Aloysius (J.H.A.)
Braverman, Sigmund
Bramley, Matthew Fredrick
Brock (Slomovitz), Phil
Broemel, Carl William
Brudno, Ezra
Cafarelli, Carmela E.
Carabelli, Joseph
Cassels, John Lang
Cassesa, Dominic
Cerri, Nicola
Chaloupka, Aloysius W.
Champa, Frank A.
Chisholm, Henry
Claasen, Edo Nicholaus
Clark, Maurice B.
Clemens, Charles Edwin
Clowser, Jack
Cohen, Gustave M.
Corlett, Selene
Crosser, Robert
Cudell, Frank (Franz) E.
Czolgosz, Leon F.
Dall, Andrew (Jr.)
Dall, Andrew (Sr.)
Dawe, Charles Davis
DeCapite, Michael
Deharrack, Charles Peretz
Demaioribus, Alessandro Louis "Sonny"
Demore, Matthew
DePaolo, Louis
DeSauze, Emile Bials
Dick, Marcel
Dinardo, Antonio
Einstein, Ruth
Eisenman, Charles
Feder, Mark
Finkle, Herman
Finkelstein, Louis
Frasch, Herman
Frey, Franz (Frank) Xavier
Fricke, Otto L.
Friedland, Abraham Hayyim
Furdek, Stephan
Genuth, David L.
Gilmour, Richard
Gittelson, Benjamin
Glasser, Otto
Glass, Myron E.
Goldblatt, Harry
Gollman, Julius
Goldman, Solomon
Gombos, Zoltan
Gottwald, Frederick Carl
Graber, Belle (Isabel) Taylor
Grdina, Anton
Grill, Vatroslav J.
Grossman, Isador

Halle, Moses & Manuel
Hanulya, Joseph R.
Heise, George
Hellerstein, Herman Kopez
Herkomer, John
Hessenmueller, Edward
Hoffman (Hopferman), Isaac
Hopferman, Simson
Horvath, Helen
Hovorka, Frank
Hruby, Frank, Sr (IV)
Ivanusch, John
Jicha, Joseph W.
Jirouch, Frank L.
Jirsa, Ferdinand "Ferd"
John, Henry J.
Jones, David L. & John
Joseph, Moritz
Kaim, Jamil (James)
Kalisch, Isidor
Kalish, Max
Kappanadze, Jason R.
Katan, Maurits
Katan, Anny Rosenberg
Kern, Frank J.
Ketteringham, George H.
Klonowski, Stanley J.
Kniola, Michael P.
Kobrack, Herbert L.
Kohanyi, Tihamer
Kolaszewski, Anton Francis
Koller, John Joseph
Kollin (Kolinsky), Abraham
Koudelka, Joseph Mary
Kundtz, Theodor
Kurdziel, August Joseph "Gus"
Landy, Rachel
Lazar, Alma Trebel
Ledbetter, Eleanor Edwards
Levine, Manuel V.
Lindstrom, E(chel) George
Lodzieski, Stefan (Stephen)
Loebell, Ernst
Logan, Walter
Lorenz, Carl
Lynch, Frank
Machol, Michaelis
MacLeod, John James
Margolies, Samuel
Martinek, Joseph
Matzen, Herman N.
Mayer, Jacob
Michelson, Albert Abraham
Mitermiler, Andrew Robert
Moncol, Andrew John
Mooney, Michael Patrick
Mueller, Ernst W.
Mueller, Jacob
Mural, Katherine
Nadas, John B.
Nassau, Jason J.
Nicola, Benjamin (Benedetto) D.
Norweb, Raymond Henry
O'Malley, Patrick
Orlikowski, Bernard E.
Osika, Charlotte
Pankuch, Jan "John"
Parsons, Kate
Peixotto, Daniel Levi
Peppercorn, Beryl
Petrash, Louis
Pirc, Louis J.
Plank, Emma Nuśchi
Porath, Israel
Puehringer, Ferdinand
Quayle, Thomas
Quintrell, Mary Corinne
Rappe, Louis Amadeus
Ratner, Leonard
Ratner, Max
Regnatz, Caroline/Caroline Obelz
Remenyi, Joseph
Reynolds, James A.
Richardson, John Newton
Ring, Emil
Risko, John "Johnny"
Rock, Frederick
Rocker, Samuel
Rose, Benjamin
Rosenblum, Max
Rosenthal, Samuel
Rosenwasser, Marcus
Ruetenik, Herman J.
Sadataki, Mary Hata
Sampliner, Herman
Sapirstein, Jacob J.
Sauer, Augusta "Gustie" Veera
Sawicki, Joseph F.
Schandler, Hyman
Schauffler, Henry A.
Schmidt, Leo Walter
Schmitt, Jacob W.
Schrembs, Joseph
Schubert, Orlando V.

Schwan, Heinrich Christian
Sebian, Thomas B.
Semenoff, Nikolai Prokofievitch
Shapiro, Ezra Zelig
Silbert, Samuel H.
Silver, Abba Hillel
Smetona, Antanas
Smithknight, Louis
Snajdr, Vaclav
Sokoloff, Nikolai
Sollman, Torald Herman
Spira, Henry
Spitalny, Maurice
Spitalny, Phil
Stempuzis, Joseph
Sullivan, Jeremiah J.
Sundquist, Gustaf Adolf
Svoboda, Frank J.
Szell, George
Tamas, Istvan
Thieme, August
Thorman, Simson
Titus, Sigmund Alexander
Torbenson, Viggo V.
Toth, John, Jr.
Vadnal, Frank L.
Vlchek, Frank J.
Von Baeyer, Eric
Walsh (Walasiewicz), Stella (Stanislawa)
Watkins, Samuel "Sammy"
Weideman, John Christain
Weil, Helen Kahn
Weil, Julius
West, Thomas Dyson
Wiesenfeld, Leon
Wilde, Joseph
Wilson, John
Winton, Alexander
Wolf, Frederick C.
Wolfenstein, Martha
Wolfram, Charles J.
Zevin, Ben D.
Zlamal, Oldrich
Zorach, William
Zorman, Ivan

## LABOR

Bandlow, Robert
Cassesa, Dominic
Davy, William McKinley
DeGrandis, Paul J., Jr.
Demore, Matthew
Donahue, Mickey
Fenster, Leo
Foran, Martin A.
Friedman, Allen
Harrison, Marvin Clinton
Hayes, Max S. (Maximilian Sebastian)
Lee, William Granville
Murphy, Edward F.
O'Malley, Patrick
O'Meara, James E., Jr.
Peppercorn, Beryl
Pollock, Samuel
Presser, Jack (Jackie)
Presser, William E.
Reynolds, James A.
Ruthenberg, Charles
Taylor, Richard S.
Toth, John, Jr.
Turner, James K.
Tussey, Richard B.
Wical, Noel
Williams, Whiting
Witt, Peter
Young, Dallas M.
Young, Merrill A.

## LAW

Addams, George Stanton
Allen, Florence Ellinwood
Andrews, Sherlock James
Arter, Charles Kingsley
Artl, Joseph A.
Backus, Franklin Thomas
Baker, Newton Diehl
Baldwin, Charles Candee
Barber, Gershom M.
Barr, John
Battisti, Frank Joseph
Beach, Clifton Bailey
Benedict, George A.
Benesch, Alfred Abraham
Bickford, George P.
Bingham, Flavel W.
Blythin, Edward
Boardman, William Jarvis

Bolton, Thomas
Breitenstein, Joseph C.
Briggs, James A.
Brough, John
Brown, Lloyd Odom
Burke, Edmund Stevenson Jr.
Burke, Thomas Aloysius
Burton, Harold Hitz
Byers, Edgar S.
Cadwell, Darius
Cannon, Austin Victor
Case, Leonard, Jr.
Celebrezze, Frank D.
Chaloupka, Aloysius W.
Chase, Russell N.
Clark, Harold Terry
Clarke, John Hessin
Coon, John
Cowles (Cowls), Samuel
Crowell, John
Crowley, Joseph Herron
Cushing, William Erastus
Davis, Harry Edward
Day, William L.
Dempsey, James Howard
Duncan, William McKinley
Dunmore, Walter T.
Eastman, Harry Lloyd
Ferrell, Frederic Leonard
Fisher, E. Burke
Flynn, Eileen Eleanor Finlin
Ford, David Knight
Ford, Horatio
Ford, Horatio Clark
Freedheim, Eugene Heitler
Fricke, Otto L.
Friebolin, Carl David
Gahn, Harry C.
Garfield, James Rudolph
Gassaway, Harold T.
Gillespie, Chester K.
Ginn, Frank Hadley
Goldenbogen, Ellen May Dursching
Goulder, Harvey Danforth
Green, Howard Whipple
Grossman, Isador
Grossman, Mary B.
Hadden, Alexander
Hadden, John Alexander, Jr.
Hahn, Edgar A.
Handrick, Gertrude M. (Foran)
Harrison, Marvin Clinton
Hayward, William Henry
Heggs, Owen L.
Herbert, Thomas John
Herrick, Myron Timothy
Hessenmueller, Edward
Holmes, Allen C.
Hoover, Earl R.
Hopkins, Willard Dean
Hostetler, Joseph C.
Howe, Frederic C.
Hoyt, James Madison
Ingalls, David Sinton, Jr.
Joseph, Emil
Kelley, Alfred
Kollin (Kolinsky), Abraham
Kuth, Byron D.
Lechowick, Margaret (Troughton)
Levin, Albert Arthur
Levine, Manuel V.
Loeser, Nathan
Lybarger, Donald Fisher
McCord, Grace Bernardina Doering
McGannon, William Henry
Marshall, Lycurgus Luther
Martin, Alexander H.
Maschke, Maurice
Meyer, Edward S.
Miller, Raymond Thomas
Minor, Norman Selby
Mooney, Michael Patrick
Morgan, Daniel Edgar
Murphy, John Patrick
Nicola, Benjamin (Benedetto) D.
Ollendorff, Henry B.
O'Meara, James E., Jr.
Parsons, Richard C.
Payer, Harry Franklin
Payne, Henry B.
Payne, Lawrence O.
Peixotto, Benjamin Franklin
Perry, Samuel V.
Petrash, Louis
Polk, Franklin A.
Pridgeon, Louise Johnson
Rankin, Alfred, M.
Ranney, Rufus P.
Reavis, John Wallace "Jack"
Rice, Harvey
Rosa, Storm
Rose, H. (Horace) Chapman
Rose, William Grey
Sanders, William Brownell

507

Sawicki, Joseph F.
Shapiro, Ezra Zelig
Sidlo, Thomas L.
Siegel, Richard H.
Silbert, Samuel H.
Smith, Charles Henry
Spalding (Spaulding), Rufus
Squire, Andrew
Stage, Charles Willard
Starkweather, Samuel
Taft, Kingsley Arter
Tayler, Robert Walker
Throckmorton, Archibald Hall
Titus, Sigmund Alexander
Tod, David
Vail, Harry Lorenzo
Vail, Herman Lansing
Van Aken, William Russell
Vickery, Willis
Wade, Edward
Walter, Paul William
Wembridge, Eleanor Harris Rowland
Westropp, Lillian Mary
Weygandt, Carl
White, Charles W.
White, John Griswold
Willey, John Wheelock
Williamson, Samuel
Willson, Hiram V.
Woldman, Albert A.

## LIBRARIES AND MUSEUMS

Baldwin, Charles Candee
Baldwin, Samuel Prentiss
Barr, John
Brett, William Howard
Britton, Gertrude Haskell
Cathcart, Wallace Hugh
Chapin, Herman M.
Colket, Meredith Bright, Jr.
Crawford, Frederick Coolidge
Cutter, Annie Spencer
Dittrick, Howard
Dixon, Ardelia Bradley
Dunkle, David A.
Eastman, Linda Anne
Fawick, Thomas L.
Feiss, Paul Louis
Gaines, Ervin J.
Gebhard, Bruno
Goetz, Bernice
Goodman, Alfred Thomas
Hawgood, Belle Dibley
Johanneson, Eric
Kirtland, Jared Potter
Ledbetter, Eleanor Edwards
McKelvey, Dorothy Marks
Palmer, William Pendleton
Power, Effie Louise
Rauschkolb, Ruth (Robishaw)
Richardson, Lyon Norman
Shepherd, Dorothy G. Payer
Shera, Jesse Hauk
Smyth, Anson
Snow, Dorcas Lavina
Taylor, (Howard) Lester
Tyler, Alice S.
Vormelker, Rose L.
White, John Griswold
Whittlesey, Charles W.
Williams, Arthur Baldwin
Williams, Edward Christopher

## MEDICINE

Ackley, Horace A.
Albl, Michael Albert
Allen, Dudley Peter
Allen, Peter
Ashmun, George Coates
Atkinson, William Henry
Barricelli, Giovanni Alfonso
Beck, Claude Schaeffer
Bill, Arthur Holbrook
Bishop, Robert H., Jr.
Bolt, Richard Arthur
Bolton, Frances Payne
Bond, Douglas Danford
Broadbent, Birdsall Holly
Bundy, LeRoy N.
Bunts, Frank E.
Canfield, Martha Ann Robinson
Cassels, John Lang
Casto, Frank M.
Cerri, Nicola

Claasen, Edo Nicholaus
Clement, Kenneth W.
Crile, George, Jr.
Crile, George Washington, Sr.
Cushing, William Erastus
Cushing, William Erastus
Cushing, Henry Kirke
Cutler, Elliot Carr
Davis, Sylvester Sanford, Jr.
Delamater, John
Dittrick, Howard
Dupertis, C. Wesley
Elwell, John Johnson
Freedlander, Samuel Oscar
Friedman, Harold J.
Gardner, W. James, Jr.
Garlick, Theodatus A.
Garlock, Anna Jansen Cordon
Garvin, Charles H.
Gebhard, Bruno
Gerber, Samuel R.
Gerstenberger, Henry John
Giddings, Helen Marshall
Giddings, Mary
Gitlin, David
Glasser, Otto
Glover, Vera Abagarl
Goldblatt, Harry
Goodman, Lester
Graber, C. Lee
Hadden, John Alexander, Jr.
Ham, Thomas Hale
Hamann, Carl August
Hart, Albert Gailord
Hartman, Charles A.
Hellerstein, Herman Kopez
Hertz, Marguerite Rosenberg
Hodgins, Agatha C.
Horton, William P.
Hudson, Charles Lowell
John, Henry J.
Katan, Maurits
Katan, Anny Rosenberg
Kelley, Samuel Walter
Kern, Frank J.
Kinzer, Gertrude C.
Kirtland, Jared Potter
Knapp, Harold Jennings
Koller, John Joseph
Lambright, Middleton Hugher, Sr.
Landy, Rachel
Leach, Robert Boyd
Lenhart, Carl H.
Leonards, Jack R.
Long, David
Lower, William Edgar
MacDonald, Calvina
MacLeod, John James
Mannix, John R.
Marcus, Sarah
Marine, David
Merrick, Myra King
Metzenbaum, Myron
Mills, Joshua
Ostendarp, Carol Anne
Owen, James Alexander
Page, Irvine Heinly
Parsons, Kate
Peixotto, Daniel Levi
Perkins, Roger Griswold
Phillips, John
Plank, Emma Nuschi
Prentice, Walter M.
Purnell, Edward Ward
Rammelkamp, Charles Henry, Jr.
Rauschkolb, Ruth (Robishaw)
Robb, Hunter
Robb, Isabel Adams Hampton
Rosa, Storm
Rosenwasser, Marcus
Rowland, Amy Farley
Salisbury, James Henry
Sihler, Christian
Skeel, Arthur J.
Sollman, Torald Herman
Sones, F. Mason, Jr.
Spenzer, John George
Strickland, Benjamin
Sutler, Martin Randolph Delaney, Jr.
Taylor, (Howard) Lester
Todd, Thomas Wingate
Toomey, John A.
Towslee, Lillian Gertrude
Tuckerman, Jacob E.
Tuckerman, Louis Bryant
Turnbull, Rupert B., Jr.
Von Baeyer, Eric
Waite, Frederick Clayton
Walters, Reuben W.
Wearn, Joseph T.
Weber, Gustav C.E.
Wiggers, Carl John

Wood, Harlan Goff
Woodruff, Mabel Alice

## MILITARY

Ambler, Henry Lovejoy
Ambler, Nathan Hardy
Ashmun, George Coates
Baesel, Albert E.
Barber, Gershom M.
Barnett, James
Barton, Thomas C.
Bauder, Levi F.
Bliss, Stoughton
Bohm, Edward H.
Brooks, Oliver Kingsley
Brown, Fayette
Cadwell, Darius
Clark, Merwin
Clingman, Andrew R.
Corcoran, Michael
Corlett, William Thomas
Crane, Orrin J.
Creighton, William R.
Crowell, Benedict
Cushing, Henry Kirke
Devereux, John H.
Dowling, James
Elwell, John Johnson
Fitch, Jabez W.
Foster, William Adelbert
Frazee, John N.
Frey, Franz (Frank) Xavier
Garfield, James Abram
Gleason, William J.
Halloran, William L.
Hampson, James B.
Hard, Dudley Jackson
Hart, Albert Gailord
Hartman, Charles A.
Hayr, James
Hayward, William Henry
Herrick, John French
Hinman, Wilbur F.
Hughes, John Arthur
Ingalls, David Sinton, Jr.
Ingraham, Timothy
Johnson, Earle Levan
Keller, William G.
Kidd, Isaac Campbell
King, Woods
Leggett, Mortimer Dormer
Leland, Jackson Miller
Lynch, Frank
McClelland, James M.
McQuigg, John Rea
Meyer, Edward S.
Mitchell, Theodore
Molyneaux, Joseph B.
Orndorf, Harry Westley
Petrarca, Frank J.
Pierce, Lucy Anne Boyle
Prentice, Walter M.
Richardson, William R.
Richman, Samuel
Rock, Frederick
Sanford (or Sandford), Alfred S.
Sanford, Julius R.
Senter, George B.
Shields, Joseph C.
Smith, Charles Henry
Smithknight, Louis
Spangler, Basil L.
Stone, Silas Safford
Streibler, Martin
Stupka, Laddie
Sundquist, Gustaf Adolf
Thayer, Lyman C.
Towle, John R.
Walters, Reuben W.
Wiley, Aquila
Williams, LeRoy Withrow
Zimmerman, Charles X.

## NEIGHBORHOODS

Barry, Frank T.
Bolles, James A.

## POLITICS AND GOVERNMENT

Addams, George Stanton
Allen, John W.
Armstrong, William W.
Artl, Joseph A.
Babcock, Brenton D.

Babka, John Joseph
Backus, Franklin Thomas
Baehr, Hermann C.
Baker, Newton Diehl
Baldwin, Norman C.
Baldwin, Samuel S.
Barber, Josiah
Beach, Clifton Bailey
Beidler, Jacob A.
Bemis, Edward W.
Bender, George Harrison
Benesch, Alfred Abraham
Bernon, (Bernstein) Maurice
Bernstein, Harry
Bielen, Casimir
Bingham, Flavel W.
Bingham, William
Black, Louis
Blee, Robert E.
Blythin, Edward
Bolton, Chester Castle
Bolton, Frances Payne
Bolton, Thomas
Boyd, Albert Duncan "Starlight"
Breitenstein, Joseph C.
Briggs, James A.
Brough, John
Brown, Jere A.
Brown, Russel S.
Brownell, Abner
Buhrer, Stephen
Bulkley, Robert Johns
Bundy, LeRoy N.
Burke, Thomas Aloysius
Burnham, Thomas
Burten, Lonnie L., Jr.
Burton, Courtney, Jr.
Burton, Harold Hitz
Burton, Theodore Elijah
Byers, Edgar S.
Cadwell, Darius
Cain, Frank C.
Carabelli, Joseph
Carr, Charles Velmon
Case, Leonard, Jr.
Case, William
Castle, William Bainbridge
Celeste, Frank Palm
Cermak, Albina
Clapp, Nettie Mackenzie
Clifford, William H.
Coates, William R.
Cooley, Harris Reid
Coon, John
Crosser, Robert
Crowell, John
Davis, Harry Edward
Davis, Harry Lyman
DeGrandis, Paul J., Jr.
Demaioribus, Alessandro Louis "Sonny"
Dewald, Louise
Dockstadter, Nicholas
Dykstra, Clarence Addison
Farley, John Harrington
Feighan, Michael Aloysius
Finkle, Herman
Fitzgerald, William Sinton
Fleming, Thomas Wallace (Tom)
Fleming, Lethia Cousins
Flint, Edward Sherrill
Foote, John A.
Foran, Martin A.
Friebolin, Carl David
Gahn, Harry C.
Gardner, George W.
Garfield, James Abram
Gassaway, Harold T.
George, Clayborne
Gerber, Samuel R.
Giddings, Joshua Reed
Gillespie, Chester K.
Gongwer, W. Burr
Gray, Joseph William
Green, Howard Whipple
Hadden, John Alexander (Sr.)
Hanna, Marcus Alonzo
Hatton, Augustus Raymond
Hay, John Milton
Hayward, Nelson
Heggs, Owen L.
Herbert, Thomas John
Herrick, Myron Timothy
Herrick, Rensselaer Russell
Hessenmueller, Edward
Hilliard, Richard
Hoadley, George
Hodge, Orlando John
Hopkins, William Rowland
Horton, William P.
Humphrey, George Magoffin

Huntington, Samuel, Jr.
Ingalls, David Sinton, Jr.
Ireland, Robert Livingston, Jr.
Ireland, Thomas Saxton, Jr.
Irwin, Josephine Saxer
Jackson, Perry B.
Johnson, Tom L.
Kelley, Alfred
Kelsey, Lorenzo A.
Kirtland, Jared Potter
Klementowicz, Bronis J.
Kniola, Michael P.
Kohler, Frederick
Kurdziel, August Joseph "Gus"
Lausche, Frank A.
Long, William Frew
Lord, Richard
Lynch, Frank
McGhee, Norman L., Sr.
McKisson, Robert Erastus
McQuigg, John Rea
Marshall, John D.
Marshall, Lycurgus Luther
Maschke, Maurice
Masters, Irvine U.
Miller, Raymond Thomas
Mills, Joshua
Moley, Raymond
Morgan, Daniel Edgar
Mosier, Harold Gerard
Mueller, Jacob
Myers, George A.
Ness, Eliot
Norweb, Raymond Henry
Orlikowski, Bernard E.
Otis, Charles Augustus, Sr.
Owen, James Alexander
Parsons, Richard C.
Payer, Harry Franklin
Payne, Henry B.
Payne, Lawrence O.
Payne, Nathan Perry
Pelton, Frederick W.
Perkins, Joseph
Pomerene, Atlee
Porter, Albert S.
Pyke, Bernice Secrest
Quayle, Thomas
Rainey, Sherlie Hereford
Riddle, Albert G.
Rose, H. (Horace) Chapman
Rose, William Grey
Rumbold, Charlotte Margaret
Russell, Jack Paul
Ruthenberg, Charles
Salen, Charles P.
Scovill, Philo
Senter, George B.
Sifleet, William J.
Smetona, Antanas
Stage, Charles Willard
Standart, Needham M.
Starkweather, Samuel
Sullivan, Jeremiah J.
Svoboda, Frank J.
Sweeney, Martin L.
Tenesy, Rose L. Gerak
Tod, David
Townes, Clayton C.
Townsend, Amos
Vail, Harry Lorenzo
Van Aken, William J.
Van Aken, William Russell
Wade, Edward
Waitt, Maude Comstock
Walker, William Otis
Walter, Paul William
Weeden, John T.
Whittlesey, Elisha
Wigman, John B.
Willey, John Wheelock
Williams, Geraldine
Wing, Marie Remington
Witt, Peter
Wood, Reuben
Zangerle, John A.
Zimmerman, Charles X.

## PUBLIC SAFETY

Birns, Alex "Shondor"
Black, Hilbert Norman
Celebrezze, Frank D.
Chadwick, Cassie L.
Clifford, Louis I.
Coach, Richard J.
Crawford, Frederick Coolidge
Czolgosz, Leon F.
Day, William L.
Delaney, John (Jack) F.
Fitch, Jabez W.

Frazee, John N.
Graul, Jacob
Greene, Daniel J. "Danny"
Harney, Harrison Hannibal
Kohler, Frederick
Minor, Norman Selby
Ness, Eliot
O'Mic, John
Schmitt, Jacob W.
Wallace, George Alexander Leroy

## RECREATION AND POPULAR CULTURE

Ball, Ernest R.
Beeman, Edwin E.
Bertman, Joseph
Boiardi, Hector
Bramley, Matthew Fredrick
Browne, Charles Farrar (aka Artemus Ward)
Carroll, Gene
Champa, Frank A.
Corrigan, Laura Mae
Dandridge, Dorothy
DaSilva, Howard
Ellsler, Effie
Ellser, John Adam
Fisher, Edward Floyd
Freed, Alan
Freeman, Ernest (Ernie)
Gentry, Minnie Lee Watson
Glass, Myron E.
Hamilton, Margaret
Humphrey, Dudley Sherman II
Katz, Meyer Myron "Mickey"
Kaye, Sammy
McLean, Phil
Manry, Robert N.
Marsh, W. Ward
Mintz, Leo
Meyers, Pierre "Mad Daddy"
Neff, Earl J.
Newman, Joseph Simon
Penfound, Ronald A. (Captain Penny)
Perry, Eleanor (Rosenfeld-Bayer-Perry)
Pickus, Abe
Sansom, Arthur B. (Art), Jr.
Siedel, Frank
Sissle, Noble
Spero, Herman Israel
Spitalny, Maurice
Spitalny, Phil
Stair, Patty
Stinchcomb, William Albert
Tambo Tambo
Tebelak, John Michael
Vadnal, Frank L.
Watkins, Samuel "Sammy"
Wolf, Frederick C.
Zaboly, Bela (Bill)
Zamecnik, John S.

## REFORM, CHARITY AND PHILANTHROPY

Adams, Almeda C.
Addison, Hiram M.
Aiken, Samuel Clark
Ali-Bey, Omar
Badger, Joseph
Baker, Edward Mose (Max)
Baker, Henry M.
Baker, Newton Diehl
Baldwin, John
Barnett, James
Barry, Frank T.
Battisti, Frank Joseph
Beard, Charles Augustine
Beaumont, Louis D.
Begin, Floyd L.
Bellamy, George Albert
Bemis, Edward W.
Bernon, (Bernstein) Maurice
Bicknell, Warren
Bingham, Charles W.
Black, Louis
Black, Morris Alfred
Blanchard, Ferdinand Q.
Blossom, Dudley S.
Blossom, Emily Elkins
Bohn, Ernest J.
Bole, Roberta Holder

Bolton, Charles Chester
Bolton, Chester Castle
Bolton, Fanny Mann Hanna
Bolton, Frances Payne
Bolton, Kenyon C.
Bond, Robert L.
Boyer, Willis Booth
Britton, Brigham
Britton, Gertrude Haskell
Brown, Anna V.
Brown, John
Brush, Dorothy Adams Hamilton
Bryant, Eliza
Burten, Lonnie L., Jr.
Burton, Harold Hitz
Byers, Edgar S.
Cadwallader, Starr
Campbell, Marion Winton Strongheart
Carr, Charles Velmon
Case, Leonard, Jr.
Case, Leonard, Sr.
Chadsey, Mildred
Chase, Russell N.
Chief Thunderwater
Clark, Harold Terry
Clement, Kenneth W.
Coakley, John Aloysius
Comoceda, Charlotte
Conners, William Randall
Cooley, Harris Reid
Corcoran, Charles Leslie
Corlett, Selene
Craig, Lillian
Crawford, Frederick Coolidge
Cunin, John R.
Dalton, Henry George
Dauby, Nathan
Day, William Howard
Delaney, Ralph David
Demmy, Olean Wells
Dively, George Samuel
Drury, Francis Edson
Dumoulin, Frank
DuPont, Zara
Durden, Edward
Eaton, Cyrus Stephen
Einstein, Ruth
Eisenman, Charles
Fagan, Harry A.
Fenn, Sereno Peck
Fenster, Leo
Ferrell, Frederic Leonard
Fesler, Mayo
Finkelstein, Louis
Fitch, Sarah Elizabeth
Flynn, Eileen Eleanor Finlin
Foote, John A.
Foster, Claud Hanscomb
Freedheim, Eugene Heitler
Freiberger, Isadore Fred
Friedman, Max R.
Fritzsche, Alfred
Gannett, Alice
Gaylord, Gladys
George, Zelma Watson
Giddings, Joshua Reed
Gitlin, David
Goff, Frederick H.
Goldhammer, Samuel
Gordon, William J.
Greve, Bell
Gries, Lucile Dauby
Gries, Moses J.
Gries, Robert Hays
Grossman, Mary B.
Gund, George
Haas, Vincent P.
Hadden, Marianne Elizabeth Milliken
Halle, Salmon Portland
Hanna, Leonard C.
Harkness, Anna M. (Richardson)
Harrison, Marvin Clinton
Hart, Albert Bushnell
Harvey, Kate Benedict Hanna
Hauser, Elizabeth
Hayes, Max S. (Maximilian Sebastian)
Henrietta, Sister
Herrick, Maria M. Smith
Herzog, Bertha Beitman
Holden, Liberty Emery
Holly, John Oliver, Jr.
Holmes, Allen C.
Horvath, Helen
Howe, Frederic C.
Hunter, Jane Edna (Harris)
Huntington, John
Hurlbut, Hinman B.
Ignatia, Sr. Mary
Ingalls, David Sinton, Jr.

Ireland, James Duane
Ireland, Margaret Allen
Irwin, Josephine Saxer
Jackson, James Frederick
Jackson, Perry B.
Jelliffe, Rowena Woodham
Jelliffe, Russell W.
Jennings, Elizabeth (Eliza) Wallace
Jennings, Martha F. Holden
Johnson, Tom L.
Jones, Carlos L.
Jones, Myrta L.
Kelley, Horace
Klaiman, Ralph
Klunder, Bruce W.
Koklowsky, Albert, S. T.
Kulas, Elroy John
Lazar, Alma Trebel
LeBlond, Charles Hubert
Leimkuehler, Paul Elmer
Leonard, William Andrew
Levin, Albert Arthur
Levine, Manuel V.
Lewis, Robert Ellsworth
Lipscomb, James Samuel
Lucas, Charles P., Sr.
McBride, Lucia McCrurdy
McCullough, W. Thomas
Magee, Elizabeth Stewart
Mandelbaum, Maurice J. (Moses)
Marks, Martin A.
Martinek, Joseph
Mather, Elizabeth Ring Ireland
Mather, Flora Stone
Mather, Samuel
Mather, Samuel Livingston
Mather, William Gwinn
Mayo, Leonard Withington
Mellen, Edward J., Jr.
Meyette, Grace E.
Mitchell, L. Pearl
Montgomery, Anzo
Morgan, Daniel Edgar
Moriarty, Elaine M.
Murch, Maynard Hale
Nash, Helen Milliken
Norton, David Z.
Norton, Laurence Harper
Norweb, Emery May Holden
Ollendorff, Henry B.
Payne, Oliver Hazard
Perkins, Anna "Newspaper Annie"
Perkins, Edna Brush
Perkins, Joseph
Pierce, Lucy Anne Boyle
Pollock, Samuel
Poutney, Richard Irving
Prentiss, Elisabeth Severance Allen
Prentiss, Francis Fleury
Prosser, Dillon
Putnam, Mildred Olive Andrews
Putnam, Peter Andrews
Rankin, Alfred, M.
Ratner, Leonard
Ratner, Max
Rawson, Barbara Haas
Rawson, Louise R. Barron
Reavis, John Wallace "Jack"
Reinberger, Clarence Thompson
Revelt, Richard D.
Rockefeller, John D.
Rogers, Margaret Marie Harden
Rose, Benjamin
Rouse, Benjamin
Rouse, Rebecca Cromwell
Ruthenberg, Charles
Saltzman, Maurice
Sampliner, Herman
Sapirstein, Jacob J.
Schmitt, Dorothy
Schmitt, Ralph S.
Schott, Harold C.
Severance, Caroline M.
Severance, John Long
Severance, Louis Henry
Sherwin, Belle
Shurtleff, Glen K.
Silver, Abba Hillel
Smith, Albert Kelvin
Smith, Dorothy
Smith, Harry Clay
Snow, Jane Elliot
Spalding (Spaulding), Rufus
Stanton (Day Sessions), Lucy Ann
Stone, Amasa
Stone, Morris Samuel
Sutler, Eleanore Marguerite Young
Sutphen, Paul Frederick
Taylor, Richard S.
Thome, James A.
Turner, Carrie Stark
Tilley, Madison

Tracy, Florence Comey
Tracy, Jane Allyn Foote
Trenkamp, Herman J.
Treuhaft, William C.
Tuckerman, Louis Bryant
Urban, Helen E.
Wade, Edward
Wade, Jeptha Homer II
Wadsworth, Homer C.
Wagner, Margaret W.
Walton, John Whittlesey
Weil, Helen Kahn
Weil, Julius
White, Thomas H.
Williams, Edward Mason
Williams, Katherine Withrow
Wing, Marie Remington
Wise, Samuel D.
Witt, Peter
Witt, Stillman
Wolf, Edith Anisfield

## RELIGION

Adams, Seymour Webster
Aiken, Samuel Clark
Akram, Wali A.
Bailey, Horace Charles
Barry, Frank T.
Bedell, Gregory Thurston
Begin, Floyd L.
Benn, Luther
Bentley, Adamson
Bird, Philip Smead
Blanchard, Ferdinand Q.
Boehm, Charles
Breed, Walter
Brewster, William H.
Brickner, Barnett Robert
Brown, Russel S.
Buck, Florence
Burton, Lewis
Canfield, Sherman Bond
Cohen, Gustave M.
Cooley, Harris Reid
Cooley, Lathrop
Corcoran, Charles Leslie
Delaney, Ralph David
Dowell, Dorsey Maxfield
Dumoulin, Frank
Fagan, Harry A.
Farmer, James
Farmer, Meribah Butler
Farrelly, John Patrick
Furdek, Stephan
Garfield, James Abram
Genuth, David L.
Gilmour, Richard
Gittelson, Benjamin
Goldman, Solomon
Goldner, Jacob
Gries, Moses J.
Haas, Vincent P.
Hagan, John Raphael
Hanulya, Joseph R.
Haydn, Hiram Collins
Henrietta, Sister
Hoban, Edward Francis
Hoffman, Flarra B.
Horstmann, Ignatius Frederick
Ignatia, Sr. Mary
Issenmann, Clarence G.
Johnson, Clara Lucil
Jurgens, William A.
Kalisch, Isidor
Kappanadze, Jason R.
Klunder, Bruce W.
Koklowsky, Albert, S. T.
Kolaszewski, Anton Francis
Koudelka, Joseph Mary
LeBlond, Charles Hubert
Leonard, William Andrew
Ludlow, Arthur Clyde
McFadden, James A.
McIlvaine, Charles Pettit
McKenney, Thomas E.
McKinney, Wade Hampton
Machol, Michaelis
Malone, Emma Brown
Malone, J. Walter
Margolies, Samuel
Mayer, Jacob
Mihalek, Emil J.
Moncol, Andrew John
Montgomery, Anzo
Moran, Francis T.
Murdoch, Marian E.
Navin, Robert B.
Nearon, Joseph R.
Nowak, Abraham
Odenbach, Frederick L., SJ
Phillips, Charles Henry
Porath, Israel

Prescott, James Sullivan
Prosser, Dillon
Rappe, Louis Amadeus
Rogers, Warren Lincoln
Rosenthal, Rudolph M.
Rouse, Benjamin
Rouse, Rebecca Cromwell
Ruetenik, Herman J.
Russell, Ralph
Schauffler, Henry A.
Schrembs, Joseph
Schwan, Heinrich Christian
Sebian, Thomas B.
Settle, Glenn Thomas
Silver, Abba Hillel
Smith, Frank A.
Smith, Herald Leonydus
Sutphen, Paul Frederick
Tello, Manly
Thome, James A.
Trenkamp, Herman J.
Tucker, Beverley Dandridge
Weeden, John T.
Wey, Alexander Joseph
White, Moses
Whitehead, Eaton
Wolsey, Louis
Zlamal, Oldrich

## SCIENCE

Allyne, Edmund E.
Frasch, Herman
Glennan, Thomas K.
Hovorka, Frank
Loebell, Ernst
Mabery, Charles F.
Michelson, Albert Abraham
Miller, Dayton Clarence
Morgan, Garrett A.
Morley, Edward Williams
Nassau, Jason J.
Odenbach, Frederick L.
Prutton, Carl F.
Shankland, Robert Sherwood
Smith, Albert Kelvin
Smith, Albert W.
Wickenden, William E.
Zapf, Norman F.

## SPORTS

Albritton, David
Atkins (Nusbaum), Larry (Law-
    rence)
Averill, Howard Earl
Bang, Edward F. "Ed"
Bertman, Joseph
Bock, Joseph Courtney
Britton, Charles Schuyler II
Brock, (Slomovitz) Phil
Brown, Paul E.
Browne, Mary Kendale "Brownie"
Burke, Edmund Stevenson Jr.
Burkett, Jesse Cail "Crab"
Carter, Wilfred Carlyle "Whiz Bang"
Chandler, Neville (Nev) Albert Jr.
Chapman, Raymond Johnson "Ray"
Clowser, Jack
Cobbledick, Gordon
Cofall, Stanley B.
Coveleski, Stanley Anthony "Stan"
Deutsch, Samuel H.
Devereux, Henry Kelsey "Harry K."
Dunn, Daniel A. "Danny"
Easter, Luscious "Luke"
Fairfax, Florence Bundy
Ford, Leonard "Lenny"
Friedman, Benjamin "Benny"
Gardner, George W.
Graney, John Gladstone "Jack"
Gries, Robert Hays
Hamilton, Alexander J.
Haskell, Coburn
Heisman, John William
Hennig, Edward A.
Jacobs, David H.
Jirsa, Ferdinand "Ferd"
Joss, Adrian "Addie"
Kilbane, John Patrick "Johnny"
Kuth, Byron D.
LaJoie, Napoleon "Nap"
Lechowick, Margaret (Troughton)
Lewis, Franklin Allan "Whitey"
McAuley, Edward J. "Ed"
McBride, Arthur B. "Mickey"
Manning, Thomas Edward "Red"
O'Donnell, James M.
O'Neill, Francis Joseph "Steve"
Owens, Jesse (James Cleveland)
Paige, LeRoy Robert "Satchel"
Reed, J. Elmer

Risko, John "Johnny"
Robison, Frank DeHaas
Rose, Irving S. "Nig"
Rosenblum, Max
Roudebush, George Milton
Sanchez, Genevieve
Sewell, Joseph Wheeler
Smith, Elmer John
Smith, William T. (Wee Willie)
Sockalexis, Louis Francis "Chief"
Somers, Charles W.
Speaker, Tristram "Tris"
Stouffer, Vernon Bigelow
Sutphin, Albert C. (Al)
Thompson, Donald Scougall
Trosky (Trojovsky), Harold Arthur
    "Hal"
Trueman, James R.
Van Horn, Frank R.
Vosmik, Joseph Franklin "Joe"
Walsh (Walasiewicz), Stella
    (Stanislawa)
Wambsganss, William (Bill Wamby)
Waterfield, Robert "Bob"
Wenham, Frederick L.
Wirtz, John J.
Young, Denton True "Cy"

## SUBURBS

Alger, Henry
Barnard, Maxwell ("Max") Vosper
Benedict, Daniel
Bentley, Adamson
Burrows, George Howard
Cahoon, Joseph
Cain, Frank C.
Celeste, Frank Palm
Chamberlain, Selah
Church, Henry, Jr.
Goldenbogen, Ellen May Dursching
Graber, Belle (Isabel) Taylor
Graber, C. Lee
Greve, Louis William
Jones, Carlos L.
Jones, Paul K.
Kelley, Datus
Lodzieski, Stefan (Stephen)
McKelvey, Dorothy Marks
McQuigg, John Rea
Majerus, Lawrence (Larry Madge)
Rainey, Sherlie Hereford
Sifleet, William J.
Snow, Dorcas Lavina
Van Aken, William J.
Van Aken, William Russell
Waitt, Maude Comstock
Zimmerman, Charles X.

## TRANSPORTATION

Alexander, William Harry
Allen, John W.
Austin, Wilbert John
Baker, Walter C.
Bradley, Alva
Britton, Charles Schuyler II
Brough, John
Burke, Stevenson
Campanaro, Dorothy M.
Case, William
Crawford, Frederick Coolidge
Davies, Thomas D.
Devereux, John H.
Duncan, William McKinley
Eaton, Cyrus Stephen
Engel, Albert John
Everett, Henry A.
Farmer, James
Flint, Edward Sherrill
Hubbell, Charles H.
Hurlbut, Hinman B.
Jordan, Edward Stanlaw "Ned"
Kelley, Alfred
Lee, William Granville
McKay, George Perry
Mandelbaum, Maurice J. (Moses)
Moore, Edward W.
Peck, Elihu M.
Peckham, George Grant Guy
Pomeroy, Alson Horatio
Quayle, Thomas
Rhodes, Daniel Pomeroy
Robison, Frank DeHaas
Schmunk, Walter George
Standart, Needham M.
Stone, Amasa
Thompson, Charles Edwin
Torbenson, Viggo V.
Van Sweringen, Oris Paxton & Man-
    tis James
White, Rollin Charles

White, Rollin Henry
Wieber, Charles L.F.
Winton, Alexander
Witt, Peter
Witt, Stillman
Wright, Walter Benjamin
Young, Dallas M.

## WOMEN

Adams, Almeda C.
Allen, Florence Ellinwood
Ames, Lydia May
Arbuthnot, May Hill
Babin, Victoria (Vitya) Vronsky
Baer, Alice Dorothy
Bage, Helen
Baldwin, Lillian Luverne
Beckwith, Ada Bel
Bell, Myrtle Johnson
Bickford, Clara L. Gehring
Blossom, Emily Elkins
Bole, Roberta Holder
Bolton, Fanny Mann Hanna
Bolton, Frances Payne
Bolton, Sarah Knowles
Bourke-White, Margaret
Braverman, Libbie Levin
Britton, Gertrude Haskell
Brooks, Minerva Kline
Brown, Anna V.
Browne, Mary Kendale "Brownie"
Brush, Dorothy Adams Hamilton
Bryant, Eliza
Buck, Florence
Butler, Margaret Manor
Cafarelli, Carmela E.
Campbell,    Marion    Winton
    Strongheart
Canfield, Martha Ann Robinson
Cermak, Albina
Chadsey, Mildred
Chadwick, Cassie L.
Clapp, Nettie Mackenzie
Clifford, Carrie Williams
Comoceda, Charlotte
Corlett, Selene
Corrigan, Laura Mae
Coyle, Grace Longwell
Craig, Lillian
Cutter, Annie Spencer
Dandridge, Dorothy
Deike, Clara L.
Demmy, Olean Wells
Devine, Margaret Crile Garretson
Dewald, Louise
Dixon, Ardelia Bradley
DuPont, Zara
Dyball, Adelaide
Eastman, Linda Anne
Einstein, Ruth
Ellsler, Effie
Evans, Dina Rees (Doc)
Fairfax, Florence Bundy
Farmer, Meribah Butler
Fitch, Sarah Elizabeth
Fleming, Lethia Cousins
Flynn, Eileen Eleanor Finlin
Forsyth (Myers), Josephine
Fox, Beatrice Wright
Fuldheim, Dorothy
Gannett, Alice
Garlock, Anna Jansen Cordon
Gaylor, Verna Frances
Gaylord, Gladys
Gentry, Minnie Lee Watson
George, Zelma Watson
Gerfen, Elizabeth H.
Getz, Hester Adelia
Giddings, Helen Marshall
Giddings, Mary
Gilchrist, Marie Emilie
Glover, Vera Abagarl
Goetz, Bernice
Goldenbogen, Ellen May Dursching
Gordon, Helen
Goulder, Grace Izant
Graber, Belle (Isabel) Taylor
Green, Virginia Darlington
Greve, Bell
Gries, Lucile Dauby
Grossman, Mary B.
Guilford, Linda (Lucinda) Thayer
Hadden, Marianne Elizabeth Milli-
    ken
Hamilton, Margaret
Handrick, Gertrude M. (Foran)
Harkness, Anna M. (Richardson)
Harvey, Kate Benedict Hanna
Hauser, Elizabeth
Hawgood, Belle Dibley
Henrietta, Sister
Herrick, Maria M. Smith

510

Hertz, Marguerite Rosenberg
Herzog, Bertha Beitman
Heydemann, Lily Carthew
Hodgins, Agatha C.
Hoffman, Flarra B.
Horvath, Helen
Hudson, Jean Roberta
Hughes, Adella Prentiss
Hull, Jessie (Jesse) Redding
Hunter, Jane Edna (Harris)
Ignatia, Sr. Mary
Ingham, Mary Bigelow (Janes)
Inman, Amie G. Steere
Ireland, Margaret Allen
Irwin, Josephine Saxer
Janicki, Hazel
Jelliffe, Rowena Woodham
Jennings, Elizabeth (Eliza) Wallace
Jennings, Martha F. Holden
Johnson, Clara Lucil
Jones, Myrta L.
Joseph, Helen Haiman
Katan, Anny Rosenberg
Keeler, Harriet Louise
Kelly, Grace V.
Kinzer, Gertrude C.
Kovell, Margaret N.
Landy, Rachel
Lawrence, Wilhelmina Price
Lazar, Alma Trebel
Lechowick, Margaret (Troughton)
Ledbetter, Eleanor Edwards
Long, Juliana (Julia) Walworth
McBride, Lucia McCrurdy
McCarthy, Sara Varley
McCord, Grace Bernardina Doering
McCormick, Anne (O'Hare)

McKelvey, Dorothy M.
McKenney, Ruth
McKinney, Ruth Berry
MacDonald, Calvina
Magee, Elizabeth Stewart
Malone, Emma Brown
Marcus, Sarah
Martin, Mary Brown
Mather, Elizabeth Ring Ireland
Mather, Flora Stone
Merrick, Myra King
Meyette, Grace E.
Mitchell, L. Pearl
Moriarty, Elaine M.
Mural, Katherine
Murdoch, Marian E.
Nash, Helen Milliken
Norton, Georgie Leighton
Norweb, Emery May Holden
O'Neill, Cordelia L.
Osika, Charlotte
Ostendarp, Carol Anne
Parsons, Kate
Perkins, Anna "Newspaper Annie"
Perkins, Edna Brush
Perry, Eleanor (Rosenfeld-Bayer-Perry)
Pierce, Lucy Anne Boyle
Power, Effie Louise
Prentiss, Elisabeth Severance Allen
Price, Grace Finley
Pridgeon, Louise Johnson
Pyke, Bernice Secrest
Quintrell, Mary Corinne
Rainey, Sherlie Hereford
Ransom, Caroline L. Ormes
Rauschkolb, Ruth (Robishaw)

Rawson, Barbara Haas
Rawson, Louise R. Barron
Redinger, Ruby Virginia
Regnatz, Caroline/Caroline Obelz
Robb, Isabel Adams Hampton
Robertson, Josephine (Jo) Wubben
Robeson, Lila Pauline
Rogers, Margaret Marie Harden
Rouse, Rebecca Cromwell
Rowland, Amy Farley
Rumbold, Charlotte Margaret
Sadataki, Mary Hata
St. Andrews, Helene
Sanchez, Genevieve
Sauer, Augusta "Gustie" Veera
Schmitt, Dorothy
Schulte, Lauretta (Oberle)
Scranton, Irene Hickox
Severance, Caroline M.
Shaw, Elsa Vick
Shepherd, Dorothy G. Payer
Sherwin, Belle
Sinclair, Jo
Smith, Dorothy
Snow, Dorcas Lavina
Snow, Jane Elliot
Stair, Patty
Standiford-Mehling, Ethel
Stanton (Day Sessions), Lucy Ann
Stashower, Hildegarde Darmstadter
Strong, Eleanor Painter
Sutler, Eleanore Marguerite Young
Taylor, Sophia Elizabeth Strong
Tenesy, Rose L. Gerak
Thornton- Silver, Eugenia
Towslee, Lillian Gertrude
Tracy, Florence Comey

Tracy, Jane Allyn Foote
Turner, Carrie Stark
Turner, Rachel Walker
Tyler, Alice S.
Urban, Helen E.
Vormelker, Rose L.
Votipka, Thelma
Wagner, Margaret W.
Waitt, Maude Comstock
Walker, Hazel Mountain
Walsh (Walasiewicz), Stella (Stanislawa)
Walters, Claire A.
Webb, Ella Sturtevant
Weil, Helen Kahn
Welter, Katherine J. Kessler
Wembridge, Eleanor Harris Rowland
Westropp, Clara E.
Westropp, Lillian Mary
Whitaker, May Tarbell Cannon
Whitley, R. (Rousara) Joyce
Wickham, Gertrude Van Rensselaer
Wieder, Judith Marx
Williams, Geraldine
Williams, Katherine Withrow
Wilson, Ella Grant
Wing, Marie Remington
Winter, Thelma Frazier
Wolf, Edith Anisfield
Wolfenstein, Martha
Woodruff, Mabel Alice
Woolson, Constance Fenimore
Young, Agnes Brooks
Zhun, Ellen Marie Stempien

# Index

Entries in this index are largely limited to names of individuals, places, and corporate entities within Cuyahoga County, Ohio. There are two major exceptions to this policy. The index also includes the names of institutions of higher learning in the United States which were attended by individuals who are the subject of an entry in this volume. In addition, the index includes references to most Ohio geographic place names that are found within the volume.

Corporate entities and governmental agencies (boards, committees, etc.) are indexed under their variant name forms as used in the text; as these are not consolidated, researchers should check all name forms for an organization when using this index.

Entries are keyed to the page number of any article in which they appear. Boldfacing of page numbers indicates a complete article on the indexed individual.

Baker & Hostetler, 21–22, 229, 412
Baker Motor Vehicle Company, 22, 479, 483
Baker Rauch & Lang Company, 22, 483
Bakery and Confectionery Workers, Local 19, 360–361
Baldwin, Caroline, 24
Baldwin, Caroline Sophia (Prentiss), 22–23, 24
Baldwin, Charles Candee, **22–23**, 24
Baldwin, Charlotte, 23
Baldwin, Edward, 24
Baldwin, Eliza, 23
Baldwin, Elizabeth, 23
Baldwin, Ellen, 23
Baldwin, Elsie, 192
Baldwin, Emily, 24
Baldwin, Hannah (Northrup), 24
Baldwin, Henry, 23, 24
Baldwin, Henry P., 23
Baldwin, Hulda, 23
Baldwin, John, **23**
Baldwin, John (son of John Baldwin), 23
Baldwin, Joseph, 23
Baldwin, Julia, 24
Baldwin, Lilian Converse (Hanna), 24
Baldwin, Lillian Luverne, **23**
Baldwin, Lucretia, 24
Baldwin, Martha, 23
Baldwin, Mary, 23
Baldwin, Mary (Candee), 22–23
Baldwin, Mary (Chapel), 23
Baldwin, Mary (daughter of Norman C. Baldwin), 23
Baldwin, Mary H. (Palmer), 23
Baldwin, Milton, 23
Baldwin, N.C., 23
Baldwin, Newton, 23
Baldwin, Norman A., 23
Baldwin, Norman C., **23**
Baldwin, Philander, 24
Baldwin, Rhoda (Boughton), 24
Baldwin, Rosanna (daughter of John Baldwin), 23
Baldwin, Rosanna (Meloy), 23
Baldwin, Samuel (father of Samuel S. Baldwin), 24
Baldwin, Samuel Prentiss, 22–23, **24**
Baldwin, Samuel S., **24**
Baldwin, Sarah, 24
Baldwin, Sarah (Camp), 24
Baldwin, Seymour Wesley, 22–23
Baldwin, Smith S., 24
Baldwin, Stephen, 23
Baldwin, Susannah (Adams), 23
Baldwin Bird Research Laboratory, 24
Baldwin Filtration Plant, 9, 442
Baldwin Institute, 23, 25–26, 239
Baldwin University, 23, 202–03, 275, 315, 319
Baldwin University Law School, 178, 460
Baldwin-Wallace College, 12–13, 23, 32, 79, 96, 97, 99, 100, 147, 162, 194, 195, 202–03, 225, 270–71, 297, 371, 377, 397–98, 424, 452, 465–66, 476–77, 485
Ball, Aaron, 24–25
Ball, Alice, 24–25
Ball, Anna (Kocker), 24
Ball, Ernest A. (son of Ernest R. Ball), 24
Ball, Ernest Adelbert, 24
Ball, Ernest R., **24**
Ball, Florence, 189
Ball, Florence (daughter of Webb C. Ball), 24–25
Ball, Florence I. (Young), 24–25
Ball, Grace A., 130
Ball, Jesse Mae (Jewett), 24
Ball, Maude (Lambert), 24
Ball, Roland A., 24
Ball, Ruth Mary, 24
Ball, Sidney Ann (Clay), 24–25
Ball, Sidney Y., 24–25
Ball, Webb C., **24–25**
Ball, Wilma, 24–25
Ball Park Mustard, 41
Ballanchine, George, 228–29
Baltimore College of Dental Surgery, 435
Bamberger-Reinthal Co., 373
Bancroft, George, 203
Bandlow, Barbara (Kachel), 25
Bandlow, Caroline, 25
Bandlow, Henry, 25
Bandlow, Karl, 25
Bandlow, Lissing, 25
Bandlow, Robert, **25**
Bandlow, Robert (son of Robert Bandlow), 25
Bandlow, Walter, 25
Bang, Betty, 25
Bang, Charles, 25
Bang, Charles (son of Edward F. Bang), 25
Bang, Edward F. "Ed", **25**
Bang, Ernest, 25
Bang, Regina, 25
Bang, Rose, 25
Bang, Rose (Schneider), 25
Bank of Berea, 357
Bank of Buffalo, 203
Bank of Cleveland, 153, 264–65
Bank of Commerce, 344, 350, 332
Bank of Henry Spira, 427
Bank of Lake Erie, 488–89
Banker's Club of Cleveland, 436
Bankers Surety Co., 332
Banks-Baldwin Law Publishing Compny, 111
Banting, F.G., 300
Baptist City Mission Society, 85
Baptist Meeting House, 139
Baptist Minister's Conference of Cleveland and Vicinity, 472–73
Barber, Abigail (Gilbert), 26
Barber, Abigail G. (daughter of Josiah Barber), 26
Barber, Alice (Cass), 26
Barber, Arthur, 25–26
Barber, Clarence, 25–26
Barber, Earnest, 25–26
Barber, Epiphras, 26
Barber, Gershom M., **25–26**
Barber, Harriet, 26
Barber, Huldah Lavinia (Seeley), 25–26
Barber, Ida, 25–26
Barber, Jerusha, 26
Barber, Josiah, **26**
Barber, Josiah, 286
Barber, Marion, 25–26
Barber, Orpha, 25–26
Barber, Phineas, 25–26
Barber, Sophia (Lord), 26
Barber, Sophia L. (daughter of Josiah Barber), 26
Barber, Stephen, 26
Bardoun, Allen E., 26
Bardoun, Anne E. (Prudek), 26
Bardoun, Donald F., 26
Bardoun, Frank J., **26**
Bardoun, Louis, 26
Bardoun, Mary Plantner, 26
Bardun Mortgage and Investment Co., 93–94
Barkwill, Ernest S. (residence), 400
Barnard, Carlotta, 26
Barnard, Jane, 26
Barnard, Jay, 26
Barnard, Lena, 26
Barnard, Margaret, 26
Barnard, Maxwell "Max" Vosper, **26**
Barnard College, 430
Barnett, Carrie M., 27
Barnett, George, 27
Barnett, James, **27**, 221, 496
Barnett, Lanny, 27
Barnett, Laura, 27
Barnett, Maria H. (Underhill), 27
Barnett, Mary (Clark), 27
Barnett, Mary C., 27
Barnett, Melancthon, 27
Barnum, David, 27
Barnum, Frank Seymour, **27**
Barnum, Jeannette May, 27
Barnum, P.T., 441
Barnum, Virginia (Lambert), 27
Barnum, W. Hamilton, 27
Barr, Delia M., 27–28
Barr, John, **27–28**
Barr, Nellie, 27–28
Barr, Suzanna, 27–28
Barr, Thomas, 27–28
Barricelli, Gian Piero, 28
Barricelli, Giovanni Alfonso, **28**
Barricelli, Lucia (Cangelicri), 28
Barricelli, Orfea Malpezzi, 28
Barricelli, Pietro, 28
Barron, Elizabeth Carpenter, 370
Barron, William, 370
Barry, David W., 28
Barry, Edwin, 189
Barry, Frank McArthur, 28
Barry, Frank T., **28**
Barry, Martha Isabel, 28
Barry, Mary K., 28
Barry, Sarah Prince McArthur, 28
Barstow, Annie Borland, 202
Barstow, Lois Catherine (Buhrer), 71
Bartlett, C.B., 455
Bartlett, Mrs. Edwar T., II, 108–09
Bartlett, Virginia (Bedell), 36–37
Barton, Thomas C., **28**
Base Hospital No. 6, 114
Basic Ceramics Co., 958
Basil, Lillian (Cahill), 79
Bassett, Franklin, 428–29
Bates, Benham, 28–29
Bates, Charlotte (Young), 28–29
Bates, Cornelia, 28–29
Bates, Eusebra (Wade), 463
Bates, Francis, 28–29
Bates, Katherine, 28–29
Bates, Kenneth F., **28–29**
Bates, Winnette (Litchfield), 28–29
Bath, OH, 99
Battista, Bruce, 29
Battista, Joseph, Jr., 29
Battista, Joseph "Pipp", **29**
Battista, Margaret (Chiocchio), 29
Battista, Mary Lou, 29
Battisti, Eugene, 29
Battisti, Frank Joseph, **29**
Battisti, Gloria Joy (Karpinski), 29
Battisti, Jennie (Dalesandro), 29
Battle of Antietam, 217
Battle of Atlanta, 289
Battle of Cedar Creek, VA, 211–12
Battle of Chickamauga, GA, 221
Battle of Chippewa, 203
Battle of Corinth, 418
Battle of Ft. Donelson (TN), 277–78
Battle of Missionary Ridge, 485
Battle of Pickett's Mills, 202
Battle of Secessionville, 142
Battle of Shiloh, 481–82, 485
Battle of the Bulge, 278
Battle of Vera Cruz, Mexico (1915), 233–34
Battle of Winchester, 109
Bauder, Arthur, 29
Bauder, Blanche, 29
Bauder, Eliza (Phillips), 29
Bauder, Elizabeth (Page), 29
Bauder, Frank, 29
Bauder, Levi, 29
Bauder, Levi F., **29**
Bauder, Theresa, 29
Bauder, Walter, 29
Baum, Mary (Shera), 411
Bay Village, OH, 79, 312, 401
Bay Village Historical Society, 79, 234
Bay Village Presbyterian Church, 234
Bayer, Ann, 351–352
Bayer, Leo G., 351–352
Bayer, Oliver Weld, 351–352
Bayer, William, 351–352
Bayless, Bertha (Snyder), 29–30
Bayless, David, 29–30
Bayless, Jean (Poser), 29–30
Bayless, Margaret (Falke), 29–30
Bayless, Robert, 29–30
Bayless, Ronald, 29–30
Bayless, Thomas, 29–30
Bayless, William, 29–30
Bayless, William Neville, **29–30**
Bayless, William Niven, 29–30
Bayless-Kerr Advertising Agency, 29–30
Bayne, William M., 17
Bea-Taylor, Judith Saltzman, 395
Beach, Adelaide (Thow), 30
Beach, Chisholm, 30
Beach, Clifton Bailey, **30**
Beach, Emily C. (Wiggin), 30
Beach, Israel Bailey, 30
Beach, Janet (Chisholm), 30
Beach Cliff (Rocky River), 30
Beach School, 30
Beachwood, OH, 129, 164–65, 493
Beard, Alison, 30
Beard, Aria (Thomas), 30
Beard, Chappell, 30
Beard, Charles Augustine, **30**
Beard, Hilary, 30
Beard, Jonathan, 30
Beard, Peggy (Lanton), 30
Bearings, Inc. ., 112, 400–01
Beaufait, Doris (O'Donnell), 30–31
Beaufait, Dorothy (Johnson), 30–31
Beaufait, Elaine, 30–31
Beaufait, Hazel, J. (Krauss), 30–31
Beaufait, Howard, Jr., 30–31
Beaufait, Howard G., **30–31**, 39–40
Beaufait, Janis, 30–31
Beaufait, Louis, 30–31
Beaumont, Dudley, 31
Beaumont, Helene M. (Thomas), 31
Beaumont, Louis D., **31**, 284
Beaumont School, 335
Beaux-Arts Institute of Design (New York), 87
Beaux-Arts Institute of Design (Philadelphia), 128
Beavis, Benjamin R., 324
Beazle, Barbara (Widder), 483
Beck, Charles, 31–32
Beck, Claude Shaeffer, **31**, 114, 484
Beck, Ellen (Manning), 31
Beck, Henry J., 31–32
Beck, Hildegarde, 31
Beck, Johann Heinrich, **31–32**, 161–62, 304, 318, 378, 392
Beck, Kathryn, 31
Beck, Martha, 31
Beck, Martha (Schaeffer), 31
Beck, Mary Blanding (Fellar), 31–32
Beck, Mary Ellen, 31
Beck, Rebecca (Butter), 31–32
Beck, Simon, 31
Beck String Quartet, 31–32
Becker, Virginia (Blanchard), 47
Beckwith, Ada Bel, **32**
Beckwith, Alida (Haight), 32
Beckwith, Belle N. (Norton), 32
Beckwith, Charles G., **32**
Beckwith, Clara L. (Sullivan), 32
Beckwith, Edwin W., 32
Beckwith, Havel, 32
Beckwith, Raymond N. Ellis, 32
Beckworth, Arthur, 202
Bedell, Barbara, 36–37
Bedell, Edna B. (Eckhardt), 36–37
Bedell, Gregory Thurston, **32**
Bedell, Gregory Townsend, 32
Bedell, Julia (Strong), 32
Bedell, Penelope (Thurston), 32
Bedell, Virginia, 36–37
Bedell Company, 36–37
Bedford, OH, 37, 172, 280, 392, 406, 477–78, 485–86
Bedford & Cleveland Railway Company, 143–44
Bedford Electric Light Company, 172
Bedford Heights, OH, 320
Bedford Methodist Episcopal Church, 37
Bedford Roller Mills, 172
Bedford Township Board of Trustees, 37
Bee Life Insurance Company, 47
Bee Line, 47
Beech Brook, Inc., 61, 126–27, 328
Beecher, Henry Ward, 60
Beecher, Lyman, 285–86
Beeman, Edwin E., **32–33**, 480
Beeman, Harry L., 32–33
Beeman, Julius, 32–33
Beeman, Lester A., 32–33
Beeman, Margaret, 32–33
Beeman, Mary Cobb, 32–33
Beeman Chemical Company, 32–33
Beeman's Pepsin Gum, 32–33, 480
Begin, Floyd L., **33**
Begin, Peter, 33
Begin, Stella MacFarland, 33
Beidler, Dudley, 33
Beidler, Hannah, 33
Beidler, Israel, 33
Beidler, Jacob A., **33**
Beidler, Joseph, 33
Beidler, Mabel, 33
Beidler, Mary, 33
Beidler, Mary (Latshaw), 33
Beiswenger, Hoch, Arnold & Associates, 200
Beitman, Emanuel, 219
Beitman, Molly, 219
Bel Geddes, Noman, 310–11
Bell, Alice (McGhee), 295
Bell, Archie, **33–34**, 227
Bell, Caree, 34
Bell, Charles, 34
Bell, Denise, 34
Bell, Edward, 34
Bell, Georgia F., 120
Bell, L. Frank, 34
Bell, Marie (Westbrook), 34
Bell, Myrtle Johnson, **34**
Bell, Nolan (son of Nolan D. Bell), 34
Bell, Nolan D., **34**
Bell, Robert, 34
Bell, Rowena, 34
Bell, Russell, 34
Bell, Samuel A., 33–34
Bell, Sarah Jane (Soden), 33–34
Bell, Viola, 34
Bell Telephone, 482–83
Bell Telephone Laboratories, 272
Bellamy, Alice, 34–35
Bellamy, Betty, 34–35
Bellamy, Christopher, 35
Bellamy, Clara (Horn), 34–35
Bellamy, Edward, 35
Bellamy, Emma (Sanderson), 35
Bellamy, Ester, 34–35
Bellamy, George Albert, **34–35**
Bellamy, Jean Dessel, 35
Bellamy, Joan B., 35
Bellamy, John, 35
Bellamy, John S., II, 35
Bellamy, Laura, 34–35
Bellamy, Lucy (Stow), 34–35
Bellamy, Marguerite Scott (Stark), 35
Bellamy, Marie Laura (Parker), 34–35
Bellamy, Mary (Mitchell), 35
Bellamy, May, 35
Bellamy, Nicole B., 35
Bellamy, Paul, **35**
Bellamy, Peter, **35**
Bellamy, Richard K., 35
Bellamy, Sheila J., 35
Bellamy, Stephen P., 35
Bellamy, William, 34–35
Belle Vernon-Mapes Dairy Co., 33
Bellefaire, OH, 38, 138, 323, 474
Bellefontaine, OH, 80
Bellefontaine and Indianapolis Railroad, 65
Bellevue, OH, 206–07, 460
Belmont County, OH, 441–42
Beloit College, 469
Bemis, Alice L., 35–36
Bemis, Annie L. (Sargent), 35–36
Bemis, Daniel W., 35–36
Bemis, Edward W., **35–36**
Bemis, Lloyde E., 35–36
Bemis, Mary W. Tinker, 35–36
Bemis, Walter S., 35–36
Ben, **36**
Ben Venue Laboratories, 280
Benade, Arthur H., **36**
Benade, James Martin, 36
Benade, Judith, 36
Benade, Martin, 36
Benade, Miriam McGaw, 36
Benade, Virginia Lee (Wassall), 36
Bender, Anna (Sir), 36–37
Bender, George, 123–24
Bender, George Harrison, **36–37**, 73–74, 274–75
Bender, Joseph, 36–37
Bender Avenue St. Club, 134
Bendix, Max, 285
Benedict, Allison, 37
Benedict, Amos, 37
Benedict, Ann (Stone), 37
Benedict, Catharine, 37
Benedict, Daniel, **37**
Benedict, Darius, 37
Benedict, George, 37
Benedict, George A., **37**, 68–69, 105, 207
Benedict, Harriet, 37
Benedict, James, 37
Benedict, Judson, 37
Benedict, Julius, 37
Benedict, Mary, 37
Benedict, Phinamber, 37
Benedict, Ralph, 37
Benedict, Randolphus, 37
Benedict, Sarah (Rathbone), 37
Benedict, Sillock, 37
Benedictine High School, 453
Benes, Clara, 37–38
Benes, Dorothy Jean, 146
Benes, Grace, 37–38
Benes, Jerome H., 37–38
Benes, Joseph M., 37–38
Benes, Josephine (Nowak), 37–38
Benes, Matilda, 37–38
Benes, Matilda F. (Nowak), 37–38
Benes, W. Dominick, 27, **37–38**, 231–32, 318
Benesch, Alfred Abraham, **38**
Benesch, Bertha (Federdian), 38
Benesch, Friedlander, Coplan & Aronoff, 38
Benesch, Helen (Newman), 38
Benesch, Isidore J., 38
Benham, Alice (Bellamy), 34–35
Benham, General Henry W., 142
Benjamin, Charles H., **38**
Benjamin, Ellen (Fairfield), 38
Benjamin, Samuel E., 38
Benjamin Rose Hospital, 464
Benjamin Rose Institute, 127–28, 385–86, 464
Benn, Bernard, 38–39
Benn, Estella (Moss), 38–39
Benn, Luther, **38–39**
Benner, Wallace, 187–88
Bennett, Alice Bennett, 116
Bennington College, 369–370
Bennis, Clurie (Williams), 487–88
Bentley, Adamson, **39**
Bentley, Benjamin, 39
Bentley, Charles, 460
Bentley, Emily, 39
Bentley, Laura, 39

515

517

518

524

530

531

543

544

545